The Bristol and Gloucestershire Archaeological Society
Gloucestershire Record Series

Hon. General Editor

Christopher Elrington, M.A., F.S.A., F.R.Hist.S.
formerly General Editor of the
Victoria History of the Counties of England

Volume 8

Ralph Bigland
Historical Monumental and Genealogical Collections
Relative to the County of Gloucester

Part 4: Uley–Yate
Introduction and indexes

RALPH BIGLAND
HISTORICAL, MONUMENTAL AND GENEALOGICAL COLLECTIONS RELATIVE TO THE COUNTY OF GLOUCESTER

PART FOUR:
ULEY–YATE
INTRODUCTION AND INDEXES

Edited by Brian Frith

The Bristol and Gloucestershire Archaeological Society

1995

The Bristol and Gloucestershire Archaeological Society
Gloucestershire Record Series

© The Bristol and Gloucestershire Archaeological Society

ISBN 0 900197 40 4

Produced for the Society by
Alan Sutton Publishing Ltd., Phoenix Mill, Far Thrupp, Stroud, Glos. GL5 2BU
Printed in Great Britain by WBC Limited, Bridgend

CONTENTS

	Page
List of plates	vi
Collation of editions	vii
Foreword	ix
Introduction, by Brian Frith	xi
Uley	1365
Uphatherley	1370
Upleaden	1371
Upton St. Leonard's	1373
Prinknash, addendum	1380
Walton Cardiff, addendum	1380
Walton Cardiff	1381
Wapley and Codrington	1383
Washbourn Great	1386
Washbourn Little	1387
Welford, addendum	1388
Welford	1389
Weston-upon-Avon	1390
Westbury in the Forest [Westbury on Severn]	1393
Westbury upon Trim	1405
Redland (hamlet to Westbury upon Trim)	1416
Shirehampton (hamlet to Westbury upon Trim)	1417
Westcot	1421
Icomb	1422
Westerleigh	1423
Weston Birt	1429
Weston Subedge	1430
Whaddon	1433
Wheatenhurst, commonly called Whitminster	1435
Widford	1441
Whittington	1442
Child's Wickham	1446
Wickwar	1449
Willersey	1457
Winchcombe	1461
Winrush	1480
Winston	1483

Winterbourn	1486
Witcombe	1492
Withington	1495
Wolstone	1503
Woodchester	1505
Woollaston	1513
Wormington	1517
Wotton-Underedge	1521
Yanworth	1542
Yate	1543
St Phillip & St Jacob, Bristol	1553
St Georges [Bristol]	1577
Indexes, by Irene Wyatt	
Persons	1585
Places	1761
Occupations and offices	1813
Causes of death	1819

LIST OF PLATES

Westbury upon Trim	1406
Monuments in Westbury upon Trim Church	1414
Wheatenhurst	1436
Whittington	1442
Coton brass in Whittington Church	1444
Stone figures in Whittington Church	1445
Wickwar	1448
Winchcombe	1462
Withington	1496
Withington Parsonage	1500
Woodchester	1506
Wotton-Underedge	1520
Thomas, 4th Lord Berkeley, and Margaret his wife	1523
Yate	1544

COLLATION OF EDITIONS

The table below collates the page-numbers of Parts 1–3 of this reprinted edition with those of the original edition.

This edn.	Orig. edn.	This edn.	Orig. edn.	This edn.	Orig. edn.
Part 1	Vol. I	Part 2	Vol. 1	Part 3	Vol. II
pages	pages	pages	pages	pages	pages
1–119	1–119	459–527	441–509	889–891	235–237
120	plate	528	plate	892	plate
121–151	120–150	529–556	510–537	893–907	238–252
152	plate	557	plate		
153–154	151–152	558–565	538–545		Vol. III
155	plate	566	plate		
156–188	153–185	567–588	546–567	908–911	253–256
189	plate	589	plate	912	plate
190–195	186–191	590–593	568–571	913	257
196	plate	594	plate	914	plate
197–218	192–213	595–628	572–605	915	258
219	plate	629	plate	916	plate
220–221	214–215	630–642	606–618	917–925	259–267
222	plate			926	plate
223–242	216–235		Vol. II	927–941	268–282
243	plate			942	plate
244–291	236–283	643–646	1–4	943–955	283–295
292	plate	647	plate	956	plate
293	284	648–672	5–29	957–967	296–306
294	plate	673	plate	968	plate
295–296	285–286	674–693	30–49	969–984	307–322
297–298	285–286 [bis]	694	plate	985–986	322*–323*
299–311	287–299	695–697	50–52	987–989	323–325
312	plate	698	plate	990	325*
313–325	300–312	699–711	53–65	991–997	326–332
326	plate	712	plate		
327–355	313–341	713–741	66–94		
356	plate	742	plate		
357–440	342–425	743–773	95–125		
441	plate	774	plate		
442–456	426–440	775–789	126–140		
457–458	plates	790	plate		
		791–827	141–177		
		828	plate		
		829–873	178–222		
		874	plate		
		875–876	223–224		
		877	plate		
		878–887	225–234		
		888	plate		

Volume III of the original edition does not have numbered pages after p. 332 except for pp. 349–360, corresponding to pp. 1015–1021 and 1023–1027 in the present present reprinted edition.

This edn.	*Orig. edn.*		*This edn.*	*Orig. edn.*
Part 3	Vol. III		Part 3	Vol. III
pages	parishes		pages	parishes
998	(plate)		1148	Stanley Pontlarge
999–1000	Quedgley		1149–1151	Stanton
1001–1003	Queinton		1152–1154	Stanway
1003–1005	Quenington		1155–1160	Stapleton
1006–1008	Randwick		1161–1162	Staunton near Newland
1009	Rangeworthy		1163–1165	Staverton
1009–1011	Rendcomb		1166–1169	Stinchcombe
1012–1013	Great Rissington		1170–1172	Stoke Giffard
1013	Little Rissington		1173–1177	Stone
1014	Wick Rissington		1178	(plate)
1014–1017	Great Rissington &c.		1179–1187	Stonehouse
1018–1020	Rockampton		1188	(plate)
1021	Rodborough		1189–1197	Stow
1022	(plate)		1198	Stowell
1023–1027	Rodborough (cont.)		1199–1202	Stratton
1028–1033	Rodmarton		1203	Stroud
1034–1035	Rudford		1204	(plate)
1035–1039	Ruerdean		1205–1218	Stroud (cont.)
1040–1041	Saintbury		1219–1221	Sudely
1042–1043	Cold Salperton		1222–1223	Sutton under Brailes
1044–1047	Sandhurst		1224	Lower Swell
1048–1052	Saperton		1224–1225	Upper Swell
1053–1054	Saul		1225–1228	Lower and Upper Swell
1055	Seisencote		1229	Swindon
1056–1064	Sevenhampton		1230	(plate)
1065	Shenington		1231–1233	Swindon (cont.)
1066–1069	Sherborne		1233–1238	Taynton
1070–1074	Shipton Moyne and Dovel		1239	Tetbury
1075	Shipton Oliffe		1240	(plate)
1076	Shipton Solers		1241	Tetbury (cont.)
1077–1078	Shipton Solers and Oliffe		1242	(plate)
1079	Shurdington		1243–1245	Tetbury (cont.)
1080–1081	Lower Siddington		1246	(plate)
1082–1083	Siddington St. Mary's and St. Peter's		1247–1253	Tetbury (cont.)
1083	Side		1254	(plate)
1084–1087	Siston		1255–1259	Tetbury (cont.)
1088	Lower Slaughter		1260	(plate)
1085–1091	Upper Slaughter		1261–1263	Tewkesbury
1091–1093	Lower and Upper Slaughter and Eyford		1264	(plate)
1094	(plate)		1265–1285	Tewkesbury (cont.)
1095–1102	Slimbridge		1286	(plate)
1103–1104	Snowshill		1287–1293	Tewkesbury (cont.)
1105–1112	Chipping Sodbury		1294	(plate)
1113	Little Sodbury		1295–1309	Thornbury
1113	Old Sodbury		1310	(plate)
1114	(plate)		1311–1314	Thornbury (cont.)
1115–1119	Old Sodbury (cont.)		1315–1317	Tiberton
1119–1123	Chipping, Little, and Old Sodbury		1318–1323	Tidenham
1124	(plate)		1324–1329	Titherington
1125–1127	Southrop		1329–1331	Todenham
1128	(plate)		1332–1335	Todington
1129–1132	Standish		1336–1339	Tormarton
1133	King's Stanley		1340–1346	Tortworth
1134	(plate)		1346–1348	Tredington
1135–1140	King's Stanley (cont.)		1349–1351	Turkdean
1141	Stanley St. Leonards		1352–1356	Turley & Haw
1142	(plate)		1357–1363	Twining
1143–1147	Stanley St. Leonards (cont.)			

For the parishes from Uley to Yate the list of contents and list of plates (above) similarly provide a collation with the pages of the original edition.

FOREWORD

The publication of the present volume completes the re-issue in four volumes of *Bigland's Gloucestershire Collections*. With the addition of two previously unpublished sections, the inclusion of previously unused illustrations, and the provision of an introdcution and comprehensive indexes, the *Collections* are now far more accessible, and in a fuller form, than at any point between the issue of the first parts, for 22 parishes beginning with the letter A, in 1786 and the publication in 1889 of the volume including Yate, alphabetically the last parish in the county. The original edition was in awkward folio-sized sheets; this new edition, in reduced photographic facsimile, can be consulted and shelved more conveniently. For some further points the reader is referred to the foreword of each of the three preceding volumes.

The introduction below describes the nature of the *Collections* and the circumstances in which they were compiled and first published. The four volumes of the present edition will be of great value primarily to parish historians and family historians. They will also interest students of social and cultural history. The people memorialised in the church and churchyard inscriptions which form the major part of the work range from the wealthiest of aristocrats through the landed gentry, the professional classes, merchants, and tradesman (the middling classes being the most heavily represented), to servants and labourers. They offer, for example, numerous instances of social relationships, of naming practices, and of attitudes to death and the dead. The phrases used to commemorate the dead may be elegant, or learnedly Latin, or euphuistic, or bathetic. The inscriptions remind the reader of the high level of child mortality, and of the frequency of death at health resorts such as Cheltenham, Bath, and Clifton. They reflect the strongly localised nature of society in the seventeenth and eighteenth centuries, while at the same time recalling the links of Gloucestershire people with London and more distant parts of Great Britain, and indeed with the far corners of the world.

Acknowledgements
The editor of the four volumes of Bigland's *Collections* in the present series wishes to acknowledge with gratitude the help which he has received from a number of sources. The late Irvine Gray gave a detailed account of the Bigland family and of the work of Ralph Bigland in an article in the *Transactions of the Bristol and Gloucestershire Archaeological Society*, volume 75 (1956). Gray's successor as County Archivist, Mr. Brian Smith, who had begun further work on Bigland's *Collections*, generously lent the present editor his notes, which were of great use, and gave much encouragement. Mr. David Smith, the present County and Diocesan Archivist, initiated the re-issue of Bigland's work and was general editor of the Record Series over the period in which the first three volumes of the *Collections* were published; he gave invaluable advice and encouragement, and did much to make the editor's task easier. Mr. E. F. M. Prince of Tetbury has written about Bigland and collected much material for the study of his

work; he has deposited notes and numerous photocopies in the Gloucestershire Record Office and has kindly allowed the material to be quoted from freely. The *Bibliographer's Manual of Gloucestershire Literature* sets out in great detail the problems and complexities of the printing and publication of Bigland's *Collections*. The staff of the Gloucestershire Record Office, and in particular Mrs. Kate Haslem and her colleagues in the Search Room, have given endless help in ways that made working in that office a pleasure.

The Society is indebted to the kindness of Mr. L. J. Hill, who has greatly added to the value of the present edition by allowing the previously unpublished inscriptions from the churches of St. Phillip and St. Jacob, Bristol, and St. George, Bristol, to be included in the present volume. The work of Mrs. Irene Wyatt in undertaking the enormous task of indexing the *Collections* has greatly increased the usefulness of all four volumes; separate indexes of persons, of places, of occupations and offices, and of causes of death are included in the present volume.

The Society also expresses its deep gratitude to Mr. Brian Frith for his work in editing the reprint of Bigland's *Collections*, the value of which is enhanced by Mr. Frith's illuminating introduction included in the present volume.

CHRISTOPHER ELRINGTON
General Editor, Gloucestershire Record Series

INTRODUCTION

Ralph Bigland's massive *Historical, Monumental and Genealogical Collections relative to the County of Gloucester* is one of the most remarkable works to have been published for the county. No other county has anything comparable. To those interested in genealogy and heraldry or in local history it is an important source. Bigland did not share the normal eighteenth-century view that parish and county history should notice the epitaphs only of the nobility and gentry. He attempted the most unusual task of recording all the inscriptions, grand or humble, inside and outside, of the parish churches of Gloucestershire. (He did not collect inscriptions from any of the nonconformist chapels in the county.) It is the inclusion of the epitaphs for the more humble folk that makes his work so valuable today. Many of the inscriptions are no longer legible, and some were difficult even for Bigland and his helpers to read, being in high or dark corners of a poorly lit church or overgrown in a churchyard.

Bigland's early intention was to produce an updated version of Sir Robert Atkyns's *Ancient and Present State of Gloucestershire*, published in 1712, and to include the epitaphs which Bigland himself had collected, together with a *Genealogical Account of all the Principal Families in the County*. His work in the College of Arms delayed his plans, so that when Samuel Rudder brought out his *History* of the county in 1779[1] Bigland decided to confine himself to publishing the epitaphs, together with genealogical tables of many families. He included historical notes for the several parishes, but in a less ambitious form than originally intended. The editors of the later sections of the work added much historical matter, including the devolution of estates, the church, population, and taxation, and Sir Thomas Phillipps added some pedigrees seemingly of his own compilation. Bigland's own genealogical tables never appeared. Bigland also planned to include tricks of the coats of arms of the principal county families, but the plan was discontinued after the first volume of the original edition. The coats of arms that were published are reproduced at the end of each of the first two volumes of the present edition. Today the value of Bigland's work lies mainly in the inscriptions which in profuse number form the bulk of the *Collections*.

Having laid careful plans for his great work, Bigland died before any of it appeared in print. The work began to be issued in unbound parts in 1786, and the first 22 parts were published as two volumes in 1791 and 1794, covering 180 parishes in alphabetical order as far as Newent. Further publication was delayed, apart from the inclusion of the Gloucester inscriptions in T. D. Fosbrooke's *History of Gloucester* in 1819, until 1838 when a part was issued that included another 18 parishes, as far as Pauntley. The remaining parishes, as far as Yate, were issued in parts in a confused

---

[1] Samuel Rudder, *A New History of Gloucestershire* (Cirencester, 1779); reprinted 1977.

way between 1870 and 1889, to form with those issued in 1838 what may be regarded as Volume Three of the original edition of the *Collections*.[2]

The importance of monumental inscriptions to the genealogist and the local historian has been discussed by Donald Steel and by the late Frederick Burgess.[3] Burgess says that the earliest memorials were made of wood, but no such examples have been recorded for Gloucestershire. He also says that few churchyard inscriptions survive from the sixteenth century or the early seventeenth, and implies that few were ever erected. Fosbrooke commented that Bigland's inscriptions were 'truly valuable because they relate to that period when the mutilation of them is considered legitimate, by sextons, workmen, and school-boys.'[4] Latin inscriptions were widely used until about the end of the seventeenth century and continued well into the next century. They seem to have been confined to the families of the more important inhabitants, and presumably meant little to most country parishioners.

Ralph Bigland and his family

Those who wish fully to study the ramifications of the Bigland family will find details in a paper by Irvine Gray,[5] which nevertheless leaves unanswered a number of questions about the antiquary himself. It is by no means clear why Bigland embarked on a work devoted entirely to Gloucestershire, for none of his roots were there. Perhaps the strongest reason was that his wife came from Gloucestershire, and his son lived in the county all his life. The Bigland family came from Westmorland: Ralph's father Richard was born at Bigland Hall, near Kendal, in 1658. Richard, a lawyer of Gray's Inn, in 1708 married Mary, daughter of Ralph Errington of Newcastle-upon-Tyne. Their son Ralph was born on 29 January 1711/12 and baptised on 30 January at St. Dunstan's, Stepney.

When Ralph Bigland was only thirteen years old his father died. Of his education we know nothing, and neither Oxford nor Cambridge can claim him. The future herald and antiquary seems to have started his career as a cheesemonger; he was probably apprenticed to a Mr. Olive, of New Crane, Wapping, where he was living with his master in October 1731. The trade in cheese took him to the Low Countries, where he spent much time. In May 1745, during the War of the Austrian Successsion, Bigland was in Flanders selling cheese, almost certainly to the British contingent of the allied army. He watched the battle of Fontenoy, from a safe distance, and in his letters wrote of what he saw of the conflict.[6]

In the late 1730s and early 1740s he was copying epitaphs in the Low Countries. He later remarked that the epitaphs there often gave genealogical information beyond that which one would expect to find in epitaphs in England and Scotland. His study of continental inscriptions formed the basis of ideas which he published in 1764,

[2] The complicated sequence of the publication of the various parts of the *Collections* is set out in detail in F. A. Hyett and W. Bazeley, *Bibliographer's Manual of Glos. Literature*, vol. i (1895), pp. 31–44.

[3] Donald Steel, *National Index of Parish Registers* (Soc. of Genealogists, 1966), vol. 1; Frederick Burgess, *English Churchyard Memorials* (Lutterworth Press, 1963).

[4] T. D. Fosbrooke, *An Original History of the City of Gloucester* (1819), p. vi. The book was reprinted in 1976.

[5] Irvine Gray, 'Ralph Bigland and his Family,' *Transactions of the Bristol and Glos. Arch. Soc.* vol. 75 (1958), pp. 116–33.

[6] G.R.O., E. F. M. Prince papers, R.O.L. G.3, the source for references in this introduction to Bigland's letters.

suggesting that parish registers should include certain items of information.[7] His ideas were sensible and ahead of their time; few have been adopted.

In the early 1730s Bigland's mother's brother-in-law, John Stodart of Newcastle, had helped to compile a pedigree of his mother's maternal family, the Babingtons, to prove a claim to certain coalmines at Heaton (Northumberland), the results of which were to help the family fortunes. Bigland spent much time in making additions to his pedigree and became a genealogical enthusiast, spurred on by inducements other than the financial rewards of his uncle's researches. The cheese trade continued to keep him reasonably prosperous. He lived for a while at Leith in Scotland, and about 1748 seems to have been supplying warships with cheese.

It was probably the cheese trade that took him to Gloucestershire, where he met John Wilkins, a substantial Frocester farmer and supplier of cheese. At Frocester on 13 June 1737 Bigland, then described as of the city of London, married Wilkins's daughter Anne.[8] Their son Richard, later to play a leading part in publishing his father's work, was born on 3 April 1738. When he was only a few months old his mother died: it has been stated that she was only 22, but the Wilkins monument at Frocester gives her age as 25.[9]

Still travelling in connection with his business, Ralph Bigland would have had difficulty in bringing up his young son. His father-in-law, writing to commiserate with his loss, offered to look after 'dear Dicky' at Frocester, and Richard lived there the rest of his life. He was well looked after by his grandparents. His father's visits were, it seems, limited: when his son was about nine, Ralph Bigland wrote from Leith, 'I am pleas'd to hear he is grown taller. I must own I could delight to see him, but the distance is so great its not easily done.' At the same time he reported that the people in Scotland were good cheese eaters.

For Richard's education his grandparents sent the boy to the rector of Duntisbourne Rouse, Edward Ford, and his wife Elizabeth. Ford wrote on 19 December 1749, 'Master Bigland . . . is . . . as fine a boy as any in England,' a cheering opinion for his father. Ralph Bigland's concern for the formation of his son's character shows in a letter which he wrote from York Place, Battersea, on 2 June 1753. He advised his son, then fifteen, 'Behave with civility and good manners to every individual person . . . even with your grandfather's servants . . . but never make yourself too familiar or free with servants. For you must always think within yourself that you are better than them.'

Nowhere in his letters to his son and his father-in-law did Ralph Bigland hint that he was considering a fundamental change of occupation. Writing to Richard from Battersea on 12 February 1757 he did not mention that he was about to abandon the cheese trade, but eleven days later he took up his duties as Bluemantle Pursuivant at the College of Arms. He may have been helped and encouraged in making the move by the duke of Norfolk, for the Howards had 'for many years patronised my late

---

[7] Ralph Bigland, *Observations on Marriages, Baptisms, and Burials, as preserved in Parochial Registers, with Sundry Specimens of the Entries of Marriages, Baptisms, &c., in foreign Countries,* London, 1764. G.R.O., R.O.L. H.1. The G.R.O. copy has some alterations in Ralph Bigland's hand. In this treatise Bigland quotes an entry in Frocester parish register recording Queen Elizabeth's visit in 1574, which he states was a 'literal copy'. Surprisingly his copy does not exactly follow the original.

[8] G.R.O. P153 IN 1/2.

[9] Above, part 2, p. 631.

father and his family.' His new career had been foreshadowed not only by his work on the Bigland family pedigree and on the epitaphs in the Low Countries but also by his embarking, about 1750, on his great Gloucestershire undertaking.

From the time of his election to the College of Arms his genealogical interests grew, and he went through all the heraldic offices, becoming Garter Principal King of Arms in 1780. His notebooks and pedigrees are a testimony to his great enthusiasm for a herald's work and he was undoubtedly an ornament to the offices which he held, working conscientiously at his duties. Acording to Sir Anthony Wagner, most of Bigland's papers were left to his nephew and namesake 'who added to them and whose executor sold the whole to the College [of Arms] in 1839. Of forty-nine volumes, twenty-five are mainly the elder Bigland's and comprise pedigrees, copies of monumental inscriptions, abstracts of wills and an interesting collection of heraldic bookplates'.

On 29 September 1758 Ralph Bigland, a widower for nearly twenty years, married for a second time, at St. Michael's, Crooked Lane, London, his wife being Anna, daughter of Robert Weir. She died in 1766; Ralph's son Richard, away in Frocester, learnt of her death only through a third party. Richard's grandfather, the worthy John Wilkins, had died on 9 March 1758, aged 64. Much to Ralph Bigland's disappointment, Wilkins left Richard only £200 in money. Writing to his son some eleven days after Wilkins's death, Ralph said 'I was in hopes he would have left you some more money, for £200 is but a small matter to begin the world with in business. However, as your grandfather has been kind enough to give you the house with all its furniture, and the land you mention, take it all together it is a pretty thing . . . and with God's blessing and a good wife by and by, I hope you will do very well. But of all things I recommend and am quite of Mr. Wilkins's opinion that you offer your services to Mr. Oatridge [Richard's uncle][1] and I have no doubt if they will please to accept of you, but they will allow you I hope at least £50 per annum which with your income from your other sources, will for the present afford you a comfortable subsistence'.[2]

Thus, with his son well set up in Gloucestershire, Bigland was able to pursue his work at the College of Arms, as an outstanding herald, genealogist, and artist, with a vast amount of material by him, collected for publication, and with yet more to be gathered in. He also had the use of the considerable library of the College. He was, in many ways, a contented man, and even before taking on his heraldic duties he wrote to Richard on 12 February 1757, 'I thank God I am not without being respected in the world, which is my happiness. I have nothing else to boast of and this I depend more upon than anything else.' Later, his office at the College presumably made him even happier.

Something which did disturb Ralph Bigland in his later years was the behaviour of his adopted son, Ralph Owen, a son of Ralph Bigland's sister, Elizabeth Maria. Ralph Owen changed his name from Owen to Bigland,[3] a change which later caused confusion between uncle and nephew, pursuing, as they did, similar occupations and interests. The elder Ralph managed to get the younger into the College of Arms, and

---

[1] Miles Oatridge, of Coaley, married Sarah, another daughter of John Wilkins, 11 December 1746, at Frocester. G.R.O. P153 IN 1/2.

[2] John Wilkins in his will also left Ralph Bigland £20, and the same sum to his other sons-in-law, Arthur Jepson of Bristol and Miles Oatridge.

[3] Born 1 May 1757, he took the name and arms of Bigland 21 Oct. 1774.

the younger Ralph, knighted in 1831, died in 1838 also as Garter King.[4] In his younger days the nephew lived with his uncle, and was a cause of anxiety and annoyance. Writing to his son Richard at Frocester, the uncle recounted the young Ralph's misbehaviour, and reported, 'That night I knew [that] he lay not in his usual bed, upon which Molly said to him the next day, You did not lie at home last night. His answer was to her that he was married, since which he has lain no more with us. However, he dines with us daily. Nancy does not know it yet, but she observed that her Cousin Ralph is not with us as he used to be, what can be the reason of it? He has every day since been assiduous writing at Mr. Heard's[5] till 8 or 9 at night, which is the same as for myself. I am so angry with him and so discomposed at the thoughts of it that sometimes I hardly know what I am doing, so that at present I had rather have him out of my sight than in it. He daily grows worse and worse'.

In spite of family worries, Ralph Bigland continued his busy working life right to the end, and died in his room at the College of Arms on 27 March 1784, his great work on Gloucestershire incomplete and unpublished. He had made his will on 24 May 1782[6] and in it requested that 'as soon as conveniently after I die my body to be put into a strong coffin made of English oak of one inch thick, and I desire that my body may not be too hastily buried but kept at least ten days prior thereto'. The oak coffin was to be put into another coffin made of lead 'about ten pounds weight to the superficial square foot'. If he died in London he wished to be buried in Christ Church, Newgate Street, where his parents were married, and in the same vault as his former colleague, Peter Dore, Norroy King of Arms.[7] If the fee for burial there was likely to exceed £5 he wished to be buried in St. Stephen's, Walbrook. If he died in Gloucestershire he wished to be buried in the body of the cathedral 'in a brick grave or vault' covered as before described and with a 'black Namur marble grave stone (which of all stones are most durable and never scale)'. He left £100 to the poor of Frocester, later invested in ground called Wet Mead in Coaley. He left a similar sum to George Bigland, of Bigland, Lancashire, 'the worthy chief of our family', together with a number of other bequests, and the bulk of his estate went to his son Richard in Frocester. He did not forget his genealogical friend, the Revd. William Holwell of Thornbury, to whom he left 5 guineas to buy a ring. Holwell seems to be the only person whom he remembered in his will for helping with the *Collections*, which suggests that Holwell was one of the few local people, perhaps the only one, to give any appreciable assistance to Ralph Bigland. Holwell's help may have been greater than the other evidence implies.

---

[4] *The Bigland Pedigree Index* (Harleian Soc. Publications, new series, vol. 9, 1990) refers to the pedigrees in the genealogical MSS. of Sir Ralph Bigland in the College of Arms, and implies that the nephew was a man of considerable stature, whose genealogical production 'stands today as being of far greater importance than the activities of his better known namesake.' Of the 49 volumes held by the College, four specifically relate to pedigrees, and Volumes XIX and XX relate to Gloucestershire families. It is said that a Mr. Chinn, clerk to Ralph Bigland, had the MS. of the pedigrees, but in 1845 Sir Charles Young, Garter King, had them.

[5] Later Sir Isaac Heard (1730–1822), Garter King on the death of Ralph Bigland in 1784.

[6] P.R.O., PROB 11/1115 (P.C.C. Rockingham 187).

[7] Peter Dore, F.S.A., born at Little Hinton, Wilts., died 27 Sept. 1781 aboard the East-Indiaman *Dutton* at Gravesend.

Although Bigland did not die in Gloucestershire it was there that he was buried, in the north aisle of Gloucester cathedral on 8 April 1784. His son, obviously proud of his father, later erected an elaborate memorial, which sets out considerable genealogical information, fitting for one who had been such an enthusiast for genealogy. The memorial also put into practice suggestions which Ralph Bigland had made years before when deploring the paucity of information often to be found on memorials in this country, unlike those which he had admired in the Low Countries. Ralph Bigland wrote an inscription for his own epitaph. It was found slipped between the pages of the copy of the *Collections* in the library of the Bristol and Gloucestershire Archaeological Society, given by Mr. Geoffrey Sanders. The inscription in the cathedral follows Ralph Bigland's draft almost word for word, but where it reaches 'Richard Bigland of Frocester' it omits, perhaps because of Richard's modesty, the 'Esqr.' which Ralph had intended to put after his son's name. The inscription continues 'He married secondly Anna, daughter of Robert Weir of Douglas in Scotland by whom he had two children who did not survive him'. That differs from Ralph Bigland's draft, where he had written 'by whom he had no issue.' It is possible that the draft was written before the children were born. The inscription also gives details of other families from which Ralph Bigland was descended, such as the Erringtons and the Babingtons. The fine memorial is a concentration of genealogical and biographical matter unlike all the others around it. It is a fitting monument for one who was a giant of a genealogist and herald.[8]

Loosely attached to the monument was the badge of Garter, clearly to be seen on the engraving in Fosbrooke's *History of Gloucester*. (The plate was the gift of Bigland's nephew, then Norroy King of Arms.) The badge was stolen some years ago, discovered for sale in a local shop, and bought back by one who recognised it. At the time of writing it is on display elsewhere in the cathedral, not in its rightful place. Bigland's arms, exemplified in 1760, are given as quarterly with crescent for difference: (1) azure, 2 ears of big (wheat) for (Bigland); (2) argent, 2 bars with 3 scallops in chief gules (Errington); (3) argent, 10 roundels gules (Babington); (4) or, a fret sable (Ward). Crest: on a torse or and azure a lion passant looking backwards gules and holding in the dexter paw an ear of big or. Motto: *Gratitudo* (over crest).[9]

By the time of his father's death Richard Bigland was well established and living in Frocester Court, and he could be regarded as a man of Gloucestershire. Probably his visits to London were rare, but when in 1765 he did go there to see his father he was taken seriously ill and his father said that it took four, five, or six people to be constantly with him in order to keep him in bed 'he was so strong and outrageous', with relapse after relapse, but the nature of the illness is not clear. Richard Bigland married Mary Raymond of Thornbury, by whom he had three daughters. Before his marriage Richard Bigland wrote to his father, 'Her name is Raymond . . . well respected and esteemed. Her fortune I am pretty well assured from good authority is above £2,000 independent, having no father or mother.' They were married on 29

---

[8] Richard Bigland paid £224 6s. for the funeral 'and all demands', the receipt signed by William Lyne being dated 28 June 1785. Gloucester cathedral received £2 'for the funeral of Ralph Bigland Esqre . . . in the body of the church': G.R.O. D936 A 1/8.

[9] *The College of Arms* (London, 1963). The College has a portrait of Bigland as Somerset Herald, by Richard Brompton (d. 1782). It is reproduced in *Transactions of the Bristol and Glos. Arch. Soc.* vol. 75, facing p. 120.

October 1768 by licence in St. Mary de Lode, Gloucester, when she was described as 'of the College Precincts'.[1] Aged nearly 46 when his eminent father died in 1784, Richard was locally a man of some consequence. Like his father and grandfather he was active in the cheese trade and had become a considerable authority on the subject. William Marshall (1745–1818) in his *Rural Economy of Gloucestershire*, first published in 1789, referred to all the cheese produced in the Vale of Berkeley as being purchased 'by what are called "cheese factors", though in reality, CHEESE MERCHANTS. About the whole production of the Vale of Berkeley passes through the hands of two men: MR. BIGLAND of FROCESTER, and MR. HICKS of Berkeley.' Marshall derived his information about the manufacture of cheese in that district from details gleaned at Frocester, where cheese was produced as well as collected. He tells us that he visited the dairy of Mr. Bigland, 'the man most capable of giving me information in every department of the subject. As proprietor of a dairy of more than fifty cows the business of a dairy farm is familiar to him. And, as a man of science, he has paid more attention to the minutiae of the art . . . than any other man.'

Of Richard's three daughters, two lived to adulthood: Anna-Maria married Ambrose Gilbert King, a cheese factor of Bristol, and Clarence (born the year that Ralph Bigland became Clarenceux King of Arms) married Daniel Ellis Saunders of Gloucester. In spite of his leading position in the cheese trade, Richard seems to have been declared a bankrupt on 12 April 1797. Most of his property is said to have been bought up by his son-in-law, Ambrose King. Richard Bigland was buried at Frocester on 27 August 1810, where his wife had been buried on 17 August 1792.[2] The Biglands of Gloucestershire kept in contact with their northern relatives. A daughter of a cousin of Ralph Bigland, Mary Stodart, married Henry Garlick of Frocester, and the Garlicks' daughter Mary married Drinkwater Scott Hayward of Frocester, from whom numerous descendants stemmed. One descendant was a Mrs. Evill of Chepstow, who *c.* 1950 possessed Ralph Bigland's Garter seal and tabard.

The editing and publication of the Collections
By the time of Bigland's death in 1784 the bulk of the work was presumably ready for publication, at least in the form which Bigland intended. That form omitted much of the additional material found particularly in the parishes towards the end of the alphabet. It was Bigland's son Richard who, though neither a genealogist nor an heraldic expert, set about getting his father's work into print. With the help of the Revd. James Dallaway, he updated a number of points, and the first of 22 parts, covering the six parishes Abenhall to Alderton, appeared in 1786. Dallaway did most of the editorial work, at Richard Bigland's expense, and they brought out Volumes One and Two in 1791 and 1794, covering 180 parishes. That was an excellent start, but publication then lapsed.

Richard Bigland's attempts to finalise the work for publication suffered many delays. The Revd. William Lloyd Baker of Uley expressed a wish to see the proof sheets for Mitcheldean before they were published, and Bigland duly sent them to him, on 1 October 1789, adding 'any corrections or additions that Mr. Baker can make would be highly acceptable, and gratefully acknowledged.' No such amendments were acknowledged, and the reason for Baker's interest in the Forest parish is not apparent. Offers and failures of other outside help probably delayed publication.

[1] G.R.O. P154/12 IN 1/11.
[2] G.R.O. P153 IN 1/3.

By 1794 the collaboration between Bigland and Dallaway was not a happy one. Acrimonious letters in the *Gloucester Journal* of 27 January, 17 February, and 10 March 1794 stated that Richard Bigland had 'liberally paid' Dallaway for making 'extracts &c.' and refuted Dallaway's claim to own Ralph Bigland's unpublished papers. Dallaway wrote from the College of Arms as if employed there, but although he often worked there he held no official position in the College at the time. Richard Bigland pointed out that Dallaway had been 'hospitably entertained under the friendly roof of my cousin Ralph Bigland, Richmond Herald.' He also referred to a loan of £50 which he had made to Dallaway, who kept postponing repayment. Dallaway said that he must defer further work on the Bigland papers as he had taken a post (as chaplain) at the Porte, in Constantinople; he had entrusted the papers to someone well qualified to carry on the work, but that person's identity was not revealed. In any case, Richard Bigland objected to the arrangement.

Dallaway, born in Bristol on 20 February 1763, was 23 when Bigland's work began to appear in print. The son of a banker who lived for a time at the Fort at Rodborough, Dallaway received his early education at Cirencester grammar school and proceeded to Trinity College, Oxford. He lived for a while in Gloucester, and took the degree of M.B. at Oxford in 1794. At some point he seems to have been secretary to the Earl Marshal, through whom he secured ecclesiastical livings in Sussex. On 26 June 1800, when described as of the parish of St. Benedict, near Paul's Wharf, London, he married, at St. Michael's church in Gloucester, Harriet Anne Jefferis (or Jefferies), daughter of Alderman John Jefferies of Gloucester.[3] He died in 1834. He achieved distinction as a topographical and miscellaneous writer,[4] and, notwithstanding his disagreement with Richard Bigland, as a young man he was effective in getting a large part of Ralph Bigland's *Collections* published.

The editors were fortunate in having as printer and publisher John Nichols (1745–1826), himself an author and antiquary and the publisher of the *Gentleman's Magazine* from 1778. After the printing of the earlier parts of Bigland's *Collections*, a fire at his London premises in 1808 destroyed all the remaining copies of the work.[5] Some criticism of the factual information in the early parts of the *Collections* appeared in the *Gentleman's Magazine* for 1791, signed 'D.H.',[6] and in the same journal for 1793 'Glevensis' defended the work against more wide-ranging critics and added, 'Useless as the compilation is declared to be, it is acknowledged by several practitioners in the law resident in Gloucestershire, that they have been enabled to clear up titles to estates solely by consulting these sepulchral tables.'[7] One of the critics seems to have been Sir John Sinclair, possibly he of that name (1754–1835) who was the first president of the Board of Agriculture and is credited with having introduced the words 'statistics' and 'statistical'.

After Richard Bigland and Dallaway the next person to edit Bigland's Gloucestershire papers was the Revd. Thomas Dudley Fosbrooke (1770–1842), in compiling his history of the city of Gloucester. He had been approached by John

---

[3] G.R.O. P154/14 IN 1/9.

[4] *D.N.B.*

[5] By a strange coincidence, almost a century earlier a fire at William Bowyer's in London destroyed most of the stock of Sir Robert Atkyns's *Gloucestershire*.

[6] Vol. lxi (part 2), p. 725, citing errors and doubts about Elkstone church, some Berkeley monuments, and a figure at English Bicknor.

[7] Vol. lxiii (part 2), p. 687.

Nichols to continue, perhaps in a more modest form, the work begun by Richard Bigland and Dallaway, but he decided to limit himself to a history of the city which would incorporate the epitaphs which Ralph Bigland had amassed for Gloucester. The book appeared in 1819, printed by John Nichols and Son,[8] and the inclusion of the inscriptions greatly added to its value. Fosbrooke stated 'The epitaphs collected by Mr. Bigland form a MS octavo volume, in a neat small hand, written on both sides, *four inches thick!*[9] Genealogy was his study, and pedigrees are title-deeds, which, if it was a general custom, as among Jews (and Arabians, in reference to horses) to preserve in families, the suitors in chancery would be diminished one half. To have given all the epitaphs in full, would have ruined the book, by excess of heavy matter, or enormous price . . . Eulogies, no longer of interest, because the parties are forgotten, are sometimes suppressed.' The suppression is regrettable, but Fosbrooke set out many of the inscriptions at length. It is doutbful that any of them would be in print without Bigland's work, and some of the churches and burial grounds have since disappeared, together with their monuments.

John Nichols acquired the other unpublished material collected by Ralph Bigland, and either he kept it elsewhere than in his printing house or it came to him after the fire of 1808, which would otherwise have destroyed it. Having failed to enlist subscribers to the publication of the remainder of Bigland's work, he found a ready purchaser in Sir Thomas Phillipps, the antiquary and manuscript collector. Phillipps was born at 32 Cannon Street, Manchester, on 2 July 1792, the illegitimate son of Hannah Walton, the father being a wealthy cotton manufacturer, Thomas Phillipps, who not only acknowledged the boy as his son, but did all that he could to help him make his mark in the world. The father bought estates on the Worcestershire–Gloucestershire borders, including Middle Hill at Broadway, and sent his son to Rugby and Oxford. At 26 the son succeeded to his father's estates, and in 1821, through the influence of his father-in-law and the duke of Beaufort, he was created a baronet at the age of only 29.

From an early age Phillipps collected historical manuscripts and books, and collecting became his obsession. He set up a private printing press at Middle Hill, and there he printed a variety of antiquarian items. Later he moved to Thirlestaine House in Cheltenham, to accommodate his enormous collection of books and manuscripts, and it was there the he died in 1872.[1] Subsequently, over many years, his lifetime's collections were sold. The Bodleian Library maintains a list of the whereabouts of all manuscripts known to have formed part of the Phillipps collection. His handwriting was and is difficult to decipher, but is immediately recognisable, as are many of his bound volumes of manuscripts, enclosed in boards, all covered with a particularly drab brown or blue paper. Phillipps also compiled many pedigrees, mostly concerning families in the north of the county, and some of these may well have been based on the work of Ralph Bigland. Phillipps also issued a number of parish registers in copies of very doubtful quality.

From his Middle Hill Press Phillipps in 1838 published what were known as the

---

[8] John Nichols was joined by his son John Bowyer Nichols (1779–1863) from about 1796.

[9] Preface, p. v. The MS. octavo volume presumably related entirely to the city of Gloucester.

[1] He was buried at Broadway, Worcs. For Phillipps see A. N. L. Munby, *Portrait of an Obsession* (Constable, 1967).

Bigland Continuations, 50 copies of the *Collections* relating to 18 parishes, from Newington to Pauntley. It was not the finest of printings, being on poor paper, and the parishes were reprinted in 1886. In 1870 Phillipps had resumed the work of publishing the *Collections*. What he called the second issue incorporated much extra historical matter, gathered by himself from sources which he had acquired in the course of his avid collecting. When he died in 1872 he had reached as far as the parish of Rendcomb.

Phillipps requested his executor, Samuel Higgs Gael, to supervise the further publication of Bigland's work, and seven more parts appeared between 1873 and 1889. Gael, a barrister and J. P., was born at Charlton Kings in 1808, son of John Gale and Susanna (née Higgs). Why he changed the spelling of his name is not clear. He wrote brief accounts of Dowdeswell church and Stowell House and park, and died at Charlton Kings on 17 September 1887. The editing of the *Collections* for the parishes from the Rissingtons to Yate was done by T. Fitzroy Fenwick,[2] a grandson of Phillipps, whose mother had been left the whole of Phillipps's library. Some of the later parts included notes, but not monumental inscriptions, for certain parishes, such as Icomb, which had been added to Gloucestershire under the Act of 1844.[3] Although it had been announced that the further parishes of St. Phillip and St. Jacob, Bristol, and St. George, Bristol, together with an index, would be published, that was never done. The manuscript material for the parishes from Newington to Yate and for the two unpublished Bristol parishes was sold at Sotheby's in 1967 and is now in the possession of Mr. L. J. Hill, of Weymouth, who has permitted the material for the two Bristol parishes to be printed at last in the present volume. Publication of the parishes from Abenhall to Yate had taken more than 100 years to be complete, yet only now can the *Collections* be said to be complete in print.

Gathering the information

It is not clear how Bigland organised the work of collecting and copying the vast number of inscriptions which form the main body of his work, or who compiled the other information included for each parish. Nor is it clear how much he undertook himself: copying tombstone inscriptions in churchyards and dark corners of churches is very much a fair-weather task, and a time-consuming one. Bigland had been an avid copier of epitaphs over many years, both in England and abroad, but there is little evidence of what he did in Gloucestershire. Presumably he did a considerable part of the work, but he evidently had helpers in the county upon whom he relied for careful copying and compilation. For one man by himself, especially for one engaged on work outside the county, the task would have been overwhelming.

From Bigland's correspondence we know that he was in Gloucestershire only occasionally.[4] Evidence that he had numerous contacts at his disposal is lacking, but

---

[2] Thomas Fitzroy Phillipps Fenwick, M.A., of Thirlestaine House, Cheltenham, born 30 Aug. 1856, son of the Revd. John Edward Addison Fenwick, late vicar of Needwood, Staffs., who married 4 July 1848 Katherine Somerset Wyttenbach, youngest daughter and coheir of Sir Thomas Phillipps.

[3] Cf. *Glos. and Bristol Atlas* (Bristol and Glos. Arch. Soc. 1961), p. 24.

[4] In Thornbury 23 Oct. 1766 he certified the death in 1726 of the Thornbury surgeon Peter Dore: G.R.O. P330 IN 1/4. At Eastleach Turville 24 Sept. 1770 he witnessed a marriage: G.R.O. P130 IN 1/3. Perhaps he was in that part collecting inscriptions.

one or two are known to have been willing and able to supply reliable material. Probably the most productive was William Holwell, vicar of Thornbury from 1762. He died there at the age of 72 and was buried on 17 February 1798. Holwell's contribution is recorded briefly in the *Collections* under Thornbury.[5] A manuscript volume in Gloucester Library (in Sir Thomas Phillipps's unmistakable binding) of parish notes for Bigland includes monumental inscriptions in Holwell's hand. In his covering note of 23 June 1767 Holwell wrote 'You see I am willing to help fill your new book. Your son was so kind as to call the very day I was at Acton [? Iron Acton].' Holwell also sent notes to Sir Isaac Heard at the College of Arms. Possibly he also sent inscriptions from other parishes in the Thornbury area.

Another known helper was the Revd. H. G. Dobyns Yate, of Bromsberrow. As late as 1780 Bigland, then Clarenceux Herald, wrote to him from London, 'Owing to my being lately engaged in the neighbourhood of Bristol, I have not long returned to this place. . . . I never advertized publickly my intentions of reprinting Sr Robert Atkins History, with additions, but owing to the encrease of business in this office, I could not get on with it so fast as I once intended and Mr Rudder having forestall'd me, I shall now so model my publication and make it more an history of the inhabitants of the shire itself, yet some acc't of the shire itself I shall give.' The pedigrees or histories of the inhabitants never appeared, though Sir Thomas Phillipps included some pedigrees in the later volumes; how far they were the work of Bigland we do not know. His letter to Dobyns Yate continued, 'I should be glad to be inform'd to what saint Bromesberrow church is dedicated & when built and by whom? Who is lord of the manor, the present incumbent, when instituted, the respective patron & name. When doth the parish register begin? An extract of the first marriage, baptism, and burial, or any particulars relative [to] your family.' If Bigland enquired in this way of every parish, he used a vast amount of other people's work, and of varying quality and reliability.

A person who played some part, though after Bigland's death, was Barak Longmate (1768–1836), a London genealogist and draughtsman. He helped many antiquaries with their work, including the printer and publisher John Nichols. About 1801 Longmate made notes concerning churches in Gloucestershire, with the intention of bringing out a continuation of Bigland's *History*, but he abandoned the idea after the fire at Nichols's printing works in 1808. No doubt through Nichols, Longmate's notes eventually passed into the collections of Sir Thomas Phillipps, and Longmate's material was very probably incorporated in the later parts of the *Collections*. Longmate evidently copied inscriptions from several Gloucestershire churches. A note relating to the memorial for the Parker and Leigh families at Pucklechurch says 'This was omitted in Longmate's copy'.[6] That suggests that he had been commissioned to add to the material already collected.

Of the large amount of Bigland's correspondence that survives, there is little that relates to the work for which he is chiefly remembered. In his preface to the first volume, written when he was Garter King of Arms and therefore about 1780, he said that he had begun collecting monumental inscriptions 'about thirty years ago. . . . Though I term it a laborious task, yet it was not an unpleasant one to me, as it tended to encrease my knowledge in that branch of science which has become my profession, and had always been my delight, and likewise furnished me with an agreeable amusement during the leisure hours which I passed in the country.' All we know of

---

[5] Above, part 3, p. 1313.
[6] Above, part 3, p. 996.

Bigland's method of taking down inscriptions is in his letter of 1765 to thank the antiquary George Allen[7] for details of certain inscriptions (not from Gloucestershire), which were well set out and won Bigland's admiration: 'I generally take my inscriptions on three sheets of paper, stitched together, in order to be bound when a sufficient number is collected.'

Acknowledgement of contributors who helped the later editors by updating and extending the information occurs here and there in the *Collections*, though it is not obvious who they were. In the nineteenth century the county had an increasing number of antiquaries, who were sometimes called upon to help with local knowledge. For instance, Canon Samuel Lysons (1806–77) supplied information on patrons, incumbents, and other matters for Rodmarton, of which he became rector in 1833. Canon David Royce (1817–1902), a great collector of books and manuscripts on local history, supplied information on Stow and the Swells, and possibly other parishes in that district. Help with information on Tetbury came from a solicitor of that town, 'Mr. Paul, Junr.', who has not been identified: the Revd. Alfred T. Lee, in his *History of Tetbury* (1857), acknowledged help from Messrs. J. T. and R. C. Paul; Alfred Henry Paul, a Tetbury solicitor born in 1809, wrote on the Paul family in *Gloucestershire Notes & Queries*; and Roland W. Paul wrote on Gloucestershire and Bristol matters. Canon William Bazeley, rector of Matson for nearly 50 years, who died on 12 July 1925 aged 82 at Charlton Kings, contributed notes on Upton St. Leonards and Prinknash. The Revd. F. Bond gave information on the Hungerfords of Windrush. R. Mullings who helped with the parishes of Southrop and Stonehouse seems to have been Richard Mullings (d. 1 Sept. 1877) of the Cirencester legal family and one of the earliest members of the Bristol and Gloucestershire Archaeological Society; in his will he mentioned his many books, paintings, and prints, his antiquarian deeds and manuscripts, and his law books. Slimbridge has supplementary notes supplied by the Revd. Dr. Bloxham, who has not been certainly identified. Walter Lawrence Lawrence (1799–1877) of Sevenhampton and Sandywell Park supplied some of the extensive information on Sèvenhampton; he was the son of William Morris M.P. but changed his name to Lawrence on 25 August 1875.

For some of the later-published parishes the inscriptions were updated by adding those made since Bigland's time, but increasingly the historical information outweighed the inscriptions. Bigland himself had for some places drawn extensively on historians of a much earlier date. For Berkeley and its neighbours he was able to quote 'from the valuable manuscripts of Mr. Smyth'.[8] He also used the manuscript collections of 'the late Mr. Prynne,[9] from which extracts are with great candour permitted by the present possessor, Dodington Hunt Esq.' Some of the preliminary notes to the parish of Northleach are taken from the writings of the much despised Abel Wantner (? 1639–1714), the Gloucester-born antiquary.[1]

---

[7] George Allen (1763–1800), of the Grange, Darlington, a lawyer who collected MSS. and printed some on the private press which he set up in 1768: *English County Histories: a Guide*, ed. C. R. J. Currie and C. P. Lewis (Alan Sutton, 1994).

[8] John Smith or Smyth (1567–1641), steward of the Berkeleys, author of *Lives of the Berkeleys* and of *Men and Armour*, much used by Gloucestershire genealogists.

[9] John Prinn or Prynne (1661 or 1662–1735), lawyer and antiquary, steward of the manor of Cheltenham.

[1] Contemporary historians said that Wantner was 'busie medling in things beyond his station' and 'very little qualify'd for this work.'

Extraneous information

Bigland sometimes included in the introduction to a parish material with little genealogical, heraldic, or historical significance. At Clifton, for example, he referred to the 'infinite variety of curious plants, many of which are peculiar to this soil', growing near the 'clifts'. A lengthy footnote gives a list of the plants, taken 'from a late publication which we adopt.' The list gives the Latin and common names, and says where the plants occurred and in which months they flourished. No other parish has so much botanical detail, though Minchinhampton has a shorter list and a description of the fossils of the district. Under Cirencester we read that in Oakley tithing 'in various parts of these vast woodlands the truffle and other vegetable productions are found.' There are details about the growing of tobacco in Winchcombe, where it 'was first planted in England.' For other parishes there are notes on archaeological sites, and the footnotes refer to rare and learned works, to which, no doubt, Bigland had access in the College of Arms. For Bromsberrow he notes that the parish register records a comet of 1680 'the taile of which was like the blade of a sword'; another comet, two years later, was 'not so formidable,' though it was the one which Halley predicted would return in 1758.

Some of the extraneous items were added by later editors. For instance, the dimensions of the Boddington Oak are taken from a *Practical Treatise on Planting, &c.*, published in 1785, after Bigland's death. For Coates a lengthy discourse on Merino sheep, taken from the travels of 'the ingenious and accurate Mr. John Talbot Dillon',[2] will have had limited interest for the average British antiquary or genealogist. There is a useful and interesting list of portraits which were then to be seen at 'the very ancient mansion at Southam', which Bigland regarded as 'certainly the oldest dwelling-house in this county.' Details are likewise given of the portraits in the mansion house at King's Weston in Henbury, together with lists of Roman coins found in Henbury in the years 1708, 1712, and 1768.

The sporadic inclusion of material of marginal relevance was probably influenced by the particular interests of the people who helped to compile the *Collections*. Bigland wrote that the reader would find in the course of the work 'some few things deserving of notice, which have hitherto passed unobserved. I would not have the reader expect that all the parishes should be equally important or amusing. This, from the nature of things, cannot be. Some must be short and barren as to matter, while others, it is hoped, will make amends.' Certainly the information is sparse for some parishes, such as Norton and Pitchcombe. Some of the places late in the alphabet have relatively full treatment because they were of interest to Sir Thomas Phillipps, who added pedigrees sometimes set in the type used at his Middle Hill Press. Much of his additional information evidently came from the enormous collections of deeds and manuscripts for which he is best remembered.

Reliability of the text

A work as extensive as the *Collections* inevitably contains errors and omissions. It is impossible to be sure about inscriptions that have gone since Bigland's day and were omitted from his lists. That there were omissions is certain. The little chapel of Winson, for example, had interments in its burial ground, but being dependent on Bibury it is dismissed in the *Collections* with the words that it 'has a small chapel, but

---

[2] Later Sir John Dillon, Bt. (1740?–1805), traveller and historical writer: *D.N.B.*

no monuments of consequence.' The implied judgement went against Bigland's intentions and suggests that it came from a contributor whose enthusiasm was relatively weak. At Swindon, near Cheltenham, some four slabs covering vaults under pews near the west end of the south aisle have inscriptions not recorded by Bigland. They may have already been inaccessible in the eighteenth and nineteenth centuries. Many other churchse had hidden epitaphs some of which may remain out of sight to the present day. At Tewkesbury some epitaphs are recorded only in the briefest form, and others are mentioned only by surname; it is noted that checking the names was a lengthy and difficult process process because the church was then being restored, suggesting that the list was updated about 1875. In the restoration of that year 'much of the flagging has been removed in the choir, transepts, and chancel, and thus the means of verifying Bigland's account of the flat stone inscriptions taken away. The nave is boarded off and used for public worship, but it is entirely covered with matting and chairs, &c. Inscriptions on the flat stones cannot be got at to be read.' At Westbury-on-Severn the latest of the recorded stones for the Colchester family is dated 1860, and we are told baldly 'In the church yard are later monuments to other members of this family.' Conscientious recorders may have made every effort to locate epitaphs and read the lettering, but some epitaphs may have been only partly visible and therefore not copied. The less conscientious may have missed or ignored epitaphs.

Gravestones were destroyed or removed after Bigland's time, as before it.[3] In 1691 Robert Crew of Dursley was brought before the Gloucester consistory court accused of 'taking away severall grave stones out of the chancell and converting them to his own proper use.' He admitted that he had taken away one stone and was ordered to bring it back, but whether he did so and whether he had removed others is unrecorded. In May 1819 Pauline Carter of Tewkesbury wrote to the bishop of Gloucester that the sexton of Tewkesbury had removed a gravestone belonging to her family and sold it to John Roberts for £2 10s. and that it was taken to 'the stone cutter to be done for Roberts.'[4] In 1847 the churchwardens of Painswick were accused of removing pews, the pulpit, and gravestones from that church.[5]

The original Preface to the *Collections* includes a note by, presumably, Richard Bigland, that the work was brought down to the year 1781. It was intended that monuments put up since Ralph Bigland's death 'such as can be collected in due course' should be added or put in an appendix, but no appendix appeared. After Ralph Bigland's day the compilation and updating of the material seems to have become less enthusiastic and less thorough. Details for the parish of Whittington, apparently through confusion with Withington, and for Sevenhampton came near to being omitted.

A check of the epitaphs against the corresponding burial registers reveals some discrepancies. The well known epitaph at Berkeley for Dicky Pearce, the earl of Suffolk's fool, suggests that he was buried there on 18 June 1728, but the burial register gives the date 18 June 1725. As the stone was replaced in 1823, with the incorrect date upon it, it is uncertain whether the error was the transcriber's, the

---

[3] The many flat-stones, with inscriptions still remarkably legible, to be seen in the garden of the Old Manor at Twyning appear to have been brought from a Worcestershire church, and none were from Twyning church.

[4] G.R.O. P329 CW 5/8.

[5] G.R.O. B4/1/2036.

printer's, or even the carver's. Misreadings are not totally avoidable, and can arise from confusing 4 with 1, 6 with 9 or 0, 3 with 5. Since the copying was the work of more than one person, the level of care and of skill at deciphering the lettering varied. Some errors are not easily explained: at Little Rissington the inscription for Mary, wife of Robert Glyn the rector, says that she died on 8 June 1668, whereas the register has her burial date as 11 June 1682.

The number of errors seems to be greater for the parishes issued later, where editorial scrutiny was not as thorough as in the first two volumes. Moreover, the updating of the inscriptions in the mid nineteenth century is disappointing: enthusiasm for that side of the work evidently diminished, as the amount of historical information that was included increased. It should also be noticed that the quality of printing varied considerably over the years, being lowest in Phillips's time.

The carvers
An army of stonemasons was kept busy carving the monuments. Most of the work was done by local men, but for the more elaborate monuments inside churches sculptors of national repute were used. John Flaxman carved Barbara Bourchier's epitaph at Newent, while Grinling Gibbons's work is to be seen at Great Badminton, along with that of Rysbrack. Frederick Burgess suggested that many local carvers had 'some considerable degree of education, over and above their craft skill. Some have been identified as parish clerks and schoolmasters as well.' In Gloucestershire there is little evidence to support the idea, and had they been well educated their errors would have been fewer. Some of the local carvers can be identified, as in Painswick churchyard, where excellent work is attributed to John Bryan and members of his family.[6] In a wide area around Stroud many inscriptions were made on bronze plates attached to stone monuments, and the lettering is often skilfully executed. Sadly, the plates can become detached through weathering, and some have disappeared.

The illustrations
Bigland says in his Preface that he used 'able artists' to illustrate his work, and the engravings are an important feature. The view of Newent church is the last of those commissioned by Bigland that were included in the *Collections* as first issued. The nineteenth-century editors used other, contemporary illustrations. The views prepared for Bigland but not used in the *Collections* were published separately,[7] and are now included in their intended place for the first time in the present edition.

Bigland himself was the artist for the views of Frampton-on-Severn, Great Barrington, and St. Briavels, while his granddaughter Clarence Bigland drew the views of the chapel at Frocester and the Jenkinson monument at Hawkesbury. For most of the work Bigland employed the highly regarded engraver Thomas Bonnor, a Gloucestershire man. About the artist and engraver Thomas Ravenhill, who produced views of a number of the churches, little is known, but he seems to have been a local man, and may have been an apprentice or collaborator of Bonnor. The name Ravenhill occurred often in the eighteenth century in the area of Elmore, Harescombe, and

---

6 David Verey, *Gloucestershire* (Pevsner's *The Buildings of England*, Penguin, 1970) has a useful section on church monuments, pp. 45–50 in each volume.

7 *A Collection of Proof Prints, engraved for Bigland's History of Gloucestershire as well as those published in that Work, as of those that were Engraved & never published* (c. 1803).

Haresfield, and several children named Thomas Ravenhill were baptised in those parishes. Thomas Ravenhill did the illustrations of the churches in that area, including Haresfield, Quedgeley, and Standish, besides others elsewhere. His work is of a quality worthy to be associated with that of Bonnor.

The views of Badgeworth and Bourton-on-the-Water were the work of T. Pinnell, almost certainly the man who is best known for the Hall and Pinnell Plan of Gloucester of 1780. His views of Badgeworth and Bourton were engraved by H. Mutlow and T. Woodman; Mutlow was probably Henry Mutlow, son of Thomas Mutlow, a Gloucester tailor. He was apprenticed from the Blue Coat school (Sir Thomas Rich's) to a Middlesex engraver, William Darling, in 1770, and became a freeman of Gloucester in 1780, when living at Snow Hill, London.[8] The figures in Berkeley church were drawn by John Carter (1748–1817), described as a draughtsman and architect, who was the artist for illustrations of Gloucester cathedral in 1809.[9]

The cost of employing artists such as Thomas Bonnor was not negligible, given the number of plates. While we do not know how much he or Ravenhill was paid for his work, there is an indication of the cost of other work which Bonnor undertook: Countess Talbot paid him £35 for his view of Barrington Park in Gloucestershire, an engraving somewhat larger than Bigland's plate of the church there.[1] In a letter of 30 June 1769 to George Allen, Ralph Bigland mentioned the cost of an engraving: 'The plate cost about £48; including the first drawing, a correct one for the graver, for which we paid nine guineas, and two guineas for drawing the arms: the remainder to the different engravers for their execution of the work. Upon the whole it is dear enough: but we could not get it cheaper. Good gravers will be paid for what they do.' In the same letter he stated, 'The paper I had for our plate I buy of one Mr. Boydell, one of the first if not the only importer of the proper paper for the copper-plate work in London. It comes chiefly from France; the English made it too smooth or fine for it.'[2]

Some of the illustrations of the earlier parishes appeared in two versions. While the main part of each view is essentially the same, there are slight variations in some of the minor figures. The *Manual of Gloucestershire Literature* notes seven such variants. For instance, the view of Avening church published in Volume One has a dog between the two horses in the foreground, and the plate is unsigned. The variant plate has a man instead of the dog and is signed by T. Ravenhill. The plate of Beverstone in Volume One has a cow standing in the lower left-hand corner, whereas in the variant the cow is lying down. The variant plate of Cheltenham church has, among other minor changes, a man on crutches, absent from the view in Volume One.

The illustrations used by the nineteenth-century editors are in general inferior to the earlier ones. The view of Sevenhampton church has, just visible in the lower left-hand corner, the word 'Graphotype', the name of an American method of printing from a wood block, invented about the year 1869; it is the only one of its kind in the *Collections*.

---

[8] *Freemen of Gloucester* (Glos. Record Series, vol. 4, 1991), p. 158.
[9] *D.N.B.*; *Some Account of the Cathedral Church of Gloucester* (Soc. of Antiquaries, 1809).
[1] The information comes from an interesting case in King's Bench which Bonnor brought unsuccessfully in 1781 against the proprietors of the *Westminster Magazine* for pirating his work.
[2] G.R.O., E. F. M. Prince papers, R.O.L. G.3.

The heraldry

A major part of Bigland's undertaking was that of including the arms of the monuments recorded. The heraldic information in the *Collections* was later brought together and published by Francis Were of Tatenhill near Burton-on-Trent.[3] Were's motives were, first, that the available index to Bigland was very confused and did not cover the parishes from Newent to Yate, and secondly that often the paint had been rubbed off the shields when a church was restored; many shields had become so faded or grimed as to change the meaning. (He suggested that sculptors should hatch the stone surfaces for the various tinctures, which would not prevent correct painting afterwards.) Were did much to interpret the arms and to gather the material so that locating families and their arms is comparatively straightforward. His comments are an important addition to the *Collections*, and he produced useful indexes to personal names and places. There are errors and questionable opinions in his article, which has become dated but is nevertheless most useful. Few genealogists have much knowledge of heraldry, and advice on copying memorial inscriptions is seldom helpful on recording heraldic information. Nevertheless, to ignore or misinterpret the evidence of armorial bearings on monuments is culpable.

BRIAN FRITH
May 1995

---

[3] *Transactions of the Bristol and Glos. Arch. Soc.* vol. 28 part 2 (1905).

ULEY.

THE CHURCH consists of Nave, and Chancel with a low embattled Tower, on the North Side, therein one Bell, and a Gallery round the Church and an Organ, it is dedicated to St. Giles. [The Church has been rebuilt. The Gallery is taken away and Aisles, Spire, &c. are added.]

THE PRESENT LORD OF THE MANOR.

The Right Honble. the Earl of BERKELEY.

Revd. Mr. .... PARTRIDGE, *Rector.*

INSCRIPTIONS IN THE CHURCH.

CHANCEL.

ON FLAT STONES.

Near this Place lies interr'd
the Body of HENRY PEGLER,
of this Parish, *Gent.*
who died 12 day of August 1695,
Aged 85 Years.
He gave a parcel of Land and
10£. in Money to the Vse of
the Poor, of this Parish for ever.
Also the Body of HESTER, his Wife,
who died the 28 day of Nov. 1694,
Aged 69 Years.

Here lyeth the Body of
Mrs. ELIZABETH HART,
2nd. Wife of *Mr.* WILLIAM HART,
Minister, of this Parish,
who departed this Life, the
23 of December, Ano. Do. 1715.

PSALM ye 116.

Return unto thy Rest, O my Soul.

Reader 'tis Wisdom every day to dye,
Consider Death and next Eternity.

In Memory of
HESTER, the Wife of PHILIP HILL,
of the City of *Worcester*, *Gent.*
who died March 30, 1722.

In Memory of
ROBERT SMALL,
who died 28 day of June 1733,
Ætat. 48.
Also of ELIZABETH, his Wife,
who died July 19, 1757,
Aged 72 Years.

In Memory of
ANNE, Daughter of ROBERT and
ELIZABETH SMALL,
who died January 15, 1746,
Ætat. 37.

Here resteth the Body of
WILLIAM, the Son of GEORGE
SMALL, of *Yuley*, *Clothier*,
and three Sons, ob. Infants, *viz.*—
WILLIAM, who died 8 Mh. 1682.
JOHN, who died 27 July 1685.
SAMUEL, who died 9 Decr. 1685.

In Memory of
HANNAH, the Wife of WILLIAM
HAYWARD, of the Parish of *Bisley*,
Clothier, who died February the 7th.
1724.

NAVE.

ON MONUMENTS.

Arms:—Argent, a fess dancette
Sable, betw. three Cornish Choughs
proper.

Near the South Door lyeth the
Body of TIMOTHY THOMAS, *Gent.*
who died June 21, 1746,
Aged 35 Years.
Also two Sons named JOHN;
First died March 3, 1739.
Second died January 27, 1744,
both Infants.
TIMOTHY THOMAS,
died January 12, 1794, Aged 54.
And with his daughter SUSANNAH,
who died an Infant, is buried
in the same Vault.

Arms:—Azure on a Chevron be-
tween threefleurs de Lis Or, three
Mullets round pierced of the first
GYDE. *impaling*—Sable three Cin-
que foils slipt, and on a Chief dan-
cette Or, three Annulets Gules.
Crest:—Out of an Earl's Coronet
Or, three Ostrich feathers Gules.

Near this Place lyeth the Body of
GEORGE GYDE, *Clothier*,
who died September 8, 1743,
Aged 48 Years.
Also three Daughters named HESTER,
First—died Decr. 4, 1718,
Aged Eleven Weeks and four days.
Second—August 8, 1721,
Aged fourteen days,
both Infants.
Third—April 19, 1724,
Aged 3 Years, and three Weeks.
Also of ANNE, Relict of
THOMAS GYDE, who died
March 21, 1751, Aged 57.

Behind this Wall lyes
the Body of JOHN EYLES,
Aged 91 Years,
and the first that ever made
Spanish Cloth in this Parish.
This Monument was erected by
M. BAYLEY, *Gent.* of *Wreisden*,
1731,
I. E.

Arms:—Gules, a Chevron vair
between three Crescents Or. DOR-
NEY. *impaling* Azure a Chevron
compony Or, and Azure, between
three birds Argent.

In Memory of
EDWARD DORNEY, *Gent.*
who died Sept. the 24, 1700,
Ætat. suæ 30.
Also of ELIZABETH DORNEY,
his Widow,
who died Jany. 1, 1732,
Ætat. suæ 61.

ON FLAT STONES.

MARY, the Wife of *Mr.* WILLIAM
VEEL, of *Simonds Hall* in the
Parish of *Wotton*, and Daughter of
Mr. TIMOTHY GYDE,
of this Parish, was here interred
the 17 day of February 1709-10.
TIMOTHY GYDE,
Ob. Decemb. vi, MDCCXXII,
Ætat. 83.

In Memory of
WILLIAM HALLING,
of this Parish, who died
April 24, 1730, Ætat. suæ 71.
And also of ELIZABETH, his Wife,
who died Oct. 14, 1732, Ætat. 77.

Here lyeth the Body of
ANNE, the Wife of SAMUEL
WENT, of this Parish, *Clothier*,
who departed this Life, ye
21 of April 1763, Aged 52.
Also the Body of the said
SAMUEL WENT, *Clothier*,
who departed this Life,
Nov. 5, 1771, Aged 56 Years.
Likewise MARY, wife of
THOMAS WENT, their Son,
Daughter of the late *Alderman*
JOHN BAYLEY, of the City of
Gloucester.
She died Sept. 15, 1779,
Aged 32 Years.
Words are wanting to express
her real worth.

Here lyeth the Bodies of
GEORGE SMALL, *Esqr.*
and MARGARET. his Wife.
He died Decr. 18, 1758,
Aged 81 Years.
She died July 24. 1742,
Aged 59 Years.
Here also are interred the Bodies of

JOHN FOYLE SMALL, *Esqr.*
and MARY, his Wife,
and THOMAS, their Son.
He died December 21, 1761,
Aged 52 Years.
She died Decr. 25*th.* 1755,
Aged 44 Years.
The Son died an Infant.
Here also lyeth Buried
JOHN SMALL, *Esqr.* their Son,
who died January 6, 1778,
Aged 30 Years.

———

Here lies
JOHN WRIGHT, Son of ROBERT
WRIGHT, of the *Ridge* in the
Parish of *Wootton under Edge,*
by ALICE, his Wife, Daughter of
WILLIAM and ELIZABETH HALLING,
of this Parish. He died
Jany. 3*rd.* 1786, Aged 77 Years.

———

Here lies the Body of the
HESTER GYDE,
who died May 4, 1743,
Aged 84 Years.
THOMAS GYDE,
died Sept. 8, 1743, Aged 48 Years.

———

TIMOTHY THOMAS, *Gent.*
1746.
TIMOTHY THOMAS,
1794.

———

Here rest ye Remains of the
Revd. THOMAS GREGORY, A. M.
who discharged with unwearied
diligence the pastoral Office of
the Church 39 Years.
He was released from his Labours
and Afflictions, June 30, 1778,
Aged 62 Years.
Also three Children died young.
Also SUSANNAH, his relict.
who departed this Life,
Sept. 27, 1789, Aged 73.
The *Revd.* JOHN GREGORY, A. M.
Rector of this Parish,
and Son of the above mentioned
THOMAS GREGORY,
died Augt. 12, 1793,
Aged 49 Years.
Also MARY and ELIZABETH,
Daughters of the said
JOHN GREGORY,
MARY, died July 11, 1789,
Aged 9 Years.
ELIZABETH, died Decr. 27, 1789,
Aged 17 Years.

———

ON A BRASS PLATE.

Here resteth the Body of
JOSEPH JOINTZ, *Gent.*
who departed this Life,
April 2, Anno Dom. 1696,
Ætatis suæ 82.

———

CHURCH YARD.

ON TOMBS.

In Memory of
WILLIAM HOLBROW, *Senr.*

of this Parish, *Gent.* who died
Febr. 23, 1730, Ætat. suæ 84.
Also of MARY, his Wife,
who died Sept. 14, 1683,
and of 2 of his Children;
viz.—MARY and JAMES,
who died in the first Year
of their Age.
Also in Memory of 3 Children of
WILLIAM HOLBROW, *Junr.*
and MARY, his Wife,
viz—WILLIAM, MARY and
ELIZABETH, who died Infants.

———

In Memory of
ANTHONY HOLBROW, *Clothier,*
who died May 19, 1729.
Ætat. suæ 67.
Also ANNE, his Daughter,
who died 22nd. July 1729,
Ætat. suæ 33.
Likewise of 3 of his Children,
ANNE, DANIEL and KATHERINE.
In Memory of
ELIZABETH, the Relict of
ANTHONY HOLBROW, who died
Febr. 8, 1754, Ætat. suæ 86.
In Memory of
WILLIAM, Son of ANTHONY
and ELIZABETH HOLBROW,
who died May 13, 1748,
Ætatis 56.
And for JOHN, the Son of
ANTHONY HOLBROW,
who died 24 May 1730.
In Memory of
WILLIAM HOLBROW, *Clothier,*
who died .... 1741.

———

In Memory of
CHARLES BARNES, of this Parish,
Clothier, who died Decr. 24, 1731,
Aged 48 Years.
Also of MARY, his Wife,
who died Jany. 11, 1731,
Aged 53 Years.
And for 3 of their Sons,
viz.—CHARLES, JAMES and HENRY.

———

Sub hoc marmore
Mortales deponuntur Exuviæ
MARIÆ GREGORY, uxoris
Reverendi THOMÆ GREGORY, A.B.
Filiæ natu minoris CAROLI BARNES,
hujus,
Loci olim Pannificis. Quæ in primo
Puerperio surrepta, optimo juventutis
Flore, ex hac vita placide decessit, Spe.
Melioris quam Virtus et vera Pietas
Morienti expectasse dederant.
Obiit Men. 10, Anno Dom. 1744,
Ætat. 22.

———

In Memory of
THOMAS JACKSON,
who died August the 15, 1756,
in the 62 Year of his Age.

———

To the Memory of
JOHN POYNTZ,
who had two Horses killed under
him at the Battle of *Marston Moor,*
fighting for the Liberties of his
Country, ...
....

JANE, Wife of ONESIPHORUS PAUL,
who died May 26, 1747,
Aged 41 Years.

———

Sacred to the Memory of
SARAH, the Wife of RICHARD
HOPKINS, of *Dursley.*
She died Febr. 15, 1782, Ætatis 63.
Also three of his Sons by
SARAH, his second Wife, *viz.*—
RICHARD, died April 13, 1786,
Aged 1 Year and 11 Months.
CHARLES FREDERICK,
died April 22, 1786, Aged 6 Months.
RICHARD, died April 15, 1794,
Aged 6 Years and 5 Months.
Here lye the Remains of
RICHARD HOPKINS, of *Dursley,*
who departed this Life,
Febr. 21, 1801, Aged 77 Years.

———

Erected to the Memory of
JOHN PRICE,
who departed this Life,
July 23, 1795, Aged 47 Years.

———

Here lie the Remains of
ELIZABETH, Relict of the
Revd. JOHN MAULE.
Vicar of Ringwood, Hants.
and Daughter of WILLIAM and
ANNE HOLBROW, of this Parish,
who died Nov. 14, 1784,
Aged 63 Years.

———

Sacred be this Memorial to
CORNELIUS HARRIS,
of *Wotton-under-Edge,*
who died May 1, 1776,
Aged 51 Years.
MARY, his Wife, who died
May 2, 1783, Aged 55 Years.
ROBERT, their Son, who died
May 11, 1770, Aged 18 Years.
WILLIAM, their Son, who died
June 18, 1783, Aged 29 Years.
THOMAS and DANIEL,
who died in their Infancy.

———

Erected to the Memory of
ANN, the Wife of CORNELIUS
HARRIS, who died May 27, 1759,
Aged 53 Years.
And also of ALICE, their Daughter,
who died June 8, 1763,
Aged 21 Years.
THOMAS and DANIEL, Sons of
CORNELIUS HARRIS, *Junr.*
THOMAS, died March 20, 1756,
Aged 21 Weeks.
DANIEL, died Febr. 16, 1762,
Aged 26 Weeks.

———

In Memory of
THOMAS KNIGHT,
who died June 16, 1794,
Aged 53 Years.
THOMAS, Son of THOMAS and
HANNAH KNIGHT, who died
Decr. 16, 1773, Aged 6 Years.
Also JAMES, their Son, who died
June 20, 1794, Aged 32 Years.

In Memory of
SAMUEL SOULS and ELIZABETH,
his Wife. He died June 5, 1757,
Ætat. 77 Years.
She June 3, 1763, Ætat. 82 Years.
Also WILLIAM, their Son,
died June 11, 1747, Ætat. 37 Years.
Also of ELEANOR, Wife of
DANIEL HALLING, of the Parish
of Cam, who died April 11, 1770,
Aged 52 Years.
Also of SARAH, Wife of
THOMAS GREENING,
Daughter of SAMUEL and
ELIZABETH SOULS.
She died June 22, 1774,
Aged 48 Years.

In Memory of
WILLIAM FOTMAN,
of this Parish, Maltster,
who died September 29, 1793,
Aged 69 Years.
ANN, the Wife of WILLIAM
FOTMAN, who died Jany. 25, 1789,
Aged 62 Years.
ANN, their Daughter,
died April 25 1768, Aged 7 Years.

In Memory of
JOHN ANDREWS, of this Parish,
Maltster, who died June 23, 1769,
in the 66 Year of his Age.

In Memory of
JANE, the Wife of JOHN ANDREWS,
of this Parish, Maltster,
who died May 5, 1754,
in the 44 Year of her Age.
MARY, the Daughter of
JOHN ANDREWS,
who died May 11, 1740,
Aged 2 Months.
ELIZABETH, their Daughter,
who died June 28, 1746, in the
5 Year of her Age.

in Memory of
JOHN WHEELER, of this Parish,
Yeoman, who died Oct. 18, 1774,
Aged 36 Years.
ELIZABETH WHEELER,
his Widow, who died
March 18, 1789, Aged 77 Years.
JOHN, the Son of JOHN WHEELER,
who died July 17, 1672.
Also DANIEL WHEELER,
Clothier, Son of JOHN WHEELER.
He died Augt. 20, 1711,
Aged 26 Years.

In Memory of
JAMES WHEELER, of this Parish,
who departed this Life,
Jany. 18, 1726, Ætat. 45.
ELIZABETH, his Wife,
who died July 6, 1752, Ætatis 52.
In Memory of
NATHANIEL LLOYD, Clothier,
who departed this Life,
January 24, 1764, Aged 45 Years.

In Memory of
THOMAS WENT, of this Parish,

Yeoman, who died Nov. 26, 1772,
Aged 72 Years.
HESTER, his Wife, who died
Oct. 24, 1769, Aged 63 Years.
ANN, their Daughter, who died
March 1, 1757, Aged 15 Years.
SAMUEL WENT,
of this Parish, Yeoman,
who died Augt. 24, 1743,
Aged 74 Years.
ANN, his Wife, who died
Sept. 17, 1751, Aged 77 Years.
SARAH, Daughter of
SAMUEL WENT, Junr.
who died Nov. 9, 1752,
Aged near 3 Years.

To the Memory of
NATHANIEL CHANCE, Son of
DANIEL and ANNE CHANCE,
late of Dudbridge in this County,
who died Oct. 3, 1705,
Aged 33 Years.

ON FLAT STONES.

In Memory of
NATHANIEL ALWAY, who died
Decr. 25, 1771, Aged 39 Years.
SAMUEL, Son of NATHANIEL and
ANNE ALWAY, who died
April 29, 1770, Aged 15 Years.
Also four of their Children that
died in their Infancy.

In Memory of
HESTER, Wife of SAMUEL NICHOLS,
of this Parish, who died
the 18 of Nov. 1750, in the
46 Year of her Age.

This Stone is erected to preserve
the Memory of JOHN WALL,
of Tyley in the Parish of
Wotton under Edge,
who died Nov. 15, 1775,
Aged 64 Years.

THOMAS PEARCE,
departed this Life, ye 17 of
Febr. 1779, in the 65
Year of his Age,
ANN, the Wife of THOMAS
PEARCE, departed this Life,
23 of April 1781, in the
58 Year of her Age.
WILLIAM PEARCE, Son of
THOMAS and ANN PEARCE,
departed this Life, in ye Year 1751.
THOMAS PEARCE, Son of
THOMAS and ANN PEARCE,
departed this Life, in ye Year 1761,
both in their Infancy.
JOSEPH PEARCE, Son of
ANN and THOMAS PEARCE,
departed this Life, 19 of Mar. 1769,
in the 20 Year of his Age.

In Memory of
ROGER LORD, who died
Sept. 3, 1765, Aged 72 Years.
Also ESTHER, his Wife,
died Febr. 17, 1765, Aged 70 Years.
Also MARTHA, Daughter of
WILLIAM and ESTHER LORD,
died Oct. 21, 1766, Aged 3 Years.

[Supplementary Tablets put up in
the Church since Bigland's time.]

ON TABLETS.

Sacred to the Memory of
JAMES SLADE, Esqr.
R. N. Admiral of the Blue,
who fell asleep, Oct. 25, 1846,
Aged 79 Years,
and was interred in the Vault beneath.
Also of CHENEY, his Wife,
who deceased Febr. 15, 1830,
and was buried at Wellington
in Somersetshire.
And five of their 7 Children,
(to whom this Monument is also
erected) who died before their
Father and were interred as below:
CHENEY ELIZABETH,
Aged 14, at Falmouth.
HENRY JAMES,
Aged 21, Midshipman of
H. M. S. Tewcar, drowned
off the Coast of Africa.
LOUISA SOPHIA,
Aged 16, at .... Devon.
HENRY SOTHERON,
Aged 18, at Wellington.
HARCOURT ROE,
A. B. of St. Peter's College,
Cambridge, Aged 26, in the same
place as his Father.
Also are here deposited the
Remains of their beloved Aunt
Mrs. SOPHIA ROE,
who died A. D. 1840, Aged 79.
The two surviving Daughters
who erected this tablet record
with thankfulness that they
all died in the faith.
HEB. xi. 13.

Near this spot lieth the Body of
ELIZABETH DORNEY,
of Bencombe,
who died April 9, 1846,
Aged 90 Years,
the last descendant of an antient
family in the male Line.
She was a faithfull and pious
Church Woman,
A gentle and liberal Neighbour;
She forgot not to do good,
and to distribute and walk
humbly with her God.
This Monument is erected by her
grateful and affectionate Kinsman
the Revd. JOHN HARDING.
Arms:—DORNEY.

In a Vault at the entrance of the
Chancel from the body of the
Church are interred the Remains of
MARY, the beloved Wife of the
Revd. WILLIAM LLOYD BAKER,
of Stoutshill, in this Parish.
She died Febr. 5, 1819, leaving
Issue only THOMAS JOHN-
-LLOYD BAKER, of Hardwick Court,
near Gloucester, Esqr.
She was Daughter and sole surviving
Heiress of the Revd. JOHN LLOYD,
who was Rector of Ryton,
in the County of Durham,
son of the Revd. WILLIAM LLOYD,
Chancellor, of Worcester,
and Grandson of the
Revd. WILLIAM LLOYD,
one of the Seven Bishops sent
to the Tower by King JAMES, II.
1688, JOHN LLOYD, was the only
male Descendant of the Bishop,
who left Issue now surviving,

But from the female part of the family there are many Branches of the names of SOLE, SANDYS, WHARTON and BAKER.
The *Revd.* WILLIAM LLOYD BAKER, died June 24, 1830, Aged 78, and lies in the same Vault, He was the youngest and only surviving Child of the *Revd.* THOMAS BAKER, who died *Vicar of Bibury*, in this County in the Year 1755, by MARY, Daughter of the above named *Chancellor* LLOYD. He was descended from the BAKERS formerly of *Boresly*, but now of *Waresley* in *Co. Worc.*

IN CHANCEL.

To the Glory of God:
In Memory of
Revd. WM. LLOYD BAKER, M. A.
who died 24 June, 1830.
A Benefactor to the Pastoral good of this Parish.

Their Works do follow them.

Arms:—1. Azure on a fess Or, 3 Mulletts Gules, between 3 Swans Necks, Or, rayed and beaked Gules.
2.—On a canton Argent, A Chev. between 3 Black-birds Sable, each holding a Worm gules.

Sacred to the Memory of
JOHN BARNES GREGORY,
of this Parish, *Captain* in his Majestys 56th. *Regiment of Foot*, who died 7 Decr. 1846, Aged 68 Years.

To the Glory of God:
In Memory of his Servant
JANE BARNES GREGORY,
born March 5, 1784, died May 1, 1872.

Daughter of the
Revd. JOHN GREGORY,
who died 1799, and Grand-Daughter of the *Revd.* THOMAS GREGORY, who died 1778, Successively *Rectors* of this Parish.

EDWARD DORNEY,
who died Sept 1700,
Ætat. suæ 30.
And of ELIZABETH DORNEY,
his *Widow*, who died Jan. 7, 1731,
Ætat. suæ 67.

DORNEY:—*as before.*

TIMOTHY THOMAS,
1746.
TIMOTHY THOMAS,
1794.
MARY, his Relict,
died Nov. 20, 1809, Aged 62.

THOMAS WENT, of this Parish, who died 6 Decr. 1806, Aged 61 Years.
MARY, his first Wife, Daughter of JOHN BAYLEY, *Alderman* of *Gloucester.* who died 1779, Aged 32.
Also Infant Daughter of THOMAS and ANN WENT, who died March 1786.
ANNE, 2nd. Wife of THOMAS WENT, who died at an advanced Age, July 13, 1834.
WILLIAM WENT, Nephew of THOMAS WENT, who died Nov. 6, 1806, Aged 27.

In Memory of
JOHN LLOYD SMALL, *Esqr.*
who died Decr. 24, 1761.

Near this place lie the Remains of the *Revd.* THOMAS GREGORY,

M. A. *Rector* of this Parish, 19 Years. He departed this Life, June 20, 1778, Aged 62.
Also of SUSANNAH, his Relict, She departed this Life, Sept. 1, 89, Aged 73 Years.
Also their 3 Children, who died Young.
[*see Flat Stones in Nave.*]
Also to the Memory of MARY PATTERSON, of *White Hill*, in the County of *Durham*, who died
....
Also of ELIZABETH GREGORY, his Sister, who departed this Life, July 1806, Aged 70 Years.
They were Nieces of the above THOMAS GREGORY.

CHURCH YARD.

ON A BRASS PLATE ON A FLAT STONE.

Sacred to the Memory of
ROGER RUTTER *alias* RUDDER, eldest son of JOHN RUDDER, of *Uley*, buried Aug. 30, 1771, Aged 84 Years.
Having never eaten flesh, fish, nor fowl, during the course of his long life.
By LYDIA, his first Wife, Daughter of JOHN HILLIER, of *Cam*, he had Issue one Son, SAMUEL RUDDER, born at *Uley*, Dec. 2, 1726, who died March 15, 1801.
and lies buried at *Cirencester*, in this County, leaving three Sons, and two Daughters SAMUEL, MARY, ELIZABETH, RICHARD, and WILLIAM.
This plate is inscribed to the Memory of their grandfather, by SAMUEL and WILLIAM RUDDER, of *Birmingham*.

N. B.—But few of the Flat Stons Inscriptions remain in this Church.

HEAD STONES.

	Died.		Aged.		Died.		Aged.
Elizabeth, Wife of Josiah Talboys	1 March	1723	56	William, their Son	21 Jany.	1738	40
Josiah Talboys	19 Decr.	1747	85	Thomas, their Son	8 June	1793	68
Joseph Tilley	10 Oct.	1775	63	Mary, his Wife	1 Nov.	1794	67
Elizabeth, his Wife	20 Oct.	1773	60	Ann, Wife of Edward Roberts	29 Sept.	1796	34
William Tilley	30 April	1771	50	William, their Son	12 July	1791	4
Hannah, his Wife	18 Febr.	1795	77	William Harris	16 Decr.	1782	38
John, Son of John Adey	26 Nov.	1773	29	Hannah, Wife of Joseph Yewen	26 July	1763	57
David, his Son	14 Aug.	1772	33	Aaron Sims	17 Decr.	1752	67
Edward Nichols	18 Jany.	1785	49	Abraham Hill	26 Febr.	1788	80
John Garlick	18 Oct.	1781	61	Hester, his Wife	23 Sept.	1767	71
Dinah, his Wife	20 April	1769	49	Mary, Wife of George Burt ...	22 July	1786	78
William Knight	21 Nov.	1764	77	Thomas Knight	26 Sept.	1756	42
Mary, his Wife	11 Sept.	1757	71	Daniel Rudder	28 Jany.	1775	49
John, their Son	10 Aug.	1740	34				

Supplementary Notes as to I.—*Devolution of Estates.* II.—*Church.* III.—*Population, Taxation, &c.*

I.—*Estates:*

In this Parish is Uley Bury Hill, the site of a Roman Encampment inclosing a space of about 40a. and fortified with a double Entrenchment along the edge of the Hill, here Coins of the latter Empire have been found.

On brow of a Hill about a quarter of a mile East-ward, of Uley Bury, on a spot covered with Beech Trees is a Cairn of about 120 feet long and 80 or 90 broad. It is heart shap-

ed. Its entrance led to a passage into which three kistvaens opened. Its Walls of thin stones were 5 feet high covered with flat stones. It was opened 1821, and several Skeletons were found mostly lying East and West. This was a British sepulchre.

Uley was at the time of the Conquest parcel of the great Lordship of Berkeley. "In Eudlege 2 Hides."
Domesday Survey.

To Berkeley Lordship Uley Manor still belongs.

Several Sub-Fees were created:—

Edw. iii—Maurice Berkeley, second son of Maurice, Lord Berkeley and Ancestor of the Berkeleys of Stoke Giffard, received the Grant of one Estate.

1 Hen. vii.—His descendants held until Sir William Berkeley was attainted for adhering to King Richard iii The Estate coming by this attainder to the Crown was granted to Jasper, Duke of Bedford, in tail male. But 4 H. 7. a Crown Grant in Reversion was made to Sir Wm. Berkeley.

see "Stoke Giffard."

Bassett's Court:—

Sir Anselm Bassett, m. Margaret, a Daughter of Thos Lord Berkeley, and received a Gift of this Estate for her portion. It passed to their Heir general who took the name of Bassett.

Edw. ii.—Edmund Bassett, died seized of Lands in Ewely, Owlepen and Camme.

The Daughter and heir of William Bassett, of Uley, married .... Westcombe, and the Estate was sold in parcels about the middle of the 18th. century.

Fox Grove Wood.

William Bassett, of Uly Manor, and Edw. Bassett, Esqr against Saml. and J. Cadle, W. Rowland, and Margery Adams, a suit concerning a Lease.

Chanc. Proceedings, Eliz B. b. 31 No. 5.

Estate of Stout's Hill:—This belonged to John de Stouteshull.

1746.—Timothy Gyde, was Owner. (see Ch. Inscript.)

Revd. Lloyd Baker, by purchase.

His son the late Mr. Thomas J. Lloyd Baker, resided here 1829, 1830, And during the time improved the Poor Law Administration of the Parish by good Workhouse Management. This family hold the Estate still and other Lands.

White's Court is a reputed Manor, but the Manor house is demolished and on its site are Buildings of various Owners.

Peglers Lands:—

1690.—Pegler to T. Small of Nailsworth, Clothier.

1735.—John Long, from G. Small, of London, son of John Small, Brother and Heir of said Thomas, and Thomas, eldest son of said John.

Part One:—

1748.—Timothy Gyde, from John Long.

Other Part:—

1735.—John Long and Edward Jackson, from Children of John Long.

1785.—Robert Harris, of Wotton-under-Edge, Clothier from John Long.

1795.—John Harris, son of Richard Harris.

James Harris, Clothier, married Mary Lloyd, their son and Heir was James Lloyd Harris, who held a Mill and Estate here. He by Will 1815, devised his Estates to Richard Donovan of Tibberton Court, in trust to sell, the Proceeds to be for the benefit of his daughter Honoria Donovan. In 1819, the surviving Trustee conveyed the Estates to Samuel Peach.

Westcote, was another Sub-Manor in Uley.

Peter de Ewley.

Part:—Robert, Lord Berkeley, from Ewely.

Priory of Bradenstoke, by his Gift.

After the dissolution of the Priory:—

R. Andrews and Nichl. Temple, by Crown Grant.

Other Part:—

Henry Berkeley, 5th. son of Thomas, Lord Berkeley.

A Capital Messuage and 94a. Land:—

27 Edw. i.—Thomas de Gloucester, Plaintiff.
Walter de Lude, (Ludlow.) Deforciant. Fine.

17 Edw. ii.—Hawise, the Widow of Walter de Glouc. Inq. ad quod dam. 6 E. iii. She gave it to Evesham Abbey.
Claus. Roll.

It passed to ....

Bencomb:—

1 Ric. i.—Peter de Ywly, held: John de Bencomb.

Agnes, his Daughter, married John Poyntz.
see Church Inscriptions.

The family of Dorney, was long settled here and at the Green Uley.

1543.—Will at Gloucester, of R. Dorney.

Of this family was, the famous parliamentarian Town Clerk of Gloucester, 1646; who was removed by the Royal Regulation Comrs. 1662, but reappointed 1667, and continued till his Death 1674. Also Thomas Dorney, who lived at the House on the Green, temp. Jac. i. and Henry, his son, who was born at Uley, 1613. Both remarkable for evangelical piety, and Christian usefulness. The "Divine Contemplations and Spiritual Breathings" of Henry, was published after his Death 1634, and a 2nd. Edition in 1773, with a preface by the Revd. Wm. Romaine. see an interesting Memoir of Hen. Dorney, in Stratford's "Gloucestershire Worthies."

The Estate passed to the family of Small and by the Will of Sophia Small, Spinster, 1776; to Samuel Peach, who 1785, settled it on his Wife Christina, for her separate use, Samuel Peach, Junr. was her son, and upon her death intestate 1791, the Estate was conveyed to him by the Trustees, It was a small Estate and is now partley subdivided.

The Holbrows had Mills and an Estate here. (see Ch. Inscriptions) William Holbrow, who died 1741, had been High Sheriff of the County. C. Holbrow Stanton, holds Hyde Hill.

Other Lands belong to the Owners of the adjoining Estates of Oldpen, Kingscote, to the latter Uley Bury.

H. 1. Geo. ii.—Phelps Purnell. Plaintiff.
T. Purnell, J. Purnell, gen. Evans, and ux. Deforciants. Fine.

E. 8. Geo. ii.—Joseph Truelove. Plaintiff.
And Fowler, and Wife, and Andrews, and Wife.
Deforciant. Fine.

Rudhall the famous Gloucester Bell founder had property here, Also the Ancestors of S. Rudder, of Cirencester.

1776.—At the County Election, the following Voted for Freeholds at Uley.

Austin, Edward.
Carter, Joseph.
Cave, Thomas.
Colborne, John.
Dauncey, George.
Ferribee, John, Senr.
French, John.
Fisher, Joseph.
Gregory, Rev. John.
Do. Thomas.
Gyde, Timothy.
Garlick, John, Junr.
Hawker, Thomas.
Harris, John. (2)
Holbrow, John, Esqr.
Jackson, Charles.

Lord, (2) James. William.
Long, (3) Nathaniel, John. Thomas.
Martin, William.
Pearce, Thomas.
Robins, (2) Edwd., Thos.
Rudhall, Abraham, of Gloc.
Smith, (2) Aaron. Joseph.
Sprat, (2) Aaron. Samuel.
Souls, Samuel.
Small. John, Esqr.
Thomas, Timothy.
Trotman, William.
Terret, William.
Went, Samuel.

II.—Church.

The Benefice is a Rectory in Dursley Deanery.

Pope Nicholas Tax. £7. 6 s. 8 d.
Kings Books, 12 3 4
Glebe 86 a.

Advowson:—

Roger, Lord Berkeley.

Priory of Leonard Stanley, by his Gift, with Tythes of 30 a. of Land.

After the Dissolution of the Priory.

The Crown.

List of Incumbents and Patrons:—

Rectors.	Patrons.
Anthony Everdyn, L. L. B. resd. 1541.	
1541.—Henry Wells, or Willis, deprived for Matrimony 1554.	Hugh Evans.
1554.—George Byrche.	Queen Mary.
Thomas Mainrearinf, B. D. resigned 1612.	
1612.—James Dalton, B. D.	King James.
1638.—Sir Herbert Croft, Bart. Afterwards Bp. of Winchester.	King Charles.
1638.—Edward Onslowe.	do.
1667.—William Heart, B. A.	King Charles, ii.
1709.—John Jackson, M. A.	Queen Anne.
1717.—Rice Williams.	King George.
1724.—Edward Loggin Griffin, L. L. B.	do.
1729.—John Tyndale.	do.
1747.—Thomas Shellard, M. A.	King George, ii.

1748.— Thomas Gregory, B. A.   King George, ii.
1773.—John Gregory, M. A.   King George, iii.
1793.—Thomas Esbury Partridge, M.A.   do.

There are several Nonconformist Chapels, And there are Day and Sunday Schools.

Charities 10 £. Yearly Value.

III.—*Taxation, Population, &c.*

Iweleghe, Subsidy Roll, 1 Edw. III. 1327.

De Walto Seymond, xiii s. iii d. q.
' Johne. Symond, vii s. vi d. ob. q.
' Nicho. Lovecoke, v s. iiii d. ob.
' Johne. de Benecumbe, v s
' Johne. de Luyde, vi s. i d. ob.
' Walto. atte Yate, iiii s. v d.
' Robto. Broun, iiii s. v d. q.

De Willmo. Topyn, ii s· vii d. ob. q.
' Johne. Jolyff, xii d.
' Johne. Spyleman, vi d.
     prob. Sma. l s. iiii d.

Acreage 1492 a.

Population 1831,—2641. 1851,—1327. 1871.—1156.

In 1815. Annual Value of Real Property 4472£.

1875. Rateable Value 3758 £.

1833-4-5. Average of three Years Expenditure on Poor 1408 £.

In Dursley Union.

The Clothing Trade flourished here for a considerable period. Besides the Names of Small. Gyde, Harris, Holbrow, there were other Manufacturers as Went, Eyles, Sheppard: which last was the chief. The trade has died out. Several of the Mills are used for other industries.

CCLXXVI. (A.)
or 281.
UPHATHERLEY.

THE CHAPEL DEMOLISHED.

Notes as to I.—*Devolution of Estates.* II.—*Church* III.—*Population, Taxation, &c.*

I.—*Estates:*

Uphatherley in Dudston and Kings Barton Hundred, is a distinct parochial Place for Civil purposes. Like Shurdington which it adjoins, it was a Chapelry of the Church of Badgeworth. The Chapel Building has long been demolished, but the Inhabitants repair and probably erected the Hatherley Aisle of Shurdington Church, in whose Church Yard they have Burial Rights.

It is noticed as a Hamlet of Shurdington, by Atkyns, Rudder and Rudge, but no notice of it having been taken by Bigland under Badgeworth or Shurdington it is here inserted.

The Manor was part of the King's Barton Estate of St. Peter's Abbey Gloucester.

4 Edw. iii.—The Archbp. of York, by Grant, from the Abbot.

Hen. viii.—The Crown, by Grant from the Archbp. of York.

Edw. vi.—Sir Thomas Chamberlain, by Grant from the Crown with Churchdown.

Gwinnett, of Shurdington, by purchase. One of the family was Lord of Manor, 1800.   *(Rudge.)*

Messuage 80 a. of Land. 2 a. of Wood. 1 a. pasture and 15 s. Rent.—

18 Edw. ii —Henry, of Hatherley, held under a Mortgage from Robert of Prestbury.   *Inq. ad quod Dam.*

Between these persons a long and sharp contention prevailed as stated under Prestbury.

Robert of Prestbury's Name occurs in the *Subsidy Roll.* 1 Edw. iii. for Uphatherley.

The Estate came afterwards to H. Miners.

He gave a Messuage late of Edward and another late of Richard and the grove called Benaore, between them, and Land called the Butts, &c. to Roger A'Wood, by service of 2 s., and A'Wood, subenfeoffed his Sister Liana of Hatherley, who (1200.) gave a House and Kitchen Garden, and 1 a. Land to the Church of Hatherley.

And the residue of the Lands, she gave to Winchcomb Abbey for its Infirmary subject to the feudal services. This grant was confirmed by H. Miners, Lord of the fee. And (1220.) Meliandra, Daughter of Roger of Compton and Mother of Liana, released her Dower therein. And Isabella, Heir of H. Miners and her Husband Jeffery Longfield, released theis feudal services to the Abbey.

         Winchcomb Abbey Cartulary.

40 Eliz.—Roger Norwood, *Plaintiff.*
William Shalke, *Deforciant.*   *Fine.*

In later times the chief Proprietors are or were Messrs. Pickernell, Winterbotham, Tickell, &c.

II.—*Church:*

Of the Chapel of Uphatherley, part of the Walls remains.

The Chapel and Tythes of Shurdington and Uphatherley and South Hatherley, belonged to the Nunnery of Usk, Monmouthshire.

Tythes:

37 Hen. viii. 1546.—James Gunter, and Walter Lewis, by Crown Grant.

22 Eliz. 1580.—John Fernham, by Crown Grant. Afterwards they passed to Jesus College, Oxford.

III.—*Taxation, Population, &c.*

Uphatherleye, Subsidy Roll, 1 Edw. III. 1327.

De Robto. de Prestebury, iiii s.
' Thom. de Hatherleye, xii d. q.
' Henr. Ermyte, vi d.
     prob. Sma. v s. vi *d. q.*

Acreage 524 a.

Population 1831,—21. 1861,—68. 1871,—50.

1815.—Annual Value of Real Property £520.

1875.—Rateable Value £1341.

1833-4-5.—Average of three Years Expenditure on Poor £48.

In Cheltenham Union.

UPLEADEN.

UPLEADEN.

T HE C HURCH is small consists of a Clancel and Nave, with a low Wooden Tower, at the West-end, and therein one Bell. It is a Curacy.

PRESENT LORDS OF THE MANOR, DAEN AND CHAPTER, OF *Gloucester*.

Revd. THOMAS DAVIS, *Curate.*

INSCRIPTIONS IN THE CHURCH.

CHANCEL.

ON A MONUMENT.

Underneath Lyeth the Body of
JOHN MARSHALL,
of this Parish, *Yeoman*,
who departed this Life.
13 Febr. 1766, Aged 61 Years.
Also ANNA, his Wife,
who died Sept. 6, 1774,
Aged 72 Years.
Also Underneath lieth the Body of
SARAH, Daughter of WILLIAM
WHITE, by MARY, his Wife,
She departed this Life,
Sept. 25, 1768, Aged 3 Years.

ON A SMALL STONE, SOUTH WALL.

In Memory of
ANNE, the Wife of EDWARD
FARMER, of *Highleadon*,
who died 22, 1785, Aged 90.

ON FLAT STONES.

Here lyeth the Body of
JOHN KAYSE, *Gent.*
who departed this Life, the
7*th.* day of August,
Anno Dni. 1622.
Also ANNE, the Wife of
JOHN KAYSE, *Gent.*
who departed this Life, the
3*rd.* day of November,
Anno Dni. 1639.
Buried 6 Sounes one Daughter,
I. K., W. K., G. K., T. K.,
R. K., R. K., Si. K.

Here resteth the Body of
Mrs. ANNE HOOKE,
Daughter of *Mr.* JOHN KEYSE,
who departed this Life, the
24 day of January 1663.

Here lyeth the Body of
ALICE WATTS, *Widow*,
late Wife of JOHN WATTS,
of *Lassington*, who departed
this Life, 27*th.* day of August,
Anno Dni. 1662.
Here lyeth the Body of
WILLIAM WATTS, of this Parish,
Yeoman, who died the 16 day of
Jany. 17..., Aged 90.

Here lyeth the Body of
MARY, the Wife of
WILLIAM WATTS, *Senior*,
who departed ys Life, the
21 day of September 1681.

Here lyeth the Body of
WILLIAM WATTS, who died
the 17 day of July, 1677.
Also MARY, the Wife of
WILLIAM PALMER, of this Parish,
Yeoman, who was here buried
the 19 day of Sept. A. D. 1715,
Aged 31 Years.
Also the Body of WILLIAM
PALMER, of this Parish,
Husband of the aforesaid who
was here interred the 12 day
of Sept. 1735, Aged 54 Years.
Also 3 of their Children,
viz.—JANE, ANNE and PHILIP,
who died in their Infancy.

Here lyeth the Body of
WILLIAM CLARKE, *Yeoman*,
whe was buried the 5*th.* of
November 1684, Aged 90.
Also the Body of
WILLIAM CLARKE,
late of this Parish, *Yeoman*,
who departed this Life, the
19 of March 1720, Ætat. 29.

In Memory of
DANIEL FOWLER, late of this
Parish, who left this Life,
November the 4*th.* A. D. 1712,
Ætatis 21.

Through Childhood safely having got
And unto Youth being come,
Just like a flower I was crop't
And sent to my long Home.

To the Memory of
RICHARD DREW, *Gent.*
who lieth here interred
October 30*th.*
Anno Dni. 1714,
Ætatis 48.
Also in Memory of
HESTER, his beloved Wife,
who was here buried Sept. the
1*st.* 1728, Aged 63.

Till by the Trump of God,
They shall be awakened unto Judgment
here lies sleeping the Bodies of
MATTHEW MORRIS,
late of this Parish, *Yeoman*,
who departed this Life,
January 25*th.* A. D. 1712,
Aged 56 Years.
Also JOAN, the Wife, of the above
MATTHEW MORRIS,
died Febr. 13, 1712, Aged 38.
And JOHN, the Son, of the aforesaid
MATTHEW and JOAN MORRIS,
who died March 13, 1713,
Aged 5 Years.
Likewise the Body of SARAH,
the Daughter of WILLIAM HALE,
of the Parish of *Hartpury*, *Yeoman*,
who died March 7, 1712,
Aged 16 Years.

NAVE.

Here lyeth the Body of
JOHN JONES, of this Parish,
and departed this Life, the
3*rd.* of May 1746, Aged 63 Years.

CHURCH YARD.

ON TOMBS.

Here lyeth the Body of
the late CHALES JONES,
of this Parish, *Yeoman.*
who was buried June 26*th.* 1734,
Aged 46 Years.
CHARLES JONES, his Son,
who died April 18, 1757,
Aged 29 Years.

Here under are interred the
Bodies of ROBERT MAYO, of the
Parish of *Minsterworth*, *Yeoman*,
and MARTHA, his Wife.
He died May 8, 1734, Aged 55.
And She MARY, the 2*nd.* 1730,
Aged 53 Years.
Also two of their Daughters, *viz.*—
SARAH, died Sept. the 16, 1730,
Aged 28 Years.
And MARY, who died the 2*nd.*
of Jany. 1743, Aged 28, and was
the Wife of DAVID MADDOX,
of *London.*

HEAD STONES.

	Died.	Aged.		Died.	Aged
Thomas Holder	12 April 1759	59	Mary Fluck	9 Jany. 1750	70
William Holder	28 Decr. 1829	71	John Vinot	2 April 1797	32
Alice Holder	6 Febr. 1757	84	Thomas Vinot	19 Apr. 1791	5
Jane, Wife of Thomas Morris	30 May 1729	39	George Broadstock	31 Jany. 1768	5
Mary, Daughter of John and } Hannah Broadstock ... }	25 August 1752	20	William Benton	5 Nov. 1778	
			Elizabeth, Wife of Thos. Phelps	15 Jany. 1767	42
John, their Son	6 May 1759	24	William, their Son	3 Jany. 1758	2
Daniel Wilkes, *Yeoman*	26 Jany. 1766	55	John, their Son	2 May 1767	14
Johanna, his Wife	31 March 1763	45	William, their Son	4 June 1767	2
Daniel Wilkes, their Son	2 June 1765	20	Emanuel, their Son	 1775	6m.
Anne Wilkds, their Daughter	2 Decr. 1765	8	Thomas, their Son	2 April 1786	36
Sarah, Wife of Isaac Barker	22 Decr. 1760	60	George Wilson	3 May 1767	50
George Wilse	4 Sept. 1761	40	Sarah, his Wife	4 Sept. 1761	40
Anne, his Wife	3 Mary 1767	30	William Lane	7 Nov. 1787	59
Thomas Fluck	21 Sept. 1744	...	Mary, his Wife	8 Jany. 1778	35

Supplementary Notes as to I.—Estates; II.—Church; III—Population, Taxation, &c.

I.—*Estates* :

Leden in Botelowes Hundred :—It had 4 Hides : Culture 10 Plow Tillages, 2 in Demesne and 8 in Villenags, (8 Villons and 2 Bordars.) Four Serfs; A Mill of 4s. 10a. Meadow. A Wood 2 miles long and 2 furlongs broad. It was worth scarcely 30 s.

St. Peter's at Gloucester, held it as parcel of Rodeford.
Lomesday Survey.

15 Edw. i.—Claim of the Abbot to freewarren allowed on Quo Warranto.

After the dissolution of Monasteries.

John Arnold, by Crown Grant.

37 Hen. viii.—Sir Nicholas, son and heir.
Rowland, his son, by descent.
Dorothy, his Daughter and Heir.

1608.—Sir Thomas Lucy, her Husband.

1711.—Thomas Brown, Alderman of Gloucester.

1719.—Mrs. Broxline. (*Rudder.*)

Manor, Courtfarm, &c.—Mr. Hodges.

Estate.—Mr. De Visme.

The Hay :—Mr. Beale, since Mr. Beale Cooper.

Drews. *see Church Inscriptions.*

Mr. Hyett.

Other Estates :
46 Edw iii.—John Mortymer, *Junr.*
Dom. de Castel Frome, Utlagatus.
Inq. post Mort. No. 42.

Among the early Wills at Gloucester, are the following of Persons of Upleadon.

Rock, 1597; Holliday, 1598.

Fine :—
32 Geo. ii.—Samuel Serjaent, Clerk, *Plaintiff.*
Richard Green, and Wife Esther, *Deforciants.*

1776.—*In the Election for Gloucestershire, the following voted for Freeholds in Upleadon.*

Cother, William.
Halford, Thomas.
Palmer, James.
Phelps, Thomas.
Vaughan, John.
Wilkes, William.
Wood, John.

II.—*Church.*

Impropriation of Church :—

Abbey of Gloucester. After the dissolution.

33 Hen. viii.—Dean and Chapter of Gloucester, by Crown Grant.

Curacy : Patron, Bishop of Gloucester.

List of Curates and Patrons of Upleaden.

1576	—Roger Shough.	Bishop of Gloucester.
1610.	—John Hutchins.	Do.
1713.	—......... Rudge.	Do.
1619.	—......... Barker.	
1625.	—......... Harris.	Bishop of Gloucester.
1628.	—Simon Jones.	Do.
1662	—John Green.	Do
1668-1701.	—William Mallett.	Do.
171·	—Daniel Bond.	Do.
1712.	—Nathaniel King.	Do.
1763.	—Samuel Sergeaunt,	Do.
1782.	—Thomas Davies.	Geo. iii. by Lapse.

1554.—Roger Low, was the Minister at Bishop Hooper's Examination, He was wholly unable to answer any question directly. The Number of Communicants was then 80.

III.—*Taxation, Population, &c. of Upleaden.*

Ledene, Subsidy Roll, 1 Edw. iii. 1327.

De Johne le Stonheware, xxi d. ob.
' Laur. de la Hay, xviii d.
' Hugon le Frend, xvii d.
' Henr. Fymon, xix d. q.
' Willmo. de la Hale, ii s ii d.
' Felic. de la Smith, xii d.
' Nicho. de Waryhulle, xii d. o.
' Alic. la Smyth, xii d.
' Johne Aylzot, xvii d. q.
' Sywardo Michel, ix d.
' Johne atte Roke, xii d.
' Henr. le Bonde, iiii s.
' Willo. atte Hay, iii s.
' Johne le Portma. iii s.
prob. Sma. xxiiii s. ii d. o.

Upleaden, Subsidy Roll, 8 Jac. i.

Jonh Clerke, ... *Bonis.*
Richd. Crowse, ... *Terr.*

Assessors :

John Keyse.
John Hayward.
Roger Jelf.
Wm. Twynning.

Acreage 1207. *a.*

Population 1831,—241. 1851.—237. 1871,—255.

In 1815. Annual Value of Real Property 1571 £.

1875.—Rateable Value £ 2485.

1833-4-5. Average of three Years Expenditure on Poor £ 166.

In Newent Union.

UPTON St. LEONARDS.

UPTON S^{T.} LEONARD'S.

THE FREEHOLDERS:—LORDS OF THE MANOR.

THE CHURCH consists of a Nave, Chancel and North Aisle, and a Gallery and an embattled Tower at the West-end, in which are five Bells. The Church is dedicated to St. Leonard. It was restored in the Year 1850.

BISHOP OF GLOUCESTER, PATRON OF THE CHURCH.

ON THE GALLERY AT THE WEST-END:

GILES COX, formerly of *Ablodes Court, Gent.* having by Will given the Residue of his Estate to certain Persons therein nominated his Executors to be by them bestowed and employed in pious and Charitable Uses:—

It appears by indenture, dated in the Reign of King CHARLES the 1st. that a part of the rents and profits thereof the proportion 3 £. 6 s. 8 d. was then appointed to the parish of *Upton St. Leonard's,* to be paid yearly on the 1st. day of May for the relief of such poor labouring householders dwelling in the said Parish both Men and Women as shall stand in most need thereof and who do not receive relief from the rest of the Inhabitants, nor are Beggars from Door to Door, nor haunters of Alehouses, nor disorderly persons but of good and honest conversation.

This Gallery was erected Anno 1757. [It is now taken away.]

The *Revd.* CHARLES BISHOP, *Minister.*

RICHARD BURRUPP, and THOMAS RODWAY, *Church Wardens.*

JOHN WELLS, and HENRY TURNER, *Church Wardens,* 1792.

ON AN ATCHMENT.

Quarterly.—Gules and Azure a Cross flory Or.—SNELL. *impaling*—Gules on a Bend Or, three Martlets Sable.—BRABAZON.

Crest:—a Fox statant proper upon a Lamb couchant Argent, behind them the holy Cross Gules.

INSCRIPTIONS.

ON A HANDSOME MONUMENT IN SNELL'S CHANCEL.

At the sides the Arms and Crest as the Atchment.

O Gracious God ! Dear Redeemer. !
have mercy on Me now and ever
was
The fervent Prayer of
SR. THOMAS SNELL,
In his Life
And humble Confidence
at his Death
which happened the 13*th.* day
of March 1754,
in the 64*th.* Year of his Age.

SR. THOMAS SNELL,

of *Whitley Court,* in this Parish, *Knt.* in his Life Time caused this Tomb to be erected and by a Deed, (inrolled in the High Court of Chancery,) dated the 9*th.* Day of May in the Year of our Lord 1746, did grant to the Feoffees of the Manour of *Upton St. Leonard,* and to their Successors a Rent Charge of Six pounds yearly on his Lands and Tenements in the same for ever. *In Trust,* in the first Place to be applied to the keeping clean and perfectly in Repair this Tomb and all and every part thereof Together with the Building over it and all Things relating to the same which are comprised within the Dimensions contained in the Faculty, granted for that Purpose. And with the Surplus to put poor Children, (born in this Parish,) apprentice at the Discretion of the said Trustees pursuant to the Deed above mentioned, which he hopes they will charitably perform, and that God will bless them evermore.

CHANCEL.

ON FLAT STONES.

In Memory of
the *Revd. Mr.* LAURENCE PAYNE,
Minister of this Parish,
who died August 24, 1751,
Aged 80 Years.
Here lyeth the Body of
BENJAMIN, the beloved Son of
the *Revd.* LAURENCE PAYNE,
Minister of this Parish,
who died April the 29th. 1740,
Aged 4 Years and 6 Months.

Arms:—Sable, ten Plates 4, 3, 2, and 1, on a Chief Argent, a Lion passant Ermine.—BRIDGEMAN.

In Memory of
JOHN, the Son of *Sir* JOHN
BRIDGEMAN, of *Princknash* in the

County of *Gloucester, Knight,*
who departed this Life, the
20*th.* day of May, Ao. 1646.
Also here resteth the Body of
ANNE, second Daughter of
Sir JOHN BRIDGEMAN, *Knight,*
who departed this Life,
September the 24, A. D. 1647.
Also in Memory of
CHARLES BRIDGEMAN,
who was buried the 23 day of July,
Anno Domini 1721.

Here was buried the Body of
ELIZABETH ATKINS,
the Wife of RICHARD ATKINS,
who deceased the 27 day of
May, Anno D. 1559.
Also here lyeth the Body of
SUSANNA ATKINS, the Wife of
JOHN ATKINS, and Daughter of
RICHARD and ANNE ATKINS,

whose soul resteth in the
Lord and was separated
from the Body the 5 of October,
Anno Domini, 1588.

Here lyeth the Body of
VINCENT HUSSEY,
son and Heyre unto
Sir RICHARD HUSSEY, of *Crygion*
in the County of *Montgomery, Knight,*
who married with
ELIZABETH BRIDGEMAN,
eldest Daughter of
Sir JOHN BRIDGEMAN, of *Princknash* in the County of *Gloucester,
Knight,* who died the
20*th.* of April 1638.
Here lyeth DOROTHY, Wife of
HENRY DAUNT, *Gent.*
and Mother to the
Lady FRANCES BRIDGEMAN,
deceased the 9*th.* of March
1656.

Here resteth the Body of
GYLES ROBINS, Yeoman,
who died 6th. day of January 1626.
Here resteth ANNE, first Wife,
of GILES ROBINS, afterwards
Wife of THOMAS ATKINS,
who was buried the 20 of Aug. 1669,
Aged 74 Years.
Here also lyeth MARGARET,
the Daughter of THOMAS ATKINS,
and ANNE, his Wife,
untill clothed with immortallity,
She died the 2nd , and was buried
the 21 day of August 1669.

In Memory of
WILLIAM ACTON, of this Parish,
Gent. who departed this Life,
the 17 of May 1719,
Aged 82 Years.
Also here lyeth the Body of
MARY, his Relict and since
Wife of SAMUEL COLE,
of Painswick, Clothier,
who departed this Life, the
21 Febr. 1744, Aged 79 Years.

NAVE.

ON A TABLET.

Sacred to the Memory of
ANN, the beloved Wife of
JOHN SMITH,
(late School Master in this Parish,)
who died January 9, 1794,
in the 51 Year of her Age.
To Husband, Children,
and this World Adieu,
O Think O think how near
Death is to you.

ON FLAT STONES.

Arms:—Argent, a Cross Sable,
a tressure of Flear de Lis, between
four Mullets pierced of the second.
ATKINS. *impaling* per pale ....
a Lion rampant. ....

Here lies the Body of
ELIZABETH LYNDON, Daughter of
Capt. CHARLES LYNDON,
by ELIZABETH, his Wife.
He was Son of the late
Judge LYNDON, of the Kingdom
of Ireland, who died April 15, 1735.
Also the Body of
Mrs. ANNE ATKINS, Daughter of
ROBERT ATKINS, Gent.
by ANNE, his Wife,
who died Nov. 3, 1737.

Arms:—as the last.

Here lyeth the Body of
RICHARD ATKINS, of this Parish,
Gent. who died April 6, 1639.
Also the Body of THOMAS ATKINS,
Son of THOMAS ATKINS, Gent.
and ANNE, his Wife, and
Grandson of the above said
RICHARD ATKINS,
He died Nov. 13, 1677, Aged 49.
Likewise the Body of ROBERT
ATKINS, of this Parish, Gent.
and ANNE his Wife,
who departed this Life.
He March the 26, 1702, Aged 62.
And She Sept. 14, 1716,
Aged 75 Years.

In Memory of
SARAH GASTRELL, Wife of
RICHARD GASTRELL, of this Parish,
who departed this Life, the
21 day of July 1754, Aged 45.
Also JOHN, their Son, who departed
this Life, the 17 day of June 1752,
Aged 2 Years.

ON BRASS PLATE.

This Plate is inscribed to keep
the Memory of
JAMES GASTRELL, late of the
City of Gloucester, Baker,
(the Son of RICHARD GASTRELL,
of this Parish, Gent. by SARAH,
his Wife.) He departed this Life,
30th. day of March 1793, Aged 51.

CHURCH YARD.

AGAINST THE TOWER.

*This Tower was repaired and the
Pinnacles first erected in the Year,*
1745.
Sir THOMAS SNELL, Knt. ⎫ Church
and ⎬ Wardens.
RICHARD FRANKIS. ⎭

AGAINST THE SOUTH WALL.

Underneath lies the Body of
EDMOND JOHN SCOTT HILTON,
Son of JOHN HILTON,
of the City of Gloucester, Gent.
and CAREW, his Wife,
He died April the 2nd. 1716.

ANOTHER.

Beneath this Place lies
interred the Body of
SAMUEL SMITH,
of this Parish, Yeoman,
who died Nov. 16, 1763,
Aged near 69 Years.
ELIZABETH, his Wife,
died Oct. 12, 1789, Aged 78 Years.
RICHARD, his Son, was buried
in his Infancy.
ANN, the Daughter of SAMUEL
SMITH, who died August 12, 1765,
Aged 19 Years.

UNDER THE LAST.

Beneath
are interred the remains of
THOMAS, the Son of THOMAS
and MARY SMITH, Grandson of
the above SAMUEL and
ELIZABETH SMITH,
He died July 6, 1792,
Aged 19 Years.

ON TOMBS.

In Memory of
JAMES SMITH, of this Parish,
he died June 12, 1787, Ætat. 77.
ROBERT his Son, died Oct. 27, 1789,
Aged 46 Years.
MARY, the Wife, of JAMES SMITH,

who died Febr. 15, 1751-2,
Aged 32 Years.
Also two of their Children,
DANIEL and MARY, lie here.
Likewise SARAH, second Wife of
JAMES SMITH,
who died March 5, 1786,
Aged 80 Years.
Near this Tomb lie three
Clildren of ROBERT and MARY
SMITH, Grand-children to
JAMES and MARY SMITH,
who died in their Infancy.

In Memory of
DANIEL SMITH, of this Parish,
Yeoman, who died Aug. 15, 1755,
Aged 81 Years.
Also of MARY, his Wife,
who died Sept. 16, 1741,
Aged 61 Years.
Also MARY, their Daughter,
died 6 Sept. 1751,
Aged 38 Years.

In Memory of
THOMAS SMITH, of this Parish,
who departed this Life, the
22 of Febr. 1745, Aged near 80.
ELIZABETH, Wife of THOMAS
SMITH, who died the
4th. of April 1748, Aged 76.

In Memory of
JOHN CARWARDINE, Senr.
of this Parish, Yeoman,
who departed this Life, the
16 Decr- 1761, Aged near 45.
SARAH, his Wife,
died July 21, 1757, Aged 43.
ANNE and ELIZABETH, their Daus:
ANNE, died April 14, 1759,
Aged 10 Years and 10 Months.
ELIZABETH, died Jany. 27, 1761,
Aged 7 Years, and 7 Months.

Here lies the Body of
WILLIAM RODWAY, eldest Sonne
of JOHN RODWAY, Yeoman,
he deceased Jany. the 31, 1693,
Aged 51 Years.
Also ANNE, the Wife of
WILLIAM RODWAY,
She deceased April the 22, 1676.
In Memory of
ISABELL, the Wife of WILLIAM
RODWAY, of this Parish, Yeoman,
She departed this Life,
Decr. 18, A. D. 1734,
Aged 86 Years.

Here lyeth the Body of
THOMAS RODWAY, Senior.
of this Parish, He departed
this Life, Jany. 25, 1795,
Aged 79 Years.
ANNE, his Wife, who departed
this Life, April 28, 1775,
Aged 59 Years.

Here lyeth the Body of
JOHN RODWAY, Yeoman,
who died January 27, 169..,

Aged 90 Years.
Also the Body of JOANE, his Wife,
who died 1693,
Aged 78 Years.

To the Memory of
THOMAS RODWAY, Son of
JOHN RODWAY, of this Parish,
Yeoman, he died 15 Jany. 1788,
who lived and died a Batchelor,
Aged 41 Years.
Uuder this Tomb lieth the Body of
THOMAS RODWAY, *Senr.*
of this Parish, *Yeoman*,
who died the 22 of Nov. 1761,
Aged 83 Years.
Also the Body of ANNE,
the Wife of the said THOMAS
RODWAY, who died the 15 of
Febr. 1769, Aged 84 Years.

In Memory of
ROBERT GRIMES, of this Parish,
who departed this Life, the
4 July 1740, Aged 60 Years.
MARY, his Wife, died Decr. 5, 1757,
Aged near 75.
ANNE BAKER, (Sister of MARY,
the Wife of ROBERT GRIMES,)
who departed this Life, the
8 March 1746, Aged 61.

Beneath this Tomb,
are interred the remains of
SARAH, the Wife of RICHARD
FRANKIS, *Yeoman*, who died
23 May 1773, Aged 66 Years.

Here lyeth the Body of
ELIZABETH, the Wife of JOHN
BISHOP, and Daughter of
WILLIAM FRANKIS, of this Parish,
Yeoman, who departed this Life,
25 day of October 1767,
ELIZABETH, the Daughter of
JOHN and ELIZABETH BISHOP,
late of this Parish,
who departed this Life, the
11 day of May 1775,
Aged 12 Years.

In Memory of
WILLIAM FRANKISS,
of this Parish, who was buried
October the 8, 1713,
Aged 76 Years.
Also ELIZABETH, his 1st. Wife,
who was buried Febr. 19, 1674,
Aged 36 Years.
Also of WILLIAM FRANKISS,
Son of RICHARD FRANKISS,
of this Parish, *Yeoman*,
who died 24 of December 1755,
in the 22 Year of his Age.

Uuderneath this Tomb lieth
buried the Body of JOHN, Son of
RICHARD FRANKISS
of this Parish, *Yeoman*, by SARAH,
his Wife who died 22 Jany. 1768,
Aged 29 Years.

In Memory of
WILLIAM FRANKISS, of this Parish,
Yeoman, he deceased Nov. 16, 1735,
Aged 70 Years.
Also ANNE, his Wife, who died
the 16 day of November 1735,
Aged 76 Years.

In Memory of
RICHARD FRANKISS, of this Parish,
Yeoman, who departed this Life,
Jany. 26, 1748, Aged 52 Years.

Here resteth the Body of
ANNE, the Wife of HENRY ROBINS,
who died the 28 day of Septem.
164...

Vita sapientis est meditatio
immortalitatis,
To the Memory of
ROBERT TAYLOE, who deceased
the 2 day of Sept. 1656,
Aged 70 Years.
Here lyeth the Body of
JAMES TAYLOE, Sonne of
ROBERT TAYLOE, who deceased
the 13 day of March 1654.

Here lyeth the Body of
THOMAS DAVIS, of this Parish,
Yeoman, who departed this Life,
Jany. 11, 1709, Aged 71 Years.
HESTER, Wife of THOMAS DAVIS,
died May 1, 1718, Aged 60.

To the Memory of
WILLIAM NURSE, of this Parish,
Yeoman, who deceased the
17 of September, 1686,
Aged 74 Years.

Here lyeth the Body of
JOHN NURSE, of this Parish,
Yeoman, who died May 10, 1697,
Aged 54 Years.

In Memory of
ELIZA, Wife of THOMAS BAYLEY,
of this Parish, *Yeoman*,
who died Aug. 29, 1701,
Aged 54 Years.

Here resteth the Body of
GYLES BINGLEY, *Yeoman*,
who was buried 18 Jan. 1643.
Also DANIEL BINGLEY, Son of
GYLES BINGLEY, who was
buried the 18 Oct. 1643.

In Memory of
GILES BINGLEY, of this Parish,
Gent. who was buried the
20 day of Augt. 1705.

Also of DANIEL BINGLEY, his Son,
who was buried the 5 of May 1720,
Aged 42 Years.
Also of MARY, Widow of
GILES BINGLEY, of this Parish,
Gent. who departed this Life,
Nov. 14, 1732, Aged 76 Years.

In Memory of
ROWLAND FREEMAN, of this
Parish, *Gent.* who departed this Life,
June 4, 1715, Aged 71 Years.
Also of ELIZABETH, the Wife of
ANTHONY FREEMAN, of this Parish,
Gent. who departed this Life,
March the 22 1713, Aged 19 Years.
In Memory of
EDITH, the late Wife of
THOMAS FIELD, of the City of
Gloucester, *Gent.* and Daughter of
ROWLAND FREEMAN,
of this Parish, who died
Nov. 4, 1698, Aged 23 Years.

Here lyeth the Body of
ROBERT FREEMAN, *Senr.*
of this Parish, *Yeoman*,
who departed this Life,
Oct. 7, 1769, Aged 84 Years.
Also WILLIAM and JAMES,
Sons of ROBERT FREEMAN, *Junr.*
(by ALICE, his Wife,)
who died Infants.

JOAN, the Wife of ROBERT FREEMAN,
died May 9, 1752, Aged 57 Years.

Here lyeth buried the Body of
THOMAS ATKYNS, he died the
20 day of Decr. 1673,
Aged 89 Years.
Also the Body of MARGARET,
the first Wife of THOMAS ATKYNS,
She died 29 Sept. 1625.

Here lieth interr'd the Body of
RICHARD OCKOLD,
who died the 2 day of Nov. 1657,
Ætat. 67.
Resurgam.

Hic Recondita est Terrena Pars
HENRICI OCKOLD, *Gen.*
olim attornati ad legem nuper
Civitatis *Gloucestriæ*, majoris.
Lberis chari, amicis fidi, vicinis
benigni, omnibus benevoli, et probis
probati. Qui Obiit Aug. 24 die
Anno Salutis nostræ 1669, Æt. 58.
Here lyeth the Body of
RICHARD OCKOLD, of this Parish,
Gent. who died March 7, 1689,
Aged 55 Years.

In Memory of
JUDITH, the Wife of RICHARD
OCKOLD, of this Parish, *Gent.*
who deceased Sept. 20,
A. D. 1699.
Also HENRY, the Son of RICHARD
OCKOLD, by JUDITH, his Wife,
died Novem. 18, Ao. Dni. 1675,
Aged 13 Years.

Arms:—per Chevron 3
Martlets counter changed. LOGGINS.

Here lyeth the Body of
MICHAEL LOGGINS, *Gent.*
who died 17*th.* day of Febr.
Ano. 1645.

In Memory of
ELIZABETH, Daughter of JOHN
KEMBLE, who departed this Life,
the 6 of Jany. 1766, Aged 33.
In Memory of
HENRY KEMBLE, of this Parish,
who died Oct. 7, 1770,
Aged 77 Years.

In Memory of
JOHN WELLS, of this Parish,
who died December 4, 1758,
Aged near 50 Years.
THOMAS, Son of JOHN and
SARAH WELLS,
died July 5, 1769, Aged 18.

ON FLAT STONES.

JANE, Wife of THOMAS WEBB,
died July 27, 1752, Aged near 84.

ANNE, Wife of GEORGE BULLOCK,
of *Hardwick*, died Feb. 22, 1758,
Aged 55 Years.

CHARLES, Son of JOHN and ANNE
HIGGS, of *Barnwood*, died the
6 of Jany. 1766, Aged 21 Years.

SARAH, Wife of RICHARD BURROP,
of the Parish of *Painswick*,
died July 14 1767,
Aged near 46 Years.

ANNE, Wife of WILLIAM ABLE,
died February 19, 1763.

ANNE, Wife of JOHN FIELD,
died the 23 of March 1754,
Aged 68 Years.

JOHN BAMFORD,
died 10 Oct. 1742, Aged 72.
ELIZABETH, his Wife,
died 7 May 1729, Aged 60.

RICHARD WHITEHORN,
of this Parish, *Yeoman,*
who departed this Life,
11 day of July 1780,
Aged 47 Years.
ANNE, Wife of RICHARD
WHITEHORN, who resigned her
Soul to God, 27 June 1779,
Aged 46 Years.

WILLIAM BULLOCK,
of ... ... *Marches,*
who died Decr. ..., 1751,
Aged near 80 Years.

THOMAS GARDNERS,
late of this Parish, *Carpenter,*
who departed this Life,
May 1, 1780, Aged 69 Years.

ANNE, the Wife of WILLIAM
GARDNERS, late *Clerk*, of this Parish,
who departed this Life,
August 16, 1767, Aged 77.
ELIZABETH, Wife of THOMAS
GARDNERS, of this Parish,
Carpenter, she departed this Life,
May 6, 1773, Aged 63.

WILLIAM FIELD,
of *Sneedham* in this Parish,
died March 5, 1791, Aged 83.

JOHN FIELD, of *Gloucester,*
(Son of WILLIAM FIELD, of
Sneedham,) died Decr. 4, 1789,
Aged 48 Years.

WILLIAM FIELD, of this Parish,
who died Aug. 3, 1776,
Aged 35 Years.
BETTY, his Daughter, died
April 22, 1773, Aged 5 Years.
MARGARET, his Daughter,
died Decem. 29, 1778,
Aged 2 Years.

THOMAS WITCOMB, of this Parish,
Yeoman, who departed this Life,
Decr. 4, 1790, Aged 72 Years.

WILLIAM WITCOMB,
of this Parish, *Yeoman,*
who departed this Life,
June 2, 1741, Aged 58.
MARY, his Wife, who departed
this Life, July 1, 1742, Aged 47.
MARY, the Wife of THOMAS
WITCOMB, *Yeoman,* who deceased
May 26, 1733, Aged 29.
SARAH, Daughter of THOMAS
and MARY WITCOMB, who died
March 6, 1761, Aged 9.
Also MARY, the Wife of
THOMAS WITCOMB, who died
Decr. 20, 1776, Aged 45.

WILLIAM GOSCOMB,
of the Parish of *Matson, Yeoman,*
who departed this Life, the
9 day of Febr. in the Year 1744,
Aged 60 Years.
MARY, his Wife,
who departed this Life,
11 day of June 1772,
Aged 76 Years.
JAMES, the Son of WILLIAM
GOSCOMB, by MARY, his Wife,

who was buried 6 day of August
in the Year 1721, Aged 21 Weeks
and 4 days.
MARY, their Daughter,
who departed this Life, the
7*th.* day of Oct. in the Year 1730,
Aged 3 Years and 3 Quarters.
THOMAS, Son of WILLIAM and
MARY GOSCOMB, who departed
this Life, May 16, 1757,
Aged 33 Years.

ANNE BROWN,
and SUSANNA MATHEWS,
both Widows, Daughters of
SAMUEL BROAD,
late of this Parish, *Gent.*
ANNE, died Decr. 8, 1750,
Aged 76 Years.
SUSANNA, died July 17, 1732,
Aged 53 Years.
Also JAMES, the Son of
SAMUEL MATHEWS,
who died Oct. 1740, Aged 2 Years.

SARAH, Wife of WILLIAM
TAYLOR, of the Parish of
St. Michael in the City of
Gloucester, and Daughter of
JOHN and MARY KEMBLE,
of *Brockworth.*
She departed this Life,
4 day of August 1777, in the
45 Year of her Age.

JOHN KEMBLE, *Yeoman,*
who departed this Life, the
29 day of August 1775,
Aged 78 Years.
MARY, Wife of JOHN KEMBLE,
of *Brockworth,* who died
9 day of Jany. 1781,
Aged 77 Years.

HANNAH, the Wife of THOMAS
CHANDLER, of the Parish of
Painswick, who died Nov. 14, 1797,
Aged 52 Years.
Also MARGARET KEMBLE,
late of the Parish of *Brockworth,*
who died 6 day of Febr. 1791,
Aged 56 Years.

JAMES WITCOMB,
who departed this Life, the
19 May 1798, Aged 48 Years.

JAMES WITCOMB, *Senior,*
who departed this Life, the
17 Sept. 17, 1798, Aged 73 Years.
MARY WITCOMB,
Daughter of the above,
died in her Infancy.

(*Additional Inscriptions in Church
since Bigland's time.*)

M. S.
ANN, Wife of SAMUEL SMITH,
late *School Master* of this Parish,
who died Jany. 9, 1794,
in the 51*st.* Year of her Age.

M. S.
JAMES HODGE BYLES, *Esqr.*
of *Bowden Hall*, in this County,
who died 23 Jany. 1837,
Aged 62 Years.
He was a faithful Servant of God,
Excellent in every relation of Life
He lived esteemed and loved,
and died sincerely and deeply
lamented.

ON FRANKIS' STONE.

SAMUEL, son of WILLIAM and
ELIZABETH FRANKIS,
who died May 23, 1773,
in 66 Year of his Age.
ANN, their Daughter, Wife of
JOHN BRIDGES,
of the City of *Gloucester*,
who died Sept. 1793, in the
59*th.* Year of his Age.
JOHN BRIDGES,
of the City of *Gloucester, Gent.*
who died Jany. 11, 1801, in the
54*th.* Year of her Age.
RICHARD, Son of the above,
RICHARD and SARAH FRANKIS,
of this Parish, *Yeoman*,
who died Nov. 10, 1800, in the
64*th.* Year of his Age.
ANN, his beloved Wife, who died
July 4, 1837, in the
88*th.* Year of her Age.
HENRY, Son of RICHARD and

ANN FRANKIS, of the
City of *Gloucester, Baker*,
who died June 16, 1801, in the
24*th.* Year of his Age.

This Tablet is erected to the
Memory of FRANCES, Relict of
BENJAMIN HYETT, *Esqr.*
of *Painswick House*, in this County.
She was the only Child of the late
Sir THOMAS SNELL,
of *Sailsbury Hall*, in the County
of *Herts* and of *Whitley Court,*
in this County, *Knight.*
She died leaving no issue,
A. D. 1768.
And her remains are interred
in this Chancel.
And of PETER SNELL, *Esqr.*
Youngest son of
VYNER SNELL, B. D.
Rector of *Duddington Marsh,*
Wimblington, and Bennack in
the *Isle of Ely*, and Nephew of the
above named *Sir* THOMAS SNELL,
whose Estates in the City and
County of *Gloucester*, he inherited.
And was many years resident at
Whitley Court, and afterwards
at *Cheltenham*, where he died,
A. D. 1814.
AGNES, his beloved Wife,
survived him, and died at an
advanced Age in 1819.

They departed in the comfortable
hope of the Gospel Covenant
which is promised to the true Believer,
And their remains are deposited
in this Chancel.

M. S.
JAMES STEERS,
of *Bernard Street, Russel Square,*
London, Esqr. F. R. S.
who died at *Cheltenham,*
31 July 1817, in the
61 Year of his Age.
This Tablet is erected by his deeply
afflicted Widow FRANCES,
Daughter of PETER SNELL, of
Whitley Court, in this County, *Esqr.*
In whose Vault in this Chancel the
Remains of her lamented Husband,
are deposited.

Arms :—Or, a mullet gules.
impaling SNELL.

A Memorial Window to MARY,
Wife of JAMES ACKERS, of
Prinknash Park,
who died Decr. 17, 1848, Aged 37.

There is a
Another to JAMES, eldest son of
JAMES and MARY ACKERS,
who died Xmas. day 1859,
Aged 23 Years.

HEAD STONES IN CHURCH YARD.

	Died.	Aged.		Died.	Aged.
Sarah, daughter of Joseph and Mary Carwardine	30 Nov.	1799	21	James Cook	... . in 1742	22
Thomas Carwardine	5 Oct.	1796	61	William Webb	3 Jany. 1781	47
Thomas Carwardine	6 May	1740	50	William Witcomb, *Senior.* ...	2 Sept. 1707	70
Mary, his Wife	14 Sept.	1789	81	Elinor, daughter of Richard and Elinor Burrup... ...	15 Febr. 1728	21
Mary, Wife of James Cole ...	29 Apr.	1790	68	Elinor, Wife of Richard Burrup	6 June 1729	44
Mary, Wife of Thomas Marsh ...	23 Nov.	1796	62	Richard Carpenter	31 Decr. 1796	83
Ann, daughter of Henry and Elizabeth Turner	27 Nov.	1795	21	Mary, his Wife	22 Febr. 1759	78
				John Field	5 Febr. 1759	37
John Print, son of Henry and Elizabeth Turner	25 Augt.	1778	5 wk.	John Pool	18 Nov. 1789	41
				John Harris	11 Mar. 1764	81
Mary, Wife of Henry Kemble	16 July	1786	82	Mary, his Wife	10 April 1782	92
Henry Kemble	7 Oct.	1770	77	William Gardner	11 Nov. 1765	68
John, son of William Wathen	19 Decr.	1771	21	Mary, his Wife	7 Jany. 1761	76
William Wathen	24 Nov.	1767	62	John Collorick	5 Sept. 1797	61
Ann, Wife of John Hams ...	5 Nov.	1760	70	John Jones	3 Nov. 1783	69
John Hams	28 April	1748	74	Elizabeth, his Wife	14 Sept. 1769	57
Thomas, his Son	15 June	1747	26	George Bullock	10 Decr. 1785	68
Elizabeth, Relict of John Carill	24 May	1756	27	Susannah, Wife of John Wells...	11 Febr. 1796	57
Jane, Wife of Thomas Webb ...	22 Febr.	1754	55	Thomas Tinnell	8 Febr. 1776	57
Thomas Carwardine	5 Febr.	1794	45	Sarah, Wife of Thomas Marston	8 July 1793	82
John Gibbs	8 Oct.	1771	65	Beata Griffin	20 April 1790	59
Joyce, his Wife	10 June	1780	73	Edward Randle	14 Oct. 1765	62
Mary Dearlove	17 Sept.	1773	40	Thomas Rodway	17 May 1775	64
Elizabeth, Wife of Daniel Gardner	21 Febr.	1769	32			

Supplementary Notes as to I.—*Devolution of Estates.* II.—*Church.* III.—*Taxation, Population, &c.*

I.—*Devolution of Estates :*

Upton in Barton Hundred, was a member of King's Barton Manor and was Terra Regis. It contained one Hide, and had 4 Men. (*i. e.* free men.) Alwin the Sheriff had been over this Estate [in King Edward's time.] Hunfrid, held it (at the Survey, but no Rent is stated.) *Domesday Survey.*

There are several Hunfrids named in the Survey as Tenants. In Numbers 68, 70, 71., three are named in succession and are distinguished as the Chamberlain, De Medehall and the Cook. De Medehall, was Tenant of Wotton, a place near to this, and of the three he probably is the one meant. But there might have been a fourth Hunfrid, or Humphry. St. Peter's Gloucester, held at the Survey, other

members of King's Barton as Barnwood, Tuffley, Morwent. Upton, was probably the farthest upland part of the cultivated Tract under the Woods or wastes which were not computed as taxable.

A Virgate of Land granted in serjeanty under Render of 200 Arrow Heads yearly—

15 Edw. i.—Walkelin de Fabrica. *Plac. Com. Gloc.*

3 Edw. ii.—The Manor or chief fee passed to the Abbot and Convent of St. Peter Gloucester, by Crown Grant.
This Abbey had acquired Lands here before:—
3 Edw. ii.—From John le Broke, William de Snedham, and many others.
The Abbey granted a Sub-fee to the Earl of Arundel ;

on whose attainder it was forfeited to the Crown, and 1330. 5 Edw. iii. was granted to Richard de Monmouth. It afterwards came back to the Arundel family.

temp. Hen. v.—The Abbey also made Grants of Kynsbury and other Lands in favour of divers Persons.

26 Hen viii—The Lay Property of the Abbey is thus enumerated in the *Valor Eccl'us.*

	£.	s.	d.
Rents of Assize	43	10	6
Farm of site of Manor	0	56	8
150a. in Prinknash Park	100 s.		
Farm of a Stone Quarry	12 s.		

After the dissolution—

The chief Manor was granted to Lord Cobham, whose descendant was attainted.

2 Jac. i —Walter Pye and Wm. Beal, by Crown Grant.

1603.—It was purchased by contributions of the Freeholders and conveyed to Trustees. (Roberts. Osborne, Gwinnett and Wood,) for the Use of the Freeholders.

1632.—The site of the Manor was conveyed by the Trustees to John and George Bridgeman.

The Trustees or Feoffees have been renewed from time to time. They hold the Lordship, the soil of Roads and the Commons, and keep a Court Leet.

Prinknash, 190a. is a manerial Estate. It will be described below separately.

Snedham, Messuage and ¼ Virgate of Land in Upton and 2a. Land and 4s. Rent in Snedham.

Abbot of Gloucester, from W. de Snedham.

Manor of Snedham:

Sir W. Nottingham, by purchase.

Abbot of Gloucester, by his Gift.

The Corporation of Gloucester, held lands here. qy. these? There are Remains of the Moat about the Toft or Site of Snedham's House:

Other Estates:

It may be convenient to notice these according to their situation:

1.—In The Village about the Church.
2.—Along the Road from Gloucester to Painswick.
3.—Along the Road called the Portway to Cranham.
4.—In the Cross Ways between the Roads.

1. Ockold's End:—an Estate here was long in the antient family of Ockold.

see Subsidy Roll, 1 Edw. iii. *& Church Inscriptions.*

Afterwards of Hyett—

T. 9. Ann.—T. Mathews and B. Hyett, *Plaintiffs.* John Bridgman, *Esqr.* Liston, Osbaldeston, and Ockold, *Gentlemen.,* Catharine and Ann Ockold, and others, *Deforciants. Fine.* of a Messuage 30 a. of Land and 40 a. pasture in Upton St Leonards and Westbury.

A Mill here belonged to Ockold's Estate.

St. Leonard's Court, a new erected Mansion on Land part of Ockolds Estate, has passed through several Names:—Parsons, Pearson, Ancrum.

Valley Farm:

This belonged to the Carwardines for many generations.

1263.—Grant by the Abbey to Kerwardyn, of Lands in Upton, *Regist. St. Peter, and see Subsidy Roll.*

Poole farm :—Mr. Wells.

2. Along the Road to Painswick, are:—

Saintbridge which belonged to Atkyns and afterwards to the Raikes' family.

Opposite to Saint Bridge House grounds is Church or Chapel Haye the toft of a Church; and above that the traces of a Moat indicating the site of a House which belonged to De Mattesdon.

see Subsidy Roll, 1 Edw. iii.

Grove Court Manor:

Messuage (a fine half timbered house) 160a. Land, Mill, &c. grant in serjeanty (40 days service of an Archer) yearly:

Ralph de Marleberg; Sibilla, daughter and heir, married 1st. Rays. 2nd. De la Grave, Robert Rays, by descent, son and heir of Sibilla, by her first Husband.

Clause Rolls, 9 Hen. iii.

10 Edw. ii.—Sibilla de la Grave, died seized of Lands here. Thomas de la Grave, by descent, (Nephew and heir,)

Escheat.

16 Edw. iv.—Nevil, Lord Abergavenny, then for some time in the Berkeley family. Richard Walter, in the last century. At *Rudder's* time in the name of the present Proprietor Blissett.

Brimpsfield:—a farm belonging to St. Bartholomew's Hospital Gloucester.

There are Farms belonging to Lord Sydney, one heretofore of the Robins family.

Others are partly in this and partly in Matson Parish.

3. The Road to Cranham is called Portway a name common to Roman Vicinal ways.

At the foot of this Road is the Manor farm late Mr. Vansittart's since Mr. B. Hunt's.

Gastrell's farm is near Portway. This Name no doubt is that of the former Owners whose name (Gastrell.) occurs *in Church Inscriptions,* and is still flourishing in the Neighbourhood. It now belongs to Mr. Ackers.

4 In the Crossways Northwards:—

Bowden Hall, at first called Creed's place, this has passed through the successive ownerships of Campbell, Jeffery, Byles, Vansittart, and Hunt. It is now Mr. Dearman Birchall's, and the Estate attached to it is much enlarged.

Whitley Court Estate:

Sir Thomas Snell, by purchase.

1746.—Indenture (inrolled) between Sir Thomas Snell, Knight, and Henry Toye, Esqr.

Afterwards Peter Snell, Esqr. *see Church Inscriptions.*

The now Owner, Willyams, is a Representative of this family, but the mansion is used as a farm house.

The Upper Mill is part of this Estate.

Other farms are:—

Pincot farm :—Mr. Ackers.

Starvehall farm:—Mr. Hyett.

Hill farm:—Cox's Charity. Lately sold to Mr. Fryer.

Kinsbury farm:

A Grant was made by Abbey of Gloucester, to Robert, son of Philip of Kynemersbury, of a House at Upton with Land at Uudercomb.

This farm (which once had a moated grange) belongs to Mr. Blissett.

In the Cross ways southwards between the Roads are Farms and Lands called Crow's Nest, Cudhill, &c.

1814.—An Inclosure Act, 54 Geo. iii. passed for inclosing Lands in Upton St. Leonards and several adjacent Places Matson, Tuffleigh, Barnwood, Wooton, and others.

The Awards under this Act and under the Annual Inclosure Act 1861, 24 & 25 Vic. 1866, are inrolled in Office of Clerk of the Peace.

1776.—*At the County Election the following Voted as Free-holders in Upton St. Leonards.*

Abel, John.	Howell, John. *Esqr.*
Ashmead, William.	Hyett, Nicholas, *Esqr.*
Barnes, B.	Long, George.
Beavan, Thomas.	Mosley, James.
Bishop, William.	Marston, Thomas.
Brown, Thomas.	Morris, John.
Campbell, Robert, *Esqr.*	Perring, Richard.
Carpenter, Joseph.	Rea, William, *Gent.*
Carwardine, (2) Jos., John.	Rodway, Thomas, *Senior.*
Chandler, Richard, *Gent.*	Smith, (2) Geo., James.
Cother, Thomas.	Snell, Peter, *Esqr.*
Field, William.	Turner, Henry.
Frankis, (2) Hen., Benj.	Wells, (2) Charles, John.
Helps, Richard.	Watkin, William.

Of these names several still remain; but "Frankis" has disappeared.

II.—*Church :*—

The Rectory was appropriated to the Abbey of St. Peter's Gloucester, who had the Nomination of the Vicar or Curate.

Farm of Rectory of Upton, £10. 0. 0.

Deduction :—Allowance to Curate 118 s. 11 d.

Valor Eccl'us.

Hen. viii.—After the dissolution of Monasteries, the Impropriation was granted to the Dean and Chapter of Gloucester; and the Nomination of Curate to the Bishop.

Endowment

1781, 1792.—The Curacy has been augmented out of Queen Ann's Bounty by Benefactions and Lot ...... 400 £.

Incumbents:—

.... Thomas, was the Curate or Minister at the time of Bishop Hooper's Examination. He learnedly answered the Questions put. The Number of Communicants was 206. The Bishop of Gloucester was Patron.

Mr. Abbot, was Vicar or Curate in the time of Sir Robert Atkyns.

Mr. Bishop, in the time of Rudder.

Mr. Samuel Commeline, in the time of Rudge.

The Ecclesiastical District of St. James, Gloucester (Pop. 1881, 8695.) comprises parts of the Parishes of St. Catharine; Mary de Lode; St. Michael; and Upton St. Leonards.

III.—*Taxation, Population, &c.*

Vpton, Subsidy Roll, 1 Edw. III. 1327.

De Willmo. le Conestable. xxii d.
' Raduo le Palmer, xxii d. ob. q.
' Willmo. Hynderlinge, ii s. iiii d.
' Willmo. Phelip, xv d. q.
' Johe Short, xxi d. q.
' Matill. Curteys, vi d.
' Johne de Yareforde, ix d.
' Elia de Byleye, ix d. ob. q.
' Walto. Short, xvi d.
' Rico. Adames, xiii d. q.
' Johe. le Bonde, ix d.
' Robto. Okholt, xii d. ob q.
' Rico. de Whaddon, xxii d. ob.
prob. Sma. xvii *s.* iiii *d. o.*

Sendebrugge, Subsidy Roll, 1 Edw. III. 1327.

De Pho. le Hayward, x d.
' Henr. le Daunsare, xv d. ob. q.
' Johe. le Daunsare, vi d. p.
' Willmo. Vggel, xiiii d. q.

Adhuc Sendebrugge.

De Robto. atte Buedelesmull, xv d.
' Galfro. Piscatore, ix d.
' Robto. Foket, ix d.
' Johe. Wymond, x d. ob.
' Willo. Gerald, vi d.
' Thm. de Mattesdon, ii s. iii d.
prob. Sma. x *s.* i *d. o. q.*

Snedham, Subsidy Roll, 1 Edw. III. 1327.

De Nicho. le Murye, xxi d.
' Rico. Axtel, xxi d.
prob. Sma. iii *s.* vi *d.*

Acreage 2974 *a.*—
whereof about 1820 *a.* pasture.
800 *a.* in commonfields
200 *a.* arable Inclosures.
90 *a.* Wood.
56 *a.* River and Wastes.
7 *a.* Common of pasture.

1815.—Annual Value of Real Property £ 5320.

1861.—Rateable Value £ 6304.

Population 1831,—898. 1861,—1035. 1871,—1173.

1833-4-5.—Average of three Years Expenditure on Poor £ 233.

In Gloucester Union.

36 & 37. Eliz.—Decree to quiet possession of Lands.

10 Jac.—Decree as to Tenure of Lands here.
Exchequer Records.

Some Parcels of Dudston Manor are in this Parish.

There is a place called Bondend in Upton where once stood a farm House and now stands an Alms House. In the Subsidy Roll, 1 Edw. iii. (above) among the Tax Payers is John le Bonde, a name denoting servitude.

A Deed of manumission by the Abbey of John Bonde, is in the Register of Abbot Braunche.

OCKOLD, OF UPTON St. LEONARD'S.

Philip de Ockolde. = ...

William de Ockolde, circa 1263-1268. — Sibilla. = William Cruste.

Robert Ockolt, Subs, Roll 1 Ed, iii, 1327.

Richard Ockold, = Agnes Robins. married at Upton, 18 Jany. 1542. buried 26 Decr, 1566.

John. bapt. 6 Augt. 1544. died an Infant. — John, bapt. 1 Nov. 1545 burd. 8 Jany. 1546. — Agnes, bapt. 2 April 1551. burd. 26 Dec. 1566. — Richard, bapt, 20 Nov. 1552. — Thomas, burd. 31 Oct. 1618. = Sibilla, burd. 1634. — John, bapt. 20 Decr. 1562.

Thomas, burd. 8 Jany. 1589. — Richard, bapt 24 Oct. 1591, marr. 14 Jan. 1610, died 2 Nov. 1657. = Elizabeth Winchcombe. — Judith, bapt. 23 Febr. 1590. — Elizabeth, bapt. 5 Augt. 1593. — Prudence, bapt. 15 Febr. 1594. — Catherine, bapt. 17 April 1598. burd. 2 Febr. 1600.

Robert, bap. 28 July 1614. burd. 1 Aug. 1614. — Henry, bap 4 Jany. 1611. Mayor of Gloucester, 1668. burd. 26 Aug 1669. = Margaret.

Elizabeth, born 2 March 1633. — Richard. born 11 March 1634. died 7 March 1689. = Judith, daughter of John Osbaldeston, of Shadlington. She died 20, & burd. 22 Sept 1699. — Mary, bap. 11 Mh. 1637. burd. 8 Ap. 1648. — Thomas, bapt. 2 Sept. 1644. — Charles. bapt 23 March 1645 burd. 29 Febr. 1719.

John Bridgeman, of Prinknash, & Nympsfield. burd. 3rd. June 1729. = Catherine, died 10 Oct. 1744, Aged 79. Will proved at Gloucester, 17 Jany. 1744-5. — Richard Tooker, of Bristol, = Frances, bapt. 18 June 1667. — Henry, burd. 20 Nov. 1675, æt. 13. Henry, bapt. 2 Febr. 1675. burd. 12 Oct. 1680. — Mary, bapt. 5 March 1667. burd. 16 Oct, 1689. Anne, bapt. 23 Nov. 1673. — Richard, bapt. 21 Apr. 1677. burd. 29 January 1749. = Mary. — .... Longbottom. = Priscilla, bap. 27 May 1684. — Joane, bap 1670. Margaret.

Sir Francis Fust, of Hill, Ancestor of H. Jenner Fust, Esqr. (See Fosb. Glouc.) = Frances, marr. at Gloucester Cathedral, Sept. 28, 1724. — Thomas Wheeler. Ment'd in Cath. Bridgeman's Will. = Mary. — Jane.

PRINKNASH,

ADDENDUM.

PRINKNASH, has been already mentioned (*No.* 206) the only information given being that it had a private Chapel. It was then extra pa1ochial. But it has lately been made a Pa1ish of itself for rating. This circumstance added to its local ecclesiastical connexion with Upton renders it proper here to give a fuller account of the place.

Prinknash *or* Prinkenedge, (a name which describes the situation of the place on the Brink or edge of the Hill, the letters P and B being interchangeable,) was probably a clearance in the great Beech Wood, (Buckholt) which extended from Birdlip to Painswick and Upton.

1121.—Gifts of Land in Buckholt, by Elias Giffard, to Gloucester Abbey.

In the History of the Abbey, (*Vol.* i. *p.* 63, *of the Record Publications.*) in divisions or bonndaries of the possessions of the Abbey in Buckholt are thus given :—Brimpsfield.) Ledencome divides as far as Alcamsode (Alcomb's Wood.) Between the Archbishop (of York and us Wycombsede. Cooper's Hill.? Between us and Roger de Chaundos, (Lord of Brockworth) the Way divides (there is still a way traceable here leading from Portway *see* "Upton" to the ancient camp on High broadridge) Between us and Payne Fitz John, (Lord of Painswick) from Salcomb's Brook as far Idel's bridge. Between the King, (Lord of Upton St Leonard's) Elgar of Kenemsbury, (Kimbury in Upton) and us from Prinknashe, as far as the Beech Tree whereon the Robber was hung, Between us and Ernulph de Mattesdon, (Matson) Prinknash as far as Idelbarrow, (in Pope's Wood) There is a Mill, This division made in the Year when King Henry (i.) married Adeliza, (1121.) Some of these Boundaries can be still traced and reasonable conjectures made as to others.

The House and Park of Prinknash, are of later date The Register speaks of the Abbots Manor of Prinkenashe but whether by that they claimed, as such Bodies were wont to do, manerial Rights over the whole tract granted, does not clearly appear. 1555, they obtained the right of free Warren in Prinknash, (Manor. ?) and hence probably a Woodward's house arose here About that time Prinknash proper was made extra parochial. At the beginning of the 16*th.* century, the Abbot had a residence here and a Park.

The Valor Eccl'us Upton (which see) mentions 150 *a.* in Prinknash Park, but there might be other Land part of the site of the Manor. The extraparochial privilege did not extend byond the House and Park. It had a private Chapel consecrated about 1625, although for ecclesiastical purpous the Place is considered to be in Upton St. Leonard's After the surrender of the Abbey and its possessions to the Crown, the Mansion of Prinknash with the Park, Mill, &c in the County of the City of Gloucester, were granted,

36 Hen. viii —to Edmund Briggs, (Brydges) son and heir apparent of John Briggs. Knight, and Dorothy Braye, Gentlewoman, in special tail male.

The marriage took effect and the Grantees descendants (Lords Chandos,) held for three Generations. It then passed by purchase to Sir J. Bridgeman, who also acquired the Reversion from the Crown. It remained in that family until the Purchaser's grandson John Bridgeman, (who married Catharine Ockold, *see* Ockold Pedigree,) died without issue, having by Will 1729, devised the Estate in divers Limitations in tail, the last being to Henry Toy, his cousin who came into possession on the death of the Widow 1744 Thence 1770. John Howell, by purchase, His son T. B. Howell, and grandson T. J. Howell, successively.

Mr. James Ackers, by purchase *see Ch. Inscriptions.*

Horace Walpole, visited this Hause 1774, which pleased him.　　　*Gent. Mag. Vol.* LXXV. *p.* 898.

A feudal relation betwen Prinknash and Brimpsfield was maintained; as the constablewick of Brimpsfield Castle was kept up after the forfeiture of J. Giffard, and destruction of the Castle. It passed by Crown Grant to the Duke of Clarence and his descendants the Mortimers and family of York. The Cognizance of Elizabeth of York, Queen of Henry VII. is on the Hall Cieling of the House.

1651.—Among the Names of Persons charged to provide Horses and Arms for the Commonwealth are:—

1.—The Lady Bridgeman and her Grand child the sonne and Heire of George Bridgeman, deceased, and Mr. Heavingham Bridgeman, Guardian of John Bridgeman, One Horse. 2.—Mr. Robins, One Horse and Armes 3.—Mr. Atkins, of Tuffliegh, One Horse and Armes. These persons were connected with Upton. Atkins, compounded for his Estate. Laurence Singleton, (whose Heir, Robins married) and Edward Nourse, of Matson ? were Parliamentarians.

1882. { Area 224 *acres.*
{ Rateable Value 321 £.

(Thanks are due to the Revd. W. Bazeley, *for the* Ockold *Pedigree and other aid in the Notes on Upton and Prinknash.)*

WALTON CARDIFF,

ADDENDUM.

284.

WALTON CARDIFF Manor: Nash in his History of Worcestershire under "Bredon" speaking of the Reades says that they were a Gloucestershire family and seem to have acquired their property in Worcestershire by marriage with a Co-heir of the Lord Beauchamp, of Powick; and that their Pedigree is to be seen in Vincent's Collection in the Herald's College, London.

Giles Read, was Sheriff of Gloucestershire and Worcestershire, He was a Man, says Nash, much respected in his time.

The Reads were the principal Inhabitants of Mitton in Bredon, and there was their Chief House.

In the Church of that Parish there were several Monuments to the memory of Members of the family.—1577, to William Read, of Mitton and his Wife Kath. and Son, 1611, to Giles Read, and his Wife Katherine, by birth Greville. On this Monument are the Arms of Read, quartering Greville, Arden, and Beauchamp, of Powyk. And 1623, to a Daughter of the said Giles and Katherine.

Merton Meadow :—In Brewers "Beauties of England" under Blaize Castle near Bristol, in a Notice of the Harford family its Owners it is mentioned that Archdeacon Richard Harford, (M. A. of Oxford, 1544.) a Member of Merton College, gave a Meadow in Walton Cardiff, to that College.

WALTON CARDIFF.

One mile from Tewkesbury.

No BURIALS.

1.—*Estates :*

Walton Church and Village are situate at the intersection of two very ancient Roads, one the Rudgeway from Tredington towards Bredon's Hardwick, the fords over the Carrant and Avon, &c (part as some suppose of the Roman Rycknield way:) (*Allies' Worcestershire Antiquities*, 418.) the other the Bentham way, from Tewkesbury to Home down Natton, Oxenton, &c When these were the only Roads in the named directions, the Village lay more in the way, than from the substitution of Roads at higher Levels, it now does. It had twelve Subsidy Payers in 1327, from which we may infer that its population was then as great as at present. It is by some stated to be a portion of Tewkesbury Parish. But on what grounds does not appear, the right of Burial there being insufficient. The Charter to Tewkesbury of Jac. the second would have included it in the Borough "whether it were within or without the Parish." But this was a stretch of prerogative and never acted on.

In Domesday Survey, Walton is mentioned as a member of Tewkesbury Manor, then *terra Regis* but late of Queen Matilda and at the conquest Brietric's. It contained three Hides and was in the Hands of a Radchenister, a sort of military tenant.

Tewkesbury with its Members was soon afterwards granted to the Earls of Gloucester, and temp. Hen. ii. one of them granted a subfee in Walton to William de Kerdiff, a name indicating his connection with another great possession (Cardiff and its Castle,) of those Earls, and which hence became distinctive of this Walton from other places (the retreats of the antient British from the Saxon Invaders) so called.

In the family of De Kardiff, the estate continued some centuries.

Edw. ii.—Paulinus de Kerdiff, died seized of the hamlet of Walton near Tewkesbury, leaving William, his son and heir. *Inq. post mort.*

13 Edw. iii.—Edwd. de Kerdiff, and Wife Johanna, were seized.

By marriage of the heir general it passed into another name—Bassett, and thereby the place became Walton Bassett. From this family it passed into that of Gunter, and then to Berow, or Barrow.

1 Mar.—Thomas and Margaret Berow, held, And 5 Eliz.—John Berow, production of whose title to the Manor of Walton Cardiff, otherwise W. Bassett, was required by the Crown. *Pasch. Recorda 5 Eliz. Rot. 87.*

But De Kerdiff's was not the only Manor. The possessions of Monasteries grew around them and in this place Tewkesbury Abbey acquired Tythes and Lands and as was usual denominated their Lands a Manor.

This Manor of Walton Kerdyff, was held thus :—

6 Ric. ii.—W. de Chesterton, H. Greyndour.

2 Ric. ii.—Pet. de Wodemancote, R. de Underhill.

A Moiety of this Manor :—

7 Ric. ii.—William de Chesterton, John Apperley, H. Best, and Pet. de Wodmancote, to Tewkesbury Abbey. *Inq. ad quod dam.*

While this Estate remained in mortmain there was little confusion between it and the lay Manor, but when it was turned into a lay fee, it soon became a matter of doubt to which Manor to refer the entries in Records relating to Walton or the Manor of Walton.

Another source of confusion here, as in many other places, is referring the entries in Records relating to the chief or paramount Manor to the sub-fee held of it. Thus Entries in Inquisitions post Mortem, of fees in Walton, Edw., iii. H. Audley and Margaret, his Wife, 4 Hen. iv. Edw., Earl of Stafford, 38 and 39 Hen. vi. Henry, Duke of Buckingham, have been referred to the sub-Manor whereas they relate to the chief seignory of Tewkesbury.

Walton Cardiff Manor :—

2 Edw. vi.—Sir Thomas Heneage, and Wife Catharine, and Lord Willoughby, held Walton.

3 Edw. vi.—They gave it in Exchange to the Crown.

7 Edw. vi.—It was granted to William and John Read. *Originalia 1 Par Rot. 76.*

1608.—Giles Read, was Lord of the Manor, and in 1658, Foulke Read.

The extent of the Cardiff lay Manor is not known; and indeed it is difficult to say which of the existing farms or estates in the Village was the Manor place

In the Register of Tewkesbury Abbey 138; it is recorded that they had impleaded Wm de Kerdiff, of the Chantry of the Chapel of Walton, and of a certain way in his Meadow towards Walton which was adjudged by discreet Men to the Abbey as was set forth in the Cyrograph made between them and him.

From this it appears that there was a Chapel at Walton and a Chantry in it. The Chapel was no doubt where the present structure stands and the late stood. To that the date of 1658, is ascribed, but the mouldings in its Windows were evidently fragments of tracery from an older Building. The Chantry in the primitive Chapel suggests that the family of De Kerdiff, were resident here. And it is not improbable that the ruins now in heaps covered by turf adjacent to the Chapel and the Moat near to its sides shew the site of the House.

The reference to the Road for the Abbey through De Kerdiff's Meadow, and the circumstance that the fields above the Chapel Meadow were called (from the Owner who succeded Kerdiff,) "Bassett's" Wood Grounds (being at one time covered with Wood,) strengthen the supposition that this Land was part of demesne.

Of the County Historians Sir R. Atkyns, named the Reads at having been Lords of the Manor, (apparently the lay Manor,) but he deduced no subsequent Title from them, Rudder, said that the Manor was in the Corporation of Tewkesbury, thus merging the subordinate in the paramount Manor.

Smithsend, was a family of repute which came here about the time of Jac. i. the *Inquisition port Mort.*, 4 Car. i. on N. Smithsend, shows that their Estate was not the Manor, but as Forbroke, suggests (on what grounds is not stated) the Manor might have been afterwards added.

Monumental Records of the Smithsends, have been found in Ashchurch, Tewkesbury and Twyning Churches. Their Estate came to Elizabeth Smithsend, the surviving Daughter of a Nicholas Smithsend, (who married Mary Romney,) and heiress of the family. She by Will, 1832, gave it to her Cousin Robert Phelps, since which it has changed hands several times. So have the other Estates here by Sales, but in their Sale particulars, no mention is made of a Manor.

4 Car. i.—Lands in Walton Cardiff, Fiddington, Tredington, Tewkesbury :—Nicholas Smithsend, who died 12 Jac i. leaving Nicholas, his son and heir, who married Elizth. Graves, and died 3 Car. i. leaving Nicholas, his son and heir, aged 12 years. *Inquisition post Mort.*

Smithsend's was a Brick House. But there were 2 or 3 ancient timber Houses one of which was on the Ecclesiastical Manor and is now destroyed, and several Cottages.

Jeynes, Symonds, and Grevile, or Lilington, were Owners of Houses here and Lands thereto.

Sir Robt. Atkyns, mentions Mr. Symonds, as having a good House and Estate in this place.

1701—Symonds then of Pengethly, Herefordshire, to T. Sparry, of Holdfast, Worcestershire and afterwards of the Mythe, Tewkesbury. His descendant sold to Longmore and from Longmore's Devisees, Gael, by purchase.

Greviles or Lewis' Lands included the Chapel grounds.

1745.—Lewis and Wife Elizabeth, late Elizth. Grevile, sold in the lue time of her Father C. Grevile, M. D. (her mother was Lilington,) to the Revd. Somerset Jones, of Ticenham, (which see) His Daughter and heir married James, and in her Widowhood devised to Revd. Wm. Seys, who was on the County Voters Register, 1804. His son sold the House and part of the Land to Long; and the Chapel grounds, &c. to Longmore, which from his devisees, came by purchase to Gael.

Ecclesiastical Estate : To return to this:—

It appears by the *Valor Eccl'us.* that under the Ecclesiastical Manor customary Tenants held whose Rents of assize were 9 £. and 4 d. and that the farm of a Meadow was worth 68 s. and 8 d. The customary Tenants must have been numerous. and as there are none such now known. the Copyholds of this Manor must have merged in the Estate which was in possession of the Abbey at the dissolution.

Lands late of Tewkesbury Abbey, a separate Manor:— Thomas Sheldon, and Laurence Poyner.

Subsequently the Estate passed to the ancestors of the Earls of Essex, and long continued in the Essex family, but was sold a few years ago, and subsequently was parcelled out.

The House was on the opposite side of the Road to the Chapel Ground. On its Close was a public Watering place the Boat pool, so called from affording accomodation for keeping Boats, an important matter in a place subject from the confluence of Brooks, to floods and until lately without a Bridge.

Its Lands:—Almonds (Haman's) Hill, Benthams, &c near Tewkesbury, the Gastons in the Village, the Rudgeway pieces in that Road. There were 2 Rent charges one of 2 £. another of 3 £ yearly which might have been part of the old Rents of Assize altho' of the Farms charged therewith (Stone's or Martins) one is said to be in Fiddington, which might perhaps be explained by the circumstance of the Homestead being in Fiddington.

Hamond or Home Downs, is a tract of Land, long in debate between Ashchurch and Walton Parishes.

As to ,Rates the Walton Occupiers by Vestry Resolution gave up the Claim of their Parish. But as to Tythes Awards were made to the Tythe Owners of both Parishes, and thus these Lands became doubly burdened with Tythes a manifest wrong, yet said to be irremediable.

This was formerly part of Warwick's Lands (*see* Tewkesbury, Sodbury, &c.) and came to the Crown.

Edw. 6.—Sir Thomas Seymour, of Sudeley, by Crown Grant.

After forfeiture by his Attainder, the Crown.

18 Eliz.—Sir Christopher Hatton, by Crown Grant.

The Devolution to the following the now Owners of Land here is not traced back—Umble, Roberts, Merton College and others.

Nor the Lande of the following heretofore Owners traceable.

Fines: H. 30 Eliz.—J. Kemmett and R. Hiet.
T. 3 Geo. i.—Thomas, Lord Mansell,

Escheat: 3 Car. i.—R. Cotton.

Among the early Wills at Gloucester, are the following of Persons of Walton Cardiff.

1545.—W. Hawling.
1598.—Stephen Green.

1776.—*In the Election for Gloucestershire, the following voted for Freeholds in Walton Cardiff.*

Bradstock, Rowland. (the Vicar.)
Smithsend, Nickolas.
Sperry, Thomas, *Senr.*

II.—*Church.*

Rectory Impropriate in Tewkesbury Abbey. After its dissolution Crown Grants of Tythes parcel of the Rectory:— *viz.*—Hay Tythe in Nether Gaston, to F. Morice and Thos. Phillips, In trust for Sir W. Ryder.   *Originalia.*

Other Tythes:—
To Thomas Sheldon and Lawrence Poyner.

Other Tytdes:—
7 Edw. vi.—To Daniel and Alexander Perte.

Vicarage:
1658.—Grant of Small Tythes.
1653.—Trial at Law and Decree concerning Tithes.
                Exchequer Records.

List of Incumbents and Patrons of Walton Cardiff.

1662.	Richard Wilks, of Tredington.	All Soul's College, Oxon.	
1681, 1701.	Robt Wriggan, of Tredington.	Do.	do.
1706.	John Mathew, of Tewkesbury.	Do.	do.
1732.	John Sayer.	Do.	do.
1750.	William Palmer.	Do.	do.
1773.	Rowland Bradstock.	Do.	do.
1786.	Oliph Leigh Spencer.	Do.	do.
1787.	Henry Willoughby Bertie.	Do.	do.
1794.	Edward Williams.	Do.	do.

Sir Robt. Atkyns, says that the Incumbents in his day was appointed by All Souls College, Mr. Symmonds and Mr. Smithsend.

1874.—The Chapel was rebuilt.

III.—*Taxation, Population, &c. of Walton Cardiff.*

Walton Kerdiff, Subsidy Roll, 1 Edw. III. 1327.

De Rico. Balkereue, xxii d.
‘ Cristin. Bastard, xx d.
‘ Willo. Baldwyne, xii d.
‘ Willo. Rolves, ii s. o.
‘ Nicho. Bonde, xii d.
‘ Johe Dauy, xxii d.
‘ Willo. Jones, xxii d.
‘ Nicho. Taundy, xviii d.
‘ Henr. Coke, xii d.
‘ Nicho. Dauy, xx d.
‘ Willo. Felice, iii s. iiii d.
‘ Willo. de Kerdyf, ii s.
        prob. Sma. xxs. ixd. o.

Walton Cardiff, Subsidy Roll, 19 Jac. i.

Nicolaus Smithsed, in ter.	... ...	£2	5	4
Henric. Edwards in ter.		1	2	8
Rob'tus. Fletcher, in bon.		3	5	0
	Som 13 s.			

Acreage 650. a.

Population 1831,—57. 1851.—60. 1871,—68.

In 1815. Annual Value of Real Property 1424 £.

1875.—Rateable Value £ 1424.

1833-4-5. Average of three Years Expenditure on Poor £ 40.

In Tewkesbury Union.

Of the Salt Wells common hereabout, those of Walton at one time were much resorted to, And a Well Room was built in the adjacent Stow Road, but the Waters are now disregarded.

In this Village are Lands called Puck Pits, and Imp'y Meadow.

WAPLEY AND CODRINGTON.

THE PRESENT LORD OF THE MANOR;

[Sir GERALD CODRINGTON.]

THE CHURCH is small consisting of a Chancel, Nave and a small Aisle on South side, which is the burial place of the CODRINGTONS. The Church is dedicated to Saint Peter, and is in the Deanery of Hawkesbury. It has a Tower and therein 5 Bells. [It was restored 1862.]

INSCRIPTIONS IN THE CHURCH.

IN THE SOUTH AISLE,

IS AN ALTAR TOMB AND ON A FREESTONE TABLET THIS INSCRIPTION:

Hic jacet JOHES. CODRYNGTON, *Armiger*, qui Obiit novo die Mensis Octobris, Anno Dni. Mo. CCCCo. LXXVo. cujus Ætat. erat die quo Obiit CXI. annor. V. mensium vii. dierum Cuj, aiè pr. picet. De. Amen.

ON FLAT STONES.

Here lyeth the Body of JOHN CODRINGTON, of *Codrington, Esqr.* who departed this Life, the 25 of September, Anno Dom: 1670, Aged Seventy Years.

Here lyeth the Body of JOHN CODRINGTON, the 2nd. son of JOHN CODRINGTON, of *Codrington, Esqr.* who departed this Life, the 6th. day of July, Ao. Dom. 1674.

Here lyeth the Body of *Capt.* WILLIAM CODRINGTON, 3rd. son of JOHN CODRINGTON, of *Codrington, Esqr.* who departed this Life, the 20 day of December, 1696.

ON MONUMENTS, SOUTH SIDE OF THE NAVE.

Here lyeth the Body of THOMAS HOOPER, of this Parish, *Gent.* who departed this Life, the 8th. day of September, Anno Dom. 1675, Aged 47. ANN HOOPER, uxor posuit. ROBERT HOOPER, son of ROBERT HOOPER, *Gent.* and JOHANNA, his Wife, died ... day of Decr. Anno Domini 1637, Ætat. suæ XIX.

SCUDAMORE GODWIN, Vicar of *Wapley* and Rector of *Filton,* near *Bristol, Gloucestershire,* Buried in 1702, Aged 57.

RICHARD GRIGMOND OSELAND, *Gent. Attorney* from *Malmsbury,* Buried 1769, Aged 38 Years.

EDMUND WILLS, Curate of this Parish, and a Native of *Carlile* in the County of *Cumberland,* was buried July 30, 1801, Aged 29 Years.

[*Several of Flat stone Inscriptions not found 1881.*]

CHURCH YARD.

Erected to the Memory of ISAAC HIGHNAM, of this Parish, *Yeoman,* who died March 9, 1776, Aged 61 Years. ANN, his Wife, who died May 8, 1781, Aged 63 Years. Also of Six Children of ISAAC HIGHNAM, and ANN, his Wife, who all died in their Infancy, Underneath the Stone adjoining this Tomb was Interred the Body of MARY, the Wife of JACOB HIGHNAM, of this Parish, who died August 30, 1791, in the 39 Year of her Age.

Here lyeth the Body of JOHN JEFFERY, of this Parish, who departed this Life, Jany. 21, 1736, Aged 56 Years. HANNAH, his Wife, who died May 31, 1713, Aged 36 Years, and 9 Months. Also here lyeth the Bodies of GRACE and HANNAH, Daughters of JOHN and HANNAH JEFFERY, who died Infants. Also JOHN, Son of JOHN and HANNAH JEFFERY, who died June 30, 1706, Aged 10 Months.

Here lyeth the Body of JOHN JEFFERY, *Junior,* who departed this Life, 15 Febr. 1730, Aged 28 Years.

Here lyeth the Body of JOHN JEFFERY, who died July 14, 1730, Aged 81 Years. GRACE, his Wife, who died Aug. 26, 1709, Aged 57.

Here lyeth the Body of NATHANIEL, the Son of NATHANIEL, and MARY OSBORNE, of this Parish, who departed this Life, Decr. 16, 1759, Aged 20 Years, 6 Months & 3 Weeks. MARY OSBORNE, of this Parish, *Widow,* who departed this Life, the 12 day of Decr. 1792, in the 88 Year of her Age.

To the Memory of RUTH, Wife of JOHN GODWIN, and Daughter of WILLIAM and RUTH WICKHAM, of this Parish, who died the 28 day of July 1789, in the 46 Year of her Age.

To the Memory of WILLIAM WICKHAM, of this Parish, *Senior,* who died March 17, 1790, Aged 87 Years. RUTH, his Wife, died April 24, 1774, Aged 67 Years. HARRY WICKHAM, of this Parish, *Junr.* their Son, died Decr. 12, 1775, Aged 2 Years.

In Memory of DANIEL HIGGS, *Yeoman,* He died Jan. 26, 1730, Aged 66. ELIZABETH, his Wife, She died March 18, 1723, Aged 60.

Erected to the Memory of GRACE, the Wife of CHARLES OSBORNE, of this Parish, She died Nov. 1, 1785, Aged 68 Years. The above CHARLES OSBORNE, who died the 14 day of Feb. 1791, Aged 72 Years.

In Memory of DANIEL, the Son of CHARLES, and GRACE OSBORNE, of this Parish, who died Sept. ye 6, 1768, Aged 19 Years.

In Memory of

JOSEPH OSBORN, late of *Says Farm*,
in the Parish of *Westerleigh*,
who departed this Life, the
10 day of May 1790,
Aged 37 Years.

Here lieth the Body of
WILLIAM SHIPP,
of this Parish, *Senr.* who died
16 day of March 1736, Aged 58.
MARY, Wife of WILLIAM SHIPP,
of this Parish, *Senr.* who died
the 1 day of July 1734,
Aged 63 Years.

Here lyeth the Body of
SIMON SMITH, *Yeoman,*
who was buried May 17, 1693.

Here lyeth the Body of
EDWARD HANCOCK, *Yeoman,*
who died April 21, 1713,
Aged 46 Years.
Also SARAH JEFFERY, who died
March 11, 1763, Aged 89 Years.

Here lieth the Body of
STEPHEN HANCOCK,
who died August 29, 1758,
in the 41 Year of his Age.
Also HANNAH, his Widow,
late Wife of JOHN MOSS,
who died April 25, 1773,
Aged 63 Years.

In Memory of
BETTY, Wife of WILLIAM
CULLURNE, and Daughter of
HENRY and ELIZABETH WHITE,
of this Parish, who died
Oct. 31, 1770, Aged 22 Years.
WILLIAM CULLURNE,
their Son, who departed this Life,
16 day of Sept. 1787, in the
18 Year of his Age.

Under this Tomb lieth the Body of
JOSIAH HIGGS, of this Parish,

who departed this Life,
20 day of April 1771, in the
70 Year of his Age.
SARAH, his Wife, who died
9*th.* day of August 1774,
Aged 71 Years.

In Memory of
HANNAH, Daughter of JOSIAH
and ELIZABETH HIGGS,
of *Chipping Sodbury*, who died
12 March 1782, in the 22
Year of her Age.
Likewise ELIZABETH, Wife of
JOSEPH HIGGS, of *Chipping Sodbury*,
who died the 10 day of Jan. 1785,
in the 55 Year of her Age
MOSSES, their Son, died April 22,
1794, in the 23 Year of his Age.
Also JOSIAH, their Son,
who died Decr. 11, 1765,
Aged 2 Years.
Also JOSIAH, their second Son,
who died Nov. 16, 1770,
Aged 5 Years.

To the Memory of
SAMUEL WICKHAM, *Gent.*
of the Parish of *Westerleigh*,
who died Jan. 28, 1792,
Aged 50 Years,
MARY, the Daughter of
SAMUEL and SARAH WICKHAM,
who died April 9, 1784,
Aged 20 Years.
Also ELIZABETH HIGGS WICKHAM,
who died March 13, 1773,
Aged 9 Weeks.
Also JAMES WICKHAM, *Gent.*
who died March 13, 1799,
Aged 32 Years.

In Memory of
THOMAS HARBERT, of this Parish,
who died Oct. 10, 1782,
Aged 78 Years.
MARY HARBERT, Widow of the
aforesaid THOMAS HARBERT,
who departed this Life,
the 23 day of February 1795,
Aged 85 Years.

ON FLAT STONES.

JAMES, Son of JACOB and
MARY HIGHNAM,
who died Jany. 3, 1782,
Aged 10 Months.

ROBERT, the Son of ROBERT,
and ELIZABETH BRISTOW,
of this Parish, who departed
this Life, Jany. 21, 1768,
in the 21 Year of his Age.

JOHN FOWLER, of this Parish,
who departed this Life, March 22,
Anno { Dni. 1703,
{ Ætatis 77.

(Additional Inscriptions since
Bigland's time.)

ON OSELAND's TABLET.

Also to the Memory of
HANNAH, Wife of the aforesaid
R. G. OSELAND,
who died 27 January 1830,
Aged 94 Years.

ON TABLETS.

Sacred to the Memory of
Revd. CHARLES RICHARD WARD,
M. A. 33 Years Vicar of this Parish,
who died 22 day of March 1858,
Aged 58 Years.

Sacred to the Memory of
Revd. HORATIO JAMES, M. A.
Vicar of this Parish,
Honorary Canon of *Ripon* and
late Vicar of *High Harrogate,*
Yorkshire. He departed this Life,
Nov. 15, 1876, in the 71*st.*
Year of his Age.
He was for 44 Years a faithful
earnest and successful Minister
of the Gospel of Christ.

HEAD STONES.

	Died.	Aged.		Died.	Aged.
Ann, Wife of Joseph Sturge ...	24 May	1779	70	Henry Carter	16 Nov.	1784	66
George James	15 Sept.	1757	81	Mary, his Wife	14 April	1778	69
Mary, his Wife	3 July	1727	36	Thomas Brookes	18 Decr.	1775	61
Joan, Wife of Isaac Serjent ...	8 Jany.	1770	50	Jane, his Wife	6 July	1753	35
James Pullin	2 July	1768	67	Hannah, their Daughter	1 Nov.	1775	22
John, his Son	7 Aug.	1795	22	Richard Brown	13 March	1762	73
William Reaey	15 Sept.	1769	52				

Supplementary Notes as to I. Devolution of Estates. II. Church. III. Population, Taxation, &c.

1.—*Estates :*

Betune (Bitton) contained 36 Hides and was terra Regis:
It had 2 Members Wapley and Winterborne. Culture:—In
Demesne 5 Carucates. In Villenage (41 Villans, 29 Bor-
dars.) 45 Carucates. There were 18 Serfs. A Mill

One Hide:
The Bishop of Constance, held of St. Laud, and Aldred
under him. Culture:—In Demesne 1 Carucate. Two Serfs,
had another. It was worth 20 *s.* (Yearly.) *Domesday Survey.*
One Hide:
Radulph de Berchelai, held of the Crown, and Godric

under him. Culture:—1 Carucate in demesne, 4 Serfs.

It was worth 20s. (Yearly.) *Domesday Survey.*

Wapley and Codrington Manor:

Hen ii.—Radulph Fitzstephen, by Crown Grant, under Rent of 11£.

Stanley Abbey, Wilts. by his Gift.

1292.—The Abbey, taxed at Seven Carucates, &c. in Codrington, whose Annual Value was £13 11 8.
Pope Nich. Tax.

John de Codrington, by purchase from the Abbey by Crown Licence Subject to the 11£. Rent to the Crown.

In 1608, Simon Codrington, was Lord.

John Codrington, Esqr. was High Sheriff of Gloucestershire, 1638; and a John Codrington, Esqr. was with Sir Robert Cook, and Sir John Seymer, Knights, the Stephen's (Nathl., Edward, John,) and others who sided with Parliament in the great Civil War appointed by Ordinance of Lords and Commons, 1643, a Committee for Gloucestershire of Sequestrators of Delinquents Estates.

Settlement by Fine, by John Cotherington and Wife Alice, on themselves and their sons Humphry, John, and Thomas, with Remainder to Margaret Besiles, late Wife of Sir Peter Besiles, in tail.

The Heiress of the family, married Sir Rich. Bamfylde.

1776.—Sir Charles Warwick Bamfylde, by descent.

Sir C. W. Codrington, by purchase.

Sir Gerald Codrington.

Stanley Abbey:—still named as Owners in Chief.

26 Hen. viii—Codryngton in Com. Glouc.

(Wigorn Dioc.) Rents of Assize 11£. *Valor Eccl'us.*

After the dissolution it was granted to Simon Codrington, at 11£. fee farm Rent.

2 Messuages and Lands:

12 Edw. iv.—J. Stanshaw, died seized.

12 Hen. vii.—John and Humphry Stanshaw, Brothers.
Escheat.

As to this family *see* "Yate.)

Cantelupe's Lands:

St. Augustine Hospital, of Bristol, by Gift of Roger de Cantelo.

After the dissolution of the Hospital. The Dean and Chapter of Bristol.

There are Wills of the following Persons of Wapley and Codrington.

At *Worcester*:—

1538.—Atkyns, William.
1538.—Belsyre, Christofer.
1539.—Code, *or* Pool, Richard.

At *Gloucester*:—

1544.—Bampton, R.

1776.—*In the Election for Gloucestershire, the following* *voted for Freeholds*:—

Moses Higgs, Richard Stokes.

II.—*Church.*

Vicarage:

26 Hen. viii.—In Rents and farm and tithes (beyond 8s. 8d. paid for cenage and proxies) £7 18 0.
Valor Eccl'us.

Of the Monument to John Codrington, an engraving will be found in Lysons' Antiquities of Gloucestershire.

The great Tythes were commuted at 35£. The Viracial or small Tithes at 340£. There are 2½ a. Glebe.

A payment of 9£. Yearly is made to the Vicar of Yate.

At Codrington a Chapel was built by Stanley Abbey, for the sole use of the Grange there. It is standing but disused.

List of Incumbents and Patrons:—

Rectors.	Patrons.
1548.—Urian Nayse.	
1549.—Thos. Brierhurst.	D. Broke, &c.
1575.—Thos. Cadle.	Giles Demery.
1586.—John Mascoll.	do.
1622.—James Latymer.	John Stokes.
Walter Osborne.	Hen. Stokes.
1662.—Geo. Nicholson.	King Charles ii.
1666.—Robt. Paine.	Jno. Stokes.
1669.—Scudamore Godwyn.	Do.
1702.—Samuel Godwyn.	B. Codrington.
1705.—John Pill.	Do.
1738.—Wm. Wickham.	John Codrington.
1760.—Francis Gold.	Sir Richd. Bamfylde, Bt.
1781.—Henry Willis.	Henry Stephens.
1794.—Edmund Willis.	Jane, Dowager Lady Bamfylde.
1804.—Thos. Hardcastle.	Sir C. W. Bamfylde.
1804.—Arthur W. Shakespeare.	Do.
Horatis James.	
1862.—Girdleston, Charles.	
Richard Ward.	
W. Winter Gibbon.	

III.—*Taxation, Population, &c.*

Wappelegh, Subsidy Roll, 1 Edw. iii. 1327.

De Gilb. de Stanshawe, iis. iiiid. o.
' Joachym atte Wode, ix d. q.
' Willo. Donning, x d.
' Rogo. atte Vyne, ii s. i d.
' Johe. atte Wode, xii d.
' Walto. de Wappelegh, xiiii d. q.
prob. Sma. viiis. iiid.

Codrynton, Subsidy Roll, 1 Edw. iii. 1327.

De Rogo. le Monck, xii d. ob.
' Robto. atte Noreharde, xix d. o.
' Cecilia Pyn, viii d. o.
' Hugon. Wat'schop, vv d.
' Raduo. Pyn, viii d. o. q.
' Nicel. Sewy, xv d. q.
prob. Sma. viis. ob.

Acreage 2448 a. of which about 41 are Common or Waste.

Population 1831,—253. 1861,—358. 1871.—335.

In 1815. Annual Value of Real Property 4828£.

1875. Rateable Value 3823£.

1833-4-5. Average of three Years Expenditure on Poor 89£.

In Sodbury Union.

WASHBOURN GREAT.

CCLXXIX.
or 286.

WASHBOURN GREAT.

Mr. BERKELEY CRAVEN, LORD OF THE MANOR.

Revd. Mr. RICHARD DARK, *Rector.*

THE CHURCH a small building consists only of a Chancel and Nave, with a Wooden Turret in the middle, therein one Bell. It is dedicated to St. Mary and has divine service performed once a fortnight.

On the outside on the east end of the Chancel "JAMES CARTWRIGHT, did new build up this Chancel in Anno Dom. 1642."

INSCRIPTIONS IN THE CHURCH.

CHANCEL.

ON FLAT STONES.

JOHN FERRIS, from *London, Gent.* was buried here December the 2nd. 1758, Aged 50 Years.
MARY, Wife of WILLIAM NOKES, who died . ...
Aged 99 Years,

Here lies the Body of
JAMES CARTWRIGHT, *Gentleman,*
Deceased the 19*th.* of January 1613.

NAVE.

ON FLAT STONES.

Here lyeth the Body of
ELIZABETH WEST,
She was the Daughter of
JONATHAN and ELIZABETH WEST,
Gent. She was buried the 9*th.*
day of July 1751, Aged 72 Years.

Here lieth the Body of
ANNE BAYLIS,
Deceased the 8*th.* of October 1708,
Aged 72 Years.

Mr. WILLIAM JONES,
of *Codrington,* and two Sons,
who departed this Life,
in March 1729.
Also in Memory of
Mrs. ANNE STEPHENS, of
Ashton under Hill, who departed
this Life, October 24, 1753,
Aged 83 Years.
Also the Body of ANNE, the
Wife of RICHARD DAUNCE, of
Greet in the Parish of *Winchcombe,*
who departed this Life, the
3 of March, A. D. 1778,
Aged 73 Years.

Here rest in hopes of a Joyful
resurrection the Body of
THOMAS MARTIN, of this Place,
(but a Native of *Ashton under Hill,*)
who departed this Life, the
22 day of January, A. D. 1787,
Aged 41 Years.
Also in Memory of
CHARLES, the second son of
THOMAS and HESTER MARTIN,
who departed this Life, the
6 day of July, A. D. 1787,
Aged 10 Months.

[*Supplementary Tablets put up in
the Church since Bigland's time.*]

SLAB AGAINST WALL.

In a Vault are laid the Remains
of the *Revd.* EVAN BEAVAN, *Clerk,*
late *Incumbent,* of this Parish,
who died Jany. 2, 1837,
Aged 69 Years.
Also of SARAH BEAVAN,
Relict of the above, who died
June 11, 1841, Aged 57 Years.

OPPOSITE.

Beneath this Place lie the
Remains of ESTHER MARTIN,
Relict of the late THOMAS MARTIN,
who departed this Life, the
29*th.* of April 1801,
Aged 42 Years.

Lo where this silent marble weeps
A friend, a wife, a mother sleeps,
A heart within whose sacred cell
The peaceful Virtues loved to dwell,
Affection warm, and faith sincere,
And soft humanity were there.
In agony, in death, resigned
She felt the wound she left behind,
Till time shall every grief remove,
With life, with memory, with love.

Also WILLIAM, son of THOMAS,
and ESTHER MARTIN,
who departed this Life, the
1*st.* September 1797,
Aged 18 Years.

HEAD STONES.

	Died.	Aged.		Died.		Aged.
Elizabeth, Wife of Phillip Parsons, and late Wife of Richard Webb, ...	23 July	1728	66	John, son of John and Ann Welch	9 March	1757	37
Anne, Wife of Thomas Norris Heming, ...	6 April	1738	37	Ann, Wife of Edward Roberts	6 July	1776	51
Thomas Norris Heming	4 Febr.	1757	57	John, son of Edward and Ann Roberts	12 June	1771	21
Elizabeth, Wife of Isaac Heming	19 March	1795	38	Ann, the Wife of John Martin	19 April	1795	40
Ann Welch	28 Oct.	1792	66	Mary, the daughter of Thomas and Hannah Alcock ...	2 Nov.	1784	59
William, son of George and Mary Farrow	28 Jany.	1759	10	Alice, Wife of James Alcock ...	11 July	1727	47
George Yeomans	4 Febr.	1757	53				
Mary, his Wife and late Wife William Kaye	25 Decr.	1794	79	*Other Inscriptions in the Church Yard to:—* TEALE, MERRYMAN, PEART, AICOCK, HEALE, DAY, MARTIN, MATHEWS, ALLEN, WALSH, HEMING, BARROW, DRINKWATER, PROBERT, SMART, &c.			
Ann, Wife of John Welsh, *Senr.*	30 May	1776	80				
Ann, Wife of William Matthews	21 May	1785	64				

Supplementary Notes as to I.—Estates ; II.—Church ; III.—Population, Taxation, &c.

I.—*Estates :*

Washbourn is one of those places says *Rudder* "of which there is but little mention." Yet it is mentioned in a very antient Charter of A. D. 780, whereby Offa, King of Mercia, gave to the Church of Bredon, (which his grandfather Eenulf, had erected) Thirty-five acres of which 5 manses were situate at Teothrigtun, (Teddington.) upon the

Banks of the Brook called Cerent, (Carrant.) ten Cassats lay at Wassanburan, (Washbourn.) adjacent East on Geolosaford and West on a spring called Gyting broc, (Guyting Brook) ten Manses at Codeswellan, (part of Cutsdean.?) upon the mountains, of the Wiccians and ten at Nortun, (Northway.) near a Brook called Tyrl, (Turl)

Dugdale Monast. Kemble Codex Anglo Saxon.

The natural Boundaries of the Brooks, Carrant and Turl still remain, and they retain their Names Guyting Brook is not adjacent, but the stream through Washbourn to the Carrant Brook is probably meant by it.

Washburn, contained 3 Hides. Culture:—In Demesne two plow tillages. In Villenage (6 Villans.) three Plow tillages. There was one Bordar, Serfs and one Bond Woman. Its Value 60s. yearly.   *Domesday Survey.*

Washbourn was then part of the possessions of Tewkesbury Abbey.

26 Hen. viii.—Great Washbourn:

Rents of Customary Tenants £11. 13s. 11d.

Rent of Grove called Horn Grove, as demised to Wm. Cartwright, 6s. 8d.   *Valor Eccl us.*

Ph & M.—Ann Fortescue, Widow of Sir Adrian Fortescue and his Heir Males, by Crown Grant.

Starkey, by Purchase, from Fortescue's Heir Male.

William, Lord Craven, by purchase.

An Inclosure Act, was passed 49 Geo. iii. at that time the Hon. H. A. B. Craven, was Lord of the Manor.

1812.—The Award of F. Phelps, after making Sale and Tithe Allotments, allotted the residue to H. A. B. Craven, and his Lessees.

Other Estates:—

1 Hen. vii.—Fines of Free Suitors payable to the Crown.

Richard Saunders, for Lands called Wasbarne 2d. (*Sherborne MSS. extracted by Fosbrooke, Gloucestershire, ii. 291.*

Messuage and 80 a. Land:—

E. 8. Geo. ii.—Hayward and Whitaker, were *Plaintiffe*, and John Darke, and R. Larke, *Deforciants.*   *Fine.*

There is a Will at Gloucester:—

1604.—Deaves, of Washborn.

1776.—*At the County Election, the* Revd. R. Darke, *Voted for a Freehold at Washbourn.*

II.—*Church:*

The Rectory was granted to the Lord Cardinal, by Act of Parliament, Its Value £9 8s. 8d.

To the Crown by his Attainder.

Grant by Queen Mary to Fortescue, with the Manor.

1776.—Richard Darke, was Impropriator.

1809.—H. Fowke, was Impropriator of the Great and small Tithes at the Inclosure, and they were exchanged for Land. The Tithe Allotment to be equal to one fifth of the arable and one ninth of the grass Land. By the Award of F. Phelps, 1812, validated by Act 9 Geo. iv. c. 23. seven Allotments were made in lieu of Tythe.

1813.—H. Fowke, by Will devised to Trustees (Revd. W. G. Maxwell, and E. W. Jones,) for Sale.

List of Curates and Patrons of Washbourne.

1548.—Ralph Rocheford.
1562.—William Bancks.
1570.—Robert Byckley.
1572.—Richard Hooper.
1580.—John Roberts.
1586.—William Grevestock.
1625.—Richard Hooper.
1642.—Ralph Dutton.
1661.—William Jones.
1681.—Lebbeus Lunn.
1721.—Francis Lamb.
1721.—George Roberts.
1785.—John Darke.   John Darke. *Patron.*
1788.—Joseph Biddle.
1797.—Richard Darke.
1810.—W. Geo. Maxwell. Henry Fowke. *Patron.*

III.—*Taxation Population, &c. Washbourn.*

Wyssebourn, Subsidy Roll, 1 Edw. III. 1327.

De Henr. Matheu, ii s.
' Sarr. de Wassheboure, xviii d.
' Julian Chapma. ii s.
' Rico. Balle, ix d.
' Rico. Baldrich, xvi d.
' Johe. Inthehale, xix d.
' Rico. Swon, vi d.
' Matill. Knyt, xxiii d. q.
' Nicho. Mey, ii s. vi d.
          prob. Sma. xiiii s. id. q.

Washborne, Subsidy Roll, 8 Jac. i.

Tym. Cartwright, Bon. iiij.
W. Jones.
H. Reade.
Jane Hill.
J. Okaye.
T. Cartwright, in ter j la.

Acreage 624. a.

Population 1831,—87.   1861.—83.   1871,—115.

In 1815. Annual Value of Real Property 1215 £.

1875.—Rateable Value £1122.

1833-4-5. Average of three Years Expenditure on Poor £33.

In Winchcomb Union.

ADDENDUM.

WASHBOURN LITTLE.

I.—*Estates:*

Little Washbourn was a hamlet of Overbury, from which it is two Miles distant. It was in Worcestershire but is now part of the County of Gloucester.

It is said in *Nash's Worcestershire* to have been parcel of Bredon Manor, and that its ancient Possessors were a knightly family here resident and hence named. From this family or its descendants through heirs general and sundry subsequent possessors it came to Mr. Gist, by purchase, and was joined to the Wormington Grange Estate. *see "Wormington."*

II.—*Church.*

The place has a Chapel without a Yard. Its right of burial is at Ashton-under-Hill.

Tythe:

The Tythe of a Yard of Land belonged to St. Faith Overbury.

III.—*Taxation, Population, &c.*

Acreage 449 a.

Population 1831,—51.   1861,—28.

1815.—Annual Value of Real Property £910.

1881.—Rateable Value £538.

1833-4-5 —Average of three Years Expenditure on Poor £19.

In Winchcomb Union.

WELFORD,

ADDENDUM.

Welleford in Deerhurst Hundred, contained 15 Hides, With 5 other Vills all in that same Hundred, it constituted a Manor which at the time of the Survey belonged to the Abbey of St. Dennis, near Paris, of which Deerhurst Priory was a Cell: The Vills were Welford, and near it, Contone, (Little Compton,) 12 Hides, and Preston (on Stour,) 10 Hides. Hockinton, (Uckington) and Starventon (Staverton,) these two (near Cheltenham.) And Colne (St. Dennis,) and its hamlet Caldicot, near Northleach. Of these scattered members the only ground of connexion was monastic ownership. Culture: the Manor had 15 Carucates in Demesne and 39 in Villenage (75 Villans and 12 Bordars.) There were 38 Bondmen. 4 Mills of 40 s. 36 a. of Meadow. And a Wood 2½ miles long and 1 mile 2 quarters broad. Of the above Lands 5 Freemen held 4½ Hides. To the same Manor belonged 2 Hides and ½ beyond the Severn.

From Domesday Survey.

St. Dennis held 2 Carucates of Land.

Rents of Assize	£ 7 9 s.	0 d.
Villenage, Predial Work	3 14	0

Pap. Nich. Tax.

At the suppression of alien Priories:—

Part (I mors Welford,) passed into lay Hands.

The Beauchamp family held Lands here which passed into the name of Stapleton, and from that by purchase to J. Greville, who died seized 23 Hen. vi. From whom by descent Sir E. Greville.

Edw. iv.—Other part granted to Tewkesbury Abbey:

Rents of Assize of free and customary Tenants Yearly	£19 4	2¼
Perquisites of View of Frankpledge and Manor Court	12 11	¼
Farm of Demesne Lands	5 6	8
Two Mills	4 6	8
Several Fishery in Avon Water	0 13	4

Deduct Fees:—Bailiff 10 s. Auditor (Tyndale) 3s. 10d. Steward 2 s. Receiver 2 s =17s. 10d.

Remains Clear £ 29 5 s. 11½ d. *Valor Eccl'us.*

Edw. vi.—After the dissolution, William Willington, by Crown Grant.

Margery, his Daughter and Heir, marr. Sir Ed. Greville.

The Parcels united forming the Manor Estate:

1608. Leonard Cranfield, Earl of Middlesex, by Purchase from Sir Edwd. Greville.

1674.—His Daughters and Coheirs:

One married Charles, Earl of Dorset, and had this Estate by partition. From whom the Earls and Dukes of Dorset. *See* Patrons of Rectory.

1806.—George John Frederick, Duke of Dorset, (a Minor, was Lord at the passing of the *Inclosure Act.*)

1815.—He died (from a fall from his horse while hunting in Ireland,) unmarried. His Estates descended to his Sisters and Coheiresses. But the titles of Duke and Earl of Dorset and Viscount Sackville, went to Charles, the 5th. and last Duke and on his death unmarried became extinct.

The Representative of the family—Lord Buckhurst, (a Title of earlier creation than those above mentioned) holds the Dorset Estates here and at Weston-on-Avon.

Freemens Estates:

31 Hen. ii.—Ralph of Welleford, paid a fine of 2 marks for having his Plaint in the Kings Court, against the Prior of Deerhurst. *Mag. Rot.* 10a. Gloc.

5 Hen. iii.—This Estate then was in the name of Hoese and Wife, by purchase.

10 Ric. ii.—Sir T. West, died seized of Lands at Welleford, called a Manor. *Esch. No.* 52.

42 Geo. iii.—An Act for inclosing Lands here.

The Award under the Inclosure Act was made in 1802, and enrolled in the Office of Clerk of Peace 1822.

The Allotments are small. The Rector received an Allotment in lieu of Tythe from Allottees of Land; and Annual Rents in respect of other tenements.

1776.—*At the County Election the following Voted as Free-holders in Welford.*

Alcock, William.	Hancock, Joseph.
Atkins, Robert.	Hughes, John.
Badson, (2) Richd., Wm.	Izod, John.
Bromley, Thomas.	Mosely, Thomas.
Bennet, Joseph.	Milward, William.
Barlow, Charles.	Redding, William.
Green, Joseph.	Smith, Robert.
Hollyoke, John.	Sale, Thomas.
Holtham, (2) John, Henry.	Shutter, J. (*Shuter, Ch. Ins.*)
Hill, Samuel.	Strapy, John.
Haines, Thomas.	Silvester, William.
Harris, (2) Joseph, John.	Welch, (2) John, Wm.
Hunt, Samuel.	Wakefield, William.

II.—*Church:*—

Church Rated at	£ 15	0	0
Portion of the Abbot of Tewkesbury	1	0	0
Portion of Prior of Deerhurst in Tythes	1 6		8

Pap. Nich. Tax.

Valor Eccl'us. £ 29 15 10.

The Church was restored by Lady De la Warr.

List of Incumbents and Patrons of Welford.

Incumbents.	Patrons.
1548.—Richard Quene.	G. Owen, and Sir Ralph Sadler.
1554.—John Williams.	" "
1562.—John Wood.	" "
1581.—Philip Jones.	Lewis Grevil, Esqr.
1592.—Edward Vernon.	Edward Grevil.
1631.—Jenkin Bown.	" "
1667.—William Izard.	Edward Paston.
1679.—John Paston.	" "
1689.—James Smith.	Earl of Dorset.
1692.—Richard Talbot.	" "
1712.—Edward Astley.	" "
1765.—John Thomas.	" "
1771.—Joseph Green.	Duke of Dorset.
1790.—John Hunt.	" "

The Sacrist of Tewkesbury Abbey had a Pension from the Rector of Welneford, 20s. *Valor Eccl'us.*

III.—*Taxation, Population, &c.*

Welneforde, Subsidy Roll, 1 Edw. iii., 1327.

De Rico. atte Strete, iii s. vi d.
' Galfro. Cauel, xii d.
' Johe Broun, xviii d.
' Galfr. de Welneforde, iiii s. i d. q.
' Margia. Wylkynes, ii s.
' Willo. Muridale, xii d.
' Georg. atte Groue, vi s. viii d.
' Cecilia Wyllyames, iii s. iii d. o.
' Robto. de Mersshton, vi d.
' Willo. Cauel, vi d.
' Johe Aldewyne, xii d.
' Gregor. Wyllames, iii s. vi d. o. q.
' Rico. Spye, vi d.
' Rogo. Skynnar, xvi d. o. q.
' Robto. atte Hulle, vi d.
' Johe Newema. iii s. i d. q.
' Willo. Geffe, xv d. o.
' Walto. de Cantilupe, vii s. v d. o. q.
' Alic. Bor. xviii d.
' Nicho. Lymeseye, vi d.
' Walto. Hycon, vi d.

prob. Sma. xlv *s.* iiii *d. o. q. pbat.*

Acreage 1705 a.

Population 1831,—669. 1861,—627. 1871.—634.

In 1815. Annual Value of Real Property 2718 £.

1881. Rateable Value 3103 £.

1833-4-5. Average of three Years Expenditure on Poor 304 £.

In Stratford on Avon Union.

WELFORD.

T H E Church consists of a Chancel, Nave, South, and North Aisles, with a Gallery over the West End, and part of the North Aisle, and a high Tower at the West-end, therein Six Bells.

HIS GRACE THE DUKE OF DORSET, LORD OF THE MANOR.

REVD. MR. JOHN HUNT, RECTOR.

BENEFACTIONS.

JOHN FRECKLETON, gave to the Poor of this Parish, Thirteen Shillings, and four pence, for ever. He also gave Six Shillings, and Eight Pence, to the Church for ever, to be paid out of Millhams.

THOMAS MILLS, gave to the Poor of this Parish, Three Pounds a Year, to be paid Quarterly for ever. He also gave Three Shillings, and Four pence, towards the repairs of the High Ways of this Parish for ever.

(For another Charity see the Stone against the Church in the Church Yard)

INSCRIPTIONS IN THE CHURCH.

CHANCEL.

MARIA ASTELEY, Infans hic Sepulta Obiit a natali vicessimo die Novembriis A. D. 1629. Qui dedit abstulit.

Here lyeth the Body of FRANCIS HALFORD, Gent. who departed this Life, the 20th. day of March 1697.

Here lieth in hopes of a Crown of Righteousness the Body of Mr. ARTHUR FLETCHER, late of Paxford, in the County of Worcester, who finished his Course, May 5, 1774, in the 71 Year of his Age.

NAVE,

FLAT STONES.

(Verge Church Text.)
Hic jacet dns.
WALTHERUS WILLIAMS, quondam Rector, isti. ecclie, qui obiit die .... mensis Augusti Anno dni. M'CCCC'LXXXIIII, Cuj'. Aie ppiciet. deus Amen.

Here lyeth the Body of ANNE JAKEMAN, the Wife of WILLIAM JAKEMAN, Gent. and Daughter of WILLIAM DOD, of Preece, in the County of Salop. Gent. Shee departed this Life, August 13, 1725, Aged 50 Years.

Here lyeth the Body of WILLIAM JAKEMAN, who departed this Life. the 11 day of February Anno Dom. 1635, Aged 70 Years.

CHURCH YARD,

ON A MONUMENT AGAINST THE SOUTH WALL OF THE CHANCEL.

Underneath is ye Grave of RICHARD RAWLINGS, of Welford, who by Will bearing date ye 22 day of October, 1727, did give 3 pounds per Annum charged upon his half Yard in Welford, (one Moiety whereof to be paid every half Year.) For ye Maintenance of a School Master there for ever to teach 8 poor Boys, of ye Parish Read, and Write English, to instruct them in the Church Catechism in the use of Figures, and to make them ready Accountants.

This Little Charity the Founder gave To Excite the Rich, who larger substance have, To increase his Fund, and so respect his Grave.

TOMBS.

In Memory of KATHARINE, Wife of WILLIAM SALEY, (? SEELEY.) Died 13 Sept. 1764, in the 29 Year of her Age. In Memory of JOAN, the Wife of THOMAS WEAVER, died April 7, 1764, in the 24 Year of her Age. (now gone in 1872.)

Here lieth interred the Bodies of WILLIAM MILWARD, Gent. and ANNE, his Wife, the former

---

departed this Life, July 15, A. D. 1669. the latter died May 25, 1682, Also JOSEPH, their Son.

S. H. M.
Novissimum Domini adventum præstolantur Mortales exuviæ THOMÆ MILWARD, Generosi, filii natu 2di. WILLIELMI, et ANNÆ MILWARD, Hujusdem Parochiæ,

....

(The rest chipt off.)

Underneath this Tomb, lieth the Body of JOHN HEWES, Gent. who departed this Life, 14 of June 1787, Aged 82.

Here lyeth the Body of THOMAS MILBURN, Died April 16, 1781, Aged 44 Years.

In Memory of RICHARD HUDSON, who died April 25, 1792, Aged 73 Years.

In Memory of ELIZABETH, the Wife of JOHN HOLTHAM, who died July 10, 1777, Aged 59 Years. Also JOHN HOLTHAM, who died June 29, 1789, Aged 71.

HEAD STONES.

	Died.		Aged.		Died.		Aged.
John Harris	3 May	1789	60	Lidia, Daughter of John, and Elizabeth Lane	1 Mar.	1794	20
Elizabeth, Daughter of John and Elizabeth Harris	1 Apr.	1796	15	Elizabeth, Wife of John Vincent	3 Jan.	1796	46
Elizabeth, Wife of Wm. Bennett	21 Oct.	1792	42	John Allcock	20 Apr.	1728	67
Elizabeth, Wife of James Bennett	10 Decr.	1757	33	Sarah, Wife of Thomas Edkins	24 May	1779	44
Henry Holtham	6 July	1749	56	Susanna, Wife of Thomas Hornby	6 Oct.	1750	53
Rebecca, his Wife	19 Febr.	1760	64	William Parker	8 Sept.	1793	62
Henry Holtham	19 Mar.	1789	67	Elizabeth, his Wife	3 Mar.	1784	42
Thomas Bentley	4 Nov.	1759	67	John Hodgkins	18 May	1799	56
Susanna, his Wife	21 Mar.	1762	69	William Wells	5 Aug.	1753	49
Thomas Compton Silvester ...	26 Apr.	1798	63	John Wells	5 Nov.	1757	23
Joseph Harris	31 May	1797	60	John Winn	7 Oct.	1780	53
John Shuter	10 July	1797	90	Ann, Wife of John Winn ...	28 Mar.	1794	48
Mary, Daughter of John, and Mary Shuter, and Wife of Thomas Edkins ..	13 Sept.	1793	33	Thomas Hunt	6 Aug.	1773	39
				Mary, Wife of John Hunt ...	21 June	1787	99
				Sarah, Wife of Mathew Mills	4 Nov.	1788	43

	Died.	Aged.		Died.	Aged.
George Milles	4 Jany. 1746	39	John Cooper	18 May 1760	43
Bridget, Wife of George Mills	7 Oct. 1768	48	Elizabeth, Wife of Wm. Cooper	6 April 1764	74
Joseph Hancox	18 May 1795	68	William Cooper	8 April 1786	63
John Winn	17 Oct. 1780	53	John, Son of Thomas Bromley, and Elizabeth, his Wife	7 Jany. 1772	31
Ann, Wife of John Winn ...	28 Mar. 1794	48			
William Currier	3 Jany. 1748-9	24	Thomas Bromley	16 Jany. 1711	61
Nathaniel Moore	30 June 1772	78	Philadelphia, Daughter of William, and Mary Bennett	1 Jany. 1775	21
Mary, his Wife	25 Dec. 1792	92			
Edward Moore	16 Feb. 1712	49			

To the Memory of Edward Holtom, late of ye Parish of Welford, who in his own defence received his mortal wound soon resigned his soul to God upon the 20*th.* day of November 1690.

CCLXXXVII. *or* 292. WESTON-UPON-AVON.

THE Church a small building dedicated to All Saints, consists of a Chancel, and Nave, and a low Tower, at the West-end, containing one Bell.

DUCHESS DOWG. OF DORSET. LADY OF THE MANOR,

DR. JAMES DAVENPORT, RECTOR.

Memorandum, March ye. 24, 1688.

This Parish Church of Weston upon Avon, in the Co. of Glouc. was by the order of the Rt. Hon'ble. Charles, Earl of Dorset, and Middlesex, repaired.

Wm. Lane, of Evesham, Junr. in the Co. of Worc. Plumber, new cast the Leads, and in consideration of 36 £. to him in hand paid, hath obliged himselfe, his Exors. Admon. and Assigns in a Bond of 100 £. to Charles, Earl of Dorset, and Middlesex, his Heirs, Exors. Admors. or Assignes that the said Wm. Lane, his Exors. Admors. &c. or some of them will from time to time, and all times hereafter during the space of 50 Years next ensewing the date hereof well, and in good, and sufficient repaire, maintaine, and keep the Leads of the said Church of Weston, at their own proper Cost, and Charge.

John Williams, of Childes Wickham, in the Co. of Glouc. Carpenter, repaired the Timber Work, of the said Church, and for, and in consideration of 22 £. to him in hand paid for which consideration aforesaid, the said John Williams, hath bound himself, his Exors. and Admors. to the Right. Hon'ble. Charles, Earl of Dorset, and Middlesex, his Heirs, Exors., and Admors., &c. in a bond of 100 £. That the said John William his Heirs, Exors. Admors., or Assignes, or some of them shall, and will from time, to time, and at all times hereafter during the space of 50 Years, next ensuing the Date hereof, uphold, maintain, and keep in good, and sufficient repair the Roof of the said Church of Weston, with Timber, and Carpenters Work at their own proper Cost, and Charges. That succeeding Generations might not be ignorant hereof this Table was here placed, by the Order, and Care of,

MARTIN CAPRON, Church Warden.

INSCRIPTIONS IN THE CHURCH.

CHANCEL,

ON A FLAT STONES.

(*very much chipped off.*)

Is a Greek Inscription to THOMAS BILLSY, and ELIZABETH,

....

(*but it is now impossible to decipher it.*) (*now quite gone* 1872.)

M. S.

Reverendi viri JOHANNES TRAPP, Art Mag.
Ædis Christi, Oxon. quondam Alumni Et hujus Ecclæ.
per annos plus minus triginta vicarij, Opera quidem non vicaria Sed Sedula, et sua In conscionibus, in scriptis, in animarum cura Diligentissimus Sacris humanisq. literis, et quod majus, est Virtutibus instructissimus In barbaro sæculo doctus, malo bonus, Iam vitæ satur
Hic juxta
Fidelissimæ conjugis ... ectos cine ...
Senex ....
.... LXÆ ....
Posuit.

M. S.

Domnæ. SUSANNÆ, Filiarum Do'ni. admodum Hon'di. LEONELLI MIDDLESEXIÆ, Comitis Dom'na. Anna Conjuge susceptarum natu minoris Cujus rediviva semina sub spe futuræ immortalitatis amplissimâ hic humo mandabantur Sextities xxii.

An. } reparatæ Salutis MDCXXXVI. } Ætatis suæ V.

Mens vis ingenij vigor venustas vix quis crediderit fuere quanta ni maturiûs hic reponerentur Mutant maculas intentiones Cædendoque acies acuta cedit Dotes quas levitas morti dederet Mors Christi merito dabit vigere.

Here lieth the Body of MR. THOMAS PEART, who departed this Life the 30 October Ano. Dom. 1702, Being in the 53 Year of his Age.

Here lies in Expectation of a Joyful Resurrection the Body of the REVD. CHARLES DAVENPORT, of *Wadham College, Oxford,* He died July 19, 1777, Aged 24.

ON A BRASS PLATE, with the Effigy of a Man in Armour with a Sword by his Side, with a long beard, and his hands joyned in prayer, his head resting upon an helmet, and *Crest*; upon a wreath a Grey hounds head coupt collared, and on his surtout are repeated the following *Arms, viz. Quarterly* 1, & 4. ...... on a Cross within a border engrailed nine balls .... 2 ....
a fess counter compony ....
3. per pale, and per fess dancette .... in the first quarter a Cressant.

Hic situs est JOANNES GRIVILLUS, eques auratus, Milcoti olim dominus qui fatum implevit Ano. redemptionis humanæ, Supra millesimum quingentesimum quadragesimo sexto, Edvardi vero sexti Anglorum regis Secundo Calendis Decembris.

ON A BRASS PLATE, exactly like the last, and same Arms.

Hic situs est EDVARDUS GRIVELLUS, eques auratus, Milcoti olim dominus; qui fato concessit pridie natalis, Christi, Ano. Salutis humane

quinquagesimo nono supra,
Millesimum, et quingentesimum
Imperante tum Anglis,
Serenissima Regina Elysabetha
ann. jam alterum.

NAVE.

ON FLAT STONES.

Here lyeth the Body of
ELIZABETH, the Wife of
JOHN WARREN,
who daparted this Life, the
20*th*. of April, A. D. 1691,
Ætatis suæ 67.

Hic situs est
Dominus JOHN WARREN,
In Parochia de *Waltham Holy Cross*,
in argo *Essexia*, nat.
vir erat sinceri, et erecti in rebus
sacris animi,
......iæ, et expositæ erga amicos
comitatis,
......ga omnes integerrimæ semper,
et plane Antiquæ probitatis
nulli mortalium gravis
...... Iie mensis Maii 16*o*.
Ao. } Dom. MDCLXXX*o*.
} Ætatis LXI*o*.

Here lieth interred
the Body of MARY JAKEMAN,
eldest Daughter of
THOMAS JAKEMAN,
and of MARGARET, his Wife,
who departed this Life,
Febr. the 7*th*. Ano. Dom. 1685-6,
Aged 20 Years.
Here lieth the Body of
SUSANNAH LADBROOK,
She died October ye. 7*th*. 1736.
Sister to the aforesaid
MARY JAKEMAN,
Aged 61 Years.

Here lyeth the Body of
MARGERY, the Wife of
ROBERT FAWDON,
who departed this Life, the
5 day of January, Ao. Don. 166....

Round the Stone in Ca, ts.

Here lyeth the Body of

ROBERT FAWDON, *Gentleman*,

Hic jacit ....
rationibus Aulam ... .
Cælestem ascendit ....
rediturus abi ....

In Memory of
ELIZABETH, the Wife of
JOSEPH GREENALL, of *Milcot*,
who departed this Life,
August ye. 30, 1748, Aged 64.

In Memory of
HENKLEY GREENALL,
who departed this Life,
Sept 26, 1756, Aged 34.

In Memory of
JOSEPH GREENALL, of *Millcot*,
who departed this Life,
Nov 26*th*. 1772, Aged 78.

In Memory of
WILLIAM GREENALL, of *Millcot*,
who departed this Life, the
24 of Nov. 1779, Aged 40 Years.

In Memory of
WILLIAM GREENALL, of *Millcott*,
who died Jany. 18, 1786,
Aged 61 Years.

(*Supplementary Note of an Additional
Monument since Bigland's time.*)

[ON SOUTH WALL OF NAVE,
ON A BRASS PLATE.

Arms:—Sable, three tombs Argent, on each a cross of passion,
Crosslet Calvary Sable.

To the Memory of
JOHN TOMES, *Gent.*
late of *Weston Sands* in this Parish,
eldest Son of JOHN and ANN TOMES,
of *Marston Sicca*, and SARAH,
his Wife the Daughter of
WILLIAM and REBECCA BAYLIES,
of *Welford*. He died Jany. 15*th*. 1864,
Aged 72 Years.

She died at *Weston Sands*,
January 18*th*. 1870, Aged 78 Years.
Also of JOHN TOMES, the eldest
Son of JOHN and JANE TOMES, of
Cavendish Square, London, and
Grandson of the above JOHN, and
SARAH TOMES. He died at
Weston Sands, Jany. 15*th*. 1845,
Aged 3 Years.
The above JOHN and SARAH,
with their Grandson were buried in
the Family vault, near the South-wall,
of the Church.]

CHURCH YARD.

ON A MONUMENT AGAINST THE SOUTH SIDE OF THE CHURCH

Here lieth the Body of
MARY MEDES, ye. Wife of
THOMAS MEDES, *Senr.*
She was buried May the 26,
A. D. 1708.
Nere unto this Place lieth the
Body of SUSANNAH MEDES, the
Wife of THOMAS MEDES,
of this Parish, *Junr.* who died
Jany. 13, 1717, Aged 15.

ON TOMBS.

Here lyeth the body of
THOMAS MEDES, *Senr.*
who departed this Life, the
13 of Febr. A. D. 1681.

Here lyeth the Body of
BENJAMIN MEDES, of this Town,
who departed this Life,
May 28, 1729, Aged 37 Years.

Here lyeth the Body of
PHILADELPHA NEWMAN,
Daughter of BENJAMIN, and
PHIADLEPHIA MEDES,
who departed this Life,
Mar the 2*nd*. 1761,
Aged 35 Years.
MARY, the Daughter of
THOMAS MEDES, and MARY,
his Wife, who departed this Life,
Febr. 25 1683, Aged 12.

HEAD STONES.

	Died.	Aged.		Died.		Aged.
Alice Palmer, of *Milcot*, Mother to the Wife of Nathaniel Edden ...	26 Aug.	1738	81	Hannah, Wife of Thos. Adkins	17 June 1782	82
				Thomas, Son of John and Mary Adkins	16 July 1788	26
Nathaniel Edden, of *Milcot*	12 May	1737	69	Robert Salman	18 Febr. 1755	57
Mary, Wife of Nathaniel Edden, of *Millcote* ...	13 Nov.	1743	66	David Wesson	18 Oct. 1800	79
				Mary, his first Wife	18 Decr. 1752	29
Henry, their Son	10 Oct.	1729	14	Mary, his second Wife	10 Oct. 1791	57
Joseph, their Son	9 Aug.	1727	6	Thomas Wesson	28 Febr. 1745-6	71
John Field	13 May	1787	35	Mary, his Wife	7 Jany. 1742-3	60
Thomas Adkins	31 Oct.	1788	95			

Supplementary Notes as to I.—Devolution of Estates. II.—Church. III.—Taxation, Population, &c.

The principal Estates in Welford and Weston upon } turies, the Parishes adjacent, and the Livings consolidated,
Avon, having been united in Ownership for nearly 3 cen- } it is deemed convenient to keep together the Notices of

these Places in the order assigned by the late Sir Thomas Phillipps, although it be not strictly alphabetical. *see Notes prefixed to* "Welford."

I.—*Estates:*

Westone in Widelie Hundred contained 3 Hides (geldable) and one free of tax. Culture: Four Carucates 2 in Demesne and 2 in the Hands of 5 Villans and a Priest. It had been worth 20 s. and then was worth 40 s. (Yearly) The Church of St. Mary of Evesham, held it
Domesday Survey.

They acquired by the Gift (716.) of Ethelbald, King of the Mercians, this Estate under the name of "Uuestona juxta Avenam" It was part of 25 Manses thus given to the Church in Ethom.

The Parishes of Welford and Weston on Avon, both contain Land of Warwickshire namely Bickmarsh and Little Dorsington part of Welford parish and Milcot part of Weston on Avon Parish.

The area of Weston in Gloucestershire, is set down as 918 a. add to this Milcot and the quantity is so much greater than the registered 4 Hides of Evesham Abbey as to lead to the inference that there must be some further Title, or that there were extensive wastes, or it might be flats or sands in the River to account for the difference. Sir R. Atkyns, does adduce a broader Domesday Title, but it is by misplacing the entries relating to this Weston and Weston Subedge

15 Edw. i.—The Abbey of Evesham claimed a Court Leet jurisdiction.

49 Edw. iii.—J. Rouse, and others sued on behalf of that Abbey. This paramount fee is considered to have passed to the Crown on the dissolution of Monasteries.

A subfee was created in Sir Thomas West and another in Regnauld. Sir Thos. West's fee is not traced.

Regnauld's fee passed by Marriage to Stapleton and thence by sale (*see Lsch.* 23 H. vi. *No.* ....) to John Greville, from him a son John, who married Joyce Cokesey, from them Thomas Greville. alias Cokesey This is one of the two Manors of Weston, the other being Weston Maudit, the origin of which is not ascertained nor are its limits shewn in the public Documents. But Maudit Lord Hanslape, held temp. Hen. iii It is stated in a Record of 10 Eliz. (*Mich. Records.*) that Weston Maudit. was then held of the Crown as of the Abbey of Winchcomb It is clearly a suborDinate fee; but the paramount Lord may have been misstated for Evesham. The Heir general of Maudit married Beauchamp, of Elmley, who 2 Edw. i. subenfeoffed Langley, who 18 Edw. ii. with his Wife and eldest son and his Wife, made a Settlement under which Peto, took as Heir general, From him W. Greville, in which family it continued for several generations unto the aforesaid Sir E. Greville, who sold both Manors to pay off Incumbrances. In the printed Abstract of Chancery Proceedings temp. Eliz. several suits by Dame Margaret Hawkins, against Sir E. Greville, to realize mortgage Securities are recorded. The Earl of Middlesex, a large Creditor became the Purchaser of the Greville Estates and the devolution from him is given under Welford. Of the Mansion House of the Grevilles at Milcote, there are some vestiges, as also of a Castle built by Lodowick Greville, but never completed.

Of the other Properties at Weston upon Avon, few Notices are found in public Documents. Only one freeholder voted at the Great County Contests of 1776 and 1811. In the later Voter's Registers occur the name of Baylies, Tomes, and others mentioned in the *Church Inscriptions.* And in the 1876, List of Voters the honored Name of "West" occurs.

A Farm and an Island called the Yame Robt. Rouse, held; from whom William and John Rouse. 8 H. vi. *No.* 35. *Esch.*

II.—*Church.*

There was a Church here before the Conquest.

The Advowson belonged to the Bishop of Worcester, who granted the great Tythes to the Nuns of Whitstan.

The Impropriation belongs to the Lord of the Manor.

Weston super Avon Vicaria:

In Rents and farm with others Profits and Tythes above 6s. 8d. to the Archdeacon and 12d. cenage £7 14 5.
Valor Eccl'us.

The Vicar has 25 a. Glebe.

List of Incumbents and Patrons of Weston upon Avon.

1540.—George Vyll or Fill.	
1556.—William Bounde.	Edward Grevyl, Knt.
1559.—William Cartrite.	
1560.—William Casemore,	Lewis Grevyl.
1568.—Thomas Woodward.	" "
1571.—William Catheral.	" "
1585.—Philip Jones.	" "
1592, July.—Thomas Heath.	Edward Grevil.
1592, Dec.—John Rutter.	" "
1593.—Stephen Hall.	" "
1639.—John Trapp.	Lionel, Earl of Middlesex.
1670.—Josias Simcox.	" " "
1681.—John Johnson.	Charles, Earl of Dorset.
1659.—Thomas Willes.	" " "
.......—Gabral Barodale.	Lionel, Duke of Dorset.
1736.—Joseph Green.	" " "
1772.—David Davenport.	" " "
1774.—James Davenport.	" " "

At Bishop Hooper's Examination George Fill, was Vicar. Commandments: He knew their number and where written but could not repeat them correctly. Belief—he knew and could rehearse the Articles, but could not prove them. Lords Prayer—He could repeat, and knew when and by whom given. The Number of Communicants was 23.

The Aisle in which many of the Greville family are buried was a Chapel dedicated to St. Ann.

The Welford Register begins 1561.

The ancient names there are Canning, Holtham, Cartrite, Millard. 1684. Old Porter died 109 Years of Age.

The Register of Weston on Avon begins 1685. The ancient Names are Bartlett, Cotterell, Durham. John Grevel, was there married 1602. In 1745, Edward Bennet, and Elizth Buggins alias Burgoigns, were married.

Benefactions:

Thomas Mills, charged his Estate in Welford with 3 £. a Year for Poor. And 3s. 4d. for Highway Repairs of Weston.

17 Jac. i.—John Frekelton, gave out of Milham Close, 13s. 4d. to the Poor of Welford, for ever. And 6s. 8d. to the Church for ever.

1721.—Richard Rawlins, charged his half Yard Land in Welford with 3£. per annum to a School Master to teach 8 poor Boys to read and write and to keep accounts.

T. Eden, by Deed gave his Houses and Land (30 a.) at Mangotsfield and Houses in St. Mary Radcliffe and St. Thomas Bristol, to Trustees to apply the Rents to maintaining Schools for the Poor in the Parishes of Pebworth, Weston Subedge and Weston upon Avon, Old Stratford and Newbold.   *Charity Inquiry Commiss.* 21 Report.

III.—*Taxation, Population, &c.*

Weston super Abonam, Subsidy Roll, 1 Edw. iii., 1327.

De Robt. le Coke, xvi d. q.
' Johne. le Skinnar, xviii d.
' Willmo. Matheu, xxii d. q.
' Willmo. Abovethetoune, ii s. ii d. ob.
' Johne. de Westone, ii s. xi d. ob. q.
' Henr. Joce, viii d.
' Hugon. le Newman, ii s. ob.
' Thom. atte Floddre, xviii d.

   prob Sma. xiiii s. i d. q.

Weston Mauduyt.

De Elia atte Pirie, iii s. iii d.
' Agnete la Neuman, xxi d. q.
' Nicho. la Baxtere, ii s. x d.
' Johne. Dod, ii s. x d. q.
' Regin. de Dersintone, xv d. ob. q.
' Thom. le Gardiner, xviii d.
' Johne. Godhine, xiii d.
' Agnete Lolle, xii d. ob.

   prob. Sma. xv s. ix d. q.

Acreage 918 a. in Gloucestershire.
Population 1831,—102.   1861,—137.   1871,—144.
1815.—Yearly Value of Real Property £1833.
1882.—Estimated Rateable Value £ 1574. in Glouc.
1833-4-5.—Three Years Average Expenditure on Poor 94£.

In Stratford on Avon Union.

WESTBURY IN THE FOREST.

[WESTBURY ON SEVERN.]

.... COLCHESTER, *Esqr.* is Lord of the Manor, He has an elegant House called *Westbury Court*, built in the Modern Stile and on pediment over the Attic story are the *Arms* of COLCHESTER, *impaling* three Crescents. [This House now taken down.]

Revd. RICHARD WETHERILL, *Vicar.*

THE OLD CHURCH with a handsome Wooden Spire at the West-end is yet standing in the Church Yard and is used as a School and Vestryroom. It is dedicated to St. Peter, and contains six Bells.

The new Church was built in 1530, in the same Church Yard for the use of the Parishioners It stands a considerable distance from the other, and therein divine service is performed. It consists of a Chancel, Nave and two Aisles supported by pillars. It is dedicated to the Virgin Mary.

BENEFACTIONS:

JOHN YOUNG, of *Ley,* gave by Will seven pounds a year one moiety for a parish Schoolmaster, the other for Sermons for ever.

The Church Lands let for 4£ 16 s. yearly were given by a person unknown, and are applied towards the repairs of the Church.

Several tenements adjoining the Church Yard and the Church House were given by persons unknown for the use of poor of this Parish.

The House, Garden and Orchard adjoining to the King's common pound usually let at forty shillings a year were given by a person unknown for the use of the Parish for ever.

A tenement near the above granted on lease formerly to THOMAS COOK, and now occupied by TOBIAS COWLES, was left by a person unknown for the use of the Parish for ever.

CORNELIUS DRAPER, gave one piece of inclosed land in *Huntley,* now let to JAMES DRINKWATER, at forty shillings a year to be given to the poor.

JOSEPH BAYSE, gave the Interest of ten pounds, (the principal now lying in the parish Stock.) to be given in Bread to the poor of *Elton* Tithing.

JOSEPH HOLSTEAD, of *Ley, Gent.* gave the Interest of twenty pounds, for the education of two Boys at the School.

JOHN MAYN, of *Staintway, Gent.* by Will gave several parcels of Free Land in *Walmore's Hill,* and one Rudge, and forehead of Leaseland during the residue of his term, of the yearly value of 1£. 2s. 6d. to buy Coal for the Poor in November Yearly.

A Chief Rent of three shillings and eight pence, on a tenement now belonging to JOHN SEIR, was given to the Poor of this Parish, by a Person unknown.

Mrs. ELIZABETH EVANS, gave twenty pounds, the Interest to be given yearly for ever to the Poor of this Parish.

[Additions to the Benefaction Table.

12.—The *Revd.* WILLIAM BOUGHTON, Vicar of *Blockley, Worcestershire,* bequeathed 200£. the Interest to be applied in repairing the Monuments erected in this Church to the memory of members of his family, and the Remainder for the Comfort of the Poor as the Vicar should think best.

13.—*Miss* ANN BOUGHTON, of *Bourton House,* in this County, Sister of the above WILLIAM BOUGHTON, bequeathed 100£. the annual Interest for establishing a Charity School or in aid of any already formed in this Parish, so as the same be of the Established Church.

14.—*Mr.* BENJAMIN MAYO, gave by Will to the Minister and Churchwardens 100£. the Interest in aid of the School establishment for educating poor Children.]

INSCRIPTIONS IN THE CHURCH.

CHANCEL.

ON MONUMENTS.

Memoriæ NICHO. ROBERTS, *Arm.*
quondam hujus
Manerij Dni Qui Mortalitatem
exuit 19o. Jan. 1636.
Hoc qualecunque charissimi Avunculi,
Meritis quam longe impar
Sacrat. voluit
E sorore Nepos
RICHUS. COLCHESTER, *Arm.*
Modernus ejusdem Manerij Dns.
25 Julij 1642.

Arms on each side of this Inscription.
1 Per pale Or, and Gules a Lion rampant Sable :—ROBERTS.
2 Or, a Chevron between three Estoils Gules :—COLCHESTER.

Arms :—COLCHESTER, *as before,*
impaling Argent, three sinister hands coupt at the wrist, Gules: MAYNARD.

Dominæ ELIZABETHÆ COLCHESTER,
Uxoris DUNCOMB COLCHESTER, militis
Filiæ JOHAN. MAYNARD,
Equitis Aurati
Servien. ad Legem et Regis Consiliarij
in Lege peritissimi,
Cineribus Sacrum.
Vitæ Sanctimoniâ
Morum suavitate et candore,
In rebus Oeconomicis Peritiâ
Charitate erga Pauperes,
Medicamentis erga infirmos
Præceptis erga Errantes,
Clementiâ erga Ignorantes
In se omnium benevolentiam
conciliantis.
Sed Eheu ! per multos annos

varijs morbis et cruciatibus conflicta
Tandem Animam immaculatam
Deo reddidit Septemb. 19o. 1681.
Filios duos, tres Filias, Superstes
reliquit moriens.
Optimæ Conjugi Amantissimus
Maritus,
Hoc posuit monumentum.

Arms :—COLCHESTER, *as before,*
impaling MAYNARD, *as before.*

Deo opt. max. sacrum
ut laudetur in
Piâ Memoria
DUNCOMBI COLCHESTER, Eq. aurat:
Qui obijt May 25to. A. D. 1694,
Æt. 65.

Hic (ut olim Solomon) in vijs
cordis sui
Pede heu libero nimis Ambulans.
Non infructuoso tandem Experimento
didicit,
Vana omnia præter numinis cultum.
Fximiis naturæ dotibus pollens
Munera publica non unius generis obivit
nec sine Laude sæculi.
Sola defuit Matura Sanctitas
Sed morbo tandem velut nuncio
cœlitus misso admonitus,
Quicquid supererat Vitæ
Id totum Pietatis studiis impendit.
Nec sufficere sibi ratus Privatam
Pœnitentiam
Omnibus quotquot Exemplo suo
nocuisse videri poterat
Pœnitentiam etiam suam notam
esse voluit,
Non metuens de Famâ, nec moratus
Dicacem Improborum hominum
stultitiam
Rem etiam in Templis publicari
curavit ipse,
Novo et singulari exemplo
Se vivum præstans omnibus
Maxime Dierum Vanitatis suæ socijs,
Illustrissmum Generosæ pœnitentiæ
monumentum.
Etiam mortuus loquitur, Lectorem
serio monens
Deum sibi quam citissme Amicum
conciliet,
Quem Asylum omnes optabunt,
Maynardus Colchester,
F. natu maximus,
Hoc marmor Patri
P.
Nec non Lorithæ, sorori
Charissimæ quæ diu Languens
Piâ Curâ ægrotantis Patris,
Mortui Pesiderio,
Terrenorum omnium Tædio
ad Cœlestem patrem migravit
Maij 10 mo. Ao. Dni 1696,
Æt. ......

Arms Colchester, as before,
impaling—Argent, on a bend Sable
a Cross Crosslet fitché Or Clarke.

Near this Place are deposited the
precious Remains of
Maynard Colchester, Esqr.
deceased honourably descended
being the eldest Son of
Sir Duncomb Colchester,
late of this Parish by Elizabeth,
Daughter of Sir John Maynard,
decd. one of the Lords Commissioners
of the Great Seal of England.
But much more honourable and
worthy to be had in everlasting
Remembrance for those truly noble
Qualities which by the Grace of
God he was early possessed of and
persevered in to the last, and
whereby he was enabled to discharge
with great Judgment,
inflexible Integrity and undaunted
Courage the several
Offices and Trusts which without
seeking he was called to by his
Prince and Country and to devise and
do many great and liberal Things
for the Honour of God and good
of mankind, having been
a principal Founder, and Supporter
of the Societies for
Reformation of Manners and
promoting Christian knowledge
by Charity Schools, of which he set
up, and maintained several at his own
Charge, and likewise one of the first
Members of ye Society for

propagating the Gospel in
Foreign Parts and a generous
Encourager of that and many
other good designs.
This Excellent Person was strictly
pious Himself and zealous to
promote true Piety in others
within his reach, especially in
his own Family and was thought
to have been so singularly
happy herein as to have
overpaid the Debt of Filial
Duty and Gratitude by being
an Instrument of Spiritual Life
to him from whom he had only
Received that which was Natural.

He was an affectionate Husband,
a tender and carefull Parent,
a kind and faithfull Friend,
a true Lover of all good Men,
tho' differng from him,
and ready to every good Work.
particularly those of Charity
to ye Poor and distressed,
For whom he yearly set apart
a large Proportion of his Income
which was strictly tho' secretly applied
to the most useful Charities.
This Christian Hero was
exercised for many
Years with almost constant
sickness and the most acute pains
which he bore with exemplary
Patience and an entire submission
to the Divine Will and Pleasure,
and at length joyfully resign'd
up his Pious Soul into the Hands
of his faithful Creator and
merciful Redeemer ye 25 of June
1715, in the 51 Year of his Age,
leaving 3 Daughters:—Anne, Jane,
and Elizabeth, by Jane, the only
Daughter of
Sir Edward Clarke Knt.
decd late Lord Mayor of London,
his loving and dutifull
Wife and now mournful
Widow.

Arms of Colchester, as before.

In Hopes of a happy Resurrection
near this Place lies the Body
Maynard Colchester, Esqr.
Nephew and Heir of
Col. Maynard Colchester,
to whose Memory a Monument
is erected. He was Grandson to
Sir Duncomb Colchester,
and Great grandson of that eminent
Lawyer, and Friend
to the Constitution and Liberties
of England,
Serjeant Maynard.
He retained thro' Life with his own
Choice and Judgment,
an hereditary Affection for the Laws,
the Religion and Civil Rights
of Englishmen,
as Established by the Revolution.
From this Principle, he ever
manifested a firm Attachment
to the illustrious House of Hanover,
and the Protestant Succession,
particularly during the Rebellion
in 1746, and approved himself by his
Conduct at all Times a vigilant,
active, and prudent Magistrate
and a friend to Society.
In private Life, he was a good
Christian, a kind Father and
indulgent Master, was cautious and
discerning in his choice of Friends,
and steady and unchangable towards
them when chosen.

His whole Character did Himself
and Family honour, and
needs not Praises, but deserves
Imitation,
Died May 25th, 1756, Aged 53.

On Flat Stones.

Here resteth the Body of
William, the son of Roger
Taylor, Senr. of Rodley, Gent.
who departed this Life, the
21st. of March 1721,
Aged 15 Years.
Here resteth the Body of
Anne, the Daughter of
Roger Taylor, Senr.
late of Rodley, Gent.
who departed this Life, the
18 day of March 1732,
Aged 31 Years.
Also Mary, Daughter of Roger
Taylor, Junr. of Rodley, Gent.
who departed this Life, the
24 May 1745, in 6 Year of her Age.

Here lyeth the Body of
Mary, the Wife of Roger Taylor,
Senr. of this Parish,
who departed this Life,
March 3, 1639.
Here lyeth the Body of
Anne, Wife of William Taylor,
of this Parish, Gent. and Daughter
of Jeremiah Hiet,
who departed this Life,
3 April 1655.

In Memory of
William, the Son of Roger Taylor,
of Bury Court, in this Parish. Gent.
who died March 31, 1656.
Roger, Son of the said William,
who died March 21, 1685,
Aged 31 Years.
Roger Taylor, the Son of the said
William, who died March 31, 1685,
Aged 31 Years.
Also Roger Taylor, of
Bury Court, Gent. who died
April 5, 1727, Aged 51 Years.
And of Mary, the Widow of said
Roger Taylor, who died
June 1, 1753, Aged near 79.

Here resteth the Body of
John Alberton, of Elton, Gent.
who departed this Life, the
20 of Nov. 1713, Aged 53 Years.
Also Mary, the Wife of
John Aylberton, of Elton, Gent.
who was interred Jany. 5th. 1721,
Aged 85 Years.
Also Joan, Daughter of the above,
who was buried May 9, 1756,
Aged 87 Years.

Here resteth the Body of
Mitchel Aylberton,
of this Parish, Gent.
who departed this Life,
April 13, 1743, Aged 47 Years.
Also in Memory of Anne, his Wife,
who departed this Life,
May the 15, A. D. 1758,

Aged 59 Years.
Also six of their Children.

Arms:—Gules a Chief Argent,
on the lower part thereof a Cloud,
the Sun's resplendent rays issuing
thereout proper.—LYSONS.

Hic jacet Corpus
GULIELMI LYSONS, de *Lay*,
infra hanc Parochiam, *Gen.*
Qui obiit 26 Januar.
Anno { Domini 1693,
{ Ætatis 65.

Hic jacet Corpus
JACOBI LYSONS,
Pannarij Qui obiit
Die Junij 10o.
Anno. { Ætatis suæ 73,
{ Domini 1702.

In Memory of
HANNAH, the Wife of STEPHEN
MALSON, of *Moyeshill, Gent.*
who died 9 Decr. 1728.
Here lyeth the Body of
STEPHEN MALSON, of *Moyeshill,*
Gent. who departed this Life,
January the 20, 1712,
Aged 45 Years.
In Memory of
ELIZABETH, Daughter of STEPHEN
MALSON, aforesaid, *Gent.*
late Wife of RICHARD EDWARDS,
of *Gloucester, Gent.*
She died 5 Oct. 1733.
Also of MARY, Daughter of
STEPHEN MALSON, who died
Jany. 16, 1705, Aged 11 Years.

Hic requescit
In spe gloriosæ Resurrectionis
Corpus MARIÆ Conjugis
ARNOLD de le GRANGE,
infra hanc Parochiam, *Generosi,* quæ
Obijt 20 die Augusti,
Anno { Domini 1647,
{ Ætatis 73.
Abi Viator
et Nov......... Contemplar.

In Memory of
JOSEPH BATE, who died the
29*th.* of August 1721,
Aged 44 Years.

[*But few of the Flat stone Inscrip-*
tions are now visible.]

CHURCH YARD.

ALTAR TOMBS.

Here lyeth the Body of
JOHN, the Son of PHILIP HAMPTON,
of *Elton,* who departed this Life,
12*th.* of December, Anno 1688,
Here lyeth the Body of
PHILIP HAMPTON, of *Elton,*
who departed this Life, the
16*th.* of November, Anno 1662.

Arms:—Argent, a Chevron bet-
ween three Cinque foils Gules.
Crest:—a Wolfs head erased
Sable. HAMPTON.

JOHN, the Son of HENRY HAMPTON,
was buried January the 18*th* 1539.
JOHN, the Son of JOHN,
was buried Oct. 4, 1570.
And also JOHN, his Son,
was buried February the 15*th.* 1635.
Also PHILIP, Son of JOHN,
was buried November the 16*th.* 1662.
Also THOMAS, the Son of PHILIP,
was buried July 24*th,* 1707.
Also MARGARET, his Wife,
and THOMAS, their Son.
Also THOMAS, the Grandson of
THOMAS, who was buried
November the 21*st.* 1712.
PHILIP HAMPTON, of *Bosley, Gent.*
And also ANNE, his Wife,
Daughter of THOMAS SYMONS,
of *Clearwell, Esqr.*
lie buried here.
He died Sept. 11, 1728.
She died December 12, 1745.
Also MARY, their Daughter,
Wife of WILLIAM RAYMOND, *Esqr.*
She died August 14*th.* 1749,
Also six Children of
WILLIAM RAYMOND, *Esqr.*
by MARY, his Wife,
lie buried here.

[*see Thornbury Inscriptions as to this*
family.]

M. S.
JOSEPH FLUCK, of *Broken Cross,*
in this Parish, *Yeoman,* who died
Febr. 12, 1790, Aged 56 Years.
Also SUSANNA, his Wife,
who died July 5, 1786,
Aged 64 Years.
SUSANNA, their Daughter,
who died an Infant.

In Memory of
WILLIAM CADLE,
of *Poultons Hill* in this Parish,
who departed this Life,
Decr. 23, 1792, Aged 61 Years.
Also of ELIZABETH, the Daughter of
WILLIAM and ANN CADLE,
of this Parish, who died
the 13 of March 1766,
Aged 1 Year and 6 Months.
And also ANN, their Daughter,
who died 27 of Oct. 1787,
Aged 2 Years.

In Memory of
RICHARD CADLE, of *Poulton's Hill,*
who died April 12, 1738,
Aged 47 Years.
Also RICHARD, his Son,
who died July 24, 1742,
Aged 9 Years.
Also ANN, his Daughter,
died Nov. 9, 1757, Aged 21 Years.
Also ELIZABETH, Wife of the
aforesaid RICHARD CADLE,
who died April 12, 1771,
Aged 69 Years.
In Memory of
ANN, the first Wife of
RICHARD CADLE, Daughter of the
Revd. Mr. WILLIAM MAYO,
formerly Rector of *Blaisdon,*
who died Oct. 27. 1729,
Aged 40 Years.

In Memory of
JOHN, the Son of
JOSEPH and SUSANNA CADLE,
who died March 13, 1724,
and SARAH, the Daughter of
JOSEPH and SUSANNA CADLE,
who died April 28, 1788.
And ABIGAIL, their Daughter,
who died August 15, 1731.
HESTER, Daughter of the
aforesaid Parents, who died
March 2, 1738.
Also of JOSEPH CADLE, of
Long Croft in this Parish,
who died June 12, 1745,
Aged 49 Years.
SUSANNA, his Widow, who died
March 13, 1767, Aged 70 Years.

In Memory of
JOSEPH CADLE, of *Long Croft*
in this Parish, who died
Oct. 19, 1774, Aged 53 Years.
HANNAH, his Sister and Wife of
SAMUEL ELLIOT,
died March 18, 1769,
Aged 40 Years.
Also MARY, his Sister, and Wife of
JOHN CUMMINS,
died Jany. 14, 1778,
Aged near 53 Years.

In Memory of
ELIZABETH, the Wife of JOHN
CADLE, of this Parish,
who departed this Life,
15 of Nov. 1759, Aged 21 Years.
And also of their two Children
that died in their infancy
and are also buried here.

To the Memory of
THOMAS CADLE, of this Parish,
who died 24 of March 1790,
Aged 48 Years.
Also WILLIAM, Son of
THOMAS and SUSANNA CADLE,
he was buried at *Blaisdon,*
the 24 of March 1780,
Aged 7 Years.
Also PHEBE CADLE.
She died 24 of Decr. 1783,
Aged 47 Years.

Sacred to the Memory of
RICHARD HOOK,
who departed this Life, the
11 Jany 1793, Aged 70 Years.
Also ANNE, his Wife,
died Jany. 9, 1791, Aged 82 Years.

Here resteth the Body of
JOANE, Wife of WILLIAM PRICHET,
who departed this Life, the
3 of March 1733.
Here lyeth the Body of
WILLIAM, the Son, of WILLIAM
and JOANE PRICHET,
who departed this Life, the
22 Jany. 1729.
Here rests also the Body of
WILLIAM PRICHET, *Senr.*
of this Parish, who departed
this Life, the 15 day of Decr. 1739,
Aged 40 Years.

1395

Likewise here resteth the Body of
ANNE, Wife of the abovesaid
WILLIAM PRICHET, and late Wife of
RICHARD HOOK, of this Parish,
who departed this Life, the
9 Jany. 1791, Aged 82 Years.

MARY, the Wife of JOSEPH FLUCK,
who died Decr. 27, 1770,
Aged 63 Years.
JOHN FLUCK, Senr. of Northwood,
died April 5, 1726, Aged 63.
Also SIBBLE, his Wife,
was buried here.

In Memory of
JOHN, Son of THOMAS HARPER,
of Northwood, by MARY, his Wife,
who died May 1, 1769,
Aged near 21 Years.

In Memory of
THOMAS HARPER, of Northwood,
Senr. who died May 22, 1748,
Aged 67 Years.
Also MARY, his Wife,
died August 17 1717,
Aged 34 Years.
ELIZABETH, his Second Wife,
died Febr. 15, 1720,
Aged 33 Years.
Also MARY HARPER, Wife of
THOMAS HARPER, of Northwood
in this Parish. She died
Febr. 23, 1781, Aged 66 Years.
Also the above THOMAS HARPER,
who died April 10, 1785,
Aged 73 Years.
ANN, Daughter of THOMAS HARPER,
by ANN, his Wife, who died
Sept. 24, 1774, Aged 4 Months.
ANNA-MARIA, their Daughter,
died Jany. 21, 1781, Aged 7 Months.
Six Children of THOMAS HARPER,
Senr. buried here:
JOHN, died June 4, 1736,
Aged 22 Years.
SIBLE, died Jany. 20, 1742,
Aged 16 Years.
THOMAS, died Nov. 17, 1713.
JAMES. died April 6, 1723.
MARY, died March 17, 1708.
MARTHA, died April 5, 1723.

In Memory of
JOHN POWELL, of this Parish,
who died May 7, 1738,
Aged 52 Years.
HANNAH, his Wife,
died Febr. 1, 1733, Aged 36.
Also ESTHER, Wife of JOHN POWELL,
died Nov. 6, 1771, Aged 37 Years.
Also HANNAH, their Daughter,
died Decr. 7, 1762, Aged 7 Weeks.

Here lyeth the Body of
SAMUEL, the Son of JOHN VERY,
who departed this Life,
June 1, 1722, Aged 19 Years,
6 Months.
Also the Body of JOHN VERY,
late of Lay, who departed this Life,
Oct. 1, 1704.
MARY, his Wife, who departed
this Life, Sept. 27, 1734.

In Memory of
WILLIAM BELLAMY,
of Bollow in this Parish,
who died Jan. 24, 1775,
Aged 48 Years.
Also HANNAH, his Wife,
died Decr. 9, 1792, Aged 65.
Also WILLIAM, their Son,
died May 16, 1777, Aged 27.
Also THOMAS, their Son,
died Febr. 10, 1797, Aged 29.

Here resteh in Expectation of a
Glorious Resurrection the Body of
ANTHONY MANN,
who departed this Life, the
8 of Sept. A. D. 1708,
Æt suæ 46.

To the Memory of
THOMAS, the Son of ISAAC
WILLIAMS, of Northwood, by
ELIZABETH, his Wife,
died March, 25, 1761, Aged 27.
Also SARAH, their Daughter,
died Oct. 1, 1736, Aged XI Weeks.
Also of ISAAC WILLIAMS,
of Northwood in this Parish,
who died May 15, 1779,
Aged 76 Years
Also ELIZABETH, his Widow,
died March 2, 1785, Aged 78 Years.

In Memory of
THOMAS BADGER, of this Parish,
who died Nov. 28, 1781,
Aged 83 Years
PRUDENCE, his Wife, who died
April 1, 1753, Aged 56 Years,
Also THOMAS, their Son,
died March 5, 1745, Aged 4 Years.
Likewise THOMAS, their Son,
died Febr. 28, 1735, Aged 1 Year.

Sacred to the Memory of
JAMES WILKINS, of this Parish,
He died the 15 of May 1784,
Aged 57 Years.
Also THOMAS and WILLIAM,
his Sons:
THOMAS, died Oct. 11, 1763,
Aged 4 Years.
WILLIAM, died Oct. 1766,
Aged 8 Years.
Also MARY, Daughter of
JOHN WILKINS, of Stantway
in this Parish, by MARY, his Wife,
She died Sept. 18, 1798,
Aged 11 Weeks.
Near this Place lie the Remains of
ELIZABETH, the Wife, of JAMES
WILKINS, of this Parish,
who departed this Life, the
2 of Sept. 1787, Aged 66 Years.

Here rests the Body of
MARY, the Wife of THOMAS
YOUNG, of this Parish, Gent.
and late Wife of
ROBERT LAWRENCE,
She departed this Life, May 30,
A. D. 1743, Aged 44.

In Memory of

SAMUEL SELWYN, Yeoman,
who died Jany. 31, 1760,
Aged 64 Years.
Also MARTHA, Daughter of
SAMUEL SELWYN, by RACHEL,
his Wife, who died March 22, 1769,
Aged XI Years.
RACHEL, Daughter of SAMUEL
SELWYN, by DEBORAH, his Wife,
who died August 10, 1775,
Aged 12 Weeks.
Also SAMUEL, their Son,
died May 17, 1776, Aged 10 Days.

In Memory of
JOHN MALSON, of Rodley
in this Parish, who was buried
April 16, 1732.
Also RICHARD AIKLEY,
who was buried March 6, 1732,
Aged 50 Years.
Also MARY, Wife of JACOB
WINTLE, of this Parish,
who was interred Decr. 28, 1749,
Aged near 40 Years.
Also five Children of JACOB
WINTLE, by MARY, his Wife,
were buried here.
Also JOHN WINTLE, of this Parish,
Son of the said JACOB and
MARY WINTLE,
He departed this Life,
July 12, 1768, Aged 35 Years.
Also the above named
JACOB WINTLE, Senr.
of the Parish of Minsterworth,
who died March 24, 1717,
Aged 78 Years.

In Memory of
RICHARD WINTLE, of Stantway,
who died March 23, 1744,
Aged 47 Years.
Also MARY, Wife of RICHARD
WINTLE, of Stantway,
who departed this Life, the
24 June, A. D. 1768,
Aged 46 Years.
Also RICHARD, the Son of
JONATHAN WINTLE, by ANNE,
his Wife, who died Nov. 30, 1774,
Aged nine Weeks.

To the Memory of
JONATHAN WINTLE, of Stantway,
in this Parish, and SARAH, his Wife,
He died May 17, 1731,
Aged 60 Years.
She died Nov. 16, 1760,
Aged 86 Years.

Here rest the Bodies of
JOSEPH MORWENT, of this Parish,
Gent. who departed this Life,
the 11 of Febr. A. D. 1645,
and of SARAH, his Wife,
who died the 4 of Nov. 1660.
Erected at the proper Charge of
JOSEPH MORWENT, of Tetbury,
in this County, Gent.
in Memory of his Parents.

In Memory of
JOHN BAKER, Senr.
late of Broadoak, in this Parish,

who died Febr. 28, 1780,
Aged 72 Years.
Also of SARAH, his Wife,
who died Nov. 23, 1786,
Aged 74 Years.

In Memory of
JOHN BROWN, of *Elton* in this
Parish, who died Oct. 6, 1781,
Aged 83 Years.
MARY, his Wife, who died
April 13, 1768, Aged 57 Years.
Also Six of their Children,
were buried here.

To the Memory of
JOHN BROWN, of *Elton* in this
Parish, who departed this Life, the
29 of March 1789, Aged 54 Years.

Here rests the Body of
FRANCIS LAUNDER, of *Elton*,
who departed this Life, the
3 of Mach 1725, Aged 80 Years.

Here resteth the Body of
JOSEPH HOULDSTEAD, of *Lay*,
who departed this Life, the
Oct. 16, 1722, Aged 71 Years.

In Memory of
JOHN NEWTON, of *Northwood*,
in this Parish, who died
April 28. 1772, Aged 69 Years.
Near this Place are deposited
the Remains of SARAH NEWTON,
Relict of *Mr.* JOHN NEWTON,
of *Northwood*, in this Parish.
She died May 27, 1791,
Aged 83 Years.

In Memory of
JOHN ADAMS, late of *Newneham*,
Mariner, who departed this Life,
Dec. 21, 1753. Aged near 54.
Also THOMAS ADAMS, of *Bolley*,
Mariner, who departed this Life,
March 25, A. D. 1761,
Aged near 55.
Also MARY, Wife of the abovesaid
THOMAS ADAMS of *Bolley*,
Mariner, who departed this Life,
Febr. 21, 1778, Aged 65 Years.
Also the Remains of
JOHN, Son of THOMAS ADAMS,
by SARAH, his Wife,
who departed this Life, March 19,
A. D. 1771, Aged 8 Years
and 2 Months.
Likewise WILLIAM, Son of the
abovesaid THOMAS ADAMS,
of *Newnham*, by SARAH, his Wife,
who died June 27, A. D. 1770,
Aged 3 Years and 4 Months.
Also JOHN, Son of THOMAS ADAMS,
of *Bolley*, by MARY, his Wife,
who died Febr. 11, 1759,
Aged 24 Years.
Near this Tomb lie Remains of
THOMAS ADAMS, of *Newnham*,
who departed this Life,
Oct. 27, 1795, Aged 59 Years.
Also JOHN ADAMS, Son of

THOMAS and SARAH ADAMS,
who died 28 May 1799,
Aged 25 Years.

In Memory of
JOHN DOWDING, of this Parish,
who died Nov. 26, 1752,
Aged 80 Years.
Also MARY, his Wife,
who died Febr. 4, 1730,
Aged 58 Years.
And two of their Children.
In Memory of
THOMAS DOWDING. of this Parish,
who died Oct. 14, 1784,
Aged 81 Years.
Also ELIZABETH, his Wife,
She died March 8, 1747,
Ætat. 35.
Two of their Children, are likewise
buried here.

In Memory of
JOHN POPE, of *Elton* in this Parish,
who died Sept. 3, 1780, in the
80 Year of his Age.
Also the Body of JANE, the Wife of
the aforesaid JOHN POPE,
of *Elton*, in this Parish,
who departed this Life,
March 21, 1708, Aged 76 Years.
Also JOHN, Son of WILLIAM
POPE, by MARY, his Wife,
who died July 25, 1779,
Aged 16 Months and XI Days.

In Memory of
RICHARD CONSTANS,
of the *Grange*, who died
Febr. 8, 1681.
Also SARAH, his Daughter,
who died Nov. 10, 1682.
Also ABIGAIL, the Wife of
RICHARD CONSTANS,
of the *Grange*, and late of
RICHARD CANNOCK, of *Elton*,
She died 11 of Nov. 1760,
Aged 56 Years.
Also the Body of JOANE, the
Wife of RICHARD CONSTANCE,
of the *Grange*, who departed
this Life, Jany. 15, in the
Year of our Lord 1711.
Here lyeth the Body of
RICHARD CONSTANCE, of the
Grange, who died May 19, 1746,
Aged near 42 Years.

In Memory of
THOMAS CONSTANS, of the
Grange. Also ELIZABETH, his Wife.
He died May 2, A. D. 1742,
Aged 43 Years.
She died Oct. 1, A. D. 1761,
Aged 85 Years.
Also ANN, Wife of EDWARD
WALTER, and Daughter of
the above mentioned THOMAS and
ELIZABETH CONSTANCE,
who died March 21, 1732,
Aged 24 Years.
Also in Memory of
THOMAS CONSTANCE,
of the *Grainge* in this Parish,
who departed this Life,
Aug. 12, 1789, Aged 74 Years
Also DOROTHY, Wife of ADAM
ROBINSON, and Sister of the

above mentioned THOMAS
CONSTANCE, who died July 11, 1733,
Aged 28 Years.

Erected to perpetuate the Memorial
of JAMES FRYER, of *Stantway*,
in this Parish, He died
July 25, 1779, Aged 67 Years.
Also of ELIZABETH, his Wife,
who died March 18, 1782,
Aged 60 Years.

In Memory of
MARY, the Daughter of JAMES
and ELIZABETH FRYER,
of *Stantway* in this Parish,
She died April 11, A. D. 1760,
in the XX Year of her Age.

Sacred to the Memory of
PEREGRINE SYMS, late of *Elton
Farm* in this Parish,
who departed this Life, the
24 February 1796, Aged 53 Years.

Sacred to the Memory of
JOSEPH POWEAL, of *Broadoak*
in this Parish, *Shipwright*,
He died 25 Dec. 1755, Aged 85.
ELIZABETH, his Wife,
died June 21, 1789, Aged 75.
THOMAS POWEAL, *Shipwright*,
Son of JOHN and ELIZABETH
POWEAL, who died ye 9 of April 1795,
Aged 47 Years.

Near this Place rest the Bodies of
SARAH, Daughter of JOHN and
ELIZABETH PLEYDELL, of *Rodley*,
who died May 7, 1765,
Aged 29 Years.
Also HANNAH, the Daughter of
THOMAS BENNETT, of *Rodley*,
by ANN, his Wife, who died
Nov. 28, 1782, Aged 14 Years.
MARY PLEYDELL,
died June 24, 1794, Aged 62 Years.
JOHN PLEYDELL, of this Parish,
died April 7, 1747, Aged 71 Years.
ELIZABETH, Wife of JOHN
PLEYDELL, died Dec. 10, 1769,
Aged 62 Years.

In Memory of
THOMAS, Son of FRANCIS and
ELIZABETH CRUMP,
died Febr. 8th. 1748, in the
22 Year of his Age.

To the Memory of
JOHN MAYO, of this Parish,
who after the faithful discharge
of his Duty as a Servant for
sixty Years, departed this Life,
Febr. 1, 1786, Aged 77 Years.
Also ROBERT MAYO, of this Parish,
who died July 4, 1785, Aged 67.
Also ESTHER, the Daughter
of the above ROBERT MAYO,
by SARAH, his Wife,
died March 6, 1769, Aged 4 Years.
Also another ESTHER, their Daughter,
died Decr. 10, 1773, Aged 2 Years.

Also Ann, their Daughter,
died May 12, 1777, Aged 15 Years.
Also Mary, their Daughter,
died Jany. 28, 1785, Aged 10 Years.

In Memory of
Rachel, the Daughter of Henry
Carpenter, by Joan, his Wife,
who died Sept. 28, 1759,
Aged 26 Years.
Also Joan, his Wife, and late Wife to
Robert Carpenter, of this Parish,
who died 6 of Nov. 1768,
Aged 72 Years.
Robert Carpenter, of this Parish,
died Febr. 7, 1749, Aged 64 Years.
Henry Carpenter,
died Aug. 3, 1738, Aged 40 Years.
Elizabeth, Daughter of Henry
and Joan Carpenter,
died Nov. 28, 1730, Aged 5 Years.

In Memory of
Thomas Bennett,
of Chaxhill in this Parish,
who died May 16, 1767,
Aged 53 Years.
Near this Tomb lie the Remaine of
Daniel, the Son of Daniel
and Susanna Bennett,
of Chaxhill in this Parish,
who died Decr. 26, 1795,
Aged 8 Years.

Here rest the Bodies of
Thomas Bennett, of Chaxhill,
Yeoman, who departed this Life,
the 1st. day of April, Ao. Dom. 1754,
in the 74 Year of his Age.
Also William Bennett,
Son of the above said Thomas
Bennett, Yeoman, who died
7 of Febr. A. D 1742,
Aged 41 Years.
Likewise Bridget, the Wife of said
William Bennett,
who departed this Life,
July 7, A. D. 1751.
In Memory of
Henry Hart, of Northwood,
He died Nov. ye 22, 1712.

Here rests the Body of
Richard Hall, of Stantway,
who departed this Life,
Oct. 17, 1728, Aged 79 Years.

In Memory of
John Baker, the Elder, of Broad
Oak, who departed this Life,
Aug. 25, 1757, Aged 83 Years.
Also Jane, his Wife,
died Dec. 4, 1735, Aged 66 Years,
and two of their Children,
who are buried here.
Likewise the Body of
John Baker, of Broadoak,
Junior, and Grandson of the
above said John Baker,
who departed this Life,
March 18, 1780, Aged 34 Years.
Also Elizabeth, the Daughter of
Edward Jackson,
by Jane, his Wife, of Broadoak,
who died April 30, 1763,
Aged 4 Years.

In Memory of
Hannah, the Wife of George
Smith, of the Parish of Lidney
in this County and Daughter of
Samuel Harvey, of this Parish
by Hannah, his Wife,
who died October 7, 1775,
Aged 37 Years.
Also Sarah, second Wife of
George Smith, Yeoman,
of Purton in the Parish of Lidney,
and Daughter of Samuel and
Hannah Harvey, of this Parish,
who died June 15 1792,
Aged 47 Years.

In Memory of
Samuel Harvey, of this Parish,
who died April 3, 1768,
Aged 66 Years.
Also Daniel Harvey, of this Parish,
who departed this Life,
May 24, 1775, Aged near 40 Years.

In Memory of
Thomas Brassington,
late of Cleeve in this Parish,
who departed this Life, the
11 day of June in the Year 1778,
Aged 60 Years.
Also Elizabeth, Daughter of
Thomas and Ann Brassington,
who died Sept. 4, 1773,
Aged 7 Years.

In Memory of
Joseph Boughton, of Rodley, Senr.
buried Oct. 22, 1760.
Also John Loughton, his Son,
buried Oct 15, A. D. 1769,
Aged 51 Years,
Also Ann, the Wife of the above-
said John Boughton, Junr.
late of Rodley, who departed
this Life, the 15 day of June in
the Year 1778, Aged 55 Years.
Also Joseph, the Son of Joseph,
and Sarah Boughton,
of Rodley in this Parish,
who departed this Life, the
16 of Oct. 1797, in the 21
Year of his Age.
In Memory of
Joseph Boughton, the Younger,
of Rodley, who died Decr. 18, 1756,
Aged 36 Years.
Also Mary, the Wife of Joseph
Boughton, the Elder, of Roaley,
who died June 21, 1728.
Also Mary, the Wife af
Joseph Boughton, the Younger,
of Rodley, who departed this Life,
June 3, 1757, Aged 59 Years.

In Memory of
Joseph Ayleway,
of the Heald in this Parish,
He died Nov. 3, 1779,
Aged 78 Years
Also Thomas Ayleway,
of the Heald, He died July 15, 1734,
Aged 69 Years.
Also Mary, the Wife of
Thomas Ayleway,
She died Oct. 1, 1727,
Aged 79 Years.
Thomas Ayleway,

Nephew, of the above Thomas
Ayleway, and Brother to the
aforesaid Joseph Ayleway,
He died June 16, 1750.
Aged 52 Years.

In Memory of
Robert Gough, of this Parish,
Yeoman, He died Oct. 6, 1792,
Aged 61 Years.
Also Deborah, the Wife of
Robert Gough,
of Rodley in this Parish,
She departed this Life, Mh. 26, 1778,
Aged 47 Years.
Also Sarah, Daughter of Robert
Gough, by Deborah, his Wife,
died Oct. 5, 1768, Aged 8 Weeks.

Here rest the Bodies of
Sarah, the Wife of John
Wilcocks, of Cleeve, and late
Wife to William Dier,
She departed this Life, Febr. 1, 1724.
Aged 74 Years.
Also John, their Son, who died
Febr. 25, 1693.
Also Ann, their Daughter,
who died March 5, 1681.

In Memory of
Abigail, the Daughter of
William Phelps,
and Wife of William Richardson,
who died Oct. 2, 1766,
Aged 46 Years.

Here rest the Body of
Mary, the Wife of Joseph
Boughton, of Rodley, Senr.
who was buried March 7th. ye
Year 1708. Also Joshua Matson,
who was buried the 18 of
April in 1731.

Here rest the Bodies of
Joshua Matson, of this Parish,
Gent. who left this Mortal Life,
the xth. of November, A. D. 1697,
Ætat. suæ 79.
Also of Jane, his Wife,
who died the 29 of Decr. 1693,
Aged 76 Years.

Here lyeth the Body of
Thomas Crump, of Rodley,
who departed this Life,
Jany. 21, 1721, Aged 90 Years.

In Memory of
Newton Braban, of Rodley,
and Ann, his Wife,
He died August 15, 1755,
Aged 55 Years.
She died December 21, 1742,
Aged 39 Years.

Here rest the Bodies of
Mr JOHN NEWTON, *Gent.*
who died March 20, 1702,
And of ELIZABETH, his Wife.

Underneath lie interred
the Remains of
THOMAS HAWKINS,
of this Parish, who died the
8 of May 1787, Æt. 52.

In Memory of
THOMAS HAWKINS,
also ELIZABETH, his Wife,
He died April 6, 1748, Aged 45.
She died August 3, 1767, Aged 71.
THOMAS, their Grandson,
died March 5, 1767, Aged 11 Years.
Here rests the Body of
HENRY KING, of this Parish,
who departed this Life,
Jany. 11, 1727, Aged 71 Years.
Also in Memory of
SARAH, Daughter of HENRY KING,
who died March 14, 1723.

Underneath are deposited the
Remains of THOMAS WINTLE,
of *Rodley* in this Parish,
who died Nov. 13, 1785,
Aged 63 Years.
Also SARAH, his Wife,
who died May 13, 1787,
Aged 60 Years.
Also JAMES, Son of THOMAS and
SARAH WINTLE, who died
Oct. 29, 1784, Aged 24 Years.
ELIZABETH and ELIZABETH,
their Daughters died Infants.
Also WINTLE, Son of HENRY
and ELIZABETH KING,
who died July 13, 1746,
Aged 20 Years.

Sacred to the Memory of
SARAH, Wife of SAMUEL CANNOCK,
who departed this Life,
April 30, 1797, Aged 50 Years.

In Memory of
ISAAC HALL, of this Parish,
who died Febr. xith. 1771,
Aged 66 Years.
Also ANN, his *Widow*,
She died Aug. 20, 1773,
Aged near 70 Years.
Also ABRAHAM HALL,
who died Augt. 4, 1784,
Aged 53 Years.
JACOB, Son of ISAAC HALL,
by ANN, his Wife,
died April 3, 1743, Aged 9 Years.
JOSEPH, their Son, who died
June 17, 1744, Aged 8 Years.
To the Memory of
JAMES, Son of JAMES and HANNAH
TBIGG, of this Parish,
He died the 22 of June 1790,
Aged 10 Months.

In Memory of
LANCELOT CANNOCK, of this Parish,

Also SUSANNA, his Wife,
He died Jany. 9, 1767, Aged 77.
She died Decr. 31, 1766, Aged 62.
At the feet of this Tomb
rest the Bodies of RICHARD
CANNOCK, *Senr.* of Elton,
who departed this Life,
July 6, 1786, Aged 42 Years.
Also JOYCE, Wife of DAVID ALLAN,
died Dec. 11, 1732, Aged 27.
Also THOMAS, their Son,
died Nov. 21, 1734, Aged 4.
Also GEORGE, Son of GEORGE
and ELIZABETH RUDGE,
died Sept. 9, 1753, Aged 10 Weeks.

To the pious Memory of
RICHARD CANNOCK, *Senr.*
of *Elton*, Also MARY, his Wife,
He died Decr. 10, A. D. 1768,
Aged 71 Years.
She died Decr 6, A. D. 1747,
Aged 47 Years.
Also LANCELOT CANNOCK, *Senr.*
of *Elton*, died Jany. 18, 1732,
Aged 80 Years.
ELIZABETH, their Daughter,
buried Oct. 24, ... (*no date*.)
Aged 27 Years.
Also RICHARD, Son of RICHARD,
and MARY CANNOCK, buried here.
In Memory of
RICHARD, the Son of RICHARD
CANNOCK, *Senr.* by MARY, his Wife.
He died April 21, A. D. 1771,
Aged 33 Years.

In Memory of
JOHN PLAISTED, of this Parish,
He died Febr. 1, A. D. 1759,
Aged 64 Years,
Also MARY, his Wife,
who departed this Life,
Sept. 29, A. D. 1763,
Aged 51 Years.

(*Additional Inscriptions in Church
since Bigland's time.*)

MAYNARD COLCHESTER, *Esqr.*
Ob. Aug. 1787, Æt. 57.
RICHARD COLCHESTER, *Esqr.*
Ob. Decr. 9, 1782, Ætat. 44.
JOHN COLCHESTER, *Esqr.*
Ob. Jany. 5, 1801, Ætat 59.
Near this Place lie interred the
Remains of JOHN COLCHESTER,
Esqr. who died June 5, 1801,
Aged 59 Years.
Also of ELIZABETH, his Wife,
She died Febr. 9, 1827,
Aged 70 Years.

Having passed a long life in the
invariable practice of every social and
sacred duty she fell asleep in Christ
full of days and honour.

Also of MAYNARD COLCHESTER,
Born July 25, 1785.
Died March 30, 1860.
Also HELEN COLCHESTER,
Born March 31, 1787.
Died June 26, 1860.
Also of ARABELLA COLCHESTER,
Born September 12, 1792,
Died December 7, 1860.

*In the Church Yard are later Monu-
ments to other Members of this family.*

NAVE.

ON FLAT STONES.

CHARLES WETHERALL, M. A.
Priest in Christ's Holy Catholic
Church, at *Staunton* in the
Diocese of *Worcester*,
Died Nov. 18, 1843,
Aged 34 Years.

HENRY WETHERALL,
died in his Infancy, Dec. 5, 1812.

NORTH AISLE.

ON FLAT STONE.

JOHN YOUNG, of *Lay*, Gent.
Died 1691, Aged 35.

*Several other Stones to persons of
this family.*

ELIZABETH, Wife of THOMAS
CRUMPE, of *Staunton*,
and Daughter of .... WINTLE,
of *Routey*, and ELIZABETH, her
Daughter, who died 12 Jany. 1657,
Both buried in one Coffin,
M [Mother] Aged 25 Years,
D [Daughter] Aged 8 Days.

ON A TABLET.

Sacred to the Memory of
WILLIAM MAYO of *Gatwick*,
in this Parish, *Gent.*
Son of JOHN MAYO, and
ELIZABETH, his Wife,
who departed this Life,
21 April 1785, Aged 55 Years,
and who with the following
Members of his Family,
lies interred in this Church:
RUTH, his Wife, Daughter of
JOHN PLEYDELL,
and ELIZABETH, his Wife,
Died 8 Nov. 1804, Aged 75.
Their Children:—ELIZABETH,
died 17 June 1761, Aged 10.
JOSEPH, died 25 June 1764,
Aged 3 Years.
JOHN, died 12 Aug. 1795,
Aged 45 Years.
JEREMY, died 8 April 1828,
Aged 68 Years.
ANN, Wife of RICHARD CARTER,
Gent. who died at *Chaxhill*,
12 Jany. 1830, Aged ....
JOSEPH, died at *Bollow* in this
Parish, 7 Feby. 1834, Aged 69.
BENJAMIN, their youngest
and last surviving son, died at
Boy's Court Bollow, 15 March 1844,
in his 73rd. Year.
ELIZABETH, their youngest and
last surviving Daughter the Wife,
of THOMAS HARVEY, of
Routey in this Parish,
died 5 August 1845, in her
74th. Year.
MARY, Wife of the aforesaid
BENJAMIN MAYO, and Daughter of
FRANCIS PICK, and ....
his Wife, died 22 Aug. 1838,
Aged 70 Years.
RUTH, the Wife of ROBERT MORRIS,
Daughter of the above
BENJAMIN and MARY MAYO,
died at *Gloucester*, 26 April 1831,
Aged 23 Years.

RUTH MAYO MORRIS,
their infant Daughter, died 3
May 1831, Aged 19 Days.
HARRIETT CARTER, only Daughter
of the above RICHARD and ANN
CARTER, died at Arlingham,
1 Oct 1837, Aged 38 Years.
The above THOMAS HARVEY,
died 7 Oct. 1845, Aged 66 Years.
To the Memory of
HENRIETTA, only Daughter of
ROBERT and MARY MORRIS,
of Hyde near Newnham,
Born Jany. 8, 1836,
Died Jany. 15, 1850.
Also of HARRISON HUGH,
Son of FRANCIS PICK and
ELLEN MORRIS,
Born Oct. 18, 1863,
Died Jany. 29, 1866.
Also of JOSEPH HARVEY,
late of the City of Gloucester,
Solicitor, eldest son of
THOMAS and ELIZABETH HARVEY,
who died July 18, 1855,
Aged 46 Years.
Also of ROBERT MORRIS,
late of Hyde, who died
Nov. 20, 1863, Aged 68.
Also of ANN, Wife of BENJ.
HARRISON MAYO, who died
Decr. 15, 1873, Aged 63.

———

To the Memory of
WILLIAM, Son of WILLIAM and
JANE WELSH, of London,
and Grandson of JOHN WELCH,
late of Hardens in this Parish,
who died at Fort Malborough,
in a respectable appointment under
the Hon'ble East India Company,
Aug. 31, 1791, Aged 18.
Also of ROBERT, their Son,
who died June 28, 1776,
Aged 1 Year.

———

Sacred to the Memory of
ANN LANE, who died Dec. 1, 1848,
Aged 58 Years.
She was Daughter of WILLIAM
MAYO, Gent. who died
July 16, 1832.
Also of WILLIAM MAYO LANE,
who died in his Infancy.

———

SOUTH AISLE.

ON TABLETS.

Near this Place lie the Remains of
RICHARD PLEYDELL,
of this Parish, late of the Parish
of Lairw in the County of

———

Monmouth, who died Nov. 25, 1809,
Aged 63 Years.
Also MARY, his Daughter,
who died Jany. 18, 1805,
Aged 26 Years.

———

Near this Place lie the Remains of
THOMAS SINDERBY,
of Pope's Hill, who lived much
esteemed, and died deeply lamented
March 9, 1812, Aged 60 Years.
Also of HANNAH, his Wife,
who died March 25, 1837,
Aged 78 Years.

[There is a Monument on outside
Wall to .... Sinderby.]

———

CHANCEL.

ON TABLETS.

Sacred to the Memory of
Mr. JOHN BOUGHTON. of Adsett,
who died 9 March 1811,
in the 89th. Year of his Age.

———

In Memory of
Mr. JOSEPH BOUGHTON, Merchant,
late of Broad Oak in this Parish,
who departed this Life.
April 14, 1782, in the 62nd.
Year of his Age.
And of JANE, his Wife,
who died Febr. 18, 1794,
Aged 64 Years.
Likewise ELIZABETH, their
Daughter, who died Aug 9, 1795,
Aged 27 Years.
Also of JOHN, their Son,
who died 2 Febr. 1802,
Aged 41 Years.

———

JANE, the Wife of JOHN WINTLE,
and Daughter of JOSEPH and
JANE BOUGHTON, of Broad Oak,
where she died after a long
and severe illness, 25 Sept. 1797,

———

Sacred to the Memory of
FREDERICK BOUGHTON,
Lieutenant in the Royal Navy,
who died at Macao in China,
5 Sept. 1817, Aged 23 Years.

———

To the Memory of
SUKEY, Wife of WILLIAM MAYO,
who died 2 May 1827,
Aged 70 Years.
And of WILLIAM MAYO LANE,
Son of JOHN and ANN LANE,
who died 25 Jany. 1821,
Aged 1 Month.

———

ON FLAT STONES.

WILLIAM MAYO, of Gatwick,
in this Parish, Son of
WILLIAM and SUKEY MAYO,
who died August 24, 1837.
HANNAH, Wife of WILLIAM
MAYO, beforenamed, who died
Nov. 2, 184... Aged 47 Years.

Likewise of the aforesaid
WILLIAM MAYO,
who died 16 July 1832,
Aged 77 Years.

———

MEMORIAL WINDOWS TO:

CHARLES ASGILL LEGG,
Born 1848, Died 1866.

WILLIAM CRAWLEY, M. A.
and MARY CATHERINE,
his Daughter.

JOSEPH BENNETT,
and THERESA FRANCES, his Wife,
and CAROLINE FRANCES,
ANTHONY, and HENRY,
their Children, A. D. 1866.

JAMES SYMS, who died
Sept. 16, 1843, Aged 73 Years.
MARY, his Wife, who died
June 8, 1845, Aged 62 Years.
Erected by her 2nd. Daughter,
CAROLINE ELIZABETH.

———

ON THE CILL OF THE WINDOW
IN NORTH AISLE ON A BRASS PLATE.

JOHN BOUGHTON,
Born 17 June 1819,
Died 26 October 1761.
ELIZABETH ALICIA BOUGHTON,
Born 17 Febr 1849,
Died 9 Febr. 1850.
WILLIAM BOUGHTON,
Born 1 August 1830,
Died 13 April 1854.

———

HEAD STONES.

	Died.		Aged.		Died.		Aged.
Tobias Cowley	7 Nov.	1779	77	Sarah, Wife of William Terrett,	29 Aug.	1795	59
Elizabeth, his Wife	24 Nov.	1761	42	Richard Gainey, ...	6 Febr.	1764	56
Tobias, their Son	2 June	1798	49	Martha, his Wife, ...	8 Febr.	1770	70
Thomas Tole, ...	17 June	1777	84	William Phelps, Senr.	5 May	1768	74
Joseph Marshall, ...	10 Decr.	1758	57	Mary, his Wife, ...	5 May	1757	70
John Worgan, ...	21 July	1770	84	Jean, Wife of William Handman,	27 Augt.	1764	77
Ann, his Wife, ...	25 Decr.	1777	92	John Calow, ...	12 Febr.	1668	...
John Thomas, ...	11 May	1770	64	Joan, his Wife, ...	18 Decr.	1714	..
Martha, Wife of John Wood, ...	17 Oct.	1779	65	Giles Farmer, ...	...	1785	6
Thomas Shaw, buried	30 Jany.	1741	...	Ann, his Wife, ...	15 July.	1771	45
Mary, his Wife, buried	30 March	1758	68	Margaret, his 2nd. Wife, ...	12 Sept.	1782	68

HEAD STONES.

Name	Died	Aged	Name	Died	Aged
James Lodge,	14 Oct. 1755	53	John Smith,	27 Sept. 1779	62
Sarah, Daughter of James and Mary Lodge,	20 May 1743	6	Elizabeth, his Wife,	22 Febr. 1776	76
Mary, Widow of James Lodge,	30 July 1765	63	John Selwyn,	16 May 1749	70
Isabell Clark, *Widow,*	16 Jany. 1747	63	Elizabeth, Wife of John Selwyn, late Wife of Thomas Frame,	5 May 1760	55
Elizabeth, Wife of Richard Elton, and late Wife of Robert Cowley,	24 April 1776	57	Jacob Selwyn, *Senr.*	8 Jany. 1765	61
Richard Elton,	10 April 1764	61	Mary, Wife of John Potter,	27 Augt. 1798	62
Hannah, Wife of John White,	7 Oct. 1764	63	Elizabeth, Wife of Joseph Siers, *Senr.*	21 June 1785	52
Samuel White,	7 July 1753	69	Philip Charles,	7 Augt. 1790	60
Mary, his Wife,	25 March 1755	58	Elizabeth, his Wife,	19 Decr. 1780	46
John Adams,	21 May 1731	63	Anna, Wife of William Charles,	6 Nov. 1737	69
Ann, his Wife,	15 April 1730	54	Ann, Wife of John Wilce,	6 April 1792	32
Thomas Davis,	8 Jany. 1792	60	Thomas Sterry,	15 Decr. 1784	58
Hannah, his Wife,	23 July 1777	45	Samuel Sterry,	31 May 1755	61
John Roberts,	4 April 1776	58	John Palmer,	9 April 1783	53
Ann, his Widow,	27 April 1777	73	William Grindon,	18 June 1780	63
Thomas Sargent,	14 Oct. 1783	80	Ann, his Wife,	30 Jany. 1780	61
Elizabeth, his Wife,	11 Augt. 1760	68	James Clarke,	5 Augt. 1792	63
Hannah, Wife of Richard Sargent,	6 Decr. 1776	55	Elizabeth, Wife of Joseph Thomas,	22 March 1772	61
Ann, Wife of Thomas Richards,	7 Nov. 1773	84	Hannah, Wife of John Bennett,	27 June 1780	53
Thomas Kilford,	20 July 1716	84	Giles Pope,	17 April 1769	74
Joseph Kilford,	28 Decr. 1782	62	John Hodgson,	14 July 1790	64
Jane, his Wife,	4 Nov. 1789	66	Betty, his Wife,	25 Oct. 1796	60
John Cadle,	8 Oct. 1760	43	Richard Cox,	13 March 1764	27
Hannah, his Wife, late Wife of John Stone,	19 Febr. 1781	54	Joseph, Son of Joseph Garney, of this Parish, by Mary his Wife,	22 March 1755	20
John Machin,	3 July 1770	76			

Supplementary Notes as to I.—*Estates ;* II.—*Church ;* III.—*Population, Taxation, &c.*

I.—Estates :

Westbury is situate on the westbank of the River Severn, which there pursues a winding course and expands to the width of an estuary near Newnham.

It is a large parish (8000 a.) including not only Westbury proper; but several Hamlets of Elton; Boseley; Adsett; Cleeve and Stantway; Northwood and Overley; Nether Ley, and Rodley.

There are six Entries relating to Westbury in *Domesday Survey.*

1.—Westbury, was terra Regis. It contained 30 Hides, whereof in culture were 5 Plough tillages in Demesne, and 28 in Villenage, (32 Villans, 15 Bordars,) 1 Serf.

The Farm or Rent in King Edward's time was one Night [*i. e.* Lodging and Entertainment for the Court for 24 Hours. see Bitton.] After King Edward's time and 4 Years of King William's 6 Hides were taken off. [as to these see the entry as to Chire, Clifton, &c. below.] But for the remainder the Sheriff paid the whole Rent.

2.—Half a hide of Land and half a fishery in Westberie Hundred; Alvin the Sheriff held, and gave it to his Wife, But this belonged to the King's farm in Westberie. William Gozenboded, holds.

3.—Manor of Three Hides in Westbury Hundred: Culture: One Plow tillage in Demesne, 4 in Villenage, (4 Villans, 3 Bordars.) 2 Serfs. This had been worth 60 s. but was then only worth 50 s :—Alwold, held and paid Tax. Durand the Sheriff holds.

[The Survey also gives an account of six Hides in Chire, (which appears to be in Salesmanbury Hundred.) 10 hides in Clifton; and 8 Hides in Newent, and Kingston, (the latter place in Herefordshire;) which belonged to the Abbot of Cormeilles, Osborn and Fitz Richard, respectively. The connection between Westbury and these Lands it is not easy to trace. It may be that the six Hides taken off Westbury, were alienated to the same Grantees as Newent, &c.]

4.—In Westberie Hundred :

Staure, (Stairs Newnham,) One hide, not taxed: Ulfeg, held in King Edward's time, William Fitz Baderon, holds.

Two Virgates and a half with One Villan and 1 Bordar, worth 3 s. The said Wm. Fitz Baderon, holds and Wiannock his Ancestor held; but the County affirms that this Land is held of the King's Demesne farm in Westberie.

5.—The men of the County say that Sapina, lies in Westberie, in King Edward's farm.

6.—In Westberie Hundred, Walter Balistarius, holds Rodelie of One Hide taxed. Tovi, held it. Culture : 1 Plow tillages in demesne and 2 in Villenage (2 Villans. 4 Bordars.) It was worth 40 s. but at the Survey only 10s.

Of these in order :

i.—The Crown Estate of Westbury.

Hen. ii.—Roger De Mynors, by Crown Grant.

William, his son, by descent; Henry, his son, by descent. He had three Daughters, Coheiresses—Isabella, marr. Longchamp, Basilia, marr. Bourghall. Elizabeth. m. Gamage. The Manor was held in shares, and the Estate allotted in partition. The descent of the Manor is stated in a *Quo Warranto Proceeding in the Hundred Roll*, 15 E. 1.

Isabella's Lot passed to Bourghall, subject to a subfee, and after some intermediate hands passed to Greyndours and from them to Walwyn, and Baynham who married Alice Walwyn, Heiress of the family.

It continued in the Baynhams for several Generations.

Of this family was John Baynham, who was burnt in Smithfield, 1532, for holding and promulgating Protestant Faith. He had been persuaded to recant but repented, and after undergoing much cruel treatment at the hands of the Chancellor Sir Thomas More, (himself afterwards a sufferer for conscience sake,) was executed as a relapsed Heretic.

Next to Sir John Dutton. From whom to Nicholas Roberts ; Cæsar, by descent, left no issue, and was succeeded by his Uncle Giles, Brother of Nicholas.

1641.—Indenture of settlement by Giles on Richard Colchester, of Gray's Inn, his Nephew, *i. e.* Son of his Sister Alice.

This Manor extends over several parts of the Parish.

The Court House, the Seat of the Colchester family, stood in Westbury proper tything where the Church and Village are. It is noticed as a "large House." by *Atkyns*, who gives a plate of it and of the Church. And Shaw, in his Tour in the West of England, 1789; says that it is "a fine old Mansion with formal Gardens and pieces of Water." The House had been rebuilt in 1735, (*Rudder, Rudge.*) It was pulled down some Years ago, by the Trustees of Mr. Maynard Colchester, but the Gardens, Canals, and Summer Houses remain. The family reside at the Wilderness, Abbenhall.

In Isabella's share the Subfee of a Messuage 260 a. Land :

44 Hen. iii.—Nich. de Bath, whose Estate passed to his Daughters and Coheirs :—Alice, married De Supy, Elizabeth, married .... Anne.

Basilia's continued in the Bourghalls for a long period. see "Boresly."

Bourghall's Manor was acquired by Maynard Colchester, two thirds in 1749, of Small of Woodchester, and the remaining one third in 1756, of Clutterbuck. These Vendors were Heirs of Mitchell.

Gamage's share :

Nicholas Gamage, had Daughters and Coheirs :—

Elizabeth Wife of Pedewerdin, Eufemia, Wife of Pembridge, who sold to Helyon.

As little more is heard of the entire Manor of Mynors in Westbury, it is probable that the manerial rights over the Lands in the several Lots went with them.

2.—Alvin's half hide, &c.: *Rudder*, says that this is "Dunny" in Minsterworth, but there was a Dunny in Westbury.

3.— Durands' Westbury Estate came to Bohun, by heirship. Durand's Heir was Milo Fitzwalter, Earl of Hereford, and Margaret, the Heiress of the family married Humphry de Bohun.

Bohun's Estate in Westbury was part in the Village and part in Boresley. Durand, the Sheriffs' Manor of three Hides in Westbury Hundred, is considered to have lain on the Newnham side.

A subfee reputed a Manor, was held of De Bohun, and Wife, by J. Mareshel. This was subdivided into shares held by Aylesford or Aynesford, (19 Ric. ii.) and Milborn.

A Subfee under John de Bohun, of a Messuage 260 a. Land, &c.:

20 Edw. ii.—Nich de Bath.

46 Edw. iii.—Hump. de Bohun, died seized of the chief fee.

Gilb. Talbot, Ph. Ann and Walter Soulier, (Solers.)held.
Esch. No. 10.

4.—The Estates held by Fitzbaderon, at the Survey continued in the family and name, for three generations when they were possessed by De Sapy, and from his Coheirs, went to Talbot, Earl of Shrewsbury.

33 Eliz.—George Talbot, Earl of Shrewsbury, had a Manor here. *Esch.*

The name Badern or Bathern, is still here about and Margaret Bathern, conveyed Land to M. Colchester.

Land and Rent.—

John Arthur, and Gef. de Morshall, held of Gilbert Talbert, by 11s.

5.—Sapina, is not identified.

6.—Rodley will be spoken of below under Tythings.

Of the supplementary information to be given concerning Estates in Westbury, some can be assigned to properties in particular tythings. But many entries relate to properties in more tythings than one, and some refer to Westbury generally, but where there cannot now be distinguished.

Adsett, Cleeve and Stanteway, are one tithing.

The name Lysaune, (Lysons) occurs in the *Subsidy Roll*, 1 Edw. iii., and subsequently on *Church Inscriptions*. And "Revd. S. Lysons," County Election 1811.

In later times occur as Proprietors the names of Phillips and Bellany, (W. Phillipps and Thomas Gylford, against John Bellamy, *Chancery Proceedings* temp. Eliz.)

Bullock and Boughton,—East. 8 Geo. ii. Joseph Boughten, *Plaintiff*., and Hawkius and Bullock and Wife, *Deforciants. Fine*. Bennett, *County Election*, 1776. Hyett, *County Election*, 1811. Beald, *Church Inscriptions*, and Mayn, held Lands.

The Colchester family acquired Lands here by purchase from divers persons, and by exchange with R. I. Townsend, &c.

Stanteway farm belonged to the Aylbertons.

1708.—Mary Aylberton, only Daughter and Heir of Samuel Aylberton, of Stanteway, Gent. to John Aylberton, of Newnham. It passed in Moieties—½ Joseph Aylberton, who sold to Sir Duncomb Colchester. ½ Mitchell Aylberton, who sold to Maynard Colchester.

Chaxhill a hamlet at the Minsterworth end of Westbury Parish and on the high Road from Gloucester to Newnham, Here flourished a family called from their Lands Chexshill, Part of which Lands were acquired by the Abbey of Flaxley. Tewkesbury Abbey, also had possessions here.

Subsequently Hampton and Baynham, were chief Proprietors.

1545.—Hampton's Will at Gloucester and *see Church Inscriptions* as to this family.

13 Car. i.—Philip Hampton, acquired Lands here from Sarah Baynham, Daughter and Heir of Daniel Baynham, late of the Grange Westbury. And 14 Car. i.—from Brether.

1697.—Col. M. Colchester, purchased Lands here of Mary Drewett, and Philip Hampton.

Lands here and in other parts of Westbury, were for some centuries held in the name of Bullock, from which to Baylis and Broom.

Other Proprietors here were Barrow, 1744. Biddulph and Coppinger, 1738.

Bollow, south of the Church is in this Tything.

Boresly is considered to have been part of Burghall's Allotment.

Lands here passed through the Names of Helyon, Ralegh, and Arnold, whose Daughter and Heir, marr. Lucy. Ric. ii. Sabyn, had Land here. This Name as well as that of "Sapy" has some resemblance to "Sapina." Sir T. C. Boevey, holds a farm here.

Elton :—is a populous place in Westbury.

The Court house here was for a long period the residence of the Aylbertons a family of repute. The heir general marr. Chinn, and Col. M. Colchester, purchased Lands from Chinn and Draper.

Netherley, was in Gamage's Allotment. Of part of the Estate Gamage enfeoffed Helyon. From which name into that of Ralegh.

Lysons acquired from Raleigh, 20 and 21 Eliz. James Leeson, was *Plaintiff*., and Simon Ralegh, *Deforciant*, in a *Fine*.

As to the rest of the Estate one of the heirs general married Pembridge, under whom a Subfee was created in Nicholas Gamage, who left 3 Daughters and Coheirs, marr. to Billing, Arthur and Fitzhugh, respectively.

Lands here were acquired by Flaxley Abbey. After the dissolution, Sir A. Kingston, from whom Sir Bryan Tuke; from him R. Andrews and Wife, who conveyed by fine to Wilmot, who (2 Mar.) died seized.

Cellar's Mount :—was parcel of the possession of Lanthony Abbey, near Gloucester, and was reputed a Manor. After the dissolution, it passed to Reeve and others; from them to Roberts, and from him to Colchester.

Farms in Lower Ley, belonged to Anthony Ellis; from him to James Wood, of Gloucester, from him to John Surman Surman, of Swindon, from him to Major and Mrs. Surman, of Tredington, and others his Devisees.

Another farm there was in the family of Barrow and passed thence to Barrow Evans.

Aston's Court, a house and Estate in this part of Westbury, called from the family resident.

3 Hen. iv.—William de Aston, an idiot was seized.

There was an Estate in the Ley, held of Butler, Earl of Ormond.

Overley and Northwood :—Northwood was part of De Bath's Estate, &c. and came subsequently to the Aylbertons.

Walmore :—was a Manor acquired by Flaxley Abbey, from Pichard, and others. After the dissolution of Monasteries, Sir A Kingston, from whom Clarke and Boevy.

Edw. ii.—Poulton was an ancient Proprietor "Poulton's Hill." At Yate, also held Lands here.

The Grange Court Estate, consisted of a Manor in Walmore and Lands in Over Ley and Northwood. It was in the Baynhams, afterwards Arnold, then for a considerable period in the Name of Kemp, whose Heir General, mar. Radcliff, Earl of Newburgh. From their Descendants to Leslie.

Upper Ley :—Peglar's farm 44½ is an Estate given for charitable purposes by Mrs. Katharine Boevey, a Lady whose benevolence is recorded in stone in the Church of Flaxley and in Westminster Abbey.

There were Lands here of St. Mary's Chantry. After the suppression. 10 Jac. Sir A. Cope, by Crown Grant.

The Probyn family held a Manor Estate and Mill here.

Rodley, is the name of a tything, or part of the Parish of Westbury. It is also the name of an Estate and Manor which comprises some tenements in other parts of the

Parish and also in Newnham. Rodley tything is the projection of Land beyond the River Line, of which Land probably Walter Balistarius, was the Proprietor at *Domesday Survey*. And it has been enlarged by accretion.

It is said in an *Inquisitio post Mortem*, of 4 Edw. i that Rodley was of the antient demesne of the Crown, (Westbury?) and that it belonged to Richard Talebot, who paid to the Crown 42£. Yearly Rent with profit of the Water.

In 1154, Roger, Earl of Hereford, was Owner; and it passed to H. de Bohun, by Marriage with Margaret, the Heir general of Roger.

1 John.—The Crown by Surrender of De Bohun. Simon Mountford, Earl of Leicester, by Crown Grant. On his attainder and forfeiture, Edmund, Earl of Lancaster, 2nd. son of King Henry iii. had a Grant and he died seized of it. His son Henry, Earl of Lancaster, succeeded. but he was taken in arms against King Edward ii. and was executed.

10 Edw. iii —His son Henry, was restored and created Duke of Lancaster ; and in his favor his Estate was made a County Palatine. He died 35 Edw. iii. Blanche, his Daughter and ultimately sole Heiress married John of Gaunt, who in her right had the Title and Estates of the Duchy. Their only son succeeded. When he became King. (H. iv.) the Palatine Estates would have merged in the Crown, but they were kept distinct by special Enactment and have so continued, and hence much of the local history of Rodley has been preserved in the Records of the Duchy of Lancaster.

Rodley Manor continued in the Crown until 1625, when it and Bury Court House, and the Fishery of Unlawater in the Severn parcel of the Duchy of Lancaster, passed by Grant under the Great Seal of England and Duchy Seal to Robert, Lord Carye, and Henry Carye, Knight. his son and heir apparent and their Heirs under a Rent of 48 £.

1633.—John Young, by purchase.

Bury Court, passed to Pleydell. And One fourth of Unlawater fishery was by Young demised for 1000 Years to Rush, at a Rent of 55 shillings. The Manor afterwards passed into the family of Guise, which still holds it.

While in the hands of the Crown, Leases and Grants were made to divers persons and are mentioned in the Headings in the Chancery of the Duchy.

3 Eliz.—Wynell, Tenant of the Rodley Manor, against' the Deputy of Sir H. Jerningham, High Steward.

By Wynell is probably meant Wintle an antient local Name in Westbury, Newnham, &c.

1545.—Will of Wintle, at Gloucester.

Wightwarden field and Flaxhay;

24 Elizth.—............ Wintle, *v.* Hyett & others.

Land called Bays Court in Rodley Manor:—
Attorney General, *v.* John Gwyllym.
Lands:—John Gwylliam, *v.* Cecily Bowley.

Messuage and Lands :—
Stephen Oakley, *v.* John Guyllim.
Duchy Chancery Proceedings.

Of this family was Guillim, Author of the Book of Heraldry, who was born in this Parish and lived at Minsterworth.

Malsons's Court and Moy's Hill, were Estates of the family of Malson. *see Church Inscriptions.*

1546.—Will of J. Malson, at Gloucester.
Fines. 29 & 30, & 31 Elizth.—Maldson and Williams.
Malson, *Junior.* and Harris.
Trin. i. Geo. ii.—Malson, *Widow.* and Pickering.
Crumps Estate :—*see* County Election 1776.

Longcroft and other Lands belonged to the families of Cadle, and Hartland.

The Abbot of Gloucester, had by Crown Grant, temp. Hen. i. a Wood and fishery at Rodele in Westbury to find a Lamp, in memoriam of Robert, the King's Brother.

In Pope Nicholas Taxation this property of the Abbey is described as a Mill, Fishery and 3 Carucates of Land. Part of their possessions in Dunny were exchanged for Lands in Sandhurst and Erlingham.

It appears by the Subsidy Roll, 1 Edw iii, that amongst many others, Mandevil, Bass or Bays, Boregast, Polton, Holkeley, Holt, Vyell, had taxable property here.

1776.—*At County Election there voted for Freehold*

Lands in Westbury Tything:

Allway, Joseph.	Hart, (2) John, Richard.
Baldwin, John.	Hawkins, Thomas.
Bellamy, Samuel.	Higgs, Thomas.
Bennett, (2) Anthony, Wm.	Kedley, John, *Clerk.*
Bovy, Crawley T.	Littleton, William.
Bowyer, Samuel.	Lodge, Thomas.
Broadstock, Solomon.	Newton, William.
Boughton, (2) Joseph, John.	Pettat, Thomas.
Bund, Thomas.	Phelps, William.
Cadle, (3) Thos. Wm. Josp.	Plaisted, Thomas.
Colchester, Maynard.	Pope, (2) Joseph, John.
Constance, Thomas.	Powell, Joseph.
Crump, Francis.	Pritchard, (2) Thos. John.
Dobbs, James.	Sargeaunt, William.
Dowding, (2) Thos. John.	Taylor, Roger.
Farmer, Samuel.	Trigg, (2) William, Wm.
Fluck, Joseph.	Wallbank, Samuel.
Fowle, William.	Waters, Thomas.
Hall, Abraham.	Wilkins, James.
Harper, Thomas.	Williams, (2) James, Isaac.
Harris, Philip.	Wintle, Thomas.

1776.—*Freeholders voting for Lands in other Tythings:—*

Adsett:—Jones, Thomas.

Cleeve:—Badger, Thomas.

Lower Ley:—Hooke, Richard.

Upper Ley :—Hayward, Sam. and Oakey, John.

Bollow:—Bellamy, (2) Robert, William.; Cooke, John; Newton, Robert; Wintle, James.

Elton:—Packer, Daniel; Sinderby, George.

Rodley.—Winniatt, James, White, George.

And for Westbury in Duchy Hundred:—

Badger, William.	Hanman, William.
Bathone, Robert.	Harris, (2) Henry, Thomas.
Bellamy, William.	Hiller, Robert.
Brabant, James.	Mayo, William.
Brown, William.	Ryder, (3) Thomas, William,
Cannock, (4) Richard, Samuel,	Thomas.
Launcelot, William.	White, Samuel.
Elliott, Samuel.	Wintle, Jonathan.
Freame, Thomas.	Young, John.
George, Robert.	

There are various manorial Distinctions of Lands Rents and payments as Reeve Land and Tithing Land Dowager Rents, &c. which cannot be accurately shewn.

There are several Awards for Inclosure of open fields and commonable grounds in Westbury and its Tythings.

1. Under a provisional Order of the Inclosure Comms. 1848, and Award 1851, of Commonfields and Meadows in Adset, Bollow, Chaxhill, Cleeve, Ley, Northwood, Rodley, Stantway.

By this, intermixed Lands and by Exchange some old Inclosures were thrown into Allotments awarded to Bennett, (32 a.) Boughton, (16 a.) M. Colchester, (143 a.) Hartland, Mayo, B. H. (Bays Court.) Mayo, R. W. Countess of Newburgh, and P. H. Howard, and Sir T. R. Gage, Bart. (24 a.) Wintle, (Robert, John, Samuel, William;) R. L. Townsend, Evans, C. B. and his Guardians, and several others.

Ways were set out to the Allotments and Provision made for their repairs, in some cases by contributions in parts of a pound.

The inclosed Land included the Marshes of Rodley, the Vicarage Meadows, Walmore, Wilmore, &c. Dinney, Dumble, Worden Hill, Clayfield, &c.

2. Under a Provisional Order and Award 1861, of Stroudfield and Elton Meadows.

3. Under a Provisional Order and Award of 1871, of Walmer Common.

The Awards of these Inclosures are inrolled in the Office of the Clerk of the Peace at Gloucester.

II.—*Church.*

The Church of Westbury, with its Chapels of Newnham and Minsterworth in the Forest Deanery Hereford Diocese was taxed on ... ... 53£. 6s. 8d.

And the Portion of the Vicar in the same at 6 13 4

Westbury Church had Portions:—

1lb. Incense from Chapel of Ruardean	13	4
Rector's Portion in Mitchel Dean	2	0
And in Abbenhull	2	0

Pap. Nichol. Taxat

In 18 Edw. i.—Nicholas Bathon, levied a fine of West-bury Manor with Advowson of Church to Anselm Guise.

Impropriation :

Vicars Choral of Hereford Cathedral had in spirituals (inter alia) Rectory of Westbury, Co. Glouc. demised to Thomas Glynn, Esqr. at per Year, £ 44.   *Valor Eccl'us.*

1839.—Rectorial Tythes were commuted for the Tythe Rent Charge of £ 555.

Vicarage :—Present net Value 261£.

In Rents and Tithes beyond payment 2s. 4d. for W. Gamage's Obit 7s. 4d. to Archdeacon for Cenage £20 2 10

Folchers Chantry :—beyond Chief Rents of 10s. 4d. to W. Colley, 7s. 2d. to G. Raleigh, 6d. to Lanthony Priory 13s. 4d. to Poor to pray for Folchers soul. *Ibid.*
     Valor Eccl'us.

The Advowson was in De Bohun, who subenfeoffed the Bishop of Hereford.

3 Ric. ii.—Lichfield Cathedral from Bishop of Here-ford and others.

1554.—The Vicars Choral of Hereford.

List of Incumbents and Patrons of Vicarage now in Forest Deanery, Gloucester Diocese.

Incumbents.	Patrons.
1544.—Richard Sheriff.	Vicars Choral Hereford.
1559.—Richard Yatton.	
1566.—Henry Mynde.	
1580.—John White.	Do. do.
1603.—Stephen Bowlton.	
1605.—Gabriel Walwyn,	
Henry Bradford.	
1626.—John White Osgood.	
1660.—Thomas Godwyn.	Do. do.
1669.—John Hulet.	
1713.—Richard Russell.	
1739.—Thomas Carpenter.	
1763.—Joseph Guest.	Do. do.
1765.—John Kidley.	
1798.—Richard Wetherell.	

Nothing now remains of the old Church at Westbury, but the Tower.

Walmer is called a separate Rectory.

1 Eliz.—Wilmot, died seized of Walmer Manor and Rectory and Lands in Adsett, &c.

There is no Chapel at Walmer.

Additional Benefactions, for Schooling and Clothing:—

1650.—J. Young, gave Lands in Westbury and Close in Huntley called Deans.

1722.—Holstead's Gift of 20 £. in augmentation of School fund.

For Bread :—C. Draper.   *For Coal:*—J. Mayo.

There are several places of Worship of Dissenters.

A Board School has been established under the Elementary Education Act.

III.—*Taxation, Population, &c.*

Among the persons who compounded for their Estates in the great Civil War was Anthony Arnold, of Westbury, Gent. (*see* Grange Court, Estate.) His Assessment was 414£. (a Year.) The largest Estate charged in the County was John Dutton, Esqr. of Sherborne, 5216 £.

Subsidy Roll 1 Edw. iii., 1327.

HUNDR. DE WESTBURY.

Villot. de Rodleye.

De Rico. fil. Rici. de Heydon, Le Isabell. Mody, xii d. x s.
' Simon. Mey, ii s.
' Rogo. Holte, ii s.
' Johe. Tuyles, vi d.
' Rico. Scorye, xii d.
' Benedict. Vounar, vi d.

' Elen. Holkeleye, x s.
' Adam Knat, vi d.
' Johe. Allehale, xii d.
' Willo. Vyel, ii s.
' Alic. Fylote, xii d.
' Adam Berde, vi d.

De Rogo. Hirdeman, ii s.
' Rico. Berde, viii d.
' Robto. de Chaxhulle, vi d.
' Henr. Zouge, x...
' Thom. Blount, ...
' Henr. Holkeleye, xii d.
' Thom. Bonde, ...
' Johe. Heydon, ...
' Willo Beneger, ...
' Willo. atte Pirie, ...
' Henr. de Rodleye, ...
' Johe. de Polton, ...
' Henr. Whinekel, ...
' Robto. Kege, ...
' Rico. de la ...., ...
' Hug. Dan..., ...
' Nicho. Shephurde, ...
' Walto. de Cly..., ...

De Petronell. Cole, ...
' Johe. atte Grene, ...
' Alexo. Basse, xii ...
' Music. Marcy, vi d.
' Rico de Wyke, ...
' Elen. atte ....,
' Johe. Kyng..., ...
' Cecil ....,
' Elen. B....., ...
' Thom. W......, viid.
' Hen. ...., ...
' Rico. ...., ...
' Johe. de Wyke, ii s.
' Johe. atte Grene, xii d.
' Rico. Billyng, xi s.
' Willo. fil. Fabre, vii s.
          xi d. o. q.

prob. Sma. xxma. *Ville de Rodleye*, li s. iii d. q.

Westbury, Cu. Hamell Ouerleye et Nethleye,

De Rogo. Jourdan, vi s.
' Willo. fil. Fabr. xii d.
' Willo. de Combe, vi d.
' Henr. Felch, xviii d.
' Rogo. ...e Hulle, xii d.
' ....e, vi d.
' Willo. ...., ii s.
' .... Solers, vi d.
' .... Elemor, vi d.
' ....on, ix s. i d.
' ...., vi d.
' Johe. atte Broke, ii s.
' Rogo. de Borughulle, iii s. vi d.

De Rico. Louwyn, vi d.
' Willo. Taillor, ii s.
' Raduo. Bongham, vii d.
' Is. Bonghan, ii s.
' Adam Bonghan, xii d.
' Henr. Baldewyne, vi d.
' Alic. de Astone, vi d.
' Laduo. atte Broke, viii d.
' Rico. Boregast, ii s.
' Amicia. Pope, xii d.
' Emma. Wodema. vi d.
' Willo. Inthefelde, ii s.
' Adam Saundres, xviii d.

Adhuc .... Bur. cum Hamell de Ouerleye et Nethleye.

De Willo. Borgast, ii s.
' Robto. Charlet, vi d.
' Willo. de Prestebur. ii s.
' Henr. Skynnar, ii s.
' Walto. Louecoke, vi d.
' Will. Gamages, vi s. viii d.
' Agr et. de Arderne, xii d.
' Alic. Budel, vi d.
' Willo. Holt, iiii s.
' Idania Maunduill, xviii d.
' Johe. Bruyn, vi d.
' Johe. Maundeuill, ii s.

De Robt. Frewyne, ii s.
' Rico. Coppe, vi d.
' Walto. Maundeuill, iii s.
' Johe. Hamull, xii d.
' Walto. Broun, ii s.
' Stepho. Whytema. iii s.
' Juliana Dauy, ii s.
' Cecilia Longe, iiii s.
' Adam atte Broke, xii d.
' Henr. Pope, vi d.
' Josep. de Hokkeleye, vii s.
' Johe. Smyth, iii s.

pbat. Sma. iiii li. xvi s. xi d.

Chirchamme Cu. Hamell Bolleye et Rodele, inter alios.

De Is. de Dunnye, xii d.
' Johe. de Dunnye, ii s.

Hamell de Northwode.

De Agn. de Polton, xx d. q.
' Willo. Cage, xii d.
' Petr. Regn, vii d. q.

De Johe. Helewys, xii d.
' Walto. Crabbe, xii d.

prob. Sma. v s. iiii d. o.

Acreage 8025 a.

Population 1801,—1680. 1831,—2032. 1871,—2495.

1815 —Annual Value of Real Property £9293.

1875.—Rateable Value £ 19426.

1863-4-5.—Average of three Years Expenditure on Poor £ 855.

In Westbury Union

In the Civil War Westbury House, was at first a Post taken by the Parliament. It was lost to Sir John Wintour, the Royalist General (through Treachery, says Corbet, of an officer;) and the House and Church strongly fortified, 1644, May 7—25, Col. Massie, the bold, and energetic Governor of Gloucester, with 2 Regiments of Horse and 900 foot displaced the King's Garrison out of Church and occupying it with his own Men made the Enemy in the House yield themselves Prisoners of War. He then attacked the adjoining Garrisons of Little Lean and Newnham with equal success.

Westbury is under a Local Board of Health, and a large portion in the Lower Level of the Commission of Sewers.

CCLXXXII. or 289. WESTBURY upon TRIM.

THE CHURCH is very large and handsome consisting of Chancel, Nave and two Aisles and a beautiful Tower at the West-end adorned with pinnacles, therein six Bells. It is dedicated to the Holy Trinity.

ON THE GALLERY.

The Gallery was erected at the sole expence of SAMUEL EDWARDS, *Esqr.* of *Cotham*, in the Year, 1794. [now taken down.]

BENEFACTIONS:

Mrs. BETTY HOLLISTER, by Will gave to the Minister and Church Wardens of the Parish of *Westbury upon Trim*, One Hundred £. the Interest thereof to be applied in the following manner, first, as often as there shall be occasion to amend and repair the Tomb Stone of her father CHARLES HOLLISTER, &c. in the Church Yard, and the remainder to be distributed to the Poor of the said Parish Yearly for ever.

GEORGE WEBB, *Esqr.* by Will gave to the Minister and Church Wardens of the Parish of *Westbury upon Trim*, the Sum of Two Hundred £. the Interest thereof to be distributed to the Poor of the said Parish Yearly for ever.

Mrs. MARY INNYS, by Will gave to the Minister and Church Wardens of the Parish of *Westbury upon Trim*, Two Hundred £. the Interest thereof to be divided amongst poor House keepers of the said Parish not receiving Alms by 10*sh.* to each for ever.

Mrs. ANNE HORT, gave by Will to the Minister and Church Wardens, One Hundred £. the Interest thereof to be applied in the following Manner, 20 *s.* to the Minister for preaching a Sermon, on the 20*th.* of January, and the remainder to be distributed in Bread to the Poor, the same day yearly.

EDWARD COULSTON, *Esqr.* gave One Hundred £. towards perpetual Augmentation of a Maintenance for the Minister of *Westbury upon Trim*, which with 120 £. given by several of the Parishioners and others, and 200 £. Queen Ann's bounty, made 420 £. and were laid out in Lands to the Value of 20 £. a year and settled for ever.

Lady CATHARINE, Wife of *Mr.* THOMAS CANN, gave 20 £. the Interest to poor Widows as ROBERT CANN, *Esqr.* shall think fit during his Life, afterwards as the Minister and Church Wardens shall think fit in the Tythings of *Stoke Bishop* and *Westbury*.

Captain JOHN SELF, of *Bristol*, gave 30 £. the Interest to the Minister for two Sermons to be preached on the 3*rd.* Sunday in March and the 3*rd.* or 4*th.* Sunday in November for ever.

Mr. WILLIAM WHITE, of *Coat*, gave 10 £. the profit to be distributed among Six Poor people of the Tything of *Westbury upon Trim*, on the 29*th.* of September, for ever.

Mrs. MARY WEBB, late of *Southmead* in this Parish, gave 10 £. the Interest to be paid for a Sermon to be preached the Sunday before Lady day, Yearly for ever.

THOMAS ELBRIDGE, *Esqr.* of *Coat*, gave One Hundred Pounds £. the Interest whereof to be applied in the following manner, 20 *s.* to the Minister for preaching a Sermon on the 30*th.* day of January and the remainder to be distributed to the Poor in Bread on the same day Yearly.

1730.—THOMAS TILLADAM, of *Stoke Bishop*, *Gent.* left to the Church Wardens, of *Westbury* Parish, the Sum of 20 £. the Interest thereof to be given Yearly to the Poor casual sickly people of the said Parish not receiving any other Alms.

1756.—EDWARD WADE, gave 15 *s.* payable Yearly out of Lands at *Alveston*, to be distributed to the Poor in 4*d.* Loaves on Good Friday, Yearly for ever.

MARY WHITE, gave 20 £. the Interest thereof to be distributed to the Poor of *Westbury* Parish, Yearly for ever.

1686.—*Mrs.* KATHERINE RUTLAND, *Widow*, Relict of *Mr.* EDMUND RUTLAND, sometime Minister of this Parish, deceased gave 50 £. the Interest thereof to be paid yearly unto the Minister who should preach Six Sermons on six certain Days. viz.—St. Thomas's day, New Year's day, Twelfthday, Good Friday, Holy Thursday and All Saints day.

The said *Mrs.* RUTLAND, gave also 10 £. the Interest thereof to be distributed amongst the poor of this Parish, on Good Friday Yearly for ever.

1715.—THOMAS HORT, *Esqr.* some time Mayor of the City of *Bristol*, gave the sum of fifty Pounds, the Interest thereof to be paid—10 *s.* for a Sermon and the remainder to be distributed to the Poor the 19 of November, Yearly for ever.

ANTHONY HILL, gave to the Poor of the Parish, 20 £. the profits of it Yearly to be paid for ever.

Mr. EDWARD HAINES, *Gent.* gave to this Parish, 20 £. the profits thereof to be distributed to the Poor Yearly for ever.

Mr. ROBERT WOOD, *Gent.* gave to the Poor of this Parish, 10 £. the profits of it Yearly for ever.

Mr. JOHN MORGAN, *Gent.* gave 5 £. the profits thereof paid to this Parish, Yearly for ever.

Mr. JOHN WASHBOROW, gave 4 £. to the Poor of this Parish, the profits thereof to be paid Yearly for ever.

Mrs. ELIZABETH HELLEN, gave to this Parish, 5 £. the profits thereof to be paid Yearly for ever.

Mr. EDMUND RUTLAND, late Minister of this Parish, gave 5 £. to the Poor in Cole, for ever.

Mr. WILLIAM BURGIS, gave a dozen sacks of Cole, to 5 or 6 poor house holders in the Villiage of *Westbury and Cote*, Yearly for ever.

Mr. HUMPHREY BROWN, sometime *Alderman* of the City of *Bristol*, gave to the Poor of this Parish, 40 *s.* and 10 *s.* for a Sermon, Yearly for ever.

Mr. ROBERT KITCHIN, sometime *Alderman* of the City of *Bristol*, gave to this Parish, Six shillings and 8 pence, to the Poor, and Six shillings and 8 pence, for a Sermon, Yearly for ever.

WESTBURY upon TRIM.

John Knight, *Esqr.* gave 10 £. the use of it to be given to the Poor of this Parish, in Coal, Yearly for ever.

Sir Robert Yeamans, *Knight and Baronet*, gave 20 £. the profits thereof to be given to the Poor of this Parish, weekly in Bread for ever.

Mr. William Cooke, second son, of John Cooke, *Doctor of Phisic*, of the Parish of *St. Michaels*, who died 13 day of March 1717-8, gave to the Poor of this Parish, 10£. the profit thereof to be given in Bread, in 2*d.* loaves to the Poor on Christmas day, for ever as the Parish Officers think proper.

1728.—Thomas Moore, *Esqr.* late of *Coat* in this Parish, gave 50£. the Interest thereof to be laid out by the Church Wardens in Clothing Poor House keepers of the Tything of *Coat* only, on the 4 of January, Yearly for ever.

ON THE GALLERY.

1797.—George Grant, gave to the Minister and Church Wardens of the Parish of *Westbury upon Trim*, the Sum of 200 £. the Interest thereof to be applied in the following manner, *viz.*—One Guinea, to the Minister for preaching a Sermon on the *5th.* day of November. 8*s.* to the Clerk of the Parish. 10 *s.* to the Ringers and the remainder to be distributed to 6 of the most infirm and poorest of the Parishioners whether receiving Parish Pay or not on some day in the same month of November, Yearly for ever.

ON ATCHMENTS.

1.—Argent, on a Chevron Sable between three Eagles heads erased Azure, three Cinque foils of the first. Jackson.

Crest:—a horse current Argent, gutteè de sang.

2.—Azure fretty Argent, on a fess Gules, three Leopards faces, Or, (with baronets hand.)—Cann, *impaling* Azure a frett Or, on a Chief of the second a Lion passant of the first.—Jefferies.

Crest:—out of a Mural Crown Gules, five Ostridge feathers Argent and Azure.

3 —Per bend Ermine and Ermines a Lion rampant Or —.............. *impaling*. Argent, three Bars and on a Canton Gules a Cross Argent. .... *On an Escutcheon of pretence Quarterly* 1 and 4, Or, a Lion rampant Sable. .... 2 and 3, Argent, a fess between three Annulets Sable.—..............

Cres:—a Demi Lion holding a Castle Argent.

4 —Argent, on a Chevron, between three Cinque foils, another Argent.—Harmer.

Crest:—an Arm vested Azure, cuffed Argent, holding in the hand proper, two rose-branches vert, one arching to the right, and flowering on the Top with a White rose, the other to the left, in the like manner with a red rose.

INSCRIPTIONS IN THE CHURCH.

CHANCEL.

At the South West Corner, upon an Altar Tomb, lies the Effigy of a naked Man in Stone without Arms or Inscription but is said to be intended for *Doctor* Carpenter, *Bishop of Worcester, in* 1443.

On Monuments.

Arms:—In a Lozenge Argent, three pales Gules, on a Canton of the second a Spur Or, within a border engrailed Azure.—Knight. *impaling* Or, on a Canton Sable a Tigers head erased of the field. Jacob.

Near this Place resteth the Body of Mary, eldest Daughter of John Jacob, late of *Norton* in the County of *Wilts. Esqr.* who in the 16*th.* Year of her Age, and of our Lord 1666, was by him given in Marriage unto Giles Hungerford, of *Wellow* in the County of *Somerset, Esqr.* who in the Year 1668, died and left her enceint with Giles, who lies near her. In 1681, She was married to John, eldest Son of Sir John Knight, of *Temple Street* in the City of *Bristol*, who in the Year 1684, departed this Life, by whom she had one Son, who caused this Monument to be erected to her Memory, who approv'd herself the best of Parents and of Friends

who always did her Duty to God, and her Neighbour, lived belov'd and died on the 15 day of August 1717, by all lamented. Underneath lyes Anne, Daughter of Jacob Knight, of *Southmead* in this Parish, *Esqr.* by Anne, his Wife, who came into this World Nov. 17 1715, and was called to Rest May 29 1716. Near this Place lyeth the Body of Giles Hungerford, Son and Heir of Giles Hungerford, late of *Wellow* in the County of *Somerset, Esqr.* Descended from the Hon'ble. House of Hungerford, of *Farley Castle*, in the said County. He married Martha, eldest Daughter of John Jacob, of *Norton* in the County of *Wilts. Esqr.* By whom he had Issue only this Son, who died the twenty third day of August, in the one and Twenty Year of his Age, Anno Domini 1689.

Arms :—Sable two bars Argent, and in Chief three Plates.—Hungerford.

Arms of Knight, *as before, impaling.*—Or, a fess wavy between Six Billetts Sable.—Dowdeswell.

Crest:—a Demi Eagle out of a mural Crown Or.

Juxta tumulatur Corpus Jacob Knight, de *Southmead, Armigeri* Filij Johannis Knight,

Armigeri natu maximi Johannis Knight, *Militis,* Vico de Temple Civitate *Bristol, Olim habitantis.* Uxorem duxit Annam Dowdeswell, Filiam Caroli Dowdeswell, *Armigeri,* de *Forth Hampton Court, Com. Gloc'tr.* Filios reliquit quatuor Johannem, Thomam, Jacob, and Carolum, In piam Memoriam Patris Patriæ dignissimi, Erga Parentes piissimi Mariti amantissimi, Filiisque indulgentissimi, Hoc erigi jussit Monumentum Vidua Superstes Obijt pridie Idus Julij M.D.CCXX. Ætat XXXVII. Jacob, tertius Filius supradict. Jacob Knight, Obijt 28 Nov. 1726, Æt. 9.

Arms Knight, *as before, impaling* Dowdeswell, *as before, in a Lozenge.*

Near this Place lieth Interred the Body of Ann Knight, Relict of Jacob Knight, *Esqr.* of *Southmead* in this Parish and Daughter to Charles Dowdeswell, *Esqr.* of *Forth Hampton Court* in the County of *Gloucester,* She was an Affectionate Wife, and a Most indulgent Mother to her Children, who out of a Strict and just Regard (due to her Memory,) Caus'd this Monument to be erected. Obiit 20 September 1736, Ætatis suæ 47.

1   2   3

Near this Place lies the Body of
JOHN HENLEY, late of the *Red
Lodge*, in the City of *Bristol*, *Esqr.*
descended from an ancient Family
in the County of *Somerset*,
He married MARY, the eldest
Daughter of HENRY FANE,
Son of *Sir* FRANCIS FANE, *Knight*
of the *Bath*. He was an affectionate
Friend, a Charitable Benefactor
to the Poor, and was greatly esteemed
and regarded by all his acquaintance,
He departed this Life, the
31 day of December 1733,
in the 59*th*. Year of his Age.

Arms:—Azure, a Lion rampant
Argent, ducally crowned Or. within a border of the second charged
with Torteuxes.—HENLEY. impal-
ing Azure three Gauntlets Or.—
FANE.

ON FLAT STONES.

Here lyeth the Body of
GEORGE FREKE, the Son of
PHILIP FREKE, of the City of
Bristol, *Merchant*, who died the
20 day of October, 1691.

Here lyeth interred the Body of
Dame ABIGALE YEAMANS,
Relict of *Sir* ROBERT YEAMANS,
Knight and Baronet,
late of *Redland* in the County of
Gloucester, who departed this Life,
the thirty first day of August,
MDCCXXVI.
Here likewise lyeth the Body of
Mrs. HANNAH THYNN,
Sister of the *Lady* YEAMANS,
who departed this Life, the
eighteenth day of January,
MDCCVII.

To the Dear Memory of
ANNE, Wife of HENRY FANE,
of *Bristol*, *Gentleman*,
who departed this Life, the
26 day of July 1721.
And also ANNE and ELIZABETH,
two of their Children,
ANNE, died the 11 day of May 1709,
Aged two Weeks.
ELIZABETH, died 31 of Jany. 1720,
Aged 10 Weeks.
Here lies interred the Body of
HENRY FANE, of the City of
Bristol, *Gentleman*.
He departed this Life, on the
19 day of December 1726,
in the 58 Year of his Age.

Here lyeth the Body of
WILLIAM PARKER, A. M.
late *Minister* of this Church,
He died Febr. 9, 1740-1,
Aged 26 Years.

Here lie the Remains of
SAMUEL CRESWICK, D. D.
late Dean of the Cathedral Church
of *Wells*, who departed this Life,
Jany. 14, 1766, Aged 72 Years.

4

Arms:—... three standing Bowles, (or Cups) out of each a Boars
head coupt.—BOWLES. *impaling*
...... three Roses ......

Crest:—a demi Boar ...... pierced
thro' the Chest with an Arrow ...

In a Vault under the Marble
are interred the Remains of
MARY, the beloved and lamented
Wife of *Major* RICHARD BOWLES,
She died May the 10, 1757,
Aged 54 Years.

Here lyeth the Body of
ELIZABETH, the Daughter of
ARTHUR BALLARD, *Mariner*,
by RACHEL, his Wife,
who departed this Life, the
11 of July, Anno 1727,
Aged near 15 Years.
Also here lyeth the Body of
RACHEL, the Wife of ARTHUR
BALLARD, who departed this Life,
the 28 of April 1737,
Aged 67 Years.

Arms:—(Argent,) on a fess (Sable)
three Stagsheads erased (Or.)
Crest:—a Stags head erased.—
BRADFORD.

Here lyeth the Body of
MARY, the Wife of WILLIAM
BRADFORD, of the City of *Bristol*,
Gardiner, who departed this Life,
the 9 day of November 1764,
in the 66 Year of her Age,
Also the Body of
WILLIAM BRADFORD, (*Clerk*.)
Son of the above, who died
6 Febr. 1765,
in the 31 Year of his Age.

NAVE.

ON A MONUMENT AGAINST A
PILLAR FACING THE PULPIT.

Arms:—PerChevron Argent, and
Sable three Elephants heads erased
counterchanged.—SAUNDERS. im-
paling Or. a fess between three
Wolves heads coupt Sable. HOWE.

Near this Place lies interred
WILLIAM SAUNDERS,
of *Coat* in this Parish, *Esqr.*
who served the Office of *High
Sheriff*, for the Counties of
Brecon and *Gloucester*,
and departed this Life,
Nov. 16, 1739, Aged 63 Years.
And also PETER SAUNDERS,
Esqr. his Son, who died May 9*th.*
1743, in the 35 Year of his Age,
And was *High Sheriff*, for the
County of *Brecon*, at the time of
his decease.
To whose Memory this Monument
was erected by MARY SAUNDERS,
Relict of the aforesaid PETER.

ON FLAT STONES.

Hodie mihi cras tibi.
Here lyeth the Body of
WILLIAM BATEMAN, of this Parish,
He deceased the 17 of June 1633.

5

Hic
repositum quicquid mortale
reverendi admodum viri,
GULIELMI STONE,
nuper hujus Ecclesiæ, nec non
Comptoniæ,
Pastoris dignissimi.
Vir
integerrimæ vitæ,
Eruditionis, in omni genere, singularis.
Pietate secundum Deum,
maxime conspicuus.
diffusa in homines, Benevolentia
et Charitate,
non minus insignis
Gravitate, mira quadam Comitate,
condita, Spectabilis.
cæteris ad sacram Functionem,
cunctis, Virtutibus ornatus.
Qui, postquam Evangelium summa,
tum Constantia,
tum diligentia, quadraginta, et
sex circiter ann.
fidelissime prædicâsset,
Mortem obijt
4to. Febij. Anno
Salutis nostræ ⎱ MDCCXXIII,
Ætatis suæ ⎰ LXXIII.

ELIZABETH, Wife of DANIEL
SAUNDERS, *Merchant*,
dyed Febr. 11, 1742,
Aged 32 Years.
SAMUEL JACOB, *Merchant*,
died June 17*th* 1743,
Aged 63 Years.
ELIZABETH, Relict of SAMUEL
JACOB, dyed April 8, 1744,
Aged 64 Years.
CHRISTOPHER TWYNIHOE,
Merchant, who died May 26, 1744,
Aged 24 Years.

Here lyeth the Body of
JOHN CUFFE, of this Parish, *Gent.*
and JANE, his Wife,
He deceased March the 27, 1620.
She deceased April the 27, 1648.
Here lyeth the Body of
THOMAS, the Son of JOHN CUFF,
of this Parish, *Gent.*
who departed this Life, the
9*th*. day of June, Ao. Dom. 1689,
Aged 75 Years.

In Memory of
WILLIAM WHITAKER, *Esqr.*
Merc. of *London*, 1759.

Here lyeth Buried the Bodie of
JOHN HIAT, *Yeoman*,
who departed this Life, the
30*th*. of April, Ano. Domini,
1600.

Here lyeth interred the Body of
JOHN, the Son of WILLIAM
WALTER, of this Parish.
He decessed the 5*th*. day of
November 1650.
Here lyeth the Body of
MARY, the Daughter of
WILLIAM WALTER, of this Parish,
She died 17 day of March, 1657.

6

Here lyeth the Body of
MARY, the Wife of CHARLES
WIETT, who departed this Life,
the 22 day of January 1743,
Aged 39 Years.
Also CHARLES, Son of the above,
who died 18 Nov. 1759,
Aged 17 Years.

Here lyeth the Body of
WILLIAM WALTER, of this Parish,
He died the 21 of May 1647.
Here lyeth the Body of
RICHARD WALTER,
Son of the aforesaid WILLIAM
WALTER, who departed this Life,
11 of November, Ann. 1673,
Aged 40 Years.

Here lyeth the Body of
ANN, the Wife of Mr. WILLIAM
WALTER, who died the
26 of Sept. 1652.
Also the Body of RICHARD
WALTER, who died March 23, 1700,
Aged 36 Years.

Here lyeth the Body of
JOHN WASBOROW, of Sherhampton,
in this Parish, Yeoman,
who died the 27 day of Oct. 1656.
Also CHARITY, the Wife of the
aforesaid JOHN WASBOROW,
who died the 3 day of October 1679,
Aged 78 Years.

Here lyeth the Body of
CHARITY, the Wife of
Mr. GEORGE P......, Gent. (defaced.)
of Shirehampton, who departed
this Life, the 15 day of
....
Also the Body of MARGARET
STOAKES, of Shirehampton,
Widow, who died the 23 day of
Augt. Anno D. 1693,
Aged 55 Years.
Also the Body of ELIZABETH,
the Daughter of MARGARET
STOAKES, Widow, who died
the 16 of April 1687,
Aged 24 Years.

Here lyeth the Body of
Mr. WILLIAM STAINER,
of this Parish, who departed
this Life, Febr. 26, 1695,
Aged 41 Years.
Also REBECCA, the Daughter of
Mr. THOMAS ELDRIDGE, Mercht.
and Grandaughter to the aforesaid
Mr. WILLIAM STAINER,
who departed this Life,
June 3rd. 1710, Aged 4 Years,
and 3 Months. Also the Body of
Mrs. JOAN STAINER, Relict of the
abovesaid Mr. WILLIAM STAINER,
who died Jany. 1744,
Aged 84 Years.

Here lyeth the Body of

DOROTHY RISHTON, Widow,
Daughter of MARTIN FOLKES, Esqr.
of Hillington in Norfolk.
She died at Stoke Bishop. in this
County, 18 Febr. 1761,
Aged 43 Years.

In Memory of
ELIZABETH RICH, of the City of
Bristol, who died Jany. 21, 1745,
Aged 64 Years.
Also of Mr. SAMUEL RICH,
of the City of Bristol, Merchant,
who departed this Life, the
27 of August 1765, Aged 53 Years.

Here lyeth the Body of
JOHN WASBOROW, the Younger,
Yeoman, who departed this Life,
the 4 day of February 1612.

Here lieth the Body of
ROBERT GATES, who departed
this Life, Decr. 6, 1766,
Aged 70 Years.
Also of DOROTHY GATES,
who died Aged 87 Years, 1768.

NORTH AISLE.

ON MONUMENTS,

Memoria æterna erit justus.

Here lye buried the Bodyes of
MILES WILSONE,
late of Redland, Gent. and of
ELIZABETH, his Daughter,
maryed some time to ROGER
REVELL, Gent. which twayne as
they lived and dyed in the
Faythe of Christ Jesus, so do they
lye Here buried together Untill
the Time of the Cominge. of oure
Mercyful Saviour Christ Jesus which
comminge we hope for as she did
to be shortly even for his Elects
sake as he hath promised.

Arms:—Per Chevron .... in
Chief two Castles and in Base a
fleur de Lis ....—REVELL.
impaling Quarterly 1 and 4, Gules
a fess between three Lozenge Cus-
sions Argent, Tassled Or. WILSON.
2 & 3, ... a Chevron ...... betw.
three Boars heads coupt ....

ELIZABETH REVELL,
deceased the 28 of July 1581.

Arms.— Quarterly 1 and 4,—
WILSON, as before. 2 and 3. ......
a Chevron ... ... between three
Boats heads coupt ....

MILES WILSON,
decased the 13 of April 1567.

UNDER AN ARCH IS THE EFFIGY
OF A MAN IN ARMOUR, AND
THIS INSCRIPTION AND ARMS.

Arms. Quarterly 1 and 4, Gules
a Saltire vair between four Mulletts Argent.—HILL.
2. Gules a Lion rampant Or.

---

debruised by a Bend Ermine.—
HALTON.
3. Sable a Bend Or. between six
Fountains.
Crest:—a Demi Leopard guard-
ant Argent, Spotted Gules collared
Or.

Here under lieth interred the
Bodie of Sir RICHARD HILL,
of Redland Courte in this Parish,
Knight, who deceased the 29 day
of May in ye Yeare of our
Lord God 1627, Aged 70 Years.

(Under this Monument on a Grave
Stone is the like Inscription.)

OVER THE VESTRY DOOR.

In Memory of
JOHN LONG, of this Parish,
Malster, who departed this Life,
ye 17th. of November 1754,
Aged 77 Years.
Also of ANN LONG,
Sister to the above who departed
this Life, the 5th. of July 1786,
Aged 81 Years,

Arms:—Azure three Gauntlets Or.
FANE.
Crest:—Out of a Ducal Coronet
Or, a Bull's head Argt. pied Sable
Armed Or, charged on Neck with
a rose Gules barbed and seeded
proper.

Sacred to the Memory of
HENRY FANE, Esqr.
Son of HENRY FANE, Esqr.
of Bristol, and Brother to THOMAS,
the Eighth Earl of Westmorland,
who died 31 May 1777, Aged 74.
He served the Offices of State with
Integrity and Represented the
Borough of Lime Regis, in four
successive Parliaments.
He was Exemplary in the duties
of Religion, Sincere in his profession
of Friendship and Charitable
without ostentation.

Near this Place in the Chancel
are deposited the Remains of
NICHOLAS and ANN JACKSON,
of Snead Park, in this Parish,
His early days he desin'd to the
Study of the Law in the Middle
Temple, where he passed his time
in the Society and Friendship
of some of the Wisest and Worthyest
Men of that Age, ever beloved
and Esteemed, His own Abilities
and the Candor and Liberallity
of his Mind and the exemplary
purity of his Manners would have
made him an Ornament to public Life,
but the peculiar Modesty and Virtue,
of his disposition determined
to a private one.
He was a great lover of Learning and
Learned Men, Himself not unlearnt.
In 1725, he retired into the Country
and on the 20th. of January in that
Year he married ANNE, eldest
Daughter of Sir THOMAS CANN,
of Stoke Bishop, a person every
way deserving, greatly endowed with
those qualifications of true Worth
and Virtue that serve to render the

7   8   9

female Character respectable, heigthened by the graces of the sweetest and evenest Temper of Mind and the most engaging manners. These Valuable Tallents, She exerted with a pious and unremitting attention in promoting the Houour of an entirely beloved Husband, and in cultivating the welfare and happiness of their Offspring:—
ROBERT, born 2 July 1727.
NICHOLAS, born 10 Feb 1728.
KATHERINE ANN. born 20 Feb. 1729.
MARY, born 21 Febr 1730.

NICHOLAS JACKSON, Senior, died 9 May, 1752, Aged 61.
ANN, his Wife, died 25 May 1762, Aged 71 Years.
KATHERINE ANN, the eldest Daughter, died Nov. ... 1751, at Overbury in Worcestershire where She lies buried.
NICHOLAS, died 22 March 1779.
ROBERT JACKSON, Esqr. of Snead Park, died 16 July 1781. In whom were united the Social the Moral and the Christian Vertues. A greeable to whose desire and to whose Memory this plain Monument is erected by his ever grateful and Affectionate Sister
MARY JACKSON,

Arms:—JACKSON, as before. impaling CANN, as before.

ON FLAT STONES.

Arms:—Azure, a Bend Or, between three Spears heads Argent.
—.............
Crest:—an Arm embowed Azure holding a ...... (broken off.)

Fuit THOMAS TILL-ADAM, hujusce Parochiæ Generosus, cujus Exuviæ prope subjacent, Objit Jan. 18, 1731, Ætat. 57.

In Memory of
SAMPSON YEOMAN, of this Parish, Yeoman, Objit 26 Oct. 1747. Ætat. 71 Years.
Also of ANN, the Wife of SAMPSON YEOMANS, Junr.
Objit 3 June 1751, Ætat. 30,
SAMPSON YEOMANS, Junr. of this Parish, who departed this Life, the 24 day of Aug. 1756, Aged 48 Years.

In Memory of
SARAH, Wife of JOHN TAYLOR, of this Parish, She died Decr. 27, 1740, Aged 32 Years.
SARAH, their Daughter, died Jany. 3, 1740-1, an Infant.

Here lyeth the Body of
WILLIAM MARTIN,
He died the 28 of July 1695.
Also the Body of ESTHER, the Daughter of WILLIAM MARTIN, buried the 30 of November 1705.
Likewise here lieth the Body of ANNE, the Wife of JOHN RUSCOMBE, of the City of

Bristol, and Daughter of the above
WILLIAM MARTIN,
of Redland Court, in the County of Gloucester, Gent. who departed this Life, the 15th. of January 1726.
Also Mrs. DOROTHY MARTIN, Sister of the above mentioned, Gentleman, was here buried April 29, 1732.

Arms:—Per pale dancette Argt. and Gules four Lions rampant counter charged, on a Canton of the second a Lion passant guardant of the first:—ELLSWORTH.
Crest:—Seven Ostridge feathers per pale Argent and Gules, out of a ducal Coronet Or.

Under this Marble Stone lies interred the Body of Sir RICHARD ELLSWORTH, late of the City of Bristol, Knight. who departed this Life, the 21 Day of Febr. Anno Dom. 1684, Ætatis suæ 64.

Here lye Interr'd the Bodyes of
PETER and EDWARD, second and third Sons of Sir RICHARD ELLSWORTH, late of the City of Bristol, Knt. and Nephews unto Sir RICHARD HILL. EDWARD, died 30 day of July 1677, in the 17 Year of his Age. and PETER, 26th. day of Sept. 1682, Aged 24 Years.
Resurgamus ad lucem in Christo.

Here lyeth the Body of
WILLIAM MARTIN,
of Realand Court, who departed this Life, the 13th. day of Jany. 1711-12, Aged nigh 60 Years.
Also here lyeth the Body of WILLIAM, his Son, who died the 8th. of May 1680, Aged 18 Months.

Arms:—Azure two Bars Gules.
MARTIN. impaling Gules two Bars Argent, on each 3 Mascles Gules.
GEERING.
Crest:—a Greyhound sejant.

Here lies the Body of
MARGARET, Wife of WILLIAM MARTIN, Redland Court, Gent. Daughter of GREGORY GEERING, of Denchworth in the County of Bucks. Gent. ob. Febr. 18o. An. 1721-2, Ætat. 62.

To the Memory of
Mrs. AMY MARTIN, Daughter of
WILLIAM MARTIN,
of Redland Court, Gent. who departed this Life, 14 of May 1760, Aged 74.

ALEXANDER EDGAR, Esqr.

died Febr. 2, 1792, Aged 58 Years.

Here lyeth the Body of
ELIZABETH, the Wife of JOHN ENGLAND, Merchant, of the City of Bristol, who departed this Life, January first 1694, Aged 72 Years.

Here lyeth the Body of
ANN, the Wife of JONATHAN SKUSE, of St. Augustin Parish, Bristol, who died the 25 of March 1730, Aged 49 Years.
Also here lyeth the Body of JONATHAN SKUSE, of St. Augustin, Bristol, who departed this Life, the 27 day of Febr. 1740, Aged 66 Years.

THOMAS HORT, died ......
(other part hid by a pew.)
Also here lyeth the Body of BRIDGETT, the second Daughter of the aforesaid THOMAS HORT, She departed this Life the 6 day of October 1692.
Also here lyeth the Body of THOMAS HORT, Junior, who departed this Life, 24 August in the Year 1721, Ætatis suæ 62.

Here lyeth the Body of
MARY, the Wife of GEORGE WEBB, of this Parish, who departed this Life, 24 May 1716, Aged 69.
Near this lyeth the Body of JONE WEBB, of this Parish, who departed this Life, the 19 of August, 17..4, Aged about 63 Years.
Also JANE BACKWELL, of this Parish, who departed this Life, the 6 of Sept. 1711, Aged 56 Years.

In Memory of
JOHN BULL, of Midsummer Norton, in the County of Somerset, Gent. who died the 7 of Nov. 1725, Aged 50 Years.
Also BRIDGET HASULTON, of this Parish, who died 19 of Decr. 1754, Aged 58 Years.
Near this Place lyeth the Body of ANN BAKER, who departed this Life, the 3 day of Sept. 1759, Aged 27 Years.

Here rests the Body of
JOSEPH FLOYD, of this Parish, who died January the 20, 1716-17, Aged 62 Years.
Also here lyeth the Body of SAMUEL, the Son of JOSEPH FLOYD, who died the 24 of Nov. 1732, Aged 33 Years.
Here rests also the Body of MARY FLOYD, the Wife of SAMUEL FLOYD, of this Parish,

10   11   12

who departed this Life,
7 Jany. 1763, Aged 63 Years.

In Memory of
JOHN SPENCER, of the Parish,
of *St. Philip* and *St. Jacob,*
Malster, who departed this Life,
the 17 of June 1738,
Aged 57 Years.
Also the Body of JOSEPH
BUCKLAND, of the above said Parish,
who died the 9 day of April 1763,
in the 55 Year of his Age.
Likewise the Body of MARY,
DAUBENY, Wife of GILES DAU-
BENY, of the City of *Bristol,*
She departed this Life,
10 April 1772, Aged 44 Years.
ANN, relict of JOSEPH BUCKLAND,
died 7 Jany. 1776, Aged 76.

To the dear Memory of HANNAH,
the Wife of JOHN BARTLETT,
of *Shirhampton* in this Parish,
who departed this Life, the
27 day of February 1711,
Aged 30 Years.
Also here lyeth JOHN BARTLETT,
Son of JOHN and HANNAH
BARTLETT, who departed this Life,
the 10 of November 1712,
Aged 3 Years.

M. S.
The *Reverend* RICHARD GREGORY,
of the Parish of *St. Michael,*
Bristol, who departed this Life, the
10 of Augst 1758, Aged 47.
MARY GREGORY,
Wife of the above, who departed
this Life, the 5 of Decr. 1790.

Here lyeth the Body of
MARY, the Wife of
WILLIAM ENGLAND,
who died the 21 of July 1726,
Aged 56 Years.
Also here lyeth the Body of
WILLIAM ENGLAND,
of *Shirhampton,* who died
11 of Oct. 1729, Aged 60 Years.

Here lyeth the Body of
CHRISTOPHER SMITH,
of *Shirhampton* in this Parish, *Gent.*
He died the 17 March 1742,
Aged 58 Years.
Also KATHERINE, the Wife, of
J. SMITH, of *Shirhampton,*
She died April 15, 1704,
Aged 44 Years.

MARY and ANNE GOLDINGHAM,
1699.
Resurgam.

THOMAS TILLADAM,
Jany. 18, 1731.

SOUTH AISLE.
ON MONUMENTS.

Arms:—Per fess: in the upper
part Azure, 3 Bars Or, over all a
Swan Argent, in the lower part
Argent, a dun hill Cock Gules,
impaling Argt a bend wavy Sable,
in Chief 3 dunghill Cocks Gules
2 and 1.

To the eternall Memorye of
his deare Mother M. ROSELARGE,
Widdow, and Daughter to
WILLIAM COOKE, of *Hampshire,*
who haveing lived vertuesly
LXXX Yeares, departed most holy
to God August XXIX,
A. Dni. 1610.

Arms:—Sable, a Lion rampant
Or, between three Scaling ladders
Argent.—JEFFERIS.

Near this Place lyes interred
the Body of WILLIAM JEFFERIS,
of *Pen-Park* in this Parish, *Esqr.*
whose Industry and Integrity
in Mercantile Affairs procured
him an Ample Reward.
having gone thro' the Offices of
Magistracy in the City of *Bristol,*
with great Reputation.
He died the 17*th.* day of April 1752,
in the 61 Year of his Age.
Also ANN, sole Daughter and
Heiress of the above
WILLIAM JEFFERIS,
Born the 21 of Aug. 1723,
Married the 30 of March 1752,
to JOHN HARMER, then of the
City of *Bristol, Merchant,* and
Died the 9 of July 1765.
The Sincerity of her Heart in all
the Actions of her Life, illuminated
by the practice of every commend-
able Virtue, deservedly procured her
the Affection and Esteem of Relations,
Friends and Acquaintance, and the solid,
Hope of a more glorious Reward
in a Life of Immortality.

Arms:—Argent, on a Chevron,
between three Annulets, Gules, another of the field.—HARMER, *impaling* JEFFERIS, *as before.*

AGAINST A PILLAR.

Near this Monument is interred
the Body of *Mrs.* EMMA SMITH,
Wife of JAMES SMITH,
of the *Island of St. Christopher, Esqr.*
who departed this Life, at *Stoke
Bishop* in this Parish,
the 15 day of March 1767,
Aged 52 Years.
Her Demeanour in the several
Characters of Wife, Parent and
Friend was such as gained her
Universal Esteem here, and the tenor
of a Life, spent in exemplary
religious Duties, Charity and
Benevolence, gave her such Fortitude
and patience in her last lingering
Illness as promises a blessing
hereafter.

Arms:—Per Chevron Azure and
Or. two Estoiles between a Crescent
Argent.—PIPON.

Near this Monument Lies interred
the Body of JAMES PIPON,
of *London, Merchant,*
who departed this Life, at the
Hot Wells, Bristol, the 12 June 1759,
Aged 48 Years.
He was the 5 Son of JOSHUA PIPON,
*Esqr. Lieutenant Bailly Chief
Magistrate of the Island of Jersey.*

Arms:—Per pale Or. and **Argent**
a Lion rampant Sable, between Six
Cross Crosslets fiché Gules.—
PHELPS, *impaling* Or, a fess be-
between three wolves heads erased
Sable.—HOWE.

Near this Place are interred
the Bodies of WILLIAM PHELPS,
Esqr. and MARY, his Widow
and Relict, both late of *Cote* in this
Parish. He died the tenth day of
August 1763, Aged 43 Years.
She died the first day of Jany. 1764,
Aged 53 Years.
This Monument is erected to their
Memories in pursuance of the
Directions of the said MARY, in a
Codicil to her Will.

Arms: Quarterly 1.—Argent, a
Dragons head erased Vert, in his
mouth a Sinister hand Gules.—
MORGAN. 2.—Gules, three Castles
MORGAN. 3.—Gules three Chev.
Argent.— .... 4.—Azure, a
Chvron betw. three Griffins heads
erased Argent.—JENNINGS.

In a Vault beneath are deposited
the Remains of *Mr.* JAMES MORGAN,
of the City of *Bristol, Druggist,*
who died the 11 of August 1780,
Aged 66 Years.
He was the Youngest Son of
JOSHUA MORGAN, *Esqr.*
of *Llanwenarth* in the County
of *Monmouth.* Eminent in Trade,
he pursued his occupation with
Credit to himself, and when nature
had her Course accomplished,
as a bright example he bequeathed
A fair and unblemished reputation
To the World,
In the same Vault also rest
together with three of their Grand-
children, who died in their Infancy.
the Mortal parts of ANN, his Wife,
Who by patient continuance in
well doing sought for happiness
in Immortality. She departed
this Life, 13 January 1787,
Aged 70 Years.

To the Memory of
Mrs. ANN HORT, of *Cote* in this
Parish, who departed this Life,
on the 11 of January 1782,
Aged 84 Years.
This Monument in Gratitude
is erected by her Cousin,
HENRY GOODWIN, *Esqr.*

Sacred to the Memory of
JAMES CROSS, *Esqr.* of *Clifton,*
in this County who died
June 27, 1791, Aged 51 Years.

13   14   15

Near this Place lies interred the
Body of MARY CHARITY KNIGHT,
born in the *Island* of *Antiqua*,
She departed this Life, at the
Hot Wells, the 14 June 1771,
Aged thirty Years,
She lived esteemed and
died lamented.

ON FLAT STONES.

Loe here the Corps of RICHARD
HEINS, not dead but leyed to rest,
Untill the Lord shall Call from
Grave, the Bad and eke the best.
Amongest which number of Elect
he certes hath a part,
Because he allwayes hoped thereon,
and that through Christes Deserte.
His Lyffe did shew forth Fruite of
Fayth, his Wordes deserved no blame,
He loved God and Neighbours both,
his Deedes confirm'd the same.
Four Sons, six Daughters he brought
forth by DOROTHY VEEL, his Wyffe,
God send to them on Earth his Grace,
in Fyne immortal Lyffe.
Obiit 6 Octob. Ano. Dom. 1583,
Ætatis suæ 74.

Here lyeth the Body of
MARY, the Wife of THOMAS
RICHARDSON, of this Parish,
Merchant, who departed this Life,
the 29 day of May, Anno 1689.
Also of WILLIAM, Son of the said
THOMAS RICHARDSON,
who departed this Life, the
15 July 1691.
Here also lyeth the Body of
JOYCE, the Wife of THOMAS
RICHARDSON, of this Parish,
Merchant, who departed this Life,
the 13 day of January, Ano. 1717-8.
Also here lyeth the Body of
the said THOMAS RICHARDSON,
of this Parish, *Merchant*,
who departed this Life, the
4th. day of November, Ano. 1722,
Aged 75 Years.

Here resteth the Body of
MARY, the Wife of NATHANIEL
HUTTON, who deceased the
3 of July 1727, Aged 47 Years.

Here resteth he Body of
NATHANIEL HUTTON,
of this Parish, who deceased
the 2nd. day of August 1727,
Aged 46 Years.

Here lieth the Body of
THOMAS HAINES, *Gent.*
who deceased the 23 day of April
in the Year of our Lord, 1604.

In the Middle of the same Stone.

Memoriæ æternae viri optimi
Patris sui colendissimi
THOMAS HAINSIJ, *Generosi.*
Chare Pater tua sancta fides tua
maxima virtus
As...... ruit cœlo teque
Animamque tuam.

16

Corpus in hoc tumulo conditum,
mea circa parentum ad tua juncta
pijs ossibus ossa cubents Pietatis
ergo posuit RICHARDUS HAINSIUS,
Filius.

Here lyeth the Body of
ELIZABETH, the Daughter of
ANTHONY HORT, of this Parish,
who departed this Life, the
6th. day of January 1675.
Also here lyeth the Body of
JOHN HORT, of this Parish,
Gent. who departed this Life, the
24 of Decr. 1714, Aged 62 Years.
Also near this Place lyeth the
Body of THOMAS HORT, *Esqr.*
sometime *Mayor* of the City of
Bristol, who departed this Life,
ye 14 of July 1715, in ye
57 Ye. r of his Age.
Here also lyeth the Body of
THOMAS HORT, Son of THOMAS
HORT, of the City of *Bristol*,
Merchant, who departed this Life,
the 3rd. day of March 1718-19,
Aged 29 Years and 6 Months.

In Memory of
JOHN BREWSTER, Son of
CHARLES and AMELIA BREWSTER,
of Newgate Street, London,
who died at Clipton, 30 Sept. 1790,
Aged 25 Years.

JOSEPH LAWSON, *Esqr.*
of *Southampton Street, London*,
died July 10, 1797.

To the Memory of
SARAH the Wife of WILLIAM
TREGO, of this Parish,
Ship Wright, who died the 10 of
Sept. 1744, Aged 70 Years.
Also here lyeth the Body of
WILLIAM TREGO,
who departed this Life, on the
11 day of May 1750, Aged 80 Years.

Here lyeth the Body of
WILLIAM PULLINGS,
of this Parish, who departed this
Life, the 11 day of October in the
Year of our Lord 1732,
Aged 40 Years.

UNDER THE BELFRY ON A
FLAT SSONE.

GEORGE POULSON,
died April 3, 1793, Aged 67.

CHURCH YARD.

ON A TABLET AGAINST THE
SOUTH WALL.

JOHANNES COOK. *Med. D......*
Practicus haud infelix, mortis mille
vias quotidie spectans, Hoc
domicilium Cryptum sibi Suisque.

17

---

fiere curavit. Vixit Ann. LVI,
Mens. X. D. XIII.
obiit Febr. XIX, MDCCXVI.

ANOTHER AGAINST THE EAST END
OF SOUTH AISLE.

To the Memory of
CHRISTIAN, the Wife of THOMAS
TAYLOR, of the Parish of *Henbury*,
Yeoman, who departed this Life,
13 Febr. 1781, Aged 28 Years.
CHRISTIAN, Daughter of the above,
who died April 8, 1781,
Aged 3 Months.

ALTAR TOMBS.

In Memory of
JOHN BOWBRIDGE, of the Parish
of *Northpetherton* in the County
of *Somerset*, who died the 16
of March 1769, Aged 81 Years.
JANE, his Wife, died 15 March 1774,
Aged 84 Years.
Also REBECCA HUCKELBRIDGE,
Daughter of the above who died
15 of April 1782, Aged 74 Years.

In Memory of
HANNAH, late Wife of THOMAS
BAYLIES, of *Stroud*, and Daughter
of JOSIAH, and HANNAH JONES,
who departed this Life,
11 of May 1796, Aged 30 Years.

In Memory of THOMAS, the Son
of JOSEPH, and MARY TEDDER,
of this Parish, who died
the 23 of October, 1753,
Aged near 21 Years.

Here lyeth the Body of
JOMN HARRIS, of the Parish of
Clifton, Lime-burner,
who departed this Life,
24 Jany. 1767, Aged 52 Years.
SARAH, his Wife, who departed
this Life, 25 Febr· 1767,
Aged 56 Years.
Also SARAH, Wife of WILLIAM
HARRIS, who died 10 Febr. 1767,
Aged 26 Years.

Here lyeth the Body of
WILLIAM POWELL,
of the *Out* Parish of *St. James's*
in the City of *Bristol*, who died
18 Nov. 1751, Aged 40 Years.

In Memory of
RICHARD ROGER, of this Parish,
Yeoman, who departed this Life,
the 10 day of Oct. 1740,
Aged 63 Years.
Also EASTER, his Wife,
who departed this Life, the
14 July 1762, Aged 73 Years.
Also EASTER, their Daughter,
who died Nov. 11, 1721, in the
8 Year of her Age.

18

RICHARD, their Son, who died
Jany. 16, 1729, Aged 5 Years.
Also of FRANCIS ROGER,
who died 8 July 1762,
Aged 39 Years.
ESTER and EMELA, died Infants.

Beneath this Tomb are interred
the remains of
ABRAHAM SAUNDERS, Junr.
Merchant in Bristol,
who died 22 of Febr. 1758,
Aged 52 Years.
MARY, his Relict, died the
19 of Nov. 1766, Aged 55 Years.
Also Captain GEORGE SAUNDERS,
Son of the above ABRAHAM and
MARY SAUNDERS,
died 14 June 1776, Aged 41 Years.

Here lyeth the Body of
JOHN NORMAN, of the City of
Bristol, Merchant, who departed
this Life, the 19 of May 1733,
Aged 49 Years.
ANN. his Wife, and Daughter of
Captain GEORGE WEBB,
of this Parish, who departed
this Life, the 15 of September 1732,
Aged 45 Years.

Here lyeth the Body of
MARY, Wife of OBEDIAH WEBB,
of the Parish of Long Ashton
in the County of Somerset, Esqr.
who departed this Life, the
4 day of Decr. 1726,
Aged 40 Years,
Also OBEDIAH WEBB, Esqr.
who departed this Life,
14 Decr. 1741, Aged 57 Years.

Arms:—Or, a Cross quarterly
counter charged Gules and Sable,
in the first quarter an Eagle displayed of the Second.—WEBB.

Here lyeth the Bodies of
EDMUND HUNT, of Shirhampton,
and also ANN, his Wife,
and most of her family.
Here lyeth the Body of
JANE, the Wife of PETER HUNT,
of Shirhampton, Yeoman,
who departed this Life, the
25 of December 1723, Aged 29.

Here lyeth the Body of
CHRISTIAN LEWIS, of ys. Parish,
who departed this Life, the
28 of April, 1740, Aged 61 Years.
Also two of his Children.
And ANN, his Wife, who died
11 May 1767, Aged 81.

In Memory of
JOHN TAYLOR, of this Parish,
Yeoman, who lies buried here,
He left this transitory Life,
on the 29 day of March 1768,
Aged 68 Years.
ANN, his Wife, who died
Decr. 28, 1779, Aged 62 Years.
SAMUEL TAYLOR,

of this Parish, Yeoman,
died 6 Sept. 1796, Aged 41.
Also of four Children of the said
JOHN TAYLOR, by SARAH,
his Wife, who died in their Infancy.
Also SAMUEL, Son of the above
JOHN TAYLOR, by ANN, his
second Wife, who died 3 Febr. 1734,
Aged 8 Years.
Also ANN, Wife of Capt. JOHN
HOWELL, and Daughter of
JOHN and ANN TAYLOR,
who died 26 Oct. 1771,
Aged 21 Years.
JAMES, Son of JAMES EDWARDS,
of the City of Bristol, Apothecary,
by MARY, his Wife,
(Daughter of JOHN and ANN TAYLOR,)
lies near this Tomb interred.
He died 2 Febr. 1772,
Æt. 2 Years and 7 Months.

In Memory of
JANE LEWIS, Relict of GABRIEL
LEWIS, Esqr. of Lanishen in the
County of Glamorgan,
who died the 11 of Nov. 1752,
Aged 64 Years.

HARRY, the Son of the Revd.
MOUNTRICH HILL and CATHERINE,
his Wife, was buried here
May 26, 1756, Aged 32.
And MOUNTRICH, the eldest Son,
was buried Feb. 13, 1764,
Aged 15 Years.

Here lyeth the Body of
LEONARD MANSEL,
who departed this Life,
April 7, 1737, Aged 54 Years.
Also THOMAS MANSELL,
who departed this Life,
Decr. 15, 1746, Aged 6 Years.

In Memory of
JOHN HOULDER, of this Parish,
Malster, who departed this Life,
10 of Febr. 1766, Aged 79 Years.
ELIZABETH, his Wife,
who departed this Life,
7 Nov. 1772, Aged 73 Years.
Also two of their Children,
MARY, the eldest,
died 10 of April 1732,
Aged 1 Year, and 7 Months.
MARY, the youngest,
died the 20 of Sept. 1734,
Aged 2 Weeks and 1 Day.
Also ANN, their Daughter,
died 4 Jany. 1748-9, in the
14 Year of her Age.
MARY, Wife of THOMAS
GWILLIAM, of this Parish, Malster,
who departed this Life, the
25 of May 1795, Aged 79 Years.

Here lyeth the Body of
JAMES JOSHAM,
who died 4 of March 1764,
Aged 41 Years.

Here lyeth the Body of
SUSANNA, the Daughter of

WILLIAM and SARAH WORRELL,
late of Stoke Gifford,
now of this Parish, who departed
this Life, 29 day of Jany. 1726-7,
in the 19 Year of her Age.
Also THOMAS, Son of the abovesaid
WILLIAM and SARAH WORRELL,
who departed this Life, the
21 day of Decr. 1728,
Aged 22 Years.

Here lyeth the Body of
WILLIAM WORRELL, of this Parish,
who departed this Life, the
9 day of March 1729,
Aged 55 Years.

ON FLAT STONES.

Beneath this Stone are deposited
the Remains of WILLIAM REEVES,
who died May 9, 1800,
Aged 47 Years.

Under-neath this Stone are
deposited the Remains of
HENRY ARTHUR EDWARDS, Esqr.
(Youngest Son of JOHN and
CORNELIA EDWARDS,) of Machynleth
in the County of Montgomery,
who died in the 19 Year of his
Age at Bristol Hot-Wells,
August 5, 1797.

BETTY GARDNER,
who died 1 May 1754,
Aged 48 Years.
PHILLIP GARDNER,
died 10 of Augt. 1755,
Aged 50 Years.
HESTER LINFIELD, of the Parish
of St. James's Bristol,
died 15 August 1764, Aged 66.
BETTY HAYNES, of the Parish
of St. James's Bristol,
.... (no date.)
Also ANN GARDNER, of the
Parish of St. James's Bristol,
who died 22 Sept. 1778,
Aged 76 Years.

NATHANIEL GARDNER,
the Son of SAMUEL GARDNER,
of Stroud, in the County of Glouc.
who died 23 of March 1771,
Aged 29 Years.

HANNAH, Wife of JOHN FOX,
Taylor, who died Decr. 19, 1792,
Aged 30 Years.
Also two Children died in
their Infancy.
GEORGE, Son of JOHN and
ELIZABETH FOX, died in his Infancy.

CHARLOTTE-MATILDA STILES,
Wife of CASTER STILES,
died 16 Febr. 1797, in the
31 Year of her Age.
JOHN WHEELER,
who departed this Life, the
Oct. 11, 1793, Aged 42 Years.

19   20   21

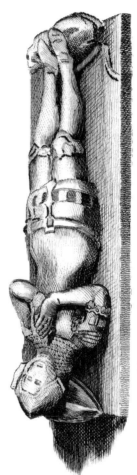

1414

JOHN PRICE, of the Parish,
who died 20 May 1790,
Aged 28 Years.
Also WILLIAM LEE, who died
6 August 1798, Aged 66 Years.

JOSEPH BARAM, who died
18 May 1777, Aged 36 Years.
MARY, his Wife, died 16 Jan. 1794,
Aged 54 Years
Two of their Children,
died in their Infancy.
ANN CUMMINGS,
died 15 Jany. 1791, Aged 21.

[Supplementary Notices of Tablets put
up in the Church since Bigland's time.]

ON MONUMENTS.

EUNICE MORGAN,
who died 1815, Aged 34.
JOHN CROSS, Esqr of Clifton,
who died 1791, Aged 51.
SARAH, his Relict,
who died 1821, Aged 82.

Sir HENRY LIPPINCOTT, Bart.
of Stoke in this Parish,
who died 1781.
And Dame KATHARINE LIPPINCOTT,
his Widow, who died 1797
Sir HENRY CANN LIPPINCOTT, Bart.
their only Son, who died ... 1829.
In compliance with whose Will this
Monument is erected.

Arms:—Quarterly 1 & 4, per fess
counter embattled Gules & Sable 3 Tal-
bots statant guardant Argent, two and
one.—LIPPINCOTT.
2 & 3, CANN, as on Atchment.

FRANCIS SAVAGE,
who died 1845, Aged 56.
LOUISA WALKER SAVAGE,
eldest Daughter of the above and
JULIA LOUISA, his Wife,
who died 1845, Aged 19.
JULIA LOUISA SAVAGE,
who died 1857, Aged 56.
ELIZABETH JENNINGS,
who died 1803, Aged 68.

Arms:—In pale: i. Argent, six
Lions rampant Sable 3, 2, 1.
ii. Argent, a hawk displayed Or. In
Chief 2 mullets Argent.

JOHN YATE, of Sneed Park,
erected by his Son in Law and
sole surviving Daughter,
He died 1819, Aged 67.
JOHN SAYER,
died 1834, Aged 63.
His Wife CHARLOTTE, Daughter of
JOHN CROSS, died 1850, Aged 74.
ELIZABETH, their Daughter,
died 1827, Aged 17.

22

ANN, Wife of HENRY WOOD,
Esqr. who died 1814, Aged 65.
ISABELLA, 2nd. Daughter of
the said HENRY WOOD,
who died 1828, Aged 85.

NAVE.

ON FLAT STONES.

CHARLES PITMAN, Esqr.
of Chigwell, Essex. who died 1835,
Aged 48 Years.

ELIZABETH, Wife of the
Revd. ROBERT FORSTER,
Curate of this Parish,
who died 1809, Aged 38.

JOSEPH THOMAS WAUGH,
Professor of Rhetoric Gresham
College, eldest son of JOSEPH WAUGH,
who died 1807, Aged 42.

NORTH AISLE.

ON MONUMENTS.

In Memory of
WILLIAM, Son of JOHN and
CHARLOTTE TAYLOR,
who died 1835, an Infant.
ELIZABETH. Mother of said
JOHN TAYLOR, who died 1839,
Aged 75 Years.
SAMUEL EDWARD, Son of JOHN
and CHARLOTTE TAYLOR,
who died an Infant.
Their Daughters :—
JEMIMA, who died 1845, Aged 19.
KEZIA, who died ....
EMILY, Wife of HENRY M. PARKES,
She died 1852, Aged 26 Years.
And CHARLOTTE ANN,
who died 1861, Aged 42 Years.
JOHN, their Son, who died 1866,
Aged 41 Years.
Also the said JOHN TAYLOR,
who died 1868, Aged 85 Years.

MARY ANN BARNET,
of Stoke in this Parish,
who died 1846.

ON FLAT STONES.

MARY BOWRON, Wife of WILLIAM
BOWRON, late of Nevis,
and Daughter of GILBERT
HAMILTON, of Georgia,
who died 1818, Aged 41.

23

JEREMIAH HILL, Esqr.
of Downhouse, who died 1831.
MARIA, his Wife, who died 1820.
JEREMIAH, their Son, who died 1857.

SOUTH AISLE.

ON FLAT STONES.

THOMAS HOOPER RIDDLE,
of Hencroft, who died 1848,
Aged 54 Years.
THOMAS HOOPER, his son,
(buried in St. Paul's Bristol,)
Erected by ELIZABETH RIDDLE,
his Mother.

RICHARD, eldest Son of
Revd. RICHARD SYMES, M. A.
Rector of St. Werburgh, Bristol,
who died 1838, Aged ... Years.
ANN, his Wife, 3rd. Daughter of
EDWARD BOWLES, of Frampton,
who died 1840, Aged 77 Years.

SAMUEL BOWDEN,
who died 1834, Aged 74.
MARY ANN BOWDEN,
who died 1840, Aged 79.

Three Children of GEORGE BOWLES,
BRIDGET, CATHERINE, FRANCES.

Arms in pale:—i. Azure, 3 Escallops Or. ii.—Azure 3 Boar's
Heads couped.

HAMELL, Wife of GEORGE HILL-
HOUSE, of this Parish. died ......
MARY WALKER, his 2nd. Wife,
who died 1820, Aged 31.
GEORGE HILLHOUSE,
who died 1848, Aged 70.

ON FLAT STONE.

....................,
who died 1793, Aged 25.
WILLIAM LAWSON,
who died 1797.

CANYNGE CHAPEL.

ON FLAT STONES.

RICHARD HAYNES, of Wyck,
who died 1726, Aged 69.
CATHERINE, Wife of JOSEPH
JACKSONS, of Sneed Park,
who died 1707, Aged 40.
Three of their Children,
died Infants.

24

HEAD STONES IN CHURCH YARD.

	Died.		Aged.		Died.		Aged.
Isaac Jones, ...	30 Dec.	1790	63	James Barratt, ...	28 Jany.	1776	56
James Parsley, ...	8 July	1768	63	Mary, his Daughter, ...	26 Sept.	1792	16
Mary, his Wife, ...	29 Oct.	1766	63	Randall Rogers, ...	13 May	1776	50
John Paul, ...	20 Aug.	1780	81	Eleanor, Wife of John Morgan,	21 Sept.	1792	47
Walter Holmes, ...	17 Nov.	1782	60	Abraham Webb, ...	21 July	1777	..
Mary Price, ...	13 Aug.	1798	67	Mary Church, ...	16 June	1784	63
George Stone, ...	4 March	1786	56	Josiah Jones, ...	10 Aug.	1793	70
Betty, his Wife, ...	11 March	1780	75	Edward Wheeler, ...	7 Nov.	1775	48

1415

INDEX TO CHURCH INSCRIPTIONS.

	Col.		Col.		Col.		Col.
Backwell, Jane,	12	Gardner, Mathew, Philip,		Knight, Ann, Spinster,	2	Saunders, Elizabeth,	6
Baker, Ann,	12	Betty, Ann,	21	Do. Ann, Relict of		Savage, Francis and Julia	
Ballard, Elizabeth,	5	Gates, Robert,	8	James Knight,	3	Louisa-Walker,	22
Do. Rachael,	5	Do. Dorothy,	1	Do. James,	2	Sayer, John Wife Charlotte,	
Baram, Joseph and Mary,	22	Goldingham, Mary Ann,	13	Do. Mary Charity,	16	and Daughter Elizth.	22
Barnet, Mary-Ann,	23	Gregory, Richard,	13			Skuse, Ann, Jonathan,	12
Bartlett, Hannah,	13	Do. Mary,	8	Lawson, Joseph,	17	Smith, Christopher, Kathr.,	13
Do. John,	13	Gwilliam, Mary,	20	Lenfield, Hester,	21	Do. Emma,	14
Bateman, William,	5			Lee, William,	22	Spencer, John,	13
Baylies, Hannah,	18	Haines, Thomas,	16	Lewis, Christian and Ann,	19	Stainer, Wm., Wife Joan,	7
Bowbridge, John, and		Harmer, John, Ann,	14	Do. Jane,	20	Stiles, Charlotte, Matilda,	21
Wife Jane,	18	Harris, John & Wife Sarah,	18	Lippincott, Sir Henry and		Stoakes, Margt., Elizabeth,	7
Bowden, Saml., MaryAnn,	24	Do. Sarah, Wife of Wm.	18	Wife Katherine, and		Stone, William,	6
Bowles, Mary,	5	Hasulton, Bridget,	12	son Sir Hen.-Cann,	22	Symes, Ann, Richard,	24
Do. Bridget, Catherine,		Haynes. Betty,	21	Long, John, Ann,	9		
Frances,	24	Do. Richard,	24			Taylor, Sarah, Dau Sarah,	10
Bowron, Mary,	23	Heins, Richard,	16	Mansel, Leonard, Thos.,	20	Do. John, Ann, and	
Bradford, Mary,	3	Henley, John,	4	Martin, William, Esther,	10	Samuel,	19
Do. William,	5	Hiatt, John,	6	Do. Dorothy, Wm., (2)		Do. John and seven	
Brewster, John,	17	Hill, Sir Richard,	9	Margaret, Amy,	11	Children,	23
Buckland, Joseph,	13	Do. Harry Mountrich,	20	Morgan, James,	15	Do. Elizabeth, his Moth.	23
Do. Ann,	13	Do. Jeremiah and Wife		Do. Eunice. Wife Sarah,	22	Tedder, Thomas,	18
Bull, John,	12	Maria & son Jeremiah,	24			Thynn, Hannah,	4
		Hillhouse, George & Wives		Norman, John, Wife Ann,	19	Till-Adam, Thomas,	10
Cook, John,	17	Hamell and Mary,	24			Trego, William, WifeSarah,	17
Creswick, Dr. Samuel,	4	Hort, Thomas,	12	Parker, William,	4	Twynihoe, Christopher,	6
Cross, John and Sarah,	22	Do. Bridget,	12	Phelps, Wm, & Mary,	15		
Do. James,	15	Do. Thomas,	12	Pipon, James,	15	Walter, John, Mary,	6
Cuff, Thomas,	6	Do. Thomas, Junr.	6	Pitman, Charles,	23	Do. William, Richard,	
Cuffe, John, Wife Jane	6	Do. Elizabeth, John,	17	Poulson, George,	17	Ann,	7
Cummings, Ann,	22	Houlder, John, Elizabeth,		Powell, William,	18	Wasborough, John, Charity,	7
		Mary, Ann,		Price, John,	22	Do. John,	8
Daubney, Mary,	13	Howell, Ann,		Pullings, William,	17	Waugh, Joseph Thomas,	23
		Hucklebridge, Bebecca,	18			Webb, Mary,	12
Edgar, Alexander,	11	Hutton, Nathaniel, Mary,	16	Reeves, William,	21	Do. Jone,	12
Edwards, James,	20	Hungerford, Giles,	2	Revell, Elizabeth,	8	Do. Obediah, & Mary,	19
Do. Henry Arthur,	21	Hunt, Edmund, & Jane,	21	Rich, Elizabeth,	19	Wheeler, John,	21
Eldridge, Rebecca,	7	Do. Ann,	19	Do. Samuel,		Whitaker, William,	6
Ellsworth, Sir Richard,	11			Richardson, Thomas, and		Wiett, Mary, Charles,	7
Do. Peter,	11	Jackson, Nicholas,	11	Mary, Joyce, Wm.,	16	Wilson, Miles,	8
Do. Edward,	11	Do. Ann, Katharine,		Riddle, Thomas, (2)	24	Wood, Henry, Isabella,	22
England, Elizabeth,	12	Ann, Nicholas, (son.)	10	Rishton, Dorothy,	8	Worrell, Susann,	20, 21
Do. Mary and Wm.	13	Do. Robert,		Roger, Richard, (2)	18, 19	Do. Thomas, William,	21
		Do. Catherine,	24	Do. Ester, (2)	19		
Fane, Ann,		Jacob, Samuel,	6	Do. Francis, Licharn,	19	Yate, John,	22
Do. Henry,	4	Do. Elizabeth,	6	Roselarge, M...	14	Yeaman, Abigail,	7
Do. Henry,	9	Jefferis, William,	14	Ruscomb, Ann,	22	Yeames, Sampson, & Wife	
Floyd, Joseph, Saml., Mary,	21	Jennings, Ann,	23			Ann, Sampson, Junr.	10
Forster, Elizabeth,	23	Joshua, James,	20	Saunders, Abraham, Mary,	19		
Fox, Hannah, George,	21	Knight, (late Hungerford,		Do. George,	19	And see "Head Stones."	
Freke, George,	4	by birth Jacob,) Mary,	1	Saunders, William, Peter,	5		

REDLAND;

HAMLET TO WESTBURY UPON TRIM.

THIS HAMLET lying a considerable distance from the Parish Church MR. COSSINS, in 1740; built a Chapel for the use of the Inhabitants which he endowed with Lands worth about 130 £. per Ann. It is built of free stone, the entrance at the West-end. It has one Bell under a handsome rotunda.

In a small Vestry room on the right of the entrance, over the door is the following Inscription on a Marble Tablet.

THIS CHAPEL, Built at the expence of JOHN COSSINS, Esqr. and by him endowed, was opened Oct. 5th. 1743.

ON A HANDSOME MARBLE MONUMENT, IN THE SAME ROOM.

In a Vault under the Communion Table are deposited the Remains of :—

Mrs. ANNE INNYS,	NICHOLAS MARISSAL,	Mrs. MARY MARISSAL,	JOHN COSSINS,	Mrs. MARTHA COSSINS,
(Sister to Mrs. Cossins,)	of Edmonton, Esqr.	his Wife,	of Redland Court, Esqr.	his Wife,
who died December 5,	who died Aug. 29,	(Sister to Mrs. Cossins,)	Founder of the Chapel,	Daughter of ANDREW
MDCCXLVII,	1739,	who died Septmb. 9,)	who died April 19,	INNYS, of Bristol,
Aged 69 Years.	(brought from Christ	MDCCLVII,	MDCCLIX,	Gent. who died
	Church in Middlesex,	Aged 66 Years.	Aged 77 Years.	Febr. 11, MDCCLXII,
	December ...,			Aged 74 Years.
	MDCCXLVII,)			
	Aged 52 Years.			

Arms:

Arms:—In a Lozenge Quarterly 1 & 4. Argent, three Estoilés Azure —INNYS. 2 —Gules 3 Boars heads coupt Or.— ABERCHERDER. 3.—Or. 3 Bars nebullée Gules.— LOVELL.	*Arms:*—Azure a Chevron between three Cover'd Cups, Or.— MARISSAL. *impaling* Quarterly 1&4.Azure a Lion rampant Or. goutté de sang and ducally crowned Gules.—COSSINS. 2 & 3.—Argent, on a bend Sable, 3 Owls, of the first SAVILLE.	*Arms:*—In a Lozenge, the same Coat as last.	*Arms:*—Quarterly 1 & 4. COSSINS, 2 & 3. SAVILLE. impaling Quarterly 1&4 INNYS, 2.—ABERCHERDER. 3.—LOVELL.	*Arms:*—the same as the last in a Lozenge.

ON A NEAT MARBLE MONUMENT.

Arms :—Quarterly 1 & 4, INNYS. 2.—ABERCHERDER. 3.—LOVELL.

Crest:—a Grey hounds head coupt Argent, collared Azure.

Motto:—Bona Spero.

To the Memory of
JOHN INNYS, *Esqr.* of *Redland Court,* (Brother of *Mrs.* COSSINS,)
who died 27*th.* October 1778, Aged 83 Years.

3 Coats at Bottom.

1.—INNYS, *impaling:*—Argent, two Bars Gules.
2.—INNYS, *impaling:*—Argent, on a Chevron Sable three Cups Or.
3.—Argent, on a Chevron Sable three Cups Or. *impaling* Sable a Cross between four fleur de Lis, Or.

CHAPEL YARD.

HEAD STONES.

	Died.		Aged.		Died.		Aged.
Francis Ward, ...	10 July	1797	53	Jane, Wife of John Marshall, *Esqr. of Armagh in the Kingdom of Ireland.* ...	3 June	1802	60
Rev. William Embury Edward, late *Minister* of this Parish	11 July	1797	37				
Mary Daubney, ...	26 March	1803	27	Maria-Catharine Temple, Daughter of *Lt. Col.* Richard Temple, and of his Wife Frances	11 June	1802	...
Elizabeth Quin, ...	4 Augt.	1795	16				
Mary-Ann Wilson, Wife of John Wilson, *Junr. Esqr.* of *Tokenhouse Yard, Lond.*	8 Sept.	1798	27				
				Wm.Hepburn,*Esqr.* of this Parish	11 Dec.	1791	77
Lady Conolly King, ...	18 Sept.	1800	60	Oliver Peard, *Esqr.*	(*no date.*)		

SHIREHAMPTON;

HAMLET TO WESTBURY UPON TRIM.

A SMALL CHAPEL consisting of a Nave, and Chancel and a Wooden turrett at the West-end, therein one Bell.

BENEFACTION TABLE.

Mrs. HONOUR BODMAN, of *Shirehampton,* gave 20 pounds the Interest whereof to be paid by the Chapel Warden, of Shirehampton, to the Minister of this Parish for Preaching a Sermon in the Chapel at Shirehampton, on the first day of January Yearly for ever. She likewise gave 30 pounds more, the Interest whereof to be distributed by the Chapel Warden and Overseer of the Poor of Shirehampton, at their discretion, among the said Poor of Shirehampton, on the said first day of January Yearly for ever.

1769.—*Mr.* HENRY BODMAN, of *Bristol, Gent.* by his Will gave the sum of 90 pounds for the purpose following viz. the Interest of 30 pounds to the Poor of *Shirehampton,* on 22*nd.* day of February Yearly for ever. And the Interest of 30 pounds for a Sermon at this Chapel, on the same day for ever. And also the Interest of 30 pounds, towards addit. ional Service every other Sunday at this Chapel, as long as the same shall continue to be performed.

1741.—*Mr.* CHRISTOPHER SMITH, of this Tything, gave 40 *s.* per Ann. 20 *s.* of which to the Minister for preach. ing a Sermon at the Chapel on Good Friday, and the other 20 *s.* to the Poor of the said Tything (frequenting divine Service,) in Bread, on the above day Yearly for ever.

1744.—*Mrs.* JOAN SAINER, of this Tything, gave 75 pounds, the Interest thereof as follows (viz.) One Guinea Yearly to the Minister of *Westbury,* for Preaching two Sermons one on the 15*th.* of January at *Westbury,* the other on Holy Thursday at this Chapel and the remainder of the Interest to be distributed to the Poor of *Westbury,* by the Chapel Warden and Overseer of the Poor of this Tything, Yearly for ever.

1747.—*Mr.* WILLIAM ASHLEY, of this Tything, gave 10 pounds, the Interest thereof in Bread to the Poor of the said Tything on the 2*nd.* of February Yearly, for ever.

1752.—*Mr.* PETER HUNT, of this Tything, gave 20 pounds, the Interest thereof to the Poor of the said Tything in Bread, on Easter Monday Yearly, for ever.

INSCRIPTIONS IN THE CHAPEL.

ON A MARBLE MONUMENT, AGAINST
THE NORTH SIDE OF NAVE.

Near this Place
are interred with his Ancestors
the Remains of
HENRY BODMAN,
late of *Bristol, Gentleman,*
He died the 21st. of June 1768,
Aged 69 Years.
Also of *Mr.* JOHN SMITH,
late of this Place, *Gentleman,*
who died 29th. of March 1778,
Aged 44 Years.
MARY BODMAN,
Obt. 13 January 1795,
Aged 72 Years.

ON A PLAIN MARBLE AGAINST
THE SOUTH WALL.

This unadorned Stone
is erected to the Memory of
MARY YATES, of *Sneed Park,*
(late of *Donnington,* in the
County of *Salop.*) *Spinster,*
who departed this Life, the
31st. December 1799,
Aged 49 Years,
And lies interred in a Vault
in the Porch of this Chapel.

ON FLAT STONES.

Here lyeth the Body of
ABRAHAM BODMAM, *Senr.*
of *Shirehampton,*
who departed this Life, the
17 January 1710, Aged 60 Years.
Also the Body of
ABRAHAM BODMAN, *Junr.*
the Son of ABRAHAM and
HONOUR BODMAN,
who departed this Life, the
15 of June 1703, Aged 17 Years.
Likewise here lyeth the Body of
ABRAHAM, the Son of JAMES
BEVAN and ANNE, his Wife,
of *Clifton,* in the Co. of *Gloucester,*
who departed this Life, the
5 of January 1727, Aged 6 Years,
and 11 Months.
Likewise here lyeth the Body of
HONOUR, the Wife of ABRAHAM
BODMAN, of *Shirehampton,*
who departed this Life, the
29 day of January in the Year 1733,
Aged 73 Years.
Here also lieth the Body of
HONOUR, Daughter of the above
ABRAHAM and HONOUR BODMAN,
who departed this Life,
22nd. of July 1742, Aged 53 Years.

Here lyeth the Body of
JOHN THOMAS, of the City of
Bristol, Son of JOHN THOMAS,
of *Shirehampton,*
who departed this Life, the
24 of July 1736, Aged 69 Years.
Here also lyeth the Body of
MARY, Wife of JACOB COOK,
of this Place, *Neice* to the above
JOHN THOMAS,
who departed this Life,
22nd. of April 1753,
Aged 57 Years.
Likewise here lyeth the Body of
the above JACOB COOK,
who died 11 July 1765,
Aged 71 Years.

Here lyeth the Body of
ELIZABETH WILLIS,
of this Parish, who died the
8 of September 1727,
Aged 57 Years.

Underneath this Stone lieth
the Body of ABRAHAM LEWIS,
Mariner, born in the City of *Bristol,*
formerly a *Sea Commander* in this
Port, and lately *Haven Master*
in the said Port, who departed
this Life, on the 25th. of July 1752,
Aged 81 Years.

Here lyeth the Body of
JOHN THOMAS, *Gent.*
of this Parish, who departed
this Life, 9th. February 1683.
Also here lyeth the Body of
JOAN, the Daughter of JOHN
and ANNE THOMAS,
who departed this Life, the
16 January 1683, Aged 21 Years.
Also here lyeth the Body of
MATHA, the Daughter of
JOHN and ANNE THOMAS,
who died 8th. September 1683,
Aged 12 Years.
Also here lyeth the Body of
ANNE, the Wife of the said
JOHN THOMAS,
who departed this Life,
29 October 1695, Aged 53 Years.

Here lyeth the Body of
HENRY CORAM, of this Parish,
who died the 21st. of January 1763,
Aged 47 Years.
Here lieth the Body of
JOHN HILL, of this Parish,
Yeoman, who died the

16th. September 1740,
Aged 42 Years.

WILLIAM GABITAS,
died August 23rd. 1713,
Aged 51 Years.
MARY GABBITAS, Relict of the
above died 5th. March 1796,
Aged 46 Years.

CHAPEL YARD.

ON AN UPRIGHT STONE.

Her Under Hurister
Legemet Af. St. Christet
NIELSEN SANDWIGEN,
fou PAA SANDWIGEN,
lied A Ben Dal I Noigi
Den XXVII September 1734,
Dod I Hougiod Den XI.
(*P. S.—More of it but sunk into the
ground impossible to make out.*)

ON TOMBS.

In Memory of
SARAH BODDLEY,
who died suddenly the
26 of January 1765,
Aged 47 Years.

In Memory of
SARAH, Wife of JOSHUA POWER,
of the City of *Bristol,*
who died 13 September 1745,
Aged 31 Years.
Also of MARY BOON, of this Parish,
who died 29 July 1748,
Aged 30 Years.
Also of SARAH WILLIS,
of this Parish, who died the
10 of September 1740,
Aged 17 Years.
Also of JOAN SEAGER, of this
Tything, who died the
3 of February 1764,
Aged 56 Years.

ELIZABETH TOMLINSON,
Wife of WILLIAM TOMLINSON,
Haven Master,
died 2 Febr. 1802, Aged 62 Years.
Their Infant Daughters.
FRANCES, died June 14, 1788,
ANN, died April 9, 1795,
And also SAMUEL and ELIZABETH
SAYER, ... (*No date.*)

HEAD STONES.

	Died.	Aged.		Died.	Aged.
Simon Harding	7 June 1788	26	Hannah, Wife of John Smily, Mariner, and Daughter of George Tomkins, ...	11 April 1762	25
Also George, the Son of Geo. and Susan Ely, ...	30 Sept. 1793	31	John Smily, her Son, ...	3 Aug. 1766	6
Mary, Wife of James Willington, (of the Parish of *Wotley. Somerset,*) and Dau. of Francis & Susan Harding.	10 Jany. 1799	33	George Tomkins, of *Axminster, Gt.*	16 Febr. 1772	61
			Martha, his Wife, ...	27 June 1771	71
George Thomas, (of this P.) *Pilot.*	1 Dec. 1766	76	Wheeler Tomkins, Son of the said George Tomkins, ...	25 Febr. 1773	39
Mary Knight, (*Spinster.*)	2 Nov. 1783	42	Nicholas Johnson, ...	24 June 1765	74
Sarah Bodily, ...	1 Jany. 1763	49			

William Davies, (late of Lamp-lighters Hall.)	4 Oct.	1790	45	Capt. John Shaw, Haven Master,	20 Decr.	1796	80
Edward Collins, of this Parish,	4 Nov.	1792	35	Arthur Long, of this Parish, ...	8 Oct.	1738	38
Edmund Turberville, of the Parish of Twinning, Co. of Glauc. Esqr.	2 March	1802	73	Grace, Wife of David Jones, of this Parish, Yeoman,	16 Nov.	1743	45
Bethea, his Wife, ...	26 June	1790	49	Also the above David Jones, ...	29 Sept.	1765	66
John, Son of John and Mary Brown, of this Parish, ...	11 June	1743	23	Ellanor Scott, Daughter of Hellen and William Scott, Esqr. Merchant, late of Newcastle upon Tyne, ...	26 April	1789	16
Mary, Wife of John Brown, Senr.	26 July	1760	75	Joseph Partridge, Esqr. Capt. in ye 46st Regt. of Invalids, and 3rd. Son of Henry Partridge, Esqr. of Buckenram Hall, Co. Norfolk.	21 Oct.	1788	75
Mary, Wife of William Price, of the Parish of Westbury,	8 Jany.	1776	58				
Mary Palmer, of this Parish, ...	10 Decr.	1786	41				
Sarah Slye, ...	3 Mar.	1792	...				
Ann, Wife of John Shaw, Haven Master, ...	23 Sept.	1792	67	Harriet Barton, ...	20 Oct	1797	21
Also 2 of their Sons Infants,	(No date.)			Susannah Allen, ...	17 Oct.	1800	68
Also Mary Shaw, Sister of Capt. John Shaw, ...	30 Decr.	1793	78				

Supplementary Notes as to I.—*Devolution of Estates.* II.—*Church.* III.—*Taxation, Population, &c.*

1.—Devolution of Estates

Westbury upon Trim, is situate in the line of a Roman Road, and in Pen Park Westbury is a deep hole considered to have been a Lead mine worked by the Romans. (*see Bristol and Gloucestershire Archaeological Society's Transactions.* iv. *page* 320.) In Anglo Saxon times, we learn that Offa King of Mercia, about the years 791—796, gave Lands *i. e.* six Manentes at Westbyrig, (Westbury) and twenty Manentes at Henbyrig, (Henbury) to the Church at Worcester (St. Mary's) with the Rights wherewith King Ethelbald had given the Lands to Offa's grandfather Eanwolf. (*Kemble's Codex Angl. Sax. Diplom.* i. *page* 202. And here was a Monastery endowed with Lands there by Ethelric, son of Ethelmund, concerning the rights over which Monastery and its Lands a dispute arose between Hubert, the Bishop of the Church at Worcester, and the religious Community at Berkeley which was referred for settlement to the synod held at Cloveshoo 824, under Beornwulf, King of Mercia and Archbishop Wulfrith. The decision was that the Lands should revert to the Church of Worcester. And so it appears by the Domesday Survey, they did, for by this or some other Title that Church, held here large possessions.

The Church of St. Mary of Worcester, held and holds Huesberie, (Westbury) in Bernintreu Hundred. It contained 30 Hides. As to Culture, there were two Carucates in Demesne and 8 in Villenage, (8 Villans and 5 Bordars.) There were 4 Serfs and one Bond Woman. To this Manor belonged these Members:—Henbury, Redwick, Stoke, Giete, (Yate,) In these were 9 Carucates in Demesne and 26 in Villenage. (27 Villans and 2 Bordars.)

There were 20 Serfs. 2 Bond Women, Also 20 Coliberts who had 10 Carucates. There was a Mill of 20 *s.* Value (Yearly.) To this Manor also belonged six Radchenisters who had eight Hides, and in Culture Eight Carucates. They (the Radchenisters,) were inseparable from the Manor.

In Bristol were 2 Houses rented at xvi pence. Of these Lands Turstin Rolf's son held 5 Hides in Auster Cliff; Gislebert Thoroldson, held 3 Hides and ½ in Compton; Constantine held 5 Hides in Ictun, and Osborn Giffard, held five Hides and yielded no service. In these Lands were five Carucates in Demesne and 12 in Villenage, (16 Villans. 12 Bordars.) and there were Eleven Serfs.

In King Edward's (Confessor's) time the whole of this Manor was worth 24£. At the time of the Survey it was worth £29 14s. 6d. yearly. *Domesday Survey.*

The religious Community or College who had the Manor &c. here was some time lay at others regular but under the Bishop of Worcester's Jurisdiction in whose Diocese Gloucestershire then was.

1288.—By Bishop Godfrey Giffard, it was made collegiate consisting of a Dean and Prebendaries. Wickliffe, was prebendary there temp. Edw. iii.

Bishop Carpynter, was a native of this place and was buried in a mortuary chapel under the Chancel of Westbury Church. He was a great Benefactor to the College.

The possessions of the College are thus stated in the *Valor Eccl'us.* of 26 Hen. viii.

26 Hen. viii.—Manor of Westbury:

Rents of Assize of Customary Tenants Yearly, 63s. 4d.			
Farm of Manor Yearly	46	8	
Farm of the demesne Lands in Thirdland, (Redland.) ... ... }	44		

Rents of Assize of Lands and Tenements in Canford ... ... }	57	4	
Less 13s. 4d. Fee to W. Veel, Bailiff yearly leaving clear £9 18 0			
And the staff and their stipends thus			
12 Choristers 43s. 4d. each together 26 £.			
Dean (John Barlow,)	63	16	8
5 Prebendaries: (J. Bell, T. Barlow, R. Hopwood, W. Burley, T. Wasteft,) received 40s. each. ... ... }	10	0	0
Sub Dean: (Leodwick Jonys,)	10	0	0
Chaplain: (W. Colyns.)	8	0	0
Golde.	10	0	0

Valor Eccl'us.

35 Hen. viii.—The Manor of Westbury, after the dissolution of Monasteries passed to Sir Ralph Sadlier, by Crown Grant and continued in the family until sale in 1675, by Walter, Lord Aston, a descendant of the Heir General, Gertrude Sadlier, to T. Yate, and Gregory Gearing. It appears by *Church Inscriptions* that W. Martin, mar. Gearing's heiress.

1680.—Sir Samuel Astry, by purchase. He left three Daughters Co-heirs; Elizabeth, marr. to Sir J. Smyth, Diana, marr. to Richard Orlebar, and Arabella, marr to Lord Suffolk. Orlebar's One-third share passed to Colston, by pur chase, and Arabella's one third share to her sister Smyth, by Will, of which half was retained by Smyth's descendants, and the other half sold to Colston's Heirs, bringing the Division into moieties, of which subsequently Edwards, and Lord Middleton and Colston became Possessors.

The College Buildings were strong, with Battlements, Corner and Central Towers. They passed from the Sadlier's by sale.—And the Hobhouse family long resided there.

John Hobhouse, Esqr.   *County Election,* 1776.
Sir B. Hobhouse, succeeded him.   To him—
Sir J. C. Hobhouse, who became Lord Broughton.

Part of the Buildings still remain, particularly the Tower, and are incorporated with the modern additions.

Stoke Bishop, a hamlet of Westbury, belonged to the See of Worcester, as distinguished from the College property. 1 Edw. vi.—The Crown by exchange, Sir Ralph Sadlier, by Crown Grant. Soon after Sir Robert Yeomans.

see "*Church Inscriptions.*"

Margaret, his sister and heir married William Cann, Alderman of Bristol, 1662, Their descendant Sir Robert Cann, Bart. built the Manson of Stoke Bishop. Of this, there is a View in Atkyns' History, the Public Road then ran near the front of the House, but was afterwards diverted.

Sir T. Cann, Knight, son of Sir Robert, by 2nd. Marrage succeeded to the Baronetcy but died without Issue. His sister and ultimately heir married Jefferies.

Robert Cann Jefferies, their son, then acquired the Estate but dying unmarried, it went to his sister who married Lippincott and Sir H. Cann Lippincott, held.

Church Inscriptions.

Redland or Thirdland was part of the demesnes of Westbury Manor.

Tewkesbury Abbey in a *Quo Warranto Proceeding*, 15 Edw. i. alleged Title hereto by gifts of Robert Fitzhamon, (*see* "Tewkesbury.") and Confirmation of Kings Wm. ii. & H. i.

The Rate Payer "Thridland," in the *Subsidy Roll,*

1 Edw. iii. took his Name from this Place.

After the dissolution of Monasteries, 6 Edw. vi. Egion Wilson, by Crown Grant. Egion Wilson, his Wife Dorothy, and son Miles, levied a *Fine* to John Foxton

1567.—Miles Wilson, died. His Daughter Elizabeth, married R. Revell.

The names of Sir Richard Hill, Gearing and Martin. appear in "*Church Inscriptions*" as Owners of Redland Court, Manor, &c. In 1734, Cossens possessed.

1776.—John Innys Baker, and Slade Baker, voted as Freeholders at the County Election

Redland Court, was rebuilt by Cossens. It is a handsome substantial Edifice of the last Century style. It belonged to Seymour, in "Rudge's" time.

Sneyd Park:—This was once a Grange and Park of the Bishop of Worcester It passed to the Crown, Edw. vi by Exchange, and from that to Sadlier, as before noted. By Sadlier's Heir general it was sold to Nicholas Jackson, and in Atkyns time Joseph Jackson, was Owner. The View given by Atkyns shows the House and a tract of ground stretching from the Road to the Severn, stiff but quaintly laid out. The Park was afterwards cut up into farms, and since has become the site of numerous Villas.

Cote House and Estate:—is a large turretted mansion, 1711.—it belonged to Mr. Saunders.

1742.—Mr. Phelps, who married his Widow succeeded, and Mr. Thomas, acquired it by purchase from the Widow.

1777.—It was held by Mr. John Webb, M.P. for Gloucester. 1796.—It had passed to Mr. Joseph Wedgwood, of Etruscan fame.

1806.—To Sir Henry Protheroe, and afterwards to Philip Protheroe, M.P. for Bristol.

Cotham House:—belonged to the Edwards family who were large Proprietors in Westbury. They took the name of Freeman, (of Batsford.)

South Mead:—St. Mary Magdalene, Nunnery, Bristol held, *Subsidy Roll*, 1 Edw. iii. Before the dissolution the Prioress granted a long Lease to the Haines family some of whom were Deans of the College, *see* "*Ch. Inscriptions.*"

36 Hen. viii.—The Reversion by Crown Grant, was obtained by J. Haynes, through Trustees; Mr. Baker, by purchase from Haynes; Mr. Knight, from him, *see* "*Church Inscriptions,*" From whom Joshua James, and Mr. Jones, successively.

Other Proprietors in Cote, were the Horts, to which family are several "*Church Inscriptions.*",

At Say Mill, were extensive Docks (now disused) at the entry of the Trim Brook into the Avon.

Rowles Scudaimore, Esqr. had a House and Estate here.

Shirehampton, on the Avon, a populous hamlet of Westbury.

1811.—Lord De Clifford, was Lord of the Manor.

Land Holders:—Lord De Clifford, P. W. S. Miles, (Penpole House.) J. Langley and others.

51 Geo. iii. c. xviii.—An Act of Parliament passed for inclosing Warths, Marshes Commons and Wastes in Westbury on Trym, Henbury, (including Weston) and Compton Greenfield, under which Allotments were made to Lord de Clifford, (Penfold Hill,) and others.

Award dated ...... in Clerk of Peace Office. Gloucester.

Here are the Avonmouth Hotel; Port and Pier Railway. Convalescent Hospital, 1860.

1776.—*At the County Election, the following Voted as freeholders in Westbury.*

Andrews, Jesse.	Leg, William.
Collins, Abraham.	Lee, William.
Edwards, Wm.	Lowle, (2) Benjamin, John.
Hardwick, Thomas.	Newman, Henry.
Harris, (2) Joseph, Stephen.	Parsley, Thomas.
Hart, George.	Page, John.
Harmer, John.	Partridge, Charles.
Hancock, *Rev.* Benj.	Pople, Thomas.
Hobhouse, John.	Saunders, Thomas.
Hookham, James.	Seager, (2) John, John. *Junr.*
Jones, Josiah.	Stretton, Thomas.
Jackson, Robt. *Sneyd Park.*	Thomas, (3) George, Thomas,
Kemp, Thomas.	Samuel.
Knatchbull, Norton, *Babington, Somerset.*	Thriftell, Edward.
	Tombs, Nicholas.
Llewellin, Richard.	Webb, (2) Wm., Samuel.
Lewis, Samuel,	Willis, William.

1776.—*Voted as Freeholders in Shirehampton.*

Davis, Mark, *Junr.*	Saunders, Thomas.
Dobbins, John.	Seager, John.
Hill, Benj.	Thomas, (2) John, Samuel.
Miller, Michael, *Junr.*	Wilding, John.

Gunpowder Works.

1776.—*Voted as Freeholders for Stoke Bishop.*

Baker, Slade, *Junr. of Oxford.* John Innys.

II.—*Church.*

The Living was a perpetual Curacy now a Vicarage, the Impropriators after the dissolution were Fane, Henley, Edwards, Edwards Freeman and Colston.

Augmentation of the Living by Donation Edward Colston, 100 £. others 120 £. Queen Ann's Bounty 200 £.=420£. laid out in Land.

A Ministers Fund of 732 £. raised for additional Duty in the Church.

No List of Curates is given in the History but there appears:—1723.—William Stone, Subsequently M. Ray, T. Broughton, Richard Carrow.

The Church has a porch on the south side over which is a Parvise or Chamber with Windows in the external Walls and a fireplace. This Room has a place for an opening to look into the Church, and connected with it are steps of descent into a mortuary or vault below the Church. The Room was probably intended for the use of a Chantry Priest.

For additional Duty in the Chapel of Shirehampton a Benefaction of 30 £. was given by Henry Bodmin, the Dividends to be paid to the Minister.

Shirehampton has long had a Chapel of Ease, now a Church with an ecclesiastical District and Vicarage, worth 37 £. Yearly. The Church consists of Nave, Transept, North Aisle and Chancel, Porch, Turret with two Bells. Register dates from 1727.

Stoke Bishop, is a Vicarage of 350 £. Yearly and Ecclesiastical District. The Church of the date 1860, consists of Nave, side Aisles, Apse, Children's Chapel, Organ Chamber. It has a Tower and Spire.

There are Wesleyan and Baptist Chapels, National Boys, Girls, and Infants Schools, British School, and School of Art in Westbury.

Near the Church is a large modern building erected at Cost of Mr. St. Vincent Ames, of Cote House, for a Music Hall and Reading Room, and with Curators House.

III.—*Taxation, Population, &c.*

Westbur. cu Hamelett, viz., Stoke and Hampton, Subsidy Roll, 1 Edw. iii.

De Priorissa bte Mar Magdalen, iii s. viii d. o.	De Robto. Jordan, vii d. q.
' Thm. de Ellebighe, iis. vd.o.	' Willo. Masoun, xxii d. q.
' Adam atte Hay, xvii d. o.	' Ad. le Parcare, iii s. iiii d.q.
' Rico. de Blakeneye, xv d.	' Thm. Somer, ii s. i d. o. q.
	' Willo. Tridelaunde, x d. q.

Adhuc Westbu. &c.

De Willo. Longe, xxi d. q.	De Hugon. Dauy, vi d.
' Walto. atte Pyle, iiii s. viii d. o.	' Walto. Hemy'ge, xiii d.
' Willo. Lambard, vi d. o.q.	' Robto. atte Pleystude, ii s. iiii d. q.
' Wal. de Asshton, viii d.o.q.	' Johe. le Foghelere, vi d.
' Thm. Sely, vi d.	' Johe. Elyot, vii d. q.
' Robto. atte Ston, vii d.	' Willo. Warr. vii d. o. q.
' Thm. Richema. vi d. o. q.	' Johe. Celar. vi s. viii d. q.
' Johe. Joye, viii d.	' Robto. Hemy'ge, viii d.
' Thom. Dammesele, vi d.	' Willo. de Auene, xvid.o.q.
' Hemingge atte Cote, xiiid. o. q.	' Willo. Hykedon, ii s. vi d.
' Willo. Godefray, xiiii d. q.	' Johne le Rede. xvi d. o. q.
' Robt. Fouke, xix d. o. q.	' Willo. Gregory, ii s. i d. q.
' Thm. Batyns, vi d. o. q.	' Willo. le Botiller, ii s.
	' Geoc. Reynny, x s.

prob. Sma. lxiiii s. i d. o. q.

Acra 4582 £.

Population 1831,—4263.	1871,—13,374.
Westbury hamlet, 1515.	8329.
Shirehampton, 420.	731.
Stoke Bishop, 2328.	1995.

1815.—Annual Value of Real Property 7605 £.

1882.— Rateable Value, £ 36,794.

1832-3-4.—3 Years Average Expenditure on the Poor of the Parish in Gloucestershire, 1318 £.

WESTCOT.

THE CHURCH is a Rectory in the Deanery of Stow, it hath a handsome Tower adorned with pinnacles at the West-end.

Dr. THOMAS BROOKES, *Rector and* LORD OF THE MANOR.

INSCRIPTIONS IN THE CHURCH.

ON FLAT STONES.

Here lyeth the Body of
LAURENCE MACE, of *Westcott*,
in the County of *Gloucester*,
who dyed the 9*th*. day of June
in the Year of our Lord 1707,
and in the 70*th*. Year of his Age.

Here lyeth the Body of
EDITH MANSELL, the Wife of
Revd. ROBERT MANSELL,
of *Charlton Kings* in the County of

Gloucester, who dyed the 10 day of
March, in the Year of our Lord
1690, and in the 66*th*.
Year of her Age.
Also ELIZABETH, Wife of
LAURENCE MACE, and Daughter of
ROBERT and EDITH MANSELL,
who departed this Life, the
13 day of June A. D 1720,
Aged 74 Years.

PORCH.

There is an Inscription on a stone to
B. BARRAN, *Esqr.* who died 1692.

CHURCH YARD.

ON A TOMB.

In Memory of
JOHN RALEIGH, who died
Febr. the 10, 1727, Aged 70 Years.
Also CATHERINE, his Wife,
who died June ye 13, 1706,
Aged 36 Years.
In Memory of
ELIZABETH, th Wife, of
JOHN RALEIGH, *Junr.*
She died Jany. 19, 1763,
Aged 73 Years.

HEAD STONES.

	Died.		Aged.		Died.		Aged.
Thomas Hathaway, ...	26 Febr.	1762	68	Elizabeth Johnson, ...	13 May	1751	48
Daniel Hathaway, ...	14 Febr.	1770	71	William Hathaway, ...	11 Decr.	1782	78
Elizabeth, Wife of Thos. Spuritt,	21 April	1763	66	Mary, Dau. of John & Sarah Rose	21 June	1788	18
William, Son of William and Mary Wright, ...	24 Febr.	1738	21	Mary, Wife of William Rose, ...	19 Decr.	1779	63
				Richard, their Son, ...	4 May	1779	22
John, Son of John & Emme Cotte.	22 March	1742	78	William Rose, ...	21 Sept.	1771	69
John Willks, ...	4 Decr.	1740	63	Hains Woodman, ...	27 Sept.	1769	87
John Layt, ...	26 June	1769	63	Elizth., Wife of Hains Woodman,	13 Nov.	1742	60
Elizabeth, Wife of John Willks,	23 Jany.	1735	60	Thomas Horkins, ...	2 Oct.	1747	42
John Layt, ...	9 Febr.	1745	68	Thomas, Son of Thomas and Anne Horkins, ...	2 Febr.	1743	27
John Johnson, ...	13 Jany.	1782	82				
Margaret, his Wife, ...	16 April	1785	72				
William, Son of Thomas and Margaret Johnson, ...	12 Oct.	1780	35				

Supplementary Notes as to I. *Devolution of Estates.* II. *Church.* III. *Population, Taxation, &c.*

In Domesday Survey, four Manors called Icomb, (three of them in Gloucestershire and one in Worcestershire,) are entered. Two of the Gloucestershire three, are said in the County Histories to be the Tythings or Hamlets of Combe Baskerville, and Westcote proper, and constitute the Parish of Westcote, an account of which here follows, the other two comprise Icomb in Gloucestershire, and Church Icomb in Worcestershire, and an account of these two will be subjoined to Westcote, but it seems doubtful from the Quantities whether the present parish of Westcote of 1500 acres does comprise the whole area of the first 2, the Quantity together of which would be more than Westcote, and whether rather part should not be given to the 3rd. or Gloucestershire Icomb, whose acreage is 650a.

In Salmanesburie Hundred, 1. Icoumbe, contained two Hides taxed. Culture: two Carucates in Demesne and One in Villenage, (2 Bordars and two Villans,) Four Bondmen and 3 Bond Women. It is worth 40s. (Yearly,) and is geldable Haldene held (before the conquest.) Roger de Laci, next held, and Ralph, after (at the survey.)

2 Icunbe, contained Ten Hides (taxed:) Culture: Three Carucates in Demesne and Seven in Villenage, (12 Villans and two Bordars,) and there were 8 Bondmen. It was and worth 6£. Ralph de Todeni, held and Roger of him.
Domesday Survey.

As to the 3rd. or Gloucestershire Icoumb, see 'Icoumb below." The name "Coumb" in Pop. Nich. Tax, included all in Comb Baskerville and Westcote, in the Subsidy Roll, 1 Edw. iii. the name "Comb Baskerville" is used for the same place (part for the whole) and so likewise is "Comb Westcot," in the Nonæ Roll.

The Baskerville family had the lands of Coumb, soon after the Conquest, and it is thought that it was Ralph Baskerville, who held under De Laci, at D. Survey 9 E. ii. Sir Walter Baskerville, was Lord of "Coumb." Bernard Barkerville, when he became a Monk in St. Peter's Abbey, Gloucester, gave to it 1 Hide of Land in Combe, and the gift was confirmed by Walter and Robt. Baskerville, in Abbot Hamelins, time about A.D. 1148. The Baskerville's Dwelling Place was near Gatcomb, and according to tradition there were a Village and Church adjoining it. The House, Church and Village have disappeared, probably when the family left to reside at Icomb place. Notices of Rectors of Combe Baskerville, have been found in Documents; and the Rector of Westcote holds a plot of ground near the supposed site of the Baskerville Church, which plot he considers to have belonged to it. The supposition is not unreasonable, and supports the notion that the Rectory and Church were transferred to the Wescote Proper hamlet.

In the Baskerville family Coumb and Westcote Manors continued until 1 Edw. vi. when James Baskerville sold to T. Sheldon, of Beoley. 1668. His descendants Ralph and George Sheldon, sold this estate in parcels:—

Site of Combe Baskerville Manor and Gatcemb to Barnard from whom B. Barran, who died 1692. (*Church Inscriptions.*) His daughter and heiress carried it to Sir Thos. Littleton, by Marriage. Enfranchisements were made to Harte, Mace, and other Copyholders or Lease-holders. Westcote Manor House, and what remained of Westcote Manor, with the advowson passed successively to .... Dr. Owen, Revd. T. Williams, Dr. Brooks, and Mr. Pantin. Gatcomb, was subsequently sold to Mr. Powell Snell, and by him or his son to Bennet, ... and it has since passed to Mr. Nicholls.

1776.—*At the County Election there Voted as Free-holders in Westcote.*

Bennet, Thomas.
Cook, Richard.
Chapman, William.
Gisborne, Anthony.
Huggins, Samuel.
Johnson, Thomas.
Mayhill, Thomas.
Mace, Lawrence.
Roberts, Joseph.
Stayte, William.
Turner, Francis.

The Names of Chapman, Stayt and Turner, occur in the Poll List for Westcote, at the Election 1811.

No inclosure has been made of the open commonable Lands, although one was attempted some years ago.

II.—*Church.*

Westcote Church is supposed to have been built out of the materials of Comb Baskerville Church. It consists of a Nave, Chancel and Porch with a Tower at the West-end The Chancel and Vestry have been lately rebuilt.

List of Rectors and Patrons of Wescote.

1648.—Dr. Edw. Baskervyle.   Domina Baskervyle.
1566.—Richard Baskervyle.   Walter Baskervyle.
1574.—John Shephard.   Queen Elizabeth.
1577.—Richard Stone.   William Childe.
1629.—Edward Loggin.   John Loggin.
1673.—Thomas Owen.   "   "
1719.—John Davis.   "   "
1742.—Francis Warneford.   Abigail Turvill.
1753.—Thomas Williams.   Mrs. A. Surmon.
1766.—Thomas Brookes.   Thomas Williams.
1774.—Joseph Godwin.   "   "
1775.—Thomas Brookes, D.D.   Thomas Brookes, *Clerk.*
1814.—Thomas Pantin.   "   "
....   William Pantin.
                             J. Wickliffe Pantin.

At Bishop Hooper's Examination Dr. Baskerfeld, was Rector, but was non resident; Garret Grenow, was then Minister, he answered the questions put by the Bishop except that of proving the Articles of Belief. Dame Baskervyle, was then Patroness. and the number of communicants was 56.

There is Village School House lately built near the Church. It is supported cheefly by the Rector. There is a Wesleyan Chapel.

III.—*Taxation, Population, &c.*

Combe Wescote, Subsidy Roll, 1 Edw. iii., 1327.

De Simon de Strode, xiii d.
" Robto. Richard, xii d. ob.
" Willmo. Budde, ix d.
" Willmo. Hulles, xiiii d.ob.
" Thom de Iccumbe, v s.
" Johne. & Willmo. de Iccumbe, v s.
" Rogo. Gurgan, xviii d.
" Willmo. Jarmeyn, ix d.
" Raduo. de Wylton, xv d.
" Robto Inthehurne,xiiiid.q.
" Will.Geffes, iii s. vi d.ob.q.
" Raduo. Robyn, xiiii d.
" Johne atte Welle, ix d.
" Willmo. Skyl, xii d. ob.
De Agnet. Wyllis, xii d.
" Johne. atte Welle, ii s. iii d. ob. q.
" Agnet. q. fuit ux. Nichi. Hugges, xii d.
" Henr. Hugyn, xv d
" Robto Geffes, ii s. i d.
" Hugon. Hulles, xx d.
" Johe. Stephen, xiiii d.
" Robto. Smert, vi d.
" Johne. le Coupere, xii d.
" Luc. de Westhalle, ix d.
" Willmo. Upclive, ix d
" Adamaro Pauncefot. v s. vi d.

prob. Sma. xliiii s. ii d.

Acreage 1495 a.

Population 1831,—188.   1861,—240.   1871,—236.

1815.—Yearly Value of Real Property £1834.

1882.—Estimated Rateable Value £ 2053.

1833-4-5.—Three Years Average Expenditure on Poor 87 £.

In Stow-on-the-Wold Union

ICOMB.

I.—ICOMB (PLACE) AND II.—CHURCH ICOMB.

I.—ICOMBE, is a Poor Law Parish, but no account of it was given in its order owing probably to the circumstance that the Church of Icomb, was then in another County. Now however both Icombes are in Gloucestershire, and it is proper that an account of them should be given.

1.—Icomb in Salemanesburie Hundred (Gloucestershire,) contained two Hides taxed. Culture: Two Carucates in Demesne and 1 in Villenage, (2 Villans and 2 Bordars.) six Bondmen and Women. It was worth 30s. and at the Survey 40s. Yearly.

Durand, the Sheriff held and Walter, of him.
Domesday Survey.

The names of the principal Possessors in the Subsidy Roll, 1 Edw. iii. are Ehaunt, Hamwell and Statherne, the last paying the largest Scot (5s.) This name may be "At the Herne," a name taken from the place of residence. It is written "In the Hurn" in Westcote, Subsidy Roll.

6 Edw. iii.—Roger Blacket and Wife Margaret, held parts of Icomb which Thomas de Icomb, formerly held. Whether, Roger or Margaret derived Title by succession from Thomas de Icombe, does not appear. But the De Icombs, were large Payers here as by the Combe Wescote List in Subsidy Roll, 1 Edw. iii. above given, appears: By the marriage of the Blacketts' Heiress Anne, the House and Estate passed to Roger Baskerville, Lord of the adjacent House and Manor of Combe Baskerville. As to them, *see* "*Church Monuments.*"

From them it passed to Milborn, in like manner. He died leaving only Daughters, to one of whom it went by co-heirship and partition. She married Whitney, of Herefordshire. They were succeeded by Cope, of Oxfordshire, Wm. Cope, "*Church Monuments.*" Henry Cope, was Possessor at Sir R. Atkyns' survey.

1776.—Richard Cope Hopton, of Canon's Frome Herefordshire, was Owner at the County Election.

The Revd. John Parsons Hopton.

Mr. Hambidge, by purchase.

At Rudder's Survey the family were non resident, and the House was occupied by a farmer as it has been ever since, a circumstance to which it owes its preservation. As to this House, *see* "Transactions of Bristol and Gloucestershire Arch'l. Socy. Stow Meeting, 1882."

II.—CHURCH ICOMB, late in Worcestershire.

St. Marys, Worcester, held at Icomb, One hide for the victualling of the Monks. Cultnre: 2 Carucates, and four amongst 4 Villans and 2 Bordars. There were 4 Serfs with 2 Carucates, and 12a. of Meadow. *Domesday Survey.*

Hen. viii.—The Crown by surrender.

Edw. vi.—The Dean and Chapter of Worcester, by exchange with the Crown.

The only freeholds in this Place were the Dean and Chapters Estate, and the Lands of the Rectory. But there were Copyholds for Lives (3 in possession and 3 in reversion with Widows freebench) under fines arbitrary and subject to heriots on death. There is a Court House at which Courts Leet for the Manor were held.

II.—*Church :—*

It consists of a Nave, Chancel, South Transept and Tower therein 2 Bells. The transept was a Chapel or Chantry to the Virgin, endowed by Sir Simon Mylborn. It was the burial place of the Blacket family. It contains a fine effigy of Sir John Blacket, Knight, who died 1431, and his Wife.

The Arms on the Knights tomb are quarterly 1 and 4 a Bend between six trefoils fitché slipped vert for Blacket. 2 & 3, Gules three Battle Axes in pale Or, for Hacklwyt.

Under the Arch in the transept is a slab with matrices which it is supposed were for figures in brass of Ralph

Baskerville and Anne (Blacket,) his Wife.

There are Church Inscriptions on a Monument and Tombs to William Cope, of Icomb, Gloucestershire, Esqr. and Lady Elizabeth Cope, his Wife, Daughter of Fane, Earl of Westmorland. William Cope, died 1691. Lady Elizabeth, died 1669. They had Issue two sons Henry and William and two Daughters—Elizabeth, who married T. Whitney, of Whitney, Herefordshire and Ruchel.

List of Incumbents.

6 Edw. vi.—W. Wye.
.......—......... Willet, was Rector for forty Years.
      He died in 1656.
1662.—Thomas Owen.
1718.—Dennis Payne.
1724.—Thomas Miles.
1733.—Thomas Jenner.
1763.—Thomas Pixell.
1782.—John Harward.

6 Edw. vi.—Houselling Population, 80.

Rectory £6 18 6   Valor Eccl'us.

The Rectory Value 130 £. yearly with Residence.

It had some Glebe.

The Chantry Estate was valued at £6 15 10. in the Valor signed by Bishop Latimer. It was leased to J Lee.

Charities:—10 £. yearly of the 20 £. Yearly by Gift of Col. Cope. see "Stow on the Wold."

III.—*Taxation, Population, &c.*

De Rico. Aperel, xviii d. q.
  * Robto. Capellano, vi d.
  * Elia Eliaunt, ii s.
  * Johne. de Hamwelle, ii s. ob.
  * Johne. Statherne, [At the Hern.] v s.
      prob. Sma. xi s. o. q.

Area 1136 a. whereof Gloucestershire 650 a.

Population :

		1831.	1861.	1871.
Church Icomb,		148.	152.	....
1776, 18 families.				
Gloucestershire Icomb.		...	12.	....

1815.—Annual assessed Value of Real Property in Church Icomb, 618 £.

1882.—Rateable Value County Rate:
  Church Icomb, £681.
  Gloucestershire Icomb, £842.

1833-4-5, Average of three Years Expenditure on Poor Both places :—Icomb, Glouc. 14£.
      Church Icomb, 57 £.

In Stow Union.

WESTERLEIGH.

THE CHURCH is in the deanery of Hawkesbury and is annexed to Pucklechurch. It is a neat building consisting of a Chancel, Nave and Aisles divided by a row of handsome pillars; A neat Gallery at the West-end and a high Tower adorned with Battlements and pinnacles, therein six Musical Bells. On the Gallery "This Gallery erected 1771. Robert Hathaway, and Robert Bryant, *Church Wardens.*" [Now taken away.]

Revd. George Swayne, Rector.

Hugh Smith, *Esqr.*, *Lord* Middleton and Edward Francis Colston, *Esqr.* Proprietors of the Manor.

Annual Account of Marriages, Birth, and Burials, in this Parish.

A. D.	Bir.	Mar.	Bur.	A. D.	Bir.	Mar.	Bur.	A. D.	Bir.	Mar.	Bur.	A. D.	Bir.	Mar	Bur.
1780	42	2	20	1785	57	14	39	1790	41	15	24	1795	48	5	27
1781	41	8	24	1786	57	4	32	1791	52	14	15	1796	50	6	29
1782	53	5	30	1787	38	11	41	1792	41	6	40	1797	55	7	19
1783	41	8	28	1788	50	8	29	1793	54	7	34	1798	62	9	33
1784	40	8	19	1789	55	12	31	1794	63	5	38	1799	48	11	25

BENEFACTIONS TO THE CHURCH AND POOR.

Mr. Edward Hill, in the Year 1619, gave 100 £. since laid on the Purchase of Freehold Lands that now produce about 14 £. a Year, whereby 3 £. is to be paid Yearly for preaching 10 Sermons. 10 £. 10 s. distributed to the Poor on Candlemas day and the Remainder applied towards apprenticing Children. Days appointed for the Preaching of *Mr.* Edward Hill's Ten Sermons :—January—the first ; February—second ; Second Sunday in Lent ; Palm Sunday ; Easter Monday ; Whitson Monday ; Sunday before Midsummerday ; August the fifth ; All Saints day ; St. Stephens day.

Mr. Robert Nailor, 1702; by his Will, charged a certain Tenement and Lands, at *Acton*, with the payment of 5 £. Yearly for ever, for apprenticing a Boy of this Parish.

Sir John Smith, *Bart.* 1715; in compliance with the Charitable Intention of his *Lady* whilst living, charged part of this Manor with the perpetual payment of 20 £. a Year, for endowing two Schools in this Parish to instruct 20 Children Yearly in reading and the Church Catechism.

The *Revd.* Thomas Prigg, *Clerk,* late of this Parish in 1686, gave a large Silver Flaggon Cup and Plate for the Communion.

1726.—*Mr.* Arthur Trewman, Gave ...... 20 £.   1729.—*Mr.* Elias Dolling, the Younger, Gave ...... 5 £.

1730.—*Mr.* John Middleton, Gave ...... 5 £.   1737.—Mary Vowles, Gave ...... 5 £.

To be distributed to and amongst the Poor, at or soon after the Death of the Donors respectively.

1736.—*Mr.* Alexander Ready, Gave .... 5 £.

[Daniel Deverell, gave a Legacy of 220 £. for apprenticing poor Children of the Parish.]

INSCRIPTIONS IN THE CHURCH.

CHANCEL.

ON MONUMENTS.

Arms:—Argent, a fess wavy between three Lions' jambs erased & bendways Sable.—CLENT. *impaling* Or. a fess Gules between three Elephant's heads erased Sable.—FOUNTAIN.

Near this Place is interr'd EDWARD CLENT, *Esqr.* Son of LITTLETON CLENT. of *Knightswick* in the County of *Worcester, Esqr.* He married ELIZTH. Daughter of ANDREW FOUNTAIN, of *Narford* in the County of *Norfolk, Esqr.* and Sister to *Sir* ANDREW FOUNTAIN, *Knt.* By her he had two Sons and two Daughters, of whom ELIZABETH, only survived him. He died lamented by all who knew him September the 19, 1735, Aged 58 Years.

To the Memory of ELIAS DOLLING, of this Parish, who departed this Life, the 18*th.* day of Sept. 1728. Aged 55 Years.

Arms:—Per pale Argent, and Gules a Lion rampant Sable.—ROBERTS. *impaling* Sable a Bend Argent, on a canton of the second, a Leopard's face, of the first.

In Memoriam THOMÆ ROBERTS, *Armigeri,* hujus Manerij dudum Domini, Qui objt. Anno Domini 1673, Julij 26 o. Ætatis suæ 49 o.

Arms:—Argent, a Lion rampant regardent Azure, between three Trefoils slipt Vert.—PRIGG.

Exuvias Mortalitatis suæ infra deposuit RICHARDUS PRIGG, *Gen.* nuper de Civitate *Bristol,* Pharmacopæus. Vir apto præditus Ingenio, Fortuna eminens, Arte sua præstans, Amicorum Solatium dum vixit, Mortuus, Suspirium. Natus fuit in hac Parochia, Denatus vero in Civitate prædicta,
Anno. { Ætatis 65, Salutis nostræ, 1723.

Arms:—Ermine a Saltire Gules. JONES. *impaling* ROBERTS, *as before.*

To the Memory of his Dear Mother *Mrs.* MARY JONES, Wife of WILLIAM JONES, *Esqr.* and Daughter of THOMAS ROBERTS, *Esqr.* Lord of this Manor. Shee deceased October 22*nd.*
Anno. { Domini 1661, Ætatis suæ 38.

A tender Mother and a Loving Wife, Composed of Meekness, free from Pride and Strife, That lived unspotted, modest, just and kind, The Poor relieved with a willing mind, Such was this matron whilst she liv'd on Earth, Who also brought Twelve Children to their Birth, Five went before, Shee left behind her seven, God grant they meet their Mother all in Heaven.

THOMAS JONES, filius posuit.

ON BRASS PLATES ON FLAT STONES.

P. M. RICHARDI HOLLISTER, eximii Ecclesiæ Alumni et Columeniæ qui objit. Maij 10o. 1659, Æt. 47. Epitaphium Vir virtute virens, Christi pugil, alter Elias, Prudens, fidus homo, jam requiescit humo. Mater humus domus est, tenebrosa nocte, sed orto, Sole, datur sanctis luce tenenda Domus.

Here lyeth the Body of *Mrs.* MARY JONES, Wife of WILLIAM JONES, *Esqr.* and Daughter of THOMAS ROBERTS, *Esqr.* Lord of the Manor.

Here lyeth the Body of *Capt.* JOHN ROBERTS, *Esqr.* sometime Lord of this Manor, who deceased the 15 of June, A. D. 1624, being Aged 69 Years.

Here lyeth the Body of *Mrs.* SARAH SWAYNE, of this Parish, *Widow,* who died May 14, 1728, Aged 67 Years.

ON FLAT STONES.

Here lyeth the Body of THOMAS ROBERTS, *Esqr.* late Lord of this Manor, who deceased the 16 of Febr. An. Di. 1655, being Aged 72 Years.

Here lyeth the Body of HENRY ROBERTS, *Gent.* Son of the aforesaid THOMAS ROBERTS, who deceased the 16*th.* day of May, An. Dni. 1654, being Aged 29 Years.

In Memory of ELIZABETH, Wife of JOHN GULLOCK, *Gent.* who died

Decr. 20, 1728 Aged 76 Years. Also of FRANCES, Daughter of John and ELIZABETH GULLOCK, who died June 8, 1736, Aged 1.

STEPHEN, Son of WILLIAM CLARKE, *Esqr.* of *Serridge* in this Parish, was interred here 24 February 1770, Aged 7 Years, and 7 Months. Also SUSANNA CRESWICKE PEARSON, Daughter of SAMUEL PEARSON, of *May's Hill* in this Parish, who died 17 of January 1799, Aged 20 Weeks.

Here lyeth the Body of JOHN USHER, of this Parish, *Gent.* who deceased Augt. 6, 1658, being Aged 82 Years.

Here lyeth the Body of *Mrs.* MARIE USHER, the Relict of JOHN USHER, late of this Parish, *Gent.* She deceased Febr. 6, A. D. 1669, Æt. suæ 87.

Here lyeth the Body of *Mrs.* URSULA BACK, of *Exeter* in the County of *Devon.* who deceased June 12, 1676.

NORTH AISLE.

In Memory of MARY, Wife of HENRY WICKHAM, who was buried the 7 of Nov. 1753, Aged 93 Years.

Here lyeth the Body of WILLIAM HOLLISTER, of *Blackberries,* who deceased the 12 day of May 1627, of his Age 84. Also of JOANE, late Wife and *Widow* of the said WILLIAM HOLLISTER, who died the 17 day of February .... of her Age 7...

In Memory of DANIEL, Son of DANIEL and HANNAH WHITE, of the Parish of *St. Stephen* in the City of *Bristol,* who died 25 August 1749, Aged 7 Months. Also HANNAH WHITE, who died 15 July 1751, Aged 24 Years. Also DANIEL WHITE, who departed this Life, March 1, 1786, Aged 62 Years.

THOMAS HOBBS, 1700. SARAH HOBBS, 1719.

Here resteth the Body of
JACOB HOLLISTER, *Yeoman,*
who deceased the 3 day of
November, Ano. Dni. 1622.
Also the Body of ANNE, the
Daughter of JACOB and ELIZABETH,
HOLLISTER, of *Nibley* in this Parish,
who died 2 January 1722, in the
63 Year of her Age.

Here lyeth the Body of
HANNAH, the Wife of
JOHN COOK, of this Parish,
Yeoman, whe died Febr. 11, 1747,
Aged 44 Years.

Depositum SAMUELIS PILL,
Nuper ex hac Parochia, Gen.
qui obijt Sept. A. Dni. 1676,
Ætatis suæ 52.
Perit Matri
non vita sed mortalitas,
ELIZABETH PILL, (SamueleDefuncto,)
per Annos 26 Vidua matrona fidelis,
ob. Maij 19o. 1702.

Under this Stone lieth interred
the Body of RICHARD DAVIS,
of this Parish, *Yeoman,*
who died April 28, 1743,
Aged 80 Years.
Also MARY, Daughter of the said
RICHARD DAVIS,
by HANNAH, his Wife,
who died 2 Nov. 1731,
Aged 3 Years and 8 Months.
Also under this Stone was buried
THOMAS, the Son of *Revd.* Mr.
JOHN PILL, who died Jany. 4, 1718,
in the 17 Year of his Age.
Also JOHN DAVIS, of this Parish,
who died July 1, 1775,
Aged 44 Years.

In Memory of
MARY, Daughter of EMERSON
and ANN GERISH, who died
Aug. 10, 1782, Aged 5 Years.
ANN, Wife of the said
EMERSON GERISH,
who died July 29, 1797,
Aged 43 Years.

In Memory of
MARGARET, Daughter of EMERSON
and ANN GERISH, of this Parish,
who died March 7, 1788,
Aged 12 Years and 6 Months.

In Memory of
JAMES HOWELL, Son of
NICHOLAS and CATHERINE HOWELL,
of the Parish of *Praston* in the
County of *Somerset,*
who departed this Life,
Jany. 11, A. D. 1724,
Aged about 44 Years.

SOUTH AISLE.

ON FLAT STONES.

Here lyeth the Body of
URSULA the Wife of

THOMAS ROBERTS, *Esqr.*
of this Parish, who died
Nov. 18, 1676.

Here lyeth the Body of
ARTHUR TREWMAN,
of this Parish, *Gent.* who died
26 Decr. 1651, Aged 52 Years.
Also the Body of SAMUEL TREWMAN,
Son of ARTHUR TREWMAN, *Gent.*
He died 31 March 1707,
Aged 86 Years.
Here lyeth the Body of
ARTHUR TREWMAN, *Gent.*
who died 2 of March 1726,
Aged 48 Years.

Here lieth the Body of
.... second Wife of
SAMUEL TREWMAN,
of this Parish, *Yeoman,* who died
16 May An. Dn. 1702, Ætatis 83.

Here lyeth the Body of
THOMAS COOK, of the Parish of
Frampton Cotterell,
who departed this Life, the
15 day of June 1739,
Aged 49 Years.
Also MARTHA, Wife of THOMAS
COOK, who died 21 August 1740,
Aged near 50 Years.

Hic jacet JOHANNES EDMONDS, *Gen.*
de *May Hill,* Qui obijt 24o. Maij,
Anno Dni. 1707, Ætatis 64.

ON A BRASS PLATE.

Here lyeth the Body of
GEORGE USHER, of this Parish,
Gent. who departed this Life, the
fourth day of June, A. D. 1702,
Ætatis suæ 84.

CHURCH YARD.

ON TOMBS.

This Tomb is erected to the
Memory of ANTHONY BROWN,
the Elder Gent. He died
Jany. 4, 1758, Aged 71.
Also EDITH BROWN, his Wife,
She died 21 Oct. 1754, Aged 82.

In Memory of
ANTHONY BROWN, *Gent.*
died 30 Nov. 1749,
Aged 37 Years.
Also two of his Children,
by MARY, his Wife, JOHN and
MARY, who died Young.

Here lyeth NATHANIEL FRIEND,
Senr. (Son of JOHN FRIEND,)
who died May 21, A. D. 1680,
Æt. suæ 84.
ALICE, late Wife of NATHANIEL
FRIEND, *Junr.* who died
Aug. 31, 1680, Ætatis 53.

Here lyeth the Body of
WILLIAM BELSIRE, of this Parish,
who died 1 Decr. 1730,
Aged 36 Years.
Depositum JONATHAN SIMONDS,
nuper ex hac Parochiâ qui obijt
Augt. 9o. A. D. 1762, Æt. 30
ROBERT SIMMONDS,
was likewise buried under this Tomb,
7 Sept. 1763, Aged 52 Years.
HESTER, *Widow* of the above said
ROBERT SIMMONDS, was buried
13 Sept. 1765, Aged 74 Years.

In Memory of
ROBERT SEYMOUR,
who died 26 May 1743,
Aged 64 Years.
Also PRICE SEYMOUR, Son of
ROBERT SEYMOUR, who died
18 July 1737, Aged 36 Years.
Also of SARAH, Wife of
THOMAS SEYMOUR, of the Parish
of *St. Nicholas, Bristol, Woollen
Draper,* who departed this Life,
the 10 of July 1751,
Aged 51 Years.
Also the remains of the said
THOMAS SEYMOUR,
who died 19 July 1773,
Aged 64 Years.
Also of MARTHA, Daughter of
THOMAS and ANN SEYMOUR,
who died in 1763, an infant.

Beneath this Tomb here lyeth
the Body of WILLIAM PARKER,
of *French hay* in the Parish of
Winterbourn, who departed this Life,
Nov. 21, 1751, Aged 48 Years.
MARY PARKER, *Widow and relict*
of the said WILLIAM PARKER,
who died Febr. 19, 1784,
Aged 79 Years.
WILLIAM, their Son, who died
March 21, 1732, Aged 16 Weeks.
Also ANN, Daughter of
WILLIAM and MARY PARKER,
who died 8 June 1757,
Aged 17 Years.
Also of SARAH, their Daughter,
who died in 1760, Aged 22 Years.

Here lieth the Body of
JOSEPH GIBBS, of this Parish,
who died the 13 of March 1753,
Aged 47 Years.
Also SARAH NICHOLAS, *Relict* of the
JOSEPH GIBBS, who died
27 May 1770, Aged 62 Years.
Also HANNAH, their Daughter,
who died in 1746, an Infant.

In Memory of
WILLIAM GIBBS, of this Parish,
Malster and Baker, who died
11 of December 1777, Aged 42.
HANNAH GIBBS, his *Widow,*
who died Jany. 12, 1783,
Aged 47 Years.

In Memory of
THOMAS ANDREWS,
of *Chipping Sodbury,* who died
the 30 of April 1746, Aged 31.
And of ELIZABETH, his Wife,

Daughter of JOHN ALSOP,
of this Parish, *Yeoman*, who died
Febr. 20, 1744, Aged 29 Years.

In Memory of
JOHN ALSOP, of this Parish,
Yeoman, who died 29 Jany. 1756,
Aged 77 Years.
MARY, *Widow and relict*, of
JOHN ALSOP, died 11 Febr. 1771,
Aged 85 Years.

WILLIAM ALSOP, of this Parish,
died 27 Decr. 1768, in the
60 Year of his Age.

RACHEL, Wife of JOHN ALSOP, *Junr.*
buried 13 June 1748, Aged 49.
JOHN ALSOP, was buried the
14 June 17..., Aged 58 Years.

Deposited under this Tomb is the
Body of JOHN WICKHAM,
of this Parish, *Yeoman*,
who died Decr. 13, 1772,
Aged 71 Years.
MARTHA, Wife of JOHN WICKHAM,
buried 24 Febr. 1740,
Aged about 45 Years.
Also of MARY, Daughter of
JOHN and ANN WICKHAM,
who died in 1758, an Infant.

Near this Tomb lieth the Body of
WILLIAM HUMPHRIES,
of this Parish, who was
buried the 10 of Febr. 1750,
Aged 33 Years.
THOMAS HUMPHRIES, the *Elder*,
who died the 1 Sept. 1729,
Aged 54 Years.
And of SARAH, his Wife,
who died 20 April 1746,
Aged 72 Years.
ELIZABETH, Daughter of THOMAS
HUMPHRIES, by SARAH, his Wife,
buried 20 May 1741,
Aged 39 Years.
MARTHA, Wife of JACOB COPE,
Daughter of the aforesaid
THOMAS HUMPHRIES,
by SARAH, his Wife, who was
buried 4 Febr. 1743,
Aged 31 Years.
Here lyeth the Body of
AMEY, Wife of JOSEPH MILLETT,
of this Parish, who died
30 April 1747, Aged 58 Years.

Uuner this Tomb lyeth the Body
of WILLIAM JAMES, *Senr.*
who was buried Oct. 25, A. D. 1726,
Aged about 68 Years.

Underneath lie the Body of
ABRAHAM HIGHNAM,
of this Parish, *Gent.*
He was buried 9 October 1756,
in the 77 Year of his Age.
Likewise EDITH, Wife of
ABRAHAM HIGHNAM, *Gent.*

who was buried 14 July 1749,
in the 70 Year of her Age.
ELIZABETH, Wife of THOMAS
BAYLIS, of this Parish,
who died July 4, 1793, Aged 49.
EMMA, their Dughter, who died
May 19 1792, Aged 4.

In Memory of
ARTHUR PARKER, who was
buried March 28, 1736,
Aged 72 Years.
Also of JOHN PARKER,
who was buried Decr. 23, 1739,
Aged 32 Years
Also of ELIZABETH PARKER,
Widow, who was buried 6 Augt.
1752, Aged 59 Years.
In Memory of
ISAAC PARKER, of the Parish,
of *Tytherington*, who died
24 May 1794, in the
85 Year of his Age.
Also of MARY, Wife of ISAAC
PARKER, who was buried
Jany. 25, 1744 Aged 32 Years.

In Memory of
ELIZABETH, *Relict* of JOHN PORTER,
of *Almondsbury*, Daughter of
ARTHUR and ELIZABETH PARKER,
who died May 21, 1767,
Aged 72 Years.

In Memory of
THOMAS SMALCOMB,
who was buried 25 Oct. 1744.
Also of ELIZABETH, his Wife,
who was buried 4 day of May 1714,
Also of SARAH, their Daughter,
who was buried in May 1748,
Aged 47 Years.
MARY, her Sister, was buried 1710,
Aged 20 Years.

WILLIAM PRIGG,
1643.
ELEANOR, his Wife,
1628.
Here also lye the Bodies of
THOMAS PRIGGE, *Yeoman*,
Son of WILLIAM PRIGGE, aforesaid
who deceased Nov. 2, 1676,
Ætatis 59.
SARAH, Daughter of THOMAS
PRIGGE, died May 26, 1674,
Aged 22 Years.
Also of MARY, the *Relict* of
THOMAS PRIGG, buried Nov. 9,
1717, Aged 93 Years.
Also of ELIZABETH PRIGG,
of *Titherington*, who died
28 Decr. 1773, Aged 86 Years.
SAMUEL, Son of WILLIAM PRIGG,
died 3 May 1725, Aged 39 Years.
THOMAS, Son of WILLIAM PRIGG,
died 14 Nov. 1743, Aged 60 Years.

THOMAS BAYLIS, to whose
Memory this Tomb is erected
was buried 23 June 1744,
Aged 43 Years.
HANNAH BROWN, Daughter of
ROBERT BAYLIS, of this Parish,
by SARAH, his Wife,
born 5 Sept. 1758, }
died 22 Mar. 1766. } buried here.

In Memory of
ROBERT BATTEN, of the Parish
of *Iron Acton*, *Yeoman*,
who was buried here the 18 Febr.
1745, in the 53 Year of his Age.

Here lies
JOHN PARKER, of this Parish,
who died April 22, 1701.
Also the Body of TABITHA,
the Daughter of the aforesaid
JOHN and ANN PARKER,
who died 4 June 1759,
Aged 72 Years.

Here lyeth the Body of
THOMAS, the Son of THOMAS
DEVERELL, *Junr.* of the Parish
of *Wapley*, *Yeoman*, by HESTER,
his Wife, who was buried
19 July 1719, Aged 16 Weeks.
Here also lyeth a second Son,
of the same Name as above,
who died 30 June 1776,
Aged 55 Years.

Here lyeth the Body of
ELIZABETH, late Wife of
THOMAS DEVERELL, of *Wapley*,
Yeoman, who died June 4, 1717,
Aged 58 Years.
Also THOMAS DEVERELL,
of this Parish, Son of the above
THOMAS and ELIZABETH DEVERELL,
who died Oct 24, 1741,
Aged 47 Years.
Also HESTER, Wife of the above
THOMAS DEVERELL,
who died March 17, 1769,
Aged 76 Years.

Here lyeth the Body of
MATTHEW RODBORN,
of this Parish, *Yeoman*,
who died Febr. 20, 1744,
Aged 67 Years.
ELIZABETH, his Wife,
died June 7, 1761, Aged 78 Years.

In Memory of
THOMAS MIDDLETON,
of this Parish, *Yeoman*,
who died Nov. 25, 1729,
in the 75th Year of his Age.
ANNE, his Wife was buried
Febr. 27, 1701, in the
39 Year of her Age.
In Memory of
SAMUEL VOWLES, *Apothecary*,
of the City of *Bristol*, Son of
SAMUEL and MARY VOWLES,
of this Parish, who died
5 March 17..., Aged 20 Years.
MARY, Wife of FRANCIS OWEN,
of the City of *Bristol*, and
Daughter of SAMUEL and
MARY VOWLES, who departed
this Life, 30 Nov. 1769,
Aged 36 Years.

Here lyeth the Body of
THOMAS GREGORY,
who was buried 27 Febr. 1749,
Aged 70 Years.

ELIZABETH, *Widow* of THOMAS
GREGORY, who died March 12, 1758,
Aged 80 Years.

ARTHUR GREGORY,
died Sept. 28, 1773, Aged 74 Years.
Also SUSANNAH, his Daughter,
died August 1, 1770,
Aged 20 Years.
THOMAS, his Son, died an Infant.
HANNAH, Daughter of ARTHUR
and PHEBE GREGORY, of this Parish,
died 20 March, 1756,
Aged 22 Years.
ELIZABETH, their Daughter,
died December 8, 1759,
Aged 21 Years.

Here lieth the Body of
THOMAS, the Son of DANIEL and
SUSANNAH DEVERELL, of this
Parish, who died 26 Febr. 1787,
in the 40 Year of his Age.

Here lyeth the Body of
DANIEL DEVERELL, of the Parish
of *St. Nicholas, Depford* in the
County of *Kent*, a Native of this
Parish, who died 15 March 1783,
Aged 34 Years.

Here lyeth the Body of
DANIEL DEVERELL, of this Parish,
who died April 18, 1789,
Aged 66 Years.

In Memory of
THOMAS NEALE, of this Parish,
who departed this Life,
Febr. 22, 1799, Aged 76 Years.
ANN, his Wife, died July 22, 1790,
Aged 65 Years.
MARY, their Daughter, died
Dec. 26, 1794, Aged 22 Years.

In Memory of
WILLIAM PULLIN, who died
July 30, 1767, Aged 71 Years.
Also MARY, his second Wife,
who died Decr. 28, 1767,
Aged 80 Years.
Likewise DAVID JONES, who died
Febr. 15, 1798, Aged 78 Years.
Also MARY, his Wife, who died
Jany. 10, 1782, Aged 52 Years.

In Memory of
JONATHAN GRIFFIN, of this Parish,
Yeoman, who departed this Life,
June 16, 1789, Aged 79 Years.
SARAH, his Wife, who died
Augt. 19, 1790, Aged 80 Years.
GRIFFIN GIBBES, of this Parish,
Grandson of the said JONATHAN
GRIFFIN, *Yeoman*, who died
June 20, 1790, Aged 40 Years.
SARAH, Daughter of GRIFFIN GIBBS,
by MARY, his Wife, died
July 13, 1793, Aged 20 Weeks.
And JONATHAN GRIFFIN GIBBS,
their Son, who died Oct. 24, 1794,
Aged 20 Weeks.

In Memoriam
THOMÆ DE SANCTO MAURO,
Civitatis *Bristoliensis, Generosi,* Filii,
ROBERTI DE SANCTO MAURO,
qui obiit 19o. Jul. A. D. 1773,
Ætatis suæ 64.
Etiam MARTHÆ, Filiæ supra dicti
THOMÆ DE SANCTO MAURO,
et ANNÆ Uxoris ejus, qui
obiit 22o. Decembris, A. D. 1763,
Ætatis suæ 3.
GEORGIUS PENROSE DE SANCTO MAURO,
filius THOMÆ DE SANCTO MAURO,
hoc monumentum ante delapsum
restauravit. A. D. 1786.
In Memoriam
ROBERTI DE SANCTO MAURO,
parochiæ hujus *Generosi,* qui
obiit 26 Martii. A. D. 1743,
Ætatis suæ 61.
Etiam PRYCE DE SANCTO MAURO,
Civitatis *Bathoniæ, Generosi,*
Filii ejus qui obiit A. D. 1757,
Ætatis suæ 36.

Arms:—Or. on a Cross Azure
between four Ermine spots Sable,
five Mulletts, Argent.
Crest:—a Cock Argent, legged &
beaked Gules.

Sacred to the Memory of
SARAH, Wife of ROBERT BAYLIS,
of the Parish of *Stapleton,*
(late of this Parish,)
whose remains are deposited under
this Tomb,
She died Sept. 6, 1800, Aged 64.
Sincerely regretted by her Relatives,
and Friends for those Virtues which
constituts the true Christian.

In Memory of
ANN, Daughter of DANIEL and

HANNAH ROLPH, of this Parish,
who died Febr. 24, 1746,
in her Infancy.
HANNAH, their Daughter,
died June 1, 1757, Aged 4 Months.
BETTY, their Daughter, who died
Jany. 21, 1778, Aged 22 Years.
Also the aforesaid DANIEL
ROLPH, *Yeoman,* died Decr. 4, 1786,
Aged 70 Years.

In Memory of
THOMAS HATHWAY, *Senr.*
of this Parish, *Yeoman,*
who departed this Life,
Sept. 15, 1789, Aged 79 Years.
MARY, his Wife, died Jany. 2. 1790,
Aged 60 Years.
ELIZABETH, Wife of JOHN PARKER,
and Daughter of THOMAS and
MARY HATHWAY, of this Parish,
died Oct. 3, 1791, Aged 50 Years.

To the Memory of
SARAH, the Wife of ISAAC PARKER,
of this Parish, who died
Febr. 3, 1764, Aged 52 Years.

In Memory of
ROBERT DREW, who died
March 24, 1780, Aged 48 Years.

In Memory of
CHARLES EDWARDS, of this Parish,
who died May 20, 1788, Aged 33.
MARY, Daughter of the aforesaid
CHARLES EDWARDS, by ANN,
his Wife, died Oct. 2, 1779,
Aged 8 Weeks.
RODNEY, their Son, died
Decr. 25, 1795, Aged 15 Years.

Beneath this Tomb were interr'd
the remains of ANN, the late
Wife of SAMUEL BELSIRE,
she died the 23rd. day of Jany. 1781,
in the 67 Year of her Age.
Also the aforesaid SAMUEL BELSIRE,
of this Parish, died the 6th. day of
Novr. 1787, in the 76 Year
of his Age. SAMUEL, their Son,
died June 7, 1760, Aged 12 Years.

To the Memory of
SAMPSON COOK, of this Parish,
who died Augt. 4, 1794,
Aged 59 Years,

HEAD STONES.

	Died.		Aged.		Died.	Aged.
John Holder	25 Febr.	1788	66	Julinn, his Wife	27 April 1781	64
Mary, his Daughter and Wife of William Kinard	28 Nov.	1791	34	Elizabeth Powder, *Spinster* ...	18 Sept. 1800	55
				William King	30 March 1801	23
John Turner	19 Nov.	1756	72	Mary, Wife of Daniel Crease	19 Decr. 1792	81
Mary, his Wife	24 Sept.	1763	75	Robert Wright	7 Sept. 1775	80
Mary, Wife of George Short ...	30 Jany.	1775	56	Elizabeth, his Wife	7 Oct. 1778	81
Joseph Cook	30 Jany.	1757	84	Thomas Parker	3 March 1761	65
Mary, his Wife	2 May	1754	66	Ann, his Wife	19 Sept. 1769	55
Isaac Dixon	24 Augt.	1783	68	Betty Llewellin	19 May 1796	57
Catharine, his Wife	12 Decr.	1779	72	John Wait	28 Oct. 1789	62
Charles Hill	29 Jany.	1761	73	James Dando	25 Oct. 1771	45
Elizabeth, Wife of William Higgs	20 July	1767	36	Elizabeth, his Wife	6 May 1772	80
Thomas Isaac *Junr.*	30 March	1777	84	Charles Hale	29 March 1780	59
Hannah, his Wife	29 Sept.	1774	71	Hannah, his Wife	26 April 1780	24
Sarah, Wife of Charles Godwin	5 Oct.	1792	76	William Llewellin	12 Jany. 1785	78
Edward Russell	10 March	1792	60	Sarah, his Wife	2 Decr. 1775	68
Betty, his Daughter	24 March	1796	29	Stephen Alsop	17 Febr. 1787	71
Sarah, Wife of John Vowles ...	24 Sept.	1727	82	Elizabeth, his Wife	8 Febr. 1793	82
John Vowles	12 April	1770	42	William Alsop	27 Decr. 1768	60
Ann, his Wife	8 May	1777	53	Mary, his Wife	21 Jany. 1791	79
John Sheal	10 Jany.	1794	83	William Russell	3 Febr. 1775	70

WESTERLEIGH.

I.—*Estates :*

Westerleigh was a member of the great Manor of Pucklechurch, which belonged to Glastonbury Abbey.

The Bishop of Bath and Wells, acquired, by way of barter for certain episcopal rights the Manor of Westerleigh, of the Abbey.

King Edward vi. by exchange with the Bishop.

2 & 3 Ph. & M.—Sir Nicholas Pointz, by Crown Grant.

John Roberts, by purchase from Pointz

In the Roberts' family, it continued for several generations. *see Church Inscriptions.*

M. 18 Eliz.—John Roberts, gent. was *Plaintiff.*, and Thomas Chester, *Deforciant, in a Fine.*

Easter 28 Eliz.—Earl of Ormond, was *Plaintiff.*, and George Roberts, *Deforciant, in a Fine.*

From Roberts, by marriage with the Heiress, to Jones. *see "Church Inscriptions."*

1680.—Samuel Astry, by purchase.

1708.—His three Daughters and Coheiresses succeeded: 1. Elizabeth, married to Sir John Smyth, of Long Ashton, Bart. 2. Diana, married to Richard Orlebar. 3. Arabella, married to Earl of Suffolk. From them the devolution was as the Manor Westbury upon Trym, which see.

The "Park" belonged to Whitmore.

May's Hill great House and Say's Court Farm belonged to the Manor Estates; the first is still in the name of Smyth and the latter in that of Colston.

Surridge Messuage, Orchard, Wood, &c. 1 Edw. iii. John de Shyrugg, paid to the Subsidy.

6 Hen. vii.—Richard Foster, Esqr. son and heir of Rd. Foster, of Little Sodbury, held; From him John Walshe;

1548.—Hugh Denys, from Sir John Walshe, and Morys, his son and heir, by Ann Poyntz. In the Denys' family it passed in succession to John, Henry, John, and Wm. Denys.

14 Eliz.—John Dennis, obtained a Grant from the Crown of the Chapal of Westerleigh, and a Messuage called Sherwick, (Surridge.) William Dennis, left Daughters Coheiresses.

1769.—Sir Alexander Cuming, and Wife Elizabeth, one of them took the Surridge Estate by Partition.

1770.—Clarke, of Surridge, is named in "*Church Inscriptions.*"

Several places can be identified with Names in the *Subsidy Roll* 1 Edw. iii.

Wooton End :—Nich. de Wotton.

Nubley or Nibley :—John de Nubbeley, Hollister, of Nibley and Blackberries, occurs in *Church Inscriptions* and in *Wills, at Gloucester* 1601, 1603.

Henfield farm :—Alan de Enefeld.

Stover :—Thomas atte Stow.

Blackleaze : Walter Blacklegh.

1556.—Thomas Were, and 40a. Land.

Rodford farm :—

1 Edw. iii.—Thomas and Edward Rodford.

Wickham :—is an antient name here.

1544.—Robert Wicam, *Wills at Gloucester*, and *see Ch. Inscriptions.*

Kendalshire was the name of a Common.

Coal Pit Heath is a Colliery District.

18a. of Heath held of the Bishop of Bath and Wells:

7 E. iii.—Walter Gasslyne.

William, his son and heir.   *Esch.*

20 Edw. iii—William, died leaving Juliana, Wife of George de Stawell, his sister and heir.

1655.—Among the Compounders for their Estates in the time of the Common Wealth was Richard Hobbs, of Westerleigh, and *see* "Tytherington.

T. 13 Geo. i.—Thomas Edwards, levied a fine of Lands in Westerleigh.

The family of Belsire, was seated here and at Yate.

1776.—At the County Election only three Freeholders of Westerleigh, voted namely Adderley, George, Nicholls, Gregory, and Tucker Arthur.

1811.—At the County Election, only two Westerleigh, Freeholders, voted, namely Cole Richard, and Parker Robert.

The greater part of the Parish is in the possession or under Lease for Lives or Years from the Lords of the Manor and in the Registers of County Voters since the Reform Act of 1832, the Lifeholders form a numerous class, 32 in 1832.

II.—*Church :*—

It is a Chapelry to Pucklechurch.

Crown Grant of Chapel of Westerleigh, to John Dennis, (*see* above.)

Patrons : Dean and Chapter of Wells.

List of Incumbents and Patrons of Pucklchurch, Westerleigh and Abston.

Incumbents.	Patrons.
1548.—Henry Bancks.	Dean and Chap. of
1578.—William Billing.	Wells.
1594.—John Trubshaw.	Do.
1579.—George Edwards.	Do.
1635.—Thomas Poel.	Do.
1663.—John Knowles.	Do.
1697.—Barthol. Mountford.	Do.
1684.—Henry Dutton.	Do.
1695.—John Davis.	Do.
1704.—Henry Berrow.	Do.
1724.—Henry Gandy.	Do.
1768.—George Swayne.	Do.
1778.—George Swayne, *Junr.*	Do.

Coal pit Heath is an Ecclesiastical district formed under the Church Building Acts consisting of part of Westerleigh and part of Frampton Cotterell. It is a Vicarage of the Value of 150£. a Year, in the Patronage of the Bishop of the Diocese.

III.—*Taxation, Population, &c.*

Westerleigh, Subsidy Roll, 1 EDW. iii., 1327.

De Robto. .... s. vi d.	Rico. atte Assh, xxi d.
Rico. atte Lude, viii s. vid.	Willo. Nicholes, vi d.
Johe de Nubbeleye, xii d.	Nicho. de Wotton, xx d.
Alic. Est, xviii d.	Alano de Euefeld, xx d.
Dulcia Vppehull, iiii s.	Johe. Hope, xii d.
Alic. Carpenter, ii s. iii d.	Johe. atte Venne, vi d.
Nicho. de Radeforde, ii s.	Adam Reol, vi d.
Johe. Parch. vi d.	Thom. atte Stor. ii s. vi d.
Thom. de Radeforde, vi s. ix d.	Thom. Okeford, ii s. vi d.
Adam Andreu, xii d.	Johe. Lyner, vi d.
Rogo. Willam, vi d.	Willo. atte Style, vi d.
Johe. atte Strete, vi d.	Robto. Pitman, vi d.
Willo. Ferthinge, vi d.	Thom. atte Berewe, xii d.
Thom. Walt's. iiii s. iii d. ob. q.	Johe. atte Berewe, xii d.
Walto. Blackb'gh. ii s.	Thom. Peris, xii d.
Thom. Chaynel, xvi d.	Rico. Dudemor, iii s. iii d.
Johe. de Shyrugg, ii s.	Jul. Shirugg, vi s. iii d.
Johe. Roy's. ii s. ii d.	Thom. atte Hulle, iiii s.
Alic. la White,ii s. i d.ob.q.	Willo. Corpe, vi d.
Willo. Haywadeby, xvi d.	Johe. de Thist'le. iii s. vi d.
	Thom. Thist'le. iii s. vi d.

prob. Sma. iiii *li.* v s. x *d. ob.*

Acreage 3860 a.

Population 1801,—1582. 1831.—1709. 1871,—1469.

In 1815. Annual Value of Real Property 10,889 £.

1882.—Rateable Value £11,133.

1833-4-5. Average of three Years Expenditure on Poor £859.

In Chipping Sodbury Union.

Edward Fowler, Bishop of Gloucester, was born in this Parish, the son of the Minister or Curate here, 1632. He was educated at the College School, Gloucester and of Corpus Christi College, Oxford. He was ejected for Nonconformity from a Benefice he held, but afterwards conformed and became, 1678, Rector of All Hallows' Bread Street and Vicar of St. Giles Cripplegate, London. He refused to read the Declaration of James ii. for Liberty of Conscience 1691, He was appointed Bishop of Gloucester, on the deprivation of Frampton, the Non Juror. He died, 1714, at Chelsea and was buried at Hendon.

He published several Works. Amongst them are the "Design of Christianity" reprinted in the Tracts of Bishop Watson. "Libertas Evangelica." Sermons:—Thanksgiving on the King's (William iii.) escape from Assassination, 1690. And at Guildhall Chapel on the Victories of Ld. Marlborough, 1706. Tracts:—On the Church of England, symbolizing with the Church of Rome. On the Papists objecton against Scripture for its obscurity.

WESTON BIRT.

THE Church consists of a Chancel, Nave, and two small Cross Aisles, and an embattled Tower at the West-end, containing two Bells.

MR. HOLFORD, LORD OF THE MANOR,

whose house is on the South side of the Church Yard.

Revd. ... . SAVAGE, *Rector.*

INSCRIPTIONS IN THE CHURCH.

CHANCEL.
FLAT STONES.

Here lyeth the Body of
WILLIAM STILL, late *Rector* of
Weston Birt, who departed this
Life the 17 day of December
Annoq. Domini 1694, Ætatis 65.
Here also lies the Body of
FRANCES STILL, *Spinster*,
daughter of the *Revd.* JOHN STILL,
who died the 22 day of January
A. D. 1739, in the 78*th.*
Year of her Age.

Here lyeth the Body of
CARISTOPHER LEE, late *Rector*
of this Parish, who was buried the
1*st.* day of March 1654.

CHURCH YARD.
ON A MONUMENT AGAINST EAST
WALL OF THE CROSS ISLE.

Before this Place lieth interred
the Body of BETTY, the Wife of
STEPHEN TUGWELL, of this Parish
who departed this Life, the
15 day of September 1768,
Aged 51 Years.
STEPHEN TUGWELL, of ys. Place *Yeoman,*
Died 12 May 1771, Aged 60 Years.
STEPHEN TUGWELL,
Grandson of the above, died in
London, 3rd. day of Decr. 1796,
Aged 17 Years.

TOMBS.

Under this Tomb resteth the Body
of ROBERT ANDREWS, *Yeoman,*
who departed this Life the
14 day of February 1714,
Aged 61 Years.
Also the Body of RACHEL, the
Daughter of ROBERT, and MARY
ANDREWS, who departed this Life
the 4*th.* day of April 1720,
Aged 24 Years.

In Memory of
THOMAS DREW, who died
May the 26, 1744, in the 90*th.*
Year of his Age.
Also MARY, his Wife, who died
May the 17, 1691, Aged 45.

THOMAS LUDLOW, *Gent.*
died June 4, 1755, in the
62 Year of his Age.

Here lieth the Body of
THOMAS DREW, who departed
this Life the 13 day of August 1760,
Aged 81.
2 *Pet. Ch.* III, 2.
ANNE DREW, *Widdow,*
who died Dec. 26, 1761,
Aged 71 Years.

Here lieth the Body of
THOMAS HILLAR, *Yeoman,*
who deceased five, and twentieth
of April 1643.
Here resteth the Body of
WILLIAM HILLAR, *Yeoman,*
who departed this Life,
21 Dec. 1722, Aged 71 Years

ELIZABETH, Wife of DANIEL
PRIER, died the 20 of May 1761,
Aged 69 Years.

Here lieth the Body of
REBEKAH, the Wife of ARTHUR
WOODROFE, who died
22 September 1766, Aged 74 Years.
Here lyeth the Body of
ARTHUR WOODROFE, who died
Jany. the 2*nd.* 1775, Aged 77 Years.

MARGERY, Wife of THOMAS
MINCHIN, and late Wife of
WILLIAM HILLAR,
died 10 March 1729, Aged 63 Years.

JEREMIAH MINCHIN,
died August 6, 1761, Aged 70 Years.
HANNAH, Wife of JEREMIAH
MINCHIN, died 26 March 1769,
Aged 84 Years.

ELIZABETH, Wife of JOHN BALL,
died the 20 of May 1761,
Aged 69 Years.

Here lyeth the Body of
JAMES, the Son of WILLIAM,
and ELIZABETH CORNELEY,
who died the 17 of July 1744,
Aged 18 Years, and Six Months.

In Memory of
JOHN CORNLEY, late of *Cowhill*
in the Parish of *Thornbury,*
in this *County,*
who died 16 September 1796,
Aged 54 Years.

In Memory of
ELIZABETH, Wife of JAMES
CORNELEY, of ys. Place,
who died 3 March 1778, Aged 75.
ROBERT, Son of JOHN, and
MARY CORNELEY, of *Thornbury,*
in this *County*
He died 7 April 1778,
Aged 6 Years.
JAMES, their Son, died 14 Mar. 1781,
Aged 5 Years, and 11 Months.

In Memory of
JAMES CORNELY,
who died 2 Sept 1775,
Aged 77 Years.

In Memory of
ANNE, Daughter of JAMES,
and ELIZABETH CORNELY,
who died 6 November 1769,
Aged 34 Years.
SARAH, and ELIZABETH,
their Daughters. SARAH, died
ye. 30 July 1733, Aged 4 Years.
ELIZABETH, died 31 Dec. 1738,
Aged 1 Year, and 10 Months.
Here lyeth the Body of
ALDOM, the Son of
JAMES, and ELIZABETH CORNELY,
who died 2 January 1744,
Aged 5 Years.
Also DINAH, the Daughter of
JAMES, and ELIZEBETH CORNELY,
who died 19 of Febr. 1745,
Aged 10 Months, and 2 Weeks.
Also MARY, their Daughter,
died 25 Oct. 1750, Aged 7 Years.

In Memory of
THOMAS GATER, who died
15 July 1758, Aged 78 Years.
ANNE, his Wife, died 17 Nov. 1755,
Aged 79 Years.
WILLIAM, Son of THOMAS, and
ANNE GATER, died 1 Sept. 172...,
Aged about 2 Years.
THOMAS, their Son, died 18 Nov. 1726,
Aged 17 Years, and 6 Months.

STEPHEN TUGWELL, 1771.
ANNE, Daughter of WILLIAM,
and ANNE TUGWELL, died
15 Jany. 1783, Aged 6 Months.
Also BETTY, their Daughter,
died 3 Dec. 1788, Aged 3 Years,
and 9 Months.
BETTY TUGWELL, 1768,

HEAD ETONES.

	Died.		Aged.		Died.		Aged.
Samuel Emley	17 Oct.	1789	74	John Ball	10 Jany.	1772	65
Anne, his Wife	13 Febr.	1785	73	Mary, his Wife	28 Sept.	1787	73
				Ruth, their Daughter ...	... .	1761	25

WESTON SUBEDGE.

WESTON SUBEDGE.

THE Church consists of a Chancel, and Nave, with a Wooden Screen that divides them. It hath a Tower at the West-End, containing one Bell. It is dedicated to St. John the Baptist. Under the King's Arms is painted "The Gift of Mr. Edward Tasker, of London, born in this Parish," and on the Gallery over the West-end, "This Church was repaired, and beautified in the Year of our Lord 1795. William Smith, and James Sansom, *Ch. Wardens*"

On the South Side of the Chancel is a small male figure (about two feet long,) with his feet against a dog, under a small Arch: there is also a similar figure opposite.

LORD OF THE MANOR ....
Revd. JOHN PEELEY, *Vicar, and Patron.*

INSCRIPTIONS IN THE CHURCH.

CHANCEL.

ON A MONUMENT AGAINST THE NORTH WALL.

Arms, Azure three Lions rampant Or.
FIENNES.—*impaling* Argent, on a Chevron between three Cinque foils Gules a Leopards face Or, between two Bezants.

H. S. E.
PHARAMUS FIENNES, L. L. D,
GULIELMI, VICECOMITIS SAY, et SELE,
Nepos;
Collegii Winton Socius;
Hujus Parochiæ Rector.
In quâ Domum Dei, et Rectoris,
Illam vasis deauratis;
Hanc Ædificiis Hortisq; cultissimis
(Hospitalitate vero magis,
et Liberalitate,)
Utramque suâ suorumqus pietate,
et moribus sanctissimis
Ornavit
Populum sibi concreditum
Fideliter docuit
Prudenter rexit,
Unice amavit
Obiit 4to. die ... Ao. {Dni. MDCCVIII.
{Ætatis LXII.

FLAT STONES.

On a Brass Plate, fixed to a blue marble Stone, is the figure of a Man, habited with a Cloak over the shoulders, and a Sword, with a beard, and muff round his neck.

Old Text.

Here lyeth the Body of
WILLIAM HODGES,
who maried the Daughter of
Sir GEORGE THROGMORTON,
of *Kellington, Knyght*, and was the *Widdow* of JOHN GYFFORD, of *Weston-under-Edge, Esquire*:
who departed this Life, the xxiii of August, 1590.

Here lyeth the Body of
RICHARD COOPER, *Rector of Weston Subedge*, he departed this Life, the 11 day of February 1666.

ON A BRASS.

Hic jacet Maria, conjux
CHARISSIMA RICI. COOPER,
Rectoris de Weston-Subedg,

filia, vero, JOHANHIS GOODWIN, de *Combe, Generosi*, quæ obiit xxx. Junij. An. Dom. 1660, Ætatis suæ XXV.

Here lieth the Body of
MARY, the Wife of RICHARD COOPER, She was borne the 7 of May 1635, and died the last day of June 1660.

(*Defaced.*)
Hic jacet MARG(ARET,) uxor
THOMÆ FAWCET, *Rectoris*
Ecclesiæ de *Aston-Subedge*,
quæ pie, et placi (*de in*)
Domino obdormivit xxii. (*die*)
Januarii, Anno Dom. (16)24.

Hic jacet EDWARDUS BALLARD,
qui Ingenio et Doctrina Sortem suam superavit eruditus, 15 die Aprilis religioso ex...............
(*Rest broken off.*)

Here lyeth the Body of
MARTHA BALLARD, *Widow*, late Wife of EDWARD BALLARD,
She departed this Life the 3 of June 1658.

H. S. E.
JOHANNES BALLARD, M. B.
Vir per-quam doctus, Artisq;
præsertim Apollineæ, quam summâ cum laude successuq;
admodum felici exercebat.
Peritissimus Anatomiam, Chymiam, Herbas, adeo calluit, ut nemo magis Dignus, qui vel Galenum Ætate superaret. Nondum annos Septuaginta natus, Oxonii (inter Musas, et literatos sibi gratissimos,)
animam efflavit, Maij 2, Anno Dom. 1678, Ætatis suæ 66.

ROBERTUS DERHAM,
GULIELMI, et ELIZABETHÆ,
Filius Pijssimus, pater charissimus
Amicus integerrimus, has Exuvias die Dni. Calendarum Maij
Ao. Dni. 1683, Æt. suæ 35.

NAVE.
FLAT STONES.

Here lyeth the Body of
ANNE, the Wife of THOMAS
PHILLIPS, who departed this Life
February the 4, 1718, Aged 38.

Here lyeth the Body of
ANNE, the Wife of WILLIAM
RICHMOND, died the 27 of May
1696, Æt. suæ 66.

CHURCH YARD.
TOMBS.

In Memory of
WILLIAM RUSSELL, who departed
this Life, 18 Sept. 1698,
Aged 51 Years.
Also of HANNAH, his Wife
who departed this Life, 24 of
October 1737, Aged 83 Years.
And of THOMAS, their Son,
who died young.

To the Memory of
JOAN, the Wife of PIERCY GROVE,
of *Middle Norton* in this Parish,
who was struck by Almighty God
with an incurable disease, which she
submitted to with a Christian
Resignation, and died Lamente d
on the 6 day of January 1754,
Aged 59.
Also of MR. PIERCY GROVE, of
Norton, who suddenly departed
this Mortal Life, Aug. 22, 1757,
in the 71*st*. Year of his Age.

In Memory of
MR. JOHN GROVE, late of *Poden*,
Son of MR. PIERCY GROVE,
by JOAN, his Wife, who departed
this transitory Life the 5 day of
March 1764. Aged 44 Years.

FLAT STONE WITHIN IRON PALLISADES.

In hopes of a joyful resurrection
lyeth the Body of MOSES BENNET,
who departed this Life, 16 day of
Octr. 179... Aged 84 Years.

HEAD STONES.

	Died.	Aged.		Died.	Aged.
John Horn, of *Weston-Park* in this Parish ... ... }	2 Sept.	1796	51	Ann Rimel	12 Aug.	1741	71
Joseph Wheatley	13 May	1692	35	Samuel Rimel, Son of John, and Ann Rimel ... ... :	11 May	1789	17

	Died.		Aged		Died.		Aged
John Stringer	12 Mar.	1728-9	58	Rebecca Drury	14 Mar.	1785	69
William Smith	31 July	1784	73	Richard Read	12 Aug.	1762	56
Elizabeth, his Wife	23 Feb.	1774	62	Elizabeth, Wife of Richard Read	11 June	1765	60
John Drury, *Gent.*	26 Apr.	1769	56	George Horton	17 Apr.	1750	58
Mr. James Laud	31 Oct.	1711	58	Ralph Dutton	5 Febr.	1792	78
Benjamin Drury	23 Nov.	1760	40	Elizabeth, Wife of Ralph Dutton	25 Nov.	1769	29
John Drury	5 May	1742	72	John, Son of Ralph, & Elizth. } Dutton ... ... }	5 Aug.	1779	16
Elizabeth, his Wife, daughter } of John Shipton ... }	26 Apr.	1754	74	William James	6 Oct.	1781	73
Henry Drury	10 Oct.	1727	60	Margaret, his Wife	30 Nov.	1784	73
Joanna, his Wife	7 Aug.	1729	...	Thomas Horne	21 Sept.	1786	75
Henry Drury	3 May	1771	52	Sibill, Wife of Thomas Horne	21 Mar.	1780	67
James Drury	18 Dec.	1789	77	Joseph, Son of Joseph, and } Susanna Clark ... ... }	10 Oct.	1796	28
Hannah, his Wife	16 Nov.	1779	65				
Edward Wasing, of *Norton-on-the-Hill* ... ... }	18 May	1759	32	Esther, Wife of John Clark, } & Daughter of Samuel, } & Eleanor Wheatly }	6 Febr.	1794	31
Mary, Wife of William Horton, of *Aston-Subedge* }	14 Dec.	1781	55	Mary, Daughter of Joseph, } & Susanna Clark }	23 Oct.	1784	21
Robert Drury	7 July	1742	70	James Clark	13 Jany.	1795	76
Mary, his Wife	27 Aug.	1738	55	Jane, his Wife	10 Mar.	1784	69
Edward Drury	4 May	1743	65	Thomas James	10 Dec.	1727	82
Mary, Wife of Edw. Drury, *Senr.*	15 Dec.	1767	91	Mary, his Wife, & Daughter } of Thos. & Eleanor Yeates }	1 May	1711	66
Edw. Son of Edw. & Mary Drury	28 June	1768	62				
John Drury	19 Nov.	1788	72				

Supplement by *Sir T. P.*

Descent of the MANOR of WESTON-SUBEDGE.

In 1084, Ansfrid de Cormeilles held this Manor ⊤ ..... Neice of Walter de Lacy
with many others in Gloucestershire.

Richard, 1125. ⊤ .....

Richard, 1166. ⊤ Beatrix

Walter, 23 H. 2. ob 2 H. 3. 1218. ⊤ Albreda de Marmion,

Richard le Brun. ⊤ **Albreda,** d. & coh.

John, 23 H. 3.

Hugh Gifford, de Boyton, ⊤ Sibilla, Co. Wilts. 1 H. 3.   d. & coh.

Robert le Archer, ⊤ Alicia, had Stoke, from | d & coh. him called Stoke Archer.

Alicia, ↔ Godefrid de d. & coh. Craucombe.

Isabella, — Simon de Solers, d & coh. 20 H. 3.

Colin le Archer.

Margaret, ⊤ Walter de Stoke, d. & coh. | of Stoke.

Walter, eldest. Archbishop of York, held Weston. ob. 7 E. 1. 1279.

2 Godefrid, Bishop of Worcester, held Weston. ob. 20 E. 1. 1302.

3 William, held 3 carucates ⊤ Katharine, d. of .... *(It is probable she was a Pinkney.)* in Boyton. Succeeded to | She presented to Sherston Pinkney, Co. Wilts. in 1314 Weston.

John, æt 32, 30 E. 1. held Weston. ⊤ ....

John, æt. 19, 13 E. 2. ⊤ Joan. — Thomas le Boteler,

John, æt. 6 months. 1 E. 3. ⊤ ....

Elizabeth, d. & heir. at 4, 29 E. 3. o. s. p. 35 E. 3. 1362.

William Giffard. ⊤ ....

Sir John, of Weston. ⊤ Mary, d. & heir of Walter Whithers, | of Newnham Padox, Co. Warw,

John, 13 H. 4. 1412. ⊤ ....

John, of Weston Subedge, 23 H. 6. ⊤ Matilda

Robert, ↔ Joanna. o. s. p. 25 H. 6.

John, æt. 17, 25 H. 6. 1447. ⊤ ....

John, æt. 26, 18 E. 4. 1479. ⊤ ....

Sir William, of Ichull, Co. Hants. & of Weston Subedge. ⊤ Eleanor, d of Sir John Padet,

John, 1531. ⊤ Joan, d of Henry Bruges, of | Newbury, Co. Berks.

Ann. ↔ Thomas Goddard, of Upnam, Co Wilts.

John. ⊤ Elizabeth, d. of Sir George Throkmorton. ↔ William Hodges.

George, 1577. This George Gifford was Knighted, and sold the Manor about the year 1623. He had 3 brothers William, John, and Richard.

William. John. Richard.

Inquis. ad qd. Damnum NICHOLAI LE CHAMBERLEYN, *et* AGNETIS, *uxoris ejus,* Ao. 29 E. 1. A. D. 1301.

Inquis. capta coram Rico. Talbot, tunc Vice-Com. Glouc. die Sabb. prox. post fest. S. Hilar. Ao 29 R. Edwdi. per 12 Jur. viz. Wm. de Aston, Ric. la Banck, Joh. de Aston, Johem. de la Grene, Wm. de Cestria, Henr. Beaumont, Johem. de Mukeltone, Adam de Dersintone, Gilbert. de Ilmendone, Nicholaum de Schireburne, Ranulphum de Whetekyn, et Nichum. de Staveleye, juratores, Qui dicunt per sacru. suum quod non est ad dampnum, nec prejudicium Regis, nec aliorum quorumcumque, licet Rex concedat Nicholao le Chamberlayn, et Agneti uxori ejus, quod ipsi 1 mess. et 1 virgatam terræ cum pertin. in Weston subtus Egge, de quibus Ven. Pater, Godefridus Giffard, Epus. Wygorn. qui illa de dno. Rege tenuit in Capite, per cartam suam prædictos Nicholaum, et Agnetem, sine licentia Dni. Regis feoffare liceat tenere, et habere possint eisdem Nicho. et Agneti, et heredibus ipsius Nichi. de dno. Rege, et heredibus ejus inpetuum, per eadem servicia quæ predictus Epus. ea de dno. Rege tenuit. Dicunt etiam quod pdca. mess. et terræ cum pertin. valent per Ann. dimid. marc. in omnibus exitibus. Dicunt etiam quod Manerium de Weston Subtus Egge, et Norton, ultra predca. messuag. et terram, remanent eidem Epo. et Epus. tenet dca. Maneria de dno. Rege per servicium militare, viz. pro 1 feodo, et dimid. et valent per ann. in omnibus exitibus 40 £. In cuj. rei testimonio predci. Juratores sigilla sua huic Inquisitioni apposuerunt.

Descent of Chamberlain's Estate in Weston-Subedge.

An Estate in this Parish was granted by Godfrey Giffard, Bishop of Worcester, the Lord of the Manor, to his Chamberlaine, Nicholas de Camera, which descended to the Harward Family, as in the following Pedigree.

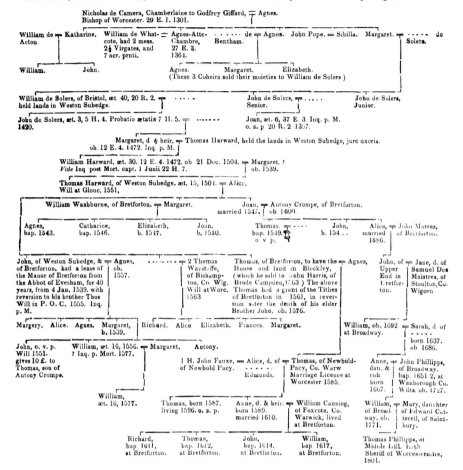

WEST LITTLETON,

see *LITTLETON, No.* CLXV. *Vol. II, p.* 173.

CCXC.
or 295.

WHADDON.

THE **C**HURCH is a strong building, consisting of a Chancel and Nave with an embattled Tower at the Westend, therein five Bells. It is dedicated to to St. Margaret and is a Curacy in the Deanery of Gloucester. [The Church was restored 1855.]

SAMUEL PEACH, *Esqr.* LORD OF THE MANOR.

Mr. JOHN JONES, *Curate.*

INSCRIPTIONS IN THE CHURCH.

CHANCEL.

ON A MONUMENT.

Near this Place lie the Remains of
WILLIAM and MARY MATHEWS,
of the *Hamlet of Tuffley.*
He died April 11*th.* 1720, Æt. 20.
She died Nov. 12*th.* 1728, Æt. 52.
Also in Memory of
Mr. WILLIAM MATHEWS,
who died May 6*th.* 1761,
Aged 58 Years.
SARAH, his Wife, who died
March 18*th.* 1770, Aged 69.
And the *Revd.* WILLIAM MATHEWS,
their only Son, who died
June 4*th.* 1764, Aged 36 Years.

ON FLAT STONES.

[*No Flat Stones* 1881.]

Underneath this Stone in a Space
between it and the Wall on which is
a Monument erected to their Memory
are deposited the Remains of
WILLIAM and MARY MATHEWS,
WILLIAM and SARAH MATHEWS,
And the *Revd.* WILLIAM MATHEWS,
Also of DANIEL MATHEWS,
who died Decr. 24, 1780.
And ELIZABETH MATHEWS,
who died August 22, 1786.

Here lyeth waiting for the
Resurrection of the Just the Body of
RICHARD WOOD, *Gent.*
He departed this Life in the true
Faith the 15 day of Jany. 1651,
Aged 61 Years.

Here also lyeth the Body of
MARY, the Wife of RICHARD
WOOD, *Gent.* who departed this Life,
the 13*th.* of December 1663,
Aged 72 Years.

Arms:—...... a Chevron engrailed
.... between three Fleur
de Lis. WOOD. *impaling* a Lion
rampant.

Arms:—......... a Chevron *......*
between three Lions heads *.........*

impaling .... a Chevron engrailed *......* between three Fleur
de Lis WOOD.

Here lyeth the Body of
MARGARET, the Wife of
ANTHONY DEWXELL,
late of the City of *Gloucester, Gent.*
the only Daughter of *............*
WOOD, of this Parish, *Gent.*
who departed this Life, the
6 day of January 1674,
Ætatis 60.

Here was buried the Body of
THOMAS ROBINS, *Yeoman,*
who departed this Life,
the 17 day of June,
Anno Domini 1610.

Here lyeth the Body of
.... Daughter of *............*
and ALICE ANDREWS, of *Stonehouse,* who departed this Life, the
... of May 1584.
Also two Sons WILLIAM and
ANDREW WAYT.

CHURCH YARD.

ON MONUMENTS AGAINST THE
SOUTH WALL.

In Memory of
ANNE, the Wife of JOHN PARKER,
of this Parish, *Yeoman,* who died
February the 21, Anno Dom. 1754,
Aged 37 Years.

In Memory of
ROBERT BEARD, who died the
28*th.* day of Jany. 1724,
Aged 59 Years.
Also of MARY, Daughter of
ROBERT BEARD, who died
March 1, 1721, in the
3*rd.* Year of her Age.
Also MARY, his Wife,
died 5 August 1755,
Aged near 84 Years.

In Memory of
RICHARD CHELL,

of this Parish, who died
the 18 day of February 1724,
Aged 53 Years.
Also of MARY, the Wife of
RICHARD CHELL, who died the
3*rd.* day of May 1754, Aged 84.

ON A MONUMENT AGAINST
NORTH WALL.

Near this Place lyeth the Body of
JOHN SMITH, of this Parish,
Yeoman, and of MARY, his Wife,
He died Nov. 28, 1745, Aged 55.
She died Sept. 9, 1759, Aged 68.
Also of MARY, their Daughter,
who died in her Infancy.

ON TOMBS.

Underneath this Place lye two
Children of WILLIAM and
JANE COPNER, of *Haresfield,*
HANNAH, died 21 July 1720,
and WILLIAM, died 11 July 1723,
both in their Infancy.

In Memory of
MARY, the Wife of RICHARD
TOWNSEND, of the Parish of
Standish. She died Sept. 23, 1741,
Aged near 95.
Also near this Place lye SARAH
and JOANNA, Daughters of the
abovesaid.
Also of WILLIAM TOWNSEND,
of the Parish of *Standish, Yeoman,*
who died June 16, 1752,
Aged near 73.

In Memory of
MARY TREDEAG, late of *Minchin-Hampton,* who died July the
15, 1755, Aged 22 Years.

Here lyeth the Body of
MARY, the Daughter of
RICHARD CHELL, by MARY, his
Wife, who died in her Infancy.

In Memory of
ALICE, the first Wife of
JONATHAN AVERY, of this Parish,
Yeoman, who departed this Life,
2 July 1735, Aged near 60 Years.
MARTHA, Daughter of JONATHAN,
and ALICE AVERY, departed
Jany. 6, 1729, Aged 14 Years.

Here lies interred the Body of
DANIEL PROUT, and also of
CATHERINE, his Wife, also
JONATHAN PROUT, Son of the above
who died June 23, 1768,
Aged 84 Years.

HESTER PROUT, died in October
1762, Aged near 66 Years.
REBEKAH PROUT, died 21 Sept.
1765, Aged 67 Years.

In Memory of
JOHN MERRETT, of this Parish,
Yeoman, who died the 30 day of
March 1720, Aged 71 Years.
Also of JOYCE, the Wife of
JOHN MERRETT, who died
14 June 1725, Aged 64 Years.

BRASS PLATE ON FLAT STONE.

Beneath this lieth the remains of
Mr. SAMUEL WATHEN,
of this Parish, who died
June 28, 1786, Aged 63 Years.

ON FLAT STONE.

In Memory of
JANET, Wife of JOSEPH HARRIS,
of this Parish, *Yeoman*,
She died Adril 21, 1782,
Aged 63 Years.

HEAD STONES.

	Died.		Aged		Died.	Aged
John Whitehorne, of the Parish of *Upton St. Leonards.*	22 Aug.	1767	76	Sarah, his Wife	10 June 1748	65
Mary, the Wife of John Whitehorne, of the Parish of *Upton St. Leonards,* and Daughter of Humphry Harris, of this Par.	8 Nov.	1761	72	Sarah, Daughter of William and Sarah Baldwin ...	28 June 1726	...
				Hester, their Daughter	15 Augt. 1726	...
				Hannah, Wife of William Fluck, and Daughter of Joseph, and Sarah Harris, of this Parish, *Yeoman.*	13 Jany. 1J43	39
Eleanor, their Daughter	8 Nov.	1761	35			
Humphry Harris, of this Parish, *Yeoman*	8 Oct.	1717	65			
John, his Son	23 Nov.	1725	30	Thomas Harris	18 Jnly 1760	27
Thomas Harris, of the Parish of *Upton St. Leonards,* Son of Humph. Harris, of this Par.	29 Oct.	1749	32	Richard Banford	15 March 1760	51
				Mary, his Wife	14 Sept. 1757	90
				Prudence Aldridge, their Daught.	24 April 1778	30
				Daniel Browning	21 March 1796	81
Humphry Land	2 April	1688	53	Martha, his Wife	4 April 1793	78
Joan, his Wife	7 Febr.	1704	70	John, their Grandson	17 Augt. 1795	21
William Baldwin, of *Tufley Court, Yeoman*	9 Nov.	1720	61			

Supplementary Notes as to I.—*Estates;* II.—*Church;* III.—*Population, Taxation, &c.*

I.—*Estates:*

WADUNE in Dunestane Hundred contained 5 Hides. Culture: 5 Carucates in Demesne, 5 in Villenage, (one Villan 7 Bordars.) Worth in King Edward's time 8 Pounds and at the Survey 100 shillings.

Durand, the Sheriff held: Five Brothers held it for five Manors, they might go where they would, and they were equal.

For subseqent Devolutions, *see* "Moreton Valence, *No.* CLXXVIII.

Sir William Dorrington, by purchase; Sir Samuel Eckley, by purchase.

John Small.

1776.—Sophia Small, Spinster. By her Will, Samuel Peach.

1785.—Settlement by Samuel Peach, on his Wife Christiana, for her separate use and with power of appointment in her.

1792.—Conveyance by the surviving Trustee of the settlement to Samuel Peach, eldest son, and heir of Christana Peach.

Whaddon Manor:

1808.—1. S. Peach. 2. L. Wilson, Deed to lead Uses of a Fine to S. Peach, in fee.

1809.—Fine levied.

1815.—Will and Codicils of Samuel Peach.

Mr. D. Long, by purchase.

II.—*Church.*

Impropriation:

Prebend in Hereford Cathedral.

Bishop of Hereford, 13 £. 6 *s.* 8 *d. Pope Nich. Tax.* in the Hands of Lesees who presented the Curates.

1841.—Joseph Pitt, Impropriator.

1840.—Tithes commuted: Award 172£. 12 *s.* 6 *d.*

The Vicarage was rated at 12 £. 10 *s.* and returned at 33£. 5 *s.*

By an Order in Council, dated 22 of May 1840, pursuant to the Act of 1*st.* and 2*nd.* Vict. ... The Vicarage of Brockthrop of which the Dean and Chapter of Gloucester, were Patrons, and the Perpetual Curacy of Whaddon, of which the Prebendary of the Prebend of Moreton and Whaddon belonging to the Cathl. Church of Hereford, was Patron, were united; the Patron of Whaddon to present for the fourth turn of every four turns and the Patrons of Brockthrop, for the first three turns of every four turns for ever.

List of Incumbents.

1840.—The Rev. Francis Turner James Bayley, A.M. was presented to the Curacy of Whaddon, on the cession of the Revd. Robert Smith, the previous Incumbent.

Charities:

Out of Giles Cox's Charity of 100£. per ann. *see* "Badgworth." and Mary Harris's Estate of 60£. per ann. Whaddon, has part.

III.—*Taxation, Population, &c.*

Whaddon, Subsidy Roll, 1 Edw. III. 1327.

De Willmo. Hankin, xiiii d. q.
‘ Johne le Cumper, xv d.
‘ Marger. le Cumper, ix d.
‘ Rico. Dabetot, v s. ob.
‘ Thom. le Clerke, ix d.
‘ Thom. le Cumper, ix d. ob.
‘ Johne de Horsforde, xiiii d.
‘ Juliana Cumper, vi d.
‘ Johne Bruggema. ix d.
     prob. Sma. xii *s.* ii *d. q.*

Acreage 727 *a.*

Population 1831,—152. 1861,—125. 1871.—127.

In 1815. Annual Value of Real Property 1204£.

1882. Rateable Value 2515 £.

1833-4-5. Average of three Years Expenditure on Poor 110 £.

In Gloucester Union.

WHEATENHURST;

COMMONLY CALLED WHITMINSTER.

THE CHURCH consists of a Chancel and Nave, with a High Tower at the West-end with battlements and four Bells. The Church is dedicated to St. Andrew, there is a Gallery at the West-end.

In the East Window are two Shields of Arms on painted Glass, both alike :—Sable a Lion rampant Or. And in the North Window of Chancel are the remains of a Painted Head of our Saviour.

On an Atchment (over the porch door) on the South Wall of Nave is a Shield.

Quarterly 1 *and* 4.—Sable on a Bend Argent, three Roses Gules, in the sinister chief point a Chess rook Argent. SMALL.

2 *and* 3.—Gules three Books clasp'd close Or, ... *impaling* Argent, a Lion rampant Sable ducally crowned Gules. *Crest:*—On a Chessrook Argent, a Wren proper. [Not there 1883.]

Mr. CAMBRIDGE, LORD OF THE MANOR.

BENEFACTIONS.

The Memory of the Just is Blessed.

Mrs. DOROTHY BAYLEY, *Spinster,* of the City of *Gloucester,* in her last Will, bearing date March 2, 1726, and proved at *Gloucester,* July 23, 1729, left one Moiety of an Estate called *Jackson Farm,* in the Parish of *Wheatenhurst,* in the County and Diocess of Gloucester, to the Bishop and Dean of *Gloucester,* for the Time being for ever, for the Use and Behoof of an Episcopal Priest to be nominated by them to officiate in the Parish Church of *Wheatenhurst,* aforesaid, the Minister is to do his Duty according to ye Rubrick and Canons to read Prayers on Wednesdays, Fridays and Holy Days and to chatechise the Children every Week, not doing it slightly but taking care to make them understand the Church of England Chatechism.

This Table was erected in the Year 1783, *by* JASPER SELWYN, *Curate.*

INSCRIPTIONS IN THE CHURCH.

ON A MONUMENT AGAINST THE NORTH WALL OF CHANCEL.

Arms. Quarterly 1 *and* 4. *quarterly* Or. and Azure, four Roe Bucks Counterchanged.—LLOYDE. 2 *and* 3 Argent, a quiver Gules banded and replenished with Arrows Or, between three Pheons Sable:LLOYDE.
Crest:—a Stags head erased Or.

Near underneath rest the Bodies of THOMAS LLOYDE, *the Elder, Esqr.* who departed this Life, the 15 October Anno 1658, Aged 70. whose first Wife was REBECCA, Daughter of THOMAS HYNSON, *Esqr.* Also MARGARET, his second Wife, Daughter of LEONARD JEFFERYS, *Esqr.* who departed this Life, April 24*th.* Anno 1643. Also THOMAS LLOYDE, *the Younger, Esqr.* with ELIZABETH, his Wife, Daughter of *Sir* THEOBALD GORGES, *Knt.* She departed this Life, April 16, Anno 1666. Aged 43, and He departed this Life, October the 14*th.* Anno 1668, Aged 49. Also ANNE, the Wife of GEORGE LLOYDE, *Esqr.* Daughter of GILES PAYNE, *Gent.* who departed this Life, Septem. 10, Anno 1670, Aged 44. Also PHILLIPPA, a 2*nd.* Wife, Daughter of WALTER PARKER, of *Lyssell* in the County of *Wilts. Esqr.* died the 29 August 1696. Also GEORGE LLOYD, *Senr. Esqr.* who died March 15, 1703, Ætat. 80.
UNDERNEATH.
EDMOND, the Son of GEORGE and ANNE LLOYDE, died the 29 Septm. 1670, Aged 4 Years. ELIZABETH, Daughter of GEORGE LLOYDE, *Junr. Esqr.* and ELIZABETH, his Wife, died March 23, 1680, Aged 4 Years.

ELIZABETH, a 2*nd.* Daughter, died Aged 6 Months, and RADAGUND, 3*rd.* Daughter of GEORGE and ELIZABETH LLOYDE, died Nov. 15, 1699, Aged 13 Years.

ON A MONUMENT IN THE CHANCEL WITH A FAMALE FIGURE KNEELING RESTING HER HEAD ON HER LEFT HAND AND A BOOK IN HER RIGHT.

Arms:—LLOYD, *impaling* Azure a Chevron between three Suns Or. HINSON, *on each side the Arms of* LLOYDE *and* HINSON, *single.*

Here lyeth REBECCA, Wife of THOMAS LLOYDE, *Esqr.* Daughter of THOMAS HINSON, *Esqr.* by ANNE, the Daughter of *Lady* SPRING, Daughter of MARGARET, *Countess of Bath,* She deceased the 16 of day of February 1625.

Virgo modesta fuit; pia mater;
et optima Conjux.
Sed Parcas pietas flectere tanta nequit.
Victa tamen vivit; gentisque insignia,
soles,
Occiduos, mutat splendidiori sole.

ON FLAT STONES IN CHANCEL.

Here lyeth the Body of RICHARD LLOYDE, *Esqr.* who deceased the 20 day of January, Anno Domini 1612.

Here lyeth the Body of MARGARET BYRD, the Wife of RICHARD BYRD, *Esqr.* who deceased the 15 day of May 1621.

Here lieth the Body of GEORGE LLOYD, Son of GEORGE LLOYD and ELIZABETH, his Wife, Daughter of WILLIAM BAYLEY, *Esq.* who departed this Life, the 19*th.* day of November, Anno Domi. 1719.

Here resteth the Body of THOMAS LLOYD, *the Younger, Gent.* late of the City of *Gloucester,* who departed this Life, the 25 of July, A. D. 1690, Ætat. suæ 57.

Here lyeth the Body of WILLIAM LLOYD, *Gent.* who departed this Life, 3 of January, A.D. 1711.

Here lyeth the Body of REBECCA, Wife of THOMAS LLOYD, *Esqr.* Daughter of THOMAS HINSON, *Esqr.* who was interred 1625. Also here lyeth the Body of RADAGUND LLOYD, the beloved Daughter of GEORGE LLOYD, *Esqr.* and ELIZABETH, his Wife, Daughter of WILLIAM BAYLEY, *Esqr.* who departed this Life, the 15 November, Anno Domini 1699, Ætat. suæ 13.

Here lyes the Body of GEORGE LLOYD, who departed this Life, the 11 of April, A.D. 1712. Aged 70 Years and 15 days. To the Memory of ELIZABETH LLOYD, who departed this Life, the

WHEATENHURST.

Bonnor del. et Sculp.

12 December, A. D. 1732,
Ætat. suæ 82.

Here resteth he Body of
ELIZABETH, the Daughter of
GEORGE LLOYD, *Esqr.* and
ELIZABETH, his Wife,
who departed this Life, the
23 of March, Anno Dn. 1680,
Aged 4 Years.

Here resteth the Body of
ELIZABETH, the Daughter of
GEORGE LLOYD, *Esq.* and
ELIZABETH, his Wife,
who departed this Life, the
ix day of August, Anno Dn. 1689,
Aged 6 Months.

Here lyeth the Body of
ANNE BAYLY, Wife of JOHN BAYLY,
who deceased the 21 day of October,
.... Years.

In Memory of
RICHARD, Son of JASPER SELWYN,
of *Matson, Esqr.* and father of
the *Eldest* JASPER, who died
about the Year 1660, Aged about 50.

Here lieth interred the Body of
JASPER SELWYN, *Gent.*
who departed this Life,
in October, Anno Dom. 1690,
Aged 66 Years.
Also of JASPER SELWYN,
of *Frampton,* Son of ye above and
JOAN, his Wife.
He died May 21, 1733,
Aged 72 Years.
She in December 1764, Aged 94.
Also of JASPER SELWYN, late *Clothier,*
of *Cam,* Son of ye above and
ELEANOR, his Wife.
He departed April 9, 1777, Aged 74.
She May 20, 1778,
Aged near 80 Years.

In Memory of
ROSAMUND, Wife of WILLIAM
HOLBROW, late *Clothier,* at *Uly,*
Daughter of JASPER SELWYN,
by JOAN, his Wife, who departed
this Life, April 13, 1776,
Aged about 84 Years.
Also of SARAH and ELIZABETH,
their Daughters, SARAH, died
August 10, 1739, Aged 21 Years.
and ELIZABETH, August 28, 1735,
Aged 16 Years.

Sacred to the Memory of
JOHN BRAY, of *Frampton,*
who died April 9, 1697,
Aged 84 Years.
Also
SARAH, Wife of JOHN BRAY,
Daughter of JASPER and JOAN
SELWYN, who departed this Life,
July 19, 1768, Aged 58.
Also of MARY, their Daughter,
who died July 3, 1768,
Aged 27 Years.

Also of ELIZABETH, Grand-daughter
of the above JOHN BRAY,
who died Augt. 13, 1801,
Aged 26 and was interred at
St. Mary's Manchester.

ON A MONUMENT IN THE NAVE.

Arms:—Azure two Ears of Big
Or.—BIGLAND. *impaling* Or. on a
Chevron between three Foxes heads
erased Gules three fleurs de Lis of
the first.—Fox.

Near this Place lies the Body of
GEORGE BIGLAND, of *Bigland,*
in the County Palatine of
Lancaster, Esqr. who died in this
Parish (upon his Return from
Bristol, where he had been for the
Recovery of his Health.)
On the 19*th* day of Sept. 1752,
Aged 49 Years.
He married MARY, only Daughter of
JOHN FOX, of *Whitehaven,*
in the County of *Cumberland, Gent.*
by whom he left Issue
two Sons, *viz:*
GEORGE and THOMAS.
Psalm. cii. *vers.* 23.

NAVE.

ON FLAT STONES.

Here resteth the Body of
MARY, the Wife of JOHN BROWNE,
of *Kingston St. Michael* in the
County of *Wilts.* who departed
this Life, the first day of Febr. 1684.

Here lies the Body of
JOSEPH COOKE, of *Helsington*
in the County of *Salop.*
who was here interred the
15 of November, 1706.

In Memory of
RUTH, ye Wife of JASPER SELWIN,
Clerk, perpetual *Curate* of this Parish,
Daughter of JOHN ALEXANDER,
of ye City of *Gloucester,* by
CATHERINE, his Wife,
who departed this Life,
June 21, 1765, Aged 55 Years.
Also of CATHERINE, their Daughter,
who died Sept. 14, 1765,
Aged 5 Months and 11 days.
Also of the *Revd.* JASPER SELWYN,
Curate, of this Parish, Son of
JASPER and ELEANOR SELWYN,
who died June 26, 1787,
being entered into the
63 Year of his Age.
[*Most of the flat stones are removed
or the inscriptions obliterated.*]

CHURCH YARD.

ON A MONUMENT AGAINST
THE PORCH.

In Memory of
JOHN TOWNSEND, of the Parish,
of *Standish,* Yeoman, who died
July 24, 1739, Aged 66.
Also MARY COOK,

died Jany. 11, 1737, Aged 19 Years.
All you that are Spectators here,
Prepare for Death, the Time draws near.

SUSANNA, the Wife of JOHN
TOWNSEND, of *Standish, Yeoman,*
died March 10, 1744-5,
Aged 69 Years.

ON TOMBS, FLAT STONES, &c.

In Memory of
SAMUEL HAWKINS, of this Parish,
Senior, Son of JOHN HAWKINS,
of *Burclear* in *Hampshire,*
who died May 26, A. D. 1740,
Aged 77 Years.
Also of JANE, his Wife, and
Daughter of WILLIAM LYE,
of *Stonehouse,* who died
5 May 1731, Aged 67 Years.

In Memory of
SAMUEL HAWKINS, of this Parish,
Clothier, who died March 25, 1763,
Aged 67 Years.
And of JUDITH HAWKINS,
who died January the 1, 1763,
Aged 59 Years.

To the Memory of
HENRY HAWKINS, of this Parish,
Clothier, who died Febr. 10, 1777,
Aged 45 Years.
Also two Children of HENRY, and
ELEANOR HAWKINS, SARAH, died
June 30, 1767, Aged 10 Months.
HENRY, died Febr. 21, 1770,
Aged 1 Year and 10 Months.

In Memory of
JOHN HOLDER, of the Parish
of *Frampton, Clothier,* who died
Sept. 8, 1737, Aged 31 Years.
Also of THOMAS HOLDER,
who departed this Life, the
x Decr. A. D. 1698, Æt. suæ 34.

Hic jacet in Tumulo Quicquid
mortalitatis THOMÆ SAUNDERS,
Applicavit (*Gloucestriæ* a Parochiâ
Johannis Baptisti in urbe *Herefordiæ*)
Chirurgiæ. Mortuus est vicessimo
tertio die Augusti Annoque Dom. 1715,
Vixit annos 71.

Man's like a Glass of Water fill'd
with Ivory Walls about,
His Glass is crack'd, his Water's spilt
so soon is Life runne out.

In Memory of
CONSTANTIA, the Wife of
THOMAS SAUNDERS,
who departed this Life, the
6 of March 1726, vixit annos 72.
Phil. 3, *Chap.* 20.

Here resteth the Body of
SAMUEL, the Son of JOHN HALL,
Scnr. who departed this Life,
Jany 20, A. D. 1704, Æt. suæ 69.
In Memory of
JOHN HALL, of this Parish,

Junr. Clothier, who departed this Life,
October the 7th. A. D. 1702,
Ætat. suæ 69.
Here resteth the Body of
SUSANNA, the Daughter of
JOHN HALL, *Senr. Yeoman*,
who died October 8, 1703, Æt. 78.

In Memory of
DANIEL HALL, late of this Parish,
Clothier, who departed this Life. the
4 day of March, A. D. 1713,
Ætat. suæ 77.

In Memory of
ANSELM BAILY, *Yeoman*,
who departed this Life, the
11 December, 1690.
Also of SARAH, the Wife of the
said ANSELM, who departed
this Life, the 3 1722,
Aged 84 Years.
NATHANIEL BAILY, of this Parish,
died December 8, 1743,
Aged 30 Years.
In Memory of
ELIZABETH, the Wife of WILLIAM
BAILY, *Senr* of this Parish, *Yeoman*,
who died Febr 2, A. D. 1744,
Aged 62 Years.
Also of WILLIAM BAILY, *Senr.*
late of this Parish, who died
Decr. 30, 1754, Aged 81 Years.
Here lieth the Body of
DANIEL WILKINS,
who departed this Life,
March 13th. 1742, in the
64th. Year of his Age.
JOHN, DANIEL and JOHN,
his Children, died Infants.

In Memory of
WILLIAM BENNET, of this Parish,
who departed this Life,
Decr. 3, A. D. 1751, in the
61 Year of his Age.

In Memory of
SAMUEL KING, *Senr.*
who died May 5, 1777, in the
88 Year of his Age.
Also two Daughters of
SAMUEL and ANN KING:
ANN, died July 7, 1775,
Aged 30 Years.
MARY, died August 16, 1776,
Aged 40 Years.
In Memory of
ANN, Wife of SAMUEL KING, *Senr.*
of this Parish, who departed
this Life, the 7 of Jany. 1769,
in the 61 Year of her Age.
Also two of their Children,
THOMAS, who died in his Infancy.
SARAH, who died 3 of Febr. 1754,
in the 6 Year of her Age.
Also in Memory of DANIEL, son of
SAMUEL and ANN KING,
who died Decr. 3, 1774,
Aged 22 Years.
WILLIAM, the Son of SAMUEL
and ANN KING, died June 2, 1783,
Aged 43 Years.
HANNAH, his Wife, Daughter of
JOHN FRYER, late of this Parish,
died July 5, 1785, Aged 42.
WILLIAM, their Son,
died June 7, 1793, Aged 26.
CHARLES, their Son,
died June 3, 1795, Aged 20.

In Memory of
RICHARD LEWIS, of this Parish,
who departed this Life,
May 19, 1784, Aged 31 Years.
Also of JAMES, his Son by
ELIZABETH, his Wife.
He died Oct. 29, 1783,
Aged 2 Months.
To the Memory of
RICHARD LEWIS, of this Parish,
Vitualler, who died Apr. 3, 1775,
Aged 46 Years.
Also of ANN, his Daughter,
who died Nov. 27, 1773,
Aged 6 Months.
Also to the Memory of
MARY, the Wife of
RICHARD LEWIS, who departed
this Life, July 23, 1780,
Aged 40 Years.

In Memory of
JOHN HILL, who departed this Life,
Febr. 14, 1670, Aged 70 Years.

In Memory of
JOHN COWLES, of this Parish,
who departed this Life,
Febr. 12, 1758, Aged 54.
Also of IZZARD, his Wife.
who departed this Life,
December 8, 1779, Aged 67 Years.
In Memory of
WILLIAM, the Son of JOHN and
ESTHER COWLES, *Senr.*
who departed this Life,
May 2, 1774, Aged 15 Weeks.

The young from death cannot be free
Old age ther's no one sure to see.

Also in Memory of the
aforesaid JOHN COWLES, *Yeoman*,
who departed this Life,
March 1, 1794, Aged 84 Years.
Also of ELEANOR, Daughter of
JOHN and ESTHER COWLES,
who died December 22, 1784,
Aged 2 Years and 4 Months.

In Memory of
DANIEL HEWLETT, of this Parish,
Carpenter, who died June 1, 1749,
in the 64 Year of his Age.
Also of MARGARET, the Daughter of
EDWARD WARNER, and 2nd. Wife
of DANIEL HEWLETT,
who died 22 of May 1713,
in the 50 Year of her Age.

In Memory of
THOMAS NEALE, of this Parish,
Yeoman. Son of SIMON NEALE,
of the Parish of *Stone*,
who died April 2, 1745, Aged 56.
Also SARAH, his Wife, Daughter of
WILLIAM BULLEY, of the Parish
of *Frampton*, who died
March 28, 1746, Aged 52.
WILLIAM, Son of THOMAS NEALE,
died the 24 of August 1739,
in the 20 Year of his Age.

In Memory of
JOSHUA KING, of this Parish,
who died 20 February 1729,
Aged 57 Years.

Also of SARAH, the Wife of
JOSHUA KING, who died
Nov 5, 1735, in the
66 Year of her Age.
ANNE, Daughter of JOSHUA KING,
died Febr. 9, 1704, Aged 8 Years.
MARY, Daughter of JOSHUA KING,
died June 22, 1734, in the
31 Year of her Age.

Here resteth the Body of
SUSANNA, the Daughter of
JOHN HARRIS, late of this Parish,
Senr. who departed this Life, the
first of Dece. Anno 1694,
Ætat. suæ 25.

In Memory of
ALICE, the Wife of JOHN HARRIS,
of this Parish, *Yeoman*, and
Daughter of GEORGE and MARY
PARK, of this Parish.
She departed this Life,
11 July 1723, Aged 35 Years.

To the Pious Memory of
JOHN CARVER, of this Parish,
who died 16 Augt. 1708, Aged 44.
Also the Body of TIMOTHY,
his Son, by MARGARET, his Wife,
who near this Place lieth interred
August 15, 1708, Aged 8 Years.

In Memory of
ROBERT CARESFIELD, *Yeoman*,
late of this Parish, who died
April 16, 1731, Aged 31 Years.

ROGER RAPIER, of this Parish,
who died May 12, 1748,
Aged 60 Years.

WALTER PAINE, of this Parish,
Yeoman, died 6th. July 1727,
Aged 71 Years.
MARY, Wife of WALTER PAINE,
died January 7, 1730, Aged 77.
ELIZABETH BIRT, Sister to the said
MARY PAINE, who died
May 5, 1728, Aged 67 Years.
MARY, Wife of THOMAS PERRY,
died March 25, 1762, Aged 60.
THOMAS PARRY.
died July 16, 1770, Aged 73.

In Memory of
WILLIAM PARK, of this Parish,
Son of EDWARD PARK,
by DEBORAH, his Wife, who died
.... Aged 63 Years.
Also several of the Children of
JOSEPH PARK, by MARY, his Wife,
viz.—HANNAH. JANE, EDWARD
and SUSANNAH.
GEORGE PARK, of this Parish,
Yeoman, who died Febraray 4, 1719,
Aged 34 Years.
ELIZABETH, his Wife,
died May 25, 1742, Aged 58 Years.

In Memory of
JAMES PARKER, of this Parish,
Yeoman, who departed this Life,
Aug. 24, 1736, Aged 62 Years.
Also of ELIZABETH, the Wife of
JAMES PARKER, who died
8 Febr. 1729, Aged 54 Years.
DANIEL, their Son, died
1 May 1718, Aged 5 Weeks.

In Memory of
ELIZABETH, Wife of JOHN COWLES,
of the *City of Gloucester*,
and Daughter of JOHN PARK.
She died April 20, 1746,
Aged near 29.
SARAH, Daughter of GEORGE
and ELIZABETH PARK, of this
Parish, died Jany. 31, 1747,
Aged   Years.

In Memory of
JOHN ALLISON, of this Parish,
who died the 16 December 1739,
Aged 50 Years.

Remember man as thou go'st by,
As thou art now so was I,
As I am now so thou must be
Therefore prepare to follow me.

(*Additional Inscriptions in Church
since Bigland's time.*)

CHANCEL.

JASPER SELWYN, of *Dudbridge*,
died Nov. 1829, in the 69
Year of his Age.
MARY, his relict, died
22 June 1866, Aged 67.

Sacred to the Memory of
WILLIAM JENKIN, of *Frampton
on Severn*, *Perpetual Curate*,
of this Parish, He died 7, Jan. 1813.
His sorrowing Widow in testimony
of a Union of 29 Years of unceasing
harmony hath caused this Tablet
to be placed in the same holy Edifice,
where he promulgated the Precepts
that he religiously observed.
ELIZABETH JENKIN,
the Widow of the above,
died Nov. 28, 1831.

In a Vault near this place repose
the Remains of JANE, the relict of the
Revd. EDWARD PARSONS, A.M.
late of the City of *Bristol*,
and daughter of *Captain* NATHANIEL
PITT, formerly of *Whitminster House*,
in this Parish. She died in *Bristol*,
on 29th day of August 1869,
Aged 86 Years.

NAVE.

Sacred to the Memory of
SAMUEL and THOMAS KING,
last surviving sons of SAMUEL
and ANN KING, a family long
resident in this Parish, universally
respected and esteemed.
THOMAS KING, died at his Residence
in the Vicinity of *Bath*,
Decr. 5, 1804, in his 63 Year,
and was buried at *Wolley*,
near that City.
SAMUEL, died 13 August 1812,
Aged 75 Years,
Whose Remains with two of his
Children :—THOMAS and ANN,
lie in the adjoining Church Yard.
THOMAS, died 13 March 1806,
Aged 34 Years.
ANN, died 23 July 1810,
Aged 43 Years.
MARY, Relict of the above
SAMUEL KING,
died 11 April 1819, Aged 82.
SAMUEL, Son of SAMUEL and
MARY KING, died March 30, 1829,
Aged 54 Years.
(*As to this family see Inscriptions
in Church Yard.*)

NORTH AISLE.

ON A TABLET.

In Memory of
CHARLES OWEN CAMBRIDGE, *Esqr.*
of *Whitminster House* in this Parish,
an active Magistrate for the
County of *Gloucester*,
Beloved by all his surviving
Relations and Friends
Of sincere and unaffected piety
Kind and charitable to the Poor,
And respected by all who knew him.
He died the 29 day of June 1847,
in the 95th Year of his Age.
Also of
CATHARINE CAMBRIDGE,
Wife of the above,

---

who unceasing in her Charities
to the Poor,
And endeared to all by her very
many Virtues,
Died the 24th day of Oct. 1835,
Aged 84 Years.

ON A BRASS PLATE ON THE WEST
WALL OF NORTH AISLE.

Extract from the Will of
RICHARD HODGES CARTER, *Esqr.*
late of the City of *Gloucester*,
who died 6th of Sept. 1868,
and was buried at *A lingham*.
By which [Will] he directed the sum
of £200. to be invested in the name
of the Minister and Church Wardens
And the interest thereof to be given
away on Christmas Eve in every
year to such deserving Poor of the
Parish not receiving Parochial Relief
as the Minister and Church Wardens
should in their discreation think ex-
pedient.
ANTHONY ELY, *Minister.*
JOHN GRAY,   ) *Church*
BENJM. HILL,) *Wardens.*

ON A BOARD.

Mr. DANIEL CRUMP,
by his Will proved in 1877, gave
100 £. to be invested in the 3 per
Cent Annuities the interest to be distributed in February yearly without
regard to religious belief.

A BOARD ON THE WALL OF THE
NORTH AISLE.

Records that the Church was enlarged in 1842, and by which means 100
additional sittings were obtained and
a Grant of 30 £. was given by the
Society for building Churches. 90 of
the sittings were declared free and
unappropriated. The provision for
Church accomodation previously to
the enlargment was 103 sittings, of
which number 80 were free.
ANTHONY ELY, *Minister.*
RICHD. MARTIN,) *Church*
JOHN BREWER.) *Wardens.*

HEAD STONES IN CHURCH YARD.

	Died.		Aged.		Died.	Aged.
John Bailey, ...	22 Sept.	1797	59	Susanna, Wife of Jos. Townsend,	10 March 1744-5	69
Mary, his Wife, ...	10 Decr.	1786	53	Mary, Wife of Samuel Weight,		46
James Bailey, ...	22 Decr.	1797	46			

Notes as to I.—*Devolution of Estates.* II.—*Church.* III.—*Population, Taxation, &c.*

I.—*Estates*:

Witenherst contained 5 Hides taxed.
Culture:—One carucate in demesne; A Priest, two Villans and six bordars with 5 Carucates; There were 3 serfs;
A Mill of 16s., and 10a. of meadow. It was worth 30 shillings, but had been worth 100 shillings [Yearly.]

It had belonged to Brictric, [a King's thane temp. the
Confessor] He mortgaged it to Hardinc, who was then in
possession. [It is put under "Lands of King's Thanes."]
Domesday Survey.

The Manors:

1.—Geoffrey Fitzpeter, held one which passed by
marriage of his Daughter to the De Bohun family, and
by partition between the Co-heirs of that family, King
H. v. (in right of his Mother,) and Ann, Countess of
Stafford, it was assigned to the King, who by private
Act 9 Hen. v. *Rot. Parl.* annexed it to the Duchy of
Lancaster. It long continued in the Crown as part of the
Duchy Estates.

Wheatenhurst Manor, Mills, &c. are mentioned in

the Duchy of Lancaster Chancery Proceedings, Vol iii. 35 Eliz in a suit of Richd. Birde, the Queens Lessee of the Manor. against Richard Frewen, A right of Way from the Queens Mills through Frampton was in controversy with Clifford and others. *Vol.* ii. & iii. 35 Eliz. The claims of Lessees under King Hen viii were put in question.

These were subsequently Paper Mills. *Rudder.* They have been taken down, but the ruins of the Walls, sluices, &c remain.

Theffgrove is mentioned in the Duchy Chancery Proceedings 1, & 2. Ph & Mary. (Commission to survey it.) *Vol.* ii. *pp.* 38, 159, 209

This included what is now called Whitminster Grove, near the Road to Eastington.

W. Bayley, by Crown Grant, to be held of the Manor of East Greenwich. From his son and heir William Bayley, it passed by purchase to Sir Samuel Eckley, whose Brother took by devise 1712.

The Estate purchased under the Trusts of Accumulation and Investment of the Will of Mr. Henry Bengough, which Trusts continued for near half a century in this place included the Manor and Estate of Fitzpeter.

2.—A large House near the Church and Estate was held by the Abbey of Gloucester, who called it a Manor and in course of time it acquired manorial Rights. *Rudge.*

1703.—Richard Byrd.

Crown Leases were granted to Byrd, the Reversion was afterwards acquired by that family.

Bird's Daughter Sybill, carried the Estate to Lloyd by Marriage.

This Estate afterwards came into the family of Cambridge, by purchase

Richard Owen Cambridge, was born here 1717. His father a Turkey Merchant of London. married a Miss Owen. Richd. O. Cambridge, married Miss Trenehard, and resided here for some years after his Marriage in the large house Having a taste for landscape gardening and much skill in mechanics and navigation he laid out his grounds ornamentally and made the Stroudwater Brook which ran through them (parallel to which the Stroudwater Canal was afterwards made) navigable for pleasure Boats towards the Severn. Frederick, Prince of Wales and his Princess, (Parents of George iii.) when on a Visit to Lord Bathurst, at his seat near Cirencester in 1750, were agreeably entertained by Mr. Cambridge, at dinner on one of his Boats on the Severn; the dinner being dressed in a large Barge attached to the Boat Of this Entertainment, an account is given in the Gentleman's Magazine 1750; July, by Cave the Printer and Editor, who was his guest. "He kept me" says Cave, "one night and took me down part of his River to the Severn, where I sailed in one of his boats and took a view of another of a peculiar make having two keels, or being rather two long Canoes connected by a floor or stage. I was then towed back again to sup and repose. Next morning he explained to me the contrivance of some Waterfalls which seem to come from a piece of Water which is four feet lower."

The Prince also visited Lord Ducie, on this occasion, at his seat near Dursley. He (the Prince) manifested great interest in the Clothing industry, and appreciated the cider of the country "Gloucestershire Champaign" he called it. He was so well received as to promise a future Visit which he never lived to pay, *see* "George the iii, his Court and family," *Vol.* i. *page* 82. Mr. Cambridge, soon afterwards removed to Twickenham, opposite Richmond, in Surrey, near the Villa late of Pope whose grotto he had helped to adorn. He died in 1802, Aged 86.

His Works the chief of which was the "Scribleriad" a satirical mock heroic poem, 1751, and "Wars in India between England and France" were republished by his son George Owen Cambridge.

Another son C. O. Cambridge, resided here in 1842, and died 1848.

All (but Saul farm,) of this Estate was sold to Mr. H. H. Wilton, who enlarged the House.

Jackson's farm:
1727.—Dorothy Bayly, Spinster, died seized.

The Bishop and Dean of Gloucester, In Trust as to one Moiety of profits for the Curate of Wheatenhurst and as to the other for the Rector of Frethern, by her Will

Parklands
Mr. Martin; Mr. Gray.

Saul farm, is partly in Wheatenhurst and Whitminster

Court, belonged to this Estate. It is now owned by Henry Pickard Cambridge.

The name of Clifford of Frampton, occurs in proceedings in Chancery in relation to Questions of Lands and rights in Whitenhurst:—Clifford, (James) against Clifford, (Hen.) Robyns, and others: Bill to be relieved from Settlement affecting Frampton and Swindon Manors and Lands in Whetenhurst, &c. *Proc'gs. in Chan. temp.* Q. Eliz.

1776.—*At the County Election, the following Voted as freeholders in Wheatenhurst.*

Harris, Joseph.	Martin, Richard.
Hawkins, Henry.	Ropier, John.
Hewlett, Daniel.	Selwyn, Jasper.
King, (2) Daniel, Samuel.	

II.—Church:

The Impropriation belonged to the Abbey of Bruton, Somersetshire, by the Gift of .... *Pat.* 45 Edw. iii.

It had belonged to the alien Priory of Troar.

On dissolution of Monasteries it was granted away. Mr. Lloyd; Mr. Selwyn; Mr. Cambridge; Mr. Aldridge, Mr. Ely, Mr. Bengough, were subsequently Patrons.

Vicarage Endowment:
Payment by the Abbey, beyond 6s 8d, paid to the Archdeacon and 2s. for cenage. } £7. 11s. 4d. *Valor Eccl'us.*

Mr. Smith, was Incumbent in *Sir R Atkyns, time.*
Mr. Selwyn, was do. in *Rudders, time.*
Mr. Hawkins, was do. in *Rudges, time.*
Revd. A. Ely, Benefaction Table.
W. Jenkin. *Church Inscriptions.*

There is a Vicarage House in the populous part of the Village.

Charities to the amount of £ 68. 11s. 7d. yearly.—
Abraham Elton.
Dorothy Bayley, *see* "Church Inscriptions,"
R. H. Carter; D. Crump; *see Benefaction Tables.*

A School House near the Vicarage was built by the last Cambridge, and is still supported.

Part of Wheatenhurst is in the Framilode Ecclesiastical District which comprises parts of Moreton Valence, Standish, Frethern, Saul, Arlingham and Eastington Parishes also, and has a population of about 650, with a Church of the date 1854.

At Bishop Hooper's Examination Rutter was Rector, the King Patron, the No. of Communicants 100. The Rector answered all the Questions except that of proving the Articles of the Belief.

III.—*Taxation, Population, &c.*

Wheatenhurst, Subsidy Roll, 1 Edw. iii., 1327.

De Com. Herford, vii s. vii d.
' Johe. Muchele, xii d.
' Rico. Broun, ii s. ob. q.
' Pho. Palme. xv d.
' Matill. Meriot, ii s. viii d. o.
' Agn. Messag. xv d. o.
' Rogo. atteHull, ii s. iii d. o. q.
' Raduo. Trocy, ii s. ix d. q.
' Willo. Whithorn, ii s. i d. q.
' Walto. Whithorn, ii s. i d. q.
' Robto. Rolues, ii s. ix d. ob.
' Willo. Walkere, xv d.
' Walto. Haiward, iii s. ix d. o. q.
' Walto. de Wynhull, xviii d.
' Willo. Willing, xxi d. ob. q.
prob. Sma. xxxvi *s. ix d. ob.*

Acreage 1217 *a.*

Population 1801,—287. 1831.—411. 1871,—**423.**

In 1815. Annual Value of Real Property 2048 £.

1882.—Rateable Value £ 2395.

1833-4-5. Average of three Years Expenditure on Poor £ 151.

In Wheatenhurst Union.

The Stroud Water (Thames and Severn), and the Berkeley and Gloucester Canals pass through this place. And here the Stroudwater Canal intersects the Gloucester and Berkeley Canal. The Stroudwater brook ran near

Whitminster House. It was on this Brook that R. O. Cambridge's navigation were made, and some vestiges may still be seen of them. It would seem that they suggested the scheme of improving the navigation of the Brook by means of connecting the Mill Ponds by short Canals and lifting the contents of the Boats to the different Levels. This was said to be the invention of Mr. Bridge, of Tewkesbury. Dean Tucker, wrote in the Papers of the Day approvingly, April 1760. but Fosbroke, ridiculed it after it had been tried and abandoned.

A private Act was passed 7 George i., for discharging part of the Estate of Richard Cambridge, Esqr. in the County of Gloucester, from the uses and limitations contained in his marriage settlement and for settling another estate in the County of better value to the same uses.

CCXCV.
or 300.
WIDFORD.

THE CHURCH is a Rectory and was in the Deanery of Stow, [in Gloucester Diocese.] The Building is very small consisting a Chancel and Nave with a Turett in the Middle containing one Bell. In the Chancel is a Piscina, and the Kings Arms painted 1679. There are the remains of a Mansion House in this Parish, belonging to the FETTYPLACES now in ruins.

CHARLES FETTYPLACE, *Esqr.* LORD OF THE MANOR.

Revd. Mr. HUGGINSON, *of Alscot, Rector.*

INSCRIPTIONS IN THE CHURCH.

CHANCEL.	CHURCH YARD.
ON FLAT STONE.	ON A HEAD STONE.
Here lyeth the Bodye of .... FETTYPLACE, who deceased the 28 of December, Anno Domini 1612.	In Memory of SIMON TURNER, and his two Wfves, He was buried March ... 1755, Aged 74 Years. (*The rest defaced.*)

Supplementary Notes as to I.— *Devolution of Estates.* II.— *Church.* III.— *Taxation, Population, &c.*

I.—*Estates:—*

This Parish late in Gloucestershire, (in the Lower Division of Slaughter Hundred.) is now for all purposes, in Oxfordshire, by which it is wholly surrounded.

Widforde in Berinton hundred, two Hides. Culture, 2 Carucates in Demesne and two in Villenage, (4 Villans and 3 Bordars.) There were 4 Bondmen; 8 a. Meadow and one Mill of 10 s. It was worth in the Confessors time 40s. at the survey 60 s. Yearly.

St. Oswald, of Gloucester held. And Ranulf, held of that saint.   *Domesday Survey.*

It was afterwards in the hands of the Archbishop of York. And a century later it became a lay fee and was for some generations held by the Lords Lovel, the heir general of which family married the Duke of Norfolk, or. whose attainder it was granted, 36 Hen. viii. to Withepol and others. It was next held by Harman, from whom by marriage to Johnson, and Harman Johnson, held 43 Eliz. 1686. It came by purchase to Sir Edmund Fettiplace, whose coheir Diana, who married Robert Bushel, And Ann Fettiplace, who married Lucy. Thomas Fettiplace, the son of Robert acquired the entirety: Robert, his son took from him and Charles Fettiplace, succeeded.

3 Jac ii.—Grant of Free Warren in Widford to Sir E. Fettiplace.

The Estate came by purchase to Lord Redesdale.

At County Election 1776, Voated as a Freeholder here.

John Martin, *Clerk.*

II.—*Church:—now in Oxford Diocese.*

List of Incumbents and Patrons of Widford.

Incumbents.	Patrons.
1548.—John Nott.	
1562.—Thomas Damport.	
1572.—Thomas Nichols.	.... Johnson, *Esqr.*
Robert Bygge.	William Johnson.
1590.—T. Afflett.	
1600.—Thomas Haines,	Harman Johnson.
1602.—Robert Rose.	
1612.—T. Burbage.	
1617.—Thomas Haines.	Edward Johnson.
1625.—Christopher Glyn.	
1642.—William Braekston.	
1643.—William White.	Charles I.
1662.—Daniel Cowley.	Elizabeth Johnson.
1726.—John Ellens.	G. Fettiplace.
1759.—James Rees.	Do.
1765.—Hen. Belf.	Do.
1770.—John Martin.	Do.
1787.—Thomas Eden.	Loxdale.
1792.—W. M. Higginson.	Williams.
Michael Wyatt.	
1812.—William Raine.	

The Advowson has gone with the Manor.

The Rectory is rated at 58s. 10d. in *Valor Ecclus.*

The Tithes in 1839, were commuted for a Corn Rent which produces about 80 £. Yearly.

Ann Pitts, by Will 1715, gave 1200£ to be laid out in Land, the Rents after paying 30£. a Year to a School Master at Swinbrook, to be applied to the Repairs of the Churches of Swinbrook and Widford.

Out of Sir G. Fettiplace's Charity, this Parish has £5 18 8 Yearly for clothing for the Poor and for preaching a memorial sermon.

III.—*Taxation, Population, &c.*

Wydeforde, Subsidy Roll, 1 EDW. iii., 1327.

De Johne. Colly, xii d.
  ' Matill. Colly, xvi d.
  ' Rico. le Walkare, ii s. ii d.
  ' Johne. Devote, xii d.
           prob. Sma. vs. vid.

Acreage 879 a.

Population 1831,—51. 1871,—47.

1815. Yearly Value of Real Property £642.

1882.—Estimated Rateable Value £.......

1833-4-5.—Three Years Average Expenditure on Poor 64£.

In Witney Union.

At Widford Mills, the manufacture of Paper has been carried on for a long period, formerly by Hatton and lately by Milburn.

CCXCVII. WHITTINGTON.

THE Church consists of a Chancel, Nave, South Aisle, and a South Chancel, *or* Tracy's Chancel, which was built by the family of the Cottons. It is a small structure with a low wooden turret in the Middle; therein is One Bell, Under an Arch between the two Chancels are two figures in Stone, lying cross legged with their hands upon their Swords, at the feet (of one) is a Lion couchant: (and of the other, a dog.) (They have each) a Shield upon the left Arm, bearing this Coat, *viz.* six Lozenges 3. 2., and 1., and a Label of five points. There is also another figure (in stone) of a female lying along in the South Aisle, with the three following Coats 1. (in an arcade of stone) Six Lozenges (with Label) as before.—2. Barry of Six.—3. as the first.

On an Atchment, (*now gone* 1870.) there are these Arms.

First.—Quarterly 1, and 4. Or, between two bendlets, Gules, an Escallop in the dexter chief point, Sable.—TRACY.

2nd.—Azure, a Cross crosslet fitché Or. *3rd.*—Sable, a bend Ermine, between two Cotizes flory, & counterflory, Or.—KECK.

Arcade On an Escutcheon of pretence, Quarterly, 1, and 4. Vert, a fess between three Roses, Argent.—DODWELL of *Sevenhampton.*—2, and 3. Argent, three Bars Gules a Canton of the second.—FULLER.

LADY OF THE MANOR MRS. TRACY.

REV. GEORGE WASEY, M. A. RECTOR.

(LORD OF THE MANOR 1870. WALTER LAWRENCE LAWRENCE, ESQR.)

(REV. ANTHONY COCKS LAWRENCE, RECTOR, 1870.)

INSCRIPTIONS IN THE CHURCH.

CHANCEL.

NORTH SIDE.

ON A BLACK FLAT STONE, LET INTO
THE WALL.

To the Memory of
BARBARA, and WILLIAM INGRAM,
the beloved Children of JAMES INGRAM,
Dr. of Divinity, and ABIGAIL, his Wife
BARBARA, deceased March 25, 1650.
aged ......
WILLIAM, left this Life,
March 25, 1651. Aged 7.

Heere sleeping lye two Rarityes
Both dainety Jewells of rich Price
Which Natvre caus'd to be refin'd
Then sent to Heaven to be enshrin'd.

MONUMENT ON THE SOUTH SIDE,

Arms. Ermine, on a fess Gules three
escallops Or., INGRAM, impaling
Barry of ten, Argent, and Azure,
over all a Lion rampant Gules. BARNS.
(*This shield now lies broken off*, 1870.)

In Memoriam
Viri admodum literati
Morum, et Religionis integerrimi.
JACOBI INGRAM,
Qui S. S. Theologiæ merito Doctor
Hujusce Parœciæ Pastor fidissimus
Ecclesiam decoravit
Vitam cum Morte mutavit
Anno ⟨Ætatis suæ 70,
     ⟨Domini 1670.

Juxta quem Sepultus jacet
Filius ejusdem natu maximus

JACOBUS INGRAM,
Cujus morum probitas simplicitas
suavitas
Effecit
ut omnibus lugubre desiderium reliquit
Jan. 20,
Anno ⟨Ætatis suæ 36,
     ⟨Domini 1678.

Hand procul positum est
Quod reliquum MARGARETÆ,
Dris. INGRAM filiæ,
ANTONII BARNS, Imo. deinde ROBTI. SHRAT.
Conjugis
Lumina condidit Id. Maijs
Anno ⟨Ætatis suæ 52,
     ⟨Æræ Xnæ. 1692.

In Charissimam Memoriam
MARGARETÆ BARNS, ANTONII, et
MARGERATÆ, prolis unicæ, quæ præ-
propera Patris Morte orba, antequam
nata, relicta matri tristissimæ solamen
nimis breve præbuit, variolis nempe
correpta immatura morte
Quinto Novemb. expiravit,
Anno {Ætatis suæ 7,
{Domini 1677.

ON A BRASS PLATE, WITH THE
FIGURE OF A MAN, HIS WIFE, AND
CHILD. (*Another figure has been on it
but is now gone, also the Arms.*)

Here lyeth the Boddyes of
RICHARD COTON, Esquier, and
MARGARET COTON, his Wife.
He decessed the nine, and twentyth
daye of Maye in the Thyrd, and fowrth
Yeare of the Reygne of Kinge Phillypp,
and Queene Marye, Ao. Domini, 1556,
and the sayd MARGARET decessed
the ...... daye of May in the fyrst
Yeare of the Reigne of our soveraigne
Ladye Queene Elizabeth, Ao.Dom.1560.

MONUMENT AGAINST THE
NORTH WALL.

Sacred to the Memory of the
Reverend WALTER THOMAS, M. A.
late Rector of this Parish,
who departed this Life the 13th. day
of June. in the Year of our Lord
One Thousand seven hundred, and
Ninety nine, and in the Sixty Sixth
Year of his Age.

His unassuming Manners, and
Amiable Behaviour to all Mankind
within his Acquaintance, endeared
him to them while living, and
caused his Death to be universally
regretted.

FLAT STONES.
In Memory of
THOMAS HACKETT, Rector of this
Parish, who departed this Life the
10 Feb. in the Year of our Lord 1717,
in the 60th. Year of his Age.

In Memory of JONE HACKETT,
Wife of THOMAS HACKETT, Rector
of this Parish, who departed this
Life the 4th. of Feb. 1712,
Aged 76 Years.

In Memory of the
Revd. CHARLES RICH, 19 Years Rector
of this Parish. He died Dec. 1779.
(*There are also Inscriptions on the
Grave Stones of*
MARGARET SHEAT.&MARGARET BARNES.)

TRACY'S CHANCEL,
OR
SOUTH CHANCEL.

Arms, Quarterly.—1, & 4, Or, betw.
two Bendlets Gules an Escallop in
the dexter chief point Sable. TRACY.
2. Azure a Cross crosslet fitchè Or,
.... 3. Sable, a Bend Ermine
between two Cotizes flory counterflory Or KECK.—On an E cutcheon
of Pretence, Quarterly 1, & 4. Vert,
a fess between three Roses, Argent.
DODWELL.—2, & 3, Argent, three
Bars, & a Canton Gules. FULLER.
(*This Shield now missing,* 1870,)

To the Beloved Memory of
THOMAS TRACY, Esq. of *Sandywell*,
in Gloucestershire, youngest Son, of
JOHN TRACY, Esq. of *Stanway*,
in the said *County*, who deceased
June 24th. 1770, Aged 53.

This excellent Man was distinguished
in Private Life,
By an uncommon Sweetness of Temper,
and Benevolence of Heart,
And possessed in an eminent degree
those social, and amiable Virtues,
Which not only procured him the Love
of his Relations, and intimate Friends,

But the universal Esteem of all
His Acquaintance.
He was unanimously chosen by his
Country in two succeeding Parliaments to represent the
County of Gloucester,
which important trust he discharged
with the strictest Integrity,
and disinterested Zeal.

He married MARY, only Daughter,
and Heiress of
Sir WILLIAM DODWELL, Knt.
And had by her one only Son,
DODWELL TRACY, who died
(from his amiable Disposition, and
distinguished Parts,) of the most
promising Hopes.
But these, alas ! were blasted, when,
in the flower of his Age, he was
snatched from the Arms of his
afflicted Parents, and Friends,
Jan. 11, 1768., at Paris, on his
return from his Travels,
in the 21st. Year of his Age.

MARY, their lamenting Wife, and
Mother placed this mournful Testimony of Her tenderest Affection
to her Dear Husband
and her beloved Son.
Their Remains are deposited in the
TRACY Vault at *Stanway*.

ON A PLAIN STONE, AGAINST A
PILLAR OF THE TRACY CHANCEL.

To the Memory of
JOHN TAYLOR, who died
August 9th. 1775.
He lived Servant in the Family at
Sandywell,
above twenty Years,
and discharged his Duty with
Honesty, and Fidelity,
and during a long, and painful Illness
was an excellent Example of Patience,
and Resignation to the Will of God,
Worthy to be imitated in every
Station of Life.

HERE LYETH THE BODDYES OF RICHARD COTON ESQVIER
AND MARGARET COTON HIS WIEFE HE DECESSED THE NI-
NE AND TWENTYTH DAYE OF MAYE IN THE THYRD AND
FOWRTH YEARE OF THE REYGNE OF KINGE PHILLYPP AND
QVEENE MARYE ANNO DOMINI 1556 AND THE SAYD
MARGARET DECESSED THE   DAVE OF MAYE IN
THE FYRST YEARE OF THE REYGNE OF OVRE SOVERAIG
NE LADYE QVEENE ELIZABETH ANNO DOMINI 1560

ON A MONUMENT AGAINST THE
ARCH BETWEEN THE TWO CHANCELS.

WILLIAM SIMON,
late of this Parish, Gent.
a Master Extraordinary of the
High Court of Chancery.
Departed this Life the 28th. day of
March in the Year of Lord 1784,
Aged 74 Years.
In his profession Honest, and
Attentive to the interest of his Clients.
Sincere in his Friendship,
In Temper, Cheerful, and Benevolent,
Beloved in his Neighbourhood,
whilst living, and
Universally lamented in his Death.
This Stone was erected to his Memory
by his
Executrix, and Residuary Legatee.

ON A PLAIN MONUMENT AGAINST THE
NORTH WALL OF TRACY'S CHANCEL.

Near this Place lieth the
Body of ELIZABETH SPOONER,
who departed this Life
Feb. ye 18, 1763.
Aged Ninety Years.
That the Memory of so worthy,
and just a Person may not be lost to
Posterity, Mrs. TRACY
has erected this Monument, in whose
Family she lived, as Housekeeper,
Seventy Years.

Well done thou good, and faithful Servant,
Enter thou into the Joy of thy Lord.

ON A MONUMENT AGAINST
A PILLAR IN THE NAVE.

To the Memory of
RICHARD THAYER, who was buried
in the Chancel, and GEORGE, the
Son of RICHARD THAYER, was
buried near this Arch, the
First of November, Anno Dom. 1639.

RALPH THAYER,
the Author of ys Table
was buried under ys Arch,
ye 1st. day of Januarye 1673.

JOANNA, ye Wife of GEORGE SMITH,
his Nephew, was buried ye
1st. day of Sept. 1674.

Hee being no longer worthy her to haue,
Shee lyeth now Interred by my Graue.

ON A MONUMENT OPPOSITE THE LAST,

Under this Arch
Resteth the Bodyes of
JOHN EBSWORTH, and DORCUS,
his Wife, DORCUS was buried the
28th. April 1731, Aged 69 Years.
JOHN, was buried the 28 April 1733,
Aged 75 Years.

CHURCH YARD.

ON A TABLET AGAINST THE
NORTH WALL.

To the Memory of
GILES WATKINS, *Gent.*
Some time Curate of ys Parish,
who was buried 7th. Feb. 1690.

By Doctrine, and Example He
Taught men how to live, and how to dye
He led the way, and speaks tho' dead
To all that they the same Steps tread
Kneel at their Prayers, be diligent
Their Parts perform, and be intent
At Sermon, that in time they may
To Heavenly Joys find out the way.

TOMBS.

In Memory of ANNE, the Wife
of RICHARD POWELL, who died
Jan. 6th 1762, Aged 68 Years.

Here lyes interred
THOMAS YOUNGE, who departed
this Life the 27 of July 1648,
and JEMIMA, his Wife who
was buried the 13th. of May 1642.

In Memory of
HENRY ARKELL, of *Whittington,*
who departed this Life
Aug. 8, 1759. Aged 77 Years.
Also ELIZABETH, his Wife,
She died Decr. 20, 1777, Aged 84.
Also of SAMUEL, Son of
HENRY, and ELIZABETH ARKELL,
who departed this Life the
31st. Aug. 1766, Aged 42 Years.

Here lie the Bodies of
WILLIAM BOURTEN, and ESTHER,
his Wife.
He was buried March 2, 1738,
Aged 60 Years.
She was buried Sep. 22, 1763,
Aged 99 Years.

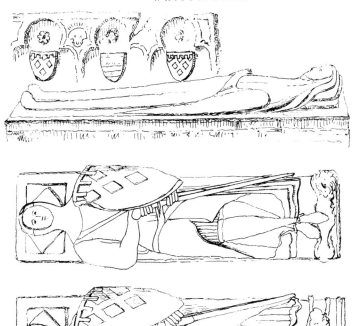

Also WILLIAM JOHNSON, who was buried July 6, 1742, Aged 50 Years. Also two Daughters of WILLIAM, and ANNE JOHNSON.

Here lyeth the Body of CHARLES HURST, being Parson of *Whittington* 23 Years, buried the 23 of June, Anno 1629.

Here lyeth the Body of EDWARD JOYNES, who was born at *Naunton*, and deceased at

Puckham, the 20 day of October Anno Domini 1675.

In Memory of WILLIAM ARKELL, of *Postlip*, second Son of HENRY, & ELIZABETH ARKELL, of *Whittington*, who died Sept. 9, 1779, Aged 63 Years.

In Memory of SAMUEL ARKELL, of *Wally Farm* in this Parish who departed this Life June 1st. 1781, Aged 84 Years.

AGAINST THE EAST END OF THE CHURCH.

Here ....
the Bodies of EDMUND WOOD, who was buried the 8th. of March Anno 1621. WILLIAM WOOD, the Sonne of EDMUND WOOD, was buried, by him, the last of June Anno 1611. (*sic in* Bigland's *MSS.*)

(*Now* 1870 *gone.*)

HEAD STONES.

	Died.	Aged.		Died.	Aged.
Elizabeth, wife of John Freeman, of *Cherrington*.	21 Feb. 1772	43	John, Son of Thomas, and Rachel Crook.	12 May 1783	22
Thomas, son of Samuel, and Alice Arkell, of *Walley*.	4 Oct. 1762	23	Robert, Son of Robert, and Eleanor Crook.	28 Dec. 1758	22
Richard Powell, of *Whittington*.	11 Dec. 1749	66	Hannah, Daughter of Henry, and Elizabeth Arkell.	11 Oct. 1756	20
Elizabeth, Wife of Joseph Probert.	13 May 1747	48	Thomas, Son of John, and Sarah Fletcher.	28 June 1770	26
Mary, Wife of John Browne.	16 Jan. 1720	39	John, Son of Thomas, and Mary Fletcher.	15 June 1796	25
James Wixoey.	14 Nov. 1792	76	John Taylor.	9 Aug. 1775	...
Eleanor, his Wife.	1 March 1770	55	Ann, wife of William Mustoe.	10 Mar. 1769	49
Mary, Wife of Jno. Shill, and daughter of Thomas, & Rachel Crook.	4 June 1792	22			

The Parish was inclosed under an Act passed 32 Geo. 3. 1792. for inclosing Commonable Lands in Whittington, Shipton Solers, Shipton Oliffe, and Dowdeswell.

At Sierford is one of the Spring heads of the Colne River.

Near Sierford in a field called Wicombe, under the surface, are remains of a Roman Military Station, It was partly exhumed in 1863, and many Roman relics were discovered. (*See an Account of them in the Gentleman's Magazine for Nov.* 1863, & *Jan.* 1864.) *S. G.*

CHILD'S WICKHAM.

THE CHURCH is a Vicarage in the Deanery of Campden, and *Mr.* FERMOR, is patron. It is built in form of a Cross, and has a handsome spire at the West-end, therein five Bells. In the Chancel Window inpaled on Glass, this Coat, Gules a fess between six Cross crosslets Or.—BEAUCHAMP, and on some Bricks .... three Chevrons Or.

.... FERMOR, of *Tusmore*, in *Oxfordshire*, is LORD OF THE MANOR.

Revd. DANIEL JONES, *Vicar.*

This parish being a peculiar, the Bishop, and Arch-Deacon are entertained at the Manor-house, where, by custom, the Lord provides his visitors, "with a Cake, a loaf, a pound of butter, a quarter of a sage cheese, a quarter of a plain cheese, a dozen of Ale, and six bottles of strong beer." Another custom of this Manor has been immemorially observed at Whitsuntide, when the Lord orders "a certain quantity of malt for ale, to be given away, and flour to make Cakes. At the same time, every one that keeps a cow, sends curds; others send sugar, plums, and flour; and the landholders contribute sixpence each : from this fund every poor person in the parish may receive a quart of ale, a cake, a piece of cheese, and a cheese cake."

BENEFACTIONS.

Mr. SAMUEL WHARTON, sometime Sherriff of *Bristol*, Son of TIMOTHY WHARTON, Vicar of this Parish, gave 27£. to purchase Lands for the use of the poor of this Parish of St. Thomas's day yearly for ever. 1683.

INSCRIPTIONS IN THE CHURCH.

CHANCEL.

ON FLAT STONES.

Here lyeth the Body of
ROBERT WISE, who died the
seventh of September in the
Year 1727, Aged 55.
Also the Body of MATTHEW, the
Son of ROBERT WISE, he died
4 July 1751, Aged 24.
Also ELIZABETH, the Wife of
ROBERT WISE, buried 16 of Sept.
1747, Aged 74 Years.
ROBERT WISE, *Gent.*
Son of the above ROBERT, and
ELIZABETH, who departed this Life,
the 21 July 1775, Aged 62.

Here lyeth the Body of
ROBERT WISE, and ANNOR,
Son, and Daughter of
ROBERT WISE, and ELIZABETH,
his Wife, ROBERT, departed this Life,
3 Decr. in the 7 Year of his Age 1707.

Round the verge Capitals.

Here lyeth the Body of
ANNE SHELDON, the Wife of
WILLIAM SHELDON, *Gent.*
who deceased the xxv. of March,
Anno Domini 1638.

ON A STONE AGAINST THE EAST END.

Here lyeth the Body of
JOHN DROREE,
who deceased the 29 day of Septem.
Anno Dom. 1658, Aged 59.

NAVE.

ON FLAT STONE.

Here lyeth the Body of
JOHN PERRIN, *Surgeon*, Son of
WILLIAM and MARY PERRIN,
who departed this Life, the
8 day of April 1780, Aged 37.

ON A MONUMENT AGAINST THE WALL OF NORTH CROSS AISLE.

In Memory of
WILLIAM PERRIN, *Gent.*
He died 22 of Nov. 1793,
Aged 84.

ON A MONUMENT BY THE LAST.

Near this Place lies the Remains of
THOMAS PERRIN, *Gent.*
who departed this Life,
March 6, 1786, Aged 44 Years.

Also two Children of THOMAS
PERRIN, by CATHARINE, his Wife,
THOMAS, died Nov. 10, 1776,
Aged 3 Months.
MARY, died Nov. Jany. 7, 1783,
Aged 4 Years.

CHURCH YARD.

ON TOMBS.

In Memory of
MARK SMITH, who died
June 12, 1759, Aged 47 Years.
Also of WILLIAM SMITH,
who departed this Life,
February 15, 1773, Aged 42 Years.
Also of ELIZABETH, the beloved
Wife of *Mr.* WILLIAM SMITH,
She departed this Life,
May 16. 1769, Aged 34 Years.
Also two Children of
WILLIAM and ELIZABETH SMITH,
who died in their Infancy.

Here lyeth the Body of
ROBERT WARNER,
who departed this Life, Apr. 20, 1762,
Aged 71 Years.
Also the Body of SARAH, the
Wife of ROBERT WARNER,
who died March 26, 1759,
Aged 52 Years,

HEAD STONES.

	Died.		Aged.		Died.		Aged.
*Mary Lane, ...	12 Oct.	1744	133	Hannah, Wife of Richard Smith.	13 Jany.	1794	85
Elizabeth, Wife of Richd. Perrin,	5 July	1751	70	Mary, Daughter of Richard			
Richard Perrin, ...	23 June	1729	66	and Hannah Smith, and	27 Febr.	1777	26
Thomas, Son of Richard and Elizabeth Perrin, ..	6 Febr.	1733-4	24	Wife of John Newbury,			
				William Dobbins, ...	19 Sept.	1790	61
Thomas Perrin, ...	14 Febr.	1696-7	83	Ann, Wife of John Mason, ...	16 Decr.	1779	26
Jane, his Wife, ...	27 Oct.	1706	83	Elizabeth, Daugh. of Michael and Ann Fisher, ...	18 June	1783	18
Lydia, Wife of Mark Smith, ...	11 Sept.	1758	67				
Thos. Fisher, of this Town, *Yeoman.*	12 April	1761	73	Michael Fisher, ...	25 Sept.	1782	61
Ann, his Wife, ...	26 July	1763	77	Ann, his Wife, ...	31 Oct.	1769	63
Mary, Daughter of Thomas and Ann Fisher	26 July	1759	42	Ann Harris	16 May	1714	70
				Margaret, Wife of Stephen Fisher,	23 Sept.	1775	39
Michael, Son of Michael and Ann Fisher, ...	11 July	1773	15	William Fisher, ...	23 Augt.	1789	75
				Elizabeth, his Wife, ...	6 Aug.	1771	53
Mary, their Daughter, ...	8 Febr.	1767	4	James, Son of William and Elizabeth Fisher, ...	2 Sept.	1786	41
James Fisher, ...	6 Febr.	1737	53				
Jane, his Wife, ...	1 July	1747	61	Mary, Wife of Stephen Fisher,	20 Decr.	1798	58
John Dame, ...	8 Aug.	1760	72	John Gibbes, ...	23 Sept.	1684	54
Ann, Wife of John Dame, ...	15 May	1752	57	William Hitch, ...	2 Decr.	1692	...
William Dance, of this Parish,	27 Oct.	1709	36	Thomas Izod, Late of Broadway,	1 Sept.	1780	77
Richard Smith, ...	15 June	1777	64	Anthony Beard, ...	16 June	1751	64

*[It appears by the Register that she was baptized in 1618, the daughter of a poor Man. If born in that Year 1618, she would have been 126 in 1844.]

Supplementary Notes as to I. *Devolution of Estates.* II. *Church.* III. *Population, Taxation, &c.*

I.—*Estates:*

Child's Wickham, this name as "Childeswicwon" occurs in a Saxon Charter, dated in 706, of grant by Alric, son of King Osher, to St. Mary's Ethom, (Evesham,) of Land (viii. Manentes,) and the name "Wicwona" (Wykwan) occurs in a Charter of 709, of Grant by King Kenred, to the same Church of three manses here. (*Kemble Codex Anglo Sax. Diplom. Nos.* LVII and LXI) But Wykwan, singly was in use for several centuries; And then the distinctive name "Child's" was resumed and has since been continued. How and when it became a Lay fee does not appear, but Evesham Abbey were not Owners at the Conquest.

Wicwene in Gretstane Hundred, contained 10 Hides taxed Culture: Three Carucates in demesne and 12 in Villenage, (32 Villans and 10 Bordars;) One serf. Two Mills of 10s. each, and 10a. of Meadow.

In Winchcomb there was one Burgess paying 16d. It had been worth 12£. and then was worth 16£. (Yearly.)

At the Survey R. Despenser held; but Baldwin, was a former Owner, [whether Saxon or not, does not appear.]
Domesday Survey.

Robert Despenser, died without issue leaving his Brother Urso D'Abitot, the oppressive Sheriff of Worcestershire, his Heir. Urso, had a son Robert and a Daughter Emmeline The son was banished from the realm, and the Daughter became the Heiress of her Father and Brother. She married William de Beauchamp.

53 Hen. iii.—William de Beauchamp, died seized of this Manor held in Capite and of Land (arable) 360a. Value at 4d. per acre. Meadow 16a. at 3d. per acre, pasture 3a. at 2s. per acre, of £6. 3s. 1d. Rent of Free Tenants. 119s. Rent of Neifs. Out of this, 20£. Rent was payable to the Chantry of Elmley Castle. *Escheat 53 Hen. iii.*

9 Edw. ii.—Guy de Beauchamp, Earl of Warwick, held.

After several descents in that Name, it passed to Nevil, Lord Latimer, by marriage with the Heir general; and by like means from Nevil to Sir William Cornwallis, 1608; It then came to the Sheldons, by purchase, and from them it went to the family of Fermor, who held at the Inclosure Act, 1761.

From the Fermors the Manor Estate passed to Mr. T. Phillipps, by purchase, and from him to his son the late Sir Thomas Phillipps, Bart. by Will.

Other Tenements:—

The Abbot of Winchcomb, had one hide in Wicquean.
Domesday Survey.

London Close, &c.

Stratford, had Lands here, part of which 1568, was sold to Stephens, and from that Name went in 1666, to Fermor.

1669.—Jacketts Close and Bromsgroves Lands:
1320.—Bromsgrove, was a Subsidy payer.

Murcot was a Hamlet and Chapelry.

St. Peter, of Gloucester, had Land here (12a.) by Gift of Wm. de la Mare, confirmed by Margt. Bohun.

1761.—The Inclosure Act, passed. By the Award Allotments were made to Land and Tithe Owners in Childs Wickham and Murcot:—

		a.	r.	p.
W. Fermor, Esqr. Impropriator.		391	3	7
Do.	Land Owner	34	2	16
Do.	...	972	2	8
Do.	... ...	0	3	21
Do.	... ...	5	2	32
T. Webb,	... ...	73	0	30
M. Fisher,	... ...	5	2	36
J. Inglis,	... ...	7	0	5
M Johnson, (Leaseholder,)		49	0	6
Broadway Common,	... ...	8	1	7
J. Hervey,	... ...	21	2	17
A. Hyatt,	... ...	4	0	21
R. Tinkler,	... ...	4	0	21
J. Gibbs,	. ...	11	3	13
W. Perrin,	... ...	45	0	2
T. Warner,	... ...	32	1	29
R. Smith,	... ...	20	0	5
R. Drinkwater,	... ...	5	1	19
J. Smith,	... ...	0	1	7
Church	... ...	1	0	14
Poor	... ...	1	3	0
W. Vale,	... ...	1	0	21
		1697	1	3

Warner's Land passed to Sir Thomas Phillipps, by purchase.

The following Names of Owners are mentioned in Fines of Lands here:—

21 Geo. ii.—Osburston.
23 Geo. ii.—Durham.
26 Geo. ii.—Cartwright.
28 Geo. ii.—Beard, (Murcot.)
20 Geo. ii.—R. Warner, from R. Hyatt and Wife.

1776.—*At the County Election the following Voted for Free-holds in Childs Wickham and Murcot.*

Burgess, Robert; Fisher, (3) William, James, Michael; Gibbs, John; Groves, John; Harvey, John; Hyatt, Henry; Mallet, John; Perrin, Thos.; Phillips, John; Poultney, John; Quarrell, John; Smith, (3) John, Ric., Thos.; Warner, Thos.

Perrins and Warners now belong to Mr. Morton.

II.—*Church.*

The Advowson belonged to the Manor till given by Guy de Beauchamp, to Bordesley Cistercian Abbey by which it was appropriated. They had a grange here. Since the dissolution of Monasteries the Impropriation has gone with the Manor Estate.

1303.—The Vicarage was endowed by the Bishop of Worcester, with Tythes of Wool, Milk, and small Tythes.

By the Inclosure Act 73 acres of Land were given to the Vicar in lieu of Tythe. There is Vicarage House and Orchard. The Living has been augmented by Queen Ann's Bounty and money payments given in lieu of Tithes on certain old Inclosures here.

List of Incumbents and Patrons of Childs Wickham.

Incumbents.	Patrons.
Michael Wharton.	
1607.—William Smith.	Bishop of Gloucester
1609.—Thomas Gyles.	R. Sheldon.
Timothy Wharton.	Do.
1700.—Richard Gregory.	Fermor.
(*from Atkyns.*)	
R. Burgis (*Ruader.*)	Do.
H. Barnard. (*Rudge.*)	Do.
Sheldon, Price, Hood,	
Harding.	

At Bishop Hooper's Examination W. Semys, was Vicar, the King Patron, the No. of Communicants 20. The Vicar answered all Questions except proof of Articles of the Belief.

Murcot, had a Chapel long since demolished.

1553.—The last Incumbent W. Bilson, or Pierson, had pension of £2 10s. per Year.

III.—*Taxation, Population, &c.*

Wykewane and Morcote, Subsidy Roll, 1 Edw. iii. 1327.

De Alicia atte Brugge, ii s.	De Cecilia Hobbekines, ii s. id.
xi d. ob	Rico. le Treuman, iii s. iii d.
Raduo. Tod, iii s. ix d. ob.	Matillda Douces, ii s. q.
Rico. Berde, iii s. x d. ob. q.	Willmo. Hondys, ii s. ix d.
Bobto. de Aldeward, xx d.	ob. q.
Johne. atte More, ii s. iiii d.	Will. Whytinge, iiii s. id.
Robto. Lruwery, iiii s. ob. q.	Alicia Hethe, iii d. vd. ob.
Robto Broun, xx d.	Rico. Aykewe, xvi d. q.
Willn.o. Joce, vi d.	Will. Toddes, iii s. iiii d. ob.
Warino de Spellesbury,	Johne. Ingelard, xii d.
iii s. vi d.	Will. Abovetoune, xv d. ob.
Robto. Rolves, ii s. vi d.	Willmo. Berde, vs. ii d.
Willmo Jurdan, iii s. ob. q.	Willmo. Kembe, iii s.
Johne. le Wariner, v s. x d.	Walto. Inthehaie, iii s. iiii d.
Willmo le Treuman, ii s. xd.	Willmo. Reynald, ii s. ix d.
Raduo. Tod, vi d.	Robto. Baroun, iii s. iii d. ob.
Johanna Berde, ii s.	Nicho. Baroun, xxi d. ob. q.
Thom. Fereman, ii s. vd. ob.	Juliana Sulewed, ii s. ixd. ob.
Nicho. le Yonge, ii s. vii d.	Edytha Russell, xxii d. q.
ob. q.	Stepho. Gilbert, iii s. vd.
Rico. Phelippes, iii s.	Johne. Gerard, ii s. viii d.
iiii d ob.	Thom. Kinge, ii s. viii d. ob.
Johne. de Bremesgrove,	Rico. Hardinge, ii s. id. q
xxiii d. ob.	Johne. Blyke, ii s. vii d.
Willmo. Hodde, iiii s. ixd. q.	Rico. Sampson, ii s. ix d.
Nicho. Honuys, ii s. vi d.	Agnete de Westone,
Matilldis Toddes, xx d. q.	iii s. iii d.
Rico. le Bedel, xix d.	Walto. de Westone, ii s. i d. q.
Alicia Rogers, xviii d.	Rico. de Westone, xx d. q.
	prob. Sma. vi li. xiiii s. vi d. o.

Acreage 1821a.
Population . 1801,—351. 1831,—415. 1871.—463.
In 1815. Annual Value of Real Property 2289£.
1882. Rateable Value 2882£.
1833-4-5. Average of three Years Expenditure on Poor 300 £.
In Evesham Union.

John Wykewan, prior of Evesham, was elected Abbot of same 1435.

WICKWAR.

WICKWAR.

THE CHURCH dedicated to St. Mary, is a Rectory in the deanery of Hawkesbury, it is a hand some structure standing upon an eminence a little distance from the Town, and consists of two Chancels (one belonging to the Parish, the other to the Minister.) Nave and North Aisle, with a high Tower at the West-end adorned with pinnacles containing six Bells. It is said that it was built by one WOOLSWORTH, an eminent *Clothier*, of this Town, who also built a house at the pool in the bottom near the Church, against the east-end of which house is a Stone carving of St. John the Baptist, in an erect posture with his left hand pointing towards the Church and over him this inscription in antient characters: .... "STE. JOHES. BAPTISTA. ORA."

Underneath the figure.

"In the yere of oure Lorde God Mᵒ. CCCCᵒ. IIII, score and XVI, trinete. Monday XXII day of May."

The Town governed by a Mayor, thirteen Aldermen and two head-boroughs. There is a free Grammer School in the Town, founded by *Mr.* ALEXANDER HOSEA, who when an Apprentice, in this Town, committing a fault for fear of correction set out for *London*, where he acquired a large fortune. He afterwards settled in this his native Town. The Grammer Master's Sallery is 28 £. per Annum and a house to live in. *Revd. Mr.* THOMAS COOKE, was *Master* (in 1801.) There is also a free School for teaching Children to read and write, endowed with 10 £. per Annum and a house for the *Master*, (who was the *Clerk* in 1801.) [Hosan's School House has been lately rebuilt.]

Lord DUCIE, LORD OF THE MANOR.
Revd. THOMAS COOKE, Rector.

BENEFACTIONS. (*printed on a Board.*)

Mr. EDWARD YATE, of *Malmesbury, Wilts.* gave by Will in 1722, the sum of 80 £. in trust, the interest thereof to be applied to the purpose of apprenticing poor Boys of the Parish of *Wickware* and *Yate*, in *London*, and not else where by the Trustees.

Mrs. ELIZABETH HICKES, *Widow*, of *Mr.* JOHN HICKES, of this Parish, gave by Will in 1724, the sum of 20 £. to be laid out in the purchase of Land, and in the mean time to be placed out at interest by the Rector, Churchwardens and Overseers of the Poor. The Rent thereof to be given to such inhabitants of the said Parish as the Rector, Church-wardens and Overseers shall think proper in manner following, One moiety on the feast day of St. Mathias, and the other on St. Mathew's at the Church Yearly for ever.

Mr. WILLIAM HOBBS, *Clothier*, by Will in 1747, gave the sum of 30 *s.* Yearly payable out of a dwelling house in this Town to be laid out by the Rector and Churchwardens in Coats for three poor Cloth-workers of this Parish, on St. Thomas's day Yeasly for ever.

Mrs. ELIZABETH HICKES, *Widow*, of *Mr.* NATHANIEL HICKES, of this Parish, gave by Will in 1782, the sum of 200 £. the interest thereof to be laid out in Gowns and Shifts for ten poor industrious Widows or other poor house-keepers of *Wickwar*, not receiving Alms, whom the Trustees shall approve of, on St. Thomas's day Yearly for ever.

(Benefactions painted on the Gallery et the West-end.)

HENRY CAM, *Gent.* gave in the 17*th.* Year of the Reign of James the 1*st.* a Messuage in the Borough of *Wickwar*, the rent thereof to be applied to the purpose of apprenticing poor Boys of this Parish by the Rector, Church-wardens and Overseers.

ALEXANDER HOSEA, *Citizen*, gave by Will in 1683, the sum of 600 £. which was laid out in the purchase of certain Lands and Houses for the present Charity Schools in this Town, and by a Codicil in his Will in 1684, ... gave for the purchase of an Estate for the support of the said School which Estate consists of two houses in *Holborn, London*, and are in the possession of the *Mayor* and *Aldermen* of the Borough of *Wickwar*, as Trustees of the said Charity School.

Mr. and *Mrs.* SPIRT, gave 2 £. a Year payable out of a dwelling house in this Town, one half to be given to the poor of this Parish, by the Rector and Church Wardens on the feasts of Mathias and St. Mathew in equal proportions the other Moiety to the Rector of the said Parish for a Sermon to be preached on each of the aforesaid feast days Yearly for ever.

Mr. and *Mrs.* WOOLFORD, left 4 £. a Year payable out of a Freehold Estate in the Parish of *Charfield* in this County, to be given to the Poor of this Parish, by the Rector, Churchwardens and Overseers, Yearly on the Monday before Christmas, for ever.

ARTHUR PROUT, of the Parish of *Cromhall*, gave by Will in 1712, a close of Ground called *Cooks Leaze*, and also 20 £. to be placed out at Interest for the purpose of buying and delivering a Cloth coat each to 5 poor Men and a Cloth coat or Gown each to 5 poor Women of this Parish not receiving Alms, as shall be approved of by the Rector, Church Wardens and Overseers on Christmas Yearly for ever, the Rest (if any) to be distributed in Bread to the same poor Persons and such other poor of the said Parish not receiving Alms, as shall be approved of as above.

INSCRIPTIONS IN THE CHURCH.

CHANCEL.

ON MONUMENTS.

To the Memory of
WILLIAM GILES, of *Westend*,

within this Parish, *Esqr.* who dyed the 29*th.* day of September 1750, Aged 80 Years.

This Monument was erected by WILLIAM SPRINGET, of *Alderley*, in the County of *Gloucester, Gent.*

Out of a due Regard to his deceased Grandfather.

Arms:—Azure a Chevron Or. between three Castles towered Argent. —GILES.

Armes:— Argent, a Bend wavy Azure between two Hawks (or Hobbys) proper.—HOBBS, *empaling* Sable a Unicorn passant Or. on a Chief Argent, three July ? Flowers Gules.

In Memory of
GEORGE HOBBS, Son of WILLIAM HOBBS, (*Clothier,*) by SARAH, his Wife, He died Sept 5*th.* 1740, Aged 21 Years.
Also of the said WILLIAM HOBBS, who died Febr. 23, 1747-8, Aged 55 Years,
And SARAH, his Wife, who died May 6, 1754, Aged 72 Years.
Also of JOHN, the Son of the aforesaid WILLIAM and SARAH HOBBS, who died June 3rd. 1759, Aged 35 Years.
Also of WILLIAM HOBBS, Son of the aforesaid WILLIAM and SARAH HOBBS, He died June 8, 1778, Aged 63.

Here lieth the Body of
MARY WORRALL, *Widow,* who was the Wife of THOMAS WORRALL, Rector of *Oldbury-upon-the-Hill,* in this County. She departed this Life, the 17*th.* and was buried the 20*th.* day of February A. D. 1694, Aged 71. Here also lyeth THOMAS WORRALL, the Son of THOMAS and SARAH WORRALL, who departed this Life, the 5*th.* of Nov. 1710.

Near this Place lyeth the Body of
WILLIAM WORRALL, *Clothier,* who died Nov. 6, 1735, Aged 66. Also ELIZABETH, his Wife, died February the 14, 1738, Aged 68 Years.
Also ELIZABETH, their Daughter, and Wife of WILLIAM GREEN, of this Parish, died January 22*nd.* 1763, Aged 63 Years.

Arms:—Gules a fess wavy between 3 fleur-de-Lis, Or.—HICKS.

Near this Place are deposited the Remains of JOHN HICKES, *Gent.* Son of JOHN and ELIZABETH HICKES, of *West-end.* He departed this Life, 1 Augt. 1639, Aged 66 Years.
Also ELIZABETH HICKES, Wife of the said JOHN HICKES, She departed this Life, the 28 Oct. 1754, Aged 84.
Also of NATHANIEL HICKES, *Esqr.* Son of DANIEL and MARY HICKES, of Cam, in this County. He departed this Life, 25 of Febr. 1776, Aged 64 Years.
Also of ELIZABETH HICKES, Wife of the said NATHANIEL and Daughter of JOHN and ELIZABETH HICKES, of *West-end.* She departed this Life, 24 March 1782, Aged 75.

ON FLAT STONES.

THOMAS RUSSELL, of this Parish, *Yeoman,* was buried under this Stone, August the 21

in the Year 1723, Aged 74.
Also in Memory of
WILLIAM RUSSELL, of this Parish, *Yeoman,* who was buried the 12 day of October 1747, in the 59 Year of his Age.

In Memory of
GEORGE, the Son of WILLIAM HOBBS, *Clothier,* and SARAH, his Wife, who died the 5*th.* day of September 1740, Aged 21 Years.

Sub Hoc Tumulo
Condientur Cineres
WILHELMI PROUT, *Clerici,*
Hujus Municipii
Archididascali
Obiit Octavo die Julij,
Anno Domini 1733*o.*
Ætatis 37.

S. E.
1683.
T. E.—1696.
Here lyeth the Body of
JOHN EDWARDS, of this Parish, who was buried Augt. 10, A. D. 1728, Aged 42 Years.
Also the Body of SARAH AISH, *Widow,* first the Wife of JOHN EDWARDS, and since of WILLIAM AISH, of this Parish, She died the 18*th.* day of January 1756, Aged 70 Years.

Hic requiescit Corpus viri
reverendi Magis. OBADIAH HIGGINS, in artibus Magistri, et hujus Parochiæ ....
(*the rest defaced.*)

Hic jacet Corpus viri
Reverendi GULIELMI PROUT, hujus Parochiæ Ludimagstri qui libenter animam afflavit die 25 Octobris, Anno Dom. 1729, Ætatisq. suæ 34. Requiescunt etiam Walh., Eliz. and Maria, Liberi prædict.

In Memory of
MARY, the Wife of SAMUEL BARDOE, of the City of *Bristol,* who died 13*th.* September 1758, Aged 44 Years.
Also of JOHN WOODMAN, of this Parish, who died 29*th.* April 1760, Aged 78 Years.
Likewise three Children of JOHN KING, by REBECCA, his Wife, who all died in their Infancy.
Also the above JOHN KING, of this Parish, who died 3 Decr. 23, 1780, Aged 36 Years.

ON A BRASS PLATE.

Here resteth the Body of

DANIEL PROUT, *Burgess* of the Borough of *Chipping Sodbury,* and Son of ARTHUR PROUT, of *Cromwell Ligon,* who departed this Life, the 15 day of Sept. Anno Domini 1724, Ætatis suæ 59.

In Memory of
ARTHUR PROUT, of this Town, who was buried 4 Febr. 1733, Aged 46 Years.
Also of SARAH PROUT, his Wife, who died 29*th* of October 1750, Aged 61 Years.
And also of BENJAMIN HOCKLY, who died the 21 April 1760, Aged 52 Years.
And of SARAH, Daughter of BENJAMIN and ELIZABETH HOCKLY, who died the 5*th.* of March 1748, Aged 4 Years and 9 Months.
ELIZABETH, his Wife, who died May 9, 1786, Aged 70.
Also ARTHUR, Son of ARTHUR and MARY HOCKLEY, and Grandson of the aforesaid BENJAMIN and ELIZABETH, who died 17 of Nov. 1790, Aged 6 Days.
Also WILLIAM, Son of BENJAMIN and ELIZABETH HOCKLEY, who died 12 December 1796, Aged 63 Years.

Here lies the Body of
MARY, Wife of WILLIAM HOBBES, *Junr.* who died Nov. 1, 1744, Aged 21 Years.
Also MARY, their Daughter, who died in her Infancy.
Likewise HENRIETTA, his Second Wife, who died March 4, 1756, Aged 32 Years.
Also THOMAS, their Son, by the said HENRIETTA, who died April 17, 1759, Aged 5 Years.

H. S. E.
JOHANNIS BIDDLE, hujus Parochiæ per quadraginta. et quatuor fere annos Rector, obiit. 25*o.* Februarij MDCCXXXIII*o.* Ætatis LXXVII*o.*

In Memory of
WILLIAM HOBBS, of *West-end, Clothier,* He died June 8, 1778, Aged 63 Years.
Also of JOHN HOBBS, He died Febr. 22, 1766, Aged 14 Years.
Also MARY, Wife of WILLIAM HOBBS, who died Sept. 9, 1796, Aged 64 Years.

NAVE.

ON MONUMENT.

Arms:—Sable a Lion rampant doublequed Ermine:—STOKES.

Near this Place are deposited the Remains of THOMAS STOKES, *Gent.* of this Parish, who died 5*th.* April 1762, Aged 86 Years.

Also EDWARD STOKES,
Younger Son of the above
THOMAS STOKES,
who died 12 April 1791, Aged 73.

BRASS ON FLAT STONE.

ALEXANDER DORNEY, the *Younger*,
of this Parish, *Gent.* was here interred,
He departed this Life, the
17 Oct. 1668, (*On his Mont. it says
he died 21 Sept. 1668.*)
Aged 38 Years.
SARAH, the Wife of THOMAS STOKES,
Senr. of this Parish, *Gent.*
formerly the *Widow* aud *Relict* of
ALEXANDER DORNEY,
abovenamed was likewise here
interred. She died on the Eighth
(*Mont. says she died* 10 *Mh.* 1721)
day of March 1721, in the
94*th.* Year of her Age.

Obiit, non Obiit Virit.

NORTH AISLE.

ON MONUMENTS.

Arms:—STOKES, *as before*, impaling,—HICKES, *as before.*

Near this Monument
In the burying Place of her
Ancestors lies interried the Body
of ELEANOR, late the Wife of
THOMAS STOKES, of this Parish,
Gent. and second Daughter of
JOHN HICKES, *the Elder*, formerly
of *West-end* in this Parish,
Gentleman, deceased by ELIZABETH,
his last Wife, also deceased
who was a Daughter of
WILLIAM OLDISWORTH,
of *Coln Rogers* in this County,
Esquir long since deceased.
She departed this Life, the
24 day of July 1754,
Aged 75 Years.

Arms:—Argent, on a fess between three Mascles voided Sable,
as many Cinque foils of the first.
PURNELL. *impaling* HICKES, *as
before.*

Sacred to the Memories of
Mr. JOHN PURNELL,
late of the *Pool House* in this Parish,
Gent. and of JANE, his Wife,
who was the Youngest Daughter
of JOHN HICKES, of *West-end*,
in this Parish, *Gentleman*,
by ELIZABETH, Daughter of
WILLIAM OLDISWORTH,
of *Coln Rogers* in this County, *Esqr.*
Mr. PURNELL, died August 16, 1726,
Ætatis 46.
His Wife dyed Apr. 5*th.* 1743,
Ætatis 60.
JOHANNES PURNELL, S. T. P. et
Novi Collegij in *Oxon.*
Custos,
Ecclesiæ item Appropriatæ de
Cwmdu. Com. Brecon.
et dioc Menevensis Rector
Optimis Parentibus
P. C.

ON A PLAIN STONE LET INTO
THE WALL.

Vnder This sTone lyeTh The Body of

ROBERT SPERT, of *Wickware*
in The CounTy of *Glouc. Esqr.*
who deparTed This Life, The
27*th.* day of OcTober, A. D. 1638.
VT David JonaThæ morTem deflexiT
amanTis
Sic fleo decessum chare mariTe Tuum
Spes Tamen una maneT cælo nos esse
sodales.
PerpeTuisque bonis absque dolore frui.

(*All Capitals but the letter T much
larger than the others.*)

Underneath this Stone
lyeth the Body of
SAMUEL NIBLETT, of this Parish
and *Alderman* of this *Borough*,
who departed this Life, the
6*th.* day of May 1735,
Aged 54 Years.

ON A TABLE OF COPPER,
AGAINST THE SOUTH WALL.

Arms:—Azure a Chevron between
three Dolphins Nayant Or. DORNEY.

In a Vault
Beneath the Opposite Alley
lye interred the Remains of
ALEXANDER DORNEY,
the *Younger* of this Parish, *Gent.*
He died Sept. 21, A. D. 1668,
in the 38*th* Year of his Age,
leaving behind him SARAH, his Wife,
and by her two Daughters, *viz.*
ELIZABETH and JANE.
the aforementioned SARAH,
afterwards the Wife of
THOMAS STOKES, (younger Son of
SAMUEL STOKES, formerly of
Stanshaw Place in the Parish of
Yate in this County, *Gent.* by
ISABELLA, his Wife, third Daughter of
SAMUEL CODRINGTON,
heretofore of *Dodrington* in this
County, *Esqr.* both long since deceased.
lyeth also interred in the above
mentioned Vault,
She died March ye tenth 1721,
in the 94 Year of her Age,
leaving behind her the before named
ELIZABETH and JANE, as also
THOMAS, her Husband, and
by him one Son only *viz:*—THOMAS.
THOMAS, the Father lyeth also
interred in the aforesaid Vault as
likewise the said ELIZABETH and
JANE, who respectively departed
this Life, in the following Order,
viz:—THOMAS, died August 12, 1732,
Aged 87 Years.
JANE, died April 24, 1738,
Aged 75 Years.
ELIZABETH, died October 7, 1745,
Aged 86 Years.

Sacred to whose Memory this
Monument was here placed by the
aforementioned THOMAS, the Son,
Nov. 7, 1753.

Arms:—Sable a Lion rampant
Ermine, in dexter Canton point a
Mullet for difference.—STOKES.

Crest:—a Demi Lion Ermine.

ALTAR TOMB ON FREESTONE WITH
INSCRIPTION IN THREE COMPART-
MENTS.

M. S.

Gulielmi Filij natu maximi

JOHANNIS HICKES, hujus Parochiæ
Generosi,
Qui obijt
Jan. 14o. Anno Domini 1674,
Ætatis suæ 21.
Hoc, ò Viator marmore Conditæ
charæ recumbent Exuviæ brevem
Viventis Optantisqo Vitam
Præcoce Cœlum Anima Petentis
Musarum Almunus jam fuit lertibus
Præfectus sacris quas sstudis pio
Atq. Aure quam fida receptas
Oxonij Coluit Parentis
Sedsprevit Artes vah nimium Breves
Vitamque longam Credidlt heu Brevem,
Tristisq Plenum Errore multo
Ipsum Hellcona Scatere vidit.
M. S.
JOHANNIS HICKES,
hujus Parochiæ *Generosi*,
Qui arthritico morbo confectus
mortem libenter oppetit
In explorata fide beatæ resurrectionis
Mensis Julij decimo quarto die
Ano. Salutis millesimo
sexcentesimo nonagesimo quarto
Ætatis suæ septuagesimo.
H. S. J.
Juxta mariti Exuvias ELIZABETHA
HICKES, Fil. GUL. OLDISWORTH,
de *Coln Rogers*, in Com. *Glouc.
Armigeri*,
Ob. Sep'ris. 6*to.* A. D. 1727, Ætat. 81.
Dum cœlum habet animam
Sub hoc Tumulo hypogœum
Caros conservat cineres
MARIA, Filiæ JOHANIS et
ELIZABETHÆ HICKES,
maximæ piæ Virginis
Quæ immedicabilibus Variolis laborans
placide in Christo obdormivit
Octobris die Vicesimo sexto
Æra Christi
Millesima septingensima undecima
paulo post anos quadriginta impleverat.

ON A MONUMENT AGAINST A PILLAR.

Arms:—Argent, three Gates Gules,
2 and 1.—YATE. *impaling* HICKES, *as
before.*

Near this Monument
is interred the Body of
ELIZABETH, the Wife of EDWARD
YATE, of *Malmsbury* in the County
of *Wilts. Clothier*, and Daughter of
JOHN HICKES, of this Parish,
Gent. by SYLVESTER, his Wife,
who departed this Life,
16 day of October, Anno Dom. 1721,
Ætatis suæ 67.

ON MONUMENTS AGAINST THE
NORTH WALL.

Arms:—Sable a Lion rampant
Argent.—STOKES. *impaling Quarterly*
1 & 4, Or. on a Canton Azure a Griffins head erased ...... 2 & 3, Gules
on a Bend Argent three Mullets Sable.
Crest:—a demi Lion Argent.

Sacred to the Memory of
SAMUEL STOKES, of this Parish,
Gent. who died 31 Jany. 1773,
Aged 60 Years.
He was endowed with all the social
Virtues of a Tender Husband,
sincere Friend and a true Christian.
This Monument
erected by his Widow as a Testimony
of her Affectionate Regard to his
Memory.
Also MARTHA, Widow of the afore-

said SAMUEL STOKES, who died
17 of June 1791, Aged 66 Years.

PAINTED UPON A BOARD.

Arms:—PURNELL, *as before, im-
paling* HICKES, *as before.*
Crest:—a Talbot sejant resting
his foot upon a Shield Argent.
(*Underneath painted in Caps.*)
Mr. PURNELL, ob. Aug. 16, 1726,
Ætatis 46.
Mrs. PURNELL, ob April 5, 1743,
Ætatis 60.

ON FLAT STONES.

Underneath lie interred the
Remains of JAMES FOWLER, of
this Town, *Mercer*, who died
Oct. 26, 1798, Aged 74 Years.
Also MARTHA, his Wife,
died Sept. 22, 1791, Aged 80 Years.

Here lies a rare Example of much
goodness, *Mr.* JOHN PURNELL,
late of *Poole House* in this Parish,
who died August 16,
Anno } Salutis } 1726,
          } Ætatis } 46.
He was a Zealous Member of the
Church of England, a loving Husband,
a tender Father, a kind Relation,
a generous Friend,
Always acceptable to the Rich
and Liberal to the Poor,
Injurys between others
He easily reconciled,
His own as readily forgave
a Blessed Peace-maker,
He was through the whole Cours
of his Life,
A Sincere Christian without
Ostentation
And a Lover of all Mankind
without desire of Praise.
Reader
Go Thou, and do likewise
That Thou' mayest rest in peace
and Rise in Glory.
Also THOMAS, his Youngest Son,
died Augest 6, 1728,
Aged 4 Years and 9 months.

Underneath this Stone lyeth
the Body of SAMUEL NIBLETT,
Alderman, of this Borough,
who departed this Life, the
21 of Sept. 1781, Aged 63 Years.

Here lyeth SARAH, the Wife of
SAMUEL NIBLETT,
who died Nov. 9, 1765, Aged 90.

CHURCH YARD.

ON MONUMENT & TOMBS.

Here lyeth the Body of
JOHN TOMES, the *Elder*,
who departed this Life, the
29 day of December 1668.

Here lyeth the Body of
JOHN TOMES, *Junior*,
who departed this Life, the
28 day of July, Anno Domini 1666,
Ætatis suæ 26.
Also the Body of
MARY GEERING, late Wife of
THOMAS GEERING,
and formerly Wife of JOHN TOMES,
who departed this Life, the
...... day of July, A. D. 1698.

ON A HANDSOME WHITE MARBLE
TOMB, ENCOMPASSED WITH IRON
PALLASADES.

Here lies SARAH, the Wife of
DANIEL WOODWARD,
of the City of *Bristol, Merchant*,
and Daughter of THOMAS
SPRINGETT, *Esqr.* of *Grosmond*
in the County of *Monmouth*,
by SARAH, his Wife,
who
(dear to her Relations
Valuable to her Acquaintance
Charitable to the Poor,
Pious towards God)
Died 13 of June 1749, Aged 31,
and has left a Name behind her
more lasting than this Marble
can perpetuate.
Also her two Daughters
ELIZABETH and SARAH, ELIZABETH,
being interred with her Aged 11 days,
And SARAH, the 6 day of January
following Aged 7 Months.
Also two of her Brothers
JAMES and GILES,
JAMES, was buried Nov. 22, 1746,
Aged 11 Months.
GILES, January 25th. 1733,
Aged 12 Years.
Here also lieth interred the
Body of WILLIAM WOODWARD,
Son of DANIEL WOODWARD, *Esqr.*
and the said SARAH, his Wife,
He died the 3 day of May 1754,
Aged 6 Years.

Arms: at one end—... ... ... three
Oak leaves .... *impaling* per fess
.... a fess wavy between three
Cresscents counter charged.

[*see Inscription in Chancel to the above*
SARAH WOODWARD, *and her Father*
WILLIAM GILES.]

Here lyeth the Body of
DANIEL OSBURN, who died
Sept. 21, 1719, Aged 52 Years.
Also MARY, Wife of DANIEL
OSBURN, who died Nov. 23, 1719,
Aged 63 Years.
DANIEL, their Son, died
Decr. 27, 1759, Aged 60 Years.
and SARAH, his Wife, died
Decr 3, 1764, Aged 82 Years.
In Memory of
JOYCE, the Wife of JOHN COX,
of *Tytherington*, and Daughter of
DANIEL OSBURN, of this Parish,
who departed this Life,
March 12, 1730, Aged 29 Years.
Also ARTHUR OSBURN COX,
their Son, died May 26, 1731,
an Infant.

Here lyeth the Body of
CHRISTOPHER ANDREWS,
of this Parish, who departed this
Life, the 25 day of Decm. 1679.
Also the Body of MARY ANDREWS,

the Wife of CHRISTOPHER ANDREWS,
who was buried August the
first 1698.
RICHARD, the Son of CHRISTOPHER
and MARGARET ANDREWS,
was buried May 27th. 1768,
Aged 71 Years.
CHARLES, Son of JOHN ANDREWS,
by ELIZABETH, his Wife, died the
9th. day of January 1754,
an Infant.

Here lyeth the Body of
CHRISTOPHER ANDREWS, *the Elder*,
of this Parish, *Yeoman*,
who departed this Life, the
16th. day of September,
Anno Dom. 1669.
Also the Body of
JOHN ANDREWS, *Yeoman*,
his Son, who departed this Life, the
1 day of May in the 76
Year of his Age and in the
Year of our Lord 1702.
Also the Body of
HANNAH, late Widow of the above
JOHN ANDREWS, who was buried
Nov. 1, 1704, Aged 93 Years.
Also the Body of ELIZABETH,
the Daughter of JOHN and HANNAH
WEBB, formerly of *Iron Acton*,
who was buried the 28 of Febr. 1753,
Aged 47 Years.
Also HANNAH, relict of the said
JOHN WEBB, and Daughter of
JOHN and HANNAH ANDREWS,
who exchanged this Life, in
hopes of a happy Immortality,
April 22, 1768, Aged 93 Years.

To the Memory of
Mrs. MARY ANDREWS, *Spinster*,
who exchanged this Life, in full
hopes of Immortality,
June 23, 1749, Aged 79 Years.

In Memory of
CATHARINE, the Wife of
SAMSON CARY, of *Wotton*,
who departed this Life,
May the 1st. 1742, Aged 32 Years.

To the Memory of
HENRY HARFORD, of this Parish,
and of ELIZABETH, his Wife,
He died April 28, 1767,
Aged 82 Years.
She August 28, 1759,
Aged 78 Years.
Also JOHN, their Son,
died Jany. 1st. 1745, Aged 34.
Also of MARTHA, the Wife of
JOHN HARFORD, of the Parish
of *Westerleigh*, who died
Sept. 18, 1731, Aged 73 Years.
Likewise to the Memory of
HENRY, Son of HENRY and
ELIZABETH HARFORD, of this Parish,
who died 16 of Nov. 1781,
Aged 64 Years.
ANN, Widow of the said
HENRY HARFORD, above mentioned.
She died 3 day of Jany. 1791,
in the 73 Year of her Age.
Also of HANNAH, Widow of
SAMUEL TIMBERMAN,
and Daughter of HENRY HARFORD.
Senior, She died the 27 day of July
1800, Aged near 82 Years.

In Memory of
BETTY, Wife of JOHN LOVEGROVE,
of the City of *Bristol*, and
Daughter of SAMUEL and HANNAH
TIMBERMAN and Grand-
Daughter of HENRY and ELIZABETH
HARFORD, who died Febr. 23, 1777,
Aged 79 Years.
Underneath this Tomb
was interred the Body of
CHRISTOPHER, Son of NICHOLAS
and BETTY ANDREWS, late of
Frampton Cotterell in this County,
who died 11 day of August 1793,
Aged 47 Years.

Here lieth the Body of
HENRY CAME, *Gent.*
who was gathered unto his
Fathers in Peace and was buried
in good age and died the 14 of
April 1620.
Uxor
Chare. vale. conjux. quamvis. mors.
Vincula fregit
Conjugii. fido. cordis. Amore. sequar.
Maritus.
Chara. vale. conjux. quam vis. nos.
dividitatrox
Mors eadem pariter reddet amica
brevi.

Here lyeth the Body of
NEBUCHADNEZZER PROUT,
who died April 23, 1692.
Also of ROBERT, his Son,
who died Febr. 19, 1690.
Also of CHRISTIAN, his Daughter,
who died Oct. 29, 1689.
Also MARY, Daughter of
ARTHUR PROUT and SARAH,
his Wife, who died April 20, 1717.
Also of ROBERT, Son of
ARTHUR PROUT and SARAH,
his Wife, who died .. ..
Also of ROBERT, Son of ARTHUR
PROUT, of *Cromhall*, who died
the 18 of May 1679.
In Memory of
THOMAS, Son of THOMAS and
ELIZABETH STURGE, of *Oveston*,
who died Decr. 5, 1760,
Aged 22 Years.
Also in Memory of
MARY WOODMAN, Relict of
JOHN WOODMAN, of this Parish,
Yeoman, who died Sept 26, 1768,
Aged 76 Years.

In Memory of
JOHN SOMERS, of *Southwood*,
in this Parish, and MARY. his Wife,
who were buried:
JOHN, April 9, 1710, Aged 63.
MARY, April 25, 1715. Aged 63.
Also of JOHN, Son of the said
JOHN and MARY SOMERS,
was buried March 18, 1734,
Aged 60 Years.
And of ALEXANDER, his Son,
by CHRISTIAN, his Wife,
was buried Oct. 10, 1710.
And of CHRISTIAN, late Widow
of the said JOHN SOMERS,
who was buried the 15 day of
December 1736, Aged 71 Years.
Here likewise lies interred the Body
of JOHN SOMERS, of this Parish,
Junr. Son of JOHN and CHRISTIAN,
his Wife, who departed this Life,
11 Oct. 1750, Aged 49 Years.

Here likewise lies interred the
Body of JANE, the Daughter of
JOHN and CHRISTIAN SOMERS,
and Relict of WILLIAM RUSSELL,
of this Parish, who departed this Life,
24 of Sept. 1776, Aged 72 Years.
In Memory of
MARY, Relict of WILLIAM SOMERS,
Senr. who died Jany. 8, 1734,
Aged 68 Years.
Also of ELIZABETH, their Daughter,
who died April 17, 1716,
Aged 16 Years.
Also of WILLIAM SOMERS, *Junr.*
who died Oct. 6, 1756,
. ged 52 Years.
Also of two more of their Sons
WILLIAM and MOSES, and of SARAH,
their Daughter, who all died young.
Likewise was Interred the
Body of SARAH, the late Widow
of the aforesaid WILLIAM SOMERS,
Junr. who died April 8. 1794,
in the 92 Year of her Age.

In Memory of
JOSEPH FOORD, *Junr.*
who died Nov 13, 1765,
Aged 66 Years.
Also eight of their Children,
who died in their Infancy.
MOSES FOORD, *Senr.*
died March 8, 1723,
Aged 58 Years.
HANNAH, his Wife,
died Decr. 3, 1710, Aged 37.
Also two of their Sons,
who died in their Infancy.
MARY, Relict of the above
MOSES FOORD, who died
Nov. 15, 1794, Aged 84 Years.
Also MOSES FOORD, the Son of
MOSES and MARY FOORD,
who died July 5, 1793, Aged 49.

Under this Tomb rest the Ashes of
THOMAS RUSSELL, of this Parish,
Yeoman, who departed this Life,
the 28 of July 1663, Aged 45 Years.
Also ELIANOR, his Wife,
who died Sept. 4, 1701,
Aged 82 Years.
Also TOBIAS RUSSELL, *Junr.*
who exchanged a Temporal for
an eternal Life, on May 13, 1702,
Aged 22 Years.

In Memory of
JASPER MORSE, of this Parish,
who was buried May 18, 1718,
Aged 67 Years.
Also EDITH, his Wife, who was
buried May 18, 1718, Aged 58.
Near this Tomb lieth the Body of
ANNE MORSE, Widow of this Parish,
who departed this Life,
1 Oct. 1738, Aged 67 Years.

Here lyeth the Body of
ANNE, the Wife of EDMUND WATTS,
of *Wickwar*, who died the
20 day of November, 1650.
Also the Body of
Mr. ABIGAIL HIGGINS, late Wife of
Mr. OBADIAH HIGGINS,
Minister, of this Parish,
who exchanged this Life,
for immortality the 13 day of
November 1675.

Uxor
Chare. vale. conjux. quamvis. mors.
vincula. fregit.
Conjugii. fido. cordis. Amore. sequar.
Maritus.
Chara. vale. conjux. quam. vis. nos.
dividit. atrox.
Mors. eadem pariter redde amica
brevi.

Here lies interred SARAH CALVERT,
who (after a faithful Service of
above 40 Years in one Family,)
departed this Life, Nov. 16, 1771,
Aged 67 Years.

In Memory of
JOHN TOWNSEND and MARGARET,
his Wife,
MARGARET, died 23 March 1690,
Aged 38 Years.
JOHN, died 10 October 1632,
Aged 79 Years.
JOHN, their Son, died 14 July 1748,
Aged 64 Years.

Here lyeth the Body of
MARGERY BROWNING, Widow,
who departed this Life,
27 August 1681.
Also the Body of WILLIAM
THOMAS, of the Parish of *Tetbury*,
was buried August 28, 1823.

Here lieth the Body of
Mr. JAMES WILKINS, *Attorney-at-
Law*, who died 31 March 1729,
Aged 46 Years.
Also ANNE WILKINS, Relict of
the said *Mr.* JAMES WILKINS,
who died 8 Decr. 1759, Aged 73.

Here lieth the Body of
Mr. ROBERT PLOMER,
who died Febr. the 2nd. 1746,
Aged 67 Years.

In Memory of
MARY, Wife of THOMAS DINING,
who died August 31, 1760,
Also of ANNE, their Daughter,
who died Aug. 16, 1759,
an Infant.
Also in Memory of
MARY and CHRISTIAN, Children of
THOMAS and MARY HICKS,
who both died in 1726, Infants.

To the Memory of
JOHN BURNELL, who died
March 1723, Aged 40 Years.

Here lyeth the Body of
ANNE, the Wife of HENRY
SHIPMAN, of this Parish, *Junr.*
who died Sept. 23, 1733,
Aged 38 Years.
Also MARY, their Daughter,
was buried Decr. 20, 1719.
Also three Children of the said
HENRY SHIPMAN, by MARY

his Wife, *viz:*—CHRISTOPHER, CHARLES and ALICE, who all died Young.
Also of WILLIAM, Son of HENRY SHIPMAN, of this Town, *Gent.* who was buried 18 April 1753, Aged 8 Weeks.
Also the Body of HENRY SHIPMAN, *Senr.* who died 21 April 1750, Aged 58 Years.
Also JOHN, HENRY and WILLIAM, Children of his Son HENRY, of this Town, *Gent.* who all died Young.
In Memory of HENRY SHIPMAN, *Attorney-at-Law*, who died Febr. 28, 1763, Aged 45 Years.
Also of ANNE, Daughter of WILLIAM and ELIZABETH ROACH. and Grand Daughter of the said HENRY SHIPMAN, who died Young.

Here lieth under this Tombe the Body of RICHARD HICKES, of this Parish, who departed this Life, the 31 Oct. 1678, Aged 49.
Also the Body of ELEANOR HICKES, of this Parish, who died the 27 of April 1706, Aged 71 Years.
Also Wife of ELIZABETH, Wife of MATHEW CREW, who was buried Nov. 4, 1720, Aged 83 Years.
Also the Body of MATHEW CREW, of *West-end, Clothier*, who departed this Life, 10 April 1726, Aged 74 Years.

In Memory of DANIEL POCLE, of this Parish, who died the 15 of May 1738, Aged 52 Years.
And of JUDITH, his Wife, who died 26 Nov. 1747, Aged 69 Years.
Also in Memory of one Son, and two Daughters of DANIEL, and JUDITH POOLE, who were buried near this Tomb:
JUDITH, 14 Febr. 1734, Aged 20 Years.
DANIEL, 31 October 1745, Aged 29 Years.
MARY, 22 April 1746, Aged 33 Years.
Also near this Tomb was buried the Body of THOMAS POOLE, of this Parish, who departed this Life, the 25 Oct. 1756, Aged 33 Years.

In Memory of HANNAH, Daughter of NATHANIEL and HANNAH WITCOMB, of this Parish and Wife of EDWARD JONES, of *Westerleigh*, who died 20 December 1762, in the 45 Year of her Age.

Sacred to the Memory of WILLIAM SOMERS, of *Pinkney* in the County of *Wilts*. who died July 5, 1787, in the 39 Year of his Age.
Also ELIZABETH, his Daughter, died in her Idfancy.

This Tomb is Erected to preserve the Memory of LAZARUS SOMERS, who died Decr. 8, 1771, Aged 36.
Also beneath this Tomb was interred the Body of WILLIAM SOMERS, Son of the aforesaid LAZARUS SOMERS, by BETTY, his Wife, who departed this Life, the 29 day of April 1799, in the 50 Year of his Age.

In Memory of ELEANOR, the Wife of WILLIAM BROWN, of this Town, She died Jany. 29, 1800, Aged 43 Years.
Also of MARY, his Daughter She died Decr. 31, 1799, Aged 61 Years.

This Memorial inscribed to CHARLES BROWN, of *Gearing-frith*, in the Parish of *Yate, Yeoman*, who died Jany. 15, 1799, in the 54 Year of his Age.
Also BETTY, his Daughter, who died Oct. 21, 1786, Aged 4 Years and 6 Months.

Sacred to the Memory of WILLIAM CANTER, of this Parish, *Gent.* who departed this Life, the 5, June 1797, Aged 66 Years.
Also of ESTHER, his Wife, who departed this Life, the 4 Oct. 1759, Aged 33 Years.
Also of ANNE, his second Wife, who departed this Life, Decr. 23, 1790, Aged 69 Years.
Also three Children, who died in their Infancy.

In Memory of STEPHEN, Son of WILLIAM and SARAH MORLEY, of this Parish, who died August 9, 1775, in the 4 Year of his Age.
Also of ALICE, their Daughter, who died Decr. 7, 1784, in the 19 Year of her Age.
And EDWARD, their Son, who died April 22, 1785, in the 12 Year of his Age.
Likewise in Memory of the said WILLIAM MORLEY, abovementioned who died the 11 day of July 1792, in the 58 Year of his Age.
Also of SARAH and THOMAS, their Daughter and Son, She died June 10, 1795, in the 15 Year of her Age.
And he the third day of Sept. 1785, in the 13 Year of his Age.

ANNE HANBURY, obiit 10 of April 1792.

In Memory of CATHERINE, Wife of RICHARD BARBER, of this Parish, who died Febr. 18, 1763, Aged 34 Years.
In Memory of RICHARD BARBER, of this Parish,

who died April 16, 1786, Aged 64 Years.
ALICE, Relict of RICHARD BARBER, who died August 19, 1800, Aged 81 Years.

WILLIAM MYNETTS, of *West-end*, in this Parish, who died 13 day of Febr. 1791, and BETTY, his Wife, who died the 1 day of June 1791, Aged 74 Years.

Sacred to the Memory of *Mrs.* JANE PARKER, who after a long and painful series of Illness which she with most Christian fortitude firmly endured departed this Life, in hopes of a Joyful Resurrection on the *6th.* day of December 1784, in the 44 Year of her Age.

In Memory of HANNAH, the Wife of STEPHEN BARBER, of this Parish, and Daughter of JOSEPH and ELIZABETH CULLIMORE, late of *Tortworth*, who died the 3 day of April 1786, in the 22 Year of his Age.

ELIZABETH, Daughter of the *Revd.* JOSEPH WILLIAMS, and ELIZABETH, his Wife, died an Infant, Sept. 25, 1788.
JOSEPH, their Son, died Febr. 25, 1791, Aged 4 Years.
MARGARET, their Daughter, died Nov. 14, 1792, Aged 15 Months.
JOSEPH, an Infant, died Nov. 19, 1792.
THOMAS, the Son, died Jan. 29, 1793, Aged 7 Years.

In Memory of ELIZABETH, the Wife of WILLIAM BARBER, of the Parish of *Charfield*, and Daughter of JOHN and HESTER HOPKINS, of the Parish of *Kingswood, Wilts.* who departed this Life, 6 Jany. 1690, Aged 24 Years.
CHRISTIAN, the Daughter of WILLIAM and MARGARET BARBER, died August 28, 1794, Aged 6 Months.

In Memory of HENRY GRIFFIN, of this Parish, who died April 23, 1778, Aged 59 Years.
ELIZABETH, his Wife, died 21 day of Decr. 1786, in the 67 Year of her Age.

(*Supplementary Note of an Additional Monument since Bigland's time.*)

In Memory of WILLIAM HOBBS, *Esquire*, of *West-end* in this Parish, who died July 8, 1860, Aged 71 Years.

1454

Also of ESTHER, his Widow,
who died Jany. 16, 1866,
Aged 83 Years.
Also of WILLIAM HOBBS, *Esqr.*
of *West-end*, Son of the above named
who died Sept. 7, 1863,
Aged 54 Years.
Also of HENRIETTA PERRY HOBBS,
Daughter of the first named
WILLIAM and ESTHER HOBBS,
who died Sept. 15, 1870,
Aged 53 Years.

ADDITIONAL INSCRIPTIONS ON
STOKES MONUMENT.

ELIZABETH STOKES, Daughter
of the above THOMAS STOKES,
died 6 Oct. 1810, Aged 96 Years.
JOHN SUMERS,
of this Parish, *Malster*,
died Febr. 28, 1763, Aged 73 Years.
Also HANNAH, his Wife,
died Oct. 29, 1768, Aged 68 Years.

A MEMORIAL WINDOW
for
CHAS. EDW. OAKLEY, M.A. B.C.L.
for 7 Years Rector of this Parish,
died Sept. 16, 1865,
And of the *Lady* GEORGINA-MARY-
LOUISA, his Wife,
died October 10, 1667.
St John, xvii 24.
[*see "Tortworth."*]

CHANCEL.

WILLIAM BARBEN, Son of
WILLIAM and RUTH BARBER,
of *Southwood*, 12 Years Superintendant
of the Sunday School of this Church
and afterwards missionary Catechist
in the Diocese of *Brisbane,
Queensland, Australia*,
fell asleep in Jesus, Nov. 21, 1860,
Aged 38 Years.
This Tablet is erected to his beloved
Memory by the *Revd.* G. E. OAKLEY,
Rector of Wickwar.

IN CHURCH YARD.

Inscriptions:—To WHITE, FRANKLIN,
WATTS, LOVELL, LOWE, CHANDLER,
HARFORD, MINETT, DORNEY, COOK,
IRVING.

.... ILES, of the Parish of *Yate*,
died 1746.
PARK, BICK, DAW, BROWN, FORD,
PARKER, TOWNSEND, JONES, SOMERS,
FLETCHER, FOWLER, PLAISHER,
CLIFF, ARNOLD, SHIPP, KELSAY,
EVEREST, BARNAM, SHIPWAY, JAMES,
TILL, BISHOP, RANDOLPH, POWELL,
HOPCINS, HOBBS, COX, MORTON,
BARKET, BARBER, AYFORD,
WILLIAM HIGGS, 1876.
ARABELLA HIGGS, *St. Pauls, Bristol.*
SARAH ANN HIGGES, 1847.
HANNAH HIGGS,
of *Chipping Sodbury.*
ELIZABETH, *Dowager Countess of*
MASSAREANE.
CULLIMORE, PHILLIPS, GLOVER,
THICK, MORLEY, BROWN, CANTER,
WITCOMB, VIVICK, REDDY, MARMAN,
PULLEN, ATKINS, JOHN, 1800.
KIRBY, ALLEN, ANDREWS, FOWLER,
AMOS, POOLE, COOKE, HAINES.

HEAD STONES IN CHURCH YARD.

	Died.		Aged.		Died.		Aged.
William White, ...	20 Nov.	1747	50	Esther, Wife of James Summers,	3 Febr.	1791	70
Thomas Hale, ...	10 July	1771	52	Mary, Daughter of Thomas Poole,	1 Febr.	1776	20
Ann, Daughter of John Rugg,	15 March	1775	15	Sarah Cook, ...	14 Oct.	1781	82
Betty, his Daughter, ...	8 July	1783	31	John Cook, ...	... ...	1745	62
Nicholas Andrews, ...	9 March	1781	55	Jane, his Wife, ...	... ...	1754	68
Hannah, his Wife, ...	17 Febr.	1779	56	John Sherman, ...	17 Jany.	1742	31
Daniel Rodway, ...	7 April	1788	48	John Reuch, ...	20 Oct.	1764	86
John Brokenborough, ...	19 April	1774	81	Robert Webbley, ...	... ...	1857	...
Elizabeth, his Wife, ...	1 August	1770	63	Elizabeth, his Wife, ...	... ...	1754	...
William Hollway, ...	8 Oct.	1770	68	James, their Son, ...	4 April	1788	42
William Hollway, ...	1 July	1771	74	Sarah, Wife of Thomas Goulter,	13 Sept.	1800	67
John Jones, ...	1 June	1746	18	Henry Rickets, ...	7 Decr.	1737	42
Ann, Wife of Richard Low, ...	22 Decr.	1773	80	William Green, ...	8 August	1766	65
Nehemiah Philpot, ...	12 May	1782	57	Daniel Rodway, ...	27 April	1788	48
Robert Lovell, ...	29 Febr.	1780	51				

Notes as to 1.—*Devolution of Estates.* II.—*Church.* III.—*Population, Taxation, &c.*

1.—*Estates :*

In Bachestanes Hundred Wicken, (Wickwar.) contained
4 Hides. Culture: in Demesne 4 Carucates, and Nine in Villenage, (9 Villans and 14 Bordars.) There were 5 Serfs. Of
Meadow 20 *a.*, of Wood, a quarentain. Its Value yearly was
7 £.

In King Edward's time, three Men of Brictric, son of
Algar, held it for three Manors, they were free to sell as
they would. The Queen (Matilda, Wife of William Conqueror, gave this and Acton Manor to Hunfred the Chamberlain, who held at the Survey. *Domesday.*

Whether this revengeful Queen held only a Life grant
herself of these Lands of the unfortunate Brictric, or how
otherwise but so it was, these came to the Crown, and by
King John, were given to a De la Warr, which family long
held them.

9 Edw. ii.—John le Warr, and Reg. le Warr. *Fine.*

From that family to Sir Robert Ducy. In which family
it continues still. *see* "Tortworth."

Lands in Wickwar :

8 Hen. vi.—J. Newton, and Wife Joan, Settlement in
tail. *Fine.*

28 Hen. vi.—W. More, from John son of J. Newton.
Fine.

Pool House, Wickwar, was built by Woolworth, 1796.
see "Lysons' Antiq. Gloucestershire, *Plate* xxviii."

My. 27 and 28 Eliz.—H. Baynham, *Plaintiff.* and W.
Woolworth, *Deforciant.*

T. 20 Eliz.—Hen. Cambe, *Plaintiff.* and Wm. Wol-
worth, *Deforciant.*

My. 29 and 30 Eliz.—Thos. Neale, *Plaintiff.* and John
Ivye, *Deforciant.* *Fine.*

Lands in Wickwar:

Andrew Sudenhum.

12 Edw. ii—J. and J. Howes, by Grant at the annual
Rent of Two Pounds of Wax.

3 Edw. ii.—Fine between Roger and Alice Burbaste.

Bagstone, formerly Bachestane, whence the name of the
Hundred:

An Estate here belonged to Dodenham, *see* "Subsidy
Roll, 1 Edw. iii."

A Messuage and Meeting House called Bow Rooms
and the Gardens called Dodenhams in Wickwar, were part
of the Town and Church Lands of Chipping Sodbury.

1838—The Wickwar, Cromhall and Tortworth Inclosure Act passed Under which an Award was made dated
5 June 1841, and enrolled in the Office of Clerk of the Peace
1841. There were 90 *a.* of common field Land and 600 *a.* of
Commons and waste Lands to be inclosed.

Earl Ducie, was Lord of the Manor but the Rights of
Lord Segrave, as Lord Royal of Cromhall, are saved.

A manerial Allotment of one-eighth part of the Land in
Wickwar, was made to Earl Ducie The other Allotments
were numerous (90) but except those to Earl Ducie, Mr.
Miller and Mr. Rolph, each of small extent.

Mines and Minerals under the Allotments were reserved
to the Lord; but Stone Quarries, &c. to belong to the Land
Owners. Six Recreation (public) Allotments were made to
the Lord, 5 of not quite an acre each, and the 6*th.* somewhat
more.

The following Farms and Places are named in the Award:
Kites Nest, Sweet House Farm, Barbers Court, Cow, Shippen Farm, Bockney, Woolfends.

1776.—*At the County Election, the following Voted as freeholders in Wickwar.*

Andrews, (2) Christopher,	Jno. Hobbs, William.
Barber, Richard.	Jayne, William.
Bick, Nichl.	Jobbings, Francis.
Canter, William,	King, John.
Cole; Norman Samuel.	Limbrick, William.
Edwards, Richd.	Neal, Robert.
Fortune, John.	Niblett, Samuel.
Fowler, James.	Somers, William.
Galraway, Francis.	Springett, William.
Hale, William.	Shoote, Revd. Henry.

II.—*Church :*

The Rectory was in Rents and farm and Tythes £11. 14s. 9d. over and above 6s. 8d. to the Archdeacon for cenage and proxies and 13d. yearly Rate of the Bishops Visitation charge 3s. 4d. every third year less 1d. and a pension of 6£. to George Colyer, Clerk. *Valor Eccl'us.*
Colyer, had been Rector, and the pension was doubtless for life only. The amount reckoned in the Living is now between 400£. and 500£. and there are a Rectory House and 70a. of Glebe.

The Advowson was long appendant to the Manor. It was severed therefrom about a century ago; but has since been reunited.

List of Incumbents and Patrons of Wickwar.

Incumbents.	*Patrons.*
15d5.—T. Bishop.	
Geo Collier.	Lord De la Warr.
1559.—Wm. Jones.	
1583.—Fcis. Yate.	Queen Elizth.
H. Bishop.	
1615.—Tobias Higgins.	T. West.
1647.—Obadiah Higgins.	W. Edwards, &c.
1668.—Eleazar Marshall.	Sir W. Ducie, Bart.
1678.—Samuel Edwards.	William, Visct. Down.
1684.—James Kirkman.	E. Moreton.
1690—John Biddle.	E. Moreton, *Junr.*
1734.—John Fortune.	Wm. Giles.
1777.—John Chester.	J. Chester.
1801.—Thomas Cook.	Thos. Cook.
T. Everest.	

At Bishop Hoopers' Examination George Colier, was not examined not being a resident in the Diocese.

Laurence Giles, the Minister and Head School Master, there, was examined and found to be a learned Man ably answering all the Articles enumerated.

It appears by this, that there was a Grammar School here before the foundation of Alexander Hosea. The name of Gyles, was of local repute.
The Number of Communicants was 400.

Charities:—

1683.—Alexander Hosea, of London, (a native of Wickwar,) by Will gave 600£. for a public Charity School, (Grammar.) Also the House called the Swan at the Corner of Gray's Inn Lane, London, to the Corporation of Wickwar.

The Income of the Endowment is said to be now 136£. a Year.

1869 —a new Scheme was framed by the Charity Commissioners vesting the management of the School and its property in the Lord of the Manor, the Rector and Church-Wardens, and the Mayor, and two Aldermen selected by the Corporation from their body.

The School House and Masters House have been recently rebuilt.

17 Jac. i.—A House in Wickwar, given for Apprenticeing poor Boys, was vested in Trustees, Rector, Church Wardens and Overseers.

1722.—E. Yate, by Will gave 8£. the Interest to apprentice poor Boys of Wickwar and Yate in London, by Trustees. It is invested in Stock.

Sermons:—Spirts Gift £2. a Year, Half for poor, as Trustees, the Rector, Church Wardens and Overseers thought fit. The other half to Rector, for preaching 2 Sermons.

Gift to the Poor Woolford's £4. a Year out of farm in Charfield, Trustees the Rector, Church Wardens and Overseers.

1712—Prouts Gift :—Cook's Leaze Close in Wickwar. and 20£. the Rents and Interest for Coats and gowns to ten poor Men and Women in Wickwar. The 20£. was invested in stock.

1724.—Elizth. Hickes, gave 20£. the Interest to poor old Inhabitants, invested by Trustees

1747.—Hobbs gave 30s. out of a Dwelling House, for Coats for 3 poor Cloth Workers in Wickwar, selected by Trustees.

1782.—Elizth. Hickes, gave 200£. The Interest to poor Widows of Wickwar, or poor Housekeepers of Wickwar, not almsfolk.

1807.—T. Summers, gave 10£. Stock the Dividends to buy Bread for the most deserving Poor of Wickwar.

There are Baptist and Wesleyan Chapels, and a National School.

III.—*Taxation, Population, &c.*

Wykewarre, Subsidy Roll, 1 Edw. iii., 1327.

De Johne de la Warre, viii s.		De Henr. Squyer, ii s. o. q.	
' Johe. Adekyn, xviii d o.		' Simon Suthinton, vi d.	
' Willo. Mulleward, ii s. xd.		' Johe. atte Cornere, xii d.	
' Rico. Harry, iii s. v d. q.		' Rogo. Denys, iii s. ii d. q.	
' Johe. Gros, xii d.		' Johe. le Machoun, vi d.	
' Andr. Tydenham, iis. viiid		' Johe. Denys, xix d. o. q.	
' Robto. Herries, vi d.		' Henr. Inthehurne, xii d.	
' Johe. de Chilton, iis. xd. o.		' Johe. Hope, xii d.	
' Robto. Baroun, iii s. xd. o.		' Willo. Mom'ay. ii s.	
' Johe. Wassemere, xii d.		' Johe. le Reue, xii d.	

prob. Sma. xlis viid. ob.

Acreage 2280 a.

Population 1801,—765. 1831.—972. 1871,—902.

In 1815. Annual Value of Real Property 4347£.

1882.—Rateable Value £6224.

1833-4-5. Average of three Years Expenditure on Poor £415.

In Chipping Sodbury Union.

The Clothing trade was at one time carried on extensivaly. Among the early Clothiers here, the Names of Giles, Springett and Adeane, Hicks, Hobbs, Morton, are in the Parish Records.

West-end was the Chief Seat of this Industry. It is now entirely discontinued.

In and near to the Boundary Brook, traces of the Mills may be found.

Wickwar, is a large Parish, 10 miles in compass. The Town of Wickwar, has a corporation of a Mayor and 12 Aldermen. Its Market House was built at the beginning of this Century.

Wickwar, is within the Low Level of the Commission of Sewers for the County of Gloucester.

WILLERSEY.

T H E Church is a Rectory, in the Deanery of Campden. It is dedicated to St. Peter, and is built in the form of a Cross, with a Tower in the middle, containing Six Bells. The founder of it is supposed to lie buried in a Nich in the Chancel, now covered by a pew. A neat Altar piece, with the Ten Commandments, with a brass Plate fixed to it, on which is engraved "This Altar Piece is the Gift of John Scott, Gent. son of the late Rector of this Parish, A. D. 1784.

.... Winnington, Esqr. Lord of the Manor.

Revd. William Scott, Rector, and Patron.

INSCRIPTIONS IN THE CHURCH.

CHANCEL.
FLAT STONES.

Hic jacet Ricardus Gregory, Hujusce Parochiæ per viginti ferme annos, vigilantissimus, et inculpabilis Rector. in Uxorem Castitatis non temerandæ Maritus, In Liberos Pietatis haud vulgaris Pater, Inter omnes Summi acuminis, et innocui leporis audivit comes. Is erat, quem imitari, Quem pro meritis laudare, Impares sumus. Sat Famæ, sibique Vixit, Ecclesiæ vero, et amicis, parum. Quid multa. Hoc Corporis Ergastulo solutus In certissimam meliois ævi spem Gregorius Gregoreo,

Obiit sexto 9bris. Anno { Ætat. 46, { Dom. 1718.

Hic deponuntur Ossa Catharinæ, Matris istius Ricardi Gregory, Quam bonus tandem Deus satis annosam, scilicet octogenariam, Testo Lychnocaiæ quæ fuit in. MDCCXX. E Mortalitatis tenebris In lucem suam cælestem vocavit.

In Memory of
Grace Scott, Wife of the
Revd. John Scott,
who departed this Life Feb. 14th.
in the Year of our Lord 1751,
Aged 36.
Having first discharged the Duties of
a good Wife, tender Mother, and
sincere Friend.
Also Jane Susanna, only Daughter
of the above Revd. John, and

Grace Scott,
who died Nov. 3rd. 1752, Aged 4 Years.
Also Mary Combe, who departed
this Life August 5 1775, Aged 70.
A most Exemplary Character, both
as a kind Sister, and indulgent Aunt,
Also the Revd. John Scott, Rector
of this Parish who died Nov. 18 1776,
Aged 54.
A good Father, and strictly honest Man.

In this Buriall also lieth the Body
of Thomas Ballard, ye Son of
Thomas Ballard, and Joane, his Wife.
Hee departed this Life the 2nd day of
May in the Year of our Lord 169 . .
Aged 78 Years.

NAVE,
On a FLAT STONE within a PEW

William Ferdinand Cottrell,
nè a Nantes 26 Avril 1791. Mort.
24 April 1793.
He pleased God, and was beloved of him,
So that living amongst Sinners, he was
translated, yea, speedily was he taken
away, lest that Wickedness
should alter his Understanding, or
deceit beguile his Soul.

FLAT STONE IN THE PORCH.

Here lyeth the Bodies of
John Ballard, and Josiah Ballard,
Sonnes of Thomas Ballard, & Joane,
his Wife. John Ballard,
died December ye. 7th. 1675.
Here also lyeth ye. Body of
Jonathan Ballard, in this Buryall.

CHURCH YARD.
ALTAR TOMB.
In Memory of
Mr. Richard George, Merchant,

who was truly eminent for
his sincere love to God
his humble Faith in Christ,
And the Practice of universal Holiness.
In consequence of which
his dying moments were calm, & serene,
and in his Hopes of immortal Glory
just, and unshaken.
He died April 14th. 1757, Aged 69.
Near this Place lies also
the Body of his Son in Law,
Mr. Francis Grove,
who died Jan. 2nd 1758, Aged 28,
of the Small Pox.

The Bodies of John Durham,
and Alice, his Wife, who, having
lived Comfortably in Marriage
39 Years, leaving Issue six Sonnes,
and three Daughters, rest here
in the Lord, expecting a Joyful
Resurrection.
He departed this Life 24 June 1636,
Aged 63.
Shee departed this Life 9 April, 1662,
Aged 84.

To the Memory of
Thomas Durham, Gent.
late of Comb, in the Parish of Campden
who departed this Life the
13 day of April 1726, Aged 55.

Beneath this Stone lieth the Body
of Mary Harris, who departed this
Life the 26 day of October 1783,
Aged 53 Years.
Also in Memory of Elizabeth, Wife of
William Morris, daughter of the
above Mary Harris,
who departed this Life the
31 day of Oct 1785, Aged 29 Years.

HEAD STONES.

	Died.		Aged.		Died.		Aged.
William Huggett, of *Willersey Quarry in this Parish.*	27 March	1757	44	Lionel Lampitt,	27 Sept.	1792	92
Anthony Roper,	8 Oct.	1727	90	Ann, his Wife,	17 Feb.	1782	79
William George. Gent. of this Place,	15 Mar.	1762	31	Thomas Stephens,	26 Nov.	1795	71
Thomas Mansell,	6 Feb.	1780	59	Mary, his daughter,	10 April	1796	16
William Moseley,	27 May	1801	86	Hannah Stephens,	18 April	1796	7
Sarah, his Wife,	11 April	1799	81	Thomas Ashwin,	6 Sept.	1798	65
Thomas Hiatt,	7 Nov.	1788	56	William Gibbs,	7 June	1777	75
Elizabeth, his Wife,	12 April	1797	7	Hannah, his Wife,	9 Dec.	1741	...
Ann, wife of Lionel Hiatt,	24 May	1775	67	Thomas Hopkins,	29 Aug.	1760	70
Anthony. son of Lionel Hiatt,	3 Sept.	1754	25	Mary, his Wife,	6 Jan.	1740	60
Mary, daughter of Henry, and Ann Garfield,	5 Jan.	1799	18	John Drury,	16 Nov.	1782	78
				Elizabeth Hopkins,	13 May	1781	60
				Elizabeth, Wife of William Drury,	10 June	1781	82
Ann, Wife of Thomas Ashwin, Senr.	17 April	1764	56	Elizebeth, Wife of James Durham,	4 April	1670	...

WILLERSEY.

A Sketch of the Pedigree of DURHAM, per T. P.

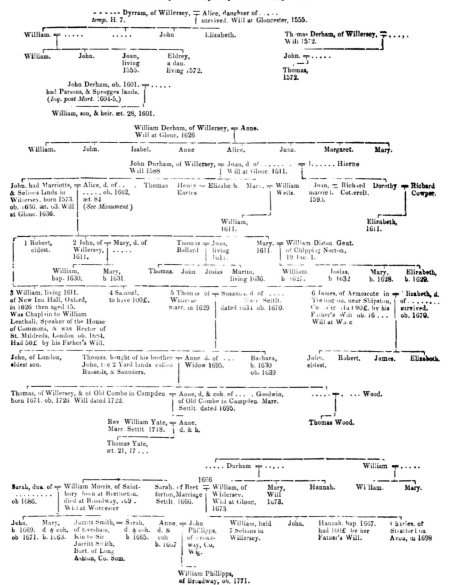

[*Inscriptions in the Church since Bigland's time.*]

MURAL TABLETS IN CHANCEL.

In Memory of
JOHN SCOTT, *Clerk*, M.A.
Rector of *Willersey*,
only Son of WILLIAM SCOTT, M.A.
Rector of *Bletchingdon, Oxon.*
He died Nov. 18, 1776, Ætat. 54.
GRACE, his Wife, died
Febr. 14, 1751, Ætat. 36
JANE SUSANNA, their only Daughter,
died Nov. 3, 1752, Aged 3 Years.
MARY COMBE, Sister of GRACE SCOTT,
died Aug. 6, 1755, in the
39*th.* Year of her Age.
They were all buried in a vault beneath.

In Memory of
JOHN SCOTT, *Gent.*
who departed this Life,
Sept. 22, 1788, Aged 36 Years.
Also JANE and SUSANNA SCOTT,
the beloved Daughters of the
Revd. WILLIAM SCOTT,
and JANE, his Wife.
The former died July 11, 1803,
Aged 24 Years.
The latter died Aug. 22, 1803,
Aged 15 Years.
LAMEN. III. 20-21.

Dedicated for a Memorial of the
Revd. WILLIAM MOULD,
Rector of *Chatiscombe, Devon.*
And Curate of *Aston Subedge,*
who died April 17, 1839,
in his 76*th* Year.
And of MARY, his beloved Wife,
the Daughter of the

Rev. WILLIAM SCOTT.
She expired 12 July 1835,
at the Age of 53.
"We look for the resurrection of the
dead and the life of the world to come."

Sacred to the Memory of
WILLIAM SCOTT, A. M.
36 Years Rector of this Parish,
who departed this Life,
Jany. 17, 1813, Aged 66.
And of JANE, his affectionate Wife,
who died Jany. 17, 1826, Aged 69.
REV. XIV. 13.

NAVE.

Beneath are deposited the Mortal
Remains of *Mr.* WILLIAM STOKES,
late of *Willersey*, and
DEBORAH-ELLEN, his Wife.
He departed this Life,
May 26, 1838, Aged 43.
She died Nov. 6, 1836, Aged 31.
Also EMILY-SARAH, their Daughter,
who died in her Infancy.
Also FRANCIS ELINOR,
Last surviving child of the above
who died at Oxford,
And was buried here, May 23, 1844
Aged 13 Years.

MEMORIAL WINDOW IN THE CHANCEL.

In Memory of
CHARLES AUGUSTUS HAND,
Captain of the 63*rd.* Regiment,
Aged 30 Years.

PHILLIPPA CHALLOT HAND,
his Wife, Aged 22.
And PHILLIPPA WORGAN HAND,
their only Child, Aged 3 Months.
Who perished together in a storm
at Sea, Febr. 11, 1862.
The *Revd.* JOHN HARTLAND WORGAN,
Father of PHILLIPPA CHALLOT HAND,
erected this memorial.

CHURCH YARD.

ON HEAD STONES.

To the Memory of
HANNAH RIMELL, Wife of
THOMAS RIMELL,
Farmer of this Parish, who died
Nov. 19, 1843, Aged 42 Years.
Also SARAH, Aged 11.
MARY, Aged 8.
ANN, Aged 5.
ELIZABETH, Aged 1.
DAVID, Aged 3.
Five Children who with
ELIZABETH JOSEPHS,
Aged 50 Years.
Perished at the awful fire which happened on that night at *Willersey*,
and whose mutilated remains are here
buried together.

In the Churchyard are memorials
to JOSEPHA, Wife of
WILLIAM BURCH GALE,
who died May 13, 1877,
and JOHN HOUGHTON GIBBON,
late Rector of this Parish,
who died 13 Augt. 1883.

The Church has been lately restored; few if any of the Flat stones are now visible. A new Vestry was built and the neat Altar Piece has has been taken away.

There is a New Font, the Gift of the WARNFORD, Trustees.

The old Font is in the Rectory Garden.

BENEFACTIONS.

1840.—The *Honble. Miss* ANN RUSHOUT, of *Northwick Park*, £100. in three per cent consols Dividends in blankets for aged dwellers in the parish who, if possible, are not receiving parochial relief, to be given on Christmas Day by the Clergyman and Overseers of the Parish.

HENRY COOPER, M. A. { JOHN BURROWS, } *Overseers.*
Rector.　　　　　　　{ JOHN MOSELEY, }

Supplementary Notes as to I.—*Devolution of Estates.* II.—*Church.* III.—*Taxation, Population, &c.*

I.—*Estates* :
A. D. 709.—Kenred, King of Mercia and Offa, Governor of the East Angles, gave to St.Mary's, in Homme (Evesham) sixty seven Mansas on either side of Aven River, whereof seven were in Willerseia.
Kemble Anglo Sax. No. ... Diplom.

A. D. 714.—Behrthulf, King of Mercia, gave to same ten "Manentes" in Willerseia. *Ibid. No. ....*

Willersie, contained 8 Hides one of which belonged to Wiquenna, (Wickham.) Culture :—Three Carucates in demesne and six among 16 Villans. 4 Bordars and a Priest. Two Bondmen. There was a little Meadow. It had been worth 4£. and then was worth 100 shillings. St. Mary of Evesham, held it. *Domesday Survey.*

Hen. iii.—Gave a Charter confirming this possession to Evesham Abbey.

15 Edw. i.—In Quo Warranto their Right was allowed.
After the dissolution, Crown Lessees:—W. Fowler, Roper and Bate, held.
4 & 5 Ph. & My.—Sir J. Bourne, by Crown Grant.
19 Eliz.—Anthony Bourne. Richd. Hobby and Wife, by purchase, from Bourne, And 1608, form Hobby. Kettleby, by purchase. 1771, E. Winnington, by purchase.
1811.—Sir T. Winnington, Bart. voted for Chief Rents here. *County Election Poll Book.*

Other Estates :—
Willersey Bartram.
36 Hen. viii.—J. Cook and Saml. Wrothe, by Crown Grant. *Orig.*
Land :—
Wm. Yate, held.
15 Car. i.—Elizth. his Daughter and Heir. *Esch.*

Venours Lands 53 a. in Willersey Banbury.

1825.—Averill, to Sir Thomas Phillipps, Bart.

The Ashwin, family were Proprietors here for a long period.

Yard Land late Parsons and Spraggs.—

The Durham or Derham family were ancient Proprietor 30 Eliz John Derham, is the highest Subsidy Payer. Will at Gloucester.

2 Jac. i.—John Derham, died seized leaving William his son and heir.   *Esh*

The Revd. W. Whitehead, who had married Joyce Durham, held, their Daughter married Stokes and in 1848, Stokes' Descendant sold the Estate to Warner and others.

Of this family was probably the Revd. W. Derham. author of Physics Theologicum.

Roper's Estate passed out of that name to Lampet and others.

Marriotts Land:—

Mariot, in named in Subsidy Roll, 1 Edw. iii.

Setton Land :—

Other Owners:—Ballard, Hyatt, Hopkins.

8 £. Rent charge to Pendrell, out of (......) Farm.

10 £. Rent charge to Shipton Poor cut of another farm.

1767.—The Inclosure Act passed for inclosing over 1000 a. of Common fields, Commonable and Waste Lands, At the time of the Act and Award under it, Francis Winnington, was Lord of the Manor, he is mentioned among Proprietors as arising a Stone Quarry, but he received in respect of his Right to the soil of the Commons an allotment of 15 a. Nathl, Ryder, Esqr. had an allotment of 89 a. Sir John Cotterell, of 175 a. Whitechurch, of 78 a. Venour, of 55 a. Ashwin, of 30 a and several others.

Ryders Estate.—

N. Ryder, was created Baron of Harrowby, Co. Lincoln in 1776. It appears by the inscription on the Monument to the Memory of his father Sir Dudley Ryder, Lord Chief Justice, K. B. in Grantham Church, Lincolnshire, that in 1756, Sir D. Ryder, had the Royal Warrant for creating Lord Harrowby, but that he died before the Patent could pass leaving his only son by Anne Newnham, of Strentham, Surrey.

1776.—*At the County Election the following Voted for Freeholds in Willersey.*

Ashwin, (3) Thomas, Thomas, *Junr.* John.
Andrews.
Bird, Martin, *Esqr.* (*Nottingham.*)
Baldwin, Richard.
Collett, Richard.
Dunn, Thomas.
Emms, Thomas.
Gibbs, William.
Hopkins, William.
Hyatt, (2) Lionel, Sylvester.
Jones, Piercey.
Rastall, John.
Whitechurch, (2) Samuel, William.
Warner, William.
White, John.

II.—*Church.*

Impropriation:—

28 Yard Lands, subject to payment to Rector of 8 Bushels of Wheat 8 Bushels of Barley, 8 Bushels of Beans, And of 8 Yard Lands, the Rector had all the Tythes.

By the Award under the Inclosure Act:—Ann George, the Impropriator received Allotments of 145 a. 28 a. and 27 a. in lieu of her Tythes.

The Rector had 83 a. in lieu of his Tythe, and he Rent Charges from Tenements, having no allotment Lands.

The Value of Rectory 154 £. a Year.   *Rudder.*

A List of Rectors and Patrons of Willersey.

1548	Robert Lyster.	
1554.	Thomas Hybbot.	Grantee of Abbey.
1559	Richard Hunt.	J. Bourne.
1559.	R. Lysturston.	Queen Mary.
1570	Henry Hunt.	J. Bourne, Knt.
1630	W. Hunt.	T. Billey.
1630.	George Sandys.	T. Sandys.
1630.	Henry Prosser.	King & Queen.
1701.	Richard Gregory.	J. Astley.
1718.	J. Dean.	Do.
1733.	W. Bell.	William Yate.
1735	Robert Goodhall.	T. Yate.
1741	W. Bell.	
1745.	W. Sanderson.	Jane Scott.
1748.	John Scott.	Do.
1777.	William Scott.	W. Scott.
1813.	Benj. Preedy.	W. Preedy.

There are National School Rooms lately built. On the Gable are Lord Harrowby's Arms

The Register Books only go back to the beginning of the 18th. Century. But there are in the Bishops Registry, Gloucester, Transcripts of the older Registers.

III.—*Taxation, Population, &c.*

Wylardseye, Subsidy Roll, 1 Edw. III. 1327.

De Willo. Pake, xxiii d. o. q.	De Agnet. Amyeen, iii s. v d.
Willo. Cloper, ii s. xi d. ob.	Matill. Everard, ii s. iiii d. o. q.
Willo. Jordan, ii s. iii d. ob.	
Regin. Athelard, ii s. xi d. ob. q	Thom. Roberdes, iii s. v d.
	Johe Hugin, xxiii d. o. q.
Nicho. Hayel, ii s. i d.	Thom, Bate, ii s. i d. q.
Thom. Inthehale, iii s. o. q.	Walto. Wethe, xx d.
Alic. la Smythes, xxii d. o.	Robto, Wethe, xviii d. o.
Willo. Marioten, ii s. ii d.	Nicho. Wethe, iii s. iiii d. o.
Willo. Geffreis, iii s. q.	Nic. Symondes, ii s. iii d.
Ranulph. Wilkines, ii s. x d. o. q.	Thom. Rosen, xviii d.
	Clar. Matheus, viii d. ob.
Rico. Binesard, ii s. iii d.	Willo. atte Forde, iiii s. vi d. ob. q.
Emma Jannen, iii s. i d. q.	
Johe. Russel, iii s. vii d. q.	Willo. atte Pastone, iiii s. ii d. o. q.
Agn. la Persones, ii s. ixd. q.	

prob. Sum. lxx s. ii d.

Willersey, Subsidy Roll, 30 Eliz.

Anthony Roper,	Bon. £4.	6 s. 8 d.
John Derham,	" 5.	8. 4.
R. Emmes,	" 4.	6. 8.
W. Derham,	" 4.	6. 8.
John Sytche,	" 3.	5. 0.
T. Ballard,	" 3.	5. 0.
J. Haydon,	" 3.	5. 0.
T. Ashwin,	" 3.	5. 0.

Sum 48 s. 4 d.

J. Tracy, H. Rainsford.

The Name of Emms, is still here.

Acreage 1173 a.

Population . 1801,—273. 1831,—327. 1871.—405.

In 1815. Annual Value of Real Property 1843 £.

1882. Rateable Value 2103 £.

1833-4-5. Average of three Years Expenditure on Poor 100 £.

In Evesham Union.

WINCHCOMBE.

THE Original Denomination of this Town proceedeth from the Hill, on which it is built, for Winch signifies Hill, the additional name Combe, is taken either for that the Town *stands upon the very Brow or Combe* [*which it does not*] of the Hill, or else from the ancient Castle which was formerly built there called Combs Castle.

THE RIGHT HON. LORD RIVERS, THE PRESENT LORD OF THE MANOR.

It is remarkable that Tobacco was first planted in England in this Parish, and Yielded a considerable profit to the Inhabitants, until they were restrained by Act of Parliament. Its seed is smaller than Mustard seed, it is sowed upon a hill Bed three Yards high in horse dung in March, then some fine earth sifted upon it, the seed is mixed with ashes, About the latter end of May, they make fresh Beds and replant it. The third time when 'tis as dry as a Cabbage, they plant it again in a Garden. In July they gather it and string it, and hang it up in the House to dry and then roll it up.

The Old Parish Church of Winchcombe, was destroyed by an accident of Fire. The Parishioners then had the East-end of the Abbey Church for their Parish Church. But William Winchcombe, (who was Abbot, 1452.) was instrumental to the building of the present structure.

THE CHURCH is in the Deanery of Winchcombe, to which it gives its name. It is a spacious building consisting of a Chancel, Nave and North and South Aisles with an embattled Tower at the West-end, containing Six Bells and a Ting Tang. The body of the Church is ornamented with battlements and pinnacles and on the buttresses are monstrous caricatures of human and animals heads. On the South side is a porch, The nave is separated from the Chancel, by a large Gallery and a carved screen below it, The Altar is detached from the Wall, covered with an antient, but once magnificent carpet, embroidered with a border of Saints. There is a good Organ. At the West-end, is kept in the Church a Fire Engine, with this Inscription painted on it "Built by Philips, of London, at the Voluntary contribution of Winchcomb, 1789." On a large brass chandeleir is this Inscription. "The Gift of JOHN MERRYMAN, to *Winchcombe Church*, 1759." On the South side of the Chancel are the remains of rich carved stalle with a pisscina, On the Arch at the West-end of the Nave is written "KEN'WULPH. KING of West Saxons, Founder, of *Winchcombe Abbey*, built this Church, Anno Dom. 800."

On the Wall of the Belfry is thus Painted.

He that presumes a Bell to ring.	A current Groat he straight must pay
With Hat, Crevat, or Spurs to ging,	Before that he doth go away.
Must a Groat pay, for that Offence,	He that presumes to fight or sweare,
Before that he do goe from hence,	Must pay the like or Punish here.
Another thing I do you tell	One thing more I must say to You
Is due from him that turns a Bell,	The forfits made, are the Clark's due.

On the Font which is Octagon of Stone painted like Marble.

N.H., N.E., C. W., 16-34.

[The Church was lately restored. At such Restorations the Galleries were taken away, the Flat stones were nearly all covered with paving Tiles. It has Open seats or benches. The Organ is put at the east end of the South Aisle and the Vestry at the east end of the North Aisle.]

BENEFACTIONS.

GEORGE TOWNSEND, of *Lincolns Inn, Esqr.* gave three Shillings in Bread to be distributed every Sunday among the Poor of this Town that come to hear Divine Service, Anno Dom. 1683.

Mr. THOMAS COMPERE, *Citizen of London,* Gave one Hundred and Fifty Pounds, the Produce thereof to be dsitributed every Sunday among the Poor of this Town that come to hear divine Service, Anno Dom. 1715.

THOMAS MERSEY, *Church Warden,* 1729.

A. D. 1685.

GEORGE HARVEY, Gave two Acres of Land to be Lett and sett by the Bayliffs of this Town, the Rents and profits to be disposed at their Discretion among the Poor of this Town Yearly for ever.

A. D. 1693.

Lady JULIANA TRACY, Gave sixteen Ridges of Land the Rents and Profits to be laid out in Coats and Gowns and delivered to the poor of this Parish upon Christmas day, Yearly for ever.

A. D. 1743.

JOHN HARVEY, Gave Ten Pounds the Interest of it to be disposed of by the Bayliffs among the Poor Widows, of this Borough.

A. D. 1752.

ANNL BLABY, Gave Fifty Pounds to purchase Land, the Rents and Profits to be disposed of on the Saturday before Easter day Yearly for ever, at the discretion of Her Executor joyntly with the Consent and Approbation of the Bayliffs, Church Wardens and Overseers to such Poor Families of this Parish, as do not receive Alms not exceeding the Sum of one Shilling and Sixpence to any one Family.

THOMAS MERRYMAN,
JOHN GREENING. } *Church Wardens,* 1764.

WINCHCOMBE.

J. Kendall F. Del. I. Foot

CHANCEL.

On Monuments.

A MURAL MONUMENT WITH THE FIGURE OF A MAN IN ARMOUR KNEELING WITH A BOOK B' FORE HIM AGAINST THE NORTH WALL.

Arms:—Argent, a Chevron betw. three Cocks Gules on a Chief Sable, three Spears heads of the first, the points embreced of the second,— WILLIAMS, *impaling* per pale and per Chevron Argent, and Sable between three Martlets counter charged.

Crest:—a Cock, *as in the Arms.*

This is the Effigies of THOMAS WILLIAMS, *Esqr.* of *Cornden,* the second Son of *Sir* DAVID WILLIAMS, *Baronet,* of *Gwer Newett in Brecknockshire,* one of his *Majesties Judges in West-minster,* who was buried here the 28 day of May in the Year, 1636.

ON A BLACK MARBLE SLAB ADJOINING THE LAST.

D. S.

THOMAS WILLIAMS, Filius et Hæres DAVIDIS WILLIAMS, *Arm* de *Cornden,* prosapiam a nob'nous, et principibus viris longa serie de-ductam, et illustrem legum et pietatis studiis vlterius illustravit ; Obijt Septem. viii o. Ano. 1669.

ON FLAT STONES.

Hic jacet HESTER, dilectissima uxor THOMÆ WILLIAMS, nuper de *Cornden, Armigeri,* obijt duodecimo Junij 1674.

H. S. E.
Vir insignissimus,
DAVID WILLIAMS, *Arm.*
de *Cornden ;*
Tam Suis quam Atavorum virtutibus vere nobilis
Et fi seris Nepotibu pie celebrandus, Numerosæ prolis pater charissimus, Famulorum clemens justusq Dominus, Nec Laboris plus quam par exigens Neq minus premij rependens.
Non sibi, Suisq solum Quin et Alijs Regi, Reip. Ecclesiæ, Deo. natus Utriusq. Juris quâ Ecclesiastici quà Civilis
Cu. pessimis periculis ad Exitiu. fere colluctantis
propugnator et Vindex.
Sic diû vixit vir bonus commne. Bonum, Honoribus, æque ac Annis plenus.
At! at! Extremæ tandem senectutis, Gravissimo sanè morbo depressus, Summaq. spe fretus Resurrectionis Beatæ,
Lubens ac lætus occubuit, Importuniom relinquens sui desiderium, Grande pietatis, et virutum omnium Exemplar
Jnn. xviij o. Ano. Dni. 1698, Ætat. suæ 85.
Hinc disce vivere Viator
Hinc oisce mori.

In Memory of
CAREW WILLIAMS, *Gen.*

1

Son of DAVID WILLIAMS, *Esqr.* of *Cornden,* who died May the 19*th.* 1722, Aged 68 Years.
Here also lyeth the Body of MARY, the relict of CAREW WILLIAMS, *Gent.* who departed this Life, the 20 day of April. Anno Domini 1730, Aged 68 Years.

ELIZABETH WILLIAMS, of *Cornden, Gentlewoman,* buried July the 13*th.* 1713.

ON A BRASS PLATE.

D. S.

Jacet hev jacet THOMAS MARKLEVS, Vir vere Bonus, erudite Pius Ecclesiæ Anglicanæ Lucerna, Resplendens allis Lumen, et vitam Largiendo propriam absumsit Denatus Maij xvi. Anno Christianatis MDCLXXI.
Also here lyeth the Body of CICELY MARKLEY, *Gen.* Relict of THOMAS MARKLEY, *Gen.* sometime Minister of this Place, She departed this Lite, the 29 of July 1706, Aged 75 Years.
Here lyeth the Body of RICHARD ROBERTS, Vicor of this Parish, 15 Years, who departed this Lite, the 11 day of May, Anno Dom. 1793, Aged 43 Years.

Here lyeth the Body of JONE, the Wife of THOMAS YEARDINGTON, who was buried the 20 Sept. 1668.

Hic jacet HENRICUS THORNE, hujus Ecclesiæ Minister, fuit 44 Ano. obiit 29 o. die Aprilis, Anno Dom. MDCCXVIII.
Here lyeth the Body of HESTER, the Wife of HENRY THORNE, late Minister of *Winchcomb,* who departed this Life, the 29 of December, Anno Dom. 1723, Aged 86.

Here lieth the Body of ELIZABETH, the Wife of JOHN HARVEY, who was buried July 10, 1717, Aged 25 Years.
Also the Body of FRANCES YARDINGTON, who died 20 July 1730, Aged 67 Years.
Also here lieth the Body of WILLIAM, the Son of THOMAS and SUSANNA YARDINGTON, who died 23 Nov. 1741, in the 20*th.* Year of his Age.
Also FRANCES, the Daughter of THOMAS and ANN COMPTON, of *Bishop's Cleeve,* who died January the 22, 1750, Aged 10 Weeks.

Near this Place lieth the Body of

2

SUSANNAH, the Wife of THOMAS YARDINGTON, *Yeoman,* who died the 25 of June, A. D. 1758, Aged 70 Years.
Also the Body of THOMAS, his Son, by SUSANNA, his Wife, who died the 13 day of June 1765, Aged 12 Years.

Here lieth the Body of *Mr.* JOHN PHILLIPS, *Senior,* of *Greet,* who was buried the 4 of August 1721, Aged 80.
Also the Body of JOHN PHILLIPS, of *Greet,* Grandson of the above, who died June 7*th.* 1765, Aged 62 Years.
And also here iieth the Body of JOHN PHILLIPS, (He was a native of *Greet* in this Parish,) the eldest Son of JOHN and ANN PHILLIPS, of the same place, who departed this Life, the 19 day of Febr. in the Year of our Lord 1801, Aged 74 Years.

Hic jacet ELIZABETHA, Uxor JOHANNIS THORNE, *Senr.* quæ Decimo Octavo die Aprilis, objit 1679.
Hic quoque jacet EDMUNDUS THORNE, A. M. *Socius Coll. Oriell, Oxon.* Sepultus decimo octavo die December 1711.
Sub eodem lapide conditur EM. RAINSFORD, Relicta EDMUNDI RAINSFORD, A. M. Obiit vicesimo die Maij. Anno Christi 1741.

Hic jacet EDMUNDUS RAINSFORD, Pastor hujus Ovilis in Expectatione Supremi illius diei et qualis ille fuit iste dies indicabit Obijt XXVIII. die Mensis Maij MDCCXXVI.

Arms:—Argent, a Bend plain between two Cotises engrailed Sable —WHITFIELD.
Crest:—Out of a Palisadoed Crown, Argent, a stags heads Or.

Here lyeth the Body of SAMUEL WHITFIELD, *Gent.* Son of JOHN WHITFIELD, *Esquire,* of *Maidenhead* in *Berks.* who departed this Life, January the 27*th.* 1710, Aged 34 Years and 3 Months.
Also ELIZABETH, the Relict of SAMUEL WHITFIELD, who died August the 22, 1719.

ON BRASS PLATES.

Hic depositæ sunt Exuviæ ANNÆ, filiæ JOHANNIS BLABY, Obiit die quato Januarii, Anno Æti. MCCLIV.

Hic jacet
ELIZABETHA, uxor amicissima

3

GULIELMI HARVEY,
Clerici triduo labore defessus
obstetricantis manus vix et ne vix
quidem auxilio tertiam enixa sobolem.
modestiæ ceterarumque ; virtutum
encomijs alicubi satis elandatam æq.
piam ac quietam, (Anno Ætatis plus
minus tricesimo Sexto.) intermisit
animam Maij Quart. Anno Christianæ
Redemtionis, MDCLXXXV.

Hic jacet GULIELMUS HARVEY,
Rector de *Burlingham*, qui mortem
oppetiit tricesimo die Martij
Anno Domini, 1686.
Sub ... ... *(defaced.)*
fuit HENRICUS HARVEY,
filius natu min............
spei juventis ob Octob. die
vecesimo quarto Ano. Dni.
MDCCIII.

Hic jacet CAROLUS BROADWAY,
Gen. Obijt 27 die May 1716.
Also FRANCES, his Wife,
was buried the 10 of February 1729,
Aged 73 Years,

Here lyeth the Body of
EDWARD BEALE BROADWAY,
Son of CHARLES BROADWAY, *Gent.*
who departed this Life, the
29 of April 1722, Aged 2 Years.
Also the Body of MARY, the Wife
of CHARLES BROADWAY,
who died the 22 of April 1730,
Aged 36 Years.
Also FRANCES, Daughter of
CHARLES and DEBORAH BROADWAY,
who died Jany. 6, 1739,
Aged 40 Years.
Hic jacet CAROLUS, Filius CAROLI
BROADWAY, *Gen.*
Obiit 2 o. die Julij Auo. Dom. 1780,
Ætatis suæ 92.

In Memory of
WILLIAM DOBBINS, *Senior,*
of this Town, who was buried
July 10. 1691.
Also of FRANCES DOBBINS, *Widow,*
who was buried here Oct. 26, 1712.
Also of
WILLIAM DOBBINS, *Junior,*
who departed this Life,
September the 18th. 1743,
Aged 57 Years.

Here lyeth the Body of
WILLIAM GOWER, *Gent.*
who died the 21 day of Nov. 1753,
Aged 49 Years.
Here lyeth the Body of
MARY, the Wife of WILLIAM
GOWER, *Gent.* who died
the 27 day of February 1750,
Aged 62 Years.

NAVE.

ON A BLACK STONE AGAINST,
AN ARCH NEAR THE WEST-END.

Near this Place in a Vault

4

built at his own Expence lies
the Body of JOHN LUCAS,
Obt. 21st. of March 1773,
Aged 66 Years.

ON FLAT STONES.

JOHN LUCAS, of *Shudely,* Senior,
was buried the 15th. day of March,
1689.
Also MARY, the Daughter of
JOHN and ANNE LUCAS, of *Shudely,*
who died in her Infancy,
Febr. ye 26, 1716.
Also JOHN LUCAS,
buried ye 9 of August 1736,
Aged 60 Years.

In Memory of
WILLIAM, the Son of JOHN
and ANNE LUCAS, of *Shudely,*
who departed this Life,
February the 1st. 1729,
Aged 9 Years.
Also ELIZABETH, their Daughter,
who dyed May 7, 1749,
Aged 24 Years.

In Memory of
MARY, the Daughter of
JOHN and SUSANNA LUCAS,
buried the 9 August, 1735.
Also REBECCA, their Daughter,
who departed this Life,
May ye 31st. 1748, Aged 7 Years.

JOHN, the Son of JOHN and
SUSANNA LUCAS, died the 17th.
of March 1748, in the 15th.
Year of his Age.
Also SUSANNA LUCAS,
died the 2 of Nov. 1749,
Aged 46 Years.

Here lyeth the Body of
THOMAS FYEEMAN, *Gent.*
of *Greet,* who departed this Life,
the 21 day of Octr. Anno Dom. 1728,
Aged 58 Years.
Also in Memory of
JOHN, his Son, who died
the 15 April 1744,
Aged 36 Years.
Also here lieth the Body of
ELIZABETH, the Wife, of
THOMAS FREEMAN,
who departed this Life, the
6 Nov. 1750, Aged 74 Years.

Here lyeth interred the Body of
THOMAS FREEMAN, of *Greet*
in this Parish, *Gent.* Son of
THOMAS and ELIZABETH FREEMAN,
late of the same place.
He departed this Life, the
26 day of May in the Year 1770,
Aged 67 Years.
Also MARY, Wife of THOMAS
FREEMAN, aforesaid who was
Daughter of GEORGE and ELIZABETH
RICHARDS, late of *Kinsham* in ye
County of *Worcester.*
She departed the Life,
10 of Febr. 1799, Aged 81 Years.

5

Here lieth the Body of
THOMAS MAISEY,
of this Town, who departed this
Life, the 11 day of Sept.
A. D. 1758, Aged 71 Years.
Here also lieth the Body of
ELIZABETH, the Wife of
THOMAS MAISEY,
who departed this Life, the
27 day of January, A. D. 1766,
Aged 76 Years.
Here also lieth the Body of
ANNE, the Daughter of
THOMAS and ELIZABETH MAISEY,
who departed this Life,
the 17 day of Nov. A. D. 1770,
Aged 45 Years.
Also MARY, Daughter of
THOMAS and ELIZABETH MAISEY,
and Wife of ABRAHAM BYRCH.
of *Cheltenham* in this County,
who departed this Life, the
7 day of May 1777, Aged 47 Years.

ELIZABETH BIBY,
buried July the 1st. 1706.

Here lyeth the Body of
MARGARET, the Wife of
JOHN CARPENTER, of *Gretton,*
buried 11 Sept. 1710.
Also ANNE, the Daughter of
JOHN and ALICE GREENING,
of *Gretton,* buried the 20 April,
Anno 1725, Aged 14 Years.
Also THOMAS, the Son of
JOHN and ALICE GREENING,
of *Gretton,* buried Jany. 30, 1730-1,
Aged 24 Years.
Also JOHN DOBBINS,
buried the 8 of Febr. 1743-4,
Aged 68 Years.

Here lyeth the Body of
JOHN CARPENTER, of *Gretton,*
buried 20 June 1721.
Also MARGARET, his Daughter,
was here buried the 13 April 1695.
Also ALICE, the Wife of JOHN
GREENING, and Daughter of
JOHN CARPENTER, of *Gretton,*
was buried the 12 Jany. 1728-9,
Aged 47 Years.
Also in Memory of
JAMES, the Son of JOHN and
MARGARET GREENING, of *Gretton,*
who departed this Life, the
28 March 1738, an Infant.
Also in Memory of
JOHN GREENING, of *Gretton,*
who departed this Life,
Jany. 20, Anno Dom. 1739-40,
Aged 29 Years,

In Memory of
HENRY, the Son of
JOHN and ALICE GREENING,
of *Gretton,* buried 24 March 1727-8,
Aged 15 Years.

In Memory of
JOHN TOMES, of *Standley,* who was
was buried the 26 day of July 1738,
Aged 89 Years.

6

MARY, the Daughter of WILLIAM and SARAH HOOPER. buried the 1*st.* September 1717.

In Memory of
Mr. JOHN STAITE, of *Irely*
in the Parish of *Hailes*,
who departed this Life,
Jany. ye 19*th.* 1726, Aged 43 Years.
Also here lieth the Body of
ANN, the Daughter of JOHN STAITE,
who departed this Life, ye
25 of May 1729, Aged 6 Years.
Also here lieth the Body of
ANNE, the Relict of JOHN STAITE,
who departed this Life, the
7*th.* of Nov. 1737, Aged 54 Years.

Here lyeth the Body of
WILLIYM FRANCIS, of *Stanley*,
and MARY, his Wife. He was
buried Sept. 10*th.* Anno Dom. 1727.
She was buried July ye 22,
Anno Dom, 1720, Aged 60 Years.

ON A BRASS PLATE.

Here lieth the Body of
FRANCES, the Wife of JOHN
SUMMERVILL, buried Nov. the 12.*h.*
1724, Ætatis 72.

ON FLAT STONES.

In Memory of
FRANCES, the Wife of EDWARD
MATHUS, of *Greet,* who departed
this Life, May ye 10*th.* 1764,
Aged 77 Years.

Here lyeth the Body of
MARY, the Wife of RICHARD
MARTEN, of *Gretton,* who was
Interred ye 26 Aug. 1696.
Also here lyeth the Body of
RICHARD MARTEN, of *Gretton,*
buried 12 April 1711, Aged 81.
Here lyeth the Body of
ANTHONY MARTEN, of *Gretton,*
who departed this Life,
Decr. 28, 1732, Aged 63 Years.
Also here lieth the Body of
MARGARET, the Wife of
ANTHONY MARTEN,
who departed this Life,
9 Sept. 1754, Aged 78 Years.

Here lyeth the Body of
WILLIAM TOMBS, *Mercer,* in
Winchcombe, who departed this Life,
ye 6 day of May, Anno Dom. 1718.
Aged 34 Years.
Also here lieth ANNE, the Wife of
JOHN TOMBS, of *Standly,*
who was buried the 20 day of
March 1733-4, Aged 78.

Here lyeth the Body of
JONE, the Daughter of JOHN and
ANNE TOMBS, of *Standly,*
and Wife of JOHN HARVEY,
buried the 22 April 1726,
Aged 39 Years.

7

In Memory of
WILLIAM STAITE, who died
the 8 day of April, A. D. 1766,
Aged 57 Years.
Also in Memory of
MARGARET, the Wife of WILLIAM
STAITE, who died the 14 day of
May 1773, Aged 54 Years.
Near this Place lieth the Body of
ANNE BAYLIS,
who departed this Life, the
23 day of April 1770,
Aged 45 Years.

In Memory of
JOHN MARTEN, of *Gretton,*
who was buried the 7 of July 1742,
Aged 36 Years.
Here also lyeth the Body of
ANTHONY MARTEN, of *Gretton, Junr.*
who was buried the 23 June,
1718.

In Memory of
RICHARD MARTEN, of *Greet,*
who departed this Life,
8 of Febr. 1765, Aged 98 Yeors.

In Memory of
ANNE, the Wife of
JOHN DISTON, of *Dixton,*
who departed this Life,
24 Febr. 1728, Aged 41 Years.

Here lieth the Body of
THOMAS STAITE, late of
Frampton in this Parish,
He departed this Life, the
12 day of July in the Year 1766,
Aged 68 Years.

Here lieth the Body of
JAMES CARPENTER, of *Gretton,*
Senr. who was buried the
15 day of December,
Anno Domini 1691, Ætat. 72.

He took great care and paines
His right for to defend,
And did agree with all Mankind
Before his Life did end,
He now in Peace lies downe
to the comfort of his friends,
Hoping to live eternally
in joy that never ends.

Also JAMES, the Son of JAMES
CARPENTER, of *Gretton, Senr.*
who was buried the 4 of Nov. 1724,
Also here lieth the Body of
JAMES, the Son of JOHN and
ALICE GREENING, of *Gretton,*
who departed this Life, the
7 of Jany. 1730-1, Aged 25.
Also JOSEPH GREENING,
who died 1752.

Here lieth the Body of
MARY, the Wife of WILLIAM
BLABY, who departed this Life, the
16 day of January 1730,
Aged 38 Years.
Also WILLIAM BLABY,

8

was buried Febr. 4, A. D. 1755,
Aged 63 Years.

Here lieth the Body of
ANNE, the Wife of WILLIAM
CANING, She was buried the
11 May Ano. Dom. 1716,
Also here lieth the Body of
WILLIAM CANING,
He was buried the 27 of September,
A. D. 1729, Aged 68 Years.
Here lieth the Body of
ANNE, late Wife of WILLIAM
CANNING, who departed this Life,
the 19 of Nov. in the Year 1752,
Aged 34 Years.

Here lieth the Body of
NICHOLAS PEARSON,
who departed this Life, the
26 day of February, An. Dom. 1674.
Here lieth the Body of ELIZABETH,
the Wife of JOHN BLABY,
who departed this Life, ye
22 of May 1739, Aged 73 Years.
Also here lieth the Body of
JOHN BLABY,
who departed this Life, the
6 day of Novr. Anno Dom. 1748,
Aged 72 Years.
MARY, second Wife of WILLIAM
BLEBY, *Junior,* And an Infant
Daughter buried April 4, 1776.
And also WILLIAM BLEBY,
Baker, of this Town,
who departed this Life,
Oct. 13, 1795, Aged 55 Years.

Here lieth the Body of
GEORGE, the Son of NICHOLAS
PEARSON, who departed this Life,
the 30*th.* day of July,
Ano. Dom. 1675.
Also here lieth the Body of
ANNE, the Wife of WILLIAM
BLEBY, buried 29 May 1730,
Aged 60 Years.
Also HANNAH, the Wife of
WILLIAM BLEBY, *Junr.*
who was buried Jany. ye 31, 1766,
Aged 28 Years.
Likewise ANNE, their Daughter,
who died in her Infancy.

Here lieth the Body of
GEORGE BARKSDALE,
of this Town, who was buried
the 24 of May 1725,
Aged near 74 Years.

Here lieth the Body of
MARY, the Wife of GEORGE
BARKSDALE, who died ye 25 of
March 1727, Aged 63 Years.

RICHARD DAUNCE,
died the 2*nd.* day of Deca. 1748
Aged 76 Years.
ELIZABETH ASHLEY,
died Aug. 22, 1789,
Aged 81 Years.
ELIZABETH RAYER,
died June 4, 1800, Aged 67 Years.

9

1465

ON A BRASS PLATE.

Under this lieth the Body of
ELIZABETH, the Wife of
RICHARD DAUNCE, of *Greet*,
buried October ye 7, Anno 1727.

ON FLAT STONES.

Here lieth the Body of
ELIZABETH, the Wife of
EDMUND HICKS, who was buried
the 16 day of February,
Anno Dom. 1665.

Here lieth the Body of
RICHARD SMITH, *Baker*,
of *Winchcombe*, who died
the 25 day of December 1712.
Also here lyeth the Body of
MARGARET, the Wife of
RICHARD SMITH, who was
buried the 21st. of February 1726,
Aged 78 Years.
Also here lieth the Body of
WILLIAM SMITH, *Baker*, of this
Town, who departed this Life,
the 18 day of Sept. A. D. 1734,
Ætatis suæ 75 Years.
Here lieth the Body of
ANNE, the Daughter of JOHN
and ANNE PRESTON,
who departed this Life, the
17 day of August 1747,
Aged 9 Years.
Also WILLIAM, their Son,
died the 5th. day of August, 1749.

MARGARETA WELD, conjux
GUIL. BARKSDALE, virgo
uxor Vidua non æmula
ad plures Obijt Decem. 28,
An. Sal. 1674,
Æta. 73. Usque quo Domine.

Hic jacet MARGARETA,
Marito Suo GUIL. WELD, *Gen.*
Desideratissima,
Ob. Jan. 11, An. Sal. 1673, Ætat. 31.
Hâc MARGARETA, nulla Gemma,
carior. In te Domine speravi.

Here lieth the Body of
Captn. JOHN DARKE, of the *Abbey*,
who departed this Life,
the 15 of August Anno Dom. 1727,
Aged 68 Years.
Also here lieth the Body of
MARGARET, the Wife of
Capt. JOHN DARKE,
who departed this Life,
10 day of May 1717.

Here lieth the Body of
ROBERT, the Son of
JOHN SMITH, *Baker*, of this Town,
and of HESTER, his Wife,
He departed this Life,
Augt. the 29, 1713, Aged 21 Years.
I. S.
1728.
Also here lieth the Body of
SARAH STAITE,
who departed this Life, the
3 day of Jany. 1767, Aged 44.

10

In Memory of
ANNE, the Wife of
JOHN MERRYMAN. *Junr.*
who departed this Life,
the 26 of Novr. 1753,
Aged 26 Years.

In Memory of
JOHN STRATFORD, of *Millham-Post,
Gent.* who departed this Life, the
17 of October, 1752, Aged 80.
Here also lieth the Body of
ANNE, Relict of the above said
JOHN STRATFORD,
who died September ye 18, 1765,
Aged 69 Years.

Here lyeth the Body of
MARGARET, Wife of JOHN
GREENING, of *Gretton* in this
Parish, *Gent.* who was Daughter
of DANIEL and JUDITH REEVE,
of the same Place. She departed
this Life, at *Hampton* in the County
of *Worcester*, 23 of May 1793,
Aged 61 Years.

Here lieth the Body of
WILLIAM STAITE, of *Frampton*
in this Parish, who departed this
Life, the 23 day of December 1775,
Aged 75 Years.
MARY, his Wife, who departed
this Life, 24 of Febr. 1777,
Aged 69 Years.
Also ELIZABETH, Daughter of
WILLIAM and ANNE COOK,
of this Town, who departed this Life,
the 11 day of April 1774,
Aged 1 Year and 3 Months.
Also BETTY, Daughter of
WILLIAM and ANN COOK,
who departed this Life,
the 21 day of March 1778,
Aged 9 Months.

Here lieth the Body of
JOHN PRESTON, *Senr. Baker*,
late of this Town,
who departed this Life,
the 1st. of Jany. 1789,
Aged 82 Years.
Also ANNE, Wife of JOHN
PRESTON, who departed this Life,
the 8 of March 1793, in the
80 Year of her Age.

In Memory of
DINAH, Daughter of JOHN and
ANN MERRYMAN, who died
Febr. 16, 1762.
Also JOHN MERRYMAN,
who departed this Life,
10 of Nov. 1780, Aged 49 Years.
In Memory of
ANN MERRYMAN, Second Wife of
JOHN MERRYMAN,
who departed this Life, the
16 of April 1797, Aged 63 Years.

ON BRASS PLATES.

Here lyeth the Body of
CHRISTOPHER MERRETT,

11

interred ye 9 of January 1624,
And of AWDREY, his Wife,
(Remarried to THOMAS HAWKINS,)
Buried ye 7th. of September 1654.
Hoc Posuit Pietatis ergo
RICHARDUS MERRETT,
CHRISTOPH. et ANDRIANÆ,
Primogenitus.

Hic etiam jacet idem RICHARDUS,
Cœlebs (Si quis alius) vitæ integræ,
Obijt xix. Martij Ano Æræ
Christianæ MDCLXX,
Ætatis LXIV.
Honoris Gratitudinisque Causa hoc
addidit
CHRISTOPHORUS MERRETT, nepos.

Here lieth the Body of
HARWOOD, the Son of HARWOOD
and MARY HARRIES, of this Town,
He departed this Life, the
20th. day of May in the Year 1751,
Aged three Months and one Day.
Also here lieth the Body of
... ...
HARWOOD and MARY HARRIES,
who departed this Life, the
2nd. day of May 1756,
Aged nine Weeks.

In Memory of
ROBERT FLETCHER, *Junr. Gent.*
late of *Postlipp* in the Parish of
Winchcombe, who died 26 July,
Anno Dom. 1722. Aged 46.
Also in Memory of DINAH,
the Wife of ISAAC BAYLISS, of
Postlipp in this Parish,
who died the 11 day of Augt. 1748,
Aged 47 Years.
Also of HESTER ARKELL, of
Cockbury in the Parish of
Bishop's Cleeve, the beloved Wife
of WILLIAM ARKELL, late of
Postlip aforesaid, and Daughter
of the said ISAAC and DINAH
BAYLISS, She died Sept. 2, 1791,
Aged 65 Years.

In Memory of
ISAAC BAYLISS, late of *Postlip*
in this Parish, who departed this Life,
Augt. 7, 1759, Aged 58 Years.

NORTH AISLE.

ON A HANDSOME MONUMENT
AGAINST THE NORTH WALL.

To the Memory of
WILLIAM SMART, M. D.
late of this Place, who departed
this Life, the 4th. day of Jany. 1768,
in the 68 Year of his Age.
Also COLLIS SMART, his Wife,
who departed this Life, the
16 day of August 1772, Aged 65.
This Monument was erected by
their Nephew BAPTIST SMART,
as a sincere
tho' small proof of his Affection.

Arms:—Or. a Chevron between
three Pheons Sable.—SMART. im-
paling Quarterly 1 & 4, Or. a Qui-

12

ver and Arrows erect Gules betw.
3 Pheons Sable.—................
2 and 3 Gules a Chevron between
three Leopards faces Or. ....

ON ANOTHER MONUMENT.

In a Vault near this Place
lie enterred the remains of
JOHN NIND, who departed this Life,
Febr. 13, 1767. Aged 54 Years.
Also SARAH, his Wife,
who departed this Life,
July 16, 1780, Aged 62 Years.
Also three of their Children, viz.—
EDMOND. died April 13, 1747,
Aged 3 Years.
SARAH, died Febr. 25, 1752,
Aged 2 Years.
HUGH JAMES, died Decr. 18, 1759,
Aged 1 Year.

BRASS ON FLAT STONES AGAINST THE
EAST-END.

Here lieth buried the Bodie of
MARGARET CRUMPE, Widow,
late Wife of WILLIAM CRUMP,
and Daughter of
FUIKE DANGERFIELD, of Naunton,
and BRIGITTE, his Wife,
who departed this Life, the
12 day of February in the Year
of our Redemption 1647.
Her virtuous and Charitable Life, is
a good Pattern for others Imitation.
T. D.

Here at the end of this Isle,
near her Mother Mrs. MARGARET
CRUMP, lieth the Body of
BRIDGET, late Wife of
EDWARD SLAUGHIRE,
of Winchcombe, Gent. who departed
this Life, the 14 of March 1652,
of her Age 42.
MARK V. verse 39.

AGAINST THE NORTH WALL
DEPICTED ON A BOARD.

Hic jacet
Pia et Generosa Fœmina
SUSANNA, THO. JAY, Filia
Uxor GEORGII MILLY, Gen.
Olim GUALT. CHARLTONI,
Ex quo reliquit Gualt.
M. D. MARIAM et SUSANNAM, Sibi
Superstites, Obiit Mai xxiii,
Anno Salutis MDCXLIX, Ætat. LVII.

Est mihi qui mortis vim
Vicit Fortis Jesus ......
Dixit, et ad Mortem
Sic properare juvat.

AGAINST THE NORTH WALL.

In Memory of
MICHAEL BROADWAY, Apothecary,
who departed this Life,
April the 6th. 1728, in the
40 Year of his Age.

AGAINST A PILLAR, DEPICTED
ON A BOARD.

Near this Place lieth what was

Mortal of MARY, the Wife, of
HARRY NEWMAN (and late Wife
of JOHN COLEMAN,) from
which her immortal part was
seperated the 6th. day of November
1768, after 45 Years Union.

ON FLAT STONES.

Here lieth the Body of
HANNAH, the Wife of SAMUEL
FREEMAN, of Gretton, Gent.
who departed this Life, the
12 day of Sept. 1788,
Aged 82 Years.
Also SAMUEL FREEMAN,
of Gretton. Gent. who departed
this Life, March 1, 1789,
Aged 88 Years.
He was brother of THOMAS FREEMAN,
of Greet, Gent.

In Memory of
RICHARD, Son of JOHN and
ANNE MERRYMAN, who departed
this Life, 27 of May 1760,
Aged 17 Years
Also RICHARD, the Son of JOHN
and ANNE PERRIN, who departed
this Life, 18 of Decr. 1778,
Aged 2 Years.
And also JOHN MERRYMAN, Senr.
who departed this Life,
Febr. 4, 1780, in the 74
Year of his Age.
MARY MERRYMAN, Wife of
THOMAS MERRYMAN,
died May 8, 1788. Aged 57 Years.
Also THOMAS MERRYMAN,
Son of the above JOHN MERRYMAN,
who died Augt. 25, 1793,
Aged 57 Years.
Also ANNE MERRYMAN, Wife of
the above JOHN MERRYMAN,
died Oct. 30, 1793, Aged 86 Years.

JOHN BATSFORD, Senior,
buried September 3rd. 1688.

SARAH RONE,
buried April the 3rd. 1666.
Here lieth the Body of
WILLIAM CURTIS,
who departed this Life, the
24 day of January, A. D. 1761,
Aged 90 Years.
A loving Uncle and a trusty friend
who loved his Kinswoman truly
to his end.

Here is interred the Body of
DAVID HARVEY, who was buried
the 11 of October 1700,
Aged 63 Years.
Also ANNE, his Wife, buried
September the 30, 1713, Aged 89.
Also Mr. ANTHONY MERCHANT,
buried September the 7th. 1730,
Aged 66 Years.
Also the Body of JANE, the Wife of
ANTHONY MERCHANT, Gent.
who departed this Life, the
24 Jany. 1741, Aged 76 Years.

Here lieth the Body of
ANN, the Wife of RICHARD HARVEY,
Gent. who departed this Life,
20 Febr. 1764, Aged 75 Years.
Also the Body of
RICHARD HARVEY, Gent.
who departed this Life, the
21 day of December 1764,
Aged 81 Years.

Here lyeth what was Mortal of
MARY, the Wife of GEORGE GILES,
from which her immortal parts
was seperated the 1 day of
April 1770, after 30 Years union.

Here lieth the Body of
MARY SLAUGHTER, Gentlewoman,
buried June the 30, Ano. Dni. 1717.

Here lieth the Body of
WILLIAM CARPENTER,
of Gretton, who was buried the
27 September 1693.
Also ELIZABETH, the Wife of
WILLIAM CARPENTER,
who was buried the 16 day of
September, Ano 1706.
Memento mori
Also WILLIAM, their Son, was
buried here June the 14th. 1726,
Aged 47 Years.

Here lieth the Body of
ELIZABETH, the Daughter of
ROBERT and DOROTHY CARNALL,
of Greet, who departed this Life,
Nov. 1, 1730, Aged 78 Years.
Also here lieth the Body of
WILLIAM, the Son of WILLIAM
and MARY CARNALL, of Greet
in this Parish, who departed
this Life, 19 of Jany. in the
Year of our Lord 1784,
Aged 58 Years.

Here lieth the Body of
MARY, the Daughter of
WILLIAM and MARY CARNALL,
of Greet in this Parish,
who departed this Life, the
7 day of Augt. in the Year of our
Lord 1798, Aged 75 Years.

In Memory of
FERDO. JONES, who died
April 15, 1793, Aged 63 Years.
Also ELIZABETH, Wife of
JOHN JONES, who died Ap. 12, 1792,
Aged 25 Years.
Also three Children of
JOHN and ELIZABETH JONES.

Here lieth the Body of
ANNE, the Wife of THOMAS PHILLIPS,
(of Greet,) who departed this Life,
18 of March 1781, in the 37
Year of her Age.
Also two Children died Infants.

Here lieth the Body of

13 14 15

ROBERT CARNALL, of *Winchcombe*,
who departed this Life, the
the 12th. day of November,
Ano. Don. 1728, Aged 74
Also here lieth the Body of
WILLIAM CARNALL, of *Greet*,
the *Elder*, who departed this Life,
ye 29 day of February, in the
Year of our Lord 1741,
Aged 48 Years.
MARY, Wife of WILLIAM CARNALL,
who departed this Life,
April 8, 1775, Aged 73 Years.

Here lieth the Body of
DOROTHY, the Wife of
ROBERT CARNALL, of *Greet*,
who was buried the 25 of July
1695.
Also ALICE, the Daughter of
ROBERT and DOROTHY CARNALL,
who was buried May ye 13
in the Year 1724.

Here lieth the Body of
MARY, the Daughter of
ROBERT and DOROTHY CARNALL,
of *Greet*, and Wife of
THOMAS CURTIS, of *Pre sbury*,
who departed this Life,
Sept. 29, in the Year 1727,
Aged 81 Years.

Here lieth the Body of
JOHN SKIP, who was buried
June the 5. Ano Domi. 1697.
Also HENRY, the Son of EDWARD and
MARGARET THORNE,
He departed this Life, the
15 of September, 1729,
Aged 29 Years.

Here lyeth the Body of
ANNE, the Wife of ANTHONY
HULLS, who was buried the
14 day of September, Anno
1701, Her Age 32.
Here lieth the Body of
EDWARD THORNE,
who departed this Life, the
22 day of March 1732-3,
Aged 67 Years.

Here lyeth the Body of
JOHN STAITE, of *Gretton*,
Buried January the 20th.
Also here lieth the Body of
WILLIAM, the Son of JOHN STAITE,
who departed this Life,
the 12 day of Decr. 1717,
Aged 70 Years.

Here lyeth the Body of
ANNE STAITE, the Daughter of
WILLIAM STAITE, of *Gretton*,
who departed this Life,
the 17th. day of October,
Anno Domini 1698.
Also ANNE, the Wife of
WILLIAM STAITE,
was here buried the 22nd. March,
Ani. Dni 1702.
Also JOHN, the Son of
WILLIAM STAITE, was buried
October the 27, 1713.

Here lyeth the Body of
ANNE STAITE, *Widow*,
of *Frampton* in this Parish,
She died the 14 of Febr. 1727,
Aged 60 Years
Also near this Place lieth
ROBERT, her Husband.

Here lieth the Body of
WILLIAM STAITE, of *Gretton*,
who departed this Life, the
26 of July 1721, Aged 26 Years.
Also here lieth the Body of
ELIZABETH, Daughter of
WILLIAM STAITE,
who departed this Life, the
27 of August 1721,
Aged 1 Year.
MARY, Daughter of
ROBERT STAITE, of *Gretton*,
buried the 5 of May 1742.

Here lieth the Body of
ELEANOR, the Wife of
JOHN STAITE, of *Gretton*,
who departed this Life,
August 10, 1731, Aged 31 Years.

Here lieth the Body of
BENJAMIN ALLEN,
who departed this Life, the
29 day of July, A. D. 1761,
Aged 45 Years.

Here lieth the Body of
MARGARET WHITHORNE,
who was buried ye 11 day of
December in the Year 1722.
Also here lieth the Body of
MARGARET. the Wife of
EDWARD THORNE, *Gent.*
who was buried the 1st. day of
March in the Year 1738, Aged 74.
Here also lieth the Remains of
EDWARD THORNE, of this Town,
Gent. who departed this Life, the
23 day of November in the Year
1767, Aged 61 Years.

Here resteth in hope of a
Joyful Resurrection the Body of
JAMES NIND, *Yeoman*,
of *Todington*,
who departed this Life. the
3rd. day of Febr. in the Year 1766,
Aged 65 Years.

In Memory of
ANN PHILLIPS and JOICE GODDARD,
Grandmothers to the present
JOHN PHILLIPS, of *Greet*,
Likewise SUSANNA PHILLIPS,
his Mother was here buried
ye 11 day of March 1721,
Aged 56 Years.
Also ANN, the Wife of
JOHN PHILLIPS, was here buried
the 11 day of September 1749.
Aged 45 Years.
Likewise SUSANNAH, his Daughter,
was here buried the 4 day of
September 1749, Aged 17 Years.

Also here lieth the Body of
Mrs. MARY NIND, Wife of
Mr. WILLIAM NIND,
late of *Brockhampton* in the Parish
of *Sevenhampton*, and Mother
of the above named ANN PHILLIPS,
She departed this Life, the
3rd. day of September 1705,
Aged 68 Years.
And also here lieth the Body of
THOMAS PHILLIPS, of *Sudely*,
who departed this Life,
2nd. day of May 1797, in the
85 Year of his Age.

Here lieth the Body of
MARY, Wife of RICHARD DAUNCE,
of *Greet*. She was buried in the
Year of our Lord 1702.
Also here lieth the Body of
EDMUND, the Son of JOHN and
SARAH NIND, of *London*,
who departed this Life, the
13 day of April in the
Year of our Lord 1747,
Aged two Years and seven Months.
Here also lieth the Body of
SARAH NIND, of *Todington*,
who departed this Life, the
2nd. day of December
in the Year 1750.
Also SARAH NIND, Daughter of
JOHN and SARAH NIND,
who died Febr the 25th. 1752,
Aged 2 Years.
Also HUGH JAMES NIND,
Son of JOHN and SARAH NIND,
who died December the 18th. 1759,
Aged 1 Year.

Here lyeth the Body of
SARAH PEARSON, who died
the 25 of December 1663.
Also THOMAS TOBBINS,
buried the 18 of of July 1689.
Also EDWARD TAWNY,
buried the 29 of July 1703.
Also ELIZABETH, Wife of
WILLIAM CURTIS, *Periwig-Maker*,
of this Town, who departed this
Life, the 19 of June 1726,
Aged 28 Years.

SARAH, the Wife of GERVIS
BRADGATE, died January the 30,
1731.
Here lieth the Body of
GERVIS BRADGATE,
who was buried the 4 of September,
1743, aged 65 Years.

ON BRASS PLATE.

Under this Stone lie the Bodies of
JOHN MOWTLOW, *Gent.*
and LUCY, his Relict,
He departed this Life, the
28th. day of April 1693.
She the 17 day of November 1720,
Hee Aged 34. Shee 63 Years.

ON STONE.

Also the Body of
Mr. THOMAS TRAVEN,
late of this Parish, who departed
this Life, the 1st. October 1746,
Aged 70 Years.

16   17   18

1468

In Memory of
REBECKAH, the Wife of
WILLIAM COMPTON, *Senr.*
who departed this Life, the
12 day of July 1733,
Aged 60 Years.
Also in Memory of
WILLIAM COMPTON, *Senr.*
who departed this Life, the
16 day of May 1743,
Aged 69 Years.
Also here lieth the Body of
CHARLES, the Son of WILLIAM
and REBECKAH COMPTON,
who departed this Life, the
28 day of August, A. D. 1768,
Aged 52 Years.

Here lieth the Body of
JOHN THORNE, *Senr.*
who departed this Life, the
8*th.* day of April in the Year 1690,
Aged 90 Years.
Also here lieth the Body of
SUSANNAH, his Daughter,
who was buried the 25 day of
April in the Year 1724.
Here also lieth the Body of
JANE, the Wife of JOHN SMITH,
and Daughter of WILLIAM and
REBECKAH COMPTON,
who departed this Life, the
5 day of January 1748-9,
Aged 35 Years.

here lieth the Body of
MARY, the Wife of WILLIAM
COMPTON, who departed this Life,
the 19 of August 17...,
Aged 37 Years.
Here lieth the Body of
WILLIAM COMPTON,
who departed this Life, the
5 day of .... 1747.

ON BRASS PLATE.

Here lieth the Body of
Mr. FRANCIS LEACH,
Citizen and Stationer, of *London,*
who died 24 May 1707,
in the 43 Year of his Age.
In Memory of
Mrs. ELIZABETH MOWTLOW,
Wife of HENRY MOWTLOW.
dyed the 3 of .... 17...,
Aged 48 Years.

Here lieth
MARY MOWTLOW,
who died the 10 day of February,
1674.
Here lieth the Body of
ANNE, the Daughter of HENRY
MOWTLOW, who died the 4*th.* day of
May, Ano. 1690.

Here lieth the Body of
ELIZABETH, the Daughter of
WILLIAM and REBECKAH COMPTON,
who departed this Life, the
3 day of May 1749, Aged 38 Years.

SOUTH AISLE.

ON MONUMENTS.

19

Arms:—Azure a fess wavy betw.
three Lions passant Or.—HAWES.

Intra sacros Hosce parietes
Juxta reconduntur Exuviæ
THOMÆ HAWES,
viri desideratissimi:
Filij natu secundi
Revdi. SAMUELIS HAWES, A. M.
Ecclesiæ *Budbrook,* juxta *Warwicu.*
Vicarij:
Qui vocatus in Familiam
THOMÆ, *Comitis* COVENTRIÆ,
Prænobilis Domini A censibus
Ejusq; post mortem, Comitissæ dotariæ,
indefessâ Diligentiâ, illibatâ justitiâ
et eodem in cœteris vitæ tenore
pariter inservijt.
Hoc insuper Disce Lector, Ac imitare
Inter varias vitæ et officij curas
Deum jugi et eximia pietate coluit
et omnes Morum Elegantiâ demeruit,
Obijt Jany. 9, 1700, Ætat. 39.

Jacet non procul intra hos parietes
JOHANES WARREN, de *Greet,*
Lapidis huni Monumento
Pressus et Oppressus
sepulchro ipso situ et pulvere sepulto.
Vir qui dum vixit
Pietate in Deum, Caritate in proximu.
Alijs præcerior in Cœlum surrexit
Prcinde ne tam carum
Tam omnibus desideratum nomen
Omnium pedibus conculcetur
Hic suffigi curavit,
JOHES. FILIUS.

Arms:—Argent, a Cross Gules,
between four Roses of the second,
seeded Or, barbed Vert: TROTMAN.
Crest:—a Garb erect Or, banded
Or, company Argent and Azure between two Ostridge feathers Argt.

Near this Place lieth the Remains of
GEORGE SCANDERBIG TROTMAN,
Attorney-at-Law, who departed
this Life, 25 Sept. 1793,
Aged 22 Years.

Near this Place are deposited
the Remains of ANN, Wife of
JOHN TROTMAN and Daughter of
JAMES MASON, who departed
this Life, Sept. 26, 1787,
Aged 48 Years
She was Iminently distinguished by
a faithful discharge of the Duties of
Domestic Life,
Displaying a bright Example of Conjugal and parental affection;
And being endowed with
meekness and benevolence of
Disposition joined to a strict integrity
of Conduct,
She supported a Character of no less
estimation in Social Life,
among those who had the experience
of her Virtues:
As a sincere Tribute of Affection
and Gratitude to the Memory of
departed Worth this Monument
is Erected by her Surviving Consort.

Arms:—TROTMAN, *impaling* Or.
three Mullets within a double Tressure Gules.—MASON.

ON A STATELY BLACK MARBLE TOMB
INCLOSED WITH IRON RAILS.

20

Here lyeth interred the Body of
Mr. EDWARD BEALE, *Gent.*
of this Parish, who departed this
Life, November the 28, 1737,
Aged 67 Years.

Here lie the Bodies of
RALPH BEALE, *Gent.*
and ELIZABETH, his Wife.
Also GEORGE, the Son of ROBERT
and ELIZABETH BEALE, *Goldsmith,*
and *Citizen,* of *London,*
He was here buried 14 of June 1740,
Aged 65 Years.
[This Tomb was taken away at the
restoration of the Church.]

Here also lieth the Body of
THOMAS SKAY, of this Town,
Baker, who departed this Life, the
31 of July 1756, Aged 64 Years.
Also the Body of FRANCES, the
Relict of THOMAS SKAY,
who departed this Life, the
17 of April 1760, Aged 66 Years.
Also the Body of ANN,
the Wife of GEORGE SKAY,
of this Town *Baker,*
who departed this Life, the
17*th.* day of October 1762,
Aged 29 Years.

ON FLAT STONES.

Here lieth the Body of
ANNE HARVEY, *Senr.*
buried the 13 day of May 1715.
Also GILES, the Son of JOHN
HARVEY, buried 19 day of
May 1730, Aged 64 Years.
Also the Body of JOHN HARVEY,
Senr. late *Bailiff* of this Town,
He departed this Life, the
7*th.* of May 1751, Aged 76 Years.

Here lieth the Body of
ANNE, the Wife of GILES HARVEY,
who was buried Decem 4*th.* 1720,
Aged 49 Years.

Here lieth the Body of
GEORGE HARVEY,
who departed this Life, the
14 day of November 1686.
Also FRANCES, the Wife of
GEORGE HARVEY,
who died 5 of April 1701.
Also the Body of ANNE, the Wife
of JOHN HARVEY, *Senior,*
who was buried the 23 Aug. 1722,
Also in Memory of JOHN SKAY,
who died the 21 of Decemb. 1763,
Aged 28 Years.

Here lieth the Body of
HENRY HARVEY,
buried March 14, 1677.
Also FRANCES, the Daughter of
THOMAS LORINGE, and Wife of
HENRY HARVEY,
who departed this Life, the
9 of January 1720-1, Aged 91.
Here also lieth the Body of
ELIZABETH HARVEY,
who died the 15 day of Nov. 1765,
Aged 99 Years.

21

In Memory of
THOMAS and WILLIAM, Sons of
HENRY and FRANCES HARVEY,
THOMAS, was buried the 16 of
Nov. 1724, in the 60 Year of his Age.

JOHN HARVEY, *Baker*,
Buried the ... day of July,
Anno Dni. 1703.

SARAH, Wife of JOHN HARVEY,
war buried the 18 day of Sept.
1654.

In Memory of
ANNE, the Daughter of HENRY
and FRANCES HARVEY, and Wife of
WILLIAM BROADWAY, *Gent.*
She died the 16 of July 1729,
Aged 70 Years
Also of
WILLIAM BROADWAY,
who departed this Life, the
1 day of December 1745,
Aged 84 Years.
Also in Memory of
THOMAS HARVEY, *Gent.*
who died June 11 1785,
Aged 70 Years.
HELEN HARVEY, *Widow*,
of THOMAS HARVEY, died
July 4, 1794, Aged 57 Years.
EDWARD HARVEY, second Son,
of THOMAS and HELEN HARVEY,
died Decr. 14, 1795, Aged 35 Years.

Here lieth the Body of
Mr. JOHN ROSE, who died
January the 29th. 1716,
Ætat. 50.
Also ELIZABETH, the Wife of
JOHN ROSE, who departed this
Life, the 4 day of X'ber. 1720.

Here lieth the Body of
ABIGAIL BLISS, who was buried
the 29 day of June in the Year
1741, Aged 60 Years.

In Memory of
JAMES HARRIS, *Malster*,
who was buried the 24 of
Sept. 1727, Aged 77 Years.
ELIZABETH, Wife of JAMES
HARRIS, was buried May the 2, 1726,
Aged 80 Years.
ELIZABETH, their Daughter,
was buried tho 13 of May 1703,
Aged 20 Years.

Here lyeth the Body of
WILLIAM HUMPHRYS,
who departed this Life, the
3 day of March 1732, Aged 48.
Here also lieth the Body of
MARY, the Wife of
WILLIAM HUMPHRYS,
who departed this Life, the
21 of October 1733.

22

In Memory of
HENRY HASLAM, *Senr.*
buried March the 3, 1736.
Also SUSANNA, the Daughter of
HENRY HASLAM,
was buried November 17, 1737.
Also ELIZABETH, tbe Daughter
of HENRY HASLAM, was buried
November the 17, 1737.
Also ELIZABETH, the Daughter,
of HENRY HASLAM, *Senr.*
buried October the 21, 1734.

Here lieth the Body of
HENRY SMITH, *Baker*,
of this Town, who died the
19 of July 1724, Aged 35 Years.
Also ANN, the Relict of
HENRY SMITH, who died
15 of Febr. 1758, Aged 73 Years.
Also of HESTER O'KEASEY,
Daughter of the above HENRY
and ANN SMITH, who departed
this Life. Dec 30, 1793,
Aged 75 Years.

Mortales hic jacent Reliquiæ
ELIZABETHÆ NEWMAN,
uxoris JOHANNIS NEWMAN,
dilectissimæ,
Obijt Novembris die Vicessimo 2do.
Anno Salutis 1747, Ætatis 64.
Also here lieth the Body of
GEORGE NEWMAN, Son of
JOHN and ELIZABETH NEWMAN,
who departed this Life, of
29 of Sept. 1775, Aged 57 Years.
Also of JOHN NEWMAN, Son of
GEORGE and MARY NEWMAN,
who departed this Life, the
15 of October 1793,
Aged 47 Years.

H. S. E.
JOHANNES NEWMAN,
Amicis Amicissimus
Omnibus Honestis Deplorandus,
Obijt Jan. 6o.
Anno Salutis 1759, Ætatis 72.
Also in Memory of
HARVY and JOHN, Sons of
JOHN and MARY NEWMAN,
HARVY, died July 28, 1779,
Aged 16 Months.
JOHN, died August 2, 1779,
Aged 5 Years and 10 Months.
Also MARY, Wife of GEORGE
NEWMAN, who died Nov. 21, 1779,
Aged 57 Years.
Also WILLIAM, Son of JOHN and
MARY NEWMAN, who died
Decr. 4, 1791, Aged 8 Months.

Here lyeth ABIGAIL, the Daughter
of GEORGE and MARY NEWMAN,
who was buried July 19, 1749.

In Memory of
WILLIAM, the Son of WILLIAM
and DINAH WOOD, who died
the 19 day of August 1780,
Aged 2 Days.
Also DINAH, the Wife of
WILLIAM WOOD.
She departed this Life, the
9th. day of August 1783,
Aged 33 Years.

23

Also WILLIAM WOOD, Grandson of
BENJAMIN WOOD, *Gent.*
who died (greatly lamented) the
19 day of Decr. 1783, in the
29 Year of his Age.
Also DINAH-SUSANNAH WOOD,
their Daughter, who departed
this Life, Aprl 21, 1785,
Aged 1 Year and 10 Months.
Hic jacet
EDMUNDUS THOS. BROWN, *Gen.*
Obiit 5o. Die Augusti,
Ano. Dom. 1733, Ætatis 85 Ann.

This Stone is laid here as a
Memorandum of the dissolution of
THOMAS WHITE, (of this Town,)
whose mortal part was seperated
from its union the 16 day of
January 1792, Aged 55 Years.
Also in Memory of
ELIZABETH, the Wife, of
JERVIS WHEATLY, Daughter of
THOMAS and HERODIAS WHITE,
who departed this Life, at
Nottingham, the 13 day of
October 1796, Aged 35 Years.

In Memory of
SAMUEL SMITH, *Baker*,
late of this Town,
who departed this Life, the
13 of Febr. 1788, Aged 66.
Also of RICHARD, Son of
SAMUEL and SARAH SMITH,
who departed this Life,
Dec. 3, 1787, Aged 26 Years.

Here lieth the Body of
ELIZABETH, Wife of JOHN PAGE,
(She was the Daughter of
JOHN and ELIZABETH NEWMAN,)
who departed this Life, the
13 of April 1786, Aged 73 Years.

In Memory of
THOMAS, the Son of THOMAS, and
HANNAH FISHER, who died
the 19 of September 1777,
Aged 5 Years and 10 Months.
Also ANN, their Daughter,
who died March 23, 1779,
Aged 4 Months.
Also HANNAH, their Daughter,
who died Febr. 8, 1781,
Aged 1 Year.
Also PAUL, their Son, who died
May 26, 1787, Aged 2 Years.

CHURCH YARD.

ALTAR TOMBS.

This Tomb was erected to the
Memory of BENJAMIN WOOD,
of this Town, *Gent.*
who lies enterred beneath the same,
He departed this Life, the 22 day of
July Ao. Dom. 1786, iu the
87 Year of his Age.
Also SUSANNA, his Eldest Daughter,
She died Sept. 3, 1745,
Aged 25 Years.
Also of SUSANNA, his Wife,
who departed this Life, the
5 of May 1748, Aged 63 Years.

24

And also of MARTHA, his Youngest
Daughter, and the Wife of
THOMAS WILSON.
She died May 15, A. D. 1750,
Aged 27 Years.
In Memory of
BENJAMIN WOOD, of *Greet*,
who departed this Life,
Febr. 18, 1739, Aged 64 Years.
Also of ANN, his Daughter,
She died April 22, 1723,
Aged 5 Years.
And also of ANN, his first Wife,
who was buried Oct. 31, 1724,
Aged 56 Years.
Here lie the Remains of
WILLIAM WOOD, *Surgeon*,
(et eruditus fuit artibus liberalibus,)
the only Son of
BENJAMIN WOOD, *Gent.*
He departed this Life, the
17 day of Jany. Anno Dom. 1755,
Aged 30 Years.
Also ANN, his beloved Wife,
She died Oct 16, 1774,
Aged 56 Years.
And also BENJAMIN, their first
born Son, was buried the
1st. of Febr. 1754, Aged 3 Years.
In Memory of
WILLIAM MATHEWS *alias* PAGE,
of *Greet*, who departed this Life,
the 10 of June 1715,
Aged 78 Years.
Also of MARTHA, his Wife,
She died 26 of Jany. 1730,
Aged 77 Years.

Here rests in hopes of a joyful
resurrection the Body of
SAMUEL BAYLIS,
who departed this Life,
26 day of December A. D. 1772,
in the 79 Year of his Age.
MARGARET, his Wife, who
departed this Life, Jany. 17,
A. D. 1730, Aged 25 Years.

In Memory of
ROBERT, the Son, of ROBERT
and MARY BAYLIS, of
Pigglesworth in this County,
who died the 2nd. day of March 1800,
Aged 6 Years.
Also in Memory of
HESTER, the Daughter of
ROBERT and MARY BAYLIS,
who died the 30 day of June 1800,
Aged 1 Year.

Here lieth the Body of
LYDIA DURHAM,
who was buried Sept. 5, 1736,
Æt. 34 Years.
JOHN DURHAM, of *Postlip*,
died Febr. 2, 1760, Aged 60.
JAMES, the Son of
JAMES and LYDIA DURHAM,
died Decr. 24, 1758, Aged 26.
HESTER DURHAM, relict of
JOHN DURHAM,
died 27 day of Nov. 1777,
Aged 71 Years.

In Memory of
ANNE, the Wife of
WILLIAM REYNALDS, *Surgeon*,

25

who died April 1st. in the Year 1772,
Aged 49 Years.
Also of THOMAS, their Son,
who died March 18 in the
Year 1783, Aged 18 Years.
Also of WILLIAM, their Son,
who died Oct. 18 in the
Year 1785, Aged 25 Years.
Also MARY, their Daughter,
who died Jany. 23 in the
Year 1788, Aged 36 Years.

Here lieth interred
ELIZABETH, Wife of JOHN TARRAN.
She died Oct 12, A. D 1757,
Aged 35 Years.
Also MARY, late Wife of
JOHN TARRAN, who died
March 13, 1798, in the 76
Year of her Age.
In Memory of
JOHN TARRAN, who died
March 19, 1800, in the 80
Year of his Age.
MATTHEW, Son of JOHN and
MARY TARRAN, who died
July 25, 1759, Aged 32.
MARY, his Wife, who died
March 29, 1768, Aged 71.
Also of THOMAS TARRAN, who died
March 20, 1771, Aged 71.
And of JOHN, Son of JOHN and
ELIZABETH TARRAN, who died
March 7, 1778, Aged 21.

Arms:—...... or a Chevron betw.
three Castle ...... a pair of Compas-
ses open ....

Here rests in hopes of a joyful
resurrection the Body of MARY,
the Daughter of LEWIS and SARAH
BRADLEY, of *Sudely Manor*,
and Wife of EDMUND SMITH,
who departed this Life, the
30 day of March in the Year 1780,
Aged 68 Years.

To the Memory of
ELEANOR, the Wife of ANTHONY
ROGERS, of the Parish of *Sudely*,
She was Daughter of LEWIS and
SARAH BRADLEY, of *Sudely Manor*,
who died March 11, 1798,
Aged 78 Years.

This Tomb was erected to
the Memory of JOHN ROGERS,
of *Cornaean*. He was eldest Son of
ANTHONY and ELEANOR ROGERS,
of *Wadfield Farm* in the Parish
of *Sudely*, who died Dec. 4, 1785,
Aged 33 Years.

In Memory of
GEORGE THORNE, *Gent.*
who departed this Life, the
18 of May 1747, Aged 69 Years.
Also of ELIZABETH, his Wife,
She was Daughter of
THOMAS LORINGE, of *Haimes.*

*The following Words she desired might
be inserted on her Tomb, viz.*—
"Here lies the Head that thought
the Church was made for the living
and not for the Dead."

26

She departed this Life, the
12 day of April 1743.
Arms:—Argent, a fess Gules be-
tween three Lions rampant Sable.
—THORNE. *impaling Quarterly*
Argent & Gules a Bend engrailed
Sable —LORINGE.

Here lieth the Body of
THOMAS MARTEN, of *Sudely*,
who departed this Life, the
27 day of September 1712,
Aged 67 Years.
Also in Memory of
WILLIAM MARTEN,
who departed this Life,
January 25, 1758, Aged 80 Years.

Here lieth the Body of
ALICE, the Wife of RALPH PEASON,
who was buried the 4 of April 1668.

Here lieth the Body of
FRANCIS, late Wife of
NICHOLAS GEARAD,
who departed this Life, the
8 day of October, A. D. 1669.
Also EDITH, the Wife of
NICHOLAS GEARAD,
buried September 30, 1630.
Also EDWARD, JOHN, MILCENT
and MARGARY, Children of
NICHOLAS and EDITH GEARAD.

Here resteth in hope of a joyful
Resurrection the Body of
JOHN SPENCER, of this Parish,
Yeoman, who departed this Life,
20 day of April 1728,
Aged 70 Years.

In Memory of
THOMAS SMITH, of *Langley*,
who departed this Life, the
22 day of October 1759,
Aged 79 Years.
Also in Memory of
SARAH, the Daughter of
THOMAS and MARY SMITH,
who departed this Life, the
30 day of January 1743,
Aged 33 Years

Here lieth the Body of
LEWIS BRADLEY, of *Sudely Manor*,
who departed this Life, the
18 September, A. D. 1735,
Aged 62 Years.
Also SARAH, his Wife,
who departed this Life, the
19 of March, A. D. 1743-4,
Aged 61 Years.
Also ANN, Daughter of
LEWIS and SARAH BRADLEY,
who departed this Life, the
14 Jany. A. D. 1744-5,
Aged 25 Years.
Also here lieth the Body of
EDWARD COLE, of *Sudely Manor*,
Buried August 9th. 1709

27

1471

ON A STONE OVER THE CHANCEL
DOOR SOUTH SIDE.

In Memory of
JOHN PHILLIPS, of *Greet, Gent.*
within this Parish,
who departed this Life, the
8 day of August, Anno Domi. 1728,
Aged 61 Years.
Also in Memory of
WILLIAM, the Son, of JOHN and
ANN PHILLIPS, Grandson of
the above named.
He departed this Life, the
9 day of Febr 1744,
Aged 5 Years and 11 Months.

ON A STONE AGAINST THE EAST-END
OF SOUTH AISLE.

In Memory of
WILLIAM, Son of HENRY and
MARGARET YARDINGTON,
who died November 24, 1719.

ON ANOTHER.

In Memory of
ANNE, the Wife of
ROBERT STAITE, of *Gretton,*
who was buried the 4 of Sept.
1727.

In Memory of
ROBERT and MARY,
Son and Daughter of JOHN and
ELEANOR STAITE, of *Gretton,*
buried 28 of February 1725.
Also ROBERT, the Son of
THOMAS and .... TAYLOR,
was buried December 26, 1724.

*(Supplementary Notices of Additional
Monuments since Bigland's time.)*

CHANCEL.

In Memory of
DOROTHY FREEMAN,
Daughter of THOMAS and MARY
FREEMAN, of *Greet* in this Parish,
She died August 11, 1818,
Aged 66 Years.
Her Sister MARY FREEMAN,
died June 4, 1821, Aged 75.
Their Sister ELIZABETH,
died Jany. 25, 1827, Aged 79.
This Monument is erected as a
grateful Tribute to the Memory of
the departed Sisters, by direction
of the late
THOMAS HALE, of *Greet, Gent.*
who died April 25, 1851, in his
79*th.* Year.

ANN, Wife of WILLIAM STEPHENS,
of *Cubberley,* Daughter of
JOSHUA and ANN BAYLIS,
of this Place, died Oct. 7, 1811,
Aged 39 Years.
WILLIAM STEPHENS,
formerly of *Cubberley,* late of
Sandford, near Cheltenham,
died March 17, 1823,

28

In Memory of
NATHANIEL LLOYD, *Gent.*
High Bailiff of this Town,
And a Resident at *Postlip* and
Winchcombe, upwards of 40 Years.
He died 14 July 1845, Aged 75.
He was buried at *Abinghall,*
where his Ancestors lie.

ON REREDOS.

In Memory of
MARY-ANN, the beloved Wife of
WILLIAM GATES ADLARD,
who died Oct. 29, 1876, at
Postlip Hall.

NORTH AISLE.

In a Vault near this Place
lie the Remains of
JOHN WORSFOLD, *Esqr.*
many years a resident of the
Island of Montserrat,
who died Augt. 20, 1811,
Aged 45 Years.
Also of MARY, his Wife,
who died Febr. 9, 1816, Aged 56.

Sacred to the Memory of
SUSANNA, Wife of RICHARD
MATHEWS, of *Greet,*
died Sept. 16, 1813, Aged 46.

Sacred to the Memory of
the *Revd.* WILLIAM DURHAM,
who died Febr. 4, 1819, Aged 63.
Also of ELIZABETH, his Wife,
who died Augt. 14, 1814, Aged 78.
Also SARAH DURHAM,
who died Decr. 14, 1814,
Aged 17 Years.
Also of HESTER ANN DURHAM,
who died June 17, 1854.
Also of MARY DURHAM,
who died Decr. 24, 1860.

In a Vault near this Place
lie the Remains of
JOHN BAYLIS, Son of
ROBERT and MARY BAYLIS,
of *Winchcombe,* who died
Augt. 19, 1825, Aged 33 Years.
Also the above ROBERT BAYLIS,
who died Nov. 19, 1855, Aged 68.
Also MARY, his Wife, who died
May 18, 1855, Aged 69 Years.
MARGARET, Wife of THOMAS
PHILLIPPS, died 1810.

Arms:—Gules on a bend engrailed, Or, between two castles, Or, three
trees proper.—BAYLIS.
Crest.—An arm embowed sable
holding a Javelin, Or.

SOUTH AISLE.

SUSANNAH WOOD, Daughter of
WILLIAM WOOD, *Surgeon,*
of this Town, and ANN, his Wife,
died 1843, Aged 91 Years.

29

ANN, her Sister Relict of
EDWARD THOMAS BROWN,
and afterwards of SAMUEL SMITH,
both of this Parish,
died ....

ON JOHN AND ANN TROTMAN'S
MONUMENT.

Also of JOHN TROTMAN,
who died 1802, Aged 79 Years.
And three Daughters of
JOHN and ANN TROTMAN,
viz.—MARY, who died Nov. 29, 1820,
Aged 55 Years.
ANN, who died Decr. 4, 1820,
Aged 52 Years.
SUSANNAH, who died in her Infancy.
Also WILLIAM TROTMAN,
who died March 24, 1850,
Aged 87 Years.
Also JANE TROTMAN, who died
Jany. 31, 1859, Aged 64 Years.

Deposited in a Vault near this place
are the Remains of
PAUL ASHMORE, who died 1790.
SUSANNAH, his Wife,
died 1802, Aged 57 Years.
ELIZABETH, Wife of ANDERSON
ASHMORE, of *Yardley, Worc.*
died June 1833.
ANDERSON, Son of PAUL and
SUSANNAH ASHMORE,
died 1837, Aged 72 Years.
THOMAS, Son of PAUL and
SUSANNAH ASHMORE,
died 1838, Aged 76 Years.
ANDERSON, Son of PAUL and
ELIZABETH ASHMORE, died 1832.
WILLIAM, Son of ANDERSON and
ELIZABETH ASHMORE,
died 1848, Aged 50 Years.
PAUL, Son of ANDERSON and
ELIZABETH ASHMORE, died 1830.

JOHN TIMBRELL, *Esqr.*
born at *Winchcombe,* 16 July 1762,
died at *Kentesh Town,*
10 Sept. 1844.

AGAINST A PILLAR.

Sacred to the Memory of
MARY, Wife of WILLIAM BEST,
Daughter of JOHN and ANNE
TIMBRELL, died Augt. 13, 1826,
She was—but words are wanting
to express what she was,
Think what a good Wife ought to
be—and She was that.

Beneath this Tablet are deposited
the Remains of
THOMAS WILLIAMS, *Esqr.*
for many Years an eminent Solicitor,
Resident at the *Abbey House,*
in this Parish.
Also of SARAH, his Widow,
A Lady whose sense of Religion
was of the purest kind and who
passed a long life in the affectionate
Esteem of all who knew her.

30

THOMAS SMITH, of this Parish,
died 1824, Aged 82 Years.
MARY ANN, his Wife, Daughter of
ARTHUR and ANN HEAVENS,
died 1844, Aged 70 Years.

MARY, the eldest Daughter,
who died 1821, Aged 21 Years.
ROBERT MAGGS, who died 1832,
Aged 19 Years.

her Memory will ever be cherished
by a fond Mother and surviving Friends
To whom in the Hour of their
affliction, she left the consoling hope
of reunion in a better world.

JOHN MAGGS, late of *Cheltenham*,
and formerly of *Hinton Blewett*,
Somersetshire, died 1816,
Aged 44 Years
SARAH, relict of the above,
died 1846, Aged 75 Years.
Two Sons and two Daughters,
died in their infancy.
ANN COX. 2nd. Daughter of
the above, died Jany. 30, 1819,
in her 17th. Year.

In a Vault at the North West corner
of this Church lie the Remains of
ANN, only Daughter of
Mr. FRANCIS JAMES,
who died 22 May 1826.
After a short but very severe illness,
she was snatched away
in the prime of Life, and bloom of youth,
Endeared to all who knew her
for the purity of her heart and
amiability of her disposition,

CHURCH YARD,
ON BRASS PLATE.

In affectionate Rememberance of the
Revd. JOHN RIDOUT HARVEY, A. M.
Vicar of *Winchcombe*,
and Rector of *Sudeley* 36 Years,
who died Jany. 1871,
Aged 63 Years.

31   32   33

HEAD STONES.

	Died.	Aged.		Died.	Aged.
Eleanor, Wife of Daniel Lacey, and Daughter of William and Philip Pensome,	23 Sept.	1751	56	Isaac Restall,	11 Jany.	1754	81
Daniel Lacey,	11 Nov.	1762	72	Charles Coats, buried in the Ch.	27 Decr.	1768	...
Eleanor, Wife of Richard Bell, and Daughter of John and Mary Smedley,	17 Oct.	1717	...	Philip Harbert, buried.	10 April	1771	83
				Ann Staite, of *Gretton*, buried,	10 April	1771	84
Richard Bell,	28 Sept.	1759	75	Nicholas Sisum, buried,	16 April	1771	95
Mary, Wife of William Merryman, and late Wife of Richard Hughs,	14 Febr.	1736	60	John Barakle, buried,	16 April	1771	74
				Joan, Wife of Charles Coats, burd	3 May	1771	89
John Best, buried,	2 Jany.	1720	...	Thomas Sebritt,	15 June	1771	79
John Johnson, of this Town, *Fishmonger*,	28 June	1745	36	John Greening, buried,	3 Nov.	1771	99
Ralph Ireland, late Keeper of *Stancomb Wood*,	22 June	1762	63	Thomas Williams, buried,	18 Nov.	1771	78
				Hannah Hill, buried,	5 Febr.	1772	...
John Badger, of *Gretton*,	27 Oct.	1767	72	John Allen, buried,	31 Decr.	1769	97
Elizabeth, the Wife of Edward Rayer, *Senr.*,	11 June	1758	61	William Cull, buried,	28 Oct	1772	84
				Margaret, Wife of Richard Bell,	24 Febr.	1773	83
John Yate, Interred,	5 April	1680	...	John Lucas, of *Sudely Castle*,	25 March	1773	65
Mary, Wife of Joseph Clarige,	6 June	1754	63	Ann. Wife of Jonathan Taynton,	2 Jany.	1798	65
Robert Cull, buried,	26 March	1718	...	Richard Howman,	24 July	1798	52
Margaret, Wife of Samuel Baylis,	17 Jany.	1730	25	Mary, Wife of David Harvey,	5 Decr.	1789	33
John Philpott, of this Town, *Blacksmith*,	26 Oct.	1718	50	Elizabeth, Wife of David Harvey,	30 July	1785	33
				Francis Ward,	19 July	1776	76
John Harvey, late *Bayliff*, of this Town,	5 Nov.	1744	44	Jane, his Wife,	23 Febr.	1797	76
William Ashley,	12 April	1762	69	Jane, Wife of William Timbrell,	21 Augt.	1794	49
Scanderberg Trotman,	6 Febr.	1752	52	William Timbrell,	15 Jany.	1800	53
William, the Son of Scanderberg and Edith Trotman, who died in the Plains of *Scorburgh*, near *Duchland*, *Germany*,	23 Nov.	1760	38	Edward Mason,	6 Jany.	1776	60
				Mary, his Wife,	4 May	1758	..
				John Roberts,	16 Augt.	1786	68
				Susanna, his Wife,	25 Augt.	1781	70
Mary, Wife of John Bibby, and Daughter of Edward Jones,	23 Nov.	1760	103	Mary, Wife of James Roberts, and Daughter of Samuel and Mary Jones,	22 Decr.	1792	41
John Newman, buried,	18 Jany.	1727	...	Samuel, Son of William and Ann Rayer,	14 Oct.	1756	54
Susanna, Wife of John Newman, buried,	10 May	1733	...	Ann, his Wife,	10 Oct.	1781	85
Thomas, their Son,	16 April	1755	57	Richard Best,	5 June	1793	80
Isaac Skillern, *Senr.*	16 Nov	1766	58	Elizabeth, his Wife,	30 March	1778	79
Ann, Wife of Isaac Skillern,	18 April	1764	60	John Bell,	21 April	1785	01
Israel Slatter, of *Frampton*,	29 March	1725	72	Mary, his Wife,	22 Augt.	1774	62
Edward Morris,		1769	52	Alice, Wife of John Ivins,	8 Nov.	1793	59
James Harbert,	15 Decr.	1755	73	Joseph Slatter,	16 June	1786	82
David Harbert,	18 April	1769	62	Ann, his Wife,	2 April	1732	43
Joseph Hedges,	31 Jany.	1773	71	Israel Slatter,	22 Sept.	1752	89
Catharine, Wife of Edw. Wontner,	26 Sept.	1727	35	John Brown,	15 June	1794	54
Joseph Batsford, *Senr.*	11 Nov.	1717	58	Mary, Wife of David Harvey, and Daughter of James and Elizabeth Harbert,	17 March	1795	74
Jane, his Wife, buried	9 Oct.	1726	63	William Heavens,	4 April	1755	57
Richard Spencer,	11 May	1767	45	Elizabeth, his Wife,	1 Nov.	1782	...
Thomas Collett,	11 Jany.	1767	74	James Page,	1 Nov.	1789	68
Hannah, Wife of Thos. Collett,	20 June	1746	46	Samuel Jones,	22 June	1793	84
William Savage,	18 Febr.	1721	57	Mary, Wife of Samuel Jones,	24 May	1778	60
Ann, his Wife, buried,	12 Decr.	1726	...	Thomas Collett,	11 Jany.	1767	74
Abraham Darke,	13 Decr.	1732	45	Mary, Wife of Thomas Skinner,	20 Oct.	1764	78
Nicholas Sisum, *Senr.*	25 Oct.	1728	75	Thomas Skinner,	27 Oct.	1772	81
Paul Sparrow, *Senr.* of *Sudely*,	12 Decr.	1743	75	William Staite,	24 Dec.	1794	63
Robert Matthews, of *Greet*,	7 Oct.	1724	55	Robert Matthews,	30 July	1788	65
John Cull, of *Nunton-field*,	20 Augt.	1769	74	William Matthews,	4 Sept.	1795	74
Elizabeth, wife of Benjamin Marten, of *Hambury Bridge* in the Parish of *Winchcomb*	7 Nov.	1725	39	Paul Sparrow,	16 June	1773	67
				John Allington,	27 July	1778	70
				Judith, his Wife,	13 Mar.	1770	...
				Daniel Dobbins,	25 Nov.	1785	69
				Mary, Wife of John Cull,	2 Jany.	1781	78
				William Greening,	9 June	1770	60

34   35

HEAD STONES.—continued.

	Died.		Aged.		Died.		Aged.
Sarah, his Wife, ...	22 May	1798	81	Richard Hughes, ...	4 Augt.	1791	78
Anthony Greening, ...	17 Oct.	1778	61	Richard Hughes, ...	8 March	1893	82
Margaret, his Wife, ...	8 May	1797	70	John Right-Hall, ...	13 Oct.	1798	57
Richard Staite, ...	12 March	1794	65	Grace, Wife of Samuel Hall, ...	20 June	1764	54
John Staite, ...	12 March	1754	55	Sarah. Wife of John Wright-Hall,	13 March	1793	52
Ann, his Wife, ...	13 March	1739	38	Elizabeth, Wife of Richd. Newman	4 Decr.	1790	81
Michael Tyler, ...	3 Oct.	1770	79	Henry Butler, ...	20 May	1794	85
Thomas Staite, ...	13 Jany.	1793	82	Mary, his Wife, ...	25 Augt.	1788	85
Ann, his Wife, ...	14 Jany.	1781	62	Mary, their Daughter, ...	10 July	1800	66
Mathias Brown, ...	29	1794	74	Phillip Breaks, ...	12 May	1786	67
Mathias Brown, ...	21 April	1782	61	Richard Beauchamp, ...	21 Decr.	1785	70
Margaret, relict of the late Richard Bell, ...	22 Febr.	1773	84	William Savage, Senr.	24 May	1785	89
				Sarah, his Wife, ...	2 Jany.	1775	77
William Cull, ...	5 June	1795	62	William Johnson, ...	13 April	1729	58
Margaret, Wife of John Cull, ...	30 Nov.	1780	73	Sarah, his Wife, ...	13 Febr.	1750	76

[*Since the Church was first visited in order to copy the Inscriptions things have been removed from the South Transept, And such removal has disclosed the following Inscriptions:—*

ON A FLAT STONE.

ARABELLA BANCKS, died 5 July 1805.
ARABELLA BANCKS, died 3 April 1851, Aged 82.
HENRY SMITH, (of *Greet,*) Gent. died July 1831.

BEALE's Tomb *has not been restored. Nearly all the flat stone Inscriptions in the Church are covered over.*]

Supplementary Notes as to I.—*Devolution of Estates.* II.—*Church.* III.—*Taxation, Population, &c.*

1.—*Estates :*

WINCHCOMBE is a small town of between one and two hundred acres in area, in a large parish which consists of the town and of the hamlets or places of Sudeley tenements, Gretton, Greet, Postlip, Corndean, Frampton, Naunton, Cotes, Langley and Cockbury, altogether 6496 acres.

The town stands upon very antient foundations. In and about it, are vestiges of Roman occupation, and of the dwellings, roads, camps, and earth works of the prehistoric period. In Saxon times it was the chief town of the Kings of Mercia. The Royal Residence was probably that afterwards known as the Castle, which was situate in Cole Street on one side of St. Peter's Church, lying between the fees of the King and Tho. de Saint Vallery. The spot is not now exactly ascertained.

It was a Walled town, and was surrounded with Woods, the defence of a British town, and which in later times also served as recreation and hunting grounds, to the inhabitants and their neighbours. It had a Liberty around it, for we find it recorded that Bartholomew de Sudeley, took two men with the dogs of Robert de Crupes, (who was of *Whittington*,) and those of Robert de Dowdeswell, (who was of that place,) out of the Liberty. *Rot. Hund.* Edw. i. Gloucestershire. This was for the chase of great game.

In Saxon times King Offa, built a Nunnery here; and A. D. 800. King Kenulf, founded a Benedictine Monastery which (with a short interval when it was secularized,) long continued increasing in possessions and power, and the Abbot in time attained the Mitre, (A. D. 1265.) and became a spiritual lord of parliament.

The town was exempt from the Hundred Jurisdiction, being a shire of itself until the time of King Canute, when it was annexed to Gloucestershire.

Winchcomb was at one time a place of large business. Much of it extended towards Sudeley and along the way to Corndean. The brook or river Isborne ran through the middle of the town, and on it were mills and wharves, of fullers, clothiers dyers, tanners. No Merchant of Winchcomb, is however mentioned in Domesday Survey. or in the Nonæ Rolls; although in the latter, Merchants of Stow, Tewkesbury and Cirencester, are mentioned. But it is the only borough in the County besides Gloucester and Bristol, mentioned in Domesday Survey.

The Town is a borough by prescription, and has a Charter of fairs and markets granted by Queen Elizabeth. It is governed by two Bailiffs, and they take ten assistants, from among whom the Bailiffs are chosen at the Court Leet Yearly.

The place became much decayed. This was due to several causes. Mercia ceased to be a Kingdom, and the Court went away. The palace or Castle was not destroyed for some centuries. It was here probably that Joan of Acre, Daughter of King Edward i. and Wife of De Clare, Earl of Gloucester,

(in whose Custody the Royal Castle would be) gave birth to Gilbert, their only child, who was slain at Bannockburn. (*Florence of Worcester*, notices that he was born at Winchcombe.)

Leland the Antiquary of the Reformation period speaks of Winchcomb as "of old a mighty large town." But this was merely by tradition, for even then the only tokens that remained of the Buildings of the old Town towards Sudeley were traces of a Ditch and the foundations of the Walls.

Queen Elizabeth's charter of fairs speaks of the great decay of the Borough, and that the Inhabitants were not able to support and repair it for the great poverty that reigned among them.

The situation of the place had something to do with its decline. Standing in vallies off the steps of the Cotswold range, having bad Roads and a stiff soil all about it, it was a place difficult of access except by Horses and Mules, and when pack horse conveyance gave place to carriages of burden, places in the plains were more resorted to for traffic than in mountainous situations neglected.

The Abbey flourished sometime after the general decay of the town. Like other great ecclesiastical bodies, it concentrated the wealth of its possessions in its chief seat, to the benefit of the town. Their rule over their dependents was somewhat rigorous; and their Registers record contentions, with the people of the town and the secular clergy of the parish. In Mrs. Dent's, "Winchcomb," (an interesting work to which the writer is indebted for much information,) it is remarked, *p.* 100. "In the midst of so much piety it is sad to see how nearly every page of the same record (Abbey Register,) is marked by accounts of disputations over such things as Wax tapers, &c."

When the Abbey was dissolved, its possessions were divided amongst many grantees, and the profits dispersed in several channels. The town was then reduced to what, it still continues to be, an Agricultural Mart.

We proceed to make Notes on the Estates in the Parish distributed under the Names of the places where they are situate (to wit) 1. The Town or Borough, 2. Abbey Demesnes, 3. Sudeley Tenements, 4. Greet, 5. Gretton, 6. Cotes and Thorp, 7. Postlip, 8. Corndean, 9. Woods, 10. Frampton and Naunton, 11. Langley, 12. Cockbury.

And then take those Notes which are referrible to the Parish generally, or to more than one of the places in it.

1.—The borough of Winchcomb rendered in King Edward's time 6£. farm rent Of this Earl (King) Herald had the third penny that is 40 s. It afterwards with the hundred of the Vill rendered 20£. Durand the Sheriff added to it 100 s. (Rent.) Roger de Ivry, 60 s. Then three hundreds were annexed to it and the rent increased to 28 £.

Dom. Survey.

Under several other manors and places, in the Survey

mention is made of their having Burgages in Winchcomb, as Broadwell, Oxenton, Alderton, Worcester, Hereford, (in respect of Prestbury.) St. Dennis, Paris. (in respect of Deerhurst,) and also under the Landholders—Gozenboded, Rog. de Laci, Roger de Lueri, Robert Despencer, Ferrers.

A Survey of a somewhat later date than Domesday is given by Sir H. Ellis, in his "Introduction to Domesday Book," and copied into the Transactions of the Bristol and Gloucestershire Archæological Society, *Vol.* 4. which furnishes some further particulars of Winchcomb & its Burgate Tenants, viz. the Bishop of Worcester, had 1: Abbey of St. Dennis, (Deerhurst,) 1; the thane Alwold, 1; Fitzhamon, (Tewkesbury, 5; De Cormeil, 2. and a Mill, (Postlip;) Herald 10, and 2 Vills, (Gretton, Greet,) Wallery and Hugh Lacy, 1; Lacy, Solers, Lane, Robert Lacy, Froisselew, 1, each or 5 together. Gozenboded, Sau-saye, Loughborn and Bellheim, 3 each or 12 together, De Ferrrer and the Abbot of Evesham, 2 each, (4 together) The King had geld of all these. In Roger Ivry's time the Rent was 10£. and then 21£. numbered, and the Sheriff had 20s. *"de rogatu."*

Herald to Boteler, see "Sudeley."

9 Edw. iv.—In a Fine of lands of Toddington, Greet and Gretton, Richard, Earl Rivers and others were Plaintiffs and Ralph Boteler, Deforciant.

T. St. Vallery, had a fee near the Church.

Abbey Register

1199.—Wm. de Sucia, or Saussay, (Salices.) late Ward of Pet. de Widendun, obtained the recognition of his Title to ⅓ Virgate of Land in Winchcomb. *Rot. Obl.* 25.

The Hundred of the Vill is spoken of; but somewhat later the Borough was deemed to be in Kittesgate, and the Hamlets in Holford and Gretstane Hundreds.

Ric. ii.—The Abbey of Winchcombe, had a grant of these Hundreds from the Crown, renewed by Hen. vi. Edw. iv. and Hen. vii.

1485.—In the Rental of these Hundreds the Abbot accounted for Fraunton and Newton, Potteslipp and Cotes, the Rent of Winchcomb, (paid by the Serjeant of the Vill) is put at 33 s. 4½.

9 Edw. ii —The Borough Manor was in the Crown.

Leland, mentions the Lord Harrington, as having acquired the Lordship of Winchcombe, by marriage with the heiress of the Lord Bonnewell, of Devonshire. This is not traceable.

In 1608.—It was a Crown Manor.

1730.—Dr. Lloyd, held in fee or under a long Lease.

Soley and Cox, married his Daughters and Heirs by his 1st. Wife Poulden.

George, Lord Rivers, by purchase from Lloyd's heirs.

2.— Abbey Demesnes:

The site of the Abbey was outside the Borough in Gretstane Hundred. The Abbey and its Buildings, Land for Garden, Orchards, &c. acquired the Title of the Abbey Demesnes and got to be a reputed Manor To this, other Tenants of the Abbey came as Suitors and paid their Rents and services.

The Abbey by advancing money and every means which prudence could suggest enlarged their possessions, and their Registers mention a great number of messuages and small Estates aliened to the Abbey. *Fosbrooke, p.* 347.

Philip of Tuoington, Harold Lord Sudely and others of that family were large Benefactors of Lands in and about Winchcomb to its Abbey.

10 Edw. i. *No.* 33.—W. Scrupes, alias de Crupes, pro. Abb. de Wynchecumbe. *Inq. ad q. dam.*

After the dissolution. Scite of the Abbey and Demesnes. In Common Estates 312 a. Broad and Hollow Meadow 105 a. Closes and Leazows (exclusive of Corndean the Amery (almonry) Farm,) and the Woods— Humbly Ho and Deep Wood.—

Thomas, Lord Seymour, by Crown Grant. After his attainder—

1504. 1 Mar —Sir John Bridges, Lord Chandos, by Crown Grant. It continued with the Title through Edmund, Giles, Grey, William and George successively Lords Chandos.

1645.—Grey. Lord Chandos, in his Composition with the Common Wealth Commissioners rated the Scite and Demesnes of the Abbey, with Rowell and Sudely Manors at 211£. Rent.

George, Lord Chandos, by Will devised this Estate to his 2nd. Wife Jane Savage, who survived him and married

twice afterwards. By Will she gave it to her 3rd. Husband, Pitt, afterwards Lord Rivers.

The Abbey House and Site afterwards belonged to Dr. William Smart, and after him to his Nephew Baptist Smart, By the latter, a part of the Building was let to the Parish of Winchcomb for a Workhouse.

The House was taken down by Mr. Thomas Williams, Part of the Buildings remained and were occupied by him.

The Abbey Revenues was subject to doles on the anniversaries of the Founder—King Kenulph and of the Abbots—R. Kidderminster, W. Wickwan. W. Wynforton.

And to Alms and Pensions given by Dame Johanna Huddleston, relict of Sir John Huddlestone, and for payments to the Master of the Grammar School, &c.

Other Crown Grants were made of Lands, &c. in Winchcomb, late of the Abbey —

35 Hen. viii.—Toft and Lands, to Andrews and Temple.
36 Hen. viii—Do   do. to Andrews and Hysley, Of Premises belonging to the Sexton of the Abbey.—

30 Eliz.—Edward Downying and Myles Dodding, by Crown Grant, to be held of East Greenwich Manor, at Yearly Rent of £12. 9. 5.

3.—Sudeley Tenements :—

The Rectory Manor of Sudeley: the Rector is Lord. Copyholds for 3 Lives were granted under this Manor. On which this Tenure, considerable part of Winchcomb Town was built.

34 Hen. viii —Clement Tyler, Nicholas Skynn, Geo. Boydon, Wr Skynn, John Hall, W. Banast, W. Hicks, John Clarke, Bartelmew Fosse, R. Trewman, W. Sandell, Phylp Pytts, Lawrence Milton, R. Tyler, H. Ryez, Humfry Burton, occur in the Muster Roll.

As to Inclosure, *see* "Greet."

4.—Greet :—

The ancient possessors here were the Knights Templars by De Lacy's Gift, to whom temp. Henry iii. 1237, a Court Leet, was allowed.

1812.—At the Inclosure Act, C. H. Tracy, was Lord of the Manor.

7 Ed. ii.—John de Greet, was Plaintiff, and John Attewode, was Deforciant, in a Fine of Lands at Greet.

19 Jac. i.—Edmund Benbow, William Carnall and John Phillips, were Subsidy payers. The families of Dance, Warren, Carpenter and Freeman, were large holders here.

10 Gul. iii.—Anne Dance, demised lands in Greet, to Richard Dance, for 1000 Years. Richard Dance, acquired lands of Carpenter, by purchase.

In 1682, David Warren, exchanged lands called Hales, in Greet, with Richard Dance.

At the Muster 34 Hen. viii. the names of James, Pendocke, Chappell, Benbow, Townsend, Southam, were returned.

Hayles Abbey, had Lands here;

2 Mar.—After the dissolution, Russell and Brockton, by Crown Grant.

Fines:—

22 Chas. ii.—Hands from Philips.
23 Geo. ii.—A Fine levied by W. Smart.
16 & 17 Geo. ii.—T. and E. Freeman to Tombs.

The Mill belonged to Pardington.

Milham Post Manor and Farm, belonged to F. P. Stratford.

The Farm : Joshua Baylis, Robert Baylis, Robert Baylis, his son held successively.

M. W. Smith, by purchase.

Other farms are Littleworth, Park, &c.

In Greet and Sudeley Tenements under the Inclosure Act, 52 Geo. iii. allotments of Land were made in lieu of Tythe to the Vicar of Winchcomb, and also road allotments, and sale allotments, Estate allotments were made to the Messrs. Freeman, 12 for freeholds and 5 for Copyholds of Sudeley Rectory Manor, to R Baylis, 10 for freeholds and 1 for copyhold estates. To T. Fisher, 4 allotments. To W. Staite, 12 copyhold allotments. To Wells and Wood, 8 allotments. Newman, 6. Grammar School trustees 5, and to Phillips, Moss, Dobyns, Bancks, Williams, Moore, Sexty, and several others, various allotments. The award under in this Act is in the Office of Clerk of the Peace.

5.—Gretton Manor:

The ancient possessors were the Knights Templars.

Roger de Dicklesdon, held one hide here.

Fines :—

5 Edw. ii.—John de Besemantel.
Robert de Vikersman.
15 Edw. iii.—John de Besemantel,
Thomas de Bassford.

2 Ric. ii.—Swinbrook Land, 18 a.—John Wotton.

8 Jac. i.—J. Tracey, to J. Stratford.

The names of Staite, Greening, Nanfan, and Yardington, occur as owners.

1 Hen. vii —The fines of free suitors for Gretton: Alice Dobbs, for lands called Mohant and Maberly in Gretton, viii d. Richard Grice, for a tenement in Gretton, xii d. John Norrice, for his tenement in Gretton, xii d. *Rental for Kiftsgate in Holford and Gretstan hundreds.* temp. H vii.

The Names in the Muster Roll. 34. Hen. viii. for Gretton, are Smith, Greenyng, Stayte, Teynton, Curtis, Trewman, Hardyng, Hyde and others.

Subsidy Roll, 9 Jac. i.—the Names of the payers are John Carpenter, Henry Greening, John Dobbins, William Hide, Henry Tayneton.

Stratfords Estate, 7 Edw. vi. John Stratford, died seized of tenements in Winchcomb, part held of Sudeley Manor and part of the King, as of his county of Hereford, of a messuage and four virgates of land in Greet and the Wood there, and three Messuages in Gretton, held of Sudeley Manor, and in Sudeley, the Sklat House, held of Sudeley Manor, Henry Stratford, being his grandson and heir. *Inq post Mort.* This family long held.

54 Geo. iii *Chap. xxviii private.*—An Act for the Inclosure of open and common fields, commons and wastes in Gretton Hamlet in Winchcomb Parish, George, Lord Rivers, Lord of Manor of Gretton, C. H. Tracy. Patron of the living, J. J. Lates, Vicar of Winchcomb Owners of land: C. H. Tracy, T. Ashmore, J. Cole, C. Fawdry, T. Wells.

Tithe owners were: Wm. Stephens, J Staite, J. Cooke, Elizabeth Lovesy, T. Williams, who received allotments of two-ninths of arable, one-ninth of pasture land, and for want of land had compensation in money.

Lady Hereford's lessees allotments were to be put near Stanley farm.

The Award is in the Parish Chest.

There is an Estate in Gretton of Chipping Campden, Charity Grammar School of the endowment of Edward Conynges.

6 — Cotes and Thorp belonged to the Abbey, and were granted to Lord Chandos afterwards.

7 —Potesley, a tything of Gretstan Hundred (now Kiftsgate Hundred, Lower Division.) Three Hides taxed; Culture: Two Plow Tillages in Demesne, and two in Villenage, (3 Villans and 5 Bordars,) A Wood one Mile long and one broad. It was worth 100 s. now 4 £.

Alfrid de Cormeliis, held it at the Survey, Godric had held it.   *Domesday Survey.*

Cormeilles' heir general, married Poher, and his Daughter and heir, married Solers, a family which long held William Solers, built the Chapel of Ease, (now dilapidated,) Whidendun, was the heir general of Solers.

27 Ed. i.—W. Poteslip, a felon was found to have a Virgate of Land here held of Solers.   *Inq. ad quod dam*

The Broadway, family held the Estate, (whether the chief fee, or a sublee,) for several generations, and built the fine Tudor Mansion here. On a Chimney piece in this House, are the Arms of Broadway, a chevron between 3 Pine Cones slipped,) BROADWAY. *imparing* a chevron between 3 Plants. The Letters G. A. b. are carved and date 1614. Giles Broadway, held in 1614. His wife was Anne Carter.

34 Hen. viii.—In the Muster Roll for Potteslyp, occur the Names of Edmund Bradway, Gent. Henry Acton, Thomas Dyp (tithingman,) Thomas Butteler, John Batt, and R. Comper.

The chief fee or Manor came to the Abbey of Tewkesbury, by

After the dissolution of Monasteries,—Stroud, Earl and Paget, by Crown Grant.

Ralph Cotton, by purchase.

The Manor and Broadways and Cottons Estate.—

3 Wm. iii.—Thomas, Lord Coventry.   *Fine..*

His descendants held until the sale to Mr. W. S. Evans Chapel :—The Solers family, endowed the Chapel with the Tythes of their Demesne Lands. But the Abbey of Winchcombe, also had Tythes here which after the dissolution came to Sir Thomas Seymour, by Crown Grant.

This is a place famous for the abundance and good quality of its Water. Advantages which brought here the paper-making trade nearly two centuries ago. The Durham family long carried it on, and resided in the Manor House. *see Church Inscriptions.*

The effect of the Works on the quality of the Water has been noticed under "Todington." It is a blot on the beauty of this Valley. A newly erected Mansion, near the Mills attests however the flourishing condition of the Trade.

8.—Corndean, was parcel of Sudeley Manor. Bruern Abbey, by Gift of Otwell de Sudeley ; Winchcomb Abbey acquired it by exchange, and here was formed a park for their Abbot. Its Value yearly 20 £ *Valor Eccl'us.*

After the Dissolution :—Lord Chandos.

1615.—George, Lord Chandos ; Composition on Sequestration of his Estates in the Common-Wealth time has this Item yearly Rent of Corndon farm in Sudely, held by Lease for "Lives and now in the tenure of Mrs. Hester Williams."

The Knightly family of Williams, appears by this to have held the Lease for Lives. This was converted into a fee afterwards.

It passed in succession through Montagu, Blizard, and Comper. The name of Comper occurs in the Muster Roll, 34 Hen. viii. for Postlip, and *see* "Bledington." as to that family.

The Coheiresses of the Compers, married Hicks, Knight and Davis. It soon after came into the possession of Swinburn, Thomas Swinburn, of Birmingham, married a daughter of Anthony Rogers, of Winchcomb, his son Thomas of Corndean, held in 1842.

9.—Deep Wood and Humble-bee-how, are extensive Woodlands to the South-end of Corndean, "Sarscomb" Closes, are near it.

The Abbey of Winchcomb, held this property. After the dissolution. Lord Chandos, by Crown Grant, whence as Sudeley.

10.—Frampton and Naunton, are near to Stanley Pontlarge, but are in Winchcomb Parish.

Winchcomb Abbey, held in Fremlinton :—

2 Carucates Yearly worth	£3	0	0.
Rents of Assize	0	12	8
Staurum.	1	10	0

Pope Nich. Tax. £5 2 8.

Frampton was kept in the Abbots hands for Husbandry, Value 60 £.   *Valor Eccl'us.*

After the Dissolution :—Butler and Petit, by Crown Grant. Sheldon, by purchase.

Tracy, of Stanway, by purchase.

34 Hen. viii.—In the Muster Roll, for "Fraunton," occur the Names of John Boyd and John Greyn.

Newetone in Gretstanes Hundred, contained 3 Hides & a half. Culture: In demesne 3 Plow Tillages, with 3 serfs in Villenage, (2 Villans.) one plow tillage and there may be yet six more. It is and was worth 40 s. The Church of Wincelcumbe holds, and two Knights hold of the Abbot.
Domesday Survey.

After the Dissolution :—

7 Edw. vi.—Tracy and Wife Elizabeth, by CrownGrant.

11.—Largley, a farm :—Edward, Earl of Cornwall.

Hailes Abbey.

After the Dissolution :—Maurice Sheppard.

Richard Houghton, by marriage with Sheppard's daughter and heir.

Richard Freeman, by purchase.

Lord Redesdale, by Will of T. E. Freeman.

Largley Hill, belonged to the Abbey of Winchcomb. After the dissolution :—Lord Chandos.

12.—Cockbury in Winchcomb Parish, was held of the fee of the Earl of Hereford and contained four Virgates.

R. Pontelarch, *see* "Whaddon."

After Hailes Abbey held.

After the dissolution :—Somerville, by Crown Grant. Afterwards Lord Coventry, as Postlip.

Stony Cockbury, a farm partly in the Parish of Winchcombe, and partly in Southam in Bishops Cleeve, was held for two centuries, by the family of Rogers, of Dowdeswell.

There are no Monumental Inscriptions in the Church of earlier date than 17th. Century: Therein occur the names of Slaughter, Merrett, Barksdale, Weld, Jay, Beale, Broadway, Williams, (Corndean,) Dance, Stratford.

In the 18th. century occur the names of Smart,(Abbey) Durham, (Postlip,) Wood, Harvey, Baylis, Freeman, (Greet,) Thorn, Trotman, Timbrill, Newman, Staite, &c.

In the 19th. century Williams, (Abbey,) Bancks, &c.

We learn from the Subsidy Roll, 1 Edw. iii Gloucestershire, the Names of the chief Trades then here: Le Webb Le Smyth. Palfreyman. Parchmanter. Hooper, Sklater. Taillur, Kimbare, Miller. Joly and Petit, denote persona Shireburn, Braundon, Stowe, Teynton, places.

Winchcombe Parish Fines:
19 Edw. iii.—John Attwood. William de Foateweys.
50 Edw. iii.—R. Crese, H. Clement.
40 Edw. iii.—H. Walton, T. Moryn.
27 & 28 Eliz. Fine.—Warne, to Burton
M. 29 & 30 Eliz Fine.—J. Throckmorton. to Forster.
M. 29 & 30 Eliz Fine.—R. Bartlett, to T. Conway.
M. 28 & 30 Eliz Fine.—Tracy and Culpepper.
H. 30 Eliz. Fine.—N. Kirkham, and J. Battel.

E. 6 Geo. i—Martin, *Plaintiff* Humphrys, Thomas, and Peter Ethelbert, *Defoliant*.

2 Geo. ii—Edward Gale, *Plaintiff*. Hartlebury, Nicholls, Timbrell, and Sturmy, *Deforcants*.

1776.—*At the County Election, the following Voted as freeholders in Winchcombe.*

Baylis, (2) Thomas, *Stroud*, Joshua, *Peylesworth*
Bell, Edward.
Berch, Alexander.
Best, (2) William, Richard.
Blabey, William.
Blake, Philip.
Bradled, William.
Brown, Mathew.
Brockhurst, Thomas.

Carnall, William.
Claridge, Joseph.
Cook, (3) Mich., Jona, Wm.
Cull, John.

Dobbins, (3) Jno.,Thos.,Danl.
Durham, William, *Postli*.

Freeman, (2) Samuel, Wm.

Goore, Henry.
Greening, (2) Richard, John, *Langley Farm*.

Harrington, Samuel.
Harries, Harward.
Heavens, John.
Hervey, Thomas.
Hill, William
Hughes, (3) Richd. ,Jas.,Wm.

Johnson, John.

Lucas, John, *Sudeley*.

Mayer, (2) William, Thomas.
Matthew, Robert.

Merryman, (3) John, William, Thomas.

Pacey Thomas.
Page, James.
Phillips, ... (3)
Philips. .... (2)
Pierson, Thomas.
Pidgeon, Edward,

Rayer, R.
Reynalds, William.
Roberts. Anthony.
Rogers, Anthony.
Do. Edward, of *Lincoln's Inn, for Cockbury*.

Savage, William.
Smith, Samuel.
Staite, (2) Richard, Thomas.
Stephens, Benj
Sumerfield, John.

Taynton, John.
Tanner, William.
Timbbrell, (2) Henry, John.
Troughton, George.
Trotman, John.
Townsend, (3) George, ...

Tustin, John.

Warren, ...
Webb, John.
Wodvin, Simon.
Williams, Richard.

Yardington, (2) Hen., Thos.

II.—*Church:*

In the time of King Hen. vi. the Abbey took the Church of which the townsfolk had the use, and in the way of substitution assigned for them a very small chapel. But the Parishioners with the aid of their powerful Neighbor Lord Boteler, of Sudeley, built the present Church the size, and beauty of which shew what was their idea of the sort of Church accommodation the Parish required.

In puritan days, and it would appear thenceforward until the recent "restoration" (1872.) the Communion Table stood in the Chancel with seats about it for the Communicants. Deerhurst Church had or until recently had a similar arrangement.

Rectory:

Winchcomb with Chapel, 14£. *Pope Nich. Tax.* Crown Grant, at Rent of £12. 9. 6. and subject to Repairs of Chancel.

24 Eliz—Tithes portion of Sir Ct. Hatton, by Crown Grant.

Another portion.
4 Jac. i.— Sir John Fortescue, and Richard Tomlins.

Great Tithes:—
1820 —George, Lord Rivers, with an Indemnity against the Rent reserved on the Crown Grant.

Vicarage:—Appropriation by Pope Urban, Bull.
Valor Eccl'us.
Vicars portion 6£. *Pope Nich. Tax.* Patron Ld. Sudeley.

List of Vicars and Patrons of Winchcombe.

Vicars.	Patrons.
1541 —George Roo.	The King.
1562 & 65.—Richard Coxe.	"
1566.—Robert Johnson.	"
1576 & 80 —William Symmous.	"
1584.—Thomas Moreland.	"
1588.—Richard Perirechief.	"
1589.—Richard Bowland.	"
1596.—Valentine Blake. *Master of the Town School.*	"
1619.—William Gorton.	"
1621.—John Geaves.	"
1522.—John Bespath.	"
1642.—William Wallington.	"
1661 —Thomas Markeley. *see Church Inscription.*	"
1671.—Henry Thorne, *see Church Inscriptions.*	"
1715.—Edward Rainsford.	"
1726.—Thomas Skieler.	"
1757.—John Taylor.	"
1774.—John Henry Williams, John Weeks Bedwell.	Lord Tracy.
1778.—Richard Roberts.	"
1793.—John James Lates. *see Church Inscription.*	Lord Tracy.

George Roo, was Minister at Bishop Hooper's Examination. He answered well as to the Commandments, he could say but not prove the Articles of Belief. He knew the Lords Prayer and by whom given, but not where it was written. There were 700 Communicants in the Parish.

In the List of Vicars Christopher or Carshew Helme, who was Minister under the presbyterian Church Government is not mentioned. He held a disputation with Clement Barksdale. Rector of Sudeley, on the points in debate between the old and new Church Discipline in Winchcomb Church.

1653.—He and other Ministers humbly remonstrated with the Lord General Cromwell, against assuming the Royal Title.

Greet :—The Chapel here was demolished about 1815.

Gretton :—Chapel here taken down and a new Church built 1868.

There were Chantries in Winchcomb Church to St. Mary and St. Nicholas, the latter Chapel was the Burial place of the Boteler family.

III.—*Taxation, Population, &c.*

Winchcombe, Subsidy Roll, 1 Edw. iii., 1327.

De Johe. Aldrinton, iii s.	De Willo. Kembare, vi d.
' Rico. Frend, ii s.	' Johne. de Teynton, ii s.
' Robto. le Webb, xviii s.	' Willo. Jolyf, xii d.
' Robto. le Smith, xii d.	' Walto. Stowe, ii s.
' Rudno. Palefrayman, xviii s.	' Willo. Momelard, iii .
	' Henr. Addy, ii s.
' Johne. Thorstayn, xiiii d.	' Johe. Molendinare, vi d.
' Johne. Cheltenham, xii d.	' Robto. Petyt, ii s.
' Johne. Braundon, xviii d.	' Henr. Jabel, xii d.
' Johne. Parchmenter, xx d.	' Johe. Parfay, ii s.
' Thom. Taman, xii d.	' Johe. Croy, ii s.
' Rico. Shirebuarn, xiii d.	' Petr. Wyshaud, xii d.
' Henr. Hopere, ii s.	' Walto. Jelemay, xiii d.
' Willo. Skiattare, vi d.	' Walto. Saltere, xii d.
' Raduo. Nouchard, xii d.	' Willo. Pysleye, ii s.
' Johe. Tallur, xii d.	' Walto. Reyner, xii d.
' Johe. Sey, ii s.	' Raduo. Turnour, ii s.
' Thom. atte Hulle, xvi d.	' Walto. Scott, xii d.
' Rico. Malemon, iiii s.	' Thom. Coleman, xii d.

De Robto. Frend, x d.
' Raduo. de Gretton, viii d.
' Johne. Leggare, vi d.
' Henr. Keys, ii s. vi s.
' Agnet. Winter, vi d.
' Johe. Benne, xii d.
' ...... Anketild, xii d.
' Edith Sturdy, xii d.
' Rico. Blebury, viii d.

De Henr. atte Celer, sub-tax.
xii d.
' Johne. Maltman, sub-tax.
xii d.
' Thom. Carpenter, sub-tax.
xii d. Sm. iii s.

prob. Sam. xxma. ville
Wynchecombe, cu. tax.
iiii li. xiii s.

Sma. xxmæ. ville Wynche-
comb, iiii li. x s.

Wynchcombe, Subsidy Roll, 19 Jac.

John Barksdall,	Bon.	£ 3.	5. *Tax.*
John Cowell,	"	3.	5. "
Christop. Merrett,	Ter.	3.	5. "
Ric. Harvey,	Bon.	5.	3. "
John Harvey,	"	2.	5. "

Sum. 28.

Greote, Subsidy Roll, 1 Edw. iii., 1327.

De Rico. Dastyn, v s. xi d.
' Robto. de Wotton, xx d.
' Will. de Wotton, xxii d. q.
' Johne. Bisshop, xiiii d.
' Ingrameo de Greote, xii d.

' Will. Gerveys, xiiii d. ob q.
' Johe. atte Grene, xli d.
' Robto. Bubel, ii s. viii d. ob.
prob. Sma. xvi s. vi *d. o.*

Gretton, Subsidy Roll, 1 Edw. iii., 1327.

De Rogo. le Warde, xx d. ob.
' .... Mohand, vi d.
' ......e atte Grene, xiiii d.ob.
' ...llmo. Ingelard, vi d.
' ..... Notervile, xiiii d. ob.
' ..... Bubel, xix d. ob. q.

' ......to Ayleward, xv d.ob.q.
' ...... Notervyle, vi d.
' ...... Snop. vi d.
' ..... Hobckines, xxi d.
' ...... de Bracebrugge, xxd.
... Sma. xii s. vi d.

Frenlyntone and Nauntone, Subsidy Roll, 1 Edw. iii 1327.

Le Willmo. Gilben, ix d.
' Willn.o. Mayou, vi d.
' Willmo. Hikeman, vi d.
' Rogo. Mayou, vi d.
' Joh Nethewarde, iiii s. ix d.
' Taundy, iii s. iiii d. (*sic.*)
' Rico. le Eyr, xxi d.

' Henr. Bonere, xxiii d.
' Margeria de Aldrintone,
v s x d. ob. q.
' Alicia Perkines, ii s.
' Rico. Boner, iii s.
prob. Sma. xxiiii s. v *d. o.*

Acreage 6406 *a.*

Population 1801,—... ... 1861.—2937.
1831.—2514. 1871,—2993.

In 1815. Annual Value of Real Property 1334 £.

1882.—Rateable Value £ 14,170.

1833-4-5. Average of three Years Expenditure on Poor
£ 1307.

In Winchcombe Union.

In the Civil War part of the Army under Lord Essex, for relief of Gloucester, was for some time quartered in Winchcombe under the protection of SudeleyCastle, then held by the Parliamentarians. After the King's departure from Gloucester and Essex's retreat to London, part of the Royal Army marched from Campden and went and plundered Winchcomb. The possession of Sudeley Castle enabled the people of Gloucester, to move forward by way of Winchcomb, Evesham and Warwick, London-wards.

Tobacco was planted here and the cultivation flourished. An Act for prohibiting the growth of Tobacco in England, was passed in the Common Wealth Time, and in 1662, it was renewed. It was found necessary in 1667, to send a body of Life Guards from London, to spoil the Tobacco plantations at Winchcombe. *Pepys' Diary.*

This retired place produced some Men of Learning as well after as before the Monks had departed:—Clement Barksdale, (already noticed) was a Native of the Place. He was the Author of the Poem "Nympha Libethris" or Cotswold Muse, and the "Memorials of Worthy Persons," in 3 *Vols* 1661, 1662, 1670, and other Works. He died Rector of Naunton, near Stow, 1687.

Merrett, Chrr. born at Winchcombe, 1614, of Gloucester Hall and Oriel College, Oxford, 1642, M. D., practised in London, and was Fellow and Censor of Physicians College, F. R. S. He died 1695, and was burd. at St. Andrew's Holborn. His Works are:—"Character of a Compleat Phy-

siciarl or Naturalist," London. "Art of Glass (Neri.) Tr. 1662. 8*vo.* Acts of Parliament, Charters, &c. relating to College of Physicians, 1660. "Pinax Rerum naturalium Britt. continens Vegetatilia &c. in hac Insula reperta," 1665. "Frauds and Abuses of Apothecaries." 1669. "Self Convictions Enumeration of Railings against the College of Physicians," 1670.

Eccles, Richard, Curate of Cleeve, a Presbyterian Covenanter after the restoration residing there, died 1686, at Gretton and was buried at Cleeve. He wrote "Sermons." "Christ exalted and Wisdom justified, 1659."

In the "Colleetanea Topograpica Genealogica" Nichols, Lond. 1835. Vol. ii. No. ii. p. 16-39 is a List of the Charters in the Winchcombe Cartularies in the possession of Lorn Sherboren:—*viz.* 73. in Registrum A, 181 in Registrum B, and 75. in Registrum D. This List or Abstract was communicated by Sir T. Phillipps, to the Editors of the Colliectanea.

There are Chapels of Baptist and Wesleyan denominations in Winchcombe The Baptist Union Chapel is a new building in the Gretton Road, the old Chapel in the Lane is shut up That has historical interest in connection with the Revd. John Foster, the Author of the Essays:—"On a Man's writing memoirs of himself;" "On Decision of Character;" "On the application of the term Romantic;" On the aversion of men of taste to Evangelical Religion" He was the Pastor or at least a missionary Preacher or Teacher of the flock meeting there in the early part of the century. The "Friend" to whom the Essays were addressed in a series of Letters was a Lady of Bourton-on-the-Water; and she after a mode of courtship quite original became his Wife. He was not the pastor of Bourton, but he made a circuit to the Villages round about it and amongst others Winchcombe. The circumstance of his ever having visited this place seems to be now forgotten but may with advantage be recalled to remembrance. He does not speak highly of the religious condition of Winchcombe, in his Correspondence.

Addendum as to Chantries:

In the Transactions of the Bristol and Gloucestershire Archl. Society, *Vol.* viii. *p.* 229. a List is given of the Certificates returned under the Commission issued Anno 2 Ed. vi. for the Survey of Chantries within the County under Statute 1 Edw. vi.

That for Winchcomb, states that there were 800 Houseling People in Winchcomb.

Our Lady's Chantry founded by Richard Chamberleyn, and others by Crown Licence temp. Hen. iv. and endowed by Feoffmsnt with Land of 9 £. 6 s. Yearly Value, (subject to Reprises of 19 s. 10 d. and payment to poor of 12 s. yearly,) to maintain a Priest to pray for the souls of Richard, his Children and others. Sir Arthur Butterworth, the incumbent had a living of 7 £. yearly thereout. It had Ornaments of 33 s 2 d. Value.

To maintain Two Tapers to burn before St. Nicholas Image in the Church, an acre of Land of 8 d. yearly Value had been given.

At Gretton was a Chapel of Ease, endowed with Land of 64 s. 4 d. yearly Value, subject to reprises of 4 s. 6 d. of it the Incumbent was Richard Freeman, whose stipend was 53 s. 4 d. yearly and he had a pension of 6 £. 13 s. 4 d. yearly for Life out of the dissolved Abbey of Winchcomb.

The Statute 1 Edw. vi. alleges in its Preamble that the vain doctrine of Purgatory and masses satisfactory to be done for them which be departed had been upholden by Chantries &c.; and that their possessions ought to be converted to better uses. Those possessions were therefore vested in the Crown, and Commissioners were appointed to survey them. Out of the Chantry revenues the Com'rs. might assign salaries to Grammar School Masters and Additional Curates in large Towns; Life Pensions to the Chantry Incumbents, and costs of maintaining Sea Banks, &c. Among the Com'rs. so appointed were Richard Pate, the Founder, (out of Chantry Lands, granted to him) of the Grammar School at Cheltenham, and of the Almshouses there and at Gloucester, and Thomas Sternhold, one of the Authors of the old metrical Version of the Psalms of David.

Index to Names on Inscriptions.

INDEX to NAMES on INSCRIPTIONS.

	Coll.
Adlard, Mary-Ann.	29
Allen, Benjamin,	17
Arkell, Esther.	12
Ashley, Elizth.	9
Ashmore, Paul & Susan,	
Thomas, their son.	
Anderson & Elizabeth,	
Wm. & Paul, their s.	30
Batsford, John.	14
Do. Joshua. *headst.*	
Barksdale, George & Mary	9
Do. Margaret,	10
Baylis, Isaac & Dinah,	12
Do. Ann,	8
Do. Samuel & Margt	25
Do. Robert & Hester,	
son & dau. of Robt.	
and Mary.	25
Do. Robt. & Mary,	
and John, their son,	29
Beale, Edw. Ralph & Eliz.	
George.	21
Best, Mary.	30
Biby, Elizabeth.	6
Bleby, John, Mary, Elizth.	8
Do. Anne.	3
Do. William.	9
Do. William & Hannah.	9
Blaby, Mary & William.	8
Bliss, Abigoid, ...	
& see "Benefactions."	22
Bradgate, Gervis, Elizth.	
Charles.	18
Bradley, Lewis, Elizabeth.,	
Ann, Mary.	27
Broadway, Chas. & Francis.	
Edward Beale, Charles	
and Francis ond Chas.	
their sons.	4
Do. Michael.	14
Do. Ann.	22
Do. William.	22
Brown, Edward, Thomas,	
Ann, *Relict.*	24
Do. *remarried to* Smith.	30
Byrch, Mary.	6
Canning, Ann, William.	9
Carnall, ... of *Greet.*	9
Do. Elizth., Mary, Wm.,	15
Do. William & Mary.,	
Robert, Dorothy,	
Alice and Mary.	16
Carpenter, of *Gretton,*	
and Daughter, John	
and Margaret.	
Do. James.	
Do. James and Mary.	
Do. William & Elizth.	
and son William.	15
Cole, Edward.	27
Cook, Betty.	11
Compton, Francis.	2
Do. Wm. and Rebekah	
and son Charles, Jane	
(Smith.) Wm. & Mary,	
Elizabeth.	19
Crump, Margaret.	13
Curtis, Mary.	16
Do. Elizabeth.	18
Daunce, of *Greet,*	
Richard, Robt. & Wife.	9
Do. Mary.	18

	Coll.
Diston, Anne. of *Dixton.*	8
Dobbins, Wm. & Frances,	
and William, *Junr.*	4
Do. Thomas.	18
Durham, of *Postlip, &c.,*	
John and Hester,	
James and Lydia,	25
Revd. Wm. & Wife,	
Sarah, Hester, Ann,	
Mary.	30
Fisher, Thomas & Hannah,	
Children of—Thomas,	
Ann, Hannah, Paul,	24
Fletcher, Robert, *Junr.*	12
Francis, William & Wife.	7
Freeman, of *Greet—*	
Thos. & Elizth. (1725.)	
Mary & Thomas, their	
son (1770.) John.	5
Do. Dorothy, Mary,	
Elizabeth.	58
Do. of *Gretton—*	
Hannah, Wife of	
Samuel, Brother of	
Thomas, of *Greet.*	14
Gearad, Fnarcis & Edith,	
Wives of Nicholas	
and Children.	27
Giles, Mary.	15
Gower, William & Mary	4
Greening, of *Gretton—*	
John and Wife Alice,	
Daughter Margaret,	
srns Thomas, James,	
John & Henry.	6
Do. James, Joseph,	8
Do. John.	11
Hale, Thomas.	28
Harris, Thomas, Harward	12
Do. James & Elizth.	
and daughters.	22
Harvey, Elizth., William.	2
Do. Henry.	4
Do. Jone, Wife of John.	7
Do. David & Ann.	14
Do. Richard & Frances.	15
Do. George & Ann,	
Henry, Giles & Ann,	
and Elizabeth.	21
Do. Henry & Frances	
son & daus.	22
Do. Thos. & Helen	
sons., John & Sarah.	
Do. *Revd.* John Ridout	33
Haslum, John & daurs.	23
Hawes, *Revd.* Thomas.	8
Hicks, Elizabeth.	10
Hooper, Mary.	7
Hulls, Ann, Wife of Anth.	16
Humphrys, Wm. & Msry.	22
James, Ann.	32
Jones, Ferd. & Elizabeth,	
Elizth. Wife of John	
& Children.	15
Leach, Frances.	10
Lloyd, Nathl.	29
Lucas, of *Sudeley—*	
John, (Fcis.) Mary,	
William, Elizabeth,	
Rebecca, Susnna.	5

	Coll.
Maggs, John, Sarah, Mary.	31
Do. Robert.	32
Markley, Thos. & Cicely.	2
Maisey, Thomas & Wife	
and Daughter.	6
Matthews, of *Greet—*	
Frances.	7
Do. Richard.	30
Do. *alias* Paul & Martha	25
Marten, of *Gretton—*	
Richard, Mary, Anth.	
Margaret.	7
Merryman, John, *Senr.*	
& Anne, Ric. their s.	
Dinah, Thos. & Wife	
Mary.	14
Merrett, Christopher Rich.	
& Andrew.	11,12
Meachant, Anthony & Jane.	14
Milby, Susanna.	13
Mowtlow, John & Lacy.	18
Do. Ann, Elizabeth.	20
Do. Mary.	20
Newman, Mary.	14
John & Elizth., Geo,	
& Marg, Abigail,	
Wm., Harry, John.	23
Nind, John & Sarah, &	
3 Children	13
Do. James.	17
Do. Mary, Hugh, James,	
Edmund, Sarah.	18
Okeasey, Hester.	23
Page, Elizabeth.	24
Perrin, Richard.	14
Pearson, Thomas.	1
Do. George.	9
Do. Alice.	27
Phillipps, John, *Senr.*	
John, *Junr.* John, son	
of John & Ann.	15
Do. Ann, Wife of Thos.	15
Do. John & Ann.	17
Phillips, John, of *Greet.*	
William.	28
Preston, John & Ann.	10
Do. Ann, William.	11
Rainsford, Edmund, *Pastor*	
and Emma.	3
Rayer, Eliz.	9
Reynalds, William, Thos.	
and Mary.	25
Roberts, Richard, (*Vicar.*)	2
Rone, Sarah,	14
Rose, John & Elizth.	22
Rogers, Eleanor, John,	
Anthony.	16
Skey, John.	16
Do. Thomas & Frances,	
George.	21
Slaughter, Bridget.	13
Do. Mary.	15
Smart, William & Collis.	12
Smith, Richard & Wife,	
William, Robert.	10
Do. Jane, (b. *Compton.*)	19
Do. Henry & Aon.	23
Do. Samuel, (*Baker.*)	
Richard.	24

	Coll.
Smith, of *Langley—*	
Thomas, Sarah.	27
Do. Thomas & Mary Ann.	31
Spencer, John.	27
Staite, Edw. of *Gretton—*	
John. & son William.	16
Do. William & Anne,	
son John, & Daughter,	
Do. Robert, Mary, his	
Daughter, Eleanor,	
Wife of John.	17
Do. Ann.	25
Do. Robert & Mary.	28
Staite, of *Hailes—*John,	
& Ann, Daughter Ann	7
Do. William & Margt.	8
Do. Sarah.	10
Staite, Thos. of *Frampton*	8
Do. William & Mary.	11
Do. Robert & Ann.	16
Stephens, William & Ann.	28
Stratford, of *Millham Post*	
John, Ann.	11
Summervill, Frances.	7
Taylor, Robert.	28
Tawny, Edward, Elizth.,	
John, son.	18
Tarran, John & Mary.	
John, Mathew & Mary,	
Thomas.	26
Thorne, Henry, (*Minister.*)	
Hester, his Wife.	2
Do. Elizabeth, Edmd.	3
Do. Edmd. Hen.	16
Do. Edward & Margaret.	17
Do. John & daur.	20
Do. George & Elizth.	26
Timbrell, John.	...
Tomes, John.	6
Do. William, Ann,	
Wife of John.	7
Traces, Thomas.	18
Trotman, G. Scunderbrg,	20,34
Do. John & Ann.	20
Do. 3 Daughters Wm.	
& Mary, Wm. & Joan.	30
Warrin, John, of *Greet.*	20
Weld, Margaret.	10
Wheatley, Elizth.	24
White, Thomas.	24
Whitfield, Samuel & Eliz.	3
Whithorne, Margaret.	17
Williams, Thomas, (Sir D.	
W's. son.) Thomas,	
D. W's., Hester, Dd.,	
Carew, Mary, his Wife,	
Elizabeth.	1
Do. Thomas & Sarah.	30
Wilson, Martha.	25
Wood, Benjamin, of *Greet*	
Do. Dinah, Wife & Dru.	23
Do. William, (*Surgeon.*)	
Do. William & Ann.	23
Do. William, Dinah,	
Susanna.	24
Do. Susanna.	29
Worsfold, John & Mary.	29
Yardington, Jone.	2

WINRUSH.

WINRUSH.

THE CHURCH is in the Deanery of Stow, and is a Vicarage. It consists of a Chancel, Nave, with a small Aisie and Hungerford's Chapel, on the Southside, with a Gallery at the Westend also a Tower at the same end containing six Bells.

.... BURT, *the present Vicar.*

CHARITY GIVEN TO THIS CHURCH.

Half a yard Land, let at three pounds ten shillings a year.

INSCRIPTIONS IN THE CHURCH.

CHANCEL.

ON FLAT STONES.

MICHAEL MILLS, the Son of
HENRY MILLS,
Minister, of *Shipton,* was
interred the 2nd. day of
September 1684.
Non abite sed Libate non an.ituntur
Anime premittuntur tantum.

MARY, Daughter of HENRY HURST,
Parson of *Borton-on-the-Water,*
Wife of MICHAEL MILLS,
Vicar of *Windrish.*

Christus mihi vita.
I liv'd to dye I dy'd to live again
A glorious Life for ever to retain,
With Christ my Lord who once for
me did dye,
That I might live with him eternally.
Make hast my Soul fly thou with
angels' Wings,
To worship and adore the King of
Kings.

Mihi mori lucrum.
All yee that live consider yee must
dye
And turn to Earth and Dust as well
as I.
Mors sceptra ligonibus æquat.

NAVE.

ON FLAT STONES.

In Memory of
ELIZABETH, the Wife of
THOMAS BROAD, *Junr.*
who died Decr. the 31st. 1733.
Also near this Place
lyeth the Body of
THOMAS BROAD, *Junr.*
Son of THOMAS BROAD, *Senr.*
And MARY, his Wife,
who died May the 7, 1739,
Aged 15 Days.

In Memory of
THOMAS BROAD, *Gent.*
who died Decr. the 13, 1744.
Also near this Place,
lyeth the Body of
THOMAS BROAD, Son of THOMAS
BROAD, and ELIZABETH, his Wife,
who died March the 6, 1748,
Aged 58 Years.

Here lies interred the Body of
WILLIAM FAUDERY,

Son of WILLIAM FAUDERY,
of *Safford* in *Oxfordshire,*
buried Jany. the 24, 1748,
Aged 77 Years

In Memory of
THOMAS BROAD, *Gent.*
who departed this Life,
Nov. 20, 1770, Aged 77 Years.
Also of MARY, his Wife,
who departed this Life,
Nov. 5, 1772, Aged 59 Years.
Also of JOHN BROAD,
Son of the above, who departed
this Life, Febr. 7, 1772,
Aged 26 Years.

SOUTH AISLE.

ON A FLAT STONE.

In Memory of
MARY, and ELIZABETH, Daughters
of THOMAS and MARY BROAD,
MARY, died June 17, 1794,
Aged 51 Years.
ELIZABETH, died Decr. 13, 1797,
Aged 54 Years.

CHURCH YARD.

ON A TABLET AGAINST THE
SOUTH SIDE OF TOWER.

Near this Place are deposited the
remains of ELIZABETH, the Wife of
THOMAS JACKSON,
who died Oct. 4, 1797,
Aged 58 Years.

ON A TABLET NEAR THE LAST.

Near this Place lie the Remains of
JAMES and ESTHER,
Son and Daughter of THOMAS
and ELIZABETH JACKSON,
JAMES, died Oct. 14, 1774,
Aged 2 Years and 6 Months.
ESTHER, died Oct. 19, 1792,
Aged 12 Years.

ALTAR TOMBS.

In Memory of
RICHARD NEWMAN,
and ELIZABETH, his Wife,
And also NATHANIEL and JAMES
NEWMAN, and ELIZABETH,
the Wife of JAMES BAKER,
with her Babe,

the Grand Children and Children of
NATHANIEL and ANN NEWMAN.
RICHARD, was buried April 27, 1708,
Aged 82 Years.
NATHANIEL, Oct. 30, 1699,
Aged 1 Year.
JAMES, Febr. 12, 1719,
Aged 12 Years.
ELIZABETH, March the 5, 1723,
Aged 31 Years.
In Memory of
ANTHONY NEWMAN,
he died August the 24, 1756,
Aged 61 Years.
Also NATHANIEL, Son of
ANTHONY NEWMAN, by MARY,
his Wife, died in his Infancy.
ANN, Daughter of NATHANIEL
and ANNE NEWMAN, and Wife of
JOSEPH JACKSON, died in Childbed,
Febr. 26, 1732, Aged 23 Years.
NATHANIEL NEWMAN,
Father to ANTHONY NEWMAN,
on the other end of this Tomb,
died Decr. 27, 1741.
ANN, his Wife, Jany. 3, 1735,
both died in advanced Age.
In Memory of
MARY, the Wife of HENRY NEWMAN,
She died Febr. 16, 1784,
Aged 69 Years.

Here lieth the Body of
ANNE, the Wife of JOHN NEWMAN,
the Daughter of HERCULES,
and ELIZABETH HITCHMAN,
who departed this Life, the
3 of September, T. H. 1713,
Ætat. suæ 36.

Here lieth the Body of
WILLIAM TRINDER,
who departed this Life,
June 13, 1677, Aged 67 Years
and 5 Months.
Here lieth the Body of
JANE, Wife of WILLIAM TRINDER,
who departed this Life,
June 10, 1684, Aged 71 Years
and 5 Months.
WILLIAM, was the Son of
THOMAS TRINDER, of *Spelsbury* in
Oxfordshire.
He married JANE, the Daughter of
JOHN BROAD, of this Parish.
Here lieth the Body of
THOMAS, the Son of WILLIAM
and JANE TRINDER,
who was buried April 26, 1727,
Aged 38 Years.
Near this Place lies the Remains of
WILLIAM TRINDER,
who died Decr. 29, 1785,
Aged 78 Years.

Here lieth the Body of
MARGERY, Daughter of THOMAS
and ELIZABETH BROAD,
Wife of WILLIAM MORSE,
who died March 25, 1748,
Aged 48 Years.
Also in Memory of
2 Daughters of WILLIAM and
MARGERY MORSE, they were
baptized by the name of HANNAH,
and buried in the Chancel,
in their Infancy.
Near this Tomb lieth
HANNAH, the Daughter of
WILLIAM and MARGERY MORSE,
She died Oct. 24, 1754,
Aged 15 Years.

In hopes of a glorious Resurrection
here lyeth the Body of
JAMES BRADSHAW, Yeoman,
Son of EDWARD and ELIZABETH
BRADSHAW, who after 2 Years
and 6 Months sore affliction patiently
submitted to the fatal stroke of
Death on May the 12, 1730,
in ye 39 Year of his Age.
Non hodie quod heri.
He was a Man of probity and Judg-
ment, a faithful Friend,
A Loving Brother,
And a kind Husband to his Wife,
with whom he left the care of
erecting this Tomb.
In Memory of
MARY, the Wife of JAMES

BRADSHAW, Yeoman, who died
May 10, 1764, Aged 71 Years.

In Memory of
JOHN TRINDER, Senr.
who died April 7, 1762,
Aged 57 Years.
In Memory of
MARTHA, the Wife of JOHN
TRINDER, who died Aug. 13, 1744,
Aged 39 Years.

Underneath are deposited the
Remains of ANN, Wife of
ANTHONY JACKSON,
She departed this Life,
April 22, 1797, Aged 29 Years.
And also SUSANNA, their Daughter,
who died May 14, 1798,
Aged 22 Months.

Underneath lie the Remains of
ELIZABETH PRATT, Wife of
JAMES PRATT,
She died Augt. 30, 1788,
Aged 66 Years.

(*Additional Inscriptions in Church
since Bigland's time.*)

ON THE WALL OF SOUTH AISLE.

Under the passage near this
Monument lye devoted to God
and his Redeemer the Remains of
THOMAS BROAD, *Gent.*
deposited with those of his Ancestors,
He was the last male descendant
of a respectable family of that name
who held the *Pinchpool* Estate in
this Parish many centuries,
He died the *4th.* day of May 1810,
Aged 70 Years.

Near this Place lie the Remains of
THOMAS JACKSON,
who died Oct. 18, 1812,
Aged 74 Years.
Also of ELIZABETH, his Wife,
who died Oct. 9, 1797, Aged 58.

In Memory of
MARY and ELIZABETH, Daughters of
THOMAS and MARY BROAD,
MARY died June 17, 1794,
Aged 51 Years.
ELIZABETH, died Dec. .. , 1797.
Aged 53 Years.
Also of HANNAH, their Daughter,
who died Jany. 15, 1814,
Aged 67 Years.
Another Daughter, died 1810.

HEAD STONES.

	Died.		Aged.		Died.		Aged.
William Newman, ...	8 Febr.	1758	48	Thomas Tilling, ...	7 Nov.	1734	69
Elizabeth, his Wife, ...	26 Decr.	1772	67	Kezia, Wife of John Lay, ...	28 April	1768	67
Also two of their Children:—				Robert Hands, *Junr.*	15 Oct.	1727	63
Elizabeth and Anne, twins }				Ann, Wife of John Duffel, ...	31 Augt.	1755	3
both died in their Infancy. }				John Dancey, ...	9 Decr.	1778	24
Joseph Jackson, ...	27 April	1760	52	Ann, Wife of Thomas Gorten }			
John, Son of Jos. & Ann Jackson,	7 Oct.	1767	11	and Relict of John Dancey, }	15 Nov.	1780	36
James, Son of Thomas and }	14 Oct.	1774	2	Sarah, Wife of Thomas Gorten,	5 March	1788	38
Elizabeth Jackson, ... }				John Mills, ...	30 March	1773	47
John Mills, ...	30 March	1773	47	Mary, Wife of Walter Howell,	14 Jany.	1778	57
Francis Carpenter, ...	28 April	1786	71	Elizabeth, Wife of Edw. Howell,	1 Sept.	1780	70
Martha, Wife of FrancisCarpenter,	25 Jany.	1794	72	Thomas Gorten, *Senr.* ...	22 Sept.	1795	69
Edward Bradshaw, ...	24 Febr.	1766	72	Hannah, Daughter of Thomas }			
Jane, Wife of Ed. Bradshaw, *Senr.*	1 Jany.	1767	67	and Hannah Gorten, ... }	6 May	1787	24
John Jackson, ...	25 Sept.	1770	35	Mary, Wife of Dennice Wadley,	5 March	1766	78
James Harwood, ...	2 June	1777	67	Francis, Son of Paul & JaneSmith,	20 Oct.	1752	48
Mary, Daughter of John and }				Susanna, Wife of Robt. French,	14 Jany.	1793	34
Ann Jackson, ... }	23 March	1775	12	Thomas Jackson, ...	25 Nov.	1779	55
Sarah, Wife of James Harwood,	21 Decr.	1765	60	Sarah, Wife of Thomas Jackson,	21 Augt.	1760	51
Henry Simson, ...	2 Augt.	1755	65	William, Son of John and }			
Cornelius, Son of William and }				Margaret Poulton, ... }	10 Sept.	1758	28
Mary Wiltshire, ... }	13 May	1747	42	Benjamin, Son of Joseph and }			
Jonathan Ford, ...	5 March	1784	36	Ann Jackson, ... }	10 Febr.	1779	27
William Corbett, ...	10 Augt.	1750	...	Mary, Daughter of Edward }			
John Brain, ...	25 July	1755	41	and Jane Bradshaw, }	10 Sept.	1759	23
Jane, his Wife, ...	11 May	1782	72	Rowland Jackson, ...	17 Febr.	1782	88
John Green, ...	15 Decr.	1775	78	Mary, his Wife, ...	25 Decr.	1786	82
Joan, Wife of John Large, ...	7 Febr.	1771	70	Jone, Wife of Robert Hands, ...	30 Sept.	1684	...
Martha, Wife of John Green, ...	2 Oct.	1738	25	William, Son of Edward and }			
Stephen Green, ...	6 Decr.	1735	67	Elizabeth Tilling, ... }	12 April	1751	17
Joan, his Wife, ...	1 Augt.	1736	63				

Notes as to I.—*Devolution of Estates.* II.—*Church.* III.—*Population, Taxation, &c.*

I.—*Estates :*

Windrush anciently Wenric, is the name of a Village, and also of a stream formed by the confluence near it, of two Brooks one from Swell, Naunton and Rissington, the other from Farmington, Sherborne, &c. The stream probably derives its name from the place, there being nothing in its attributes of a winding rustling character having allusion to Water.

Wenric appears in Anglo Saxon records. In the way of Royal Gifts, occur King Offa's to Duddo, An. 779, King Kenulf to Winchcombe Abbey, King Edward's (Confessor,) Grants and Charters to same (*see Monasticon,* **Vol.** 2. 301.)

Bliss' Edition. Winchcombe Abbey Chartulary, Kemble Anglo. Sax. Charters, &c.) Grants from private persons Bolle, Wenric, &c. (Winchcombe Chartulary.) Inwinsburg. named as a boundary in the Saxon Charters may perhaps mean Swinbrook.

Domesday Book contains five Entries relating to Wenric: But two of these are in duplicate. They both agree as to the holder of the subfee being Elsi de Ferendone, but in one it is stated that he held under the King, in the other that he held under the Abbey of Winchcombe, to whom Bolle a former Saxon Owner had given it, they also agree in the Quantity, 3½ Hides; in the Culture, 5 Carucates in demesne and 1 in Villenage, (1 Villan 7 Bordars.) and in the number of Serfs (10.) in there being a Mill and half of 12s. 6d. Value, and in the general Valuation of 8£. They agree too in the account of the former Saxon Owners, Wulfric, Tovi and Lewin who were resiants free to go or stay and who held as for three Manors, Wulfric, holding 2 Hides, Tovi 5 Virgates, and Lewin one Virgate of Land. In the way of explanation of the variation as to the chief Lord there is the statement in the Survey that this manor which Elsi, held of the Abbot was wrongfully put into Salemansbury Hundred after Bolle, was dead. But was afterwards assigned to Bernintone (Barrington.) Hundred by the Verdict of the Jury of that Hundred.

Other two Entries relate to the Estate of Roger de Laci: In Bernintone Hundred he held and Ralph of him Wenric containing two Hides whereof in Culture were one Carucate in Demesne and one in Villenage (3 Villans and 2 Bordars.) Of Serfs 5. A Mill of 5s. and 2a. of Meadow. Its Value formerly 100s. then 4£. The same Roger held in the same place and Hugh of him:—One Hide and 1 Virgate, whereof in Culture, 1 Carucate in demesne, Two Bordars, One Serf. A Mill of 3s. and 8a. Meadow ... Value late and present 24s., This Estate had been held by Goderic, one of King Edwards thanes.

The fifth Entry is of Land (1 Hide and 1 Virgate,) held of the King in Gersdone (subsequently Gretstan,) Hundred, Culture:—One Carucate. Four Serfs, Its worth was and is 20s. In Saxon (King Edward's) times, Chetel held and continued to hold at the Survey.

In Nom. Villarum temp. 9 Edw. ii. the names of the Lords of the Vill of Wenric are the Abbey of Winchcombe, William Pynchpole and Robert le Moris

Winchcomb Abbey subgranted part of its Manor to Frinlinton or Frampton.

Winchcomb Abbey, held its Manor until the time of the dissolution. In the Valor Eccl'us. the Wenric Estate is computed with Sherborne, (which see.) The Almoner of the Abbey is said to have 12s. out of the Rents of Wenric.

After the dissolution:—Christopher Allen, by Crown Grant.

6 Edw. vi.—Thomas Dutton, by purchase from Sir Christopher Allen and Wife Ethelreda.   Fine

Pynchpole applied to a person is a nick name after the Saxon manner. What the patronymic of W. Pynchpole, was does not appear. This Estate was long held by this family and then passed to Broad, named in the Subsidy Roll, 40 Eliz. and in an inscription in the Church to Thomas Broad, who is said to be the last male Representative of his family.

Maris and Lay, or Lan Maris, was a hamlet or Vill in Winrush.   Rot. Fines 13.

6 Edw. i.—John Delamer,
Robert Le Marys, (his son and heir.)   Inq. p. Mort.
Le Mary's is still the name of a farm here.

The Hungerford family it appears by Sir Robt. Atkyns, had a good seat and large Estate in this Parish.

Sir John Hungerford, of Down Ampney, by his Will in 1524, left to Edward Hungerford, of Winrush, his 2nd. son, all his Sir John's sheep at 1 untesborne and Winrush. Edwd. married Margaret St. John, and died about 1531, they left George, their eldest son, who died in 1597, leaving by Katherine Fabian, Edward, who married Katherine Hugford, and died in 1611, leaving Edward, his eldest son, who married Mary Farren, and died 1645, leaving Edward, who married Mary Cotten, or Calton, and died 1705, leaving Edward, (who died without Issue 1749.) and five Daughters of whom Mary, married 1st. George Morgan, of Bristol, and 2ndly, in 1708, Henry Brett, of Cowley. Jane, who married John Bradley, and three Spinsters. This Edward Hungerford, about 1718, sold the Windrush Estate, to Richard Bigg, of Wallingford, Esqr. and Richard Bigg by Deed of that date yielded to Edward Hungerford, the right of burial

for himself, his relations and posterity in St. Mary's Chapel in the Parish Church of Windrush.

Lands in Wyke and Winric, belonged to Robert Mortimer, Earl of March, & the Berefords, held a sub fee from him.

3 Hen. vi.—R. Bereford and his Wife Philippa, held this Subfee.

The Duttoo family acquired eome of these Estates.

Lanthony Abbey had possessions here which might have been derived from the De Lacis' Benefactions to that Church

Among their possessions at Wenrich was the Advowson.

De Lacy, had Lands at Risington, a parish near. These and other Lands in this Hundred passed to Burnell, whose Co-heiress married Edmund Hungerford. If part of Burnell's Estate lay in Wynrich it might have come to the Hungerfords, through this marriage.

1655.—Windrush Mill. was granted by Cary, Viscount Falkland, to Sir Edmund Bray.

1776.—At the County Election, the following Voted for freeholders in Windrush.

Broad, Thomas.
Bradshaw, Edward.
Guest, George.
Hands, Thomas.
Moss, Thomas.

The Sherborne and Windrush Common fields and Downs, Inclosure Act passed, 17 Geo. iii. Award dated 1778,

James Dutton, Esqr. was the Impropriator of the Church and received for his Tythe on the allottable Lands an Allotment of 143a. 3r. and for Tythe on ancient Inclosures an allotment of 16a 3r. 20p.

The Vicar received for his Tythes in the fields and Downs, several Allotments containing together near 140a.

Estate Allotments were made for Commonfield Rights: Eight to James Dutton, Esqr. together over 650a. Four to Thomas Broad, Esqr. together above 260a. Three to Edmund Bradshaw, together near 250a.

And Other allotments to Mary Guest, Thomas Hands and others; and an allotment of 10a. was set out for Fuel for the Poor and vested in the Vicar, Church Wardens and Overseers.

II.—Church:

There is no Presbyter mentioned in Domesday for this Parish

Lanthony Abbey had the Rectory by the Gift of Roger de Lacy, Earl of Hereford and it was appropriated to them.

Farm of pasture for Sheep in Wynrishe 33s. 3d.

As Rector of Wynrish:—the Abbey had the Farm of Hay Tythe demised to Thomas Brygg, for 4£. 10d. yearly.

Farm of two portions of small Tythe demised to Hugh Ellington, Vicar 20s. Issue of Wool the 26s. 8d. and price of Lamb Tythe 56s. yearly in hand.   Valor Eccl'us.

The Church of Windrush, was taxed at 3£. 6s. 8d.
Pope Nich. Tax.

The Vicar returned his Vicarage as endowed with 34a. Arable and 17a. af Meadow Land of 17£. Yearly Value.

The ninth Sheaf, fleece and Lamb, was taxed at 20 marks.   Nona Roll.

Tythe of Garb and Hay, Wool and Lamb and Personal Tythe and Oblations at 12s.

Tythe of a Mill 2s.

Tythe of Pork, Veal, Milk, Eggs, Hens, Honey and Wax 10s. 8d.   Valor Eccl'us.

The Impropriation after the dissolution of Lanthony Abbey was granted to Sir Christopher Allen.

List of Vicars and Patrons of Windrush.

Vicars.	Patrons.
John Drury.	
1551.—Edmund Catterall.	Queen Mary.
1554.—Thomas Rawlyns.	Do.
1564.—John Harris.	Queen Elizabeth.
1567.—Nicholas Jones.	Do.
1572.—William Jones.	Do.
1578.—Peter Geast.	Do.
1599.—William Jackson.	Do.
1617.—John Lesley.	William Dutton.
1647.—Robert Rowden.	Do.
1660.—John Lesley, restored.	Do.

Michael Mills, *(Inscription.)* William Dutton.
1684.—William Hughs. Sis Ralph Dutton, Bart.
1687.—John Bradley. Do. do.
1711.—David Gwynn. John Dutton,
1714.—John Fifield Do.
1754.—Richard Rice, ceded 1771. James Lenox Dutton.
   T. Meyler. *see* "Sherborn." Joseph Twyning.
1776.—Do. *consolidated with Sherburn.*
1793.—Thomas Birt. Lord Sherborne.
1806.—David Roderick. Do

The Vicar of Windrush, Sir John Drury, was accused by Roger Dodds, for that when he Dodds, came first to him to be his servant, he sware him upon a booke to keepe his Counsels in all things, and after that he shewed him a certain woman in his House who he saide to be his Wife; counselling more over the said Roger Dodds, upon an embring day to suppe with bread and cheese saying that which goeth into a man's soule to a man's soule, but that which goeth out of the bodie defileth both body and soule. He taught him the A B C to the intent that he should have understanding in the Apocalyps wherein he said that he should perceive all the falsehood of the World and all the truth. He told him when he had been at the Ladie of Worcester, and at the flood of Hayles, which had cost him xviii pence, that he had done as an ill husband that had ploughed his land and sowen it, but nothing to the purpose: For he had worshipped mans handicworke and cast away his Money which had been better given to the poore, for he should worship but one God and no handy worke of man. When the People would offer Candles where he was Vicar to Marie Magdalene, he would take them and say they were fooles that brought them thither. *Foxe's Book of Martyrs.* The Vicar was ignominiously punished, 761.

Church Table :—Charity given to this Church being half a Yard Land for ever let at £3. 10*s.* a Year Title immemorial possession This consists of 10*a.* of which 8*a.* are arable and 2*a.* parture It is under the management of the Church Wardens. Rent 20£. applied to Church Repairs It was mortgaged about for 20 years to raise 250£. laid out for new roofing and pewing the Church.
21 *Charity Inquiry Rept. p.* 184. *temp.* 1829.

III.—*Taxation, Population, &c.*

Winriche, Subsidy Roll, 1 EDW. iii., 1327.

De Johne. le Veysyn, xii d.
' Robto. Bone, xiiid.
' Willmo. in Angulo, xx d.
' Johne. Abraham, vi d.
' Willmo. Lammare, xvi d.
' Adam Mille, iiii s. vi d.
' Galfro. Saunders, ix d.
De Agnet. Kun, iii s. vii d.
' Johne. Bone, xviii d.
' Robto. le Mareys, xviii d.
' Johne. Elys, ii s.
    prob. Sma. xx *s. o.*

Windrush, Subsidy Roll, 30 Eliz.

Katharine Hungerford, in bon. 6£ 10*s.*
Edward Broadstowe, in bon. 3. 5.
John Broade, in bon. 3. 5.
    sma. £13.

Acreage 1729 *a.*

Population 1801,—371. 1831,—291. 1871.—266.

1815. Yearly Value of Real Property £2015.

1882.—Estimated Rateable Value £1806.

1833-4-5.—Three Years Average Expenditure on Poor 254£.

In Northleach Union.

Bradley, who married Jane Hungerford, was the father of the Astronomer. *see* "Sherborne."

An acknowledgment is due to the Revd. F. BOND, for Information concerning the Hungerford family.

WINSTON.

CCXCXI.
or 304.

THE CHURCH consists of a Chancel and Nave, with a low Tower at the West-end, therein two Bells. It is a very small building dedicated to St. Bartholomew, it is in the deanery of Stonehouse.

.... SANDYS, *Esqr.* PRESENT LORD OF THE MANOR.

Revd. Mr. LONGDON, *Rector.*

BENEFACTIONS.

Mr. THOMAS MUGLETON, (who lies buried in *Miserden Church,*) gave by Will, 15 Shillings yearly Rent to the Poor of this Parish, and it is paid by the Overseers of *Duntsborne Abbots.*

INSCRIPTIONS IN THE CHURCH.

CHANCEL.

UPON A WHITE MARBLE TABLET AGAINST THE SOUTH WALL.

Upon the ingenious and judicious Artist *Mr.* JOHN HAVILAND, Sonne of that Reverend Proffessor, and Dispencer of God's word
Mr. JOHN HAVILAND, sometimes Incumbent here at *Winston,*
Anag
JOHN HAVILANDE,
Hold'ay in Heav'n
Obijt Novem. 10 An. Dni. 1638.

None printed more and erred less in Print,
None led a Life that had less Errors in't

None had a State that did more Good with it,
None lesse appearing and more full of Wit
Nons lesse affected to Phantastick Fashion,
None more addrest to Christian Compassion
None better known to the Misstry of his Art,
None of a stronger Braine, a cleaer Hart,
Well has he finish'd then his Pilgrim Race
Who ever liv'd of Form, and died in Case
This constant impreze then shall seal his Grave,
Each year my Works must new Impressions have.

EPITAPH.

A Matrice, gave my Life, a matrice gain
And Earth's the matrice that does me contain.

ON FLAT STONES.

Here lyeth the Body of
Mrs. JOANE WEBB,
the chaste Wife of
Mr. FRANCIS WEBB, of *Winston,*
She piously departed this Life,
Jany. the 8*th.* 1645,
Aged 54 Years.

EPITAPHIUM, MERITO SUUM.

Virgo nupta prius, postquam matrona
    pudica
Uni juncta viro, dum tibi Vita manet,
Tam caste vivans, Tu sancta Exempla
    dedisti,
Fœmineum castum, sic foret, omne
    genus,
Post mortem triplici solaris prole mari-
    tum
Vt. sint virtutis Stemmata viva tuæ.
ST. JOHN, Chap. xi.
Jesus said unto her I am the Resurrec-
tion and the Life.

Here lieth ye Body of
Mr. FRANCIS WEBB, Mr. of Arts,
and Rector of ys Parish 29 Years,
who departed June ye 7, 1648,
Aged 64.

VV ltum quis stantem? certum quis
    poscit amicum
E x animo sanctum Pastorem, et ad
    omnia doctum,
B iblia sacra suis et Vitâ et voce
    tenentem
B elle nôvos contra Doctores bella
    gerentem
V icinis gratum poscis? vis denique
    charum
S anctis FRANCISCUS, sanctus fuit
    omnia WEBBVS.

Here lyeth the Body of
the Revd. THOMAS EGERTON,
Rector, of this Parish 41 Years.
who was here buried Febr. the
24th. 1741-2, Aged 67 Years.

Here lyeth the Body of
HESTER, Daughter of the
Revd. THOMAS EGERTON,
and MARY, his Wife,
She died the 23rd. of Febr. 1738.

Mrs. ALICE HAVILANDE,
Widow, was buried here the
16 of April A. D. 1648,
Aged about 90 Years.

Here resteth the Body of
Sir WILLIAM SPARROWHAWKE,
Knight, who was buried the
7th. day of May, Anno Domini 1573.

NAVE.

ON FLAT STONES.

In Memory of
ELIZABETH, the Wife of
JOHN HAVILAND, (Malster,)

who died Febr. the 27, 1773,
Aged 50 Years.

In Memory of
JOHN HAVILAND, (Malster,)
who died Sept. 28, 1786,
Aged 65 Years.

CHURCH YARD.

ON ALTAR TOMBS.

In Memory of
JOHN HAVILAND, Senr.
of this Parish, Yeoman,
who died the 5 of April,
Ano. Domi. 1742 Agd 75 Years.

Here lies the Body of
RICHARD HAVILAND, Senr.
of this Parish, who died
Oct. the 7. 1758, Aged near 64.
In Memory of
FRANCES, the Wife of
WILLIAM HAVILAND,
of the City of Gloucester,
late of this Parish.
She died Sept. 22, 1766,
Aged 33 Years
SUSANNA, Wife of RICHARD
HAVILAND, of this Parish,
She died March the 5, 1789,
Aged 89 Years.
SUSANNA, Daughter of JOHN
and MARY HAVILAND,
died Oct. 18, 1771, Aged 89.
Also three Children, who died
in their Infancy.

In Memory of
FRANCIS HAVILAND,
of this Parish, Yeoman,
who died October the 24, 1746,
Aged 82 Years.
ELIZABETH, his first Wife,
died in January 1737,
Aged 76 Years.

To the happy Memory of
THOMAS LIMBRICK, Carpenter,
and MARY, his Wife of this Parish.
He died January the 29, 1739,
Aged 80 Years.
She died Septem. 17, 17...,
Aged 40 Years.
Also of HUGH, CHARLES, JAMES,
and ALICE, their Children.

In Memory of
JOHN DANCER, of the Parish
of Painswick, Yeoman,
who departed this Life,
October the 15, A. D. 1737,

Aged 71 Years.
SUSANNA, Wife of JOHN DANCER,
Yeoman, died the 18 day of June,
Ano. Dni. 1720, Aged 58 Years.

Here lyeth the Body of
WILLIAM SINGLETON, of Stroud,
who died in Jany. Ao. Do. 1747,
Aged 71 Years.
Also his Father, Mother and Sister.

In Memory of
JOHN ABELL, Senr.
Interred March 3, 1745, Aged 51.
JOHN, his Son, Interred
Nov. 22, 1747, Aged 17.
JANE, his Daughter, Interred
Febr. 11, 1735, Aged 7.
MARY, the Wife of JOHN ABELL,
Senr. who died August 2, 1776,
Aged 76 Years
COMFERT, Daughter of
WILLIAM ABELL and JANE,
his Wife. died Decr. 18, 1778,
Aged 11 Months.

Sacred to the Memory of
MARGARET, the Wife of EDWARD
HAVILAND, who died
March 16, 1776, Aged 35 Years.
Also three of their Children:
MARTHA, died Febr. 26, 1777,
Aged 6 Years.
JAMES and MARGARET, died Infants.
Also ANNE, the Wife of EDWARD
HAVILAND, of this Parish,
who departed this Life,
April 23, 1793, Aged 45 Years.

BRASS PLATE ON FLAT STONES.

In Memory of
RICHARD BROWN,
(late of Stockwell in the Parish
Cowley, Yeoman.)
He departed this Life, the
6 of Decr. 1790, Aged 77 Years.

This Plate Perpetuates
the Memory of MARY, Wife of
JOHN BRUNSDEN,
of this Parish, Yeoman,
who died Nov. 14, 1765,
Aged 35 Years.

(Additional since Bigland's time.)

A Tablet to the Memory of the
Revd. JOHN LONGDEN, Rector,
who died 1808.

HEAD STONES.

	Died.		Aged.			Died.		Aged.
Mary, Wife of John Haviland, ...	19 Decr.	1780	44	William, Son of William and } Elizabeth Williams, ... }		6 April	1729	27
Nicholas Cross, ...	2 Febr.	1783	65					
Hannah, Wife of Nicholas Cross,	3 Oct.	1770	40	Thomas Abell, Senr.		4 Nov.	1769	71
Mary, Wife of William Bowley,	10 Febr.	1770	72	William Abell, ...		27 Nov.	1724	60
John, Son of William Browne,	27 March	1735	30	John Abell, ...		4 Mar.	1742	80
Susanna, Relict of John Haviland,	2 Nov.	1739	43	Eleanor, his Wife, ...		7 Jany.	1731	41

1484

Supplementary Notes as to I. *Devolution of Estates.* II. *Church.* III. *Population, Taxation, &c.*

I.—*Estates:*—

Wynston in Bradley Hundred is often mistaken; Records for Winson, near Bibury.

Wineston in Bradlege Hundred, contained 5 Hides taxed. Culture:—Four Carucates in Demesne and 5 in Villinage, (9 Villans. 4 Bordars.) There were 10 Bondmen and Women. A Mill of 7s 6d. (Rent,) 15a. of Meadow. It had been worth 8£. then 7£.

Ansford de Cormeleis, held and in (Saxon.) times Edric Leuric and Elvic, had held for 3 maners. *Domesday Book.*

The same Survey informs us that Ansfrid, had married a Daughter of Walter de Lacy and receved this and Duntesborn (Abbats,) by his Gift before the Survey.

6 Edw. iii.—Wynston Manor:—Simon de Solers, *Plaintiff* and Thomas de Solers, *Deforciant,* in a *Fine.*

As to the descent from Cormelius, to Solers, *see* (Shipton Solers

It was in the Mortimer family and came to the Crown temp. Hen. vii. by their forfeiture.

Hen. viii.—The Countes of Downe and Ann, Wife of T. Howard, were parties to a Fine of Lands in Brimpsfield, Winston and Bisley.

Edw. vi.—It was acquired by the Hungerford family' who long held it.—It was afterwards purchased by the Sandys family, (*see* "Brimpsfield, and Miserden." and in 1778.—was mortgaged.

1820.—The Mortgage became vested in George Elwes, whose Daughter and only Child Emily Frances, married Thomas Duffield.

1833.—Under a foreclosure suit the Sandys Estate at Winstone containing 700a. was sold by Order of the Court of Chancery. to the Revd. Edward Reed, who had married Barbara Sandys.

1859.—J. W. Lyon, by purchase.

1862.—Sir John Rolt, Knight, by purchase.

Other Estates:—Mr. William Haviland, of this Parish purchased in the Year 1777, of Samuel Sandys, Esqr. a Farm of about 176 *acres*:—It continued in the Haviland Family 'till about 1800, in which year it was purchased by Mr. William Stephens, and in the year 1833, it was vested in William Penn Gaskell, by purchase.

Fines:—

45 Edw. iii.—John le Haye; R. Churcheye.

20 Edw. iii.—John de Acton; Reg. de Stoke; John le Brun.

14 W. le Eyr; John de Whitleby.

33 Edw. i.—John de Acton; Nich. le Archer.

32 Edw. i.—R. de Barton; W. de Barton;

M. 18 Eliz.—L. Eyton. *Plantiff.* Anthony Corbet, *Deft.*

1782, 22 Geo. iii.—Winstone Common fields (770a.) Inclosure Act passed. Saml. Sandys, Esqr. was Lord of the Manor and the Revd. J. Longdon, Rector, to whom an Allotment in lieu of Tithe was given.

1776.—*The following Voted as Freeholders in Winstone, at the County Election.*

Abel, William.
Bronsden, John.
Cross, Nicholas.
Haviland, John.
Haviland, John, *Junr.*
Longden, John, *Revd.*
Williams, William.

II.—*Church.*

The Advowson is in the Lord of the Manor.

Rectory Value of £4 13 4.   *Pope Nich. Tax.*

Portion of Priory of Hereford, in Tythe 13s. 4d.   *Valor Eccl'e.*

Rectorial Glebe 80a.

1841.—Tithe Apportionment.

Rent charge 199£. inclusive of 16£. Rent charge on Glebe.

There is a Parish School House, built 1835.

List of Incumbents and Patrons of Winston.

Incumbents.	Patrons.
1548.—Hugh Somner.	
1553.—William Sparhawke, *see Church Inscriptions.*	Athony Hungerford.
1573.—John Haviland, *see Ch. I.*	John Hungerford.
1619.—Francis Webb, *see Gh. I.*	
1648.—W. Eldridge,	Miles Sandys.
1679.—Henry Heane,	Miles Sandys.
1701.—Thomas Egerton, *see Ch. I.*	Edward Sandys.
1742.—Thomas R ards,	Barbara Sandys, *Widow.*
1742.—John Longdon,	Do. do.
1808.—Fredrick Wm. Holder.	
......—............ Hayward,	J. Rolt, Esqr.

III.—*Taxation, Population, &c.*

Winstone, Subsidy Roll, 1 Edw. iii. **1327.**

De Alan. Brounynge, iii s. viii d. ob.
' Rico. Robynes, xii d. q.
' Johne. Houwes, xviii d.
' Henr. le Saman, ii s. iii d. ob. q.
' Edith. atte Grove, xvii d. ob. q.
' Walto. Kolves, xviii d. ob.
' Robto. Hamound. xiiii d. ob.
' Rogo. de Solers, xiiii s. ii d.
' Henr. Perys, xxiii d.
' Johne. Bernard, ii s. vi d. q.
' Rogo. le Bas, xx d ob.
' Walto. Wyllam, iii s. iii d. ob. q.
' Johne. le Kynge, ii s. viii d. ob.
' Henr. Inthehurne, ii s. xi d. ob.
' Johne. atte Grene, ii s. ii d. q.
' Isabell. Prattes, x d.
' Felicia de Zaneworth, ii s. v d.

     prob. Sma. xxxvii *s.* vi *d.*

Acreage 1437 a.

Population 1801,—143. 1831,—164. 1871.—227.

In 1815. Annual Value of Real Property 1486£.

1852. Rateable Value 1531 £.

1832-3-4. Average of three Years Expenditure on Poor 38 £.

In Cirencester Union.

Land of 8d. yearly was given to find a Lamp, which 8d. was given to the Poor.

A stock of Sheep, worth 4s. to find 2 Tapers. *Certificate of Chantries under the Commission,* 2 Edw. 6.

WINTERBOURN.

WINTERBOURN.

T HE CHURCH is large consisting of a Chancel, Nave, and Aisle and Chapel on the North, It is uniformly pewed. It hath a Gallery at the West-end, a high Tower on the South side adorned with pinnacles and a handsome Spire on the top, containing six Bells, and a Vestry on the same side. The Church is dedicated to St. Andrew. The advowson thereof was given by ELIAS BOY GIFFARD, to the Abbey of *Gloucester*, in the Reign of King STEPHEN. It is a Rectory in the Deanery of *Bristol. St. John's College, Oxford*, are Patrons who always pre- sent the oldest Batchelor to the Living. Under an Arch between the Chancel and Chapel is the figure of a Man in Complete Armour, and cross Legged, his hands in a supplicating posture, and a sword by his side, his head rests upon a boars head collared, with a ducal Crown, and at his feet a Lion couchant, and alongside is the effigy of a Lady in loose Robes her hands in a supplicating posture and her feet resting upon a Dog, these are supposed to represent some of the BRADESTONE family, there is a brass-plate in the Chancel of a Lady, but the Inscription is worn out, there is also in this Chancel an Effigy of a Man in Armour with his head resting upon a Ram and at his feet a Lion conchant and a Lady by his side, it is supposed for FOKERAM, the proprietor of *Stourden.*

An old Statue of a Woman in Stone, lies in the Belfry.

In the West Window are the two following Coats:—Gules a Chevron between eight Crosses patté Or. within a border Argent:—BERKLEY, *impaling* Azure, three Chevrons interlaced and a Chief Or. .... 2 Azure two Bars Argent within a Border of second.

In the West Window at the end of North Aisle the Arms of BERKLEY.

Mr. PROBYN, LORD OF THE MANOR.

Revd. Mr. S. PARKER, *Rector.*

BENEFACTIONS TO THE POOR OF THIS PARISH.

1.—HUGH BROWN, *Esqr.* gave 5 s. in Bread weekly on every Sunday after divine Service for ever, to be distribut- ed by the Church Wardens and Overseers of the Poor together with whom the owner of his Mansion called *Winterbourne, Court*, should appoint, unto such labouring Persons Parishioners there as do not receive any other Alms, or pay from the said Parish, and such as constantly resort to the said Parish Church, 1691.

2.—WILLIAM BAYLY, *Esqr.* sometime Sheriff of *Bristol*, born in this Parish, gave 50 £. the Interest thereof in Bread to poor Housekeepers of the Parish that should not receive Alms and constantly frequent this Church, to be divided equally between them on 26 of December, for ever.

Mr. RICHARD BLAKE, of the City of *Bristol*, *Gent.* gave to the Minister and Church Wardens of this Parish, the sum of Fifty £. to be laid out at Interest, &c. the Interest arising therefrom to be laid out in Bread and given to the Poor of this parish at Christmas for ever.

INSCRIPTIONS IN THE CHURCH.

CHANCEL.

ON MONUMENTS.

Arms:—Argent, on a Bend en- grailed Or. three Eagles display'ed Sable.—BROWNE. *impaling* Paly of six Argent and Sable, three Eagles displayed counter-changed. WHIT- COMB.
Crest:—Out of a Mural Crown Argent, a demi Eagle displayed Sable.

M. S.

HUGOHIS BROWNE, *Nuper,* de *Winterbourne Court,* *Armigeri,* qui obijt primo die Septembris Anno Domini Millesimo Sexcentesimo nonagesimo primo, Ætatis suæ Quadragesimo Septimo. Hoc amoris sui Pignus Charissima Conjux Posuit Monumentum. Here also lyeth the Body of ANN BROWNE, Wife of the above named HUGH BROWNE, *Esqr.* who died the 19 of March, 1725.

Sacred to the Memory of the *Reverend* EDWARD DAVIS, A.M. Prebendary of *Landaff*, whose Remains are deposited near this Place, He departed this Life, Jany. 13, 1789, Aged 79 Years.

Near this Place lieth Intered the Body of the late *Mr.* THOMAS MOUNTJOY, *Surgeon*, late of *Whiteshill* in this Parish, who departed this Life, the 22 day of April 1797, in the 64 Year of his Age. He was noted thro' England, Ireland and Wales for his Knowledge and success in curing the discases of Weakly and Ricketty Children and Ruptures which he practiced successfully for 40 Years, from an Original Receipt which had been in the family for near 200 Years. As a token of Gratitude this Monu- ment was erected by the Directions and at the Expence of

Mr. JAMES WILKINSON, *Surgeon*, of *Rotherham* in the West Riding of the County of *York*, and MARY WILKINSON, his Daughter two of the Executors.

M. S.

Viri optimi et Ornatissimi Patris sui colendissimi JACOBI BUCK, *Armigeri*, Qui in Domino Placide obdormivit, An. Do. CIↃIↃCXIIo. Martiq XIIIo. Ætatis LXVIo. Quod Bruti statuæ subscripsit Roma Sepulchro Inscribam Patrio; Viverat, opto Pater. Sed Patris pietas, procul esto dissita mundo Hinc rapuit patrem restituitque Deo Piet ergo lugens posuit MATTHÆUS BUCK, filius et Hæres.

Here lyeth the Body of
WILLIAM BURGES,
of this Parish, *Gent.*
who departed this Life, the
24 of September 1705,
in the 78 Year of his Age.
Here lie the Remains of the
Reverend NATHANIEL MOORE, L.L.D.
late *Rector* of this Parish,
Born 9 of November 1744.
Died 6 Nov. 1798.

In Memory of
AMY, the Wife of THOMAS SYMES,
Esqr. of this Parish, Daughter of
EDWARD BRIDGES, of *Keynsham*
in the County of *Somerset, Esqr.*
descended from the noble Family
of the *Lord* CHANDOIS, *Baron* of
Sudely Castle in the County of
Gloucester, who though her
Extraction was Honorable, yet by her
Examplary Life and Manners
became an honor to her Family
and after 17 Years spent in her
minority and 20 Years in Wedlock
in which interval she was mother of
twelve Sons and four Daughters,
changed this mortal State for an
immortall the 30 of April 1662.
Here also lyes the Body of
THOMAS SYMES, of this Parish, *Esqr.*
Son of JOHN SYMES, of *Ponsford*
in the County of *Somerset, Esqr.*
who deceased the 22 day of
Januarij 1669, Aged 48 Years.
Here also lyes the Body of
BENJAMIN, Son of THOMAS SYMES,
Esqr. and AMY, his Wife,
who deceased August the 12, 1662,
Aged 6 Months.
Here also lyes the Body of
ELIZABETH, Daughter of THOMAS
SYMES, and AMY, his Wife,
who deceased the 18 of January,
.... (*no date of the Year.*)
Aged 19 Years.

Arms:—Azure three Escolleps
in pale Or.—SYMES. *impaling* Argent, on a Cross Sable, a Leopards
face Or.—BRIDGES.

Here under lyeth the Bodys of
HENRY and PHILLIPA GUISE,
Son and Daughter of HENRY GUISE,
of this Parish, *Esqr.* who departed
in March and August last 1672.
Hic jacet PHILLIPPA GUISE,
uxor HENRICI, et Soror
Sir THOMÆ BRIDGES, de *Keynsham,*
Qui obiit Octo. Die (Febr. 1674.)

Sacred to the Memory of
ARTHUR TURNER, of this Parish,
and MARY, his Wife, whose
remains are deposited near this Place,
He died April 12, 1785, Aged 72.
She died October 20, 1781, Aged 61.
Also of their Children:
THOMAS, who died May 10, 1747,
Aged 6 Weeks.
SARAH, who died April 13, 1757,
Aged 15 Years.
ARTHUR, who died Sept. 12, 1762,
Aged 25 Years.
MARY JONES, who died
April 14, 1778, Aged 26 Years.
And of another of their Children,
who died in its Infancy.

THOMAS, who died March 24, 1793,
Aged 43 Years.
SUSANNAH JONES, who died
June 24, 1786, Aged 8 Years.

ON FLAT STONES.

Here lyeth the Body of
JOHN HICKES,
of the City of *Bristol, Merchant,*
who departed this Life,
June 7, 1704, in the
50 Year of his Age.
Beneath this Stone are also
deposited the Remains of the
Reverend EDWARD DAVIES, A.M.
who departed this Life,
January 13, 1789.

Here lyeth the Body of
THOMASINE CALLOWHILL,
who departed this Life, the
8 of December 1713,
in the 78 Year of her Age.

Here lies in hopes of a Blessed
Resurrection the Body of the
Reverend EDWARD WARNFORD, B.D.
late fellow of *St. John's College,
Oxford,* and 18 Years *Rector*
of this Parish, He departed this
Life, the 7*th.* day of February 1795,
Aged 59 Years.

Arms:—Argent, a Chevron Sable
between a Black-amoors head affrontè
proper.—GRIFFITH. *impaling* Ermine
on a Chief. .... 2 Griffins rampant respectant. ....
Crest:—a Buck's head cabosed.

Hic sepulta jacet Maria,
CHRISTOPHORI GRIFFITH,
de *Winterbourn, Generosi,*
Charissima conjux,
Terræ corpus, Deo animam restituit,
Octavo calendarum Februarij,
Anno Salutis MDCCXVII,
Ætatis suæ XLVIII.
Sub hoc etiam Quiescunt Tumulo,
Filius JOHANNES Filiaque MARIA,
Impuberes.

Aams:—......... on a fess ....
between three demi hares ....
three Roundlets.

Here lyeth the Body of
THOMAS HAYNES, *Gent.*
who departed this Life,
the 5 of March 1713,
Aged 53 Years.
Here also lyeth the Body of
SARAH, the Wife of the late
THOMAS HAYNES,
who departed this Life, the
21 of September 1728,
Aged 57 Years.
Likewise ELIZABETH PORTLOCK,
Widow, Daughter of the said
THOMAS and SARAH,
who died the 6 Febr. 1756,
Aged 49 Years.

Hic jacet
ELIZABETHA GRIFFITH,
filia Unica
GULIELMI GRIFFITH,
de *Bristol, Merchant,*
Obijt Mensis Augusti XIIII,
Ano. Christi MDCXLVI,
Ætatis suæ XXVIII.

Arms:—GRIFFITH, *as before,*
impaling Argent, on a Cross Azure
five Lozenges Or.
Crest:—a Buck's head cabosed.

Here lyeth the Body of
MARY, Wife of CHRISTOPHER
GRIFFITH, of this Parish, *Gent.*
(one of the Daughters and coheirs of
LOFTUS BRIGHTWELL, late of
Padworth in the County of *Berks.
Gent.*) who died the 7 day of
March 1748, Aged 58 Years.

Hic inhumatar est
JOHANNES GRIFFITH,
Rector de *Winterborne,*
per quinqueginta Annos,
Obiit Vicessimo quinto
die Januarij 1697,
Ætatis suæ 86.

Here lyeth the Body of
JOHN GIBBS, *Esqr.*
late of *French Hay* in this Parish,
who died December. 28, 1758,
Aged 70 Years.

ON A BRASS PLATE.

Arms:—Per fess nebulé Argent
and Sable three Bucks attires fixed
to the scalps counter changed.—
BUCK. *impaling* .... on a Bend
.... three Mullets ....

Here lyeth the Body of
MATHEW BUCK, *Esqr.*
who deceased the 17 of Sept.
Anno Dom. 1631.

Allthough the Subject of these fatall
Rymes
(This MATHEW,) lived in the Cus-
tome of the times,
Reader thou must (like him) before
thou diest
Leave the Worlds Custome for to
follow Christ
And then his Censure shall shutt up
thy Storie
Hee that did rise to Grace shall rise
to Glorie.

Here lyeth the Body of
THOMAS BUCK. *Esqr.*
Lord of this Manor,
who deceased the 14 day of April,
Anno Dmi. 1658, Æt. 47.
ROM. 8. v. 18-19.
Arms: of BUCK, *impaling* ....
a Saltire ....

Here lyeth the Body of
Mrs. ANN BROWNE,

by her first Husband
CHARLES WILLIAMS, *Esqr.*
some time *Sheriffe* of ye City of
Bristol, who died 11 of April 1730,
Aged 50 Years.

Here lyeth the Body of
Mrs. ANN BROWNE,
Widow of her second Husband
HUGH BROWNE, *Esqr.*
of *Winterborne Court*,
who died the 19 of March 1725,
Aged 82 Years.

In a Vault beneath this Tomb
are deposited the Remains of
FRANCES, the Wife of
EDMUND PROBYN, *Esqr.*
Lord of this Manor,
who died Sept. 6, 1799,
Aged 68 Years.

NAVE.

ON FLAT STONES.

Here under lyeth
Captain RICHARD HUDSON,
sometime of this Parish,
who deceased Sept. 25,
Anno Dom. 1679.
Also here lyeth ALICE, his Wife,
who deceased April 25, 1683,
Ætatis suæ 64.

Arms:—Argent, three Torteaux
and on a Chief Gules, a Mullett
.... BAYLY.
Crest:—Out of a ducal Coronet
a Horse's head.

Here lieth the Body of
THOMAS BAYLY, of this Parish,
Gent. who departed this Life, the
30 of May 1726.
Also of ELIZABETH JANE,
Sister to the said THOMAS BAYLY,
who departed this Life, the
11 Decmbr. 1728.

Under this Stone is interred
MARY PERRY, *Spinster*,
Daughter of THOMAS PERRY,
formerly of this Parish, *Gent.*
deceased, who died 20 Febr. 1749,
Also HUGH PERRY, Son of the
abovesaid THOMAS PERRY,
who died 27 March 1767,
in the 69 Year of his Age.

Under this Stone lyeth the
Body of CALEB JESSE, late of
this Parish, *Gent.*
who departed this Life, the
14 day of June 1756,
Aged 28 Years.
Also the Body of PHILLIS, late
Widow and Relict of the said
CABEL JESSE, but afterwards the
Wife of RICHARD LOW,
the Younger of this Parish,
Felt Maker, who departed this Life,
May 19 1761, Aged 33 Years.

Here lyeth the Body of
ANN ELDRIDGE, of this Parish,
Spinster, who died 17 Oct. 1763,
Aged 70 Years.

ON A MARBLE MONUMENT
AGAINST THE WALL.

Beneath are deposited in the
hopes of a Joyful and Blessed
Resurrection the Remains of
JOHN DEVERELL, *Esqr.*
of *Clifton* in the County of *Gloucester*,
who died April 3, 1797,
Aged 72 Years.

In him was comprised every Christian Virtue,
To his Memory his very disconsolate
and Afflicted Widow has inscribed
this Marble.

NORTH AISLE.

ON FLAT STONES.

Under this Stone lies the Body of
MARTHA, Daughter of WILLIAM
and FRANCES NICOLLS,
of this Parish, who died
Jany. 2, 1763, Aged 5 Years.
Also of EDWARD, their Son,
who died Febr. ye 17, 1767,
in the 3 Year of his Age.
Also of FRANCES, their Daughter,
who died 21 Oct. 1767, in the
14 Year of her Age.
Likewise SAMUEL, their Son,
who died the 15 May 1779, in the
20 Year of his Age.
Also WILLIAM, their Son,
who died the 9 of Sept. 1790,
Aged 34 Years.
Also the aforesaid WILLIAM
NICOLLS, of this Parish,
who departed this Life,
6 Jany. 1792, Aged 66 Years.

Underneath lie the Remains of
JOHN RICHARDS, of this Parish,
Junr. who died 18 May 1756,
Aged 45 Years.
Also of ELIZABETH, *Widow of*
JOHN RICHARDS, aforesaid
who died Jany. 15, 1767, in the
52 Year of her Age.

Here lieth the Body of
Lieutenant JOHN PAYNE,
who married MARTHA, the Daughter
of JOHN BRINSTORP,
Wine Merchant, of the City of *Bristol,*
He departed this Life, the 15 day of
June 1750, Aged 33 Years.

Here lies interred the Body of
ISAAC PAYNE, *Gentleman,*
who departed this Life,
ye 12 of March 1773,
Aged 36 Years.
BETSEY GRIFFITH PAYNE,
his Daughter, died Dec. 23, 1768,
Aged 4 Months and 3 Weeks.
CHRISTOPHER GRIFFITH PAYNE,
his Son, died Sept. 14, 1772,
Aged 1 Year and 4 Months.

This Inscription to his Memory
is put, by his *Widow,*
FRANCES PAYNE, 1787.

Under this Stone lie
interred the Remains of
FRANCES HALL, *Relict* of
MATHEW HALL, late of ye City of
York, Gent. and Mother to
FRANCES PAYNE, of this Parish,
who departed this Life,
Nov. 4, 1786, in the
87 Year of her Age.
This Stone is put to her Memory
by her only surviving Daughter
the above FRANCES PAYNE.

CHURCH YARD.

ON TOMBS.

To the Memory of
ISAAC WEBB, who died
20 Febr. 1774, in the
54 Year of his Age.
Also WILLIAM, JOHN and JACOB,
his Children, by SARAH, his Wife,
died Infants.

Here lyeth the Body of
THOMAS HITCHINS,
who died Augt. 7, 1731,
Ætatis suæ 58.
Here also lies the Body of
ELIZABETH, Daughter of THOMAS
HITCHINS, aforesaid who departed
this Life, Febr. 1, Ao. 1728-9,
in the 20 Year of her Age.

Here lyeth ABRAHAM MILLS,
of *Mangotsfield,*
who died 5 April 1723,
Aged 26 Years.
SARAH, his Wife, (Daughter of
JOHN CAMBORN,) died July 5, 1770,
Aged 78 Years.

Under this Tomb lie interred
the Remains of ROBERT TUCKER,
who died 26 June 1771,
Aged 51 Years,.
SARAH, the Wife of ROBERT
TUCKER, of this Parish, Yeoman,
who died 20 June 1762,
Aged 42 Years.
ROBERT TUCKER, *Junr.*
died 7 Nov. 1774, in the
31 Year of his Age.

In Memory of
ARTHUR TUCKER, who died
May 22, 1760, in the
83 Year of his Age.
JANE, his first Wife,
died Febr. 10, 1743, Aged 21.
ELIZABETH, his second Wife,
died Decr. 31, 1766, Aged 22.
SARAH, his third Wife,
died 24 April 1733, Aged 34.
With Several of his Children
who died Infants.

1488

Here lieth the Body of
ROBERT TUCKER,
Also of ANNE, his Wife,
He died May 3, 1720,
Aged 72 Years.

Here lieth the Body of
JOHN TUCKER, of this Parish,
Yeoman, who died Sept. 1, 1739.
Aged 29 Years.
Also ANNA, his Daughter,
Aged 10 Days.

Here lieth the Body of
ROWLAND PRIGG, of *Stanley* within
the Parish of *Winterborn*,
who departed this Life, the
22 day of May Ano. Dm. 1628.

SARAH, Daughter of ARTHUR
TUCKER, *Junr.* of this Parish,
Yeoman, died 13 April 1777,
in the 15 Year of her Age.
Also ARTHUR, Son of
ARTHUR TUCKER, by MARY,
his Wife, died Sept. 21, 1762,
in the 25 Year of his Age.

In Memory of
WILLIAM MAGGS, of this Parish,
who died March 24, 1798,
Aged 61 Years.
Also of MARY, his Wife,
who died 5 June 1798,
Aged 59 Years.

Near this Tomb lies the Body of
EDWARD UNDERWOOD,
of this Parish, who died
Jany. 18, 1740, Aged 73 Years.
Also MARY, his Wife, who died
April 8, 1748, Aged 72 Years.

Under this Stone lie the Remains
of HESTER, Wife of JONATHAN
EVANS, of this Parish,
who died May 6, 1783, in the
69 Year of her Age.
Also three of their Children,
who died in their Infancy.

To the Memory of
NATHANIEL COOK,
of the Parish of *Frampton Cotterell*,
who died Sept. 29, 1760,
Aged 44 Years.
Also of WILLIAM, his Son,
who died in his Infancy.
Also of THOMAS MORGAN,
of the Parish of *Frampton Cotterell*,
who died July 1, 1790,
Aged 56 Years.

Here lieth the Body of
WALTER RAINSTORPE,
of this Parish, *Gent.*
who departed this Life, the
21 March, Ano. Dom. 1714,
Aged 69 Years.

To the Memory of
CHRISTOPHER EDMUNDS,
of the City of *Bristol*,
who died 15 March 177...,
Aged 55 Years.
Also in Memory of ANN, Wife of
DANIEL CRIBB, of *Redland* in the
Parish of *Westbury upon Trim*,
in this County, *Yeoman*,
and late *Widow*, of the said
CHRISTOPHER EDMUNDS,
who died 36 August 1775,
Aged ...3 Years.

Sacred to the Memory of
MARY, Wife of GEORGE COLE,
Junr of this Parish, *Mason*,
who died in Childbed,
24 Febr. 1781, in the
23 Year of her Age.
To the Memory of JOHN, Son of
RICHARD and ELIZABETH COX,
of this Parish, who died
6 July 1781, Aged 2 Years.

Here lieth the Body of
MATHEW HALL, of this Parish,
Carpenter, who departed this Life,
the 3 day of October, 1749,
Aged 54 Years.

Here lyeth the Body of
THOMAS PERRY, of this Parish,
Gent. who died May 2, 1744,
in the 53 Year of his Age.
Also of SAMUEL and HENRY,
Sons of the abovesaid
THOMAS PERRY, *Gent.*
SAMUEL, died the ... day of
Jany. 1719, Aged 11 Months.
HENRY, died 22 August 1730,
Aged 6 Months.
Also MARY, the Wife of the said
THOMAS PERRY, who died the
1 July 1766, Aged 80 Years.

Underneath this Stone lies the
Body of JOHN PAYNE, of
French Hay in this Parish,
who departed this Life,
9 Febr. 1766, Aged 36 Years.

FLAT STONE.

In Memory of
ANN BISP, Wife of JOHN BISP,
of the City of *Bristol*,
who departed this Life,
29 March 1795, Aged 39 Years.

---

*(Supplementary Notices of Additional
Monuments &c. since Bigland's time.)*

*The Church was restored 1878, It has
a Round headed Door South and on
the Chancel Wall is a mural Painting
in Fresco, of a Knight praying.*

MEMORIAL WINDOW IN SOUTH
TRANSEPT UNDER TOWER.

LOUISA AGNES TANNER,
who died 1853, Aged 36 Years.
AGNES LOUISA TANNER,
who died 1854, Aged 10 Years.

NAVE.

Monuments to:—
Mr. W. RICHARDS,
and *his* two Wives.

And to *Mr.* PURNELL.

Under an Arch in the Wall of the
Chapel is a Tomb and
thereon is a recumbent figure with
a Dog at the feet, said to be of
STANTON, of *Stourden*.

CHANCEL.

ON A BRASS PLATE.

In Memory of
JOHN WALKER JONES,
who ministered 22 Years in this Parish.
The Eastern Wall of the Chancel
was rebuilt by him, and the Reredos,
and the Painted Window given
by his affectionate Widow.

M. S.
WILLIAM PARRY, *Gent.*
who died 1807, Aged 85 Years.
Also MARY, his Wife,
who died 1816, Aged 83 Years.
WILLIAM PARRY, M.D.
their Son, who died 1808,
Aged 34 Years.
THOMAS PERRY, their Son,
who died 1826, Aged 74 Years.
MARY KATHERINE, their Daughter,
who died 1844, Aged 67 Years.
Revd. J. W. JONES,
who died in 1849, Aged 60 Years.
ELIZABETH PERRY,
who died 1850, Aged 90 Years.
MARY ANN, *Widow* of the above
Revd. J. W. JONES,
who died 1862, Aged 77 Years.

ON NORTH WALL.

In Memory of
THOMAS WHITFIELD, B.D.
Formerly Tutor of *St. John's College,
Camb.* & 7 Years *Rector* of this Parish,
who died Febr. xvi, MDCCXXXIV,
in the LXIX, Year of his Age.
If unpretending kindness of
Heart, steadfastness of friendship,
And firmness of purpose
Based upon the Principles
And illustrating the influence
of the Gospel,
Are worth the contemplation of
the sober Christian
Peruse, digest reflect,
And Imitate.

ON SOUTH WALL.

SARAH, Wife of *Revd.* EDWARD
DAVIES, A. M. and Daughter of
.... THOMPSON.

ON SOUTH WILL.

SARAH, Wife of Revd. EDWARD DAVIES, A.M. and Daughter of .... THOMPSON.

ON FLAT STONES.

GEORGE MARTIN, Gent. of Stapleton, who died 1837, Aged 65 Years.

ON EAST SIDE OF CHANCEL ARCH, ON BRASS PLATE.

MARY, Youngest Daughter of the Revd. JOHN CHOLMELEY, woh died at Winterbourne, 1816, Aged 2 Years.

EMMA CHRISTIAN, the beloved Daughter of SAMUEL and SUSAN BRICE, who died 1826, Aged 25 Years.
RICHARD DAUBENY BRICE, who died 1855, Aged 59 Years.
SAMUEL BRICE, who died 1816, Aged 19 Years.
EDWARD DAUBENY BRICE, who died 1824, Aged 21 Years.

SAMUEL BRICE, Senr. Gent. 1848. His Wife SUSANNAH, who died 1841, Aged 61 Years.

In Memory of GEORGE MARTIN, Gent. who died Nov. 2, 1837, Aged 65 Years. In an lubarious and honorable course Life, He uniformly displayed great Energy of Mind, combined with strict integrity of purpose. His Widow had this Monument erected as a testimony of regard for her late Husband, and an affectionate record of his Loss.

Also of SARAH BEVAN, Relict of the above GEORGE MARTIN, who died the 14 April 1861. This is erected dy her 2nd. Husband, WILLIAM BEVAN, of Stapleton, As a tribute of his Affection for a beloved Wife, whose integrity, singleness of Heart, and unostentatious piety Endeared her to him in life, And whose lamented Death, He feels as an irreparable loss.

ON NORTH WALL.

M. S. ARTHUR TUCKER, of this Parish, And MARY, his Wife, He died April 1786, Aged 72. She died ...... 1784, Aged 68. Also 8 of their Children.

RACHEL, the Wife of GLENCAERE GUN CUNINGHAM, Esqr. who died 1872.

SOUTH TRANSCPT.

ON A TABLET.

In a Vault beneath are deposited the Remains of WILLIAM FREEMAN, late of Frenchay, formerly of Bristol, Merchant, wdo died 1832, Aged 75 Years. ANN, his Wife, who died 1797, Aged 67 Years. ELIZABETH FREEMAN, his Sister, who died 1802, Aged 77 Years, CAROLINE MARSHALL, Sister to ANN FREEMAN, who died 1780, Aged 49 Years.

HEAD STONES.

	Died.		Aged.		Died.		Aged.
Samuel Shillum, of the City of Bath.	16 June	1783	40	Richard Prevett, ...	12 Decr.	1770	68
				Thomas Ricketts, ...	9 Decr.	1780	86
William Shillum, ...	3 May	1773	67	Catharine his Wife,...	15 May	1773	82
Christian, his Wife, ...	1 April	1780	75	Richard Low, ...	27 Jany.	1784	85
Thomas Rickards, ...	7 Febr.	1785	66	Rebecca, his Wife, ...	24 April	1760	88
Mary, his Wife, ...	23 Febr.	1780	62	Elizabeth, Wife of John Sargeant,	20 Oct.	1723	61
Sarah, Wife of John Knapp, ...	27 Sept.	1792	69	Elizabeth Jones, ...	20 Nov.	1789	83
James Summerell, ...	3 Nov.	1782	80	Mary, Wife, of Robert Jonos,...	7 May	1779	55
Sarah, his Wife, ...	15 July	1780	74				

Supplementary Notes as to I.—Devolution of Estates. II.—Church. III.—Taxation, Population, &c.

1.—*Estates:*

Winterbourne is a large Parish, comprising the tithings of Winterbourne and Hambrook with French-hay or Froomshaw, and in respect of Estates the Manors of Winterbourne, with its outlying Members Hampton and Patchway," (in Almondsbury Parish,) Hambrook, Stourden, &c. and for Ecclesiastical purposes the Mother Church, and the new District Churches of French hay and Winterbourne Down.

There are two entries in Domesday Survey, relating to this Place. 1.—Winterbourne and Wapley conjoined, (as to Wapley, see No. CCLXXVIII.) stated in Domesday Survey to be Members of the Manor of Betun, (Bitton.) Culture of Britton:—In Demesne there were 5 Carucates. In Villenage, (4 Villans and 29 Bordars,) 45 Carucates:—There were 18 serfs, and there was a Mill. It was terra Regis, and in the time of the Confessor rendered the farm of One Night, (Lodging &c. for the Court,) and still did so at the Survey.

2.—Hambrook, of which hereafter.

2 Ric. i.—As to Winterbourne, By Grants from the Crown and subfees created by Crown Grantees. Fitzstephen held; from or under whom Bradston and his Wife Agnes, took and held a manerial estate for a fee in tail male. This family took their name from the Estate they held in Berkeley Parish. They had Estates at Horton and other places in the County; and for some generations they were summoned by Writ to Parliament as Barons of the realm, they held the Estate here till the time of Queen Elizabeth, in whose reign there was a Chancery suit in the family in which Robert Bradston, was Plaintiff, and Anthony and Elizabeth Bradston, John Green, alias Collyer, and Roger Talbot, were Defendants.

Chancery Proc'gs. Eliz. B. 6. 5. 11. 16.

Other part of Fitzstephen's possessions here passed to Walsh: 9 Hen. iii Walsh, held divers Messuages in Winterbourne, of the King's Gift. Ralph Walsh, held afterwards and had two Daughters his Coheirs, one was married to Wrokeshull, and the other to R. de Hadley.

22 Hen. vii.—John Walsh, and others held a Moiety of Lands in Hambrook by purchase from Richard Forster.

Another subfee in part of the Waste of the Manor of Winterbourne, of 3 Water Mills, &c. was acquired by Walter de Gaselyn or Catlyn, who left William, his son and heir, and a Daughter Juliana. William, dying without issue. Juliana succeeded. She married Geoffery Stawell, who conveyed to Hydon or Haddon.

9 Edw. ii.—In Nomina Villarum the following are given as Lords of the Vills in Winterbourne,—Ralph de Hadley, Galf. de Mohun, John de Brokenburo', Henry de Haddon. and C. de Cernie.

Hadley and Mohun, are mentioned in the Subsidy Roll, of 1 Edw. iii.—and also Ph. de Cerne, and John de Brokenborrow, the last is the name of a Manor in Almondsbury Parish. Haddon, the remaining Name we have seen before under the form of Hydon.

About the time of Henry vii or viii. Anthony Poyntz, acquired from Haddon.

From Poyntz the Estate passed to Buck, which family

held for several generations, (*see Church Inscriptions.*) From the last to Browne, by purchase; and from that family to Jones, in 1712. from his grand-daughter and heir in 1779. to her Husband the Revd. T. S. Whalley, who subdivided the Estate:—The Manor to Probyn, and from him to Parry. by Devise and from Parry to Brice and Cox, by purchase

Like the Hanbury Estate of Sir Samuel Astry, the Poyntz, Lands here appear to have passed in moieties, one to Sir John Smyth, and his descendants the other moiety to the Daughters and Coheirs of Thomas Edwards, who married respectively Lord Middleton, and Alexander Colston.

H. 13 Geo. ii.—Diones Gibbes, Esqr *Plaintiff.*
Francis, Lord Middleton, *Defor.* *Fine.*

The Court House is near the Church, The handsome Gateway &c. was built by Sir J. Smyth.

Part of Winterborne, (perhaps Ridgway,) appears to have been in Giffard's fee *i e.* Stoke Giffard.

13 Edw. ii.—Manor of Winterborne juxta Stoke, to P de Gomeldon.

There was a suit in Chancery temp. Elizth. by Richard Barkley, and Matthew Smith, Esqr against Roger Jones, and Richard Moon, for performance of an Award of Lands here. *Chanc. Proc'gs.* Eliz. B. 6. No. 23, 33.

Crossley House in Winterborn, belonged to the family of Faukes.

2.— Hambrook :—In Domesday Book is this Entry: In Swinshoved Hundred, the Bishop of St. Laud, of Constance, held Hanbree; and Osulf, under him. Algar, held it in King Edward's time and was free to go It contained Two Hides Culture. In Demesne two Carucates and in Villenage two Carucates, Two Serfs and 6 a. Meadow, It was worth 100 s. then 60 s.

Hambrook and Froomshaw. (Frenchay.)

43 Edw. iii.—Fine by Foliott, of Bristol and Wife to Richard le Cock, and Wife Juliana.

Hen. iii —Thomas Moreton, Esqr. died seized of Hambrook Manor, leaving Sir Robert Moreton, son and heir who died seized, 14th. Hen. viii.

There was a Subfee of Bradstone's Manor in Hambrook, of a Messuage. Carucate of Land and 10 s. Rent in Sir Robt. Ashton, which became by Marriage the property of Westou Teysant.

Stourden was a subfee. It consisted of a Carucate and 2 Virgates of Land with two Cotterells or Serfs.

41 Hen. iii —Two Brothers Fokeram, held it. William, left two Daughters, one of whom married Tregoz; from whom De le Riviere, took who is the largest Subsidy Payer in Hambroke, 1 Edw. iii The Moieties of the Daughters were reunited in Sir R. Brooke, from whom Stanshaw descended, and Poyntz took from him.

Baylee Harding and Wife Juliana, took Lands from Poyntz.

1830.—An Act for inclosing 185 *acres* of Common Lands and commons of Winterborne Down, Wadleys End, Cloister Common. Hambrook, Black Pits, Hicks Common. 1831, Award of Commissioners was made under it, and it was deposited in the Office of the Clerk of the Peace, 1831. John Wadham, was Lord of the Manor. 203 Allotments. Sir John Smyth, the largest Allottee. Queen Elizabeth's Hospital Bristol, next-heads, 8 public and 14 private were set out, Sale Allotments were made.

II.—*Church:*

The Parish is in the Diocese of Bristol and was in Dorset Archdeaconry, now Gloucester and Bristol Diocese.

The Advowson of the Rectory was long united to the Manor in the Hands of Giffard and Bradston, one of whom was founder of the Chantry in the Church of which the last Incumbent was Robert Rastall. This Wardenship or Chantry was founded for 2 Priests. Its profits was valued at 11 £. *Valor Eccl'us.*

The Lands thereof were granted by King Edw. vi. for years to W. Denys, Esqr. *Chanc. Proe'gs.* Eliz. B. 6. 7.

Patron of Rectory, St. John's College Oxford.

Rectory. £... *Valor Eccl'us.*

French hay in Winterbourne is an Ecclesiastical District with Winterbourne Down, another.

Charities:

1741.—............ Silcocks, gave 50 £. the Interest to Minister for preaching 4 Sermons a Year.

50 £. the Interest to teach poor Children of parents not paupers, paid by Representatives of Christopher Griffith, Executor of Silcocks, and afterwards given to the National School.

1691.—Hugh Browne, of Winterborne Court, gave by Will 5 s. for Bread weekly to poor persons not paupers commonly resorting to the Parish Church, the 5 s. charged on Tenements in Mangotsfield Parish.

1720.—William Bayley, gave by Will 50 £. the Interest for Poor not Paupers. (*Lost.*)

.....—Gregory Bush, (*Minister.*) gave by Will 50 £. the Interest for poor Housekeepers not Paupers frequenting the Church.

1826.—William Richards, gave by Will 200 £. in stock to Rector and Churchwardens, 20 s. for preserving his Vault. 5 £. in Bread for Poor not in the Workhouse.

1771—Richard Blake, gave by Will 50 £. to Minister and Church Wardens the interest laid out in Bread. (*Lost.*) *18th. Charity Inquiry Com'rs. Report, p.* 330.

III.—*Taxation, Population, &c.*

Winterbourn, Subsidy Roll, 1 Edw. III. 1327.
De Adam atte Luyde, **xx** d. o.
' Johe. Wade, **xv** d.
' Willo. Campe, **xx** d.
' Willo. de Holurst, **xxii** d. o.
' Johe. Adames, **xii** d.
' Thom. atte Hurn, **xii** d. o.
' Willo. Dype, ii s. ii d.
' Johe. de Came, **xxi** d.
' Robto. Campe, **xviii** d.
' Rogo. atte Croyce, **xii** d.
' Nicho. atte Hull, **xviii** d.
' Walto. atte Lepeyate, iii s. i d. o.
' Walto. P'trich, **xviii** d.
' Johe Temes, **xxi** d. q.
' Margia. le Mohoun, **xviii** d. o.
' Pho. de Cerne, ii s. viii d.
' Adam atte Fortheie, **xx** d.
' Willo. Hogyn, **xviii** d.
' Galf Segar, **xiiii** d.
' Robto. Hikkes, **viii** d.
prob. Sma. **xxxii** *s. o. q.*

Hambroke, Subsidy Roll, 1 Edw. iii., 1327.
De Rico. de la Riuer, iii . iiii d.
' Johe. Aueray, ii s.
' Johe. de Hambrok, ii s.
' Adam Homypyn, ii s. vi d.
' Nicho. Mussegros, **xii** d.
' Johe. Richardes, **xviii** d.
' Simon Frema. viii.
' Willo. Hompyn, ii s.
prob. Sma. **xv** *s.*

Hempton Wodelond et Petshawe de Wynt'bourn, Subsidy Roll, 1 Edw. iii., 1327.
De Johe. de Brokeneb'we, iii s. vi d. o.
' Laur. Pesshoun, **xii** d.
' Willo. atte Wode, **x** d.
' Regin. Pesshoun, **xviii** d.
' Willo. Lyngyur, **xii** d.
' Johe. Fabro, **viii** d.
' Walto. Austyn, **xviii** d.
' Willo. Henries, **viii** d.
' Alic. Denis, ii s.
' Willo. Widewesson, **xii** d.
' Willo. Kynge, **xviii** d.
prob. Sma. **xiii** *s.* **xi** *d. o.*

Subtax.
De Henr. Chann, **xii** d.
' Ric. Pesshoun, **xii** d,
Sma. ii *s.*
prob. Sma. toti. hundr. cum tax subt. **x** *li,* **xviii** *s.* **xi** *d. ob.*

Acreage 3112 *a.*

Population 1801,—1592, 1831,—2889. 1871.—3234.

In 1815. Annual Value of Real Property Winterbourne and Hambrook, 4347 £.

1882. Rateable Value 12,278 £.

1832-3-4. Average of three Years Expenditure on Poor 1255 £.

In Barton Regis, (late Clifton) Union.

THE **C**HURCH a small building dedicated to St. Mary, consists of a Chancel, Nave, and North Aisle, with a Stone Tower, at the West-end containing two Bells.

Sir WILLIAM HICKS, *Bart.* LORD OF THE MANOR.

Revd. Dr. NASH, *Rector:*

ATCHMENTS, 1:—Gules a fess wavy between three fleur-de-Lis Or, on the fess a crescent Gules:—HICKES. *impaling* Argent, a fess engrailed Sable gutteé Or, between three Wolves heads erased of the second collared of the third:—HOWE.

Crest:—a Stags head coupt Or, gorged with a Chaplet of Roses Gules.

2.—HICKS, *as before, impaling* Argent, two Bars, Azure, and in Chief three Pelletts.—WATTS.

Crest:—as before.

INSCRIPTIONS IN THE CHURCH.

CHANCEL.

ON A MARBLE MONUMENT.

Arms:—Gules a fess wavy between three fleur-de-Lis Or, on the fess a Crescent Gules.—HICKES, *impaling* Argent, a fess engrailed Sable gutteé Or, between three wolves heads erased of the second collared of the third.—HOWE.

Crest:—a Stags hd. coupt Or, gorged with a Chaplet of Roses Gules.

Near this Place
lies interr'd the Body of
Sir MICHAEL HICKES, *Kt.*
Younger Son of
Sir WILLIAM HICKES, *Baronet,*
of *Beverston Castle* in this County,
who departed this Life,
May 4*th.* in the Year of our
Lord 1710, and the 65*th.*
Year of his Age.
Near whom is reposited the Body of
MICHAEL HICKES, his 3*rd. Son,*
who died an Infant.

See Ag'd experience submits to
Death,
And Infant Innocence resigns its
Breath,
Happy the Soul whose first Essay
of Praise
Is joined in concert with the
Heavenly Layes,
Much happier those whose virtuous
acts engage
A Weight of Glory for a Load of
Age.

Near this Place lyeth
Dame SUSANNA, Relict of
Sir MICHAEL HICKS, *Knt.*
and Daughter of *Sir* RICHARD
HOWE, of the County of
Surrey, Knt.
She died November 1724.
Here also lyeth MICHAEL, the
Son of HOWE HICKS, *Esqr.*
and MARY, his Wife,
He died 6 March 1721,
Aged 9 Months.

ANOTHER MONUMENT.

Arms:—HICKES, *as before.*
impaling. Argent, two Bars Azure,
in Chief three Pelletts.—WATTS.

Near this Place
resteth what was mortal of
HOWE HICKS, *Esqr.* Son of

Sir MICHAEL HICKS,
He died Febr. 12, 1726,
Aged 38 Years.
Here also lie the Remains of
MARY, Relict of HOWE HICKS,
Esqr. and Daughter of
JEFFRY WATTS, *Esqr.*
of the County of *Essex,*
She died Augt. 6, 1728,
Aged 36 Years.
Here also lieth HOWE HICKS,
Son of HOWE HICKS, *Esqr.*
and MARTHA, his Wife, and
Grandson of the above
HOWE HICKS, *Esqr.*
He died Jany. 4, 1744-5, in the
5*th.* Year of his Age.
In Memory of
SUSANNA ELIZABETH HICKS,
Daughter of HOWE HICKS, *Esqs.*
and MARTHA, his Wife,
She died June 17, 1747,
Aged one Year and 23 days.
Here also lyeth MARY HICKS,
Daughter of HOWE HICKS, *Esqr.*
and MARTHA, his Wife,
She died July 30*th.* 1758, in the
15*th.* Year of her Age.

ON FLAT STONES.

Here lyeth MARY WILLIAMS,
Daughter of HOWE HICKS, *Esqr.*
and MARY, his Wife,
She died Febr. 14, 1755,
Aged 35 Years.

Sir MICHAEL HICKS.
MICHAEL HICKS, an Infant.
HOWE HICKS, an Infant.
Here lies HOWE HICKS, Son of
WILLIAM HICKS, *Esqr.*
and JUDITH, his Wife,
He died June 13, 1787, Aged 1.
Here also lieth CHARLES HOWE
HICKS, fourth Son of MICHAEL
HICKS, *Esqr.* and HENRIETTA-
MARIA, his Wife,
He died May 29, 1788,
Aged 8 Weeks.

Dame SUSANNA HICKS,
MICHAEL HICKS, an Infant.

HOWE HICKS, *Esqr.*
and MARY, his Wife.

Here rests the Body of
MARY HICKS, who departed
this Life, 30 day of July 1758,
in the 15 Year of her Age.

Tho few her years, She not untimely
died,
Who richly was with heav'nly Gifts
supplied
Thus GOD decrees—when ripe for
Heav'n the Soul,
Quits her terrestrial house, without
controul
Of Youth, Physicians Care or Par-
ents Love,
T'enjoy her blest Abode prepar'd
above.

Here also rests the Body of
HENRIETTA HOWE HICKS,
Daughter of HOWE HICKS, *Esqr.*
and MARTHA, his Wife,
She departed this Life,
March 16, 1768, in the
16 Year of her Age.

Here lieth the Body of
MICHAEL, Son of *Sir* MICHAEL
HICKS, *Knt.* and SUSANNA,
his Wife, who in innocence of
Childhood, departed this Life,
Jul. iii, MDCLXXXIX.

NAVE.

ON FLAT STONES.

Here lieth the Body of
FRANCIS LIGON, Sonn of
WILLIAM LIGON, of *Marsfield,*
Esquire, who deceased the
12 November, Anno Dni, 1601,
At the Charges of Grace his Wife.

Here resteth the Body of
KATHARINE, who was the Wife of
WILLIAM LIGON, *Gent.*
40 Years,
She fell asleep July 30, 1679,
Aged 71 Years.

Here resteth the Body of
WILLIAN WEBLIN, *Yeoman,*
who died 15 May 1659,
Ætat. suæ 73.

(Additional Inscriptions in Church since Bigland's.)

ON TABLETS.

Sacred to the Memory of
Sir HOWE HICKS, *Baronet.*
Son of Howe HICKS, *Esqr.*
of this Place, who departed this Life,
April 9*th.* A. D. 1801,
Aged 78 Years.
Also of *Lady* HICKS.
Daughter of the *Revd.* J. BROWNE,
Rector of Cubberley.
who departed this Life,
May 4, 1802, Aged 86 Years.

Arms:—Per pale. 1. HICKS,
2. On a fess gules. 3. Chess Rooks
Or. In Chief 3 Martlets.—BROWNE.

Sacred to the Memory of
Sir WILLIAM HICKS, *Baronet.*
of this place Son of the late
Sir HOWE HICKS, *Bart.*
who departed this Life,
on the 23 day of Oct. 1834,
Aged 80 Years.

Also to the Memory of
ANNE RACHEL, Relict of the
above named *Sir* W. HICKS, *Bart.*
And eldest Daughter of
THOMAS LOBB CHUTE,
of the *Vine* in the County of
Southampton, Esqr.
She died on 13 day of April 1839,
Aged 84 Years

Sacred to the Memory of
Sir MICHAEL HICKS HICKS BEACH,
Baronet, M. P. of *Williamstrip Park,*
in this County,
He died on the 22 of Nov. 1858,
Aged 45 Years.

Sacred to the Memory of
WILLIAM HICKS HICKS BEACH,
Esqr. who died on the 7*th.* of
August 1844, Aged 33 Years.
He was the only Brother of
Sir MICHAEL HICKS HICKS BEACH,
Baronet, of Williamstrip Park

in this County, And great Nephew
of *Sir* WILLIAM HICKS, *Bart.*
of *Witcombe Park.*

In Church Yard.

ON RAISED TOMBS.

HEATHER HICKS BEACH,
Born August 22nd. 1870.
Died April 7th. 1880.
"He shall gather the Lambs
in his Arms."

In Memory of
JOB TOMBS,
who died 1868, Aged 75 Years.
With this equivocal Epitaph.

"Praises on TOMBS, is time vainly
spent,
A Man's good name is his best
Monument."

HEAD STONES.

	Died.		Aged.		Died.		Aged.
Elizabeth, Wife of John Holliday, of this Parish, ...	12 Jany.	1742	67	Ann, Wife of Henry Wilson, ...	26 April	1791	70
John Hulbert, *Mason*, ...	8 Nov.	1765	51	Thomas Gregory, ...	13 Oct.	1797	69
Margaret Holliday, ...	7 Nov.	1775	89	Barbara, his Wife, ...	26 Jany.	1797	75
William Hunt, ...	23 Decr.	1787	67	John, their Son, ...	13 Sept.	1759	7
Hannah Hunt, ...	1 Augt.	1790	76	Joseph, their Son, ...	10 Nov.	1779	19
John Rider, ...	23 Jany.	1789	81	Giles Tombs, ...	8 Febr.	1784	78
Jane, his Wife, ...	22 Augt.	1777	71	James Ballinger, ...	22 May	1799	68
Henry, their Son, ...	15 Nov.	1775	31	Ann, his Wife, ...	18 July	1788	57
Mary, Wife of William Freeman,	23 June	1791	60	James, their Son, ...	7 April	1786	21
Thomas, Son of John and Sarah Penson, ...	16 May	1799	26	William Pugh, ...	31 Oct.	1798	85
				Elizabeth, his Wife, ...	1 March	1785	67
				John Hydon, ...	... .	1775	...

Notes as to I.—*Devolution of Estates.* II.—*Church.* III.—*Population, Taxation, &c.*

The parish of Great Witcombe, lies mainly in the wide comb or valley to the south of the Irmin Street, a British and Roman Way, and extends on eastwardly beyond the Birdlip and Brimpsfield Ridge. That way is a distinctive feature of the spot, and the white stone of its surface, was considered by Sir Robt. Atkyns, as explaining the name of the Village as spelt Whitcombe. On the opposite side of the Village was the "Green street" and in Saltcombe the Saltway, both ancient roads; and on this side at a place pleasant for residence and good for out look into the Vale stood a Roman Villa, the Remains of which were accidentally brought to light in 1818. These were described in the Archæologia. Vol. xix, by Mr. Samuel Lysons, and in the Transactions of the Bristol & Gloucestershire, Archæolog'l Society, 1879-80, page 34. Beech Plantations cover the Hills here as they do about Woodchester, a great Roman Station. The Romans understood their use for charcoal burning; which business was carried on here—perhaps in the Romans time and for ages after. At the foot of the woods are meadows through which, completing the rural scene, ran a brook derived from the numerous springs of water issuing from the cliffs and flowing down the valley to Horsebury bridge. But these Waters are now carried by Pipes into the great reservoirs here formed for the Water Supply of Gloucester City.

This Place has the addition of "Great" to its name, to distinguish it from "Little" Witcombe, a hamlet in Badgeworth Parish, but not situate in a comb at all.

I.—*Estates:*—

Before Domesday Survey the Priory of St. Oswald of Gloucester, held Churchdown, of which this Great Witcombe was a member. That Body had mortgaged its possessions to the Archbishop of York, who held at the Survey, though not without challenge by the Archbishop of Canterbury; and the fierce disputes between these Prelates neither Pope nor King could allay.

Under the head of Lands of Thomas the Archbishop, (of York,) is this Entry in Domesday Book:—

Archbishop Stigand, (Canterbury,) held Circesdun, (Churchdown,) 15½ Hides. In demesne, were 2 Carucates, in Villenage, (18 Villans & 5 Bordars with Seven Radchenisters.) 30 Carucates. A Wood half a league long and broad. It had been worth 13£. then 12£. *Domesday Survey.*

Witcombe formed part of the Archbishop of York's Barony of Churchdown. *Harl. MSS.* 438.

Under the Act 37 Hen. viii. cap. 16. an exchange was effected by the Archbishop and King Henry viii.

Sir T. Chamberlayne, took Churchdown and its members by Crown Grant, and held in 1608. In a Copy of Court Roll, of the Manor of Churchdown, Lands in Witcombe, were granted to Ridler, otherwise Gregory, for three lives the grantee, his wife during chaste viduity, and his son. The name Gregory remained long here.

1612.—Sir John Chamberlaine, mortgaged the Manor Mansion, and Estate of Witcombe to Dame Elizabeth Hickes, of Ruckholt, Essex, widow of Sir Michael Hickes, Secretary to Lord Burleigh, for securing £2,200. Dame Elizabeth Hickes, obtained a decree of foreclosure; and in 1616, Sir J. Chamberlaine, and his trustees conveyed the Witcombe Estate to her absolutely. In this latter deed is a grant of bond men and bond women with their "sequels." a rare instance at so late a date of reference to villans regardant, in a conveyance of Lands, but probably inserted merely from an old Precedent. This Lady's Name of birth was Colston. She died in 1634. William, her eldest son by Sir Michael, was made a Baronet, 1619. He married a daughter of Lord Paget, and died in 1680, leaving 2 sons, William and Michael. Sir William, the eldest son resided in Essex. Michael, the 2nd. son, married a Daughter of Sir Richard Howe, of Surrey, (*Church Inscr.*) and appears to have pos-

sessed Witcombe. He had a son Howe, who levied a Fine 6 Geo. i. 1708, and made a settlement of this Manor and Estate. He married Mary Watts, of an Essex family, and died in 1728. He had a son, afterwards Sir Howe Hicks, Bt.
Church Inscriptions.

1798.—Land Tax £ 46, 6s. was redeemed by Sir Howe Hicks, the Estate on this occasion was generally described thus :—

Manor of Witcombe, the Park, 100 a. Arable 41 a. Wood 160 a. Three farms 100 a., 213 a. 46 a., Several Closes of pasture, the Black Horse Inn.

To Sir Howe Hicks, succeeded his eldest son Sir William; and to him his only Child Lady Cromie, the present possessor.

Subsequently acquired were—

Witcombe farm :
This Estate was in the hands of the family of Hellow for many generations.
On a large Oak Table which is at Witcombe Park, are the Letters R. H. 1619.
Over the stone Chimney piece of the Sitting Room, the same Letters R. H. 1665. On the West end of the House the Line Memor esto brevis ævi R. H. 1619.
Over the Front door "Love the truth, Sin God doth hate ; And be content, with thine Estate.
It is probable that this Estate was acquired with the Advowson.

Capels farm :—this belonged to the Machyn fam'ly a name met with in the Subsidy Roll, 1 Edw. iii. In 1659, it was the property of Alderman W. Caple, of Gloucester, and with other Estates settled by him in the Way of Jointure on his son's Wife Margaret Clutterbuck, with it went the Whitehorse Inn, at Horeebury Bridge and a Messuage purchased by Capel, of William Stonehouse, Esqr.

The farm was purchased by Sir W. Hicks' Trustees. The Inn also came after intermediate Ownership to them. Also the Lands of Gregory and Nash and others in like manner so that the Manor and these Estates with the Rectory Land and Reservoir sites of the Corporation of Gloucester, comprize the Parish.

II.— *Church.*

Kips Picture in Atkyns' Gloucestershire, shews a Wooden Turrett to the Church. In 1749, the Tower was rebuilt in stone.
The Living is a discharged Rectory, Rated at £4 6s. 0d. in the Kings Books.
By the Apportionment under the Tythe Commutation Act £132 5s. 9d. is awarded to the Rector in lieu of Tythes.
The Priory of St. Oswalds, Gloucester, had a Portion of 13s. 4d. out of the Rectory. *Pope Nich. Tas.*
4 Edw. i.—Hayles Abbey, had a portion.
Gt. Witcombe Register dates back to 1575, It records that Margaret Giles, Gentlewoman, was buried 1595; John Machin, in 1596 ; William and John, sons of Francis Ligon, Gent. 1598-9 ; and others of that family to 1680 ; John Escombe, Gent. 1723.

1654.—Nathl. Winter, of Cirencester and Elizabeth Hone, of Gt. Witcombe, were married before Edmund Collett, J. P. Mayor of Gloucester, according to Act of Parliament.

1713.—Jonathan Castleman, marr. Susan, Lady Hicks. 1724, She died.

1766.—John Pettat, of Stonehouse, Clerk. married Martha Hicks.

List of Incumbents and Patrons of Witcombe.

Incumbents.	Patrons.
1575.—John Lloyd.	R. Hands.
1638.—Thomas Lloyd.	Wm. Ero, D.D.
1669.—H. Hill.	R. Payn, Senr.
1678.—John Clark.	Chas. Hellow, of London, Gent.
1681.—John Abbott.	R. Fielding, M. D.
1734.—John Browne.	Howe Hicks, *a Minor* by B. Hyett and John Browne, his Guardians.
1737.—Thomas Thache.	Howe Hicks.
1769.—Thomas Nash.	Do. do.
1826.—T. G. H. Freston.	Sir W. Hicks.
T. M. Browne.	Trustees of Sir W. Hicks.
1839.—C. R. Pettat.	Do. do.
1845.—J. R. Trye.	Do. do.

Charity Gifts :—
1607.—5 £. Thomas Hellow.
1616.—5 £. Isabell Bubb.
1630.—1 £. Thomas Nelmes.
    1 £. Richard Sparkes.
    8 £. William Mills.
    20 £. Giles Cox, Interest for 2nd. poor not Paupers or Beggars.

III.— *Taxation, Population, &c.*

Magna Whytecombe, Subsidy Roll, 1 Edw. iii. 1327.
De Johne de Whytecombe, xii d. ob.
' Johe. Sely, x d.
' Rico. de Salcombe, xiiii d.
' Henr. Lyne, xx d. ob.
' Galfrido Mogge, xii d. ob. q.
' Gilbto. Keys, xvi d.
' Henr. Alfrid, xii d. ob.
' Johne Gernun, xv d. ob. q.
' Thom. Strene, vi d.
' Willmo. Machyn, xiiii d.
' Willmo. Keys, xviiid. q.
    prob. Sma. xii s. viii d. q.

Birdlip is a Roadside Village on the Table land, In the accounts in the 1st. Volume of Brimpsfield and Cowley Parishes, it is stated that so much of Birdlip, as lies on the North side of the Great Roman Road is in Cowley, and the part on the South side is in Brimpsfield Parish. On the high road towards Painswick, branching from the above, the East side is also in Brimpsfield Parish and the West in the Parish of Witcombs. On that side the Blackhorse Inn, is situate.

The Roman Road up the ascent was in so very bad condition in Sir R. Atkyns' time that it was made turnpike in order that it should be maintained by tolls. But the Act was allowed to expire.

By an order of the Court of Quarter Sessions, Michaelmas 1719; three Justices, (Cocks, Crawley and Lye.) were deputed to enquire into the liability to repair the Gloucester and Cirencester Road from the Upping stone, at the foot of Birdlipp Hill to Horseperry bridge. The committee examined witnesses and reported 19th. Oct. 1719, that for three score years last past, except for a few years when the highway was repaired out of the profits of the late turnpike, Badgworth, and Witcomb Magna, had jointly stoned it, load for load of stone in the said part of the high way, and those parishes ought to do the repairs jointly and in equal shares.

But the Road from Gloucester to Cirencester, was again made turnpike, and so continued until the abandoment of the Turnpike system.

Estates:—Under Cowley, *Rudder*, notices that Richard de Bradelep, gave 2 a. of Land in Cowley, for the Brethren of Saint Bartholomew in Gloucester, and in the Subsidy Roll, 1 Edw. iii. among the Payers in Little Whitcomb, a William de Briddelep, is named.

Whether the house of this family was on the Hill, or in the Vale may be doubted. In Sir R. Atkyns, time there were 9 Houses in Birdlip. The Hill Houses were chiefly Inns for the rest and resort of travellers and their Beasts.

No Notes are at hand of the devolution of Estates here except as part of the Farms. But at the County Election 1776, two Freeholders of Brimpsfield resident at Birdlip, voted namely Pitt and Welsh. For Cowley there was no freeholder the Land there being Church Leasehold.

A Company of Volunteer Infantry was formed in the Year 1798, under the command of Wm Hicks, Esqr. afterwards Sir W. Hicks, They are said by a contemporary topographer (Ruff) to have acquitted themselves with credit as regards their duty and discipline. But after the treaty of Amiens they were disembodied, receiving the thanks of the King, George iii.

Acreage 806 a.

Population 1801,—119. 1861,—165.
    1831.—174. 1871,—181.

In 1815. Annual Value of Real Property 954 £.
1882.—Rateable Value £ 1549.
1833-4-5. Average of three Years Expenditure on Poor £ 66.

In Cheltenham Union.

WITHINGTON.

THE CHURCH is dedicated to St. Michael, in the deanery of Winchcombe, is built in the form of a Cross, in the middle a Tower adorned with pinnacles and battlements and furnished with six Musical Bells, there is a small South Transept or Chapel belonging to the Compton estate, which is the burying place of *Lord* CHEDWORTH's family. [There was a Gallery, taken away at the restoration of the Church, 1872.]

Bishop of WORCESTER, LORD OF THE MANOR AND PATRON.

Revd. BENJAMIN GRISDALE, *Rector.*

ATCHMENTS.

1.—Or, a fess between three Wolves' heads couped Sable a Crescent, *for diff.*—HOWE.

2.—HOWE, *as before.*

Crest:—On a Wreath a dexter Arm in armour, erased below the elbow, lying fessways, holding in the hand a Scymeter erect proper, hilted and pomelled Or, pierced through a boar's head coupt Sable. Supporters—Dexter a Lion, Argent, pelleted armed and langued, Gules, Sinister an Angel proper, the face in profile, with brown hair, habited crimson the under garment Azure, Wings Argent.

Motto:—"Justus et propositi tenax." *This is set up for Lord* CHEDWORTH.

3.—Argent, on a Bend Sable three Cinque foils Or, on a Chief of ths second a Lion passant of the first. .... *impaling* Argent, a Chevron between three Apples Gules.

Crest:—Out of a ducal Coronet Or, a demi Lion Argent, holding a fleur de Lis, of the first. *There are also two bannerols with the Arms of* HOWE.

4.—Argent, on a fess Azure three Lozenges Or.—FIELDING, *impaling* Sable three Estoiles Argent, with a Crescent for difference within a bordure engrailed Or. [*These Atchments are taken away.*]

A TABLE OF BENEFACTIONS.

WILLIAM OSBERNE, D. D. Rector of this Parish, gave 100 £. for the apprenticing poor Children

JOHN RICH, *Esqr.* gave 100 £. for Apprenticing poor Children.

ROBERT FIELDING, M. D. gave 20 £. to the Parish for Charitable uses.

JOHN GILMAN, Rector of this Parish gave 20 £. for Charitable uses.

Lady HOWE, Relict of *Sir* RICHARD HOWE, *Bar't.* gave a service of Gilt Plate, for the Communion Table.

CHARLES FIELDING, *Gent.* gave 20 £. to this Parish for Charitable uses.

JOHN HAYWARD, Rector of this Parish hath vested One Hundred pounds Old S. S. Annuities in the names of Certain Trustees the Interest thereof to be yearly distributed at the Church Porch to the Poor in Bread, one half on the 15 day of March and to be called the *Carswell Bread*, and the other half on the 15*th.* day of September and to be called the *Guiting Bread*, in memory of his two most excellent Wives B. SOUTHBY, of *Carswell, in Berkshire*, and ANNE HAYWARD, of *Temple Guiting*, in this County.

[*Additional:*—JOHN SMITH, *Esqr.* late of *Owdswell*, gave 100 £. the Interest to be distributed in Coats to the Poor. 1847.—*Mrs.* ROGERS, of *Foxcote*, gave 200 £. to this Parish, for charitable Uses.]

INSCRIPTIONS IN THE CHURCH.

CHANCEL.

ON MONUMENTS.

Arms:—*Quarterly.* Azure and Ermin, a Cross engrailed Or.—OSBERNE, *impaling the same.*

Memoriæ sacrvm
viri reverendi GILBERTI OSBERNE,
S. S. T. B. Præbendarij Ecclesiæ
Cathedralis *Gloucest.*
Nec non Rectoris de *Withington,*
Qui cum in Temporibus plus quam
difficillimis,
Egregi m Charitatis exemplar grandeq.
Fidei specimen edidisset et in omnibus
Vitam ....
egisset.
In Beatorum consortiu lubens secessit.
ANNA (*Dni* RICHARDI OSBERNE,
Baronetti, de *Knockmon Hiberniæ,* filia
mœstissima Relicta
Amoris in defunctum conjugem,
et Mœstitiæ pignus
Hoc lacrymis humidum erexit marmor.
Obijt Febr. 16, Ætat suæ 56,
salut 1656,
E...................

ON A SMALL TABLET BELOW.

Disce ab hoc uno esse mori beatum

Vita cujus Mors erat, et sepultus
Prædicat, vivens moriens vocetur
Jure sacerdos.
Norma vivebat pietatis ; hoc stet
Marmor ut possint homines futuri
Scire, verum hic pessima sæclá ferre
Ecclesiasten.

Arms:—OSBERNE, *as before.*

Si hóes tacuerint, lapis hic clamabit
vitam
Mortemq. perinde imitanda viri
clarissimi
GULIELMI OSBERN,
Qui antiquâ prosapiâ ortus ; Literis
Humaniorib. imbutus, in academiam
Oxoniensem,
Ascitus, in socium Omn : An. creatus;
S. Theologiæ
Doctoratu insignitus, in Canonicum
Residentiar.
Ecclesiæ Sarisburiensis ascriptus; in
Rectorem
Hujus Ecclesiæ electus; cujus curâ
fideliter
Obeundâ, Seniô tandem confectus;
annos plus
Minus Octoginta natus ; denatus est
1o. Aprilis
Anno Dni. 1646.

ON A BRASS PLATE AGAINST THE WALL.

Vita Christ. mori Lucrum.

Vbi sistis jacet SYBILLA, uxor
ROBT. KNOLLIS, *Gen.*
Artisq. mag.
Stirpe pat. ex generoso Owenorum
Monæ insulæ Nat. ex
Antiq. nobilissaq. Barckleyorum
Fam. orta cujus pietatem
prudàm cas. Fidemq. conjugalem
hocæs poster, cumen.
dat imitandas 1614, Sept. 25,
mortem. cu. vitâ commutavit
Lect. Pio.
Es. qd. cra. qd. sum fueris, tu scripta
legendo
Sis memor ipse me. sis memor ipse tui.

ON FLAT STONES.

[*The Flat stones are removed outside and most of them placed erect against the south Wall.*]

Here lyeth the Body of
EDWARD, the Sonne of GILBERT
OSBERN, hee died April 25, 1657.

WITHINGTON.

J. Ravenhill del J. Smith

Arms:—OSBERN, *as before, impaling the same.*

G. O.
Here lyeth the Body of
GILBERT OSBERN,
who departed Febr. ye 16, 1656.

Here lyeth the Body of
ELIZABETH, the Wife of the
Right Reverend Father in God
JOHN THORNBURGH,
Lord Bishop of *Worcester,*
who died Primo Maij,
An. Dom. 1627.

Here lyeth the Body of
GRACE, the Daughter of
GILBERT OSBERN.
Shee died July 25, 1665.

Arms:—Argent, on a fess Azure
three Lozenges Or.—FIELDING,
impaling .... a Cross raguly.
Crest:—a palm Tree proper
charged with a Lozenge Or.

M. S.
ROBERTI FIELDING,
M. D. Et Col. Med. Lond. Soc.
Ob. Maij XXII, A. D. MDCCIX,
Æt. LXXXVII.
Arma portabat patriæ Saluti
Hunc Salus trivit patriæ togatum
Et piis ar.i is inimica fata
Arte premebat
Res tamen fluxæ haud tenuere totum
nam suæ morbis animæ vacavit
Vita cum cedat medicusq. quod
dat EUTHANASIAN.

Arms:—FIELDING, *as before,* with
a Crescent for differnce, *impaling*
.... a Chevron between three
Etoiles.
Crest:—FIELDING, *as before.*

Here lyeth ye Body of
CHARLES FIELDING,
of the *Inner Temple, London,*
Gent. youngest Son of
ROBERT FIELDING, M. D.
who died the 15 of Decemb. 1737,
in the 63 Year of his Age.

Here lye the Bodies of WILLIAM
and LUCY, the Son and Daughter
of GEOFREY WALL and DOROTHEA,
his Wife.
WILLIAM, departed this Life,
August the 25, 1687, and
LUCY, Jany. the 29, 1697.

JOHN, the Son of JEFFREY WALL,
Clerk, by DOROTHY, his Wife,
died July the 10, 1686,
Aged 5 Weeks and 3 Dads.

Hic Lapis tegit exuvias Annæ
JOHANNES GILMANNI,
(hujus Ecclesiæ Rectoris,)
Per annos 54, Uxoris Piæ Castæ,

Charæ, Beatam Resurrectionem,
Obijt 4 die Maij,
Anno Incarnat I. C. 1711,
Ætat. 77.

Hic jacet
Defunctus vitæ Curis atq officiis,
JOHANNES GILMAN, M. A.
Vir multa Virtute venerandus
Benevolentissimus Amicus
Sanctissimus Parens
Conjux .... fidelissimus
Gregis commissi Pastor vigilantissimus
Sine superbia doctus sine simula-
tione pius,
Collegij Ænei Nasi apud Oxonienses
quondam
Socius,
Rector hujus 'arochiæ constitutus
est iis Temporibus
Cum neque Regem Britannia nec
Ecclesiam haberet
Fuit-tamen per omnes Temporum
Vices ....
Et Regum fidelis subditus
Et Optimæ matris observantissimus
Filius
Condit hoc saxum,
Quicquid filius potuit mori
Tum denuo in Vitam renovandum,
Quum dux salutis æternæ
Strenue Militiæ functum
Coronâ Gloriæ triumpham decorabit
Obijt 18 die Maij,
Anno Chr. 1716, Ætat 83tio.

NAVE.

ON FLAT STONES.

[*Now removed against the Wall outside.*]

In Memory of
ELIZABETH, that was the Wife of
WILLIAM LOOKER,
who left this mortal Life, the
15 day of Febr. 1707,
Aged 83 Years.
In Memory of
WILLIAM LOOKER, *Gent*
who left this Mortal Life, the
20 day of January 1720-1,
Aged 88 Years.

Here lyeth interred the Body of
ELIZABETH, the Wife of
RICHARD EYCOTT, of *Cirencester
Mercer,* (and Niece of MARY
WILKINSON, of this Parish, *Widdow,*)
who departed this Life,
the third day of June 1721,
O. S. ob. June 7, 1789,
Æt. 71.

Here lyeth the Body of
GILES POWELL, *Gent*
who departed this Life,
May the 30, Anno Dom. 1746,
Ætatis suæ 56.
Here lyeth the Body of
ELIZABETH, the Wife of
GILES POWELL, *Gent.*
who departed this Life,
January 20, 1774, Aged 81 Years.

Here lieth the Body of
MARY, the Wife of JOHN RANDALL,
and MARY, his Daughter,

MARY, his Wife, departed this Life,
the 31 day of Decr. 1700.
MARY, his Daughter,
died one day after.
JOHN RANDELL,
died the 8*th.* day of July,
Anno Dom. 1710, Æt. 32.

Here lyeth the Body of
JOSEPH LONGFORD, of this Parish,
Yeoman, who on the 23 day of
Febr. 1699, in the 63 Year of
his Age, left this mortal Life, in
hope of a glorious Resurrection-

Here resteth the Body of
SIMON LONGFORD, *ye Younger,*
Son of NICHOLAS LONGFORD, and
YIDDETH LONGFORD,
who departed this Life, the
16*th.* day of April, An. Do. 1695,
Aged 53 Years.
SAMUEL LONGFORD,
Obijt 27o. February, An. Dni. 1710,
Ætat. 70.

Here Resteth the Body of
NICHOLAS LONGFORD, of *Foxcot,*
who departed this Life, the
4 day of April, Anno Dni. 1648.
Here also Resteth the Body of
EDITH LONGFORD, his Relict,
who departed this Life, the
18*th.* day of December 1648.
SAMUEL LONGFORD, *Gent.*
ob. 10o. Ap. 1712, Ætat. 28.

IN A SMALL ISLE ON THE SOUTH
SIDE IS A HANDSOME MARBLE
MONUMENT.

[*Removed and reerected in the Nave.*]

Arms:—Or. a fess between three
Wolves heads coupt Sable.--HOWE.
im aling per pale Azure and Gules
a Cross bottoné fitché between four
fleurs de Lis, Or.—RICH.

BRIDGETT, one of the Daughters of
THOMAS RICH, of *North Cerney,*
in this Co of *Gloucester, Esqr.* one
of the *Masters* of the Highe Courte
of Chancery and ANNE, his Wife
one of the Daughters and Coheirs
THOMAS BOURCHIER, of *Barnesly,*
in said County, *Esqr.* the 23rd. of
July 1620, was married to JOHN
HOWE, of *Little Compton,* in this
Parish, *Esqr.* Nephewe and Heire
of *Sir* RICHARD GROBHAM, of
Great Wishford, in ye County of
Wilts. Knt. deceased. With whome
She lived a vertuous and loving
Wife, 21 Years and a XI Months.,
and had Issue 9 Children, (*viz.*)—
First RICHARD GROBHAM HOWE,
born the 28*th.* of August 1621,
who married LUCIE, one of the
Daughters of Sir JOHN ST. JOHN,
of *Lyddiard Tregoze,* in the said
County of *Wilts. Knt. and Bart.*
2ndly.—JOHN GROBHAM HOWE,
born ye 25 of Jauuary 1624, who
married ANNABELLA, one of ye
Daughters and Coheirs of EM-
ANUEL, late *Earl* of SUNDERLAND,
3rdly. December. ye 4, 1626,
SUSANNA, was borne, who married
JOHN ERNLE, of *Berry Towne* in
the said County of *Wilts. Esqr.*

4thly. the third day of March 1629, THOMAS GROBHAM HOWE, was born.
5thly. the 13 day of June 1630, WILLIAM HOWE, was born, Slain at Limbrick in the Kingdom of Ireland.
6thly. the 4th. of March 1632, ANNA HOWE, was born, who died very younge and lyeth heere buryed.
7thly the 21 day of December 1633, ELIAABETH HOWE, was borne now the Wife of THOMAS CHESTER, of Aunsbury in this County, Esqr.
8thly. the 22 of October 1635, GEORGE HOWE, was borne, who dyed younge and lyeth buried at Wishford, in ye Vault. 9thly. the 27 of November 1637, CHARLES HOWE, was borne.

And on the 15 day of June 1642, Annoquæ Ætatis 46, left them to the protection of the Almighty and her owne Mortality to this Earth expecting a joyfull Resurrection.

CHURCH YARD.

On Altar Tombs.

In Memory of
MARY, Wife of JAMES LAWRENCE, of this Parish, Yeoman, who died Oct. 29, 1726.
In Memory of
JAMES LAWRENCE,
who died May 4, 1735, Aged 55.

Here resteth the Body of EDMUND LAWRANCE, the Sonne of EDMUND LAWRANCE, who deceased this Life, the 3rd. day of February 1655.

Here resteth in hope of a glorious Resurrection the Body of ANTHONY ROGERS, of this Parish, who departed this Life, Nov. 30, A. D. 1742, in the 80 Year of his Age.
Also in Memory of ANNE, his Wife, who departed this Life, Aug. 15, 1750, Aged 81.
In Memory of
ELIZABETH ROGERS, who died Jany. 28, 1753, Aged 18 Years.

Here resteth in hope of a Glorious Resurrection the Body of EDMUND LAWRENCE, who departed this Life, Oct. 21, 1758, Aged 82.
Here resteth the Body of the Wife of EDMUND LAWRENCE, who departed this Life, July 27, 1761, Aged 71 Years.
Here lyeth the Body of GILES LAWRENCE, who deceased the 17 of November 1658.

In Memory of
THOMAS BURROWS, who died July 13, 1768, Aged 75 Years.
In Memory of
CATHERINE, Wife of THOMAS BURROWS, who died July 28 1767, Aged 58 Years.

MARY, Daughte. of JOHN and CHRISTIAN LAWRENCE, of Witcomb, in this County, 21 Decr. 1762, Aged 4 Years.

In Memory of
RICHARD SAVERY, of this Parish, Yeoman, who departed this Life, 7 June 1738, Aged 65 Years.
ANNE, Wife of RICHARD SAVERY, who died Sept. 4, 1754, Aged 74.

In Memory of
THOMAS JACOB, Yeoman, of this Parish, who departed this Life, the 12 July 1730, Aged 69 Years.
In Memory of
JOSHUA, Son of THOMAS JACOB, who died Febr. 10, 1731, Aged 81 Years.
Also SUSANNA, Wife of JOHN YOUNG, Junr died Oct. 30, 1779, Aged 76 Yeras.

Here lieth the Body of SIMON YOUNG, Yeoman, who departed his Life, June 27, 1772, Aged 65 Years.

Here lyeth the Bodie of ROBERT WHITTERNE, Senr. who deceased the 8 day of June, 1667.
Here lieth the Body of ROBERT WHITTERNE, Junr. who was buried the 2nd. day of October 1712, Aged 72 Years.

In Memory of
EDMUND LAWRENCE, and CATHARINE, his first Wife, He was buried the 16 day of August 1711, and CATHARINE, his Wife was buried 22 Nov. 1696.
And also CATHARINE, their Daughter who was buried near this place the 9 of November 1697.
In Memory of
JOAN LAWRANCE, who died Nov. 20, 1734, Aged 74 Years.

To the Memory of
HENRIETTA-MARIA, Relict of GREGORY RUSSELL, who died Jany. 22, 1786, Aged 80 Years.
Here resteth in hope of a Joyfull Resurrection the Body of SARAH, Wife of JOHN RUSSELL, who died June 10, 1781, Aged 40 Years.

Here lieth interred the Body of JOHN WOOLLEY, Gent. who departed ys. Life, March 10, 1695.
And also ELIZABETH, the Relict of the said JOHN WOOLLEY, who died July 21, 1726, Aged 67 Years.

JOHN, the Son of JOHN WOOLLEY, Gent. died 30 July 1762, Aged 63 Years.
JOHN WOOLLEY, Gent. died 2 Febr. 1749, Aged 73 Years.
Also BARBARA, Relict of THOMAS WOOLLEY, Gent. who departed this Life, March 7, 1684.

In Memory of
RICHARD SAVORY, who departed this Life, Decr. 18, 1788, Aged 54 Years.
Also of ARABELLA, his Daughter, by ELIZABETH, his Wife, who died August 31, 1789, in the Seventeenth Year of her Age.
Here lie the Remains of all that is mortal of ELIZABETH, Wife of RICHARD SAVORY, who went to a better Life, the 15 of September 1780, in the 43 Year of her Age.

To the Memory of
THOMAS COLLETT, who having for many Years Faithfully discharged the Office of Steward for several respectable Gentlemen, departed this Life, Augt. 14, 1783, Aged 49 Years.
Also ANNE, his Wife, who died May 7, 1786, Aged 58 Years.

On Flat Stones.

To the Memory of
ROBERT MASON, who departed this Life, March the 30, 1796, Aged 73 Years.

Underneath lie the Remains of ROBERT WILSON and MARGARET, his Wife, She died ...... 29, 1760, Aged 40 Years.
He died Jany. 25, 179... Aged 81 Years.
Also JOSEPH, Son of the above, died May 20, 1762, Aged 24 Years.

(Additional since Bigland's time In the Church.)

Near this place lieth the Body of the Revd. BENJAMIN GRISDALE, A. M. 37 Years Rector of this Parish, and Vicar of Chedworth, He died June 18th. 1828, Aged 84 Years.
Also of ELIZABETH, his Wife, who died Jany. 15th. 1830, Aged 61 Years.
Yea though I walk through the Valley, of the shadow of death I will fear no evil. for thy Rod, and thy staff they comfort me.

In Memory of
CAROLINE SARAH, Daughter of the Honble. GEORGE GUSTAVUS CHETWYND TALBOT, Rector of

this Parish, and of EMILY SARAH, his Wife, Born 28th. Jany. 1847, and died 11th. 1850. "Suffer little children to come unto me and forbid them not for of such is the Kingdom of Heaven."

MEMORIAL IN EAST WINDOW.

To the glory of God and affectionate remembrance of EMILY SARAH, Wife of the *Honble.* GEORGE GUSTAVUS CHETWYND TALBOT, *Rector* of this Parish, b. July 28, 1815, d. Nov. 31, 1876, Also of CAROLINE SARAH, born Jany. 28th 1847, died April 11th. 1850, and EMMA FRANCIS, born Sept. 14, 1852, died Dec. 31, 1875, then Daughters.

Stones now put out side the Church.

Here lie the Remains of THOMAS LOOKER, (*Yeoman.*) who died Nov. ye 1st. 1785, Aged 52 Years.

GILES ROGERS, *Gent.* died 1813. MARY ROGERS, *Widow,* who died 1847.

Here resteth the Body of THOMAS MUSTO, who departed this Life, Augt. 29th. 1684.

In Memory of JOHN EYCOTT, *Gent.* whose Remains are deposited near this place, he died June 7th 1789, Aged 71 Years.

In Memory of *Mr.* W. DAVIS, late of *Marsdon* in the Parish of *Rendcombe,* Son of HALISON and MARTHA DAVIES, of *Cranham,* who died 31 Decr. 1814, Aged 70 Years,

His remains are interred acording to his own request in the Church Yard of this Parish.

In a Vault near this spot are deposited the remains of JOHN JONES, of *Withington House,* who died August 20th. 1834, Aged 79 Years. Also of MARY, his beloved Wife, who died Decr. 30, 1830, in the 70 Year of her Age. This tablet is erected by their Children as a public testimony of their respect and affection to the Memory of Parents who having as it is hoped fallen asleep in Jesus, will be numbered among the faithful the day of his reappearance.

At the West End out side on a flat stone.

Underneath lye the Remains of ROBERT, son of ROBERT BAYLIS, and MARY, his Wife, He died Aug. 10, 1840, Aged 34 Years.

[*Outside the Church near the South Wall of the Chancel is a recumbent figure with a Dog at the foot. This was brought from the Shrubbery at the Rectory.*]

HEAD STONES.

	Died.		Aged.		Died.		Aged.
Joseph Burrows, ...	11 March	1717	68	Thomas, Son of Michael and Mary Ballinger, ...	8 May	1784	19
Mary Burrows, ...	23 March	1735	48	Mary, Wife of Joseph Horlick,*	4 Jany.	1791	36
William Burrows, ...	10 April	1749	64	Henry Wilson, ...	8 Decr.	1783	55
Joseph Burrows, ...	30 Oct.	1766	76	Joseph Wilson, ...	8 July	1757	76
Thomas Burrows, ...	2 April	1759	48	Anna, his Wife, ...	10 June	1757	76
Judith, Wife of John Burrows,	1 Jany.	1745	69	Mary, Wife of Jacob Davis, ...	10 Oct.	1745	26
John Burows, of this Parish,	28 Decr.	1743	70	Jacob Davis, ...	25 May	1790	76
Richard Burrows, ...	16 Nov.	1769	81	Martha, his Wife, ...	15 Sept.	1799	71
Margaret, his Wife, ...	9 Decr.	1782	81	Maria, Wife of Joseph Midwinter,	17 April	1798	19
William Burrows, ...	22 Sept.	1791	57	Thomas Looker, ...	24 April	1781	51
John Young, of this Parish, Yeoman	12 Jany.	1754	77	Robert Shill, ...	4 June	1785	83
Eleanor, Wife of John Young, ...	3 Jany.	1756	80	Elizcbeth, his Wife, ...	14 Febr.	1775	84
John Young, of this Parish, Yeoman, ...	12 Jany.	1753	77	John Hooper, ...	23 Augt.	1780	63
Bernard Bellinger, ...	8 Jany.	1773	83	Elizabeth, his Wife,...	19 Augt.	1775	47
Margt. Wife of Bernard Ballinger	8 May	1762	70	Ann, Wife of John Fern, ...	21 July	1789	40
William Brassington, ...	16 Nov.	1764	76	William Faulks, ...	31 August	1754	62
Mary, Wife of WilliamBrassington	7 Decr.	1755	72	Ann, his Wife, ...	15 Sept.	1786	65
Elizabeth, Daughter of William and Mary Brassington, ...	15 March	1754	33	Elizabeth, Wife of John Jonas,	22 Sept.	1792	76
Thomas, Son of John and Susanna Young, ...	26 Jany.	1755	31	John, Son of John and Rebecca Faulks, ...	31 July	1786	24
Edmund Lawrance, ...	9 May	1713	79	Ann, their Daughter, ...	22 May	1784	30
Thomas Bateman, of this Parish,	17 Febr.	1737	25	John Field, ...	4 May	1792	47
Gregory Russell, ...	6 Sept.	1755	63	William Dickenson, ...	1 Augt.	1790	66
William Goodrich, ...	28 Oct.	1729	18	Rachel, his Wife, ...	27 May	1789	65
William Goodrich, ...	13 Jany.	1759	80	Joseph Sherwood, ...	25 May	1776	75
Margaret, Wife of Wm. Goodrich.	22 Nov.	1710	39	Ann, his Wife, ...	19 Jany.	1784	78
Ann Walker, ...	5 Sept.	1798	31	William, their Son, ...	30 Augt.	1773	29
Mary, Wife of Joseph Turner,	19 Febr.	1793	70	Anthony Holland, ...	1 Nov.	1781	74
William Wiltson, ...	8 Nov.	1784	50	Dorothy, his Wife, ...	18 Nov.	1791	72
John Bishop, ...	3 Sept.	1791	41	William Jones, ...	26 Augt.	1772	53
Martha, Wife of John Blake, ...	3 April	1772	48	Richard Jones, ...	12 Febr.	1793	70
Thomas Bubb, ...	27 April	1782	78	Gilbert Jones, ...	19 Jany.	1790	67
John Cook, ...	9 April	1789	80	Elizabeth Harding, ...	26 Sept.	1783	13
Elizabeth, Wife of Thomas Bubb,	9 Oct.	1783	84	Samuel Hoins, ...	5 May	1750	25
Jane, Wife of Robert Sly, ...	14 June	1729	50	Richard Hathaway, ...	16 March	1777	59
Bartley Wilson, ...	21 Jany.	1793	57	Mary, his Wife, ...	1 Sept.	1785	66
Ann, Wife of John Collett, ...	26 April	1777	61	Thomas Collett, ...	12 Novr.	1761	72
Charles Bellinger, ...	2 Nov.	1781	63	Sarah, his Wife, ...	27 May	1772	83
John Clarke, ...	23 Sept.	1790	47	Edward Humpheris, ...	24 April	1743	38
				Edmund, Son of Edmund and Ann Humpheris	28 June	1770	35

* With this *Epitaph:*—In One thousand seven hundred and ninety one, I was delivered of a son, After which my time was short, Before from Life, I did depart, A Husband young I left behind, For him another Wife to find, As good as I, He'd ask no more, Before his fleeting Life is o'er.

WITHINGTON PARSONAGE, BUILT BY THE REVEREND
JOHN HAYWARD, NEAR SIXTY YEARS RECTOR,

To Thomas Hayward Esq.r the Plate is inscribed by his Obliged and Obedient Servant R. Bigland.

1500

Supplementary Notes as to I. *Devolution of Estates.* II. *Church.* III. *Population, Taxation, &c.*

Estates :—

Withington is an extensive Parish, stretching from the brow of the Hill of Ravensgate and Rossley, near Cheltenham Hundred to Compton Park, near Northleach, and across from the Valley of the Coln, to the near side of that of the Churn stream. It comprises the Hamlets, tythings or places of Owdswell, Foxcote, Cassey Compton, Bruern or Little Colesborn, and part of Pegglesworth. Rossley, once a Hamlet has lately been annexed to Dowdeswell.

The summits of the Hills shew traces of British Occupation, and near the Village, and at Foxcote are Roman Remains. Those near the Village were of a Roman Villa and are described in the 18th Volume of Archæologia. p. 118.

The Subsidy Roll of 1 Edw. iii. in the List of Subsidy Payers records in their Names the following Places of abode: Foxcote, Upcote, Huldcot, (Hilcot) Thornden, Attwell, Attbridge.

Widendune in Wacrescombe Hundred, contained 30 Hides, of which 3 never paid tax. The Church of Worcester, held. Culture, two carucates in Demesne and 7 in Villenage. (16 Villans. 8 Bordars.) Six Serfs. 10 a. of Meadow. A Wood one mile long and half a mile broad.

Conton, (Compton.) 1 Carucate, and in Villenage another (2 Villans. 2 Bordars.) 2 Serfs a Mill of 5s.

In the same Manors 4 Radchenisters had 2 Hides and 2 Yard Lands. In Culture, two Carucates. A Priest had half a Hide and 1 Carucate. In Gloucester Town, 4 Burgesses paid 7½ d. In Fuscote, (Foxcote.) Morinus, held 3 Hides of the Land of W. Manor. In Colesborne and Willcote, (Hilcot?) Anschitel, held 2 Hides. In Dowdeswell and Pecleford, (Pegglcworth) 4½ Hides. In Nate, rave, (Notgrove) Schelin, held 5 Hides. And in Aston. Brogo, held 10 Hides.

Domesday Survey.

15 Edw. i.—The Bishops Right to Court Leet and Warren in Withington admitted. *Quo Warranto*

The Bishop of Worcester, held at Wythendon, in Yearly Revenue of Rents Assize 8 £. 2 Carucates worth 1 £. each Year. A Dovehouse 6 s. A Water Mill 1 £. 10 s. Pleas and Perquisites of Court 1 £. 10 s. *Pope Nich. Tax*

Foxcote—One of a family named from this Place, Elias de Foxcote, gave Land in Windrush, to Winchcomb Abbey.

One of the Botelers, of Sudeley gave an Estate here to Westbury College, near Bristol.

26 Hen. viii.—Westbury College, held this Manor of Foxcote, consisting of Rents of Assize 23s. 8d. Farm of Manor, 4 £. 6s. 8d. This was subject to a Chief Rent to the Manor of Guyting. *Valor Eccl'us.*

This Manor came to the Ansell family. (*Inclusure Act.*)

The Manor House is standing but is divided into Cottages. Allotments were made for this Estate at the Inclusure.

Foxcote House Estate:—One Yard Land in Foxcote and half a Yard Land in Owdswell, about 143 a. James Whitehead, held in 1628. Nicholas Longford, by purchase. He died 1648. *Church Inscriptions.*

Nicholas Longford, in 1646, made a settlement under which his son Richard, took. Richard's Widow and 3 Daughters Coheiresses sold 1732, to Giles Powell, of Frogmill.

1746.—Giles Powell, the Son by devise of his Father and confirmation of the Revd. J. Powell, his fathers heir.

1762.—Robert Rogers, by purchase of the Assignees of Giles Powell, the son who had become Bankrupt.

1776.—By Robert Rogers' Will his Widow for Life, with Remainder to his son Giles Rogers, in fee.

1813.—Giles Rogers, died having devised to his Widow Ann, for Life, with Remainder to his Nephew William Rogers, in fee. 1831, the Nephew sold this Remainder to Edmund Stephens, who in 1847, on the Widows Death entered, and 1857, devised to his Son William.

The Foxcote House Estate had One Yard Land in Withington, and half a Yard Land in Owdswell, modern gives 140 a. of which 1a. 1r. 7p. in Dowdeswell.

Late Reece's other part of Longford's.

1720.—John Longford, made a Settlement on his Marriage with Elizabeth Trye, on her for life and their Children in tail. There were 3 Daughters of the 3 Marriage:

1.—Mary, who married John Trye, and had Issue C. B. Trye, and others.

2.—Elizabeth, who died without issue. And 3. Catharine, She and C. B. Trye, barred the entail, and by Partition Deed 1786, the Estate passed to Catharine, which she by Will devised to her Niece Mary Trye Reece, who 1819,

married T. Y. Lister, and died 1820, without issue. T. Y. Lister, died 1829. Mary Trye Reece's Heir on the part of her Father was her Uncle, and on the part of her Mother the son of C. B. Trye, 1847. After some Litigation these Heirs compromised their conflicting Claims, and the Estate was sold to Mr. Troughton.

22 Geo. ii.—In a Fine of Lands at Wythington, John Longford, Clerk. was Plaintiff and Susan Peachey, Widow, William Peachey, Esq. and Susan and Mary Ann Peachey, Spinsters, and Carpenter and Wife. were Deforciants.

Owdswell, farm containing 156 a. near Andoversford, belonged to Studley Priory, Co Warwick, 1558, Francis Hayden, by Crown Grant

1697.—William Lawrence, of Little Shurdington, by Will devised to Littleton, son of his Cousin Robt Lawrence, n tail Littleton Lawrence, died 1740, and his eldest surviving son Robert, barred the entail in 1718. He died having devised to his son William, in fee. 1820, William died having devised his Estate to Trustees for his only son William Edward Lawrence.

1837 Under the Trusts of this Will the Estate was sold to Fulwar Craven, Esqr. who by Will devised the same to his Daughter. She married Captn. Colquit Goodwyn. By the Inclosure Award, Allotments amounting to 98 a. were made to the then Owners for Rights of Common and other rights.

There was a Chapel here.

Pegglesworth, is partly in Withington and partly in Dowdeswell It was part of the Templars Estate. See "Quo Warranto 15 Edw. i." Joan, the Widow of John Huddleston, Knight. obtained in 7 Hen. vii. a pardon for aliening without licence the manor of Temple Guyting, Guyting Poer, Dowdeswell, Pekelworth, and other Estates to John Daston.

About 1600, John Dutton, Esqr. held. From him Theophilus Brereton, of Turkdean. Gent. 1753. Nicholas Harris, of Worcester, from that name 1660, to Mr. Ridler, who left 3 Daughters, who married respectively Jones, Wade, and Cambridge. This Estate came to Wade. *Rudge.*

Rossley Bottom, is a flat meadow once apparently the bed of a Lake, at the end of which towards Colesbourn, might have been the ford over the Water, and except on the overflow Winter torrents a streamlet.

There were Remains of a Chapel at Pegglesworth.

Little or Cassey Compton, this Hamlet is named from its Proprietors the Casseys see "Deerhurst" Hen. vii John Cassey, died seized, leaving William, his son and Heir, who died 1512, His son and Heir Lionel, died without issue. 1555, Robert, brother of Lionel, succeeded him and married Elizabeth, and 1545, Robert, died leaving Henry, his son and heir by Elizabeth, which Henry, married Dorothea Fettiplace, 38 Eliz. Thomas, was his son and Heir, then 37 years of age.

This House and Park was the seat of the Howes, before they purchased Stowell, and Compton passed with the last Lord Chedworth's Estates here to Sir William Scott, by purchase, see "Stowell."

Hilcot, Moreplats, Cottwell, Halwood alias Keyswood: held in capite at 6 s. Rent:

1636, 1 Eliz.—William Lawrence, died seized, leaving Richard, son of Edward, who died 5, and 6 Ph. and M. his Heir Robert, was son of William, of Yanworth.

Part:—Dodwell, by purchase.

Mrs. Lightbourne. *Inclosure Award.*

Other Part:—10 a. Wood, Ayle Wood.

M. 42 Eliz.—Fine between W. Higges, *Plaintiff.* Edward Lawrence. and Wife Agnes, *Deforciants.*

Bruern Coppice:

1611, July 5. Release by Richard Lawrence, of Wythin. *Yeoman.* to W. Higges, of Stepney, Middx. then or late of London, *Merchant.*

At the Well south of the Village and near the Coln is supposed to have stood the Old Town where the Remains of the Roman Villa above referred to were discovered in 1811. Thorndean, Elwell and Upcote are between the Village and Foxcote.

Fulford farm is on the opposite Bank of the Coln.

Upcote had belonged to Rich, of Upper Dowdeswell, but at the Inclosure is belonged to Mr. Elwes.

Bruern Wood belonged anciently to the Abbey so named. It passed afterwards to the family of Roberts, of Cold Salperton and Cheltenham. Above Foxcote near the Old Gloucester Road is St. Pauls Epistle a British Barrow.

At Little Colesbourn was a Chapel the Revenue of which augments the living of Withington.

The Rector of Dowdeswell, had at Pekelsworth 7½ a. of Land and half an acre of pasture in right of his Church.

St. Bartholomew's Hospital, Gloucester, had Lands here That Charity was reformed by Decree of the Court of First Fruts and Tenths, 3 Edw. vi.

Staple farm was one Dr. Fieldings, in right of his Wife. It belonged to Mr. Elwes, at the Inclosure.

Needleshole farm, near Pegelsworth, belonged to the family of Rich. of Upper Dowdeswell. At the Inclosure Sir Charles Pole, held it, and in this Name it was in 1867.

The Inclosure Act was passed in 1813. The Award dated .... is in the Shire Hall Office, Gloucester.

Among the Land Owners named therein are Sir W. Scott, Pole, Elwes, Mrs. Lightbourne, (Hillcote, Wood,) Mrs. Hester Rogers.

1776.—*At the County Election the following Voted for Freeholds in Withington.*

Ballinger, Michael.
Collier, John.
Kimber, William.
Rogers, Robert.
Savoury, James.
Turner, Joseph.
Wilson, Robert.
  Do. Bartley.
Young, Simon.

II.—*Church:*

The Confirmation in A. D. 774, of Milred, Bishop of the Wiccii, (Worcester,) of the Land of the Monastery at Widiandun which was situate on the West side of the River Tillnoth, containing 21 manentes, which Land Osber, Sub Regulus of the Wiccii, had, with the consent of King Ethelred, given to Dun, She with the consent of Egwin, gave it to her Daughter Erother, the Abbess who surrendered to Bishop Milred And that Bishop delivered it to the Abbess Ethelburga, the Daughter of King Alfred, on condition that at her death, it should go to St. Peter's Monastery at Worcester, according to the command of King Alfred.

Kemble Anglo Sax. Diplom. Vol. i. *No.* cxxiv.

A Nunnery was founded at Wydandun, by Ethelred, King of Mercia. It was made a cell to Worcester, A. D. 774.
Tanners Notitia Mon. Dugd. Monast.

John Lawrence, Rector returned Four Virgates of Land adjoining the Rectory; A Messuage and Virgate of Land at Foxcote; One Virgate at Owdeswell; One Virgate at Little Colesborne; One Virgate at Bowood; One Virgate at Blackold End; One Virgate of Giles Chalf; 106 s. 8 d.; And in Tythe of Blade, Hay, Alterage and other Emoluments £ 24. 13s. 4d. Al together 30£. *Valor Eccl'us.*

List of Incumbents and Patrons of Withington.

Rectors.	Patrons.
1548.—John Lawrence.	King Edw. vi.
at Bishop Hooper's Visitation.	
1567.—John Pedder.	R. Smith.
1571.—John Bullingham.	
Bp. of Gloucester, in 1581.	
1581.—Thomas Knolles.	Queen Elizabeth.
1584.—John Atkins.	
1591.—	
1601.—Thomas Knolles.	
1614.—William Osborne.	
1634.—Gilbert Osborne.	Arthur Duck, H. V.
died 1656.	Prebend. Glouc. Ch. Inscrip.
	Nicholas Vicary.
1660.—John Gilman.	Chas. ii.
Church Inscriptions.	
1716.—R. Smalbrook,	
after Bp. Bristol, an Option.	
1732.—John Hayward,	King Geo. ii.
died 1791.	
1791.—Benj. Grisdale,	
Option in Caroline Cornwallis.	

This Parish and that of Dowdeswell, constitute the ecclesiastical Peculiar of Withington—a Jurisdiction exempt from the Archdeacons Visitation. The Rector of Withington had power of granting Probate of Wills of Testators and Letters of Administration to the Effects of Intestates dying within the Peculiar, such as Bishops have in their Dioceses.

The Wills titus collected in the Rectors Registry contain many particulars of interest concerning persons and property in the locality. But the Jurisdiction has been abolished, and the Wills, &c. removed to the Registry at Gloucester.

III.—*Taxation, Popul'n, &c.*

Wydindone, Subsidy Roll, 1 Edw. iii., 1327.

De Johne. le Whyte, ii s. vi d.
' Henr. de Chaddresleye, xiii d. q.
De Johne. Osbarn, ii s.
' Johne. Capel, xii d. ob.
' Johne. le Neuman, vi s. x d. ob. q.
' Walto. le Mulleward, xvi d.
' Willo. Upthehulle, xvii d. ob.
' Stepho. Inthehale, ii s. v d.
' Rico. Upthehulle, vi d. ob.
' Johne le Newman, jun. ii s. iiii d.
' Willmo. Morbel, xix d. ob. q.
' Walto. Iver, ii s. iiii d.
' Henr. le Holdare, xvi d.
' Johe. Beyondethhtoun, xiiii d. ob.
' Johne. Russel, iiii s. viii d. ob. q.
' Johne. atte Stable, x d. ob.
    prob. Sma. xxxiii s. ix *d.*

Oldeswelle.

De Priore de Stodleye, v s. ix d.
' Willmo. de Culne, xix d
' Walto. atte Brugge, viii d. ob.
' Johne de la Mare, vi s. q.
' Silvestr de Huldtcote, xv d. ob. q.
' Johne. le Bereare, xv d. ob. q.
' Thom. Cole, iii s. iiii d. q.
' Thom. de Foxcote, iii s. xi d. q.
' Sibilla Gerard, iiii s. iii d.
' Johne. atte Welle, xiii d. ob.
' Johne. Crossum, vi s. vi d. ob.
' Willmo. de Thorndene, xvii d.
' Gunnilda de Tdorndene, xix d. ob.
' Christian de Upcote, iii s. q.
    prob. Sma. xlii s.

Withington, Subsidy Roll, 30 Eliz.

Richard Laurence,	terr.	5 £.	6s. 8d.
Ric Laurence, of *Foxcot*,	terr.	5 £.	4s.
Richard Philpes,	bon.	10 £.	10 s.
John Laurence,	bon.	8 £.	8 s.
William Fawx,	bon.	6 £.	6 s.
William Harbert,	terr.	20 £.	16 s.
Edmund Laurence,	bon.	3 £.	3 s.
R. Bateman,	bon.	3 £.	3 s.
Richard Whitehorn,	bon.	3 £.	3 s.
Joan George, *Vid.*	bon.	4 £.	4 s.
Thomas Laurence,	bon.	3 £.	3 s.
Richard Longford,	bon.	3 £.	3 s.
Richard Collins,	bon.	3 £.	3 s.
			Som 59 s.

Acreage 6071 a.

Population 1801,—572. 1831,—743. 1871,—768.

1815. Yearly Value of Real Property £4384.

1882.—Estimated Rateable Value £5197.

1883-4-5.—Three Years Average Expenditure on Poor 429 £.

In Northleach Union.

This account of Withington is imperfect. The Parish is large, and the information requisite to frame its history difficult to collect. And even if it could be procured the narrow limits of this Work would preclude its insertion in full. Topographical matter is slowly gathered, and subsequent Inquirers may be usefully and agreeably employed in adding to the stock.

WOLSTON.

WOLSTONE.

THE CHURCH is small consisting of a Chancel, Nave an Aisle on the North side And a Tower at the West-end with battlements, containing three Bells and a Tinkler, It is dedicated to St. Martin, and was rebuilt in 1449, Within the Altar space is a figure of a Man lying at length in a Clergyman's habit, but no inscription remains. [The Church was restored in 1873. In rebuilding a part thereof some fragments of Roman Archetecture were discovered supposed to have belonged to a Pagan Temple.]

The Right Honble. Lord COVENTRY, LORD OF THE MANOR.

Revd. Mr. SOUTHHOUSE, *Rector:*

INSCRIPTIONS IN THE CHURCH.

CHANCEL.

ON A FLAT STONE RAISED ON FOUR LARGE PILLARS.

Here Sleepeth the Body of
of that *Reverend Divine*
Mr. JOSHUA ELYOTT,
who was 34 Years, and upwards
Rector of this Parish.
He was of eminent Parentage of
ingenious education a Master of Arts
and Fellow of Oriel College in Oxford.
He lived a Peace Maker among his
Neighbours and Friendly to all,
He was a Valiant Assertor of sound
Doctrine to his Dying Day and
on the 28 day of November, 1652,
He exchanged his earthly tabernacle
for an Heavenly Mansion,
Aims Cyrony of eight.

ON A SMALL BLACK MARBLE MONUMENT AGAINST THE WEST-END.

Near the FONT lieth Interr'd the
Body of *Mrs.* ELIZABETH BISHOP,
late Wife of the *Revd. Mr.* BISHOP,
Rector of this Parish,
who departed this Life,
Febr. the 18*th* A. D. 1765,
Aged 68 Years.

ON FLAT STONES.

Here was buried the Body of
JOHN ROBERTS, the *Elder*,
Husband of KATHERINE ROBERTS,
Aged 62 Years,
who departed this Life, the
15*th* of October, Anno Dni. 1650.
Here lieth the Body of
his Sonn JOHN ROBERTS,
who was buried February the Tenth,
1682.
Here lyeth by her Loving Husband
KATHERINE, the Wife, of
JOHN ROBERTS, Senr.
Shee was buried the 29 day of Aug.
Anno Dom. 1660.

NAVE.

ON A FLAT STONE.

This is the Burial Place belonging to
the *Revd. Mr.* BISHOP,
Rector of this Parish,
Here lieth the Body of
CECIL BISHOP, Son of
Mr. N. BISHOP, *Merchant*,
of *Bristol*, who died May the 14*th*.
1766.

CHURCH YARD.

ON TOMBS.

Here lyeth the Body of
EDMUND BOOTH, of *Prescott*,
who departed this Life, the
10 day of March 1704.
Also here lyeth the Body of
MARY, the Wife of EDMUND BOOTH,
who departed this Life, the
13 October 1702.
In Memory of
ANN BOOTH, who died the
28 day of July, A. D. 1768,
Aged 88 Years.
Here lyeth the Body of
ANN, Relict of JOHN BOOTH,
who departed this Life, the
2nd. day of September,
Anno Dom. 1727.
Also here lieth the Body of
EDMUND BOOTH, *Junior*,
late of *Prescott*, who departed
this Life, December the 21, 1751,
Aged 69 Years.

Here was buried the Body of
MARY, the Eldest Daughter of
JOHN VICKARS and HANNAH,
his Wife, the Wife of JOHN
ROBERTS, *Senior*, who departed
this Life, the 21 day of
February in the Year of our
Lord 1689, Aged 46 Years.
Also here lieth the Body of
RICHARD ROBERTS, of this Parish,
who departed this Life, the
21 day of January 1749,
Aged 60 Years.

In Memory of
HENRY ROBERTS, of *Prescott*,
who departed this Life, the
7*th.* day of June, A. D. 1754,
Aged 60 Years.
In Memory of
RICHARD ROBERTS, of *Prescott*,
Senior, who departed this Life,
March the 25, A. D. 1721,
Aged 67 Years.

This Tomb was erected
to the Memory of JOHN ARKELL,
who departed this Life, the
44*th.* day of August, A. D. 1761,
Aged 52 Years.
Also in Memory of
ANN, his beloved Wife,
who departed this Life, the
23 day of Feb'y. in the Year 1789,
Aged 67 Years.

In Memory of
THOMAS ROBERTS,
late of *Gotherington* in the
Parish of *Bishops Cleeve*,
He departed this Life,
Decr. ...... 1794, Aged 76 Years.

*(Supplementary Notices of Additional
Monuments &c. since Bigland's time.)*

IN CHURCH.

In Memory of
the *Revd.* ALEXANDER LUDERS,
who died on the 24 March 1851,
Aged 62, and whose remains
are placed in a Vault on the
North East side of the Church
Yard. Also of MARGARETTA
PENELOPE, his Wife, daughter
of the *Revd.* THOMAS BRADSTOCK,
Rector of *Birlingham*, in the Co.
Worcester, born Febr. 16, 1792,
died April 3, 1875.

NAVE.

In Memory of
ELIZABETH, relict of THOMAS
PEACEY, *Esqr.* of *Pardon Hill*,
She died March 5, 1840,
Aged 68 Years.
WILLIAM, eldest Son, of the above
named THOMAS and ELIZABETH
PEACEY, who died at *Newburgh*,
North America, Febr. 15, 1836,
Aged 33 Years.
THOMAS PEACEY, their youngest
Son, died June 6, 1839,
Aged 29 Years.
JOHN FREEMAN PEACEY,
their second Son, died Aug. 17, 1870,
Aged 64 Years.
ELIZABETH, their Daughter,
relict of EDWARD FRICKER, Esqr.
of *Cheltenham*, died April 20, 1880,
Aged 75 Years.

HEAD STONES.

1503

HEAD STONES IN CHURCH YARD.

	Died.		Aged.		Died.		Aged.
John Wythe, of *Monmouth*, Son-in-Law of *Edmund Booth, Senr.* late of *Prescot*,	26 Febr.	1748	27	Mary, ...	8 Oct.	1759	2
				William Arkell, ...	2 Nov.	1760	42
				Thomas Arkell, ...	18 Febr.	1736	63
Martha Gwatkin, 2nd. Daughter of William and Martha Gwatkin, born at *Nether Town* Co. *Hereford*, and second Cousin to Edmund Booth, late of *Prescot*, ...	8 May	1748	38	Judith, his Wife, ...	24 May	1745	66
				John Arkell, ...	14 Aug.	1761	62
				John Finch, ...	16 Febr.	1776	74
				Elizabeth, his Wife, ...	6 April	1777	90
				Richard Roberts, of *Prescott, Senr*	25 March	1721	67
Richard Roberts, *Senr.* of this P.	23 Decr.	1728	55	Margaret, Wife of John Robins, *Senr.* and Grandaughter of John Greening, of *Woolston, Gent.*	1 Oct.	1785	60
Anne Roberts, *Widow*, late Wife of Richard Roberts, ...	19 May	1668	...				
Mary, Wife of John Roberts, of *Woolston*, ...	22 Mar.	1705	...	John Robins, *Junr.* late of the Parish of *St. John's Southwark London, Druggist.* ...	17 Sept.	1782	34
John Roberts, of *Woolstone*, ...	14 Aug.	1715	...				
John Roberts, ...	3 Febr.	1771	48	John Robins, ...	3 Febr.	1781	40
Katherine Roberts, *Widow*, of *Woolstone*, ...	1 Febr.	1694	...	Richard Roberts, ...	1 Nov.	1793	80
Mary, Wife of Richard Shipway	11 July	1765	42	Mary, Wife of Charles Nind, late of *Gotherington* in the Parish of *Bishop's Cleeve*,	23 Jany.	1800	52
Children of Ric. & Mary Shipway.							
Elizabeth, ...	14 Sept.	1759	6	Mary, Wife of Richard Roberts,	6 Oct.	1778	73
Richard, ...	15 Sept.	1759	4				

Supplementary Notes as to I.—*Devolution of Estates.* II.—*Church.* III.—*Taxation, Population, &c.*

I.—Estates:

Wolstone was part of the possessions of Deerhurst Priory which was a cell of St. Dennis of Paris. I do not find it mentioned by name in Domesday Survey. Temp H.iii. the Priory had 22 s. Rents of Assize here. After the forfeiture of Alien Priories. Wolstone was granted to Tewkesbury Abbey, and after the general suppression of abbies, Sir W. Throckmorton, acquired it by Crown Grant.

1630.—Lord Keeper Coventry, by purchase; and in that family it still continues.

7 Geo. ii.—Fine of Lands at Wolston, levied by Brook Bridges, Esqr.

Dumbleton *Plaintiff* the Parson of Aldrinton, *Deforciant.* Same *Plaintiff* Alfred Conquest, *Deforciant.*

PRESCOT, has been already noticed *No.* CCII. as an extra parochial place. It is now a Parish. But as there are Inscriptions in the Church and Church Yard of Wolstone, which furnish evidence of Inhabitants of Prescot, there buried, it seems not improper to add here further information of the latter place.

The Abbot of Tewkesbury, had the Manor and two Plow tillages. *Domesday Survey.*

1545.—Walter Comptou, by Crown Grant after the general dissolution of Monasteries. The Estate passed to Tracy, of Stanway, and it is said to have been purchased at several times by Lord Ellenborough.

Other Land Owners were, Vicaris, (*Church Inscr.*) and *see Subsidy Roll*, 30 Eliz. Wolston; Booth, *Church Inscr.* from whom Delabere; Arkell, of Greet, Washborn, (*Rudge.*) Peacy, of Pardon Hill, Roberts.

1776.—*At the County Election, the following Voted for freeholds in Wolston.*

Richard Hobbs; Thomas Roberts; John Washbourn.

And for Prescot:—

James Lawrance & William Minett, of *Prescote.*

II.—Church.

Advowson of Wolstone, is annexed to the Manor.
The Glebe about 30a.

1767.—Part of the Glebe was given in exchange for other Land by the Patron and Rector with consent of Bishop Benson, to Henry Collett, Esqr.

Tythe Commutation Rent charge 133 £.

A messuage and Lands was given for maintaining the Church. Vicaris, Heir of surviving Trustee v. Pope. *Chancery Procys. temp. Eliz.*

List of Incumbents and Patrons of Wolstone.

1536.—H. Darke.
1582.—N. Keak.
1613.—J. Kay.
"   —W. Powell.
1618.—Joshua Elliott.
"   —Edward Rogers

1661.—Martyn Pindar.   Lord Coventry.
1684.—J. Applebee.   "
1690.—Philip Bound.   "
1720.—Henry Jones.   "
1724.—Walter Jones.   "
1783.—Richard Bishop.   "
"   —Hugh Lawrence.   "
1795.—Edward Southouse. "

III.—Taxation, Population, &c.

Wolstone, Subsidy Roll, 1 Edw. III. **1327.**

De Willo. Balle, iii s. i d.   De Agn. Wykewane, iiis. xd.q.
' Johne. atte Putte, vi d.   ' Johe. Droys, vi d.
' Henr. Alured, iii s. ii d. q.   ' Rico Swalewe, ix d. o. q.
' Alic. Kent, xii d.   ' Henr. Yonge, xii d.
' Willo. Pygas, vi d.   ' Alic. Jannes, iii s. ix d.o.q.
' Alic. Goldyng, xii d.

Adhuc Wolston.

De Hewelina Ballard, vi d.
' Walto. de Leden, xxi d.
' Walto. Frensshe, vi d.
' Eugenea Mulward, iii s. iii d. o. q.
' Matill. Wade, xii d.
' Walto. Broun, ix d.
' Pho. Persoun, xii d.

    prob. Sma. xxviii s. o. q. pbat.

Prescote, Subsidy Roll, 1 Edw. III., 1327.

De Rico. atte Hasele, xv d.
' Thm. Rede, xx d. o. q.
' Robto. Masoun, ii s. ii d. q.
' Jone. Masoun, xii d.
' Thm. atte Welle, vi d.

    prob. Sma. vi s. viii d.

1546.—Robt. Vicaria, Will at Gloucester.

Wolstone, Subsidy Roll. 30 Eliz.

Will'us. Vicaresse, in oon. £3.   5 s. *Tax.*
Joh'es. Robertes, in bon.   3.   5.
Nicholaus Uffemore, ln bon.   3.   5

Acreage Wolston 774 a. and Prescot 485 a.

Population:—
Wolston, 1801.—83, 1831,—92. 1871.—89.
Prescot, 1801.—33, 1831,—51 1871.—60.

In 1815. Annual Value of Real Property Wolstone £1486. Prescot £686.

1882. Rateable Value Wolstone 1568 £. Prescot 802£

1832-3-4. Average of three Years Expenditure on Poor Wolstone 2 £. Prescot 18£.

Wolstone in Tewkesbury Union.

Prescot in Winchcombe Union.

The Tirl Brook rises near this place dividing Wolstone, from Gotherington and running through Pamington, Ashchurch and Walton Cardiff, where it flows in to the Swilgate near Tewkesbury.

WOODCHESTER.

THE CHURCH consists of a Chancel, Nave, and a small Aisle on the South side with a low Tower at the West end containing six Bells. It is dedicated to St. Mary. [Taken down. A new Church built on a different site.]

FRANCIS MOBETON, *Esqr.* LORD OF THE MANOR.

Revd. PETER HAWKER, *Rector.*

HATCHMENTS.

1.—Argent, on a Cross Sable, a Leopard's face Or.—BRIDGES. *Crest:*—an Anchor erect Or.

2.—Argent, three Bars Wavy Azure.—BROWNING. *impaling* BRIDGES, *as before.*

3.—Argent, on a fess Azure, three Cross crosslets Or, in base three Ermine spots (with a Baronets hand.)—*Sir* .... PAUL, *Bart.* impaling Gules two Chevrons between three Martlets Argent.—PEACH. *Crest:*—a Leopard's head proper erased perfess Gules.

4.—PAUL, *as before with baronets hand. impaling, Quarterly*—1, and 4, Azure three Lozenges Or.—FREEMAN, 2 and 3, Sable on a fess between two Lions passant guardant Argent, three Crescents Gules.

5.—Per fess nebullé Azure and Argent, three Antelopes heads erased counter charged, armed Or.—SNOW, *impaling* PAUL, *as before.*

BENEFACTIONS TO THE PARISH.

Mr. NATHANIEL CAMBRIDGE, of *Hamburgh, Merchant,* gave in A. D. 1699, *Saintloe School* in the Parish of *Hampton,* for teaching Boys of this Parish. And *Mr.* RICHARD CAMBRIDGE, of *London, Merchant,* gave in A. D. 1709, 100£. as an augmentation to the said School.

Mrs. ELIZABETH SEYS, gave in A. D. 1705, 400 £. to be laid out in an Estate the profits of which to be divided between three Poor Women or more, for teaching poor Girls to read and work, and the poor Women are to be appointed by the Trustees who are to advise with the Chief of the Parish in appointing them ; which Money with 215 £. Interest is since laid out on two Estates, one in the Tything of *Ham Fallow* in the Parish of *Berkeley,* the other called *Hipp's Hill* in the Parish of *Wheatenhurst,* both in this County.

ROBERT BRIDGES, *Esqr.* gave in A. D. 1722, 500 £. to be laid out in an Estate, the Profits of which to be applied to teach Poor Boys to read English and to Write, also to Cloath and to put out apprentice every Year one Boy, and for teaching and putting out apprentice Yearly a greater number of Boys if the Profits of the Estate will allow it which Money (except 20 £.) is since laid out on two Estates at *Wheatenhurst,* in this County.

Mr. RICHARD CAMBRIDGE, of *London, Merchant,* gave Anno Dom. 1729, 20£. the Interest of which to be disposed of at the discretion of the Overseers.

PAINTER IN THE BELFRY.

Mr. JOHN BOX, of this Parish, *Blacksmith,* gave Anno Dom. 1761, the Treble Bell, belonging to the Peal:—SAMUEL MARTIN, WILLIAM KIRBY, THOMAS BROWNING, GEORGE DAVIS, WILLIAM WOOD, JOSEPH HODDINOT, *Ringers.*

INSCRIPTIONS IN THE (OLD) CHURCH.
[*Many of these are removed to the New Church.*]

CHANCEL.

On a handsome raised Tomb with a Lady and Gentleman lying along under a Canopy supported by pillars. She has a ruff round her Neck, and a dog at her feet. He is in Armour. In front of the Tomb are seven Male Children kneeling and at the end are three Female Children kneeling. This Tomb was sett up for *Sir* GEORGE HUNTLEY, *Knt.* of *Frocester,* and his *Lady,* with these *Arms over the Canopy but no Inscription, Quarterly* 1.—Argent, on a Chevron between three stags heads coupt Sable, as many bugle Horns stringed of the field. HUNTLEY. 2.—perpale .... 3.—...... ..... on a fess .... three Balls .... in Chief three Mullets .... and in base three Balls, ... 4.— ... ... on a fess a spear's head .... in Chief three Balls ...... and in Base a Pheons head .... *Impaling Quarterly* 1, & 4, Azure, six Mullets, Or. 2, & ...... three fleurs de Lis, ... and A Label of three points ... . 3 Argent, on a Chevron Azure between three pheons heads ...... a pheons head.

ON A MARBLE MONUMENT, ON THE NORTH SIDE.

Arms:—Argent, on a Cross Sable a Leopard's face Or.—BRIDGES. *impaling the same.*
Crest:—An Anchor erect Or.

To the Happy Memory of ROBERT BRIDGES, *Gent.* and ELIZABETH, his Wife, who after their being married together near 50 Years, departed this Life, She on the 5 of April, He on the 12 of May, Anno Dom. 1648, leaving Issue behind them 3 Sonnes :—JOHN, HUMPHRY and RICHARD, and one Daughter MARGARET, married to EVAN SEYS, *Esqr.*

ON A HANDSOME MARBLE MONUMENT AGAINST THE SOUTH SIDE.

Arms:—BRIDGES, *as before.*

Near to this Place is deposited all that is Mortal of ROBERT BRIDGES, *Esqr.* who departed this Life, the

6 day of March, 1722, Aged 72. In Memory of whom this Monument was erected and of his Bro'. in Law, *Mr.* RICHARD HICKS, and JANE, his Wife, Sister of the said *Mr.* BRIDGES, who lies in the Chancel of this Church. Also near to this Place lies the Body of *Mrs.* ELIZABETH BROWNING, Sister to the said ROBERT BRIDGES. *Esqr.* who departed this Life, December 4, 1733.

ON A SMALL MONUMENT IN THE CHANCEL, NEAR THE PULPIT.

M. S.
JOHANNIS KING, A. M.
Hujus Ecclesiæ Rector.
Ob. 4o. Julij, Anno Dom. 1723*mo.*
Ætat. suæ 70*mo.*
ELEONORÆ KING, *Viduæ ejus,*
Ob. 31*mo.* Jan'rij. Anno Dom. 1728*o.*
Ætat. suæ 72*do.*
Omnia mors æquat.

WOOD CHESTER.

ON A MONUMENT AGAINST THE
EAST WALL.

Arms:—Gules two Chevrons
between three Martlets Argent.—
PEACH. *impaling* Argent, on a fess
Gules between three Martlets
Sable as many Escollops Or.

Crest:—a demi Lion rampant
per fess Ermine and Gules ducally
crowned Or.

Sacred to the Memory of
NATHANIEL PEACH, *Esqr.*
of *Bownham's House* in the Parish
Rodborough, who departed this
Life, 2nd. of May 1788, Aged 39.

AGAINST THE SAME WALL IS A
MONUMENT OF WHICH THE DESIGN
IS TWO GENII HOLDING UP A
SKELETON.

Arms:—PEACH, *as before*, impaling Azure, a bend embattled between two Unicorns heads erased
Or.—PEARSE.?

This Monument is erected
in Memory of
NATHANIEL PEACH, of this Parish,
Clothier, who died August 19, 1719,
Aged 43 Years.
MARGARET, his Wife, who died
Oct. 18, 1741, Aged 58.
Also DEBORAH, Wife of
NATHANIEL PEACH, Son of the said
NATHANIEL and ELIZABETH PEACH,
and Sister to SAMUEL PAUL,
of *Rodborough, Esqr.*
She died May 16, 1765, Aged 58.
Also NATHANIEL PEACH, *Esqr.*
third Son of the said NATHANIEL
and MARGARET PEACH, and
Husband to the said DEBORAH.
He died the 25 of Dec. 1780,
Aged 68 Years.

Arms: at bottom PEACH, *as before*,
impaling Argent, on a fess Azure,
three Cross Crosslets Or. in base
three Ermine spots.—PAUL.

NEAR THE LAST.

Arms:—PEACH, *as before at top and*
bottom.

This Monument is Erected
in Memory of
EDWARD PEACH, late of *Ebley*
in this County *Clothier*,
eldest Son of NATHANIEL and
MARGARET PEACH,
He died July 5, 1770,
Aged 68 Years.
Also of JOHN PEACH, late of the
City of *Bristol, Merchant*,
second Son of the said NATHANIEL
and MARGARET PEACH,
He died at *Bath*,
September 20, 1774, Aged 63.
Likewise WILLIAM GAINSFORD
PEACH, of *Rooksmore, Esqr.*
Nephew to the above EDWARD
and JOHN PEACH, He died at
Wootton-under-Edge, the 14 day
of April 1785, Aged 42 Years.

ON FLAT STONES.

Arms:—BRIDGES, *as before*, in
a Lozenge.

Here resteth the Body of

ANNE BRIDGES, (Daughter of
HUMPHREY BRIDGES, of this Parish,
Gent. deceased) who departed
this Life, June 4, Ao. D'ni. 1703.

H. S E.
JANA RICHARDI HICKES,
Generosi, filia obijt
14mo. die Martii
Anno Ætatis 1mo.
Anno Domini 1687.

Arms:—BROWNING, *as before.*

Here resteth the Body of
JOHN BROWNING, *Gent.*
(being ye only Son of STEPHEN
BROWNING, of *Coaley* in this
County *Gent.* deceased,) by
ELIZABETH, his Wife,
who departed this Life,
August 25, Anno Dom. 1667,
Ætat. suæ 22.

ON BRASS PLATE.

In Memory of
PETER, the Son of PETER
HAWKER, Rector of this Parish,
died Febr. 25, 1767.
An Infant 6 Months old
JOHN HAWKER, who died
21 Jany. 1771.
An Infant twin 3 Months Old.
HANNAH HAWKER,
who died 11 Oct. 1779.
An Infant one Month Old,
HANNAH, Wife of PETER HAWKER,
Rector of this Parish,
died June 20, 1797, Aged 62.

NAVE.

ON FLAT STONES.

Here lieth the Body of
NATHANIEL PEACH, *Clothier*,
who died August 22, 1719,
Aged 43 Years.
Also MARGARET, his Wife,
who died Oct. 20, 1741,
Aged 54 Years.

Here lieth the Body of
EDWARD TOWNSEND,
of this Parish, *Clothier*, 2nd. Son of
EDWARD and ELIZABETH TOWN-
SEND, of *Alleston* in the County
of *Warwick*, who died the
19th. day of August 1711,
Aged 24 Years.

ON A MONUMENT AGAINST THE
WEST-END OF NORTH AISLE.

Arms:—Sable on a Chevron engrailed between six Crosses patteè
Or, three fleur-de-Lis Or.—SMITH,
impaling .... a Bear rampant
muzzled ....
Crest:—a Falcon Close.

Underneath lie the Remains of
JAMES SMITH, *Gent.*

who departed this Life,
Febr. 7, Anno Dom. 1757,
Ætatis suæ 72.
Affliction sore, long time I bore,
Physicians were in vain
Till God did please Deth should me seize,
To ease me of my pain.
Also the Remains of
MARY, relict of the above
JAMES SMITH, *Gent.*
who departed this Life,
Sept. 23, 1762, in the 62 Year
of her Age.

CHURCH YARD.

ON ALTAR TOMBS.

To the Memory of
CATHARINE, *Lady* PAUL,
second Wife of
Sir ONESIPHORUS PAUL, *Bart*
Eldest Daughter of FRANCIS
FREEMAN, of *Norton-mal-reward*
in the County of *Somerset, Esqr.*
She departed this Life,
20th. day of October 1766, in ye
56 Year of her Age.

SUSANNA PAUL, Daughter of
GEORGE PAUL, L. L. D.
Obiit 18 May 1767,
Ætatis suæ 43.

In Memory of
RICHARD CAMBRIDGE, *Esqr.*
who died the 10 of Febr.
Anno Domini 1756,
Ætatis 73.
MARY, his Wife, died the 20th. of
May 1761, Ætatis 72.

Here lieth the Body of
SARAH, the Wife of THOMAS
ROGERS, of this Parish,
who died March 6, 1765, in the
81 Year of her Age.

Under this Tomb lie the Remains
ELIZABETH, Wife of THOMAS LAND,
Daughter of THOMAS and SARAH
ROGERS, of this Parish,
who departed this Life, the
4 May 1765, Aged 40 Years.

EDMUND BROWNE, *Esqr.*
died 9 day of Febr. 1731,
Aged 52 Years.
EDMUND BROWNE, *Esqr.*
Son of the late EDMUND BROWNE,
Esqr. died August 30, 1754,
Aged 30 Years.

In Memory of
FRANCIS MANNING, of the Parish
of *Minchin Hampton, Clothier*,
who departed this Life,
Jane 11, Anno Dom. 1727,
Aged 78 Years.
Here lyeth the Bodie of
HESTER, the Wife of FRANCIS
MANNING, of the Parish of

Minchin Hampton, Clothier,
who died August 13, 1715,
Aged 78 Years.

In Memory of
ELIZABETH, the Wife of DANIEL
FOORDS, who died the 29 day of
March 1709.
Also of DANIEL FOORDS,
who died the 19 day of Decr. 1723.
Also of JOHN, the Son of
DANIEL FOORDS, who died the
13 of Jany. in the 24 Year
of his Age 17. . 3.

Here resteth the Body of
THOMAS DEANE, *Clothier,*
who deceased November 16, 1701.
Mathew 24, 44.
Here resteth the Body of
SARAH, the Daughter of THOMAS
YATES, and Wife of THOMAS
DEANE, *Clothier,* who deceased
the 28 of Sept. 170...
Romans 8, 18.

In Memory of
DEAN PAUL, *Esqr.*
He died Novr. 17, 1761,
Aged 51 Years.
Also of ELIZABETH, his Wife,
and Daughter of JOHN ANDREWS,
of *Stonehouse, Gent.*
She died Augt. 4, 1741,
Aged 37 Years.
Also of ANNA, his second Wife,
and Daughter of JOHN SELF,
of *Cirencester, Gent.*
She died Sept. 7, 1745,
Aged 61 Years.
In Memory of
MARGARET PAUL, 3*rd.* Wife of
DEAN PAUL, *Gent.*
and Daughter of
PHILIP HAMPTON, *Gent.*
of the Parish of *Westbury* in the
County of *Gloucester,*
She died March 11, 1764,
Aged 59 Years.

In Memory of
JOHN SMALL, of *Rodborough,*
and ELIZABETH, his Wife,
She died July 17, 1721,
And he died March 10, 1726.

In Memory of
THOMAS SMALL, who died
Sept. 7, 1745, Aged 53 Years.
RICHARD SMALL,
Merchant of Bristol,
died May 11, 1734, Ætat. 30.

Sacred to the Memory of
RICHARD SMALL, of *Nailsworth,*
Esqr. who departed this Life,
Sept. 14, 1758, Ætat. 30.
Also of ELIZABETH, his Wife,
who died April 16, 1760, Ætat. 36.
Here also lie the Remains of
Four of their Children :—*viz.*
RICHARD, SARAH, THOMAS, and
JOHN, who all died young.

In Memory of
ANDREW HAYNES,
of this Parish, *Clothier,* who died
December the 4, 1736, Ætat. suæ 46.
Also of DEBORAH HAYNES,
Widow, who died Augt. 7, 1742,
Aged 81 Years.
In Memory of
Four Sons of ANDREW HAYNES,
Senr. :—THOMAS, died Decr. 28,
1691, Æt. 8 Months.
GEORGE, died Oct. 13, 1694,
Æt. 2 Years.
JOHN, died Febr. 3, 1715,
Æt. 18 Years.
and GEORGE, died March 23, 1719,
Æt. 23 Years.

In Memory of
BENJAMIN CAMBRIDGE,
Clothier, of the Parish of
Minchin Hampton,
who departed this Life, the
18 day of October 1703, in the
62 Year of his Age.

Here lyeth the Body of
RICHARD CAMBRIDGE, *Clothier.*
who departed this Life,
in the Faith of Christ, the 9 day
February 1676.

In Memory of
SARAH, the Wife of GEORGE
TOCKNEL, of the Parish of
Hampton, who died the 19 day of
March, Anno Dom. 1701.
In Memory of
GEORGE TOCKNELL,
of *Culverhouse,* in the Parish of
Minchin Hampton, Yeoman,
who departed this Life, the
26 day of August, 1713,
Aged 81 Years.

Arms:—Ermine on a fess embattled and counterembattled Sable
three Escollops Argent.—BROWNE.
Crest :—a Storks head out of a
Mural Crown.

In Memory of
EDMUND BROWNE, of *Lincoln's Inn,*
Esqr. Councellor at Law, late of
the Parish of *Rodborough,*
who died August ye 30*th.* 1754,
in the 36 Year of his Age.

In Memory of
ANDREW ROGERS, and SARAH,
his Wife, He died the 9 of
Nov. 1720, Ætatis suæ 78.
And She died May 29, 1723,
Ætat. 70.
And of JAMES, their Son.
In Memory of
THOMAS, Son of ANDREW ROGERS,
who died July 1, 1742, Aged 56.
In Memory of
RICHARD ROGERS, *Clothier,*
who died August 30, 1748,
Aged 60 Years.
Also of NATHANIEL, Son of
JOHN ROGERS, who died
Oct. 11, 1749, Æt. 10.

THOMAS GYDE, of the Parish of
Avening, departed this Life,
the 26 of March, Ao. D'ni. 1693,
Ætatis suæ 79.
MARY, the Wife of THOMAS GYDE,
Clothier, died the 6 of April 1706.

ANNE, the Relict of WILLIAM
MERRICK, *Esqr.* of *Weston,* in the
County of *Hereford,* died 29 of
October 1754, Aged 64.

SARAH, Wife of JAMES FORD,
died Sept. 29, 1747.

In Memory of
JOHN PEACH, of this Parish,
Clothier, who died March 1737,
in the 64 Year of his Age.

In Memory of
JOSEPH HILL, and SARAH, his Wife,
She died Jany. 5, 1718, Æt. 37.
He died April 16, 1748, Æt. 63.
ELIZABETH, second Wife, of
JOSEPH HILL, died
Decr. 23, 1722, Aged 41 Years.

JANE, the Wife of WILLIAM HILL,
died the 3 of Oct. 1748, in the
44 Year of her Age.
In Memory of
ELIZABETH, the Wife of
JOSEPH HILL, *Senr.*
who died the 29 of July in the
56 Year of her Age, 1731.
Also in Memory of
JOHN, his Son, who died
18 Sept. 1706.

ANNE, the Wife of JOHN CHURCH,
died June 23, 1711, in the 70
Year of her Age.

JANE, the Wife of
ONESIPHORUS PAUL,
died May 26, 1748, Aged 41.

To the Memory of
THOMAS PIERCE, *Clothier,*
who died the 2 of Febr. 1760,
Ætat. 64.
In Memory of
MARY, the Wife of THOMAS PIERCE,
Clothier, who died April 18, 1732,
Ætat. suæ 35.

ON A BRASS PLATE.

Here lye the Remains of
THOMAS COOK, of this Parish,
and ELIZABETH, his Wife,
She died the 4 of March 1750,
Aged 56 Years.
and He May 10, 1751, Aged 56.

Here lyeth the Body of
DANIEL GLADAM,
He died April 13, 1765,
in the 36 Year of his Age.

In Memory of
JEAN, the Wife of STEPHEN
DUDBRIDGE, of this Parish, *Clothier*,
who died 2 of Jany. 1717.

In Memory of
THOMAS CHURCHES, *Clothier*,
who died Decembr 3. 1762,
Aged 79.
THOMAS CHURCHES, *Senior*,
died in Nov. 1698, Aged 36.
and MARTHA, his Relict,
May 22, 1730, Aged 70.
and ANNE, their Daughter,
Sept. 25, 1729, Aged 39.

In Memory of
ROBERT BALL, *Senr.*
MARTHA, his Wife,
She died Decr. 14, 1701, and
He Decem. 23, 1743, Aged 79 Years,
and She 36 Years.
In Memory of
HESTER, the Wife of
ROBERT BALL, *Junior*,
who died Nov. 27, 1761,
Aged 70 Years.

Here resteth the Body of
URSULA, the Wife of RICHARD
KING, who deceased the 30 day of
July, An. Di. 1620.
In Memory of
JOHN KING, of this Parish, *Gent.*
who died March 24, 1741,
Aged 62 Years.
In Memory of
SARAH, Wife of JOHN KING,
died the 24 of Sept. 1727,
Ætatis suæ 41.
Here lyeth the Body of
ELIZABETH, the Wife of
NATHANIEL KINGE,
who deceased the 15 day of April,
Anno 1690.
Sacred to the Memory of
JOHN KINGE, of this Parish, *Yeoman*,
who died of the small pox, Sept. 11,
1794, In the 75 Year of his Age.
To the Memory of
NATHANIEL KING, *Yeoman*,
who died April 1, 1729,
Aged 84 Years.
To the Memory of
MARY, the Wife, of NATHANIEL
KING, who died the 17 of June 1711,
Aged about 63.

To the Memory of
two Daughters of NATHANIEL KING,
Senr. of this Parish, *Gent.*
ELIZABETH, the Wife of
JOHN WOOD, the Parish of *Dimmock*,
in this County, *Gent.*
Died 1 July 1671.
MARY, the Wife of HENRY BOURNE,
of this Parish, died the
14 day of October 1711.

In Memory of

ANNE, the Wife of JOHN KING,
who died Decr. 5, 1736,
Also ANNE, the Wife of WILLIAM
KING, who died Augt. 28, 1768,
Aged 49 Years.

In Memory of
ELIZABETH, the Wife of SAMUEL
CHURCHES, who died Nov. 26, 1756,
Aged 36 Years.
Also SARAH, their Daughter,
who died Decr. 15, 1756, Æt. 13.

In Memory of
RICHARD LOCKLEY, *Esqr.*
late of this Parish, who died the
10 of May 1756, Aged 38.

In Memory of
NATHANIEL CAMBRIDGE,
who died August 23, 1693,
Also of ANNE, his Wife,
who died June 6, 1747.
Near this Place lyeth the Body of
RICHARD CAMBRIDGE,
who died Jany. 1640,
MARGARET, his Wife, who died
April 1633.
MARY, their Daughter,
who died 1644.
NATHANIEL, the eldest Son,
who died Sept. 1667.
ORIANAH, his Wife, who died
Sept. 1659.
RICHARD, eldest Son of NATHANIEL,
who died Febr. 1676.
MARY, his Wife, who died
Augt. 1669.
DORCAS, Daughter of NATHANIEL,
who died 1656.
HESTER, JOSEPH, and DANIEL,
who died 1661.
MARY, who died 1676.
BENJAMIN, who died Oct. 1703.

In Memory of
JOSEPH CHURCHES, of *Saintloe*,
in the Parish of *Hampton*,
And JANE, his Wife, She died
Febr. 12, 1715, Aged near 87,
and He March 5, 1730, Aged 94.
In Memory also of MARY CHURCHES,
Spinster, Daughter of JOSEPH and
JANE CHURCHES, who died the
10 day of June 1758, Aged 84 Years.

In Memory of
JOHN SHURMUR, of this Parish,
Clothier, who deceased Sept 14, 1747,
Ætat. suæ 80.

In Memory of
THOMAS SHURMUR, of this Parish,
Clothier, who departed this Life,
March 4th 1727-8, Ætatis suæ 66.
Also SARAH, the Wife of
THOMAS SHURMUR, of this Parish,
Clothier, who died April 18, 1753,
Aged 81 Years.

In Memory of
SUSANNA WATKINS,

late of *Dursley*, *Widow*,
who departed this Life,
June 17, 1724, Ætatis suæ 85.

In Memory of
RICHARD REMMINGTON,
of this Parish, *Yeoman*,
who died March 14, 1749,
Aged 60 Years.
Also of RICHARD, his Son,
who died Febr. 16, 1746,
Aged 25 Years.
In Memory of
MARY, the Wife of RICHARD
REMMINGTON, who died Nov. 21,
1763, Ætat. 73.

In Memory of
HENRY DUDBRIDGE, of this Parish,
who died 7 of August, 1727,
Aged 72 Years

In Memory of
JEAN, Daughter of HENRY
DUDBRIDGE, who died 8 Augt. 1728,
Aged 40 Years.
In Memory of
ANNA, the Wife of HENRY
DUDBRIDGE, of this Parish, *Dyer*,
who died the 24 day of June
in the 72 Year of her Age, 1720.
In Memory of
HOLIDAY DUDBRIDGE, of this Parish,
Clothier, who died Nov. 24, 1752,
Aged 72 Years.

To the Memory of
JOSEPH DUDBRIDGE, *Clothier*,
who departed April 8, 1744,
Ætat. 78.
In Memory of
SARAH, the Wife of JOSEPH
DUDBRIDGE, of this Parish, *Clothier*,
Died the 3 of Febr. A. D. 1709.

To the pious Memory of
ANSELM DUDBRIDGE, *Clothier*,
He died Febr. 18, 1720,
Aged near 43.
MARY, his Wife, departed,
June 23, 1753, in the 73
Year of her Age.

JONATHAN CHURCHES,
Died Decr. 20, 1727.

In Memory of
CHARLES KING,
who died March 25, 1729,
Aged 46 Years.

Here lieth MARY, Daughter of
JOHN MALSON, who departed this life,
June 28, 1758, Aged 40.

Dedicated to the Remembrance of
RICHARD HEAVEN, of the Parish, of

Minchin Hampton, Malster,
and Son of SAMUEL HEAVEN,
late of the Parish of *King Stanley,*
who departed this Life, the
16 day of Sept. A. D. 1732,
Ætatis suæ 39.
In Memory of
EDWARD HEAVEN, of the Parish,
of *King Stanley,* who departed this
Life, Febr. 10, Anno Dom. 1733,
Aged 77 Years.

In Memory of
PHILIP WATHEN, and ELIZABETH,
his Wife, She died Augt. 17, 1702,
And he Febr. 12, 1702,
Also MARY, their Daughter,
died May 20, 1730,
In Memory of
WILLIAM MITCHELL,
of the Parish of *King Stanley,*
and SARAH, his Wife.
He died Jany. 15, Aged 60.
And She April 28, Aged 80, 1759.
CHARLES MITCHELL,
died August 26, 1762, Aged 42.

In Memory of
HESTER DREW, *Spinster,*
of the Parish of *Alderley,*
in this County, who died
March 16, 1755, Aged 64 Years.
WILLIAM, Son of JOHN and
HESTER DREW, departed this Life,
May 3, 1759, Aged 19 Years.

Here lieth the Bodie of
ELIZABETH CHAPMAN the Daughter
of JAMES and JANE CHAPMAN,
Buried the Fifteenth day Decemb.
Anno Domini 1518.

To the Memory of
THOMAS PAVEY, of this Parish,
Esqr. who died Decemb 9, 1794,
Aged 63 Years.
THOMAS, Son of THOMAS PAVEY,
of this Parish, *Esqr.* and
ANN, his Wife, died July 1, 1783,
Aged 10 Weeks.

In Memory of
GEORGE SMALL, of *Rodborough,*
Gent. who was interr'd here the
1st. of March 1756, Aged 48.
MARTHA. his *Widow,*
died 9 Sept. 1759, Aged 46.
Underneath are deposited the
Remains of JOHN SMALL, late of
Clapham, in the County of *Surry,*
Esqr. who departed this Life, the
18 of May 1780, Aged 65 Years.
THOMAS, their Son, was buried
16 July 1765, Aged 20 Years.

In Memory of
ELIZABETH, the Wife of JOHN
HAMPTON, who died May 15, 1771,
Aged 31 Years.
Also two of their Children,
who died Infants.
Near this Tomb lie the Remains
of WILLIAM HAMPTON,
late of this Parish, and SARAH,
his Wife. He died July 17, 1776,
Aged 70 Years.
She died Nov. 29, 1769, Aged 67.

Arms :—Argent, on a fess Gules
a Rowel Or. pierced Gules.—
HAMPTON.
Crest:—An Arm embowed habit-
ted Gules, hand proper holding a
Sword proper.

To the Memory of
THOMAS PEIRCE, *Clothier,*
ob. Febr. 2, 1760, Æt. 64.
ANN, his Daughter, died Dec. 18,
1795, Aged 68 Years.
In Memory of
MARY, Wife of THOMAS PEIRCE,
Clothier, died April 28, 1732,
Ætatis suæ 35.
MARY, their Daughter, who died
who died Decr. 3, 1726,
Aged 6 Months and 14 Days.
JOHN, their Son, died April 11.
1731, Aged 2 Months and 4 days.

In Memory of
AARON WICKES, of *Pudhill* in this
Parish, *Clothier,* who died
Nov. 7, 1750, Anno Ætatis 60.
ANNE, his Wife, died Sept. 20,
1751, Anno Ætatis 49.
In Memory of
ANNE, his Daughter,
died May 5, 1760, Aged 20 Years.
AARON, their Son, died
March 26, 1764, Aged 29 Years.
ISABELL, his Wife died Decr. 7,1771,
Ætat. 47.

To the Memory of
JOHN DREW, and HESTER, his Wife,
He died Dec. 28, 1773, Aged 82.
She died March 5, 1776, Aged 74.
WILLIAM, their Son,
died May 3, 1759, Aged 19.
JOHN DREW, who died
Nov. 12. 1778, Aged 52.
HESTER, Wife of the aforesaid
JOHN DREW, departed this Life,
Oct. 10, 1791, Aged 77.

ON FLAT STONES.

Arms :—......... an Eagle displayed
Crest :—a demi Eagle ducally
crowned.

Here lyeth interred the Body of
MARTHA, Wife of WILLIAM WEBB
Gen. of *Howcombe* in this Parish,
who died March 16, 1684,
Also of WILLIAM WEBB, *Gen.*
their Son, who died May 15, 1742
Aged 72 Years.
Also NATHANIEL WEBB, *Gen.*
of the Parish of *Avening,*
He died March 19, 1742,
Aged 33 Years.

In Memory of
HANNAH, Wife of Sir JOHN WILMOT
PRIDEAUX, of *Netherton* in *Devon-*
shire, Bart. and Daughter of
WILLIAM and ANNE WEBB,
of this Parish. She departed this
Life, 1st. day of July 1789,
Aged 32 Years.
WILLIAM, her Father, died
Jany. 27, 1790, Aged 84 Years.

In Memory of
MARY, Daughter of WILLIAM,
and MARY WELDRON, who died
Dec. 7, 1777, Aged 16 Years.
The aforesaid WILLIAM, died
April 5, 1787, in the 67 Year
of his Age.

This Memorial inscribed to
THOMAS LITTLE, of this Parish,
who departed this Life,
Oct. 30, 1798, Aged 34 Years.
JASPER, his Son, died 30 Ap. 1795,
Aged 19 Weeks.

In Memory of
JOSEPH HODDINOTT, and JOHANNA,
his Wife, She died March 8, 1790,
Aged 66 Years.
He died August 30 1791,
Aged 66 Years.

In Memory of
ELIZABETH, Wife of ROBERT
LEIGHTON, who died Nov. 4, 1791,
Aged 56 Years.

In Memory of
ELIZABETH, Wife of JOHN PRICE,
of this Parish, *Yeoman,*
died the 14 day of May 1793,
Aged 64 Years.

HEAD STONES.

	Died.	Aged.		Died.	Aged.
Walter Heaven, ...	23 May	1763	67	Mary, his Wife, ...	25 June	1770	50
Hannah, his Wife, ...	11 Sept.	1736	...	Jacob Walkley, ...	19 June	1696	42
Elizabeth, Wife of William Pegler,	18 Nov.	1772	72	John Creed, ...	12 Decr.	1738	68
Lydia, Daught. of Walter Heaven,	4 Nov.	1773	10	Mary, his Wife, ...	31 Decr.	1739	59
Benjamin Perry, ...	12 Febr.	1792	79	William Creed, ...	14 Febr.	1792	66
Mary, his Wife, ...	25 Jany.	1789	75	John Dudbridge, ...	24 June	1792	87
Martha, Wife of William Hodges,	14 June	1757	66	Mary Backer, ...	25 Jany.	1793	76
Moses Browning, ...	21 Nov.	1773	82	Joseph Hoddinott, ...	14 May	1773	77
Samuel Browning, ...	9 June	1797	75	Martha, his Wife, ...	20 May	1771	75

(Additional Inscriptions most since Bigland's time.)

OLD CHURCH YARD.

ELIZABETH EMMA, Wife of
JAMES SMITH ADAMS,
who died 1843
JAMES SMITH ADAMS, died 1860.

Arms:—2 Griffins rampant, *impaling the same.*
Crest:—A Griffin's head erased between 2 Wings.

ON BRASS PLATES.

JAMES BOULTON, died 1869.
ANN, his Wife, died 1873.

ANN, Wife of JOHN EARL,
who died 1866.
JOHN EARL, died 1873

To GEORGE MATHEW, who died 1860.
And to HARRIETT JANE, his Wife, &
Their Infant Children:—ELLEN,
JANE, HARRIETT EMMA.
ANN, Wife of GEORGE HARWOOD,
died 1862.
KIZIA, Wife of OWEN NEWTON,
died 1835.
JOHN TUCKER, died 1843.
CHARLOTTE, his Daughter, d. 1847.
MARY ANN BOULTON, died 1844.
JAMES HENRY BOULTON, died 1843.
ELIZABETH, Wife of JOHN PRICE,
died 1792.
JOHN PRICE, died 1801.
ELIZABETH, Wife of WILLIAM PRICE,
died ....
THOMAS BOULTON, of *Rodborough,*
died 1817.
CHARLOTTE AUGUSTA BOULTON,
died 1848.
JOHN ILES, died 1835.
WILLIAM LANGERFIELD, died 1856.
GEORGE, his Son, died 1862.
HARRIETT, Wife of the above,
died 1866.
WILLIAM HAMPTON, died 1862.
JOHN BOX, died 1721.
ELIZABETH, his Wife, died 1743.
THOMAS COLLETT, died 1854.
JAMES WATSON, died 1858.
MARY ANN TILEY, died 1842.
HANNAH TILEY, died 1882.
WALTER TILEY, died 1857.
HENRY DUDBRIDGE, died 1826.
HESTER DUDBRIDGE, died 1819.
ANN DUDBRIDGE, died 1820.
ANN DUDBRIDGE, died 1807.
HESTER, her Daughter, died 1814.
STEPHEN DUDBRIDGE, died 1824.
RICHARD REMINGTON, died ....
JOHN BROWN, died 1790.
HELEN BROWNING, died 1869.
JOHN KING, died 1855.
SAMUEL HARRISON, died 1834.
ELIZABETH, his Wife, and
4 Children.

In Memory of
ROBERT PAUL, *Esqr.*
Commander of H. M. Sloop
"Pheasant" who died while cruising
off Trinidad, Jany. 1805,
in the *27th.* Year of his Age, and
was buried at Grenada
His public conduct repeatedly
procured for him the admiration and
thanks of his country, and his private
Virtues alike endeared him to his
friends.

Not feigned the sorrow, nor suborned
the tear
That pays due tribute to this early bier;
Each Sailor wept, and each with misty
eye,
For his loved Captain heaved the
parting sigh.
So mourned his friends, too proud,
alas to claim
A kindred interest in his rising fame.
For his firm breast the ocean had its
charms
The war of elements, the shock of
arms
And though no stone may mark his
distant grave,
On shores where rolls the trans-
atlantic wave
Here in this vale shall memory speak
his praise
And fond affection here this tablet
raise.

CHARLOTTE, Wife of ROBERT
SNOW PAUL, of *Hill House,*
Rodborough, who died 1838.
ROBERT SNOW PAUL,
who died 1849, Aged 81.

MARY WATHEN, eldest Daughter
of WILLIAM CARRUTHERS, of
Brownhill, Esqr. Wife of
NATHANIEL PEACH WATHEN,
Esqr. of *Arlingham Court.*

This exemplary Woman had learned
to estimate all the duties of Life by
the Gospel and to practise them with
christian diligence and humility. But
the great and enduring excellence
of her character is that while her
heart was possessed with the Love
of God her Saviour, her hope of
immortality was exclusively built on
his Love to her. She fell asleep in
Jesus, April 9, 1817, Aged 44 Years.
This Monument was erected by her
afflicted husband N.P. WATHEN, who
died Decr. 18, 1846, Aged 75.

MARGARET PEACH, Daughter of
OBADIAH PAUL WATHEN,
5 Children:—ELLEN, HAWTRY,
JULIA, PEACH, ISABEL.

MARY, Wife of JOHN BINGLE,
who died 1837.
JOHN BINGLE.

ON BRASS PLATES.

MARY LONG, who died 1850.
JAMES IRONSIDE, died 1852.
ROBERT LEIGHTON, died 1831.
ANNE FISHER, died 1824.
CHARLES, her Son, died 1859.
JANE HILL, died 1842.
WILLIAM, her Husband, died 1844.
WILLIAM HILL, of *Paganhill,*
who died 1851.
ELIZABETH, his Wife, died 1848.
MATILDA RATCLIFFE, died 1841.
WILLIAM RATCLIFFE, died 1858.
SAUL HEAVEN, died 1796.
MARY, his Daughter, died 1796.
SAMUEL, his Son, died 1798.
SAMUEL, his Son, 1829.
ANN, his wife, died 1857.
SAMUEL RATCLIFFE, died 1868.
BETSY, his Widow, 1880.
WILLIAM BULFORD, died 1841.
ANN, his Wife, died 1854.
3 Sons died Infants.
ELIZABETH COOKE, died 1750.
THOMAS COOKE, died 1751.
MARY TANNER, died 1837.
STEPHEN DUDBRIDGE, died 1831.
BETTY DUDBRIDGE, died 1834.

MARIA BOULTON, died 1834.
MARY, Wife of JOHN BOULTON,
died 1844.
JOHN BOULTON, died 1846.
THOMAS BRAND, died 1814.
THOMAS HILLMAN, died 1820.
CATHERINE CARRUTHERS, died 1859.
CATHERINE WATHEN, died 1848.
JOSEPH WATHEN, died 1849.
CHRISTIANA CARRUTHERS, died 1836.
HENRY CARRUTHERS, died 1834.

ON FLAT STONES.

THOMAS LITTLE, died 1798.
JASPER, his Son, died 1795.
BENJAMIN PERRY, died 1792.
MARY PERRY, died 1789.
SARAH ORGAN, died 1815.
ROBERT HOPKINS, died 1798.
MARY, his Wife.
JOSEPH WARTNALBY, died 1834.

ON A BRASS PLATE.

NATHANIEL PEACH, of this Parish,
Clothier, died 1719.
MARY, Daughter of THOMAS and
MARY PACEY, died 1805,
Aged 49 Years.
...... Wife of JAMES HAMTON, *Gent.*
THOMAS PLUMMER DEANE,
of this Parish, *Gent.* died 1867,
Aged 65 Years

IN SOUTH AISLE NEAR THE FONT
WAS THE EFFIGY OF A
Man and Wife six Sons, 3 Daughters.

ELIZABETH COOPER, eldest Daughter
of *Sir* SAMUEL WATHEN,
died July 20, 1808. Aged 31 Years.

NORTH AISLE.

ANN MARIA DIGHTON,
Daughter of *Sir* SAMUEL WATHEN,
died October 3, 1813, Aged 28.

IN SOUTH AISLE.

BRASSES IN MEMORIAM.

JOHN WOOLRIGHT, and WILHELMINA,
EMILY and JULIA, his 3 Children.
BASIL WILLIAMS, B. D. *Priest,*
who rested on the Eve of the
Epiphany, 1862.

NEW CHURCHYARD.

ANN, Wife of ELI JONES,
ob. 1883, Æt. 73.
GEORGE PEGLER, ob. 1881.
GERALD NORTON SMITH,
ob 1882.
AMY, Wife of GEORGE PEARCE
SEROCOLD, ob 1872.
ANN WAINWRIGHT, ob. 1882.
HENRY CRITCHLEY, ob. 1820.
PRISCILLA, Wife of JAMES PEARCE,
of *Atcombe Court,* ob. 1881.
GEORGE HENRY EVANS,
Rector, ob. 1878.
CHARLES FARRINGTON EVANS,
his Son, ob. 1875.
MABY LOUISA BROWNE, ob. 1881.
HENRY MILLS, ob. 1875.
SUSAN STEVENS,, ob. 1866.
ALFRED PARSONS, ob. 1879.
CHARLES JOSEPH EARL,
ob. 1882.
CHARLES VIRGO, ob. 1882.
ELIZABETH, Wife of JOSEPH
MITCHELL, ob. 1865.
JOSEPH MITCHELL,
ob. 1869.
WILLIAM WHITE, ob. 1808.

Notes as to I.—*Devolution of Estates.* II.—*Church.* III.—*Population, Taxation, &c.*

The name of this place recalls its pristine condition of forest in the times of the Britons and early races, and the encampments therein of their invaders the Romans whose dwelling here is further evidenced by the remains of a Villa discovered under the surface of the old Church Yard nearly two centuries ago, mentioned in (Cambden's Brittaniæ, 1692, described by R. Bradley, 1722. (British Museum, Additional, MSS. 5238.) and in King's Monumenta Antiqua, and illustrated by the sumptuous work of Mr. S. Lysons, (Antiquities of Woodchester.) and in the Transactions of the Bristol and Gloucestershire Archæological Society, *Vol.* 4.

In Saxon times (710-743,) a grant of the land of three cassata in the woodland country was made by Ethelbald, King of the Mercians, to St. Peters, Worcester, confirming the gift of Bishop Wurfarth, in this and other places adjacent:—Bisley, Rodborough, Avening, Nailsworth, Theescombe. *Kemble, Anglo. Sax. Diplom.*

The Saxons and Danes left vestiges of their occupation in the wanton destruction of the works of Roman civilization so far as fire could destroy them.

The woods still remained, and their memorial yet survives in Forest Green, the name of a hamlet here in a clearance of Wood; and the trees grew and covered up the Moisture which supplied the brooks in the vallies and combs with water. When the manufacture of Woollen cloth was introduced into England from Flanders in time of Edw. iii. this neighbourhood was resorted to for water, and perhaps for Water power; and its rural condition was changed. Woods and Brooks and running waters gave place to Mill ponds and Beech Plantations, less pleasing but more profitable.

The stream running through Nympsfield Park, was let down step by step through a chain of ponds to supply the small water cloth mills in Woodchester and Inchbrook.

The Subsidy Roll for Woodchester, 1 Edw. iii. does not contain any local Clothiers Names, but that of 30 Eliz. mentions Atwood, Clutterbuck, Chapman.

The Monumental Inscriptions to the members of successive clothier families through, two or three centuries in the course of which the trade had sprung up flourished and to a considerable extent decayed, will show how the trade grew by degrees from small Water Mills to steam Power Establishments. Some of the Factories of the Cloth making trade exist, but many of the Mills have been put to other uses.

The earliest Trade Buildings might have been half timbered structures; but of those now standing the oldest are stone built with Residences attached or near thereto. The Yarn was spun in the Cottages about the Villages. Bristol was the great out port of the West of England trade It was approached by Land from Nympsfield, by the Gloucester and Bristol Road and by Water through the Severn.

In Taylors Map of the County, 1777, about 10 Mills are marked in the lmits of Woodchester, chiefly on the Brook from Spring in Nympsfield Park.

In 1788, July 20, King George iii , in the course of his stay at Cheltenham, visited Woodchester, where Obadian Paul, exhibited the processes of the manufacture of Woollen Cloth to the Royal Party.

Estates :—

As to Estates, There were two Manors here:—1*st.* Widcestre in Blacheleu Hundred, contained one hide taxed. Culture, in demesne nothing, in Villenage, (sixteen Villans, twelve Bordars,) sixteen Carucates, one Burgess in Gloucester, rendering 10*s.* a Mill of 10*s.* This Manor was, with 10 *s.* Brictric, held then, and had held in King Edward's time.

Gueda, Mother of Earl (King) Harold, held Udecestre in Langetreu hundred. Earl Godwin, bought it of Azor, and gave to his wife that she might thereof subsist while she dwelt at Berkeley, for she was unwilling to take anything (from Berkeley,) on account of the destruction of the Abbey. This land, Edward of Wiltshire, held as of his farm. But unjustly, for the County saith that it belongeu to no farm, No steward of the King gave any account of this Manor. The Manor paid 7£. *Domesday Survey.*

Woodchester and Berkeley are some miles apart by carriage roads; but no doubt there was a shorter Packway through the woods at the time of the survey. It is considered that the Countess Gueda's, objection arose from the Nuns having been expelled through the act of Earl Godwin, from Berkeley; but the expression, in the survey are, very obscure and the writer was not an impartial Historian as regarded King Harold, and his family. This Manor was on the Nympsfield side of the Parish of Woodchester.

These two Manors came to the Crown, Brictric's on his forfeiture, and that of the Countess, after her death through King Harold's forfeiture.

In the reign of Edward i. the Manor was in the hands of John Maltravers, holding under William, Earl Marshall, From Maltravers, it passed to Fitzallan, Earl of Arundel and through that family to Thomas, Duke of Norfolk, on whose attainder it reverted to the Crown.

6 Eliz.—Sir George Huntley, Knight and John Huntley, Esqr. by Crown Grant.

Sir R. Ducie, whence as Tortworth, to Henry, Earl Ducie and from the late Earl to Mr. W. Leigh, by purchase.

Other Estates :—

42 Eliz.—Stony Close, 2½ in Parsons Meadow :

Jasper Selwin, and Wife Margaret and Brother Richard, (sons of Wm. Selwin,) to Jasper Clotterbooke.

44 Eliz 1602.—Capital Messuage and site of Manor of Woodchester, and Park and Shortcomb Closes and Wood ground, &c and Advowson of Church: Geo. Huntley, Esqr. to Robt. Tayloe, of Stroude, Clothman and Robert Tayloe, Junior. The consideration or price was £1,190. "Tayloe" is an old form for Taylor. *see* "Church Inscriptions."

Robert Bridges, by purchase from Tayloe. *Rudder.*

1805.—Sir Saml. Wathen, *Rudge, History of Gloucestershire.*

Temp Wm. iii.—Obadiah Grevell, held a Messuage and Lands here.

1791.—Northways, 8 a Comyn, T. Shurmer's.

1795.—Wilkins and Halliday, Assignees of T. Shurmer, Nathl. Dyer, by purchase.

Webbs Estate: *part Freehold and part Leasehold.*
Freehold Messuage Close 28 a. Okey Leaze 10 a.

1740—John King.

1799.—John Hort, by purchase.

1890.—Nathl. Dyer, by purchase.

D Richards, by purchase.

1818.—Sale Deed to Vizard.

1810.—Rev. W. Moore, by purchase of D. Richards and Vizard.

Webb's Estate, other part freehold,—Okey Close, Northway Close 8 a. Little Northways 2½ a. &c.

1713.—Nathl. Webb.

Settlement on Marriage with Eliz. Beard.

1754.—Danl Webb, Minchinhampton, Clothier. Elizth. Webb, Widow. Nathl. Webb, her son. Edw. Webb, Children of Nathl. Webb, and Elizth. his Wife. Samuel Webb, of London, Daniel Webb, and John Webb, other Children, and Richard Brown, of Cirencester, Soap Boiler and Mary, his Wife, late Mary Webb, another Child of ditto.

And part long Leasehold:—

1731.—Bird, (7 Jac. i.) Lease to Clutterbook.

Ann Pegler, Mortgage.

1732.—Aaron Wicke, marr. Ann Pegler.

1733.—James Smith, by purchase. of both freehold and Leasehold.

Nash Estate:—Two Messuages, Gardens, 2 Orchards containing 3a. late in J. Nash's possession. A Messuage and Garden adjoining the above late in J. Barnard's pos. session during life of Elizabeth, late Wife of W. Huntley. Two New Cottages 2 s. yearly Rent out of Barnard's. 2 s, yearly Rent out of Erecroft, held for residue of a long term of years.

Isaac Smith, of Dursley, Clothier and Wife Abigail, Henry Smith, of Kingswood, Clothier and Wife Sarah, and Silvanus Lysons, of Gloucester, Gent. and Wife Mary.

John and Giles Nash, of Woodchester, Clothiers, by purchase.

1701.—Robert Bridges, of Woodchester, Gent. In Trust for Jane Hicks, his Sister.

1714.—Robert Hicks, her son to Robert Bridges.

Pudhill afterwards Park Hill:
Mr. Small. (*Atkyns.*) Wickes, *Church Inscriptions.* Mr. Cambridge. (*Rudder.*) Mr. Wade. Gordon and Wife, by Will. Rev. W. Moore, by purchase. Mr. Playne, by purchase.

Atcombe House: Mr. Haycock's, afterwards Mr. Pearce, then Mr. H. D. Clark.

Woodchester House and Mills:—Mr. Peach.
Oakley House:—Mr. Dunn's.
Southfield House:—Mr. Budd's.
Lawn House:—Mr. Woolright's.
Elmsley House:—Mr. Wilberforces'.

1776.—At the County Election the following Voted for Freeholds in Woodchester.

Beadles, Nathl.	Pearce, Samuel.
Browning, Saml.	Pavey, Thomas.
Churches, Joseph.	Remington, Samuel.
Clark, William.	Rede, William.
Drew, John.	Rodway, Thomas Wicks.
Hill, William.	Rogers, Erasmus.
Do. Richard.	Smith, Walter.
Hodges, Thomas.	Shurmur, Thomas.
Hoddinott, Joseph.	Sharp, Edward.
Harrison, John.	Snow, George.
Hawker Peter, *Clerk.*	Tyley, James.
King, John.	Webb, William.
Merrett, William.	Wood, Levy.
Price, John.	Wade, John, *Esqr.*
Peach, Nathl. *Esqr.*	Young, Robert.

II.—*Church:*

The Advowson went with the Manor until Sale of the Estate by the late Lord Ducie. It is now vested in the Trustees of the Revd. Charles Simeon. The Rectory is of the Value about (£300.) a Year in (30a.) Glebe and Tithe Rent Charge.

A List of Rectors and Patrons of Woodchester.

1521.—Richard Higdon.	
1555.—Simon Seward.	E. Arundell.
Void 3 Years.	
1561.—Thomas Freeman.	
1585.—Jasper Merriett.	Queen Elizabeth.
1587.—John Tullie.	Christopher Moody.
1609—Thomas Ferebee.	George Huntley, *Knt.*
1623.—John Ferebee.	William Huntley.
1662.—John Edwards,	Sir Wm. Ducie, Bart.
1668.—James Stansfield.	Do. do.
1723, July.—John King.	Lord Ducie.
1723, Nov.—Thomas Dibble.	Do.
1756.—Peter Hawker.	Do.
1809.—Peter Hawker.	Do.
John Williams.	Do.

There are Chapels of Protestant Dissenters, Baptists, and others, in this Parish.

About 1850, very extensive Roman Catholic Establishments were set up here viz. A Dominican Priory with Mission Church, and a Franciscan Convent with Orphanage attached. They were founded or largely endowed by Mr. W. Leigh.

III.—*Taxation, Population, &c.*

Woodchester, Subsidy Roll, 1 EDW. iii., 1327.

De Galfrido le Stedeman, ii s.
" Robto. Adam, vi d.
" Rico. Jones, ix d.
" Nicho. Llot, ix d.
" Willmo. le Shephurde, xiii d.
" Robto. Braunche, xii d.
" Henr. Caperon, xviii d.
" Rogo. le Steer, vi d.
" Al·xr. West, xi d.
" Rico. Thoms, xvi d.
" Robto. Bronegare, xii d.
" Hug. Wymond, ii s.
" Johne. Adam, viii d.
" Johne. le Huware, x d.
" Dno. Johne. Mautravers, v s.
" Edith. Cokes, ii s. ix d. ob.

prob. Sma. xxii s. vii d. o.

Woodchester, Subsidy Roll, 30 Eliz.

John Awoode, ...	*bon.*	£5.	5s.
Thomas Browning, ...	*ter.*	20.	1s. 6d.
George Hucksall, ...	*bon.*	4.	4s.
W. Kinge, ...	...	3.	3s.
Edw. Clooterbook, ...	*bon.*	3.	3s.
James Chapman, ...	*bon.*	3.	3s.
John Merrett, ...	*bon*	3.	3s.
Thomas Wilkins, ...	*bon.*	4.	4s.
Elizth. Cook, ...	*bon.*	5.	5s.
William Shillam, ...	*bon.*	3.	3s.
William Wellstead and Thomas Birde, }	*bon.*	3.	3s.
John Cole, ...	*bon.*	3.	3s.

Acreage 1202 a.

Population 1801,—613. 1831,—885. 1871.—974.

1815. Yearly Value of Real Property £2730.

1882.—Rateable Value £3656.

1833-4-5.—Three Years Average Expenditure on Poor 350£.

In Stroud Union.

CCCV.
or 310.

WOOLLASTON.

THE CHURCH consists of a Chancel, Nave, and Two cross Aisles with a Spire and Steeple in the middle in which are four Bells. [Restored about 1875.]

His Grace the DUKE *of* BEAUFORT, LORD OF THE MANOR.
Revd. JOHN PRICE, B. D. *Trinity College, Oxford, Rector:*

BENEFACTIONS.

Names of the Benefactors to this Parish as appears by their Deeds now in the Custody of the Church Wardens.

1.—HENRY NEWLAND, *Abbot of Tinterne,* gave the Church House and Green, [for Widows Lodgings,] Anno 1501.

2.—*Mr.* RICHARD CLAYTON, *of Chepstow,* gave 20s. yearly in Money to the Poor.

3.—*Mrs.* MARGARET CLAYTON, his *Widow,* gave 40 Shillings for the teaching of four Poor Boys.

4.—*Mr.* THOMAS JAMES, *Alderman of Bristol,* gave 100£. to be lent by the Church Wardens to employ poor Widows in Spinning, each Widow to have the Use of Ten pounds for Twelve Years without Interest giving sufficient security for the repayment of the principal at the expiration of that Term, 1618.

5.—*Mrs.* SMART, *of this Parish,* gave 20s. yearly in Bread, [for poor Widows and fatherless Children] issuing out of Plasterwine farm, 1685.

6.—In perpetuam singularis providentiæ memoriam *Mr.* ROBERT GRIFFITH, (durante vita) gave 40s. to be distributed yearly in Bread, on the 1st. Sunday after the 26th. of June. Benedictus benedicatur ROBERT GRIFFITH, *Rector,* 1719.

JOSEPH CRAWLEY and PHILIP WILLIAMS, *Church Wardens.*

INSCRIPTIONS IN THE CHURCH. [*Few of these now to be seen.*]

CHANCEL.

ON A FLAT STONES.

Here lieth the Body of
HENRY LLOYD,
who died the 2nd. day of ....
(*defaced.*) ....

Here lyeth the Body of
WINIFRED GWILLIAM,
who departed this Life, the
27 of October 1667.

Under this Stone buried doth Lie
The mirrour of our Parts for Charitie
Religion was her Rule, Christ was
her Guide,
A Pious life she led and so she died.

Here lieth the Body of
WALTER SKINNER,
and MARTHA SKINNER,
Son and Daughter of
RICHARD SKINNER,
WALTER, deceased the 10 Dec. 1660.
(*defaced the rest*)

Here lyeth the Body of
THOMAS BELL, *Gent.*
who departed this Life, the
13th. of May, Anno 1 om. 1705.

Here lyeth the Body of
ELIZABETH, the Wife of JOHN
DAVIS, who departed ys.
Nov. 8, 1732.

M.
CALI. RI. GRIFFITH, hujus
Eccl. Rectoris filii natu maximi
Eximiæ virtutis adolescentis qui
quod maturior esset Cœlo
quam Academiæ illuc
migravit Anno Ætatis XVIIo.
Salutis MDCCXXVIII.
Sub eodem saxo Jacet ELIZ.
Predict. R. GRIFFITH, A. M Conjux
fidelis et diligens
domi semper fuit, in
forma boma mente quam
humilis, quæ obiit nono
Aprilis Anno Ætatis XLIVo.
MDCCXXX. (*very defaced.*)

NAVE.

ON FLAT STONES.

Here lyeth the Body of
ELIZABETH, the Wife of
CHRISTOPHER SHIPMAN,
of this Parish, who departed this Life,
Febr. 1, 1654.

Here lieth the Body of
ELIZABETH, the Wife of BENJAMIN
TAYLOR, of this Parish,
who departed this Life,
October 11th. 1760, Aged 52.
A rare Example of Fidelity.

In Memory of
LOVE BARROW, Wife of
JOHN BARROW, of *Woollaston Grange,*
who died 18 May 1785,
Aged 37 Years.

In Memory of
SARAH HANMOND, of this Parish,
who departed this Life, ye
1st. of Sept. 1782, Aged 65 Years.

In Memory of
MARY, Wife of JAMES HAMMOND,
Tanner, of this Parish,
who departed this Life, on the
day of Mid. 1785, Aged 22 Years.

In Memory of
JAMES HAMMOND, of this Parish,
Gent. who departed this Life, the
8th. day of Sept. 1780,
Aged 72 Years.

In Memory of
HESTER, Relict of JAMES HAMMOND,
Gent. of this Parish,
who departed this Life, the
2nd. of December 1795,
Aged 76 Years.

In Memory of
SUSANNAH, the Wife of
THOMAS LONG, and Daughter of
JAMES and MARY WOODROFFE,
of this Parish, who died the
28 of May 1794, Aged 28 Years.

Here lieth the Body of
JOAN, the Wife of JAMES WOODROFF,
who departed this Life, the
12th. day of May in the
Year of our Lord 1682.
And also of
JAMES, the Son of JAMES, and
the above JOAN, the Wife of
JAMES WOODROFF,
who departed this Life, the
19th. day of Nov. in the
Year of our Lord 1628.
And also here lieth the Body of
MARY, the Wife of EDMUND
WOODROFF, of *Noverend* and
Relict of JAMES WOODROFF, of
Plasterwine, who departed this Life,
25 December A. D. 1776,
Aged 34 Years.

Here lieth the Body of
ANN, Wife of JAMES WOODROFF,
of this Parish, She died 20 Jan. 1689.
Also here lieth the Body of
MARGARET, the Wife of JAMES
WOODROFF, *Junr.* of ys. Parish,
She died the 5th. Decr. 1712,
Aged 72 Years.
Also MARY, the second Wife of
JAMES WOODROFF, *Junr.*
of this Parish,
She died ye 29 Nov. 1730.
Also here lieth the Body of
JAMES WOODROFF, of ys. Parish,

---

who died the 10th. of July 1750,
Aged 65 Years.
Also JAMES WOODROFF, *Junr.*
died the 18th. June 1770,
Aged 63.

In Memory of
ISAAC, the Son of JAMES, and
BLANCH WOODROFF,
of *Plasterwine* in this Parish,
who died the 12th. of Jany. 1791,
Aged 3 days.
Also THOMAS WOODROFF,
died ye 10th. of July 1793,
Aged 1 Year and 2 Months.
Also WILLIAM SMALLWOOD WOOD-
ROFF, died April the 1st. 1794,
Aged 7 Months.

CHURCH YARD.

ON ALTAR TOMBS.

Here lyeth interred the Body of
MARY, the Daughter of WILLIAM
SMART, of this Parish,
who died the 3 day of November,
Ao. 1684.

Here lieth the Body of
WILLIAM SMART, of this Parish,
who departed this Life, the
22 Sept. 1680.
ANNE, the Wife of WILLIAM
SMART, died the 13 of Jany. 1666.

Here lyeth the Body of
CHARLES GWILLAM, *Gent.*
who died the 6 day of May 1724.
Aged 87 Years.
Here lyeth the Body of
ANNE STRATFORD, who died
9 March 1712.
Here lyeth the Body of
ELIZABETH, the Wife of CHARLES
HUGHES, of *Abergavenny, Gent.*
who departed this Life, the
7 of January 1694.

Here lyeth the Body of
JANE, the Wife of HUGH CANTON,
who departed this Life, the
9 March 1698.
WILLIAM, Son of said HUGH,
and JANE, his Wife,
ob. 13 August 1670.
Also JOHN CANTON,
who died 9 June 1702.

Here lyeth the Body of
HONEST WILLIAM CLARKE,
who departed this Life, the
30 day of September 1671.

In Memory of
WILLIAM ROGERS, of this Place,
who died the 16 day of April 1763,
Aged 31 Years.
WILLIAM, the Son of WILLIAM,
and PRUDENCE ROGERS,
died an Infant.

Here lyeth the Body of
JOSEPH CRAWLEY, of this Parish,
who departed this Life, the
19 Febr. 1760, Æt. 69.

Here lies the Body of
ANNE, the Wife of ROGER
BODSMAN, of *Rodrack, Esqr.*
who departed this in Jany. 1694.

In Memory of
HENRY JONES, of this Parish,
who died Febr. 23, 1789,
Aged 55 Years.

In Memory of
WARREN SILCOKS, *Senior,*
of this Parish, who died
the 29 of Nov. 1746,
Aged 50 Years.
ELIZABETH, the Wife of
WARREN SILCOCKS, of this Parish,
who died March 29, 1779,
Aged 30 Years.
In Memory of
ELIZABETH WORGAN,
of *Plasterwine*, who departed
this Life, 4 of June 1771,
Aged 82 Years.

Here lieth the Body of
JOSEPH, the Son WILLIAM and
ELIZABETH WORGAN, of this Parish,
who departed this Life, 10 day
of October 1754, Aged 22 Years.
JOSEPH, the Son of WILLIAM and
MARY CRADDOCK, of this Parish,
who departed this Life, 3 of
July 1776, Aged 14 Years.

Near this Place lies the Remains
of ELIZABETH, the Wife of
THOMAS ALLEN, of the *Hggins* in
the Parish of *St. Briavels, Gent.*
and Daughter of WILLIAM and
SARAH WORGAN, who departed
this Life, 19 of April 1793,
Aged 73 Years.
Also in Memory of
MARY, the Wife of WILLIAM
CRADDOCK, who departed this Life,
7 Febr. 1794, Aged 60 Years.

Here lies interred the Body of
ANN, the Wife of WALTER HARRIS,
Daughter of RICHARD BARROW,
Gent. She died 20 Oct. 1786,
Aged 73 Years.
Her Grandson died in his Infancy.
RICHARD HARRIS, of this Parish,
Son of the abive WALTER and
ANN HARRIS, who departed this
Life, 27 day of Jany. A. D. 1784,
Aged 52 Years.

In Memory of
EDWARD WHITE,
who died 22 March 1782,
Aged 75 Years.
ELIZABETH, Wife of EDWARD
WHITE, *Junr.* of this Parish,

died 10 Jany. 1782, Aged 75 Years.
EDWARD WHITE, of this Parish,
died 11 August, 1730,
Aged 60 Years.
MARY, his Wife, died 13 Jany. 1745,
Aged 76 Years.
Also WINIFRED, the Wife of
WILLIAM WHITE, of this Parish,
died the 12 of November 1748,
Aged 36 Years.
Also the above WILLIAM WHITE,
who died the 9 of Febr. 1775,
Aged 63 Years.
Also PRUDENCE, the Daughter of
the above WILLIAM and WINIFRED
WHITE, Aged 10 Years.
FRANCIS and JANE JONES,
who died 6 July 1784,
Aged 1 Year and 4 Months.

In Memory of
WILLIAM HARRIS, *Gent.*
Sail Maker, of this Parish,
who died 29 June 1799,
Aged 65 Years.
In Memory of
EDWARD WHITE, of this Parish,
who died the 18 of October 1787,
Aged 51 Years.
Also MARY, *Widow,* of the above
EDWARD WHITE, and *Relict* of
RICHARD HARRIS, *Tanner,*
of this Parish, who died
Sept. 16, 1792, Aged 63 Years.
SARAH, the Daughter of
JOHN and MARY SADLER,
who died Aged 3 days.
In Memory of
RICHARD BARROW, *Gent.*
who died 23 June 1720.
MARY, the Daughter of RICHARD
BARROW, and Wife of GEORGE
BUCKLE, who died 12 Decr. 1733.
GEORGE, the Son of GEORGE and
MARY BUCKLE, who died the
16 of Novr. 1773, Aged 87 Years.
JOHN BARROW, *Gent.*
who departed this Life,
12 Decr. 1775, Aged 77 Years.

In Memory of
PRUDENCE, Wife of WILLIAM
LEWIS, of this Parish,
who died 8 day of Oct. 1799,
Aged 67 Years.
WILLIAM, the Son of WILLIAM
and PRUDENCE ROGERS,
of this Parish, died 20 Oct. 1761,
Aged 5 Years and 6 Months.
WILLIAM ROGERS, of this Parish,
who died the 16 day of April 1763,
Aged 51 Years.

In Memory of
THOMAS and JOSEPH WILLIAMS,
late of *Keynsham* in this Parish,
THOMAS, died May 26, 1785,
Aged 75 Years.
JOSEPH, died July 15, 1793,
Aged 86 Years.

In Memory of
SARAH, the Wife of JAMES WHITE,
of *Plasterwine,*
who died 14 Sept. 1769,
Aged 64 Years.
JAMES, the Son of JAMES and
SARAH WHITE, of this Parish,
who departed this Life,
4 of March, 1766, Aged 17 Years.

In Memory of
WILLIAM WATKINS, of this Parish,
who departed this Life,
17 June 1780, Aged 69 Years.
RICHARD WATKINS, of this Parish,
died 14 April 1789, Æt. 48.
ELIZABETH, Wife of WILLIAM
WATKINS, died Sept. 19, 1791,
Æt. 91.

Here lyeth the Body of
SARAH, the Wife of ABEL ADAMS,
of the City of *Bristol,*
who departed this Life, the
10 day of Sept. in the Year of our
Lord 1706, Aged 57 Years.
ELIZABETHA, Filiæ JACOBI
WOODROFE, uxor GULIELMI PROBYN,
de *Newland,* Obiit Ultimo die
Decembr. Anno Dom. 1665.
Here lyeth the Body of
JAMES WOODROFFE,
who departed this Life, Jany. 25,
Anno Dom. 1728.
Here lyeth the Body of
ELIZABETH, the Wife of EDMUND
WOODROFFE, who died 14 day of
June 1780, Aged 85 Years.

In Memory of
HENRY JONES, late of this Parish,
who died Febr. 23, 1789,
Aged 55 Years.

(Supplementary Notices of Additional
Monuments &c. since Bigland's time.)

CHANCEL.

Sacred to the Memory of
JOHN GWATKIN DOWLER,
formerly of *Thraxton* in the Co. of
Hereford, and late of the *Grange*
in this Parish, He died
2 March 1834, Aged 55.
His Remains are interred at
Monmouth.

Sacred to the Memory of
the following Children of
ANTHONY and ELIZABETH HAMMOND:
JAMES, who died 24 Aug. 1823,
Aged 39 Years.
ANTHONY, who died 28 June 1833,
Aged 48 Years.
WILLIAM, who died 5 Febr. 1837,
Aged 46 Years.
MARY, who died 11 Oct. 1865,
Aged 73 Years.

EDMOND WOODROFFE,
died Febr. 5, 1845, Aged 55.
SUSANNAH, his Wife,
died Decr. 30, 1846, Aged 37.
SUSANNAH BLAND, only Daughter
of the above, died Dec. 21, 1841,
Aged 17 Years.
The Sisters of the said EDMOND
WOODROFF:—ANNE, died March 26,
1839, Aged 30 Years. And
ELLEN JANE MOSLEY,
died July 9, 1839, Aged 36.

Sacred to the Memory of
BLANCH, the Wife of
JAMES WOODROFEE, *Gent*
late of *Plasterwyne,* died July 1881,
Aged 66, haveing survived her

Husband, who died Aug. 1822,
Aged 54 Years.

IN THE PORCH.

Over the Church Door is a Tablet
to ROBERT WARD,
who died 1825.

NAVE.

OVER THE SOUTH DOOR.

In a Vault underneath repose

JOHN and MARY SADLER WARD,
of the .... Stroud.
In Death they were united.
This Tribute of affection is erected
by their Daughter
EMMA E. PONTING.

In Memory of
ANTHONY SHIPMAN,
of this Parish, who died April 1660.
JAMES HAMMOND, Nephew of
the above, died 23 July 1660.
ANTHONY HAMMOND,
Son of the said JAMES HAMMOND,
died 3 April 1731.

JAMES HAMMOND,
Son of said ANTHONY HAMMOND,
died .... 1760, Aged 72.
HESTER, his Wife, died 2 Dec. 1725.
JAMES, Son of the said ANTHONY
and HESTER, HAMMOND,
died 17 Sept. 1829, Aged 70.
MARY, his Wife, died 15 Mh. 1785,
Aged 32.
ELIZABETH HAMMOND, Spinster,
died 6 Jany. 1834, Aged 78.
ANTHONY HAMMOND,
formerly of the Grange afterwards
of High Woolaston, died 4 Mh. 1832,
Aged 80 Years.
ELIZABETH, his Wife,
died 8 Sept. 1826, Aged 69.

HEAD STONES.

	Died.	Aged.		Died.	Aged.
James Williams, ...	21 July	1750	60	Maud, his Wife, ...	30 Augt. 1799	68
William Williams, ...	29 March	1776	82	John Jones, ...	9 June 1799	75
Tabitha, his Wife, ...	9 Nov.	1760	70	Margaret, Wife of John Jones,	5 Nov. 1766	56
Morgan Howell, ...	5 Nov.	1755	70			

Supplementary Notes as to Devolution of Estates I. Church, II. Population, Taxation, &c. III,

I.—Estates.

Woolaston in the Forest division of Westbury Hundred, stands on the north east side of the rising bank of the Severn on its higher ground runs the (late Turnpike,) Road from Gloucester to Chepstow and below that Road the Great Western Railway.

Although on the confines of Wales it was on the English side of Offas Dyke.

Odelvaston in Twiferde Hundted contained two Hides taxed. Culture: No tillage in demesne. But in Villenage 5 Carucates. (5 Villans.) There were a fishery in Severn of 5s. kent and a Mill of 40 pence rent. The Estate was worth 20s. per Year. Domesday Survey:

The great Saxon thane Brictric, held it.

After the Conquest William de Ow, or Eu, a Norman held until by adhering to the fortunes of Robert, Duke of Normandy, against William Rufus, he forfeited his Estate.

As mentioned under Tidenham this Parish was part of Lord Worcester's Estate which was granted by Vote of the House of Commons to the Lord General Cromwell; and at the Restoration returned to its former Owners. It was lately sold to Sir S. S. Marling, Bart.

The Duke of Beaufort's House called the Grange, is noticed in Chamberlin's "Angliæ Noticiæ," 1704, as one of the noblest seats in the County. In Rudder's time it was neglected; its chapel being converted into a Malthouse. It has since been restored.

There are several Hamlets or places in Woollaston.

Brookend: Gumstod:

Plaster Wyne :—Mr. Hammonds.

Fines of Lands in Woollaston were levied :—

21 Eliz.—W. Gough, Plaintiff. E. Madocks, Deforciant.
28 Eliz.—W. Gough, Plaintiff. Robt Hempsted, Defor.
W. Morris, Plaintiff. Hen. Morris, Deforciant.

T. 31 & 32, Geo. ii.—Thos. Summer, Plaintiff. Chas. Wyndham, Deforciant.

The Inclosure Act, Geo. iii. is noticed under Tidenham.

The Garden Allotment here was 15 a. The Poors Allotment 3 a. And there was set out for Road Materials one sixteenth part of the Commonable Land : Amongst the Proprietors named are the Duke of Beaufort, Messrs. Hammond, Jenkins, Woodruff.

Ancient Wills at Gloucester, of Woollaston.

1544.—Elizth. Bayse.
1545.—W. Hemsted.
1546.—Joan James.
1546.—R. Bate.

1547.—J. March.
1547.—J. Radolf.
1603.—......... Smith.

1776.—At the County Election the following Voted for freeholds in Woollaston:

Bamard, James.
Barrow, James.
Do. Thomas.
Do. Richard.
Gain, William.
Hammond, James.
Harris, Richard.

James, Morris.
Price, Joseph.
Penny, Robert, D. D. Rector.
Worgan, John.
Watkins, William.
Woodruff, Edmund.
Woodroff, James.

II.—Church.

List of Incumbents and Patrons of Woolaston, with Alvington and Lancaut.

Incumbents.	Patrons.
1548—Roger Winter, deprived 1557.	
1557.—Thomas Whitfield.	Earl of Worcester.
1562.—John Bull, deprived 1562.	Countess Worcester.
1564.—Henry Ellston.	
1580.—Henry Lloyd.	
1627.—Arnold Williams.	John Anderton.
1661.—Thomas Pugh.	Marquis Worcester.
1674.—Thomas Davis.	Do. do.
1695.—............	King W. & Q. Mary.
1696.—Robert Bell.	Lapse.
1711.—Robert Griffith.	Henry D. Beaufort.
1737.—James Meredith.	Do.
1745.—Somerset Jones.	Abp. Canterbury.
1769.—Robert Penny.	Duke Beaufort.
1732.—James Price.	Do.
1813.—Charles Bryan.	Do.

III.—Taxation, Population, &c. of Woollaston.

Acreage 3168 a.

Population 1801,—613. 1861,—971.
1831,—800. 1871,—998.

In 1815. Annual Value of Real Property 3159 £.

1882.—Rateable Value £8007.

1833-4-5. Average of three Years Expenditure on Poor £.......

In Chepstow Union.

LANCAUT, is a Chapelry of 39£. Yearly Value. Its Church is in ruins. see "Tidenham."

Of Lancaut in 1871, the Population was 9, and rateable Value 235 £.

WORMINGTON.

THE CHURCH is small dedicated to St. Catherine, or the Holy Trinity, the figure of St. Catherine with the Wheel, appears on painted Glass in one of the Windows. It has a small low Wooden Tower in the Middle containing three Bells, and an Aisle on each side of the Nave and a Chancel.

SAMUEL GIST, *Esqr.*, LORD OF THE MANOR.

Revd. JOHN DUDDALL, *Rector:*

HATCHMENTS.

1*st. H.*—*Quarterley* 1 *and* 4 party per pale Gules and Sable, On a Chevron engrailed Or, three fleur de lys Azure between 3 Swans' necks erased Argent,—GIST, *impaling quarterly* 1 *and* 4, per bend Or and vert, in chief a tree vert, in base a Seahorse regardant Argent. 2 *and* 3 Or, three Martlets closed Gules within a bordure,—WESTENRA; Or, 2 *and* 3 per Saltire Argent, and Or, two Leopards' heads counter charged in chief and base. On sides Or, two roses Gules barbed and seeded proper.—WESTENRA. *Motto.* "Resurgam."

Crest double:—A Swan's neck erased Argent, collared and labelled Gules. A demi savage proper, labelled Gules holding in dexter hand a wreath vert, in sinister hand a cross cross-let Gules.

2*nd. H.*—*Quarterly* 1 *and* 4, GIST, *as before.* 2 *and* 3, Or, three Cypress trees vert between two chains Sable bend-wise, on dexter side a wreath Sable. *An escutcheon of Pretence of* WESTENRA. *A celestial Crown and Motto in Coelo Quies.*

3*rd. H.*—Blazonry of Arms, *same as No.* 2

Crest:—*same as No.* 1. *Motto* "Benigno Numine."

4*th. H.*—Blazonry of Arms, *same as No.* 1. Cherubs at corners. *No Crest.*

INSCRIPTIONS IN THE CHURCH.

CHANCEL.

ON A PLAIN MONUMENT AGAINST THE
NORTH WALL.

Sacred to the Memory of
WILLIAM ANDERSON, *Esqr.*
who departed this Life, the
1*st.* day of January 1796,
Aged 54 Years.

ON A MONUMENT AGAINST THE
SOUTH WALL.

Near this Place lieth the Body of
JAMES PARTRIDGE,
Rector of this Church 40 Years.
i.e was buried the 11*th.* day of
July Anno Domini. 1734,
Aged 64 Years.
Also ELIZABETH, his beloved Wife,
was buried here October 12*th.* 1750.
Aged 80 Years.

UNDER THE LAST.

Here lieth the Body of
JOHN PARTRIDGE,
Parson here 28 Years,
who departed this Life, the
21*st.* day of July 1690.
Aged 63 Years.

ALONGSIDE THE LAST.

Here lieth also the Body of
MARY PARTRIDGE,
his beloved Wife, who departed this
Life, the 3*rd.* day of February,
Anno Dom. 1700,
Aged 56 Years.

ANOTHER.

Near this Place lieth the Body of
JOHN PARTRIDGE,
Rector of this Parish, 41 Years.
He was buried the 27 day of May,
A. D. 1775, Aged 76 Years.

ON FLAT STONES.

FRANCISCUS LANSTON,
Artium Magister et in Legibus,
Baccalaureus, Obijt 2 die Aprilis,
Anno Domini 1605.

Here lieth the Body of
WILLIAM DOBYNS, *Esqr.*
who deceased the 20*th.* of May,
Anno Dom. 1680.

Here lieth the Body of
MARGARET the Wife of
WILLIAM DOBYNS, *Esqr.*
who deceased the 23*rd.* day of June,
Anno Dom. 1677.

Here lieth the Body of
THOMAS PARTRIDGE,
who departed this Life,
April the 30*th.* Anno Dom. 1721,
Aged 56 Years.

ON WHITE STONE WITH THE FIGURE
OF A MAN BETWEEN HIS TWO WIVES,
WITH VERGE INSCRIPTION IN OLD
CHURCH TEXT.

Hic jacent corpora
JOHANNIS DASTON, *Armigeri,*

et CATHERINÆ, et ELEANORÆ,
uxorum ejusdem qui quidem
JOHANNIS, obijt xxiiii die mensis
Augusti Anno Dom. M°.CCCCXXXII,
et CATHERINÆ, obijt xiii. Octobr.
Anno Dom. M°.CCCCCXVII.
et ELEANORÆ, obijt xx. die Febr.
Anno Dom. M°.CCCCXXXII.
Animabus propitietur Deus Amen.

ON A BRASS PLATE.

The english on the Verge the
latin in the centre with a Woman and
Child dressed in swadling clothes lying in a Bed with the representation
of the Inside of a Room, all engraved
on a Brass Plate.

Arms at top first Coat:—Argent,
six Lions rampant Sable.—SAVAGE.
2*nd. Coat Quarterly* 1 *and* 4. Gules
on a bend Or. three Estoils Sable.—
DASTON. 2 *and* 3 .... a fess
wavy between six Billets.

Here lieth the Bodye of
ANNE SAVAGE, the Wife of
JOHN SAVAGE, of *Norbury* in the
County of *Worcester, Esqr.*
And Eldest Daughter of
RICHARD DASTON. *Esqr.*
who departed out of this Life,
the xvii day of June 1605,
being of the Age of 25 Years.

Filiolus, Conjux, Pater, effera fata
queruntur
Quæ delictam ANNAM SAVAGE,
Eripuere marito
Et primogenita DASTON, velut al-
tera Phœnix,
Dum paret illa perit, dum parturit
interit Anna
Anna animum cœlo lustris jam
quinque perfectis
In cœlum reuijt, sed terræ huic
ossa reliquit.

HENRY PARTRIDGE,
of the Age of 71,
died the 17 day of October,
Anno Dom. 1624.

JOHN PARTRIDGE,
of the Age of 78 Years,
and *Parson* here 48 Years,
died 14 day of September,
Ano. Dni. 1622.
Here lyeth the Body of
JOHN PARTRIDGE,
Aged 83 Years,
and *Parson* here 39 Years,
who died March 11,
Ano. Dni. 1661.

ON A FLAT STONE THREE FEMALE
FIGURES IN ANCIENT DRESS.

NAVE.

ON FLAT STONES.

Arms Quarterly 1 and 4, DASTON,
as before. 2 and 3. .... a fess
wavy .... between six billetts.—
DUMBLETON.
Crest:—a Reindeers head and
Neck, affronté with an Arrow run
thro' the Neck.

ANTONIUS DASTON, *Armiger*,
.... December, die Martii.
Anno Domi. MDCXLI.
.... DASTON, Filius ANIONI,
Armiger. Sepultus Decimo Quarto
die Julii Ano. Dni. 1.........
(*very much defaced*.)

Arms:—Argent, two bars wavy
Sable.—FELL.
Crest:—a Pelican feeding her
young Gules.

Here lieth the Body of
WILLIAM FELL, *Gent*.
who died the 31st. of May 1690,
Ætatis suæ 52.

NORTH AISLE.

ON FLAT STONES.

Here lieth the Body of
Mrs. REBECCA WELLS,
who departed this Life, the
14 of June 1727, Aged 24 Years.

Here lyeth
ELIZABETH, the Wife of
WILLIAM WADE,
.... Anno Dom 1632.

SOUTH AISLE.

ON FLAT STONE.

Here lyeth the Body of
JOHN MOORE,
who departed this Life, the
13 day of December,
Anno Domini 1710.

CHURCH YARD.

(NO ALTAR TOMBS.)

(*Additional since Bigland's time.
In the Church.*)

IN CHANCEL.

ON TABLETS.

Sacred to the Memory of
SAMUEL GIST, *Esqr*.
Patron of Church and Lord of Manor,
who died Jany. 15, 1815,
Aged 92 Years.

Sacred to the Memory of
MARY GIST, Daughter of
JOSIAH GIST, *Esqr*. and ANN,
his Wife, of *Wormington Grange*,
who departed this Life,
January 31, 1834, Aged 30 Years.

Sacred to the Memory of
the *Honble*. MARY ANN GIST,
the beloved Wife of SAMUEL
GIST GIST, *Esquire*, of *Wormington
Grange*, and only Daughter of
Lord ROSSMORE, of *Monaghan,
Ireland*, who departed this Life,
Febr. 14, 1844, Aged 43 Years.

Also to the Children of
SAMUEL GIST GIST, *Esqr*.
and MARY-ANN, his Wife:
MARGARIT ELIZABETH,
who died Febr. 26, 1829,
Aged 11 Months.
ELIZABETH PERKINS,
who died Oct. 2, 1821,
Aged 8 Months;
ANN, who died March 6, 1832,
Aged 5 Years;
ELEANOR AUGUSTA, who died
Decr. 29, 1835, Aged 6 Months.

Sacred to the Memory of
JOSIAH GIST, *Esqr*.
of *Wormington Grange*, and
High Sheriff of this County,
who departed this Life,
March 25, 1834, Aged 69 Years;
Also of ANN, Wife of the above,
who departed this Life,
Nov. 18, 1825, Aged 59 Years.

IN CHURCHYARD.

MARY BUMFORD, died 1820.
ALICE BUMFORD, died ....

JOSEPH PHIPPS, died 1808.
MARY PHIPPS, died 1802.
ESTHER PHIPPS, died 1806.
CHARLES PHIPPS, died 1807.

JANE STAITE, died 1872.
RICHARD STAITE, died 1874.

OSCAR WILLIAM JAYNES,
who died 1878.
WILLIAM CHARLES JAYNES,
who died 1852.

HEAD STONES.

	Died.	Aged.		Died.	Aged.
George Horniblow, ...	3 March 1757	64	John Phipps, ...	6 Dec. 1781	68
Mary, Wife of George Horniblow,	30 Oct. 1762	77	Henry Clayton, ...	23 Augt. 1783	57
Edward Aly, ...	18 Sept. 1737	71	Christian, Wife of Henry Clayton,	9 Oct. 1793	76
Joan, his Wife, ...	20 Jany. 1737	54	James Clark, ...	5 Sept. 1786	62
Sarah, Daughter of John and Anne Phipps, ...	17 Jany. 1766	17	Tapling Wheeler, ...	15 Jany. 1791	84
Charles Toney, ...	17 June 1744	66	Ann, his Wife, ...	18 Sept. 1748	66
Mary, Wife of Charles Toney,	15 May 1752	76	Elizabeth, their Daughter, ...	22 July 1745	7
Mary, Daughter of Charles and Mary Toney, ...	26 April 1752	33	Joseph, their Son, ...	20 Jany. 1749	13
Richard Salis, ...	15 April 1751	56	Benjamin, Son of John and Mary Alcocks, ...	15 Nov. 1787	17
Mary, Wife of Richard Salis, ...	15 Sept. 1740	60	William Bayliss, ...	5 Decr. 1789	65
Ann, Wife of John Phipps, ...	10 Nov. 1773	52	George, Son of William, and Sarah Bayliss, ...	21 July 1793	29

Notes as to 1.—*Devolution of Estates*. II.—*Church*. III.—*Population, Taxation, &c.*

I.—*Estates*:

Wormington is a small parish situate 5 miles North from Winchcomb. It consists of two places distinguished as Great and Little Wormington, and has one Church which is in Little Wormington.

Little or Church Wormington, is thus mentioned in Domesday Survey: In Gretestan Hundred:—

Wermetune contained 5 Hides taxed. Culture: 2 Carucates in demesne; and 2 in Villenage; Two serfs; A Mill worth 8s; 10a. of Meadow. It was worth 100s. but then (at the Survey) 4£. 1175.—Roger de Laci, held and Walter Ercoldson, of him and Edwy, had held [in Saxon times.]
Domesday Survey.

From the Lacy family it passed by Gift to the Knights Templars.

On the suppression of that Order, Little Wormington, was granted to Westbury College, near Bristol.

1 Hen. vii.—Entry in the Crown Rental of Kiftsgate Holford and Gretstane Hundreds: In Wormington, Westbury College pays for demesne Lands and Tenements 3s. 4d

Thomas Darston, for Tenements 2 0
Henry Jones, for Tenements 1 0

On the dissolution of the College in 1544, Little Wormington, passed by Crown Grant to Sir Ralph Sadler. In 1608, it belonged to John Newton, from whom it passed by marriage of a female Heir to Gwinnet, who in 1658, compounded for his Estate, then by purchase to Dobbins, (see "Church Inscriptions.") who sold it to Townsend, who devoted the greater part of his Estate to charitable uses.

1682.—George Townsend, of Lincoln's Inn, devised by his Will, a capital Messuage and site of Manor of Wormington, and 159 a. of Land to his Cousin Robert Kenrick, but the bulk of his Estate was given to Trustees to provide Exhibitions at Pembroke College, Oxford, for Scholars from the Grammar Schools of Campden, Cheltenham, Northleach, & Winchcomb. see "Statement of the Will, in the 72 Report of the Charity Inquiry Coms. Cheltenham Charities."

The Dastyn or Daston family held Lands here for several generations, and this place was sometimes called Dastyn's Wormington.

Mr. Partridge, who held the Benefice had claims on this Manor which he sold to Mr. Jefferys, who sold to Gist.

Other Estates:—
Fines of Lands in Little Wormington.
16 Hen. vi.—R. Stake, H. Aylworth.

7 Edw. iv.—W. Vance, W. Heyne.

52 Geo. iii.—The Act for inclosure of the open fields and Meadows commonable and intermixed Lands of the Parish of Wormington. It states that Samuel Gist, was Lord of the Manor and Patron of the Church and John Duddell Clerk, was Rector and entitled to the Glebe Land and Tythes It names as the Trustees of Townsend'a Charity: A. Rogers, W. Mathews, R. Miles, C. Tidmarsh, T. Nettleshipp, Geo. Kidman, and T. Symonds. The Award and the Map thereof show that the Place to be enclosed was Church Wormington. The total area of old Closes and Allotments was 510 a. The Allottees were Mr. Gist, Townsends Trustees and the Rector The Tythe Allotments were to be one ninth of the passure and one third of the arable Land to be inclosed.

The Award sets out two new Roads one to Aston Somerville and the other to Laverton, and makes provision for improving certain Water courses. The Award is at Gloucester.

1776.—At the County Election, the following Voted for freeholds in Wormington:
Nathl. Jefferys, and the Revd. Thomas Stedman.

At the Election 1811, voted.
Revd. John Duddell, S. R. Franklin.

Great Wormington, is by Atkyns and Rudder, stated to be in the Parish of Didbrook; And in the 1st. Volume of this Work under Didbrook, (No. XCIV.) Wormington Grange and its then Owner are mentioned; but the place is not said to be in the Parish of Didbrok. Fosbroke, could not find out what the connection was between the two Wormingtons, but says that they both together passed to Kenrick and Partridge, who sold it Jefferys and he to Gist, ii. Fosb. 353. They both did indeed belong to Jefferys, but Great Wormington, was by him acquired from Lord Aylmer, and Little Wormington, from Kenrick, (claiming under Townsend,) and Partridge.

Great Wormington, was a small Vill, formerly a grange farm of the adjacent Abbey of Hayles. According to monastic usage it was claimed, and in time reputed, to be a Manor of itself. Its Tythes were appropriated to that Abbey which was also appropriator of Didbrok.

How Great Wormington, came to Lord Aylmer, does not appear; but his Arms are blazoned in the Collection of the Arms of the Nobility and Gentry of the County of Gloucester, by Sir George Naylor, 1792.

26 Hen. viii.—In the Valor Ecc'tus. under Wormington Magna, the farm of the site of this Manor, with the Meadow and pasture (Except Land held of Laverton,) is stated, be in the hands of the Abbot of Hayles for Husbandry and is estimated at 20 £. Value Yearly.

It may be assumed that the Vills were originally one

Parish. The Vills were at one time more populous than in later times. see the "Subsidy Roll, of 1327," after stated.

II.—Church.

1268 —Bodenham, is named Patron, after him Chapman le Cleve, Butler and Bray, successively.

List of Patrons and Rectors of Church Wormington.

Rectors.	Patrons.
1348.—Robert Shardlow.	
1373.—Roger Jones	
1375.—Richard Bancks.	Richd. Bancks
1387.—John Partridge.	
1623.—John Partridge.	Henry Partridge.
1662.—John Partridge	Margaret Partridge.
1690 —Robert Morse.	
1694 —James Partridge.	Mary Partridge.
1734 —John Partridge.	Augustin Meadows.
1775.—Thomas Stedman.	Nathl. Jefferis.
1791 —John Duddell.	Samuel Gist Gist.

Thus Five Incumbents of the Partridge family held the Benefice for near 200 years.

1546.—At Bishop Hoopers Examination R. Sherlow, was Rector. Commandments:—He knew their number and where they were written, but could not repeat them. Belief: He knew and could repeat but not prove the Articles. Lords Prayer: He Answerd well. The Communicants were 40.

Wormynton Parva:—Land given to the finding of a lamp there. Distributed to the poore sithens lamps taken away. The yearly Value thereof iiij s. iiii d.

III.—Taxation, Population, &c.

Wormyngtone Parva, cum Lullyntone, Subsidy Roll, 1 Edw. iii., 1327.

De Robto. de Bodenham, ii s. i d.		De Walto. de Colne, ii s.	
Rico. atte Mulle, ii s. vii d. ob. q.		Robto. de Knelle. ix d.	
		Alicia de Colne, vi d.	
		Robto. Dastyn, vi s. x d.q.	
Edythea Rolves, xiiii d.		Willmo. Horsnayl, viii d.	
Johne. le Kinge,ii s.ii d.q.		Nico. le Wyse, vi d.	
Matilda Jones, ii s. i d. q.		Marg. la Carpenter, vi d.	
Robto. Wylkines, viii d.		Isabella Aleyn, vi d.	
Agnete Wyke, xv d. q.		Rico. Alein, vi d.	
Willmo. Beaufiz, viii d.		Willmo. Molendinario, vi d.	
Nich. Graunt, xii d. ob. q.			

prob. Sam. xxviii s. d. o.

Wormyntone Magna, Subsidy Roll, 1 Edw. III. 1327.

De Thom. Cole, xxi d. ob. q.		De Johne. Huggen, ii s. i d,	
Willmo. Mogge, xx d.ob q.		Robto. Brant, xvi d.	
Johne. Houwen, ii s.v d q.		Willmo. Ferthings, ii s. vii d. ob.	
Andr. Grant, xix d. ob.			
Johne, Dabat, ii s. viii d.		Willm. le Noble ii s. ix d.	
Willmo. Abraham, xii d.		Robto. Gouwer, xx d,	
Rob. de Homme, ii s. x d.		Rico. Brant, xx d.	
Petro Wyllam, ii s. xi d.		Rico. Bonde, xiii d. ob.	
Willm. Huggen, ii s. vii d. ob. q.		Rico. de Homme, iii s. i d.	
Henr. Edam, xii d.		Walto. Huggen, iii s. i d.	

prob. Sma. xl s vi d.

In the Musters for part of the County of Gloucester, 1543, Little Wormington:
John Why Hill, Const(able) was co(mmanded) to a Bill.
  b. John Freman, co(mmanded) to harnez for a bill man.
  b. Richard Hayley, co(mmanded) to harnez an archer.
  b. Henry Cottrell, co(mmanded) to a saiet.
  ad. Richard Honyburn.
  ad. William Stevyns.
  ad. John Stevyns, junr.
This Township held in redynez a horse harnez and a bill.

Acreage of Little Wormington, 521 a.

Population:—1801,—91, 1861.—79.
1831.—96. 1871.—86.

In 1815. Annual Value of Real Property 707 £.

1882. Rateable Value 612 £.

1832-3-4. Average of three Years Expenditure on Poor 47 £.

In Winchcombe Union.

WOTTON - UNDEREDGE.

WOTTON-UNDEREDGE.

THE CHURCH is very large consisting of a Chancel, Nave and a large Aisle on each side therein are also several Chantries. It is dedicated to St. Mary. It hath a high Tower at the West-end with battlements and pinnacles containing eight Bells. At the East-end of South Aisle are the Arms of the King of Denmark, viz.— Azure three Crowns Or, and in several of the Windows are the Arms of BERKELEY:—Under the Kings Arms are the Arms of TATTERSALL, viz.—Sable a Chevron between three heraldic Tygers looking at their faces in a Mirror Or. and On the Gallery the following,—"Gloria Deo Gratia Fundatoribus." [The Gallery was taken away at the Restoration 1882.]

The Right Honorable the EARL *of* BERKELEY, *the present* LORD OF THE MANOR.

Revd. WILLIAM DECHAIR TATTERSALL, *Vicar.*

BENEFACTIONS.

In thankful remembrance of the Honble. and worthy Persons, who have been Benefactors to the Parish and so that their Gifts and Memorys may not be lost or forgotten are these Tables inscribed.

Dame CATHERINE BERKLEY, *Widdow, of the* Right Honble. THOMAS, *Lord* BERKLEY, founder of a Free School in *Wotton under Edge*, with Maintenance for the Master and certain poor Scholars for ever, in the Eighth year of the Reign of RICHARD the Second, Ano. Dmo. 1385, which foundation was recovered and new settled as now is by the Care and Cost of JOHN SMITH, of *North Nibley*, the *Elder, Esqr.* in the 10th. Year of King JAMES, and supported by his Majestys Letters Patent.

Lady ANNE, *Countess of* WARWICK, Gave the new *Tolsry*, to the use of the Town of *Wotton*, the rest of the Howsing and tenements thereto belonging with the Rents thereof to the Poor of the said Town and Parish for ever, the enfeoffment of this Land is continued. The aforesaid ANNE, *Countesse of* WARWICK, in 38th. of Queen ELIZABETH, erected a large Almshouse at *Cheyney* in *Buckinghamshire*, and therein appointed two Almsfolks to come from *Wotton*, with allowance of 5£. per Ann. a piece which HENRY, Lord BERKLEY, upon the agreement with her for the Manor of *Wotton*, cofirmed to them ....

The *Right Hon'ble.* GEORGE, Lord BERKLEY, in the Year of our Lord 1626, gave the materials and Builded a Gallery in this Parish Church of *Wotton-under-Edge*.

Sir RICHARD VENN, *Knt.* and *Alderman*, of the City of *London*, who was born in this Parish, gave one Annuity of 10£. a Year for ever to the Poor of *Wotton* aforesaid to be issuing out of all his Lands within the Parish of *Wotton* and *Nibley*, aforesaid. Also he gave certain Plate. viz.—Two large Silver Flaggons for the Service of the Communion Table of the Parish Church of *Wotton*, aforesaid, besides divers other Gifts for the Benefit of the Town and poor.

The Gift of *Sir* JONATHAN DAWES :

Memorand. that *Sir* JONATHAN DAWES, *Knt.* deceased late one of the Sheriffs of the City of *London*, and son of *Mr.* ROBERT DAWES, *Clothier*, of *Wotton-under-Edge*, deceased did give the sum of One Thousand Pounds to be laid out in the Purchase of Lands and Tenements for the succor and releife of the poor of this Parish of *Wotton-under-Edge* which Money was accordingly laid out by Dame ANNE DAWES, *Relict* of the said *Sir* JONATHAN, THOMAS DAWES, Brother of the said *Sir* JONATHAN, and ROBERT DAWES, son of the said THOMAS, in the purchase of Divers lands and Tenements scituate in *Hill alias Hull*, in the County of *Gloucester*, of and from RICHARD FUST, *Esqr.* and others which Lands are also since by the Decrees of his Majestie's high Court of Chancery and other assurances in the Law settled to the use aforesaid which Decree and deeds are in the Vestry, A. D. 1678.

Likewise *Mr.* WILLIAM and *Mr.* ROBERT, Sons of *Mr.* RICHARD HIET, and MARY, Sister to *Sir* JONATHAN DAWES, *Merchant*, of *London*, gave to the Poor of *Wotton-under-Edge*, (the place of their Birth,) Six Hundred Pounds which said sum was accordingly laid out in the purchase of Lands in the Parishes of *Wotton* and *Berkley*, by *Mr.* ROBERT DAWES, and *Mr.* THOMAS, his Son, Anno Dom. 1693.

HUGH PERRY, *Esqr. Alderman*, of City of *London*, gave Lands to the Value of 50£. per Ann. and above for ever for the use of the poor of *Wotton*, aforesaid, (being born in the said Town,) he also built an *Almshouse* for 6 poore Men and 6 poore Women in the said Towne, with a Chappell for prayers and appointed a Lecture to be preached Weekly in the Parish Church of *Wotton*, and prayers to be read twise a Week to the poor in the Chappell and ordayned ye Rents of ye said Land for the maintenance of the said Guifts and did many other Charitable Works there. The deeds of the land are in the said Vestry.

ROBERT HALE, of *Alderley*, *Esqr.* gave the Reversion of a Living in *Raingeworthy*, after one Life of the value of 20£. per Ann. which is now in hand to the Use of the Poor for Ever, which Gift was settled and confirmed by the *Right Hon'ble.* Sir MATHEW HALE, *Chief Baron of the Exchequer*, his only Child. The Deeds are also in the Vestry.

MARGARET HALE, *Widdow*, gave certain Lands in Reversion to the Poor of *Wotton*, for ever, which was since bought in by the Parishioners and is worth about 7£. per Ann. lying in *Rockhampton*. The Deeds whereof are also in ye foresaid Vestry.

JOANE GOUER, *Widdow*, gave a certaine Tenement with a Close of Ground adjoyning, lying in *Bradley Street* within the Town of *Wotton*, aforesaid to the yearly value of 4£. to the use of the Poor, for ever. The Deeds of which Land are also in the said Vestry.

MARGARET MALLOWES, of the City of *London*, *Widdow*, gave a Sum of Money to purchase *Cawsey Mead* and *Mill*

Mead, within the said Parish, the Rents and profits thereof to remain for the Use of the Poor, of the said Parish, for ever 1619.

HUGH VENNE, of this Parish, *Clothier*, gave 20 s. a Year, out of certain Lands in *North Nibley*, and a Tenement in *Dursley*, of 30 s. a Year for the Use of the Poor, for ever. The Enfeoffment remains in the Vestry.

ROBERT WEBBE, of *Sinwell*, in the foresaid Parish, *Clothier*, gave 4 s. a Week to be distributed every Sunday in Bread to the Poor of said Parish for ever, and 40 s. Yearly to 40 poor householders to be paid them 12 d. a piece in Money on St. Thomas Day, yearly for ever, which he ordered by his Will, to be paid out of his farme called the Grange, a Copy of which Will is entered in the Church Booke.

The old *Almshouse and Tenements*, belonging to the Poor, Donor not known, the Enfeoffment is in the Vestry.

The *Church House* and WILLIAM WALLINGTONS *House* belong to the Church of *Wotton*. The Enfeoffment whereof is in ye foresaid Vestry.

Mrs. SARAH WINSTON, of this Parish, gave a large *Silver Paten*, for the Use of the Communion Table, A. D. 1686.

Mr. THOMAS BLAGDEN, gave a *Pulpit Ornament* of Crimson Velvet enriched with Gold. Also the said *Mr.* THOMAS BLAGDEN, at the time of his Decease which was in 1737, gave 50 £. to the *Charity School*, for ever.

1748. RICHARD OSBORNE, *Esqr.* gave for the *Ornament* of the *Communion Table*, a Cover of Crimson Velvet, enriched with Gold and also two *Silver Plates*, for collecting the Offertory.

1763, WILLIAM MOORE, *Esqr.* gave the rich *Chandelier*, that is suspended in the Middle Isle.

In the same Year *Mr.* ROBERT PURNELL, bequeathed Five Hundred and Fifty Pounds, for ever, for Bread to such Poor Inhabitants as have not received *Alms* of the Parish. Also the said *Mr.* ROBERT PURNELL, gave One Hundred Pounds, to the *Charity School.*

1765. *Mrs.* ANN MOORE, of this Parish, gave a *Silver Bread Paten or Salver*, for the Use of the Communion Table. 1769, *Mr.* EDWARD BEARPACKER, gave 100 £. to the *Charity School.*

ON THE GALLERY.

JOHANNES OKES,—In hoc oppido natus, Oxoniæ innutritus, et per annos quadraginta in Ædibus Cholmleianis, apud Vale Royale in agro Cestriensi Sacris Operatus, Pio erga Solum natale Animo, sexcentos aut plures libros huic Ecclesiæ, et 20 libras pauperibus, Moriens legavit.

THOMAS DAWES, of *Bradley*, *Esqr.* gave an Estate at *Bournstream*, worth near 30 £. per Ann. in Trust to and for the Poor of this Parish, for ever.

The *Hon'ble* COL. MORTON, gave the Timber of the *Charity Working School*, 1714.

The *Right Hon'ble.* GEORGE, Lord BERKELEY, built the *Old Gallery*, 1626.

ROBERT, *Earl* of LEICESTER, gave a *Brotherhood*, to this Parish, in his Hospital at *Warwick*, worth 20 £. per Ann. which we enjoy.

THOMAS DAWES, of *Bradley*, *Esqr.* gave a new *Fire Engine*, for the Use of this Parish.

RICHARD MEADES, *Alderman*, of this Town, gave 6 £. per Annum without any deduction to JONAH OKES, and RICHARD OSBORN, their Heirs and assigns for ever, in trust to be distributed every Michaelmas, amongst 6 *Ministers* of the *Church of England*, that do or shall Read the Weekly lecture in the Church; and the like Annuity to ROBERT WEBB and RICHARD NICOLAS, to be given to the Poor ye 2nd. of February, no Person or Family more than 5 s. nor less than **Two** and sixpence.

The feoffees of the Market by the Approbation of the *Mayor* and *Aldermen*, gave Fifty Pounds, towards the expence of recovering the *Free Grammar School*, and settling the same in Trustees; and also one Hundred Pounds towards purchasing the augmentation to the Vicarage; and likewise Fourscore Pounds, towards the maintenance of a Curate.

Mr. WILLIAM BAILEY, *Clothier*, gave 20 £. to the Poor of this Parish and 20 £. in Trust for the *Charity School*, for ever, 1721.

RICHARD OSBORN, of *Wortly*, *Esqr.* gave 3 £. per Annum, viz. 10 s. for a *Charity Sermon*, and 50 s. to the *Charity School*, so long as it is continued in the Discipline of the Church of England, as now by Law established, 1722.

Mrs. MARY BLAGDEN, of *Nind*, gave 20 £. in Trust to be distributed every good Friday, in Bread to the Poor of the Hospital, and 10 £. for the Benefit of the *Charity School*, 1723.

Mrs. SARAH WINCHCOMB, gave 40 £. to the *Old Hospital*, and 30 £. to the *Charity School*, in Trust to *Mr.* E. BAILEY, and *Mr.* S. CARY, 1773.

INSCRIPTIONS IN THE CHURCH.

CHANCEL.

BEFORE THE COMMUNION TABLE IS THE FOLLOWING IN SAXON LETTERS ON THE VERGE OF A FLAT STONE WHERE THE FIGURE OF A MAN IN BRASS HAS BEEN, NOW GONE.

Natus in hac Villa, cognomine dictus ab illà,
Qui Rector fuit hic, aptum nomenq.
sibi sic,

R. de WOTTON, jacet hic, cui cœlica dona
Impetret ipsa pulcherrima virgo Maria, Amen.

In the Centre of the Stone.

Es mihi virgo pia, Dux et Lux sancta Maria.

UNDER THE ALTAR PIECE, A FLAT

STONE ON THE VERGE THIS INSCRIPTION IN CAPITALS.

Here lyeth the Body of
Dame ELIZABETH BARKLEY,
who deceased the 2nd. of April,
Anno Domini, 1611.

MONUMENTS ON THE NORTH SIDE.

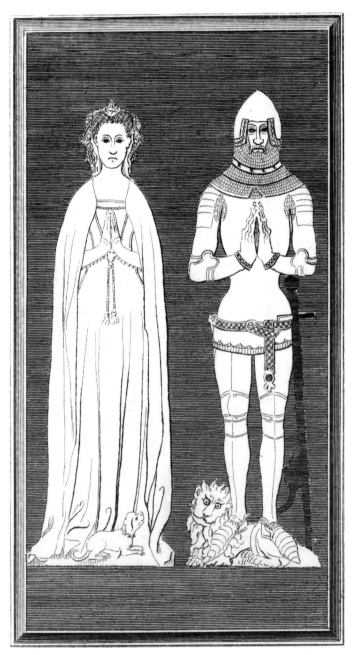

Thomas, 4th Lord Berkeley, and Margaret his wife

Arms:—Ermine a Chevron per pale Or. and Sable.—COSTER. *impaling* Or. an Eagle displayed Vert.ROUS.

Near this Place lyes interred
JANE, eldest Daughter of
Mr. THOMAS ROUS, of this Town,
and Wife of *Mr.* THOMAS COSTER,
of *Redbrooke* in this County,
who left this Life, for a Better the
7th. day of June 1721,
Aged 23 Years.
She was an obedient Daughter,
a true Friend and an excellent Wife,
She lived in the exact Practice of
Piety and Virtue and dyed with a
perfect Resignation of herself
to the Will of her Maker.

Juxta hoc Marmor,
Mortales deponuntur Exuviæ
THOMÆ ROUS, *Arm.*
cui Hoc oppidum natalem Locum dedit,
Juris Prudentiâ primos Juventutis
Labores exercuit, in Quâ currente
Ætate notabiliter
Sagacem eximiumq. se præstitit.
Hactenus, aptissime instructus ad
justitiarii munus evectus fuit, in Quo
pari, et fælicissima justitiæ,
et Misericordiæ Temperantia se gerens,
modo Mansuetudine, modo Authoritate
valens, Provinciam hanc cum Dignitate
perfunctus est.
Neque privatæ Vitæ Officiis indecoram
egit
Partem, Seu Maritum, Parentem
Amicum, aut imprimè alacrem
urbanum et facillimum,
Obiit 28o. Febr. 1737, Æt. 60.
Nec Non JANÆ, dilectissimæ ejus
uxoris quæ Marito non diu superstes
Obiit 8o, Oct. 1740, Æt. 69.

Arms:—Azure three Treefoils slipt
Argent, on a Chief dancetté Or. three
Annulets Gules.—BLAGDEN. *impaling*
Argent, on a Bend Azure three Leopards faces Or.—ADEY.

In Memory of
Mr. MARY BLAGDEN, *Widow,*
Daughter of DANIEL ADEY, *Esqr.*
of *Comb* in this Parish,
she resigned her Soul to God,
who gave it, on the ninth day of
September in the Year 1761,
Aged 75 Years.

Arms:—Argent, a Lion rampant
Sable, a Chief per fess dancette Argent, and Sable.—HYETT.
Crest :— Horses head.

To the Happy Memory
of that most prudent and Charitable
Gentleman *Mr.* ROBERT HYETT,
late *Citizen* and *Merchant,* of *London,*
who departed this Life, the
21st. day of April, Anno Dom. 1691,
at the House o *Mr.* THOMAS
THEYER, of *Rodborough,*
in this County, and lies buried
near this Place.
The said THOMAS THEYER and
MARY, his Wife, Sister and sole
Executrix of the said ROBERT,
as a Pledge of their surviving Love
and affection to the Memory of
their dear Brother have erected
this Monument.

Near also lies the Body of
Mr. JOEL CAM, *Alderman,*
of this Town, who departed this
Life, Oct. 11, 1768,
Aged 70 Years.
Also DEBORAH, his Wife,
who departed this Life,
Jany. 23, 1773.
Near this Place likewise lyeth
interred MARGARET, the Sister
of the said ROBERT HIETT,
and Wife of THOMAS WINSTON,
thrice Mayor of this Towne,
She was buried the 4th. of Nov.
A. D. 1655. in the 27th.
Year of her Age.
Here lyeth buried also THOMAS,
the Son of the aforesaid THOMAS
and MARY THEYER, who departed
this Life, Febr. 19th. A. D. 1670.

In Memoriam
THOMÆ ROUS, *Armigeri,*
E. Vicino orti
Honesti viri et preclari
In hospites Comis et Urbani
In Suos mitis et benigni
Omnibus bonis viris chari.
Rerum Indicarum Orientalium,
In quibus se maxime habuit
Scientissimi.
Quarum in Directionem
(Quam pluribus licet eam ambientibus)
Plus quam bis-decies successive
electus fuit
Ter etiam in Cathedram ipsam vocatus,
adeoq. equidem in dirigendis utilis
Ut ter in Directoribus eligendis
Positis, quorundam vaframentis
prætormissus
Singulari suffragiorum incorruptorum
consensu
(Quasi sine illo infeliciores evaderent)
Spectatam ob fidem et diligentiam
Totidem restoratus, fuit.
Sedem Indicarum orientalium
Omni Tempore
Pro viribus vindicis et fautoris
Periclitamtibus usque A. D. 1762.
Silicet incauta Pace Præcipitataque
per consilium suum et constantiam
rerum Conservatoris.
Inter opes opum minime
(ut plerumque solet) grassatoris,
Publici Commodi quam sui
appetentis
omni denique virtute præditi
Et publica et privata.
Necnon
in Memoriam MARIÆ ROUS,
Prædicti THOMÆ ROUS,
Uxoris Amicissimæ amantissimæque
Hi per spatium 34 Annorum
Felicissimo in matrimonio conjuncti
Crudeli tandem morte dissociabantur
Ille obijt 29 die Junii A. D. 1771,
Ætatis suæ 61.
Illa obijt 29 die Febr. A. D. 1781,
Ætatis suæ 67.
Amborum ossa in Ecclesia de Paroch.
vocat. *St. Mary-le-bone,*
in Comitatu *Middlesex,* tumulata
conquiescunt.
Hoc qualecumque sit Monumentum
pietatis
In Parentes desideratissimos
Posuerunt
filii illorum superstites,
A. D. 1781.

Arms:—Or. an Eagle displayed Vert.
ROUS. *impaling* Sable on a fess engrailed Argt. 3 hands Or.

Sacred to the Memory of

ELIZABETH ROUS, Daughter of
THOMAS ROUS, *Esqr.*
of *Peirsfield,* in the County of
Monmouth, died Nov. 21, 1786,
Aged 79 Years.

This Monument
is inscribed to the Memory of
ROBERT VEEL, second Son of
WILLIAM VEEL,
of *Symondshall* in this Parish,
After serving with reputation in the
Navy during four Years of the late
War, against the Enemies of his
Country, he fell a Victim to the
Climate of Bengal,
On the 30 of November 1787,
In the 25 Year of his Age.

Arms:—Argent, on a Bend, Sable
three Calves of the first, with a crescent for difference.—VEEL.

Arms:—a Rebus for the Nams
R. WEB.—Or. *impaling* Sable a Cross
moliné Or, charged in the centre with
an Annulet.—DRAPER.

Resurrectionem in
Christo hic expectat reveren:
Dn. ROBERTUS WEB,
pietate comitate, et
Charitate vix ulli secundus, ut
dives sic largus opum
qui vivus pauperes paterno amore
fovit et moriens testamento
cavit, ut in æternum e fundis
Suis viginti et sex libræ quotannis
in egenos erogarentur ita ut quatuor
solidi unoquoq die dominica
in templo finitis precibus matutinis
viginti quatuor indigentibus
Wottoniæ ubi vixit, totidemque
Regissylvæ ubi natus distribuerentur.
Hisce moribus qualis esset testatum
reliquit, monumentum, quæ sibi
in animis hominum diutius mansurum
struxit, quam hoc quod
memoriæ ejus, amoris et conjugalis
fidei ergo suis sumptibus
posuit ANNA charissima uxor,
filia RICHARDI DRAPER, *Mercatoris,*
Londinensis, quæ illa, ANNAM,
unicam filiam peperit NICHOLAO
WEB, de *Ashwick,* in Com. *Glouc.*
Gen. connubio junctam.
Obijt totius vicinæ lachrymis
defletus 14o. Jany. A. S. 1662,
Æt. 74.
ROBERTUS WEB,
O tu Rebus uber,
Te Deus Ubertim ditavit Rebus opimis.
Pauper inopsque tuis Rebus et Uber erat
Uber tuSemper nam quæ donantur egenis
Has Tecum solas semper habebis opes
Fama perennis erit præclari nominis ;
et si
In cineres abeas author, at extat opus
Cavisti prudens, jejunos qui tot alebas
Vivus, ne pereant, te moriente simul
Jam Vivant inopes, dum vivunt tuquoque vives
Rebus ut Uber eras, Rebus, et Uber eris.

M. S.
RICHARDI OSBORNE, de *Wortley, Arm.*
Quem mira Animi alacritas,
Nuda Veritas, Moresq. puri,
Charum reddiderunt ac bona flebilem,
Humanitas Egenis desiderantissimum.
Gravissimos Arthritidis cruciatus,
Per Annos quamplurimos sustinuit,
Tali constantia ac fortitudine,

4

5

6

1524

Qualem sola ministrat Virtus
Ac vere Christiana Fides.
Labefacto tandem ac devicto corpore
Animam pie et placide efflavit
Die Aprilis 28, A. D. 1749, Æt. 60.
Juxta requiescit
Quicquid terrestre fuit SARÆ OSBORNE,
Prædicti Conjugis dilectissimæ,
Ob. Jan. 25, 1742, Æt. 51.
Nec non eorum seq: Liberorum,
JOHANNIS, Infantis,
RICHARDI, ob. Dec. 12, 1723, Æt. 6.
THOMÆ, ob. Julij 25, 1736, Æt. 17.
GULIELMI, Infantis.

Arms:—Argent, a Bend between
two Lions rampant Sable.—OSBORNE.
impaling—BLAGDEN, *as before.*

ON FLAT STONES.

In Memory of
STEPHEN COMPERE,
Attorney at Law, who was interred
near this Place,
He departed this Life, the
6th. day of March, Anno Dom. 1733,
Aged 35 Years.
Also ANN, Daughter of
OFFLEY SMITH, of *Topcroft* in
Norfolk, Esqr. she departed this
Life, the 5 of July 1785,
Aged 85 Years.

Here lyeth the Body of
JANE, the Wife of NICHOLAS
HESKINS, who was buried
December 16, 1684.

Here lieth the Body of
ELIZABETH, the Wife of
EDWARD BEARPACKER,
Obijt the 27th. Jany. 1744.

Here lyeth the Body of
CHRISTIAN WEBB, Wife of
NICHOLAS WEBB, who died
April the 27, A. D. 1658.
Here lyeth the Body of
ANNE WEBB, second Wife unto
NICHOLAS WEBB,
who died September 13th. A.D. 1663,
Here lyeth the Body of
MARY WEBB, *Widow* of
NICHOLAS WEBB, *Clothier,*
who died March the 19th. A.D. 1707,
in the 43rd. Year of her Widowhood,
and 91st. Year of her Age.

JOHN, the Son of JOHN WHITE,
of *Monmouth, Gent.*
who departed this Life, the
16th. of February, A. D. 1724,
Aged 6 Months.

In Memory of
Mr. ROBERT PURNELL,
who died Augt. 20, 1763,
Aged 87 Years.

In Memory of

7

ANTHONY BAVE, M. D.
who departed this Life,
Febr. 23rd. 1737, Aged 39.
Also MARY, his Wife, who died
August 31, 1750, in the 53rd.
Year of her Age.

Here lyeth the Body of
JOANE, Daughter of RICHARD
HADDOW, of *Hampstead* in the
County of *Middlesex, Gent.*
who was buried the 7 day of July,
Anno Dom. 1686, in the 15th.
Year of her Age.

ALICIA, filia JOHANNIS PURNELL,
de *Dursley, Gen.* Uxor DANIELIS
ADY, Sepulta fuit 17 Jany.
A. D. 1690, Ætatis suæ 37.

Here lyeth the Body of
ANTHONY BLANCHAT,
of *Steeple-Aston,* in the County of
Wilts. Gent. who was buried
May the 12th. A. D. 1681.

Here lyeth HESTER, the Wife of
ROBERT WEBB,
(Neice of the Wife of ROBERT
MANDEY,) who died Feb. 13, 1691.

ARTHUR TYNDAL,
borne at *Stinchcombe, Merchant,*
of *London,* dying at *Wotton,*
Sept. the 8th. 1625, lyeth buried here.
Mrs. ANN MOORE, 1763.
WILLIAM MOORE, 1789.
JOHN COOPER, *Surgeon,*
died Jany. 14, 1788, Aged 58.

SAMPSON CARY,
died Nov. 6, 1790, Aged 76 Years.
SARAH, his Wife, died
12 of Jany. 1784, Aged 73 Years.

In Memory of
JOHN POWELL, *Surgeon,*
who was born at *Hereford,* and
departed this Life, 15 of April 1782,
Aged 43 Years.
Also SARAH, his Wife,
She departed this Life, 12 day of
May 1782, Aged 43 Years.

The *Revd.* JAMES TATTERSALL, A.M.
Vicar of Tewkesbury,
died Nov. 9, 1791, Aged 38 Years.

JOHN DAUNCEY,
died Nov. 2, 1787, Aged 51.

CHRISTIAN DAUNCEY,
died June 1, 1785, Aged 19.

8

JOHN DAUNCEY,
died April 30, 1782, Aged 13.

JOHN HUNT,
was buried here the 21 of May 1790,
Aged 68.
JOAN, his Wife, June 3, 1777,
Aged 57.
WILLIAM, their Son,
July 17, 1777, Aged 27.

NAVE.

ON A MONUMENT AGAINST A PILLAR.

Before this Place
Lyeth interred the Body of
EDWARD WALLINGTON,
of this Town *Merchant,*
who was beared to the Church.
the 22nd. day of April 1616,
by Six of his Grandsons.
All Sons to EDWARD WALLINGTON,
Mercer, by SUSANNA, his Wife,
The said EDWARD WALLINGTON,
Mercer, was interr'd
Decr. 1, 1728, Aged 82.

Arms:—Sable a Chevron between
three Tygers passant Or, looking at
their faces in a Mirror of the last.—
TATTERSALL.
Crest:—a Herald Tyger.

Sacred to the Memory of the
Revd. JAMES TATTERSALL, A. M.
Vicar of Teukesbury,
who died from a fall from his Horse,
Mar 3, 1791, Aged 38 Years.
Strength of Judgment and sweetness
of disposition, he received from Nature; to these he added the support of
sound Religious principles; and this
union of good Qualities with the best
acquirements produced an amiable
Character and an Exemplary Life.
His brothers the *Revd.* JOHN
TATTERSALL, and the
Rev. WILLIAM DECHAIRTATTERSALL,
(*Vicar* of this Parish.)
Impressed with the deepest Sorrow
for their Loss, And impelled by the
sincerest Affection and Gratitude
have caused this Monument to be
erected.

ON A MONUMENT.

Arms:—Quarterly of 6, 1 VEEL,
as before 2 Quarterly. Or. and Gules
in the first quarter a Mullet Sable.
VERE. 3.—Sable, a Lion rampant and
a Canton Argent.—KINGSTON. 4.—
Gules an Annulet between two Bars
and in Chief a Lion passant Or.—
TORRINGTON. 5.—Argent, a fess ra-
gullé between three Annulets Gules.
VYVELL. 6.—VEEL, *impaling* Argent,
three Covered Cups between semi of
Cross Crosslets Sable.—BUTLER.

MARIA, uxor THOMÆ VEEL,
filij THOMÆ VEEL, de *Alveston,*
in Com. *Glouc. Armig.* filia viro
HENRICI BUTLER, de *Henley,*
in agro *Dorcest. Armig.* immaturos
ex itineris molestijs
Gemellos enixa, non sine maximo
conjugis dolore expiravit Dec. 16,
A. D. 1658, Æt. 24.

9

Huc usque peregrina, nunc domi.
My Journey's, at an End, my
Travaile's done
I'm brought to Bed, and now
I am at home,
MARIA VEEL,
ira me Leva
Me Deus oppressit, quis a ....
at Levet ira
Me Christus VELET, liberet,
atque Levet.

1 Tim 2. 15.

ON FLAT STONES.

Here lyeth the Body of
JOHN MORRIS, of *Bristol, Baker,*
who was buried Nov. 16, 1747,
Aged 88 Years.
Also ELIZABETH, his Daughter,
and Wife of JAMES MACIE,
who was buried Oct. 21, 1747,
Aged 53 Years.

Here lyeth the Body of
ROBERT HUGHES,
who departed this Life,
Oct. 17th. 1733, Aged 57.

Also MARY, Daughter of
WILLIAM and MARY BRACKEN-
BOROUGH, who was buried
October the 19th. 1750, Aged 26.

In Memory of
MARY, Daughter of JOHN BLAGDEN,
of *Nind, Gent.* who was
buried July 15, 1723.
Also HENRY HADNOT,
was buried here February 23, 1742,
Aged 59 Years.

NORTH AISLE.

ON MONUMENTS.

H. S. E.

ELIZABETHA, filia MAURITIJ TROT-
MAN, uxor GUL. NELMES, de
Cam, cui peperit JOHANNEM NELMES,
de *Bradstone,* MARIAM ROBERTO
HESKINS, de *Wotton,* connubio
junctam; JANAM GULIELMO GARD-
INER, de *Stroude;* LYDIAM THOMÆ
DAWES, de *Bradley;* SARAM GUL-
IELMO STOKES, de *Horton,* insigne
pietatis ergæ Deum, et Charitatis
erga egenos præcipue verbi Divini
Ministros exemplar, cum vixisset
LXXV annos, supremum diem
in Domino,
Obiit Febr. XXVIº. A. D.
MDCLXXXIIº.
Hic etiam reponuntur reliquiæ SARÆ,
Uxoris GULIELMI STOKES,
de *Horton, Gent.* et GUL. NELMES,
de *Cam. Gen.* filiæ,
Obiit et Quievit Maij 24º.
Anno Æræ Christianæ 1691.
ELIZABETHÆ, eorum filia e cunabilis
ad cœlum evasit Aug. 28º. 1619,
Ætatis suæ primo.

Arms:—Azure three Mullets Ar-
gent.—DAWES.
Crest:—a Mullet between two
Wings.

D. O. M. S.
Infra deponitur quod reliquum est
RICHARDI DAWES, *Arm.*
Exhonestâ et antiquâ nostros
inter Dobunos
prosapiâ oriundi,
Coll. Wadh. Apud *Oxon.* olim alumni,
Ubi Academiâ Augustis: ANNÆ,
triumphos
Solemni ritu celebrare
ad res sublimes depingendas designatus
quam optime munus implevit.
Hinc in societatem *Templi int.* adscitus
Juri municipali operam dedit,
Atque inter Causidicos repagulares
adscriptus est
Optimus Adolescens,
ingenii acumine et gravitate spectabilis,
morum integritate et elegantiâ magis
Conspicuus,
Animi candore, et magnitudine
ornatissimus,
Pietate denique in Deum, et in
parentes observantiâ
nunquam satis laudatus
Si vivum sciveris, viator,
habes cur impensius mortuum plores
Ille 9no. Cal Jun. An.
Sal. 1712, Neanon Æt. 26.
ROBERTI DAWES,
RICARDI, jam memorati fratris
natu min.
Qui etiam optimarum artium studiis
in eadem inclytâ musarum sede
per triennium non infeliciter incubuit
fraternæ virtutis æmulus.
Sed proh. dolor. utrumque tantæ
spei juvenem,
delicias omnium, decus et ornam-
entum familiæ
(cujus nominis perpetuandi in ijs
spes sola mansit)
eadem dira variolarum pestis corripuit,
ac quicquid mortale fuit,
oblivioni et tenebras mandavit,
non nisi tubâ ultimâ revocandum
Animæ interim ad Cœlum evolarunt,
easq. occupavere sedes
Quas *Deus Salvator* Justis præparavit.
Hæc nobis indubitata fides.
Uterque enim dignus ævo in terris
extento.
nisi ad vitam istam meliorem,
festinassent
Hic 3tio. Id. Jun. An.
Sal. 1711, Æt. 22.
Hoc sepulchrale Marmor, haud
procul a quod et suas reliquias
Condi Volunt
Filijs, Nepotibus
desideratissimis
Pater, Patruus
Mæstissimi posuere.
Likewise was interred near this Place
the Body of THOMAS DAWES,
of *Bradley, Esqr.* who died the
4th. day of July, A. D. 1713,
in the 62nd. Year of his Age.
Lamented by all that knew Him,
because when living
He was doing good to all,
He was devout an Constant in
Religious Exercises
Hospitable and Generous in his House,
Kind and Charitable to the Poor,
Meek in his Temper, affable and
pleasant in his Conversation,
Courteous and Benevolent to all Men,
He was a loving Husband, a good
Master, and a faithful Friend,
But why should we praise Him
by our Words whose Works
doth praise and follow him,
And are an Example for our Imitation.

Lastly here lie reposed the only
Mortal Remains of
LYDIA DAWES,
Relict of the said THOMAS DAWES,
Esqr. who died 15 Febr. 1739,
Aged 88 Years.
Who most amiably conjugal in every
Virtue of his, as well as in her Love
towards Him not only bore a Part in
those excellent Graces that adorn'd
Him living, but after his Death, in-
grafted as it were upon her Self the
whole, Shone forth a most illustrious
Pattern of every humane and Christian Virtue. Sincerely Pious, unaffect-
edly Devout, Munificent, Hospitable,
Charitable, Affable and Courteous.
Stranger (if such thou Sh'st. be
to her Virtues) drop a Tear, Lament
the Degeneracy of the Times and
teach thy Self from this faint and too
faithless Record of her Merit, to imitate whom thou must shortly follow.

In Memory of
JOHN NELMES, of *Bradley, Esqr.*
A Worthy Pattern of Prudence,
Temperance, Integrity, and Justice,
possessing these Virtues, he discharged
the Duties of Life in the most exemplary Manner and conscious of the
rectitude of his Conduct, he bore a
long and painful Illness with that for-
titude Patience and Resignation peculiar to the true Christian. It pleased
God to release him from this mortal
State on the 15 Nov. 1742, Aged 61.
Also of ELIZABETH, his Wife,
who departed this Life,
Oct. 31. 1713, Aged 25.
And LYDIA, thier Daughter,
who died an Infant.
The Remains of ELIZABETH NELMES,
another of thier Daughters,
are also deposited near this Place,
She died the 7th. of June 1778,
Aged 68 Years.
MARY SMART, their only surviving
Daughter, as a Testimony of
affectionate Regard to their Memory
caused this Monument to be erected.
Arms:—Or. three Elm Trees pro-
per.—NELMES.

Arms:—ADEY, (*single*) *as before.*

This Monument is erected
to preserve the Memory of
WILLIAM ADEY,
of *Comb,* in this Parish, *Esqr.*
who having for several Years,
laboured under an infirm State of Body,
At length Calmly resigned up his Soul
into the hand of his Creator
on the 31st. of July 1765,
Aged 67 Years.

THOMAS GRAIL, *Medicinæ Professor,*
in Qua non,
Mediocriter versatus Galeni Methodo,
et Vestigijs maximè insistens non sine
optato Successu et applausu munus
obivit, qui etsi non toto orbi tamen
viciniæ salutifer fuit et juvamen alijs,
quod sibi præstare non Potuit præstitit; apoplexiâ laborans Vitam jun.
Vº. A. S. MDCLXIXº. Ætatis LXIº.
finivit.
In cujus memoriam uxor ejus
SARAH, filia LAURENTIJ POTS,
Mercatoribus, Angl. Metelliburgi,
Sacellani hoc monumentum.

Extrui curavit.

Here underneath interred doth lie
One that bids Thee prepare to die
I lov'd in upright Paths to go ;
Physic my Practice was, but loe
Death is too strong for any Man;
For Physick and Physician.

Also
SARAH, Relict of the aforesaid
THOMAS GRAIL,
and since the Wife of
Mr. THOMAS WINSTONE,
Thrice Mayor of this Town,
dyed the 3rd. and was buried the
7th. day of March, A. Dom. 1691,
Aged 75 Years.

Arms:—First shield —ADEY, *as
before.* impaling BLAGDEN, *as before.*
Second shield ADEY, *as before.* im-
palmy. Azure a Lion rampant Arg.
CREW.

To the Memory of
DANIEL ADEY, *Esqr.* of Comb,
who having thro' Life approved
Himself a Character of Piety,
Virtue and general Usefulness to
mankind, left this World for the
Rewards of a Better, on the 4th. of
Febr. 1752, Aged 80 Years.
To the Memory of
ELIZABETH, his Wife, who died
March 5th. 1747, Aged 52.
DANIEL, and FREDERICK,
two Sons of THOMAS CURTIS,
of the City of Bristol, Esqr.
his Grandsons, were buried here.
To the Memory also of
DANIEL ADEY, Esqr.
of Simwell, who died on the
11 of Nov. 1765, Aged 67 Years.
Mrs. BRIDGET ADEY,
the Wife of SAMUEL ADEY, Esqr.
of Simwell, was buried on the
11th. of October 1740, in the 41
Year of her Age.
Interr'd here also lye six of their
Sons and two Daughters with two
Children unbaptized, one other son
lies buried at Wickware.

M. S. *Rev. et Cl.* viri RIC. KENT,
M. A. hujus Ecclesiæ Pastoris,
qui Judicii Dexteritate, cordis
Simplicitate, doctrinæ puritate, erga
omnes humanitate Præcellentis
omnium bonorum memoria et amore
dignissimi, qui Laboribus
Pro commissi gregis incremento,
febrique longa confectus, huic
miseræ vitæ valedixit,
4to. Cal. Apr. A. S. MDCLo.
Ætatis suæ XLo.
Kantius invictus, cedere nescius olim,
non minus ac regio, nominis hujus erat.
Tempora mutantur, victa est hæc
virtus et ille,
Hæc martis jaculis, mortis at ille feris.
Octonis annis fuit admirata docentem
Wottonia, assimilem vix habitura virum.
Corpus lenta febris potuit, delere ;
vetustas
Supprimet at laudes nulla, decusque
suum.
Jam vitæ finem grandisque laboris
adeptum
Assequitur virtus, fama superstes erit.

Deare KENT, this Stone's too narrow
to set forth
Thy boundlesse Virtues and transcen-
dant Worthe,

Thou needst no monument, our Ton-
gues for Thee
An Epitaph, a Tombe our Hearts
shall bee.

In Memory of
DOROTHY, the Virtuous Wife of
JOHN OKES. of this Town, *Mercer,*
She departed this Mortal Life,
in Great Peace of Conscience
and Quietness of Mind on
Sunday the 31st day of July in the
Year of our Lord 1653, and in the
41st. Year of her Age,
giving abundant Testimony
both in her Life and Death that
her Soul now rests in Peace
with her God. Her Body lyeth
buried in the Church Yard near
adjoining to this Place, in
expectation of a Joyful Resurrection
to Glory.

Arms:—BLAGDEN, *as before.* im-
paling NELMES, *as before.*

Near this Place lies Interr'd the
Body of JOHN BLAGDEN, of Nind,
Gent. who died Feb. 25, 1741,
Aged 69 Years.
Also two of his Daughters,
LYDIA, who died an Infant,
And MARY, who died Sept. 8, 1735,
Aged 14 Years.
Also of Mr. JOHN BLAGDEN,
his eldest Son, who died on
the 10th. day of June 1750,
in the 56 Year of his Age.
Also the Body of LYDIA BLAGDEN,
Wife of JOHN BLAGDEN, Senr.
who died Augt. 10th. 1763,
Aged 72 Years.

In Memory of
MARTHA, the Wife of
JONAH OKES, of this Town, *Mercer,*
who departed this Life, the
13 of Febr. A. D. 1708, in the
46 Year of her Age.
And also of JOHN, their Son,
who died the 10th. day of May 1695,
Aged 2 Years.
Also of the said JONAH OKES,
who was buried Decemb. 22, 1742,
Aged 76 Years.
And of JONAH, another Son,
who was buried Febr. 13, 1722,
Aged 39 Years.
And of LYDIA, Daughter of
JONAH OKES, Junr. who died
Decembr. 25, 1712, Aged 5 Months.

Near this Place lyeth interred
SARAH, the Wife of JOHN OKES,
of this Town, Gent. who with
a Cheerful resignation made her
quiet and peaceable Exit on Sunday
the 13th. day of March,
Anno Dom. 1725, Aged 56.
And left Issue of her Body living
three Sons and ten Daughters.
Also ELIZABETH, their Daughter,
who died August 22, 1726,
Aged 52 Years.

Neare this Place amongst his
Relations lyeth buried the Body of

JONAH OKES, *Senr. Mercer,*
who was three Times Mayor
of this Towne, He departed this
Life, May the 19th. and was buried
May 23rd. in the 85th. Year of
his Age, A. D 1692, waiting for
a joyful Resurrection to Glory.
Sage Arborists this maxim do main-
taine,
That by transplanting, Trees perfec-
tion gaine
So OKES removed from Earth to
Heaven's blest soile
Attained Perfection free'd from Care
and toile.
Also MARY, Wife of the said
JONAH OKES, was buried
February 5th. A. D. 1704,
Aged 86 Years.

M. S. GULIELMI WILLET, filii
natu max. RADULPHI WILLET,
Generosi, qui Phthisi Laborans
Pie et placide mortale
Corpus deposuit Sep. 11, A. D. 1657,
Ætatis suæ 22o.
Anima vero fiduciâ Salutis etsi
Imprimis Languidâ
Tandem vividâ et certâ, cœlum adibat:
Quo et SUSANNÆ Sororis, PETRI et
MATHÆI WILLET,
Fratrum Animulæ, non Multo
ante translatæ
Expectant una felicitatis consum-
mationem.
One House nay Wombe these four
once had, one Grave
Theyr Bodies now, their Soules one
Heaven Have,
Death doth not them divorce, but
as they were
In Life united, now in Death they are.
In them there was what e're des-
erved Prayse.
They wanted nought could be des-
ired but dayes.
In Spring their Autumn was, Too
ripe they were
Too hopeful pious, pretty to be here,
Preservers weake are Stones, their
Names shall last
When Brasse and Marble unto Dust
shall waist.
GULIELMUS WILLET
Luget illum levius.
Hic vivus toties propter peccata dolebat
Ut madidæ Lachrymis nocte dieque
genæ:
Constiterat quocunque loco Peccata
videbat
Ante oculos habuit crimina cuncta
suos.
Non citharæ cantus, non vestes, prædia
larga
Non cordi mundi regia quicquid
habet.
Panis erant lachrymæ ; potum victum-
que perosus,
Confectus macie, funeris instar erat.
Longa referre mora est, per quot dis-
crimina, plancus
Peccato, Satana, morte, trophea tulit.
Per Christum tandem Victor, caret at-
que periodi.
Luget eum levius quisquis amicus
erat.

Arms:—Or, two Bars and in Chief
a Lion passant Azure.—GREGORY.

Near this Place lie the Remains of
EDWARD GREGORY,
Son of ABRAHAM GREGORY, S.T.P.
Born at *Gloucester,*

Educated at *Eaton School*,
afterwards Student of Christ Church
in *Oxford*.
And at the Taking of *Vigo*, under
Admiral ROOKE,
Chaplain to the *Torbay* Man of War,
Sometime Lecturer of *Allhallows*
Staining in London,
and Lastly *Vicar* of this Parish,
where he continued above thirty Years,
Indefatigable in the Duties of his
Function
Loving and beloved by his Parishioners.
At Length worn out with a lingering
Illness
He quitted this Life in Hopes
of a Better,
October 31, 17.8, Aged 62 Years.
EDWARD, ABRAHAM, THOMAS
and FRANCIS,
Out of a True Love and filial Piety
Erected this Monument,
To the Memory of their Father.
MARY, his Relict,
Obijt 7 Decr. 1774, Æt. 82.

AGAINST THE SIDE OF AN OLD TOMB.

Here lyeth the Body of
PETER BYRD, *Gent.*
who was buried the 12th. of Decr.
Ano. Dom. 1633.
Near adjoyneing him lieth the Body of
MARY, his Wife, who was
buried the 23rd. of December,
Ano. Dom. 1618.
Both at rest in the Lord.
Also SUSANNA, Daughter of
PETER BYRD, and Wife to
RALPH WILLET, was interred here
October the 29, A. D. 1686,
Aged 74 Years.
Here lyeth a BYRD, whose Body
left, his Spiritt
Ascended hath the Heavens through
the Meritt,
Of Christ his Saviour which shall
once againe
Assume the Body and e'r Blest
remayne.

CHARLES, the Son of
WILLIAM STEPHENS, B. D.
Vicar of this Parish, was laid here
Decemb. 18, A. D. 1686.
WILLIAM, another Son of
WILLIAM STEPHENS, was laid here
May 4, A. D. 1689.

Underneath this Place lies the
Body of *Mr.* ROBERT HEYWARD,
of this Town, who was buried
October 25th. 1730, Aged 47.

Arms:—OSBORNE, *as before*,
On an escutcheon of pretence Argent,
a Lion rampant Sable —WHITE.

Sacred to the Memory of
JOHN OSBORNE, *Esqr.*
of *Monks Mill*, in this Parish,
In whom were united all those Virtues
that adorn the sincere Christian.
This Monument was
Erected by his Widow ELIZABETH,
Daughter of GEORGE WHITE, *Esqr.*
of *Goodrich* in the County of
Hereford, as a Testimony of her
true Affection.

16

He departed this Life,
26 Oct. 1770, Aged 49.
Near the same Vault are deposited
the Remains of three of their
Children, RICHARD, born
Ap. 12, 1753, died May 1, 1757.
ANN, died Nov. 6, 1755,
Aged 4 Months.
GEORGE WHITE,
died June 16, 1757, Aged 4 Months.

A respectful Tiribute to
the Memory of ELIZABETH, and
ANNE OSBORNE, of *Alderley*,
Daughter of RICHARD OSBORNE,
of *Wortley* in this County, *Esqr.*
by SARAH, his Wife.
ELIZABETH, died 26 June 1780,
Aged 65 Years.
ANNE, died 13 March 1790,
Aged 63 Years.

Sacred to the Memory of
ELIZABETH OSBORNE,
(Relict of JOHN OSBORNE, *Esqr.*)
who died 1 March 1797, Aged 75.

Arms:—Gules in Chief three
Leopards faces and in base a Cinque foil Or.

Near this Place lies interred the
Remains of ROBERT HICKES, *Esqr.*
of *Comb*, he died Aug. 7, 1743,
Aged 70 Years.

Near this Place amongst her
Relations resteth the Body of
ANNA, the Wife of ROBERT KNEE,
of this Town, who departed this
Life, Nov. 29, in the 57th. Year
of her Age in the Year of our
Lord 1709.
Also ANNA, their Daughter,
was buried Nov. 3, 1689.

Depositum desideratissimæ Animæ.
RICHARDI OSBORNE,
de *Wortley*, *Armigeri*,
Ex antiquâ stirpe oriundi, juxta hunc
Locum requiescit: et requiescat, Precor,
Non, nisi Tubâ ultimâ evocandum.
Vixit omnibus charus, qui morum
Suavitatem, inconcussam Fidem, et
Sinceram Religionem, quæ in illo
Emicuerunt, venerantur, Regnante
ANNA,
Cujus memoriam nulla delebit dies
Irenarches erat incorruptus, sagax
Et strenuus, Ecclesiam Anglicanam
Summa Reverentiâ semper coluit,
Exemplo ornavit. Cum Talem
Tantumq. Virum sepultum videmus,
Quis Patriam Lector non deflebit.
Gravissimum morbum fortitudine
Vere Christianâ diu sustentavit,
Obdormivit Aug. xxiv°.
A. D. MDCCXXII°.
Ætat. LXII.

UNDER A LARGE FAIR TOMB OF GREY
MARBLE WITH TWO FIGURES EN-
GRAVED ON BRASS PLATES, WAS TILL
THE TIME, OF THE CIVILL WARS

17

THE FOLLOWING INSCRIPTION.

THOMAS, the 4th. *Lord*
BERKELEY, upon the eighth day of
July in the fifth yere of the Victorious
King HENRY the fifth, Anno 1417,
died at *Wotton under Edge*, he then
of the Age of 64 Years 6 Months,
and 8 Daies, whereof he had sat
Lord 49 Years, 1 Monthe and 5 Daies
and lived a Widdower the last 26
Yeres thereof and lyeth buried under
this Tombe with the Translated Bones
of the *Ladye* MARGARET, his Wife.
Nnnc quos certus amor primis convixit
ab annis
Junxit idem tumulus junxit idemq polus .
In Youth our Parents joyn'd our
Hands, our Selves our Hearts,
This Tomb our Bodies hath, the
Heavens our better Parts.

The *Revd.* JOHN TATTERSALL, A. M.
Chaplain in Ordinary to His Majesty,
Vicar of *Harwood* and of *Ledsham*,
Yorkshire, Died April 2nd. 1801,
Aged 50 Years.
For Hospitality, Loyalty, Learning,
Beneficence and Piety,
As a good Subject, and conscientious
Divine,
His Memory will long be revered
and honoured.
As a determined Foe to all Acts of
Oppression,
He dared by a reluctant Appeal
to the Laws of his Country,
To maintain the Cause of the Poor,
To vindicate the Rights of Himself
and his Successors
And every suit having been
decided in his favor,
He was applauded for his Perseverance,
By the Archbishop, his venerable
Diocesan
With this Strong Encomium
"SIR, you have done your Duty,"
Muse Reader, on this interesting
Character,
Admire the just Inflexibility
of his Principles,
And if thou seekest the Rewards
of Virtue, in a better Life,
Commend his Zeal:—
"Go and do thou Likewise."

ON FLAT STONES.

WILLIAM HARRIS,
was buried here Dec. 23, 1738
in the 47th. Year of his Age.
Also SARAH, Wife of JONATHAN
HARRIS, of *Stonehouse*, and
Mother of WILLIAM HARRIS,
was buried here April the 10, 1742,
Aged 79 Years.
And SARAH, the Daughter of
WILLIAM and RACHEL HARRIS,
was buried April 23, 1754,
Aged 29 Years.

In Memory of
SAMUEL TROTMAN,
who was born the 24 Aug. 1691,
and died March the 13th. 1767,
Also of HANNAH, his Wife,
who died December the 15, 1754,
Aged 39 Years.

In Memory of

18

JAMES ROGERS, *Apothecary*,
and of MARTHA, his Wife,
He died May 21, 1729, Aged 42.
She April 21, 1762, Aged 80.

In Memory of
RICHARD RUGG, *Snr.* of *Comb*,
He was buried March 21*st.* 1738,
Aged 69 Years.
Also MARY, his Wife, was buried
April 17*th.* 1751, Aged 79.

Beneath this Stone are deposited
the Remains of SARAH ADEY,
Daughter of JAMES VAUGHAN,
of *Newnton* in the County of
Wilts Esqr. and Wife of
DANIEL ADEY, *Esqr.*
She died 13 Jany. 1769,
Aged 37 Years.

In Memory of
ELIZABETH, Wife of JAMES RICHMOND,
who departed this Life,
March the 30*th.* 1755,
Aged 58 Years.
Also JAMES RICHMOND,
died Jany. the 15*th.* 1764,
Aged 69 Years.

Here lyeth the Body of
ROBERT HICKES, of *Comb, Esqr.*
who died 7*th.* day of August,
A. D. 1743, Aged 70.
Also RICHARD HICKES, his Son,
who died the 27*th.* of January 1699,
Aged 7 Weeks and 2 Days.

Here resteth the Body of
FRANCIS JOBBINS,
who was buried the 13*th.*
of April 1676.
And Also of ALICE, his Wife,
who was buried July 25*th.*
A. D. 1686.

Here lyeth the Body of
ALICE LEIGH, eldest Daughter of
WILLIAM LEIGH, of this Parish,
Gentleman, who died the 26 day of
July, Anno Dom 1649.
Here also lyeth the Body of
MARY, the Wife of FRANCIS
JOBBINS, the *Younger*, and
Daughter of WILLIAM LEIGH,
Gent. who was buried the 8*th.*
day of Jany. 1663.
And also JOHN and WILLIAM,
Sons of FRANCIS JOBBINS,
were buried Novem. 18*th.*
Anno Dom. 1685.

Here lyeth the Body of
ELIZABETH, Wife of WILLIAM
SMYTH, who was buried
November 2*nd.* 1757.

Here lyeth the Body of
ELIZA VENN, late from *Killcott*,

19

---

who was buried Aug. the 19*th.* 1704,
Aged 87 Years.

Here lyeth the Body of
THOMAS VENN, of this Parish,
who was buried June the 14, 1730,
Aged 76 Years.
In Memory of
ESTHER, the Wife of THOMAS
VENN, who died Jany. 17*th.* 1739,
Aged 87 Years.

In Memory of
MARGARETTA, Daughter of
GILES AUSTIN, *Clothier*,
who died Oct. 2, 1736,
Aged 7 Months.

H. S. E. JOHANNES BARNES,
Præfectura moriens III *id.* Jan:
MDCXCIII.

HARRY PEARCE,
33 Years *Clerk* of this Parish,
died August 12, 1761,
Aged 60 Years.
FRANCES WICHELL,
died March 25, 1769,
Aged 42 Years.
The *Revd.* OFFSPRING PEARCE, B.A.
died in *North America*,
in Decr. 1760, Aged 50 Years.
HARRY PEARCE, *Junr.*
died June 4, 1775, Aged 33 Years.
ANN, Wife of JOSEPH PEARCE,
died March 4, 1796, Aged 68.

R. OSBORNE, 1749.
S. O. 1742.
R. O. 1757.
A. O. 1755.
G. WHITE, 1757.
JOHN OSBORNE,
obiit Oct 27, 1770, Ætat. 49.

Sacred to the Memory of
ELIZABETH LEIGH, *Widow*,
who died Jany. 29, 1766, Aged 85.
Also of HESTER, her Daughter,
who died Octob. 16, 1791,
Aged 77 Years.

In Memory of
JOHN RUGG, who died
March 10, 1784, Aged 83.
LYDIA, his Wife, died Jan. 17, 1783,
Aged 73 Years.

Underneath lie the Remains of
MARY, Wife of MATHEW BIDDLE,
who died 19 May 1774,
Aged 39 Years.
Also three of their Children that
died in their Infancy.
SARAH HICKES, Sister of
Mrs. BIDDLE, who died
23 of Jany. 1775, Aged 38 Years.
MATHEW BIDDLE,
died March 21, 1781, Aged 51 Years.

20

In Memory of
ELIZABETH, Wife of THOMAS MILES,
She died June 30, 1790,
Aged 64 Years.

ELIZABETH HODGSON,
Died Decemb. 15, 1792, Aged 47.

In Memory of
MARY, the Wife of
JOHN PRICE, of this Town,
Clothier, who died Sept. 8, 1777,
Aged 71 Years.
The above mentioned JOHN PRICE,
died Nov. 18, 1786, Aged 71.

Sacred to the Memory of
MARY YEATS, Daughter of the late
JAMES and MARY YEATS,
of *Nailsworth*, in this County,
She died Nov. 30, 1783,
Aged 52 Years.

SOUTH AISLE.

ON MONUMENTS.

Arms:—ADEY, *as before.* *impaling*:—Azure en a Chevron betw.
3 fleur de Lis Or, three Mullets
pierced Sable.—GYDE.

Near this Place are deposited
the Remains of WILLIAM ADEY,
of *Uley*, in this County, *Esqr.*
whose Military Abilities exerted in
the Service of his Country acquir'd
him the Rank of *Lieut. Col.*
in the 68*th.* Regiment.
In his private Character he discharged
the Social Duties of Life with Ten-
derness and Humanity.
He died the 7*th.* of November 1763,
Aged 39 Years.
His Widow's affectionate Regard
to his Memory Caused this
Monument to be erected.

Arms: Quarterly 1 & 4.—Azure
a Lion rampant and in Chief three
Escollops Argent.—CLUTTERBUCK.
2 and 3.—Gules on a fess cotized
between six Martlets Or, three Pellets.— .... *impaling Quarterly* 1.—Gules a Chevron, betw.
three Bulls heads affronté Argent,
Armed Or.—BAINHAM. 2.—Azure
on a Chief, ... three Mullets
.... 3 —Argent, on a Bend
Sable three Eagles Or, ...
4.—Argent, a Castle Sable, ...
5 —per pale Gules, and Or, an
Eagle display'd with two heads
Vert. .... 6.—Sable a Lion
rampant Argent. .... 7 —...
on a bend ...... three Calves. VEEL.
8.—Azure four martlets and label
of three points Or, ... 9 —
a Chevron between ten Crosses
.... 10. *Quarterly.*—Or, and
Gules, in the first quarter a Lion
pas ant Sable, ... 11.—Sable
three fusils in fess Or. ....
12.—Sable a Lion rampant Or.

Here resteth the Body of
Mrs. DORCAS CLUTTERBUCK,

21

Widowe, of WILLIAM CLUTTERBUCK, late of *King Stanley*, in the Countie of *Gloucester*. *Gent.* Daughter of JOHN RAINHAM, of *Westhurie*, in the *Forest of Dean*, *Esqr.* And of MARIE BONHAM, sometime maide of Honour to *Queen* ELIZABETH, his Wife. After She had finished her Course in the Race of Pietie, Aged 84 Years, And she departed in Peace, She entered into Bliss January 20th and was here buried February the 1st. 1667. To her deare Memorie ELIZABETH, the Wife of ROBERT OLDISWORTH, of *Bradley*, *Esqr* her Daughter and Executrix erected this Monument.

ON A BEAUTIFUL MONUMENT.

Arms:—Per pale Ermine and Gules on a fess Gules a Lizard.

Sacred to the Memory of WILLIAM TASWELL, A. M. A Divine whose professional Character received a Lustre from the Elegant Accomplishments of the Scholar, The Lessons which he delivered with the most persuasive Eloquence, were illustrated by the best of All comments His exemplary Conduct. He was many years Vicar of this Parish, and of *Almsbury*, And in discharging the sacred Duties of his Office, He kept in View the pious example of his father The *Revd.* JAMES TASWELL, D. D. *Rector* of *Newington*, in *Surry.* He died the *6th.* day of August 1775, In the 67 Year of his Age. Also in Memory of DOROTHY, his Wife Daughter of Mr. .... KENNETT, of *Feversham*, in *Kent.* who in Cultivating the Qualifications which embellish and exalt the female Mind, Paid a just Attention to the Humble Offices of Domestick Life, She died 28 of Octob. 1777, Aged 63 Years.

ON RAISED TOMBS.

Ergo Domina ELIZABETHA LONG, filia natu maxima GEORGII MASTER, de *Cirencestria*, in *Com. Gloucest.* *Armigeri*, primo connubio Juncta EDVARDO OLDISWORTH, de *Bradly*, in hac parochia *Armig.* deinde GUALTERO LONG, de *Dracott Cerne*, in agro *Wilts.* Equiti aurato ex hac vita discessi, Nov. 14, Ao. S'tis. MDCLVIII, Ætatis 58 et hic requiesco at Resurgam. *At the Top are these Arms:*—1st. Gules a Lion rampant gardant Argt. supporting between his fore paws a Rose of the field leaved and Barbed Vert —MASTER. *impaling.* .... in fess three plates .... 2nd. *Coat.* MASTER, *as before.* *impaling.*—Gules three Crescents Argent, a Chief Ermine. *At the feet the following two Coats:*—1. Azure a Lion rampant and semi of Cross

Crosslets Argent.—LONG, *impaling* MASTER, *as before.* 2nd.—Gules on a fess Argent, three Lions passant gardant purpure. OLDISWORTH, *impaling* MASTER. *North Side.* .... a fess nebullè between three Cinque foils Gules .... *impaling* OLDISWORTH, *as before.* *South Side.* *Quarterly* 1.—OLDISWORTH, *as before.* 2.—Argent, six fusils in Bend Sable. 3.—Or, a Griffin Segrant Sable. 4.—Sable an Etoil Or, a Chief checque Argent, and Sable *impaling Quarter-ly* 1 and 4, CLUTTERBUCK, *as before.* 2 and 3, Gules on a fess cottized between six Martlets Or. three Pellets.—...

ON FLAT STONES.

Arms: Quarterly, 1. OLDISWORTH. 2. Argent, Six fusils in bend Sable ... 3. Or, a Griffin segrant Sable ... 4. Sable an Etoil Or, a Chief Checque Argent, and Sable.

Here was buried WILLIAM, the only Son of ROBERT OLDISWORTH, *Esqr.* who at 20 Years old died on the 23rd. of August, Ano. Dni. 1674.

Under this Stone were buried JOHN ROUS, *Gent.* who died the 15th. day of Oct. Ao. D. 1709. Ætatit suæ 61. WILLIAM ROUS, Son of the said JOHN ROUS, who dyed ye 21 day of Jany. A. D. 1683, Ætatis suæ 9. ANNE, Wife of the aforesaid JOHN ROUS, died 22 day of March 1720, Aged 72 Years JOHN, THOMAS, JAMES, and WILLIAM, Sons of THOMAS ROUS, and Grandsons of the aforesaid JOHN ROUS, died in their tender Infancy, October 30, 1703. .... April 5, 1713. April 16, 1713.

Here lyeth the Body of THOMAS, Son of RICHARD WESTFIELD, *Gent.* who was buried October 16, 1700.

In and near this Place lie the Bodies of RICHARD HIETT, Twice *Mayor* of this Town, who was buried Dec. 10, A. D. 1659, Æt. 57. MARY, his Wife, buried Mar. 28, 1689, Ætat. 79. SAMUEL, their Son, M. A buried March 7th. A. D. 1658, Ætat. 23. And JONATHAN, another Son, buried September 13, A. D. 1686, Ætat. 39.

Here lyeth the Body of RALPH DEANE, of the City of *Gloucester*, Collector of his Majesty's Excise, who was buried March 21st, in the .... Year of his Age, A. D. 1699.

In Memory of JOHN BARRY, Son of WILLIAM BARRY, of *Trigett*, in the County *Hereford*, *Gent.* who departed this Life, Oct. 5, A. D. 1718, in the 19 Year of his Age.

In Memory of MARY SMITH, late Wife of JOHN SMITH, of this Town, *Apothecary*, who died Nov. 5, 1717 Aged 95 Years.

Here Resteth the Body of SUSANNAH, Wife of EDWARD WALLINGTON, *Mercer*, who departed this Life, Dec. 14, 1725, in the 74 Year of her Age.

MARY RICKARDS, died Jany. 25, 1755, Aged 82.

In Memory of STEPHEN HUNT, and of ELIZABETH, his Wife, of this Town, He died October the 16, 174.. Aged 61 Years. She February the 15, 1740, Aged 57 Years.

In Memory of ALICE, Wife of RICHARD FRYER, who was buried here Jan. 6, 1735, Aged 45 Years. And of MARY, their Daughter, and Wife of CHARLES WALLINGTON, who was buried June 23, 1753, Aged 29 Years. Also of ANNE, their Daughter, who was buried Febr. 8, 1756, Aged 4 Years and 8 Months.

MARY, Daughter of JOSEPH and ELIZABETH COOKE, was buried Augt. 27, 1726, Aged 4 Years, and JOSEPH, their Son, was buried Jany. 30, 1735, Aged 8 Years.

In Memory of WILLIAM TOWNSEND, who died Nov. 30, 1766, Aged 55 Years. Also of ELIZABETH, his Wife, who died Sept. 17, 1772, Aged 61 Years.

To the Memory of Mr. FRANCIS HUNTRIDGE, *Surgeon*, who died Febr. 24, 1766, Aged 56 Years. Also of MARY, his first Wife, who died July 23, 1745. Also of MARY, his second Wife, who died May 11, 1756.

22   23   24

MARTHA, the Wife of JOHN FRYER,
died March 3, 1773, Aged 35 Years.
MARY, ANNE and SAMUEL,
the three Children of
JOHN and MARTHA FRYER,
who died in their Infancy.
JOHN, their Son who died,
March 3, 1784, Aged 14 Years.

CHURCH YARD.

ON A MONUMENT AGAINST THE PORCH.

Near this Place lies the Body of
JOSEPH MABBATT,
who was buried March 29, 1756,
in the 66th Year of his Age.
Also JOAN, his Wife,
who was buried Sept. the 29, 1742,
Aged 76 Years.
And SAMUEL. their Son was buried
March 28, 1711, and RICHARD,
their Son, Jany. 27, 1763,
Aged 55 Years.

MARY, Wife of WILLIAM LOCKIER,
Daughter of THOMAS and MARY
ASHBY, who died Oct. the 15, 1762,
Aged 44 Years.
Also three Children of
WILLIAM and MARY LOCKIER,
died in their Infancy.
Also WILLIAM, their Son,
died Nov. 2nd. 1768, in the
17 Year of his Age.

Near this Place lies interred
the Body of ROBERT CREW,
of this Town Gold and Silver wire
Drawer, who died July 28, 1763,
Aged 79 Years.
His Neice MARY COCKE, his Executrix
erected this Stone to his Memory.

ON A MONUMENT AGAINST SOUTH WALL.

MARY, Wife of THOMAS ASHBY,
Daughter of Mr. JOHN CLARK,
Cowley, and Grand-daughter of
Mr. ROBERT ROWDOWN,
Rector of Coberley in this County,
Died Nov. 20, 1750, Aged 67 Years.
On whose Soul God have Mercy
and grant her the joys of Heaven
for the Merits of Christ.

ON ANOTHER MONUMENT AT EAST-END OF SOUTH AISLE.

Near this Place lie the Remains of
ISAAC HODGES, Card Maker,
and of SARAH, his Wife.
He died Octob. 9, 1762,
Aged 75 Years.
She died June 7, 1759,
Aged 70 Years.
Also of ISAAC, their Grandson,
Son of ALEXANDER and JANE DOW,
(who erected this Stone
to their Memory.)
He died in his Infancy,
Dec. 18, 1758.

ANOTHER MONUMENT AGAINST THE EAST WALL OF NORTH AISLE.

In Memory of
EDMUND SMITH, died Jan. 1, 1764,
Aged 76 Years.
WILLIAM SMITH, died Dec. 18,
in the Year 1797, Aged 74.
SARAH, Wife of WILLIAM SMITH,
died June 31, 1757, Aged 28.

ON A MONUMENT AGAINST THE NORTH WALL.

Before this Place lie the Children of
RICHARD and MARY OSBORNE:
ANN, buried Dec. 21, 1686,
Aged 14 Months
WILLIAM, buried July 30, 1687,
Aged 4 Months and 3 Weeks
WILLIAM, buried June 9, 1696,
Aged 3 Weeks.
THOMAS, buried April 14, 1702,
Aged 1 Year and 8 Months.
MARTHA, buried March 18, 1708,
Aged 1 Week.
JOHN, buried October 16, 1708,
Aged 2 Years and 8 Months.
EDWARD, buried July 14, 1704.
Also ALICE, Wife of THOMAS HILL,
died Nov. 29, 1739, Aged 47 Years.
Beneath the Monument are likewise
Interred the Remains of
MARY PARBERY, Widow,
Daughter of the aforesaid THOMAS
and ALICE HILL, and Grand-
daughter of the above mentioned
RICHARD and MARY OSBORNE,
She died 25 Febr. 1801,
Aged 81 Years.

ON A MONUMENT AGAINST EAST WINDOW.

Before this Place lies the Body of
EDWARD SMITH, who was buried
Jany. 16, 1725, Aged 50 Years.
Also SARAH, his Widow,
was buried Febr. 8, 1715, Aged 51,
SARAH, their Daughter, was buried
Oct 20, 1714, Aged 19 Years.
And a Daughter of WILLIAM SMITH,
unbaptized.
Likewise ELIZABETH SMITH,
Wife of WILLIAM SMITH,
was buried Sept. 21, 1737,
Aged 40 Years.

In Memory of
WILLIAM SMITH, Saddle Tree Maker,
who died Augt. 23, 1748,
Aged 80 Years.
SARAH, his Relict, died Sep. 22, 1790,
Aged 86 Years.
Also THOMAS, the Son, of
WILLIAM HARIS SMITH,
died May 14, 1751, Aged 12.
And BROMFIELD, their Son,
who died June 19, 1775,
Aged 31 Years.
Also ELIZABETH BROMFIELD,
who died Jany. 19, 1775,
Aged 66 Years.

In Memory of
ANN, the Wife of SAMUEL
BROMFIELD, who died Nov. 30,
1783, in ye 40 Year of her Age.

ON A MONUMENT AGAINST THE SOUTH WINDOW.

Here lieth the Body of
NATHANIEL BENNETT,
who died Nov. 29, 1770, in
the 86 Year of his Age.
Also HESTER, his Wife,
died Jany. 23, 1759,
Aged 77 Years.
BENJAMIN, their Son, who died
Oct. 7, 1744, Aged 39 Years.
EPHRAIM, HESTER and EPHRAIM,
died in their Infancy.

ON ALTAR TOMBS.

JOHN WALLINGTON, of this Town,
died April 20th. 1744, Aged 58.
CHARLES and WILLIAM, his
Children, were buried here,
CHARLES, July 19, 1712.
WILLIAM, March 4, 1727.

In Memory of JOHN WALLINGTON,
late of this Parish, Clothier,
who died November the 1st, 1761,
Also of JOHN, his Son,
who died an Infant.

Here lieth the Bodye of
NATHANIEL CAPEL, Physician,
who departed this Life,
Nov. 2, 1759, Aged 56.

Against the East End of the Church
were here interred
RICHARD and MARY WALLINGTON,
MARY, Dec. 27, 1736, Aged 67.
RICHARD, Nov. 15, 1746, Aged 70.
Also were buried the Children of
RICHARD and MARY WALLINGTON,
viz —RICHARD, SAMUEL, WILLIAM
and MARY, who all died Infants.

In a Vault underneath this Tomb
lieth the Body of
Mr. SAMUEL DAWES,
who died Jany. 25, 1738,
Aged 80 Years.

M. S.
ROBERTI DAWES,
qui hujus Mundi satur,
melioris certus, in Servatorem oculos
mentis intentos habens, spretas
omnibus mundanis, nil æque ac mortis
horam expetivit votiq Compos in
Sepulcrum matris ELI BYRTON,
quod voluit hic repositus
Oct. iiijo. A. D. ......
ROBERTUS DAWES,
Deus tu es robur
Tu Deus es robur mihi contra tædia
mortis,
Scilicet infirmus corpore, mente
potens.
Contemno mundum, quoniam (soterion)
illud
Vi in oculis fidei; mors mihi munus erit.
Vita vale. Discedo libens, dimitto
servum
Nunc nunc dissolvi, supplico, pace
tua.
Cunctorum damnum lubeat mihi ferre
patique,
Quo portum teneam, salvus et esse
queam.

25

26

27

Here lyeth the Body of
ROBERT DAWES, *the Elder*,
Once Mayor of this Town,
who departed this Life, the
4 day of March 1630, Ætat. 60.
Also the Body of
.... DAWES, his Wife,
who departed this Life, the
22 day of Jan. 1654, Ætat. 67.

BRASS PLATES ON ALTAR TOMBS.

M. S.

GUILIELMI MOORE, *Senioris*,
Qui obiit Decimo nono Februarij,
Anno Ætatis suæ
Octagesimo quarto A. D. MDCCII.

CHRISTIANA, illius uxor et
HESTER, Eorum
Filiæ e periculoso mundo parius
evaserunt, illa
Decimo quarto Novembris,
A. D. MDCLVII.
Itace Undecimo Junij,
A. D. MDCLXIII.
Etiam ad Terram reversum est
Quicquid terestre fuit
GUILIELMI MOORE,
Vitam hanc pie et placide evasit
dieiquanto,
Februarij, Anno Dom. MDCCXXVI,
Ætatis LXIX.

Here resteth the Body of
SARAH, the Wife of DANIEL ADEY,
and Daughter of WILLIAM MOORE,
deceased who was buried the
10th. day of March, 1686.
Also HESTER, their Daughter,
who died in the 18th. Year of her
Age 1705.

JOHN BEARPACKER, *Clothier*,
died March 1, 1742, Aged 42.

JOHN DEMERY,
died June 2, 1762, Aged 49.
MARY, his Wife, died Jan. 11, 1748,
in the 40th. Year of her Age.
THOMAS, their Son,
died July 12, 1761, Aged 16.
And MARY, their Daughter,
died June 8, 1761, Aged 24.
HENRY, their Son,
died May 20, 1795, Aged 62.
SARAH, Daughter of JOHN DEMERY,
Junr. died March 6, 1794, Aged 62.
MARY, his Wife, died April 22, 1790,
Aged 20 Years.
Also 3 of their Children Infants.

In Memory of
BENEDICT TURNER, *Junr.*
who died Oct. the 14, 1722,
Aged 42 Years.
Also of JOSHUA EVERETT,
his *Son in Law*, who died
December the 25, 1762, Aged 55.

In Memory of
JAMES RICKETS, *Senr.* of *Bradley*,
and of SARAH, his Wife,
He died October 5, 1720, Aged 56.

28

She died October the 17, 1728,
Aged 66 Years.
THOMAS and ANN, their Children
were buried here.

This Tomb was erected to the
Memory of SARAH, the Wife of
JOHN PHILLIPS, of the *Lower
Barnes*, in the Parish of *Kings
Wood*, and Daughter of
JAMES and ELIZA RICKETS,
of *Bradley*, in this Parish,
who died Apr. 12, 1764,
Aged 33 Years.
JOHN PHILLIPS,
died Nov. 11, 1798, Aged 73.

Under and Near this Tomb
were interred the Bodies of
THOMAS WATHEN
and ANNE, his Wife,
THOMAS, died May 11, 1691.
ANNE, died April 13, 1700.
Also *Mrs.* ANNA WORKMAN,
Widow, Mother of the said
THOMAS WATHEN,
was buried April 13, 1697.

To the Memory of
ROBERT CREW, *Clothier*,
who was buried here November
the 1, 1673, Aged 74.
ARTHUR, his Son, was buried
the 19 Febr. 1671, Aged 31.
ALICE, the Wife, of ROBERT CREW,
was buried the 16th. of
December 1682, Aged 89.
MARY WITCHELL, *Widow*,
Daughter of ROBERT CREW,
was buried here November
the 8th. 1707, Aged 80.
Mrs. MARY JOBBINS, *Widdow*,
Grand-Daughter of ROBERT CREW,
was buried here October the
18, 1743, Aged 74.
Also *Mrs.* SARAH ADEY,
Grand-Daughter to ROBERT CREW,
was buried here Febr. 1, 1755,
Aged 84 Years.

Here resteth the Body of
NATHANIEL HIERON,
who was buried the 22 day of
January 1705, in the 68th.
Year of his Age.
Also NATHANIEL, SAMUEL, SAMUEL,
NICHOLAS and ROBERT,
Children of the said NATHANIEL
HIERON and EDITH, his Wife,
which EDITH, departed this Life,
the 10 day of March 1727, in the
71 Year of her Age.

In Memory of
NATHANIEL HIERON,
of this Town, who died December
12, 1775, Aged 7. Years.
And five of his Children, by MARY,
his Wife, viz.—EDITH, NICHOLAS,
SAMUEL, EDITH and LETTY,
who all died in their Infancy.

In Memory of

29

SARAH VINES, Daughter of
THOMAS VINES, of this Town,
Alderman, who died May 15, 1722,
Aged 24 Years.
Near this Place lies
THOMAS VINES, *Alderman*,
of this Town, who died
August 23, 1741, Aged 63 Years.
MARY, Wife of THOMAS VINES,
departed this Life, April 25,
A. D. 1739, Æt. 66.

If Virtue can demand the flowing
Tear
'Tis just we shed the watry Tri-
bute here;
Virtue display'd in every Scene of
Life
The Daughter, Sister, Mother,
Friend and Wife,
Nor does a false Inscription stain
this Stone
Which tells that so much Goodness
was in one.

Also ISAAC, their Son, departed
this Life, May the 10th 1739,
Aged 23 Years.

Here lyeth the Body of
RICHARD HICKES, once Mayor
of this Town, who was buried
April 23, 1703, Aged 53 Years.
Also ELIZABETH, his Wife,
was buried June 2, 1722,
Aged 72 Years.
THOMAS, their Son, was buried
Febr. 22, 1708, Aged 31 Years.

Here lieth the Body of
WILLIAM HIERON, *Gent.*
late *Lieutenant of Dragoons*, under
the Command of *General* STANHOPE,
who died August 12, 1724,
Aged 57 Years.

In Memory of
THOMAS HILL, who was buried
July the 3rd. 1727, Aged 88 Years.
ANNA, his Wife, June 4, 1729,
Aged 62 Years.
Also of ELIZABETH, Wife of
JOHN HILL BENNET,
who died Febr. 23, 1756,
in the 47th. Year of her Age.

Hic jacet THOMAS WINSTONE,
Qui hujus oppidi Prætoris
Munere Summa cum Laude
prefunctus ob. Anno Ætatis LXXI,
Salutis MDCXCIII.

Here lieth the Body of
THOMAS WINSTON,
who was buried Sept. the 2nd. 1728,
Aged 54 Years.
Also THOMAS, his Son, who was
buried December the 23 d. 1730,
Aged 27 Years
Also MARGARET, the Wife of
THOMAS WINSTON, *Senr.*
who was buried November 22, 1753,
Aged 79 Years.

In Memory of

30

RICHARD WINSTON, *Clothier*,
who was buried April 17, 1745,
Aged 40 Years.
Also RICHARD and ANNE,
his Children were buried here,
RICHARD, July 19, 1736,
ANNE, August   , 1736.
In Memory of
WILLIAM WINSTON, who died
Aug. 17, 1747, Aged 50 Years.

In Memory of
THOMAS PALSER, of *Combe*,
who was buried May 16, 1735,
Ætatis suæ 80.
Also of ELEANOR, his Wife,
who was buried Sept. 18, 1736,
Ætatis suæ 76.
Near this Place lie the Children of
HUGH PALSER, *viz.*—RICHARD,
died Sept. 6, 1724, Aged 1 Month.
And MARY, Dec. 15, 1721,
Aged 4 Years.

To the Memory of
HUGH PALSER,
who exchanged this Life, for a Better
Sept. 16, 1761, Aged 73 Years.
Also of ANNE, his Wife,
Daughter of THOMAS ORCHARD,
of *Huntingford* in this Parish,
who died Febr. 16, 1745,
Aged 60 Years.
HUGH ALEXR. Son of ROBERT and
MARY PALSER, died Febr. 6,
Aged 13 Days.

RICHARD COLLWELL, *Senr.*
was buried November 16, 1723,
Aged 72 Years.
And MARY, his Wife, June 2, 1708,
Aged 48 Years.
RICHARD COLLWELL, *Junr.*
was buried June 1, 1724,
Aged 42 Years.
JOHN COLLWELL,
died March 10, 1747, Aged 71 Years.
EDMUND COLLWELL,
died June 10, 1747, Aged 64.
ELIZABETH, his Wife,
died June 22, 1763, Aged 71 Years.

In Memory of
JOHN COLLWELL, of this Town,
who departed this Life,
August 30, 1723, Aged 89.
Also of SARAH, his Wife,
who died March 24, 1722,
Aged 78 Years.
And also of WILLIAM and RACHEL,
Children of WILLIAM and RACHEL
HARRIS, who were buried here.

In Memory of
RACHEL, Wife of WILLIAM HARRIS,
who departed this Life,
Augt. 23, 1726, Aged 37 Years.
Also of JOHN COLLWELL HARRIS,
Son of the said WILLIAM and
RACHEL, who died July 19, 1726,
Aged one Year and Six Months.

Before this Tomb lyeth the Body of
STEPHEN HUNT, *Senr.*
who died January 31, 1721,
Aged 73 Years.

Here resteth the Body of
SARAH, the Wife of JOHN SMITH,
who was buried Aug. 16,
A D. 1671.
Also SARAH, the Wife of
STEPHEN HUNT, *Senr.*
Daughter of the said JOHN and
SARAH SMITH, who was buried here
Oct. 5, A. D. 1720, Æt. 72.
Also here lyeth the Body of
JOHN SMITH, who was buried
the 9 day of October 1691,
Aged 84 Years.

Here lyeth the Body of
JOHN SAUNDERS, *Alderman,*
of this Town, who departed this Life,
Nov. 24, 1739, Aged 74.

In Memory of
EDWARD BURGE, and of ANN,
his Wife. He died July 21, 1730,
Aged 40 Years.
She March 17, 1758, Aged 60.

Here lies the Body of
SAMUEL GOODSON, of this Town,
Clothier, who was buried
Dec 14, 1731, Aged 74 Years.
Also the following Children by
MARY, his Wife: SAMUEL, buried
Nov. 5, 1705, Aged 5 Months.
WILLIAM, buried Sept. 21, 1728,
Aged 37 Years.
REBECCA, Wife of THOMAS TUDGEY,
buried Oct. 29, 1729, Aged 36.
FRANCIS, buried Sept. 5, 1732,
Aged 46 Years.
SARAH, Wife of SAMUEL GOODSON,
died October 22, 1685.

M. S.
ELIZABETHÆ SCOTT, Relictæ
THOMÆ SCOTT, hujus Oppidi, et
Filiæ THOMÆ DYRION, A. M.
Quæ obijt 6to. die Decemb.
Ann. Ætatis 83, et nostræ Salut.
MDCCXXXIX.

WILLIAM DYER, *Clothier*,
died August 13, 1740,
Aged 54 Years.
ELIZABETH, his Daughter,
died November 4, 1747, Aged 29.
SAMUEL, his Son, died
July 18, 1749, Aged 24 Years.
MARY, Wife of the said WILLIAM
DYER, died Nov. 25, 1762,
Aged 68 Years.
CHARLES DYER, *Clothier*,
died July 13, 1789, in the
60 Year of his Age.
SARAH, his Wife, died
Sept. 18, 1766, Aged 31 Years.

In Memory of
CHARLES and CORNELIUS, Sons of

EDWARD and CHRISTIAN BYE.
CHARLES, died June the 11, 1713,
Aged 16 Years.
CORNELIUS, May the 5th. 1760,
Aged 50 Years.

Near this Tomb lyeth the Body of
ROBERT YOUNG,
who departed this Life,
November 16, 1705, Aged 47.
Also the Body of ANN, his Wife,
who departed this Life,
March 7, 1738, Aged 71.

In Memory of
JOHN CARY, and of HANNAH,
his Wife. He died Nov. 27, 1726,
Aged 57 Years.
She died December 25, 1752,
Aged 83 Years.
And of Eleven of their Children.

Jacent hic Cineres
RICHARDI and JOHANNIS HESKINS,
fratrum qui obierunt Cælibes Ille,
12 Januarij A. D. 1708,
Ætatis 70, Ille A. D. 17....

Under this Tomb lyeth the Body of
WILLIAM FOWLER, *Clothier*,
who departed this Life,
Nov. 1, A. D. 1693, Aged 64.

Under this Tomb are buried
THOMAS OKES, who died the
15 of Febr. 1653, Aged 32.
And DOROTHY, his Wife, who died
May the 12, 1670, Aged 60.
Also THOMAS, their Son,
who died June 15, 1680, Aged 32.
And HANNAH, his Wife,
Oct. 10, 1700, Aged 62.
JANE, Daughter of the said
THOMAS and HANNAH OKES,
Sept. 5th. 1680, Aged 5.

Here lieth the Body of
THOMAS DAWS, *Gent.*
who departed this Life, the
11th. of Jany. 1702, in the
58 Year of his Age.
Also SARAH, his Wife,
was buried Nov. 7, 1715, Aged 74.

Hic situm est
Corpus GULIELMI OSBORN. Lanarij
Mariti ALICIÆ, sub jacentis qui bis
Prætor hujus oppidi
Obijt vicessimo nono Januarij
Annoq. Domini 1705,
Ætatis suæ 71.

In Memory of
WILLIAM MAYO, of this Town,
Goldsmith, who was buried
Febr. 28. 1740, Aged 30.
Also SARAH, his Wife and
Daughter of WILLIAM CLARK,
who was buried Aug. 25, 1740,
Aged 24 Years.

In Memory of
JOHN WALLIS, *Clothier,*
who departed this Life,
16 Oct. 1753, Aged 38 Years.

Here resteth the Body of
RICHARD NICHOLAS,
Once Mayor of this Town,
who departed this Life, the
13*th* day of May 1711, in the
46*th*. Year of his Age.
Also three of his Children,
were buried here:
MARY, A. D. 1794.
WILLIAM, A. D 1706.
WILLIAM, A. D. 1710.
Also the Body of MARY, his Wife,
who departed this Life,
November the 25, 1712, Aged 47.
Also near this Place the Body of
MARY, their Daughter, who was
buried July 8, 1747. Aged 52.
MILLECENT, Wife of FRANCIS
CURRY, and Daughter of
RICHARD NICHOLAS,
died Augst. 31, 1785, Aged 85.

Here lyeth interred the Body of
WILLIAM WIGHT, *Alderman,*
of this Town, who departed this
Life, October 9, 1730, in the
49 Year of his Age.
Also two of his Children were
buried here,—EDWARD, Febr. 1*st.*
1729, Aged 8 Years.
JOHN, Nov. 24, 1730, Aged 13.

Here lieth the Body of
WALTER YOUNG, *Clothier,* and
JANE, his Wife.
WALTER, was buried Nov. 26,
A. D. 1696. JANE, Jan. 22, 1669.
Also the Body of WILLIAM,
Son of the said WALTER YOUNG,
Feltmaker, and Citizen of *London,*
who departed this Life, the
30 day of December,
Anno Dom. 1700, Aged 35.

Here lyeth the Body of
HENRY PEARCE, who was buried
April 11, 1728, Aged 58.
Also three of his Children,
were buried here:
THOMAS, January 16, 1701,
Aged 11 Years.
ROBERT, July 22, 1730,
Aged 25 Years.
JAEL, February 19, 1734,
Aged 33 Years.
Also ROBERT, THOMAS and JAEL,
who died Infants.
Also PATIENCE, his Daughter,
was buried Febr. 6, 1742,
Aged 35 Years.
And near this Place lies
ELIZABETH PEARCE, *Widow,*
who was buried Mar. 22, 1748,
Aged 80 Years.

In Memory of
RICHARD PEARCE, *Clothier,*
who was buried July the 5*th.* 1743,
Aged 68 Years.
And SARAH, his Wife, was buried

Jany. 4, 1737, in the 71*st.*
Year of her Age.
Also of RICHARD, their Son,
who was buried July 10, 1733,
in the 23*rd.* Year of his Age.
Also of MARY, Wife of
CORNELIUS BYE, and Daughter of
RICHARD PEARCE, *Clothier,*
who died Febr. 23, 1760,
Aged 56 Years.

Under this Tomb were buried
the Bodies of HENRY and JOSEPH,
the Sons of WILLIAM FORDE, of
the *Rudge* in this Parish.
HENRY, died July the 16*th.*
A. D. 1672, Aged 22 Years.
JOSEPH, died July the 20,
A. D. 1696, Aged 36 Years.
Also HANNAH, the Daughter of
WILLIAM FORDE, and Wife to
THOMAS RUSSELL, of *Wickwar,*
was buried here May the 6*th.*
A. D. 1719, Aged 50 Years.

Near this Place lies the Body of
JAMES WATTS, Son of WILLIAM
and SARAH WATTS, who died
June 26, 1762, in the 35*th.*
Year of his Age.
Under this Tomb lies the Body of
WILLIAM WATTS, of this Parish,
who died Febr. 20, 1762, Aged 75.

In Memory of
SAMUEL HODNOT, who was
buried May the 20*th.* 1720,
Aged 72 Years.
Also ANNE, his Wife, who was
buried Decr. 21, 1726, Aged 76.
Also of FRANCIS MANNING,
who died December the 18, 1724,
Aged 29 Years.
Also the Body of THOMAS BRUTON,
who was buried March the 10*th.*
1736, in the 84 Year of his Age.

In Memory of
CHRISTOPHER WILLIS,
and of MARY and ANN, his Wives.
He died October 31, 1755,
Aged 66 Years.
MARY, died 1727,
Aged 40 Years.
ANN, died Nov. 5, 1744,
Aged 77 Years.
Also of SAMUEL SUMMERS, *Hatter,*
his Son-in-Law, who died
Augt. 22, 1754, Aged 28 Years.
Here lieth the Body of
REBECCA, Wife of HUMPHREY
MAYO, of this Town, *Goldsmith,*
and Daughter of WILLIAM OSBORN,
who died July the 7th. 1726,
Aged 52 Years.

Under this Tomb lyeth the Body of
MARY, the Wife of EDWARD
AUSTIN, who was buried the 4 day
of July, A. D. 1696, Aged 56 Years.
Also the Body of the said
EDWARD AUSTIN, *Clothier,*
was buried here Augt. the 31,
A. D. 1708, Aged 71 Years.
And three of their Sons,

also buried here
WILLIAM, January the 1*st.*
A. D. 1684.
THOMAS, June the 19*th.*
A. D. 1700, Aged 20 Years.
EDWARD, January the 2*nd.*
A. D. 1700, Aged 32 Years.

Near this Place lyeth the Body of
GILES AUSTIN, *Clothier.*
who was buried Augt 14, 1724,
Aged 52 Years.
Also six Sons and One Daughter, *viz.*
WILLIAM, buried March 19, 1726,
Aged 39 Years.
EDWARD, buried Dec. 20, 1696.
EDWARD, buried Jany. 25, 1701.
FRANCIS, buried Febr. 11, 1701.
JOHN and THOMAS,
buried March 20, 1708.
MARY, buried Sept. 9, 1711.

Under this Tomb resteth the Body of
JOSEPH BICK, *Senr.*
who was buried July the 9*th.*
1735, Aged 85 Years.
Also ELIZABETH, his Wife,
was buried Augt. 31, 1735,
Aged 77 Years.
Aan JOSEPH, MARY, JOAN and
HESTER, their Children,
were also buried here.

In Memory of
MOSES WIGHT, who was buried
Novem. 20, 1712, in the 66*th.*
Year of his Age.
And of MARY, his Wife,
who buried January 12, 1726,
Aged 77 Years.
Also of RICHARD WIGHT,
who died May 31, 1754,
Aged 70 Years.

MARY, the Wife of WILLIAM
PANTING, was buried May 8, 1738,
Aged 37 Years.
Also the *Revd. Mr.* SAMUEL
PANTING, A. B. their Son,
was buried Febr. 14, 1764,
Aged 26 Years.

In Memory of
JOHN WOOLWORTH, and ANN,
his Wife, who were buried here.
He October 6, 1756,
Aged 62 Years.
She May 22, 1759, Aged 50.
Also of five of their Sons,—*viz.*
THOMAS, March 23, 1719,
Aged 2 Years.
THOMAS, July 1, 1736,
Aged 9 Years.
......, July 9, 1736, Aged 7 Years.
WILLIAM, July 17, 1756,
Aged 4 Years.
JOHN, Febr. 14, 1756,
Aged 31 Years.
SARAH WALLIS, Sister of the said
ANN WOOLWORTH, who died
Nov. 25, 1756, Aged 70 Years.

Hic Vitæ Curriculo peracto
pariter requiescens

34   35   36

ROBERTUS et ALICIA WIGHT,
Probus, Honestus,
Casta. pia.
Conjuges inculpabiles
Annos natus LXIV ob. Feb. XXI°.
A. D. MDCCXXXV.
HÆC Quadragenaria ob. Feb. X°.
A. D. MDCCXXV.
Salvete, nobile par virtutibus
propriis Illustre
L audavere omnes Boni
Ploravere sui
Imitentur Posteri.

Under this Tomb lieth interred
the Body of WILLIAM WALLIS,
of *Wortley*, who departed this Life,
Nov. 12, 1726, Aged 44 Years.
Also MARY, his Wife, was buried
April 7, 1751, Aged 67 Years.
And three of their Children,
were here buried:
ROBERT, Sept. 2, 1717,
Aged 7 Years.
WILLIAM, June 11, 1738,
Aged 30 Years.
MARY, July 26, 1743,
Aged 31 Years.

Under this Tomb lieth the Body of
ALICE, Wife of SAMUEL COOPEY,
who departed this Life,
Sept. 7, 1729, Aged 80 Years.
And near this Tomb lieth the
Body of MARY, their Daughter,
Wife of SOLOMON HALL,
who departed this Life,
June the 9th. 1729, Aged 47.

Here lyeth the Body of
THOMAS SMYTH, who was buried
December the 25, 1736, Aged 55.
Also the Bodies of Five of
his Children,—*viz.*
THOMAS, Oct. ...., 1736,
Aged 17 Years.
JOSEPH, October 5, 1736,
Aged 12 Years.
BENJAMIN, March 21, 1736,
Aged 4 Years.
Also RICHARD and THOMAS,
who died Infants.

Here lieth the Body of
JEREMIAH OCKWELL,
who was buried October 9th. 1738,
Aged 60 Years.
And ANN, his Wife, was buried
February 27, 1731, Aged 58.

Under this Tomb resteth the Body of
CHARLES TROTMAN, *Clothier*,
who was here interred
April 9, 1714, Aged 59 Years.
Also JANE, his Wife, was buried
July 7, 1722, Aged 70 Years.

Under this Tomb lye interred
the Bodies of JONATHAN WITCHELL,
of this Parish, *Clothier*,
who departed this Life,
18 day of January 1701, in the
62nd. Year of his Age.
And MARY, his Wife, who was
interred Nov. 30, 1678.

37

HENRY WINCHCOMB,
died June 28th. 1760,
Aged 62 Years.

Here resteth the Body of
WILLIAM CLARK,
who departed this Life,
June the 30th. 1743, in the
61th. Year of his Age.
Also ELIZABETH, his Wife,
who died Jany. 19, 1745,
Aged 60 Years.
Also HARRY, his Son,
who died October 22, 1720,
in the 8th. Year of his Age.

In Memory of
JOHN HARDING, who was
buried April 9th. 1701,
Aged 67 Years.
Also of HANNAH, his Wife,
who was buried February the
24th. 1698, Aged 59 Years.

Here resteth the Body of
GEORGE HARDING,
who was buried May the 29th. 1744,
Aged 67 Years.
Also ABIGAIL, his Wife,
who was buried Dec. the 11. 1740,
Aged 60 Years.

In Memory of
ROBERT BENNET, *Senr.*
and of MARY, his Wife, who
were buried here.
He January 24. 1716, Aged 77.
and She April 17th. 1697,
Aged 63 Years.
Here resteth the Body of
ROBERT BENNETT, *Junr.*
Writing-master, in this Town
42 Years, who died
February 4th. 1732, Aged 61.
Also MARY, his Wife, who died
Sept. 24, 1757, Aged 65.
And WILLIAM, their Son,
who died an Infant.

In Memory of
JOSEPH and ESTHER COATES,
who after a Sincere Endeavour in
the Discharge of their Duty to God
their Neighbour and themselves
departed this Life. She 1st. day of
April 1757, Aged 79 Years.
He the 21 of August 1757,
Aged 72 Years.
Also near this Place lieth the
Body of SARAH, Wife of
RICHARD JEFFERYS, who departed
this Life, January the 20th. 1760,
Aged 72 Years.
Also RICHARD JEFFERYS,
who died Nov. 21, 1762,
Aged 75 Years.

In Memory of
JOSEPH WOOLRIGHT,
who died August 2nd. 1749,
Aged 43 Years.
HESTER, his relict, died
April 22, 1781, Aged 77 Years.
And of Four of his Children.

38

This Tomb was erected to preserve
the Memory of SARAH, the Wife
of WILLIAM GOWER, of the
Lodge in this Parish, and Daughter of
WILLIAM and ELIZABETH
OLDLAND, of *Woodford* in the
Parish of *Berkeley*, who died
August 3, 1775, in the 43
Year of her Age.
WILLIAM, their Son, who died
Oct. 23, 1773, Aged 12.
MATHEW, their Son, died an Infant.

MARTHA, Wife of DANIEL
DIMERY, died July 16, 1784,
Aged 59 Years
DANIEL, their Son, who died
Ap. 12, 1798, Aged 37 Years.

In Memory of
ROBERT DREW, of the Parish of
Wickwar, and SARAH, his Wife,
Daughter of THOMAS CREW,
of this Town. She died
Febr. 1, 1738, in the 38
Year of her Age.
He April 26, 1767, Aged 60.

In Memory of
JOHN BENCE, of this Town,
Bookseller, who died March 4, 1757,
Aged 47 Years.

Under this Tomb lyeth the
Remains of ELEANOR HOOK,
Wife of JOHN HOOK, of
Didmarton in this County,
died Febr. 27, 1798 Aged 73 Years.

This Memorial Inscribed to
ELIZABETH JAMES,
who died April 28, 1800,
Aged 54 Years.
She was a faithful Servant 37 Years
to DANIEL DIMERY, late of
Dersley, but now of *Stancombe*,
Yeoman, who erected this Tomb,
as a testimony of Gratitude for her
Best Services. She was the first
Claimant to the Bath Agricultural
Society, for the Bounty to industrious
Servants and received 3 Guineas.

In Memory of
DANIEL WEBB, who died
Jany. 4, 1785, in the 64
Year of his Age.
Also ELIZABETH, his Wife,
who died Febr. 8, 1755,
Aged 45 Years.
JOHN, their Son, died Jan. 4, 1783,
in the 24 Year of his Age.
HESTER, their Daughter,
died July 23, 1768, Aged 12.

In Memory of
RICHARD, Son of JOHN and
LYDIA RUGG, of *Comb*,

39

in this Parish, who died
June 8, 1756, Æt. 7.
ELIZABETH, their Daughter and
Wife of JAMES KNIGHT,
died Dec. 27, 1764, Æt. 19.
HANNAH, Daughter of RICHARD
and MARY KNIGHT,
Died Dec. 28, 1787, Aged 13 Weeks.
SOPHIA, their Daughter,
died Decr. 2, 1790, Aged 7 Years.

In Memory of
MARIAM ROSE,
who departed this Life,
Febr. 8, 1792, Aged 83 Years.

In Memory of
JAMES KNIGHT, Senr.
of the Layes in this Parish,
who departed this Life,
April 3, 1780. in the 87
Year of his Age.
SARAH, his Wife, who departed
this Life, June 3, 1779,
Aged 89 Years
BETTY, the Wife of JAMES
KNIGHT, Junr. died Decr. 10, 1772,
Aged 33 Years.
HANNAH, the Daughter of
JAMES KNIGHT, Junr.
died June 22, 1770, Aged 13 Years.

To the Memory of
CHARLES BYE, who died
Nov. 12, 1780, Aged 50 Years.
LYDIA, his Wife, who died
July 8, 1798, Aged 59 Years.
CHARLES, his Son, who died
Octob. 17, 1786, Aged 10 Years.
Also EDWARD and LYDIA,
two of their Children who
died Infants.
CHARLES RODWAY, his Grandson,
died Jany. 24, 1787,
Aged 1 Year and 6 Months.
CHARLES, Son of CHARLES and
LYDIA BYE, died Jany. 20, 1797,
Aged 34 Years.

In Memory of
JOHN LACY, of Wortley,
in this Parish, who died
April 28, 1786, Aged 72 Years.
ANN, his Wife. died Oct. 19, 1794,
Aged 77 Years.

To the Memory of
THOMAS BAYLY, who died
Decr. 8, 1721, in the 67
Year of his Age.
CHRISTIAN, his Wife,
died July 12, 1722,
Aged 66 Years.
Also CHRISTOPHER and WILLIAM
BAYLY, their Sons,
CHRISTOPHER, died May 6, 1712,
Aged 24 Years.
WILLIAM, March 12, 1721,
Aged 27 Years.

To the Memory of
CHRISTOPHER JORDON,
who died April 13, 1704,

Aged 85 Years.
CATHERINE, his Wife, died
Sept. 10, 1707, Aged 86 Years.

To the Memory of
THOMAS BAYLY, of this Town,
Clothier, who departed this Life,
Nov. 16, 1775. in the
80 Year of his Age.
SARAH, his Wife, died
Oct. 26, 1729, Aged 31 Years.
And three of their Children,
died in their Infancy.
MARY, Wife of THOMAS BAYLY,
who departed this Life,
April 16, 1755. Aged 67 Years.
Also EDWARD BAYLY, Gent.
who died April 19, 1797,
Aged 72 Years.

In Memory of
EPHRAIM HALL, Cooper,
who died Sept. 10, 1764,
in the 76 Year of his Age.
SARAH, his Wife, who died
Febr. 5, 1755, in the 77
Year of her Age.
Also of ROBERT CROOME, Watch-
Maker, who died April 1, 1768,
in the 46 Year of his Age.
And MARY, his Wife, Daughter of
EPHRAIM and SARAH HALL,
died March 15, 1770,
Aged 52 Years.
Also ANN, the Daughter of
EPHRAIM and SARAH HALL,
died May 22, 1785, Aged 66 Years.

To the Memory of
CHARLES BAKER, of this Parish,
who died Febr. 6, 1784,
Aged 91 Years.
Also JOHN, his Son, of the Parish
of Uley, who departed this Life,
Febr. 25, 1784, Aged 65 Years.
Likewise MARY, relict of
JOHN BAKER, who departed this
Life, 10 of Febr. 1786,
Aged 64 Years.

ON FLAT STONES.

Underneath this Stone lie
the Remains of WILLIAM RODWAY,
whose death was occasioned by a
Fall from his House, the 26 of
May 1801, in the 39 Year of his Age.
By his Exertion the Psalmody in
this Church was brought to a very
high Degree of Perfection and the
Choir sincerely regret the Accident
that deprived them of his Support.
Never promise yourself Safety
from the Casualties of Life, but
remember that the fatal Shafts fly
promiscuously and none can guess
who shall be next summoned to
Eternity.
Time flies. Man dies.
Prepare to meet thy God!

(Additional Inscriptions
most since Bigland's time.)

IN CHURCH.

Sacred to the Memory of

FANNY, Wife of EDWARD AUSTIN,
Esqr. of this Place,
and Daughter of DAVID RICARDO,
Esqr. of Gatcombe Park, in this
County, who departed this Life,
on the Seventeenth day of April in
the Year of our Lord, One Thousand
Eight Hundred and Twenty,
in the Twentieth Year of her Age.

"Blessed are the pure in heart for
they shall see God."

In Memory of
ISAAC AUSTIN, Esqr.
whose benevolence was universal
whose generosty was unbounded
a sincere and constant friend
an active and humaine Magistrate,
a cheerful and enlivening member
of society,
But ah! how vain all human
enjoyments! it pleased Almighty
God to snatch him from amidst his
friends in festivity and innocent
recreation, on the 11th. July 1796,
Aged 54 Years.
Also of ELIZABETH, his Wife,
who was adorned with every
Christian Virtue departed this
Life, the 31st. July 1804,
Aged 65 Years.

Arms:—A Lion passant regardant, on a chief? no colours.
Motto:—"Sua praemia laudi."

Sacred to the Memory of
L'ESTANGE SOUTHWOOD AUSTIN,
Esquire, of the Warren, in this
Parish, who after a long and most
painful illness borne with Christian
patience and resignation, died
relying only on the merits of his
Redeemer, on the 10th. day of
February 1549, in the 60th.
Year of his Age.

Deeply lamented loved and respected.

Sacred to the Memory of
WILLIAM VEEL, Esqr.
of Symondshall in this Parish,
for many years one of his
Majesty's Justices of the Peace,
for this County,
who died January 26, A. D. 1783,
Aged 62 Years.
Also to the Memory of
ANNE, his Wife, eldest Daughter
of the late STEPHEN COMPEER,
of this Town, who departed this Life,
June 17th. A. D. 1799,
Aged 71 Years.
In the same Vault are deposited
the Remains of their 4th. Daughter
ELIZABETH, who died April 28,
A. D. 1793, Aged 27 Years.
Also of their eldest Son,
WILLIAM VEEL, Esqr. M.A., F.A.S.
a Barrister-at-Law, one of his
Majesty's Justices of the Peace
and Deputy Lieutenant of this
County, &c. who died December 6th.
A. D. 1820, in the 59
Year of his Age.
And of SARAH, his Wife,
Youngest Daughter of the late
Revd. RICHARD HUNTLEY,
of Boxwell, who died Ap. 7, 1820,
Aged 51 Years.
Also of their eldest Daughter

ANN, who died Febr. 25th. 1851,
Aged 71 Years.

Arm:—On a bend 3 calves passant or, a Chevron between 3 ....
...... 3 crosses crosslets fitchee.
Crest:—a Wheatsheef or enfiled
with a ducal coronet Gu.

Sacred to the Memory of
GEORGE WASTIN, *Esqr.*
An inhabitant of this Borough,
where in the mature vigour of life.
And full enjoyment of every
temporal blessing
He was seized by the hand of death,
In the 35th. Year of his Age,
February 15th. A. D. 1815.
In his several relations as Father,
Husband and Brother,
He was tender, indulgent and
affectionate,
In his general conduct
Liberal benevolent and disinterested,
As a Citizen and a Majistrate,
Active persevering and indefatigable.

Sacred to the Memory of
JOHN COOPER, *Esqr.*
late *Surgeon* of this Town,
who surrounded by his affectionate
and sorrowing family departed this
Life, in the humble hope of Divine
acceptance through the mediation
of his Redeemer, August 27, 1827,
in the 62nd. Year of his Age.
In fulfilling the various duties of life
His Character shone conspicuously
And as Husband, Father and Friend,
His memory will long and deservedly
be cherished.
"Let me die the death of the righteous,
And let my last end be like his."
Also in Memorial of four Children :
CAROLINE, JOHN, LAURA and

43

JESSICA COOPER,
who all died in their Infancy.
Also in Memory of another Son,
JAMES COOPER,
whom it pleased the Almighty to take
in the flower of his Age,
Aged 25 Years.
"The Lord gave and the Lord hath
taken away.
Blessed be the name of the Lord."

Also of MARY, the beloved Wife,
and relict of the above named
JOHN COOPER, and Daughter of
the late WILLIAM VEEL, *Esqr.*
of *Symondshall*; in this Parish,
who died August the 25th. 1836,
Aged 67 Years.
May her Christain life example
and advices ever live in the hearts
of her affectionate children,
by whom this humble tribute to
paternal worth is paid.
"The memory of the just is blessed."

Additional Inscription at foot of
ELIZABETH ROUS,
Monument in Chancel.

From a grateful sense of
The strong Affection and the
steady friendship
Experienced through her life
and at her Death,
This testimony of the sincerest
Esteem was erected by her niece,
JANE QUICKE.

ON FLAT STONES IN CHANCEL.

Underneath lie the remains of
JAMES COOPER, *Esqr.*
who died February 13th. 1822,
Aged 26 Years.
Also of JAMES, only Child of
the above JAMES COOPER, *Esqr.*

44

and ESTHER, his Wife, who died
August 20th. 1842, Aged 20 Years.

JOHN COOPER, *Surgeon,*
died January 11th. 1788,
Aged 58 Years.

T. C. 1721.

T. R. 1737.
J. R. 1740.

In Memory of
ANTHONY AUSTIN,
*Lieutenant in the R. S. Gloucester-
shire Militia,* and Justice of the
Peace for this County,
Indefatigable in performing his duty
As an Officer,
Impartial in Administering Justice,
As a Magistrate,
A good Father and a steady Friend,
After struggling for 20 Years
with an excruiating disease
which resisted the united efforts
of the most celebrated
of the Medical Profession,
He resigned his breath
On the 14th. of December 1800,
Aged 54 Years.

SARAH, Daughter of .... ADEY,
died June ...., 1810,
Aged 50 Years.
MARGARET, Daughter of ...... ADEY,
died June 20, 1810, Aged ... Years.

Here lyeth the Body of
ANTHONY BLANCH,
of *Stepleaston*, in the County
of *Wilts. Gent.* who was buried
May the 12th. A. D. 1681.
T. B. 1737.

45

HEAD STONES.

	Died.		Aged.		Died.		Aged.
Thomas Durnell, ...	3 March	1766	27	James, the Son of Philip and Mary Dunn, ...	21 April	1782	24
Edward Holloway, ...	30 Nov.	1792	27				
Catharine, Wife of Sam. Holloway,	11 July	1800	68	William Cratle, late *School Master*, of this Parish, ...	21 April	1787	73
Stephen Humphreys, ...	26 Jany.	1766	84				
Ann, his Wife, ...	24 Decr.	1745	63	Samuel Bennet, ...	26 July	1761	50
Humphrey Humphreys, ...	12 June	1782	69	William Bennet, ...	24 July	1734	84
Hester, his first Wife, ...	11 Nov.	1744	25	Elizabeth, his Wife, ...	27 Oct.	1744	94
Mary, his second Wife, ...	17 Febr.	1765	35	Nathaniel Stinchcomb, ...	10 Febr.	1790	73
Richard Blanchard, ...	6 Jany.	1797	28	Robert Pearce, ...	28 July	1780	69
John Mathews, ...	10 March	1800	46	Mary, his Wife, ...	16 May	1775	72
James Lapley, ...	15 Jany.	1756	59	John Vebb, ...	5 April	1792	57
Mary, his Wife, ...	9 Jany.	1735	40	Thomas Witchell, ...	13 July	1756	66
Edward Hopkins, ...	24 July	1780	53	Richard, his Son, ...	23 Aug.	1755	25
Stephen Hopkins, ...	22 Decr.	1790	19	Betty, Wife of Daniel Nemes,	15 June	1756	47
Mary Heron, ...	29 March	1797	80	Betty, his second Wife, ...	24 Jany.	1783	52
Mary Brandiss, ...	10 May	1761	58	Ann, Wife of Arthur Eastmead,	12 Augt.	1755	65
Margaret, her Sister, ...	23 Nov.	1775	66				

46

47

Notes as to I.—*Devolution of Estates.* II.—*Church.* III.—*Population, Taxation, &c.*

I.—*Estates.*

Wotton under Edge, is an extensive parish in the upper
Division of Berkeley Hundred containing the Town and Hamlets of Bradley, and Sinwell, Symondshall and Combe, Wort-
ey, and Huntingford, four miles distant south of Dursley,
five miles north-east from Wickwar and nineteen miles
south from Gloucester. The soil extending over 3500 acers,
is in general of stone-brash, and in tillage, except immediately in the Vicinity of the town where it is deeper, and
affords excellent pasture and meadow.

In Vutune (Wotton.) Fifteen hides and half a virgate
were held of the Manor of Berchelai in the reign of king
William the Conqueror. (*Domesday Book.*)

Symondshall :—Half a hide in Symondshall did belong
to the manor of Berchelai in the reign of King William
the Conqueror. (*Domesday Book.*)

And the inheritance of this manor has ever since continued in the Berkeley family; but the estate was in lease
to Thomas Veel, Esqr. who is descended of very ancient
family which came into England with King William
the Conqueror.

1537

It is called a borough and has a Mayor, 11 Aldermen and 2 Constables, but sends no members to parliament. Refusing to serve the Office of Mayor in this borough is punishable by fine. In the year 1632. Richard Poole being chosen refused to serve and was fined 10£. John Leigh, was then chosen by the Steward. and refusing in like manner paid a fine of 6£. 13 s. 4 d. The legality of the Steward's imposing such fine has been determined in the Case of Thomas Laws, who was fined 10£. in the Year 1693 which he would not pay whereupon he was arrested in virtue of a Capias sued out of the Court of King's bench in Mich ae'mas term 1695. and a verdict was obtained against him at the Lent Assizes and judgment entered in the same court the Easter term in 1695.

Wotton, was burnt down in the reign of King John. and a place called the *Bunds*, is supposed to mark its ancient site.

From Kings Wood to Wotton, a praty market Towne, welle occupied with Clothiars havynge one fair longe Strete and welle buylded in it and it standethe dyvinge toward the roles of an Hill. *Leland.*

The town was the resort of Flemish Clothiers, temp. 1 Edw. iii. The Brook below the town supplied water power to fulling Mills on the Brook running by Kingswood towards Berkeley and into the Severn. As to Kingswood, *see* Vol. 3. No. .... The trade traffic was by pack horses.

Land Fines Wotton under Egge,

Walter Deruys, Miles, David Broke, Mil., Nic Wekys, Arm. and Hugh Derys, Gen.

29 Eliz. Fine.—R. Bridge, W. Phillips.

30 Eliz.—R. Bridge, T. Seaburn, als. Plomer.

29 & 30 Eliz.—Hugh Venor, J. Dorney.

Wotton, was the scene of that outrage on Law and Order which happened between William, Lord Berkeley, and Thomas, Viscount Lisle, the quarrel arose in the following manner; Thomas, fourth Lord Berkeley, left Elizabeth, an only daughter and heiress, married to Richard Beauchamp, Earl of Warwick; but by a special entail and fine set left the Estate and Lordship of Berkeley, with its appurtenances, on his Nephew James, the next heir male of his family. This Settlement produced a Law-suit between James, fifth Lord Berkeley, and Richard Beauchamp, Earl of Warwick, who in right of his wife, claimed the Berkeley Estates and violently seized Nibley and several other Manors into his own hands. He and his posterity kept possession of this Manor One hundred and Ninety two Years, for which space of time the law suit was carried on with unprecedented violence. During the continuance of this suit Thomas Talbot, Viscount Lisle, descended from the above mentioned Elizth. sent a letter with a Challenge to William, sixth Lord Berkeley, wherein he desired him to fix a time and place for deciding their title by the sword. The Lord Berkeley, by the answer appointed the next morning for the time and Nibley Green for the place of action. and both parties meeting on the 20th. of March, 1470, 10 Edw. iv. with their respective followers, amounting in the whole to about 1000 men, a furious engagement ensued, wherein about 150 men were slain, in which number was Lord Lisle himself, being shot in the mouth with an arrow by one James Hiatte, of the Forest of Dean, Lord Berkeley, after his victory hastened to Wotton, where the Lady Lisle resided, who being big with her first child, miscarried through the fright. His Lordship rifled the house, and carried away some of the furniture and many deeds and evidences which concerned the Lord Lisle's own Estate, and they remain to this day preserved in Berkeley Castle. Government was at the time prevented from taking cognizance of this violent outrage, by the Civil Wars, which raged in the kingdom during great part of the turbulent reign of Edward the fourth.

Edward, (Beaufort) Duke of Somerset, and Eleanor, his Wife, and Joan, Earl of Shrewsbury, and Margaret, his Wife, and George Nevil, Lord Latimer, and Elizabeth, his Wife, the Ladies being the Coheiresses of Thomas Talbot, Lord Berkeley, gave evidence relating to the Estate of Wotton, and other Estates of this Thomas in variance between Plaintiffs and James Lord Berkeley, which Evidence was written down and whereof Mr. Payn, of Rodborough, hath great knowledge.

Introduction in Prog's in Chancery, temp. Q. Elizabeth, p. xx. of Int Vol. 2d.

The absence of the Feoffment was attributed by Wm. Lord Berkeley, to Lord and Lady (Margaret,) Shrewsbury, being at Berkeley Castle, at her Fathers death and having ejected James, Lord Berkeley, the heir male and seized the family Documents. It was alleged on the part of the Coheires of Lord and Lady Shrewsbury, that the spoliation was atributed to the said William, Lord Berkeley, having sacked Wotton House, when Lord Shrewsbury was absent serving in the Kings Wars; they alleged that Lord Stanley, had no interest in the Lands for William, Lord Berkeley, and his Brother; for that Thomas, Lord Berkeley the Countess grandfather, that is, father to Elizabeth the Countesses Mother, was and died seized of Wotton and Symondshall, of a general Estate tail to him and the Heirs of his Body, and upon his decese the Manors descended to the said Countess his Daughter who married Lord Shrewsbury, and while he was engaged in Normandy on the King's Wars.

Rafe Gyll and Wife Jane, late Wife of G. Symons, deceased and their son William, against Brice Berkeley, and John Watershipp, Claimed under a Settlement by James Berkeley, Father of Jane, on her marriage with G. Symons. *Chancery Prog's.* 1 Vol. temp Eliz. 14.

After that fearful struggle a private Act was obtained 12 and 13 Edw. iv. (1471.) by which the Manor and Borough of Wotton under Edge, and Symondshall and Erlingham Manors were assured to William Berkeley and his Wife Johanna, paying 151£. yearly to the Viscountess Talbot, during her Life. same all other Estates.

Wotton was one of the Estates granted to William, Lord Berkeley, by King Henry vii and Heirs male of Earl and Marquis of Berkeley and Nottingham, by way of barter for these right Titles, and it appears that in 1531, while the Entail subsisted King Hen. viii. gave instructions to Thomas Cromwell, to commune with Duddley, (afterwards Lord Warwick,) and Lord Berkeley, for bringing the fee simple of the Manors into that Kings Hands. *State Papers,* Hen. viii. *Vol.* 1. *page* 81.

Free Grammer School at Wotton-under-Edge, for Master and 2 Poor Scholars, 8 Ric. ii. Founded by Katherine Lady Berkeley, Endowed with real Estate by Lady Berkeley the School was reestablished for one Master and Five or more Scholars, by Letter Patent, 20 Jas. i.

The posessions of the School were 31 houses and 162 acres and 10 perches of land, the yearly rents whereof were 21 £. 4 s. 6 d. and the value to be improved above that sum was 121 £. 17 s. 2d. They also found the value of Warren's court, a controverted part of the premises to be 38 £. 1 s. 4d. besides 48 s. and 12 s. payable out of the same. No Language but Latin to be used.

39 Geo. iii. 1799 —Act of exchange between Trustees and Nicholas Owen Smyth Owen, Esqr. of Starwell Farm in North Nibley, and 106. acres, lying in or near the parish of North Nibley, dispersedly among the Estates of Nicholas Owen Smith Owen, Esqr. These were exchanged for 133 a. 3 r. 12 p together with a House and Garden.

Charfield farm:—consisting of 40 a. 36p. purchased in 1748, for 420 £. rent at 24 £. per annum. 22 houses, all at Wotton-under Edge, except one in Newport in the Parish of Berkeley, let at the Rent of 37 £. 17 s. 6 d. and fines on a 26 Years average is 44 £.

The property in the funds so produced and which is all in the three and half per cents. amounts in that stock to 3800 £. the annual dividend being 134 £. 15 s. 0 d.

Total income 376 £. 12 s. 6 d.

Mayor, &c. Trustees:—John Jortin, Esqr. alternately to nominate the Scholars.

Mr. Nicholas Owen Smith, of Nibley Estate to nominate the Master.

John Jortin, Esqr. purchased the Nibley Estates and rights of nomination in 1799.

South Newton in Wotton-under-Edge, did formerly belong to the Lovels, whose daughter and heir married J. Sherby, son of Fras. Sherby, of Brailsford, Derby, who died in his fathers Life time and having issue George, who inherited this Manor as well as Battlebridge, Hants., Dorington, Glouc. G. created by King James.

Bradley, is a hamlet on the road to Berkeley, from Nympesfield, an antient family took its name from the place.

1 Edw. iii.—Subsidy Roll, and after them ... Dawes, held, *see* "Church Inscriptions." This Mansion is depicted Kipsplate in Atkyn's Gloucestershire. with the Road and the myde of traffic by Stage Waggons and pack horses. There are several good houses here.

Canons Court:—belonged to St. Augustin's Bristol, by Gift of Lord Berkeley.

After the dissolution of that Abbey, Dean and Chapter of Bristol, by Crown Grant.

The Nelmes' family were for a long period Leaseholders under that Body. see "*Church Inscriptions.*"

Symonds Hall :—half a hide in Symonds hill, belonged to the Lordship of Berkeley.

1547.—Symondsall : of an Estate here Joan Poyntz was Lessee in possession, and W. Barnes in reversion.

There was a free Chapel of Ease at Wortley, up Chapel Hill, with Rents to keep a Lamp alight in the Chapel here.

Of the Site of the Manor of Huntingford, Henry Ogan, Esqr. died seized temp. Eliz. leaving Johan Ogan, his Daughter and Heir.

Flower and Grayler, *Chancery Pro'gs. temp.* Eliz.

The Ridge :—belonged to Kingswood Abbey.

After the Dissolution, to Sir N. Poyntz.

This Estate was in Brereton, of which the last possessor took the name of Westfaling, see "Edgworth."(*Rudder.*)

Combe :—belonged to Bordesley Abbey.

7 Edw. vi.—After the dissolution of Monasteries to Thomas Smith, afterwards to Lord Fitzharding.

In 1875 this house was burnt and was afterwards rebuilt as it now stands. Some outbuildings escaped the destruction and have been recently removed in which underground passage and Dungeons were discovered.

1776.—*At the County Election the following Voted for freeholds in Wotton-under-Edge.*

Bence, Joseph.	Hunt, John.
Bennet, John, *Senr.*	Lacey, John.
Buckle, Cornelius.	Milward, William.
Cambridge, Thomas.	Nash, Mark.
Carey, Sampson.	Perryn, Nathaniel.
Clarke, Thomas.	Rice, John.
Cowley, Benjamin.	Ricketts, James.
Dauncey, John.	Roach, William.
Dimery, Henry.	Rugge, John.
Dyer, Charles.	Somers, Joseph.
Do. John.	Tanner, John.
Do. William.	Vines, Thomas.
Evan, Martin.	Vizard, Arthur.
Fryer, John.	Wallington, Charles.
Gunter, John.	Watts, Edward.
Hall, James.	White, Samuel.
Do. William.	Woolwright, Richard.
Harris, Robert.	Worlock, Richard.
Hill, Rowland.	

And in 1811, the following Voted.

Bencehill, Joseph.	Nelmes, Richard, *Esqr.*
Bracey, James.	Organ, John.
Brown, Thomas.	Do. Edward.
Bruton, William.	Owen, Abraham.
Do. Thomas.	Palser, John.
Clarke, Thomas.	Do. Joseph.
Cooper, John.	Do. John.
Dauncey, S. G. *Esqr.*	Do. Thomas.
Dyer, H. *Winchcomb.*	Parry, John.
Evans, John.	Pearce, Joseph.
Foxwell, John.	Pegler, John.
Gardner, Charles.	Pinnell, Samuel.
Harding, John.	Plomer, Samuel.
Do. William.	Powell, John.
Harris, Thomas.	Ricketts, Thomas.
Hill, *Revd.* Rowland.	Robertson, John.
Hook, Richard.	Smith, Isaac.
Hunt, John.	Do. Jonathan.
Lewis, *Revd.* John.	Sprague, *Revd.* Daniel.
Lloyd, Daniel, *Esqr.*	Twyford, John.
Long, William.	Vines, Mark.
Mathews, Thomas.	Webb, John.
Miles, William.	Wiles, Richard.
Mills, Richard.	Worthington, *Revd.* W.

II.—*Church.*

Wotton Underhedge Vicaria :—Valet clare in X*is.* ibm. p. annu. ultra II*s.* VIII*d.* solut. pro visit. epi. juxta rat. cujuslt. II*cii.* anni VIII*s,* & V*s.* pro sinodal. & procur. XIX £. XII *s.* IIII *d.* Xma inde. XXXIX *s.* III *d.*

Valet clare in reddit. & firm. ibmp. annu. ultra XVIII*s.* I *d.* solut. dno Regi pro capital. reddit. XII *s.* IIII *d.* Willmo. Berkeley, pro capital. reddit. & VI *d.* ob. Jacobo Berkeley, pro capital. reddit. XI £. XII *s.* VI *d.* ob. Xma inde XXIII *s,* III *d. q.*

Taxacio vicarie de Wotton under Egge facta virtute commissionis Regie emanata de curia primitiar. et decimar. directe Waltero Denys militi, David Broke, svien. ad legem, Nicholao Weykes armigero, et Huzoni Denys, generos. ut p. eandem comissionem ac certificatorium predict. comissionar. in curiam decimar. et primitiar. predict. termino Michis. anno quarto Regis Edwardi Sexti introduct. et p. decretum in ea parte p cancellarium et consilium ejusdem curie fact. plenius liquet et apparet.

Valet in quadam annuali pensione viginti marcar. in pecuniis numeratis de decano et capitlo ecclie Cath. Chri. in Universitate Oxon. modo rectoribus sive proprietar. ecclie sive rectorie. de Wotton under Egge, aut eo ·in firmarijs ibm recept. et de quadam mansione spectan. ad dcam. vicaria annui valoris III*s.* IIII *d.* Sma XIII £. X*s* Xa inde XXVII*s.* Sma. clare valor hujus decanatus CCCXLIII £. XIII *d. ob. q.*

In P. Nich. Tax :—The Church of Wotton, 85£. 6s 8*d.*

The Vicar portio 5 £. 13 *s.* 4 *d,* In King's books at 13 £. 10 *s.* net income, £ 112.

List of Incumbents and Patrons of Wotton-under-Edge.

Incumbents.	Patrons.
1544.—John Myrriman, d. 1549.	Dean & Chap. Christ Ch·rch, Oxford.
1549.—Maurice Burnet, depriv. 1554.The same.	
1554.—Philip Ap Griffith, d. 1566.	The same.
1566.—John Mower.	Robt. Biddle.
1572.—Augustin Pilsworth, ceded 1578.	
1578.—John Staunton, d. abt. 1626.	Robt. Biddle.
1626.—John Singleton, B.A. occurs 1638.	
........—Thomas Heywood, 1641.	
1642.—Richard Kent.	Dean and Chapter, Ch. Ch. Oxford.
1661.—Joseph Bowden, depriv. 1662.	
1662.—John Nant, resd. 1662.	The same.
1662.—Moore Pye, M. A. d. 1675.	The same.
1675.—Wm. Stephens, M. A. res. 1687.	The same.
........—Samuel Heron, M. A.	
1687.—Samuel Allway, d. 1704.	The same.
1704.—Thomas Stockman, M. A.	The same.
1707.—Edward Gregory, M. A.	The same.
1738.—William Taswell, M. A.	The same.
1775.—William James, M. A.	The same.
1778.—William Tattersall, B. A.	The same.
........—Thomas Clissold, M. A.	

There were several Chantry Chapels dedicated to Saint Mary, Holy Cross, St. Nicholas, St. Catherine, All Souls, one now used as a Vestry and built by Thomas, Lord Berkeley and Margaret, his Wife, daughter of Warren, Lord Lisle.

1262.—Chantry at Church Way, built by Thomas, 3*rd.* Lord Berkeley.

Relict of Thomas, the son of 1*st.* Lord Berkeley.

Thomas, Lord Berkeley and Margaret, daughter of Gerald Warren, Lord Lisle.

Chapels and Altars:—St. Mary, St. Cross, St. Luke, St. Catherine, All Souls.

Bradley Chapel now Vestry.

III.—*Taxation, Population, &c. of Wotton-under-Edge.*

Wottone Intrinc. Subsidy Roll, 1 E. iii. 1327.

De Isabell de Berkeleye, xiiii s. iiii d.
' Maur. de Chepstouwe, v s. q.
' Willmo. Godard, ii s.
' Willmo. Fycard, xii d.
' Johne. le Dyeare, ii s.
' Willmo. de Almondesbury, xii d.
' Johne. Brevel, vi d.
' Hugon. Pydus, ii s.
' Jacobo le Mulleward, ii s.
' Walto. Bonde, vi d.
' Johne. le Wese, vi d.
' Henr. Snyte, viii s.
' Adam Pynnoke, xii d.
' Willmo. le Vicory, xii d.
' Johne. le Plomer, xii d.
' Johne. de Aure, xii d.
' Elia le Bakere, xii d.
' Johne. de Hokesforde, xii d.
' Rico. le Smythe, xviii d.
' Johne. Geffrey, ii s.
' Thom. Brounynge, ii s.
' Petro. le Chepman, vi d.
' **Gregor. le Hore, xii d.**

prob. Sma. li *s.* x *d. q.*

Wottone Forinc. cum Hamellettis.

*De Isabella de Berkeleye, x s. i d.
' Reginald. Sake, v s. x d. ob.
' Adam Heysogge, v s. iii d.
' Thom. le Hayward, iii s. x d.
' Rico. atte Welle, xi d.
' Elia Reman, xii d.
' Walto atte Hulle, xvii d. ob. q.
' Thom. Fallewell, iii s. vii d. q.
' Thom. Wynegod, xiiii d.
' Elianora de Bradeleye, iii s. ii d.
' Robto, Slydewine, xviii d,
' Rico. Brounynge, ii s. x d. ob.
' Adam Josep, ii s.
' Walto. le Machoun, xvi d-
' Walto. Josep, xv d. ob. q.
' Rico. atte Broke, iiii s. xi d.
' Rogo. de Berleye, v s. i d.
' Henr. le Holdare, xv d.
' Matheo. Latyn, iiii s. iiii d. ob. q.
' Rogo. le Styward, ii s. i d.
' Abbate Sci. Augustini, vii s. ii d.
' Johanna de Kyngestone, ii s.
' Robto. atte Hall, xii d.
' Michl. Howes, xx d. ob. q.
' Walto. Saundres, iii s. ii d.
' Johne. le Skay, iiii s vii 4.
' Rogo. le Duynysshe, xv s. i d. ob. q.
' Rico. de Caumvylle, ix s. ii d. q.
' Claricia de Combe, ii. s. ob.
' Johne. atte Chirche, vi s. x d. ob.
' Nicho. Warderobe, iii s. ob.
' Willmo. Pavy, xix d. q.
' Nicho. Draysid, vi d.
' Nicho. Bernard, xiii d.
' Robto. le Shephirde, ii s. viii d.
' Johne. Cronnoke, ii s,
' Nicho. Heynes, xii d.
' Walto. Axepode, xxi d.
' Adam Edus, ii s. ix d. ob. q.

prob. Sma. vi li. xv s. i d. q.

*1327.—Isabella de Berkeley, was by far the largest Tax Payer.

Isabella, daughter of Gilbert de Clare, was the 2nd. Wife of Thomas, Lord Berkeley.

Acreage 4390 a.

Population 1801.—1587. 1851.—4224.
1831.—5482.

In 1815. Annual Value of Real Property ......£.

1882.—Rateable Value £.......

1833-4-5.—Average of three Years Expenditure on Poor £.......

In Dursley Union.

1831.—Wotton contains 4382 acres, the population is 2489, of this number only 68 families are employed in agriculture and 778 in Manufactures. There are 13 clothing mills in Wotton under Edge. The Parish is divided into Tithings.

Turnpike roads were made towards Gloucester, Tewkesbury, Sodbury and Bristol.

Tabernecle Chapel of the late Rev. Rowland Hill, is a handsome structure in a fine situation.

1556.—John Horn, was burnt at Wotton under Edge, with a Woman, for their Religion.

William Dangerfield, Sufferings Wife and Child, a honest and godly poor Man, fled from persecution but hearing that his Wife was brought to bed he went to see her. His Neighbours carried him to Prison where he was kept so long in Irons, that the Irons eat into his Flesh. His Wife with her infant of 14 days was taken to Prison and put among Thieves and Murderers, No fine. Bishop Brokes, told Wm. D. that his Wife had recanted whereupon he promised to do so too. But finding this account false he died of grief. The Wife died in Prison where also the Child was burned to death. His Mother died of Grief.

INDEX TO NAMES ON THE INSCRIPTIONS.

	Coll.		Coll.		Coll.		Coll.
Adey, William.	12	Bennett, Elizabeth.	30	Coates, Joseph & Esther.	38	Dimery, Martha, and	
Do. Sarah.	19	Do. Robt. *Senr.* & Mary.	38	Collwell, Richard, *Senr.*		Daniel, her son.	39
Do. William.	21	Do. Robt. *Jun.* & Mary.	38	& Mary, Richard, *Jnnr.*		Dow, Isaac.	25
Do. Sarah & Margaret.	45	William, their son.	38	and John.	31	Drew, Robert & Sarah.	39
Do. Sarah, Hester, her		Do. Samuel.	47	Do. Edmund & Elizth.	31	Dunn, James.	46
Daughter.	28	Do. William & Elizth.	47	Do. John & Sarah.	31	Durnell, Thomas.	46
Do. Sarah.		Berkeley, Thomas, *Ld.*	29	Compeer, Stephen		Dyer, William & Mary,	7
Ady, Alicia.	8	Biddle, Mathew & Mary.	20	Cooke, Mary and Joseph.	24	Elizabeth and Samuel,	
Do. Daniel & Elizabeth.	13	Bick, Joseph & Elizabeth,		Cooper, John.	8	their Children.	32
Do. Daniel & Bridget	13	Joseph, Mary, Joan		Do. John & Caroline,		Do. Charles & Sarah.	32
Ashby, Mary.	25	and Hester their C.	36	John, Laura 3 Child.	43		
Austin, Margaretta.	20	Blagden, Mary.	4	Do. Jessica & James.	44	Eastmead, Ann.	47
Do. Edward & Mary.	35	Do. Mary.	10	Do. Mary.	44	Everett, Joshua.	28
Do. William, Thomas,		Do. John, *Senr.* and		Do. James & Esther,			
Edward.	36	Lydia.	14	James, their son.	44	Forde, Henry and Joseph.	35
Do. Giles, William,		Do. John, Lydia and		Do. John.	45	Fowler, William.	33
Edward, Edward,		Mary.	14	Coopey, Alice.	37	Fryer, Alice, Mary & Anne.	24
Francis, John, Thomas,		Blanch, Anthony.	45	Coster, Jane.	4	Do. Martha, Wife of	
and Mary.	36	Blanchart, Anthony.	8	Cratle, William.	47	John.	25
Do. Fanny.		Blanchard, Richard.	42	Crew, Robert.	46	Do. Mary, Anne, Samuel,	
Do. Isaac & Elizabeth.	42	Brakenborough, Mary.	10	Do. Robert & Alice,		& John, their Children.	25
Do. L'Estrange S.	42	Brandiss, Mary.	46	Arthur, their son.	29		
Do. Anthony.	45	Do. Margaret.	46	Croome, Robert & Mary.	41	Goodson, Samuel & Mary,	
		Bromfield, Elizabeth.	26	Curtis, Daniel & Fredrick,	13	Samuel, William and	
Baker, Charles.	41	Do. Ann.	26	Curry, Millicent.	34	Francis.	32
Do. John & Mary.	41	Burge, Edward & Anne.	32			Goodson, Sarah.	32
Barkley, *Dane* Elizth.	3	Burton, Thomas.	35	Dauncey, John.		Gower, Sarah, William and	
Barnes, Johannes.		Bye, Chas. and Cornelius.	33	Do. Christian & John.	8	Mathew, her sons.	39
Barry, John.	24	Do. Mary.	35	Dawes, Richard.	11	Grail, Thomas and Sarah.	12
Bave, Anthony & Mary.	8	Do. Charles & Lydia,		Do. Robert.	11	Gregory, Edward & Mary.	16
Bayly, Thomas & Christian		Charles, Edward,		Do. Thomas.	11		
Christopher & Wm., sons.	40	Lydia and Charles,		Do. Lydia, relict of T.	12	Haddow, Joane.	8
Do. Thomas & Sarah,		their Children.	40	Do. Samuel.	27	Hadnot, Henry.	10
& Mary, his Wives.		Byrd, Peter and Mary.	16	Do. Robert.	27	Hall, Mary.	37
Do. Edward.	41			Do. Robert and	28	Do. Ephraim & Sarah.	41
Bearpacker, Elizabeth.		Cam, Joel & Deborah.	7	Laws, Thomas & Sarah.	5	Do. Ann.	41
Do. John.	28	Capel, Nathaniel.	27	Deane, Ralph.	23	Harding, John & Hannah.	38
Bence, John.	39	Cary, Sampson & Sarah.	8	Demery, John & Mary,		Do. George & Abigail.	38
Bennett, Nathaniel and		Do. John & Hannah.	33	Thomas, Mary and		Harris, William & Sarah,	
Hester, Benjamin,		Clarke, William & Elizth.		Henry, their Children.	28	and Sarah.	18
Ephraim, Hester and		Harry, their son.	38	Do. Mary and Sarah,		Do. William & Rachel.	31
Ephraim.	27	Clutterbuck, Dorcas.	21	her Daughter.	28		

Name	Coll.
Harris, Rachel.	31
Do. John Collwell,	31
Heron, Mary.	46
Heskins, Jane.	7
Do. Richard, Johannis.	33
Heyward, Robert.	16
Hickes, Robert.	17
Do. Robert & Richard.	19
Do. Sarah.	20
Do. Richard & Elizth. Thomas, their son.	30
Hieron, William	30
Do. Nathaniel & Edith, Nathaniel, Samuel, Samuel, Nicholas, & Robert, their sons.	29
Do. Nathaniel. Edith, Nicholas, Saml., Edith and Betty, his Children.	29
Hiett, Richard & Mary, Samuel and Jonathan.	23
Hill, Alice.	26
Do. Thomas & Anna.	30
Hodgson, Elizabeth	21
Hodges, Isaac & Sarah.	25
Hodnot, Samuel & Anne.	35
Holloway, Edward.	46
Do. Catherine.	46
Hooke, Eleanor.	39
Hopkins, Edward.	46
Do. Stephen.	46
Hughes, Robert.	10
Humphreys, Steph. & Ann.	46
Do. & Hester, 1 wife, and Mary, 2 wife.	46
Hunt, John and Joan, William, their son.	9
Do. Sarah.	32
Do. Stephen & Elizabeth.	24
Hunteridge, Francis and Mary, 1st. wife., and Mary, 2nd wife.	24
Hyatt, Robert.	4
James, Elizabeth.	39
Do. Dunn.	35
Jefferys, Richard & Sarah.	38
Jobbins, Francis & Alice.	19
Do. John & William.	19
Jobbins, Mary.	29
Jordon, Christopher.	40
Do. Catherine.	41
Kent, Revd. Richard.	13
Knee, Ann and Anna.	17
Knight, Elizabeth.	40
Do. Hannah.	40
Do. Sophia.	40
Do. James & Sarah.	40
Do. James, Junr. and Betty & Hannah, dau.	40
Lacy, John and Ann.	40
Lapley, James & Mary.	46
Leigh, Alice and Mary.	19
Do. Elizabeth & Hester.	20
Lockier, Mary, Wife of William and William, Mary & William, their Chidren.	25
Long, Elizabeth.	22

Name	Coll.
Mabatt, Joseph & Joan, Samuel & Ric. sons.	25
Macie, Elizabeth.	10
Master, George.	22
Mathews, John.	46
Mayo, Humphrey.	35
Do. William & Sarah.	35
Miles, Elizabeth.	21
Moore, Ann.	8
Do. William.	8
Do. Gulielmi.	28
Do. Christiana, Hester.	28
Do. Gulielmi Morris, John.	28
Nelmes, Elizabeth.	10
Do. John & Elizabeth, Lydia & Elizth., daus.	12
Nemes, Betty.	47
Do. Betty.	47
Nicholas, Richard & Mary, Mary, William, Wm. & Mary, their Children.	34
Ockwell, Jeremiah & Ann.	37
Oldisworth, John.	22
Do. William.	23
Okes, John.	14
Do. Jonah & Martha, John, Jonah & Lydia.	14
Do. Sarah & Elizabeth.	14
Do. Jonah & Mary.	15
Do. Thomas & Dorothy.	33
Do. Thomas & Hannah, Jane their daughter.	33
Osborn, Richard.	6
Do. Sarah, four Children. Johannis, Richardi, Thomæ and Gulielmi.	7
Osborne, Gulielmi.	33
Do. John.	16
Do. Richard, George-White and Ann.	17
Do. Elizabeth & Ann,	17
Do. Elizabeth.	17
Do. Richard.	17
Do. R., S. O., R. O., A. O., and John O.	17
Do. Ann, William, William, Thomas, Martha, John, Edwd.	26
Palser, Thomas & Eleanor.	31
Do. Richard and Mary.	34
Do. Hugh & Anne.	31
Do. Hugh-Alexander.	31
Panting, Mary, & Samuel, her son.	36
Parbeey, Mary.	26
Pearce, Harry.	20
Do. Revd. Offspring, Harry, Junr.	20
Do. Ann.	20
Do. Robert & Mary.	20
Do. Henry & Elizabeth, Thomas, Robert, Jael, Robert, Thomas, Jael, and Patience, their Children.	34
Do. Richard & Sarah.	34
Do. Richard, Richard.	35

Name	Coll.
Phillips, Sarah.	29
Do. John.	29
Powell, John & Sarah.	8
Price, John & Mary.	21
Purnell, Robert.	7
Richmond, James & Elizth.	19
Rickards, Mary.	24
Rickets, James & Sarah.	28
Do. Thomas & Anne, their Children.	29
Rodway, Charles.	40
Do. William.	41
Rogers, James & Martha.	19
Rose, Mariam.	40
Rous, Thomas.	4
Do. Thomas & Mariæ.	5
Do. Elizabeth.	6
Do. John & Ann, and William.	23
Do. John, John, Thomas, James and William.	23
Do. Elizabeth.	44
Rugg, Richard and Mary.	19
Do. John & Lydia.	20
Russell, Hannah.	35
Saunders, John.	32
Scott, Elizabeth.	32
Smith, Ann.	7
Do. Elizabeth.	19
Do. Mary.	24
Do. Edmund.	26
DO. William & Sarah.	26
Do. Edward & Sarah, Sarah, a daughter.	26
Do. William & Sarah, Thomas & Bromfield.	26
Do. Sarah.	32
Do. Sarah.	32
Do. John.	32
Symth, Thomas.	37
Do. Thomas, Joseph, Benjamin, Richard, and Thomas.	37
Stephens, Charles & Wm.	16
Stinchcomb, Nathaniel.	47
Stokes, Sarah & Elizabeth.	10
Summers, Samuel.	35
Taswell, William.	22
Do. James & Dorothy.	22
Tattersall, James.	9
Do. Revd. John.	18
Tattershall, James.	8
Theyer, Thomas, son of Thomas and Mary.	5
Townsend, Wm. & Elizth.	24
Do. Robert, Richard, and Mary.	25
Trotman, Saml. & Hannah.	18
Do. Charles & Jane.	37
Tudgey, Rebecca.	32
Turner, Benedict, Junr.	28
Tyndall, Arthur.	
Veel, Robert.	6
Do. Maria.	9
Do. William & Anne.	42
Do. Elizabeth, 4th. dau.	42
Do. William, Junr. and Sarah.	42

Name	Coll.
Venn, Eliza.	19
Do. Thomas & Esther,	20
Vines, Thomas & Mary, Sarah and Isaac, their Children.	30
Wallington, Edward, Edward & Susannah.	9
Do. Susannah.	24
Do. John & Charles, and William.	27
Do. John & John.	27
Do. Richard & Mary, his wife, and Richard, Samuel, William and Mary, their Children.	27
Wallis, William & Mary	37
Robert, William and Mary, their Children.	37
Do. John.	34
Do. Sarah.	36
Wastin, George	43
Do. William and James, his son.	35
Wathen, Thomas & Anne.	29
Web, Robert.	6
Webb, Christian.	7
Do. Anne.	7
Do. Mary.	7
Do. Hester.	8
Do. Daniel & Elizabeth, John & Hester, s. & d.	39
Do. John.	47
Westfield, Thomas.	23
White, John.	7
Do. G.	20
Wichell, Frances.	20
Wight, William,	34
Do. Edward & John.	34
Do. Moses & Mary.	36
Do. Richard.	36
Do. Robert & Alice.	37
Willett, Gulielmi.	15
Do. Susanna,	16
Willis, Christopher & Mary and Ann, his wives.	35
Winchcomb, Henry.	38
Winston, Margt. wife of T.	5
Winstone, Sarah.	13
Do. Thomas.	30
Do. Thomas & Margt. Thomas, their son.	30
Do. Richard and Richard & Anne, his Children.	31
Do. William.	31
Witchell, Mary.	29
Do. Thomas.	47
Do. Richard.	47
Do. Jonathan & Mary.	37
Woolright, Joseph & Hester.	38
Woolworth, John & Ann, Thomas, Thomas, ..., William, and John, their sons.	36
Workman, Anna.	29
Wotton, R. de.	1
Yeats, Mary.	21
Young, Robert & Anne.	36
Do. Walter & Jane, William, their son.	34

YANWORTH.

YANWORTH.

A HAMLET TO HASLETON, (see No. CXXXVI.)

YANWORTH, or ENWORTH, which is divided from HASLETON by the Parish of HAMPNETT, is by one third Part of smaller Extent. The Chapel is an inconsiderable Building, with an Aisle on the North Side, and a small Tower. It had anciently no Right of Sepulture; and in 1366, WILLIAM WITLESEY, Bishop of *Worcester*, made a Decree between the Abbot of *Winchcombe*, and the Rector of *Hasleton*, by which a Chaplain was established here.

Right Honble. JOHN, *Lord* CHEDWORTH, LORD OF THE MANOR.

Revd. ...., *Rector:*

INSCRIPTIONS IN THE CHURCH.

IN THE NORTH TRANSEPT.

ON A FLAT STONE.

Arms:—a Cross Raguly.

Here lieth the Body of
GILES LAURENCE, of this Parish,
Gent. who departed this Life,
the first day of September,
Anno Dom. 1711, Aged 50 Years.
Psalm. 37. verse 37.

.... BICKNELL,
who departed this Life, the
20 of August 1711.

[*The above now* 1888, *partially covered by pews.*]

CHURCH YARD.

ON A BRASS PLATE AFFIXED TO THE WALL ON SOUTH SIDE.

Close under this place lieth the
Body of ELIZABETH BICKNELL,
Wife of THOMAS BICKNELL,
of this Parish, who departed this Life,
August 31, 1745, Aged 53 Years.

In Memory of
THOMAS BICKNELL, *Gent.*
who died March 19, 1750,
Aged 61 Years.
By the order of his Nephew
THOMAS BRIDGES, of *Winson.*

ON TOMBS.

MARY, Daughter of ROBERT SLEY,
of *Chedworth,* 1st. Wife to
WILLIAM KILMASTER,
of *Stowell,* and 2nd. Wife to
EDWARD PALMER, of *Yanworth,*
died May 7, 1736, Aged 71 Years.
ROBERT PALMER,
died Sept. 2, 1703, Aged 93 Years.
ALICE, his Wife,
died Nov. 23, 1701, Aged 73 Years.
EDWARD, son of ROBERT PALMER,
died March 26, 1740, Aged 74 Years.
MARY, Wife of JOSEPH BURFOOT,
Senr. died Jany. 18, 1767,
Aged 72 Years.

CHARLES BICKNELL,
died Nov. 2, 1715, Aged 22 Years.
CHARLES BICKNELL,
died Jany. 16, 1719,
Aged 84 Years.
SARAH BICKNELL,
died Jany. 7, 1717.
WILLIAM BICKNELL,
died July 20, 1707, Aged 14 Years.
ELIZABETH, Daughter of
THOMAS BICKNELL, and ELIZABETH,
his Wife, died Jany. 25, 1729,
Aged 12 Years.

Additional Inscriptions since Big-land's time.

CHANCEL.

ON THE NORTH WALL.

Sacred to the Memory of
THOMAS WALKER,
who died March 6th. 1888,
Aged 67 Years.
Also of
MARY, Wife of THOMAS WALKER,
who died March 6th. 1883,
Aged 68 Years.
CHARLES WALKER,
died May 12th. 1885, Aged 34.

In a Vault adjoing lie buried
THOMAS, the Son of THOMAS and
MARY WALKER, who died
September 26th. 1850,
Aged 2 Years and 4 Months.
REBECCA WALKER,
died July 9th. 1857, Aged 13 Days.
JOSEPH HARRY WALKER,
died November 11th. 1858,
Aged 7 Days.
KATE WALKER, died
August 12th. 1861, Aged 9 Years
MARY, Wife of THOMAS ARKELL
and Daughter of THOMAS and
MARY WALKER, who died
February 23rd. 1882,
Aged 35 Years.

HEAD AND FLAT STONES

	Died.		Aged.		Died.		Aged.
Charles Blacksl, ...	1 May	1789	84	Elizabeth, Wife of Richard } Harding, *Junr.* ... }	12 July	1742	55
Joanna, Wife of Robert Barnett,	28 July	1769	82	William, Son of Richard and }			
William Cull, ...	24 Sept.	1719	...	Mary Harding, ...}	17 April	1749	37
John Cull, ...	6 Nov.	1724	74	Solomon, their Son, ...	8 Nov.	1751	...
Martha, Daughter of John Cull,	11 June	1752	21	John, Son of John and Mary } Randall, ...}	17 Febr.	1755	40
Elizabeth Turk, of *Chedgle in* } *Crudwell, Wilts.* ... ...}	12 Febr.	1790	59				
Charles Barnett, ...	10 Sept.	1747	92	Mary, Wife of John Randall, *Senr.*	20 Febr.	1759	80
John, his Son, ...	13 May	1725	26	Joseph Burfott, *Senr.*	14 August	1751	65
Robert, Son of John Barnett,	10 May	1777	72	George Laurence, ...	10 August	1719	49
Joan, Wife of Robert Barnett,	28 July	1769	82	Mary, Wife of Thomas Burrows,	18 Jany.	1736	32
Richard Harding, ...	4 Nov.	1755	84	Mary, Wife of Samuel Thomas, } and Daughter of Francis } and Mary Carington, ...}	30 Oct.	1737	25
John Harding, ...	19 May	1773	59				
Ann, his Wife, ...	4 Febr.	1771	66				

YATE.

YATE.

THE CHURCH is built in form of a Cross and hath a Cross Aisle on each side, the Chancel has also an Aisle on each side; a large Tower at the West-end containing six Bells. It is dedicated to Saint John the Baptist. The South Aisle belongs to the Lord of the Manor of *Stanshaw*, and the North to the Lord of the Manor of *Yate*.

BECKFORD CATER, *Esqr.* LORD OF THE MANOR.

Revd. Mr. HAY, *Rector.*

DONATIONS.

[*The following Benefactions are inscribed on two metals tablets on the Wall of the North Aisle.*]

1741.—Mr. WILLIAM MASON, late Rector of this Parish and *Mrs.* HESTER, his Wife, left to the Poor the Sum of £ 30.

1758 —Mr. BENJAMIN MASON, their Son, left also the Sum of £ 350. for the same Use, which said Sums are now laid out in Lands in this Parish, and the nett Produce thereof distributed at Christmas yearly to Twelve such poor Persons as have no Relief from the parish, by the Minister and Churchwardens for the Time being.

1732.—Mr. DANIEL BELSIRE, of *Hatl-end* in this Parish, left to the Poor the Sum of £ 2. 10s. 0d. to be for ever given Yearly out of that Estate at Christmas.

1732.—Mr. WELLS, of *Thornbury*, left to this Parish, the Sum of £ 63. for placing out poor Children to Apprentice, which Money is laid out on Lands in this Parish the Produce thereof to be applied to that Use by the Minister and Church Wardens for the Time being.

1760.—JOHN WALKER, *Esqr.* gave the Sum of Twenty Shillings for ever, to be paid Yearly out of his Estate and to be laid out in Bibles and Testaments by the Minister and Church Wardens, for the use of Poor Families. [*Not on the Tablet,* 1887.]

INSCRIPTIONS IN THE CHURCH.

IN CHANCEL.

ON MONUMENTS.

Arms:—Or. on a Chief Azure 3 Martlets of the first:—WOGAN.
Crest:—a like Martlet.

Juxta hunc Tumulum reconditur
urna continens cineres
HENRICI WOGAN, *Armig.*
qui natus apud *Wiston*, in Comitat
Pembroke, a familia antiquâ,
Obiit apud *Yate*, in Comitat *Gloc.*
1 die Febr. Anno Ætat. 22,
Annoq. Dei 1661.
Vivit post funera Virtus.
[Not to be found, 1887.]

To the Memory of
JOHN WICKHAM,
who died June 13*th.* 1790,
Aged 74 Years.
In testimony of her love and
Gratitude this Monument was
erected by his faithful Relict
HESTER WICKHAM.
Also in Memory of the above
HESTER WICKHAM,
who died Jany. 11, 1794,
Aged 75 Years.
[Not to be found, 1887]

ON A BRASS PLATE AGAINST THE SOUTH WALL OF CHANCEL.

1625 :
WILLIAM, died the 12 of Dec.
having lived M.-0. W.-2. D.-1.
1627 :
A Female Child, died 26 of Apr.
having lived M.-0. W.-0. D.-0.
1630 :
JAMES, died the 26 of Octob.

having lived M.-5. W.-1. D.-5.
1633 :
ANNE, died the 19 of Nov.
having lived M.-1. W.-3. D.-2.
1649 :
ELEANOR, died the 26 of Sept.
having lived Y.-14. M.-2. D.-6.

Sicut Flos sic Vita.

These were the Sonnes and
Daughters of WILLIAM and SIL-
VESTER HUCHENSON,
Whom nature in the Worlds disdaine
Shew'd unto the World and put
them upp again.
All these lye interred between the
Monuments of ELEANOR HUCHEN-
SON, late Wife of said WILLIAM,
and of EDWARD WEEKS, in ye Ex-
pectation of a joyfull Resurrection.

1638 :
WILLIAM, died the 2 of June,
having lived Y.-9. M.-6. W.-1.,
and he lies interred in ye Church
of *St. Thomas* in *Oxon.*
1641 :
JASPER, fell dead the 14 of Sept.
having lived Y.-21. W.-2.,
he lyes interr'd in the Church of
Chalberry in the Countie of *Oxon.*
1650 :
SILVESTER, mother to the aforesaid,
died the 25 ....
having lived 55 Years.
Memento Mori.
[Not to be found, 1887.]

ON FLAT STONES.

Hic in spe certa beate
Resurrectionis Jacent
ELEANOR HUCHENSON
et SILVESTRA BAYNHAM,
Mater ejus
Illa sepulta fuit 7 Julij,
Anno Dom. 1623.

Hæc expiravit 27o. Aug. et
humata fuit 4o. Sept. An. Dom. 1668,
et Ætatis suæ 89.

Here resteth the Body of
SILVESTER, Daughter of WILLIAM
HUTCHENSON, *Rector of Yate,*
late Wife of JOHN HICKES, of
West-end, who changed a holy
and humble Life, for a holy and
comfortable Death Aug. 9, 1652,
Anno Ætatis 28.
[Not to be found, 1887.]

Here lyeth the Body of
THOMAS BAYNHAM, M. A.
who lived Parson of this Parish
of *Yate,* 50 Years,
...... deceased the 29 day of Augt.
Anno Dom. 1622, having 3 Sons,
viz.,—ADAM, HENRY and EDWARD.
ADAM BAYNHAM, *Gent.*
Sagax sciens
Aged 84 Years, Son to the said
THOMAS, was Gathered to his
Fathers Ashes the 10 of April 1661.
In Memory of
MARY, Wife of *Mr.* JOHN SILBY,
of *Bradford,* and Younger Daughter
of ROBERT GODWYN, of this
Parish, *Gent.* who departed this
Life, July 16 in the 2nd.
Year of her Age, 1723.
[Not to be found, 1887.]

[ON A BRASS PLATE ON THE FLOOR
BENEATH ARCH DIVIDING THE
NAVE FROM THE S. CROSS AISLE.]

Here lieth the Body of the
Revd. RICHARD WALLINGTON,

YATE.

Rector of this Parish, who died
the 5th. of October 1764,
Aged 60 Years.

Hic jacet corpus GEORGII RAYMOND,
Generosi, filii GEORGII RAYMOND,
Arm. Natu maximi qui obiit
25o. die Augusti Anno Dom. 1677,
Ætatisque suæ Vicesimo.
Here lyeth the Body of
CHRIS. RAYMOND, Son of
WILLIAM RAYMOND, of Berkeley,
Gent. who departed this Life, the
29 day of May, Anno Dom. 1701.

Hic jacet Corpus GEORGII RAYMOND,
Armigeri, ob 16 die Mensis Julij,
Anno D m. 1694, Ætatis suæ 63.
Hic jacet corpus EGIDII RAYMOND,
Generosi, Filii secundi
GEORGII RAYMOND, Armigeri,
qui obiit 3 die Decembris,
Anno Dni 1680,
Ætatis suæ vicesimo primo.

Subter hunc Lapidem jacet corpus
ANNÆ RAYMOND,
primum uxoris, tunc Viduæ
ROBERTI BURNELL, Gent.
necnon
post ejus obitum uxoris
GEORGII RAYMOND, Arm.
necnon
Filiæ CHRISTOPHERI WEBB, Gen.
de Ashwick infra Parochiam
de Marshfield,
Baptizata fuit 23o. Februarij 1622,
nec non
Sepult. fuit 23o. Februarij 1703,
Ætatis suæ 81.

ON BRASS PLATE.

Epitaphium in obitum
JOHANIS BLAGDEN,
In Morem Prosopopæiæ
En mea vitâ brevis transit repleta
dolore;
Et Labor et mundi gloria morte
perit.
Sed spe venturæ caro nunc requie-
scit in urna,
Vitæ dum regnet civitas arce dei.
Christus in adventu renovabit vile
cadaver.
Et dabit in Cælo gaudia plena
mihi.

Job 14. 1. Ps. 16. 9-10. Phil. 3. 21.

Christus mihi vita
Et mors mihi lucrum.
JOHN BLAGDEN,
of the Parish of Yeat,
died Febr. 15, 1622, Æt. suæ 50.

TOBIAS HIGGINS, in Memoria
amantiss. amici sui JOH. BLAGDEN,
hos versiculos composuit.

Here lieth the Body of ANNE,
Daughter of JEREMIAH RUSSELL,
by JANE, his Wife, of this Parish,
who departed this Life,
28 May 1760, Aged 34 Years.
Also here lieth the Body of
JEREMIAH RUSSELL,
who departed this Life,
12 Augt. 1763, Aged 65 Years.
Also JANE, late Widow, of the said
JEREMIAH RUSSELL,
who departed this Life,

---

the 22 of March 1771,
Aged 74 Years.
[Also in Memory of
THOMAS, Son of the above JEREMIAH
and JANE RUSSELL, who died
January the 7th. 1803,
Aged 73 Years.]

[ON A FLAT STONE SOUTH AISLE
OF CHANCEL.]

Arms:—Argent, a Lion rampant
Sable debruised with a bend Gules:
— BURNELL, impaling ... a Lion
passant guardant ... ... between
three hawkes Lures.

Here lyeth the Body of
THOMAS BURNELL, Gent.
who died the 27th. of June 1694,
Ætatis suæ 45.

[ON A BRASS PLATE IN CHANCEL.]

B. P. Hic jacet ROBERTUS WALKER,
Generosus, qui obiit vicessimo tertio
die Martij Anno Dom. 1676-7,
Annoq. Ætatis suæ 39.
Memento mori
Hic peregrinus eram mundus
mihi dura noverca
Iam patriam viso terra aliena, vale.
[In mortem qui repentinam
Dum valeas, mortem pendas, me
namque valentem
Discerpsit rapida mors inimica manu.
Arms on a Brass Plate above.
Per chevron 3 elephants heads erased
armed a label of 3 points for difference.
impaling A Chevron between 3 Swans.]

Hic jacet MARIA WALKER,
Soror ROBTI. defuncti virgo quæ
Mortem obijt repentinam
vicesimo octavo die Martij,
Ano. Dni. 1678.
[On a Brass Plate immediately above are
the Arms:— Per chevron 3 Elephants
heads erased armed a label of 3 points
for difference. Beneath the Inscription,
Dum valeas, mortem pendas, me
namque valentem
Discerpsit rapida mors inimica manu.
In helth watch thou to die, for sud-
daine death,
Whiles I was well, deprived me of
my breath.]

IN NORTH AISLE OF THE CHANCEL.

This Stone was laid by
ELIZABETH HUNTER,
in Memory of her dear Mistress,
ELEANOR BRAY,
who departed this Life,
17 Febr. 1773, Aged 76 Years.

[Farewel this world of noise and strife!
From anxious cares and toils of life,
I'm here at rest, in hopes to be
With God above eternally.]

ANNE, the Daughter of
JOHN and SILVESTER HICKS,
died April 18, 1656.

UNDER THIS TABLE.

Here lyeth He, who while he

---

lived served at (but being dead lyeth
under) the Table. WILLIAM
HUTCHENSON, Minister.

Under this Stone resteth the
Body of RICHARD SAUNDERS,
late of Old Sodbury, Gent.
who departed this Life,
the 25 day of September,
Anno Dom. 1728, Æt. suæ 68.

Under this Stone resteth the
Body of GERTRUDE SAUNDERS,
[Wife of RICHARD SAUNDERS,]
of the Parish of Old Sodbury,
Gent. who departed this Life,
18 Jany. A. D. 1712, Æt. suæ 39.

P. M.
JEREMIA HIRLER, A. M.
hujus Ecclesiæ
per 26 Annos Rectoris, defuncti
3o. die Decembris,
Ano. Dom. 1685,
Ætatis suæ 60.
Emittat Dominus operarios
in Messem Suam.

Here lyeth the Body of
Mrs. PRISCILLA MASON,
Daughter of Mr. JOSEPH MASON,
of London, Gent. who died
the 23 day of March 1751,
and in the 51 Year of her Age.

Hic jacet Corpus
GEORGII MASON, Gen. de Hospitio
Lincoln. Londini, filii
GULIEMI MASON, Rector. de Yate,
Qui Sepultus erat 13 Septembris,
Anno Dom. 1724, Ætatis suæ 31.
Necnon in Memor.
JOHANNIS MASON,
secundi filii præd GULIELMI
MASON, qui efflavit animam ad
Barbados, 14o. Martij,
Ano. Dom. 1718, Ætat. suæ 24.
Hic jacet etiam Corpus
GULIELMI MASON, Junr.
qui obijt 14 Aprilis, Anno. Dom. 1739,
Ætatis suæ 33.

[Arms on separate plate above:—
Per pale a Chevron between 3 billets
impaling On a chevron, 3 roses.]

Hic jacet Corpus
Dani. BAINHAM, Generos.
qui spe certa Resurrectionis
obiit vicessimo nono die Decembris
Anno Dni. 1669, Ætat. suæ 29,
"Memento Mori."

NAVE.

To the Memory of
THOMAS BAYNHAM, Gent.
and GRACE, his Wife,
whom death separated for a Time
but now hath brought together
again into this Grave where
their Bodies lye Interred in
expectation of a joyfull resurrection,

He died Dec. 23, 1642.
She died Nov. 8. 1663.
Also of GERTRUDE, Wife of SAMUEL
ADEY, of the City of *Bristol*,
Iron-monger, and Daughter of
RICHARD SAUNDERS, of *Old
Sodbury*, *Gent.* who died
12 of June 1724, Æt. suæ 24.
And of HENRY ADEY, late of the
Borough of *Chipping Sodbury*,
Son of the said SAMUEL and
GERTRUDE ADEY, who died
Febr. 7, 1773, Aged 55
Also in Memory of JANE, Wife of
JAMES LUDLOW,
of *Chipping Sodbury*, and Daughter
of the said HENRY ADEY,
who died 29 of June 1778,
Aged 74 Years.
And three of their Children
that died in their Infancy.

ON MONUMENTS.

In Memory of
WILLIAM MASON, A. M.
Rector of this Chnrch, and
of HESTER, his Wife,
He died February 24, 1740,
Aged 84 Years.
She died August 21, 1729,
Aged 56 Years.
JOHN, their Son, who died in
Barbadoes, March 14, 1718,
Aged 23 Years.
GEORGE, their Son, died
Sept. 10, 1724, Aged 31 Years.
WILLIAM, their Son, died
April 12, 1733, Aged 27 Years.
BENJAMIN, their Son, died
Jany. 20, 1758, Aged 50 Years.
HESTER JENKINS,
their Grandaughter, died
Sept. 9, 1751.

Arms:—Per pale Or. & Argent,
a Chevron counterchanged between
three billets Sable.—MASON. *impaling* Argent, on a Chevron Gules
three Roses of the field.
Crest:—a Stagshead couped Sable
attired Or. gorged of the last.

In Memory of
RICHARD HILL,
late of this Parish, *Esqr.*
who died March the 31*st.* 1755,
Aged 59 Years.
As also of MARY, Relict of
the said RICHARD HILL, *Esqr.*
and Daughter of THOMAS ROUS, *Esqr.*
of *Wotton-under-Edge*, in the
County of *Gloucester*,
who died May the 20*th.* 1759,
Aged 53 Years.

Near this Monument lies
interred the Body of
JOHN WALKER, of *Hill House*,
within this Parish, *Esqr.*
who died the 27 day of December,
in the Year of our Lord 1760,
Aged 82 Years.

ON FLAT STONES.

Hic jacet Corpus
HODGES GODWIN, *Jun. Armiger.*
Legum Angliæ periti, Qui obiit
2*o.* die Novembris, Anno Dni. 1677,
Spe Beatae Resurection,
Ætatis suæ 40.

Hic jacet Corpus
HODGES GODWYN, *M. A. Generos.*
qui obijt 6 Julii, Anno Dom. 1677,
Ætatis suæ 87.
Also here lieth the Body of
SILVESTER, the Wife of
HODGES GODWIN,
who died 19 June 1707,
Ætatis suæ 92.

ANN, Daughter of
DANIEL and ELIZABETH RIDLEY,
was buried here the 5*th.* of
April 1751, in the 15*th.*
Year of her Age.

Arms:—MASON, *as before, impaling.*—Argt. on a Chevron Gules
three Roses of the field.

Hic jacet Corpus
HESTERÆ MASON, nuper Uxoris
GULIELMI MASON, A. M.
Rectoris de *Yate*,
quæ sepulta erat 24*o.* die Augusti,
Anno Dom. 1729, Ætatis suæ 56.
Infra jacet Corpus
Viri *Reverendi* GULIELMI MASON,
Hujus Ecclesiæ nuper Rectoris,
Qui obijt 24*o.* Febr. Ano. Dni. 1740,
Ætatis suæ 84.

Hic jacet Corpus
JOHANNIS GODWIN,
filii HODGES GODWIN, *Senr. Gener.*
qui (postquam quatuor ferme annos
in Academia, *Oxon.* Studiis operam
dedisset,) obijt 6 die Decemb.
Anno Dni. 1677,
Ætatisque suæ 22.

In Memory of
ANNE, one of the Daughters of
Mr. ROBERT GODWYN,
and late Wife of the
Revd. Mr. GILES RIDLEY,
since deceased and buried at *Stone,*
Also of ELIZABETH, Daughter of
Mr. DANIEL RIDLEY,
Son of the said GILES and
ANN RIDLEY.
ANNE, died Dec. 9, 1728.
ELIZABETH, died Oct. 20, 1736,
Aged 2 Years and 10 Months.

NORTH AISLE.

Sacred to the Memory of
CHARLES ORCHARD, of this Parish,
who departed this Life,
18 of September 1788,
Aged 67 Years.
Likewise HANNAH, Wife of
JAMES ORCHARD,
who departed this Life, the
15 day of Oct. 1789. Aged 30 Years.

ON FLAT STONES.

In Memory of
MARY, Wife of ROBERT SARGEANT,
of *Wapley*, *Gentleman*, and also
Daughter of THOMAS TAYLOR,
of this Parish, *Gentleman*,
who departed this Life, the
12 Nov. 1751, Aged 42 Years.
Also of *Mr.* ROBERT SARGEANT,

Gentleman, who was here interred
the 14 day of of Jany. 1767,
Aged 55 Years.

In Memory of
MARY, Wife of THOMAS TAYLOR,
late of the Parish of *All Saints,
Bristol*, but now of this Parish
Gentleman,
who departed this Life, the
26*th.* of June 1751, in the 79*th.*
Year of her Age.
Also in Memory of the abovesaid
THOMAS TAYLOR,
who departed this Life, the
15 day of February 1752, in the
80*th.* Year of his Age.

In Memory of
JOHN GREEN, late of this Parish,
He departed this Life, the
9*th.* of August, 1757,
Aged 76 Years.
Also in Memory of
ROSE, late *Widow* of the
above said JOHN GREEN,
who departed this Life, the
1*st.* August 1760, Aged 75 Years.
Also in Memory of ARTHUR HARTS-
HORNE, Son of SAMUEL HARTSHORNE,
Attorney at Law, in *Northampton*,
He died the 31*st.* of Dec. 1743,
in the 10 Year of his Age.
Also in Memory of CATER, the Son
of the said JOHN and ROSE GREEN,
died 22 of Febr. 1777,
Aged 54 Years.
Also three of their Children,
who died in their Infancy.

In Memory of
MARY, Wife of BARNABAS TOMAS,
of this Parish, who died the 19 of
October 1761, Aged 70 Years.
Also the above BARNABAS TOMAS,
who died August 4*th.* 1787,
Aged 91 Years.

ON FLAT STONES IN CROSS AISLE.

Here lyeth the Body of
THOMAS SMITH, of this Parish,
Gent. who departed this Life,
the 24 day of October 1714,
Aged 81 Years.

Here lyeth the Body of
SARAH, the Wife of THOMAS SMITH,
who deceased ye 13*th.* day of March,
Anno Dom. 1669.
Aged 27.
Here also lyeth ye Body of
MATHEW SMITH, *Gent.*
Son of ye said THOMAS and SARAH,
who deceased ye first day of
October, Anno Domini 1703,
Ætatis suæ 37.

Under this Tombstone lieth
the Body of RICHARD STOKES,
of this Parish, *Gent.*
who departed this Life, the
27 day of January, Anno Dni. 1721,
Aged near 80 Years.

His jacet Corpus
THOMAS BELSIRE,
qui obijt 13o. die Februarij,
Anno Domi. 1669, Annoq.
Ætatis suæ 94.
Ut Flos sic Vita.
In Memory of
HESTER BELSIRE,
Widow and Relict of RICHARD
BELSIRE, deceased, who died
the 9 day of January 1731-2.
Also the Body of
RICHARD BELSIRE, *Gent.*
only Son of the above mentioned
RICHARD and HESTER,
who died the 20 day of April 1739,
in the 17 Year of his Age.

Here lyeth the Body of
ALICE, late the Wife of
.... STOKES, ...
....
PARKER, of *Barnewood, Gent.*
by MARGARET, his Wife
Daughter of EDWARD STEPHENS,
of *Effington, Esqr.* which
ALICE, having foure Children,
viz —SAMUEL, JOHN, DANIEL,
and ELIZABETH, the 3rd. of April,
Anno Dom. 1615,
departed this Life to live
with Christ for ever.
Under this Tomb Stone
there likewise is inhumed the
Body of ISABELLA, Wife unto
SAMUEL STOKES, of *Stanshawes
Place* in this Parish, *Gent.*
She was the Daughter unto
RICHARD CODRINGTON,
of *Dodington, Esqr.* and JOYCE,
Sister unto *Sir* WILLIAM BURLESS,
of *R ckmore,* in the County of
Buckingham, who was Grandfather
unto *Sir* JOHN BURLESS, of the
same Place, *Knt. and Baronet,*
who breathed out her Soul,
the 6 day of December 1675,
leaving behind her 8 Branches,
viz.—3 Sons:—EDWARD, RICHARD,
and THOMAS and 5 Daughters:—
JOYCE, ANNE, ELIZABETH,
MARY and ISABELLA.

Arms:—.. ...... a Lion rampant
.... *impaling* .... a fess
.... between three Lions passant ....

In Memory of
ESTHER TILLIT, *Junior,*
who died 10 Nov. 1732, in the
12 Year of her Age,
and now lies buried here
near her Grandmother
HESTER BELSIRE,
late of this Parish, *Widow,*
deceased.

MARIA, quondam
JOHANNIS HICKES,
de *Winterborn, Gen.* nuper vero
THOMÆ BELSIRE,
(Juxta Sepulturæ tradito,)
Connubijs sociata, Carnis
Exuvias infra ceposuit,
Ob. 22, Die Martij,
Anno 1728,
Ætat. suæ 64.

DANIELIS BELSIRE, *Gen.*
et ELIZABETH, uxoris ejus

Qui obijt XVIo. die Julij,
Anno Salutis MDCCXXXIIo.
Ætatis suæ XLIX.

Here lyeth the Body of
MARTHA, the Wife of NICHOLAS
WHITE, of *Chipping Sodbury,
Yeoman,* Daughter of THOMAS
BELSIRE, of this Parish, *Gent.*

ON BRASS PLATES.

Hic Jacet Corpus
GABRIELIS BELSIRE,
Qui obijt 10 die Martij,
A. D. 1668, Æt. suæ 49.

Ad dextram hujus Tumuli
proxime jacet
corpus ELIANORÆ BELSIRE,
uxoris GABRIELIS BELSIRE
prædicti, Quæ obijt 28 die Octobris,
A. D. 1678.
Quæ, supersunt Cineres
RICHARDI BELSIRE, *Gen.*
hic sepultæ jacent. Anima reliquit
Corpus XIII. die Martij,
Anno Dom. MDCCXV,
Ætat. suæ LXVII.
[Part only to be found in 1887.]

Here lies interred ESTHER,
the Wife of JAMES TILLIE, *Esq.*
only daughter of
RICHARD BELSIRE. *Gent.*
deceased who died at
Pentillie Castle in *Cornwall,*
the 16 day of May, in the
38 Year of her Age. (*no Year.*)

Under this Stone lieth the Body of
JOHN and SAMUEL, Sons of
WILLIAM HOBBS,
and SARAH, his Wife,
JOHN, was buried Oct. 25, 1729,
in the 6th. Year of his Age.
SAMUEL, was buried Dec. 19, 1722,
Aged 2 Months and 14 days.
Also ELIZABETH, their Daughter,
died June 28, 1722, in the 13
Year of her Age.

Beneath this Stone are deposited
the Remains of
Mr. JAMES BAKER,
lately from the *Island of St. Kitts,*
who departed this Life the
30 of June 1796, Aged 63.
His Widow has gratefully caused
this Plate to be erected
to perpetuate his Memory.
[*On a Brass is inscribed.*
Also of ANN, Relict
of the aforesaid *Mr.* JAMES BAKER,
of *Iron Acton,* who departed
this Life, June 30th. (1833,?)
Aged 75 Years.]

In Memoriam
ELIZABETHÆ, Charissimæ nec non
Amantissimæ Conjugis
THOMÆ BELSIRE,
quæ Animam in manus,
Creatoris humillime deposuit
XXVIIIo. die Aprilis,
Anno Dom. 1694.

Infra etiam reconduntur
Exuviæ Supradict
THOMÆ BELSIRE, *Gen.*
Qui supremum efflavit Spiritum
30mo. Die 7bri.
Anno Renovati Hominis 1728,
Ætat. suæ 73.
GULIELMUS et MARIÆ,
duo eorum Liberi juxta inhumantur
Hic etiam Spe Resurrections beatæ
ELIZABETHA supradicti
THOMÆ et ELIZABETHÆ,
Filia requiescit, Obijt 25 Jan. 1738,
Anno Ætatis suæ 55.

ON A LARGE BRASS PLATE ON WHICH
ARE THE FIGURE OF A MAN BETWEEN
HIS TWO WIVES, ELIZABETH AND
AVIS :—UNDER THE FIRST WIFE, SIX
MALE CHILDREN AND UNDER THE
SECOND FIVE FEMALE CHILDREN.

Corpus ALEXANDRI STAPLES,
lapis iste tuetur, Spiritus ætherea
beatus agit Rursus supremum tuba
cum tarantantara danget Spiritui
junget mortua membra Deus.
Tercentum Sustris octodenoq;
Fluente, Bernardi, a Christo,
concidit ipse die
Saxum hoc mæsta suo ponebat ELIZA:
Marito Conjugij signum quod
pietatis erit,
22o. Augusti 1590.

CHURCH YARD.

ON A MONUMENT AGAINST
THE PORCH.

Near this Place lies the Body of
HENRY PINKETT, of this Parish,
Yeoman, who was buried the
21st. December 1729,
Aged about 74 Years.
Also KATHARINE, his Wife,
was buried near this Place.
[Not to be found, 1887.]

AGAINST THE SOUTH WALL
OF CROSS AISLE.

Underneath this Stone,
Resteth the Body of
JOHN MILLARD, *Gent.*
who for some years lived within
this Parish, and died at
Wickwarre, the 30 day of Septemb.
Anno Dni. 1688, Ætat. suæ 65.

ON ALTAR TOMBS.

Here lyeth the Body of
HENRY OCKFORD, (and ANNE,
his Wife,) which HENRY, died
the 11th. day of August 1643.
And ANNE, the 5th. of Jan. 1655.
Here lyeth the Body of
HESTER MILLARD, Daughter of
JOHN MILLARD, *Gent.*
who departed this Life, the
26th. of October 1682.
Also 3 Sons and 3 Daughters.

In Memory of
THOMAS WALLIS, of this Parish,
who died the 31 of May 1723,
Aged 65 Years.

Also HANNAH, his Wife,
who was buried the 4 Jany. 1743.
Also of FRANCES, their Daughter
who died 27 Oct. 17 . 7,
Aged 20 Years.
Also of RICHARD GRIMES,
of this Parish who was buried
2 Febr. 1732, and of MARY, his
Wife, who died Dec. 7, 1746,
Aged 58.

Here lyeth the Body of
MARY, the Wife of WILLIAM
WOODWARD, of this Parish, *Yeoman*,
who departed this Life, the
6 day of Decemb. 1715,
Ætat. suæ 68.

In Memory of
SARAH, Wife of WILLIAM SHORT,
of *Iron Acton*, *Yeoman*,
who died Dec. 11, 1722,
Aged 31 Years.
Also of WILLIAM SHORT,
Yeoman, the Son of WILLIAM
and SARAH SHORT aforesaid,
who died Sept. 11, 1719,
Ætatis suæ 28.

Here lyeth the Body of
WILLIAM SHORT, of the Parish
of *Iron Acton*, *Yeoman*,
who departed this Life,
January 21, 1713, Aged 66 Years.

Here lyeth the Body of
JOHN HARDING, of the Parish
of *Iron Acton*, *Yeoman*,
who died Febr. 5, 1726, in the
39*th.* Year of his Age.
Also JOHN, his Son,
who died Febr. 6, 1723,
Aged 1 Year and 4 Months.
Also MABELL, Daughter of
WILLIAM and SARAH SHORT,
and late *Widow*, of JOHN HARDING,
of *Iron Acton,* who departed
this Life, the 2*nd.* day of
August 1748, Aged 58 Years.
Also SARAH, Wife of WILLIAM
EGGLESE, and Daughter of the said
JOHN and MABELL HARDING,
who departed this Life, the
20 day of December 1755,
Aged 30 Years.

In Memory of
DANIEL LUTON, who died
Febr. 25, 1801, in the 84
Year of his Age.
And of BETTY, his Wife,
who died Sept. 1765, Aged 50.
DANIEL, their Son, died an Infant.

Here lyeth the Body of
THOMAS SMITH,
who departed this Life, the
6 of July 1681, Ætatis suæ 78.
Here lyeth the Body of
MARY SMITH, Wife of THOMAS
SMITH, and Sister of
JOHN BAYNHAM, who died
the 26 day of May,
Anno Dom. 1676.

Here lyeth the Body of
CATHARINE, the Wife of
WILLIAM NEALE, of this Parish,
who departed this Life,
April 29, 1740, Aged 60 Years.
Here lyeth the Body of
WILLIAM NEALE, of this Parish,
who departed this Life,
May 2, 1741, Aged 60 Years.
BENJAMIN NEALE, of this Parish,
Yeoman, died May 18, 1801,
in the 63 Year of his Age.
Also SARAH, Daughter of
JOHN and SARAH NEALE,
of this Parish, who died Feb. 23,
1777, in the 13 Year of her Age.

In Memory of
SARAH, the Wife of JOHN NEALE,
She died June 13, 1744,
Aged 38 Years.
And under this Tomb lyeth the
Body of JOHN NEALE,
who departed this Life,
May 5, 1746, in the
36 Year of his Age.
JOHN NEALE, of this Parish,
died 8 of June 1801, in the
62 Year of his Age.

Here lyeth the Body of
WILLIAM NEALE, Son of
JOHN NEALE, of this Parish,
Yeoman, who departed this Life,
Dec. 16, 1741, Aged 37 Years.
Also SARAH, Wife of the said
JOHN NEALE, who died
4 June 1754, Aged 60 Years.
Also JOHN NEALE, *Senr.*
of this Parish, *Yeoman,*
who died 27 Decr. 1761,
Ætatis suæ 84.
Also MARY, Wife of JOHN NEALE,
of this Parish, *Yeoman,*
who departed this Life, Nov. 5,
A. D. 1736, Ætatis suæ 77.

Under this Tomb lyeth the Body of
JOHN NEALE, *Senr.*
who departed this Life,
June 10, 1727, Aged 75 Years.
SUSANNAH NEALE, of this Parish,
who departed this Life, the
11 Febr. 1775, Aged 82 Years.
Here lyeth the Bodies of
ALEXANDER NEALE, and PARTISE,
his Wife. ALEXANDER, deceased
the 14 of Jany. in the Year of
our Lord 1651, Aged 63 Years.
And PARTISE, died the 21 day of Mar.
A. D. 1689, Aged 62.

In Memory of
ALEXANDER, Son of ALEXANDER
and PARTISE NEALE, aforesaid,
who died June 3, 1694,
Aged 30 Years.
Also the Body of SARAH, the Wife
of JOHN NEALE, *Senr.* aforesaid
who departed this Life,
April 12, 1728, Ætatis suæ 83.

Here lyeth the Body of
GABRIEL NEALE,
who departed this Life,
July 31, 1731, Aged 46 Years.
Also of 5 Children:—3 Sons and
2 Daughters of the aforesaid

GABRIEL and SARAH NEALE,.
Here also lyeth the Body of
SARAH, the Wife of GABRIEL
NEALE, aforesaid, who died
March 22, 1733-4, Aged 40 Years.
Also in Memory of
JOHN BROWN NEALE, Son of
WILLIAM and CATHARINE NEALE,
who died in Jany. 1716-17,
Aged 4 Years, &c.
Also of MAURICE NEALE,
late of *Chipping Sodbury,*
Son of the aforesaid GABRIEL
and SARAH NEALE,
who died 18 Sept. 1770, Aged 47.

Here lyeth the Body of
THOMAS ROLPH and ANN,
his second Wife.
He died the 30 of November 1676,
And she died the 27 of December,
1675.
ANN ROLPH, of *Cromhall, Widow,*
and *Relict* of DANIEL ROLF,
of *Iron Acton,* was interred here
November 23, 1726,
Aged near 100 Years.
Also ANN HOYLE. *Widow* and *Relict*
JOHN HOYLE, and Daughter of the
said DANIEL and ANN ROLPH,
lies here interred,
She died August 11, 1735,
Aged 54 Years.

In Memory of
THOMAS ROLPH. of *Iron Acton,*
who died 1*st.* of April 1763,
Aged 46 Years.
In Memory of
ROBERT ROLPH, of the Parish
of *Westonleigh*, who died
Sept. 25, 1751, Aged 83 Years.
Also of SARAH, *Widow* and *Relict*
of ROBERT ROLPH, who died
Novemb. 17, 1775, Aged 86 Years.

Here lyeth the Body of
ROBERT ROLPH, and ANN,
his Wife. He died the 28 day of
April 1704, Aged 66 Years.
She died the 13 day of Sept. 1701.

Here lieth the Body of
JOSEPH ROLPH,
who was buried July the 2nd. 1720,
Aged 44 Years.
Also the Body of ANN, his Wife,
who was buried Jany. the 4*th.* 1767,
Aged 84 Years.
Also the Body of MARY, their
Daughter who was buried
June 11, 1731, Aged 28 Years.
Also the Body of JOHN, their Son,
who was buried Oct. 19, 1731,
Aged 24 Years.

Under this Tomb lieth the
Body of SUSANNA PRICE, of the
Parish of *Iron Acton,*
who was buried May 19, 1737,
Aged about 75.
In Memory of
SUSANNA, Wife of JOHN WALKLEY
who died April 30, 1766,
Aged 48 Years.
Also HANNAH, their Daughter,
who died May 6, 1766,
Aged 4 Years.

Here lieth the **Body** of
SARAH, the Wife of JOHN PULLIN,
who was buried Jan. 12, 1715,
Aged 50 Years.
Here lieth the Body of
JOHN CORNWELL,
who was buried Jan. 11, 1678.

In Memory of
SARAH, Wife of EDMUND WREN,
who died June 12, 1763,
Aged 78 Years.

Here lyeth the Body of
WILLIAM STOCK, Senr.
who was buried in Febr. 1734,
Aged 81 Years.
Also ELIZABETH, his Wife,
who was buried Novem. 20, 1724.
Also WILLIAM, Son of WILLIAM
and ELIZABETH STOCK,
aforesaid who was buried in
July 1723, Aged 43 Years.

In Memory of
JOHN STOCK, Son of WILLIAM STOCK,
of this Parish, who departed this
Life, the 13 of October 1742,
Aged 60 Years.
Also of MARTHA, late *Widow*
of the said JOHN STOCK,
who departed this Life, the
18*th.* day of Novem. 1754, in
the 75*th.* Year of her Age.

Here lyeth the Body of
RICHARD BATTEN,
who departed this Life, the
3*rd.* day of January 1666.
Also of MARY BATTEN,
Wife of the said RICHARD BATTEN,
who died Febr. 17, 1661.

In Memory of
CHARLES ORCHARD,
of this Parish, who died the 12 of
May 1749, Aged near 60 Years.
Also of BRIDGET, his Wife,
who died 14 of April 1746,
Aged near 53 Years.
SARAH, Wife of GEORGE MEREDITH,
and Daughter of CHARLES and
SARAH ORCHARD,
who died April 16, 1777,
Aged 24 Years.
SARAH, their Daughter,
died June 18, 1795,
Aged 2 Years and 6 Months.
HENRY, their Son, died
Augt. 2, 1797, Aged 13 Months.

Here resteth the Body of
ALICE BAYNHAM, Wife of HENRY
BAYNHAM, of this Parish, *Gent.*
who departed this Life, the
19 May 1694.
Also ROBERT BAYNHAM,
of this Parish, who died
February the 28, 1728.

Here lyeth the Body of
MARY, the Wife of HENRY TOWERS,

---

who departed this Life,
September 27, 1713, in the
25 Year of her Age.
Also ELIZABETH, the Daughter of
HENRY and MARY TOWERS,
who died 4 February 1765,
Aged 53 Years.

In Memory of
WILLIAM TOWERS, late of *Clapton,*
who died April 28, 1768,
Aged 51 Years.
ELIZABETH TOWERS, who died
3 April 1774, Aged 77 Years.

In Memory of
HESTER, Wife of PETER HARDWICKE,
who departed this Life,
20 August 1774. Aged 42 Years.

Here lyeth the Body of
GEORGE HORT, of this Parish,
Yeoman, who departed this Life,
the 23 day of February 1704,
Aged 85 Years
Also MARY, Wife of GEORGE HORT,
who died 17 of April 1708,
Aged 76 Years.
Also under this Tomb lieth the
Body of SUSANNA, Wife of
STEPHEN FRANCOMBE,
of this Parish, *Yeoman,* who died
6 December 1755, Aged 28 Years.
Also GEORGE, Son of JOHN and
MARY FRANCOMBE, of this Parish,
who died Nov. 6, 1745, in the
19 Year of his Age.
Also here lies STEPHEN FRANCOMBE,
before mentioned, who died the
13 March 1772, Aged 46 Years.

In Memory of
WILLIAM CORBETT, Senr.
who died December 7, 1713,
Aged 80 Years.
Also of MARTHA, the Wife of
the said WILLIAM CORBETT,
who died December 6, 1713,
Aged 79 Years.
In Memory of
WILLIAM CORBETT,
who died March 22, 1729,
Aged 26 Years.
Also MARY, the Wife of
WILLIAM CORBETT, who died
April 6, 1729, Aged 25 Years.
NATHANIEL, Son of WILLIAM
CORBETT and MARY, his Wife,
who died August 20, 1743,
Aged 17 Years.

In Memory of
JONATHAN CORBETT, of this Parish,
who died the 26 of Nov. 1762,
Aged near 56 Years.
SARAH, Daughter of JONATHAN
and ELEANOR CORBETT, died the
3 of Sept. 1757, Aged near 21 Years.
ELEANOR, Wife of JONATHAN
CORBETT, who died July 8, 1737,
Aged 31 Years.

Here lies the Body of
NATHAN CORBETT,

---

who departed this Life the
3 day of Sept. 1743, Aged 46.
Also HENRIETTA, the Wife of
JONATHAN CORBETT, of this Parish,
who died the 8 of Febr. 1769,
Aged 30 Years.
Also JOHN, their Son, who died
Decr. 17, 1768, Aged 16 Years.
And three of their Children:
WILLIAM, ANNA-MARIA, & NATHAN,
who all died in their Infancy.

Here lyeth the Body of
JOAN, the Wife ef ROBERT COLT,
who died the 8 of 1716,
Aged 82 Years.
Also the Body of JONATHAN
CORBETT, of this Parish,
who was buried May 17, 1732,
Aged 69 Years.
Also the Body of MARY,
late *Widow* of JONATHAN CORBETT,
of this Parish, buried
24 Sept. 1749, Aged 75 Years.
NATHAN CORBETT, of this Parish,
who died 19 June 1770,
Aged 61 Years.
Also of NATHAN CORBETT, Son of
NATHAN and GRACE CORBETT,
of this Parish, who died
17 of March 1763, Aged 15.
GRACE, the *Widow,* of the above
NATHANIEL CORBETT,
who died April 26, 1796,
Aged 86 Years.

Here lyeth the Body of
RICHARD, Son of RICHARD HILL,
of this Parish, *Clothier,*
who died 27 July 1693.
Also of RICHARD HILL,
of this Parish, *Esquire,*
who died the 31 of March 1755,
Aged 55 Years.

ON BRASS PLATE.

Hic jacent
JOHANNES WALKER,
qui obiit 31*o.* Die Jan. Ano. 1637,
Ætat. suæ 77.
Nec Non
MARIÆ WALKER, uxoris predict.
JOHANNIS, Quæ obiit 26*o.* die Sept.
Anno Dni. 1635, Æt. suæ 58.

M. C. deceased the 18 day of
Febr. 1682.

In Memory of
THOMAS CAM, of this Parish,
Yeoman, who died 24 April 173...
Aged 51 Years.
Also of SARAH, their Daughter,
who died 14 of April 1730,
Aged 11 Years.
ELEANOR, the *Widow,* of
THOMAS CAM, who died
March 7, 1766, Aged 77 Years.
ROBERT, Son of the aforesaid
THOMAS and ELEANOR CAM,
of the Parish of *Old Sodbury,*
departed this Life, 7 day of
May 1790, Aged 63 Years.

Here lyeth the Body of
THOMAS RUSSELL, of this Parish,
Yeoman, who died 3 May 1714,
Aged 74 Years.
In Memory of
JOSEPH WOODWARD,
late of the City of *Bristol,*
who departed this Life the
20*th.* of February 1772,
Aged 55 Years.
MARY, late *Widow,* of the aforesaid
JOSEPH WOODWARD,
died Dec. 21, 1790, in the
67 Year of her Age.

Here lyeth the Body of
PETER CROOCKS, who died
8 July 1652, Also ELIZABETH,
the *Widow* of PETER CROOCKS,
who died 12 March 1683.

In Memory of
MARGARET, Wife of JOSEPH
WERRETT, of this Parish,
who died 19 March 1755,
Aged 46 Years.
The above JOSEPH WERRETT,
died April 19, 1793,
Aged 85 Years.
Also RICHARD WERRETT,
of this Parish, who died
the 28 of Decr. 1750,
Aged 79 Years.

To the Memory of
MARY, the Wife of GADDES
JONES, *Senr.*
Also MARY, the Daughter of
GADDES JONES, by MARY, his Wife
who died 14 June 1732,
Aged 15 Months.

Sacred to the Memory of
WILLIAM WINSTON, of the
Borough of *Chipping Sodbury,*
Senr. who died the 20 of Sept. 1751,
Aged 68 Years.
SARAH, his Wife, died July 6, 1757,
Aged 72 Years.
MARY, Wife of WILLIAM WINSTON,
Junr. died May 15, 1784,
Aged 72 Years.
The above WILLIAM WINSTON,
late of the Borough of *Chipping
Sodbury,* died May 24, 1793,
Aged 81 Years.

Underneath lie the Remains of
WILLIAM PEARCE, of this Parish,
Yeoman, who died Jan. 28, 1770,
Aged about 40 Years.
MARY, his Daughter by ANN,
his Wife, died Augt. 20, 1768,
Aged 1 Month and 3 days.
ANN WEEKS,
who died Jany. 16, 1795,
Aged 32 Years.

Under this Tomb lyeth the Body of
TRYPHENA FRANCOMB,
who departed this Life,
Nov. 17, 1793, Aged 57 Years.

WILLIAM, Son of STEPHEN and
SUSANNAH FRAMCOMB,
died May ..., 1779, in the
23 Year of his Age.

In Memory of
MARY, Wife of JOHN GARDNIR,
and Daughter of NATHANIEL and
GRACE CORBETT, who departed
this Life, April 30, 1785,
Aged 40 Years.

In Memory of
BETTY, Wife of THOMAS MORSE,
of *Hogsdown* in the Parish of
Berkeley, who died Aug. 18, 1798,
Aged 82 Years.
Also the above THOMAS MORSE,
who died Decr. 3, 1798,
Aged 76 Years.

---

*[Additional Inscriptions,
most since Bigland's time.*

ON BRASS IN SOUTH (CHANCEL)
AISLE.

Underneath are deposited the
Remains of JOSEPH BENDALL,
of the Parish of *Old Sodbury,*
who died the 11*th.* of Sept. 1828,
Aged 54 Years.
Also of MARY ANN, his Wife,
who died the 6*th* of May 1841,
Aged 64 Years.

We rest in hope waiting for thy
mercy, in Christ Jesus, at that
Great Day, when thou shalt
awake us out of the dust.

MONUMENT ON SOUTH WALL.

Near this Monument lies Interred
the Body of JOHN WALKER,
of *Hill-house,* within this Parish,
Esquire, who died the 27*th.* day
of December in the Year of
Our Lord 1760, Aged 82 Years.

ON MONUMENTS AGAINST EAST
WALL OF CROSS AISLE, S. SIDE.

Sacred to the Memory of
Capt. THOMAS STOKES, of
Stanshawe's Court, in this Parish,
who departed this Life,
Decr. 18*th.* 1786, Aged 80 Years,
and lies interred in this Church.
Also of SARAH STOKES,
Relict of *Capt.* THOMAS STOKES.
A Lady equally pious and benevolent
Who met the stroke of Death with
Christian fortitude, Febr. 17, 1788,
Aged 84 Years.
Also of THOMAS STOKES, *Esqr.*
their Son of *Stanshawe's Court,*
who lies interred in the same vault,
and who having filled the Office of
Magistrate with exemplary attention
and integrity, Left this world in
joyful hope of a better, the 15*th.*
of Jany. 1803, Aged 70 Years.
Also of ANN STOKES, his Wife,
who as firm in Virtue,
as full of Years,

Rests likewise in the adjacent Vault,
Having departed this Life,
August the 3*rd.* 1803, Aged 66.
Inscribed to whom and the venerable
partner of her mortal state,
This Monument witnesses the
affection of their Executrix.

"Take then these tears Mortality's relief
"And till I share your joys forgive my grief,
"These little rites a Stone, a Verse receive,
"'T is all that tender friendship now can give !

Arms:—Azure *or* Sable? a Lion
rampt. gard. double queued Argent.

In Memory of
THOMAS STOKES, *Esqr.*
of *Stanshawe's Court,* in this Parish,
who died Nov. 15*th.* 1808,
Aged 49 Years.
Also of SARAH, his Wife,
who died Oct. 12*th.* 1821,
Aged 64 Years.
Also of ANNIS, Wife of
ADRIAN STOKES, *Esqr.*
eldest Son of the above named
THOMAS and SARAH STOKES,
She died Jany. 22*nd.* 1848,
Aged 53 Years.
Beloved in Life, in death lamented.
Also of the abovenamed
ADRIAN STOKES, *Esquire,*
who died April 21*st.* 1853,
Aged 65 Years.
A Magistrate for the County and
much esteemed for his many good
qualities.

NAVE.

ON FLAT STONES.

Sacred to the Memory of
CHARLES ORCHARD,
of this Parish, who departed this
Life, the 18*th.* day of Sept. 1788,
Aged 71 Years.
Also in Memory of JAMES
ORCHARD, Son of CHARLES and
SARAH ORCHARD, *Yeoman,*
who died Febr. the 14*th.* 1798,
Aged 37 Years.
Also of SARAH, his Wife,
who departed this Life, the
27*th.* day of November 1788,
Aged 67 Years.
Likewise of HANNAH, Wife of
JAMES ORCHARD,
who departed this Life, the
15*th.* day of October 1789,
Aged 30 Years.
Also of ELIZABETH, 2*nd.* Wife,
of the aforesaid JAMES ORCHARD,
who departed this Life,
November 12*th.* 1830,
Aged 65 Years.

Beneath this Stone lie the
Remains of WILLIAM-STEPHEN
GOODENOUGH, M. A.
Forty-two years Rector of *Yate,*
who departed this Life,
March 10, 1843, Aged 66 Years.

Beneath this Stone lieth the Body of
ISAAC BENDALL, of the Parish
of *Wapley and Codrington, Yeoman,*
who departed this Life,
July 3*rd.* 1810, in the 38*th.*
Year of his Age.

"Death on a sudden seiz'd on me,
And God himself thought fit,

When we have liv'd our time on
earth,
To death we must submit."

A MONUMENT ON WEST WALL OF
NORTH CROSS AISLE.

In a Vault near this spot
Lie the Remains of HENRY-CATER,
Son of the *Revd.* HENRY J., and
FRANCES RANDOLPH,
who departed this Life,
Augt. 11*th.* 1818.
Also of CHARLES, their Son,
who died in his infancy.
Also of MARY CATER, of *Yate
House*, who died Sept 22*nd.* 1836,
Also of her Sister
FRANCES SPENCER,
who died June 18*th* 1839,
And of ANNE CATER,
Mother of the ahovenamed
FRANCES RANDOLPH,
who died Decr. 23*rd.* 1840.

*Two Stones in the North (Chancel)
Aisle are partially hidden by the
platform of Organ and a Seat: one
appears to be to the Memory of
.... BRADSHAW & Wife,
date* 1819, *Surname on the other*

---

is not visible, though the date 1819,
is.
*On a portion of a Stone near the
Organ in North (Chancel) Aisle,
appears the following:*—
Body of JOAN ....
1639.

To the Memory of
AUGUSTA MATILDA,
Daughter of JOHN and CHARLOTTE-
MARY BRADSHAW, who died
October 14*th.* A. D. 1810,
Aged 4 Months.

Near this place lie the Remains of
WILLIAM STEPHEN GOODENOUGH,
Forty-two Years Rector of *Yate*,
who departed this Life,
March 10, 1843, Aged 66 Years.

NAVE.

ON FLAT STONES.

In Memory of
JOHN GABB, Clerk.
late *Curate* of this Parish,
who departed this Life, the
25*th.* of June 177..., Aged 40 Years.

On a Brass Plate on the same Stone.

RICHARD STOKES, *Esqr.*
died the 4*th.* of June 1782,
Aged 82 Years.

On the same Stone.

HORATIO RUDGE, Son of
Mr. JAMES RUDGE, *Gent.*
late of *Cromhall*, who died
May the 24*th.* 1802, iu the 24*th.*
Year of his Age.

THERE IS A STAINED GLASS
WINDOW AT THE EAST.

To the Glory of God and in Memory
of EDMUND PONTIFEX,
by his five Sons.—ALFRED, WM.-
CHARLES, ARTHUR, DUDLEY-
DAVID, and SEPTIMUS EDMUND.

IN THE SOUTH AISLE IS A STAINED
GLASS WINDOW:—

In Memory of
WILLIAM STEPHEN GOODENOUGH,
Rector of this Parish,
ANN, his *Widow*, and FRANCES-
MARY, their Daughter,
by the three Surviving children :
WILLIAM, SOPHIA and ANN.
(*Very small portions of the old stained
Glass in the Windows remain* 1887.)

HEAD STONES.

	Died.		Aged.		Died.		Aged.
Daniel Horwood, ...	18 Sept.	1775	51	Grace, Wife of Samuel Aldous, and Daughter of William and Catharine Neale, ...	27 Febr.	1767	57
Christian, Wife of Samuel Shipp,	30 Jany.	1792	35				
Joseph Shipp, ...	7 Augt.	1767	57				
Hannah, his Wife, ...	31 May	1791	74	Stephen Allpass, ...	12 July	1797	73
James Walkins, ...	23 Oct.	1785	53	Sarah, his Wife, ...	5 Aug.	1796	80
Joseph Shipp, ...	4 Sept	1793	71	Isaac Limbrick, ...	11 July	1744	54
James Tyler, ...	29 March	1790	37	Joane Limbrick, his Wife, ...	5 Oct.	1762	60
William Boyer, ...	5 Febr.	1747	40	Samuel Long, ...	9 Oct.	1766	68
Sarah, Wife of James Tyler, ...	10 Jany.	1783	25	Ann, his Wife, ...	7 June	1766	63
Mary, Wife of William Bristow,	17 Oct.	1797	67	Richard Latch, ...	15 March	1795	70
Thomas Simmonds, ...	21 April	1752	55	John Orchard, ...	4 Oct.	1787	28

Notes as to I.—*Devolution of Estates.* II.—*Church.* III.—*Population, Taxation, &c.*

I.—*Estates.*

Fines of Lands in Yate.
E. 30 Geo ii.—Summers, *Plaintiff.*
Lockyer, Elizth. & Edw. *Deforciant.*

Ancient Wills at Gloucester, of Yate.

1542.—Wm. Dymere.
1543 —John Somers.
1544.—Richd. Ellyes.
Richd. Short.
Robt. Vealle.

1707.—Richd. Birwicks, Lord of the Manor of Yate
and of Yate Court Farm, Question of Medows, v. Mason,
Rector of Yate.

Waste Lands 656 *a.* inclosed under the Act of 1842.

**1776.—*At the County Election the following Voted for*
Freeholds in Yate.

Alpass, Stephen.
Burgum, Henry.
Clarke, William.
Clifford, Thomas.
Codrington, Robert.
Cole, Robert.

Crowther, Nathaniel.
Gould, John.
Green, Cater.
Humphreys, John.
Iles, William.
Millard, Daniel.

Neale, Benjamin.
Parker, Jacob.
Russell, John.
Stock, John.
Sturge, Nathan

Thomas, Barnabas.
Thurston, Edward.
Walker, John.
Wherreat, Joseph.
Williams, John.

**1811 —*At the Election the following Voted:*—

Alpass, Stephen.
Cole, Charles.
Do. Robert.
Godwin, John.
Goodenough. *Rev.* W. S.
Higgs, Daniel
Holloway, James.
Howell, Henry.
Ludlow, William.
Neale, John.
Pearce, John.
Smith, Benjamin.

Stokes, Adrian.
Do. Edward.
Sturge, Toby Walker.
Tayler, Samuel.
Veel, William, *Esqr.*
Werrett, John.
Do. Joseph.
Wickham, John, *Senr.*
Do. John, *Jun.*
Widcombe, Nathaniel.
Young, Thomas.
Do. William.

II.—*Church:*

List of Incumbents and Patrons of Yate.

Vicars.   *Patrons.*

1548 —At Bishop's Visitation,
... Bowlam, d. 1552.

1552, Sept. 16, Ins'd.—George Morris,
   depriv. for Ven Subscription 1572.
1572, June 28, Ins'd.—Thomas Bay- Thomas Veale,
   neham, d. 1622.   and others.
1622, Decr. 11, Ins'd.—William   Adam Bayneham.
   Hutchenson, d. 1660.
1660, July 24, Ins'd.—Jeremiah   Do.
   Horler, d. 1685.
1685, Febr. 3, Ins'd.—William   John Beyneham,
   Mason, B. A. d. 1740.   Clerk.
1741, July 4, Ins'd. Richard   himself.
   Wallington, M. A.
   d. 1764
1765, Febr. 2, Ins'd.—Thomas   William Tournay.
   Tournay, M. A. d .1795.
1795, May 12, Ins'd.—Richard-   himself.
   John Hay, B. A. res'd. 1801.
1801, July 2, Ins'd.—William   Ann Goodenough,
   Stephen Goodenough,   of *Bath*, *Widow*.
   B. A. d. 1843.
1841. ....   W S. Goodenough. ..

Tithes Comm. 685 *a*.

Glebe 154 *a*.

III.—*Taxation, Population, &c.*

Yate and Ichenton, Subsidy Roll, 1 Edw. iii., 1327.

De Johne de Wylington, viii s. iii d.
‘ Johne de Bromcroft, iiii s. vi d. o. q.
‘ Alic. de Blakeneye, xii d.
‘ Willo. le Brok, x d. o.
‘ Thm. Ady, xiii d. q.
‘ Johne atte Forteye, xix d.
‘ Thm. Gerwy, viii d.
‘ Rico. le Bostare, xiii d.
‘ Simon Russel, viii d. o. q.
‘ Walto. Kynseth, ii s. vi d. o. q.
‘ Walto. le Hert, ix d. q.
‘ Nicho. le Brode, viii d.
‘ Walto. de Stanburn, xxii d. q.
‘ Johne Broun, viii d.
‘ Thom. le Gaunt, iii s. iii d. o. q.
‘ Rogo. Osward, vi d.
‘ Robto. Morgan, viii d.
‘ Willo. Gewy, viii d. o. q.
‘ Johne Wyth, xv d. o.

‘ Hugon Betherigge ,ii s. v d. o,
‘ Edith atte Wode, x d. o. q.
‘ Thom. atte Nasshe, xix d. o.
‘ Thom. Dollinge, xxii d. o. q.

Adhuc Yate and Ichenton.

De Willo. Stincescombe, xv d.
‘ Pho. le Slegh, xiii d. q.
‘ Robto. Godgrom, viii d.
‘ Thom. atte Heth, xxii d. o. q.
‘ Robto. atte Hulle, xviii d.
‘ Thom. le Carte, xv d.
‘ Walto. le Swon, vi d.
‘ Willo. atte Burcholte, viii d.
‘ Thom. Bonebroke, xii d.
‘ Thom. Upehulle, v s. iii d.
‘ Rogo. Raybon, v s. o. q.
‘ Rogo. le Gay, xxi d.
‘ Johne Wynebeke, ii s.
‘ Willo. le Holdare, vi s. ix d.
‘ Galfro. fil. Johane, vii s. o.
‘ Rico. Heynes, vii s. q.
‘ Johne fil. Johane, iii s.
‘ Thom. Jones, iii s. iii d.
‘ Juliana Barry, iii s. ix d. o. q.
‘ Rogo. Dauy, ii s. o. q.
‘ Rogo. Bolt, ii s. v d. o. q.

    prob. Sma. iiii *li.* xix *s. q.*

Acreage 4040 *a*.

Population 1801,—...   1831,—.... 1871.—....

1815. Yearly Value of Real Property £....

1882.—Rateable Value £....

1833-4-5.—Three Years Average Expenditure on Poor ... £.

In Sodbury Union.

1801.—Houses 126. Inhabited 123. Families 138. Males 342. Females 312. Total 654.

1811.—Houses 137. Inhabited 131. Families 138. Males 346. Females 371. Total 717.

1831.—Houses 171. Inhabited 165. Families 180. Males 427. Females 397. Total 824.

APPENDIX

The sections which follow for the parishes of St. Philip & St. Jacob and St. George, Bristol, have never before been published. They have been transcribed by Mrs. Mary Campbell from drafts marked up for printing and are included by kind permission of their owner Mr L. J. Hill.

CLXXXXIX St PHILLIP & St JACOB, BRISTOL

T he Church consists of a chancel & North Chancel called St Mary's Aisle, Nave, North & South Aisles, with a Gallery at the West end & over the North Aisle, a square Tower embattled therein eight Bells. The Pulpit & font are richly Carved and the Royal Arms, God save the Queen 1704.

Mrs Bolton principal Lady of the Manor
Thomas Chester Esq. Lord of the Manor of the Hundred of Barton Regis
James New Vicar

ATCHMENTS IN THE CHURCH

1   Pally of six Or and Gules on a Bend Sable three Mullets Or ELTON Impaling Azure a Sword erect & point upwards Argent pomelled Or between two Lion rampant respectant Or. Crest an Arm embowed holding a broad sword all proper.
2   ELTON as before Impaling Barry of six, Or, & Azure, an Escutcheon Ermine on a Chief of the first three Pallets of the second, between two Esquires bandexter & sinister of the second MORTIMER.
3   Azure three Boarsheads erased Argent   Impaling Argent on a fess Gules three Mullets Or.
    Bend a Human Heart Gules surmounted by two Arms conjoyed in fess proper CUBIT

Painted on a board against a Pillar opposite the Mayors' Seat with A Royal Crown, & Royal Arms, Bristol Arms, Sword, Mace etc.

Thomas Stephens	1668	Edmond Mountjoy	1718
Thomas Laston	1682	Edward Foy	1730
William Jackson	1688	Nathaniel Foy	1772
Arthur Hart	1689	John Bull	1780
Thomas Hort	1712	Edward Price	1782
Henry Whitehead	1714		

BENEFACTIONS TO THE POOR OF ST PHILLIP & JACOB

Mr EDWARD COX 8£ per Annum to Poor & 4£ for eight Sermons yearly for Ever.

Mr Alderman KITCHEN Gave 40 shillings per Annum to householders who is Poor for Ever

Mr Alderman HARRINGTON Gave 40 shillings per Annum to the Poor for Ever.

Mr Alderman CLEMENTS Gave 30 shillings per Annum to the Poor of the Out Parish & 10 shillings for a sermon on the first of January for Ever.

Mr FRANCIS GLEEDE of this City Gave 40 shillings per Annum to the Poor to be paid quarterly for Ever.

Mr WILLIAM BURROUGHS Gave 20 shillings per Annum to the Poor for Ever.

Mr THOMAS FARMER Gave 50£ the profit thereof to the Poor for Ever

Mr WILLIAM CURTES Gave 50£ the profit to the Poor for Ever.

Mr ABRAHAM BIRKINS Gave 5s per Annum to the Poor in Bread for Ever.

Mr JOHN HARFORD Gave 5£.15s.4d. per Annum to the Poor for Ever.

Mr TIMOTHY PARKER Gave 5£ the profit thereof to the Poor in Bread yearly for Ever

Mrs MARY BOUCHER & her Daughter Mrs JONE LANGTON Widdows Gave Lands for the Payment of Xs a peice to 52 poor Widdows of this City yearly for Ever of which this In Parish hath a proportion.

1685 Mr JEREMY HOLLOWAY of this City Merchant Gave 30£ the Profit thereof to the Poor of the In Parish yearly for Ever.

1686 Mr SAMUEL HALE Merchant 10£ the profit thereof Weekly to the Poor in Bread for ever, and Also the Interest of 230£ towards the placeing apprentice poor children in seven Parishes in this City of which this Parish is one.

1687 Sir WILLIAM CANN, Knt & Bart Gave 100£ to 4 Parishes in this City Whereof this Hath a Quarter Part, the Profit thereof to Be Distributed to the Poor the 8th of January for ever.

1688 JOHN LAWFORD Esqr sometime Mayor & Alderman of this City Gave 50£ the Profit thereof to the Poor of the In Parish Yearly in Bread for Ever,

1689 Mr WILLIAM SCOTT Gave 10£ the Profit thereof to the Poor of the In Parish yearly for Ever.

1689 Mrs ELIZABETH PITTS Widdow of this Parish Gave 20£ the Profit thereof to the Poor of the In Parish yearly for ever.

1715 FRANCIS FULLER M.D. Born in this Parish & late Resident in London Gave 334£.10s.2d. the Profit thereof to be Distributed According to his Will to the Poor of the Inn Parish.

1716 WILLIAM JACKSON Esqr sometime Mayor & Alderman of this City Gave 50£ the profit thereof to such Poor in Cole of the In Parish not Receiving Alms.

1716 WILLIAM WHITTINGTON Esq. of Stapleton Parish gave 100£ for the purchasing Lands the Rents whereof are to be Distributed Yearly to such Poor Inhabitants of the In Parish as receives no Weekly Pay.

1690 Mr EDWARD TILLY of this City Gave 100£ to 4 Parishes whereof the In Parish hath a Quarter Part the Profit to Be Given to the Poor Weekly or ever.

Mr EDWARD TERREL Gave 50£ the profit thereof to the Poor of the In Parish for ever.

1692 Mr HENRY MERRETT sometime Sherrif of this City Gave 50£ the Profit thereof Weekly in Bread to the Poor of the out Parish for ever.

Doctor SHERMAN Gave 9£.10s. the Profits to the Poor of this Parish for ever

JOHN BROWN Labourer Gave 10£ the Profit to the Poor of this Parish for ever.

1695 Mr WALTER STEPHENS Gave 3£.13s.4d. per Annum to be Distributed to the Poor of the In Parish Weekly for ever.

1701 Mrs BARBARA MERRETT Widow Gave 30£ the Profitts of it yearly to the Poor of the out Parish for ever.

HERBURT VAUGHAN E. Esqr Gave 10£ the Use thereof to the Poor of the In Parish for ever.

1720   Mr WILLIAM VIGOR of this City Gave 20£ the Interest whereof to Be Given to the Poor of the In Parish in Bread on the 2nd of Feby yearly for ever By the Churchwarden of this Parish.

1720   Captn JAMES SMITH Gave 3£.8s.4d yearly for ever for the Preaching 2 Sermons one on the 4th of Jany the other on the 9th of May & for Bread to the Poor of the out Parish Yearly and 25£ More to the out Parish and 12£.10s. to the In Parish the Interest Whereof to be Given Yearly in Bread to Poor housekeepers not Receiving Alms, at the Discretion of the Churchwardens Respectively.

1720   Mr HENRY GIBBES of this City Gave 10£ the Interest thereof to the Poor of this Parish for ever.

           HENRY WHITEHEAD Esqr Sometime Mayor & Alderman of this City Gave 40£ the Profits thereof to be Disposed of by the Churchwardens to the Poor house Keepers of the In Parish Not Receiving Alms on Candlemas Day yearly for ever.

           Mr ANTHONY WHITEHEAD of this Parish Gave 20£ the Profits thereof to Poor house-keepers of the out Parish Not Receiving Alms on the first Day of May yearly for ever.

1726   Mrs CHRISTIAN BLACKBURN Widow Gave 25£ for two Sermons on Ash Wednesday & Good Friday in the Afternoon yearly for ever.

1728   Mr WILLIAM WELCH Mr DANIEL SHEWRING, & Mr JOHN PITMAN Gave 20£ the Profits to Poor housekeepers of the out Parish on the 8th of March Not Receiving Alms.

1727   Sir ABRAHAM ELTON of this City Baronet Gave 50£ the Interest thereof to be Paid Viz. 20s. Part thereof to the Minister for preaching a Sermon on the first of May if not on a Sunday but if so on the Day following & the Residue to Be equaly Divided Between 10 poor Housekeepers Within the out Parish Not Receiving Alms for ever.

           Also a Close of Ground Leading to Gloucester Road the Rents thereof for teaching poor children to read for ever, of the out Parish.

1729   Mr JOSEPH COLEBROOK of the out Parish Gave 10£ the Profits to be Distributed to the Poor of the out Parish in Bread on the 16th Day of October yearly for ever.

1730   Mr JOHN JAYNE of this City Marriner Gave in his Life time two tenements in Cheese Lane the Profits thereof for the Cloathing as many poor Men & Women Being freemen & widows of freemen of this In Parish as the Clear Rents shall amount to on Michaelmas Day yearly for ever.

1705   ISAAC DAVIS Esq sometime Sherrif of this City Gave 50£ the Profits thereof to Be Given to the Poor of the in Parish Weekly in Bread for ever.

1708   Mr JOHN EDWARDS of this Parish Wheelwright Gave 50£ the profits thereof to be given to 10 Poor housekeepers not receiving Alms on the 27th Day of Jany yearly for ever.

1709   Mr NICHOLAS WHITEING of this Parish Gave 10£ the Profits thereof to the Poor of the out Parish for ever.

1712   Mrs ELENOR BAYLY Widow of the out Parish Gave 20£ for the use & Benefit of this Church to be Disposed of at the Discretion of the Present Churchwardens.

1715   JOSEPH JACKSON Esq Sometime Alderman of this City Gave 40s yearly to the In Parish for the Benefit of their Poor & 4£ yearly to the Poor of Castle Precincts for ever.

1712   Mr SAMUEL PERRY Gave 5£ to the out Parish for Binding out an apprentice (Not upon the Alms) to a free tradesman in this City yearly for ever.

1733   Mrs DIONESS GIBBS in Memory of her Brother Mr HARRINGTON GIBBS Merchant of this City Gave fifty Pounds the Profits thereof to Be Deposed of as followeth. Twenty Shillings to the Minister to preach a Sermon on the 20th Day of Septr in the afternoon if not on a Sunday if so on the Day following and the Remainder to Be Distributed By the Churchwardens in Bread to the Poor of the out Parish on the same Day yearly for ever.

1734   Captn JOHN ROUSE of this Parish Merchant Gave 20£ to the Churchwardens for the time being of the out Parish the Profit thereof to be Given to the Poor of the said Parish In Bread on the 27th of August yearly for ever.

1727   Mrs ALICE JAMES Widow Gave 20£ the Interest thereof to Be Given in 12d Bread to the Poor of this Parish not receiving Alms on Christmas Day yearly for ever.

1751   October Gave By an unknown hand the Sum of twenty pounds the Profits thereof to be Given to the Poor of the out Parish at the Discretion of the Churchwardens.

1754   Mr JAMES OSWALD late of the Parish of St Stephens in this City Soap Maker Gave 10£ the Interest to Be Given to the Poor of the Parish in Sixpenny Bread on Candlemas Day for Ever.

1754   GILBERT BARCROFT Senr Gent of this Parish Apothecary Born Sept 11th 1684 & Died Jany 11 1754 Gave to the Poor of the In Parish 20£ the Interest thereof to Be Given to Poor housekeepers on Sept 11th in 6d Bread by the Churchwarden for Ever.

1755   Mrs LAETITIA BARCROFT in Memory of her Dear Deceased Husband GILBERT BARCROFT Senr Gent Gave of her own free Will these 3 Tables.

1754   Mr HUGH HENRY Gave 50£ towards the Beautifieing this Church which was laid out Accordingly.

1757   Mrs ANN TAYLOR Relict of the Revd JOSEPH TAYLOR (formerly Vicar of this Parish) By her Will Gave to the Churchwardens &c of the In Parish 100£ the Interest thereof to be Divided amongst Poor Women of the said Parish on the second Day of December yearly for ever, in manner By the said Will Directed.

1767   Mr SAMUEL STOKES of this Parish Attorney at Law Gave by his Will the Sum of 100£ to the Churchwarden of the In Parish to be placed forth at Interest and the Interest to be by him Distributed yearly on the 20th Day of March amongst the Poor Inhabitants of the same In Parish for ever.

1777   Mr MARK NOBLE Gave 20£ the Interest Thereof to be Given to the Poor of the out Parish yearly.

1793   Mrs MARY BLAGDEN Gave 100£ the Interest thereof to be given yearly to such Poor Widows resident in or Belonging to the Parish of St Phillip & Jacob in the City of Bristol.

INSCRIPTIONS IN THE CHURCH

ON MONUMENTS IN THE CHANCEL

Arms Pally of six Or & Gules on a Bend
Sable three Mullets Or ELTON Impaling
Argent two Chevrons between three
Martlets Gules PEACH

In Remembrance
of
Her Piety
Filial Obedience
Conjugal Affection
Integrity of Heart
and
Amiableness of Manners
This Monument is erected
by
ISAAC ELTON the younger Esq
to SARAH his Wife
Daughter of Mr SAMUEL PEACH
Merchant of this City
who died universally
lamented
the 13th Dec 1763 In the 22d Year of her Age

In Memory also of the above named
ISAAC ELTON Esq
who departed this Life the 31st of March 1790
Aged 51

Arms Azure six Lions rampant Or VIGOR.

Near this Place lyeth the Body of
WILLIAM VIGOR of this Parish Gent
who died 26 day of Feb AD 1719
In the 60 Year of his Age
In Memory of whom his loving Wife FRANCES
hath erected this Monument
Also DOROTHY and FRANCES two of their Daughters
Also WILLIAM their Son who died 19 of June AD 1733
Aged 33 Years
FRANCES Wife of Wm VIGOR the elder died 4 day of Jany AD 1738
in the 77th Year of her Age
JOHN VIGOR of the Parish of St Mary Redcliff
in this City Gent Eldest son of the said
WILLIAM VIGOR the elder by FRANCES his Wife
He died 18th of March 1754
Aged 58 Years
Also ELIZABETH the Wife of the said JOHN VIGOR
she Died 21 day of Decr AD 1756 Aged 60 Years
WILLIAM son of the above JOHN VIGOR
Died 14th
of October 1777
Aged 56 Years

In Memory of
SAMUEL KENT
of this City Merchant
who departed this Life the
16 of August 1741
Aged 62
He was strictly Pious, remarkable
Upright, Punctual in His dealings,
Zealous in God, Sincere in
Friendship, & Cheerful in Conversation
whose death was greatly lamented
by all who knew Him

Arms per Pale Argent & Sable a Saltire
Counterchanged KENT

In Memory
of HENRY APTHORPE Esq.
of Boston in New England
Merchant
who died at the Hott Wells
July 10 1762
In the 25 Year if his Age

In Memory of
ANN the eldest Daughter of SAMUEL FOX
of this Parish Gent who Departed this Life 28 May
Anno Dom 1722 Aged 5 Years
& 7 Months
Near this Stone lies the said SAMUEL FOX who
departed this Life ye 14 day of Octr
Anno Dom 1727
in the 55 Year
of his Age

Sacred to the Memory of
THOMAS EVANS BULL
of this Parish Gent
eldest surviving Son
of the late JOHN BULL Esq
and MARY his Wife
who departed this Life the
9th day of November 1799
Aged 39 Years

Arms Gules an Escutcheon Argent, with an
Orle of Mullets Or, CHAMBERLAYNE
Impaling Azure a fleur de Lis Or & a
Canton Ermine CLARKE

In Memory of THOMAS ye Son
of THOMAS and MARY CHAMBERLAYNE
who died ye 10 of October
1731 Aged 22 Weeks
Also of THOMAS GUNTER their 3d
Son who died the 19th of
October 1735 Aged 9 Weeks
Also of EDWARD PYE their 2d
Son who died the 3d December
1741 Aged 8 Years & 7 Months
Also of MARY the Wife of
THOMAS CHAMBERLAYNE who
died the 17 of July 1747 In the
50 Year of her Age
Likewise of THOMAS CHAMBERLAYNE Esq
Husband to the said MARY
who died 28 of March 1749
Aged 57 Years

Arms Quarterly 1s 4th Argent a Lion
rampant Sable BARCROFT 2 Sable
three Lions passant in pale Argent
.... 3d Quarterly 1 & 4 Argent on
a saltire Gules a Cressant of the first GERARD
2 Sable a Lion rampant Argent crowned
Or ....3d Quarterly.......... within
a Border Azure charged with Plates

GILBERT BARCROFT
of this Parish
Apothecary son
of JOHN BARCROFT of Barcroft
Hall in Lancashire Esq By
CHARLOTTE his Wife daughter of
the Hon Sir GILBERT GERARD of
Brasserton Hall in the Nth Ride-
ing of Yorkshire Baronet and
Grand Daughter of the Right
Reverend Father in God
JOHN COSIN late Lord
Bishop of Durham, Erected
This Monument in memory of his two Children
buried underneath February 8th
1722
Also SARAH his Wife
died July ye 28 1744 Aged 59
Also DEBORA ye Wife of
GILBERT BARCROFT Junr 1746
Also GILBERT BARCROFT Junr 1752 Aged 31
Also GILBERT BARCROFT
Senior Aged 71

Arms Sable a Lion passant Argent TAYLOR
Hanc juxta Columnam
jacent reliquiae
JOHANNES TAYLOR nuper de hac
Parochia Generosi, et ELIZABETHAE
Uxoris hujus
File Obiitt 8 die Januarii 1677 AEtatis suae 50
Necnon ELIZABETHAE TAYLOR Uniqua corum
filiae quae obiit 14 die Maii 1728
AEtatis suae 55

FLAT STONES

On this Stone cut a Dog & Cross Bow
inscription round verge

Here lyeth the Body
of THOS PYTLEY Symtime Keper of
the Forest of ....
.. the last of October Anno Domini 1596

On a Brass let into the stone above

In Memory of EDWARD TRISSELL
of this Parish Gent who departed
this Life 12 March 1789 Aged 56

Arms Argent on a Chief Sable two Boars heads coupt
Argent TAYLOR Impaling ..... a Chevron
between three Griffins' heads erased

Crest a Fox statant Or

H.S.E.
JOSEPHUS TAYLOR AM Hujus Ecclesiae
per XII Annos Vicarius cum Duabus
Filiabus Infantibus Obiit XXVII
die Octobris Anno 1723 AEta XLVI
Also ANN TAYLOR here interred
Daughter of the above named JOSEPH
TAYLOR who was of a Virtuous disposition
died 2 of December 1747 Aged 29

Arms Per Chevron Argent & Azure three Mullets
counterchanged DAY Impaling Pally of
six Or & Gules on a Bend Sable three
Mullets Or ELTON

Crest

Hic jacet ELIZABETHAE Amibalis
Uxor PATRI DAY Armigeri Pia
filia ABRAHAMI ELTON Baronetti
Quae in ipso flore vitae decidit
morte immatura omnibus
praeterquam Sibi et deo Quam
in Spem immortalitatis
Religise Coluit obiit sexto die
November 1718 AEtat 26

Here lyeth the Body of Capt JAMES
SMITH of this Parish who departed
this Life 9 day of May 1720
ELIZABETH his Wife died 4 Jany 1717
ELIZABETH her Daughter died 6 Augt 1714
Also Mr JAMES SMITH the Elder
died the 24 day of October 1719
Also ELIZABETH Wife of Mr JACOB SMITH
who died 28 of Feb 1724 Aged 33
Years & 1 Month JACOB BAKER SMITH
died 11 Sept 1800 Aged 48 Years

Arms Argent on a Bend Azure three Dolphins
embowed Argent FRANCKLYN Impal
ing .... a Lion rampant between
six quarterfoils ... between two
flanches Ermine

Crest a Dolphin embowed

Here lyeth the Body of Mr RICHARD
FRANCKLYN of this City Merchant
who departed this Life 10 Jany AD
1711 AEt 60. MARY his Wife who departed this Life July 1 1719 Aged 54 Years
Also Mr PHILLIP FRANCKLYN brother
to ye above who departed this Life
the 3 of Nov A.D. 1710 AEt suae 53
Also the Body of WILLIAM FRANCKLYN
of this City Merchant who departed
this Life 29 Decr 1719 AEt 57
Mrs MARY FRANCKLYN sister of the
above said three Brothers who died
21 of May 1729 AEt 69

To the Memory of MARY the Wife
of Mr JEREMIAH HILL Merchant
of this Parish who departed this Life
the 24 day of January 1778 in the
55 Year of her Age

Here lyeth the Body of ELIZABETH CAPEL
who departed this Life the 21st of Octr
1749 Aged 49

Mr RICHARD NORTHCOTE of this Parish
Malster Departed this Life the 8th of
April 1800 Aged 75 Years

Here lyeth the Body of Mr ISAAC
ELTON of the Parish of St Stephen in
this City who departed this Life 23 of
October 1714 Aged 54 Years
Also 2 of their daughters both of which
were baptized MARY

In Memory of THOMAS CARY AM
Vicar of this Parish who departed this
Life the 30 day of Oct 1711 Aged 61
Also WILLIAM CARY AM son of the
above named THOMAS CARY who was
likewise Vicar of this Parish & departed
this Life 21 of Jany 1759 Aged 70
PENELOPE CARY Widow of the said
WILLIAM CARY who departed this Life
10 day of May 1760 Aged 70
PENELOPE CARY younger daughter of the
said WILLIAM & PENELOPE CARY who
departed this Life 14 day of July 1764
Aged 41

ANN CARY the elder daughter of the
said WILLIAM & PENELOPE CARY who
departed this Life the 2 of Sept 1795
Aged 76

Here lyeth the Body of Mr JAMES
HARRIS of this Parish who departed
this Life August 10 1700 Aged 63 Years
MARY his Wife died June 2 1701
Aged 71 Years
Also of Mr JAMES HARRIS their Son
who died Decr 23 1687 Aged 23 Years
MARY their Daughter died Decr 6
1688

Here lyeth the Body of ROBERT WHATLEY
of ye Castle Precincts Grocer died
August 9 1740 Aged 58 Years
Also four Children of EDWARD WHATLEY
of the Castle Precincts who died in
their Infancy
Also MARY SMITH of the said Precincts
who died the 17 of Jany 1770 Aged 70 Years
Also MARY the daughter of the said
EDWARD WHATLEY who died the 27 of
August 1776 Aged 20 Years
Also the said EDWARD WHATLEY Esq.
& one of the Aldermen of this City
who died 7 Nov 1779 in the 64
Year of his Age

Here lyeth the Body of Captn JOHN
WALKER of this Parish Merchant
who died 12 July 1722 Aged 63 Years
Also JAMES BOWYER & SARAH his Wife
are here interred with ten of their Children
Likewise MARY Widow of WILLIAM EDMOND
STOUNE Esq of Cambuswallace in Scotland
late Captain in the 27 Regiment who
died Decr 13 1781 Aged 59 Years

Here lyeth the Body of JOHN ARGIER
who departed this Life the 2 of July
1760 Aged 83 MARY his Wife
died .. of Jun: 1716 Aged ..

Here lyeth the Body of JOHN ROUSE
of this Parish who departed this Life
the 28 of August 1755 Aged 41 Years

THOMAS EVANS of this Parish Gent
died 12 March 1772 Aged 62
Also of MARY EVANS of this Parish
Widow of the above THOMAS EVANS
died 13 Nov 1791 Aged 79 Years
Also THOMAS EVANS BULL of this
Parish Gent grandson of the above
died 9 of Nov 1799 Aged 39

Here lyeth MARY the Wife of HENRY
TONGE of this Parish who departed
this Life the 6 of June 1717 Aged
33 Years also two daughters

Here lyeth JOHN NAYLOR of this
Parish Distiller who died July 2
1793 Aged 46 Years

Here lyeth the Body of HENRY MERRIT
Younger of this Parish Goldsmith
who departed this Life the 12 day of
June 169. In the 40 Year of his Age

Beneath lies Interred MARY PROVIN
died Decr 26 1748 AEt 62
JOHN PROVIN died 26 Decr 1748 AEt 64
JOHN WASHBORNE his Nephew died 16
March 1753 AEt 38
CHARLES COUPLAND died 31 Decr 1756
MARY COUPLAND died 1 April 1759 AEt 2
MARY WASHBORNE relict of JOHN WASHBORNE
died March 24 1768
MARY TAYLOR daughter of JOHN WASHBORNE
relict of CHARLES COUPLAND & Wife of WALTER
.... of the Parish of St Thomas within
the City who died 14 August 1780
Aged 44 Years
WALTER TAYLOR 1781

St MARY'S ISLE

ON MONUMENTS

Here lyeth the Body of HENRY MERRITT Esq
sometime Sherriff of this City an Inhabitant
of the out Parish, to the Poor of which He was
a Benefactor who departed this Life the 11th
of September Ano Dom. 1692
in the 71 Year of his Age

Arms Azure a Lion rampant & a semi of
roses Or WARREN Impaling Argent
three Battle Axes in fess Sable
Near this Monument
lyeth ye Body of THOMAS WARREN
Gent of this Parish, who departed
this Life ye 23 day of January
Anno Dom. 1722 Aged 68
And Also ye Body of
JANE WARREN eldest daughter of
THOMAS WARREN who departed
this Life ye 25 day of Decemr 1712
Aged 1 year
And Also ye Body of
THOMAS WARREN Junr Gent
who died July 3d 1736 Aged 22
Jesus Saith unto her
thy Brother shall Rise Again

Arms Or two Calves Gules cottised Or FOY
Impaling Sable a Lion rampant Argent
[ ] first Wife and Azure fretty
Argent on a fess Gules three Leopards
Faces Or CANN second Wife

To Him
whose Memory will be preserved to Posterity
for his Virtues
more durable than by the inscribed Marble
JOHN FOY Esq
Senior Alderman of this City also in the Commission of the Peace
for the Counties of Gloster & Somerset
Filial Piety, and tender Witnesses of his last Scene
have erected this Monument
To fill the Measures of his Worth, & say
he clos'd it like the Righteous Man
in Peace & Resignation
Jany 19 1771
NATHANIEL FOY EDGAR Esq his Grandson obiit 11 June following
ALEXANDER EDGAR Esq Commissinary of the Stores for the Royal Engineers Department
second Grandson of the aforenamed JOHN FOY Esq died at the Island of St Domingo
on June 22 1796 Aged 27 Years
ROBERT CANN EDGAR Lieutenant in the 57th
Regiment, who died in the West Indies August
7 1796 AEtatis 26

ON TWO ALTER TOMBS ON BRASS VERGE

Here under lieth Buried the Bodie of
MARY the first Wife of EDWARD COX Merchant who leaving this World entered into Eternall
life the 11 day of March Ano Dni 1620
Cor 15.19. If in this life only we have hope in Christ we are of all men most miserable

---

ON THE OTHER TOMB

Under this Stone is laid to rest the
Bodie of MARY the second Wife of EDWARD COX Merchant, who Lying downe this
Tabernacle attained immortalitie
October the 24 Ano Domini 1623 Christ both in Life and Death is advantage

---

OBLATE STONES

Here lyeth the Body of Liftinant
Corranell WILLIAM SHARDISH of
Vergenia who departed this materail
Life 21 day of November 1668 Aged
46 Years

NAVE

ON MONUMENTS

To the Memory of WILLIAM JAMES
of this Parish
who died Feb 5 1787
Aged 75
Also
ELIZABETH his Wife
who died Feb. 13 1798
Aged 78

In Memory of
JOHN JAMES of Shelwick
in the City of Hereford who died 12 Feb 1762
Aged 82 Years
Also of
The Revd EDWARD EVANS JAMES
son of WILLIAM and ELIZABETH JAMES
of this Parish who died 8 Jan 1771
Aged 23 Years
And three others of their Sons & three Daughters
who all died in their Infancy
also
of WILLIAM their Son
who died in the East Indies 1777
Aged 25 Years

FLAT STONES

In Memory of NATHANIEL Son of
JOHN & ANN GARNISTON who died
13 Oct 1747 Aged 18 Years
JOHN GARNISTON died 19 Jan. 1752
Aged 68 Years
ANN his Wife died 17 April 1754
Aged 52 Years
ROBERT son of ROBERT & SARAH GORDON
died 8 Sep 1759 Aged 11 Months
Also SARAH daughter of the said
ROBERT & SARAH GORDON who died
8 Feb 1774 Aged 12 Years
Also the said SARAH the Wife of
ROBERT GORDON who died 6 Augt 1777
Aged 45 Years

E. LAVERS died August 6 1795
Aged 36 Years
JANE WEBB died April 26 1798
Aged 63 Years

Here lyeth the Body of ELIZABETH
the Wife of WILLIAM CHILD who
died 3 Feby 1762 Aged 46 Years
Also WILLIAM CHILD Gent of the
Parish of St Augustines Glass
Manufactorer who died 30 Jany
1781 Aged 70 Years

Arms ... three fleur de Lis .. BIRCH
Crest a Fleur de Lis

Here lyeth the Body of
MARY the Wife of JAMES BIRCH
of this Parish who departed this
Life 5 March 1719 Aged 53

Sacred to the Memory of
MARY KINDON Wife of SAML: KINDON
who departed this Life 20 Octr 1779
Also of THOMAS KINDON son of the
aforesaid SAML & MARY KINDON who departed
this Life 15 June 1800 Aged 23 Years
Also of HESTER, GEORGE & HENRY KINDON
Children of the aforesaid SAML & ANN
KINDON his Wife who died in their
Infancy
Also of SAMUEL KINDON Husband of
the aforesaid ANN who departed this Life
13 Jany 1801 Aged 54 Years

In Memory of ELIZABETH the Wife
of JOHN WHITEWOOD who died 24 of
April 1754 Aged 54 Years
Also of the said JOHN WHITEWOOD who
died 7 Nov 1775 Aged 76 Years
Also MARY WHITEWOOD daughter
of the above JOHN & ELIZABETH WHITEWOOD
who died May 7 1797 Aged 59 Years

In Memory of MARY PASSEY who
died 21 Jany 1773 Aged 2 Years &
11 Months Also THOMAS PACKER
PASSEY who died 6 Decr 1776 Aged
8 Years – Also MARY PASSEY who
died 19 of Dec 1776 Aged 3 Years & 5 Months
Also THOMAS PASSEY father of the
above who died 18 June 1785
Aged 66 years
Also SAMUEL PASSEY son of the
above THOMAS PASSEY who died
21 Jany 1794 Aged 22 Years

NORTH AISLE

FLAT STONES

Here lyeth the Body of DANIEL BAYNTON
of this Parish (Surgeon) who died Augt
25 1755 in the 48 Year of his Age
Also PETER & HANNAH two of his Children
died
Pe: 12 Nov: } 1748 Aged { 8 Years
Ha: 30 Dec: } 1748 Aged { 3 Years

Also SARAH their daughter she died
28 June 1756 Aged 7 Years
Also MARY wife of the above said
DANIEL BAYNTON who departed this
Life the 4 of Feb 1761 Aged 53 Years

MARY the Wife of Doctor BAYNTON
1749
Also here lies the Body of WILLIAM
BAYNTON of this Parish (Surgeon)
who died 25 Feb 1775 Aged 57

Under this Stone is the Remains of
.... LURY many Years ....
of the Castle Precincts who departed
this Life the 7 of March 1789 Aged 51

Here lyeth the Body of SAMUEL HODGES
of this Parish of this Parish
Glass-bottle Maker who died August
15 1752 Aged 44 Years
HANNAH daughter of the above SAMUEL
HODGES who died August 12 1753
Aged 9 Years

Here lyeth the Body of THOMAS SMITH
son of WILLIAM & ELIZABETH SMITH of
Kingswinford in the County of Stafford
who departed this Life the 2d day of
July 1733 Aged 18 Years

SOUTH AISLE

ON MONUMENTS

NEAR
this Place
lyeth the Body of
MARGARET daughter of JOHN & MARGARET JAMES
of this Parish who died ye 14th
of Octr 1750 Aged 2 years
ALSO
JOHN son of the above died
the 13 of Octr 1753 Aged 4 years
ALSO
MARY daughter of the above died
17th May 1757 Aged 7 Years
ALSO
of MARGARET JAMES mother of the
above who died March the 8th 1776
Aged 58 Years
ALSO
of the said JOHN JAMES
Gent Husband of the above MARGARET JAMES
who died May the 17th 1778
Aged 63 Years

Arms Azure three Treefoils slipt Argent
on a Chief dancette Or three annulets
Gules BLAGDON Impaling Argent a
Chevron between three Griffins heads
erased Sable FOX

Crest a Lamb Trippant Argent

Sacred
to the Memory of
THOMAS BLAGDEN
of this City Esqr
and MARY his Wife

He was the second Son of
JOHN BLAGDEN of Nind in Wiltshire Esqr
by LYDIA NELMES his Wife
And died the 12th of May 1794
Aged 77 Years
She was one of the daughters of
SAMUEL FOX Gent of this Parish
And died the 1st of January 1792
Aged 72 Years

Arms Argent on a fess engrailed between three
Mullets Azure, an Anchor Or between
two Bezants GOMOND Impaling
Argent on a Chevron Azure between
three Lions rampant proper, an Anchor
Or between two Bezants OSWALD

Sacred to the Memory
of Mr SAMUEL OSWALD
of the Parish of St Stephens
in the City of Bristol, Soap Maker
who died the 15th March 1754 Aged 66 years
Also
EDMUND GOMOND Esq of the said Parish
of St Stephens Merchant
who died 19 February 1784 Aged 71 Years
And MARY his Wife
daughter of the aforesaid JAMES & SARAH OSWALD
who died 2d March 1782 Aged 66 years
Also
six of their Children Viz

				Yrs	Mons
SARAH GOMOND who died	5th Decemr	1741	Aged	0.	7
ELIZABETH ———————	30 Decem	1744	——	0.	10
JAMES —————————	11 July	1748	——	6.	0
ELIZABETH ———————	24 June	1752	——	0.	6
SARAH —————————	30 April	1753	——	4.	7
MARY —————————	31 March	1765	——	18.	2

Sacred to the Memory of ANN
Wife of RICHARD NELMES Esq
of the City of BRISTOL
and only daughter of THOMAS BLAGDEN Esq
who departed this Life
16th December 1789
Aged 33 Years

Arms Or three Oak Trees eradicated at
the roots proper NELMES Impaling
BLAGDEN as before

FLAT STONES

In Memory of HESTER Wife of
JAMES GULLEY of the Castle Precincts
who died 9 Decr 1737 Aged 34
Also of GRACE the Wife of THOMAS GUEST
of the out Parish of St Phillip & Jacob
who died August 9 1738 Aged 74 Years
Also of the said THOMAS GUEST who
died 14 of Feb 1740 Aged 68 Years
Also the said JAMES GULLEY who
[died] the 10 of Feby 1775 Aged 76 years
And of one Son & two Daughters of
the said JAMES & ESTHER GULLEY who
died in their Infancy

CHURCH YARD

ON A MONUMENT AGAINST NORTH WALL

Under this Place lyeth the Body
of ELIZABETH, RICHARD, MARY, JOHN
Sons & daughters of THOMAS
HEAD of the Castle Precintes
Freemason, JOHN died May 3 1687
Also MARGARET CROOM my Sister
September 27 1662

TOMBS

Here lyeth the Body of NICHOLAS
HIERON of this Parish who dep-
arted this Life 26 day of June
1697 Aged .. Years
SARAH his Wife who departed this
Life 21 of April 1710 Aged 78
In this Vault resteth NICHOLAS HIERON
of this Parish who died June 26 1697
AEt 65 SARAH his Wife who died
April 21 1713 AEt 78 SAMUEL son
of NICHOLAS & SARAH HIERON who died
unmarried Jany 4 1726 AEt 68
NICHOLAS second Son NICHOLAS & SARAH
HIERON who died unmarried Feby
27 1749 AEt 78 ELIZABETH daughter
of NICHOLAS & SARAH HIERON who died
unmarried June 25 1696 AEt 34
MARGARET daughter of NICHOLAS &
SARAH HIERON & Wife of JOSEPH LUFFE
who died August 5 1724 AEt 56
SARAH daughter of NICHOLAS & SARAH
HIERON & Wife of JOHN REDDISH who
died Decr 29 1745 AEt 81

SAMUEL Son of JOHN & SARAH REDDISH
who died Oct 9 1742 AEt 53 – SARAH
Wife of JAMES SHARPELL & daughter
of NICHOLAS REDDISH second Son of
JOHN & SARAH REDDISH who died Oct
10 1791 AEt 71

In Memory of PETER ROYNON of
this Parish who departed this Life
10 of May 1750 in the 67 Year of his Age
Also four Grand Children Sons &
Daughters of GEORGE & HANNAH LEWIS
Mariner

SARAH		(NB		17	
GEORGE	}	blank on	{	1	} Months
ELIZABETH		the Stone)		7	
JOHN				..	

ANN LEWIS died Jany 15 1766 Aged 19 Years
GEORGE LEWIS died 9 of Sept 1766 Aged .. Years
Also MARY ROYNON who departed this
Life July 4 1768 Aged 75 Years

To the Memory of five Children of
JOHN & ANN DUNN of this Parish
BETTY GIBSON DUNN their Daughter
died 23 Feby 1778 Aged 2 Years & 7 Weeks
BETTY GIBSON DUNN their Daughter
died 1 August 1781 Aged 2 Years & 6 Months
WILLIAM DUNN their Son died in June
1789 Aged 4 years & 6 Months
THOMAS DUNN their Son died 1 June
1798 Aged 11 years & 6 Months
JOHN DUNN their Son died 18 Jany
1801 in the 20 Year of his Age
JOHANNA HOWSE Mother of the above
ANN DUNN died 16 Nov 1800 Aged 76

In Memory of EDWARD TRISSSELL
of this Parish who departed this
Life the 16 of November 1741
in the 42 Year of his Age
Also three of their Children that
died in their Infancy

In Memory of ANN
Daughter of JAMES & MARY SIMMOND
of the out Parish of St Phillip & Jacob
who Departed this Life Decr 12 1767
Aged two Months
Also the above JAMES SIMMONS
who departed this Life Decr 2 1772
in the 39 Year of his Age

Also JAMES Son of JAMES SIMMONS
who died 7 August 1784 Aged 20 Years
Also MARY wife of the first mentioned
JAMES SIMMONDS who died the 14
Sept 1784 Aged 46 Years

Here lyeth MARY the Daughter
of JOHN & ELIZABETH TEAGUE who
died the 27 of May 1767 Aged 79 Years
JOHN Son of JOHN TEAGUE Senr
Aged 6 Years He died 15 Sept 1769
ELIZABETH Wife of ..... TEAGUE
obiit 2 Feb 1768 Aged 57 Years

In Memory of JOHN Son of JOHN
& ELIZABETH PIDDING who died 22
of Feby 171. ELIZABETH Wife of
THOMAS PIDDING died 8 July 1734
THOMAS PIDDING died 9 Oct 1744
JOSHUA ROBOTHAM died 21 May 1763
Aged 46

Here lyeth the Body of JOHN
WOOD of the Castle Precints
who departed this Life the 4 of
Novr 1763 in the 69 Year of his Age
ANN his Wife who departed this
Life Octr 14 1737 Aged 34 years
MARY his second Wife with two
of their Children who died ye 10 of
April 1752 in the 50 Year of her Age
Also THOMAS Son of the said JOHN
WOOD who departed this Life 12 of
June 1764 Aged 29 Years

Here lyeth the Body of WILLIAM
JAMES who departed this Life
10 of July 1770 Aged 17 Years
WILLIAM JAMES born 12 Decr 1781
died 2 April 1783
Also of four Sons & four Daughters
of SAMUEL & MARY JAMES who
died in their Infancy
MARY Wife of SAMUEL JAMES
who died 10 of March 1779
Aged 46 Years

In Memory of THOMAS LEWIS
who died 25 of April 1782 Aged 68 years

MARY his Wife died 20 of March
1797 Aged 84 Years
BENJAMIN Son of the above died
21 of April 1791 Aged 34 Years

In Memory of ELIZABETH the
Wife of JOHN TOMLINSON who
died the 1st of August 1765
Aged 53 Years

ON FLAT & HEAD STONES

	Died		Aged
Ellis Payne Glass Maker of this Parish	16 Nov	1782	39
Elizabeth Martin of this Parish	16 Oct	1779	60
William Long of the Out Parish of St Phillip & Jacob	11 Mar	1799	74
Ann his Wife	15 Dec	1797	76
Daniel Broome	.. July	1734	2
Hester Whatley	31 Oct	1745	54
Thomas Whatley	9 Dec	1749	74
Hester Broome Grand daughter of the above Daniel &			
Hester Broome	12 Oct	1762	17
Thomas Broome their Son	1 March	1766	32
Also three of their Children			
Francis Broome daughter of the above Daniel & Hester			
Broome	3 Jany	1771	60
Hannah daughter of William & Sarah Tyler	9 Jan	1793	20
Richard Mathews of the out Parish	12 Dec	1727	40
Alexander Pinney of Castle Precincts Mariner	26 Feb	1727	48
John & Esther son & daughter of Alexander & Mary Pinney			
Esther	10 May	1608	12 [sic]
John	6 Jan	1716	10
Richard Gills of this Parish	10 May	1762	–
John Short	3 Dec	1785	65
Ann Lowder grand daughter of the above John Short	3 Oct	1796	26
Thomas Edwards Lowder son of William & Ann Lowder	26 Sept	1796	1 & 9 Months
Diana Nichols	15 Nov	1796	80
Sarah Wife of Edward Jones of this Parish Export			
[Supervisor?]	24 Feb	1790	48
David Jones	14 July	1796	50
Ebenezer Barnett	13 Nov	1775	56
Elizabeth his Wife	15 Feb	1775	75
John Woodward	17 Nov	1788	53
Sarah sister to the above John Woodward	16 July	1795	69
Earl Pearce of this Parish Potter	28 May	1795	51
Thomas Bird	28 Nov	1787	42
Richard his Son	11 Sept	1796	15
Ann Wife of James Thomas & relict of the aforesaid Thomas			
Bird	14 Augt	1799	57
John Webb of this Parish	21 July	1789	54
John Webb Son of John & Mary Webb	23 July	1790	27
Likewise three of their Children who died in their Infancy			
Mary Williams	24 June	1794	35
Francis Walker of this Parish	20 April	1787	66

	Died		Aged
Elizabeth Wife of Thomas Mason of this Parish	17 July	1775	44
Elizabeth Stephens		1783	1 & 9 Months
Sarah Widow of William Green	12 July	1793	76
John Bentenshaw of Denton in Lancashire	3 Sept	1781	46
Joseph Neal		1780	70
M. Fletcher		1781	6
Mary Wife of William Birte House Carpenter of the out Parish of St Phillip & Jacob	29 Mar	1750	40
Richard Brown		1769	28
Mary Birte		1769	29
Sarah Fry		1772	28
Thomas Birte		1776	33
William Birte	16 Jan	1783	72 & 9 Mths
Stephen Lambert late Supervisor of Excise in this County	14 Augt	1783	58
Elizabeth Wife of Nathaniel Radmore Officer of Excise	15 May	1782	26
William Son of Thomas & Ann Pole of the Parish of St Nicholas	6 Mar	1782	–
John Curtis Grocer	25 Feb	1710	61
Sarah his Wife	6 Jan	1732	82
Mary, Joseph, Elizabeth & Catherine Fargus they died in their Infancy Sons & daughters of John & Ann Fargus of the Castle Precincts			
Margaret daughter of John & Ann Fargus died in her Infancy			
John William Conney grandson to the said John & Ann Fargus	6 Feb	1798	2 & 1/2
William Son of Sampson & Sarah Avard	7 May	1791	5 Months
Thomas Avard	16 Sept	1794	2
Benjamin Dyer of this Parish	10 March	1792	50
John Evans of this Parish	12 Jan	1787	49
Catherine Evans Mother of the above	12 Oct	1788	88
Jenny Wife of John Crane of this Parish	10 Sept	1788	22
Jane Wife of Richard Parsons of this Parish	14 April	1772	44
Rachel second Wife of Richard Parsons	26 Sept	1787	54
Thomas Ferris of this Parish	20 Jany	1792	51
Joanna the daughter of William & Joanna Curtis of the Parish of St Nicholas	23 March	1777	4 & 3 Months
Abraham Page of this Parish Shalloon & Stuff Maker	13 May	1733	33
William Sheppard	5 Augt	1787	52
Mary Davis	12 Augt	1789	32
John Son of John & Sarah Hopkins of this Parish	22 Feb	1757	2
Hannah their daughter	6 Augt	1759	2 & 4 Months
John Holliday	13 June	1800	67
Richard Jones of this Parish Gent	19 June	1800	62
Methusalem Rice many Years an Officer of Excise within this City	10 April	1787	47
Mary daughter of Joseph & Mary Cox of this City Butcher	7 June	1786	21
John Child	25 Sept	1790	74
Richard Child his Son	29 March	1791	48
Henry Powell of this Parish Copper Refiner	19 April	1745	59
Sarah Crinks grand daughter of Henry Fowler	30 Dec	1748	4 & 4 Months
Samuel Powell Copper Refiner son of Henry Powell	10 Jany	1753	28
Sarah Wife of Henry Powell	19 April	1770	81
Ann Crinks of Crewshole in the Parish of St George	5 Jany	1793	73
John Lewis	10 Oct	1790	37

	Died	Aged
Kitty daughter of the above John Lewis	19 July 1791	2 & 9 Months
Elizabeth Lewis Sister of the aforesaid John Lewis	7 Dec 1791	31
Margaret relict of John Reilly Sugar Refiner of this Parish	21 April 1795	50
Hannah Wife of Thomas Hardwick of this Parish }	26 Feb 1778	47
The above Thomas Hardwick	13 May 1778	35
Sarah daughter of Isaac & Eleanor Newton of this Parish	30 April 1800	5
Susanna Wife of George Gwinnett of this Parish	25 Jany 1794	65
Thomas Sandell	31 Jany 1795	81
Martha his Wife	22 Dec 1766	46
Sarah Robbins of this Parish Widow	22 May 1771	70
Miss Margaret Kimpland her Daughter	13 March 1795	60
Thomas Rookeby Esq of Arthingworth in Northamptomshire who died at Clifton	7 Sept 1796	73
John Stephens	31 March 1796	48
Mary-Ann Stokes	30 April 1790	29
Thomas Cooper	11 April 1794	31
Elizabeth Payne	18 May 1789	60
Henry Payne Glass Maker & Husband of the above	21 July 1792	63
Sydenham Osborne	24 June 1791	45
John Tomlinson of this Parish Malster	22 Nov 1785	72
John Carter Malster	21 Dec 1779	62
Mary his Wife	3 Jany 1780	63
Nathaniel Arthur Carter their Son	in 1759	–
Thomas Son of Thomas & Ann Rawlings of this Parish	16 Sept 1796	18
Thomas Evans of the out Parish of St Phillip & Jacob Tyler & Painter	15 Jan 1794	40
Sarah Garland of North Nibley in the County of Gloucester widow	3 May 1784	78
Thomas Williams of the out Parish of St Phillip & Jacob	5 March 1757	45
Sarah Wife of Ralph Hopkins of this Parish	7 Feb 1801	44
Giles Bennett of this Parish	4 Oct 1799	49
Ann his Wife	15 March 1797	45
Mary Moore wife of Joseph Moore Pump Maker	in 1794	47
Joseph Pendry	4 June 1759	–
Ann daughter of William & Ann Ball of St Phillip & Jacob	10 June 1786	4
Mary Ann Ball	25 April 1792	5
George Ball	7 May 1793	4
Lydia daughter of Thomas & Mary Nutt of this Parish Butcher	19 July 1778	2
Mary their daughter	6 May 1781	4
Ann Nutt above mentioned	7 March 1794	54
Richard Handford Brick Maker of this Parish but late of Temple Parish	24 Oct 1799	73
Robert White	22 Decr 1749	35
Mary Rumley of this Parish	5 March 1740	57
Edward Rumley of this Parish	27 Jan 1760	72
five Children of Henry & Mary Bowen died in their Infancy Also the above Henry Bowen of the Parish of Christ Church Haberdasher	30 May 1765	50
Alice Savage	3 June 1788	–
Thomas son of Evans & Ann Watkins	10 Decr 1785	13
George Leare, Gardner	26 April 1789	48
Ann his daughter by Ann his Wife	12 Decr 1787	22
Thomas Murch	8 July 1792	48
Jane his daughter by Ann his Wife	6 Decr 1784	2

	Died		Aged
Mary Wife of John Parkinson	25 April	1799	37
Ann Whiting Wife of Thomas Whiting of this Parish	1 Jany	1795	38
Also two of their Children Thomas Whiting Aged 2 years & Mary Ann Whiting Aged 4 years			
James Fagg	2 May	1746	44
Hester his Wife late Wife of Francis Dutiland	2 July	1765	63
James Fagg their Son	3 May	1745	10
Ann daughter of the said James & Esther Fagg Wife of Thomas Lidiard	7 March	1762	51
Ann Fagg Lidiard their daughter in her infancy	in 1761		
John Whitford of this Parish Baker	25 Nov	1797	59
Charles Morgan of this Parish	30 April	1774	38
Ann his daughter died in her infancy			
{John Pickett, Charles Collings, Jacob			
{Marman and Nicholas Blackborn	7 March	1772	72
Mr John Stansbury one of the recruiting Officers of the Honble East India Company & many Years Serjant Major of his Majesty's 34 Regt who discharged himself by his good behavior up the Streights of France the West Indies and North America	26 April	1790	58
Elizabeth his Wife	7 March	1794	56
Hannah Room of Birmingham	25 July	178.	70
William Gotley of this Parish Butcher	20 June	1773	33
St John Allen Britte Gotley son of William & Elizabeth Gotley	28 June	1775	3 & 7 Months
Albena Meriah Gotley their daughter	5 June	1779	9
Robert Jacob	21 June	1693	44
Joan His Wife	10 Oct	1713	65
Henry Hine	2 Dec	1765	53
Alice his Wife	29 April	1756	54
Job Flook	2 Nov	1800	29
Joseph Phippen	1 Decr	1748	50
Edward Jecock	12 June	1778	54
Ann his Wife	9 April	1761	46
Sarah Duffett	14 March	1794	38
William Pool	9 Jan	1778	60
John Attwood	29 Augt	1778	60
Joseph Short	21 Decr	1773	26
Mary Wife of William Shute	27 Janr	1747	53
Ann Paglor	30 April	1799	61
Thomas Cook	12 Oct	1755	60
Thomas Booth	20 Oct	1783	37
Francis Callan	15 Sept	1790	28
John Kidson	2 Sept	1781	66
Thomas Core	8 Jany	1792	53
Elizabeth Wife of Con: Bowen	12 Jany	1738	55
Thomas Holloway	29 July	1765	30
Daniel Holloway	25 Nov	1784	21
Joseph Holloway	16 March	1785	33
Betty Wife of John Beaven	18 Oct	1768	32
Betty Law their daughter	5 Oct	1792	30
Arthur Dart	19 May	1762	68
Mary his Wife	5 Oct	1739	39
John Atcherley	11 July	1777	52
William Roach	26 Feb	1782	57

	Died	Aged
John Hooper	22 April 1779	26
William Hope	6 Decr 1767	37
Robert Butt	3 April 1765	63
Elizabeth his Wife	11 Decr 1753	63
Robert Prichard	14 Oct 1772	19
Thomas Purner	11 Augt 1764	54

ST GEORGES

T his is a newly erected Parish, it was formerly part of the out Parish of St Phillip & Jacob, in the City of Bristol (a perticular Account may be seen in Mr Rudders History of Gloucester). The Church is very neat plain building seventy feet long by sixty broad, it consists of a Chancel Nave & two aisles, supported by two rows of free Stone pillars, the Chancel is very small with a Venetian Window over the communion table, at the West end is a large square Tower, seventy two feet high containing two bells.

INSCRIPTIONS IN THE CHURCH

In the Chancel on the North side of the East end is the following table

BENEFACTIONS

1756
The Right Revd JOSEPH BUTLER
late Lord Bishop of Bristol gave
Lands in fee to the amount of 400 pounds towards the endowment of the Vicarage and to the
Vicar thereof and his Succeessors
forever. He was the first that recommended the building this Church
and obtained the Act of Parliament
for separating and dividing the
Parish of Saint George from that of
Saint Phillip and Jacob and greatly pro-
moted that pius undertaking but
died before the completion thereof
THOMAS CHESTER Esqr Knight
of the shire of the County of Glocester and Lord of this Manor was
likewise a great promoter of this
pious undertaking and gave towards
augmenting the Vicarage several Lands in fee
to the amount of
four hundred pounds and upwards
and on part thereof this Church and
the Vicarage house have since
been erected by the generous Contributions
of Sundry other well disposed
Christians
The porch and the North and South
entrance of this Church was the gift of
Mr MOSES UNDERWOOD of
this Parish Gent 1788

CHANCEL

FLAT STONES

In Memory of JUDITH Wife of
JOHN WALTON of this Parish
who entered into the Joy of her Lord
the 16 November 1793 Aged 59 Years
ALSO
of Mr JOHN FRANCIS WALTON
Sinner saved by the Merit
of the adorable JESUS who entered
into Glory 19 March 1794
Aged 53 Years
Wak'd by the Trumpet sound I from my Grave shall rise
Behold the Judge with glory Crown'd and see the flaming skies

---

In
Memory
of SARAH the Wife of DANIEL CRIBB who died
the 5th of December 1756
Aged 38 Years
Also
MARY his second Wife
who departed this Life
the 5th of March
1768 Aged 32 Years

Here lieth the Body of
GEORGE MARTIN of the Parish
of St Philip and Jacob in the
County of Gloucester, who died
the 20th of February 1800
Aged 59 Years

NAVE

FLAT STONES

In Memory of
NATHANIEL HODGKINS
of this Parish
who departed
this Life
August 2d 1793
Aged 48 Years

In Memory of
CHARLES POWELL
who departed
this Life
Novr 13 1792
Aged 82 Years

In Memory of JOHN
Son of
MOSES UNDERWOOD
of this Parish Gent
by REBECKER his Wife who
died Feby 16 1773 Aged 17 Years
Also the Body of Mrs
REBECKER UNDERWOOD of this Parish Wife of
MOSES UNDERWOOD, Gent
who departed this Life the
18th July 1783 Aged 61 Years
Likewise the above
MOSES UNDERWOOD, Gent
who died the 19th Decr 1795
Aged 75 Years
Also THOMAS UNDERWOOD, Gent son of the
said MOSES UNDERWOOD, who died the
16 Novr 1801. Aged 41 Years
And MATTHEW
Son of the said Mrs UNDERWOOD who died
the 3d April 1802 Aged 48 Years

In
Memory of JAMES SEVEIR
Son of JAMES & HANNAH
SEVEIR who died 11 of January
1780 Aged 8 Months
Also ANN their Daughter
Ob. 17 Nov 1788 AEt 7 Years, 3 Months
Also
HANNAH the Wife of
JAMES SEVEIR Obt Oct 19 1789
AEt 37
Also ANN FORD SEVEIR Daughter
of JAMES & ANN MUNSLY SEVEIR
Obt 4th Jan 1792 Aged 16 days
Also FREDERICK their Son
Obt 5 Jany 1800
Aged 14 Weeks

THOMAS WILLIS 1765
ELIZABETH WILLIS died 22 Augt
1789 Aged 82

In Memory of
REBECCA Daughter of
WILLIAM and GODSALL WEBB
Obt 7 July 1759 Aged 7 Months
Also REBECCA another Daughter
Obt 8 Nov 1760 Aged 4 Months
Also REBECCA Wife of
JOHN GORE Obt 12 Feb 1767
Aged 57 Years

Also JOHN GORE Gent
Obt 11 Decr 1778 AEt 84

GODSALL WEBB }
ELIZABETH WEBB } July 5 1784

.... TURNER Obt 2d July 1793
Aged 31 Years

HONNA COMER 1752

In Memory
of GEORGE PULLIN of
The City of Bristol
Breeches Maker who de-
parted this Life August
7th 1757 Aged 52 Years
being the first man buri-
ed in this Church
Also in Memory of
CHARLES WILCOX, Gent
who died 19 April 1788
Aged 49 Years
Also PENELOPE Wife of
the Said CHARLES WILCOX
who died 21st of January 1798
Aged 59 Years
Also ELIZABETH PULLIN
Wife of the aforesaid
GEORGE PULLIN who
died the 22d of November 1801
Aged 93 Years

NORTH AISLE

ON MONUMENTS

Near this place lieth the Body of
HONORA the Wife of WILLIAM CORNER
Officer of the Excise, and Daughter of
JOHN TOOKER Esqre of Chilcompton in
the County of Somerset, who departed
this Life the 22d day of November 1759
Aged 33

Sacred
to the Memory of
GODSALL Wife of WILLIAM WEBB
of this Parish
who died July 23d 1784
Aged 22 Years

Lifes tender blossom hastens to decay
Swift to its Goal ye winged moments flies
To mortals cries all nature Come away
And seek a happiness above the Skies?
The wise obey and in a Saviours breast
from sin and sorrow find eternal rest.

To the Memory of
THOMAS WILLIS of this Parish, Gent
and one of the Commissioners appointed by Act
of Parliament for building this Church
who died Sept.1st 1765. Aged 67 Years.
O Death
who can escape thy Shaft?
But Oh through Grace
How Pointless
By the resurrection of Jesus Christ
How wellcome are those to the faithfull
Who
Having received the first fruits of the Spirit
Groan to be delivered
From the bondage of Corruption
Into the Glorious Liberty
Of the Children of God

SOUTH AISLE

ON A MARBLE TABLET

Spe beatae immortalitatis
Infra jacet Sepulta
CHRISTIANA uxor
JOHANNIS ARMITSTEAD
De Ingleton in agro Eboracensi
Obiit Oct 24 A.D. 1772. AEtat 54
Here vita incerta est lathi nil certias hora
Atque omnes quando venerit illa latit
[ ]ors invenes rapit atque senes discrimini nullo
et redit in cinerem quod fuit ante cinis
Spiritus aeternos manet aeternumque manebit
Et Christi Auspicis Surgit ad astra Dei.

ON A FLAT STONE

In Memory of
MARY CHAPMAN Wife of
ROBERT CHAPMAN
who died 6th Augt 1770
Aged 39 Years
Also ELIZABETH her Daughter
who died Jany 2d 1771 Aged 11 Years & 6 Months
Also JOHN the Son of
MARY CHAPMAN who died Nov 27th 1771
Aged 4 Years

Also MARY her Daughter who
died the 17th of May 1784 Aged 14 years
Also ROBERT CHAPMAN
who died April 13th 1803 Aged 74 Years

CHURCH YARD

No Tombs

ON HEAD STONES

	Died			Aged
James Alcott of the Parish of St Philip & Jacob Gent	1	Sep	1778	63
Also Ann Webber his Neice	21	Aug	1793	14
Isaac Phipps of this Parish	1	Sep	1792	63
Mary his Wife	10	Mar	1798	64
Edward Lacy of this Parish	28	Mar	1782	68
Sarah his Wife	27	Sept	1801	82
Hannah Wife of Edward Lacy Junr	11	Mar	1786	33
Also the above Edward Lacy Junr	27	Jan	1787	34
Mrs Elizabeth Concannen Wife of Mr George Concannen of Bristol	17	July	1796	21
The above George Concannen	17	July	1798	29
Betty Wife of George Harding	16	Aug	1788	35
Thomas their [Son] died in his Infancy				
Joseph Roach	24	June	1774	..
Sarah Wife of Samuel Crinks & daughter of the said Joseph Roach	25	June	1778	18
Susannah Daughter of Samuel & Ann Bryant of this Parish	1	March	1769	2
Thomas their Son	15	Nov	1774	11
Ann Wife of the said Samuel Bryant	3	June	1801	68
John Son of Samuel Bryant Junr & Mary his Wife	11	Ap	1788	2
James their Son	2	Mar	1801	10
William Son of Thomas & Priscilla Lyons of the Parish of Compton Dando in Somerset	16	Feb	1771	7
Martha their daughter an Infant	2	Sept	1765	
Priscilla Lyons their Mother	9	Mar	1789	52
Edward Hawkins Senr of this Parish	27	Oct	1761	54
Betty Daughter of Robert & Hannah Milsom of this Parish	16	Sep	1751	22
Robert Millsom of this Parish	23	June	1767	64
Also Hannah his Wife	20	June	1769	63
Thomas Nicholas	17	Feb	1764	17
Mrs Martha Balland of Bristol Widow	31	Dec	1780	84
Ann Wife of Henry Davis of Bristol Linen Draper & youngest daughter of Richard Hart late of Hannam Esq	8	Feb	1760	31
Edward Greenaway of this Parish	26	Jany	1778	68
John Dearlin late of Chichester Sussex	31	Dec	1767	75
Mary Wife of Simon Briton of this Parish	25	July	1788	38
Also their Daughter Elizabeth an Infant	27	April	1788	–
Alice Stephens Widow	19	Nov	1787	66
Evan Daniel	12	Mar	1791	91
James Burgess of this Parish	10	Feb	1793	90
Martha his Wife	8	Ap	1792	74
Charlotte Wife of Richard Henderson	20	Dec	1775	53
John Henderson B.A. of Pembroke Coll: Ox.	2	Nov	1788	31
Richard the Father of John Henderson	14	Feb	1792	55

Mary Wife of John Avery of this Parish	3 May	1778	30
Henry Luton of this Parish	21 Jany	1792	41
Elizabeth daughter of Stephen & Martha Flook of this Parish	5 Jany	1790	20
Thomas Lyne of this Parish	5 June	1772	25
John Hewson of Snape in the County of York	19 Jany	1775	65
Elizabeth Dove	21 Nov	1777	45
John Southcote of the City of Bristol	3 July	1777	38
Six Children of Samuel & Betty Edwards of the City of Bristol died in their Infancy			
Also the above Betty Edwards	1 June	1783	43
Also Samuel Edwards	10 Feb	1790	47
Samuel Sweet	29 Aug	1801	46
Elizabeth Jesse Widow of this Parish	20 Jany	1779	84
George Burley of this Parish	7 April	1790	49
Ann his Daughter	7 June	1792	19
William Church	19 Jan	1784	68
James Harding of this Parish School Master	24 June	1784	78
Ann his Wife	26 Decr	1787	81
Henry their Son	29 Ap	1803	67
Martha Daughter of Edward & Ann Jones of this Parish	16 May	1785	4
The above Edward Jones	20 Oct	1787	47
George their Son	29 Ap	1788	2
Thomas Palmer of this Parish Engineer	1 Aug	1800	40
Samuel Cotton	19 Aug	1801	66
William Turser	4 Mar	1801	–
Elizabeth Kittlee	9 Mar	1798	69
Susannah Andress	15 Apr	1787	40
James Collier Sheriden of this Parish	20 Dec	1800	29
Elizabeth Daughter of Benjamin & Betty Woodward of this Parish	6 Aug	1790	24
John Hodges Glass Maker of this Parish	1 Jan	1762	77
Frances his Second Wife	5 June	1762	70
John Powell of this Parish Cooper	16 Aug	1773	36
Samuel Crinks of this Parish	20 Apr	1798	43
Francis the Son of Daniel & Ann Haskins	4 Mar	1772	22
Henry Fox of this Parish	21 Oct	1799	61
Thomas Jones of this Parish	5 Jan	1773	40
Mary Wife of Richard Hayes of this Parish Gardiner	11 Aug	1786	33
The said Richard Hayes	23 Apr	1798	65
Thomas Lawley of this Parish	17 Apr	1782	38
Joseph Brian of this Parish	30 June	1790	58
Susannah his Wife	24 June	1790	52
John Living of this Parish	23 July	1765	66
John Hicks	25 Apr	1786	60
William Kitley of this Parish	30 Oct	1765	40
Sarah his Daughter & Wife of Samuel Britten	29 Augt	1777	24
Charles Greenway of this Parish	9 June	1795	74
Robert Parsons of this Parish	19 Oct	1788	79
Ann his Wife	28 Nov	1784	85
John Tyler, of this Parish	28 Aug	1792	31
Dennis Bryant of this Parish	5 Jany	1795	40
David Davis	22 Feb	1763	61
David Son of Nicholas & Deboriah Davis of this Parish	5 July	1789	23
Hannah Wife of Joseph Pratten	2 Sep	1758	34
Sarah their Daughter	17 Jan	1764	18

	Died		Aged
Thomas Willis of this Parish	20 Nov	1770	71
Charity 2d Wife of Thomas Willes	28 June	1772	85
Jonathan Smith of this Parish	26 June	1757	40
Edward Clements of this Parish	3 Oct	1771	46
Ann daughter of Edward Spiring	29 May	1798	39
Hannah Wife of Stephen Brain of this Parish	16 May	1786	22
Dennis Rogers of this Parish	14 Jany	1766	36
Elizabeth Daughter of Philip & Mary Walker of this Parish	10 Jany	1770	10
Mary Wife of Philip Walker	24 June	1785	49
William Buckney	26 Jan	1765	52
Elizabeth Wife of Henry Roach	7 Sep	1787	58
Henry Roach of this Parish	28 Mar	1789	70
John Roach of this Parish	9 Aug	1780	74
Jane Wife of William Baynes of Hanham	19 May	1768	36
Sarah Daughter of Thomas & Mary Phipps of this Parish	18 Mar	1763	23
John Ford Junr Son of John Ford Senr & Catherine his Wife	11 Oct	1766	19
Elizabeth Wife of Robert Jenkins of this Parish	1 May	1768	73
Edward Tyler of this Parish	2 April	1781	48
Mary Wife of Edward Burgiss	22 Decr	1800	69
John Tyler of this Parish	12 May	1757	56
Hannah Wife of John Tyler	20 Sept	1759	52
Giles Smith of this Parish	27 Nov	1797	65
Giles his Son	21 Oct	1783	28
Mary Daughter of Daniel & Sarah Smith	19 May	1761	21
William Ford of this Parish Yeoman	8 Jan	1781	53
Joseph Jarvis of this Parish	20 Oct	1759	39
James Waters of this Parish	25 Dec	1791	37
Hannah Widow of Thomas Smith of this Parish	12 Dec	1766	84
Henry Crook of this Parish	11 Nov	1765	58
Mary his Wife	5 June	1763	47
Samuel Easterbrook of this Parish	21 June	1795	37
William Easterbrook	29 Mar	1766	34
Rachel relict of the above William Easterbrook late Widow of Daniel Smith	15 Dec	1787	35
James Taylor	14 June	1794	27
Joseph Willis of this Parish	24 Oct	1771	60
Henry Pearce of this Parish Blacksmith	25 Jany	1792	70
Jane his Wife	28 Sept	1796	95

INDEX OF PERSONS

* An asterisk indicates that the page has more than one reference.

Ab Eyck, John, 325 n
Abarrow, Eliz., 1251, 1255; Sir Wm., kt., 1251
Abbadeston, John de, 1086
Abbenhall (Abbenhalle), Ralph de, 244; fam., 462, 469
Abbington, *see* Abington
Abbott (Abbot, Abbits), Ann., 847; Edith, 847; Eliz., 677; Rev. Hen., 674, 675*, 677, 829, 886; Rev. John, 1494; Mary, 296, 398, 675; Sam., 847*; Rev., 1379
Abel (Abell, Able), Anne, 1376; Comfort, 1484; Eleanor, 1484; Jane, 1484*; John, 976*, 1378, 1484*; Mary, 1484; Sarah, 976; Thos., 1484; Wm., 1376, 1484*, 1485
Abercorn, Jas., earl of, 740
Abergavenny [*peerage*](Bergavenny), Anne, Lady, 520; Nevil, Lord, 1378; Lord, 520; *and see* Beauchamp, *passim*; Neville, E.
Abington (Abbington, Abyngton, Habington), Ant., 502, 505; Eliz., 505, 1256; John, 502; Nic., 502; Ric., 502; fam., 753
Able, *see* Abel
Aborn, *see* Ebborn
Abovetoune (Abovethetoune), Hen., 1150; Rog., 1127; Wm., 1392, 1447
Abrahall, Dorothy, 473; Eliz., 473*; Isabel, 473; John, 766; Markey, 473*; Mary, 473; Thos., 473*; Wm., 473; fam., 392, 469
Abraham (Abram), John, 1483; Rev. Peter, 1356; Sarah, 407*; Wm., 407*, 1519
Abyngton, *see* Abington
Ackerley, Eliz., 1194; John Hawksy, 1194; (later Chamberlayne), Joseph Chamberlayne, 1193, 1195
Ackers (Akers), Edw., 310*; Jas., 1377*, 1380; Jane, 310; Mary, 1377*; Mr., 1378*
Ackland, Ann, 1250; Eliz., 1250; Grace, 1249; Jane, 1250; Joseph, 1250; Ric., 1249*; Wm., 1250, 1258
Ackley, —, 945
Acock (Aycocks), Anne, 948; John, 1232; Joseph, 948; Mary, 948*; Rob., 948
A'Court, Kath., 329; Wm. P., 329
Acre, Joan of, 1474
Acreman, *see* Akerman
Acton (Actone), Hen., 1476; John (de), 579, 1101, 1432, 1485*; Joseph, 820; Kath., 1432; Mary, 1374; Nic., 778 n; Odo de, 1102; Rob., 493; Wm. (de), 1289, 1374, 1432*; fam., 579, 612

Adam, abbot, 359
Adam, ap, *see* ap Adam
Adam, Wm. son of, 720
Adams (Adam, Adames, Addams), Abel, 1515; Abigail, 473; Alice, 130, 738; Ann(e), 97, 220 n, 320, 413, 955, 1271, 1401; Betty 958, 963; Catham [*sic*], 137; Edm., 601*, 991; Edw., 97; Eliz., 510, 601, 955*, 1019, 1159, 1301, 1302*; Eliz. Emma, 1511; Francis, 320, 1194*; Gabriel, 601*; Geo., 842*, 1019*; Hannah, 601, 1302*; Harry, 137; Hen., 137, 517; Issard, 1126; J., 1312; Jas., 555; Jas. Smith, 1511*; Jane, 842, 1301, 1302; John, 431, 517, 598, 957, 958*, 963, 1226, 1271, 1301, 1302, 1397*, 1401, 1491, 1513; Rev. John, 515, 678; Joseph, 343; Judith, 633; Luke, 958; Margery, 1369; Mary, 517, 957*, 963, 970, 1019, 1397*; N., 633; Nat., 343, 969, 970, 1301, 1302*; Rachel, 957; Rebecca, 517; Ric., 710, 738, 955*, 959, 1020, 1379; Rob., 413, 955, 1217, 1513; Sam., 95, 957, 963*, 1312; Rev. Sam., 678; Sarah, 95, 320, 431, 957, 958*, 963*, 1397*, 1515; Susannah, 601*, 1194; Rev. T., 1027; Theophilus, 720, 1020; Thos., 510*, 550, 924, 955, 957*, 958, 959, 963, 1333, 1397*; W., 1312; Rev. Wal., 1043; Wm., 130, 515, 797, 958, 1302*, 1397; Sir Wm., 220 n; Mr., 960; —, 1020, 1121, 1256; *and see* ap Adam; Badham
Adamson, Rev. John, 820
Addams, *see* Adams
Addean, *see* Adeane
Adderley (Aderley), Ant., 1209; Edw., 33*; Geo., 1428; Hen., 1203; Isabel, 1209; Mary, 1179, 1183; Wm., 1183, 1213
Adderton, John, 858*, 986; Rev. Wal., 569
Addis (Addes), Benj., 1301; Chas., 1361; Dan., 962*, 1301; Eliz., 962, 978; John, 413, 456, 1238; Marg., 1361; Mary, 456; Rachel, 1301; Sarah, 1301; Wm., 1361*; —, 978
Addison, Rob., 413; Mr., 220 n*; —, 1102
Addy, *see* Adey
Adeane (Addean, Adean, A'Deane), Ann(e), 104*, 106, 107, 109; Christian, 106; Grace, 106; Jas., 106*, 107, 108; Joan (Jone), 107, 934; John, 104, 106*, 107*, 108, 112, 651*, 1097; Lewis, 639*; Marg., 104, 106, 639; Mary, 102, 112; Mat., 30*, 102, 104, 106*, 107*, 111, 696*, 697, 934; Ric., 106, 109, 1097; Rob., 107*; Thos., 106, 112*; Mr., 102; —, 1456; fam., 649; *and see* Dean
Adee, *see* Adey

Adekines (Adekyn), *see* Atkins

Adelred, *see* Ethelred

Aderley, *see* Adderley

Adey (Addy, Adee, Ady, Adye), Alice, 1525; Ann, 538; Bridget, 1527; Christian, 538*, 1074; Dan., 540, 696, 697, 1524, 1525, 1527*, 1529, 1532; David, 1368; Edw., 385; Eliz., 9, 622, 654, 1116, 1527; Esther, 385; Gertrude, 1546*; Hen., 9, 531, 538*, 540*, 1477, 1546*; Hester, 540, 938, 1532; Jane, 1116, 1546; John, 385*, 540*, 654, 1116*, 1368*; Judith, 538; Lydia, 540; Marg., 1537; Martha, 538, 540; Mary, 58, 385*, 538, 622, 1524; R., 1312; Ric., 938, 1116*; Sam., 1527, 1546*; Sarah, 1116*, 1529, 1532*, 1537; Swithin, 58, 59; Thos., 622*, 666, 1116, 1552; Wm., 538, 1074, 1116, 1526; Lieut. Col. Wm., 1529; Mr., 367; Mrs., 19; —, 1074, 1102, 1177, 1311*; fam., 159, 532, 538

Adhelan, John, 1288

Adkins, *see* Atkins

Adlam, Chas., 728*; Esther, 728; Mary, 728; Susannah, 728*; Thos., 728*

Adlard, Mary Ann, 1472; Wm. Gates, 1472

Adlington, Leighton, 211; Susanna, 211

Ady (Adye), *see* Adey

AElfred, *see* Alfred

Aelwold (fl. 1066), 1005

Agg (Agge), Ann, 494; Eliz., 494; Jas., 494, 986*, 1064; John, 522*; Sarah, 522*; Thos., 494

Agnes, abbess, 651*

Agrove, R., 1328

Aibrug, Edith, 1033; John, 1033; Thos., 1033

Aidewelle, Adam, 1197

Ailberton, *see* Aylberton

Ailesbury [*peerage*](Ailsbury), Chas., earl of, 25, 1080; Eliz., countess of, 123; Eliz., dau. of Chas., *see* Breuse; Mary, dau. of Chas., 25

Ailord, Eliz., 77; Wm., 77*

Ailsbury, *see* Ailesbury

Ailward (fl. 1066), 1082*

Ailway, *see* Alway

Ailworth, *see* Aylworth

Ainge, Cath.. 795; Magdalen, 1002; Lettice, 795; Mary, 385*; Ric., 385*, 793, 795*; —, 1002; fam., 792

Ainsger (fl. 1066), 1077

Ainslie, Cordelia, 1088, 1091; Geo., 1088; *and see* Ansley

Ainslow, *see* Ansloe

Airdma[n], Wm., 1314

Aisgill, Rev. Hen., 511, 513, 1021, 1041, 1126, 1127; Hester, 512; Rev. Joshua, 511, 512; Sara(h), 1041, 1126

Aish, *see* Ash

Aistell, *see* Astill

Aistroppe, John, 413

Akerman (Acreman), Anne, 982; Cath., 706; Eliz., 235, 983; Hen., 235, 332*, 891, 983, 986; Jas., 706, 982; Jane, 235; John, 235, 891*, 986; Mary, 332, Susanna, 235; Thos., 235*; Wm., 235*; —, 986

Akers, *see* Ackers

Aland, Rob. son of, 1221

Aland, John, 661; John Fortescue, Lord Fortescue, 570 n; Mary, 661; Thos., 661*

Alanson, *see* Allanson

Alared, *see* Allard

Albemarle (Alba Mara), Isabella, 1039; Kath., 1039; Matilda, 1039; Reg. de, 529; Rog. de, 529; W. de, 1039, 1168; earl of, *see* Odo; —, 1039*; earl of, *see* Odo

Albert (Allbert), Anna, 1004; Rev. Geo., 1004*, 1005; Rev. John, 613; Ric., 883

Alberton, *see* Aylberton

Albright, Rev. W., 1043

Alchorne, Anne, 1255; Edw., 1255

Alcock (Alcocke, Alcocks, Allcock), Alice, 1386; Benj., 1518; Dan., 1361; Edw., 1194; Eleanor, 1361; Eliz., 1194; Geo., 1270, 1275; Hannah, 1386; Jas., 1386; Jane, 872; John, 221, 1389, 1518; John, bishop, 745; Joseph, 818; Mary, 1386, 1518; Ric., 1281; Ric. Greening, 28; Sam., 872; Thos., 1065, 1386; Wm., 1388; —, 1386

Alcott, Jas., 1582

Aldar, *see* Alder

Alden, Edith, 208*; Eliz., 661; Hester, 1112; Jas., 1121; John, 1160; Jonathan, 661*; Rob., 1112*; Capt. Sam., 208*; Sarah, 1112*; Thos., 1121; Wm., 1121

Alder (Aldar), Eliz., 659; Jeremiah, 659; John, 1187; Mary, 659

Aldersey (Aldersay), Dan., 948; Mary, 948; Thos., 1148

Alderson, Rev. Jas., 685*

Aldern, Rev. Francis, 1228

Aldeward, Rob. de, 1447

Aldewyne, John, 1388

Aldington, Rev. Wm., 1329, 1331

Aldous, Grace, 1551; Sam., 1551

Aldred, bishop, 565, 1502

Aldred (fl. 1086), 1384

Aldridge, Ann, 70, 467; Benjamina, 1207; Edw., 201; Elianor, 70; Eliz., 1206, 1207*, 1208*; Esther, 1007; Jane, 203*; John, 203, 467*, 1207, 1209; Joseph, 1008; Mary, 70, 201, 1207*, 1209; Prudence, 1434*; R., 1005; Ric., 1206*, 1207*, 1208*, 1215; Rob., 1238; Sam., 1213, 1217; Sarah, 1207*; Stephen, 65; Thos., 70, 1207*; Ursula, 1207; Wm., 70*; Mr., 1440; —, 1185, 1203; fam., 1215

Aldrinton (Aldrintone), John, 1477; Margery de, 1478; Wm. de, 1074

Aldworth, A., 1159; Rev. Nat., 128, 319

Alein, *see* Allen

Alenare, Alice, 1335; John, 1335

Alerde, *see* Allard

Aleway, *see* Alway

Aleworth, *see* Aylworth

Alexander III, pope, 183, 544

Alexander (Alisaunder, Alysaunder, Elysander, Elysaunder), Alice, 1051*; (or Mauncel), Alice, 1052*; (or Mauncel), Ambrose, 1052; Amy, 1051; Ann, 1245; (or Mauncel), Ant., 1052; Cath., 1437; (or Mauncel), Cyprian, 1052; Dan., 1249; Eliz.,

124, 1051; Fanny, 1247; (or Mauncell), Hen., 1051*; J., 1258; Jas., 1247; John, 1051*, 1249*, 1437; (or Mauncel), John, 1051*; Martha, 124; Mary, 1249, 1250; (or Mauncel), Mary, 1052; Ric., 1051*; (or Mauncel), Ric., 1051; Ruth, 1437; S., 1250; Thos., 1051*, 1245; (or Mauncel), Thos., 1052; Wal., 1051*; (or Mauncel), Wal., 1051; Wm., 124, 1051*; Rev. Wm., 424, 681; —, 1256, 1258*; fam., 1051*; (or Mansell), fam., 1052

Aleyn, *see* Allen

Alflett, Rev. T., 1441

Alford, Rev. Rob., 508

Alfred (AElfred), king, 357, 365, 366, 1502*

Alfrid, Hen., 1494

Algar (fl. 11th cent.), 1120, 1285, 1287, 1309, 1361, 1455, 1491

Algedus, *see* Valentine

Alie, *see* Alley

Aling, *see* Ayling

Alisaunder, *see* Alexander

Allan, *see* Allen

Allanson (Alanson), Rev. Thos., 685, 1335

Allard (Alared, Alerde, Alured), Anne, 857; Gil., 1233; Hen., 1504; Jas., 1273*; John, 1165; Rebecca, 1273; Sarah, 1282; Wm., 857

Allaway, *see* Alway

Allbert, *see* Albert

Allbury, John, 1361; —, 1361

Allcock, *see* Alcock

Allebar, J. de, 1160

Allehale, John, 1404

Allen (Alein, Aleyn, Allan, Alleyn, Alleyne, Allin, Aulen), Ann(e), 111, 250, 296, 453, 950; Arthur, 454; Benj., 1468; Chris., 1068*, 1482; Sir Chris., 1482*; David, 1399; Edw., 1307; Elinor, 873; Eliz., 202, 296, 429, 886, 964, 1278, 1515; Ethel(d)reda, 1068, 1482; Frances, 429; Giles, 703*; Hannah, 825; Hen., 886; Isabella, 1519; Sir J., 1068; Jacob, 429; Jas., 250, 1082; Jane, 429; Joan, 454; Joan [? John], 1361; John, 64, 111, 296*, 800, 825, 950, 959, 1082, 1278, 1292, 1473; Rev. John, 297; Joyce, 1399; Lawr., 857; Lucia (Lucy), 453, 835; Marg., 455, 1307; Martha, 1024; Mary, 64, 429, 486, 826, 957; Mat., 873; Nic., 1519; Obadiah, 873; Phil., 111; Poulton, 1192; Prudence, 814; Ric., 296, 1354; Ric. Cooper, 1355; Rob., 453*, 454*, 957*, 1197, 1307; Sam., 197, 429, 1362; Sarah, 202, 703, 881; Susanna(h), 250, 1419; Thos., 250, 455, 741, 881, 1082, 1399, 1515; Rev. Thos., 770; Wm., 202*, 486, 826, 835, 964, 1024; —, 1386, 1455; fam., 638, 1082

Allerdyne, —, 1121

Alley (Alie, Ally, Aly, Alye), Edw., 1277, 1518; Jas., 746; Joan, 1518; Mark, 1333; Sarah, 746, 1277; W., 1290*; Wm., 1333; Rev. Wm., 783; —, 1293

Alleyn (Alleyne, Allin), *see* Allen

Allingham, Ric., 846

Allington, John, 1473; Judith, 1473

Allison, Arthur, 639; John, 639*, 1439; Millicent, 639; Penelope, 639; Ralph, 639; Ruth, 639

Alloway, *see* Alway

Allpass, *see* Alpass

Allway, *see* Alway

Ally, *see* Alley

Almond, Mary, 1110; Thos., 1110

Almondesbury, Wm. de, 1539

Alpass (Allpass), John, 176*; Mary, 176; Stephen, 1551*; Sarah, 1551

Alre, Phil. de, 985

Alric (fl. 1066), 1339, 1447

Alrich (Aylrich, Aylriche), John, 1074, 1215; Marg., 1314

Alsleye, Rob. de, 1027; Wm., de, 1027

Alsop, Amy Wallington, 824; Eliz., 1425–6, 1427; Rev. Geo., 1336; Hugh, 824; Joan, 824; Joanna, 1336; John, 1426*; Marg., 824; Mary, 823, 1426, 1427; Rachel, 1426; Rob., 824*; Sarah, 824*; Stephen, 1427; Wm., 824*, 1426, 1427; Rev. Wm., 823*; —, 824

Alston, Rob., 1384

Alured (fl. 13th cent.), 1227

Alured, *see* Allard

Aluric (fl. 1066), 1011, 1032*, 1253, 1255

Alvi (fl. 1066), 1328

Alvin the sheriff, 1401, 1402

Alward (fl. 1066), 1015, 1121

Alway (Ailway, Aleway, Allaway, Alloway, Allway, Ayleway, Ayllway, Aylway, Eylway), Ann(e), 130, 1234, 1367; Chris., 1234; Dan., 701*; Eliz., 331, 335, 746, 757*; Frances, 1234; Geo., 746; Hester, 701*, 758; J., 1203; Jas., 746; Joan, 4; John, 4, 331, 335, 701, 757, 911, 1217, 1234*; Jonathan, 130; Joseph, 1398*, 1403; Martha, 331; Mary, 130, 701, 758, 1210, 1398; Nat., 1367*; R., 1238; Ric., 130*, 387, 1234; Sam., 1367; Rev. Sam., 613, 1539; Sarah, 387, 910; T., 1237; Thos., 387*, 701, 910*, 1234, 1398*; W., 1016, 1093, 1195; Wm., 701*, 758, 1234; Mr., 1215; —, 697; fam., 1237

Alwin (fl. 1066), 990*, 1074, 1237, 1377

Alwold (fl. 1066), 1345, 1401, 1475

Aly (Alye), *see* Alley

Alysaunder, *see* Alexander

Amarson, Ric., 756; *and see* Emerson

Ambery, Alice, 193; Ant., 193*; Eliz., 194; Jane, 193; Joseph, 194; Mary, 191; Wm., 191, 193*

Ambler, Humph., 1016

Ambrose (Ambrass), Anna, 111; Geo., 923*; Joan, 923; Phil., 1008; Wm., 48

Ames, Martha, 920; Mary, 924; St. Vincent, 1420; Thos., 920*, 924

Ammenseye, Alice de, 1140

Amos, Edw., 407; Eliz., 491; Esther, 407*; Jacob, 491; Thos., 407*; Rev. Wm., 103

Amott, Hannah, 549; Jas., 549

Amphlett, Hannah, 907; John, 907, 1282

Ampney, Nic. de, 360

Amyeen, Agnes, 1460

Amyot, Edith, 1329; Rog., 1329

Anchitel (fl. 1066)(Anchitil), 1032, 1082

Ancrum, —, 1378

Anderne, Marg., 1033

Anderson, Dorothy, 995, 997; Edm., 995, 997; Rob., 796; Wm., 1517
Anderton, John, 1516
Andress, Susannah, 1583
Andreu, *see* Andrews
Andrew, abbot, 359, 1255
Andrews (Andreu, Andrewes), Abigail, 1137; Adam, 1428; Alice, 1433; Ann(e), 173, 217, 826, 965; Rev. Ant., 674, 675, 1132; Betty, 1453; Bridget, 821; Charity, 18; Chas., 486, 1452; Chris., 1452*, 1453, 1456; Dan., 103; Dorothea, 573; Edw., 833, 834; Eleanor, 826; Eliz., 453*, 454, 486, 522, 541, 677, 830, 834*, 1118*, 1180, 1367, 1425, 1452, 1508; Frances, 573; Francis, 804; Geo., 731; Hannah, 177, 332, 1184, 1452*, 1455; Hen., 702*; Rev. Hen., 1004; Hester, 1118; J., 1186; Jane, 177, 1367; Jesse, 1420; Joan, 418; Joannah, 217; John, 118, 172, 174, 217*, 418*, 453*, 454, 522, 541*, 677, 804, 1119, 1130, 1180, 1184, 1186, 1367*, 1452*, 1456, 1508; Rev. John, 1169, 1317; Joyce, 118; Marg., 1452; Martha, 418, 1119; Mary, 49, 173, 177, 741, 811, 1130*, 1184, 1367, 1429, 1452*; Maurice, 541*; Naomi, 177; Nic., 453, 1453, 1455; Pat., 413; R., 1227, 1312, 1350, 1369, 1402; Rachel, 1429; Ric., 173, 176, 332, 418, 454, 523, 670, 741, 890, 983, 1015, 1043, 1078, 1130, 1228, 1255, 1452; Rev. Ric., 89, 147; Rob., 16, 18, 826, 1118*, 1119, 1429*; Rog., 821; Sarah, 173, 418, 670, 703, 1183; Susanna, 177*, 702; Thos., 16, 177*, 217*, 603, 702, 703, 965, 1183, 1184*, 1289, 1342, 1425; Rev. Thos., 463, 571, 573*; Wm., 177, 632, 811*, 954, 1043, 1137, 1183*, 1184*, 1361; —, 1011, 1185*, 1369, 1455, 1460, 1475*
Angulo, Luke in, 1351; Wm. in, 1483; *and see* Corner
Anirwood, John, 1323
Anketild, —, 1478
Anne, queen, 23, 24, 93, 162, 180, 244*, 263, 359 n, 363, 365, 511, 561, 567, 571, 829, 865, 915, 961, 1187, 1349, 1356, 1369
Anne, Rev. Thos., 691
Anne-Holles, Wm., earl of Essex, 324
Anner, Anne, 1268; John, 1268; Mary, 1268
Annett, Nic., 1039
Ansell (Auncell), Alice, 1013; Ann, 296*; Ant., 296*; Benj., 296*; Betty, 1012; Edw., 1013; Eliz., 296; John, 1012*, 1013*; Marg., 1013; Mary, 296; Simon, 1013*, 1015; Thos., 1013; Rev. Wm., 853; —, 1015*, 1017, 1216; fam., 232, 1501
Anselm, R., 1221
Ansley, John, 923*; Martha, 923; Thos., 923; *and see* Ainslie
Ansloe (Ainslow), Eleanor, 203; Rog., 203; —, 646
Anstey (Anstee), Anne, 555; Geo., 555*; Jane, 555; John, 555*; Marg., 555; Mary, 555; Rob., 555*; —, 1147
Anstis, John, 690 n; —, 1177
Anthony, Wm., 1063
Anti (fl. 1066), 1331

Antoild, Rev. Rob., 233
ap Adam (ap Adams), Eliz., 576, 720; John, 178; John, baron of Beverstone, 1322; Sir John, 576, 720; Thos., 179, 576; Sir Thos., 720; Wm. (son of), 720; Rev. Wm., 1031; —, 1322*; fam., 179, 807; *and see* Adam; Adams; Adamson
ap David, *see* Apdavid
ap Gryffith, *see* Griffith, David ap, Rev. Phil. ap, *and* Rheese ap
ap Gwrgant, *see* Gwrgant
Ap Howell, *see* Howell, Rev. Morgan Ap
Ap Jenkins, *see* Jenkins, Rev. Edw. Ap
Aparel, Ric., 1423
Apdavid, Rev. Edw., 643; *and see* David
Apperley (Apperlegh), Eliz., 741; Hannah, 1183; Hester, 1183; Jane, 1183; John, 741, 1381; Martha, 1025; Mary, 1183*; Ric. (de), 1025, 1047; Sam., 1183*, 1186; Thos., 1183; Messrs., 1186
Appleby (Applebe, Applebee, Apulby), Rev. J., 1504; John, 690; Marg., 690; Mary, 733
Applegarth, John, 333, 504; Martha, 333
Appleheved, —, 1017
Appleton, Anne, 124
Appletree, Rog., 465
Appreece, Greg., 1201
Apsley, Cath., 363 n; Sir Peter, 363 n
Apsley, baron, *see* Bathurst, Hen. *and* —
Apthorp (Apthorpe), Geo., 331; Hen., 1557
Apulby, *see* Appleby
Apworth, Ursula, 797
Aragon, Kath. of, 252, 449, 534 n, 738, 792, 876
Aram, John, 929; Marg., 933; Mary, 929; Thos., 929; Wm., 933
Arandel, *see* Arundel
Arch, Eliz., 669; John, 669; Rob., 669*
Archar, *see* Archer
Archard, Agnes, 169; Ann, 169*; Eliz., 169*; (or Hayes), Eliz., 1248; (or Hayes), Giles, 1248*; Joan, 169; John, 169; Kath., 169; Marg., 937; N., 1201; Ric., 169*, 825; Sarah, 169; (or Hayes), Sarah, 1248; Thos., 169, 369, 825; Wm., 169, 937*, 1101; (or Hayes), Wm., 1248; *and see* Archer
Archdale, Ric., 1257
Archer (Archar, Archers), Alice, 1431; Amy, 510; And., Lord Archer, 988; Ann, 187, 510*, 1200; Chas., 1193; Chris., 1196; Colin le, 1431; David, 510*; Edw., 60, 861*; Eliz., 510, 974, 1193*; Francis, 1193; Grace, 1193; Jas., 187; Jane, 510; Joane, 861; John, 510*, 974; Marg., 510*; Martha, 388; Mary, 510; Nic. le, 1485; Ric., 510*, 1196, 1200; Rob. (le), 388, 510*, 1193, 1200, 1431; Rog. le, 1102; Sam., 1196; Sarah, 884*; Sarah, Lady Archer, 988; Sophia, 1193; Thos., 884; —, 1102; *and see* Archard; Argier; Orchard
Arden (Arderne), Agnes de, 1404; (or Collier), Anne, 905; Giles, 311 n; John, 1033; Marg., 311 n; Matilda, 1033; Thos., 905, 1033
Ardglass, earl and countess of, *see* Cromwell, *passim*

Argier, John, 1562; Mary, 1562; *and see* Archer
Ariss, Ann, 1065; Geo., 1065
Arkell (Arkayl, Arkel, Arkill, Arkle), Agnes, 1363; Alice, 1445; Ann, 636, 1075, 1091, 1503; Chas., 862; Dorothy, 772*; Edm., 339; Eliz., 1063*, 1444*, 1445*; Frances, 328; Hannah, 1058, 1445; Heary [*sic*], 772; Hen., 1064, 1093, 1444*, 1445*; Hester, 254, 1466; Jas., 133, 1225; John, 254*, 328, 772*, 1063, 1075, 1165*, 1334, 1503, 1504; Joseph, 328; Judith, 1504; Lucinda Timbrell, 1063; Mary, 317, 339, 800, 966, 1058, 1063, 1091, 1334, 1542; Rob., 317; Sam., 800, 1444, 1445*; Sapphira, 254; T., 1064, 1093; Thos., 1058*, 1063, 1064*, 1091*, 1093, 1445, 1504, 1542; W., 800, 1064; Wm., 348, 636, 966, 1058, 1064*, 1075, 1091, 1093, 1361, 1445, 1466, 1504; Mr., 1165; —, 1504; fam., 228, 1165
Arketyl, Thos., 1363
Arkill (Arkle), *see* Arkell
Armes, John, 383; Mary, 383; Sarah, 383
Armitstead, Christian, 1581; John, 1581
Armond, Rev. Rob., 198, 445
Armstrong, Rev. John, 1323
Arnald, *see* Arnold
Arnett (Arnott), Cath., 1004; Dan., 836; Rob., 1004; Thos., 1004
Arnold (Arnald, Arnill, Arnolds), Alice, 351; Ant., 1404; Betty, 1338; Dan., 1200*; Dorothy, 1372; Eliz., 450, 455, 1338; Hen., 1069; Hester, 375; Isabel, 351; Jas., 907; Jane, 1200; John, 349, 351, 352, 785, 1372; Rev. John, 421, 450, 503, 504; Joshua, 38; Mary, 38, 907, 1200, 1338*; Martha, 1338*; Neast, 871; Sir Nic., kt., 351, 893, 1372; R., 1121; Ric., 455; Rob., 455*; Rowland, 1372; Sam., 236; Rev. Sam., 236; Wm., 1338*; —, 1402*, 1455
Arnott, *see* Arnett
Arran, earl of, *see* Gore, —
Arras (Atrebatensis), Wm. of, 688 n
Arrowsmith, Anne, 385; Eliz., 903, 1269; John, 821; Judith, 821; Mary, 821, 983, 1269; Nat., 903; Obadiah, 385*, 907, 1269; Olive, 385; Sam., 328, 983; Susannah, 907; Thos., 385*; Yerrow, 1289; —, 1140, 1288
Arthur, prince of Wales, 581 n
Arthur (Arthurs, Arthuyr), Chas., 1158*, 1160; Eliz., 703, 1158; Francis, 203; Hester, 843; John, 836*, 1402; Martha, 836; Mary, 319; Rev. Ric., 515, 798; Sarah, 473, 703, 1158; Thos., 703*; Wm., 1339; —, 1402; fam., 1160
Artus, Thos., 1226; —, 1226
Arundel (Arandel, Arundell), Alianor, 1139; Alice, 1319; Ann(e), 536, 537*, 1207, 1208, 1216; Arabella, 1208; Cath., 618; Chas., 985; Dr. Dan., 1319*; Rev. Edm., 1319, 1323; Sir Edm., 1051; Eliz., 536, 537, 1143, 1146; Fream(e), 1025, 1207, 1208*, 1216, 1217; Hen., 536; Humph., 1139; Jas., 1208*, 1215, 1216*; Jane, 1025, 1207, 1208, 1213*; John (de), 388, 531*, 534*, 535, 536, 537*, 539, 618, 1139*, 1213, 1215*, 1245, 1258; Sir John, 618*; John Greg., 1207; Josiah, 531, 536; Mary, 537, 539, 754; R., 1215;

Ric., 1207, 1213*, 1215, 1218; Sam., 388, 1025, 1143, 1146, 1207, 1208, 1213, 1217; Sarah, 830, 1213*, 1245; Susanna, 388; Thos., 830, 1207*, 1217; Thos. Crozier, 1208, 1216; Ursula, 1213; Wm., 830, 1007, 1139, 1186, 1218; Rev. Wm., 1362; Mr., 1186; —, 1203; fam., 1186, 1378
Arundel [*peerage*], Hen., earl of, 1140, 1185; Jane, Lady, 1297; John, Lord, 1298; Thos., earl of, 763; earl of, 688, 1185, 1339, 1377, 1513; Lady, 1297; *and see* FitzAlan
Asbil, Geo., 891
Ascham, Rog., 346
Aschill (fl. 1066), 1015
Ascough, *see* Ayscough
Ash (Aish, Assh), John, 59; Ric. atte, 1428; Sarah, 1450; Wm., 1450
Ashbee, *see* Ashby
Ashburnham, Bertram, 1016; Wm., 719 n; Earl, 1156; Mrs., 719 n; —, 1016
Ashby (Ashbee), Ann, 703*; Geo., 703; Hen., 703; Isaac, 703; Mary, 703*, 1531*; Rob., 703*; Thos., 703, 1531*; Wm., 703
Ashcomb (Ayshcombe), Eliz., 1001; Frances, 136; John, 1001, 1227; Oliver, 1227; Sir Wm., 136; *and see* Escombe
Ashcraft (Asshecrofte), Adam, 1292; Sarah, 924; Thos., 924
Asheton, *see* Ashton
Ashfield (Aysfield), Ann(e), 1271*, 1288; H., 1063; Mary, 1296, 1311; Mic., 599, 864; Sir R., 1237; Ric., 1296; Sir Ric., bt., 1296, 1311; Rob., 599*; Sam., 1271*, 1288; Rev. Wm., 599
Ashley (Ashly, Esheley), Ant., 761; Eliz., 10, 1465; Frances, 803; Hannah, 339; Joan, 486; Job, 339; John, 10, 388, 486, 761, 803; Martha, 10; Mary, 10, 388; Ric., 10; Thos., 10; Wal. de, 311; Wm., 10, 1417, 1473
Ashman, Eliz., 751; Jas., 751; Jane, 751*
Ashmead (Ashmeade), Amy, 316; Ann, 332, 460; Eliz., 316, 339; Francis, 127, 464*; Giles, 316, 336; Hannah, 387; John, 254, 387, 460*; Marg., 336; Mary, 336, 339; Nic., 339*; Sarah, 332, 336*; Susannah, 464; T., 1083; Thos., 316*, 332*, 336*, 1083, 1289; Wm., 1378; fam., 1232*
Ashmore, Anderson, 1472*; Eliz., 1472*; Paul, 1472*; Susannah, 1472*; T., 1220*, 1476; Thos., 1472; Wm., 1472
Ashton (Asheton, Asshton), Rev. Edm., 103, 1147; John, 89; Sir Rob., 1491; Wal., 1420; *and see* Aston; Easton; Eston
Ashwell, Dan., 384; Hannah, 366
Ashwin, Ann, 1457; John, 1460; Ric., 1263; Sarah, 1263; T., 1460; Thos., 1457*, 1460*; —, 1460; fam., 1460
Asplin (Aspilon), Mary, 567; Nic., 1331; Rev. Wm., 567*
Assh, *see* Ash
Asshecrofte, *see* Ashcraft
Asshton, *see* Ashton
Asteley, *see* Astley
Astill (Aistell, Astile), Abraham, 789*; Ann, 789; Rev. John, 860

Astley (Asteley), Rev. Edw., 1223, 1388; J., 1460;
John Wolvey, 1126; Rev. John Wolvey, 1004;
Mary, 1389; Lord, 1197; —, 1126
Astman, Anna (Anne), 1236*; Eliz., 887, 899, 902;
John, 899, 902*; Rev. John, 898; Mary, 583, 887,
902*, 903; Miles, 902*, 903; Ric., 902; Sarah,
583, 902; Thos., 761, 831, 887, 902; Wm., 583*,
902, 1236
Astmer, Wm. de, 1221
Aston (Astone), Alice de, 1404; Ann(e), 74, 399,
520; Ant., 1268*; Sir Edw., 520; Eliz., 1268;
Rev. F., 1154; Gertrude, 717; John (de), 683,
1431; Rev. John de, 1031; Mary, 1214; Phil.,
1214; Sam., 74, 337*; Sarah, 683; Thos., 360,
399; Rev. Thos., 1335; Rev. Wal., 221; Sir Wal.,
717; Wal., Lord Aston, 717, 722, 1419; Wm.
(de), 1061, 1402, 1431; —, 1148; and see
Ashton; Easton; Eston
Astry, Anne, 99; Arabella, 99, 718, 724, 1419*,
1428; Diana, 99, 718, 1419, 1428; Eliz., 99, 718,
724, 1419, 1428; Lady Eliz., 98, 99*; Luke, 99;
Sir Ralph, 718; Rebecca, 718 n; St. John, 99,
724; Sam., 724, 1428; Sir Sam., kt., 98, 99, 718,
722, 1419, 1491; fam., 724, 1156
Atcherley, John, 1576
Atford, see Attford
Athelam, see Athelham
Athelard, Reg., 1460; Rob., 1005
Athelham (Athelam), John, 1292*
Athelmond (fl. 800), 770
Athelstan, king, 518
Atherton, Louisa Henrietta, 1235; Mrs., 1237
Atkins (Adekines, Adekyn, Adkins, Atkines,
Atkyns), Allc. [? Alice], 1197; Ann(e), 262, 296,
677, 1226*, 1373, 1374*; Ann Dorothy, 1226;
Sir E., 1226; Edw., 445, 525, 1226; Sir Edw.,
301, 1049, 1226; Elinor, 714; Eliz., 262, 683,
1226, 1373; Giles, 315; Hannah, 262, 1391; J.,
1226, 1227; John, 210, 296*, 1224, 1226,
1227–8, 1373, 1391, 1456; Rev. John, 1502; John
Tracy, 1226*; L. C. B.,- 1048; (Dame, Lady)
Lovise (Lovice), 1049, 1052*, 1226; Marg., 713,
1374, 1375; Margery, 296; Martha, 210; Mary,
289, 1391; R., 1220; Rev. R., 767; Sir R., 1052*,
1201, 1225, 1226* 1381, 1392; Ric., 683, 714*,
1226*, 1267, 1373*, 1374*; Sir Ric., kt., 1052;
Rob., 1052, 1226*, 1374, 1388; Sir Rob., kt., 27,
195, 271, 287, 311 n, 318, 346*, 364*, 365, 366,
444, 445, 515, 525*, 552, 556, 713, 769, 773,
778, 823, 870, 882, 913, 915*; 925, 927, 1011,
1049*, 1051 & n, 1052*, 1074, 1123, 1186, 1189,
1226*, 1284, 1312, 1345*, 1379, 1381, 1382,
1482, 1493; Sam., 262; Susanna, 296, 1373;
Thos., 262, 296, 683, 713, 1267, 1339, 1374*,
1375*, 1391*; Tracy, 1154; Wm., 210*, 289*,
1385; Lady, 1048, 1052; Mr., 1380*; —, 1378,
1401, 1419, 1420, 1455, 1519, 1538; fam., 459,
870, 1195, 1226
Atkinson, Rev. Abraham, 1348; Anne, 643; Rev.
Brian, 643*; Chris., 1269*; Eleanor, 1269*;
Eliz., 1113; Geo., 32; Sir Hen., kt., 643*; John,
35; Sir John, 945; Mary, 1269*; Rev. Nic., 1317;

Rachel, 32; Ric., 643; Rob., 643*; Sarah, 35,
1269; Thos., 1113; Wm., 32, 1269; Rev. Wm.,
31, 32; Lady, 369, 945, 1198; Rev., 121; —,
1198*
Atkyns, see Atkins
Atlee, Mary, 4; Wm., 4
Atrebatensis, see Arras
atte Berue, see Atterbury
atte Forde, see Attford
atte Watere, see Attwater
atte Welle, see Attwell
atte Wode, see Attwood
Attefeld, W., 1311; and see Field
Atterbury (atte Berue), Thos., 1027; —, bishop,
363 n
Atterton, Ann, 569; Ric., 569
Attewode, see Attwood
Attford (Atford, atte Forde), Hen., 1091; Wm.,
1460; —, 1052, 1091, 1455; and see Ford
Attwater (atte Watere), Rog., 1102; —, 1069
Attwell (atte Welle, Atwell, Atwells), Agnes, 1061;
Edw., 959; Eliz., 959; Rev. Hugh, 369; J., 1092,
1309; Jane, 1298, 1300, 1301*; John, 1061,
1298, 1301, 1309*, 1313, 1339, 1351, 1422*,
1502; Rev. Joseph, 593; Mary, 1301; R., 1092*;
Ric., 1091*, 1093, 1298, 1300, 1301*, 1540;
Rob., 1069, 1314, 1363; Thos., 1504; Mr., 487;
—, 1091; fam., 1091
Attwood (atte Wode, Attewode, Atwood, A'Wood),
Abigail, 210*; Alice, 397; And., 206; Ann(e),
977*, 984; Ant., 1334; Ciprian, 397; Edith, 1552;
Edm., 397, 977*, 1353*; Rev. Edm., 681, 682;
Eleanor, 1063, 1334, 1359; Eliz., 396, 741,
1096*, 1269; Frances, 536; Geo., 1160; Giles,
1334; Hannah, 977; Hen., 1116, 1165, 1292;
Isaac, 1168; Jas., 35*, 1168; Jane, 641, 977,
1352; Joachym, 1385; John, 159, 281, 396, 490,
536, 538, 977, 986, 1058, 1096, 1168, 1313,
1385, 1475, 1477, 1513, 1576; Marg., 760; Mary,
641, 977*, 984*, 1352, 1353; Prescilla, 490;
Ric., 906, 984*, 986; Rob., 1096*, 1292, 1363;
Rog., 1370; Sarah, 741, 905, 977, 1096; Thos.,
74, 490, 550, 1334; Wal., 1172, 1269, 1359;
Wm., 74, 167, 175, 210, 396, 641, 741*, 760,
977*, 984*, 986, 1116, 1353, 1491; Mr., 905,
1355; —, 1011*, 1140, 1169, 1334, 1512; fam.,
1011
Atwold, —, 1311
Atwood, see Attwood
Aubrey, see Awbrey
Auchor (Auckkor, Auckor), Anne, 1222; Edw.,
1222; Mary, 1222; Thos., 1222; —, 1223
Audley (Audele), H., 1381; Hen., 1201; Hugh (de),
556, 559, 1313; Hugh, earl of Gloucester, 1011;
Isolda de, 556, 559; Jane, 1082, 1199; Marg.,
556, 1381; Marg., countess of Gloucester, 1011;
Rev. Thos., 1346; —, 1201; fam., earls of
Gloucester, 556, 568, 1199
Audley [peerage], baron de, 287; and see Touchet,
Thos.
Auene, Wm. de, 1420
Aueray, see Avery

Aula, *see* Hall
Aulen, *see* Allen
Aumerle, duke of, *see* Plantagenet, Edw.
Auncell, *see* Ansell
Aungere, Wm., 1005
Auny, Rev. Joseph, 1317
Aure, *see* Awre
Aust, John, 727*; Sarah, 727
Austin (Austyn), Ant., 1537; Edw., 1369, 1534*,
    1536; Eliz., 386*, 1536; Fanny, 1536; Francis,
    1226; Giles, 1529, 1534; Isaac, 1536; Jarvis,
    386*; John, 1534; L'Estange Southwood, 1536;
    Margaretta, 1529; Mary, 386*, 595, 1534*; Rob.,
    386; Sir Rob., bt., 347; Thos., 530, 604, 1534*;
    Wal., 1491; Wm., 386, 595, 1534*; Rev. Wm.,
    463; —, 288
Avad (Avard), *see* Harvard
Avenant, Rev. Thos., 895, 897; Rev. Mr., 895
Avenbury, Maud de, 671
Avenel (Avenell), Radulph, 1238; —, 1237
Avening (Aveninge), Alice (Alys), 361, 362, 368,
    372; John, 372
Averill, —, 1460
Averis (Averiss), Dan., 975; John, 337; Mary, 730;
    Rebecca, 337; Stephen, 661; Wm., 975
Avery (Aueray), Alice, 1434; Eliz., 1025; Hannah,
    97; John, 1491, 1583; Jonathan, 1434*; Martha,
    1434; Mary, 1583; Thos., 1025; Wm., 97; Rev.,
    1217; —, 1257, 1258
Awbrey (Aubrey), Thos., 678*; Rev. Wm., 678; —,
    1339
Awdrey, Ambrose, 781; Rebecca, 781
Awfield, Rev. Rob., 128
A'Wood, *see* Attwood
Awre (Aure), Anne, 110*; Caseandrew, 110; Chas.,
    110*; Gil. (de), 101, 110; John (de), 110*, 1539;
    Mary, 110; Thos., 110
Axpode, Wal., 1540
Axtel, Ric., 1379
Aycocks, *see* Acock
Aycrigg, Benj., 1359; —, 1362
Aykewe, Ric., 1447
Ayland, Joseph, 623; Mary, 623; Thos., 623*, 1101
Aylard, Joseph, 1100
Aylberton (Ailberton, Alberton), Anne, 1394; Joan,
    1394; John, 1394*, 1402; Joseph, 1402; Mary,
    1394, 1402; Mitchel(l), 1394, 1402; Sam., 1402;
    Wm., 927*; Mr., 927; —, 927, 1394; fam., 1402*
Aylesford (Aynesford), —, 1402
Aylet, John, 496; Philopone, 496; Sarah, 496
Ayleward, *see* Aylworth
Ayleway, *see* Alway
Ayleworth, *see* Aylworth
Ayliffe, Wm., 517; —, 1202
Ayling (Aling), Eliz., 796*; J., 1328; Jas., 796
Ayllway, *see* Alway
Aylmer, John, bishop, 1223; Lord, 1519*
Ayloffe, Joseph, 561; Marg., 561
Aylrich (Aylriche), *see* Alrich
Aylway, *see* Alway
Aylworth (Ailworth, Aleworth, Ayleward,
    Ayleworth), Anne, 1301*; Ant., 689; Arthur,

1301*, 1307; Edith, 1307; Edw., 79; Eliz., 79;
    Elsabeth, 889; Frances, 1307; H., 1519; Joshua,
    944, 1042, 1190; R., 1328; Ric., 890; T., 1312;
    —, 309, 889, 1196, 1362, 1478; fam., 889
Aylzot, John, 1372
Aynesford, *see* Aylesford
Ayres, Sir Chris. 743; Jas., 812; John, 479; Reuben,
    112
Ayscough (Ascough), John 707, 1074
Aysfield, *see* Ashfield
Ayshcombe, *see* Ashcomb
Azor (fl. 11th cent.), 1512

Baber (Babor), John, 739; Rev. John, 1336, 1339;
    Mary, 739
Babington, Eliz., 223; John, 432; Sir Wm., 223
Babor, *see* Baber
Bach, *see* Bache
Bachcote, J., 1256
Bache (Bach), Rev. J., 886; Margery, 788; Thos.,
    788*; —, 1355; *and see* Back; Bake
Bachelor, *see* Batchelor
Back, Ursula, 1424; *and see* Bache; Bake
Backer, Mary, 1510
Backhouse, Jane, 1090; Marg., 1090; Rob., 313;
    Thos., 1090; Capt., 894 n, 928
Backwell, Jane, 1410
Bacon, Dorothy, 854; Eliz., 659; Sir Francis, kt.,
    324*; Rev. John, 659; Mary, 659*; Rog., 197;
    Thos., 854; —, 1067; —, friar, 648
Badam, *see* Badham
Badcock (Batecoke), Rev. John, 1217; Wal., 1197
Baddam, *see* Badham
Badern, *see* Bathern
Badger, Rev. Chas., 78, 1348; Dan., 1145*; David,
    1141; (or Badgehott), Edm., 1064; Geo., 1092;
    Giles, 1092; Rev. Jas., 89, 147; John, 1473; Rev.
    John, 1348*; Mary, 1145; Prudence, 1396; Sir T.,
    see Baghott; Thos., 1396*, 1403; Wm., 1361,
    1403; fam., *see* Baghott
Badham (Badam, Baddam), Anne, 1319; Geo., 923;
    Hannah, 1319*; Hopkin, 1319*; Wm., 736, 1323;
    fam., 1322*; *and see* Adams; ap Adam
Badnege, Hen., 381; Sarah, 381
Badsey, Sarah, 1361; Thos., 1361
Badson, Ric., 1388; Wm., 1388
Bagehott, *see* Baghott
Bagg (Bag, Baggs), Eliz., 47; Hen., 47; Hester, 47;
    John, 184; Mary, 1226; Rev. Rob., 184; Stephen,
    47; Mr., 960; *and see* Beg
Baghott (Bagehott, Baghot, Bagott), Ann(e), 982,
    986*, 1136; C., 1092*; Cath. Hester, 986; Edm.,
    see Badger; Edw., 952, 986*; Eleanor (Elinor),
    1090, 1092; Eliz., 323 n*, 324, 983, 986, 1138;
    Frances, 986; Geo., 986; Grace, 986; (later
    Delabere), Hester, 986; Hester Eliz., 986; John,
    986, 1052; Kath., 986; Kinard, 986; Rev. Kynard
    (Kinard, Kinnard), 519, 983, 1140*; Kinard
    Wm., 986; Marg., 952, 986; P., 1215; Sir P.,
    1139; Paul, 1139; Sir Paul, 1136; Ric., 1140;
    Sam. Paul, 1139; Sarah, 986; (or Badger), Sir T.,
    986; Thos., 986*; Rev. Thos., 519, 890, 1138; Sir

Thos., 986; W., 986; Wm., 392, 519, 982, 986*, 1090; Winifred, 986; —, 1064*, 1092, 1215; (or Badger), fam., 986

Baghott Delabere, *see* Delabere

Baglin, Eliz., 284; John, 284*

Bagnall (Bagnel), Benj., 1041; John, 872, 1041

Bagott, *see* Baghott

Bailey (Baillie, Baillyff, Baily, Bayley, Bayli, Baylly, Bayly, Beleye), Agnes, 1055; Alex., 109*; Allise, 1250*; Anna, 666; Ann(e), 77, 109, 171, 626, 677, 687, 730, 1000, 1131, 1437; Anselm(e), 677, 832, 1438*; Chas., 379, 1250*, 1258; Christian, 106, 107, 1536; Chris., 333, 1536; Dorothy, 625 n, 626, 1435, 1440*; E., 1522; Edw., 171, 961*, 1112*, 1536; Elenor, 1555; Eliza, 1375; Eliz., 166, 171*, 172, 212, 379, 413, 418, 419, 627, 797, 845, 961, 1112, 1155, 1250, 1435*, 1438; Eliz. Jane, 1488; Francis, 1250, 1258; Rev. Francis Turner Jas., 1434; Geo., 406; Rev. Geo., 1147, 1196; Giles, 418*; Gore, 1045; Grace, 95; Hannah, 109; Hen., 1289; Hester, 961; Isabel, 109; Jas., 166, 172, 531, 540, 662, 1439; Joan, 666; John, 81, 107, 109, 171*, 173, 412*, 419*, 597, 666*, 677, 703, 730, 845, 1055, 1365, 1368, 1437, 1439; Jonathan, 109; Joseph, 578; Joyce, 626; Leonard, 419; M., 1365; Marg., 418; Margery, 1055; Martha, 536; Mary, 77, 171, 212, 412, 419*, 578, 597, 666, 677, 797*, 887, 1000, 1045*, 1112, 1365, 1368, 1439, 1536; Nat., 1438; Rachel, 406; Radegund, 626; Ric. (le), 77*, 108, 212, 797, 845, 1238; Rob., 407; Rog., 107, 409; Ruth, 109; Sam., 211, 212*, 578, 1243*; Sarah, 49, 108*, 109, 171, 173, 407, 418*, 419, 961, 1250*, 1438, 1536; Susannah, 961; T., 976, 1063; Theophilus, 108*; Thos., 48, 49, 95*, 159, 160, 212*, 418, 419, 535, 536, 666, 797, 1375, 1488*, 1536*; Rev. Thos., 1102, 1133, 1135, 1140; Valentine, 379*; W., 1440; Wal. (le), 108, 109, 1172; Wm., 95, 109, 173*, 174, 342, 413, 418, 419, 625, 626*, 627*, 666, 687, 703, 797, 887, 1000*, 1043, 1045, 1054, 1131, 1435*, 1438*, 1440, 1486, 1491, 1522, 1536; —, 1054, 1069; (or Hodgets), —, 1092; fam., 819; *and see* Baylis

Bailis, *see* Baylis

Baillie (Baillyff, Baily), *see* Bailey

Bainam, *see* Baynham

Bainbroke, Rev. Thos., 255

Baine, *see* Baynes

Bainham, *see* Baynham

Bainton, *see* Baynton

Baion, Thos. de, 565

Baird, Dr., 327 n

Bairsbrigg, Col., 313 n

Bake, Thos., 1317; *and see* Bache; Back

Baker (Beaker), Abraham, 984; Ann(e), 100, 186, 237, 276, 963*, 984, 1222, 1375, 1410, 1547; Arabella, 637; Benj., 963; Betty, 637*; Chas., 1361, 1362, 1536; D., 1140; Dan., 240; E., 1140; Edw., 1307*, 1317, 1319; Eleanor, 1315; Elia le, 1539; Eliz., 100, 186, 781, 963, 1079, 1222, 1328, 1480; Esther, 728; Frances, 1165; Francis,

394; Rev. Francis, 603; Rev. Geo., 1004; Grace, 1298; Hannah, 728; Hester, 338, 768; J., 1232; Jas., 1480, 1547*; Jane, 100, 186, 727, 1298*, 1398; Jo[a]ne, 739; John, 55, 99, 100*, 270*, 339, 781, 820, 923*, 963, 1079, 1232, 1298*, 1315*, 1328, 1396-7, 1398*, 1536*; (or Williams), Rev. John, 1317; Sir John, bt., 44; John Innys, 1420*; Joseph, 731, 963, 1298; Lawr., 625; Rev. Lloyd, 1369; Lucretia, 1298; Lucy Maria, 186; Marg., 1165, 1315*; Martha, 781, 960; Mary, 44, 52, 55, 217, 270, 338, 728, 818, 923*, 980, 1222*, 1298, 1307, 1367, 1368, 1375, 1536; Nic., 237, 739, 1313; Phil., 47, 728*; Sir. R., 1165*; Ralph, 100*, 728; Ric., 494, 522, 637, 818, 1222*; Rob., 731; Sam., 1138, 1215; Sarah, 47, 217, 240, 456, 958, 1298, 1361, 1397; Slade, 1420*; Thos. (le), 55, 217*, 276, 637, 727, 743, 744, 818*, 980, 1101, 1258; Rev. Thos., 184, 186*, 1368; Sir Thos., 743, 1165; Rev. Thos. J., 1369; Thos. John Lloyd, 1367; Tobias, 1138; Rev. W., 1186*; Wal., 1061; Wm., 217, 456, 637, 743, 744, 768, 958, 1222*, 1223, 1298; Rev. Wm., 436, 438, 503, 804; Rev. Wm. Lloyd, 1367, 1368*; Mr., 1420; —, 1223*, 1368; (or Weaver), —, 1355; *and see* Becker; Pistor

Baladon, *see* Balun

Baldewyne, *see* Baldwin

Balding (Balden), Joseph, 270; Rob., 1218

Baldrich, Ric., 1387

Baldwin, abbot, 1355

Baldwin (Baldwyn, Baldewyne), Ambrose, 1288, 1358*; Ann(e), 90, 118, 299, 473; Beata, 299*; Benj., 118, 262, 388; Bernard, 90*, 150; Chas., 1288; Edwin, 1358*; Eleanor, 299, 796*; Eliz., 90, 118, 150, 797, 800, 1358; Frances, 90*; Geo., 299, 800, 815; Hannah, 1358*; Hen., 299*, 1049, 1404; Hester, 1434; Rev. J., 1127; Jas., 468; Rev. Jas., 1127; Jane, 1358*; John, 90*, 262, 387, 431, 815, 832, 1403; Joseph, 262*; Marg., 261; Mary, 90*, 693, 1049, 1077*; Phil., 884; Priscilla, 262; Prudence, 262*; Rachel, 1046; Ric., 90*, 261, 262, 814, 1046, 1103, 1460; Rose, 884; Sam., 1030; Sarah, 468, 796, 797, 832, 1434*; Stephen, 90, 1288, 1358*, 1362; Susanna, 90, 1333; Thos., 90, 262*, 666, 693*, 796*, 797, 1333, 1358*, 1363; Rev. W., 1125; Wm., 133, 262, 473, 602*, 1049*, 1382, 1434*; Rev. Wm., 685; —, 985, 1362*, 1447

Balis, *see* Baylis

Balistarius (*balistarius*), Wal., 612, 1401, 1403

Balkereve, Ric., 1382

Ball (Balle, Bawle), Alex., 1348; Alice, 736; Ann, 1112, 1337, 1575*; Cath., 1172*; Edm., 777*, 911; Elias, 1172*; Eliz., 736, 1182, 1429; Geo., 1112, 1575; Hannah, 250, 777, 1180; Hester, 1509; Jas., 1112; Joanna, 836; John, 250, 532, 540, 1112, 1179*, 1182*, 1185, 1348, 1429*; Capt. John, 1179; Rev. John, 1122; Martha, 1509; Mary, 540*, 777, 1179*, 1182, 1185, 1266, 1429; Mary Ann, 1575; Obadiah, 660; P., 918; Ric., 777*, 1387; Rob., 1179*, 1182, 1184, 1185, 1509*; Rev. Rob., 559, 561; Rev. Rog., 1147;

Ruth, 1429; Sam., 1180, 1182, 1337; Sara(h), 540, 777, 1182*; Thos., 324, 540, 777; Rev. Thos., 678*; Wm., 250, 540, 736, 777, 836, 1504, 1575

Ballacote, Wm. de, 1255*

Balland, Martha, 1582

Ballard, Arthur, 1408*; Dan., 1118; Edw., 1430*; Eleanor, 980; Eliz., 295, 1408; Hewelina, 1504; Jas., 886; Rev. Jas., 524; Joan(e), 1457*, 1458; John, 1430, 1457*, 1458; Jonathan, 1457; Joseph, 980; Josiah, 1457; Josias, 1458; Martha, 1430; Martin, 1458; Mary, 1118, 1191; Nic., 296; Rachel, 1408*; Ric., 1196; Sam., 295; T., 1460; Thos., 1457*, 1458*; Wm., 1191; Rev. Wm., 696; —, 864 n, 1460

Balle, see Ball

Ballinger (Ballinge, Bellenger, Bellinger), Ann, 1493; Bernard, 366, 1499*; Cath., 1058; Chas., 320, 575, 948, 1499; Edm., 800; Eliz., 644; Esther, 983; Giles, 254; Hen., 1058; Jas., 1165, 1493*; John, 340, 800; Marg., 1499; Mary, 800*, 1499; Mic., 1499, 1502; Rachel, 254; Rebecca, 317; Ric., 644, 983; Rob., 254; Sarah, 320; Thos., 317, 800, 1499; Wal., 1289; Wm., 317, 399, 800*

Balster, Jane, 923; Sam., 923

Baltimore, baron, see Calvert, Chas.

Balun (Baladon), Isolda de, 556; Rog. de, 1035; Winebald de, 556, 1035

Bamard [? recte Barnard], Jas., 1516

Bambury, see Banbury

Bamford (Baneford, Banford), Ann, 1086; Dorothea, 1247*; Edw., 1247; Eliz., 1248, 1251, 1376; Hen., 1247; Isabella, 1247; John, 368, 1248, 1251, 1376; Josiah, 1251; Maria, 1247; Martha, 1086; Mary, 780, 1251, 1434; Mat. Paul, 1248; Prudence, 1434; Ric., 1434; Rob., 1247*; Thos., 348; Wm., 780, 1086*, 1258

Bampfield (Bamfylde), Sir Chas. Warwick, 1385*; Edith, 1077; Jane, Lady Bamfylde, 1385; Mary, 1077; Sir Ric., bt., 1385*; Wm., 1077

Bampton (Bamptone), Ann(e), 794, 834; Eliz., 15; Hen., 794*, 795; Hugh, abbot, 1052*; Hugh (or Hen.) de, 359; John (de), 15, 1148; Juliana de, 1197; R., 1385; Sam., 795, 834*; Susannah, 794*, 795; —, 1017

Banast (Banaster, Banastre), see Bannister

Banbury (Bambury, Bannebury), Eliz., 1331; Ernald de, 1060, and see Ernald; Frances, 953; John, 953*; Wm., 1015, 1227; —, 1195

Banck (Bancks), see Banks

Band, Rev. Nic., 233; Rev. Wm., 427

Bane, see Baynes

Baneford (Banford), see Bamford

Banester, see Bannister

Bangor, Viscount, 1150

Banister, see Bannister

Banks (Banck, Bancks, Bankes), Arabella, 1474*; Benj., 550; Rev. Hen., 1428; Rev. John, 449; Rev. Lawr., 1104, 1149; Mary, 550; Ric. (la), 1431, 1519; Rev. Ric., 1519; Wm., 922; Rev. Wm., 1387; Mr., 1149; —, 1475, 1477

Bannaster, see Bannister

Bannebury, see Banbury

Banner, Thos., 980; Wm., 980

Banning, Eliz., 296; Hester, 124; Nat., 124; Sarah, 1194; Rev. Stephen, 19, 783; Thos., 296, 1194

Bannister (Banast, Banaster, Banastre, Banester, Banister, Bannaster, Bannyster, Banyster), Chas., 1289; Dingley, 1163; Eliz., 705, 1350*; Fredeswed, 919; Geo., 73, 483, 922*, 1349, 1350, 1355; Jane, 1349*, 1350; John, 922; Joyce, 335; Mary, 335; Ric., 335*, 799; Sarah, 73; Thos., 919, 1163; Rev. Thos., 1165, 1233; W., 1350, 1475; Wm., 468, 688*, 705, 1282, 1349*, 1350; Sir Wm., kt., 1349, 1350*

Banson, Thos., 730, 1329; Sir Thos., kt., 1329; and see Benson

Bany, Ann, 1316; Wm., 1316

Banyster, see Bannister

Barakle, John, 1473

Baram, Joseph, 1415; Mary, 1415

Barber (Barben, Barbour), Alice, 1454; Cath., 1454; Christian, 1454; Eleanor, 659; Eliz., 1454; Hannah, 1454; Jane, 1282; John, 1292; Marg., 1454; Ric., 1454*, 1456; Rog., 1147; Ruth, 1455; Stephen, 1454; Thos., 659*; Wm., 1454*, 1455*; —, 1455

Barckley, see Berkeley

Barcroft, Charlotte, 1559; Debora, 1559; Gil., 1556*, 1559*; John, 1559; Laetitia, 1556; Sarah, 1559

Bardoe, Mary, 1450; Sam., 1450

Bardsat, Alice, 1202; E., 1202

Bares, Chas., 1279; Diana, 1279; Rev. Francis, 1279; Hen., 1279; Olive, 1279

Baret, see Barrett

Barford, Alice, 422; Jonathan, 422; Mary, 422; Rev. Wm., 704

Bariatinsky, Cath. Eliz. Louisa Maria Frances, 1067; Princess Frances Mary, 1067; Prince John, 1067; Prince, 1067

Barkeley (Barkeleye), see Berkeley

Barker (Bercare), And., 588, 591, 592*, 593; Ann, 257; Cath., 257; Eliz., 845; Esther, 592; F., 257*; Isaac, 1372; J. R., 1005; Jane, 591; John, 293, 797; (formerly Raymond), John, 592; John Raymond, 593, 860; Joseph, 845*; Joyce, 845; Marg., 339; Martha, 845; Mary, 31, 257*, 592, 845, 1273; N., 1356; Rev. Peter, 1221; R., 257; Raymond, 859; Rob. (le), 73, 1198; Sam., 592, 696; Sarah, 257*, 1372; Talbot, 114; Thos., 21, 36, 257*, 339, 817; Lieut. Thos., 257*; Wm. de, 1043; Rev. Wm., 785; Mr., 859; Rev., 1372; fam., 588; (or Coverall), fam., 592

Barkerville, see Baskerville

Barkley (Barkly), see Berkeley

Barksdale (Barksdall), Chas., 891; Charlton, 891; Rev. Charlton, 704; Clement, 891; Rev. Clement, 890*, 1221, 1477, 1478; Eliz., 880*; Geo., 1465*; Joan, 891; John, 880, 1478; Margareta Weld, 1466; Mary, 891*, 1465; Mary Barbara, 880; Wm., 891, 1466; Mrs., 197; —, 1477

Barlich, —, 1093

Barlow, Benj., 1016; Chas., 1388; Rev. John, 1419; T., 1419

Barly, Dorothy, 862*; Stephen, 862*

Barnam, —, 1455

Barnard, Abigail, 752; Deborah, 752; Edw., 1028*, 1029*, 1030; Eleanor, 1028, 1244; Eliz., 398, 486, 622*, 623*, 755, 803, 1028; Ester, 1028; Rev. H., 1447; Hannah, 1319; J., 1512; Jas., 623*, *and see* Bamard; Joan(e), 1012, 1016; John, 622*, 623, 1012, 1017, 1028*, 1029, 1030*, 1137*, 1140, 1244; Rev. John, 1031; Joseph, 486, 803; Kath., 1337; Marg., 1028, 1030*; Mary, 316, 1028, 1137; Matilda, 1074; Ric., 755, 1028; Sam., 623; Sarah, 468, 486, 623*, 1028, 1029; Susanna, 1028, 1029; Thos., 398*, 468, 622, 623, 752, 1137, 1319; Wal., 1233; Wm., 486*, 622*, 1186, 1289; —, 1140, 1421, 1512; *and see* Bamard; Bernard

Barnefield, *see* Barnfield

Barnell, Thos., 1110

Barnes (Barns), Alice, 338; Ann(e), 212, 225, 539, 756*, 765, 1273; Ant., 151, 1442, 1443; B., 1378; Benj., 402, 486; Betty, 765; Chas., 1366*; Edw., 756*, 973; Eliz., 541, 974, 1269; Frances, 906; Griffin, 958; Hannah, 211, 632*; Hen., 973*, 1366; Humph., 1034; Jas., 550*, 687, 1325, 1352, 1366; Jane, 399, 973; Joan, 541*; John, 211, 212, 225, 399*, 539*, 541*, 765, 906, 1121, 1269*, 1362, 1529; Joseph, 402*, 765*, 1116; Marg., 1442, 1443*; Margery, 714; Martha, 211, 906; Mary, 151, 211, 225, 402*, 486, 550, 687*, 765*, 867, 898, 946, 979*, 1325, 1366*; Nic., 1355; Prudence, 906; Ralph, 898*; Ric., 632, 803; Sam., 632; Sarah, 973, 1269*; Simon, 979*; Susanna, 846; Thos., 211*, 846, 1273*, 1289, 1325, 1363, *and see* Berners; Tim., 338, 687*, 765; W., 1539; Wm., 151, 212, 402*, 486, 687, 765, 846, 867*, 973, 974; Rev. Wm., 1162; Woolvin, 541; Rev., 1161*; —, 985*, 1290; fam., 630

Barnesley, *see* Barnsley

Barnett (Barnet), Chas., 1542; Ebenezer, 1573; Eliz., 1573; Joan, 1542; Joanna, 1542; John, 1266*, 1542*; Mary, 1266*; Mary Ann, 1415; Rob., 1542*; Thos., 789

Barnfield (Barnefield), Anne, 423; Jas., 542; John, 660; Joseph, 752; Mary, 450, 752; Ric., 450; Sam., 660*; Wm., 423, 752

Barnolph, *see* Beornwulf

Barns, *see* Barnes

Barnsdale, Rev. John, 279, 619; Mary, 878

Barnsley (Barnesley, Barnsly), Jane, 268; John, 573*; Mary, 573; Rebecca Brereton, 130; Rev. Reg., 1228; Lieut. Sam., 573; Susannah, 573; Thos., 573*; Wm., 268; Wm. B., 130; fam., 570

Barnwood, Edm., 716*; Mary, 716

Barodale, *see* Barradell

Baron (Baroun), *see* Barron

Barow, *see* Barrow

Barr (Barre), Sir J., kt., 1238; John, 205; Rob. atte, 1069; fam., 205

Barradell (Barodale), Eliz., 983; Rev. Gabral, 1392; Kinnard, 983; Mary, 983

Barran, *see* Barron

Barre, *see* Barr

Barrett (Baret, Barratt, Barret), Alice, 1212, 1214; Ann(e), 111, 112, 1077; Arthur, 871; Dinah, 662; Eliz., 873; Geof., 1363; Geo., 662, 1077, 1238; Rev. Geo., 302; Hen., 973, 1212*, 1214*, 1217; Isaac, 1205; Isabell, 1214; Jas., 1415; Job, 296; John, 112, 873, 1212; Martha, 871, 965; Mary, 296, 464, 1212, 1214, 1415; Ralph, 872; Ric., 111, 112, 873*, 1212, 1214*; Rowena, 1077; Sarah, 660, 973; Thos., 660; Rev. Thos., 979; Wm., 965; —, 228, 1455

Barrey, *see* Barry

Barrington, Jane, 581; John, 17; Shute, bishop, 260, 581, 582, 1009;

Barron (Baron, Baroun, Barran), Adam, 1314; Ann(e), 886*; B., 1421*; Chas., 632; Eliz., 631, 887; Geo., 472*, 632*, 886*, 887; Hannah, 886*; Hester, 886; John, 886; Marg., 632; Margery, 472; Mary, 631, 632, 886*; Nic., 472, 631, 632, 1447; Rob., 1313, 1447, 1456; Sarah, 632; Thos., 631; Wm., 466; —, 1311; fam., 885

Barrow (Barow, Berewe, Berow, Berrow, Berrowe, Berrowes, Berue), Agnes atte, 1069; Ales [Alice], 811; Angeletta, 1000; Ann(e), 1000*, 1274, 1515; Cath., 958; Chas., 352; Sir Chas., bt., 102, 103, 606, 869, 872; Dan., 832; Deborah, 249; Dorety, 999; Edm., 664, 811, 813, 999, 1000; Edw., 249, 150*; Eleanor, 664, 1000*; Eliz., 664 n, 958, 999; Frauncis, 999; Geo., 103, 597, 1386; Hannah, 1274; Rev. Hen., 7, 36, 1428; Hester, 1307; Jas. (Jhamis), 999*, 1516; Jane, 597*; John (Johan)(atte), 103, 111, 250, 467, 597*, 999, 1274, 1381, 1428, 1514, 1515; Joseph, 1132; Love, 1514; Mabel, 999; Marg., 1000*, 1381; Mary, 958, 1386, 1515; Rebekah, 1274; Ric. (Rychard), 999*, 1000, 1274, 1515*, 1516; Sarah, 832; T., 1312; Thos. (atte), 103, 111, 249*, 352, 664*, 958*, 999*, 1000*, 1027, 1274*, 1381, 1428, 1516; Wal., 664 n; Wm., 250*, 958, 1386; —lett, 924; —, 1020, 1317, 1386, 1402; fam., 105, 349, 1381, 1402

Barry (Barrey), Barbara, 513; Chas., 210; John, 1329, 1530; Juliana, 1552; Rev. Martin, 263, 511, 513, 667; Rev. Ric., 206, 210*; Rob., 1355; Susannah, 513*; Wm., 1530; —, 1311; fam., 392

Barston, Eliz., 150; Ric., 150; —, 1293

Bartelot, *see* Bartlett

Barten, *see* Barton

Barter, Adam, 1069

Bartholomew, abbot, 708

Bartholomew, Francis, 1266; John, 1258; (or Smith), Hester, 1250; Mary, 48, 295; (or Smith), Ric., 1250; Susanna, 290; Thos., 48, 1266; Rev. Wm., 288, 290, 295; —, 1063

Bartlem (Bartlam), Mary, 815; Thos., 469, 873*

Bartlett (Bartelot), Agnes, 1313; Alice, 1041*; Betty, 598, 1307; Cecilia, 849; Edw., 46*, 1304*; Eliz., 46, 1063, 1304, 1307; Hannah, 46, 1411*; Joan, 1307; John, 46, 1304*, 1307, 1411*; Marg., 1304*; Mary, 211, 1477; R., 1477; Ric., 429, 849, 1226*; Rob., 598; Sarah, 204; Thos., 203, 204;

W., 1312; Wm., 598, 953, 1307, 1313; Mr., 1103; —, 1226*, 1287, 1392

Barton (Barten), Ann(e), 433, 939, 1307*; Edith, 1109; Eliz., 891; Geo., 1303; Harriet, 1419; Hen., 954; J., 1312; John (de), 433, 935, 1303, 1307, 1313; Jonathan, 1307*; Kath., 935; Mary, 1307; Priscilla, 954; R. de, 1485; Ric., 939; Sarah, 952, 1297; Susannah, 1303; Thos., 891, 1109, 1196, 1297; W. de, 1485; Wm., 210, 952; Rev., 1014

Bartram, *see* Bertram

Barwick, Dr. John, 1066; Mary, 1066; *and see* Berwick

Bas, Rog. le, 1485

Bascoe, John, 1138

Basdale, —, 890

Basile (Basiles), Marg., 1120, 1339; Sir Peter, 1120

Baskerville (Barkerville, Baskerfeld, Baskervyle, Baskeville, Baskevylle), Anne, 1423; Bernard, 1421; Dr. Edw., 1422*; Eliz., 255; Humph., 821; Jas., 1421; Jane, 643; Lawr., 671; Ralph, 1421, 1422-3; Rev. Ric., 1422; Rob., 1421; Rog., 1422; Wal., 255, 643, 1421, 1422; Sir Wal., 1421; Wm., 704; Lady, 1422*; —, 1217, 1355; fam., 255, 1421*

Baskett, John, 1330

Baskeville (Baskevylle), *see* Baskerville

Bason (Besyn), John de, 1093; fam., 392 n

Bass (Basse), *see* Bayse

Bassett (Basset), Agatha, 1350; Sir Anselm, 1369; Arthur, 613*, 1047; Chas., 1008; Edm., 1369; Edw., 1369; Eliz., 834; Gil., 1015*; John, 1047, 1197, 1214; Jonathan, 1008; Marg., 783, 1369; Ralph, 1015, 1350; Ric., 1197; Rog., 1223; T., 1091; Thos., 1015; Wm., 834, 1369*; —, 1015, 1350*, 1381; fam., 612, 783, 1015

Bassford, Thos. de, 1476

Bastard, *see* Burstead

Bastin (Baston), Ann, 316, 317; Eliz., 1058*; Esther, 174; John, 317; Mary, 1058*; Thos., 174, 316, 1058*; Wm., 317; fam., 992

Batchelor (Bachelor), Giles, 411; Honner, 841*; John, 841*

Bate, *see* Bates

Batecoke, *see* Badcock

Bateman (Batman), Anne, 434; Rev. B., 1356; Rev. Benj., 1265*; Eliz., 434, 689, 752, 1265; Honora, 1265*; Jas., 434*; Jane, 1350; John, 434, 752; Joyce, 434; R., 1502; Sarah, 212; Simon, 1350; Thos., 689, 1499; Wm., 212, 1408; Rev., 1352

Bates (Bate), Betty, 1328; Eleanor, 867; Isaac, 1319; Jas., 340; Joseph, 1395; R., 1516; Thos., 867, 1460; Wm., 1328; Rev., 1315; —, 1459; fam., 863

Bateson (Batson), Ann(e), 231*, 1103; Hen., 821; Rob., 231; Rob. Devereux, 231; Wm., 230, 231*, 272, 882, 1103; Mr., 882; —, 231; fam., 230*

Bath (Bathe), Alice, 1401; Anne, 1401; Eliz., 1401; Rev. Geo., 691; Jeff(e)ry, 366, 368, 652; Lydia, 1302; Marg., 1302; Nevill, 1302; Nic. de, 1401, 1402; — de, 1402

Bath [*peerage*], Marg., countess of, 1435; *and see* Thynne, Thos.

Bathern (Badern, Bathom, Bathon, Bathone), Marg., 1402; Nic., 1404; Rob., 1403; W., 1062*; —, 1402

Bathurst, Allen, Earl Bathurst, 363, 364*, 367, 379*, 459, 713, 806 n; Allen, Lord Bathurst, 1052, 1080, 1082; Rev. Allen, 180, 1048; Anne, 792, 806, 808; Sir B., 1082; Barbara, 795; Benj., 364*, 806*, 1080; Sir Benj., kt., 363*, 366; Lady Betty, 1083; Cath., Lady Bathurst, 363 n, 379*; Edw., 795; Sir Edw., bt., 792*, 793*, 794*; Eliz., 794*, 1080; Harriott, 1332; Hen., 364*; Hen., Earl Bathurst, 298, 360, 370, 444, 460; Hen., Lord Apsley, 364, 525, 526; John, 1048*; Lawr., 791, 795; Leonora, 1048; Marg., 794*; Mary, 792, 795; Peter, 364, 1332; Poole, 806; Dr. R., 287 n*; Rob., 792, 793*, 794*; Susanna(h), 794, 795, 806; Thos., 102, 806; Dr., 1048; Earl, 365*, 525, 806, 1048, 1050, 1052, 1082*, 1083; Lord, 368, 1082, 1440; Mr., 1080; —, 1186*; —, baron Apsley, 363 n; fam., 297, 792

Batingson, Ann, 958; John, 958*

Batman, *see* Bateman

Batsford, Jane, 1473; John, 1467; Joseph, 1473

Batson, *see* Bateson

Batt, Eliz., 203, 209; Jas., 506; John, 1476; Martha, 203; Rog., 203; Thos., 201

Battel, *see* Battle

Batteley, Rev. Oliver, 13

Batten (Battens, Battin, Batyn, Batyns), Ann, 407; Cath., 315; Rev. Edw., 613; John, 315, 499*, 1228; Mary, 499, 1549; Ric., 1549*; Rob., 1426; Thos., 1329, 1420; Wm., 407*, 1329

Battle (Battel, de Bello), J., 1477; Joan, 1051; Miles, 1051

Batyn (Batyns), *see* Batten

Baudenton, *see* Baunton

Baugh (Baughe), Alice, 1359; Anne, 1269, 1280; Constance, 1269; Edw., 1269, 1357, 1358*, 1361*, 1363; Hen. Chas., 1323; Joseph, 1280; Judith, 1358; Mary, 1280, 1357; Ric., 1358*, 1359*, 1363*; Rowland, 1363; W., 1363; Wm., 1358*, 1363

Baunton (Baudenton), Clement of, 1201; John, 74; Maud of, 1201; Stephen of, 1201

Bave (Bavey), Dr. Ant., 1525; Mary, 1525; Sam., 206

Bawl, *see* Ball

Bawn, *see* Bourne

Baxfel, Ric., 1140

Baxter (Baxtere), Anne, 1354; Chas., 567*; Chris., 287 n; Dudley, 1140; Eliz., 567*, 660; Geo., 567*, 1126; Jas., 225; John, 660; Mary, 660; Rev. Nat., 630; Nic. la, 1392; Phil., 567, 1355; Ric., 567*, 1354; Sarah, 567*; —, 925

Bayce, *see* Bayse

[Bayeux], Thos. of, archbishop, 346, 1131, 1232, 1493

Baye [? Paye], Eliz., 1058

Bayley (Bayli, Baylly), *see* Bailey

Baylis (Bailis, Balis, Baylies, Bayliss), Ann(e), 118, 138, 429, 637*, 641, 706*, 762, 1152, 1334*, 1386, 1465, 1472*; Ant., 494; Caleb,

637; Dan., 1023, 1215; Dinah, 1466*; Edw., 1034, 1353*; Eliza, 632; Eliz., 641*, 710, 1023*, 1024, 1426; Emma, 1426; Esther, 1034, 1334; Geo., 1012, 1518; Hannah, 637*, 706, 976, 1412; Hannah Brown, 1426; Harry, 706; Hen., 1353; Hester, 1353, 1466, 1471; Isaac, 706*, 710*, 1466*; Jas., 632, 822*; Jane, 138, 641, 756, 1024; (or Randall), Jane, 150; Johannah, 641; John, 118, 399, 429, 522, 756*, 974, 976*, 1150, 1151, 1152, 1267, 1273, 1334, 1362, 1472; Joseph, 762; Joshua, 1472, 1475, 1477; Ligon, 1152; Marg., 399, 1471, 1473; Margery, 494; Mark, 1334; Mary, 522, 706, 744, 756, 974, 1012, 1034, 1334, 1471*, 1472*, 1499; Matthea, 1267; Moses, 637; Pleasent, 1334; R., 1475; Rebecca, 706, 1391; Ric., 118; Rob., 637*, 641, 706, 1023, 1103, 1220, 1427, 1471*, 1472*, 1475*, 1499*; Sam., 1150*, 1151, 1217, 1471, 1473; Sarah, 822, 1150, 1151, 1391, 1426, 1427, 1518; Stephen, 762; T., 1203, 1215; Thos., 118, 138, 744*, 976, 1012*, 1023*, 1024, 1034, 1334*, 1412, 1426*, 1477; Wm., 494*, 641*, 976, 1026*; 1150, 1160, 1334, 1355, 1391, 1518*; —, 1220, 1317, 1392, 1402, 1477; fam., 546; *and see* Bailey

Baylly (Bayly), *see* Bailey

Baynam (Bayneham), *see* Baynham

Baynes (Baine, Bane), Ann, 235; Rev. Chris., 432, 599, 600 n; Eliz., 282; Frances, 235; Jane, 1584; Rev. John, 704, 705; Mary, 84, 235, 1168; Nat., 84; Ruth, 84; Thos., 84; Wm., 282, 1584

Baynham (Bainam, Bainham, Baynam, Bayneham, Baynsham), Adam, 210, 834, 1543, 1552; Alice, 462, 464, 652, 913, 997, 1039, 1401, 1549; Anne, 613, 652; Cecily (Cicely), 913, 919, 920; Dan., 1402; Dorcas, 1135, 1530; Edw., 1543; Eliz., 210, 473, 1530; Grace, 1545–6; H., 1455; Hannah, 834, 1307; Hen., 1307, 1543, 1549; Rev. Hen., 613; Isabel, 421 n; Joan(e), 919, 1039; John, 1401, 1530, 1548; Rev. John, 1552; Joseph, 652*, 1135; Margery, 464; Marie, 1530; Mary, 5*, 919, 1548; Ric., 1307*; Rob., 1549; Sarah, 5, 1402; Silvester (Sylvester), 834, 1543; Thos., 421 n, 462*, 463, 464, 473, 913, 919, 920, 1039, 1545–6; Rev. Thos., 1543, 1552; Sir Thos., 913; Wm., 5*; —, 997, 1401, 1402*, 1545; fam., 102, 807, 919, 1401; *and see* Beynon; Paynham

Bayning, Paul, Viscount Bayning, 1165*

Baynsham, *see* Baynham

Baynton (Bainton, Bayntun), Sir And., 508 n; Dan., 1567*; Eliz., 1067; Hannah, 1567; Hen., 342*; Sir Hen., 1067; Mary, 1567*; Nat., 1248*; Peter, 1567; Sarah, 1248*, 1567; Thos., 463; Thomazina, 1248; Wm., 1567; Dr., 1567; fam., 305, 341

Bayse (Bass, Basse, Bayce, Bays), Alex., 1404; Anne, 352; Eliz., 352, 1516; Joseph, 1393; Marg., 352*; Thos., 787; Wm., 352*, 789; —, 403

Bayzand (Beyzand), Abigail, 273*; Eliz., 86, 273; Hannah, 90; Isaac, 90; John, 273*; Mary, 273*; Ric., 86, 273*, 1274*, 1289; Rob., 1274; Ursula, 1274; Wm., 86; —, 1288

Bazeley, T., 1005; Sir T., 1093; Rev. W., 1380 n

Beach (Beache, Beche), Francis, 899; (later Hicks Beach), Henrietta Maria, 1005; John, 666; M., 1127; M. H. H., 1127; Sir M. H. H., 1126, 1127; Mary, 666; Phil., 1160; Wm., 1005*; —, 999, 1003

Beadle (Bedel, Bedeles), Edith, 1313; Nat., 1513; Ric. le, 1447

Beadon, —, bishop, 1169

Beak, Geo., 1127

Beaker, *see* Baker; Becker

Beale (Beal, Bele), Amy, 560; Ann(e), 315, 516, 560, 905, 1232; Bridget, 560; Cath., 560, 561, 1012, 1054; Dorothy, 904; Edith, 560; Edw., 1354, 1469; Eleanor, 1336; Eliz., 560, 896*, 899, 1248, 1278, 1336, 1469*; Frances, 560; Francis, 560; Francis Hathey, 1175; Geo., 1469; Gil., 899; Hannah, 907; Helen, 1232; J., 1054, 1202; Jas., 846; Joan, 486, 1202; John, 315, 396, 479, 638, 639, 640*, 896*, 899, 1042, 1043*, 1096, 1248, 1356; Rev. John, 103, 190, 859, 860, 898, 1336; Sir John, bt., 516; Joseph, 846; Letitia, 896; Magdelen, 560; Marg., 560; Mary, 396*, 638, 640, 846, 1042, 1043, 1096*, 1232, 1354; Miles, 190, 896*; Phil., 1175; Ralph, 1469; Ric., 486, 846*; Ric. Stratford, 396; Rob., 560*, 561, 1469; Sarah, 896*, 1175; Stephen, 896; T., 1232; Thos., 396*, 638, 896*, 905, 927, 1012*, 1232*; Ursula, 560, 899; Wm., 348, 730, 905, 907, 1096*, 1147, 1232, 1233*; 1279, 1378; Mr., 927, 1372; —, 1229, 1355, 1474, 1477; fam., 649, 709 n, 894

Beams, Wm., 524, 1121*

Bearcroft, Cath., 680; Edw., 672, 680, 894*

Beard (Beerd), Ann(e), 1007, 1031, 1034, 1143, 1146; Ant., 1446; Caroline, 1143; Chas., 1143, 1146; Charlotte, 1143; Deborah, 1143*, 1146*; Edm., 887, 1053; Eliz., 1130*, 1143, 1146*, 1512; Esther, 786*; Hannah, 1180; Hen., 438; Jas., 786*; John, 959, 1007*, 1031, 1143*, 1146*, 1147, 1217; Rev. John, 802; Joseph, 1007; Judith, 1130; Kath., 1180, 1183; Mary, 563, 573, 887*, 1007, 1034*, 1143*, 1144, 1146, 1433*; Nat., 1007, 1021, 1143, 1144, 1146*, 1180*, 1183, 1186; Ric., 413, 1182*; Rob., 1433*; Sam., 563, 887, 1007, 1130*, 1131, 1132, 1180*, 1183, 1186; Sarah, 887, 1007, 1143*, 1182*; Smart, 1007; Thos., 1143*, 1146*, 1180; Wm., 1007*, 1034*, 1180; —, 1339, 1447; *and see* Bird; Byard

Beare (Bere), Jane, 954; John, 954; Wm. (le), 954*, 1258; *and see* Delabere

Bearne, Ant., 398

Bearpacker, Edw., 1522, 1525; Eliz., 1525; John, 839, 843; Jnhn [Jonathan], 1532

Beauboys, Isabel, 1073; John, 1074*

Beauchamp, Alice,, 764; Anne (de), 763, 805, 1287; Bertha de, 1255; Edith, 1092; Eliz., countess of Warwick, 1100*, 1538*; Emma, 1219; Emmeline, 1447; Francis, 123; Guy de, earl of Warwick, 1447*; H., duke of Warwick, 1261; Hen., duke of Warwick, 763, 805; Hen., Lord Beauchamp, 123*, 1287; Isabel, Lady

Abergavenny, 1287; Isabel, Lady Warwick, 1287; Isabell(a), 1291, 1328; Iva, 1092; Joan, 1082, 1219; Joan, baroness Bergavenny, 763; John (de), 481, 1092; Joseph, 140; Mary, 123; Mary, duchess of Beaufort, 123; Nonellus de, 1255; R., earl of Worcester, 1261; Ric., 1291, 1474; Ric., earl of Warwick, 153, 158*, 763, 1100*, 1328*, 1538*; Ric., Lord Abergavenny, 1287; Sir Ric., 525, 763; Thos. de, earl of Warwick, 1195; Ursuly, 140; W. (de), 1082, 1219; W., earl of Warwick, 1219; Wm. de, 1447; Wm., baron Bergavenny, 763; Wm. de, earl of Warwick, 244; —, 1055, 1082, 1165, 1255, 1392; —, earl of Warwick, 1011, 1120; fam., earls of Warwick, 228, 255, 318, 403, 440, 500, 588, 591, 1148, 1201, 1255, 1287, 1388
Beauchamp of Powick, Lord, 1380
Beaufiz, Wm., 1519
Beaufort, Edm., duke of Somerset, 1261; Edm. de, earl of Mortein, marquis of Dorset, 119; Edw., duke of Somerset, 1538; Eleanor, duchess of Somerset, 1538; Hen. de, duke of Somerset, 119; John, 1261; John de, earl of Somerset, 119
Beaufort [peerage], Eliz., duchess of, 122; Hen., duke of, 119, 121, 123*, 125, 244, 476, 495*, 612, 713, 733, 1155, 1189, 1516; Mary, duchess of, 119, 121, 123*; duchess of, 806 n, 1155, 1156, 1172, 1189; duke of, 53, 119, 121*, 124, 125, 612, 696, 697, 732, 806 n, 823, 953, 1105, 1121, 1123, 1170, 1172, 1322, 1323*, 1336, 1339, 1513, 1516*; and see Beauchamp, Mary; Somerset, passim
Beaumont, Hen., 1431; Isabel, 612; Ph[il]. de, 1033; Sir Thos., 612; Wm., 612; Lady, see Knevet, Joan
Beaurere (Boverera), Everard, 1091
Beausiz, see Beaufiz
Beauveys, Ric., 1221
Beavan, see Bevan
Beaw, Jane, 1297; Dr. Wm., bishop, 1297
Beawdley, Wm., abbot, 605
Beche, see Beach
Beck (Becke), Rev. Jas., 230*, 1154*; Rev. Ric., 1228
Becker, Jasper, 1137; Mary, 1137; Sarah, 1137; and see Baker
Beckett (Becket), Ann, 1334; Eliz., 884; Frances, 334; Jas., 332, 334*; John, 334, 1334*; Marg., 1334; Mary, 386; Pates, 334; Ric., 332, 884; Sarah, 332; Wm., 386; —, 985; —, archbishop, 1334
Beckington, Dr. Thos., 1021*
Becoues, —, 1223
Beddis, Isabel, 112; Marg., 112; Mary, 112; Wm., 112*
Beddome, Jane, 657; Joseph, 657
Bedel (Bedeles), see Beadle
Bedford, Anne, 64, 982; Edm., 1318; Edw., 64, 315, 1115; Rev. Edw., 982; Eleanor, 315; Eliz., 847, 1115*; Rev. Hen., 1115*, 1122; Jas., 847; Jane, 64; John, 64, 815; Rev. Ric., 1318*, 1323; Thos., 836; Wm., 64; —, 1355

Bedford [peerage], Jasper, duke of, 807, 1020, 1219, 1369; Jasper, Lord Bedford, 1015; John, duke of, 244; duke of 552; earl of, 688; and see Neville, G.
Bedgegood (Bedggood), see Bidgood
Bedingfield, Rev. Edm., 394*, 395
Bedwell (Betewelle), Anne, 861*; Eliz., 597*; Francis, 861; John, 861; Rev. J. Weekes, 691; Rev. John Weekes, 309, 313, 1477; Mary, 861; Thos., 597, 679; Rob. de, 1363; fam., 859; and see Biddle
Bee, Anne, 25; Betty, 1058; Cath., 1042; Edw., 25; Hannah, 1058; J., 1043; Jas., 1063; John, 1042, 1043, 1058*; Mary, 25; T., 1064; Thos., 1058*; —, 1064
Beeke, Mr., 882
Beeley (Beely), Rev. Geo., 488; Rev. Wm., 488, 1140
Beerd, see Beard
Beeston, Rev. R., 1356
Befs [? Bess], Thos., 1314
Beggegood, see Bidgood
Beg, Thos., 1339; and see Bagg
Behrthulf, king of Mercia, 1459
Beilby, bishop of London, see Porteus
Belami (Belamy), see Bellamy
Belcher, Ann, 339, 542; Benj., 948; Chas., 657; Eliz., 317*, 542, 948; John, 542; Mary, 270, 637*, 716, 993, 1350; Ric., 270, 339, 637, 993; Rob., 542; Sam., 542; Thos., 270, 1350; Wm., 317*
Bele, see Beale
Beleye, see Bailey
Belf, Rev. Hen., 1441
Belitha, Wm., 459
Bell, Ann(e), 618, 620; Cath., 620, 1045; Edw., 917*, 1477; Eleanor, 1473; Eliz., 618, 1045, 1307; J., 1419; Jas., 811; Joan, 997; John, 1299, 1342, 1473; Rev. John, 221; Marg., 1473, 1474; Mary, 1045, 1299, 1315, 1342, 1473; Posthumus, 1045; Rev. R., 1317; Ric., 1473*, 1474; Rev. Ric., 53, 1315; Rev. Rob., 1516; Sarah, 1342; Thos., 997, 1514; Sir Thos., kt., 618; Rev. W., 1460*; Wm., 475, 618*, 620, 1045*, 1299; Rev. Wm., 500; Dr., 1160; Mr., 918, 1293; —, judge, 1033; fam., 1047
Bellamy (Belami, Belamy, Bellomey), Ann, 354*; Chris., 831; Eliz., 682; Hannah, 1396; Joan, 831; John, 682, 1402; Judith, 682; Mary, 354; Ric., 1069; Rob., 1403; Sam., 354*, 1403; T., 1195; Thos., 1396; Wm., 682, 1396*, 1403*; —, 1402
Bellenger, see Ballinger
Bellesyse, see Belsize
Bellheim, —, 1475
Bellinger, see Ballinger
Bellingham, Anne, 810; Sir Edw., kt., 810; Eliz., 810; John, 810
Bello, see Battle
Bellomey, see Bellamy
Belon, Thos., 1351
Belsire (Belsere, Belsyre), Ann, 1427; Chris., 1121, 1358; Dan., 696, 1543, 1547; Eleanor, 1547;

Eliz., 1547*; Gabriel, 1547*; Hester, 1547*; Martha, 1547; Mary, 1547*; Ric., 1547*; Sam., 1427*; Thos., 1547*; Wm., 1425, 1547; fam., 1428

Belsize (Bellesyse), Viscount, 337

Belsyre, *see* Belsire

Benbow (Benbowe), Edm., 1475; Rev. John, 1147; —, 1475

Bence, Ann(e), 701*, 846; Betty, 846; Eliz., 167; Geo., 167; Grace, 1110*; Isaac, 846*; Joan, 701; John, 701*, 846, 847, 1110, 1535; Joseph, 1539; Mary, 212, 701; Ric., 1110*; Sam., 1110; Sarah, 846; Susannah, 846, 1110*; Wm., 212*; —, 696

Bencehill, Joseph, 1539

Benche, Agnes atte, 1351

Benchmaler, —, 1017

Bencomb (Benecombe), Agnes de, 1369; John de, 1369, 1370

Bendall (Bendal), Abraham, 176; Ann(e), 70, 317, 826, 836; Dan., 284; Edw., 627; Eliz., 176, 284, 939*; Esther, 836; Giles, 1101; Hannah, 284; Isaac, 284, 1550; Joanna, 284; John, 284*, 413, 836*; Joseph, 939*, 1550; Mary, 413, 959; Mary Ann, 1550; Nat., 1168; Ric., 317, 939; Solomon, 836; Wm., 826, 836*, 1168

Bendlowe, Wm., 778*

Bendysh, Sir John, bt., 1296; Martha, 1296

Benecombe, *see* Bencomb

Benefield, *see* Benfield

Beneger, *see* Benger

Benet, *see* Bennett

Benfield (Benefield), Anne, 332, 333, 338; Edw., 338; Eliz., 332, 338, 921; John, 332*; Mary, 921; Ric., 811; Rev. Ric., 415; Sam., 917; Sebastian, 982; Rev. Sebastian, 860; Thos., 118, 333*, 338; Wm., 921; —, 985

Benger (Beneger, Bengere), John, 381*, 1005; Rob., 1005; Sarah, 381*; Thos., 381; Wm., 1404

Bengough, Hen., 1440; Mr., 1440

Benhall, —, 1093

Benne, John, 1220, 1478; —, 1220, 1225

Bennett (Benet, Benett, Bennet), Abel, 884; Abigail, 1118; Agnes, 372; Alice, 1037, 1038; And., 124; Ann(e), 539, 837, 1008, 1036*, 1037*, 1397, 1575; Ant., 1400, 1403; Benedicta, 789; Benj., 1531; Betty (Bette), 789, 1037; Bridget, 924, 1398; Caroline Frances, 1400; Cath., 757; Chas., 1037, 1337; Christian, 1021; D., 1140; Dan., 632*, 836*, 1247, 1343, 1344, 1398*; David, 1118; Edm., 923, 924; Edw., 1392; Ele(a)nor, 308, 1013*; Eliz., 616, 746, 757, 1006, 1025, 1037*, 1182, 1186, 1337, 1389*, 1392, 1531, 1537; Ephraim, 1531*; Esther, 1025; Frances, 884, 1008; Geo., 842*, 1013*, 1037; Giles, 1008, 1013, 1575; Grace, 1038, 1116, 1118; H., 1216; Hannah, 124, 611, 632, 1343, 1344, 1397, 1401; Hen., 124, 1008, 1043, 1400; Hester, 1531*; Rev. Hugh, 643; Isaac, 1247; J., 1036, 1312; Jas., 124, 473*, 1036, 1037*, 1389; Jane, 980, 1037; Joan, 1021; John, 210, 226, 372, 611, 746, 836, 1021, 1027, 1036*, 1037*, 1038, 1039, 1116*, 1118, 1187, 1401, 1539; John Hill,

1532; Jonathan, 789; Joseph, 202*, 1008, 1388, 1400; Joshua, 616; Rev. Josiah, 305, 308*; L., 1356; Lydia, 1037; Martha, 1247; Mary, 193, 202, 491, 836, 842*, 941, 959, 1009, 1025, 1037, 1119, 1343*, 1344*, 1390, 1535*; Maynard, 1037; Rev., Mic., 447; Moses, 1430; Nat., 1531; Philadelphia, 1390; R., 1255; Rachel, 1118; Ric., 491, 509, 757*, 1038, 1039, 1258, 1282; Rob., 121, 124*, 539, 1009, 1422, 1535*; Sam., 836, 1025*, 1182, 1344, 1537; Sarah, 473, 632, 746, 941*, 993; Sophia, 1025; Stephen, 837, 1043; Susan, 124; Susanna, 1398; Theresa Frances, 1400; Thos., 124, 748, 789, 958, 979, 1008, 1025*, 1038*, 1039*, 1187, 1307, 1362, 1397, 1398*; Rev. Thos., 498; Tim., 1037; Wm., 124, 188, 193, 611*, 746, 757, 941*, 980, 1006*, 1037*, 1119, 1389, 1398*, 1403, 1438, 1535, 1537; Rev. Wm., 829, 1044; Mr., 1015; —, 1017, 1052, 1174, 1238, 1261, 1282,*, 1311, 1339, 1362, 1402, 1403; fam., 236

Benshire (or Benson or Rensham), Rev. Ric., 1346

Benson, Ann, 1350; Dan., 1146; Hester, 1146; J., 1350; Jas., 1129, 1132*; Rev. Jas., 1132; Rev. John, 1129; Dr. Martin, bishop, 449, 493, 859, 1149*, 1187, 1504; Rev. Ric., *see* Benshire; *and see* Banson

Bent, John, 1054

Bentenshaw, John, 1574

Bentham, Agnes, 1432*; Eliz., 1432; Marg., 1432; — de, 1432

Bentley, Susanna, 1389; Thos., 407, 1389

Benton, Clark, 1268*, 1269; Eliz., 1268, 1269; Grace, 313; Hester, 1268, 1269; Sarah, 1269; Wm., 1269, 1372

Beoleghe, *see* Bowley

Beoleyesterte, Thos. de, 1102

Beornwulf (Barnolph, Beornulf, Beornulph), king of Mercia, 628, 1131, 1132, 1419

Bercare, *see* Barker

Berch, *see* Birch

Berde, *see* Bird

Berdoe, Marmaduke, 197

Berdone, *see* Burdon

Bere, *see* Beare; Delabere

Bereare, John le, 1502

Bereford, Philippa, 1482; R., 1482; fam., 1482; *and see* Beresford

Berenger, —, 1015

Beresford, Francis, 1227*; Mr., 92; *and see* Bereford

Berewe, *see* Barrow

Bergavenny (Bergavenay), Rev. Vincent de, 221; Wm. de, 1132; —, 1082

Bergavenny [*peerage*], *see* Abergavenny

Berghton, *see* Burton

Berkeley (Barckley, Barkeley, Barkeleye, Barkley, Barkly, Berkelei, Berkeleye, Berkley, Berohelai), Agatha, 1086; Agnes, 527; Anne, 1270*; Benj., 388; Brice, 1538; Cath., 680*, 681; Dame Cath., 1521; Chas., earl of Falmouth, 739 n; Cecilia, 1147; Ciceley, 527; Cole, 418; Edm., 908; Edw., 533*; Eliz., 1170, 1171*, 1243; Dame Eliz.,

1522; Lady Eliz., 157, 1538; Eliz., countess of Warwick, 1100*; Eliz., duchess of Beaufort, 122; Fitz Nicol, *see* Berkeley, Nic.; Frances, Lady Shirley, 162*; Mrs. Francis, 1155; Hawisia (Havisia), 527*, 908; Hen. (de), 527*, 529*, 809*, 1086, 1170, 1369; Isabel(la) (de), 1020, 1539, 1540*; J., 1255; Jas., 1538, 1539; Jane (Jeyne), 680*, 681, 1009, 1010, 1270, 1538; Joan(e) (de), 527, 1051, 1147; Johanna, 1538; John (de), 122, 265 n, 527*, 529*, 530, 533, 613, 680, 908*, 1147, 1170; Sir John, 179, 533*, 720*, 1011*; John Symes, 1170–1; Juliana, 1148; Lady Kath., 154, 156, 533; Letitia de, 618; Sir M., 1139*; Marg. (de), 265 n, 1147, 1170, 1253, 1369; Lady Marg., 154, 696, 1528; Mary, 509, 1010, 1169, 1170; Mary, Lady Zouche, 162*; Maud, 527, 1147; Maurice (de), 251, 529, 533*, 576, 773*, 1011, 1020, 1120, 1148, 1255, 1369; Sir Maurice, kt., 324, 435, 576*, 720*, 1172; Meriel (Myriell), 383, 1170; N., 1147*; Nic., 527, 737; Nic. or Fitz Nicol, 738 n; Norborne, 1171; Norborne, Lord Bot(t)etourt, 244, 327, 1170*, 1172*; Oliver de, 778 n; Phil. de, 778 n; R., 1148, 1169; Sir R., 1011*; Ralph de, 1086*, 1100, 1101, 1147, 1384; Rebecca (Rebekah), 1009*, 1010*; Ric., 612, 1159, 1170*, 1171, 1270*, 1491; Sir Ric., kt., 509*, 720*, 1010, 1170; Rob., 157, 383, 527, 529, 773, 1009*, 1010*, 1086, 1170; Sir Rob., 576; Rog. (de), 157, 414 n, 497, 527*, 529*, 533, 737, 778*, 908*, 1086*, 1100*, 1101; Sarah, 418; Sibell, 527; Susan, 1171; Thos. (de), 533, 663, 745, 775, 1051*, 1101, 1102, 1169, 1243; Lord Thos., 1100; Sir Thos. (de), kt., 162*, 163, 420 n, 576, 696, 720*; W., 1312; Col. W. Fitzhardinge, Earl Fitzhardinge, 1168; Wm. (de), 527*, 529*, 533*, 778, 908, 1086, 1101, 1538, 1539; Sir Wm., 179, 576*, 720*, 807, 1015, 1020*, 1369*; —, 1147*, 1185, 1253; fam., 39, 179, 305, 420*, 452, 497*, 511, 527 n, 532*, 533, 547, 807, 817, 908*, 1011, 1020, 1147, 1148, 1172, 1312, 1378, 1486, 1495, 1537

Berkeley [*peerage*](Barkley, Berkelei, Berkley), Augustus, earl of, 174, 244; Cath., baroness, 305; Chas., earl of, 177, 244; Chas., Lord, 162; Elenor, Lady, 1010; Eliz., Lady, 162, 163, 1253; Fred. Augustus, earl of, 161, 244, 245, 279, 415, 479, 603*; Geo., baron Berkeley, Viscount Dursley, 532; Geo., earl of, 156, 161; Geo., Lord, 153, 154*, 163, 164, 414, 533, 738*, 773, 775, 1253*, 1521, 1522; Helena, Lady, 527; Hen., Lord, 66, 162, 163, 459, 533, 738, 775, 1100, 1257, 1521; Isabella, Lady, 529, 664; Jas., earl of, 168, 174, 244; Jas., Lord (baron), 156, 157, 459, 664, 1100, 1257, 1538*; Jane, Lady, 162; Kath., Lady, 158, 162, 720*, 1538*; Marg., Lady, 1539*; Maur., Lord, 154*, 157*, 251, 509, 576, 585, 618 n, 737, 1101, 1102, 1369; Rog., Lord, 65, 158, 1101*, 1147, 1369; Thos., Lord (baron), 153, 154*, 156, 157*, 159, 161, 178, 179*, 251 n, 278*, 305, 324, 414*, 529*, 533, 737*, 738, 779 n, 1100*, 1101*, 1169, 1369*, 1521, 1528, 1538*, 1539*,

1540; Wm., Lord, 158, 530, 773, 1100*, 1538*; Wm., marquis of, 157, 618, 664; Wm., Viscount, 1100, 1101; earl of, 41, 65, 75, 156, 159*, 161*, 165, 174*, 175, 177, 740, 1095, 1166, 1173, 1174, 1365, 1521, 1538; Lord, 534, 602*, 935, 1100, 1101*, 1102, 1255, 1256, 1257*, 1259, 1538; marquis of, 1538; *and see* Fitzharding, Rob.; Howard, Kath.

Berleye, *see* Burley

Bernard, Rev. Jas., 19, 1336, 1339; John, 1029, 1123, 1197, 1485; Marg., 1074; Nic., 1540; Ric., 1197; Thos., 1356; Rev. Wm., 1356; *and see* Barnard

Berners, John, 1159; (or Barnes), Thos., 743; Wm., 360 n, 1062

Berohelai, *see* Berkeley

Berow, *see* Barrow

Berriman (Byrryman), Alice, 1195; Anne, 541, 972; Rev. Jas., 940*, 972; Joan, 940; John, 203, 541*

Berrington, Anne, 1111; Benj., 1111; John, 812; Rev. Thos., 430; *and see* Barrington

Berrow (Berrowe, Berrowes), *see* Barrow

Berry, Eliz., 70; Hen., 70; John, 884; Ric., 530; Sibble, 797; Thos., 797; Wm., 530

Berston, Rev. John, 266

Bertie (Bertic), Rev. Chas., 1047; Rev. Hen. Willoughby, 1382; Peregrine, Lord Willoughby, 852 n

Berton, *see* Burton

Bertram (Bartram), Mary, 840; Sam., 840; —, 1017

Berue, *see* Atterbury; Barrow

Berwick, Ann, 585, 1165; John, 1165; Joseph, 585, 586; *and see* Barwick

Besemantel, John de, 1476*

Besiles, Marg., 1385; Sir Peter, 1385

Bespath, Rev. John, 1477

Bess, *see* Befs

Best, Ann(e), 73, 521; Ant., 521*; Edw., 1363; Eliz., 1473; H., 1381; Hen., 1150; John, 1473; Juliana, 1290, 1291; Mary, 73, 1472; Ric., 73, 1473, 1477; Thos., 1174*, 1363; Wm., 360, 1472, 1477; —, 1363

Besyn, *see* Bason

Betenson, *see* Bettenson

Betewell, *see* Bedwell

Bethell, Cath., 207

Betherigge, Hugh, 1522

Bette, *see* Betty

Bettenson (Betenson), Albinia, 852 n, 853; Sir Edw., bt., 852 n, 853

Betterton, Ann, 597, 862; Chas., 597, 598; Edm., 510; Edw., 862; John, 368, 597, 862*, 1357; Mary, 510; Rob., 597; Sarah, 598, 862; Wal., 510

Betts, Alice, 610; Ric., 610; Thos., 1226

Betty (Bette), Anne, 514; John, 514; —, 1017

Betun, Rob. de, prior and bishop, 1060

Bevan (Beavan, Beven, Bevin, Bivans), Abraham, 730, 1418; Alice, 172; Ann(e), 730*, 1418; Arthur, 172*; Betty, 1576*; Chas., 168; Edm., 1129, 1131*; Edw., 924*, 1000*; Eliz., 160*, 172, 1131; Esther, 730; Rev. Evan, 1386; Rev. Geo., 319; Hen., 735; Jas., 1320, 1418; Jane,

169, 735; John, 730, 744, 1576; Mary, 744, 922; Sarah, 623, 826, 1386, 1490; Susanna, 1320; Thos., 172*, 623, 683, 826, 922*, 1355, 1378; Tim., 169; Wal., 169*, 172; Wm., 169, 1172, 1490

Beverley, Rev. Elizeus, 1346

Beverston, Rev. Thos., 696 n

Bevin, see Bevan

Bevington, Jeffrey, 1331; Tim., 1355

Beynon, Rev. Thos., 599; and see Baynham; Eynon

Beyondthetoun, John, 1502

Beyzand, see Bayzand

Biatte, Jas., 1538; and see Byard

Biby, Eliz., 1464

Bick (Bicke, Bike, Byck, Bycke, Byoch), Aaron, 133*, 348; Alice, 337; Anne, 133, 348, 687; Chas., 1289, 1347*, 1348; Eliz., 69*, 70, 1534; Geo., 74, 118*, 262*, 1347; Giles, 703; Hester, 1534; Jane, 70, 262*; John, 69, 118, 907, 1347*, 1348; Joan, 1534; Joseph (Josebh), 1534*; Mary, 69, 70*, 118*, 1534; Nic., 1456; Ric., 687; Rob., 337; Rev., Rob., 1217; Sarah, 70, 1347; Susanna(h), 118, 1347; Thos., 69*, 118, 984; Wm., 69*, 70*, 683, 861, 1118; —, 1054, 1292, 1348*, 1455; fam., 65

Bickerton, Thos., 730

Bicknell, Chas., 1542*; Eliz., 752, 1542*; Ric., 752; Sarah, 1542; Thos., 252, 1542*; Wm., 943, 1542; —, 1542; and see Bignell

Biddle (Biddell, Bidle, Bydell), Ann, 254; Ben, 779; Betty, 254; Dan., 701; Eliz., 959, 1014*; Esther, 254; Hannah, 1208; Jas., 254; John, 254, 305, 1014*, 1016, 1208; Rev. John, 1450, 1456; Rev. Joseph, 89, 147, 1387; Luke, 959; Mark, 959; Martha, 204, 701; Mary, 254*, 669, 701, 1014*, 1529; Mat., 1529*; Nat., 254; Ric., 254*, 669, 1014*; Rob., 1015, 1539*; Sarah, 254; Thos., 681, 683; Wm., 204; Mr., 1215; —, 1017; and see Bedwell

Biddulph, Rev. Mic., 221; —, 1402

Bidgood (Bedgegood, Bedggood, Beggegood, Buggegod), Anna, 1300; Anne, 1300, 1328; J., 1328; Jas., 1327, 1328*; John, 1172; Nic., 1300, 1307, 1312; Reg., 1172; Sarah, 1327*; Thos., 1327

Bidle, see Biddle

Bidmead, Ant., 203, 204; Eliz., 1050; Jeremiah, 203; Joan, 203; John, 203; Martha, 204; Mary, 203; S., 1052; Sam., 1050

Bien, John le, 1335

Bige (Bigg), see Biggs

Bigger, Edw., 1013; Sarah, 1013

Biggs (Bige, Bigg, Bygge), Edw., 448; Eliz., 856; J., 1216; John, 1027, 1150; Marg., 253; Phil., 531; Priscilla, 253*; Ric., 1292, 1482*; Rob., 448, 856; Rev. Rob., 1441; W., 1218; Wal., 253*; Wm., 93; Mr., 1093; —, 1216

Bigland, Geo., 1437*; Mary, 631, 1299, 1303, 1437; Ralph, 630, 631; Ric., 630, 631, 1299; Thos., 1437; Mr., 913, 915, 925; fam., 415, 558

Bigley, Rachel, 958; Ric., 958

Bigling, John, 803

Bignell, Ann, 1012; Rev. John, 643; and see Bicknell

Bigot, Hugh, earl of Norfolk, 1322; Maud, countess of Norfolk, 1322

Bike, see Bick

Bil (fl. 1066), 1077*

Bilbie, Joseph, 814

Bill, C. H., 1256

Billey, T., 1460

Billing (Billyng), Ric., 1404; Thos., 1222; Rev. Wm., 1428; —, 1402

Billingham, Ann, 907; Edw., 1237; John, 762, 1237; Joseph, 907; Mary, 1237; Wm., 1237

Billingsley (Billingsly), Sir H., kt., 1159; Rev. Nic., 103; Wm., 130; Mr., 103; —, 1086

Billsy, Eliz., 1390; Thos., 1390

Billyng, see Billing

Bilson (or Pierson), Rev. W., 1447

Bincher, E., 765; W., 765; Wm., 765

Bindon, Thos., Viscount Bindon, 771

Binesard, Ric., 1460

Binfield, Adam, 1092

Bingham, Edm., 660; Eliz., 976; John, 976; Martha, 660; Sir Ric., 885; Thos., 660*

Bingle, Anne, 133; Eliz., 133; Giles, 133; Jane, 133; John, 1511*; Martha, 661; Mary, 661, 1511; Thos., 661*; Wm., 661

Bingley, Dan., 1375*; Giles (Gyles), 1375*; Mary, 1375; Mic., 133; Rev. Mic., 508

Binning, Francis, 730

Bint, John, 1010

Binter, Wm., 1217

Birch (Berch, Byrch, Byrche), Abraham, 1464; Alex., 1477; Eliz., 923; Geo., 923; Rev. Geo., 651, 1369; Jas., 1566; Mary, 1464, 1566; Wm., 915; Rev. Wm., 221; Col., 1197

Birchall (Burchall, Burchell), Dearman, 1378; John, 836; Mary, 836; Wm., 836

Birchold (Burcholte), Rev. Thos., 1031; Wm. atte, 1552

Bird (Berde, Birde, Brid, Byrd, Byrde), Abraham, 660; Adam, 1404; Alice, 1153, 1317; Ann(e), 752, 1040, 1573; Edm., 1010; Eliz., 254*, 765; Joan, 1447; John, 254, 1362; Rev. Jonathan, 1354; Marg., 1028, 1030; Mary, 254, 1010, 1528; Martin, 1460; Peter, 1528; Randall, 1289; Ric., 254, 529*, 1028, 1030*, 1140, 1147, 1404, 1435, 1440*, 1447, 1573; Rob., 1061; Rev. S., 1289; Sam., 752, 1362; Sarah, 660; Susanna, 254, 1528; Sybill, 1440; Thos., 254, 563*, 765, 1061, 1513, 1573*; Wm., 254*, 1040, 1146, 1153, 1447; Dr., 1218; —, 1512; and see Beard; Byard

Birdlip (Bradelep, Briddelep), Ric. de, 1494; Wm. de, 1494

Birkin (Birkins, Byrkin, Byrkyn), Abraham, 1554; Eliz., 105, 107, 248; Isabel(la), 111, 932; Jas., 111*, 832; Joan, 111; John, 104, 105*, 111*; Marg., 104; Martha, 111; Mary, 105, 248; Ric., 105*, 107, 109, 110, 111, 247*, 248, 932; Sarah, 109, 832; Thos., 248*

Birt (Birte, Burt), Betty, 1025; Eleanor, 677; Eliz., 666, 887, 1438; Jas., 832, 887*; Jane (Janm),

1025; John, 49, 666, 683, 832, 887; Joseph, 1025; Josiah, 1025*; Martha, 49; Mary, 887, 1574*; Ric., 887; Sam., 677; Sarah, 832; Rev. T., 1331; Thos., 677, 1574; Rev. Thos., 919, 1069, 1324, 1329, 1483; Wm., 194, 887, 922, 1324, 1574*; Rev., 1066, 1480

Birwicks, Ric., 1551

Bis, *see* Bisse

Biscoe, John, 1140

Bishop (Bishope, Bishopp, Bisshop), Rev. Alan, 619; Alex., 1197; Alice, 254; Ann, 832, 850, 993, 1088, 1248*; Benj., 1113; Betty, 1248; Caleb, 1194, 1196; Cecil, 1503; Rev. Chas., 114, 483, 579, 639, 640, 1373; Deborah, 750; Edm., 254*; Eleanor, 1184; Eliz., 563, 1040, 1113, 1118, 1282, 1375*, 1503; Frances, 755, 1118; Geo., 1282*; Rev. H., 1456; Rev. Hen., 56, 508; Hester, 174, 254; Isaac, 254*; J. B., 583; Jas., 124, 858; Jeremiah, 967*, 1050; Joan (Jone), 1113*; Job, 567; John, 64, 174, 665, 750, 755, 993*, 1027, 1113*, 1118, 1121*, 1140, 1248, 1259, 1282*, 1375*, 1478, 1499; Jonah [? Joanna], 967; Jonathan, 562; Jordan (Jurdan), 1121, 1123*; Joseph, 976, 1289; Judith, 174; Martha, 174; Mary, 124, 133, 254, 567, 750*, 836*, 850, 1004; Mary Sophia, 1282; N., 1503; Nat., 1113; Nic., 1258; Paul, 174*; R., 1093; Rev. Ralph, 121; Rebecca, 347, 1136; Ric., 755, 832, 1088*, 1248; Rev. Ric., 1504; Sir Ric., kt., 1040; Rob., 598, 850; Sam., 563*, 836*, 1136, 1184, 1186, 1248*, 1258; Sarah, 254, 563, 750, 868, 967, 1088, 1194, 1282; Simon, 850*; Susannah, 562; Rev. T., 1456; Theodosia, 1040; Thos., 64, 133, 347*, 429, 1004, 1140, 1150, 1226*; Thos. Handy, 1215; Rev. Wal., 562; Wm., 307, 661, 803, 868, 1074, 1378; Sir Wm., 1040; Rev. Mr., 1379, 1503*; —, 1015, 1256, 1455

Bisley (Byseley, Byssheleye), John (de), 688 n, 1047; Ric., 512; Thos., 688

Bisp, Ann, 1489; John, 1489

Bisse (Bis, Biss, Bysse), Amy, 612; Anne, 604; Arthur, 782; Dorothy, 954; Edw., 612*, 615*; Eleanor, 953; Geo., 964; Jane, 612*, 615; Job, 954; Rev. John, 953*; Mary, 782; Ric., 1218; Sarah, 953; Thos., 953; Wm., 604, 964; Dr., bishop, 1258

Bisshop, *see* Bishop

Bivans, *see* Bevan

Blaake, *see* Blake

Blaby (Blabey, Bleby),Anne, 1461, 1463, 1465*; Eliz., 1465; Hannah, 1465; John, 1463, 1465*, 1473; Mary, 1465*, 1473; Wm., 1465*, 1477

Black, Rev. Geo. Chas., 161; *and see* Blake

Blackall, Chas., 1542

Blackborn, *see* Blackburn

Blackborow (Blackb[orou]gh), Ann, 1157; Geo., 1159; Martha, 1157; Mary, 1159*; Penelope, 1157; Peter, 1157; Rob., 1157*, 1159; Stephen, 1157; Wal., 1428; Wm., 1157

Blackburn (Blackborn, Blackburne), Christian, 1555; Rev. Hen., 770, 1063; John, 1266; Nic., 1576; Ric., 1063; Rev. Thos., 42

Blacket (Blaket), Anne, 1422, 1423; Sir John, 1422; Marg., 1422*; Rog., 1422*; —, 1092; fam., 1422

Blackleach (Blaklech), Mary, 997; Rev. Wm., 997

Blackley (Blacklegh), Wal., 1428; Mr., 288

Blackman, Joseph, 1357; Stephen, 1196

Blackshaw, John, 946; Joseph, 946*; Lucaser, 946; Mary, 946

Blackwell, Ann(e), 1066, 1120, 1199, 1200; Archar, 655; Chas., 320, 636; Eliz., 446, 575, 752; Esther, 1200; Geo., 575; Giles, 320, 448, 1010*; Hannah, 541; Hen., 446; Hester, 423, 752; Isaac, 147; Jane, 1200; Joanna, 97; John, 320, 446*, 637, 1200*; Jonathan, 89, 147*; Kath., 655; Martha, 655, 656; Mary, 320, 446*, 575*, 1010*, 1200*; Nat., 532; Ric., 97, 1199, 1200; Rob., 446; S., 1005, 1103; Sam., 56*, 60, 61*, 102, 364*, 678, 1005, 1066, 1103*; Thos., 320, 423*, 752; Rev. W., 1290; Wm., 446, 575; Rev. Wm., 147, 603; Mrs., 61; fam., 197, 427, 532

Blackwood, J., 1312

Blade, Ralph de, 1150

Blades, Wm. de, 1052*

Blagden, Ann, 1569; John, 307, 779, 1526, 1527*, 1545*, 1569; Lydia, 1527*, 1569; Mary, 779, 1522, 1524, 1526, 1527, 1556, 1568; Thos., 779, 1522*, 1568, 1569

Blagg (Blague), Rev. Jonathan, 668*; Mary, 668; fam., 890*

Blagrove, Eliz., 517; Marg., 795; Mary, 795*; Obadiah, 517; Thos., 795*

Blague, *see* Blagg

Blake (Blaake), Anne, 299; Rev. Edw., 1346; Eliz., 1213; Grace, 604; Johanna, 1111; John, 299, 360, 388, 515, 604*, 731, 986, 1276, 1499; Joseph, 1107*; Martha, 1276, 1499; Mary, 1107, 1213; Phil. 1477; Ric., 1105, 1107*, 1486, 1491; Rob., 1111; Sam., 1107; Sarah, 543; Thos., 1213; Rev. Valentine, 1477; Wm., 532, 543*, 671; —, 985, 1217, 1355; *and see* Black

Blakeneye, Alice de, 1552; Ric. de, 1420

Blakenham, Alice, 1126; Benedict, 1126*; Joan, 1126

Blaket, *see* Blacket

Blakeway, Rev. Edw., 603

Blaklech, *see* Blackleach

Blanc, Ric. le, 816

Blanch (Blaynch), Anne, 105, 114, 922; Ant., 1537; Benj. 52; Cath., 562; Dinah, 623; Eliz., 562*, 623; Jasper, 105*; John, 105, 558, 562, 563, 922; Rev. John, 582; Marg., 105; Marg. Adean, 105; Mary, 52, 562*; Sam., 1039; Stephen, 1039; Thos., 203, 562*; Ursula, 563; Wm., 562*, 579; Ric., 105*, 562, 623*; Thos., 1137*

Blanchard (Blanchat, Blanshard), Ant., 1525; Martha, 81; Ric., 1537; Thos., 616, 1121; Rev. Thos., 81

Bland, Susan, 296; Wm., 844, 915; —, 1362

Blandford, Eliz., 1171; Isles, 1171; Silas, 1160; Thos., 423, 1171; Rev. W., 1127

Blankfont, Sir John, kt., 1148

Blanshard, see Blanchard

Blatchley, Eliz., 981; John, 981

Blaithwait (Blathwayt, Blathwayte), Ann, 723*; Joseph, 554; Mary, 554; Thomasine, 554*; Wm., 552*, 553*, 554*, 555, 723

Blaynch, see Blanch

Blebury (Blebur), Ric., 1356, 1478

Bleby, see Blaby

Blechesden, Ric. de, 927

Bleck, see Blick

Blencowe (Blinckcoe, Blinco), Eliz., 920; Sir John, kt., 920; Lawr., 686; Ric., 779; Sarah, 779

Blenman, Eliz., 410; Wm., 410

Blennerhasset, Rev. Edw., 463

Bletchley, Ann, 846; Thos., 846; Wm., 846

Blewett (Bloet, Bluett), Ann, 608; Cornelius, 820; Eliza, 459 n; John, 459 n; Mary, 820; Ralph (de), 435, 459; Rog., 608; Wm., 927; fam., 459, 927

Blick (Bleck, Blycke, Blyke), Gabriel, 363, 1357; Jane, 182; John, 182, 984, 1447; Sybill, 1357;

Blinckcoe (Blinco), see Blencowe

Bliss (Blisse), Abigail, 1470; Ann, 1108; Benj., 1191; Chas., 118; Dan., 974; Eliz., 170, 339, 970; Geo. Brudenell, 1108; Isabella, 1201; J., 1052; Jas., 661; Jane, 446, 1336*; Joan, 348, 974; John, 118, 170*, 340*, 661, 984; Rev. John, 1251, 1257; Joseph, 348, 446; Mary, 661, 800, 970, 1191; Nat., 661*, 1108; Rev. P., 1336; Phil., 1336; Rev. Phil., 19, 498*, 613, 1108, 1336, 1339; Ric., 339, 800*, 1049; Rev. Ric., 1191, 1228; Rob., 446; Sam., 170, 661; Thos., 340, 974*, 1052; Ursula, 1049; Wm., 660, 984; Rev., 495*

Blissard, see Blizard

Blissett (Blissed), C., 1220; Hen., 1238; Mr., 1378; —, 1378

Blisson, Mary, 781; Rob., 781

Blizard (Blissard), Ann, 348; Bevil, 337; Deborah, 337; Dorothy, 884; Edm., 118; Joseph, 1288, 1289; Mary, 133, 1194; Ric., 1194, 1196*; Sam., 1288; Thos., 133, 348, 884, 1194, 1196*; W., 1195; Wm., 348*; —, 1476

Blocklei, John de, 218

Bloet, see Blewett

Blome, —, 1237

Blomer (Bloomer), Ant., 692; Cath., 692; Eliz., 567; Frances, 328, 691, 692*; Giles, 448; Hen., 328; Sir Hen., 691; John, 690*, 691*, 692*, 1127; Mary, 690, 691, 692; Ric., 567*, 1127; Wm., 369, 568, 690, 691*, 692*, 793; Mr., 369; fam., 447, 565, 691 n

Bloore, Eliz., 692*; Ric., 692*

Blount, see Blunt

Blowing (Blowen), Mary, 598; Ric., 598; Rob., 1126; Susanna, 1126; Wm., 1126

Bloxham (Bloxam, Bloxsom), Edw., 1054; Eliz., 867; John, 1282; Rev. John, 87, 88; Mary, 88; Rev. Mat., 72, 230; Thos., 867; Wm., 88; Rev. Dr., 1101

Bluett, see Blewett

Blundell, Rev. Geo., 1238; —, 1227

Blunson, Ann, 758; John, 758

Blunt (Blount), Chris., 249; Sir Chris., 1237; Edm., 602*; John, 602; Marg., 602*; Thos. (le), 1317, 1404; Willelma, 602; Wm., 602; Mr., 1011; Mrs., 347; fam.,205, 525, 833*

Blycke (Blyke), see Blick

Boarding, John, 796; Rebecca, 796

Boat, Godfrey, 1029; Mary, 1029

Bobbett, Amey, 930

Bocher, see Butcher

Boddily (Boddley, Bodily), Eliz., 1107; John, 1107; Sarah, 1418*

Bode, Peter le, 1160

Bodenham (Bodnum), Alice, 872; Eleanor, 1269; H., 1061; Hannah, 872*; Jas., 872; John, 872*; Mary, 872*; Rob. (de), 872*, 1269, 1519; Sarah, 872; —, 1519

Bodicote, John, 1015

Bodily, see Boddily

Bodisant, fam., 696

Bodman (Bodmin, Bodsman), Abraham, 1418*; Anne, 1515; Hen., 1417, 1418, 1420; Honour, 1417, 1418*; Mary, 1418; Rog., 1515

Bodnum, see Bodenham

Bodsman, see Bodman

Body, Eliz., 1030; Giles, 1249*; John, 1243; Marg., 1243; Mary, 1249; Nat., 562*, 1030, 1249*

Boevey (Boevy, Bovey, Bovy), Ann, 1165; Cath., 606*, 607; Crawley T., 1403; Kath., 1402; Sir T. C., bt., 1165, 1402; (formerly Crawley), Thos. Crawley, 606*; Sir Thos. Crawley, bt., 470, 479, 606; Wm., 606*, 607; Mr., 607; Mrs., 607; —, 1402; fam., 606

Bohemia, queen of, 158

Bohun, Edm., 671; Eleanor de, duchess of Gloucester, 927*; Eliz. de, 1014, 1051; H. de, 1403*; Hen. de, 869, 925; Humph. de, 925*, 927*, 1078, 1402*; Humph. de, earl of Hereford, 671*, 678, 851, 1309; John de, 671, 1014, 1051*, 1402; Marg. de, 301, 671, 925, 1402, 1403, 1447; Mary de, 927; Maud de, countess of Hereford, 671; Wm. de, 925*, 927; — de, 1078, 1402*, 1404; — de, earl of Hereford, 1214; fam., earls of Hereford, 214, 392*, 581, 648, 671, 672, 851, 1051, 1439; and see Boon

Bolecroft, Ric., 1314; —, 1311

Bolle, Ric., 360 n; —, 1482*; and see Bull

Boller, Capt., 928; and see Buller

Bolt (Bolte), Rog., 1552; Rev. Thos., 1257; and see Boult

Bolton, see Boulton

Bolwell, Ann, 491; Grace, 555; Hugh, 491, 555; Mary, 491*; Rob., 491*

Bomford, Alice, 1518; Mary, 1518

Bonaventura, —, 1082

Bond (Bonde), Ann(e), 412, 622, 762*, 922, 980; Chris., 917, 918, 921*, 923*, 1066; Rev. Cornelius, 586; Dan., 1027, 1217; Rev. Dan., 802, 886, 1372; David, 412; Deborah, 598; Dennis [Denise], 1129; Edm., 245, 733*, 918*, 920; Capt. Edm., 921; Eliz., 516, 622, 735*, 847, 918, 920; Emma, 931; Rev. F., 1483; Frances, 921; Frances Cellameria, 921; Francis, 921;

Geo., 917, 921*, 923; Sir Geo., 1129; Giles, 924; Hen. le, 1372; Rev. Hen., 415, 1203, 1210, 1217*; Sir Hen., 829; Jas., 847; Jane, 921*, 1066; Jemima, 921; John (le), 621*, 633, 847*, 922, 923, 1210, 1215, 1379*; Marg., 921*; Mary, 621, 733*, 762, 847, 921*, 924, 931, 1021*, 1210; Rev. Nat., 1021; Nic., 1331, 1382; Ric., 516, 622, 733*, 735, 922, 980, 981, 1210, 1519; Sam., 847, 922, 923; Sarah, 621, 633, 923*, 1210; Thos., 598, 762*, 931*, 980, 1194, 1210, 1404; Ursula, 1210; Wal., 1197, 1539; Wm., 980, 1210, 1331; Mr., 918, 1186; —, 1052, 1311; fam., 245

Bone, John, 1483; Ric., 1363; Rob., 1483
Bonebroke, Thos., 1552
Boneknight, Juliana, 1150
Boner (Bonere), see Bonner
Boneville, Luke de, 1258; Wal., 1259
Bongham (Bonghan), Adam, 1404; Is., 1404; Ralph, 1404
Bonham (Bonhome), Eva, 1259; John, 1259; Marie, 1530; Juliana, 1259; Ric., 1259
Bonion, see Bunyan
Bonner (Boner, Bonere, Bonnor), Ant., 570; Benj., 133; Edm., bishop, 1223, 1331; Eliz., 768; Geo., 570; Hen., 1478; Jane, 789; John, 865, 866; Joseph, 768, 1039; Mary, 789; Ric., 789*, 1478; Wm., 979; —, 789
Bonnewell, Lord, 1475
Bonnor, see Bonner
Booker, Eliz., 573; Thos., 573; Wm., 862
Boon, Arthur, 811; Mary, 811, 1418; and see Bohun
Boorne, see Bourne
Boote, Jnhn, 1183
Booth (Boothe), Alicia, 1150; Ann, 1503; Edm., 1503*, 1504*; John, 835, 1503; Mary, 1503; Rev. Nat., 1122; Thos., 1576; —, 1504; (or Jackson), —, 1150
Bor, Alice, 1388
Bordon (Bordunn), John, 1031, 1032
Boregast, see Burgess
Borghton, see Burton
Borkens, T., 1063*
Borless, Sir John, kt. & bt., 1547; Joyce, 1547; Sir Wm., 1547
Boroughs (Borroughs), see Burrows
Borton, see Burton
Borughulle, see Burrell
Boscawen (Boscowen), Admiral Edw., 1338; Eliz., 1338; J., 1103, 1104; Thomasina, 1104
Bosco, see Boyce; Wood
Boscowen, see Boscawen
Bosley, Joane, 871; Ric., 871*
Bossom, Ann, 468; Thos., 468*; Wm., 468
Bostare, Ric. le, 1552
Bostock, Cath., 755; Rev. Miles, 1043; Nat., 755; Rev. Wm., 691
Boston, Hannah, 337; Jas., 337*; Lady, see Selwyn, Albinia; Lord, see Irby, Fred. and Wm.
Boswell (Buswell), Elenor, 401; Rev. Geo., 1122; Ric., 1196; Rob., 401
Boswood, Eliz., 550; John, 550

Bosworth, Rev. John, 1341, 1345*, 1346; Sir John, kt., 1341; Mary, 550; Wm., 550
Boteler, see Butler
Boter, Adam, 1317
Botetourt, see Bottetourt
Botevile, see Bottevyle
Botiller, see Butler
Botte, Hen., 1363
Bottetourt (Botetourt, Bottourt), John de, 244*, 1172; Kath. de, 1172; Lord, see Berkeley, Norborne
Bottevyle (Botevile), Geof., 771; (or Thynne), Sir John, 769
Bottourt, see Bottetourt
Botyler, see Butler
Boucher, see Butcher
Bouctoun, Rob., 1154; Thos., 1154
Bouge, Rev. Wm., 870
Boughton (Boughten), Ann(e), 215*, 872, 1393, 1398; Eliz., 1400; Eliz. Alicia, 1400; Francis, 92; Lieut. Fred., 1400; Jane, 1400*; John, 215*, 1398*, 1400*, 1403; Joseph, 215, 872, 1398*, 1400*, 1402, 1403; Marg., 215; Mary, 215, 1398*; Sarah, 815, 1398; Wm., 215, 815, 1400; Rev. Wm., 1393*; Mrs., 1348; —, 1402, 1403
Bouket, Ann, 978; Jane, 978; John, 978*
Bould, Jonathan, 953*; Mary, 953
Bouldesdon, fam., 894
Boult, Jane, 187*; Mary, 187; Rob., 187*; and see Bolt
Boulter (Boultar), Jas., 693; Thos., 1282
Boulton (Bolton, Bowlton), Ann(e), 317, 1511; Arthur, 52; Charlotte Augusta, 1511; Edw., 730; Eliz., 636, 730; Grace, 722; Hen., 46; Hester, 963, 1334; Jas., 1511; Jas. Hen., 1511; John, 1334*, 1511*; Maria, 1511; Mary, 1511; Mary Ann, 1511; Patience, 1354*; Ric., 730, 963; Rev. Ric., 319; Rob., 636; Ruth, 52; Stephen, 317; Rev. Stephen, 1404; Thos., 1353, 1354, 1511; Wm., 722, 1073, 1354*, 1355; Mrs., 1553; —, 1033
Bound (Bounds), Blanche, 922; John, 1132; Rev. John, 603; Mary, 1278; Rev. Phil., 1504; Ric., 922; Thos., 922, 1278; Rev. Wm., 1392
Bourchier (Bourchiere), Anne, 298, 1497; Ant., 1147; Barbara, 898; Brereton, 129*, 130*; Chas., 898; Eliz., 129*, 130*; Martha, 129; Sarah, 129; Thos., 128, 298, 1497; Wm., 128*; Rev. Wm., 129*, 691; Mr., 159; fam., 128*, 360
Bourghall, see Burrell
Bourknygt, see Burnett
Bourne (Bawn, Boorne, Bourn), Ant., 643, 1459; Benedicta, 897*; Dorothy, 897*; Geo., 1218; Gil., bishop, 651; Hannah, 1171; J., 1460; Sir J., kt., 1459, 1460; John, 897*; Nic. de la, 1217; Phil., 651 n; Thos., 1171, 1172*; Tim., 421; W., 1323; Rev., 767; —, 1198, 1214
Bourten, see Burton
Bouverie, Charlotte, 640; Harriot, Viscountess Folkestone, 523; Jacob Pleydell, earl of Radnor, 523, 524; Wm., Viscount Folkestone, earl of Radnor, 523

Boverera, *see* Beaurere

Bovey (Bovy), *see* Boevey

Bowan, *see* Bowen

Bowbridge, Jane, 1412; John 1412; Rebecca, 1412

Bowden, Mary Ann, 1415; Rev. Joseph, 1539; Sam., 1415

Bowditch, Rev. Geo., 1127*

Bowen (Bowan, Bown), Anne, 751, 931, 933; Con., 1576; Dan., 751; Eliz., 1576; Hen., 1575*; Rev. J., 1351; Rev. Jenkin, 1388; John, 931; Mary, 1575; Prudence, 899; Rev. Thos., 37, 1350, 1351; Rev. W., 1074; Wm., 933*; Rev. Wm., 1070; Rev., 328

Bower (Bowers), Anne, 903; Christian, 898, 906; Edw., 899*, 903*; Eleanor, 903*; Eliz., 466; Hannah, 903; Hubert, 903*; J., 895*; Jas., 1112; Jane, 903; Joanna, 907; John, 899, 903, 1101; Marg., 899, 903*; Mary, 903; Meredith, 1317; Rob., 898; Thos., 466, 895, 903*, 907

Bowerman, —, 1092

Bowers, *see* Bower

Bowes, Anne Wanley, 330; Frances, 409; Geo., 409; Geo. Wanley, 330; John, 409

Bowlam, —, 1551

Bowland, Rev. Ric., 1477

Bowles, Ann(e), 1146, 1415; Bridget, 1415; Cath., 1415; Edw., 1415; Eliz., 1236; Frances, 1415; Geo., 1415; John, 1146*; Mary, 1408; Major Ric., 1408; Rev. Ric., 793; Sarah, 1146; Thos., 124; Wm., 1236*

Bowley (Beoleghe), Cecily, 1403; Edw., 344, 1082; John, 344; Mary, 1484; Sam., 1201; Sarah, 344; Thos. de, 1102; Wm., 344, 1484; —, 1201

Bowlton, *see* Boulton

Bowman, Edw., 48; Mary, 48

Bown, *see* Bowen

Bowron, Mary, 1415; Wm., 1415

Bowser, Alice, 620; Ant., 1176; Eleanor, 620; John, 620; Mary, 620; Thos., 620*, 1176

Bowyer, Jas., 1562; Judith, 658; Mary, 658; Ric., 662; Sam., 424, 579, 580, 662, 1403; Sarah, 1562

Box (Boxe), Hen., 703; John, 1505; Ric., 1256

Boxwell, Rev. Edw. de, 236

Boy, Eliz., 105, 1200; Hannah, 1304; Joan, 1304*; John, 1304; Judith, 1305; Rob., 102, 103, 105, 1303, 1304*; Thos., 1303, 1305; *and see* Boyce

Boyce (Bosco, Boyes, Boys, Boyse), Adam, 1197; Ann, 1040; Benj., 569*; Rev. Benj., 139, 565; Dinah, 569; Ella de, 1292; Geo., 118; Rev. Hudson, 1104, 1154; John, 786, 1040*; Rev. John, 1040, 1041*; Judeth, 1149, 1151; Marg., 1040*; Mary, 569*, 1041; R. E., 569; Ric., 569; Rob., 1149, 1151; Sarah, 786, 1041; Sarah Anne, 569; Thos., 1041, 1200; Rev. Thos., 56, 61; Wm. de, 1011; Rev. Wm., 1041; — de, 1237*; fam., 570, 1011; *and see* Boy; Wood

Boyd, John, 1476

Boydon, Geo., 1475

Boyer, Wm., 1551

Boyes, *see* Boyce

Boyfield, Rog. de, 870

Boyle, Ann, 598

Boylston, Edw., 1267; Chas., 1267; Frances, 1267

Boys (Boyse), *see* Boyce

Braban (Brabaen, Brabant, Braben), Abraham, 930; Ann(e), 1144, 1398; Edw., 248; Eliz., 248, 762; Jas., 1403; John, 245; Joseph, 762; Newton, 1398; Thos., 1144

Brabourne, Eliz., 104; Rob., 104

Brace, Anne, 811; Joshua, 811

Bracebrugge, — de, 1478

Bracegirdle, Rev. Edm., 643; Rev. Edw., 319

Bracey, Christian, 47*; Hester, 47*; Hezekiah, 47*; Jas., 1539; Mary, 47*, 413; Ric., 47; Sarah, 47; Stephen, 47*; Thos., 47*; Wm., 47, 413

Brachel (Brachall), Denise, 1033; Geof., 1033; John, 1033; Wal., 1033

Brackenborough, *see* Brokenborough

Bradbury, Edm., 1266; Eliz., 1266

Bradeford, *see* Bradford

Bradelega, *see* Bradley

Bradelep, *see* Birdlip

Bradey, Wm., 1053

Bradewell, —, 1195

Bradford (Bradeford, Braidford), Cornelius, 622; Eliz., 622; Esther, 622; Geo., 934; Rev. Hen., 1404; J., 1288; John (de), 622, 896, 902, 993*, 1102; Rev. John, 1165; Marg., 622, 623; Mary, 622*, 1408; Rob., 765; Thos., 622*, 934*; Wm., 1408; Rev. Wm., 1408; —, 1293

Bradgate, Gervis, 1468*; Sarah, 1468

Bradled, Wm., 1477

Bradley (Bradelega, Bradleye), Ann, 1150, 1151, 1471; Ant., 1227; Eleanor (de), 861, 1471, 1540; Eliz., 226, 584, 1038; Geo., 262, 1274; Hannah, 584, 1010*; Hen., 583*, 584; Hester, 137; Jas., 656; Rev. Jas., 861; Jane, 583, 584, 656*, 660, 1482; John, 137, 583*, 584*, 660, 1038, 1482; Rev. John, 135*, 691, 692, 1483; Joyce, 584; Lewis, 1471*; Rev. Lewis, 19, 1339; Margery, 137; Mary, 578, 583, 584*, 1471; R., 1512; Rebecca, 656; Ric., 1038; Sarah, 1471*; Rev. Stephen, 868; Thos., 467, 872; Wm., 578, 583, 584, 656*, 660*, 778 n, 1010*, 1150, 1151; Rev. Dr., 656; —, 1483

Bradshaw (Bradshawe), Augusta Matilda, 1551; Charlotte Mary, 1551; Edm., 1482; Edw., 1481*, 1482; Eliz., 1481; Idey, 569; Jas., 1481*; Rev. Jas., 263; Jane, 1481*; John, 1551; Mary, 1099*, 1481*; Peter, 1099*; Wm., 1099; —, 1195, 1551

Bradstock, John, 946*; Margaretta Penelope, 1503; Rev. Rowland, 1382*; Susannah, 946; Rev. Thos., 1503

Bradston (Bradstone), Agnes, 1490; Ant., 1490; Eliz., 1169, 1328, 1490; Rob., 1490; Thos., 1169; Sir Thos., 1169; —, 1169, 1328, 1490, 1491*; fam., 753, 1328, 1486

Bradway, *see* Broadway

Braekston, Rev. Wm., 1441

Braganza, Cath. of, 1154

Bragge (Brage, Bragg), Anne, 806; Chas., 12, 205, 612, 806, 833, 834, 835; G. D., 1226; John, 1090; Lucy, 835; Lucy Ann, 1090; Wal., 1313

Braggins, Eliz., 868

Braidford, *see* Bradford

Brain (Braine, Brayne), Abigail, 108; Ann(e), 226, 564, 886, 980; Ant., 473; Chris., 470, 1038; Dinah, 108*; Eliz., 473, 867; Geo., 108*; Hannah, 1584; Kath., 640; Kitford, 472; Ja[s]., 867; Jane, 1481; John, 226, 470, 833, 886, 980, 1481; Mary, 886; Randford, 564; Ric., 469; Ruth, 1038; Stephen, 1584; Wm., 470, 640; —, 1162

Bramble, Eliza, 304; Geo., 304; Mary, 304

Brampton, Anna, 1243; John, 1243; Ric., 1243; Rob., 1243

Bramy, Capt. Hetford, 928

Branch (Braunche), Adam, 353; Anne, 353; Jane, 353; Rob., 1513; Thos., 89, 147, 353; —, abbot, 1379

Brand, Thos., 1511; Miss, wife of Sir Rob. Kemp, 431; *and see* Brant

Brandenburg, elector of, 723

Brandis (Brandiss), Joanna, 36; Marg., 1537; Mary, 1537; Thos., 26

Brandon (Braundon), Eliz., 664; Sir Chas., duke of Suffolk, 664, 665; John, 1477; —, 1477

Brangwaine, Thos., 1220

Brant, Benj., 90*; Eliz., 90; Ric., 1519; Rob., 1519; *and see* Brand

Brany, Ensign Chas., 928

Braose, *see* Breuse

Brassington (Brassinton), Ann, 1398; Eliz., 1398, 1499; John, 429; Marg., 429, 1499*; Rev. Ric., 483, 1273; Thos., 1398*; Wm., 1499*

Brathwait, Eliz., 1191; Rev. John, 1191, 1196

Braunche, *see* Branch

Braundon, *see* Brandon

Braw, Frances, 1298; Jane, 1297; Dr. Wm., bishop, 1297, 1298*

Brawne (Brawn), Anne, 1040; Diana, 1131; Eliz., 1040*; Hester, 1131; Hugh, 1040*; Jane, 1131; Joan, 1046; John, 1040*; Rev. John, 1040; Joseph, 1131; Judeth, 1040; Sir Ric., kt., 987, 1040; Theodosia, 1040; Thos., 1046*, 1131*; —, bishop, 1040

Bray (Braye, Brays), Ann, 136*; Ashcomb, 136*; Barbara, 136*, 137, 246; Cath., 136*; Dorothy, 1380; Edm., 136*, 1012, 1015*; Capt. Edm., 134, 136; Major Edm., 136; Sir Edm., 136, 896, 1015, 1482; Edw., 136; Eleanor, 256, 1545; Eliz., 136, 1437; Frances, 136*; Giles, 136*; Sir Giles, 136*, 1015; Jane, 136*, 137, 1016; John, 77, 136, 256, 1437*; Marg., 136*; Mary, 77, 136*, 1437; Reg., 135, 136*, 137, 246, 1015; Sarah, 1437; Rev. Thos., 515, 678, 1187*; Wm., 136*, 827 n; Lt. Col. Wm., 136; Lord, 1219; —, 1519; fam., 134, 894

Braybrook, —, 1351

Braye, *see* Bray

Brayne, *see* Brain

Brays, *see* Bray

Brazier, Mary, 989

Breach (Breech), Hugh de, 985; John, 380; Marg., 380; *and see* Brerch

Breaks, Phil., 1474; *and see* Breeks; Breic; Brickes

Breakspear, Ric., 953

Breavitt, W., 1312

Brechcumbe, Hen. de, 1027

Bredon (Breedon), Rev. John Symonds, 1147; Thos., 851 n; —, abbot, 1101

Bree, Rev. Edw., 567*

Breech, *see* Breach

Breedon, *see* Bredon

Breeks, Rev. John, 1233; *and see* Breaks; Breic; Brickes

Breen, Sarah, 1249; Stephen, 1249

Breether, *see* Brether

Breghenoke, Adam, 1292

Breic, Ric., 533; *and see* Breaks; Breeks; Brickes

Bremesgrove, *see* Bromsgrove

Brent, Jane, 411; Kath., 953; Rob., 411, 953

Breoas (Breouse), *see* Breuse

Brerch, Phil., 1352; *and see* Breach

Brereton, Barbara, 574, 575; Bridget, 314; Dr. Hen., 1082*; Rev. Hen., 722; Hester, 314*, 1082; Ralph, 368; Ric., 1082; Rev. Ric., 574*, 575; Rob., 129, 314, 366, 368*, 370, 985, 1082*; Sarah, 129; Susanna, 314*; Theophila, 314; Theophilus, 313, 314*, 368, 1082*, 1501; Thos., 574*; Col., 1197; Mrs., 368; —, 1539

B[rereton], Wm., 130

Bret, *see* Brett

Brether (Breether), John, 583; —, 1402

Bretherton, Ann, 984

Brethwy, Cristian, 1069

Breton, Rev. Rob., 245, 808; *and see* Britton

Brett (Bret), Anne, 512; Arthur, 448, 512; Geo., 512*, 1010; Henrietta, 448; Hen., 447*, 448*, 502, 511, 512*, 1482; Hester, 512*; Sir Jerome, 349 n; John, 472; Joyce, 512*; Lucy, 472; Marg., 448; Mary, 1010, 1482; Rob., 512; Capt., 928; fam., 447, 511

Breuse (Braose, Breoas, Breouse, Breuouse, Brewes, Brewosa, Brewose, Bruce, Brywes), Agnes (de) 1253*, 1259; Aliva, 1253; Annora de, 1033, 1255; Beatrix, 1015, 1253; Bertha, 1253; Eliz., 1080; Geo., 1255; Isabel(l), 1253*; John de, 1253, 1256, 1259; Marg., 1253; Mary, 1253; Matilda, 1253, 1255; Maud, 1253; Peter de, 908, 1033, 1253*, 1255; Reg., 1255; Rob. de, 1015*, 1016; Thos., 1253*; W. de, 1033, 1253, 1255, 1259; Wm. de, 1033, 1253*, 1255*; Lord, 1251; —, 1253*, 1255; fam., 1253*, 1255*

Breval (Brevel), John, 1539; Thos., 1103; —, 1103

Brewer, Grace, 1348; Hester, 584; Jas., 584; John, 722*, 1439; Rev. John, 400; Joyce, 1046; Mary, 1348; Ric., 598; Sarah, 598; Thos., 1046, 1348; —, 1380

Brewes, *see* Breuse

Brewet, Marg., 1085; Thos., 1085

Brewosa (Brewose), *see* Breuse

Breynton, Rev. Rog., 1061

Brewster, Amelia, 1412; Chas., 1412; John, 1412

Brian, *see* Bryan

Briand (Briant), *see* Bryant

Briard, Anne, 1326

Brice (Brise), Chantry [? Charity], 1321; Edw. Daubeny, 1490; Emma Christian, 1490; John,

1005; Mary, 1086; Ric. Daubeny, 1490; Sam., 1490*; Susan, 1490; Susannah, 1490; Thos., 1321; Wm., 1086; —, 1328, 1491

Brickdale, John, 603; Matt., 603

Brickendine (Brickendon), Anna Caroline, 978; Rev. John, 447

Brickes, Rev. Wal., 860; *and see* Breaks; Breeks; Breic

Brickstock, Owen, 1189

Brictric (Brietric, Britric), 798, 1120, 1138*, 1285*, 1287*, 1309*, 1322, 1361*, 1381, 1439, 1455*, 1512*, 1516

Brid, *see* Bird

Briday, Sam., 1217

Briddelep, *see* Birdlip

Bridge, *see* Bridges

Bridgeman (Bridgman, Bruggema[n], Brydgman), Abel, 1195; Amey, 1159*; Anne, 1101, 1373; Benj., 1159; Cath., 1379*, 1380; Chas., 105*, 471, 1373; Eliz., 1373; Lady Frances, 1373; Geo., 940, 1378, 1380; Hen. Toye, 65, 66; Heveningham (Heavingham), 940, 1380; Sir J., 1380; Jas., 66*, 940; John, 66, 1373, 1378*, 1379, 1380*, 1434; Sir John, kt., 1373*; Mary, 940; Ric., 130; Thos., 1159; W., 1101; Wm., 940*; Rev. Wm., 1140; Lady, 1380; —, 65, 1132, 1323; fam., 102, 469

Bridger, Ann(e), 474, 1096, 1097; Arthur, 1095, 1096; Benj., 1097; Desborough (Desbrow), 474, 1097; Geo., 1096, 1097*; Joane, 1097; Sir John, kt., 427, 1125; Jonathan, 1097; Rev. Lawr., 1095, 1102; Mary, 1096*, 1336; Dame Rebecca, 427; Sam., 1096*; Theophilus, 1095, 1096; Wm., 1336

Bridges (Bridge, Bruges, Brugge, Brydges), Alice atte, 1447; Amy, 1487; Annabell, 1052; Ann(e), 138, 800, 1263*, 1377, 1507; Lady Anne (Lady Chandos), 1219; Ant., 860, 1201; Beata, 974*; Beatrix, 1051; Brook, 1504; Lady Caroline, 25; Chas., 1263*, 1281; Chris., 1355; Deborah, 661; Dorothy, 1380; E., 1355; Edm., 1219, 1380; Edm., Lord Chandos, 1219, 1475; Edw., 482, 488, 684, 1281*, 1282*, 1355, 1487; Rev. Edw. Tymewell, 1220; Sir Egerton, 1219; Eleanor, 137, 1324*; Eliz., 44, 137, 181, 331, 367, 379, 380, 421, 431, 484, 488, 862, 899, 1139, 1281, 1324, 1333, 1505*; Eliz. Allen, 1282; Esther, 538; Geo., 138, 1082, 1220; Geo., Lord Chandos, 1219, 1475*; Giles, 800, 1263; Giles, Lord Chandos, 859, 1219, 1220, 1475; Sir Giles, bt., 421 n, 684, 1051, 1263; Grey, Lord Chandos, 1051, 1219, 1475*; H., 1201; Hannah, 899; Harriet, 1282; Harry, 331; Hellen, 1282; Hen., 92, 94, 1052, 1201, 1282*, 1355, 1431; Rev. Hen., 21 255; Humph. (Humfry), 368, 379, 380, 1505, 1507; Isabel, 1355; Isabel, Lady Bruges, 421 n; J., 1219; Jas., 1101, 1160; Sir Jas., 1219; Jane, 1145, 1505, 1512; Jane, Lady Chandos, 1219*, 1475; Joan(e), 715, 1431; John, 420, 431*, 715, 899*, 974, 1220, 1263, 1281, 1355, 1377*, 1505; Sir John, kt., 570, 1380; Sir John, Lord Chandos, 449, 546, 1219, 1333, 1475;

Joseph, 974*; Kath., 1051; M., 1220; Marg., 1505; Mary, 22, 25, 862; Mary, Lady Bridges, 1263; Mary, Lady Chandos, 1219; Maud, 546, 1232; Mic., 974*; Milly, 1281*, 1282*; Phillippa, 1487; R., 1052, 1538*; Ric., 297, 421*, 738, 862, 899*, 974, 1081, 1145, 1324, 1505; Lieut. Ric., 1281; Rev. Ric., 1324; Rob., 44, 421, 1324, 1505*, 1512*; Sarah, 413, 974; Savmercal [*sic*], 661; Susan, Lady Chandos, 1219; T. de, 1356; Tacy, 899; Thos., 137*, 252, 484, 538, 546, 862*, 899*, 1232*, 1355, 1542; Sir Thos., 1487; Wal. atte, 1502; Wm., 138, 413, 431, 899*, 973, 974, 1355; Wm., Lord Chandos, 1219, 1475; Mr., 420 n, 1441; Rev., 973; —, 1232, 1288*; fam., 309, 389, 393, 1139, 1362; *and see* Briggs

Bridgewater, earl of, *see* Daubeny [*peerage*], Hen.

Bridgman, *see* Bridgeman

Bridle, Rev. John, 1221

Brierhurst, Rev. Thos., 1385

Brietric, *see* Brictric

Briggs (Brygg), Hannah, 954; Rob., 954; Sarah, 954; Thos., 1482; *and see* Bridges

Bright, Ann, 677, 722, 1038; Chas., 677; Hen, 212; Jo[a]ne, 821; John, 722*; Jonathan, 821; Josiah, 821*; Kath., 100; Martha, 832; Mary, 677; Sarah, 821; Thos., 821*, 822, 832; Wm., 677, 821

Brightwell, Loftus, 1487; Mary, 1487

Brimble, Ann, 555, 963; Hannah, 963; Jas., 212; Jacob, 963; Joanna, 555; John, 555; Mary, 212; Rob., 555; Wm., 963; *and see* Brindle

Brimscombe, Marg. de, 1021; Margery, 1027

Brimyard, Ann, 340; Joseph, 340; Wm., 340

Brinckett, Mary, 752

Brindle, John 187*; Mary, 187; Rob., 187; Sam., 187; Susanna, 948; Wm., 187, 948*; *and see* Brimble

Brinkworth, Edw., 13; Hen., 1138*; Jasper, 1138*; John, 13, 1302*; Mary, 1302*; Sarah, 1138*; —, 1054

Brinsdon, Ric., 429

Brinstorp, John, 1488; Martha, 1488; *and see* Rainstrop

Brion, *see* Bryan

Briscoe, Hester, 843; John 843; Sam., 843*; Wm., 843

Brise, *see* Brice

Bristowe (Bristow), Ann, 1327; Chas., 1327; Eliz., 1384; Mary, 586, 1551; Rob., 1384*; Wm., 1551

Briton, *see* Britton

Britric, *see* Brictric

Britton (Briton, Britten), Ann, 846; Eliz., 1582; Geo., 846; John, 1334*; Mary, 48, 1582; Rev. Ric., 198, 199, 200; Sam., 1583; Sarah, 200, 1583; Simon, 1582; Wm., 48; Mr., 1335; —, 1335; *and see* Breton

Broacher, —, 1054

Broad (Brode), Alice, 991; Anne, 1376; Elianor, 38; Eliz., 299, 1480*, 1481*; Esther, 948; Hannah, 1481; Hester, 300, 317; Geo., 946; Jane, 1480; John 231, 660, 991, 1480*, 1483; Marg., 38*; Margery, 1481; Mary, 38, 299, 300, 1480*,

1481*; Nic. le, 1552; Phil., 708 n; Ric., 660;
Rob., 299*; Sam., 317, 1376; Rev. Sam., 432,
511, 512; Sarah, 299; Susanna, 1376; Thos., 38*,
300*, 991, 1480*, 1481*, 1482*; Rev. W., 1290;
Rev. Wm., 579; —, 1011, 1482
Broadhead, Rev. Thos., 696
Broadhurst, Eliz., 622; Lydia, 622*; Rev. Mr., 622
Broadstock, Geo., 1372; Hannah, 1372; John,
1372*; Mary, 683, 1372; Solomon, 1403; Thos.,
683, 1317; Wm., 1238; —, 1317
Broadstowe, Edw., 1483
Broadway (Bradway), Alex., 534; Anne, 1470,
1476; Chas., 1464*; Deborah, 1464; Edm., 1476;
Edw. Beale, 1464; Frances, 1464*; Geo., 1333;
Giles, 1476; Jane, 296*; Lydia, 884; Mary, 296,
1333*, 1464; Mic., 1467; Thos., 884; Wm., 296*,
1470*; —, 1476, 1477; fam., 1476
Broben (Broban), Abraham, 930*; Ann(e), 872;
Edw., 934; Eliz., 930*; Jacob, 474, 930*; John,
473*, 474, 930; Jonathan, 930*; Joseph, 473;
Joyce, 930; Mary , 474, 930*; Sarah, 473; Wm.,
930, 934
Brock, Hannah, 686*; Joseph, 686; Mary, 1301;
Thos., 1301*; and see Brooke
Brockhampton, Sarra de, 1104; Wal. de, 688 n
Brockhurst, Thos., 1477
Brockton, —, 1475
Brode, see Broad
Broderwick, Anne, 1194; Eliz., 1194*; Mary, 1194;
Thos., 1194*
Brok (Broke), see Brooke
Brokenborough (Brackenborough, Brokenboro',
Brokenborrow, Brokenborrowe, Brokenbrow,
Brokenbury), Adam de, 360; Eliz., 1455; John
(de), 1455, 1490*, 1491; Mary, 1526*; Rachael,
657; Wal., 657; Wm., 1526
Bromage, see Bromwich
Bromcroft, John de, 1552
Bromedge, see Bromwich
Bromfield, Ann, 1531; Eliz., 1531; Sam., 1531
Bromiche, see Bromwich
Bromley, Eliz., 1270, 1390; Hen., 1270; John,
1390; Judith, 1362; Thos., 1388, 1390*; fam.,
1293
Bromsgrove (Bremesgrove), John (de), 481, 1447;
—, 1447
Bromwell, Eliz., 1150, 1151; John, 1150*, 1151*
Bromwich (Bromage, Bromedge, Bromiche,
Bromwick, Bromwyche), Anne, 118; Arthur,
534; Edm., 265; Edw., 619, 621; Eliz., 534, 1324;
Isaac, 265; J. Hooper, 1177; John, 266*, 1324*;
Rev. John, 415; Sir John, 266; John Hooper,
1173, 1174, 1176; Joseph, 1177; Lancelot, 820*;
Marg., 619; Mary, 1174; Priscilla, 820*; Ric.,
621, 1324; Rob., 265 n, 266*; Rog., 1355; Thos.,
266, 1177; Wal., 118; Wm., 917; Rev. Yate, 626,
820*; Mr., 918; —, 266, 1020, 1328; fam., 265,
819
Bronegare, Rob., 1513
Bronsden, see Brunsden
Brooke (Brok, Broke, Brook, Brookes, Brooks),
Adam atte, 1404; Alice, 270; Ann, 211, 270,

1119, 1247; Audrey, 474; Chas., 211; D., 1385;
David, 1539; Sir David, 1538; Deborah, 270;
Eliz., 953*, 1113, 1116*, 1119*, 1193, 1247*;
Eliz. A., 1247; Esther, 768; Fitzherbert, 1119;
Fitzherbert Hartley, 1119; Frances, 1119; Frances
Eliza, 1119*; Hannah, 683, 1113*, 1115, 1116,
1119*, 1384; Hen., 1282; Rev. Hen., 1341, 1346;
Hester, 413, 777*; Jas., 1058, 1116; Jane, 768,
1384; Joan(e), 1011, 1269; John (atte, de la, in
the), 611, 768*, 1172, 1218, 1223, 1247*, 1307,
1355, 1377, 1404; Rev. John, 421*, 579, 770,
860, 1348; Jonathan, 683; Joseph, 413, 1247,
1256; Laduo. [sic] atte, 1404; Marg., 465, 1169;
Mary, 611, 768, 777*, 873, 1058, 1116*, 1119,
1193, 1247; N., Lord Cobham, 403, 1378; Nic.,
958; Oliver, 1113, 1116*, 1119; Sir R., 1491; Ric.
(atte), 270*, 474, 851, 1113*, 1115, 1119*, 1150,
1269, 1540; Rev. Ric., 328, 853; Ric. John,
1119*; Rob., 465*, 777*, 1193, 1233; Sam., 211,
212, 465; Sarah, 212; Stephen, 873; Susan, 1169;
Susannah, 851; T., 1122; Theresa Frances, 1119;
Thos., 777*, 787, 873, 953, 1011, 1116, 1119*,
1247*, 1282, 1307, 1384; Dr. Thos., 1421, 1422;
Rev. Thos., 1422*; Sir Thos., 511; W., 1257;
Wallis, 777; Wm., 474, 893, 1116*, 1119, 1247*,
1256*, 1313, 1552; Dr., 1421; Serjt., 1123; —
(atte), 1015, 1120*, 1169, 1311; —, bishop,
1540; fam., 265, 630; and see Brock
Brooke [peerage](Broke, Brook), Anne, baroness,
628; Lord, 763, 1001; and see Greville, Sir Fulk
and Rob.
Brookman, —, 1339
Brooks, see Brooke
Broome (Broom), Dan., 1573*; Francis, 1573;
Hester, 1573*; John, 975; Lucy, 975; Thos.,
1573; —, 1402
Brossar, Hester, 624; Joseph, 624*
Brotheridge, Eliz., 74; Jane, 151; Thos., 74, 151
Brothers, Eliz., 543; Thos., 543*
Brotherton, Thos. de, earl of Norfolk, 925, 1322
Broughton, T., 1420; Lord, see Hobhouse, J. C.
Broun, see Brown
Brounynge, see Browning
Brown (Broun, Browne, Brun, Bruyn), Adam,
1102; Alex., 1289; Albreda le, 1431; Alice, 685*;
Anna, 204; Anne, 348, 413, 422, 613*, 614,
1042, 1117, 1143, 1282, 1352, 1376, 1486, 1487,
1488; Ant., 1425*; Sir Ant., 1169; Arthur, 797;
Betty, 111, 446, 1454; Blanch, 789; Bridget, 413;
Cath., 111, 348*, 1143, 1250; Chas., 49, 111*,
1143*, 1146*, 1352, 1354, 1454; Dan., 182*,
777, 1243; Dorothy, 1250; Edith, 1317, 1425;
Edm., 1507*, 1508; Edm. Thos., 1470; Edw., 42,
435*, 1012, 1250; Edw. Thos., 1472; Eleanor,
685*, 1248, 1276, 1454; Elias, 140; Eliz., 95,
110*, 182, 413, 422, 446*, 569, 658, 662, 677,
734, 800, 873, 953, 984, 1042, 1143, 1168, 1214;
Frances, 986, 1036; Francis, 613; Geo., 412, 413,
515; Giles, 1143*, 1147; Rev. H., 1226*;
Hannah, 446, 797, 1280; Hen., 348, 685*, 686*,
731, 734, 932, 1352*; Rev. Hen., 216, 1224,
1226, 1227, 1228*; Hugh, 1486*, 1488, 1491;

Humph., 13, 515, 1280*, 1282, 1405; Sir Humph., kt., 515; Isabell, 105; J., 1043*, 1078; Rev. J., 1492; Jas., 873, 1117, 1121, 1159, 1250, 1258; Jane, 575, 758, 772, 777, 1352*; Joanna, 1117; John, 110*, 115, 140*, 182, 192, 193, 333, 348*, 351, 377, 422, 425, 485*, 575*, 638, 789, 871, 878, 949*, 967, 984, 1042*, 1043*, 1064, 1150, 1168, 1243, 1248, 1258, 1292, 1352*, 1353, 1356, 1388, 1397*, 1404, 1419*, 1425, 1431, 1437, 1445, 1473, 1484, 1485, 1494, 1511, 1552, 1554; Rev. John, 421, 422*, 1494; John Beale, 1042*; John Wm., 1354; Joseph, 48*, 871, 1196; Joyce, 48*; Judith, 192; Lucy, 1169; Marg., 685, 783, 1146; Martha, 446, 658; Martha Susanna(h), 1042*; Mary, 111, 112, 193, 333, 354, 377, 382, 425, 435, 515, 569, 613*, 638, 658, 662, 685, 802, 905, 923, 1042*, 1098, 1140, 1143*, 1146, 1352, 1353, 1397, 1419*, 1425*, 1445, 1454, 1512; Mary Anne, 1042; Mary Dipper, 1354; Mary Eliz., 194; Mary Louisa, 1511; Mat., 1477; Mathias, 1474*; Nic., 1307; Sir Peter, bt., 1036; Rachel, 48; Ric. (le), 110*, 193*, 364, 377, 382, 569, 658, 677, 758, 777*, 801, 802*, 863, 923, 949*, 984, 991, 1042, 1069, 1137*, 1352, 1384, 1431, 1440, 1484, 1512, 1574; Rev. Ric., 1186; Rob., 42, 95, 204, 412, 413, 613*, 614*, 1339, 1354, 1370, 1447; Rob. Beale, 1042; Rupertia, 1226; Sam., 1143; Sara(h), 115, 351, 413, 485*, 569, 758, 772, 822, 841, 924, 1137, 1237, 1250; Sarah Eliz., 1354*; Susanna, 1042; T., 1043; Rev. T. M., 1494; Thos., 95, 111, 112, 182, 384, 421, 442, 489, 569, 802, 841*, 884, 1042*, 1043*, 1083, 1214, 1237, 1372, 1378, 1539; Thos. Beale, 638, 1042; Wal., 783, 1215, 1404, 1504; Wm., 110, 193*, 354, 446*, 485, 685*, 686*, 693*, 731, 772, 789, 822, 986, 1104, 1276, 1354*, 1403, 1454, 1484; Wm. Ant., 1354; Winifrede, 693; —, 1064, 1147, 1165, 1177, 1311, 1355, 1455*, 1491; fam., 349, 577, 684*, 1043
Browning (Brounynge, Browninge), Agnes, 1027, 1165; Alan, 1485; Alice, 1239; Alienor, see Browning, Elinour; Anne, 1251; Anselme, 832; Cecilia, 1051; Christian, 416; Cicely, 801, 1027; Dan., 543, 1434; Edw., 174, 631*; Elinour (Alienor), 602, 737; Eliz., 44, 264, 416*, 543*, 563, 670, 1071, 1210, 1214, 1505, 1507; Giles, 491*, 1210, 1214*; Helen, 1511; Hester, 563; Jane, 416, 1008; Joan (Johane), 264, 832, 1351; John, 44, 182, 414*, 415*, 416*, 531, 602*, 670, 737, 830, 890, 1027, 1165*, 1168*, 1172, 1186, 1239, 1251, 1434, 1507; (or Fitz Nichol), John, 801; Joseph, 93, 748, 1071; Judeth, 631; Lydia, 623; Margery, 1453; Martha, 1167, 1168, 1434; Mary, 174, 182, 416, 623, 1168*, 1210, 1510; Moses, 1510; Nic., 1351; R., 1027, 1101; Reg., 1169; Ric., 182, 416, 473, 530, 531, 563*, 890, 1027, 1092*, 1167, 1168, 1186, 1540; Sir Ric., 1051; Rob., 182; Rob. Day, 1008; Sampson, 543*; Sam., 174, 623, 633, 907, 1510, 1513; Sarah, 174, 182, 491, 563, 729, 832; Stephen, 415, 416, 1507; Thos., 264*, 542, 563*, 631,

729*, 832*, 1027, 1210*, 1214*, 1217*, 1505, 1513, 1539; Wm., 174, 176, 491, 531, 543, 602, 623*, 832, 1210*, 1214*, 1217, 1351; Mrs., 415; —, 630, 1074, 1169; fam., 415
Brownjohn, Hen., 812*
Brownlowe, Dame Henrietta, 448; Sir Wm., bt., 448
Broxline, Mrs., 1372
Bruce, see Breuse
Bruge (Bruges, Brugge), see Bridges
Bruggema[n], see Bridgeman
Brumston, Rev. Thos., 820; and see Brunsden
Brun, see Brown
Brunett, see Burnett
Brunsden (Bronsden), John 1484, 1485; Mary, 1484; and see Brumston
Bruselaunde (Bruselaunce), Geof., 1258; Wal., 1259
Brush, Jane, 517; Mary, 1019; Rebecca, 1019*; Rev. Thos., 1019*; Wm., 517; —, 1020
Bruton (Bruten, Brutoun), Moses, 1105; Peter, 1292; Rob., 703*; Thos., 454, 1534, 1539; Wm., 1539
Bruyn, see Brown
Bryan (Brian, Brion), Ann, 9*, 11, 300; Anna, 10; Betty, 490, 555; Chas., 8; Rev. Chas., 1516; Chris., 836; Dan., 1268; Edw., 555*; Eleanor, 202; Elias, 836, 1159; Eliz., 11, 300, 614, 845, 884*; Frances, 614; Geo., 615, 884, 1194*; Rev. Geo., 614; Grace, 1348; Guy (de), 9, 244, 555*; Hannah, 490, 555; Jas., 11*; Jane, 10; John, 8, 10*, 300*, 490*, 845, 847, 881*, 974, 1331; Rev. John, 962; Joseph, 1583; Lewis, 8*, 9*; Marg., 1348; Maria-Clemencia, 962; Mary, 9, 10*, 11, 555*, 836, 847, 881, 1159, 1194*, 1268, 1331; Oswell, 762; Reg., bishop, 195; Ric., 10, 1348; Ruth, 555; Sam., 10*; Sarah, 974*; Susannah, 1583; T., 121, 1331; Thos., 202*, 300, 884*; Rev. Thos., 783; Wm., 11*, 555*, 847; —, 395, 1017, 1216; fam., 392 n
Bryant (Briand, Briant), Ann, 996, 1582*; Betty, 996; Chas., 758; Dennis, 1583; Eliz., 10, 616; Geo., 616*; Rev. Geo., 613; Jas., 1582; John, 413, 996, 1582; Mary, 837, 1582; Rob., 996*, 1423; Sam., 1582*; Susannah, 130, 1582; Thos., 10, 210, 1093, 1582; Wm., 130, 837, 845
Brydges, see Bridges
Brydgman, see Bridgeman
Brygg, see Briggs
Bryn, D., 1055; John [? Joan], 1055
Brywes, see Breuse
Bubb, Ann(e), 132, 715, 716, 1210; Eliz., 118*, 174, 689, 1210, 1499; Geo., 1210*; Hannah, 1350; Hen., 118, 580*; Hester, 1269; Isabell, 1494; Jas., 891, 1289; Jeremiah, 132; Joan, 118; John, 118*, 132, 689, 715*, 716, 857, 1350; Mary, 105, 118, 1269; Ric., 1210; Rob., 716; Thos., 118, 1155, 1156*, 1499*; Wm., 118, 132; fam., 1160
Bubel, Rob., 1478; —, 1478
Buceles, see Buckle
Bucer, Martin, 534 n

Bucher, *see* Butcher

Buck (Bucke), Betty, 703; Eliz., 652; Geo., 108*, 616; Hans, 1312; Isabel, 810; Jas., 703, 1486; Jeremiah, 652*, 655; John, 108, 331, 652, 810, 811*; Margery, 95; Martha, 616; Mary, 331, 616, 810, 811*; Mat., 103, 108, 1487; Nat., 244; Rachel, 108, 616; Sarah, 652; Thos., 703, 814, 1487; Ursula, 652*; Wm., 811; Rev. Wm., 93, 95*; Capt., 651 n; —, 709, 1490; —, wife of Thos., 814; fam., 649

Buckhurst, Lord, 1388

Buckingham, Ann, 677; Dan., 657*; Eliz., 677; Esther, 657; Geo., 633; Hannah, 622; Jas., 633; Joan, 657; John, 657, 677; Joseph, 633; Mary, 622, 657, 677; Penelope, 657; S., 1132; Sarah, 240, 622, 633; Seymore, 622*; Thos., 622, 633*, 657*, 677, 1027; Wm., 240; —, 1311*

Buckingham [*peerage*], prince Edw., duke of, 1295; duke of, 1220; *and see* Giffard, Wal.; Grenville; Stafford, *passim*

Buckland, Ann, 1411; Joseph, 1411*

Buckle (Buceles, Buckoll, Bukle), Ann(e), 229*, 336, 587; Arthur Hart, 1083; Capel, 334; Cartwright, 315, 316; Cornelius, 1539; Diana, 336; Edith, 586, 1164; Eliz., 229, 586*, 1355*; Geo., 1515*; Hannah, 665, 1229; Hen., 586; Isabell, 316; Rev. Jas., 1083; Joan, 229*; John, 229*, 334*, 585, 586*, 1363; Mary, 229*, 315, 316*, 334, 586*, 815, 1515*; Ric., 229*, 587, 677; Rog., 676; Sarah, 586*, 1083, 1097; Thos., 229, 316, 586*, 1229; Rev. Thos., 228, 586*, 1164, 1165; W., 1362; Wal., 229, 315, 316, 585, 586; Wm., 229, 313, 316, 334, 336*, 586*, 665, 676, 1097, 1289, 1355*; Mr., 1348; —, 1288*, 1362; fam., 585

Buckler, Cath. (Kath.), 591, 595 n; John, 591 n; Sir Wal., kt., 591, 595

Bucknell, Ann, 203; S., 1213; Sam., 203

Buckney, Wm., 1584

Buckoll, *see* Buckle

Budd (Budde), Wm., 1422; Mr., 1513

Budding (Buding), Ann, 542; Anselm, 1008; Dan., 542; Edw., 981*; Eliz., 981, 1008; Geo., 562*; Hen., 542; Jas., 562; John, 981, 1217; Martha, 981; Mary, 562, 1054; Ric., 1054; Sam., 1182; Sarah, 1008, 1182; Wm., 562, 1008

Budel (Buedel), Alice, 1404; John le, 1339

Buding, *see* Budding

Budworth, Rev. Ric., 754

Buedel, *see* Budel

Buedelesmull, Rob. atte, 1379

Buggood, *see* Bidgood

Buggin (Buggins, Burgoigns), Eliz., 1267, 1392; Martha, 1267*; Mary, 1267; Rob., 1267*

Bukle, *see* Buckle

Bulbat, Wm., 1363

Bulkeley, Thos. Coventry, 195, 1217

Bull, Anne, 1081; Eliz., 96; Geo., 96*, 370, 1081*; Rev. Geo., 93, 96; Hannah, 264; Jas., 264; John, 1410, 1553, 1558; Rev. John, 1516; Mary, 1558; Rachel, 96; Ric., 264; Rev. Rob., 275, 350, 1346; Rev. T., 1043; Thos. Evans, 1558, 1563; —, 1199; —, bishop, 1082, 1258*; *and see* Bolle

Bullen, Anne, 1295

Buller, Cath., 220 n; Francis, 220 n; G., 1328; Rev. Jas., 615; *and see* Boller

Bulley (or Busli), Rog. de, 400

Bullingham, John, 302; John, bishop, 252, 1502; Nic., 221

Bullock, Alice, 584; Anne, 215, 832, 1376; Benj., 846; Betty, 832, 991*, 1316; C., 1317; Cath., 1054; Chas., 1316; Edm., 215*, 1315*; Edw., 215; Eliz., 683, 832; Geo., 215*, 1376, 1377; Grace, 60; Hannah, 716; Jas., 468; Jane, 821; Joan, 821; John, 74, 468, 821, 832, 1079; Marg., 215; Mary, 468, 846; Priscilla, 74, 1079; R., 1054; Ric., 584, 991; Rob., 832*; Rog., 60; Sam., 1234, 1238, 1316; Sarah, 468, 832; Susannah, 821; Thos., 215, 683, 1079, 1315; W., 1317; Wm., 214, 716, 832*, 1054, 1376; —, 1317, 1402*; fam., 214

Bulstrode, Francis, 1103

Bumford, John, 1258

Bumpas (Bumpass), Eliz., 88*; Jane, 88; Marg., 88; Mary, 88*, 751, 989; Ric., 88*; Thos., 989*

Bumpsted, Chris., 878

Bunce, Joseph, 506

Bund, Thos., 218, 1403

Bunting, Ann(e), 1013*; Eliz., 1013; Jane, 1013; Marg., 1068; Mary, 1013*; Ralph, 1013*; Rob., 1013*, 1068*; Thos., 1013; Wm., 1013*; —, 1015, 1017

Bunyan (Bonion), John, 1186, 1258

Burbage, Rev. T., 1441

Burbaste (Burbast, Burbastes), Alice, 1455; Rob., 1082; Rog., 1455; —, 1082*

Burben, Dorothy, 448; John, 448*

Burbridge, Thos., 429

Burchall (Burchell), *see* Birchall

Burcholte, *see* Birchold

Burcombe (Burcomb), Ann(e), 847, 1106*; Benj., 1167; Dan., 1106*, 1116*; Dorcas, 1106; Eliz., 1116; Isabella, 1110; Jane, 1106; John, 1106, 1116; Marg., 1251; Mary, 1116*, 1167*; Rob., 1106; Sam., 1106*, 1121, 1251; Sarah, 847; Stephen, 1167*; Thos., 847, 1109, 1121; Wal., 1116; Wm., 1121; —, 1121, 1122

Burder, Rev. Dr., 1217

Burdock, Ann, 203; Hester, 1008; Jane, 1008; John, 1008; Sarah, 1008; Wm., 203, 975*, 1008

Burdon (Berdone, Burdun), John, 1259; Rog., 1258; —, 1237

Burel, *see* Burrell

Bures, Hawise de, 1238; John de, 1238*

Burfield, Ann, 102

Burfoot (Burfott), Joseph, 1542*; Mary, 1542

Burford, Abraham, 16; Ann, 235, 1511; Benj., 1146; John, 941*; Joseph, 235; Mary, 16, 941, 1146; Rob., 941; W., 1092; Wm., 1511; —, 1282

Burfott, *see* Burfoot

Burge, Ann, 93, 1533; Edw., 1533; John, 381*; Mary, 381; Rob., 1127; Sam., 381*; Wm., 381*

Burgess (Boregast, Burges, Burghersh, Burghess, Burgis, Burgiss), Anne, 757; B., 1120; Caroline, 1050; Cath., 510*; Edw., 1584; Eliz., 510*, 1120;

Harry, 510*; Hester, 751; Jas., 1050, 1582; John, 208, 510, 751; Lawr., 510*; Lydia, 751, 752; Martha, 1582; Mary, 1584; Obadiah, 751, 752; Phil., 757; Rev. R., 1447; Ric., 1404; Rob., 1447; Sarah, 751, 1050; Thos., 510; Wm., 1404, 1405, 1487; Rev. Mr., 275; —, 1403

Burgh (Burgo), H., 1139, 1203, 1215; Hubert de, earl of Kent, 581; Isabel de, 1287; John de, 581; — (de), 1054, 1287

Burghall, see Burrell

Burghersh (Burghess), see Burgess

Burghill, Rev. John, 1335; and see Burrell

Burgis (Burgiss), see Burgess

Burgo, see Burgh

Burgoigns, see Buggin

Burgoyne, Dr. Rog., 374

Burgom (Burgum), Eliz., 550; Hen., 1551; John, 550*; Thos., 465, 608

Burhill, see Burrell

Burleigh, Lord, 1093, 1493

Burley (Berleye, Burleigh, Burly), Abigail, 939; Ann(e), 173, 177, 623, 1583; Dan., 623; Geo., 1583; John, 939; Rog., 1540; Ruth, 623; Sarah, 623, 1438; Sir Simon, 297 n, 325; Stephen, 173; Thos., 173*; W., 1419; Wm., 177, 563, 623*, 1438

Burlington, earl of, 220

Burlston, Martha, 1193

Burly, see Burley

Burne, John (atte)(de), 1197, 1311

Burnell (Burnall, Burnel), Alice, 1016, 1017; Anne, 1545; Edw., 1015; Hugh, 1016; Isabell de, 1350; John, 1453; Marg., 961; Maud, 1015*; (formerly Handelo), Nic. (Nickolas), 1015*; Phil., 1015; Rob., 1545; Rob., bishop, 1015, 1016; Thos., 963, 1112, 1545; Wm., 961*, 1121; —, 915, 1120, 1351, 1482*; fam., 1015

Burnett (Bourknygt, Brunett, Burnet, Burnit), Anne, 872; Cristina la, 1228; John, 868, 872*; Mary, 872; Rev. Maur., 1539; Rob., 884; Thos., 236; —, bishop, 1334

Burnley (Burnlie), Rev. John, 206, 207

Burr, D., 1323*; Rev. Hen. Scudamore, 1323; —, 1322

Burrell (Boroughulle, Bourghall, Burel, Burghall, Burhill), Adam, 1102; Basilia, 1401; Geo., 785; Gil., 1102; Rob., 546; Rog. de, 1404; —, 1401*, 1402; fam., 1401 and see Burghill

Burrop, see Burrup

Burrows (Boroughs, Borroughs, Burroughs), Ann, 881, 1079; Cath., 1498; Dan., 348; Dennis, 202*; Edm., 317; Eleanor, 348; Eliz., 586, 1164; Esther, 1079, 1307; Francis, 730; Hannah, 1307; Hester, 202; Humph., 1079; Jane, 317, 730; John, 881, 1163, 1186, 1307*, 1459, 1499*; Joseph, 1499*; Judith, 1499; Marg., 1499; Martha, 1079; Mary, 202*, 948, 1499, 1542; Rebecca, 202; Ric., 1140, 1499; Sarah, 1163; Thos., 1079*, 1163*, 1164, 1165, 1498*, 1499, 1542; W., 1092; Wm., 202, 721, 948, 1499*, 1554

Burrup (Burrop, Burrupp), Elinor, 1377*; Ric., 1373, 1376, 1377*; Sarah, 1376

Burstead (Bastard, Burstede, Bustard, Busted), Ant., 643; Cristina, 1382; Eliz., 1063*; Mary, 1063; Myles, 1061; R., 985, 1063*; Ric., 1062; Rev. Wm., 744, 1196*, 1228; —, 985, 1064*

Burt, see Birt

Burthogge, Ric., 1115; Sarah, 1115–16

Burton (Berghton, Berton, Borghton, Borton, Bourten, Byrton), Alex., 530; Ann, 1002*; Benedict, 1160; Eliz., 554, 1531, 1533; Esther, 1444; Rev. Geo., 409; Hen., 1031; Humf., 1475; Jas., 554, 1046; Joahane, 431; Rev. John, 840; Joseph, 388; Marg., 797; Octiavia, 1046; Ric., 431; Rob., 797, 848, 1002*; Rev. Sam., 534, 848, 849, 1228; Thos. (de), 18, 1011, 1032, 1533; Rev. Thos., 142, 144*, 495, 567, 630; Wm. (de), 1016, 1444; —, 1011*, 1477

Bury, Eliz., 1003; Hannah, 1003; John, 1003; Mary, 1002; Phineas, 1127; Rev. Phineas, 1127; Rebecca, 1003*; Ric., 1016; Thos., 1002, 1003*; Wm., 353

Busby, Anne, 263, 668; Benj., 884; Mary, 884

Bush (Bushe), Anna, 82; Ann(e), 83, 212, 1107*, 1108*; Dorothy, 83; Eleanor, 210*, 1107, 1108; Eliz., 83*, 1107*, 1108*; Geo., 213; Giles, 83*, 210; Greg., 1107, 1491; Hester, 846; Jas., 212, 1107*, 1108*; Johan, 945; John, 210; Joseph, 841; Martha, 83; Mary, 83, 302, 841; Paul, bishop, 452, 532 n, 577 n; Rev. S., 1127; Sam., 83*, 210; Thos., 301, 302*, 357, 945; Wm., 82, 83*, 206, 210*, 846, 1107; —, 487, 1016

Bushel (Bushell), Diana, 1441; Jane, 1317; Rob., 1441; W., 1317; Rev. W., 1317; Rev. Wm., 1317

Busher, Jane, 412; Wm., 412

Busli (or Bulley), Rog. de, 400

Bustard (Busted), see Burstead

Busteen, Mary, 90

Buswell, see Boswell

Busy, Edw., 1217

Butcher (Bocher, Boucher, Bucher), Ann, 284, 1008, 1131; Edw., 55; Eliz., 5; Lieut. Jas., 1282; Jeremiah, 1008*; Joan, 55; John, 55*, 467, 1008*, 1131*, 1186; Jonah, 418*; Joseph, 5, 1131; Josiah, 5; Kath., 1131; Martha, 418, 789; Mary, 1008, 1131, 1554; Maur., 540*; Olive, 284; Rob., 5*; Sam., 1131, 1132; Sarah, 540, 1008; Susanna, 467; Thos., 284, 467, 789, 1132; W., 1132; Wm., 592, 595, 1131*; Rev. Wm., 525; (or Robyns), fam., 852

Buter, Johne le, 1027; Rob. le, 1027; Wal. le, 1027

Butherne, G., 1323

Butler (Boteler, Botiller, Botyler, Butteler, Buttler), Alice, 1221; (Boteler a Park), Sir Almeric, 663, 672; Anna, 948; Ann(e), 973, 1239*, 1243, 1256; Edw., 1034; Eliz., 69*, 249, 663, 689, 1034, 1239, 1248*; Geo., 555*; Hannah, 490*, 1044*, 1047*; Hen., 1474, 1525; Isabel, 108, 663; J., 1256; Jas., 1034; Jane, 1243, 1248; Joan, 1219, 1431; John, 108*, 109, 201, 636, 689, 695*, 696, 870, 1044*, 1047*, 1092*, 1239, 1248; Sir John, 634, 695; Jonas, 1052, 1239, 1243, 1248; Joseph, 1248; Joseph, bishop, 1577; Kath., 1221; Marg., 756, 1306; Margareta, 1239; Mary, 69, 636, 973,

1248, 1474*, 1525; Mat., 249; Moses, 555; Rev. Nat., 1048; Nic., 119, 121, 695; Ralph, 1334, 1475; Sir Ralph, kt., 124, 1032; Ric., 490, 555, 948, 973; Rev. Ric., 66, 69*, 197; Sarah, 490, 555; Sylvester, 695, 696; T., 985; Thos. (le), 197, 201, 636, 756, 1219*, 1239, 1248*, 1431, 1476; Sir Thos., kt. 1092; W. (le), 696, 1219; Wm. (le), 109, 490*, 555, 1034*, 1074, 1102, 1292, 1420; Lord, 1477; —, 1219, 1220, 1256, 1475, 1476*, 1501, 1519; —, bishop, 1292; —, earl of Ormond, 1402, 1428; fam., 119, 121, 565, 634, 663*, 695, 748, 806, 816, 1047, 1221, 1477

Butt (Buts), Ann(e), 201, 202, 494, 802, 950*, 1241; Christian, 201; Eliz., 950*, 1577; Giles, 802; Hen., 950; Jas., 687; Jane, 803, 1024; Rev. Jeremiah, 263; John, 494, 587, 802*, 1025; Lydia, 661; Marg., 486; Martha, 661; Mary, 514, 683; Nat., 661; Patience, 950; Ric., 70*, 202, 683, 950*, 1024; Rob., 339, 486, 801, 1577; Sarah, 661, 950*; Thos., 70, 486*, 514*, 587, 1024*; Tim., 661; Wal., 654, 661*; Wm., 201*, 950

Buttal, Marg., 1004; Wm., 1004

Butterworth, Sir Arthur, 1478

Button, Dame Elinor, 681; Sir Rob., bt., 681

Buxton, Rob., 612*; Susannah, 612

Byam, Ann, 375, 1249; Hester, 1136; Sam., 1136*; Sarah, 1136; Thos. Fisher, 1249; Wm., 1136; —, 1140, 1255, 1256

Byard, Edw. Wagstaff, 1316; Hester, 1315, 1316*; Ric., 1315*, 1316*; and see Beard; Biatte; Bird

Bybury, Rob. de, 1363

Byck (Bycke), see Bick

Byckley, Rev. Rob., 1387

Byconnill, Dame Eliz., 1148

Bycote, John, 297

Bycroft, Sam., 1156

Bydell, see Biddle

Bye, Chas., 1533, 1536*; Christian, 1533; Cornelius, 1533, 1534; Edw., 1533, 1536; Lydia, 1536*; Mary, 1534

Byfar. John de, 1238

Byford, Eliz., 815; Geo., 815; Nat., 1315; Sarah, 1315

Bygge, see Biggs

Bykenor, A. de, 1039*; Alex. de, 1039; —, 1039*

Byles, Christian, 36; Jas. Hodge, 1377; —, 1378

Byleye, Elia, 1379

Byne, John, 1197

Byng, Gen., 1303

Byoch, see Bick

Byrch (Byrche), see Birch

Byrd (Byrde), see Bird

Byrkyn (Byrkin), see Birkin

Byrton, see Burton

Byryman, see Berriman

Byseley, see Bisley

Bysse, see Bisse

Byssheleye, see Bisley

Cable, Ric., 1121; Rev. Wm., 121

Cadale (Caddell), see Cadle

Caddick, Ann, 1282; Thos., 1282

Cadle (Cadale, Caddell, Cadell), Abigail, 1395; Ann(e), 1117, 1395*; Chris., 7, 36; Cyrus, 1113, 1117*, 1121; Eliz., 1395*; Hannah, 1395, 1401; Hester, 1395; J., 1369; John, 820, 1117*, 1119*, 1238, 1395*, 1401; Joseph (Josp), 1395*, 1403; Mary, 1395; Phebe, 1395; Ric., 1395*; Sam., 1369; Sarah, 1119, 1395; Susanna, 1117, 1119, 1395*; Thos., 1395*, 1403; Rev. Thos., 19, 1385; W., 1186; Wm., 1395*, 1403; fam., 1403

Cadogan, Jane, 112; Jonathan, 112; Mary, 112; Thos., 112; Wal., 112; Mr., 101

Cadurcis, see Chaworth

Cafford, Mary, 800*; Ric., 800*

Cage, Edw., 624; J. 1232; John, 619*, 624, 625, 1233; Judith, 624; Mary, 619, 625; —, 1054; (or Gage), fam., 625

Cains (Kayen), Ann, 411; Hen., 1228; Rebecca, 411; Sarah, 411*; Wm., 411*

Calbeck, Anna Maria, 1336; Chris., 1336*; John, 1336

Calcot, Ann, 1065

Caldbourn (Caldebourne), John de, 1256; Wm. de, 1258

Calder, Hen., 731; Jas., 731

Caldewell, see Caldwell

Caldicote, —, 1017

Caldwell (Caldewell, Caudwell, Chaldewelle), Anne, 976; Dorothy, 976; Jeremiah, 976; Rev. John, 1223; Rev. Joseph, 1223; Mary, 976; Wal. de, 1197; Rev. Wm., 139; —, 1017

Calixt[us] III, pope, 708 n

Callan, Francis, 1576

Callow (Callowe, Calow), Ann, 884; Rev. Benj., 1191, 1196, 1228; Eliz., 1152, 1191; Isabel, 464; Joan, 1400; John, 871, 884, 1400; Joseph, 1152; Rev. Joseph, 1152*, 1154; Mary, 1152; Ric., 1196; Sam., 884; Susannah, 871; Wm., 464*

Callowhill, Thomasine, 1487

Calmel, Peter, 848

Calmudee, Ric., 890; Vincent, 890

Calow, see Callow

Calton (or Cotten), Mary, 1482; —, 1120

Calvert, Ann(e), 754, 755; Cath., 755; Chas., baron Baltimore, 754, 755; Mat., 385; Olive, 385; Sarah, 1453

Cam (Cambe), see Camm

Camber, John, 1057, 1058

Cambourne (Camborn, Camborne), Ann, 729*; Edw., 555; John, 1488; Mary, 729; Sarah, 1488; Thos., 729*; Wm., 729

Cambray, Hannah, 1013; Mary, 1012; Ric., 1013; Rob., 598, 1012*, 1013*; Thos., 1012*; —, 1015*, 1017*

Cambridge, Ann(e), 661, 1509; Anna(h), 658, 660; Benj., 651, 1508, 1509; Betty, 20; C. O., 1054, 1440; Cath., 660, 1439; Chas., 661; Chas. Owen, 1054, 1439; Dan., 1509; Dorcas, 1509; Eliz., 655; Eusebius, 655; Geo. Owen, 1440; Hen. Pickard, 1440; Hester, 1509; Joan, 661; John, 659, 660*, 661*; Joseph, 1509; Marg., 1509; Martha, 661; Mary, 562, 661, 776, 837, 1507,

1509*; Nat., 648, 651, 655*, 776, 1505, 1509*; Orianah, 1509; R. O., 1054, 1441; Ric., 93, 562, 651, 655, 1006, 1021, 1441, 1505*, 1507, 1508, 1509*; Ric. Owen, 1440*; Rob., 837; Sam., 655*, 658; Sarah, 655, 659, 660; Stephen, 661; Thos., 837, 1539; Toby, 660; Wm., 20; Mr., 1435, 1440*, 1512; —, 1053, 1054, 1440, 1501; fam., 648, 885, 1440

Cambridge [*peerage*], Ric., earl of, 252, 1255

Camcry, And., 84; Eliz., 84*; Thos., 84*

Camden, —, 53, 98, 197, 205, 807, 1219, 1253; *and see* Campden

Came, *see* Camm

Camera, Nic. de, *see* Chamberlain, Nic. le

Camerarius, Wm., 568

Camm (Cam, Cambe, Came), Ann(e), 546, 549*, 899, 1009; Dan.; 703; Deborah, 1524; Dinah, 343; Dorcas, 549; Eleanor, 1549*; Eliz., 163, 343; Francis, 343, 703; Hannah, 17; Hen., 1449, 1453, 1455; Jas., 18, 756, 963*; Joel, 1524; John (de), 343*, 418, 419*, 546, 547, 549*, 899, 1009, 1491; Rev. John, 767; Joseph, 548*; Marg., 418, 756; Mary, 169, 548*, 963*; Rachel, 283*; Rob., 549, 1549; Sarah, 419, 1549; Thos., 17*, 18, 163, 169*, 283*, 419, 532, 995, 1021, 1025, 1549*; Wm., 284, 548*, 549, 584

Campbell, Colin, 1160; Rob., 263, 667, 713, 1378; —, 552, 1378

Campden (Campdene), Joan, 850; John, 85; Rev. John, 184; Thos., 850; *and see* Camden

Campden [*peerage*], Baptist, Viscount Campden, 288, 290, 291; Edw., Viscount Campden, 290, 291; Eliz., Viscountess Campden, 290; Juliana, Viscountess Campden, 288 n*, 290, 291*; Lord, 230 n, 324; Viscount, 1290*

Campe, Rob., 1491; Wm., 1491

Camplin, Ann, 1320–1; Rev. John, 577; Dr. Joseph, 1320, 1321; Rev. Thos., 1321; Rev. Wm., 860; Rev., 859

Camvil (Caumvylle), Ric. de, 1015, 1540

Candelarii, *see* Chandler

Caning, *see* Canning

Cann (Canne), Anne, 1409; Dame Ann(e), 100*; Lady Cath., 1405; Dame Eliz., 43; Rev. Gil., 184; Ric., 435*; Rob., 1405; Sir Rob., 100, 435, 577, 825, 1419*; Sir Rob., bt., 435; Sir T., kt., 1419; Thos., 1405; Sir Thos., 435, 1409; Wm., 1419; Sir Wm., bt., 43*; Sir Wm., bt. & kt., 1554

Canning (Caning, Cannin, Cannings, Canynge), Anne, 1432, 1465*; Eliz., 846; Endymion, 288; Jas., 846; John, 1432; Mat., 1016; Nic., 868; Ric., 1432; Thos., 854, 1362, 1432; Wm., 390, 850, 854, 1432*, 1465*; —, 1392

Cannock, Abigail, 1397; Eliz., 1399; John, 1403; La(u)ncelot, 927, 1399*, 1403; Mary, 1399*; Ric., 1397, 1399*, 1403; Sam., 1399, 1403; Sarah, 1399; Susanna, 1399

Cannon (Canoun), John, 1197; Susanna, 787; Thos., 787

Canshaw, Rob. of, 1339

Canson, Hen., 450

Canteleni, Ralph, 529

Cantelo (Cantelope, Cantelupo), *see* Cauntelo

Canter (Cantor), Anne, 1454; Eliz., 623*, 660*, 1112; Esther, 35, 1454; Hen., 1112; Hester, 836; Jas., 660; John, 1107; Joseph, 386, 623; Martha, 660; Mary, 388*, 1112; Sam., 388; Sarah, 386, 388; Solomon, 388*; Susannah, 660; Thos., 836; Wm., 35, 1454, 1456; —, 1455

Cantilope (Cantilupe, Cantilupo), *see* Cauntelo

Canton, Hugh, 1514*; Jane, 1514*; John, 1211, 1218, 1514; Thos., 1211; Wm., 1514

Cantor, *see* Canter

Cantrell, Anne, 1252; John (Jean), 1252; Wm., 1252

Canute, king, 349, 357, 475, 483, 1474

Canynge, *see* Canning

Capel (Capell, Caple), Anne, 675, 811*, 1210; Arthur, earl of Essex, 609; Arthur, Lord Capel, 123*; Chris. (Xr.), 559 n, 982*, 986*; Dan., 811, 1207, 1216, 1217; Dr. Dan., 1207; Rev. Dan., 279, 539, 886; Dorothy, 562; Edw., 726; Eliza, 983; Eliz. (Klizabeth), 653, 675, 1210, 1561; Frances, 675, 676; Gamaliel, 653; Sir Gamaliel, 653; Jas., 675; John, 811*, 1502; Marg., 982; Mary, 123*, 672, 676, 1210*; Nat., 1531; Rev. Nat., 574; Ric., 981, 982; Rev. Ric., 559, 562, 674, 675*, 676; Sam., 981, 1210*; Sarah, 982*, 1210; Sarah Susanna, 983; Thos., 1210*; W., 1203, 1494; Wm., 969*, 982*, 983, 986; Lady, 327, 1290; Mr., 1215; —, 986, 1494*; fam., 98, 547

Capellanus, Rob., 1423; *and see* Chaplin

Capelond, *see* Copeland

Capenhurst, Rev. Thos., 1102

Caperon, Hen., 1513; —, 1093

Capes, Arthur, 1282; Mary, 1282; Reuben, 1282

Capey (Capy), Alice, 100; John, 100*; Thos., 1069

Caple, *see* Capel

Caplew, John, 814

Capner, Eliz., 202; Giles, 276; Mary, 202; Thos., 202*; *and see* Copner

Capper (Cappar), R., 986; Wal., 1147; Wm., 1147

Capron, Martin, 1390

Capy, *see* Capey

Car, *see* Carr

Carbonel, T., abbot, 1132

Carby, Anne, 1004; Joshua, 1004

Cardiff (Kardiff, Kerdiff, Kerdyf), Edw. de, 1381; Johanna, 1381; Paul de, 1381; Wm. de, 1381*, 1382; fam., 1381*

Cardonnell (Cardnell), Cecil(y) de, baroness Dynevor (Dinevor), 135, 1015; W. de, 1201; Wal., 1201

Care (Kare), Rev. Bevan, 1127; Eliz., 336*, 587; John, 133*, 336; Sarah, 133; *and see* Carr; Kear

Carefield (Caresfield), Anne, 624, 666; Eliz., 624; Jane, 624; John, 624*; Mary, 624*, 666; Rob., 666*, 1438; Wm., 524, 666*

Careless (Careloss, Carles, Carloss), Alice, 1273; Rev. Chas., 128; Edw., 898; John, 898, 1273*, 1288; Jo[a]ne, 1195; Lydia, 1273; Rachel, 1273; Ric., 1288, 1289; Thos., 895, 900; Rev. Thos., 370, 371 n, 374

Carent (Karent), Alex. de, 1039; Edw., 1039; John, 1039; Margery, 1039

Caresfield, *see* Carefield

Carey (Carew, Cary, Carye), Ann(e), 1153, 1562; Benj., 1153*; Caroline, 1073; Cath., 1452; Dorothy, 1004; Eliz., 162, 596, 1153*, 1167; Sir Geo., kt., Lord Hunsdon, 162; Hannah, 1533; Sir Hen., kt., 651, 1403; Jas., 1153; John, 596*, 1004, 1289, 1533; Rev. John, 838, 840, 841; Penelope, 1561*, 1562; Reg. Pole, 1073; Rob., Lord Carye, 1403; S., 1522; Sam(p)son, 1167, 1452, 1525, 1539; Sarah, 1525; Thos., 1153; Rev. Thos., 1561*; Wm., 1153*, 1561, 1562; —, 1005, 1293

Carill, Eliz., 484, 1377; John, 484, 1377

Carington, *see* Carrington

Carisbrook, John, 1258

Carles, *see* Careless

Carleton, Rev. Gerard, 1331

Carloss, *see* Careless

Carmarthen, Lord, 1027

Carn, *see* Carne

Carnall (Carnoll), Alice, 1468; Anne, 334; Dorothy, 1467, 1468*; Eliz., 1467; Hen., 334; Mary, 1467*, 1468*; Rob., 1467, 1468*; Wm., 1467*, 1468*, 1475, 1477

Carne (Carn), Ann, 269; Edw., 360 n; Francis, 269

Carnoll, *see* Carnall

Carpenter (Carpent, Carpynter), Alice, 1428, 1464; Ann(e), 247, 800, 1034, 1250; Dorothy, 706; Edm., 800; Eliz., 247*, 337, 1398, 1467; Frances, 247; Francis, 1481*; Hannah, 282*, 1043; Hen., 1398*; Jas., 28, 337, 1043, 1465*; Joan, 1398*; John, 28, 221, 282*, 1464*, 1476; John, bishop, 360 n, 390, 403, 532, 791 n, 1092; Joseph, 388, 1378; Marg. (la), 28, 982, 1464*, 1519; Martha, 1481; Mary, 282, 388, 706, 733, 1250, 1377; Morris, 247; Rachel, 1398; Ric., 1143, 1377; Rob., 857*, 1250, 1398*; T., 1061; Thos., 337, 388*, 1015, 1478; Rev. Thos., 1047, 1404; Wm., 247*, 413, 706, 733, 1121, 1467*; Dr., bishop, 1407, 1419; —, 1047, 1475, 1501; fam., 1475

Carr (Car, Carre), Geo., 413; John de, 1147; Nic., 1363; Sir Rob., kt., 230 n*; *and see* Care; Kear

Carrington (Carington), Francis, 1542; Rev. Gerard, 147*; Rev. Gervase, 689; Mary, 1542*

Carrow, Ric., 1420

Carruthers (Caruthers), Cath., 1511; Christiana, 1511; Eliz., 1184; Geo., 1181; Hen., 1511; Hester, 971; John, 339, 1184*, 1186; Mary, 1181*, 1511; Thos., 1181; Wm., 971*, 1181, 1511; Wm. Palling, 971; fam., 971

Carswell, Mary, 1082; W. de, 1082

Cart (Carte), Hen., 1348; Thos. (de), 1278, 1552

Cartaret, *see* Carteret

Carte, *see* Cart

Carter (Cartere), Alice, 1057; Ann(e), 69, 254, 335, 1056, 1399, 1400, 1476; Dame Anne, 1057; Bryan, 704; Dan., 597*; Deborah, 26; Edw., 224*, 309*, 944; Eliz., 69*, 79, 597, 932*; Francis, 349 n*, 787; Giles, 65, 69*, 79*, 1226; Goddard, 78; Grace, 257; Henrietta, 1400; Hen.,

1384; Isaac, 212; J., 1062, 1064; Jas., 597*; Jane, 69; Joan (Jone), 70, 884; John, 69*, 79, 257, 309*, 335, 597, 884, 1056, 1057*, 1228, 1289, 1575; Joseph, 542*, 1369; Mary, 69*, 70, 220, 224*, 542, 704, 884, 1384, 1575; Nat. Arthur, 1575; Peter, 1096; R. H., 1440; Ric., 69*, 932, 1399, 1400; Ric. Hodges, 1439; Sarah, 69*, 597*, 932; Simon le, 1259; Thos. (le), 26, 69*, 70*, 254, 1259; Wal. le, 1259; Wm. (le), 69*, 70, 79, 573, 682, 1351; —, 1017, 1064, 1078; fam., 78, 309*

Carteret (Cartaret), Rev. Elias, 445*, 446; Sir Geo., 1049; Lovise (Lovice), 1049, 1052, 1226; Phil., 446

Cartwright (Cartrite, Cartwrite, Chartwrite), Alice, 879; Anne, 117, 1347; Chas., 117, 1348; Isabell, 117, 316; Eliz., 117, 1051, 1348; John, 256; Jas., 115, 116, 117*, 1347, 1348, 1386; Marg., 986; Mary, 316, 1347*; Rev. Nic., 230; Sarah, 116, 117, 1347; T., 1387; Thos., 1347*, 1348; Tim. (Tym), 316*, 879, 1387; Wm., 365 n, 1051, 1347; Rev. Wm., 1392; —, 986, 1348*, 1392, 1447

Caruthers, *see* Carruthers

Carver (Karver, Kerver), Eliz., 1263, 1279; John, 1217, 1279*, 1438; Marg., 1438; Nic., 1335; Patience, 1279; Thos., 1263; Tim., 1438

Carwardine (Kerwardyn), Anne, 1374; Eliz., 1374; John, 1374, 1378; Joseph, 1377, 1378; Mary, 1377*; Sarah, 1374, 1377; Thos., 1377*; Rev. Thos., 1016; —, 1015, 1378; fam., 1378

Cary (Carye), *see* Carey

Casamayor (Casamajor), Anne, 962; Eliz., 962*; Hannah, 962; Harriot, 962; Henrietta, 962; Hen., 962*; Lewis, 962; Lieut. Lewis John, 962; Maria Clemencia, 962; Thos., 962

Casemore (Cassmore), Rev. Ric., 1335; Rev. Wm., 1392

Cassey, Alice, 483; Dorothea, 1501; Eliz., 484, 1501*; Hen., 1201*, 1238, 1501*; John, 482, 1092; 1201*, 1237, 1501; Sir John, kt., 482, 483*; Leonard, 1201*, 1237; Lionel, 1501*; Rob., 1201*, 1237-8, 1501; Thos., 1238, 1501; W., 1201; Wm., 484, 1201*, 1237, 1501; fam., 1501

Cassmore, *see* Casemore

Casson, Rev. Abraham, 919; Anne, 919

Castello, Adrian de, bishop, 1056

Castle, Ann(e), 450, 598; Eleanor, 975; Hannah, 450; Isaac, 468; Jane, 468; Lettice, 794; Mary, 450; Ric., 794; Rev. Ric., 793, 794; Sam., 598; Thos., 450, 975; Wal., 975, 976; —, wife of Wal., 976

Castledine, Eliz., 442; Wm., 442

Castlehaven, Ann, countess of, 1221

Castleman, Chas., 422; Edw., 749; Eliz., 749*; Jane, 422*; Jonathan, 420, 421, 422*, 969*, 1494; Mary, 422*, 749*; Paul, 420, 422*, 747, 748*, 749; Susan, 1494; Susanna, 422; Thos., 749; Mrs., 748*; fam., 422

Castleton, N., 1339; Nat., 19

Caswell, Edith, 84; Rev. Sam., 81*, 84

Catchmay (Catchmayd, Catchmaye), Barbara, 246*, 735; Eleanor, 732; Dame Eleanor (Elinor), 246, 733; Eliz., 246; Jane, 246; Lodovic, 1323; Mariana, 245, 246; Ric., 248; Trac(e)y, 246*, 247, 732; Wm., 246*, 735*; (later Gwinnett), see Gwinnett; Sir Wm., kt., 245, 246, 732; —, 136; fam., 245

Cater, Abraham, 1159; Anne, 1551; Beckford, 1543; Eliz., 1159; Frances, 1551; John Wyatt, 1159; Mary, 1551; —, 1160

Catesby, Eliz., 992

Catherall, see Catterall

Catherine, princess of Holstein Beck, 1067

Catling (Catlyn), Eliz., 217; John, 217; (or Gaselyn), Wal., 1490

Catterall (Catherall, Catteroll), Rev. Edm., 1016, 1482; Rev. Wm., 1392

Caudle (Cordell), Mary, 450, 505; Rev. Sam., 452; Thos., 505, 891; Wm., 450

Caudwell, see Caldwell

Cauel, Geof., 1388; Wm., 1388

Cauntelo (Cantelo, Cantelope, Cantelupo, Cantilope, Cantilupe, Cantilupo, Cautelo), Eliz. de, 527; M., 1147; Maud de, 527, 1147; Rob. de, 527*; Rog. de, 619, 1385; Wal. de, 1388; Wal. de, bishop, 218, 221, 581, 711, 717; — de, 497, 1147, 1385; fam., 1043

Caumvylle, see Camvil

Causon, Edw., 1282; Juliana, 1282; Wm., 1282

Cautelo, see Cauntelo

Cave, Ann Collins, 941; Rev. Astley, 1209; Eliz. Martha, 1209; John, 941; Mary, 941*; Mary-Ann, 941; Phil., 1140; Sarah, 941; Thos., 941*, 1259, 1369; —, 1440*; fam., 745

Cavendish (Chavenedissh), Adam, 1259; Eliz., 1339; Eliz. Dorothy, 1170; Wm., marquis of Newcastle, 1339*; Wm., duke of Devonshire, 823; Sir Wm., 1339

Cawdron, Ann, 814

Cecil (Ceysyll, Sisil), Anne, 820; Jhoane, 1271; John, 1271, 1337; Rob., earl of Salisbury, 392, 609, 710; Sam., 296; Wm., 820; Wm., earl of Salisbury, 820; fam., 1337

Celar (Celer), Hen. atte, 1478; John, 1420

Celestine, pope, 323

Cemery, Ann, 555; Edw., 555; Patience, 555

Cerne (Cernie), C. de, 1490; Phil. de, 1490, 1491

Cestria, Wm. de, 1431; and see Chester

Ceysyll, see Cecil

Chadbourn (Chadbourne), Ann, 637; Eliz., 587; Jane, 637; John, 637; Thos., 587*

Chaddeswelle, see Chadwell

Chaddresleye, Hen. de, 1502

Chaddwell (Chadewele), see Chadwell

Chadner (Chadnor, Chodnor), Eliz., 1354; John, 1352*, 1353, 1354, 1355; Marg., 1353; Sarah, 1354

Chadock, see Chidiocke

Chadwell (Chaddeswelle, Chaddewell, Chaddwell, Chadewele), Ann(e), 140, 1015; Jane, 797; John, 1016; Simon, 1015; Stephen, 797; Thos., 140; Wm. (de), 255, 1016, 1017, 1259; —, 1216; 1226*; fam., 255*, 1015

Chadwick, Rev. Jas., 1140

Chadworth, see Chedworth [peerage]

Chaeles, see Charles

Chaldewelle, see Caldwell

Chalfandhey, John, 1313

Chaloner, Mary, 865; Sir Thos., 865

Chamar, John, 1313

Chamberlain (Chamberlaine, Chamberlayn, Chamberlayne, Chamberleyn, Chamberlin, Chaumbleyn), Agnes, 1431*, 1432*; Ann(e), 250, 952; Bickerton, 1193; Cassandra Agnes, 1193; Cath., 1032; Cecil, 1194; E., 1196, 1226; E. J., 1194, 1226; Edm., 985, 986, 1190, 1191*, 1193, 1195*, 1196, 1197, 1226; Col. Edm., 1191*; Edm. John, 346, 347, 445, 870, 1194, 1195*; Edw., 952; Edw. Pye, 546, 548*, 898, 1558; Edwin, 1193; Eliz., 548, 898, 952, 960, 1226*, 1314; Emma, 1190, 1191*; Frances, 952; Geo., 952, 1193*; Henrietta Cath., 1193; (formerly Ingles), Hen. Ingles, 1189, 1195; Humf. (Hunfrid)(the), 990, 1082, 1455; Sir J., 1493; Jas. Montague, 1191; Jane, 1249*; John, 952, 953, 1189, 1190*, 1191*, 1193*, 1195*, 1196, 1197, 1224, 1233, 1249*, 1355, 1361; Rev. John, 1191*, 1194, 1195; Sir John, 1493; Joseph, 960, 1132; (formerly Ackerley), Joseph Chamberlayne, 1193, 1195; Kath., 953, 1432; L. F. E., 1194; Leonard, 952, 1015, 1228; Marg., 666, 952*, 1432; Martha, 1193; Mary, 258, 548, 952, 1191*, 1262, 1558*; (or de Camera) Nic. le, 1431*, 1432; Sir R., 1216; Rebecca, 1249; Ric., 1478*; Sam., 538; Sarah, 1190, 1191; Sibilla, 1432; Sir T., 985, 1493; T. A., 1193; Thos., 952*, 953*, 1032, 1189, 1224, 1262, 1558*; Dr. Thos., 255, 258*; Rev. Thos., 1016; Sir Thos., kt., 434, 438, 952, 1369; (or Tankerville), Sir Thos., kt., 346; Thos. Gunter, 1558; W., 1032; Rev. W., 681; Wm., 250, 666; Admiral, 1193; Dr., 1227; —, 1195, 1226*, 1516; fam., 349, 547, 885; and see Chaumbrer

Chambers (Chambre), Agnes atte, 1432; Alex., 938; Alice, 750; Ann, 938; Elias, 846; Eliz., 656; Francis, 659, 938, 1216; Geo., 659; Giles, 750, 1258; Hester, 659*, 728, 752; Jas., 656, 659; John (atte), 839, 846; John, bishop, 609 n; Joseph, 749, 1289; Josiah, 1289; Kath., 749; Mary, 370, 846; Ric., 846, 919; Rob., 919, 996; Sarah, 659; Thos., 659, 846; W. Clutterbuck, 1216; Wal., 550*, 748; Wm., 728, 996, 1092; Mr., 369; —, 1292; and see Chaumbrer

Chamflour, R. de, 1078; Rog. de, 1078

Champagne, earl of, see Odo

Champaye, Ric., 1312

Champeneys, see Champneys

Champion, Geo., 1160; Rachel, 284; Wm., 284, 460

Champneys (Champeneys, Champneis, Champnies, Chaumpeneys), Edm., 576, 826; Edw., 46; Eliz., 45*, 47; Hen., 1311; John (de), 45*, 46, 47, 576, 741, 1296*, 1311*, 1313; Mary, 46, 1296; Ric., 1307; Rob., 47; Ruth, 1307; Sarah, 1307; Sir T. S., 1311

Chance, Anne, 1367; Anne Posthuma, 1023; Ant., 381*; Damaris, 1023; Dan., 1023*, 1186, 1367; Eliz., 1023*; Hannah, 254, 1023; Kath., 381; Nat., 1023, 1367; Sarah, 1023; Thos., 1023; Lieut. Thos., 1023; Wm., 254, 1023

Chandler (Candelarii, Chaundler, Chaunler, Chauntler, Chawnler), Ann(e), 387*, 509, 641, 1270, 1361; Barbara, 1125; Benj., 1217, 1270; Betty, 1008, 1125; Cesar, 509*; Chas. Edw., 1281*, 1288; Christian, 1064; Edw., 1008*; Eleanor, 1056, 1064; Eliz., 238*, 423, 1043, 1075, 1125, 1270; Hannah, 1376; Hester, 1008*; J., 1064; Jas., 1125, 1126; Jane, 1075*, 1125; Joan, 1125; Job, 1008, 1217; John, 238, 296, 368, 1043, 1075, 1125*, 1288; Rev. John, 432, 445, 568, 792, 1125*, 1140; Joseph, 641*, 1007, 1008, 1217; Kenelm(e), 1270*, 1281, 1288; Letty, 641; Mary, 641*, 1007, 1125*, 1127*, 1136, 1281, 1282; Nat., 1008, 1288, 1289; Phil., 369; R., 1061; Rebecca, 1271; Ric., 238, 1378; Rob., 641*; Sam., 1008, 1270; Sarah, 677, 1008*; T., 985, 1062, 1063, 1064; Thos., 423, 677, 1006, 1007, 1009, 1062, 1063*, 1075*, 1136, 1376; W., 1064; Wiering, 1008; Wilkins, 1007*; Wm., 387*, 641, 1008, 1056, 1063, 1064*, 1361, 1362; —, 1062*, 1063*, 1064*, 1455; fam., 890

Chandos (Chandois, Chaundos), Edm., Lord Chandos, 232, 684, 859, 860, 1221; Frances, baroness Chandos, 447; Frances, Lady Chandos, 1221; Geo., 358; Geo., Lord Chandos, 852 n, 1476; Lord George, 1220; Giles, Lord Chandos, 233, 252, 421, 449, 859, 860, 1220, 1221*; Grey, Lord Chandos, 1051; Jas., Lord Chandos, baron Sudeley, 23, 24, 1190; Jane, Lady Chandos, 1219; John, Lord Chandos, 92, 94, 252, 1221, 1333; Sir Lawr. de, 259; R. de, 1078; Rob. de, 819; Rog. de, 1078, 1380; Wm., 860; Wm., Lord Chandos, 1220; fam., 259, 546

Chandos [peerage](Chandois), Hen., duke of, 25; Mary, duchess of, 25; duke of, 1083, 1220*; Lady, 1220; Lord (baron), 393, 420, 704, 1219*, 1220, 1221, 1380, 1476*, 1487; and see Bridges, passim; Chandos, passim; Grenville; Grey, Eliz.

Chann, Hen., 1491

Channan, John, 472

Chansy, Sir John, 778 n

Chantrel, H., 1061; Rev. John, 783

Chapeau, Ann, 1077, 1078; David, 1077; Rev. John, 1075, 1076; Wm. Posthumus, 1078

Chaplin, John, 413; and see Capellanus

Chapman (Chepman), Alice, 662, 1201; Ann(e), 1275, 1276*; Rev. Chas., 103, 104*; Charlotte, 662; Dorothea, 1199; Dorothy, 1251; Eliz., 262*, 662, 1510, 1581; Francis, 1217; Geo., 1274, 1275; Giles, 348; Guy, 1266; Hawkins, 1201, 1256; Hen., 1251, 1256; Jas., 1510, 1513; Jane, 460, 1115, 1275, 1510; Jasper, 1199*, 1201*, 1256; Johanna, 1201*, 1256*; John, 662*, 1217, 1581; Rev. Joseph (Jos.), 145, 459*, 460, 524; Julian, 1387; Marmaduke, 1115; Rev. Marmaduke, 495, 1122; Mary, 632, 1581*, 1582;

Peter le, 1539; Rob., 1581, 1582; Sam., 1276; Sarah, 435, 662, 1266*; Susanna, 104; T., 1061; Thos., 662; Toby, 1201, 1256*; Wm., 262*, 632, 1266*, 1276, 1288, 1422; —, 1139, 1422, 1512; fam., 268 n, 523; and see Chipman

Chapone, Rev. John, 114, 1149, 1151; Sarah, 1149, 1151

Chapp, Ann(e), 1115, 1116, 1118, 1119; Edm., 488, 1115*, 1116, 1118*, 1119*, 1121; Hannah, 1115*, 1118; Jane, 1106, 1115; Jeremiah, 1115*, 1118*; John, 1115, 1118; Mary, 488, 1119; Sam., 1115

Chappel (Chappell), Ann, 1200; He. . ., 954; Hester, 954; Jas., 703; John, 506, 703, 954; Joseph, 496, 954*; Mary, 496, 954*; Nat., 954; Nic., 954; Sam., 703; Sarah, 703*; Willmot, 954; —, 1475

Chard, Hester, 780; John, 780; Mary, 780; Thos., 780*

Chardborough, John, 805; Julian, 805

Charles I, 81, 85, 164, 198, 220 n, 232, 244, 249, 286, 287 n, 291, 313 n, 317, 324*, 325, 359 n, 415, 420 n, 436 n, 440, 475, 488, 744, 748, 764, 802, 852 & n, 865, 870, 915, 959, 1021, 1197, 1293, 1340, 1356, 1369, 1441

Charles II, 2, 6, 56, 76, 78, 86, 135, 139, 180, 198, 218, 220 n, 244*, 249, 259, 288 n, 297, 313 n, 380, 420 n, 432, 440, 447, 452, 459, 476, 488, 511, 689, 704, 723, 724, 767, 783, 802, 808, 829, 853, 878, 890, 913, 1180, 1186, 1293, 1356*, 1369, 1385, 1502

Charles, prince of Wales, 324, 1120, 1206

Charles (Chaeles), Abigail, 108, 761; Ann, 226; Anna, 1401; Betty, 1153; Eliz., 108*, 1401; Frances, 1193*; Hannah, 109, 891; J., 1101; Jas., 761; Jo[a]ne, 821; John, 108*, 109, 226, 474; Joseph, 1192; Mary, 636, 762, 1193; Peter, 761*; Phil., 1401; Ric., 1149, 1153*, 1154, 1193, 1196; Ric. Smith, 636; Rob., 944, 946; Sam., 226*, 891; Thos., 636; Wm., 821*, 1192, 1401; fam., 890

Charlet (Charlett), Arthur, 798; Joane, 834; John, 192, 884; Mary, 192; Rob., 1404

Charlton (Charleton, Cherleton), Abigail, 264; Geo., 728; Mary, 891, 1467; Meshach, 264; Rice, 961; Ric. de, 360; Rev. Rob. John, 960; Susanna, 1467*; Wal., 1467; Webert de, 1255; fam., 1255

Charlwood, Ann, 1282; Benj., 637; Edw., 1282; Isaac, 1282; Mary, 226, 637

Charteris, Francis, Lord Elcho, 1153; Susan, 1153; and see Chatteris

Chartwrite, see Cartwright

Chatham, earl of, see Pitt, Wm.

Chatteris, John, 187; and see Charteris

Chaumbleyn, see Chamberlain

Chaumbrer, Ric. le, 1355; and see Chamberlain; Chambers

Chaumpeneys, see Champneys

Chaundler, see Chandler

Chaundos, see Chandos

Chaunler (Chauntler), see Chandler

Chavenedissh, see Cavendish

Chawnler, *see* Chandler

Chaworth (Cadurcis), Isabel de, 769; Pat. de, 769, 770; Payan de, 770; Sybella, 690; fam. (barons), 690, 769*

Chaxhill (Chaxhulle, Chekeshill), Rob. de, 1404; fam., 1402

Chaynel, Thos., 1428

Chease, *see* Chese

Chedder (Cheddre), Eliz., 527, 529; Ric., 527, 529; —, 1147*

Chedley, Rev. Wm., 1165

Chedworth, Thos., 895; fam., 688

Chedworth [*peerage*](Chadworth), Dorothy, baroness, 421; Eliz., Viscountess, 291; Hen. Fred., Lord, 421, 644; John, Lord, 319, 420, 421*, 434, 644, 689, 1542; John, Viscount, 291; Lord, 643, 1198*, 1495, 1501; Viscount, 272; *and see* Howe, John

Cheeke, Rev. Rob., 783

Cheeker, Eleanor, 460

Cheere, Sir H., 497 n

Cheigne, *see* Cheyne

Chekeshill, *see* Chaxhill

Chelardiston, Joan, 876; Wm. de, 876

Chell, Mary, 1433*; Ric., 1433*

Chelenhed, Adam le, 1238

Cheltenham (Cheltham), Eliz., 1169; John, 1477; Ric., abbot, 1261; Stephen de, 1032; Wal. of, 1052, 1078; Wm. de, 101, 533; —, abbot, 1291

Chepman, *see* Chapman

Chepstouwe, Maur. de, 1539

Cherche, *see* Church

Cherington (Cherrington), Ann, 387; Chas., 171; Dorcas, 800; Eleanor, 299; Eliz., 800, 1232; Geo., 299, 300; Hester, 399; Jane, 800; John, 338; Mary, 338, 984; Rev. Ric., 302; Sam., 171*, 399, 800*; Sarah, 171*, 299, 387; Thos., 171, 387, 984, 1232*; Wm., 299*, 387*, 800; *and see* Sherrington

Cherleton, *see* Charlton

Cherley, Wm., 388

Cherrington, *see* Cherington

Cherry, W., 1033

Chese (Chease), Adam, 1313; John, 413, 1313; Margery, 1259

Cheshere, Hen., 1150; John, 1150

Cheslin, Job, 1232

Chesnecot, *see* Sezencot

Chester, Anne, 333; Ant., 339; Arthur, 43; Bridget, 43; Bromley, 1160; Mrs. Bromley, 1159; Chas., 43; Dan., 332, 339*; Dominick, 43; Eliz., 43, 661, 1274, 1498; Eliz.-Lucy (Bromley), 42, 43; Geo., 43; Hannah, 616, 1150, 1151; Harry, 616; Dame Heneretta, *see* Chester, Sarah Henrietta; J., 1456; Rev. John, 259, 744*, 802, 1456; Rev. Joseph, 582, 829, 886; Lucy, 43; Mary, 43*, 332; Nat., 337*; Ric., 43, 1150, 1151, 1274; Ric. How, 43*; Rob., 1195; Sarah, 333, 337*, 339; Sarah Henrietta (Dame Heneretta), 43*; T., 1159; Thos., 41, 42, 43*, 616*, 1428, 1498, 1553, 1577; W., 1159; Wm., 43*, 1195; Wm. Bromley, 43; Mr., 1159; Mrs., 113; —, 1159, 1186, 1196; fam., 40, 1195; *and see* Cestria

Chester [*peerage*], Ric., earl of, 1091; *and see* Lupus, Hugh

Chesterton, W. de, 1381; Wm. de, 1381

Cheston, Dan., 409; Mr., 1

Chestroe, Ant., 338*; Eliz., 338; John, 338; Marg., 338; Susanna, 338; Wm., 338

Chetel, Cath., 1267; Isabella, 1267; Wm., 1267

Chetwode, Rev. Knightley, 1016

Chetwynd, Rev. Edw., 161; Rev. John, 722; Mary, 395

Chew (Chewe, Choo), Betty, 1026; Edith, 204; Eliz., 981; Rev. Jas., 440; Mary, 981; Mic., 981*; Nat., 1217; R., 1328; Ric., 204, 1026*; Thos., 1026; Wm., 708 n

Chewett, John, 813*, 815; Mary, 813; Wm., 815

Cheyne (Cheigne, Cheyney), John, 544 n; Ric., 302

Cheynynge, Rev. John, 266

Chicheley, Hen., archbishop, 1021

Chichester, Giles, 755; Mary, 755

Chidiocke (Chadock, Chidioc), Cath., 618; Sir John, 618; fam., 403

Chilcoke, Ant., 360 n

Child (Childe, Childes), Agnes, 1197; Ann, 320, 662, 1064; Anne Mary, 223; Dan., 731; Eliz., 223, 662, 716, 1566; Geo., 906; Rev. Hen., 66; Hester, 906; Joan, 731; John, 662, 1064, 1307*, 1574; Mary, 662, 731, 1307; Merrial, 257; Ric., 662, 716, 1574; Rob., 1065; Sam., 731*; Sarah, 662; Thos., 223, 662; Rev. Thos., 503; Wm., 223*, 257, 320, 731, 1160, 1422, 1566; fam., 218

Chilton, Deborah, 419; John de, 1456; Ric., 419

Chin, *see* Chinn

Chineshale, John de, 1218

Chinn (Chin), Alice, 932; Anne, 930, 1274; Edw., 894, 898; Eliz., 898, 1274; Geo., 1274; Gough, 106; Hannah, 932, 1137; Isabella, 932; John, 1137*; Jonathan, 932*; Marg., 106; Mary, 69, 105, 106, 932*, 933; Nat., 1274; Ric., 69, 930*, 933*; Sarah, 896, 932; Thos., 896, 930, 932*, 1274*; Mr., 927; —, 214, 932, 1402*

Chinnery, Sir John, 413

Chipman, Thos., 1137; *and see* Chapman; Shipman

Chirche, *see* Church

Chissold, Cath., 981; Dan., 981*

Chitts, Ann, 963; Betty, 963; Hannah, 963*; Marg., 963; Martha, 963; Wm., 963*; Wm. Thos., 963

Chitty, Wm., 1289

Chivers, Secole, 1359

Chock, Joseph, 727

Chodnor, *see* Chadner

Cholmeley (Cholmley), Ann, 560; Eliz., 521; Sir Hugh, bt., 560, 561; Jas., 521; Rev. John, 1490; Mary, 561, 1490; Nat., 561; fam., 1522

Choo, *see* Chew

Christmas, Rev. Jas., 228

Christopher, Ann, 213; —, 1020

Church (Cherche, Chirche), Ann(e), 182, 1508; Edw., 369; Eliz., 132, 1047; Hen. atte, 1047; Rev. Hen., 785; Hester, 132; Jas., 872*, 873*, 1162; Jane, 1315; John (atte), 77, 182, 872, 873*, 906, 1140, 1508, 1540; Mary, 77, 872, 1415; Meriam (Miriam), 872, 873; Molly, 729; Rebecca, 132;

Ric., 729; Sam., 338*; Sarah, 1047; Theophila,
428; Thos. (atte), 262, 428*, 485, 873, 1044,
1047; Wm., 132, 1047*, 1315*, 1583
Churchay (Churcheye), R., 1485; Ric., 1162
Churches, Anne, 1509; Christian, 660; Eliz., 1509;
Jas., 660; Jane, 1509*; Jonathan, 1509; Joseph,
633, 1509*, 1513; Martha, 633, 1509; Mary, 651,
1509; Sam., 1509; Sarah, 660, 1024, 1509; Thos.,
1024, 1509*
Churcheye, see Churchay
Churchill, Eliz., 835*; John, 50, 835; John, duke of
Marlborough, 1428; Sam., 835; Wm., 835*
Churchlep, Rev. John, 1031
Churchman, Anne, 100; Eliz., 1319; Hen., 100*;
Capt. Hen., 99; Rev. John, 279; Mary, 99; Rob.,
99*; Thos., 1323; Wal., 1319*; Mr., 99
Churn, Alice, 227; Ric., 227; Wm., 227
Chute, Anne Rachel, 1493; Thos. Lobb, 1493
Cioches, Sigar de, 688, 704
Cissor (Cissore), Rog., 1140; Thos., 1314
Clapp, Rob., 413
Clapon (Clappen), Hannah, 706; John, 706*; Mary,
706*; Ric., 706; Thos., 320
Clapton, Mary, 800; Ric., 800; and see Clopton
Clarck, see Clarke
Clare (Clara, Cleare), Amice de, 1011; Anne (de),
1287, 1357; Benj., 494; Eleanor (Elianor)(de),
591, 1082, 1120, 1287; Francis, 1357; Gil. de,
1293, 1540; Gil. de. earl of Gloucester, 297*,
391, 400, 444, 591, 889, 1011, 1195, 1261*,
1287*, 1474; Is(abella) de, 1313, 1540; Jas., 696,
699, 1328; Joan de, countess of Gloucester,
1287; John, 494; Julyana, 494; Marg. (de), 978,
1011*; Mary Webbe, 910; Maud de, 1261; R. de,
earl of Gloucester, 1093; Ric. de, 1287, 1292;
Ric. de. earl of Gloucester, 591, 823, 1255, 1261,
1287; Ric. de, earl of Hertford, 1011; [Ric. de,
earl of Pembroke], see Strongbow; Rob. de,
1293; Sybill, 1357*; Thos. (de), 244, 978; Rev.
Thos., 783; Wm. de, 1293; —, 1078, 1288, 1312;
—, earl of Gloucester and Hereford, 990, 1082,
1312, 1322, 1474; fam., earls of Gloucester, 297,
403, 426, 440, 487, 556, 568, 588, 663, 763, 859,
1011, 1120, 1228, 1287*, 1309, 1312, 1322
Clare [peerage], baron, 287; and see Nugent
Clarence, Geo., duke of, 805, 1261, 1287, 1291;
Isabel(la), duchess of, 763, 805, 1261, 1287,
1291; Lionel, duke of, 251, 252, 459; duke of
791 n, 1380
Clarendon, Lord, 358
Claridge (Clarige), Jane, 1330; John, 1330*;
Joseph, 1473, 1477; Mary, 1330, 1473
Clarke (Clarck, Clark, Clerk, Clerke), Abraham,
606*, 607; Adam, 569*; Alice, 800, 1244; Amy,
338; Ann(e), 49, 175, 241, 535, 569, 762, 931,
978, 1058, 1086, 1187, 1244, 1268, 1306; Anne,
Lady Clarke, 1281; Anne Frances, 1184; Ant.,
338; Arthur, 964*; B., 1312; Betty, 1073; C.,
1312; Charity, 442; Chas., 70, 858; Chris., 241,
1072, 1241, 1244*, 1303; Dan., 563; Deborah,
320; Dobbs, 974; Edw., 703*, 906*, 983; (or
Hobbs), Edw., 1326; Sir Edw., 1394; Eleanor,

1241, 1244; Eliz., 177, 227, 320, 337, 338*, 542,
563, 607, 640, 761, 818, 904, 906, 974, 983,
1072, 1110, 1235, 1535; Emma, 752*; Esther,
543, 1241, 1257, 1431; Frances, 569*; Francis,
499; Rev. Geo., 860; Giles, 49, 474, 1158, 1200*;
H. D., 1512; Hannah, 70, 175, 234, 535*, 633,
757*; Harry, 1535; Hen. (le), 296, 442, 830, 930,
931*, 1238; Hester, 832; Isabell, 1401; J., 1362;
J. M., 77; Jacob, 542, 543; Jas., 241, 607, 687,
1073, 1112, 1121, 1401, 1431, 1518; Jane, 165,
479, 607, 703, 761*, 800, 858, 930, 931, 974,
1235*, 1394, 1431; Jasper, 569; Joan(e), 640*,
757, 818, 832, 931; Joanna, 607; John, 51, 213,
241, 337 338*, 442, 569, 640*, 641, 757*, 777,
800, 818, 832*, 858, 906, 964, 978, 1039, 1046,
1058, 1086, 1160, 1184, 1194, 1238, 1372, 1431,
1475, 1499, 1531; (or FitzRalph), John, 985,
1060; Dr. John, 1344; Rev. John, 221, 1019,
1122, 1362, 1494; Rev. Jonathan, 744*; Jos.,
1356; Joseph, 1086, 1234, 1235*, 1431*; Josiah,
535; Josias, 531; Judith, 1194; Lifoly [sic], 174;
Marg., 77, 703, 858, 1108, 1109; Martha, 758,
1019*; Mary, 165, 175, 234*, 241, 338, 474, 479,
524, 542, 563, 569, 687, 830, 858, 903, 906, 931,
963, 964, 984, 1073, 1111, 1200, 1244, 1431,
1531; Nash Eliz., 842, 844; Rev. Nic., 1177;
Rebecca, 718 n; Ric. (le), 177, 227, 338, 563*,
640, 752*, 757, 761*, 762, 818, 974, 1217, 1221,
1244; Rev. Ric., 848; Rob., 175*, 402, 535, 543,
1108*, 1109, 1121, 1241*, 1244*, 1258; Sam.,
531*, 535*, 609, 906; Rev. Sam., 770, 1147;
Sarah, 175*, 442, 499, 633, 703, 731, 832, 1112,
1158, 1241, 1244, 1533; (or Hobbs), Sarah, 1326;
Sibilla, 569; Simon le, 1313; Sir Simon, 1281;
Stephen, 818, 1110, 1424; Susanna, 1431*;
Sylvester, 757; T., 1312; Thos. (le), 165*, 174,
175*, 234*, 338*, 524, 718 n, 752*, 842, 844,
904, 963, 978, 984, 1121*, 1232, 1235, 1434,
1539*; Thos. Knowles, 1238; W., 1159, 1356;
Wm., 77*, 165, 175, 213*, 320, 535, 543, 569*,
633, 703, 758*, 832, 858, 930, 931*, 948, 986,
1111, 1180, 1268*, 1289, 1306*, 1345*, 1355,
1371*, 1424, 1513, 1514, 1533, 1535, 1551; Dr.
Wm., 366; Madam, 1035; Mr., 607, 1039, 1255,
1355; —, 1093, 1402, 1428; (or Hobbs), —,
1328*; fam., 440, 606, 738, 1232
Clarkson (fil. Cl[er]ici), Eliz., 931; Sarah, 486;
Thos., 1140; Wm., 486, 931
Clarvoe, Mary, 442
Claville, John de, 1139*
Clay (Cley), John, 1165; —, 1323
Claydon, Joseph, 883; Mary, 883; and see Clayton
Clayfield, Eliz., 750*; Francis, 750*; Hen., 1008,
1217; Jane, 661; Joseph, 203; Patience, 661;
Rebecca, 203; Ric., 750; Rev. Rob., 829; Sarah,
1008; Thos., 661, 750; Wm., 661
Clayton, Alice, 51; Ann, 522; Christian, 1518;
Edw., 522; Eliz., 522; Hazlewood, 868; Hen.,
522, 1518*; Marg., 1513; Mary, 1334; Ric.,
1513; Susan, 51*; Thos., 1334; Dr. Thos., 51*;
—, 1029; and see Claydon
Cleare, see Clare

Cleaveley (Cleavly), *see* Clevely
Cleeveland, *see* Cleveland [*peerage*]
Clegram, W., 1053
Clemencia (fl. 1329), 1214
Clemens, *see* Clements
Clement VI, pope, 1132
Clements (Clemens, Clement), Anne, 976; Arthur,
    49; Beata, 971; Edm., 338, 976; Edw., 1584;
    Eliz., 95, 881; Rev. Gerard, 704; H., 1477; Hen.,
    881; Hester, 338; Joan, 49; John, 613; Mary,
    1079; Sarah, 881; T., 993; Thos., 881; Rev.
    Thos., 114, 1079; Tobias, 993; Wm., 49; —, 1554
Clent, Anna, 803; Anne, 871; Edw., 1424; Eliz.,
    1424*; John, 871*; Littleton, 1424; Mat., 803;
    Thos., 669; Wm., 669, 871
Cleregise, Wal., 1074
Clerk (Clerke), *see* Clarke
Clermont, Mary, 1250
Cletherow, Wm., 384
Cleve, Bart., 803; Chapman le, 1519
Cleveland, Ann, 378; John, 378*; Marg., 378; Nat.,
    378; Susanna, 378
Cleveland [*peerage*](Cleeveland), earl of, 1048
Clevely (Cleaveley, Cleavly), Eliz., 1276; Jas.,
    1276; Jonathan, 976; Mary, 338; Sarah, 338*;
    Thos., 351; Wal., 338*
Cley, *see* Clay
Cleymond, Rev. John, 394
Cliffe (Cliff), Anne, 231; Wm., 1289; —, 1455; *and
    see* Clift
Clifford (Clyfford), Alice, 618; Anne, 621, 1141;
    Anne, countess of Dorset, 720 n, 721 n; Ant.,
    620*; Cath., 617, 618; Charlotte Anne, 1168;
    Christian, 619; Dorothy, 626, 1232; Edm., 617,
    619; Eliz., 106, 620, 1141, 1194; Frances, 1193*;
    1215; Geo., 338, 1232; Geo., earl of
    Cumberland, 720 n, 721n; H., 1233; Hen. (de),
    534, 618*, 619, 621, 625, 1218, 1232, 1440;
    Hester, 338; Sir Hugh, 618; Isabel, 618, 720 n; J.,
    1227; Rev. J., 1215; Jas., 534*, 618 n*, 619,
    625*, 626, 670, 1232*, 1440; Rev. Jas., 259;
    Joan, 620; John (de), 106, 338, 558, 561, 618*,
    619, 620*, 621, 1141, 1194*, 1196, 1307*;
    Letitia, 618; Mabel, 621; Marg., 618; Mary, 558,
    561, 618, 625, 1141*, 1193, 1232, 1307*; Nat.,
    1168; R., 1198; Ric. (de), 618*, 620, 1193, 1196;
    Ric., bishop, 1016; Rob., 618; Rog. de, 529,
    1091; Rog., baron Clifford, 244; Rog. de, Lord
    Clifford, 720 n; Rosamond (Fair Rosamond),
    618*, 625, 690; Rosamund, 621*, 1141; Sarah,
    1307*; Thos., 1551; W., 1198; Wal. de, 565,
    618*, 1091; Wal., Lord Clifford, 625; (or
    FitzPons), Wal., 618; Wm., 617, 1196, 1233;
    Capt., 1189; —, 1027, 1054, 1195, 1221, 1440*;
    fam., 544, 565, 617*
Clifford [*peerage*], Lord (baron), 265 n, 278, 618 &
    n, 721*, 722, 745, 1420*; *and see* Clifford, Rog.
    (de) *and* Wal.; Southwell, Edw.
Cliffton, *see* Clifton
Clifielde, Hen., 1218
Clift, Ann, 659*; John, 658, 659*; Mary, 658, 659,
    661; Sam., 661; Wm., 661; *and see* Cliffe

Clifton (Cliffton), Edw., 1288; Hen., 73, 1267; Rev.
    Jas., 1233; John, 1267*, 1288; Mary, 1267*;
    Wm., 1267, 1288, 1289
Clinch, Chas., 597*; Hannah, 597; Sarah, 597;
    Solomon, 597; Susannah, 597; Wm., 597
Cling, Adam, 1238
Clinton (Clynton), Jordan de, 1082; R., 1092; Rev.
    Sam., 1233; Wm., 1078; Rev. Wm., 764; Wm.
    de, earl of Huntingdon, 664, 890, 1032; Lord,
    1001, 1328*; —, 1328; fam., 255, 1032
Clinton and Say, Lord, 1078
Clinton de Say, fam., 638
Clissold (Clisseld), Ann(e), 202, 981, 1144, 1245*;
    Eliz., 203, 204, 1206*; Grizel, 203; Hannah,
    1007; Jane, 203, 1008; John, 204, 1180, 1185;
    Kath., 1210*; M., 1052; Mary, 1180, 1185, 1214,
    1245; Nat., 203, 1021; Peter, 202, 203*; Ric.,
    969; Sam., 1007, 1214; Susanna, 202, 203;
    Thos., 203*, 204, 1206*, 1210*, 1211, 1218;
    Rev. Thos., 430, 910, 1539; Wm., 981*, 1008,
    1144, 1206; —, 1215
Clive (Cliue, Clyve), Adam atte, 1351; John (de),
    1288, 1292; Ric., 360, 445; Thos. atte, 1351
Cliveden, Cath., 305; Sir John, 305
Clooterbook, *see* Clutterbuck
Cloper, Wm., 1460
Clopton, Agnes, 572; Joan, 1002; Sir John, 572;
    and see Clapton
Close (Closs, Clowes), Isaac, 1172; Jas., 832; John,
    249, 250, 1054; Josiah, 793 n; Josias, 660; Mary,
    1054; Ric., 832, 1054; Sarah, 250; Solomon,
    1217; Susan, 660; Thos., 250; Wm., 264, 958
Cloterbooke, *see* Clutterbuck
Clother, Ann, 1046; Eliz., 1046; Jas., 946; Sarah,
    1046*; Thos., 1046*; Wm., 1046
Clotterbooke, *see* Clutterbuck
Cloudsley, Mary, 661; Wm., 97, 661
Clowes, *see* Close
Clunn (Clunne), Rev. Hugh, 498, 1177
Clutterbuck   (Clooterbook,   Cloterbooke,
    Clotterbooke,   Clutterbook,   Clutterbooke,
    Clutterbucke), Abigail, 620, 1137; Alis, 620;
    Anna, 560; Ann(e), 93, 560, 561, 562*, 1135,
    1136, 1145, 1206, 1216; Betty, 1143; Cath., 561,
    620, 1135; Chas., 562*; Clifford, 620; Dorcas,
    1135, 1529–30; Edith, 169*; Edm., 92, 93, 652;
    Edw., 370, 376*, 385*, 1513; Eliz., 165, 376,
    1135, 1182; Esther, 169, 1182*; Fabian, 558,
    562; Fortune, 169; Frances, 1135; Freame,
    1206*, 1216; Giles, 560*, 561; Grace, 562;
    Hannah, 560*, 561, 1135, 1143; Hen., 562;
    Hester, 339; Jas., 169, 367, 376*, 388, 524, 1135,
    1147, 1216; Jasper, 1027, 1133*, 1135*, 1136*,
    1140*, 1512; Joan, 1136; John, 161, 165, 169,
    339, 376*, 562*, 563, 1133*, 1136*, 1143,
    1145*, 1147, 1214; Josiah, 562; Rev. Lewis,
    966*; Lydia, 1135; Marg., 562, 1494; Margery,
    388; Martha, 562*, 658, 1027, 1136; Mary, 339,
    376, 385*, 558, 561, 562*, 618, 620, 621*, 749,
    1143, 1146; Nat., 558, 559, 561, 562*, 563, 618,
    620*, 1135; Peter, 172, 558; R., 618; Rebekah,
    560; Ric., 558*, 560*, 561, 562*, 618, 1133*,

1135*, 1136*, 1139* 1140*, 1143, 1145; Rob., 620; Rev. Rob., 1104; Sam., 658, 1143, 1146, 1206; Sarah, 376*, 562, 563*, 620, 621*, 633, 658, 1133, 1136; Susanna, 376*; Thos., 72, 169*, 198, 199, 370, 484, 563, 620, 658, 1133*, 1135, 1136, 1137*, 1143*, 1182*, 1206, 1216; Tobye, 749; Wal., 558; Willett, 376*; Wm., 169, 559, 560*, 561*, 562*, 620*, 621*, 633, 1120, 1135, 1143, 1530; Rev. Wm., 66; Rev., 619, 620; —, 1027, 1052, 1139*, 1402, 1512*; fam., 159, 255, 558, 649*, 672, 1136, 1140

Clyfford, see Clifford

Clynton, see Clinton

Clyve, see Clive

Coal, see Cole

Coates (Cote, Cotes, Cotte), Ann(e), 262, 880, 881; Chas., 1337, 1473*; Rev. Digby, 713; Eliz., 846; Emme, 1421; Esther, 1535; Giles, 320, 388; Hannah, 320; Hemingge atte, 1420; Joan, 1473; John, 387, 846, 878, 881*, 1421*; John, abbot, 1261; Joseph, 1535; Mary, 387, 881, 1337; Rev. R., 1121; Rev. Rob., 1106*, 1107, 1122; Sarah, 1106, 1107, 1337; Thos., 320; Walron de, 1091; Wm., 262, 880*

Cobb, John, 1231*; Mary, 677; Nat., 677; Sarah, 1231

Coberley (Cubberley), Rob., 224; W., 1123*

Cobham, Elinor (Alienour), 602*; Reg. de, 602*; Thos., bishop, 218, 221, 816; Lord, see Brooke, N.; —, 1093

Cobley, Rev. Wm., 704

Cobyndon, Joan de, 371; Ric. de, 371

Cocheye, John, 1346

Cock, see Cox

Cockayne, Mary Anne, 835

Cockbill, Hannah, 138; (or Diston), J., 1227; John, 138

Cockerell, Sir C., 1055*

Cockes, see Cox

Cockle, Ann, 657; Geo., 657; Ric., 657

Cocks (Cocus), see Cox

Code, (or Pool), Ric., 1385; Wal., 1165

Codrington (Codryngton), Agnes, 32, 496*; Alice, 696; Ambrose, 619; Anne, 454; B., 1385; Sir C. W., 1385; Chris., 496, 497, 839, 840; Dorothy, 498; Eliz., 496, 498, 499, 840; Frances (Francis), 496*; Francis, 619*; Sir Gerald, 1383, 1385; Giles, 497; Grisel, 495; Isabella, 1451, 1547; Joan, 498; John (de), 416, 496, 696, 1121, 1383*, 1385*; Joyce, 1547; Rev. Lewis, 1177; Marg., 619; Mary, 416, 619; Rachel, 454, 496; Ric., 496, 498, 555, 1547; Rev. Ric., 498*; Rob., 32, 454, 495*, 496*, 497 n, 1551; Sam., 265 n, 497, 498*, 499, 1451; Simon, 495*, 496, 1385*; Rev. Thos., 498*, 840; Wm., 497, 498*; Capt. Wm., 1383; Sir Wm., bt., 498*, 839; —, 1123, 1385; fam., 452, 495, 696, 1383; and see Cotherington

Coffrill (? Cottrill), Wm., 1003

Cok, see Cox

Coke, see Cooke

Coker, Rev. Thos., 487, 488

Cokes, see Cox

Cokesey, see Cooksey

Cokkebur, Ric., 1314

Cokks, see Cox

Colas, see Cowles

Colborne (Colborn, Colbourn, Colburn, Colebourne, Colesbourne, Colesburne), Ann, 1203, 1207; Benj., 1207; Eliz., 1207, 1208; Emma, 1211; Hugh de, 1074; John, 1009*, 1101, 1207, 1212, 1369; Joseph, 1207, 1208; Marg., 1009; Mary, 1211; Sam., 1115*; Thos., 1211*; W., 361

Colchester, Alice, 1401; Anna, 486; Anne, 1394; Arabella, 1399; Capel, 486; Dorothy, 1394; Sir Duncomb, kt., 2, 3, 788, 1393*, 1394*, 1402; Eliz., 1393, 1394, 1399; Helen, 1399; Jane, 1394*; John, 463, 470, 479*, 788, 1399*; M., 1403; Col. M., 1402*; Mary, 3; Maynard, 1, 463, 469, 915, 1394*, 1399*, 1401*, 1402, 1403; Col. Maynard, 1394; Ric., 1393, 1399, 1401; Stephen, 77*; Wm., 77; —, 1393, 1402; fam., 346, 463, 1401, 1402

Coldicoat, Jane, 88; John 88

Coldrick, Mary, 787; Salathiel, 787

Cole (Coal), Rev. And., 81, 82; Ann(e), 28, 726, 764, 765, 1026, 1148, 1182, 1209; Bart., 1313; Benj., 1180, 1182; Betty, 765; Blanch, 726; Bridget, 726*; Cath., 174; Chas., 726*, 1551; Chris., 721, 725, 726*; Edw., 1471; Eleanor, 765; Eliz., 175, 176, 699, 726*, 903*, 904, 1175; Esther, 1026; Frances, 32*, 699; Geo., 734, 1123, 1209, 1489; Hannah, 1180, 1361; Harry, 699; Hen., 575; Hester, 1175; J., 1476; Jas., 174*, 725, 1175*, 1377; Jane, 575; Joan, 174; John, 28, 174, 339, 734, 764*, 765*, 781, 903*, 1026*, 1175*, 1289, 1348, 1513; Joseph, 174*; Joyce, 82; K., 756; Kath., 1024, 1175; Martha, 734*; Mary, 174*, 726, 764, 765*, 1024, 1374, 1377, 1489; Nat., 175, 1182; Nic., 174*; Norman Sam., 1456; Petronell, 1404; Rev. Potter, 31, 32, 696, 699; Priscilla, 1213; Ric., 175, 765, 996, 1177, 1180*, 1209*, 1213; Rev. Thos., 524, 1225; Tim., 175; W., 1177; Wm., 175, 231, 429, 699, 764*, 765*, 904, 1024, 1165, 1313; —, 1052, 1148, 1355

Colebourne, see Colborne

Colebrook, Joseph, 1555

Coleman (Colman), Ann(e), 868*; Dee, 868; Eliz., 374*, 822, 1158; Grace, 822; Hen., 374; Joan, 822; John, 822*, 868, 1467; Joseph, 822; Josiah, 822; Mary, 1467; Sarah, 1158; Thos., 374*, 1477; Wm., 1158; Rev., 1083

Colen, see Cullen

Colepeper (Colepepper), see Culpepper

Coleraine [peerage], Eliz., baroness, 770; and see Hanger, Eliz., Gabriel, and John

Coles, see Cowles

Colesbourne (Colesburn, Colesburne), see Colborne

Colescombe, John 1356

Coleseye, Wal., 1356

Coley, Eliz. Fream, 623; Geo., 623; Joseph, 623; Sarah, 623; Wm., 623; Wm. Webley, 623

Colimor, *see* Cullimore

Coliues, Alice, 1339

Collabine (Cullabine), John 522*; Sarah, 522

Collard, Rev. Chris., 435

Collens, *see* Collins

Collerick (Collorick), Jas., 262; John, 1377; Rebekah, 262

Colles, *see* Cowles

Collett (Collet), Ann(e), 1091, 1498, 1499; Ant., 233, 234*, 235*, 1093; Benj., 1266*, 1288; Betty, 336; Bridget, 1266*; Caleb, 1091; Cath., 706; Charlotte, 399; Edm., 1494; Eliz., 884, 1068, 1088, 1266*, 1330; Ellin, 336; Emmit, 706; Esther, 399, 818; H., 1092; Rev. H., 1291; Hannah, 235, 818, 1068, 1194*, 1473; Harry, 1092, 1196; Hen., 235*, 394, 952, 1091*, 1092, 1266*, 1288*, 1289, 1504; Jemima, 1266*; John, 35*, 235, 336*, 399*, 431, 706, 818, 884, 889, 891, 1063, 1088*, 1089*, 1091, 1092*, 1193, 1194, 1499; John Waterworth, 1266; Joseph, 818, 1266*; Joyce, 1091; Martha, 1193; Mary, 235, 399*, 431, 598, 818, 884, 952, 1068, 1088, 1091, 1194; Par(r)is, 1091*, 1092*; Ric., 235, 598, 818, 884, 1068, 1091*, 1092*, 1460; Rob., 1068, 1092; Ruth, 818; Sam., 315, 1091*; Sarah, 35*, 818, 1063, 1088*, 1091*, 1266, 1499; Thos., 336, 399, 706*, 818, 953, 1068*, 1088*, 1089, 1091*, 1092*, 1093, 1330, 1473*, 1498, 1499, 1511; Waterworth, 1289; Wm., 235, 598, 953, 1088, 1091, 1193, 1194, 1227; Wm. Early, 598; Master, 1089 n; Miss, 1288; Mr., 1089; Rev. Mr., 965; fam., 232*, 639, 792, 1092, 1093

Colley (Colly, Coly), Matillda, 1441; John, 1238, 1441; W., 1404

Collier (Colyar, Colyer), Anne, 905; Dauid, 1314; Eliz., 781; Rev. Geo., 1456*; Rev. Giles, 85, 221; Hester, 539; John, 257, 569, 911, 1502; (or Green), John, 1490; Martha, 257, 543; Mary, 539; Nat., 543; Rebecca, 1028; Rob., 543; Sam., 257, 264; Sarah, 264; Rev. Stephen, 781, 1028*, 1031; Thos., 539*, 543; Mr., 1028; —, 1311, 1456

Collingridge, Edm., 150

Collins (Collens, Collings, Collyns, Colynes, Colyns), Abraham, 555, 729*, 730*, 1420; Alice, 669; Amey, 937; Ann(e), 729*, 857, 941, 1138*, 1307; Benj., 669*; Betty, 633*; Chas., 467, 1576; Dan., 907, 937; Deborah, 10*; Diana, 555*; Edm., 687, 1318; Edw., 730, 1419; Eliz., 283, 834, 1282, 1306; Frances, 1343; Francis, 1160; Geof., 1061; Geo., 857, 1138*; Hannah, 555; Hester, 1150, 1151, 1304, 1307; J., 1312; Jane, 1360; John, 339, 467, 542, 818, 1138*, 1140, 1196, 1282, 1304*, 1307*, 1318, 1319; Rev. John, 1313; Marg., 687; Martha, 1138; Mary, 10, 818, 907, 964, 1138, 1282; Rebecca, 555; Ric., 10*, 555*, 730, 1502; Rev. Ric., 263; Rob., 10, 633, 703; Sam., 622, 1150, 1151, 1282*; Sarah

(Saroh), 176, 339, 467, 622*, 633, 703, 1282; Selah, 555; Susanna, 1282, 1318, 1319; T., 1195, 1312; Thos., 834, 941, 1306, 1307, 1360, 1362; Tim., 176, 283; W., 633, 1312, 1419; Rev. Wal., 890; Wm., 463, 542, 555, 587, 729, 964, 1175, 1304*, 1307*; Rev., 748; —, 823, 1020*, 1062

Collinson, Rev. John, 375; Mary, 375

Collorick, *see* Collerick

Collwell, *see* Colwell

Colly, *see* Colley

Collyer, *see* Collier

Collyns, *see* Collins

Colman, *see* Coleman

Colmor, *see* Cullimore

Colne (Coln), Alice de, 1519; John de, 1127; W. de, 1147; Wal. de, 1519; *and see* Culne

Colson, Thos., 151

Colster, Ralph, 479

Colston (Coulston), Alex., 593, 596, 718, 722, 833, 834, 1491; (formerly Ready), Alex., 718; Rev. Alex., 722; Deborah, 133; Edw., 603, 718, 745, 833*, 1351, 1405, 1420; Edw. Francis, 1423; Eliz., 1493; Jane, 133*; John, 133; Joseph, 133*; Ric., 133*; Wm., 133; —, 1419*, 1420, 1428

Colt, Cath., 567; Eliz., 1067; Geo., 1067; Joan, 1549; Rob., 1549

Coltam, Alice, 1216

Colthrede, John le, 1259

Colton, Rev. Ralph, 1016

Colur, Wm., 1160

Colwell (Collwell), Dan., 1182*; Edm., 1533; Eliz., 1533; Jane, 1182; John, 1038, 1533*; Mary, 1038, 1533; Ric., 1533*; Rob., 873; Sarah, 1533; Alderman, 895

Coly, *see* Colley

Colyar (Colyer), *see* Collier

Colymore, *see* Cullimore

Colyns (Colynes), *see* Collins

Combe (Coombe), Alice in the, 1218; Clarice de, 1540; Jane, 332; Jo(h)anna, 1111*; Mary, 1457, 1459; Ric., 332; Thos., 1111*; Wm. de, 1404

Combecke, John, 708

Comber (Comer), Honna, 1580; John, 1062

Combes (Combs, Comes), Eliz., 1043; Geo., 293; Thos., 1043; Wm., 1202

Comeley, *see* Comley

Comer, *see* Comber

Comes, *see* Combes

Comley (Comeley), Eliz., 702*; Jas., 702*; Lawr., 597; Ric., 597; Sabina, 597

Commeline (Commelyne), Rev. Jas., 674, 675; Rev. Sam., 1379

Commins, *see* Cummins

Compere (Compeer, Comper, Compier, Cumper), Ann(e), 1194, 1536; Ant., 1194*, 1195; Dorothy, 642; Eliz., 1166*; J., 1194; Joan, 702; John (le), 35, 703, 1434; Juliana, 1434; M., 1194; Margery le, 1434; Mary, 702*; R., 1476; Rob., 702, 1166*; Sarah, 702*; Stephen, 702*, 1525, 1536; Thos. (le), 635, 641, 702, 1092, 1190, 1434, 1461; W., 1196; Wm., 642, 702*; —, 438*, 1092, 1195*, 1196, 1226, 1476*; fam., 1195

Compton, Ann, 1065, 1463; Lady Anne, 224; Ant., 852 n, 854; Cath., 680, 1065; Chas., 1469; Chas., earl of Northampton, 123; Dennis, 54; Dorothy (Dorothie), 681, 997; Elinor, 681*; Eliz., 1232, 1469; Eliz., countess of Northampton, 220, 224*; Frances, 1463; Geo., earl of Northampton, 224; Helen, 680; Dr. Hen., bishop, 366, 1223, 1331; Isabella, countess of Northampton, 721 n; Jas., earl of Northampton, 721 n; Jane, 54, 680, 1469; John, 681, 1065*, 1232; Mary, 1469; Meliandra of, 1370; Peter, 1311; Rev. R., 1362; Rebe(c)kah, 1232, 1469*; Rog. of, 1370; Ruth, 852 n; T., 1063*, 1064*; Thos., 360, 361, 1232, 1463; Wal., 680, 681*, 984, 997, 1287, 1504; Sir Wal., bt., 680; Wm., 680, 681*, 1220, 1469*; Wm., Lord Compton, 1351; Sir Wm., 1311; —, 1064, 1219, 1351*, 1495; fam., 680
Comyn, see Cummins
Concannen, Eliz., 1582; Geo., 1582*
Conckling, Damaris, 931; Jacob, 931*
Conestable, see Constable
Congreve (Congrave), Rev. Ric., 221; Lieut. Col., 469 n*, 927, 928, 929
Coningsby (Connyngesby), Eliz., 1059; Humph., 147; Ric., 1059
Conles, —, 1033
Conney, John Wm., 1574
Connyngesby, see Coningsby
Conoldi, Edm., 755; Eliz., 755
Conolly, Jas., 1027; T. R., 1027
Conquest, Alf., 1504; J., 1288; fam., 1288
Constable (Conestable), Ann, 1250; Eliz., 1250; Esther, 1250; John, 1250; Ric., 608; Sarah, 130; Stephen, 130; Rev. Thos., 128, 130; Wm. le, 1379
Constance (Constans), Abigail, 1397; Ann, 1397; Dorothy, 1397; Eliz., 1397*; Esther, 902; Isabell, 761; Joane, 1397; John, 902*; Ric., 761, 1397*; Thos., 820, 1397*, 1403; Wm., 761
Constant, Ann, 412, 923*; Israel, 923*; John, 249, 352; Joseph, 250; Mary, 250*; Ric., 352; Sarah, 923*; Sibill, 249; Thos., 412; Wm., 249
Constantiis, John de, bishop, 717
Constantine (fl. 1066), 1419
Consul, see Counsell
Controne, Pontius de, 1015
Conway (Conwaic), Rev. Ric., 643; T., 1477; Thos., 1126, 1127; Sir Thos., 1125
Conway [peerage], Henry, Lord, 502; Lady, 1125; Lord, 986*
Conynges, Edw., 1476
Coo, Ann(e), 1222*; Cath., 1222*; Chris., 1222*; Rev. Chris., 1222*, 1223; Eliz., 1222*; Wm., 1222
Cooffe, John, 785
Cooke (Coke, Cook), Sir A., 1054, 1132; Aaron, 176*; Abigail, 5; Amy, 303*; Ann(e), 25, 399, 434, 706*, 797, 810, 970, 971, 975*, 1006, 1153, 1344, 1466*; Benj., 975*; Benj. Josiah, 975; Betty, 456, 706, 952, 996, 1466; Bridget, 971*; Cassandra, 25; Chas., 176; Christian, 1306*; Chris., 340; (or Gibson), Comfort, 984*; Dan.,

203, 336, 587*, 981*; Dennis, 583, 785*; Dorothy, 907; Edm., 394, 1015; Edw., 121, 583, 785, 810, 872, 1157; Sir Edw., 737; Eliz., 274, 303, 587, 856, 871, 872, 933, 970, 971, 1034, 1066, 1068, 1091*, 1267, 1272, 1466, 1508, 1511, 1513, 1530; (or Minty), Eliz., 1248*; Esther, 1262; Frances, 336; Gabriel, 378; Geo., 348, 587, 662, 1150, 1152, 1153*; Rev. Geo., 1340, 1344, 1346; Giles, 857*; Habakkuk, 1289; Hannah, 47, 203, 339*, 930, 981, 1425; Henrietta, 429; Hen. (le), 303*, 304, 981, 1007*, 1091*, 1217, 1221, 1382; Rev. Hen., 142; Hester, 330, 715, 731*; Isabell, 1247; J., 1459, 1476; Jacob, 1418*; Jas., 370, 431, 440, 658, 662*, 952, 1146, 1186, 1377; Jane, 337*, 587, 616, 785, 1066, 1455; Jean, 1212; Joan, 713, 873; John, 5, 47, 231, 274*, 342, 353, 367, 456, 587*, 616, 662, 666, 706*, 713, 731, 751, 803, 805, 836, 873, 907, 922*, 930, 947, 970, 971*, 975*, 976, 984, 1019, 1153, 1247, 1403, 1425, 1455, 1499; (or Gibson, Gybson), John, 984*; Dr. John, 1407, 1412; John Taylor, 337; Jona., 1477; Joseph, 616, 846, 1427, 1437, 1530*; Josiah, 399*, 433; Judith, 1212; Juliana, 1491; Lawr., 952*; Lucy Maria, 1306; M., 1411; Marg., 339, 703, 706, 1019; Martha, 616, 715*, 1425; Mary, 133, 337, 348, 431, 433, 520, 583, 587*, 658, 706*, 803, 846, 857, 952*, 975*, 1000, 1157, 1267*, 1418, 1427, 1437, 1530; Mat., 339; Mic., 1477; Morris, 47*, 48*; Nat., 203, 706*, 1489; Penelope, 658; Rebecca, 399, 952; Reg., 1356; Ric., 348, 706, 801, 970, 971*, 972, 1006*, 1091, 1143, 1212, 1215*, 1267*, 1422, 1491; Rob. (le), 394, 429, 785, 1392; (or Minty), Rob., 1248; Rob., earl of Leicester, 394; Rev. Rob., 394; Sir Rob., kt., 520, 1385; Rog. (le), 452, 1259; Sampson, 1427; Sam., 25, 133, 313, 337*, 339, 703, 715, 1007, 1212–13; (or Minty), Sam., 1248*; Sarah, 47*, 48, 304, 616, 658, 662, 706, 922, 947, 971, 972, 975, 1006, 1007, 1143, 1316, 1455; Solomon, 658; Stephen, 801, 970; Susannah, 971*; T., 1290; Theodosia, 583; Thos., 339, 543, 662*, 706, 715*, 836, 948, 952*, 970, 984, 996, 1000*, 1006, 1226, 1314, 1353, 1355, 1393, 1425*, 1456, 1508, 1511, 1576; Rev. Thos., 214, 951, 1449*, 1456; Thos. Wm., 1066; W., 785, 1092; Wal. le, 1258; Wenman, 1066; Wm., 303, 304*, 330*, 339, 349, 350, 434, 587, 683, 706*, 715, 797, 856, 857, 871, 933, 952*, 981, 984, 986, 1019, 1034*, 1038, 1089, 1316, 1407, 1411, 1466*, 1477, 1489; Rev. Wm., 495; Sir Wm., 349; Col., 349 n, 350 n; Lord, 479 n; Miss, 1202; —, 1148*, 1292, 1455*; fam., 102, 313, 349, 350, 639; and see Coke, Lord
Cooksey (Cokesey), Joyce, 1392; (or Grevil), J., 1014; (or Greville), Thos., 1055; (or Greville), Sir Thos., 1392; fam., 311
Cookson, Rev. Joseph, 770; Rob., 1086
Cooley, Rev. Thos., 488
Coombe, see Combe
Cooper (Coopper, Coupere), A. A., earl of Shaftesbury, 1293; Alf., 1249; Amy, 1014;

Ann(e), 262, 597*, 1014, 1169, 1249; Ant., 1014*, 1068; Beale, 1372; Caleb, 273; Caroline, 1537; Dorothy, 849; E., 1287; Edw., 1023; Eleanor (Elner), 506, 700; Eliz., 317, 550, 598, 703, 849*, 1014, 1023*, 1249*, 1390, 1511; Esther, 1537; Geo., 262, 1023, 1249; Henny, 1247; Hen., 339, 848, 1041 n, 1249; Rev. Hen., 1459; Hester, 703; Jas., 506, 550*, 1537*; Rev. Jas., 161; Jane, 550, 975; Jessica, 1537; Joan, 849, 1041; John (le), 339, 758, 848, 850, 975, 1025, 1088, 1390, 1422, 1537*, 1539; Rev. John, 31, 696, 700*, 754; John Chanter, 975; John Gil., 1031; Joseph, 703*, 1247; Josepha Catherina Susanna, 1031; Laura, 1537; Maria, 1088*, 1249; Martha, 541; Mary, 335, 703*, 979, 980, 1025, 1088, 1430*, 1537; Rev. Miles, 447; Nardon, 1025; Paul, 1025*; R. B., 1054; Ric., 531, 541*, 564, 849*, 1249*, 1430*; Rob., 293, 849, 979*; Rob. Bransby, 1168, 1169; Rev. Rog., 754; Sam., 313, 314*, 335; Sarah, 541, 703, 758, 1023, 1068, 1088, 1249; Sibil, 550; Susanna, 293; Thos., 598, 979, 980, 1023, 1088*, 1244, 1249, 1575; Rev. Wal., 853; Wm., 597*, 703, 1068, 1390*; Rev. Wm., 848, 849; —, 1020*; *and see* Cowper

Coopey, Alice, 1535; Elianor, 419; Eliz., 348; Mary, 1535; Ric., 348*, 683; Sam., 1535

Coopper, *see* Cooper

Cope (Coppe), Sir A., 1402; Alice, 1250; Anne, 830; Ant., 585, 890; Eliz., 781, 832, 1073, 1297*, 1423; Lady Eliz., 1423; Grace, 1250; Hannah, 996*; Hen., 1363, 1422, 1423; Jacob, 1426; Jas., 1250; Jane, 1250; Joan, 830*; John, 830*; Jonathan, 781, 830, 1171; Sir Jonathan, bt., 697; Joseph, 1297*; Marg., 1255; Margery, 1258; Martha, 1426; Mary, 697, 781, 830, 832, 996, 1297; Nat., 781*; Rachel, 1423; Ric., 1404; Rob., 996*; Sarah, 830; Susan, 1171; Thos., 830*, 832*; Sir W., 1197; Wm., 996*, 1190, 1250*, 1258, 1422, 1423*; Col., 1189, 1423; —, 1255, 1422

Copeland (Capelond, Copland, Coupland), Chas., 1563*; J., 1061; Mary, 1563*; Rob.., 1061

Copner (Copmer), Anne, 670; Eliz., 669, 1000*; Geo., 669, 670; Hannah, 1433; Jane, 1433; John, 264, 669, 1274; Joseph, 1131; Mary, 264, 669*, 1131, 1274; Rebecca, 1274; Susanna, 1131; Thos., 1000*, 1131*; Wm., 669*, 1433*; —, 1069, 1261; *and see* Capner

Coppe, *see* Cope

Coppedethorne, Wm., 1160

Coppin (Coppynge), H., 1061; Mary, 1200; Wm., 1200

Coppinger, —, 1402

Coppynge, *see* Coppin

Copson, Rev. John, 1024*; Mary, 1024

Coram, Hen., 1418

Corbett (Corbet, Corbitt), Anna-Maria, 1549; Anne, 1001; Ant., 1485; Chris., 755; Dan., 661; Eleanor, 1549*; Eliz., 1003*; Francis, 752; Grace, 1549*, 1550; Hannah, 1002*, 1250; Henrietta, 1549; Jane, 300, 1250; John, 217,

1001, 1003*, 1088, 1250, 1258, 1549; Jonathan, 1328, 1549*; Josias, 300; Judith, 1250; Marg., 997, 1086; Martha, 752, 1003, 1549; Mary, 661, 1003, 1214, 1549*, 1550; Mic., 1001*; Sir Miles, 311; Muriel, 1002; Nathan, 1549*; Nat., 1549*, 1550; Sir Peter, kt., 1086; Ric., 1328; Rog., 634, 1328; Sir Rog., 570*; Rowland, 1250*, 1258; Sarah, 1003, 1549; Thos., 1002*, 1003, 1088; W., 1328; Wal., 997; Wm., 1328, 1329, 1481, 1549*; —, 158, 179, 263, 341, 805, 852, 855, 875, 894, 927, 928, 1328, 1355, 1404; fam., 634, 864

Cordell, *see* Caudle

Cordwainer, John, 720

Cordwell, Anne, 1275; Eliz., 1275; Rev. Wm., 1275

Cordy, Ann, 284; Bridget, 284; Chas., 284; Mary, 284; Wm., 284*

Core, Thos., 1576

Corgan, Mic., 804*

Cork (Corke), Edm., 991; Job, 79; Joseph, 79; Marg.. 810; Mary, 79, 417, 620*, 991; Ric., 417, 620; Thos., 810

Cormeilles (Cormeil, Cormeleis, Cormeliis), Albreda, 1077, 1431*; Alf. de, 1476; Alice, 1431; Ansfrid (Ansfard) de, 1077*, 1431, 1485*; Beatrix de, 1077, 1431; Lucian de, 221; Marg., 1077, 1431; Ric. de, 1077*, 1431*; Sibilla, 1431; Wal., 1077, 1431; — de, 1475, 1476

Cormell, Eliz., 765; Mary, 765; Sam., 227; Wm., 765

Cornbill, Eliz., 1193; John 1193*

Corneley (Cornely, Cornley), Aldom, 1429; Anne, 1429; Dinah, 1429; Eliz., 1429*; Jas., 1429*; John 1429*; Mary, 1429*; Rob., 1429; Sarah, 1429; Wm., 1429

Cornelius, Jas., 181; Sibella, 181

Cornely, *see* Corneley

Cornemonger, Ralph le, 1258

Corner (Cornere), Honora, 1580; John atte, 1456; Nic. atte, 1259; Sydney, 1293; Wm., 1580; *and see* Angulo

Corney, Joseph, 231; Myles, 231

Cornley, *see* Corneley

Cornock (Curnock), Amey, 937; Ann(e), 173, 176, 938; Benj., 175; Dan., 938*; Edm., 935, 938; Edw., 176; Eliz., 173*; Geo., 938; Hannah, 957; Hester, 173, 176; J., 1101; Jas., 176, 1101; Jane, 176; Joan, 173; John, 173, 175, 935, 1080, 1301; Joseph, 284; Martha, 173*; Mary, 166, 173*, 936, 938*, 1080; Nic., 173*; Rebecca (Rebeckah, Rebekah), 936*, 937; Ric., 173, 176*, 542, 937, 938; Rob., 936*, 937, 938*; Rose, 937; Sarah, 175, 176, 284, 938; Susanna, 173, 1301; T., 1101; Thos., 166, 176, 938, 957*; Wm., 173, 938, 1101, 1301; —, 1102; fam., 159

Cornewallis, *see* Cornwallis

Cornwall, Brice, 662; Chas., 662*; Eliz., 662*; Hannah, 538; Sir Ric., 1011; Thos., 662*; *and see* Cornwell

Cornwall [*peerage*], Ailmer (Ailmore), earl of, 1189, 1196; Edm., earl of, 708, 792, 1016, 1225; Edw., earl of, 1476; John (king), as earl of, 1287;

Isabel, countess of, 1287; Ric., earl of, 392, 481, 509, 707, 708*, 709, 791*, 792, 816, 1225*; Senchia (Sentia), countess of, 359, 708*, 791
Cornwallis (Cornewallis), Caroline, 681, 1502; Sir Wm., 1447
Cornwell, John, 1549; Sam., 1182; Sarah, 1182; and see Cornwall
Coroner, Cristina la, 1069; Elia la, 1069; Matilda la, 1069
Corpe, Wm., 1428
Cors, Cristina de, 1292
Corslet, Marg., 814; Morgan, 814
Cortis, see Curtis
Corvyser, Ric. le, 1258
Cosburn, Ambrose, 659*; Ann, 661; John, 661*; Mary, 659*; Rebecca, 658; Roseanna, 659; Sam., 658; Susannah, 659
Cosby, Sir M., 1322
Cosham, see Cossham
Cosin (Cosins), see Cousins
Cosley (Cosseley), Wm., 1351; —, 1043
Cossens, see Cousins
Cossham (Cosham), Betty, 1182; Ch., 1312; Eliz., 1182, 1306; Geo., 1306; John, 1182; Susanna, 1182; Thos., 1182, 1186; —, 1140, 1361
Cossins, see Cousins
Costard, Rev. Geo., 1127
Costello, —, bishop, 1062
Coster, Anne, 811*; Eliz., 920; Eugenia, 920; Grace, 920; Jas., 920*; Jane, 1524; John, 811*, 920*; Mary, 920*, 921*; Ralph, 921; Rebecca, 811; Rob., 920, 921; Sarah, 920; Thos., 920, 1524
Costlow, Joseph, 563; Rachael, 563
Coston, Edith, 1033; Wm., 1033
Cosyn, see Cousins
Cote, see Coates
Cotel, see Cottell
Coteriche, Rob., 1027
Cotes, see Coates
Cother, Joseph, 906; Mary, 906*; Solomon, 906; Thos., 906, 1378; Wm., 906, 1372
Cotheridge, Frances, 484; John, 484
Cotherington, Alice, 1120, 1339, 1385; F., 1101; Humph., 1120, 1385; J., 1339; John, 1120*, 1385*; Marg., 1120; Thos., 1120, 1385; and see Codrington
Cothier, Wm., 1316
Coton, see Cotton
Cotte, see Coates
Cottell (Cotel), Edith, 52; Ric., 52; fam., 612
Cotten, see Cotton
Cotterell (Cotterill, Cottrell, Cottrill), Alice, 1052; Ann(e), 868, 1041, 1353, 1354*; Sir Chas., 1220; Edm., 850, 1041*; Edw., 1052, 1432; Eliz., 16, 46, 1354*; Francis, 850*; Hannah, 16, 1041; Hen., 1041 [recte Cooper], 1519; Sir Hen., bt., 1041; J., 1061; Joan (Jone), 1041*, 1458; John, 1062, 1353, 1354, 1460; Joseph, 1354*; Mary, 46*, 339, 1052, 1354*, 1432; Ric., 1458; Sarah, 850*; Stephen, 46; Susanna, 16*, 46; Thos., 46*, 339*, 1041*; Wm., 16*, 46*, 721, 725, 1354*,

and see Coffrill; Wm. Ferdinand, 1457; —, 1293, 1348, 1356, 1362, 1392; fam., 287
Cotton (Coton, Cotten), Benj., 171*; Cath., 174; Dorothy, 995*, 997*; Edm., 332; Edw., 90, 174*, 924*; Eliz., 171, 436, 1063; Geo., 1015, 1302; Hen., 1302*; Jas., 174; Sir John, bt., 995, 997; Lydia, 90, 1302; Marg., 1443, 1444; Mary, 924; (or Calton), Mary, 1482; R., 1063, 1382; Ralph, 1476; Ric., 1062, 1443, 1444; Sir Rob., kt., 436; Sam., 1583; T., 1288; Thos., 432; Ursula, 1302*; —, 1476; fam., 1288, 1442
Cottrell (Cottrill), see Cotterell
Coucher (Cowcher), Ann, 97; Edw., 97; John, 1289; Mary, 858; Thos., 858*
Couchman, Lieut. Thos., 1107*
Couelege, see Cowley
Coues, Wm., 636
Couherde, Matilda le, 1335; Thos. le, 1102
Couhull (Couhulle), Felic., 1313; Not. de, 1313; —, 1311
Coules, see Cowles
Couley, see Cowley
Couling, see Cowling
Coulsey, Rev. Wal., 547; Wm., 683
Coulson, Rev. John, 297
Coulston, see Colston
Counsell (Consul), Hen., 671; Hester, 780*; Jas., 780; John, 780; Rebekah, 780; Rob., 638; Sam., 780; Thos., 780*
Coupere, see Cooper
Coupland, see Copeland
Court, Eliz., 924; John, 924, 1003; Mary, 321, 429; Sam., 250; Sarah, 250; Stephen, 429; Thos., 321, 429; Wm., 250*; Mr., 98
Courteen, Sir Wm., 1226, 1228*
Courtenay, John, 755*; Mary, 755
Courtier, Anne, 125; Eliz., 125*; Isaac, 125*; John, 125; Sam., 1121; Thos., 125, 1121
Cousins (Cosin, Cosins, Cossens, Cossins, Cosyn, Cozen), Edw., 696, 697, 700; Eliza, 696; Frances, 700; John, 1092, 1416*; John, bishop, 1559; Joseph, 413; Martha, 1416; Rev. Thos., 488; Mr., 1416; —, 1420*
Covel, John, 1033; Jule [? Juliana], 1033
Coventry, Eliz., 572; Francis, 572*; Jas., 1009; John, 1104; Mary, 273, 771; Wm., 1009*; Sir Wm., kt., 184, 1189; —, Lord Keeper, 1217, 1504; fam., 481–2
Coventry [peerage], Geo., earl of, Viscount Deerhurst, 482*; Thos., baron, 572; Thos., earl of, 123; Thos., Lord, 771, 1290, 1469, 1476; earl of, 1203, 1356; Lord, 273, 864, 1291, 1352, 1355*, 1356, 1476, 1503, 1504; and see Somerset, Anne
Coverall (or Barker), fam., 592
Coverdale, Dr. Miles, 1220
Cowarn, Hester, 90; Morgan, 90*
Cowcher, see Coucher
Cowell, Eliz., 1275; John, 1275*, 1478
Cowles (Colas, Coles, Colles, Coules, Cowls), Benj., 883*; Chas., 812; Culpep(p)er, 1064, 1263*; Edith, 45; Edw., 45*; Eleanor, 1438;

Eliz., 610, 1439; Esther, 1438*; Geo., 15; Hannah, 17; Izzard, 1438; J., 1061; Jeremiah, 814; Joan, 907; John, 118, 522, 610, 635, 812, 1263, 1438*, 1439; Joseph, 1027; Martha, 703; Mary, 522, 1278; Ric., 339; Rob., 1061; Rev. Rob., 1043; Thos., 17*, 907, 1039; Tim., 610; Tobias, 627, 1393; Wal., 1331; Wm., 703, 1278, 1438; —, 1058, 1195; fam., 635

Cowley (Couelege, Couley), Alice, 598; Ann, 598; Anna, 1315; Benj., 1539; Cath., 1097, 1099; Rev. Dan., 1441; Eliz., 70, 598, 1097, 1400, 1401; Hannah, 638; John, 70, 437, 598, 1097, 1098, 1099, 1315*, 1316; Martha, 460; Mary, 176, 598*, 1100; Ric., 598; Rob., 1100*, 1401; Sam., 633; Sarah, 282; Simon de, 529; Thos., 1097, 1098; Tobias, 1400*; Wm., 176*, 282, 460*, 598*, 633, 1097*, 1101

Cowling (Couling), Cath., 772; Eleanor, 772; Eliz., 608, 772; John, 608; Leonard, 772*; Marg., 772; Mary, 862; Thos., 772; Wal., 772; Wm., 862

Cowls, see Cowles

Cowmeadow (Cowmeade), Alex., 906; Anna, 832*; Eliz., 627; Grace, 832; John, 627, 906; Ric., 832; Thos., 832

Cowper, Dorothy, 1458; Eliz., 1458; Ric., 1458; W., 1323; Wm., 429; and see Cooper

Cowstans, see Custans

Cox (Cock, Cockes, Cocks, Cocus, Cok, Coke, Cokes, Cokks, Coxe), Abraham, 661; Alice, 1029; Ann(e), 55, 336*, 344, 438, 485*, 521, 578, 741*, 768, 826, 906, 963, 972, 1010, 1018, 1029*, 1030, 1175; Ant., 55, 203, 412; Arthur, 308, 1307*; Arthur Osburn, 1452; Betty, 203, 973; Bridget, 1249; C., 1032*, 1052*; C. W., 1033; Cath. (Catharina), 485, 521, 1029*, 1032*, 1176*; Chamberlaine (Chamberlayne), 963, 1029; Chas., 17, 118, 197, 252, 364*, 485, 518, 519*, 520, 521, 1029*, 1032, 1033*, 1216, 1306; Chas., Lord Somers, 518; Rev. Chas., 519; Chas. Wesley, 445; Charlotte, 1231; Chris., 520, 1030*; Chubb, 521; Celia, 1176; Deborah (Doborah), 1029, 1030; Dorothy, 518, 519, 520, 521, 1030; E., 1074; Edith, 332*, 1513; Edw., 332, 344*, 562, 1029*, 1030*, 1554, 1564, 1565; Rev. Edw., 19; Eliz., 46, 47*, 55, 92*, 203, 211*, 341*, 343, 396, 446, 520*, 521*, 661, 741*, 973, 1028, 1029, 1032. 1307, 1489; Eliz. Ann, 1032; Esther, 973; Frances, Lady Cocks, 520; Geo., 485, 963; Giles, 114, 131, 259, 263, 327, 336, 347, 350, 582, 667, 681, 713, 853, 1029, 1030*, 1033, 1044, 1373, 1434, 1494; Hannah, 1030; Hen., 1018; Hester, 845, 846, 1018*; Jacob, 211*; Jane, 963, 1111, 1303; John (le), 47*, 203, 240, 308, 336*, 343*, 344, 364, 396*, 485*, 519, 520*, 526, 578, 661*, 741*, 803, 906, 973*, 1002, 1018*, 1028*, 1029*, 1030*, 1031, 1032*, 1033, 1052, 1111, 1175*, 1176*, 1216, 1217, 1238, 1307, 1351, 1452, 1489; Capt. John, 1231; Rev. John, 297*, 366, 1028, 1029, 1031; John H., 1196; John Surman, 1231; Joseph, 1328, 1574; Joyce, 1452; Judith, 520*; Kath., 1265; Lawr., 485, 1279*; Marg., 1029, 1030; Martha, 661,

1029; Mary, 17, 336*, 343*, 396, 397, 408, 455*, 485*, 520, 730, 906, 963, 973*, 985, 1029*, 1030*, 1043, 1063, 1111*, 1176, 1201, 1238, 1265, 1279, 1307*, 1328, 1532, 1564, 1565, 1574*; Mat., 1028, 1029*; Millicent, 1002; Nat., 1028, 1030; Peter (de), 397, 1127; Rev. Peter, 394 & n; Rebecca, 203; Ric., 203, 233, 518, 520*, 1029, 1044, 1292, 1401, 1489; Rev. Ric., 236, 239, 1122, 1477; Sir Ric., bt., 519*, 520*; Rob. (le), 332*, 336, 521, 961, 963, 985, 1029*, 1032, 1346; Sir Rob., bt., 518, 521*, 667; Sam., 211*, 845, 846, 1249; Sarah, 240, 308, 333*, 335*, 336*, 485*, 521, 562, 768, 950, 961, 973, 1018*, 1030, 1111, 1265; Susanna(h), 46, 47, 343*, 485*, 1111; Dame Susanna, 520; T., 1312, 1348; Theodora, 1032*, 1033; Thos., 46, 47*, 55*, 336*, 343*, 384, 396, 446*, 455*, 485*, 518, 519, 600, 730*, 768*, 826, 972, 973, 1029*, 1030*, 1035, 1043, 1111*, 1121*, 1303, 1307*; (or Hayward), Thos., 610; Rev. Thos. Chamberlayne, 93, 252, 297, 1029; Tim., 203; Rev. W., 1102; Wal., 333*, 335*; Westley, 1032; Wm., 48, 112, 468, 485*, 741*, 950, 973, 1010*, 1018, 1029, 1176, 1199, 1303; Rev. Wm., 519; Rev. Wm. Hayward, 1231; Dr., 1362; Mrs., 1295; —, 327, 511, 855, 1016, 1017, 1020, 1028, 1033, 1074, 1172, 1176, 1378, 1455, 1475, 1491, 1494; fam., 159, 297, 365, 424, 788; (or Hayward), fam., 609

Coxeter, Barbara, 795; Geo., 792, 795*; Mary, 792, 795; Ric., 795

Coxwell, Anne, 185*, 186, 1349*; Cath., 186*; Chas., 185*; Rev. Chas., 128, 184*, 421, 859; Eleanor, 185; Eliz., 1349*, 1350; Hen., 1349*, 1350; John, 184*, 185*, 186*, 366, 369, 1349*, 1350; Leanna, 1349*, 1350; Mary, 185, 1349*; Rob., 1349; Sam., 369; Mr., 1082; Rev., 1079; fam., 184

Coyde, Rev. John, 498

Cozen, see Cousins

Crabbe, Wal., 1404

Cradock (Craddock, Cradoc, Cradocke, Craduck), Anne, 1095; Dan., 1095; Eleanor, 906; Eliz., 112, 431, 1036; (or Taylor), Rev. Hum., 767; Jane, 1036; John, 112, 948. 1036*, 1037, 1039; Rev. John, 767; Joseph, 431, 1515; Marg., 112; Mary, 948, 1515*; Ric., 906, 948; S., 1095; Rev. Sam., 748; Sarah, 112, 1095; Susanna, 1095; Thos., 1037; Rev. W., 1102; Wm., 112*, 1515; Rev. Wm., 1095; —, rector, 1102; fam., 205

Craft (Crafts), Betty, 950; Cath., 112; Dan., 563; Eliz., 517, 563; Hester, 873; John, 873*; Ric., 112, 517; Wm., 950

Cragg (Crag, Craggs), Ann, 507; Chris., 87; Harriot, 507; Jas., 507; (formerly Nugent), Rob., Viscount Clare, 507

Craig, Ann, 542; John, 542

Craister, Rev. John, 895; Rev. Dr., 895, 898

Crancombe, Alice, 1431; Godfrey de, 1431

Crane, Jenny, 1574; John, 1574

Cranfield, Leonard, earl of Middlesex, 1388

Cranmer [archbishop], 534 n*

Crassus, *see* Fortibus

Cratle, Wm., 1537

Craven, Berkeley, 1386; Eliz., 22, 130, 1348; Fulwar, 1501; H. A. B., 1348, 1387*; Hen. A. B., 1348; Hen. Augustus Berkeley, 982; Wm., 1348; Sir Wm., 22, 130; —, 1348

Craven [*peerage*], Wm., earl of, 228, 579*, 1348*; Wm., Lord, 346, 394, 580, 986, 1165, 1348, 1387; earl of, 228; Lord, 71, 72, 985, 1064*, 1346, 1348

Cravenhull, John de, 1238

Crawford, Thos., 1289

Crawley, Rev. Chas. Yonge, 1237; Joseph, 1513, 1515; Mary Cath., 1400; (later Crawley Boevey), Thos., 606*; Wm., 1400; Rev. Wm., 606; —, 1494

Crayle, Rev. John, 1177

Crease, *see* Creese

Creed (Creede), Alice, 727; Ann, 64; Ant., 510; Dan., 1211, 1214; Edith, 752; Edw., 727; Eliz., 510*, 730, 967; Giles, 752, 921*; Grace, 752; Hen., 64; Jas., 752; Rev. Jas., 947; John, 510, 777, 1510; John Worlock, 777; Kath., 777; Marg., 921; Mary, 752, 1510; Ric., 752; Sarah, 967*, 1211, 1214; Susannah, 921; Thos., 730, 777*, 921, 967*, 1211, 1214; Wm., 730, 752, 777, 1510

Creese (Crease, Crees, Creise, Crese, Cresse), Dan., 1427; Jas., 27, 28; John, 611; Mary, 1427; R., 1477; Susannah, 611; —, 1017

Cresby, Alice, 868; Thos., 868

Crese (Cresse), *see* Creese

Cresser, Marg., 984; Stephen, 984, 986

Cresswell, *see* Creswell

Cresswicke, *see* Creswick

Creswell (Cresswell), Ann(e), 184, 1201, 1202; E., 1202; Estcourt, 183, 184, 364, 859, 1005, 1201, 1202*; John, 486, 1270; Mary, 486; T. Estcourt, 1201; Thos. E., 1202

Creswick (Cresswicke, Creswicke), Anne, 883; Francis, 206, 208*; Geof., 208; Helen, 208; Hen., 206, 208, 883*; John, 208, 250; Mary, 208; Sam., 882, 883*; Dr. Sam., 1408; fam., 205

Crew (Crewe), Alice, 1532; And., 463; Ann, 1248; Arthur, 531, 695, 696, 1532; Bridget, 35*; Edw., 34; John, 1248; Eliz., 1454; Mary, 491, 555, 562, 797, 1532; Mat., 35*, 1454*; Milburn, 1248; Nat., 797; Rebecca (Rebekah), 35, 562; Rob., 1531, 1532*; Sarah, 1535; Thos., 491, 555, 562, 1121*, 1535; Wm., 31, 35*

Cribb, Ann, 1489; Dan., 1489, 1578; Mary, 1578; Sarah, 1578

Crinks, Ann, 1574; Sam., 1582, 1583; Sarah, 1574, 1582

Cripps (Crips), Ann(e), 130, 1215; Benj., 641; Betty, 130, 641*; Chas., 1176; Rev. Chas., 1177; Edw., 373; Eliz., 369, 373, 376*, 641*, 1012; Frances, 1215; Giles, 130, 641, 1012*; Hen., 373; Rev. Hen., 1186; John, 201, 373*, 376, 641*, 1245; Joseph, 381, 990*, 1202*, 1215; Marg., 1245, 1251*; Mary, 641*, 1012, 1245; Nat., 1244, 1251*, 1255*; R., 1139; Ric., 641*;

Sophia Eliz., 1176; Temperance, 1244; Thos., 641, 1245*, 1258; Wm., 130, 641; Mrs., 1126, 1202; fam., 365*, 1255; *and see* Crupes

Crisp (Crispe), Eliz., 840*; Ellis, 839*; Geo., 840; Mary, 840*; Nic., 839*; Sir Nic., 358; Sam., 840*; Sarah, 840; Thos., 839, 840*; Capt., 806 n; fam., 839

Crispin, Milo, 1047*

Critchet, Ric., 325; fam., 798

Critchley, Hen., 1511

Crocker (Crokare, Croker, Crooker), Eliz., 731; John, 730, 1064, 1363; Rob. le, 1363; Thos., 731*; Wm., 729*; fam., 142

Crockett (Crokett), Eliz., 762; J., 1238; Martha, 762; Mary, 1236*; Ric., 762; Thos., 1236*

Croft (Crofte, Croftes), Agnes, 1148(?); Anne, 438; Edw., 224, 1223; Eliz., 1222*; Hen., 1222*; Sir Herb., bt., bishop, 1369; Hugh, 1148; Jane, 220, 224; Jonathan, 1307; Leon, 1148(?); Lyonell, 1223; Rev. Phil. de, 221; Ric. (de), 1051, 1222*, 1223*; Wm., 1222; —, 1223*

Crokare, *see* Crocker

Croke, *see* Crook

Croker, *see* Crocker

Crokett, *see* Crockett

Crom, *see* Croome

Cromie, Lady, 1494

Cromp (Crompe), *see* Crump

Crompton (Crumpton), John, 1257; Mary, 1353; Thos., 1059*, 1062; —, 1062*, 1064

Cromwell, Anne, baroness Cromwell, 721 n; Cath., countess of Ardglass, 723; Lady Eliz., 719 n*, 721 n, 723, 724; Oliver (Lord General), 507 n, 864 n, 915, 1233, 1322, 1362, 1477, 1516; Sir Oliver, 1101; Ric., 719 n, 1322*; Sir Ric., 719 n; Thos., 1538; Thos., earl of Ardglass, 719 n; Thos., earl of Essex, 719 n*, 721 n, 723, 885, 1148; Vere Essex, earl of Ardglass, 723; Wingfield, earl of Ardglass, 719 n; —, 119, 349 n, 476, 518 n, 1322*

Crondall, Rev. Nic., 1289

Crones, Rev. Lewis, 853

Cronnoke, John, 1540

Crook (Croke, Croocks), Eleanor, 1445; Edy, 949; Eliz., 1550; Hen., 1584; John, 591, 1250, 1445; Mary, 949, 1445, 1584; Peter, 1550*; Rachel, 1445*; Rob., 1445*; Thos., 1132, 1445*; Wm., 949*, 1232

Crooker, *see* Crocker

Croome (Crom, Croom), Ann(e), 181, 386*, 456, 1342; Chas., 456; Eliz., 165, 751*; Hannah, 537; Jas., 165, 171*, 386*, 751, 1213, 1217; Jas. Fielder, 1132*; Jane, 171, 386; John, 171*, 308, 456*, 537, 751*, 752, 1132, 1331; Joseph, 456; Marg., 1570; Martha, 386*; Mary, 171*, 308, 456, 752, 1182*, 1536; Millicent, 181*; Rachel, 386; Ric., 171*, 456; Rob., 386*, 1536; Sam., 181*; Sarah, 171, 181*, 751*, 752; Thos., 171, 181*, 1182; Uzzell, 1342*; Wm., 456; Mr., 1292; —, 1082, 1342; fam., 159

Cropp, Marg., 5; Ric., 5*

Crosby, Constant, 1298; Wm., 1298

Cross (Crosse, Croyce), Ann(e), 706*, 1111, 1117; Ant., 1152*; Ant. Dix, 1152; Chas., 965; Edw., 1127; Charlotte, 1415; Eliz., 73, 466*; Eunice, 1068; Francis, 1111*; Hannah, 1484; J., 1312; Jas., 1411; John (atte), 633, 884, 1013, 1228, 1415*, 1502; Dr. John, 1146; Mary, 633, 706, 1013, 1152*; Nic., 1484*, 1485; Ric., 815; Rob. (atte), 1068, 1491; Sarah, 706, 815, 1415; Sophia, 466; Thos., 425, 706*, 1117; Wm. (atte), 466*, 706, 815, 1314; —, 1017, 1195
Crossley, Eliz., 446; Martha, 387; Rev. Rob., 446; Thos., 387*
Crossman, Ann, 48*; Eliz., 48; Geo., 48; Hannah, 731; John, 48*; Joyce, 48; Mark, 48; Thos., 731
Croucher, Jane, 496; Mary, 496*; Ric. David, 496; Rob., 496*
Crouder (Croudar, Crowder), Eliz., 48; J., 1312; Rees, 1314; Thos., 48; and see Crowther
Crowse, Ric., 1372
Crowther, Anne, 1144, 1146, 1297*; Cath., 1144; Eliz., 1297*; John, 16*, 1146*, 1297*; Rev. John, 503, 504; Marg., 16, 1144; Nat., 50, 1297, 1551; Ric., 1297; Thos., 1144; —, 1311; fam., 12; and see Crouder
Croy, John 1477
Croyce, see Cross
Crozier, Thos., 1216
Cruger (Crucer)(later Peach), Sam. Peach, 619
Crumbe, Rob., 1168
Crump (Cromp, Crompe, Crumpe), Alice, 1432; Anne, 812, 1432; Ant., 321*, 1432*; Bridget, 1467; D., 1440; Dan., 1439; Edith, 1010; Eliz., 176, 450, 873*, 1269, 1282, 1397, 1399*; Esther, 321; Francis, 353, 1397, 1403; Hannah, 958*; 963; Hester, 321; Rev. Jas., 1217; Jane, 1432; Joan, 1432; John, 176, 275, 812, 1432*; Marg., 810, 1467*; Martha, 812; Mary, 353, 800, 812; Nat., 1048; Ralph, 800; Ric., 812, 873; Rob., 958*; Sara(h), 198, 1168*, 1432; Susannah, 870; Thos., 450, 808, 810, 812*, 958*, 963, 1168*, 1269*, 1397, 1398, 1399, 1432*; Wm., 583, 958, 1010, 1269, 1432, 1467; Rev. Wm., 493; —, 1403
Crumpton, see Crompton
Crupes, Edm. de, 1061; Rob. de, 1474; (or Scrupes), W. de, 1475; and see Cripps
Cruste, Sibilla, 1379; Wm., 1379
Cryer, John, 1086
Cryklade, Ric., 1288
Cubberley, see Coberley
Cudd, Edw., 818
Cuff (Cuffe), Cath., 1052; Eliz., 765*; Jane, 1408; John, 765*, 1052, 1408*; Sarah, 765; Thos., 1408
Cuggel, Cristin, 1317
Culey, Rev. Ric., 221
Cull, Ann, 74, 976; Cath., 62; Dan., 543; Eliz., 332, 506, 1334; Esther, 975; Geo., 975, 976; Guy, 64*; John, 74, 97, 506, 543, 1473*, 1474, 1477, 1542*; Jonathan, 567; Marg., 1474; Martha, 450, 1542; Mary, 64, 339*, 399, 543*, 567, 976, 1473; Ric., 339*, 399; Rob., 62, 1473; Stephen, 450*; Rev. Stephen, 332; Susannah, 567; Thos., 97; Wm., 62*, 1473, 1474, 1542

Cullabine, see Collabine
Cullam, Ann, 797
Cullen (Colen, Cullinge), Abigail, 220 n; Sir Abr., 220 n; Joseph, 376; Matilda, 1102; Mary, 376, 1066; Sir R., 1227; Sir Rushout, bt., 1066; and see Cullurne
Culliforde, Eliz., 955; Stephen, 955*
Cullimore (Colimor, Colmor, Colymore), Ann(e), 1300, 1327*, 1343*; Betty, 963*, 1343; Edith, 1107; Eliz., 730*, 1306*, 1327, 1343*, 1345, 1454; Grace, 730; Hannah, 963, 1304*, 1343, 1454; Hen., 1327*; Hester, 1327*, 1343, 1345; Jas., 730, 1304*, 1306*, 1327*, 1343*; Johanna, 1343; John, 1300, 1304*, 1307, 1314, 1327*, 1343*; Joseph, 308, 1177, 1343*, 1345*, 1454; Judith, 1327*; Mary, 308, 1300*, 1327, 1343; Maty, 1327; Peter, 730; Ric., 1107; Rob., 730; Rev. Rob., 613; Sarah, 730, 1306, 1327, 1343*; Thos., 1343; Unity, 1327; Wm., 963*, 1306, 1327*, 1343*; —, 1020, 1121, 1311, 1346, 1455; fam., 305
Cullinge, see Cullen
Cullis, Eleanor, 1353*; Geo., 1353; Rosement, 1353; Sam., 1353*; T., 1054; Thos., 1353; Wm., 1353; —, 1054
Cullurne, Betty, 1384; Wm., 1384*; and see Cullen
Culne, Wm. atte, 1502; and see Colne
Culpepper (Colepeper, Colepepper), Alex., 688; Marg., 875 n, 880; Ric., 688; Thos., 688; Wal., 875 n, 880; —, 1477
Culter, Simon, 250
Culton (or Wootton), Ralph, 768
Cumberland, Rev. Ric. Den(n)ison, 515, 678; Susannah Willett, 1147*
Cumberland [peerage], Geo., earl of, 721 n; Hen., earl of, 721 n; earls of, 618; and see Clifford, Geo.
Cumbersome (Cumbersum), Mary, 686; Wm., 686, 1355
Cummins (Commins, Comyn, Cuming, Cumings, Cummin, Cummings), Sir Alex., 1428; Ann, 549*, 1415; Charlotte, 965; Edw., 348; Eliz., 550, 885, 1428; Hen., 1112; Jas., 965*; Joan, 885; John, 348, 885, 1395; Joseph, 550; Mary, 906, 965*, 1395; Susannah, 1112; Thos., 448, 549; —, 1512
Cumper, see Compere
Cundicote, Laur. de, 1228
Cuningham, Glencaere Gun, 1490; Rachel, 1490
Cupitt (Cupett), Jas., 111*; Milborough, 110; Ric., 110; Thos., 111; Wm., 110, 111*
Curll, see Kyrle
Curnock, see Cornock
Currier (Curryer), Anne, 315; Wal., 315; Wm., 1390
Curry, Francis, 1534; Millecent, 1534
Curryer, see Currier
Curtis (Cortis, Curtes, Curteys, Curthoys, Curtice, Curties), Ann(e), 247, 254, 666, 904, 974; Clara, 567; Dan., 615, 1527; Edith, 1157; Eleanor, 567; Eliz., 446, 543, 640, 862, 1468; Francis, 542, 543; Fred., 1527; Geo., 446, 567; Giles, 320*;

Hen., 254, 862; J., 1291; Jane, 433, 615; Joanna, 1574*; John, 143, 446*, 567, 601, 962*, 974, 1172, 1273, 1574; Jona [sic], 262; Joseph, 666; Kath., 542; Mary, 143, 320, 542, 567, 601, 884; Matillda, 1314, 1379; Nic., 962; Rebekah, 962; Ric., 433, 446, 567, 758; Rev. Ric., 1031, 1290; Rob., 854; Sam., 1193; Sarah, 262, 1273, 1574; Thos., 28, 247, 542, 543, 700, 862, 1527; Wm., 446, 884, 904, 1157, 1467, 1468, 1554, 1574; —, 1476

Curwen, Wm., 395

Custans (Cowstans), Geo., 606; Mary, 933

Cute, see Cutts

Cuthbert, Rev. And., 963*; John, 1282; Rachel, 963*

Cutler, Sir Thos., kt., 793, 1189

Cutt, see Cutts

Cutter, Ambrose, 735; Eliz., 735

Cutts (Cute, Cutt), Hannah, 284; Jas., 736*; Jonathan, 284*; Mary, 284; Sam., 284; Thos., 736; Wm., 301*; —, 1017

Cvenild the monk, 889

Cwichelm son of Penda, 649

Cynegils son of Penda, 649

Dabat, John, 1519

D'abernon, —, 1237

D'Abitot (Dabetot, Dabitott), Eliz., 977; Emmeline, 1447; Giles, 977; Ric., 1434; Rob., 1447; Urso, 1055, 1119, 1447*; —, 1055

Dacre, Isabella, 1169; —, 1169

Dacres, Ann, 1226; Arabella Boyd, 1245; Lieut. Hew Dalrymple, 1245; Cmdr. Jas. Ric., 1245; Vice-Admiral Jas. Ric., 1245; Capt., 1245

Dadge (Dage), Ann, 575; Benj., 575; Jas., 575; Joseph, 772; Mary, 575, 772; Wm., 953

Dadley (Dadlee), John, 1074; Thos., 1074

Dafter, Mary, 211; Thos., 211

Dage, see Dadge

Dahl, —, 393 n, 719 n; and see Dale

Daie, see Day

Dainty, Wm., 284

Dake, Hen., 1154; and see Darke

D'Albini, see Daubeney

Dalby, Israel, 1050; Jaques, 938; Jas., 1241*, 1243*; Jane, 1241*, 1243, 1245; John, 1363; Mary, 1050, 1241; Ric., 882

Dale, Ann, 250, 1008; Deborah, 1143–4; Edw., 250*; Eliz., 250, 999, 1144; John, 250*; Mat., 999; Maudilin, 250; Thos., 250*, 1008, 1143, 1144, 1146; and see Dahl

Dallaway, Eliza, 657; Jas., 657, 1216; Rev. Jas., 1216; John, 656, 1216; Martha, 657; Rebecca, 656; Rob., 656; W., 1216; Wm., 657, 1216; —, 1027, 1203; fam., 1216

Dalne, Gil., 1313

Dalrymple, Arabella Boyd, 1245; Gen. Sir Hew, 1245

Dalton, Rev. Isaac, 56; Rev. Jas., 1369; Ric., 801; Sophia, 801

Dalyngrich, John, 1221

Damalisaundre, Thos., 1351

Damarey, see Dimery

Dame, Ann, 1446; John, 1446*; Ric., 1150

Damedyth, Rob., 1150

Damford, Sam., 661; Sarah, 661; and see Danford

Dammarie, see Dimery

Dammesele, see Damsell

Damport, Rev. Thos., 1441

Damsell (Dammesele, Damzel), Ann, 203*; Eliz., 203; John 543; Margery, 543; Sam., 203*; Thos., 369, 1420; and see Dansell

Danbuey, Rev. Jas., 1202

Danby, earl of, 363, 365; Lord, 363; and see Danvers, Hen. and —

Dance (Daunce), Adam, 587; Anne, 1386, 1475; Eliz., 587, 1153, 1466; Hannah, 587; John, 587, 1361; Mary, 1361, 1468; Phil., 587*; Ric., 1386, 1465, 1466, 1468, 1475*; Sarah, 1361; Thos., 1361*; Wm., 1153, 1446; —, 1477; fam., 1475

Dancer (Daunsare, Dawnser), Hen. le, 1379; J. Ric., 708 n; John (le), 1379, 1484*; Rebekah, 254; Ric., 254; Susanna, 1484

Dancey (Dancy, Dansey, Daunsey, Daunsy), Amos, 1072; Ann, 1481; Arthur, 171, 175; Cath., 1077; Christian, 1525; Geo., 1369; Joan, 1072; John, 1077, 1481*, 1525*, 1539; John Thos., 108; Martha, 175; Rose, 1350; S. G., 1539; Sam., 1350; Sarah, 171, 175; —, 1078

Dando, Eliz., 1427; Jas., 1427; Jane, 836; John, 542*; Martha, 542; Stephen, 542, 836; Susanna, 542*

Dandy, Joan, 1034; Thos., 1034

Dane, Gil. de, 1172; and see Dean; Denn

Danell, see Daniel

Danet, Sir John, 870

Danford, Abraham, 538; Betty, 683; Isaac, 532; Jonathan, 662; Mary, 538; Wm., 683; and see Damford

Dangerfield, Ann, 777; Brigitte, 1467; Cath., 1187; Dan., 418, 419*, 777; Eliz., 419*, 659; Fulke, 1467; Geo., 1131*, 1511; Harriett, 1511; Joan, 1186; Joannah, 661; Joseph, 659, 661; Marg., 1467; Mary, 339, 419, 1131*; Nic., 531*, 1131*; R., 1187; Sam., 1147; Susannah, 418; Thos., 419*, 1187, 1214; Wm., 1511, 1540*; Mr., 985; fam., 415, 885

Daniel (Danell, Daniell, Daniells), Deborah, 661*; Eliz., 1088; Evan, 1582; Geo., 1046, 1047; Rev. H., 1228; Hen., 1158; Rev. Hen., 221; Jas., 1046; Joan, 1046; John, 1046; Margerie, 573; Mary, 1158*; Nat., 1046; Noble, 1046; Ric., 1323; Rob., 573, 873, 1088*; Sarah, 661, 1046; Silvester, 873; Thos., 660, 661*, 911, 1123, 1197, 1217; Wal., 1186; Wm., 573, 1157, 1158*

Danis, Dan., 387

Dankes, Honor, 1327; Ric., 1327

Dansell, Alice, 1249; Dan., 1249*; Eliz., 1249; Hannah, 1249*; Wm., 1249*; and see Damsell

Dansey, see Dancey

Danvers (D'Anvers), Arabella, 1040; Chas., 363, 364; Dorothy, 867; Eliz., 257, 258, 508 n, 1040, 1226; Hen., earl of Danby, 361; John, 257, 258, 348; Sir John, 363, 508 n; Ric., 348; Rev. Wm.,

1040; Sir Wm., 348; Lord, 368; —, 1082; —, earl of Danby, 1082

Daper, Nic. le, 1238

Darby (Darbie, Derby), Arab[ella], 727; Rev. Arthur, 722, 727; Cath., 296*; Eliz., 409; Hen., 296*; John, 296*, 409, 727; Mary, 295; Ralph, 740; Ric., 295; Sarah, 296

Darby [peerage], see Derby

Darcy, Sir A., 1313

Darch, Sam., 986; and see Darke

Darell (Dayrell), Rev. David, 1362; Lionel, 430; Mary, 572; Wal., 572

Darke (Darck), Abraham, 1473; Anne, 966; Edw., 1289; Eliz., 966, 1273; Rev. H., 1504; Hester, 984; J., 1348; John, 984, 986, 1387*; Capt. John, 1466*; Rev. John, 72, 1387; Marg., 73, 1466; Mary, 73; R., 1348, 1387; Rev. R., 1387; Ric., 73*, 966, 1387; Rev. Ric., 1386, 1387; Sarah, 984; Rev. Thos., 635; Wm., 1273*; —, 986; and see Dake; Darch

Darling, Ant., 1318*, 1319; Ric., 1318; Susanna, 1318, 1319; fam., 1323; and see Dearlin

Darly, Rev. Geo., 432

Darston, see Daston

Dart, Arthur, 1576; Betty, 175; Giles, 175; Hannah, 175; Mary, 1576; Thos., 413

Dartiquenave, Chas., 408; Mary, 408

Darwell, Cath., 1303; Cornelius, 1303; Rev. F. L., 1303; Rev. Geo., 1303

Dary, Jane, 454

Dashwood, Cath., 697; Sir Rob., bt., 697

Dassett, Edm., 1012; Eliz., 1012; Jane, 1012; Thos., 1012; —, 1017

Daston (Darston, Dastin, Dastyn), Anne, 521, 1517; Ant., 744, 1335*, 1518*; Cath., 1517; Eleanor, 1517; Geo., 743 n; John, 521, 1104, 1501, 1517; Margerie, 518; Rev. Oliver, 519; R., 1104; Ric., 1021, 1478, 1517; Rob., 518, 1519; Thos., 1519; Wm., 521, 743 n; —, 1518; fam., 519, 743, 1519

Datcheler, Adrian, 1265

Daubeney (D'Albini, Daubeny, Dawbney), Ann, 1199; And., 721, 1199; Conan, 765; Elias, 851; Ellinor, 1200; Florencia, 765; Geo., 39; Giles, 1411; Helen Mary, 1200; Rev. J., 1220; Jas., 1200; Rev. Jas., 989, 1199, 1200, 1221; (or de Todeni), Joan, 1014; John, 613*, 990; Mary, 1411, 1417; W., 990; (or de Todeni), Wm., 1014, 1050, 1051; —, 1082

Daubeney [peerage](D'Aubeney), Giles, baron, 612; Giles, Lord, 1047; Hen., Lord, earl of Bridgewater, 1047

Daunce, see Dance

Dauncey, see Dancey

D'Aungier (or Hanger), John, 515

Daunsare, see Dancer

Daunsy, see Dancey

Daunt (Daunte), Achilles, 959; Alice, 959; Chris., 959, 960*; Dorothy, 1373; Eliz., 959; Frances, 1373; Geo., 959; Gyles, 1187; Hannah, 959*; Hen., 1373; John, 959*, 960*; Rev. Kingscote, 959; Mildred, 959; Thos., 959*, 960; —, 1311

Dautry (Dawtry), Blanch, 763; Sir Francis, kt., 763; —, 1015

Dauvert, Rev. Ant., 272

Dauwe, see Dawe

Dauy, see Davy

Davenport (Devenport), Rev. Chas., 1390; Rev. David, 1392; Rev. Jas., 1390, 1392; Sam., 1065*

Daves (Davers), see Davis

David, Rev. John, 829; —, 1017; and see Apdavid

Davidson, Barnard, 1238; Eliz., 812; Grace, 1065; John, 1065; and see Davison

Davie, see Davy

Davis (Davers, Daves, Davies, Davyes, Davys), Abraham, 615*; Alice, 768, 997, 1195; Ann Susannah, 1323; Anna Maria, 1096; Anne, 10, 48, 84, 204, 337, 431*, 446, 489*, 491, 541, 703, 741, 749*, 922, 1081*, 1096*, 1097*, 1118, 1200, 1244, 1360, 1582; Barbara, 192; Betty, 616*; Catorn [sic], 146; Rev. Chas. Greenall, 1290; Comfort, 550*; Dan., 204, 446, 460, 657, 749, 1081; Dan. Drayton, 1118; Dan. Holborow, 1118; David, 931*, 1026, 1583*; Debor(i)ah, 1096, 1097, 1583; Dinah, 616; Dorothy, 353, 974; Rev. Duncomb Pyrke, 190; Eamey, 460; Edith, 633; Edm., 524; Edw., 124, 490, 491*, 797, 967, 1096*, 1227; Rev. Edw., 1486, 1487, 1489, 1490; Eleanor, 211, 1026; Eliz., 52*, 84, 248, 283*, 296, 431, 460, 491*, 614*, 622, 624, 653*, 772, 844, 873, 883, 963, 967, 1129, 1210, 1514; Eliz. Bluett, 1327; Ezza, 847; Frances, 472, 1323; Francis, 1258; Geo., 408, 492, 907, 1320, 1323, 1505; Giles (Gyles), 814, 1218; Grace, 1095; Halison, 1499; Halliday, 450; Hannah, 284, 490, 563, 702, 1037, 1401, 1425; Harri, 665; Harriett, 1185; Harriette Sarah, 1247; Harrington, 211; Hen., 614*, 1096, 1140, 1258, 1582; Hester, 622, 624, 1138, 1375; Isaac, 84*, 563, 1186, 1555; J., 1101; Rev. J., 1289; J. Lloyd, 1327; Jacob, 1138, 1499*; Jas., 245, 304, 491, 730, 815, 1129, 1320, 1323; Rev. Jas., 247*, 248; Jane, 247, 431, 815*, 967, 996, 1038, 1067, 1096, 1097; Jane Ann, 1185*; Rev. Jeremiah, 63; Joane, 1320; Joanna, 1062*; John, 90, 174, 190, 283*, 337, 431*, 437, 489, 550, 563, 616*, 633, 703*, 768, 797, 800, 815*, 844, 862, 1013*, 1038, 1096*, 1098, 1118*, 1159, 1210*, 1217, 1307, 1323, 1425, 1514; Rev. John, 7, 85, 802*, 1422, 1428; Jonas, 1096; Joseph, 431, 844*, 922; Joyce (Joice), 431, 931; Judith, 622, 741; Lewis, 963; Louisa, 1185*; Marg., 489*, 923; Mark, 1420; Martha, 52, 84, 211, 450, 700, 1323, 1499*; Mary, 10*, 52*, 84, 174, 408, 437, 491, 564, 578*, 615*, 657, 702, 749, 768, 814, 920, 981, 1013, 1024, 1096, 1097, 1106, 1185*, 1324, 1425, 1499, 1574; Mary Emma, 1185*; Morgan, 700; Nat., 749, 1217; Nic., 1583; Phil., 1160, 1172, 1300; Phillis, 797; Priscilla, 964; R., 1345; Rachel, 304; Rebekah, 296; Ric., 192, 211*, 240, 353, 489*, 622, 624*, 967*, 1024, 1425; Rev. Ric., 85, 748, 1239, 1257; Rob., 974, 1095, 1096*, 1106; Sir Rob., 997; Rob. S., 1185; Rob. Spry, 1185; Rob. Stephens, 1185*; Rog., 296*;

Rose, 703; Ruth, 703; Sabina, 64; Sacheverel, 1038; Sam., 491, 749, 981, 1324*; Sarah, 211, 284, 550, 652*, 703*, 749*, 812, 847, 1096*, 1097*, 1138, 1159, 1300, 1489, 1490; Simon, 1330; Stanfield, 1027; Stephen, 296, 1096; Susanna(h), 550, 614*, 815, 1096; Thos., 10*, 48, 52*, 54*, 97, 283, 296, 437, 472, 564, 578*, 616*, 622*, 624, 633, 652, 653, 702, 741, 748, 749*, 812, 815*, 883, 920, 924, 996, 1081*, 1096*, 1097*, 1200, 1244, 1375*, 1401; Capt. Thos., 759 n; Rev. Thos., 53, 524, 613, 793, 1177, 1348, 1371, 1372, 1516; Thos. Smith, 578; Vincent, 772; W., 1499; Rev. W., 1102; Web., 1312; Wm., 64, 284, 304*, 353, 490, 550*, 660, 703, 741, 797, 814*, 815, 862, 873, 923, 924*, 978, 1095*, 1096*, 1097*, 1138*, 1360, 1419; Rev. Wm., 1, 66, 483, 559, 904, 964, 976, 1019, 1020, 1096, 1097*, 1177; Messrs., 1186*; Mrs., 1001; —, 438, 1015, 1020, 1122, 1195, 1312, 1328, 1363, 1476; fam., 745, 1101

Davison, Ann(e), 1346, 1347; Eliz., 1347*; Hannah, 1347*, 1348; John, 339; Ric., 1346, 1347*, 1348*, 1359; Sarah, 339*; Thos., 1272; Wm., 1347*, 1348; and see Davidson

Davy (Dauy, Davie), G., 1331; Hugh, 1420; John, 1329, 1382; Rev. John, 42, 603, 722, 725; Sir John, bt., 725; Juliana, 1404; Nic., 1382; Ric., 1061; Rob., 1351; Rog., 1552; Wm., 725

Davys (Davyes), see Davis

Daw, see Dawe

Dawbney, see Daubeney

Dawe (Dauwe, Daw, Dawes, Daws, Door, Dore), Ann(e), 991, 1098, 1297, 1526; Dame Anne, 1521; Bridget, 962; Caleb, 1100; Cecilia, 730; Chas., 1100; Eliz., 10*, 543*, 962*, 991; Geo., 10, 632*, 1100; Hannah, 632, 1098; Hen., 10*; Hester, 623, 730; Jas., 632*; Jane, 991; John, 730, 836, 1069, 1216; Jonathan, 687; Sir Jonathan, kt., 739, 1521*; Lydia, 1526*; M., 411; Marg., 632; Mary, 730, 991*, 1100, 1521; Peter, 1297; Ric., 687, 991*, 1526; Rob., 821, 1521*, 1526, 1531, 1532; Sam., 623*, 1531; Sarah, 623, 632*, 836, 1533; Thos., 543*, 1521*, 1522*, 1526*, 1533, 1538; W., 1100; Wm., 632*, 730, 962*, 991*, 1098; —, 1455, 1532; fam., 255, 890

Dawkes, Marg., 339

Dawkins, Grace, 1110; Hen., 1110

Dawnay (Dawney), Rev. Hen., 56; Sir Hen. Pleydell, bt., Viscount Downe, 58; John, 364*

Dawnser, see Dancer

Daws, see Dawe

Dawson, Hester, 225; John, 225, 708 n; Letticia, 225; and see Doweson

Dawtry, see Dautry

Day (Daie), Ann(e), 133, 797, 849, 1081; Bart., 797; Bridget, 659; Dan., 660*; Edw., 1075; Eleanor, 138; Eliz., 52, 186, 797, 948*, 1560; Geo., 623; Hen., 431; Jas., 814, 957, 1081*; Jeremiah, 659*; John, 45*, 138, 369, 660, 797, 862, 948*, 957*, 1121; Rev. John, 1147; Margery, 660; Martha, 948*; Mary, 45, 138, 385, 431, 433, 656, 957, 1081; Pat., 1560; Paul, 957;

Ric., 138*; Rev. Ric., 848, 849; Richmond, 385; Sarah, 653, 796, 797, 957*, 1075; Thos., 133*, 138*, 433, 797, 1362; Sir Thos., kt., 405; Wm., 186, 321, 644, 796, 797, 948*, 1081, 1217; Rev. Wm., 1081; Rev. Mr., 1217; —, 1140, 1386

Dayare, Wal., 1292

Dayrell, see Darell

de la Bere, see Delabere

de la Fontaine, see Fontaine

de la Mare (de la Mere, de la More), see Delamere

de la Pole, see Pole

de la River (de Rivere, de la Rivers, de la Riviere, de la Riviers), see Rivers

de la Warr, see Delaware; Warr

De Visme, Mr., 1372

De Winton (or Wilkins), Wal., 1047; (formerly Wilkins), Rev. Wal., 1046

Deacon (Deakins, Deckins), Ann, 368, 378, 710; Eliz., 368; Esther, 1241; Joseph, 741; Lucy, 1334; Margery, 377, 1201; Mary, 741, 1241*; Ric., 710; Rob., 1334; Sam., 710; Simon (Symon), 368, 1201; T., 1256; Thos., 368, 377*, 378, 1080, 1201*, 1241*, 1256; W., 1256; Wal. the, 1055*; —, 1256; fam., 1201; and see Dickens

Dean (Deane, Dene), Anne, 642, 653, 1046, 1084, 1085; Capt. Chas. Meredith, 1085; Clutterbuck, 653; Dan., 176; Devereaux, 1046*; Eleanor, 1046; Eliz., 656; Eliz. Anne, 1085; Giles, 1075; Rev. H., 886; Hen., 1084, 1085; Hugh de, 618; Rev. J., 1460; Jane, 627; Geof. de la, 1035; Jeremiah, 1157; John (in la, le), 654, 656, 1005, 1197; Rev. Kenelm, 630, 1104*; Marg. (de), 1157, 1217; Mary, 639, 1046; Naomi, 641; Ralph, 1530; Ric., 708 n; Rog. de, 1217, 1351; Sarah, 653, 654, 1508; Thos., 635, 639, 641, 1085, 1508; Thos. Plummer, 1511; Rev. W., 627; Wm., 1046; Rev. Wm., 263, 626; Rev. Mr., 627; —, 1087, 1214; fam., 462; and see Adeane; Dane; Denn

Deanes, Sir Wm., 839

Dearing (Deering, Dering), Sir Edw., bt., 719 n, 723, 724; Eliz., 719 n, 723, 724; Frances, 1298; Francis, 1298; John, 841; Dame Mary, 724; Wal., 778

Dearlin, John, 1582; and see Darling

Dearlove, Mary, 1377

Deaves, —, 1387

Dechair, Rev. Dr., 1013, 1016, 1017

Deckins, see Deacon

Dee, John 906; King, 338; Sarah, 338, 906

Deedes, Cath., 1091

Deerhurst (Deorhyrste), Eliz. de, 664 n; Thos. de, 664 n; Viscount, see Coventry [peerage], Geo.; fam., 664 n

Deering, see Dearing

Deffield, John, abbot, 259

Degge, Dorothy, 98; Rev. Staunton, 98, 1139

Deighton (Dighton), Abraham, 380; Ann Maria, 1511; Francis Keyte, 400; Hannah, 561; Hen., 401; Job, 400; John, 1211; Lister, 400, 401; Mary, 388*; Nat., 388*; Ric., 400; Rev. Ric.,

400; Susanna, 1211; Thos., 380, 388; Wm., 561*;
  Rev. Wm., 559, 574
Delabere (de la Bere, Delaber), Ann(e), 333, 982,
  986; Eliz., 982; Ellen, 392; Grace, 982; Hester,
  393 n; (formerly Baghott), Hester, 986; Rev. J.
  Baghott, 114; Joan, 393 n; Joanna, 1206; John,
  323 n, 324, 325*, 333, 393 n, 394, 982, 986,
  1206; John, bishop, 392 n, 852 n; Rev. John, 135,
  313, 424; Rev. John Baghott, 519; Kinard, 392*,
  393 n*, 394, 395 n, 986; Marg., 395 n; R., 393 n;
  Sir R., 392 n; Ric., 392*, 395 n; Sir Ric., 325 n*;
  T. B., 986; Thos. Baghot(t), 195, 198, 394, 1215;
  Wm. Baghot(t), 519, 986*; —, 982, 1159, 1504;
  fam., 325 n, 392, 393 n
Delahay, Marg., 921; Wm., 920; and see Hay;
  Hayes
Delamere (de la Mare, de la Mere, de la More,
  Delamer, Delamore), Agnes, 1317; Anne, 902;
  Ciceley, 527; Geof., 1011; John, 902, 905, 1482,
  1502; Sir John, 527; Sir John, kt., 646; Maud,
  646; Peter, 1032; Petronella, 889; Rob., 778 n;
  Rog., 1093; Thos., 1091, 1093; Wm., 482 n,
  1011*, 1447; —, 1011; fam., 341, 646, 1011*
Delaware (de la Warr), Lady, 827 n, 913, 1388
Delawell, Hen., 598; Jane, 598
Deleau, Anne, 1057; John, 1057
Delmont, Lieut. Joseph Francis, 1214
Demery, see Dimery
Dena (fl. 11th cent.), 420
Denbigh, Wm., earl of, 291
Dene, see Dean
Dening, see Denning
Denly, Joseph, 1075; —, 1064
Denman, Chas., 204
Denmark, Anne of, 720 n
Denn, Ann, 677; Jane, 677; Ric., 677; and see
  Dane; Dean
Denning (Dening, Dennyng), Anne, 456; Chris.,
  456; Hester, 174; John, 174; Mary, 496; Sarah,
  174*, 496; Thos., 174*; —, 1101; and see Dining
Dennis (Dennys, Denys, Deruys, Derys), Alice,
  997*, 1491; Alicia, 997; Anne, 997; Dame Anne,
  551*, 552; Cath., 997*; Cecilia (Cicelia), 582,
  997; Cornelius, 405; Dorothy, 995, 997*; Edw.,
  553; Eleanor, 997; Eliz., 997*; Fortune, 997;
  Francis, 1165; Sir Gil., kt., 552*, 961, 997; Hen.,
  995*, 997*, 1428; Hugh, 995, 997, 1428, 1538,
  1539; Hugo, 997; Joan, 995, 997; Joanna, 997;
  John, 582, 995*, 997*, 1428*, 1456; Kath., 595 n,
  995, 997; Marg., 552, 995, 997*, 1086; Mary,
  765, 995*, 997*; Maur. (Morys), 552, 961*,
  997*, 1086, 1428; Sir Maur., kt., 997, 1159; Ric.,
  501, 552, 747, 997*; Rob., 765; Rog., 1456;
  Thos., 997*; W., 1491; Sir W., 1159; Wal., 997*,
  1087; Rev. Wal., 553; Sir Wal., kt., 552, 747,
  961, 997*, 1123, 1159, 1538, 1539; Wm., 595 n,
  995*, 997*, 1428*; Sir Wm., kt., 551*, 552*,
  553, 997*; Mr., 552*, 553; —, 1159; fam., 552*,
  748, 994, 997, 1428
Denny, Hannah, 1274; Mary, 1251, 1274; Nat.,
  1274; Wm., 1251
Dennyng, see Denning

Dennys, see Dennis
Dent, John, 1220*, 1221; John Coucher, 1220;
  Martin, 1221; Mary, 1221; Thos., 1221; Wm.,
  1220*, 1221; Messrs., 1220; Mrs., 1474; fam.,
  1220
Denton, J. J., 1091; Ric., 1186; Sam., 1050;
Denys, see Dennis
Deorhyrste, see Deerhurst
Depling, Ric., 1318
Derby, see Darby
Derby [peerage](Darby), Edw., earl of, 1296;
  Dorothy, countess of, 1296
Derham, see Durham
Dering, see Dearing
Derret, Mary, 262*; Wm., 262*
Derrick, Mary, 1159; Peter, 1159
Dersintone, see Dorsington
Deruys, see Dennis
Derwentwater, earl and countess of, see Radcliffe,
  Anna Maria and Jas.
Derys, see Dennis
Des Maistres, Jane, 1432; Sam., 1432
Descury, Eliz., 412; Col., 412
Despencer (de Spenc, de Spencer, De Spensator,
  Despenser), Adam (le), 798, 1139; Almaric,
  1139*; Edw., 1120, 1261, 1287*; Edw., Lord,
  1261; Eleanor (Elianor, Elinor), 591, 1082, 1120,
  1287; Eliz., 1120*, 1261; Gil. le, 482; Hugh (le),
  244, 251, 591, 769, 816 n, 876, 925, 1020,
  1082*, 1120*, 1287*, 1291; Hugh, Lord, 1261*;
  Isabel, 769, 1120, 1287; Isabella, countess of
  Warwick, 1261; Jeffrey, 876; Mary le, 1140; R.,
  1447; Ric., 1082, 1202, 1287; Rob., 1447, 1475;
  Thos., 1016, 1120, 1261*, 1287; Thos., earl of
  Gloucester, 357; Thos., Lord, 1082; Thurstan,
  1139; W., 1140; —, 1138, 1139; fam., 440, 588,
  690, 792, 1287; and see Spencer
D'Esterre, Laura Ann M., 1119*; Rob. Ker, 1119
Dethick (Dethek), Hen., 2; Wm., 1059
Dethridge, Ann, 1276; Thos., 1276
Deuenissh, Gil., 1314
Devalve, Rev. John, 221
Devenport, see Davenport
Deverell, Anne, 662; Dan., 308, 496, 1423, 1427*;
  Eliz., 1426*; Hannah, 496, 662*; Hester, 1426*;
  Joan, 749; John, 662*, 1488; Mary, 658;
  Susanna(h), 308, 662, 1427; Thos., 658*, 1426*,
  1427; Wm., 749
Devereux, Anne, 1237; Eliz., 544; Frances, 1332;
  Leicester, Viscount Hereford, 1332; Rob., earl of
  Essex, 1062 n, 1237*; Sir Wal., 544, 1237; Col.,
  928, 985
D'Everty (Deverty), Annora, 1039; T., 1039; Thos.
  (de), 244, 1039; —, 1039
Devonshier, Chris., 33
Devonshire, duke of, see Cavendish, Wm.
Devote, John 1441
Devys, Rev. Ric., 748
Dew (Dewe, Dewes), Anne, 333; Bernard, 333; Dan.,
  978; Eliz., 923, 978, 1162; Geo., 923*, 1162*;
  Hester, 934; John, 923*, 978; Mary, 1162; Wal.,
  978; Wm., 848, 934; —, 913, 1311; fam., 301

Dewguard, Wal., 1289
Dewxell, Ant., 1433; Marg., 1433
Dewy, Betty, 1112; Cath., 689; Jas., 1112; John, 1112; Marg., 1112; Wm., 689
Deyce, Rev. Hen., 820
Deyere, see Dyer
Deynton, Thos. de, 487, 488
Dibble, Anne, 1191; Thos., 1196; Rev. Thos., 1191, 1192, 1228, 1513
Dibdon, Hannah, 736; Isabel, 815; Morgan, 736; Solomon, 815; Wm., 736, 815
Dich (Diche), see Dyke
Dichewaya, Wm. le, 1218
Dickens (Dickins), Eliz., 951; Fred. Wm. Guy, 223; Hannah, 223; Melchior Guy, 223; Rev. Wm., 951; —, 1223; and see Deacon
Dickenson, Francis, 1016; John Vickeris, 839, 840; Rachel, 1499; Rev. Thos., 31; Wm., 1499
Dickes, see Dix
Dickham, Griffin, 1146
Dickins, see Dickens
Dicklesdon, see Dixton
Dickman, Eliz., 1031
Dicks, see Dix
Dier, see Dyer
Digby, Isabella Marg., 1160
Digger, Grace, 1194; Wm., 62, 1194
Digges (Diggs), Anne, 977; Sir D., 1290; Sir Dudley, 1293; Jane, 1353; John, 977, 978, 1353
Diggle, Ann, 1095; Rev. Edw., 1102; Dr., 1189
Diggs, see Digges
Dighton, see Deighton
Dike, see Dyke
Dillingham, Dorothy, 849; Thos., 849
Dillon, Eliz., 1327; John Talbot, 443 n; Mary, 413; Thos., 1327; —, 1288
Dilly, John, 431; Ric., 431; Sarah, 431
Dimery (Damarey, Dammarie, Demery, Dimorey, Dymere), Dan., 532, 1345, 1535*; Giles, 1385; Hen., 1532, 1539; John, 1532*; Martha, 1535; Mary, 1345, 1532*; Nic., 738; Sarah, 1532; Thos., 1345, 1532; Wal., 1043; Wm., 1345, 1551; —, 738, 1092
Dimock (Dimmock, Dimoc), see Dymock
Dimorey, see Dimery
Dinely, Barbara, 600; Edw., 438*; Eliz., 600; Rob., 600
Dinevor, see Dynevor
Dining, Anne, 1453; Mary, 1453; Thos., 1453; and see Denning
Dinwiddie, Rob., 408
Dipper, Ann(e), 484*, 1354; Eliz., 339, 1354; Hannah, 486; John, 1354, 1355; Joseph, 1353*, 1354; Joshua, 1352, 1353*, 1354*; Josiah, 1355; Mary, 1353*; Philippa, 486; Sam., 229; Sarah, 229, 1353, 1354; Thos., 339, 486; Wm., 484*, 486*
Disbon, Rev. Wm., 895
Diston (Dyston), Anne, 1465; Eliz., 1458; Giles, 257; Grace, 1065; (or Cockbill), J., 1227; John, 1465; Rev. John, 630; Josias, 1458; Mary, 257, 1458*; Rev. Oliver, 1228; Wm., 1065, 1227, 1333, 1334, 1458*; —, 1378

Dix (Dickes, Dicks), Ann, 182, 1200; Eliner, 174; Eliz., 182; Geo., 174*; Isaac, 344; Jane, 465; John, 1200; Mary, 344*; Rachel, 344; Sam., 465*; Thos., 182, 344; W., 1202; Wm., 1217
Dixon, Cath., 1427; Rev. Geo., 319; Isaac, 1427; Rev. Wm., 1121
Dixton (Dicklesdon), Edw., 367; Ric., 371; Rog. de, 1476
Dobbe, see Dobbs
Dobbins (Dobyns), Anna, 897; Ann(e), 151, 338, 1267, 1268; Ant., 641*; Benj., 47, 826*; Bridges [? Bridget], 897; Dan., 151*, 1043, 1473, 1477; Deborah, 270*, 993; Edw., 834*; Elinor, 897; Eliz., 28, 336, 338, 834, 897, 1334, 1361; Esther, 1262; Farmer, 1362; Frances, 1464; Grace, 854; Guy, 896, 897*; Hannah, 826; Hen., 854, 1262*, 1267*, 1268, 1288; Hester, 270, 897, 973, 1267*, 1268; J., 1148; Jas., 710*, 854; John, 73*, 336, 338*, 413, 895, 964*, 965, 1269*, 1277*, 1334*, 1420, 1464, 1476, 1477; Marg., 964*, 1275, 1517; Mary, 710, 950*, 964, 1043, 1267; Nat., 897; Nic., 338; Owen, 1361*; Phil., 897; Ralph, 893; Randall, 895; Ric., 28, 522, 950*; Rob. (Bobert), 267, 270*; (later Yate), Rob., 265; Dr. Rob., 993; Sam., 151, 896, 897*, 1267*, 1268, 1288; Sarah, 710, 1269, 1277*; Susanna(h), 413, 834*; Thos., 338, 1275, 1334, 1468, 1477; Rev. Thos., 1356; Wm., 519, 683*, 897*, 973*, 1361, 1446, 1464*, 1517*; —, 1043, 1148, 1288, 1475, 1519; fam., 265 n
Dobbs (Dobbe), Alex., 789; Alice, 1476; Ann, 762, 821*, 1216; Jas., 762, 1403; Jane, 821; Jo[a]ne, 821; John, 1216; Joseph, 550; Thos., 820, 821*; Wm., 354, 550, 821*; —, 1216, 1317*
Dober, John, 1363; Wm., 1292
Dobson, Rev. Bart., 689*
Dobyns, see Dobbins
Dockwray, Josias, 526; Rev. Josias, 525, 526; Rebecca, 526
Dodd (Dod, Dodds), Anne, 1389; John, 1363, 1392; Rev. Nat., 895; Owen, 337; Rog., 1483*; Wm., 1389
Dodding, D., 1093; Myles, 1475
Doddington, see Dodington
Doddridge, Anna Cecilia, 1292; Mary, 1292; Dr. Phil., 1292
Dodds, see Dodd
Dodebrugge, see Dudbridge
Dodenham, —, 1455*
Dodge, Edm., 1012; Edw., 792, 793; —, 1017
Dodington (Doddington), John, 568, 628; Sir Wm., kt., 628
Dodisham, Joan, 1160; Wm., 1160
Dodmer (Dudemor), John, 436; Rob., 436; Ric., 1428
Dodo (fl. c. 715)(Duddo), 1005*, 1153, 1285, 1287, 1291, 1481
Dodson, Mr., 985
Dodsworth, —, 157
Dodwell, Ann, 1063; Dame Anne, 1057*; Eliz., 1057; Jas., 818; Jas. Tredwell, 818; Leanna, 1349, 1350; Mary, 1064*, 1092, 1443; Dame

Mary, 1057*; P., 1064; Paul, 114, 503, 1057,
1063*, 1349; R., 1064; Ralph, 1063; Rev. Thos.,
817, 818*; W., 1063*, 1064*; Sir W., 114, 1064*,
1092; Wm., 1064*; Sir Wm., bt., 503, 890; Sir
Wm., kt., 1057*, 1063*, 1064, 1092, 1443

Doghead, Amy, 905; Isaac, 905

D'Oile (D'Oilgi, *see* Doyley

Dole, *see* Dowell

Doleman, *see* Dolman

Dolle, *see* Dowell

Dolling (Dollinge), Anne, 1115; Elias, 1423, 1424;
Jane, 1115; John, 1115*; Thos., 1552

Dolman (Doleman, Dowlman), Ann, 726; Eliz.,
1010; Geo., 1010; John, 1104; Rev. John, 726*;
Mat., 1104, 1149, 1150; Rebecca, 726*; Ric.,
1313; Sarah, 726; Thos., 1104*, 1149

Dolphin, Rev. John, 1043; Lucy Ann, 1090; Thos.
Vernon, 1090; Mr., 1093; Mrs., 1093; —, 1226*,
1362; fam., 1093

Donald, Helen, 1338; Capt. Jas., 1338

Done, *see* Dunn

Doning, *see* Dunning

Donnaldson, Rob., 413; Wm., 413

Donne, *see* Dunn

Donnynge, *see* Dunning

Donovan, Caroline Eliz., 1316; Caroline H., 1316;
Francis, 1316; Honoria, 1369; R., 1316*; Ric.,
1316*, 1369; Sarah Maria, 1316

Dooll, *see* Dowell

Door (Dore), *see* Daw

Doresewell, *see* Durswell

Dorington, *see* Dorrington

Dorman, Anne, 1046–7; John, 1046

Dormer, Cath., 330; Sir Fleetwood, kt., 325, 328,
330; Rev. John, 793

Dorne, Wm. de, 1017, 1259

Dorney, Alex., 1451*; Edw., 1365, 1368; Eliz.,
176, 1365, 1367, 1368, 1451; Hannah, 176*;
Hen., 1369*; J., 1538; Jane, 1451; Joseph, 176*,
1111*; Martha, 176*; R., 1369; Ric., 676; Rob.,
676; Sarah, 1109, 1451*; Thos., 176*, 676, 1369;
—, 1311, 1455; fam., 1369

Dorrell, Chris., 803*

Dorrington (Dorington), Ann, 1110; J. E., 1215;
John, 1110; Mary, 1110; Rebecca, 1110*; Sarah,
1110*; Thos., 1110*, 1121*; Wm., 1110*; Sir
Wm., 1434

Dorset, Jane, 139

Dorset [*peerage*], countess of, 827 n; *and see*
Beaufort, Edm. de; Clifford, Anne; Sackville,
passim

Dorsington (Dersintone), Adam de, 1431; Reg.,
1392

Dorwood (Dorwoode), Rev. Geo., 970*;
Nehe[miah], 970; Sarah, 970

Dotin, Eliz., 410; Joseph, 410

Douces, *see* Dukes

Doudin, *see* Dowding

Doughton, Rob. de, 1255

Doughty, *see* Dowty

Douglas, Anne, 249; Sir John, 249

Dounynge, *see* Dunning

Dove, Eliz., 1583

Dover, J. 1196; John, 287 n; Rob., 287; Wm. de,
1074; —, 1104

Dovey, Ann, 1046; John, 1193*; Martha, 1193;
Mary, 1046*; Thos., 486; Wm., 1046*

Dow (Dowe), Alex., 1531; Isaac, 1531; Jane, 1531;
—, 1074

Doward, Edw., 50 1303*; Mary, 924; Thos., 924

Dowdeswell, Ann(e), 610*, 1407*; Bridget, 440,
585, 586; Chas., 268, 609*, 610*, 1270, 1407*;
Eliz., 268. 610*, 641*, 1131, 1290*; Jane, 670;
John, 340, 641*; Joseph, 1130, 1131; Marg., 610;
Mary, 340, 641*, 1275; R., 1288; Ric., 585,
609*, 610*, 670*, 1270, 1293; Rob. de, 1474;
Sam., 641, 1131, 1132, 1186; T., 1064; Thos., 74,
228, 482, 483, 641, 689, 1064; Wm., 72, 440*,
565, 585, 641, 691; Rev. Wm., 1356; —, 1292;
fam., 565

Dowding (Doudin, Dowdin. Dowdyn), Eliz., 1396;
Geo., 388; Jas., 121; John, 1397. 1403; Mary,
881; Thos., 666, 881, 1397. 1403

Dowdy, Margery, 661; Rob. 661; Ric., 661*; Sarah,
661; Wm., 661

Dowe, *see* Dow

Dowell (Dole, Dolle, Dooll, Dowel, Dowle,
Dowlle), Alice, 204; Amy, 932; Anne, 931, 964;
Arthur, 176; Betty, 815; Chas., 584, 815; Edw.,
524; Eliz., 44*, 373, 1096; Giles, 298; Hannah,
176; Hester, 964; J. B. B., 1139; Jas., 204, 468*,
523, 964*; Job, 931; John, 42, 44, 46, 833, 1009;
John Baker, 44*, 1139; John Bridges Baker, 44*,
1139; Judith, 204; Mary, 44, 298, 524, 964;
Oliver, 523, 524*; Ric., 46, 49, 932; Sarah, 468*,
524, 584, 931, 931; Thos., 49, 204, 964*, 1096*,
1161, 1162; Rev. Thos., 1177; Wm., 584; fam.,
833

Dower, John, 854; Mary, 854; Priscilla, 854*; Wm.,
854*

Doweson, Rev. Thos., 184; *and see* Dawson

Dowfield, Rev. J., 1384

Dowle, *see* Dowell

Dowler, Edw., 898; John Gwatkin, 1515

Dowlle, *see* Dowell

Dowlman, *see* Dolman

Dowman, Eliz., 983; Giles, 983; Sarah, 983–4;
Wm., 984, 986

Downe [*peerage*], Frances, Visc., 630; Wm.,
Viscount, 1456; countess of, 1485; Lady, 1343;
Lord, 1343; Viscount, 58, 59, 452, *and see*
Dawney, Sir Hen. Pleydell; Ducie, Sir Wm.;
Pope, Lucy *and* Thos.

Downes, *see* Downs

Downing (Downyng), E., 1093; Edw., 1475; —,
1328

Downs (Downes), Anne, 308; Eliz., 970*; Frances,
653; Hannah, 308*; John, 308*, 969; Rev. John,
969, 970; Joseph, 308; Mary, 308; Rev. Rob., 66;
Sarah, 308; Wm., 653, 781; Rev. Wm., 66

Downyng, *see* Downing

Dowsing, Rev. Hugh, 1356; —, 1355

Dowty (Doughty), Ann, 257; Frances, 641; Mary,
641; Wm., 641

Doyley (de Oilei, de Olgi, D'Oile, D'Oilgi, D'Oyley, Doyley), Ann, 1126; C., 1126*; Chas., 184*, 1125; Christian, 1125; Eliz., 1126*; Eliz. Ann, 1126; Sir John, bt., 78; Marg., 1126*; Rob., 365, 889 n, 1016, 1033, 1351*; Rog., 889; —, 1064*; fam., 430

Drake, Alice, 711 n; Rev. Gil., 438; Priscilla, 320; Rev. R., 1289; Thos., 320

Draper, Anne, 902*, 1524; Bridget, 902; C., 1404; Cornelius, 902, 1393; Dorothy, 901; Edw., 899*, 902*; Rev. Edw., 754, 870, 901*; Eliz., 77, 896, 899*, 902, 907; John, 79, 1058, 1062; Mary, 77, 901; Ric., 902, 907*, 1524; Sam., 896*, 899; Sarah, 79; Thos., 77; Wm., 77, 906; Rev. Wm., 798; Sir Wm., 403; —, 1402

Draycott (Draycote), Eliz., 1092; Mary, 690, 691, 692; Ric., 690. 691, 692; Rog., 1092; —, 1148

Draysid, Nic., 1540

Drayton, Isabel, 552; Sir John, 552; Martha, 870; R., 1339; — (poet), 393 n, 763, 864; fam., 500

Drayzey, Mary, 174; Wm., 174

Dresser, Anna Maria, 771; Rev. Thos., 770, 771

Drew (Drewe), Alice, 473; Ann, 1250, 1429; Barbara, 1236; Dorothy, 182; Elinor, 1145; Eliz., 683, 837, 907, 1009; Frances, 1236; Geo., 473; Grace, 937; Hannah, 182, 1250; Hester, 240, 1009, 1371, 1510*; Jas., 353, 473*, 934; Jane, 906; Joan (Jone), 240, 353, 873; John, 240*, 353, 683, 937, 993*, 1236, 1250, 1258, 1510*, 1513; Jonathan, 550, 1250*; Joseph, 1217; Joshua, 907; Marg., 182; Mary, 18, 240, 540, 993*, 1236, 1429; Rachel, 1009; Ric., 1034, 1371; Rob., 18, 182, 1009, 1145, 1236*, 1427, 1535; Rog., 240; Sarah, 182, 240, 308, 353, 1535; Susannah, 934; Thos., 276, 308, 353, 550, 683, 768, 873, 906, 1176, 1429*; Wm., 182*, 240*, 532, 540, 837, 993*, 1009*, 1236, 1250, 1510*; —, 1238; fam., 236

Drewett, Mary, 1402

Drinkwater (Drinkewater), Ann(e), 761, 803, 1045, 1046; Benj., 1046; Betty, 761; Deborah, 1146; Eliz., 353, 761, 1045; Hannah, 1046*; Jas., 353, 761*, 1393; John, 789, 1146, 1164, 1197; Joseph, 803, 1045, 1046*, 1047; Mary, 1045, 1046, 1164; Olive, 338; R., 1447; Ric., 133; Sam., 338; Sarah, 133, 761; Thos., 353, 761*, 803, 1046*, 1146; Wm., 118, 511, 513, 1046*; —, 1386

Driver, Alice, 344; Betty, 1026; Chas., 96*, 97*, 716, 1052; Dorothy, 96, 97*; Edith, 344; Eleanor, 1026; Eliz., 96*, 341; Geo., 344*; Giles, 1352; Hannah, 344; Hester, 353; Jane, 504, 734, 1200, 1352; Joan, 97, 107*; John, 92, 93, 96*, 97*, 107, 203, 341, 344, 1200; Mary, 97*, 344*, 716, 734, 884*; Mat., 96*, 107*, 734; Nat., 97*; Rachel, 97; Ralph, 1200; Ric., 107, 204, 353, 1026*; Rob., 97*, 779; Sarah, 107, 1026; Ursula, 1026; Wal., 97; Wm., 504, 884*, 1026*; Rev. Wm., 503; Mr., 92*; —, 1039; fam., 91, 92, 109, 630, 648

Droree, see Drury

Droys, John, 1504

Drummond, Dr., 1160; —, 205

Drury (Droree, Druwery), Benj., 1431; Sir Drew, 1255; Edw., 1431*; Eliz., 1431, 1457; Hannah, 1431; Hen., 1431*; Jas., 1431; Joanna, 1431; John, 1431*, 1446, 1457, 1482; Sir John, 1483; Mary, 1431*; Rebecca, 1431; Rob., 1431, 1447; Wm., 1457

Dryden, —, 674 n

Dryn, Gil., 1314; —, 1311

Dubber, Mic., 517; Sarah, 517; Wm., 378

Dubberlowe, John, 1058

Dubberly, Mary, 906; Thos., 906

Ducie, Eliz., 1345; R., 1033; Sir R., 1033, 1255, 1512; Sir Ric., bt., 451*, 452, 1345, 1346; Sir Rob., bt., 451, 628, 1340*, 1345, 1455; Sir W., bt., 1345, 1456; Sir Wm., bt., 1341, 1346, 1513; Sir Wm., Viscount Downe, 452*, 630, 1345; Mr., 1345

Ducie [peerage], Arabella, Lady, 1342; Francis, Lord, 341, 452*, 628*; Hen., Earl, 1139, 1512; Marg., Lady, 1341; Mat., Lord, 451, 630, 1342; Thos., Lord, 451, 630, 1033, 1341; Lord, 305, 940, 941, 1133, 1340*, 1344*, 1345*, 1440, 1449, 1513*; and see Morton, passim

Duck, Rev. Arthur, 1502; N., 1160

Duckett, Martha, 597; Ric., 597

Dudbridge (Dodebrugge), Anna, 1509; Ann(e), 1175, 1511*; Anselm, 1509; Betty, 1511; Eliz., 1026; Hen. (de), 1217, 1509*, 1511; Hester, 1511*; Holiday, 1509; Hugh de, 1140; J., 1216; Jean, 1509*; John, 1510; Joseph, 1509*; Mary, 1509; Ric., 1218; Sarah, 1509; Stephen, 1509, 1511*; Thos., 1173; Rev. Thos., 1175; Wm., 1026; —, 1214

Duddall (Duddell), Rev. John, 1517, 1519*

Duddley, see Dudley

Duddo, see Dodo

Dudecote, Wal., 1292

Dudemore, see Dodmer

Dudfield, Ann, 1360; Barbara, 765; Betty, 765; Eliz., 765; John, 765*; Jonathan, 133; Mary, 133, 765; Sam., 765*; Thos., 765; Wm., 765

Dudley (Duddley), Ambrose, earl of Warwick, 634, 852 n; Anne, Countess of Warwick, 634; Eliz., 940*; John, 707; John, duke of Northumberland, 183, 318, 717*; Joseph, 940*, 941; Marg., 940, 941; Mary, 940*; Rob., earl of Leicester, 66, 259, 544, 848, 852 n; Sam., 940*; Sarah., 940; Wm., 940; —, Lord Warwick, 1538

Duffell (Duffeil, Duffel, Dufful), Ann, 811, 1481; Chas., 815; Jas., 815; John, 1481; Marg., 815; Martha, 601; Ric., 601*

Duffet (Duffett), Anne, 412; Geo., 412*; Sarah, 1576; Thos., 412

Duffield, Chas., 931; Emily Frances, 1485; Mary, 931; Thos., 1485

Dufful, see Duffell

Dugan, Chris., 872; Martha, 872

Dugdale (Dugdel), Elias, 708 n; Rev. Elizeus, 1196; Sir Wm., 362; —, 218, 605, 617, 1202

Dugmore, Wm., 903

Dukes (Douces), Hannah, 923; Matilda, 1447; Thos., 923*

Dumble, Ann, 1282; Geo., 1282*; —, 1382
Dumbleton, John, 231; —, 1504
Dumvile, Rog. de, 1074
Dun (fl. 9th cent.), 1502
Dun, *see* Dunn
Duncan, Rev. David, 488
Dunce, Sarah, 641; Thos., 641
Dunch, Ann, 620; Bridget, 509; Edm., 507, 509; Hungerford, 508; John, 620
Duning, *see* Dunning
Dunn (Done, Donne, Dun, Dunne), Agatha, 1272; Ann(e), 208, 569, 1571*; Betty Gibson, 1571*; Eliz., 450*; Francis, 208, 522; Hen., 250; Rev. Hen., 593, 895; Jas., 522*, 1537; John, 1016, 1272, 1273, 1571*; Mary, 250, 522, 1537; Rev. Obadiah, 449, 450*; Phil., 1537; Rev. Ric., 263, 450*; Sarah, 208*; Thos., 1217, 1460, 1571; Tobias, 208*; Wm., 177*, 569, 1571; Rev. Wm., 619; Mr., 1513; —, 1172
Dunning (Doning, Donnynge, Dounynge, Duning), Clarice, 1197; Dorcas, 809; Edm., 1150; Eliz., 810*; Geo., 813; Joan(e), 809*, 813; John, 809*, 810*, 1197; Marg., 809; Mary, 810; Rob., 1074; Thos., 808, 809*, 810*; Wm., 809*, 810*, 1385; Rev. Wm., 81; fam., 807
Dunnye, Is. de, 1404; John de, 1404
Dunsany, Ann Constance, baroness Dunsany, 1067
Dunster, —, 1311
Duntesborn, Alex. de, 1051, 1215*
Dunwallo [supposed founder of Tetbury], 1253
Dupplin, Constantia, Viscountess Dupplin, 1070
Durand, sheriff, 885, 1032*, 1055*, 1060, 1077, 1078, 1131, 1401, 1402*, 1422, 1434, 1474
Durant (Duraunt), Rev. Geo., 221; Phil., 1160
Durer, Albert, 591 n
Durford, E., 537
Durham (Derham, Dyrram), Alice, 1457, 1458*; Anne, 501, 1458*; Barbara, 1458; Chas., 1458; Dorothy, 1458; Eldrey, 1458; Eliz., 501, 1430, 1457, 1458*, 1472; Hannah, 1458; Hester Ann, 1472; Isabel, 1458; Jas., 850*, 1457, 1458*, 1471*; Joan, 1458*; John, 1457, 1458*, 1460*, 1471*; Joyce, 1460; Lydia, 1471*; Marg., 1458; Mary, 1458*, 1472; Rob., 1430, 1458*; Sam., 1458; Sarah, 1458; Susanna, 1458; Thos., 1457, 1458*; W., 1460; Rev. W., 1460; Wm., 287 n, 501, 850, 1430, 1458*, 1460, 1477; Rev. Wm., 1472; —, 1392, 1477, 1458*, 1477; fam., 1458, 1460, 1476
Durnell, Thos., 1537
Durrett, Geo., 254*; Mary, 254*; Rachel, 254
Dursley, Viscount, *see* Berkeley [*peerage*], Geo.
Durston (Durstone), Rev. John, 878, 879; Rev., 435
Durswell (Doreswell), Martha, 1342; Rob., 1342; Wm., 1346; —, 1345
Dusoul, Moses, 413
Dutfield, Joseph, 1121
Dutiland, Francis, 1576; Hester, 1576
Dutton (Duttoo), Ann Constance, 1067; Anne, 1066, 1067*; Cath., 1066; Eliz., 868, 1066, 1067*, 1431*; Eliz., baroness Sherborne, 1067; Eliz., Lady Sherborne, 1067; Frances, 1066;

Frances Mary, 1067; Rev. Geo., 820; Hen., 784; Rev. Hen., 7, 994, 1428; Sir J., 1068; Jas., 966, 1066*, 1068*, 1069*, 1186, 1482*; Jas., baron Sherborne, 1067; Jas., Lord Sherborne, 328, 667, 885, 886, 1067, 1068; Jas. Hen., Lord Sherborne, 1069; Jas. Hen. Legge, 1067, 1068; (formerly Naper), Jas. Lenox, 1066*, 1067, 1068*, 1483; Jane, 1066*, 1067*; Jemima, 1066; John, 296, 325, 369, 420, 422, 868, 944, 1015, 1064*, 1066, 1067*, 1068*, 1069, 1092, 1404, 1431, 1483, 1501; John, Lord Sherborne, 1066, 1067*, 1068; Sir John, bt., 1016, 1066*, 1068, 1401; Lawr., 1007; Lucy, 420, 422; Mary, 296, 659, 1066*; Sir R., 1125; Ralph, 296, 1066*, 1431*; Rev. Ralph, 1348, 1387; Sir Ralph, bt., 37, 885, 943, 1066, 1068*, 1132, 1189, 1483; Sir Ralph, kt., 1068*; Sarah, 659, 784, 1007; Thos., 659, 944, 985, 1016, 1062, 1066, 1067*, 1068*; Wm., 659*, 784, 868, 944, 1021, 1066*, 1067*, 1068*, 1482, 1483; Wm. Naper, 1067; —, 1064, 1351; fam., 305, 420, 1069, 1482
Duval, Rev. Phil., 1122
Dych, *see* Dyke
Duynysshe, Rog. le, 1540
Dyde, Ann, 226; Grace, 980; Rob., 226*; Thos., 226; Wm., 226, 980*
Dyer (Deyere, Dier, Dyeare, Dyere), Agatha le, 1197; Ann, 983, 1075; Arthur, 884; Benj., 1574; Betty, 317; Chas., 1533, 1539; Edw., 752*; Elenor, 1075; Eliz., 48, 90*, 296, 831, 883, 1533; Frances, 434, 883, 884; Grace, 562*, 884; H., 1539; Hannah, 752; Hen., 90*; Jas., 787; Jane, 948; Joanna, 317; John (le), 884, 1043, 1075, 1217, 1292, 1539*; Joseph, 847; Lawr., 434; Marg., 751; Mary, 90, 752, 966, 1043, 1533; Maur., 562; Nat., 751, 983, 1512*; Nic., 883*; Paul le, 1197; Ric., 90; Sam., 1107, 1533; Sarah, 787, 815, 884, 1398, 1533; Susanna, 434; Thos., 48, 90, 434, 815, 831, 884; Wal. le, 1197; Wm., 296, 884, 948, 966, 1075, 1398, 1533*, 1539; Mr., 882; Mrs., 1311
Dyke (Dich, Diche, Dike, Dych), Ann, 320; Eliz., 380; Mary, 1112; Thos., 380, 1112, 1121; Wm. (atte), 130, 1172; Rev. Wm., 488, 1335; —, 1220
Dylke, Rev. Thos., 613
Dymere, *see* Dimery
Dymock (Dimmock, Dimoc, Dimock, Dymoke), Eliz., 1008*, 1143, 1185*; Francis, 1008; Giles, 1181; Rev. Giles, 524; Rev. H., 886; J., 1185; J. D., 1186; John, 1143, 1181, 1185; Rev. John, 1186; Nat., 1183; Priscilla, 1183; Ric., 1086; Rog., 546; Sarah, 1008, 1143, 1181; Thos., 1008; Wm., 1183
Dyne, Elena, 1317; Wal., 1317
Dynevor [*peerage*](Dinevor), Lord, 1015*, 1016; *and see* Cardonnell, Cecil(y)
Dyngley, Rev. W., 1196
Dynton, Wm. de, 360
Dyp (Dype), Thos., 1476; Wm., 1491
Dyrram, *see* Durham
Dyston, *see* Diston

Eacott, *see* Eycott
Eade, Rev. John, 206
Eader, John, 1314
Eagles, Abraham, 683; Eliz., 677; Esther, 1282; Geo., 1282; Isabel, 486; John, 832; Mary, 563; Ric., 563, 1008*; Sarah, 683; Thos., 677*; Wm., 486*
Eames (Emes), Edw., 505; Eliz., 944; Jas., 505; John, 931*; Mary, 931; Parthenia, 505; Wm., 505; *and see* Emms
Eanwolf (Eanulf), grandfather of king Offa, 1386, 1419
Earl (Earle, Earles, Eorl), Amy, 1053; Ann, 1511; Chas. Joseph, 1511; Eliz., 97, 659*, 1458; Hen., 1458; John, 1053*, 1511*; Mary, 659; Ralph le, 1150; Ric., 1053*; Sam., 1053; Sarah, 1053*; Thos., 97, 370, 659*; Sir Thos., kt., 503; W., 1287, 1288; Wal., 1348; Wm., 304, 659; —, 1476
Early, Mary, 598; Rebecka, 598; Wm., 598*
Earnly, Jane, 509; Mic., 509
East (Est), Alice, 710, 1428; Eliz., 710; Hannah, 962; John, 710; Thos., 710; Sir Wm., bt., 962
Eastcourt (Eastcot), *see* Estcourt
Easterbrook, Rachel, 1584; Sam., 1584; Wm., 1584*
Easthope, *see* Esthope
Eastman, Sarah, 20*; Wm., 20
Eastmead, Ann, 1537; Arthur, 36*, 1537; Eliz., 36; Wm., 36*
Easton, Rev. John, 142; Rev. Thos., 142; fam., 721; *and see* Ashton; Aston; Eston
Easy, Chas., 662
Eatly, Benj., 687
Eaton, Bridget, 1262, 1275; Eliz., 269; Rev. Guy, 534, 754; Honora, 1265; John, 1262, 1277, 1280; Joyce, 1275, 1277; Kath., 1014; Mary, 111, 550, 815, 1280; Rev. Ric., 266*, 269*; Rob., 269; Rev. Rob., 1262*, 1263*, 1275, 1277*, 1280*, 1290*; Rev. Thos., 547; Wm., 111*; Rev. Mr., 1277; Mr., 53
Eberton, Rev. John de, 1225
Ebborn (Aborn, Eborne), Eliz., 55; Josiah, 55*; Rev. Ric., 1147; Rose, 55
Ebrington, Viscount, 571
Ebsworth, Abigail, 377; Alice, 693*; Ann(e), 598*, 693; Cath., 947*; Dorcas, 1444; Eliz., 203, 377, 693*, 1058, 1063*; Geo., 986; John, 693*, 1058, 1063*, 1444; Mary, 693, 797; Ric., 598, 693*; Rob., 1058*, 1063; Thos., 693*, 797, 947*; Wm., 777*, 693; —, 1063
Eccles (Ecles), Eliz., 1013; Hen., 1013; Marg., 1013; Rev. Ric., 1478; Rev. Sam., 1228; *and see* Egglese
Ecgwin, bishop, 1195*
Eckley, Sam., 1440; Sir Sam., 1434; Thos., 266
Ecles, *see* Eccles
Ecott, *see* Eycott
Ecton, Rev. Ralph, 764; —, 91, 147, 275, 763
Edam, Hen., 1519
Edde, *see* Eddy
Eddels, John, 660; Judith, 660
Edden (Eddon), Hen., 1391; Joseph, 1391; Mary,

1391; Nat., 1391*; Ric., 708 n; Wm., 1223; —, 1223
Eddy (Edde, Edy, Edye), Ann(e), 733, 811; Cath., 1038, 1333; Elinor, 811; Eliz., 811*; Geo., 1038; Jane, 1038; John, 733, 811*, 812*, 1038*, 1039; Rev. John, 1332, 1333, 1335; Mary, 733, 812; Nic., 730; Rob., 811*, 812; Thos., 811*, 1311, 1314; Wal., 1005; Wm., 811
Edeldred, *see* Ethelred
Eden, Constant, 1330; John, 288; Susanna, 980*; T., 1392; Thos., 980*; Rev. Thos., 1441; Wm., 980, 1330; —, 1196
Edgar, king, 863
Edgar, Alex., 40, 1410, 1564; Nat. Foy, 1564; Lieut. Rob. Cann, 1564
Edge, Ann, 1333; Joseph, 1333
Edgecoke (Edgock, Edgocke), Ric., 1357; Thos., 1363; —, 1363
Edgecomb, Alice, 1271; Edw., 1277
Edgecumbe, Lord, 252, 449
Edgell, Edw. Gould, 1282; Mary, 1282
Edginton, Betty, 1013; Edm., 1013
Edgley, Wm., 944
Edgock (Edgocke), *see* Edgecoke
Edgworth (Eggeworth), Eliz., 730; Hen., 730; Peter de, 985
Edinburgh, Capt., duke of, 1344
Edington, Wm. de, bishop, 599
Edkins, Mary, 1389; Sarah, 1389; Thos., 980, 1389*; Rev. Thos., 85
Edmar (fl. 11th cent.), 1047
Edmonds (Edmondes), *see* Edmunds
Edmund Ironside, king, 483
Edmund the Martyr, king, 1196
Edmund, bishop of London, *see* Bonner; Gibson
Edmund (fl. 11th cent.), 1201
Edmunds (Edmonds, Edmondes), Alice, 1432; Ann(e), 904, 907, 1489; Ant., 721, 898, 901*, 904; Christian, 577, 729; Chris., 903*, 907, 1489*; Dorothy, 907; Rev. Francis, 840; Jane, 901*; John, 901*, 1425; Rev. John, 1229; Lawr., 388*; Marg., 901, 903, 922; Mary, 901; Priscilla, 388*; Sam., 907; Sarah, 901; Sir T., 232; Thos., 362, 577*; Rev. Thos., 1232, 1233; Wm., 797, 922*; Mr., 927 n; —, 1432
Edney, Caleb, 837; Joshua, 837
Edric (fl. 1066), 119, 1355*, 1485
Edus, Adam, 1540
Edward the Confessor, king, 153, 157, 178, 179, 324, 358, 420, 481, 527*, 737, 745, 990, 1050, 1051, 1162, 1194, 1219, 1223, 1227, 1287, 1316, 1322, 1328, 1335, 1355, 1481*
Edward the Elder, king, 98, 649*, 1287
Edward I, 41, 178, 218, 244*, 341, 400, 507, 732, 745, 769, 819, 869, 876, 915, 1059, 1287*, 1322, 1431, 1474
Edward II, 158, 244*, 251, 357, 529, 885, 1403
Edward III, 101, 158, 244*, 251, 265 n, 278, 286 n, 305, 325 n, 359, 363, 515, 664, 1293, 1316
Edward IV, 153, 195, 205, 244, 443 n, 481, 497, 525, 570, 745, 785, 791, 792, 1123, 1189, 1255*, 1311, 1316, 1475

Edward V, 876 n
Edward VI, 184, 195, 197 n, 220 n, 225, 309, 365, 392 n, 393 n*, 434, 570 n, 671, 769, 952, 1126, 1221, 1356, 1428, 1491, 1502, 1539
Edward Prince of Wales, son of Henry VI, 570 n, 571, 1261, 1280, 1285, 1291, 1293
Edward the Black Prince, 325 n, 599 n
Edwards (Edward, Edwardes), Adam, 1339; Altheia, 387; Ann(e), 114, 117, 950, 1427; Ant., 116, 117*, 118, 132; Bart., 339; Betty, 1583*; Cath., 116, 118; Chas., 1200*, 1427*; Cornelia, 1413; D., 1140; Dan., 174; Dorothy, 213; Edw., 296; Eleanor, 847; Eliz., 49, 118, 132, 339, 367, 368, 369, 370, 375*, 768, 772, 1107, 1200, 1350, 1395; Esther, 623; Geo., 728; Rev. Geo., 1428; Giles, 514; Hannah, 728, 810, 934, 973*, 974*; Hen., 339*, 1382; Hen. Arthur, 1413; Isaac, 117, 375; Jas., 768, 1065, 1413*; Rev. Jas., 75, 76, 275, 350, 593, 853; Jane, 235, 797; John, 49, 116*, 117*, 118*, 174, 348, 387*, 514, 623, 768, 772, 810, 858, 973*, 974*, 976, 1028, 1031, 1032*, 1065, 1108, 1413, 1450*, 1555; Rev. John, 643, 1346, 1513; Joyce, 1108; Judith, 1065; Langham, 407; Marg., 768; Margery, 976, 1032; Martha, 177; Mary, 114, 117*, 143*, 339, 891, 974, 1065*, 1413, 1427; Nic., 366, 368, 370*, 375*; Nutt, 1277; Paul, 623*; R., 1121; Rachel, 387; Ralph, 1328; Ric., 117, 1395, 1456; Rob., 1107*, 1108; Rodney, 1427; Rog., 49; Sam., 213*, 721, 847, 934, 1405, 1583*; Rev. Sam., 1362, 1456; Sarah, 118, 465, 1450; Sybil, 468; Thos., 231, 235*, 718, 722, 730, 745, 768, 891, 924, 1065, 1351, 1428, 1491; Rev. Thos., 515; W., 1140, 1309*, 1456; Wal., 143*, 772; Wm., 113, 117*, 177, 728, 797, 819, 820, 898, 907, 910, 950, 1289, 1295, 1420; Rev. Wm., 1257; Rev. Wm. Embury, 1417; —, 1256, 1282, 1339, 1419, 1420; fam., 113; (later Freeman), fam., 1420
Edwards Freeman, —, 1420
Edwey, Agnes, 1313
Edwin (Edwyn), bishop of Worcester and of London, see Sandys
Edwin (Edwyn), Chas., 245*, 479*, 922
Edwy, king, 1321*
Edwy (fl. 1066), 1077*, 1331
Edwyn, see Edwin
Edy (Edye), see Eddy
Eechnam, Mary, 884; Thos., 884
Eede, Wm., 1292
Effingham, earl of, 927
Egbert, king, 40
Egby, see Eggby
Egerton, Hester, 1484; Mary, 1484; Rev. Thos., 1484*, 1485
Eggby (Egby), Chas., 540*; Dan., 540, 543*; Hester, 540; John, 540; Sarah, 543*; Wm., 540
Eggeworth, see Edgworth
Egglesby, Lieut. Wm., 928
Egglese, Sarah, 1548; Wm., 1548, and see Eccles
Eglesfield, Rob., 502
Egremont, earl of, 913

Egwin (Egwine), bishop, 21, 1502
Eikins, see Eykyn
Elaf (fl. 1066), 990*
Elborowe, see Elburrough
Elbridge, Ann, 1324, 1488; Cicely, 727; Thos., 1405; Rev. Wm., 1324*, 1329
Elburrough (Elborowe, Elbrough), Eliz., 336; Jane, 60; John, 1127; Ric., 336; Thos., 1217; Wm., 60
Elcho, Lady, 1153, 1154; Lord, see Charteris, Francis
Elder, Frances, 542
Eldon, John, Lord Eldon, 1198; earl of, 1198
Eldred, archbishop, 1047, 1131
Eldridge (Eldrige, Elridge), Ann, 847; Barbara, 138; Calvin, 847; Dan., 138; Eliz., 679, 683; Hen., 77, 303*; Hester, 353; Jo[a]ne, 77; John, 138, 303, 353*, 847; Mary, 77, 517; Mercy, 679*; Rachel, 303; Rebecca, 1409; Sarah, 524; Thos., 1409; Rev. W., 1485; Wm., 133, 300, 517, 524, 679*
Elemor, —, 1404
Elevaunt, John; and see Eliaunt
Eley (Elly, Ely), Rev. A., 1440; Rev. Ant., 1439*; Eliz., 1303; Geo., 1418*; Rev. Godfry, 1317; Jas., 1303; John, 1138, 1312; Nic. de, 221; Susan, 1418; Mr., 1440
Elfleda (fl. 981), 743
Elias, —, 1068
Eliaunt, John, 1423; —, 1422; and see Elevaunt
Eliot (Eliots), see Elliot
Elizabeth, queen, 27, 31, 40, 66, 76, 81, 121, 139, 142, 147, 161, 179, 184, 198, 214, 230, 232, 233*, 236, 246, 259, 287, 305, 319, 323 n, 324*, 325, 359, 363, 365, 367, 391, 393 n, 415, 427, 440, 447, 463, 482, 488, 503, 511, 547, 553, 556, 560, 561, 567, 571, 579, 586, 591*, 625, 639, 643*, 678, 689, 691*, 696, 709, 719 n, 748, 770, 793, 802*, 805, 829, 839, 848, 865*, 870, 878, 890, 952, 1059*, 1061, 1062, 1201, 1219, 1221, 1228*, 1233, 1238, 1293*, 1296, 1317, 1328, 1329, 1334, 1346, 1355, 1356, 1422, 1456, 1474*, 1482, 1502, 1513, 1530
Elizabeth, wife of Henry VII, 360 n
Elland, Joseph, 1214; Sarah, 1214; —, 1186
Ellebighe, Thos. de, 1420
Ellenborough, Lord, 1504
Ellens, Rev. John, 1441
Ellery, Eliz., 1111; Jane, 1111; John, 1111; Mary, 1111
Ellesmere, Lord, 1021
Ellett, see Elliot
Ellington, Rev. Hugh, 1482
Elliot (Eliot, Eliots, Ellett, Elliott, Elliotts, Ellyates, Elyot, Elyotes, Elyott), Agnes, 1073; Dan., 419; Edw. Craggs, Lord Eliot, 508; Eliz., 79, 453*, 536, 541*, 563, 993; Esther, 536*, 1182; G. H., 1185; Giles, 1115; Hannah, 419, 536, 1395; Harriot, 507; Hester, 761; J., 1186*; John, 453, 520, 541, 1104, 1150, 1182*, 1186, 1231, 1282, 1420; Rev. John, 536*, 574; Joseph, 563*; Rev. Joshua, 79, 802, 1503, 1504; Josuah, 993; Judith, 520, 541; Marg. Hughes, 1320; Mary, 116*, 427,

1008, 1115; Maur., 419; O. E., 1320; Onesiphorus, 536, 558; R., 1121; Ric., 507; Rob., 1172; Rosamond, 563; Sam., 79, 541*, 1395, 1403; Sarah, 453, 563*, 1231; Thos., 419, 761, 797, 1008, 1186, 1218, 1311, 1314; Wm., 453*, 541, 563, 1026, 1079*, 1172, 1292; Mr., 1052, 1186; —, 1079, 1185

Elliott [peerage](Eliot), Lord, 508*, 807; and see Elliot, Edw. Craggs

Ellis (Ellyes, Elys), A., 1165; Alice, 336, 338; Anna Maria, 1208; Anne, 338, 830; Ant., 1194, 1402; Chas., 810*; Christian, 1180; Mrs. Chris., 1186; Dan., 336, 513, 583, 584*, 870*, 1194*, 1196; Diana, 584; Eleanor, 382; Eliz., 338, 583*, 584*, 832, 1024, 1053, 1210, 1211, 1212, 1213; Est(h)er, 1024, 1026*; Geo., 716, 1210; Guy, 336*, 338; Sir H., 1475; Jas., 810; Jane, 810, 1194, 1235; Joan (Ioane), 810*; John, 328, 336*, 382, 1194, 1196, 1212*, 1213, 1235, 1483; Jonathan, 830, 832; Joseph, 139, 558*, 583, 584*, 832, 1180*, 1186; Marg., 584, 760; Martha, 1267; Mary, 336, 382, 1194*, 1211*; Phil., 1289; Phoebe, 583; Rebecca, 716; Ric., 584*, 1053, 1213, 1551; Rob., 1006, 1024*, 1026*, 1047, 1150, 1213, 1217; Sam., 1024, 1065; Sarah, 584, 1024, 1026, 1053*, 1210, 1211, 1213; Susannah, 513, 583*, 1194; Thos., 1053*, 1186; W., 1237; Rev. W., 1203*; Wal., 1039; Wm., 336, 338, 382, 438, 584*, 760*, 830*, 832, 1211*, 1212*; Rev. Wm., 619, 1208, 1211; Wm. Hen., 1211; —, 1015, 1165

Ellison, Hen., 1256; Mrs., 1247

Ellston, see Elston

Ellstrip (Rllstrip), Eliz., 1097, 1099

Ellsworth, Edw., 1410*; Peter, 1410*; Sir Ric., kt., 1410*

Elly, see Eley

Ellyates, see Elliot

Ellyes, see Ellis

Elmbridge, John, 870; Thos., 870

Elmes (Elme), B., 1027; John atte, 1356; Thos. atten, 1047; Wm., 491; and see Nelmes

Elridge, see Eldridge

Elsemere, see Elsmore

Elshew, Hen., 655

Elsi (fl. 1066), 829; and see Ferendone

Elsley, Joseph, 1343; Mary, 1343*; Wm., 780, 1343*

Elsmore (Elsemere), John, 915; Joyce, 768; Mary, 924; Ric., 924*

Elston (Ellston), Ann, 1348; Rev. Hen., 1516; Wm., 1348

Eltom, Fletcher, 321; Mary, 321; Sabina, 321

Elton, Abraham, 1440; Sir Abraham, 695; Sir Abraham, bt., 1555, 1560; Alice, 1034; Ambrose, 520; Ann(e), 520, 1156; Ant., 1034; Edw., 1315, 1316, 1317; Eleanor, 906; Eliz., 1401, 1560; Rev. Gil., 1315, 1317; Isaac, 1156, 1160*, 1556, 1557, 1561; John, 906; Mary, 1561; Ric., 1401*; Rowland, 1361; Sarah, 1556; Susanna, 520; Thos., 1361; Mr., 1315; —, 1256, 1258, 1316, 1362

Elvic (fl. 1066), 1485

Elvins, John, 989

Elward (fl. 1066), 990*

Elwes (Helewys), Rev. Chas., 206; Emily Frances, 1485; Geo., 1485; John, 1404; Mr., 1501, 1502; —, 1502

Elwin (fl. 1066), 1055

Ely, see Eley

Elyates (Elyot, Elyotes, Elyott), see Elliot

Elys, see Ellis

Elysander (Elysaunder), see Alexander

Embly, see Emley

Embury, Chas., 1289; John, 1288; Mercy, 679; Thos., 679*; Wm., 1288; Mr., 1362; —, 1361

Emerson (Emmerson), And., 836; Anne, 846; Eliz., 1326; Hamoys (Hamoise), 845*; Hannah, 845; Jas., 846; John, 846; Marg., 756; Mary, 844, 845*; Ric., 756, 836; Sarah, 836; Seal, 844, 845; Thos., 84, 756, 1326; Rev., 949; and see Amerson

Emes, see Eames

Emett, see Emmett

Emley (Embly, Emly), Anne, 1429; Arthur, 750; Eliz., 262; (or Ernly), Eliz., 995*; John, 124*, 616; (or Ernly), Hen., 995*; Moses, 262*; Sam., 1429; Sarah, 124; Thos., 1258

Emmerson, see Emerson

Emmes, see Emms

Emmett (Emett, Emmet, Emmitt, Emmots), Anna Maria, 1025; (or Taylor), Betty, 64; Chas., 835, 1160; Edw., 836; Eliz., 1158*; Eliz. Millett, 1158; Hannah, 836; John, 836; Mary, 835; Morgan, 592; (or Taylor), Peter, 64; Rob., 1025; Thos., 1158; Wm., 1158*, 1160

Emms (Emmes), R., 1460; Thos., 1460; —, 1460; and see Eames

Endel, Hen., 1233

Endes, Adam le, 1238

Endon, Alice, 1082; Thos., 1082

Enefield (Euefeld), Alan de, 1428*

Engehain, Alice, 898; Sir Edw., kt., 898; Isaac, 898*; and see Engham

Engel, Jas., 411

Engham, Sir Edw., kt., 900; Mary, 900; and see Engehain; Hengeham

England, Ann, 11; Bridget, 841; Eliz., 492, 1410; Geo., 492; Hannah, 780; Jas., 492; Joel, 780*; John, 731, 780, 841*, 1410; Joseph, 11*, 492*, 841; Kath., 1106; Lydia, 1143; Marg., 492; Martha, 780; Mary, 1411; Ric., 1143; Rob., 413; Sarah, 492, 731*, 780*; Thos., 780*; Wm., 780, 846, 1411

English, Betty, 752; Edw., 752; Hannah, 750; Jane, 328, 752; Rev. John, 328*, 1238; Mary, 328, 752; Thos., 752; Wm., 750

Engly, Joanna, 787; John, 413; Lucy, 413; Ric., 787

Enoch, Thos., 1086

Eorl, see Earl

Ercoldson, Wal., 1518

Erdynton, Wal. de, 1015

Erian (Erie), see Erye

Ermingham, Edw., 778 n

Ermyte, Hen., 1370
Ernald (fl. ? 12th cent.), 1060, 1061 n, *and see* Banbury
Ernesi (fl. 1066), 876, 1082, 1091, 1225, 1227
Ernesius, son of Oce, 1227
Ernle (Ernly), Eliz., *see* Emley; John, 1497; Hen., *see* Emley; Susanna, 1497
Ernulphus (Anglo-Saxon), 851
Ero, Wm., 1494
Erother, abbess, 1502
Erye (Erian, Erie), Rev. Rob., 1289, 1290
Esbury, Dan., 699*, 730; Joane, 702; Mary, 699, 702; Sarah, 699*; Thos., 699, 702*
Escombe, John, 1494; *and see* Ashcomb
Escott (Escourt), *see* Estcourt
Esheley, *see* Ashley
Eskotte, *see* Estcourt
Essewy, John, 1091
Essex, Ann, 429; Eliz., 97, 1214; Hester, 657; Jas., 1214; Jonathan, 657; Mary, 661; Ric., 661; Rob., 429; Wm., 97
Essex [*peerage*], Rob., earl of, 497 n; countess of, 230 n; earl of, 190, 311, 325, 1382; lord, 358, 759 n, 1148, 1288, 1348, 1478*; *and see* Anne-Hollis; Capel, Arthur; Cromwell, Thos.; Devereux, Rob.; Mandeville, Isabel *and* —
Essington, Eliz., 1025; Ric., 1025, 1211*; Sarah, 1211*; Wm., 1211; Capt. Wm., 1101
Est, *see* East
Estcourt (Eastcot, Eastcourt, Escott, Escourt, Eskotte, Estcot, Estcote, Estcourte), Agnes, 1073*; Alice, 380; Anna Maria, 68; Ann(e), 280, 1073*, 1343; Rev. Dan., 1127; Edith, 1071, 1074; Edm., 92, 527, 529, 783*, 1072, 1073*, 1243, 1343; Rev. Edw., 495; Sir Edw., 380; Eleanor, 1073; Eleanor Bucknall, 1073; Eliz., 307*, 1073*; Esther, 1072; Gil. de, 523; Sir Giles, bt., 364; Grace, 1251; Hannah, 981; Isabel, 1073; Major-Gen. J. B. B., 1070; Major-Gen. Jas. Bucknall, 1073; Jane, 1072, 1073*; Jasper, 1027*; Joan, 1073; John (de la), 307, 783*, 1073*, 1074, 1251; Jonathan, 1217; Juliana, 1073, 1074; Lydia, 280, 1072, 1073*; Marg. (de), 1073, 1074*; Martha, 981; Mary, 1243; Dame Mary, 784, 1073*; Mat., 280, 783, 1072, 1073*; Ralf de, 360; Ric., 1027*; Sam., 1074; Simon de la, 1073; T., 1074*; Sir T., 1258; T. G. B., 1073*; T. H. S. S., 1070; Thos., 92, 524, 527, 529, 535, 579, 783*, 1070*, 1071*, 1072, 1073*, 1074*; Sir Thos., kt., 527, 529, 530, 534, 783*, 784, 908, 1073*, 1257; Thos. Grimston Bucknall, 1073*; Wal. (de la), 783, 1071, 1073*; Cmdr. Wal. G. B., 1073; Wm., 363; Dr., 953; —, judge, 1071; —, 1074; fam., 278, 523, 579, 909, 1073, 1256
Esterfield, J., 1101
Esthope (Easthope, Estop), Ann, 172; John, 172*, 1288, 1289*; Mary, 172; Ric., 172*; Thos., 1288, 1289; Wm., 172; —, 1282
Estmat, Stephen, 703
Eston, Alured of, 1227; Wal. of, 1227; *and see* Ashton; Aston; Easton

Estop, *see* Esthope
Etell, Thos., 815
Ethelbald, king of Mercia, 1392, 1419, 1512
Ethelbert, Peter, 1477
Ethelburga, abbess, 1502
Ethelmund (fl. 8th cent.), 1419
Ethelred (Adelred), king, 1194, 1195*, 1196, 1253, 1335, 1502*
Ethelred (fl. 9th cent.)(Edelred), 1288, 1309
Ethelric (fl. 8th cent.), 1419
Ethelwold (fl. 10th cent.), 357
Etheridge, Anne, 330; Edm., 803; Eliz., 226, 637*, 858; Jas., 264, 330; John, 330, 637*, 858, 887; Mary, 226, 264; Ric., 226; Rob., 637; Susannah, 887; Thos., 486*; Wm., 226*
Etherton, Ric., 815
Etlins, Rev. John, 139
Ettry, Joel, 1159
Eu, *see* Owe
Euefeld, *see* Enefield
Eugene IV, pope, 708 n
Eure, Chas., 1262; Priscilla, 1262; Wm., Lord Eure, 1262
Evans (Evan, Evance, Evenis, Eveniss, Evens), Abraham, 815; Ann(e), 460, 627*, 751*, 752, 923, 1157; Barrow, 1402; Betty, 386, 627; C. B., 1403; Cath., 563, 1574; Chas., 869, 870*; Chas. Farrington, 1511; Cornelius, 1162; Rev. Dan., 593, 853; Edw., 563*, 623*, 736*; Eleanor, 1162; Eliz., 109, 257, 413, 550, 563, 611, 623, 815, 984, 1037*, 1393; Rev. Geo. Hen., 1511; Grace, 1162; Hen., 768, 1162; Hester, 512, 1037, 1150, 1151, 1489; Hugh, 802, 1369; Rev. Hugh, 890; Jacob, 460; Jas., 77*, 413, 563, 611, 623, 751*, 858, 1038; Jane, 369; Joan, 213, 858; John, 38, 48, 212, 386, 460*, 550, 563*, 608, 623*, 627, 963*, 1037*, 1039, 1273, 1282, 1289, 1539, 1574; Rev. John, 245*, 347, 808; Jonathan, 1489; Joseph, 752, 1037, 1149, 1150, 1151; Josiah, 1037; Rev. Lewis, 206; Lieut. Luellin, 928; Marg., 512, 997; Martha, 623, 1038; Mary, 77*, 250, 486*, 563, 622, 623*, 627*, 736, 996, 1150*, 1151*, 1162, 1563; Martin, 1539; Rev. Meredith, 493, 643; Rev. Morgan, 190; Rachel, 814; Rebecca, 1000; Ric., 257, 512, 984, 1150*, 1151*; Rob., 486; Sam., 109, 213*, 563, 623; Sarah, 486, 563*, 608, 623*, 815, 1150, 1151; Susanna, 1038; Thos., 486*, 563, 622, 623*, 627*, 631, 814, 815, 923, 924, 996*, 1038, 1150, 1162*, 1563, 1575; W. S., 1476; Wal., 1000; Wm., 250, 563*, 623*, 627, 815, 984, 997, 1162, 1186; Rev. Wm., 112, 1147; Mr., 119, 1165; Rev., 813; —, 1122, 1165*, 1369
Evanson, Rev. Edw., 1289, 1290*, 1348
Eve, Wm., 844
Evelyn, John, 1345
Evenis (Eveniss, Evens), *see* Evans
Everard (Everad), John, 1259; Matilda, 1460; T., 1101; —, 1257; *and see* Everett
Everatt, *see* Everett
Everdon (Everdyn), Alice, 1092; Rev. Ant., 1369; Thos., 1092

Everest, Rev. T., 1456; —, 1455
Everett (Everatt), Dan., 175*; Edm., 921; Eliz.,
539*; Hugh, 532, 542; Jas., 175; Jane, 411; John,
539*, 921; Joseph, 542, 741; Joshua, 1532; Mary,
174, 175, 542, 741; Ric., 160; Sarah, 175, 539;
Thos., 411*, 531, 542*; Wm., 174; and see
Everard
Evers, Matilda de, 696
Everton, Ann, 797; John, 797
Everty, see D'Everty
Evesham, Sylvester of, bishop, 426
Evett, Sarah, 411; Thos., 411
Ewe, see Owe
Ewely, see Uley
Ewett, see Hewett
Ewley, see Uley
Exell (Exall, Exel), John, 782; Mary, 499; Ric., 445 n,
499; Sarah, 782
Exeter, duke of, see Holland, John
Eycott (Eacott, Ecott), A. F., 1186; Beata, 300;
Bridget, 300; Cath., 1008; Eliz., 381, 1497; H.
C., 1186; Hen., 1008; John, 399, 1499; Jones,
381; Joseph, 300*; Mary, 598; Ric. 300, 1497;
Sarah, 300, 454, 456; Thos., 299*, 598; Wm.,
300, 454, 456
Eyett, E., 1101; Edw., 1100; J., 1101; W., 1101; and
see Hyett
Eyford, —, 1091
Eyils, see Eyles
Eykyn (Eikins), Rev. John, 599, 600; Mary, 600;
Rev. Thos., 266
Eyles (Eyils, Yeeles, Yeels, Yells), Albert, 381; D.,
182; Dan., 308; Eliz., 781, 846; Esther, 797;
John, 731, 846, 1365; Mary, 182, 308, 381, 496,
846; Ric., 381*; Rob., 846; Sarah, 741; Sam.,
781; Thos., 741; Wm., 797, 846*, 847; —, 1370
Eyloe, Eliz., 1127; Ric., 1127*
Eylway, see Alway
Eynon, Eliz., 978; Jas., 978; and see Beynon
Eynsham, —, 1093
Eyre (Eyr, Eyres, Heyr), Cornelius, 772; Francis,
424*; J. le, 1061; Sir Jervase, kt., 209; John le,
1061*; Mary, 209; Marianne, 408; Mary, 408;
Ric. le, 1478; Rob. le, 1127; Rev. Rob., 206;
Stafford, 408; Susannah, 772; Theodora, 1032*;
Thos. le, 1032, 1172; Wm. le, 1198, 1485; Rev.,
1217
Eyton, L., 1485

Faber, John, 1491; Wm. son of, 1404; and see
Smith; Smithson
Fabian, Kath., 1482
Fabrica, Walkelin de, 1377
Facey, Griffith, 815
Fader, Adam, 1314; Rog. le, 1351
Fagg, Ann, 1576; Esther, 1576; Hester, 1576; Jas.,
1576*
Fairfax, Geo., 702*; Rev. Guy, 1193; Henrietta
Cath., 1193; Mary, 702*; Sir Thos., kt., 364
Fairford, Viscount, see Hill, Wills
Fairmedow, Sir Cornelius, 1262; Eliz., 1262
Fairweather, Val., 1287

Faithorn (Faithorne), Geo., 531, 536*; Hester, 540;
Joseph, 532, 540*, 970; Martha, 540; Mary, 536,
540, 970; Nat., 540; Wm., 540
Fakel, Marg., 1197
Falconer, 706; Ric., 706
Falkland, Cary, Viscount Falkland, 1482
Fallewelle, Joan, 1102; Thos., 1540
Falmouth, earl of, see Berkeley, Chas.
Fane, Anne, 1408*; Eliz., 1408; Lady Eliz., 1423*;
Frances, 573; Francis, 722; Sir Francis, kt., 1408;
Francis, earl of Westmorland, 573; Hen., 1408*,
1409*; Mary, 1408; Mildmay, 573; Thos., earl of
Westmorland, 1409; W., 573; —, earl of
Westmorland, 1423; —, Lord Westmorland,
1043; —, 1420
Fane [peerage], Chas., Viscount, 436; Susanna,
Viscountess, 437, 804; Lady, 1331
Fanter, Sarah, 344; Thos., 344
Farail, see Farrell
Fardon, Ann(e), 641*, 710; J., 710; Jas., 641*;
John, 710; Mary, 710
Farell, see Farrell
Fargus, Ann, 1574*; Cath., 1574; Eliz., 1574; John,
1574*; Joseph, 1574; Marg., 1574; Mary, 1574
Farhill, see Farrell
Farley (Farly, Ferley), Ann, 906; Eliz., 906; John,
906; Joseph, 765; Thos., 97; Wm., 1362
Farmer (Farmor), Ann(e), 683, 1371, 1400; Arthur,
206; Dan., 74; Edw., 1034, 1371; Giles, 1400;
John, 657, 1191; Marg., 1400; Ric., 657, 1196;
Sam., 1403; Thos., 683*, 1554; Wm., 486*,
1362; —, 483; and see Fermor
Farmiloe (Farmilo), Ann, 751; Hester, 751; John,
751*; Marg., 751; Sarah, 661; Thos., 661; Wm.,
751*
Farmor, see Farmer
Farn, Sam., 1010; and see Fern
Farnell, Anne, 1085; Rob., 1085*; Sarah, 1085
Farr (Farre), Ann, 1214; Francis, 660; Hannah, 730;
Hugh, 1214*; John, 730; Marg., 1217; Mary,
489, 661, 730, 1214; Phil., 661; Stephen, 730;
Susannah, 730; T., 719; Thos., 489, 708 n, 730
Farrell (Farail, Farell, Farhill), Eliz. Isabella, 1164;
Geo., 1070, 1071; Joseph, 412; W., 1055
Farren (Farrin), Abraham, 1272*, 1277; Ann, 1272;
Comfort, 1277; Geo., 1272; Jane, 233, 235;
Martha, 1267; Mary, 1482; Sarah, 1272; Thos.,
1267
Farrer, see Ferrers
Farrin, see Farren
Farrington, Eliz., 812; Rob., 812
Fauconberg, Earl, 327
Faudery, see Fawdry
Faukes (Fauks, Faulkes, Faulks, Faux, Fauxe), see
Fawkes
Fawcet (Fawset, Fawsett), Eliz., 49; Geo., 49;
Marg., 1430; Rev. Thos., 87, 88, 1430
Fawdon, Margery, 1391; Rob., 1391*
Fawdry (Faudery), C., 1476; Wm., 1067, 1480*
Fawkes (Faukes, Fauks, Faulkes, Faulks, Faux,
Fauxe, Fawx), Alice, 1432; Ann, 1499*; Chris.,
354; Edw., 803; Eliz., 660; Hannah, 777; Hugh,

13; John, 262, 777, 1432, 1499*; Mary, 262; Rebecca, 1499; Ric., 660; Sarah, 660; Thos., 777, 1005; Wm., 1499, 1502; fam., 1491

Fawkines, Rev. Thos., 1323

Fawset (Fawsett), see Fawcet

Fawx, see Fawkes

Feast, Rob., 1131; Sarah, 1131; Thos., 1131

Fecknaham, John, 841; Mary, 841; Rev. Thos., 840, 841

Feeble, Randall, 1316

Feire, Jeffry de, 1316

Felch, Hen., 1404

Felde, see Field

Felice, Wm., 1382

Fell, Rob., 408; Wm., 1518; Dr., 1196

Felsteed, Armel Miles, 858

Felton, Joseph, 339; Lieut. Wm., 1266

Fendall, John, 275; —, 1165*

Fenn, Rev. Nic., 228, 1165

Fennell, Ric., 564; Sarah, 564

Fenner, Hen. le, 1217

Fenton, Lord, 1312

Ferce (Ferc), John atte, 1363; Hugh, 1218

Fereby (Ferebee, Ferraby, Ferrebee, Ferribee), Edm., 387*; John, 1369; Rev. John, 1513; Thos., 368; Rev. Thos., 297, 1513; —, 1216

Ferebury, Geo., 584*; John, 584; Mary, 584

Ferendone, Elsi de, 1482*; and see Elsi

Ferguson Sir Jas., bt., 410; Marg., 410

Ferich, Wal., 1238

Ferley, see Farley

Ferlinge, Ric., 1154; Thos., 1150

Fermor, Eliz., 484, 591, 592; Hen., 484; Peter, 484*; W., 1447; Mr., 1446; —, 1446, 1447*; fam., 482, 1447*; and see Farmer

Fern (Ferne), Anne, 1499; John, 1499; —, 819; and see Farn

Fernham, John, 1370

Fernley (Fernly), Ann, 781; Josiah, 781*; Mary, 782; Obadiah, 782; Rob., 782*; Sarah, 782

Ferraby (Ferrebee), see Fereby

Ferrers (Farrer, Ferrars, Ferris, Ferrour, Ferrys), Ann(e), 73*, 1237; Rev. Bart., 508; Chas., 683; Edith, 1292; Edm., 1237; Eliz., 212; Hen. (de), 364, 792; Lady Isabel, 791 n; John, 651, 652, 1288, 1386; Rev. John, 651, 652*; Moses, 683; Rog., 72, 73*; Sarah, 683; Thos., 72, 73, 1574; W., 1216, 1290*; Wm., 71, 72, 212; barons, 228; Lieut. Col., 928; Lord, 545 n; Mr., 1293; Rev., 980*; —, 1475*; fam., 1237

Ferret, John, 787; Sarah, 787

Ferribee, see Fereby

Ferris (Ferrour), see Ferrers

Ferryman, John, 1262, 1267; Mary, 1262, 1267

Ferrys, see Ferrers

Ferthinge (Ferthings), Wm., 1428, 1519

Fettiplace (Fettyplace, Fhettiplace), Ann, 1441; Cecily, 1015; Chas., 1441*; Diana, 1441; Dorothea, 1501; Sir E., 1441; Sir Edm., 1441; Elinor, 1048*; Eliz., 427; G., 559, 1441; Sir G., 1441; Geo., 427*, 428 n, 1103; Giles, 427*, 428; Sir Giles, 366, 369; John, 1015; Sir Ric., kt.,

1048; Rob., 1441; Theophila, 428; Theophilus Partridge, 427; Thos., 1441; Col., 358; Lady, 369; Mr., 370; —, 1033, 1441; fam., 424, 1015, 1441

Fewster, Anne, 1303; Eliz., 1130, 1303*; Mary, 486, 661; Sarah, 377; Thos., 661, 1303; Wm., 486, 1130

Feye, Wal. le, 1221

Ffynch, see Finch

Fhettiplace, see Fettiplace

Ficketts, Jane, 517; John, 517

Fidkin (Tidkin in error), Rev. Edw., 76, 853

Fido, Rev. Edm., 81, 84; Rev. Edw., 783; Eliz., 82; Mary, 84; Rev. Thos., 1335

Field (Felde, Inthefelde), Ann(e), 524, 1206, 1376; Ant., 1215, 1218; Rev. Benj., 87, 865, 866*; Betty, 1376; Caroline, 866; Dan., 1076*; Edith, 1375; Edw., 90, 524, 1206*, 1215; Eliz., 329, 1206; Hen., 524; Joanna, 1206; John (in the), 522, 524, 1218, 1376*, 1377, 1499; Rev. John, 1157; Marg., 1376; Mary, 522, 1076; Nic., 293, 1227, 1289; Ric., 1206, 1215; Sarah, 90; T., 1215; Thos., 524*, 1375; Wal. atte, 1314; Wm., 524, 1376*, 1378, 1404; —, 1215; fam., 218, 523; and see Attefeld

Fielder, Eliz., 1130; Geo., 1130*, 1131, 1132; Mary, 1130; Sam., 1130; Thos., 1131; and see Filder

Fielding (Fieldings), Anne, 291; Chas., 1495, 1497; Dr. R., 1494; Dr. Rob., 1495, 1497*; Rev. Rog., 754, 909; Dr., 1502; Rev. Mr., 908

Fiennes, Eliz., 1040; Ric., 1040; Dr. Pharamus, 1430; Wm., Viscount Saye and Sele, 1040, 1430; Col., 1293; and see Fines

Fifield, Eliza, 1268; Hannah, 429, 948; Jane, 429; John, 762; Rev. John, 427, 429, 1483; Mary, 884, 948; Merial, 948; Rebecca, 429; Rob., 948*; Thos., 884; Tobias, 948; Wm., 1016

Figgures, John, 227

Filder, Wm., 1258; and see Fielder

Filkin, Ric., 1250, 1258

Fill (Vyll), Edw., 730; Rev. Geo., 1392*

Filton, Elias de, 602*, 1172; Ralf de, 602

Finch (Ffynch), Anne, 766, 767, 1350; Deborah, 858; Eliz., 1333, 1504; Francis, 766; Geo., 858, 966; Hen., 766*, 767; (or Wicks), Isaac, 1200; John, 766, 966*, 1504; Mary, 1361; Ric., 1217, 1350; Rev. Rob., 798; Sam., 1361; (or Wicks), Susanna, 1200; Thos., 1333*; Rev. Thos., 678; Wm., 1333; Lady, 979; —, lord chancellor, 719 n; fam., earls of Winchelsea, 766

Finden, Rev. Wm., 525

Fines, Mr., 882; and see Fiennes

Finnimore, Rev. Jacob, 599

Fisher (Fissher, Fisshere), Abraham, 1159; Anna, 1243; Ann(e), 984, 1144, 1241, 1243, 1446*, 1470, 1511; Avice, 865; Benj., 90, 270*, 1209*, 1273; Chas., 1209, 1511; Clement, 262; Edw., 865; Sir Edw., 865; Sir Edw., kt., 864, 865; Eliz., 413, 823, 846, 1209, 1446*; Francis, 683; Geof., see Piscator; Hannah, 270, 1470*; Hen., 1209; Rev. Hen., 643; J. T., 1215; Jas., 846*, 1152,

1159, 1446*, 1447; Jane, 984, 1446; John, 353*, 823, 845, 986, 1209; Joseph, 1369; Joseph Timbrell, 1209; Joshua, 1209; M., 1447; Marg., 1209, 1446; Martha, 353; Mary, 407, 587, 715, 846, 865, 948, 984*, 1063, 1241*, 1243, 1446*; Mic., 1446*, 1447; Nic. le, 1259; P. H., 1217, 1218; Paul, 407*, 1470; Paul Hawkins, 1209; Ralph, 1292; Ric., 984; Rob., 339, 984, 986; Sam., 1144, 1209; Sarah, 845, 1275; Stephen (le), 1259, 1446*; T., 1475; Thos., 360 n, 1241, 1243*, 1446*, 1470*; Wal. le, 1259; Wm., 587, 1209, 1241, 1249, 1258, 1275*, 1446*, 1447; Rev. Wm., 817, 1223*, 1331; —, 1216, 1255, 1256; fam., 823, 863*, 865

Fishpool, Edw., 731; John, 731; Sarah, 731

Fissher (Fisshere), see Fisher

Fitch, Ann, 1119; Ric. de la, 1218; Sarah de la, 1218

Fitcher, Thos., 948

Fitchew, Thos., 304

FitzAlan (Fitz Allan, Fitz-Alan), Hen., earl of Arundel, 424, 1139; Humph., earl of Arundel, 1139; Mary, duchess of Norfolk, 1139; Thos., earl of Arundel, 763; —, earl of Arundel, 1133, 1512

FitzBaderon, John, 819; Wm., 102, 759, 805, 819, 925, 1082, 1316, 1355, 1401*; —, 1355, 1402

FitzClerk (fil. Cl[er]ici), see Clarkson

FitzEdwards, Hester, 1262; Rev. Francis, 394, 1262*

FitzHamon (FitzHaimon, FitzHaman), Mabel, 1011, 1287; R., 1261, 1291; Rob., 71, 147, 482, 568, 585, 588, 609, 1011, 1261, 1287, 1419; —, 1285, 1287, 1309, 1475

FitzHarbert, see FitzHerbert

FitzHarding (FitzHardinge), Aldena, 773, 776; Nic., 737*; Raph, 737*; Reg., 737; Rob., Lord Berkeley, 39, 41*, 75, 153, 154, 156, 157*, 178*, 278, 451*, 527, 576*, 601, 720*, 721, 737*, 745, 773*, 776, 1369, 1539; Rog., 737*; Earl, see Berkeley, Col. W. Fitzhardinge; Lord, 1539; —, 1086*, 1100*, 1101, 1295

FitzHerbert (FitzHarbert), Eliz., 289; Eustace, 289; Peter, 1255; Ric., 1227*; Rob., 15*; Sarah, 15

FitzHugh, —, 1402

FitzJohn, Payne, 1380

Fitz-Milo, Rog., earl of Hereford, 605, 778 n, 1403

FitzNichol (FitzNicholl, FitzNichols), Agnes, 738*; Alienor, 737; John, 737*, 738; (or Browning), John, 801; Kath., 602, 737; Margery (Margerie), 602*; Thos., 602, 737, 738; Sir Thos., 602*, 738*, 1172*

FitzOsbert, Hugh, 1350*

FitzOsborne, Osborn, bishop, 1328; Rog., earl, 1322*; Wm., earl, 1322*

FitzPatrick, Bernard, 413; Jane, 413; Mary, 413

FitzPeter, Geof., 1439; Wm., 1015; —, 1440

FitzPons (Fitz Pons, Fitz Ponz), Drogo, 565, 618; Osbern, 829; Osbert, 1350; Ric., 565, 618, 619, 1350*; Wal., 1126, 1198, 1350; (or Clifford), Wal., 618; —, 1350

FitzRalph, John (the Clerk), 985, 1060; Phil., 985*, 1060

FitzReyn, Phil., 1033

FitzRichard, —, 1401

FitzRoy, Rob., earl of Gloucester, 1011, 1219, 1287

FitzStephen, John, 1316; Ralph, 1385; —, 1490*

FitzWalter, Miles, earl of Hereford, 244, 671, 1032, 1060, 1402; his daughter Marg., 671, 1402; Rob., 1052

FitzWarren, Cath., 533; Thos., 533; Warren, 533; Wm., 1031, 1032

FitzWilliam (FitzWilliams), Brian, 1062; Hugh, 1237, 1238; W., 1287, 1348; Wm., earl of Southampton, 301

Fladebur, Simon de, 1292

Flagge, Wal. de, 708*

Flandricus, see Fleming

Flatcher, see Fletcher

Fleetwood (Fleetwode), Garard, 1064; Hen., 738; Jas., 221; Mary, 1225; Ralph, 1225; fam., 739

Fleming (Flandricus, Flemynge), Alard (le), 1014*, 1051*; Ann(e), 1051*; Florence le, 1014; Hen. (le), 1014, 1051; Joan (le), 1014*, 1051; John (le), 1014, 1051; Mary, 666; Rainbert, 1074; Rev. Wm., 452; Dr., 1127; —, 1051

Fletcher (Flatcher), Alice, 1034; And., 633; Ann(e), 573*, 580, 862, 970, 1150, 1151, 1330, 1359; Ant., 818; Arthur, 866, 1002*, 1330, 1389; Barnabas, 868; Rev. Basil (Bazill), 1359*, 1362; Betty, 623, 706; Chas., 1026; David, 623; Dinah, 641; Dorothy, 293, 1002*; Edm., 676, 970; Edw., 1150, 1151; Eglantine, 573; Eleanor, 1152*; Eliz., 293*, 296, 623, 641, 1010; Esther, 868; Francis, 1194; Geo., 95, 970*; Grace, 847; Harry, 862; Hen., 508, 509; Hester, 1359*; Jas., 633; Jane, 862, 1012; Jeiffry, 715; Jo., 1034; Joane, 683; John, 293, 437, 442, 580, 623*, 633, 660*, 683, 706, 1012, 1034, 1075, 1445*; Joshua, 573; Judeth, 631; Kath., 676; M., 1574; Margery, 970; Martha, 686*; Mary, 95, 437, 509, 660, 706, 883*, 1002, 1026, 1445; Nic., 293, 883*, 1152; Ralph, 1016, 1047; Ric., 386*, 437, 493, 573*, 580, 847, 1218; Rob., 296*, 641, 1010, 1152*, 1382, 1466; Rob. Warren, 1154; Rog., 862; Sam., 631*; Sarah, 442, 573, 686, 848, 850, 1075, 1445; Susanna(h), 573*, 660, 715; Thos., 87, 289, 293, 296, 573, 1012, 1445*; Wm., 573, 623, 686*, 858*, 1010, 1012, 1121; Winifred, 386; —, 36, 1015*, 1017*, 1282, 1455; fam., 218

Flexman, Hen. le, 1259

Flight, Jas., 1026; Joshua, 1025

Floddre, Thos. atte, 1392

Floid, see Floyd

Flook (Flooke), see Fluck

Flower, Ann, 211, 677; Dan., 1115; Eleazer, 677*; Eliz., 211*, 1085, 1115; Geo., 211; Hen., 1084; Hester, 677; Joanna, 211; John, 210*, 211*; Lamorack, 211; Marg., 1085*; Mary, 210, 1115; Rebecca, 211; Rev. Ric., 1085*, 1087; Susanna, 211; Thos., 1217; Wm., 616; —, 1061, 1539

Floyd (Floid), Joseph, 1410*; Mary, 1410; (or Loyde), Rev. Nic., 1317; Sam., 1410*; (or Lloyd), —, 1054; and see Lloyd

Floyer, Jas., 1312

Fluck (Flook, Flooke, Flucke, Fluke), Edith, 485; Edw., 485; Eleanor, 485; Eliz., 485, 801, 1274, 1583; Esther, 1316; Geo., 1158, 1231; Giles, 485; Hannah, 1434; Joan, 1158*; Job, 1576; John, 485*, 801, 1289, 1396; Joseph, 485, 1158, 1395, 1396, 1403; Martha, 1583; Mary, 1231, 1372, 1396; Sarah, 485*, 486; Sibble, 1396; Stephen, 1583; Susanna(h), 485*, 1395*; Thos., 486, 1372; Wm., 485*, 1158*, 1434

Fludd, Rob., 168*; Sarah, 168

Fluke, see Fluck

Flyfield, Aron, 1100; Mary, 1100*; Moses, 1100

Foaks, Ric., 611; and see Fox

Foard, see Ford

Foateweys, Wm. de, 1477

Foghelere, see Fowler

Fokeram, Wm., 1491; —, 1486, 1491

Foket, Rob., 1379

Folcher, see Folker

Foley, A., 894; And., 893, 894, 895, 896; Eliza, 1185; Rev. John, 895, 1185; Rev. Rob., 895; Thos., 479, 895; Thos., Lord Foley, 893; Lord, 893; —, 1165

Foliot (Foliott, Folliott), Gil., bishop, 1238; Hugh, bishop, 766; Reg., 985; Rob., bishop, 1060; —, bishop, 1093; —, 1491

Folker (Folcher), Ambrose, 598; Mary, 598; —, 1404*

Folkes, see Fowke

Folkestone, Viscount and Viscountess, see Bouverie, Wm. and Harriot

Folliott, see Foliot

Fontaine, Sir Erasmus de la, kt., 291; Mary de la, 291; and see Fountain

Fonte, A., 1091; Hen. de, 1043; John de, 1091; Rob. de, 1314; — de, 1091

Foord (Foords), see Ford

Foort, see Forte

Foot (Fot), Ann, 368; Geo., 211*; John, 1313; Mary, 211*; Thos., 211

Forbes, Rev. Wm., 1313

Force, Thos., 944

Ford (Foard, Foord, Foords, Forde, Fords), Anna, 241; Ann(e), 241, 624, 703, 919, 1344, 1345; Cath., 1584; Chas., 419; Cicely, 1175; Dan., 284, 419, 1508*; Dinah, 304; Rev. Edw., 228*, 525, 526; Eliz., 16, 211, 419, 454, 526, 1344, 1508; Rev. Francis, 919; Geo., 211, 1318; Hannah, 282, 1453, 1534; Hen., 241*, 249, 1534; Hester, 1175; Jas., 241, 1175*, 1345, 1508; John, 6, 211, 212, 241, 282*, 456, 551 n, 552, 906, 907*, 967, 1307, 1508, 1584*; Jonathan, 1481; Joseph, 967, 1000, 1453, 1534; Mary, 249, 282, 284, 1146, 1175, 1342, 1344, 1453*; Moses, 1453*; Naomi, 967; Rebecca, 919; Rev. Ric. Wilbraham, 1016; Sam., 417; Sarah, 212, 456*, 1508; Susannah, 906; Thos., 454, 456, 703, 1344*; W., 1312; Wm., 10, 249, 304, 456*, 624, 703, 1146, 1345, 1534*, 1584; Mr., 1185; —, 1455; —, abbot, 392; —, Lord Grey, 139; fam., 236, 558; and see Attford

Forden, Ann, 368; Wm., 367, 377

Forder, Amy, 377; Ann, 377*; Grace, 699; John, 377; Mary, 377; Thos., 377*

Fordewelle, Wal., 1074

Fording, Jas., 1132

Fords, see Ford

Forest (Forrest), Wal. le, 1259; —, 1127

Forrester (Forestar, Forester, Forrister), Anne, 413; Eliz., 496*; (or Forster), Eliz., 576; Jas., 413; Capt. John, 496; Nic., 1313; (or Forster), Ric., 576; Wm., 1005*; Sir Wm., 1005; Wm., Lord Forrester, 496; fam., 427; and see Forster; Foster

Forshew, Alice, 862; Anne, 517, 859, 862*; Edw., 862*; Eliz., 517, 862; Jane, 862*; John, 517, 859, 862*; Rob., 862; Sarah, 862; fam., 859

Forster, Edw., 1103; Eliz., 1121, 1415; (or Forrister), Eliz., 576; Geo., 920; Giles (Gyles), 544, 920; Humph., 546; Sir Humph., bt., 471; Marg., 471; Ric., 1121*, 1490; (or Forrister), Ric., 576; Rev. Rob., 1415; Susan, 920; —, 1477; fam., 770; and see Forrester; Foster

Forte (Foort, Fort), Edw., 522; Marg., 1275*; Mary, 1275; Ric., 448; Wm., 1275*; Rev. Wm., 870

Fortescue, Sir Adrian, 1120, 1169*, 1348*, 1387; Ann, 1169, 1348, 1387; Sir Francis, 1348; Sir Hen., 570 n; John Inglett, 639; Sir John, 570, 571, 1339, 1477; Marg., 1169; Rob., 571; —, 1387*; fam., 570

Fortescue [peerage], Hugh, Earl, 635; Mat., Earl, 571*; Earl, 571; Lord (baron), 571, 864, 865; and see Aland, John Fortescue

Fortey (Forteye, Fortheie, Forthey, Fortheye), see Forty

Forthington, Wal. de, 1060

Fortibus (or Crassus, le Gros), Aveline, 1120; Hawise, 1120; Wm. de, 1120*, 1123

Fortune, Anne, 937; Dorothy, 1341; Eliz., 35, 281*; Hester, 1330; John, 937*, 1456; Rev. John, 1456; Mary, 281, 937*; Rev. Moore, 936, 937*, 1329, 1331; Sarah, 936; Wal., 1341; Wm., 281, 937

Forty (Fortey, Forteye, Fortheie, Forthey, Fortheye), Adam atte, 1491; Agnes, 945; Eliz., 1046; Grainger, 1194; Hannah, 1194; John (atte), 906, 943, 1194*, 1196, 1314, 1552; Joseph, 1196; Ric., 683, 1046; Thos. (atte), 906, 945, 1069; Mr., 943

Fosbroke (Fosbrooke), —, 1082, 1123, 1177, 1196, 1255, 1309, 1321, 1345, 1381, 1441, 1519

Fosse, Bart., 1475

Foster, Alice, 273, 1052; Jas., 273; John, 273; Rev. John, 1478; Mary, 273; Ric., 1428*; Thos., 273*, 1052; Wm., 1157; and see Forrester; Forster

Fot, see Foot

Fothergill, Dr., 327 n

Fotman, Ann, 1367*; Wm., 1367*

Fouch (Fouke), see Fowke

Foulere, see Fowler

Fountain, And., 1424; Sir And., 1424; Eliz., 1424; and see Fontaine

Fowke (Folkes, Fouch, Fouke, Fukes), Dorothy, 1409; H., 1387*; Hen., 1281*, 1360, 1387; Jane, 1297; Jane Charlotte, 1360; John, 1289; Martin,

1409; Rob., 1297*, 1420; Sarah, 1281; Mr., 1362; —, 1311

Fowle, Abraham, 907; Deborah, 761; Eliz., 822; Rev. Fulwar Craven, 579; John, 760, 761, 821, 822, 1316; Josiah, 821, 1036; Judith, 658; Rev. Lawr., 760; Mary, 474, 821, 822, 1316; Rob., 761*; Sam., 762; Sarah, 762; Susannah, 761, 822; Theophilus, 658; Thos., 762; Wm., 474, 1316, 1403

Fowler (Foghelere, Foulere), Amey, 1004; Anna, 560; Ann(e), 562, 887, 1049*, 1050, 1117, 1136, 1137, 1179, 1182, 1244; Anselm, 887, 1145, 1179*, 1185; Barbara, 283; Betty, 1049; Chas., 399*, 1008; Chris., 835*; Dan., 283*, 560, 658, 1049, 1136*, 1137*, 1140, 1185, 1212, 1307, 1371; David, 1049, 1050; Edw., 302, 741, 1145, 1183, 1186; Edw., bishop, 664, 1428; Rev. Edw., 1186; Eliz., 282, 283, 344, 398, 399, 658, 661, 835*, 1004, 1136, 1212; Geo., 1049*; Giles, 398, 399, 905*; Hen., 562, 651 n, 1004, 1179, 1218, 1574; Rev. Hen., 325, 651, 860; Rev. Hen. Bond, 1348; Hester, 339, 1137*, 1315; Jas., 660, 1049, 1179, 1452, 1456; Jane, 100, 399, 658, 835, 1049; Jeremiah, 661; John (le), 182, 399, 658*, 1049*, 1244, 1313, 1384, 1420; Judith, 1183; Marg., 398; Martha, 308, 1452; Mary, 182, 399*, 623, 658*, 905*, 1049*, 1136, 1137, 1182, 1183*; Nat., 1137, 1182, 1186; Nic., 308; Rebecca, 1179; Ric., 399*, 659, 905*, 1207, 1268, 1315*; Rev. Ric., 1117; Rog., 1062; Sam., 1137*; Rev. Sam., 447; Sarah, 658, 887, 1049, 1179; Stephen, 1137, 1179; Susannah, 1137; Thos., 398, 399, 623, 658*, 835, 1049, 1182, 1183, 1186; Tracy, 1207; W., 1185*, 1187, 1459; Wm., 282, 308, 344, 399*, 1049*, 1050, 1129, 1179*, 1533; Rev., 1132; —, 1139, 1216*, 1311, 1369, 1455

Fowles, Edw., 846; John, 781; Lambert, 964; Sarah, 846; Sebbatin, 846; Susan, 1171; Sir Thos., kt., 1171

Fownes, Anne, 1076; Geo., 1076; Rev. John, 764; Joseph, 972; Sarah, 972

Fox (Foxe), Alice la, 1198; Ann(e), 486, 921, 989, 1224, 1558; C. J., 1198; Edith, 492; Edm., 999; Edw., 492; Edw., bishop, 534*; Eliz., 212, 842, 923, 999, 1413; Geo., 1413; Hannah, 1413; Rev. Help-on-High, 808; Hen., 1583; Rev. Hopwel, 810; Rev. Humph., 1290; Jas., 921*; Jane, 111, 226*, 492; Joane, 211; John, 423, 842, 923*, 1196, 1224, 1413*, 1437; Rev. John, 511; Lydia, 1569; Martha, 226; Mary, 921*, 923, 1437; Phil., 1224*; Poyntz, 211; Ralph le, 1172; Ric. le, 1258; Dr. Ric., bishop, 394*, 525, 638; Rob., 212; Sam., 486, 1558*, 1569; Sir Stephen, 1005 n; Thos., 226*; Wm., 111; —, 1123*; fam., 989; and see Foax

Foxcote, Elias de, 1501; Ric. de, 1351; Thos. de, 1502; —, 1351

Foxcroft, Rev. J., 1170

Foxe, see Fox

Foxton, Rev. Geo., 1360*, 1362; John, 1420; Sarah, 1360*

Foxwell, John, 1539; T., 1177; Thos., 1177

Foy, Edw., 1553; John, 1564; Nat., 1553

Foyle, Edw., 385; Mary, 385

Frame, see Freame

Framilesworth, Eleanor, 1103; Wm., 1103

Frampton, Anne, 60; Ely, 60; Hannah, 60; Harriette, 1245; Rev. J., 1256; Jacob, 60; John, 60; Marg., 336; Mary, 60; Rob., 336; Dr. Rob., bishop, 93, 1129, 1132, 1189, 1428; fam., 721

Francia, Francesco, 591 n

Francis, bishop of Hereford, see Godwin

Francis (Fraunceys, Frauncis), Chris., 1191; Eliz., 210; Hannah, 111; Jas., 210; John, 413, 797*; Juliana, 1259; Marg., 797; Mary, 797*, 1191, 1465; Nic., 1061; Wm., 111, 1465

Francklyn, see Franklin

Francom (Francomb, Francombe, Franckombe, Francum, Frankcom, Frankcomb, Frankcombe, Frankcome, Frankecombe, Frankum), Ann, 398, 963*; Betty, 730, 755, 823; Dan., 703; Dorothy, 125; Esther, 491; F., 1121; Francis, 124, 125*, 241, 755*, 823; Geo., 1549; J., 1356*; Jane, 1353*; John, 492, 699*, 730, 1341, 1353, 1549; Marg., 699, 1341; Mary, 491, 730, 977, 1337*, 1353*, 1356, 1549; Rebekah, 703; Ric., 125, 823, 1337*; Rob., 962; Sam., 125, 491, 836; Sarah, 125*, 491; Stephen, 1549*, 1550; Susanna(h), 1549, 1550; Thos., 1353; Tryphena, 1550; Wm., 977, 1353*, 1550; —, 398, 415, 1355*; fam., 823, 1337

Franke, see Franks

Frankecombe, see Francom

Frankis (Frankiss), see Franks

Frankland, Fred., 135; Ric., 135; T., 1015

Franklin (Francklyn, Franklyn, Fraunkelein, Fraunkeleyn), Adam, 1317; Barbara, 446; Dorothy, 446; Francis, 203; Jas., 1213; Sir John, kt., 89; Mary, 1561*; Phil., 1561; Ric., 1561; S. R., 1519; Sam., 429, 922*; Sarah, 429, 922; Rev. Thos., 121, 1348; Wm., 429, 1052*, 1223, 1316, 1561; —, 1455

Franks (Franke, Frankis, Frankiss), Ann(e), 1375, 1377*; Benj., 1378; Eliz., 1375*, 1377; Hen., 1377, 1378; John, 1375; Ric., 715*, 1374, 1375*, 1377*; Rev. Ric., 1165*; Sam., 1377; Sarah, 715, 1375*, 1377; Wal., 1058; Wm., 1375*, 1377; —, 1378

Frankum, see Francom

Frape, Anna, 623; Edw., 1099; Francis, 1099; J., 1101; John, 623, 1099*; Mary, 1099; Sarah, 623; Wm., 703, 1099*

Fraser (Freyser), Rev. John, 1228; Joseph, 1289

Fraunceys (Frauncis), see Francis

Fraunkelein (Fraunkeleyn), see Franklin

Freame (Frame, Fream, Freeme, Freme), Alice, 584, 652; Anna, 1206; Dan., 800, 1163; Eliz., 905, 1401; Hannah, 133*; Hester, 1163; J., 1216; Jasper, 905*, 906; Joan, 1163; John, 133, 450, 905*, 1163*; Judith, 837; Mary, 335, 800; R., 1216*, 1317; Ric., 1207; Rob., 652, 1207, 1218; Stephen, 837; Thos., 133, 198, 199, 450, 1206*, 1207, 1401, 1403; Wm., 166, 198, 328, 335, 370, 374, 450*, 837, 906; —, 1216*

Freckleton (Frekelton), John 1389, 1392
Frederick, prince of Wales, 349 n, 1440*
Fredericks (Frederick), F., 1323; —, 1238
Freebank, G., 1356
Freebury, Chas., 1213; John, 567; Martha, 567;
    Mary, 641; Sarah, 1213; Thos., 567; Wm., 641;
    —, 1216
Freeman (Frema., Freman, Fremon), Alice, 1375;
    Rev. Amb., 424; Anna, 143, 1360; Ann(e), 59,
    142, 383*, 615, 693, 812, 814, 1043, 1075, 1227,
    1360, 1490; Ant., 986, 1375; Rev. Ant., 114, 332,
    586; Arthur, 1226*; Barbara, 1360; Cath., 405,
    1507; Chas., 388, 1358*, 1360, 1362; David,
    296; Dorothy, 1472; E., 1475; Edith, 1375; Edw.,
    148, 615*, 1041; Ele(a)nor, 1280, 1359; Eliz.,
    143, 150, 151*, 338, 587, 1226*, 1375, 1445,
    1464*, 1472, 1490; Esther, 274; Frances, 383;
    Francis, 554, 615, 1507; Hannah, 1358*, 1467;
    Hen., 636, 1043; Jas., 659*, 814, 1197, 1375;
    Jane, 983, 984; Joan, 202, 1375; John (le), 142,
    150, 202*, 396, 429, 636*, 686, 693, 715*, 868*,
    871, 1091, 1104*, 1197, 1214, 1331, 1363, 1445,
    1464, 1519; Rev. John, 221, 1346; John Lloyd,
    383; Joseph, 660; Kennet (Kemmet, Kemmett),
    449, 484, 1262, 1267, 1360, 1362; Marg., 383*,
    871, 1358; Marg. Eliz., 143; Margery, 296;
    Martha, 563; Mary, 143, 150, 274, 429, 524*,
    554, 686, 868, 1075, 1193*, 1262, 1464, 1472*,
    1493; Meriel, 383; Mic., 891, 1226*; Priscilla,
    1262*, 1267, 1288, 1360; Rebecca, 332; Ric.,
    143*, 274, 524, 1154, 1190, 1227, 1361, 1476;
    Rev. Ric., 1478; Rob., 814, 1002, 1330, 1375*;
    Rob. Berkeley, 59; Rowland, 202, 368, 383*,
    1375*; Sam., 1467*, 1477; Sarah, 150*, 296*,
    ?1043; Simon, 1491; Susanna, 151; T., 1220,
    1475; T. E., 1476; Thos., 142, 187, 274*, 383*,
    636*, 814, 890, 891, 983, 984, 1075, 1350,
    1464*, 1467, 1472; Rev. Thos., 424, 651, 1154,
    1513; Thos. Edwards, 142*, 143*, 205, 206*,
    220, 272*; Thos. Motley, 187; W., 1195*; Wal.
    (le), 143, 1150; Wal. Edwards, 143; Wm., 148,
    150*, 151*, 187, 198, 296, 338, 434, 524*, 563,
    587, 636, 816, 864, 865, 1043*, 1120, 1193,
    1226, 1331, 1375, 1477, 1490, 1493; Messrs.,
    1475; Mr., 142, 206, 288; —, 1002, 1043, 1195*,
    1196, 1197, 1220, 1331, 1477; fam., 142, 1362,
    1475; (formerly Edwards), fam., 1420
Freeme, see Freame
Freeth (Frith), Ann, 1282; Ann King, 1282; C.,
    1282; John, 1334
Freke, Edm., 221; Geo., 1408; Phil., 1408; Ric. le,
    1259
Frekelton, see Freckleton
Freman (Frema.), see Freeman
Freme, see Freame
Fremer, Hen. le, 1217
Fremon, see Freeman
French (Frenche, Frensh, Frensshe), Betty, 1307;
    Eliz., 329*, 1307; Jas., 1275; John, 633*, 1307*,
    1369; Marg., 329; Mary, 633; N., 1061; Nic.,
    1061; R. (le), 1061, 1062; Rob., 1313, 1481;
    Sarah, 633*; Susanna, 1481; Thos. le, 1061; Rev.

Thos., 1031, 1061; Wal., 1061, 1504; Wm., 329,
    1313; —, 1017
Frencham, Anne, 903; Rev. Ric., 903
Frenche, see French
Frend, see Friend
Frensh (Frensshe), see French
Frescheville, Amicia, 876; Sir Ralph, 876
Freston, Rev. T. G. H., 1494
Fretherne (Frethern), Geof. de, 1054; J., 1195;
    fam., 625
Fretwell, Geo., 604; Mary, 604
Frewen (Frewyne), Accepted, archbishop, 559 n;
    Eliz., 1344; Jas., 1344; Rev. John, 1340; Ric.,
    1440; Rob., 1404
Frey, Jane, 35; Sarah, 35; Thos., 35*; and see Fry
Freyser, see Fraser
Fricker, Christian, 577; Edw., 1503; Eliz., 1503;
    Joseph, 577*; Sarah, 577
Friend (Frend), Alice, 1425; Edw., 540*; Eliz., 540;
    Hugh le, 1372; John, 1425; Nat., 1425*; Ric.,
    1477; Rob., 1478
Frier, see Fryer
Frith, see Freeth
Froggeforde, Thos., 1313; Wm., 1313
Frogley, Rob., 1334
Froisselew, —, 1475
Frome, Rev. Rob. de, 711 n
Fromond, Rob., 1288
Frost, Mary, 751; Wm., 751*
Fry, Celia, 837; Edw., 300; Geo., 48*, 211, 837;
    Hester, 48*, 837; John, 837; Rev. John, 704;
    Joyce, 48; Peter, 887; Sarah, 1574; Rev. Thos.,
    411; Wm., 1334; Rev. Wm., 909*; and see Frey
Fryer (Frier), Alice, 1530; Anna, 70; Ann(e), 832*,
    1531; Ant., 832; Dan., 70, 666, 1157; Eleanor,
    666, 930; Eliz., 70, 623, 1397*; Esther, 536;
    Hannah, 100, 831, 1438; Hen., 923; Jas., 1397*;
    John, 70, 388, 831, 930, 1158, 1438, 1531*,
    1539; Judith, 623; Martha, 1531; Mary, 70*, 388,
    831*, 923, 1077, 1397, 1530, 1531; Mat., 832;
    Ric., 100, 388, 1158*, 1530; Sam., 1531; Sarah,
    70, 831, 832, 1157, 1158; Susannah, 832; Thos.,
    70*, 166, 387, 536, 538, 832*, 931; Wm., 70*,
    558, 623, 831*, 832, 1077, 1186; Rev. Wm.,
    1169; Mr., 1378; Rev., 1166; —, 913; fam., 885
Fuist, see Fust
Fukes, see Fowke
Fuller, Rev. E. A., 1101, 1202; Francis, 1057; Dr.
    Francis, 1554; Mary, 543, 1057; Ric. Wyman,
    543
Fulljames, Thos., 1323
Fulman, Rev. Wm., 860*
Fulwell, Rev. Ulpian, 890
Fulwood, Rebecca, 86; Thos., 86
Furney, Hannah, 789*; Mary, 789; Rev. Ric., 488;
    Rob., 789*
Fushs, Jane, 1248; John Martin, 1248
Fussell, Mary, 10; Sam., 11; Wm., 10*
Fust (Fuist), Edw., 738, 739; Sir Edw., bt., 737,
    739*, 1208; Eliz., 520, 1208; Frances, 1379; Sir
    Francis, 739*, 740, 741, 1379; H. Jenner, 1379;
    John, 739; Sir John, bt., 520, 739*, 740*, 741,

1019; Dame Philippa, 739*; Ric., 738, 1521; Thos., 739; —, 1020; fam., 739*

Fustis, Jas., 946

Fydell, Thos., 1233

Fylote, Alice, 1404

Fymon, Hen., 1372

Fynian, Ralph, 1074; Wal., 1074

Fyrer, Rev. Chas., 1335

G., Nic. le, 1218

G—, Eliz., 919

G—me, Diana, 981; John, 981

Gaball, Rev. Ric., 1335

Gabb (Gabbe), Dan., 981; Edith, 1182; Eliz., 172*, 317, 563, 1187; Giles, 172*, 317; John, 677, 938*; Rev. John, 1551; Mary, 419*, 938, 981; Nic., 1182, 1187; Ric., 172, 1217; Sam., 419*, 938; Thos., 317, 1172; Wm., 563

Gabbett, Eliz., 467; Rob., 467

Gabbitas (Gabitas), Mary, 1418; Wm., 1418

Gabel, see Gabriel

Gabitas, see Gabbitas

Gabriel (Gabel), Rev. Ric., 1346

Gael, see Gale

Gage, Sir T., Viscount Gage, 1162; Sir T. R., bt., 1403; W. Hall, 1162; —, 1292; fam., 913, 917; (or Cage), fam., 625

Gage [peerage], Beata Maria, Viscountess, 1162; Hen., baron, 1162; Hen. Hall, Viscount, 1162; Thos., Viscount, 188, 913, 921; Lady, 1162; Lord, 913, 1161*, 1162; Viscountess, 921; and see Gage, Sir T.; Hall, Wm.

Gaie, see Gay

Gain, Wm., 1516

Gainer (Gayner), Anne, 677, 961; Benj., 398; Betty, 780; Chas., 1019; Eliz., 176, 830; Hester, 780*; John, 398, 677, 961*, 1312; Mary, 398, 961; Nic., 176; Rob., 780*; Sam., 830; fam., 603

Gainey, John, 1212; Martha, 1400; Phebe, 1212; Ric., 1400; Sam., 1212

Gainsborough, Baptist, earl of, 288*; Hen., earl of, 288; earl of, 220, 288, 570*; Lord, 287 n; and see Noel, Wriothesley Baptist

Gainsford, Capt., 928; Major, 103

Gale (Gael, Geale), Alice, 337*; Ann(e), 377, 1250; Chas., 780; Edith, 843; Edm., 337*; Rev. Edm. Estcourt, 783; Edw., 314, 317, 1477; Eliz., 337; Geo., 1250; Isaac, 843; Rev. Isaac, 783; Izard, 317; John, 316, 317, 662, 784, 1251*; Josepha, 1459; Mary, 377, 780; Prudence, 780; Ric., 597; Rob., 314, 317*; Rog., 864 n; S., 1005; Sarah, 317, 780; Thos., 377, 662*; Wm. Burch, 1459; Dr., 807; —, 1381*

Galeys, Wal., 1292

Gallop, M., 1087

Galloway (Galraway), Ann, 797; Anabell, 797; Francis, 797, 1456; Mary, 333

Gally, Rev. Peter, 275, 350

Galraway, see Galloway

Gamage (Gamages), Eliz., 1401, 1402; Eufemia, 1402; Nic., 1402*; W., 1404; Wm., 1404; —, abbot, 426; —, 1401, 1402*; fam., 392, 546

Game (Gamme), Peter, 1174; Col., 806 n

Gamon (Gamond), Ann, 486; Jas., 486*; Wm., 1010

Gamuel, Cath., 337; W., 337

Ganaway, Ric., 1119

Gandy, Rev. Hen., 7, 994, 1428

Gant, see Gaunt

Gardiner (Gardener, Gardner, Gardners), Amy, 429; Anna, 1210; Ann(e), 317, 337, 429, 762, 858, 953, 972*, 1041, 1166, 1211, 1316, 1376, 1413; Ant., 1321; Augusta Hillman, 975; Rev. Bernard, 713; Betty, 981, 1413; Chas., 953, 1539; Charlotte, 975; Chris., 657; Dan., 174, 972*, 976*, 1164, 1213, 1377; Dorwood, 972; Edith, 337*; Edith Cox, 337; Edw., 52, 337, 622*, 972, 980; Eleanor, 1210; Elisha, 1213; Eliz., 77, 541, 657, 666, 789, 976, 1041, 1137, 1213, 1321, 1376, 1377; Frances, 953; Gabriel, 429; Giles, 429, 670, 1181, 1206, 1211, 1215; Grace, 971; Hannah, 706; Hen., 972*, 1165; Jas., 35; Jas. Lambert, 337; Jane, 337, 550, 661, 670, 1050, 1526; Job, 975*; John, 337, 429*, 622*, 706, 946, 953*, 970*, 972*, 1004, 1012, 1180*, 1181, 1196, 1550; Rev. John ('J. G.'), 722, 729; Col. John Gil. Cooper, 1031; Josiah, 980–1; Luke, 969*, 972*; Marg., 972; Margery, 953; Martha, 1041; Mary, 35*, 52, 337, 429*, 789, 972*, 976*, 1004, 1137, 1180, 1181, 1377, 1550; Mat., 35; Nat., 981, 1186, 1203, 1210*, 1212, 1413; Paul, 762; Peter, 976; Phil., 1413; Priscilla, 429, 657; Ric., 946, 972*, 981, 1316; Rev. Ric., 1166, 1169; Rob., 953, 1216; Rosamund, 622; Sam., 541, 789, 972*, 976, 1413; Sarah, 229, 429*, 907, 970, 972*, 976, 1041, 1137, 1181, 1212; Stephen, 969, 971; Dr. Stephen, 534 n; Thos. (le), 317, 337*, 550, 857, 858, 907, 981, 1137, 1150, 1203, 1217, 1376*, 1392; Ursula, 52, 1321; W., 1052; Wm., 77*, 635*, 661, 789*, 891, 980, 1041*, 1050, 1181, 1210*, 1217, 1377, 1526; Rev. Wm., 1177, 1376; Wm. Hen., 975; Wm. Jas., 981; Wm. Thos., 975; Mr., 1232, 1288; Rev., 272*; widow, 1218; —, 1017, 1215, 1216

Garfield, Ann, 1457; Hen., 1457; Mary, 1457

Garine, see Gearing, Eliz. and Wm.

Garland, Edith, 174; Geo., 413; Jeane, 741; Martha, 413; Mary, 413; Nat., 741; Sam., 413*; Sarah, 1575; Thos., 174*, 413

Garlekmonger, John le, 1258

Garlick, Dinah, 1361; John, 1368, 1369; fam., 630

Garmyn, see Jarman

Garn, see Garne

Garnbury, Wm., 797

Garne (Garn), Jas., 339, 398; John, 1068; Mary, 398; Minerva, 1068; Miriam, 1068; Thos., 1068*

Garner, Hen., 847; Sarah, 203, 847; Wm., 203

Garney, Joseph, 1401*; Mary, 1401

Garniston, Ann, 1566*; John, 1566*; Nat., 1566

Garnons (Gernon, Gernons, Gernun), John, 1494; Luke, 1165; Mary, 789; Wm., 789, 1092

Garrard, Alice, 1255; and see Garrett; Gerard

Garrat, see Garrett

Garraway (Garway, Gerwy), Eliz., 1113; Jane,

1113; John, 1113*; Mary, 1113; Thos., 1552; W., 1139; —, 1139

Garrett (Garrat, Garritt), Anne, 1153; Dan., 1330; Edw., 1150, 1153; Joanna, 1330; Mary, 1330; Thos., 1330; Mr., 206; *and see* Garrard; Gerard

Garstang, Hugh, 361

Garston (Gaston), Eliz., 150; John, 150; —, 1064

Garter, Mary, 683; Wm., 683

Garton, Jas., 920; Mary, 920

Garway, *see* Garraway

Garwood, Anne, 1360

Gascoyne (Gascoyn), Claudius, 293*; Hugh, 1331; Martha, 293

Gase, *see* Gaze

Gaselyn, *see* Gasslyne

Gaskell, Wm. Penn, 1485

Gasslyne (Gaselyn), Juliana, 1428, 1490; Wal., 1172, 1428; (or Catlyn), Wal. de, 1490; Wm., 1428*, 1490

Gaston, *see* Garston

Gastrell, Anna, 1241; Ann(e), 175*, 1241, 1245, 1251, 1257; Edw., 175*; Fabian, 1251*; Gil., 1241*, 1252, 1257; Jas., 1241, 1374; Jane, 1241, 1252; John, 375, 1256, 1374; Marg., 1243; Mary, 1241*, 1243, 1245, 1251*, 1252; Rev. Miles, 1257; Ric., 375, 1251*, 1374*; Sam., 1251; —, 1241, 1378; fam., 1255*

Gate, *see* Gates

Gater, Anne, 1429*; Thos., 1429*; Wm., 1429

Gates (Gate), Dorothy, 1409; Rob., 1409; Sarah, 906, 1374*; Rev. Tim., 394, 395, 579; Wal. atte, 1197; *and see* Yate

Gaunt (Gant), Eva (Eve), 576, 720; John of, duke of Lancaster, 119*, 1316*, 1403; Maur. de, 179, 576, 720; Thos. le, 1552; fam., 40, 179, 807

Gautroun, Nic., 1356

Gaveston, Marg., 1011; —, 1011

Gay (Gaie), Benj., 736; Betty, 736; Mary, 10, 736; John, 10*, 413; Ric., 727; Rog. le, 1552; Sarah, 491; Thos., 491; Rev. Wm., 272

Gayler, Rev. Rob., 1087

Gayner, *see* Gainer

Gazard, *see* Gazzard

Gaze (Gase), Ann, 787; —, 1017

Gazzard (Gazard), Ann(e). 938, 1176; Ant., 938; Benj., 1176; Cornelius, 939; Eli, 939; Eliz., 752, 1344; Hannah, 1176; John, 1176; Nic., 752; Ric., 1176, 1344*; Sophia, 939; Wm., 938*

Geale, *see* Gale

Gearad, *see* Gerard

Gearing (Gearin, Geering, Gerin), Alex., 797; Ann, 796*; Cath., 727, 797*; Eliz., 797; (or Garine, Gernon), Eliz., 1232; Greg., 1410, 1419; Hen., 797; John, 797; (or Geere), Rev. John, 1290*; Marg., 1410; Mary, 797*, 1452; Ric., 796, 797*; Rob., 796*, 797*; Sarah, 797; Simon, 796*, 797; Thos., 727, 1452; Wm., 796, 797; (or Garine, Gernon), Wm., 1232; —, 1420

Geaste, *see* Geest

Geaves (Gyves), Rev. John, 1477; Rob., 688, 704

Geddes, Rev. Mic., 599

Gedgrom (Godgrom), Rob., 1552; —, 1017

Gee, —, 159

Geekie, Rev. Wm., 534

Geere (Geers), (or Geering), Rev. John (J.), 1290*; Dr. T., 1290; Serjt., 1197

Geering, *see* Gearing

Geers, *see* Geere

Geest (Geaste), Giles, 1290; Rev. Peter, 1482; —, 1293; *and see* Gist

Geffe (Geffes), *see* Jeffs

Geffray, *see* Jeffery

Geffreis, *see* Jefferies

Geffrey, *see* Jeffery

Gegg (Gege), Ann, 1080; Geo., 1075; H., 1052; Hannah, 388; Joan, 1033; John, 1033; Jonathan, 1080*, 1136; Rev. Joseph, 76, 440; Mary, 1075, 1080*; Rebecca, 1080; Ric., 1080; Rev. Rob., 440, 442; Sam., 388; Thos., 859, 1080*; Wm., 370, 1080*; —, 1082

Gelfe, *see* Jelf

Gelsthorpe (Gelsthrope), Alice, 501; John, 501; Thos., 501; Rev. Wm., 500, 501

Geneville (Genevil), — de, 1016, 1082

Genn, —, 1017

Genn, —, 1017

Genyns, *see* Jennings

Geoffrey son of Johane, 1552

George I, 56, 78, 136, 198, 440, 447, 459, 488, 507, 511, 561, 567, 689, 854, 1069, 1356, 1369

George II, 56, 139, 180, 198, 216, 244*, 415, 440, 459*, 488, 511, 567, 571, 586, 689, 748, 802, 829, 853, 854, 1356, 1369, 1370, 1502

George III, 56, 58, 139, 180, 198, 244, 327 n, 440, 447, 459, 488, 567, 586, 689, 748, 802, 829, 1356, 1370, 1372, 1440, 1494, 1512

George, Alice, 372; Ann(e), 55*, 70, 541, 963, 1460; Chas., 1029; Chris., 985; Edith, 1031*; Edm., 321, 1028; Eliz., 146*, 1031, 1091; Francis, 249, 250; Hannah, 55; Henrietta, 1029; Hen., 1289; Hester, 1031*; J., 1197; Jas., 145, 1031; Joan, 1502; John, 55*, 145, 146, 299, 339, 358, 364*, 372, 611, 990*, 1031, 1216, 1362; Joseph, 610; Marg., 249, 610; Mary, 55, 611; Prudence, 299; Rachel, 1031; Rebecca, 366, 368, 369, 384*, 990; Ric., 364, 367, 990 1031*, 1457; Rob., 369, 1028, 1403; Sarah, 55, 1031; Temperance, 963; Thos., 55, 70, 327, 623, 736, 963; W., 1256; Rev. W., 990, 1033*, 1216*; Wal., 960; Wm., 250, 360, 366, 367, 368, 384*, 990, 1031*, 1033, 1289, 1457; fam., 145

Gerald [de Barri](Gyraldus), 357

Gerald, Hen., 1238; Wal., 1238; Wm., 1379

Gerand, Wm., 851 n

Gerard (Gearad, Gerrard), Rev. Augustin, 1228; Charlotte, 1559; Edith, 1471*; Edw., 1471; Frances, 1471; Rev. Geo., 770, 771, 1127; Sir Gil., bt., 1559; John, 1197, 1447, 1471; Margary, 1471; Milcent, 1471; Nic., 1471*; Sibilla, 1502; Thos., 1197; —, 404 n; *and see* Garrard; Garrett

Gerin, *see* Gearing

Gerish *see* Gerrish

Gernon (Gernons, Gernun), *see* Garnons; Gearing, Eliz. *and* Wm.

Gerrard, *see* Gerard

Gerrish (Gerish), Ann, 1425*; Emerson, 1425*; Marg., 1425; Mary, 1425; Sam., 1328
Gerveys, *see* Jarvis
Gerwy, *see* Garraway
Gethen (Gethan, Gethin, Gething, Githens), Ann, 538, 539; Eliz., 538; Geo., 682, 735; Jas., 538*, 539, 543; Jane, 539, 682, 735, 923; John, 531, 538*, 539*, 1241; Lois, 543; Mary, 538, 539, 1241; Ric., 538; Sophia, 924; Thos., 539*, 924; Wm., 538; *and see* Gittings
Gewy, Wm., 1522
Ghezzi, C., 119
Ghudal, *see* Goodall
Gibbe, *see* Gibbs
Gibbens, *see* Gibbons
Gibbes, *see* Gibbs
Gibbons (Gibbens, Gibbins, Gibbon, Gybbons), Ann, 880; Ant., 880; Cath., 797; Chas., 468, 1039; Dan., 448, 797, 880; Eliz., 448; Frances, 448; J., 1027; Jane, 354; John, 174*, 354, 448, 494, 880; Rev. John, 1055; Rev. John Houghton, 1459; Joseph, 174; Sam., 1217; Sarah, 174, 880; Susan, 468; Thos., 922, 935; Rev. W. Winter, 1385; Wm., 448
Gibbs (Gibbe, Gibbes, Gibbys, Gibes, Gybbe), Alice, 293; Ann, 1002, 1013; Bart., 1187; Cath., 468; Deborah, 337; Diones(s), 1491, 1555; Eliz., 337, 467, 468, 842, 871; Eliz. Bathurst, 513*; Geo., 468; Giles, 1139*; Griffin, 1427*; Hannah, 1425*, 1457; Harrington, 1555; Hen., 842, 1555; J., 1447; Jane, 274; John, 86, 227, 231*, 337, 573, 1154, 1194, 1377, 1446, 1447, 1487; Jonathan Griffin, 1427; Joseph, 1425*; Joyce, 1377; Marg., 293; Marion, 293; Martha, 337; Mary, 1002, 1282, 1427; Phaebe, 1194; Ric., 1002; Rob., 274, 1104; Sam., 385*; Sarah, 337, 385*, 542, 1104, 1425, 1427; Thos., 231, 542, 871, 1012, 1013*; Tim., 86; W., 1187; Wm., 293, 337*, 467, 511, 513, 1150, 1233, 1289, 1425, 1457, 1460; Wroughton, 513*; fam., 511
Gibson (Gybson), (or Cook), Comfort, 984*; Edm., bishop, 1331; (or Cook), John, 984; Mary, 984; Mat., 711 n; Thos., 274, 800; Wm., 984*
Gidgell, *see* Gingell
Gidley, Bart., 994; Mary, 994
Gifford (Giffard, Gyfford), Ann, 616, 1431; Edw., 18; Eleanor, 798, 1431; Elias (Helias), 251*, 449, 1380; Elias Boy, 1486; Eliz., 1431*; Sir Geo., kt., 1431; Sir Gil., 851 n; Godfrey, bishop, 218, 221, 390, 707, 1419, 1431, 1432*; Helias, *see* Gifford, Elias; Hugh, 1431; J., 1139*, 1380; Jas., 616*; Joan, 1431*; Joanna, 1431; John, 745, 798, 1020, 1139*, 1172, 1430, 1431*; John, baron Giffard, 244, 251*, 525; Sir John, 1039, 1431; Kath., 1431; Marg., 1074, 1172*, 1185; Margery, 1187; Mary, 1431; Matilda, 1431; Osborn(e), 251, 1020, 1172, 1419; R., 1185; Reg., 1221; Ric., 1431; Rob., 1431; Sibilla, 1431; Thos., 251; Wal., archbishop, 1431; Wal., earl of Buckingham, 251; Wm., 1431*; Sir Wm., 1431; —, 1027, 1039, 1074, 1093, 1172, 1491*; fam., 251, 798, 1020, 1172, 1185*

Gignell, Dinah, 1325; Eliz., 1325; Stephen, 1325; *and see* Gingell
Gilben, Wm., 1478
Gilbert, bishop of London, *see* Sheldon
Gilbert (Gilburt), Ann(e), 412, 922; Chas., 948; Eliz., 413; Emma, 252; John, 504, 613, 1354*; Dr. John, archbishop, 252, 449*; Lawr., 685; Luke, 413; Mary, 1354*; Mat., 412*; Ric., 686; Sarah, 948; Stephen, 1447; Thos., 922*, 1172; W., 1104
Gilderd, Alice, 1197
Gilding, *see* Guilding
Giles (Gilles, Gyles), Ann, 339, 1297*; Deborah, 841; Eliz., 1012*, 1297; Geo., 841*, 1467; Rev. John, 66; Rev. Laur., 1456; Marg., 1494; Mary, 700, 1012, 1297*, 1467; Ric., 947, 1297*, 1312; Rob., 1012*; Sarah, 1297*, 1452; Rev. Stephen, 1177; Thos., 339, 1012, 1258; Rev. Thos., 571, 1447; Wm., 700, 1449, 1452, 1456; —, 1017, 1456*; *and see* Gill; Gills
Gilford, John, 797
Gilkes, John, 1289
Gill (Gille, Gyll, Gylle), Eliz., 981; Francis [Frances], 814; Jane, 1538; John, 814*; Mary, 811, 814*; Rafe, 1538; Ric., 811*, 814; Susan, 1214; Thos., 981; W., 1016, 1148; Rev. W., 1104, 1195; Wm., 1214, 1538; Rev. Wm., 1093; *and see* Giles; Gills
Gillam, Geo., 387; Lewes, 387; *and see* Gwilliam
Gille, *see* Gill
Gilles, *see* Giles
Gillett (Gillet, Gyllet), Betty, 601; Chas., 601*; Rev. Hen., 1043; Hester, 118; Jas., 601; John, 118, 601, 1268; Martha, 1013; Mary, 118, 601, 641; Rebekah, 601; Ric., 641; Sarah, 598, 641; Wm., 598, 641*, 1012, 1013*; Rev. Wm., 853, 870*, 1034; —, 1015, 1017
Gills, Ric., 1573; *and see* Giles; Gill
Gilman, Anne, 1497; Deborah, 343; Rev. John, 1495, 1497*, 1502; Rob., 343; Rev. Mr., 319
Gilpin (Gilpyn), Alice, 1015; Ric., 1015; Mr., 345 n
Gilson, Frances, 226; Jas., 226
Gingell (Gidgell), Ann(e), 616*, 1308; Cornelius, 700; Dr. D., 1308*; Dan., 1308; Eliz., 615, 1118; Geo., 1131; Hen., 887, 1113, 1115*, 1121; Jane, 1115; John, 510*, 826, 910, 1308; Joseph, 616*; Maky [?Mary], 510; Marg., 887, 1131; Mary, 510, 1115; Raymond, 1308; Wm., 615; *and see* Gignell
Girdler, Serjt., 1016; *and see* Girler
Girdleston, Rev. Chas., 1385
Girler, Eliz., 932; Ric., 932; *and see* Girdler
Gisborne (Gisborn, Gisburn), Ant., 36, 817, 818, 1422; Jane, 818; Sarah, 226
Gise, *see* Guise
Gislebert, bishop, 297, 1032, 1121
Gislebert son of Turold, 890, 1011, 1331
Gist, Ann, 1518*; Eleanor Augusta, 1518; Eliz. Perkins, 1518; Josiah, 1518*; Marg. Eliz., 1518; Mary, 1518; Mary Ann, 1518*; Sam., 1517, 1518, 1519; Sam. Gist, 1335, 1518*, 1519; Mr., 1335, 1387, 1519; —, 1519*; *and see* Geest

Githens, *see* Gethen

Gittings (Gittins), Grace, 922; Matilda, 1282; Wm., 922; *and see* Gethen

Gittos (Gittoes), Amy, 871; Eliz., 871, 1353; Rev. Jas., 871, 1353, 1356; Mary, 1353; Olive, 1354; Rob. Brown, 1354; Wm., 1353, 1354; —, 1216

Gladam, Dan., 1509

Gladwin (Gladwyn), Alice, 1194*; Anne, 891; Edw., 891*; John, 891, 1196; Rev. R., 1356; Rob., 1194; —, 1015

Glamorgan, earl of, *see* Somerset, Edw.

Glanvill (Glanville), Dorothy, 381; Geo., 381*; John de, 1139

Glaskodine, Eliz., 499; John, 499; Wm., 499

Glass (Glasse), Eliz., 237*; Ric., 237; Rev. Sam., 558

Glastonbury, Phil., 111

Glaswryght, John, 1292

Glave, Rev. Mat., 1217

Gleed (Gleede), Francis, 1554; Wm., 97

Gloucester, Hawise de, 1369; John de, 708, 1147; (or Workman), Marg., 274; Ralph of, 1033; Thos. de, 1369; (or Workman), Thos., 274; Wal. de, 915, 1369

Gloucester [*peerage*], Eleanor, duchess of, 927; Hen., duke of, 894 n; Humph., duke of, 1159; Mabel, countess of, 1011, 1287; Ric., duke of, 1219; Wm., earl of, 838, 1011, 1287; his daughter Amice or Anne, 1011, 1287; his daughters Isabel and Mabel, 1287; duke of, 1219; earl of, 1011, 1225, 1381; *and see* Audley, Hugh, Marg., *and* fam.; Bohun, Eleanor de; Clare, *passim*; Despencer, Thos.; FitzRoy; Melun, Rob. de; Milo; Woodstock, Eleanor *and* Thos. de

Glover, Anne, 1297, 1361; Hen., 820; Lawr., 644*; (or Wright), John, 321; Joseph, 1297*; Marg., 644, 1297*; Mary, 1297, 1361; Priscilla, 820; Ric., 174, 1217, 1361*, 1362; Thos., 1362; —, 1455

Glyn (Glynn, Glynne), Rev. Chris., 1441; Rev. Clement, 1200; Mary, 1013; Rev. Rob., 1013, 1016; Thos., 1404

Gnyge, John, 1292; *and see* Guyge

Goad, Cecilia, 891

Goda (Gueda), countess, 648 n; 1101, 1138*, 1219, 1335, 1512*

Godchild, Ric., 1197

Goddard (Goodard), Ann, 575, 1431; Anna, 509; Chas., 1208; Edm., 636; Edw., 509, 771; Francis, 1199; Joice, 1468; Ric., 575*; Rev. Ric., 771; Rob., 597, 771; Thos., 491, 1431; Wm., 1539; —, 537, 1064

Godeline, Juliana, 1069

Godemon, *see* Goodman

Goderic, *see* Godric

Goderich, *see* Goodrich

Godewin, *see* Goodwin

Godfrey (Godefray, Godefrey, Godfree), Ann, 429; Cath., 18*, 213; Dorothy, 897; Frances, 1010; Geo., 213, 429*; Gertrude, 18; Jas., 133; Joan, 213; John, 18*, 429*; Rev. Jonathan, 133; Sarah, 429*; Stephen, 1228; Wm., 979–80, 1420; fm., 897

Godgrom, *see* Gedgrom

Godhine, John, 1392

Godiva, Lady, 244

Godman, *see* Goodman

Godmanston, Rob. de, 1055

Godric (fl. 1066)(Goderic), 990*, 1147, 1384, 1476, 1482

Godrun (or Gythurnus)(fl. 879), 357*, 366

Godsell (Godsale, Godsall, Godschalk, Godschall), Eliz., 781, 1266; Frances, 1278; Jas., 1289; Joas, 220 n; John, 1288; Marg., 781; Phil., 1278*; Ric., 781*; Sam., 1034; Wm., 1266*; —, 1225

Godwell, John, 696 n

Godwin, earl, 156, 157, 179, 1101, 1138, 1512*

Godwin (Godwyn), Anne, 1546; Chas., 797, 1427; Deborah, 249; Eliz., 118, 194, 772, 1118; Francis, bishop, 191; Hannah, 191; Hodges, 1546*; Joan, 190; John, 15, 288, 923, 1383, 1546, 1551; Rev. Joseph, 1422; Marg., 1212; Mary, 15, 797, 923*, 1543; Nat., 1118; Ric., 191*, 194, 249, 921, 923; Rob., 772, 1543, 1546; Ruth, 1383; Rev. Sam., 603, 1385; Sarah, 1427; Rev. Scudamore, 603, 1383, 1385; Silvester, 1546; Thos., 176, 288, 1212*; Thos., bishop, 191, 1428*; Dr. Thos., 191; Rev. Thos., 190, 191, 603*, 1404; Wm., 1086; —, bishop, 609 n; *and see* Goodwin

Godwy, Rob., 1223

Godwyn, *see* Godwin; Goodwin

Goff (Gof, Goghe), *see* Gough

Goisfrid (fl. 1066)(Goiffred), 1077*, 1350

Goizenboded (Gozenboded), W., 1237; Wm., 519, 570, 634, 864, 889, 1401; —, 1237, 1475*

Gold (Golde, Gould), Ann, 996; Benj., 295; Dan., 1085; Edw., 1102; Rev. Francis, 1106, 1107, 1110*, 1328, 1385; Geo., 1361; Hen., 321; John, 203, 1551; Mary, 1106, 1107, 1110*; Ric., 918*; Sarah, 1106, 1107; Thos., 996

Goldby, Eliz., 868; Susannah, 868; Wm., 868

Goldcline, Wm., 1329

Golde, *see* Gold

Goldenham, *see* Goldingham

Goldesborough (Goldisborough), Godfrey, bishop, 1101; John, 1101; Rev. John, 1102; Mary, 845; Nic., 845*

Golding (Goldin, Goldyng), Alice, 1504; Ann, 510; Rev. Chris., 128; Esther, 1250; John, 174, 510*, 1266; Sarah, 510*; Thos., 510*, 1250*; Wm., 1339

Goldingham (Goldenham), Anne, 1411; Eliz., 722; Mary, 1411

Goldisborough, *see* Goldesborough

Goldney, Hen., 1087; Joan, 1087; fam., 403, 577

Goldsmith (Goldsmyth), H., 1201; Rob., 1292

Goldyng, *see* Golding

Gole, Ric., 1292

Golightly, Rev. John, 415; Rev. T. J., 1070

Goltzius, —, 591

Gomeldon, P. de, 1491

Gomond, Edm., 1569; Eliz., 1569*; Jas., 1569; Mary, 1569*; Sarah, 1569*

Gonner, John, 1165

Goodall (Ghudal, Goodhall), Ann, 689; John, 422, 506*, 689; Mary, 506, 689; Rev. Nic., 13; Rev. Rob., 400, 1460

Goodard, see Goddard

Goodchep (Goodcheape), Ann, 1269; Benj., 686; Dorothy, 686; Etherington, 686; Hen., 686, 1269; Thos., 687, 1354

Goode, Hannah, 905, 907; Henrietta, 905; Jas., 1039; Wm., 905, 907

Goodear, Hen., 884; Martha, 884

Goodenough, Ann, 1551*, 1552; Rev. Edm., 744; Frances Mary, 1551; Sophia, 1551; Rev. W., 783; W. S., 1552; Rev. W. S., 1551; Wm., 1551; Rev. Wm., 139; Rev. Wm. Stephen, 1550, 1551*, 1552

Gooder, Ann, 399, 401; Hen., 401; Sir Hen., kt., 401; Wm., 401

Goodhall, see Goodall

Gooding (Goodin), Ant., 850; Eliz., 850; John, 293, 850; Mary, 803, 850; Ric., 803; Susanna, 293; Serjt., 850

Goodlake, Eliz., 1231*; John Hughes, 1231*; Mary S., 1233; Thos., 1231; Thos. Mills, 1217; Rev. Thos. Wm., 1231

Goodman (Godemon, Godman), Chas., 354; Christian, 456; Chris. Woodward, 901; Dorothy, 407; Edw., 763 n; Eliz., 210*; Francis, 210*; Rev. Godfrey, 764*, 770; Dr. Godfrey, bishop, 145, 763; Jas., 456*; John, 210, 901; Thos., 406; Wm., 407, 638, 1259; —, bishop, 278; —, 392 n; fam., 392

Goodrich (Goderich, Goodrick, Goodrydge), Ann(e), 337, 982; Edw., 984; J., 1165; John, 984; Kath., 517; Marg., 1499; Mary, 317; Rev. R., 1127; Ric., 317, 984; Sarah, 984; Wal., 337; Wm., 517, 1499*; —, 985, 986*

Goodsclagh, John, 1092*

Goodson, Francis, 1533; Mary, 1533; Rebecca, 1533; Sam., 1533*; Sarah, 1533; Wm., 1533

Goodwin (Godewin, Godwyn), Abigail, 563; Ann(e), 352, 353, 1458; Rev. Austin, 230; Caleb, 1040; Capt. Colquit, 1501; Eleanor, 1162; Eliz., 962; Geo., 1162*; Hen., 1069, 1411; John, 1065, 1430; Joseph, 873; Mary, 1040*, 1065, 1210, 1430; Rev. Morgan, 808; Nat., 1040*, 1333; Peter, 1328; Rev. Ric., 817; Rob., 962, 1210*; Sam., 352, 353; Susanna, 1210; Theodosia, 1040; Rev. Thos., 1102; Wm., 563, 873; —, 1458; and see Godwin

Gooer, see Gower

Gooper, —, 288

Goore, see Gore

Gopeshill, John, 1314

Gordon, Alex., duke of Gordon, 760; Anna, 1032; Christiana, 409; Eliz. Ann, 1032; John, 833; Rob., 1032*, 1566*; Sir Rob., bt., 409; Sarah, 1566*; Wm., 403; —, 1032, 1033, 1512

Gore (Goore), Chas., 407; Dorothy, 1157; Edw., 722, 726; Eliz., 1157; Helena, 719 n, 723; Hen., 1477; Jas., 340; John, 1579, 1580; Juliana, 1160; Marg., 1157; Martha, 1157; Mary, 340; Rebecca, 1579; Ric., 407; Major Rob., 723; Thos., 1157*,

1258; Wm., 1157*; —, earl of Arran, 1103; —, 1104; and see Gower

Gorewy, Rog., 1223

Gorges, Anne, 1048; Eliz., 268, 1435; Ric., 268; Sir Theobald, kt., 364, 1048, 1435; fam., 552, 1156

Gornay, see Gurney

Gorstlett (Gosselat, Gostlet, Gostlett), John, 838, 839, 842*; Mary, 842; Wm., 839; —, 839

Gorton (Gorten), Ann, 1481; Hannah, 1481*; Jonah, 60*; Marg., 60; Mary, 60; Sarah, 1481; Thos., 1481*; Rev. W., 1043; Rev. Wm., 635, 1477

Goscomb, Eliz., 974; Jas., 1376; Mary, 1376*; Thos., 1376; Wm., 974, 1376*

Goshelin, see Gosling

Gosley, Rachel, 32

Gosling (Goshelin, Gosselin), Adam, 1160; Mary, 786; Ralph, 1150; Thos., 786

Gosselat, see Gorstlett

Gosselin, see Gosling

Gossington (Gussenton), John de, 1101, 1160; Rog. de, 1101

Gostlet (Gostlett), see Gorstlett

Goter, —, 1017

Gotley, Albena Meriah, 1576; Eliz., 1576; St. John Allen Britte, 1576; Wm., 1576*

Gottenvey, Thos., 463

Gough (Gof, Goff, Goghe, Goughe), Alice, 732; Alydea, 683; Anne, 249*; Ben., 1292; Blanch, 249, 250; Cath., 249*; Chas., 249*; Dan., 654, 659; Deborah, 1398*; Eleanor, 732; Eliz., 654, 734*; Geo., 250*, 732, 733, 734*, 919*; Geo. Gwinnett, 116; Giles, 659; Israel, 734; J., 1323; Jas., 249, 250, 734; Jane, 857; Jeremy, 43, 116; Joan, 830; Johanne, 919; John, 250, 583, 830*; Jonathan, 683; Judith, 660; Mary, 43, 249, 250*, 583, 683, 732, 733*, 734, 872; Mat., 871; Sir Mat., 245*; Ric., 732, 734, 915; Rob., 1398*; Sam., 660; Sarah, 1398; Thos., 654, 857; W., 1516*; Warren, 248, 250; Wm., 245, 249*, 250*, 683, 733*; Mr., 502, 507 n, 532 n; Mrs., 918; —, 915; fam., 145, 732

Gould, see Gold

Gouldwell, Eliz., 1051; —, 1051

Goler, Sarah, 1455; Thos., 1455

Gournay (Gourney), see Gurney

Gouwer, see Gower

Gover, —, 1362; and see Gower

Gowen, Ann, 954*; Christian, 702, 703; Joyce, 954; Mary, 702, 954; Wm., 702, 703, 954

Gower (Gooer, Gouwer), Abel, 257; Joane, 1521; Mary, 257, 1464; Mat., 1535; Rob., 1519; Sarah, 1535; Wm., 1464*, 1535*; and see Gore; Gover

Gowling, 336; John, 339

Gowsyth, Rev. John, 793; and see Gussage

Gozenboded, see Goizenboded

Grace, Geo., 531; Hen., 48; John, 543, 1172; Mary, 543; Susan, 1172; Thos., 543

Graceing (Grasing), Wm., 872, 873

Graeme, see Graham

Grafton, Eliz., 176; Peter, 176; Thos., 177; Rev. Thos., 1346; Rev. Wm., 271, 272

Graham (Graeme, Grahme), Sir Edw., bt., 1281; Eliz., 1281; Eupheme, countess of Strathern, 1281; Sir Pat., earl of Strathern, 1281; Peter, 1258; Sir Ric., bt., 1281; Sir Rob., bt., 1281; Sir Rob., bt., Viscount Preston, 1281; Sarah, 412; Thos., 1160; V. J., 1160; Wm. de, 1281; Capt. Wm., 412

Grail (Graile, Grayle), Alice, 1174; Edm., 442*, 786; Rev. Edm., 442; Eliz., 442; Esther, 786*; Ezra, 442; Rev. Ezra, 785, 786*; Rev. John, 1174; Sarah, 786, 1526, 1527; Thos., 442, 786; Dr. Thos., 1526, 1527; Rev. Thos., 785, 786*; Tim., 442

Grain, Ric., 797

Graingab, John, 1200; Sarah, 1200

Grammett, Hannah, 976; Mary, 976; Thos., 976

Grand, Rev. Peter, 553*

Grandiner, Job, 1312

Grandison, Otto de, 869; Wm., 869; fam., 544

Grange (Graung), Arnold de la, 1395; J., 1055; Mary de la, 1395; Thos., 1329

Granger, Lydia, 385

Grant (Graunt), And., 1519; Geo., 1407; Nic., 1519

Granville, Bernard, 274; Col. Bernard, 274; Sir Bevil(le), 6*, 7, 80, 274; Geo., Lord Lansdown, 6;

Grasing, see Graceing

Gratwick, Thos., 1165

Graung, see Grange

Graunt, see Grant

Grave (Graves), Anne, 867; Danvers, 867; Eleanor, 867; Eliz., 867*, 1381; Frances, 867; I., 867; John (atte), 587, 864, 867, 1238; Marg., 587; Morgan, 864 n, 867*; Ric., 864*, 867*; Rev. Ric. Morgan, 865; Sam., 864*, 865, 867; Sibilla de la, 1378; Thos. de la, 1378; Walwyn, 87*, 864 & n, 865; — (de la), 1017, 1378; fam., 863, 867; and see Grove

Gravenor, Ric., 646

Graves, see Grave

Graville, see Greville

Gray, see Grey

Grayhurst, see Greyhurst

Grayle, see Grail

Grayler, —, 1539

Grazebrook, Ann(e), 204, 1208; B., 1203; Benj., 204, 1208; Mr., 1215; —, 1027

Greatrake, Francis, 412; Mary, 412

Green (Greene, Grene, Greyn, Grnne), Adam, 810; Alice (Alis), 938, 1093; Ann(e), 352*, 354*, 387, 938, 978, 1268; Arthur, 938*; Ayliffe, 405, 406; Bridget, 97; Cater, 1546, 1551; Cath., 567; Clement, 351; Diana, 336; Diana Robella, 336; Dorothy, 895; Edith, 1004; Edm., 608*; Edw., 803; Eleanor (Elianor), 891, 895, 899, 903; Eliz., 467, 598, 706, 1450; Ephraim, 608; Esther, 1372; Frances, 693; Rev. G. W., 1329; Geo., 814; Giles, 235; Hannah, 354; Hen. (atte), 235, 818, 868, 1259; Rev. Hen., 508; Jas., 336, 856, 978; Jane, 772*, 814; Joan, 1481; John (atte, de la), 387*, 429*, 467*, 567, 706, 796, 854, 891, 922, 952, 981, 1330, 1404*, 1431, 1476, 1478, 1481*, 1485, 1546*; (or Collyer), John, 1490; Rev. John,

435, 1092, 1372; Joseph, 1388; Rev. Joseph, 878, 1388, 1392; Joshua de, 1268*; Marg., 429, 608, 1013, 1268; Martha, 352, 1481; Mary, 467, 542, 608, 706, 1004*; Nic., 868; Ric. (atte), 352*, 354, 597, 810, 1238, 1372; Rob., 1004*; Rev. Rog., 503; Rose, 1546*; Sam., 772*; Sarah, 772, 796, 983, 984, 1159, 1268*, 1574; Stephen, 1382; Susanna, 1004*; T., 1062, 1093; Thos., 429, 542*, 549, 706, 796, 938, 1159; Valentine, 864 n; Wal., 693; Wm., 97, 567, 598*, 896, 899*, 903, 983, 984, 1013, 1123, 1450, 1455, 1574; Rev. Wm., 161; — (atte), 1020, 1478

Greenall (Greenald, Greenhall), Eliz., 1391; Henkley, 1391; Joseph, 904, 1391*; (or Greenhill), Rev. Rob., 498*; Sam., 499; Wm., 1391*; and see Greenhalf; Greenhill

Greenaway, see Greenway

Greene, see Green

Greeneand, see Greenland

Greenfield, Rev. Rob., 808

Greenhalf (Grinnuf), Eleanor, 567, 796; Eliz., 796; Geo., 796; Jas., 567; Rob., 567*; Susan, 567; Thos., 567; and see Greenall

Greenhall, see Greenall

Greenhill (Grenehill, Grenehulle), Anne, 26*; Ant., 26*; J., 1061; R., 1195; Ralph de, 1027; (or Greenald), Rev. Rob., 498*; —, 1226; and see Greenall

Greening (Greenyng, Grining), Alice, 1464*, 1465; Ann(e), 28, 494, 670, 792, 793, 974*, 1464; Ant., 1474; Augustine, 637*; Dan., 1129, 1130*; Edborough, 887; Eliz., 28, 792, 887*, 1129; Grace, 637; Guy, 1173; Henrietta, 974*; Hen., 974*, 1464, 1476; Hester, 284; J., 793; Jas., 1464, 1465; Jeremiah, 670, 887*; John, 112, 792*, 1461, 1464*, 1465, 1466, 1473, 1477, 1504; Joseph, 1465; Kath., 1130; Marg., 1464, 1466, 1474; Mary, 284, 637, 1130; Nat., 815; Ric., 28*, 494*, 1477; Sam., 887, 1130; Sarah, 974, 1367, 1474; Thos., 284, 637*, 1367, 1464; Wm., 974, 1473; —, 1476*

Greenland (Greeneand), Jane, 847; John, 847*; Mary, 847; Wm., 847

Greenow (Grenow), Rev. Garret, 1422; —, 1293

Greenway (Greenaway, Grinway), Alice, 380; Chas., 1583; Edw., 1582; Eliz., 380, 1137; Geo., 803, 1137; Giles, 139*; Hen., 378; Hester, 803; Jas., 378; Jane, 425, 378, 1086; John, 380*, 1086; Rev. John, 1328; Joseph, 1086; Judith, 1137; Mary, 380, 1354; Philippa, 486; Ric., 1354; Rev. Ric., 1035; Sarah, 380; Thos., 425

Greenwell, Wm., 324

Greenwood (Greenwoode), Ann, 317; Betty, 317; Edw., 317*; Geo., 883; Hester, 317*; John, 385; Rev. Josiah, 1048; Marg., 385; Mary, 1081; Ric., 1081*; Rob., 1081; Sarah, 1081; Thos., 883, 1081; Dr., 1132; —, 1293

Greenyng, see Greening

Greet (Greote), Ingram de, 1478; John de, 1475

Gregory X, pope, 717

Gregory, Abraham, 1527, 1528; Rev. Abraham, 275, 350, 447, 452*; Ann(e), 17, 132, 317, 331,

338, 412, 1207; Arthur, 1427*; Barbara, 1493;
Cath., 338, 1457; Chas., 412*; Dan., 17*; Edw.,
204, 1528; Rev. Edw., 1527–8, 1539; Eliz., 17,
338*, 486, 1366, 1368, 1427*; Esther, 412;
Frances, 714; Francis, 331, 338, 1528; Greg. (?),
1457; Hannah, 1427; Hester, 331; Jane Barnes,
1368; Rev. Jeremiah, 163, 1081; Rev. Jerome,
161; John, 337*, 338*, 984, 1493; Capt. John
Barnes, 1368; Rev. John, 534, 711 n, 713*, 714*,
1047, 1366*, 1368, 1369, 1370; Joseph, 486,
1493; Kath., 887; Martha, 204, 338; Mary, 333,
887, 984, 1366*, 1411, 1528; Phebe, 1427; Ric.,
333; Rev. Ric., 1411, 1447, 1457*, 1460; Rob.,
132, 789*; Sam., 17; Sarah, 338, 714; Stephen,
710; Susanna(h), 1091, 1366, 1368, 1427; Thos.,
331, 338, 677, 887, 1207, 1368, 1369, 1426,
1427*, 1493, 1528; Rev. Thos., 1366*, 1368*,
1370; Wm., 338*, 1091*, 1420; Rev., 370*; —,
985, 1493, 1494; (or Ridler), —, 1493
Grendour, see Greyndour
Grene, see Green
Grenehill (Grenehulle), see Greenhill
Grenow, see Greenow
Grenville, Ric., duke of Buckingham and Chandos,
1220
Greote, see Greet
Gresham, Sir Ric., 271; Sir Thos., 271
Gretton, Ralph de, 1478
Grevel (Grevell), see Greville
Grevestock, John, 715; Rev. Wm., 1387
Greville (Graville, Grevel, Grevell, Grevil, Grevile
Grevill, Grevylle), Ann(e), 348, 628; C., 1381;
Chas., 804, 1331; Sir E., 1388, 1392*; Edw., 315,
863, 1388, 1390; Sir Edw., 311, 1055*, 1388;
Eliz., 763, 1328, 1381; Sir Fulk, 763, 1328*; Sir
Fulk(e), Lord Broke, 511, 1328; Giles, 311, 313,
325; J., 1388; (or Cooksey), J., 1014; Sir J.,
1055; Joan, 286 n; John, 348, 1014*, 1055, 1092,
1390, 1392*; Sir John, kt., 1014; Joyce, 1392;
Kath., 1380; Lewis (Lodovick), 311 n, 1388,
1392; Marg., 311 n, 1328; Margery, 1388;
Marion, 291; Mary, 315; Obadiah, 1512; Peter,
804, 1331; Ric., 1272, 1331; Rob., baron Brooke,
628; Thos., 1331; (or Cokesey) Thos., 1055; (or
Cokesey), Sir Thos., 1392; W., 1061, 1392; Wm.,
286 n*, 291*, 311 n, 313, 328 n, 1031, 1032; Sir
Wm., 328 n; Dr., 327 n; —, 1055*, 1257*,
1381*; fam., 311, 325, 570, 634, 804 & n, 1392*
Grey (Gray), Ant., 759; Rev. Ant., 1233; Eliz.,
1028; Eliz., countess of Kent, 759; Eliz., Lady
Chandos, 1219; Hen. de, 766; Hen., earl of Kent,
759, 760; J., 1061; Jane, 1337, 1338; Lady Jane,
1220; John (le), 1154, 1221, 1439; Reg. de, 759;
Rob. le, 1154; Thos., 980; Rev. Thos., 1028; Wal.
de, bishop, 390; Wm., 1045; Mr., 1440; fam., 792
Grey [peerage], Edm., Lord, 1219; Lady, 1044; and
see Ford, —
Grey de Wilton, fam., 819
Greyhurst (Grayhurst), Agnes, 217; Ann(e), 140,
818; John, 135, 139, 140*, 217*, 377, 1190,
1331; Sarah, 140; Thos., 818*; Wm., 140; —,
1196; fam., 139

Greyn, see Green
Greyndour (Grendour), Eliz., 462; H., 1381; Joan,
913, 915; Sir John, 462*; R., 1316; Rob., 462,
913, 915; fam., 462, 807, 1401
Gribble, Eliz., 683
Griber, Ann, 107; Cullins, 107
Grice, Ric., 1476
Griffen, see Griffin
Griffeth, Rhese ap, prince of Wales, 819
Griffeth (Griffeths), see Griffiths
Griffin (Griffen, Gryffin, Gryffyn), Abraham,
1353*; Rev. Abraham, 1362; Beata, 1377; Rev.
Benj., 135; Betty, 662; Edw., 1075*, 1355; Rev.
Edw., 19, 1339; Rev. Edw. Loggin, 574, 1369;
Eleanor, 308; Eliz., 455, 1206*, 1454; Esther,
455*; Geo., 1109; Giles, 455; Hen., 1454; Hester,
455; J., 1216; Jas., 542, 641*; Jane, 1075, 1353;
John, 455, 542*, 624, 1206*; Jonathan, 1427*;
Joseph, 419; Joshua, 419; Lucy, 641; Martha,
1214; Mary, 130, 455, 662, 846, 1353; Prudence,
455; R., 1101; Rob., 455*; Sam., 532, 1353;
Sarah, 662, 1353*, 1427; Susannah, 662; T.,
1216; Thos., 93, 130, 308, 455, 662, 846, 1206,
1217; Rev. Thos., 455; Wm., 455, 662; Rev.
Wm., 453, 1177; Mr., 1189; —, 515, 1216, 1355,
1356
Griffith (Griffeth, Griffeths, Griffits, Gryffith,
Gryfith), Alice, 250; Ann, 47, 250, 386, 584;
Betty, 47; Bryan, 250*; Chris., 41*, 603*, 1487*,
1491; Dan., 870; Rev. Dan., 228, 1165; David ap,
1102; Eliz., 300, 354, 468, 1487, 1514; Rev.
Evan, 31, 32; Geo., 1362; Griffit, 1162;
Guenthlien, 819; Hester, 47; Rev. Hugh, 463;
Jas., 905, 907; Rev. Jas., 895; Jane, 468, 768;
Jeffery, 927; Jeremiah, 524; John, 47, 249*,
250*, 468, 584, 708 n, 814, 1175, 1487; Rev.
John, 1487; Jonathan, 249*, 352; Joseph, 768;
Marg., 446; Mary, 249*, 250*, 386*, 468, 1162,
1487*; Peter, 814; Rev. Phil. ap, 783, 1539; Ric.,
47, 249, 386; Rev. Ric., 424, 1514*; Rob., 250*,
386, 1513; Rev. Rob., 53, 1513, 1516; Simon,
47*; Thos., 468; Tryphosa, 249; Warren, 249;
Wm., 300, 354, 1054, 1289, 1487
Grime (Grim, Grimes, Gryme), Alice, 1065; Ann,
388, 1065*; Chas., 1065*; Edw., 388; Mark, 440;
Mary, 1375*, 1548; R., 1216; Rev. R., 1202;
Ric., 1548; Rob., 1375*; Thos., 1065; Wm., 658;
—, 1032*, 1033
Grimston (Grimstone), Rev. Harbottle, 651; Jas.,
Viscount Grimston, 1072, 1073; Jane, 1072,
1073*
Grindal (Grindell), Jas., 923, 924
Grindon, Ann, 1401; Eliz., 623; Mary, 623; Wm.,
623, 1401
Grinesend, Rev. Wm., 221
Grining, see Greening
Grinnuf, see Greenhalf
Grinshaw, Anne, 1279; Benj., 1279*
Grinway, see Greenway
Grisdale, Rev. Benj., 319, 1495, 1498, 1502; Eliz.,
1498
Grnne, see Green

Grobham (Grubham), Sir Ric., 434; Sir Ric., kt., 1497
Groom, Rev. John, 1186; Sarah, 212
Grosse (Gros, Grose, Gross), Rev. Edw., 1186; Francis, 244; John, 1456; Thos., 1250; Wm. le, *see* Fortibus
Grosvenor, Mr., 894
Grove (Groue, Groves), Ann, 1297; Rev. Bendy, 214; Edith atte, 1485; Eliz., 52, 1299; Francis, 1457; Geo. atte, 1388; Joan, 1430*; John, 1238, 1312, 1430, 1447; Joseph, 1297*; Kingsmill, 1309; Marg., 1297; Mary, 1297*; Matilda atte, 1102; Piercy, 868, 1430*; Ralph, 1299; Rev. Ralph, 1297*, 1313; Ric., 1063, 1312; Rev. Rob., 1223; Sam., 1237, 1238; Stanhope, 1237; Thos., 52, 383*, 619, 1062; W., 1061; Wm., 151, 546, 1297*; Rev. Wm., 681, 682; —, 1063; fam., 618, 864; *and see* Grave
Growcutt, Eliz., 1159; Mary, 1159; Sarah, 1159; Wm., 1159
Grubham, *see* Grobham
Grundy, Ann, 550*; Edw., 550*; Lydia, 550
Gryffin, *see* Griffin
Gryffith (Gryfith), *see* Griffith
Gryffyn, *see* Griffin
Gryme, *see* Grime
Grymsby, —, 1120
Gueda, countess, *see* Goda
Guellem, *see* Gwilliam
Guelett, Geo., 923; Jo[a]ne, 923
Guerney, *see* Gurney
Guest, Ann, 473; Ant., 884*; Eliz., 473; Emm, 127; Geo., 1482; Grace, 1570; Hannah, 300, 834; Hen., 300, 1250; John, 473*; Rev. Joseph, 1404; Mary, 473, 834, 1250, 1482; Ric., 473; Rob., 834*; Sarah, 473; Theophilus, 834; Thos., 1570*; —, 493
Guilden, *see* Guilding
Guildford, Francis, earl of, 816; Lord, 1055*
Guilding (Gilding, Guilden), Cath., 270; Dan., 584*; Edw., 583; Eliz., 583; Francis, 1237; Geo., 583, 584; Joan, 1237; John, 270, 1129; Mary, 584*; Wm., 1234, 1237, 1238
Guillim, *see* Gwilliam
Guisden, Mary, 832; Thos., 832
Guise (Gise, Guyse, Gyes, Gyse), Alice, 582; Anselm, 1404; Sir Anselm, 581; Sir Chris., bt., 259, 260, 581, 582; Cicelia (Cecilia), 582, 997; Dorothea, 583*; Edw., 583; Hen., 349, 583*, 1487*; Major Hen., 582; Hester, 1044; Jane, 581; Joane (Joanne), 1044*; John, 105, 134, 252, 259*, 349, 581, 582, 583, 695, 1044*, 1236; Sir John, bt., 134, 259*, 260*, 263, 297, 349, 350*, 479, 581*, 582*, 583, 667, 681, 713, 785*, 1009, 1010, 1011, 1236; Rev. Lewis, 184; Marg., 582, 817; Mary, 583; Nic., 581; Phillip(p)a, 1487*; Rev. Ric., 1016; Rob., 581; Sylvester, 695; Theodosia, 583; Wm., 259, 582*, 583*, 997, 1236; Sir W., 1064; Sir Wm., bt., 105, 260, 297, 581, 582*, 817, 997, 1010, 1034; Gen., 349 n; Mr., 581; Sir —, 1011; fam., 259, 297*, 581, 582, 1010, 1403;

Guiswald, Marg., 861
Gulafre, *see* Gullifer
Gulley, Esther, 1570; Hester, 1570; Jas., 1570*
Gullifer (Gulafre, Gulliver), Eliz., 133; John, 133*; Thos., 133, 1077; —, 1312
Gullock, Eliz., 1424*; Frances, 1424; John, 1424*
Gundalf (fl. 1066), 1077
Gunn, Ann, 282; Sara, 1041; Thos., 282*, 1041; —, 1017
Gunning, Alice, 83; Ann, 83, 84, 492; Edm., 84; Eliz., 84, 492*; Geo., 492*; Hannah, 492; John, 80, 81, 83*, 84, 245, 492*; Mary, 212, 492*, 844, 846; Rev. Peter, 488; Rob., 83; Sir Rob., kt., 81, 479, 839; Sarah, 492*; Thos., 212, 492*, 844, 846*; Wm., 83*, 492, 847
Gunter, Alice, 369, 382; Ann, 47; Edw., 419; Hugh, 1321; Jas., 1370; John, 382, 550, 1539; Marg., 1321; Mary, 47, 578; Thos., 47*, 550*; Wm., 578*; fam., 1381
Gurgan, Rog., 1422; —, 1017
Gurnee, *see* Gurney
Gurner, Wm., 203*
Gurney (Gornay, Gournay, Gourney, Guerney, Gurnee), Anselm de, 178, 576*, 720, 775; Benj., 370; Denis (Dyonis), 1140; Eliz. (de), 370, 576, 654, 720; Eve de, 720; Frances, 867; Jas., 768*; Jane, 768*; John (de), 386*, 576, 720; Joseph, 386; Lettice, 768; Rob. de, 576; Sarah, 386; Sir Thos., 1080; Wm., 867; —, 720; fam., 178, 179, 807
Gussage, —, 1216; *and see* Gowsyth
Gussenton, *see* Gossington
Guy (Guye), Ann(e), 217, 258, 623, 1272*; Edw., 484; Eliz., 1226; Frances, 484; Jane, 1272; John, 217, 258*; Mary, 258, 623, 1272; Moses, 258*; Phil., 623; Ric., 1266, 1272; Rob., 1345; Sam., 623, 1224, 1226*; Sarah, 1266, 1272; T., 1101; Thos., 258, 623; Wm., 623, 1272*
Guyet, Rev. Rog., 1348
Guyge, Wm., 1292; *and see* Gnyge
Guyllim, *see* Gwilliam
Guyse, *see* Guise
Gwatkin (Gwatkins), Dorothy, 1296; Martha, 1504*; Wm., 1296*, 1504
Gwent, Ric., 360 n
Gwilliam (Guellem, Guillim, Guyllim, Gwillam, Gwillim, Gwillm, Gwylliam, Gwylliams, Gwyllym), Cath., 112; Chas., 1514; Eliz., 3, 1095; John, 870, 1317, 1403*; Mary, 1413; Morgan, abbot, 41; Rev. Peter, 1102; Thos., 112, 1413; Rev. Thos., 245, 808, 809; Wm., 3; Winifred, 1514; —, 1403; *and see* Gillam; Williams
Gwin, *see* Gwynne
Gwinnett (Gwinnet, Gwynnett), Anne, 513; Eliz., 117, 949, 1079; Geo., 43, 115*, 117*, 118, 133, 949, 1575; Rev. Geo., 748, 749; Hannah, 117; Hen., 1079; Hester, 133; Lawr., 1079*; Mary, 43; Ric., 118*; Sam., 133; Rev. Sam., 511, 513; Sara(h), 115, 117; Susanna, 1575; Thos., 133; Wm. Catchmay(d), 113, 115, 511, 512, 585, 1079; —, 1370, 1378, 1519; fam., 116, 511, 585

Gwrgant, Justin ap, 392
Gwylliam (Gwylliams, Gwyllym), *see* Gwilliam
Gwymalyn, —, 1069
Gwynne (Gwin, Gwyn, Gwynn), Ann(e), 1297, 1353; Rev. David, 313, 1483; Eliz., 755, 1297; J. Crowther, 1311; John, 406, 967, 1353*; Marg., 967; Mary, 169, 815; Mills, 815; Nat. Crowther, 1297; Rev. Nat., 384, 459, 460*; Ric., 169, 175*, 1297; Stephen, 815; Susanna, 175, 384, 1352, 1353; Thos., 169; Rev. Thos., 754, 755*, 1221; Rev., 967
Gwynnett, *see* Gwinnett
Gybbe, *see* Gibbs
Gybbons, *see* Gibbons
Gybson, *see* Gibson
Gyde, Ann(e), 1023, 1365; Cam, 1023; Dan., 96*; Eliz. Caroline, 1025; Geo., 1365; Hannah, 975*; Hester, 1025, 1365, 1366; Jas., 1023, 1025; John, 1023*, 1025*; Marg., 96*; Mary, 96, 1365, 1508; Nat., 1025*; Sarah, 1023, 1211; Thos., 971, 974, 975, 1023, 1365, 1366, 1508*; Tim., 1365*, 1369*; Wm., 96*, 1023, 1211*, 1212; —, 1370
Gyes, *see* Guise
Gyfford, *see* Gifford
Gyles, *see* Giles
Gyley, Rev. John, 793
Gylford, Thos., 1402
Gyll (Gylle), *see* Gill
Gyllet, *see* Gillett
Gynes, *see* Jeynes
Gyse, *see* Guise
Gythurnus, *see* Godrun
Gyves, *see* Geaves

Habgood, Jas., 777; Martha, 777
Habington, *see* Abington
Hacker, Wm., 1244
Hackett, Jo[a]ne, 1443; Rev. Thos., 1443*; —, 1309
Hackham, Eliz., 343; Rev. Nat. (Nathan), 342, 343
Hackman, Rev. Chas., 1356; Judith, 659*; Martha, 659; Rev. Nat., 659
Haddock (Haddockes, Hadock), Dorothy, 193; Edm., 733; Wm., 193
Haddon, Hen. de, 1490; (or Hydon), —, 1490*
Haddow, Joane, 1525; Ric., 1525
Hadley, R. de, 1490*; Ralph de, 1490; fam., 278
Hadnock (Hadnot), *see* Hoddinott
Hadock, *see* Haddock
Hael, *see* Hale
Haggett, Wm., 1160
Hagley, John, 1050
Hague (Hauge), Rev. Isaac, 760*
Haidens, *see* Hayden
Hail (Haile), *see* Hale
Haines (Hains), *see* Haynes
Hainger, *see* Hanger
Haiward, *see* Hayward
Hakebourne (Hawkebourne), John, 360, 361, 362
Haldene (fl. 1066), 1421
Hale (Hael, Hail, Haile, Hales, Halles, Hayel, Hayle, Inthehale), Alex. de, 709; Amy, 33, 34*,

612, 614; Anna, 33, 34; Ann(e), 34, 214, 215, 989, 1068*, 1271, 1279*, 1280*; Ant., 989*, 1068*; Betty, 1176; Chas., 1058, 1427; Constance, 1269*; Dan., 174; Deborah, 1274; Dorothy, 393 n; Edw., 34*, 151*, 1275; Rev. Edw., 438, 449; Edw. Bisse, 34*, 612, 613; Eliz., 34*, 762, 823*, 909, 1068, 1175, 1176, 1279*; Frances, 33; Francis, 1175; Gabriel, 32, 33*, 34*, 612, 614; Hannah, 1427; Harriot, 410; Hester, 627; Isabell, 1176; Jas., 762; Jane, 215, 474, 614; Jeane, 563; Joan(e), 393 n*, 1280; Joanna, 33; John, 142, 215, 683*, 762, 880, 1041, 1078, 1131, 1175, 1231, 1274, 1275, 1280, 1387; John Blagden, 30, 31, 696, 697, 778, 779; Sir John, 393 n*; Joseph, 627, 832*; 1176; Josiah, 563; Julian, 1080; Letitia, 1262; Louisa, 1208; Marg., 215, 1521; Margery, 1271, 1275; Mary, 31, 32*, 33*, 34, 393 n, 762, 823, 1058, 1138, 1175*, 1176*, 1231, 1269, 1279; Mat., 29, 30*, 31*, 32*, 33*, 34*; Rev. Mat. Blagden, 1208, 1217; Sir Mat., 1521; Sir Mat., kt. 29*. 31, 33*, 34, 612, 859, 909, 910*; Nic., 778, 1460; Patience, 1279; Rachel, 33, 832; Ralph, 1256; Ric., 1138*, 1154, 1175; Rob. (de), 33*, 34*, 215*, 762, 823*, 1061, 1521; Sam., 1176*, 1275, 1554; Sarah, 563, 683, 832, 1137–8, 1176, 1371; Sophia, 1208; Stephen, 1059*, 1062*, 1502; Susanna, 151, 989*; Thos., 1068, 1195*, 1262, 1269*, 1271*, 1275, 1279*, 1280, 1288*, 1455, 1460, 1472; Rev. Thos., 853; Sir Thos., bt., 410; Wal., 1447; Wm. (de la), 151, 215, 762, 1058, 1279, 1313, 1371, 1372, 1456; Mr., 30; —, 1238(?); fam., 29, 214, 696
Halford, Anne, 804; Benj., 951*; Francis, 1389; Geo., 804*; Hannah, 804; Jas., 787*; Joseph, 706; Judith, 951; Mary, 706, 804; Susanna, 787; Thos., 804, 1372; W., 1092; (or Hayford), Wm., 743
Haliday, *see* Halliday
Halifax (Hallifax), Rev. Rob., 1129*, 1132*; Sam., bishop, 121; Sarah, 1129
Halifax [*peerage*], Montague, earl of, 1220; earl of, 704
Halimote, Rev. Humph., 770
Haling (Halings), *see* Hawling
Halke, Rev. Wm., 829
Hall (Aula, Halle), Abraham, 1399, 1403; Alice, 1048; Amy, 464; Ann(e), 193, 446*, 757*, 921, 978, 984, 1161, 1162, 1194, 1267, 1399*, 1536; Beata Maria, 1161; Benedict, 187, 913, 917, 921*, 1161*, 1162; Betty, 601*; Caleb, 601*; Cath., 139; Chas., 52, 176, 948; Chris., 920; Cornelius, 439; Dan., 1438; E., 703; Edith, 317; Edm., 38; Edw., 4*, 703, 1161*, 1267; Eliz., 16, 20, 176, 310, 622*, 661, 837, 978, 1112, 1153, 1324; Ephraim, 1536*; Ester, 978; Frances, 1488; Geo., 16, 20, 176, 186, 941; Rev. Geo. W., 1238; Giles, 353; Grace, 948, 1474; Hannah, 1112; Hen., 917, 921*, 1161; Rev. Hen., 515; Hen. Benedict, 921; Hester, 186*, 235; Isaac, 1399*; Isabell, 353; Jacob, 1399; Jas., 736, 757, 818, 948*, 1153, 1539; Jane, 837, 1038; Joan,

464*; John, 283, 310, 584, 601, 757, 837, 913, 921*, 948*, 984, 986, 1038, 1039, 1169, 1194, 1217, 1355, 1437*, 1438, 1475; John (W)right, 1474*; Rev. John, 553; Jos., 601; Joseph, 235, 446, 1399; Lydia, 661; Marg., 756, 948, 978; Mary, 4*, 96, 187, 283, 703, 920, 941, 1535, 1536; Mat., 1488, 1489; Pauncefoote, 978*; Petty, 601; R., 1054; Ric., 16, 186, 549*, 757*, 978*, 1121, 1398; Rev. Ric., 1, 180, 181*, 415, 463, 464; Rob. (atte), 317, 549*, 622, 797, 983, 1540; Sam., 1437, 1474; Rev. Sam., 1324, 1329; Sarah, 52, 464*, 549, 948, 1291, 1474, 1536*; Solomon, 1535; Rev. Stephen, 1392; Susanna, 948, 1438; T., 1054; Thos., 20, 93, 317, 353, 446*, 679, 756, 905*, 948, 954, 978, 1112; W., 985; Rev. W., 1232*; Wal. de, 1005; Wm. (atte), 95, 96, 184, 186*, 187, 235, 442, 818, 906, 921, 941, 1048*, 1324, 1329, 1346, 1539; Rev. Wm., 93, 96; Wm., Viscount Gage, 190, 479; Mr., 918, 1189*; —, 1052, 1311; fam., 913, 917

Halles, *see* Hale

Hallewell, *see* Halliwell

Halley, Mary, 575

Halliday (Haliday, Hallidaye, Halyday), Anne, 5; Edw., 1027, 1139; Eleanor, 631; Hannah, 250; John, 308; Mary, 660; Mic., 651, 1021; Nat., 660; Ric., 5; Sam., 308, 631; Sarah, 308; Thos., 1021; Wm. (Weliam), 250, 708 n, 1027; —, 1512; fam., 649*, 1139; *and see* Holliday

Hallifax, *see* Halifax

Halling (Hallin, Hallins), *see* Hawling

Halliwell (Hallewell), J. W., 1215; Joseph Watts, 1215; Mary, 413

Hallows (Hallowes), Ann, 542; Benj., 542; Joan, 539; John, 539*; Joseph, 539; Sam., 542; Sarah, 542*; Wm., 542; *and see* Hellow; Hollow

Hallship, Marg., 1282; Patience, 1282; *and see* Holdship

Hallyng (Hallynge), *see* Hawling

Halsey (Halsy, Holsey), Alice, 1353*; Chas., 686; Dorothy, 1353*; Eliz., 858; Thos., 350, 686, 1353*; Wm., 858

Halton, Joseph, 1058; Mary, 1058; *and see* Holton

Halvesleghe, Stephen de, 1127

Halyday, *see* Halliday

Ham (Hams), Ann, 948, 1377; Eliz., 677; Giles, 677, 803; Rev. Hen., 281; Joanna, 803; John, 1377*; Rev. John, 678, 679; Sarah, 281, 677; Thos., 984, 1377; Rev. W., 1154; Rev., 678

Hambidge (Hambage), Rev. Ric., 1221; Mr., 1422

Hamblett (Hamlet, Hamlett), Ann, 584; Eliz., 584, 1004; Guy, 706; John, 1004; John H., 1004; Mary, 991; Mary Ann, 1004; Rachel, 1004; Rob., 584*, 991*, 1004; Thos., 1004; —, 1005, 1082

Hamblin (Hamlyn, Hammeline), Ant., 254; Betty, 1232; Biggs, 254; Cath., 1126; John, 1126; Mary, 254; Priscilla, 254; Rev., 788; Sarah, 254; Thos., 1232*; Wm., 254*;

Hambourne, Thos., 28

Hambrok, John de, 1491

Hamelin, abbot (Hamelyne, Hammeline), 449, 851 n, 1238, 1421

Hamilton, Cassandra Agnes, 1193; Cath., 723; Admiral Sir Chas., bt., 1193; Rear Admiral Sir Edw., bt., 1193; Gervase, 349 n; Gil., 1415; John, 406, 740, 1350; Capt. Sir John, bt., 1193; Mary, 1415; Philippa, 740

Hamlet (Hamlett), *see* Hamblett

Hamley, Wm., 413

Hamlyn, *see* Hamblin

Hammeline, *see* Hamblin; Hamelin

Hammond (Hamman, Hamond, Hamound, Hanmond), Ant., 812*, 1515*, 1516*; Eliz., 1515, 1516*; Hester, 1514, 1516*; Jas., 1514*, 1515, 1516*; John, 812, 883; L., 1317; Marg., 812*; Mary, 1514, 1515, 1516; Rob., 1217, 1485; Sarah, 1514; Wm., 1515; Dr., 990; Mr., 1516*; *and see* Hanman

Hamp, Mr., 1196

Hampden, John, 1313; Ric., 825

Hampton (Hamton), Dame Alice, 649, 654; Alvereda, 1068; Anne, 339, 1299, 1395; Edm., 486; Eliz., 486, 1063, 1510, 1511; Elyn, 654; Hen., 339, 1395; Jas., 761, 1511; John, 339, 361, 486, 649, 654, 1395*, 1510; Rev. John, 525; Marg., 215, 486, 1395, 1508; Mary, 339, 486, 1299, 1395; Nic., 778 n; Phil., 1299, 1395*, 1402*, 1508; Ric., 778; Sam., 339; Sarah, 1510; T., 215; Thos., 339, 486*, 1395*; W., 361, 1201; Wm., 1201, 1510, 1511; Sir Wm., 649 n; —, 985, 1402; fam., 649*

Hamptonel, Hen. de, 360

Hams, *see* Ham

Hamton, *see* Hampton

Hamull, John, 1404

Hamwell, John de, 1423; —, 1422

Hanborough, John, 1232

Hanbury, Albinia, 852 n; Anne, 992*, 1454; Eleanor, 1303; Eliz., 992; John, 852 n, 992; Sir John, 875 n; Judith, 1263, 1266; M., 993; Marg., 1263; Mary, 875 n; Obadiah, 1303; Thos., 992, 993; Rev. Thos., 993; Sir Thos., 992; Wm., 992

Hancks (Hanckes), *see* Hanks

Hancock (Hancocke, Hancocks, Hancox, Handcock, Handcox, Hencock), Alice, 1049, 1050; Ann(e), 49, 201, 296, 702*, 1265, 1358*, 1360; Rev. Benj., 1420; C., 1362; Cath., 1265, 1290, 1303; Chas., 1288, 1289, 1357*, 1358*, 1360; Denway, 201; Edw., 1384; Rev. Edw., 746; Eleanor, 1333; Eliz., 49, 203, 803, 862*, 1049*; Frances, 1050; G., 1303; Giles, 49, 376*, 459, 460*, 1201; Grace, 49, 386; Hannah, 1384; Harewell, 1358; Hen., 803, 862*; Isaac, 74; Jas., 386, 797, 803; Jeremiah, 459; Joan, 376; John, 49*, 201, 296, 960, 963, 1065, 1244, 1348; Joseph, 959, 1388, 1390; Judith, 803, 1358, 1360; Kath., 1358; Mary, 49, 201, 1049*, 1244, 1248, 1358*; Maur., 963; Nat., 201, 1049, 1050; Peter, 1360; Rebecca (Rebecka), 1049, 1050*, 1248; Ric., 604, 702*, 1333*; Rob., 146, 386; Sarah, 1049, 1248; Stephen, 1384; Susanna, 201; Thos., 146, 1049, 1050*, 1201, 1244, 1248, 1258; Thos. Holdham, 1244; Wal., 201, 203,

1049*, 1050; Wm., 198, 201*, 442, 702*, 803, 1050*, 1265, 1357*, 1358*; —, 585, 1201*, 1361, 1362, 1363; fam., 197

Hancon, see Hankins

Hancox, see Hancock

Hand, see Hands

Handborough, Maud, 546; Thos., 546; fam., 546

Handcock (Handcox), see Hancock

Handelo (Handeloe), Isabel de, 690; John de, 244, 426, 690, 1015*; Maud, 1015; (later Burnel), Nic. (Nickolas), 1015*; Ric. de, 690; fam., 1015

Handford (Hondford), Rev. Nic. de, 184; Ric., 1575

Handman, see Hanman

Hands (Hand, Hondys), Ann, 693; Capt. Chas. Augustus, 1459; Eleanor, 227; Rev. Hen., 427; Jo[a]ne, 1481; Mary, 693; Nic., 1447; Phillippa Challot, 1459*; Phillippa Worgan, 1459; R., 1494; Rob., 296*, 1481*; Susannah, 693; Thos., 227, 1482*; Wm., 693, 1447; —, 1475

Handy, Francis, 996; Mary, 996; Thos., 996

Hane, see Haynes

Hanger (Hainger), Dame Ann, 516; Anne, 516; Eliz., Lady Coleraine, 516; Gabriel, 517*; Gabriel, Lord Coleraine, 515*, 516, 769; Geo., 516*, 1081; Sir Geo., kt., 516*; Jane, 516; John, 517*; John, Lord Coleraine, 516; (or D'Aungier), John, 515; Martha, 517; Mary, 516

Hanis, see Hannis

Hankes, see Hanks

Hankins (Hancon, Hankin), Ann, 548*, 549, 550; D'Avenant, 1280; Eliz., 548; Geo., 550; John, 270, 548*, 549; Mary, 270, 548; Thos., 269, 546, 1159; Ursula, 548; Wm., 548*, 1434; —, 1256

Hankinson, John, 1306

Hankman, see Hanksman

Hanks (Hanckes, Hancks, Hankes), Ann, 284, 1224; Eliz., 437, 1091, 1194; Hannah, 1224; Hen., 1091*; Hercules, 1194; Isabell, 1226*; Jane, 1043; John, 437, 1043, 1194; Sarah, 1091, 1194; Stephen, 284; Thos., 1091, 1226; Rev. Thos., 1043; Wm., 636, 1224; —, 1043; and see Hunks

Hanksman (Hankman, Hunxman), John, 431; Joseph, 431*; Rev. Joseph, 890*; Mary, 431*

Hanley, Rev. Chris., 1147, 1169; Geo., 1276*; Mary, 1276; Sam., 1276, 1289

Hanman (Handman), Ann, 1000; Anselm, 583; Hester, 887; Joan, 1400; John, 583; Thos., 1000*; W., 1317; Wm., 550, 887*, 1400, 1403; and see Hammond

Hanmer, Sir John, 743, 744

Hanmond, see Hammond

Hannis (Hanis, Hanns), John 787, 1197; Mary, 1107; (or Harris), Rev. Rob., 76; Rog., 1083; Sarah, 1083; Thos., 832

Hansbey, Rev. Wm., 878

Hanslap (Hanslape), Anne, 24; Chas., 24; Eliz., 24; Marg., 24

Hanslape, Lord, see Maudit

Hanson, Rev. Hen., 1356

Hanway, —, 1001*

Harald, T., 1195; and see Harrold

Harang, Nic., 1082; Rog., 1082*; —, 1082; and see Herring

Harber, Eliz., 797; Francis, 797; John, 584

Harbert, see Herbert

Harbidge, Freeman, 1331; —, 1331

Harbord, Sir Chas., 476; and see Herbert

Harborne, J., 1154

Harbottle, Ann, 907; Wm., 907

Harbridge, —, 848

Harby, Rev. E., 1069

Harcourt (Hercourt), Agnes, 643*, 1198*; Eliz., 1350; John, 333*; Letitia Sarah Maria, 333; Rebecca, 718 n; Ric., 643, 1198, 1350; Simon, 1198; Sir Simon, 718 n

Hard, see Heard

Hardcastle, Rev. Thos., 1385

Harden, Hester, 124; Rev. Rob., 266, 268; Wm. (de), 124, 915; and see Harding

Hardeshull, John de, 244

Hardiman, Ann, 296; Thos., 296

Hardinc (fl. 1066), 1439

Harding (Hardinge, Hardyng), Abigail, 1535; Ann, 320, 416, 1031, 1158, 1542, 1583; Arabella, 1194; Baylee, 1491; Betty, 1582; Dorothea, 279; Dorothy, 280; Eliz., 416*, 543, 792, 976, 1158, 1499, 1542; Esther, 284; Frances, 761; Francis, 1418; Geo., 1535, 1582; Hannah, 555, 996, 1535; Hen., 452, 1583; Hester, 948*; Jas., 1158*, 1194, 1583; Joan, 212, 991; John, 280, 284, 320, 388, 416*, 468, 524, 543*, 796, 901, 906, 976*, 1031, 1535, 1539, 1542, 1548*; Rev. John, 1367; Jonathan, 941; Joseph, 948, 1158; Juliana, 1491; Mabell, 1548*; Marg., 901, 1030; Martha, 211*, 1158; Mary, 212, 416, 442, 468, 524*, 543, 976, 996, 1030, 1031, 1100, 1418, 1542; Maur., 416; Miriam, 796; Nic., 792; Peter, 996; Phil., 555, 996; Rebecca, 991; Ric., 36, 442, 948*, 1158, 1252, 1447, 1542*; Rob., 991; Rev. Rob., 678, 991; Rog., 211*, 212*; Sam., 284, 531, 1158*; Sarah, 36, 212, 284, 1030, 1158*; Simon, 1418; Solomon, 1542; Susan, 1418; Susanna, 212; Thos., 524*, 836, 948, 996*, 1031*, 1582; Wm., 212, 284, 523, 524, 531*, 678, 1030*, 1258, 1539, 1542; Rev. Wm., 279*, 280, 415; Mr., 280 n; Rev., 1447; —, 1292, 1476; fam., 415, 523, 745; and see FitzHarding; Harden

Hardman, Cath., 339; Mary, 1315; Sarah, 229; Thos., 1315*; Wm., 229, 339; and see Herdman

Hardwick (Hardwicke, Hardwicks), Agnes, 1105; Ann(e), 111, 1105*, 1106, 1108, 1327*; Edw., 1106; Eliz., 15, 1105, 1327; Eliz. Bluett, 1327; Eliz. Jones, 1327; Euseby, 470; Eustace, 469, 471*; Geo., 753, 1105*, 1106*, 1121; Hannah, 1575; Harriett, 1327; Harriett Priscilla, 1327; Hen., 1108, 1327; Hen. Tucker, 1327; Hester, 1549; Jas., 1105, 1324–5, 1328, 1329; Rev. Jas., 1105, 1329; Jas. Machin, 1327; John, 15, 471, 733, 907, 1121; Joseph, 1107; Maria, 1327; Mary, 5, 276, 471*, 733, 907, 1105, 1108; Mary Ann, 1327; Peter, 1105*, 1107, 1122, 1328, 1329*, 1549; Priscilla, 1327; Ric. Ayton, 1108; Sam., 1105, 1108*; Sarah, 1107; T. B., 1327;

Thos., 1323, 1327*, 1420, 1575*; Thos. Bluett, 1327; Thos. Machin, 1327*; W., 1328; Wm., 5, 276, 1105; Rev. Dr., 1324; fam., 102

Hardwick [*peerage*](Hardwicke), Phil., earl of, 325; Lord Chancellor, 78; *and see* York, Phil.

Hardyng, *see* Harding

Hare (Harre), Alice la, 1074; John le, 1074; Sam., 1136

Harefield, Jane, 284

Hareson, *see* Harrison

Harewell, Eliz., 1311; *and see* Harwell

Harford (Herford), Ann, 1452; Chas., 843; Edw., 12, 721; Eliz., 1452*, 1453; Hannah, 399, 845*, 1452; Hen., 1452*, 1453; John, 843, 845*, 1452*, 1554; John Scandrett, 718; Joseph, 1158, 1160; Marg., 843; Martha, 1452; Mary, 1158; Rev. Nat., 432, 691; Ric., 399; Rev. Ric., 1380; Sarah, 845; Thos., 843; Rev. Thos., 1031; Trueman, 1039; —, 1160, 1287, 1455; fam., 721, 1160, 1380

Harker, Rob., 1153

Harley, Rev. Wm., 1122; fam., 392; *and see* Herle

Harman, Ann, 983; Edm., 1015; Eliz., 543; Jane, 983; John, 983; Mary, 1079; Rob., 658; Sam., 1079; Sarah, 118, 658, 983; Susanna, 983; Thos., 543; Wm., 118, 1079; —, 1441

Harmer (Harmar), Ann, 1411; Eliz., 1007, 1008, 1183; Esther, 661; Geo., 1008; J., 1027; Jas., 1026*; Jane, 1008, 1183; John, 346, 661, 1007*, 1139, 1183*, 1186*, 1411, 1420; Jonathan, 1008, 1183; K., 1139;; Mary, 661; Ric., 661; Sarah, 1026; Thos., 1007–8, 1183; W., 1139; Wm., 1062, 1187; Dr., 1087

Harnage, Dorothea, 1273; Edw., 1273

Harnhull, Wm. de, 678; —, 1255

Harnons, John, 832; Sarah, 832

Harold, Earl (king)(Herald), 713, 769, 807, 1047, 1050, 1051, 1126, 1138, 1474, 1475*, 1512*

Harold, son of Radulph, earl of Hereford, *see* Sudeley

Harold, *see* Harrold

Harpe, Rev. Ric., 302

Harper (Harpur), Anna-Maria, 1396; Ann(e), 1307, 1396*; Betty, 1037*, 1307*; Eleanor, 284; Eliz., 923*, 1157*, 1396; Giles, 609; Hannah, 284, 923; J., 1062; Jas., 1396; John, 284, 1037*, 1039, 1396*; Rev. John, 76, 89, 147, 149; Kitty, 1037; Martha, 1396; Mary, 1037, 1396*; Peter, 284; Rebekar, 1157; Ric., 284; Sam., 1307; Sible, 1396; Thos., 1396*, 1403; Wm., 215, 923*, 1037, 1157*

Harptre, fam., 807

Harpur, *see* Harper

Harre, *see* Hare

Harres (Harries), *see* Harris

Harrington, Ann, 211; Betty, 211; Dionysia, 842; Eliz., 210, 842; Geo., 210, 211; John, 211, 839*, 842*; Mary, 211, 842; Sam., 1477; Thos., 142; Vertue, 842; Wm., 546; Lord, 1475; —, 1362, 1554

Harris (Harres, Harries, Harriss, Harrys, Heris, Herries), Alice, 676, 1366, 1438; Ann(e), 308,

677, 886*, 932, 985, 1026*, 1064, 1088, 1153, 1366, 1466, 1515*; Benj., 687, 886*, 887, 1361; Blanch, 812; Rev. Brian, 342*; Bridget, 868*, 976; Cath., 472, 1158*; Chas., 862*, 1158*; Cornelius, 868, 1366*; Dan., 1366*; Deborah, 981; Dinah, 70, 97; Ebenezer, 351*; Edith, 1064; Edm., 1358*; Edw., 483, 1031; Eliz., 670, 677, 734, 862*, 886*, 887, 967, 976, 981*, 1036, 1064, 1358, 1389*, 1457, 1470*; Gabriel, 513, 1186; Giles, 1015; Grace, 1088*; Hannah, 887, 1083, 1088, 1434; Harwood (Harward), 1466*, 1477; Hen., 100, 1298, 1403; Hester, 1182; Humph., 1434*; Isaac, 1172; Rev. J., 785; Jas., 472, 677, 714*, 967, 1369, 1470*, 1562*; Rev. Jas., 754; Jas. Lloyd, 1369; Jane, 137, 1158, 1180; Janet, 1434; Jenkins, 412; Jeremiah, 812; Joan, 1250; John, 54, 70, 97, 100, 118, 138*, 351*, 446, 522, 636, 670, 676, 677*, 706, 736, 749, 854, 862, 886*, 966, 967*, 976, 981*, 1031, 1039, 1065, 1083, 1180*, 1369*, 1377, 1388, 1389*, 1412, 1432, 1434, 1438*; Rev. John, 463, 1482; John Collwell, 1533; Jonathan, 1180*, 1528; Joseph, 137, 383, 660, 1388, 1389, 1420, 1434*, 1440; Kath., 100; Lovisa, 714; Marg., 137, 274, 967(?), 1026; Martha, 1158; Mary, 54*, 138*, 446, 713, 714*, 735, 736, 749, 862*, 887, 932*, 953, 1064, 1065, 1183, 1366, 1369, 1377, 1434*, 1457, 1466*, 1515, 1562*; Matthias, 735; Moses, 1088*; Nic., 1501; Pendock, 399; Peter, 138, 782; Phil., 1298, 1403; R., 1216; Rachel, 1528, 1533*; Rebecca (Rebekah), 687, 1361; Ric., 460, 862*, 967, 1026*, 1083, 1216, 1369, 1515*, 1516; Rob., 274, 976, 1366, 1369, 1456, 1539; Dr. Rob., 287, 518 n; Rev. Rob., 1020; (or Hannis), Rev. Rob., 76; Rev. Sam(p)son, 1179, 1180*, 1186*, 1187; Sam., 887, 967; Rev. Sam., 190, 919; Sarah, 351*, 383, 412, 636, 660, 967, 1000, 1036, 1180, 1361, 1412*, 1434, 1528*; Sophia, 1180*; Stephen, 1420; Susanna(h), 513, 1438; T., 1064; Thos., 97*, 137, 308*, 351*, 446, 734*, 736, 868*, 887*, 976, 985, 1036, 1047, 1064*, 1153, 1183, 1201, 1250, 1366*, 1403, 1434*, 1539; Rev. Thos., 1329; W., 1101; Wal., 1039, 1515*; Wm.. 100*, 351, 616, 660, 676, 700, 735, 868, 932*, 967(*?), 1000, 1088*, 1147, 1169, 1186, 1366, 1368, 1412, 1515, 1528*, 1533*; Rev., 1187, 1372; —, 1015, 1027, 1064, 1370, 1403; fam., 349, 482; (or Prickley), fam., 1165

Harrison (Hareson), Abraham, 661; Ann(e), 567, 1081; Cath., 379; Dame Dorothea, 375; Eliz., 932*, 1161, 1511; Geo., 932; Rev. Jas., 1103; John, 1513; Rev. John, 990*; Rev. Joseph, 370, 375, 379, 459, 991; Lewis, 296; Marg., 572, 932; Mary, 296; Priscilla, 510; Ric., 304*, 510; Rev. Rob., 840, 1031; Sam., 1511; Susanna, 304; Thos., 567, 837; Sir Thos., kt., 375*; Wm., 230 n, 304, 567, 572, 932*, 1081; Rev. Wm., 1161*, 1346; Winter, 932*; Mr., 1189; —, 591 n, 1103

Harriss, *see* Harris

Harrold (Harold), Eliz., 542*; Jas., 419; John, 40, 156; Joseph, 419; Sarah, 419*; *and see* Harald

Harrowby, Lord, 87; *and see* Ryder, Nat.

Harry, Charlotte, 167; Ric., 1456

Harrys, *see* Harris

Harshfield, —, 1087

Hart (Harte, Heart, Heort, Hert), Rev. Abel, 449; Ann(e), 1212, 1582; Arthur, 1553; Betty, 174, 1207; Chas., 175; Dan., 1212; Eliz., 1079, 1207, 1212, 1365; Geo., 978, 1420; Hannah, 841*; Hen., 1398; Hester, 978; Jas., 174; Jane, 215; Joan, 542; John, 542, 841, 1079, 1207*, 1212, 1282*, 1403; Mary, 1110, 1282*; Ric., 102, 215*, 944, 1403, 1582; Sir Ric., kt., 206; Sarah, 215, 1282; Stephen, 1110; Thos., 215*, 841*, 1207, 1217; Wal. le, 1552; Wm. (le), 7, 815, 1259, 1356; Rev. Wm., 1365; Mr., 7; —, prior, 259 n; —, 1421

Hartelbury, *see* Hartlebury

Hartgill, Mary, 765

Hartland, Beata, 468; Benjamina, 468; Eliz., 611, 760, 761, 904*; Joan, 821*; Joanna, 821; John, 904*, 1235*, 1315; Rev. John, 1217; Marg., 354; Mary, 1184; Miles, 468; N., 1290; Rev. Rob., 691; Sarah, 1235, 1315; Sarah Andrews, 468; Thos., 821*, 902, 904, 1184, 1315; Wm., 1288; Mr., 893, 894, 1288; —, 1238*, 1403; fam., 1403

Hartlebury (Hartelbury), Cath., 1271*, 1274, 1280; Eliz., 337, 1274, 1280*; Esther, 1274, 1281; Mary, 329, 337; Merrett (Menret), 1274, 1280*, 1289; Sarah, 337; Thos., 329, 1271*, 1274, 1280, 1288; Wal., 337*; Wm. Merrett, 1280; —, 1477

Hartley, Ann, 1120; Betty, 468; David, 1119*, 1120, 1122, 1123*; Eliz., 1119, 1120; Hen., 468*; Mary, 1119; Sarah, 468; W. H., 1120, 1122; W. Hen., 1123; Winchcomb Hen., 1105, 1113, 1116, 1119; —, 1121

Hartman, Rev. Paul, 1122

Hartnell (Hartnol, Hurtnol), Ann Gowling, 336; Eleanor (Elinor), 336, 814; John, 336; Wm., 814; *and see* Hurnall

Hartshorne, Arthur, 1546; Sam., 1546

Hartwell, Grace, 226; Mary, 226; Thos., 226; W., 1160

Harvard (Avad, Avard, Havard, Havford), Anne, 112; Frances, 1359; Geo., 112; John, 1359; Ensign John, 928; Mark, 843*; Mary, 623, 843*; Neast, 1289; Ric., 623*; Sampson, 1574; Sarah, 843*, 1574; Susannah, 623; Thos., 1574; Wm., 1574; —, 1288, 1289; *and see* Harward

Harvest, Geo., 1301; Mary, 1301

Harvey (Harvie, Hervey), Ann(e), 14, 332, 473, 1107*, 1232, 1467*, 1469*, 1470; Betty, 1118; Dan., 1398; David, 1467, 1473*; Edw., 1470; Eliz., 817, 1111, 1225*, 1399, 1400, 1463*–4, 1469, 1473; Frances, 14, 1469*, 1470*; Frances Charlotte, 1225; Geo., 1461, 1469*; Gideon, 817*; Giles, 331, 1469*; Hannah, 1398*; Harvey, 1118; Harvey Hill, 1118; Helen, 1470*; Henny, 1241, 1248; Hen., 1464, 1469*, 1470*; Hen. Clay, 1248; J., 1101, 1447; Jacob, 1118; Jo[a]ne, 1465; Johanna, 1111; John, 863, 1225, 1447, 1461, 1463, 1465, 1469*, 1470*, 1473,

1478; Rev. John, 13, 14*; Rev. John Ridout, 1473; Joseph, 1400; Louisa, 1225*; Mary, 752, 1111*, 1473*; Mat., 1189; Ric., 1220, 1225, 1467*, 1478; Rev. Ric., 1225, 1228; Sam., 1398*; Sam. Clay, 1241*, 1248; Sarah, 1398, 1470; Susanna, 1118; T., 1064; Thos., 752, 1399, 1400*, 1470*, 1477; Wm., 166, 168, 1107*, 1111*, 1121, 1470; Rev. Wm., 56, 1464*; Rev. Mr., 13; —, 1064, 1477

Harward, Agnes, 1432*; Alice, 1432*; Altham, 231; Anne, 1432; Ant., 1432; Joan, 1432; John, 1432*; Rev. John, 1423; Dr. Kempe, 231; Lucy, 231; Marg., 1432*; Margery, 1432; Mary, 867; Thos., 1432*; Wm., 867, 1432*; fam., 230, 1432; *and see* Harvard; Harwood

Harwell, Rev. Thos., 1196; *and see* Harewell

Harwood, Ann, 1511; Eliz., 563; Geo., 563, 1511; (or Horwood), Hester, 615; Jas., 1481*; (or Horwood), John, 615*; Lucy, 900; Ric., 900; Sarah, 1481; *and see* Harward

Hascombe (or Horsepol), Rev. Francis, 1335

Haseldine, Rev. Wm., 421

Hasele, *see* Hazel

Haselwood, Mary, 1266; Sir Thos., 1266

Haskins, *see* Heskins

Haskoll, Ann, 1273; Ric., 1273

Hasleton (Hasulton), Anne, 340; Bridget, 1410; Dan., 340

Haslam (Haslum, Hazleham, Hesleham), Eliz., 799, 800, 1470*; Geo., 439; Hen., 439, 1470*; Jas., 800; Jane, 800*; Mary, 800; Susanna, 439, 1470; Wm., 799, 800*

Hassard, *see* Hazard

Hassell, Eleanor, 1127; T., 1127; *and see* Hazel

Hastings, Bridget, 1068; Hen., 1068; Joan, 1126*; Rev. Penyston, 216; Wm. de, 1126; Woodman, 1362; Lord, 1219*; Mr., 1215; —, 1355*; fam., 255

Hasulton, *see* Hasleton

Hatch, Anne, 764; Colibery, 764; Edw., 1267, 1268, 1288; John, 90; Joseph, 1288*; Rev. Joseph, 72, 764*; Sarah, 90; Ursula, 1268; W., 1160

Hatchet, Ann, 388; Wm., 388

Hateswy, *see* Hathaway

Hatfield (Haytfield), Ann, 642; Sarah, 642*; St[ephen], 1339; Wm., 642*

Hatford, Rev. Nat., 288

Hathaway (Hateswy, Hatheway, Hathewy, Hathway, Hethewy, Hetheway), Abiathan, 637; Amy, 982; Ann(e), 637, 983*, 1224*; Beate, 777; Chris., 463; Dan., 1421; Edw., 982, 995*, 996; Eleanor, 637; Eliz., 141, 555, 995, 1053, 1224*, 1342, 1427; Frances, 995; Francis, 555*; Hen., 510, 1053*; J., 1227; Jane, 995*; John, 7, 36, 506, 983*, 986, 1087, 1342*; Justinian, 637, 1224*; Marg., 982; Mary, 995*, 1194, 1224, 1427*, 1499; Rebecca, 35; Ric., 141, 1196, 1224, 1499; Rev. Ric., 630; Rob., 995*, 1053, 1259, 1423; Sarah, 510, 995; Sibill, 1039; Simon, 321; Thos., 637, 777*, 1194, 1421, 1427*; W. (de), 1039*; Wm., 777, 984, 995*, 1307, 1421; —, 1039; fam., 245, 806, 1039

Hathemer, And. de, 1218

Hathen, Giles, 661; John, 661; Susannah, 661; Thos., 661

Hatherell (Hatherall, Hatherel, Hatherill), Abraham, 1338*; Ann, 1338; Isaac, 121; Joan, 1338; Joanna, 1118; John, 124, 1118; Joseph, 434; Mary, 1118, 1338; Sarah, 124, 1118; Wm., 862, 1118, 1338

Hatherley (Hatherleye), Hen. of, 1370; Liana of, 1370*; Thos. de, 1370*

Hatheway (Hathewy), see Hathaway

Hathey, Francis, 176, 1175, 1176; Mary, 176

Hathington, Jas., 1330

Hathway, see Hathaway

Hatman, Susanna, 1345; Wm., 1345

Hatt, John, 708 n

Hattars (Hattare, Hatters), Rob. le, 1061; —, 1062, 1064*

Hatton, Ann, 111, 112, 1184, 1231; Betty, 1231; Canaan, 611; Sir Ct., 1477; Sir Chris., 628, 711, 985, 1062, 1093, 1139, 1226, 1339, 1382; Dan., 1184; Eliz., 611, 1279; Francis, 906; Hen., 1265, 1279; John, 611*, 1046; Jonathan, 112; Joseph, 1231*; Marg., 904*; Mary, 906, 1184; Nic., 611; Phil., 111; Rob., 1039; Wm., 904, 1237; Rev. Wm., 449; —, 986, 1064, 1441

Hauge, see Hague

Haughlin, Anne, 1334

Haughton, Ann, 1281; Comfort, 1277; Eliz., 1277*; Kath., 1281; Phil., 1281; Thos., 1127; and see Houghton

Haukins, see Hawkins

Hauley, Jane, 1023; Sarah, 1023; Wm., 1023; and see Hawley

Hault, Rev. John, 452

Haunynge, John, 1363

Havanage, —, 1148

Havard (Havford), see Harvard

Haviland (Havilande), Alice, 1484*; Rev. Ant., 459; Edw., 1484*; Eliz., 1109, 1484*; Frances, 1484; Francis, 1484; Jas., 1484; John, 1483, 1484*, 1485*; Rev. John, 1483, 1485; Marg., 1484*; Martha, 1484; Mary, 1484*; Ric., 1484*; Rob., 1109; Susanna, 1484*; Wm., 1484, 1485; fam., 1485

Hawe (Haw), John de, 1356; Rev. Rob., 128

Hawes, John, 90; Rob., 884; Sarah, 884; Rev. Sam., 1469; Thos., 1469

Hawkebourne, see Hakebourne

Hawken, see Hawkins

Hawker, Alice, 486; Ann, 1006; Edw., 1082; Geo., 965, 1027, 1289; Giles, 486; Grace, 1137, 1138*, 1143; Hannah, 1027, 1507*; Hester, 1007; John, 814, 1136*, 1138, 1507; Mary, 1007, 1023, 1137, 1143; Peter, 1507; Rev. Peter, 644, 1027, 1505, 1507*, 1513*; Ric., 803, 1007*, 1136, 1137*, 1138*, 1143; Sam., 447, 1023; Sarah, 1136*, 1138; Susannah, 1137*; Thos., 1138, 1369; W., 1215; Wm., 950, 1203; Rev. Wm., 1216; —, 1027, 1139

Hawkes (Hawks), Ann(e), 171, 872, 989; Hen., 360 n; John, 171, 872; John Prinsep, 347; Sarah, 347; Thos., 989; Wm., 171*, 347, 872

Hawkesbury, Chas., Lord Hawkesbury, 697; baron, see Jenkinson, Chas.

Hawkesworth (Hawksworth), John, 51*; Ric., 50, 51*, 1121; Sarah, 51*; fam., 825

Hawkins (Haukins, Hawken, Hawkyns, Horkins), Alice, 814; And., 111; Ann(e), 111, 666*, 872, 1065, 1421; Awdrey, 1466; Betty, 616; Chas., 603; Dan., 584; Deborah, 622, 1026; Edw., 111, 1582; Rev. Edw., 198; Eleanor, 583, 622, 666, 1437; Eliz., 616, 622, 666*, 814, 872, 922, 931, 1399; Geo., 1289; Hannah, 583; Hen., 466, 922*, 947, 1010, 1086, 1437*, 1440; Isabel, 351; J., 1256; Jas., 814*, 903, 905, 922, 924, 931; Jane, 693, 1437; Jeremiah, 622, 870*, 1355*; Johanna, 624, 1201, 1256; John, 471, 622*, 624, 666, 693, 872*, 903, 931*, 993*, 1062*, 1147, 1186, 1201*, 1351, 1437; Joseph, 870*, 872, 873; Judith, 1437; Dame Marg., 1392; Mary, 55, 300, 622, 624, 666, 687, 693, 762, 931, 1010; Nat., 584, 666*, 687, 858; Rev. Nat., 583*; Ric., 55, 1026; Rob., 55; Rog., 555; Sam., 622, 665, 666, 1437*; Sarah, 622, 666*, 872, 903, 922, 1025–6, 1437; Susannah, 584; Thos., 616, 666*, 762, 931*, 1065*, 1165, 1307, 1399*, 1403, 1421*, 1466; Wm., 351, 814, 1039, 1350; Mr., 1021, 1440; —, 1214 n, 1351, 1363, 1402; fam., 440; and see Howkins

Hawks, see Hawkes

Hawksworth, see Hawkesworth

Hawkyns, see Hawkins

Hawley, Lord, 1005 n; and see Hauley

Hawling (Haling, Halings, Hallin, Halling, Hallins, Hallyng, Hallynge), Alice, 1366; Ann(e), 348, 983; Dan., 1367; Eleanor, 1367; Eliz., 338, 485*, 751*, 881, 983, 1365, 1366; Francis, 1182, 1184; Jo(a)ne, 73, 118, 1130; John, 73, 485*, 486, 881, 983*, 1116, 1265; Rev. John, 553; Judith, 486*; Lydia, 1073; Mary, 398, 750, 983, 1265; Nic., 1101; Peter, 1005; Ric., 118, 348, 1130; Ric. Vicar, 118; Sam., 486, 1265; Sarah, 716, 1184; Susanna, 1211; T., 1101; Thos., 118*, 338, 398, 750*, 983, 1102, 1211; Rev. Thos., 571; W., 1382; Wm., 118, 167, 485, 486, 716*, 1365, 1366; —, 985, 986

Hawsted, —, 1064

Hay, Adam atte, 1420; Anne, 408; Col. David, 1225; Rev. Hen., 808; John le, 1485; Laur. de la, 1372; Louisa, 1225; Rev. Ric. John, 1552; Wm. atte, 1372; Rev. Mr., 1543; and see Delahay; Hayes

Hayard, see Hayward

Haybarare, Wm., 581 n

Haycock, Ann, 1183; Chas., 1183; Eliz., 1336; Frances Mary, 1183; Joseph, 1336*; Mary, 1336*; Thos., 1183; Mr., 1512

Hayden (Haidens, Haydon, Heyden, Heydon), Ann(e), 520, 976, 1077; Bliss, 976; Sir Chris., 520; Edw., 305, 1077; Rev. Edw., 1346; Eliz., 1081; Francis, 1077, 1078, 1501; Rev. Francis, 305; Hen., 1077; J., 1460; Jas., 1081; John, 1083, 1404; Olive, 1083; Ric. de, 1404*; Rob., 1331; Sarah, 1076; Thos., 1077; Wm., 1081, 1083; —, 1077, 1078; fam., 1076

Hayel, *see* Hale

Hayes (Hayse, Heyes), Eliz., 1336; (or Archard), Eliz., 1248; Giles, 1258; (or Archard), Giles, 1248*; Jas., 494; John, 329, 932; Marg., 329; Mary, 932, 1583; Ric., 1583*; (or Archard), Sarah, 1248; Wm., 932; (or Archard), Wm., 1248; —, 1017, 1069, 1126; *and see* Delahay; Hay

Hayford (or Halford), Wm., 743

Haygarth, Rev. John 1031; Rev. John Sayer, 990; Sarah, 1031

Hayle, *see* Hale

Hayley (Heyley), Eliz., 608; Ric., 1519; Wm., 608

Haylings, John, 965; Susannah, 965

Haym, Hen., 1197

Hayman, Jacob, 730; Rachel, 730

Haynes (Haines, Hains, Hane, Hayne, Heanes, Heins, Heyne, Heynes), Ad[a]m de, 1165; Alice, 320; And., 1508*; Ann(e), 73*, 300, 460*, 596, 624, 726, 850, 857, 1010, 1084; Benj., 73; Betty, 317, 1413; Chas., 73; Chris., 1087; Rev. Chris., 834, 1084*, 1087; Deborah, 1508; Dorothy, 1412; Edith, 624; Edm., 320*; Edw., 621*, 1210, 1405; Eleanor, 850; Eliz., 383, 460, 526, 850, 1144, 1487; Frances, 73; Francis, 1262, 1268; Rev. Francis, 571; Geo., 1508*; Gil., 1069; Giles, 460*, 526; Hannah, 38, 320, 1210*; Hen., 854; Isaac, 1278*; J., 1420; Rev. J., 1084; Jas., 38, 1210; Jane, 387, 460, 906; John, 74*, 118, 300, 387, 460*, 526*, 624, 659, 849, 850*, 1069, 1217, 1335, 1344, 1508; Joseph, 623; Joyce, 1268; Lucy, 550; Martha, 202; Mary, 8, 73*, 74, 88, 526*, 596, 621, 624, 1084, 1241; N., 1202; Nat., 624, 1202; Nic., 1540; Peter, 88, 1144, 1316; Ric., 6, 7*, 36, 74, 317, 419, 526, 726, 1412*, 1415, 1552; Rog., 1329; Rosamund, 621; Sam., 211, 814, 857, 906; Sarah, 8, 460*, 624*, 1084, 1278, 1344, 1487; Thos., 8*, 51, 71, 202*, 383, 550, 623, 624*, 1049, 1218, 1241, 1388, 1412*, 1487*, 1508; Rev. Thos., 1441*; W., 1519; Wm., 73*, 74, 486, 596*, 906; —, 848, 985*, 986, 1122*, 1420, 1455; fam., 459, 619, 1420; *and see* Heane

Hayold, Ric., 1137; Sarah, 1137

Hayse, *see* Hayes

Hayter, John, 1282; Mary, 1282

Haytfield, *see* Hatfield

Haywadeby, Wm., 1428

Hayward (Haiward, Hayard, Heyward), Abraham, 111; Agnes, 639; Alice, 254*; Ann(e), 132, 254, 268, 510, 517, 563, 636, 639*, 658*, 873, 1000*, 1013, 1275, 1280, 1495; Rev. Ant., 236; B., 1495; Bathshua, 1267; Benj., 658*; Cath., 1047; Cath. Augusta, 1047; Cecily, 1309; Chas., 71, 72, 75*, 76, 639, 680, 999; Charlotte, 1231; Chris., 369; Dan., 563; Deborah, 636*; Edw., 254*, 510; Eleanor, 1000*, 1162; Eliz., 111, 112, 254, 456, 517*, 609, 610*, 611, 631, 1000, 1267, 1273; Esther, 636, 973; Frances, 117, 852 n, 999*; Geo., 546; Rev. Geo., 630*, 643, 940; Rev. Geo. Chris., 1136; Hannah, 1365; Harriott, 268; Harry, 636; Rev. Hen., 574; Hester, 563; Hopewell, 609,

610*; J., 1312; (or Westripp), Rev. J., 1147; Jane, 254, 517, 1302; Joan, 254*; John (le), 111*, 112, 254*, 517, 563, 636*, 872, 973, 1017, 1162*, 1228, 1263, 1302, 1372; Rev. John, 76, 630, 631*, 1495, 1502; Joseph, 1267, 1289; Leonard, 1192, 1193; Marg., 75, 76, 1000; Martha, 658, 872, 1301; Mary, 254*, 610, 611*, 631*, 670, 814, 873, 973, 1063, 1088, 1236, 1275, 1280; Mary Ann, 1280; Mercy, 999*; Mic., 610; Nat., 563; Packer, 610; Phil. (le), 611*, 1267*, 1379; Philippa, 611; Ric., 117, 132, 254*, 456, 639*, 670, 1088, 1302; Rob., 1233, 1292, 1528; Rog. (le), 639, 1017; Sam., 263, 449, 667, 713, 1044, 1047*, 1267, 1403; Rev. Sam., 937; Sarah, 110, 165, 1302; Sarah Eliz., 1136; Susannah, 639; Rev. T., 1069; Thos. (le), 110, 231, 517*, 610, 611, 639*, 852 n, 999*, 1000*, 1302, 1540; (or Cockes), Thos., 610; Rev. Thos., 228, 1066; W., 1044; (later Winstone), W., 1160; Wal., 1440; Wm., 75, 254*, 436, 496, 625, 636, 873, 1000*, 1140, 1231, 1236, 1267*, 1275, 1365; (later Winstone), Wm., 999; Rev. Wm., 266*, 268, 547; Rev., 1485; —, 266, 1017, 1185, 1282, 1301, 1387; fam., 346, 638; (or Cox), fam., 609; *and see* Haywood

Haywarden, Jonathan, 837

Haywood (Heywood), Eliz., 831; John, 831*, 832; Martha, 385; Mary, 385, 831, 832; Sarah, 385; Thos., 385*, 831*; Rev. Thos., 1165, 1539; Wm., 831; *and see* Hayward

Hayworth, Geo., 13

Hazard (Hassard), Arthur, 1317; Geo., 1289

Hazel (Hasele, Hazell), Ann, 1168; John, 1168; Ric. (atte), 608*, 1217, 1504; *and see* Hassell

Hazleham, *see* Haslam

Head (Hedde), Edw., 165; Eliz., 164, 1092, 1570; Hen., 1020; Rev. Hen., 161, 164*, 165; J., 1092; Joanna, 1092; John, 230, 413, 983, 1570; Joshua, 1226; Marg., 1570; Mary, 164, 165, 983, 1570; Ric., 1570; Thos., 360 n, 1227, 1570; —, 1282

Headington, Rev. Clement, 427, 798, 859

Heald, —, 1402

Heale, —, 1386

Healing, Hester, 803; John, 485; Mary, 1282; Sam., 485, 803, 1282

Heane (Hene), Ann, 1037; Caroline, 1037; Eliz., 1037*; Hen., 1037; Rev. Hen., 1485; Sir Hen., bt., 1033; Jas., 1037; Mary, 1037; Rowland, 471; Wm., 1037; fam., 469; *and see* Haynes

Heanes, *see* Haynes

Heard (Hard, Herde, Hurd), Ann, 1019; Chas., 716; Eliz., 716; Ezekiah, 562; Joan, 716; John, 369, 716, 1102, 1117; Marg., 716; Martha, 562; Rev. Ric., 534; Rob., 716*; Sam., 716; Sarah, 562, 563, 1117; Wm. (le), 562, 563, 1019, 1259

Hearn (Hearne, Hern, Herne, Hierne, Hurn, Hurne, Inthehurne, Stathherne), Adam, 1228; Edw., 4*; Hen., 1456, 1485; Jas., 412, 830; Jane, 830; John (at the, in the), 412, 1228, 1423; Rev. John, 1221; Ric., 1228; Rob., 1422; Sam., 996; Sarah, 4; Thos. atte, 1491; Wal., 1255; Rev. Wm., 31; —, 590 n, 591 n, 1422, 1458; *and see* Heron

Heart, see Hart

Heath (Heth, Hethe, Inthehethe), Alice, 1447; Eliz., 815, 1361; Jas., 815; Jane, 787; John, 1259; Martha, 543; Nic., bishop, 221, 717*, 890; Ric., 815, 1289, 1330; Sarah, 543, 1330; Susanna, 1361; Thos. (atte), 74, 543, 1552; Rev. Thos., 1392; Topp, 409; Wm., 787, 1361; (or Mayle), Wm., 895

Heather, T., 1312; Rev. Thos., 495

Heathfield, Hannah, 175; Hen., 175*; John, 169; Sarah, 175

Heaton, Rev. Rob. Salusbury, 93, 651, 653

Heaven (Heavens, Hevyn), Alice, 632; Ann(e), 632*, 1176, 1473, 1511; Arthur, 1473; Dinah, 662; Edith, 632, 1098; Edw., 632, 1027, 1510; Eliz., 240, 537, 632, 1473; Giles, 632, 662, 1137; Hannah, 1510; Hester, 677; J., 1220; John, 632*, 1098*, 1100, 1140, 1148, 1477; Joshua, 1176; Lydia, 1510; Martha, 632; Mary, 632*, 1098*, 1511; Mary Ann, 1473; Ric., 456, 632*, 677, 751, 773, 1509–10; S., 1027*; Sam., 632*, 1510, 1511*; Sarah, 537*, 632, 1137; Saul, 1511; Thos., 632*; Ursula, 632; Wal., 1510*; Wm., 532, 537*, 632*, 1473; —, 1148*; fam., 236, 392 n, 630; and see Henene

Heberden, fam., 159

Hedde, see Head

Hedges, John, 836; Rev. John, 263; Joseph, 1473

Hegun, see Higgins

Heins, see Haynes

Helewys, see Elwes

Helion (Helioun, Helyon), Peter (or Walter), 990; Rose, 990; —, 1402*

Hellen, Eliz., 1405; and see Heylyn

Hellier, Ann, 1111; Eliz., 1110*; Hen., 1110*; John, 1111, 1121

Hellow, Chas., 1494; Thos., 1494; fam., 1494; and see Hallows; Hollow

Helme, Rev. Chris. (or Carshew), 1477; Neastor, 1268; Sarah, 1268; Messrs., 1215

Helps, Alice, 847; Ric., 1378; Wm., 847

Helsam (Helsome), Cath., 844; John, 843; Mary, 843, 844; Ric., 844*; Thos., 843, 844

Helyon, see Helion

Hemming (Heming, Hemmin, Hemyge, Hemynge), Ann(e), 138, 141*, 1386; Dan., 138; Edw., 1012, 1013; Eliz., 1386; Frances, 140; Isaac, 138*, 1386; John, 501, 1012, 1086*, 1361; Joseph, 1012; Martha, 501, 1361; Mary, 138, 1086; Ric., 141*, 296; Rob., 1420; Thos., 138*, 140*, 141; Thos. Norris, 1386*; Wal., 1420; Wm., 1086, 1361; Wm. Hampton, 1086; —, 1386

Hempsted (Hemsted), Rob., 1516; W., 1516

Hemyge (Hemynge), see Hemming

[Henchman], Humph., bishop, 1223

Hencock, see Hancock

Henderson, Charlotte, 1582; John, 1582*; Ric., 1582*; —, 1017, 1256

Hendy, Thos., 1087; Wm., 1238

Hene, see Heane

Heneage (Heneg), Cath., 556, 1381; Thos., 556; Sir Thos., kt., 838, 1381; Wm., 1314; —, 1311

Henene, Hen., 1233

Hengeham, Rev. Ralph, 593; and see Engham

Henley, John, 1408; Mary, 1408; Wm., 708; —, 1420

Henor, —, 1017

Henries, see Henryes

Henrietta, queen, wife of Charles I, 852 n

Henry I, 244, 301, 323, 359, 364, 365, 367, 515, 527*, 663 n, 769, 829, 927, 990, 1201, 1259, 1287

Henry II, 41, 153, 154, 157, 178, 278, 443 n, 475, 482, 527*, 529, 533, 546, 576, 605 n, 609, 688, 690, 720*, 737*, 773*, 809, 927, 1139, 1334

Henry III, 30, 37, 50, 179, 244*, 255, 275, 278, 357, 502, 544, 576, 684 n, 707*, 708 n, 717, 791, 792, 816, 885, 1159, 1403

Henry IV, 357, 362, 363, 365, 367, 544, 893, 1316, 1403

Henry V, 245, 324, 436, 648, 927*, 1316*, 1439

Henry VI, 147, 153, 244*, 481, 570 n, 571, 1291, 1316, 1475

Henry VII, 318, 325 n, 360 n, 361 n, 392, 481, 576*, 591, 1101*, 1123, 1159, 1201, 1287*, 1291, 1293, 1316, 1380, 1475, 1538

Henry VIII, 37, 91, 131, 178, 263, 278, 286, 341, 349, 392, 414, 430, 436, 445 n, 451, 482, 544, 552, 568, 605 n*, 612, 651, 695, 709, 720, 738, 753, 764, 778, 785, 817, 829, 943, 952, 1159, 1221*, 1238, 1261, 1287, 1290, 1295, 1335, 1348, 1356, 1440, 1493, 1538

Henry IV, king of France, 1048

Henry, prince, 220 n, 341, 502, 1120

Henry, bishop of London, see Compton

Henry, prior, 1339

Henry, Hugh, 1556; Wal., 1197

Henryes (Henries), John, 1061; Ric., 1348; Wm., 1491

Hentelone, John, 1154

Henwood, John, 413

Heo, Chas., 598; Hannah, 598

Heort, see Hart

Heose, see Hussey

Hepburn, Wm., 1417

Herald, see Harold

Herbarwe, Hen., 1363

Herbert (Harbert, Herberd, Herebard), Ann(e), 446, 1013, 1249; Ant., 524; Chas., 597*, 598; David, 1473; Deborah, 59; Edm., 974*; Edw., 446, 1249*; Edw., Lord Herbert, 445 n*; Eliz., 446, 485, 597, 999, 1249, 1473; Esther, 597; Lady Frances, 1033; Hannah, 953, 974, 1013, 1083; Harry, 598*; Rev. Hen., 793; Jas., 1473*; Jane, 881, 974; Joan, 1062; John, 348*, 598, 772, 884*, 907; Rev. John (de), 228, 1165, 1225; Marg., 880*, 881, 1249; Martha, 772; Mary, 217, 337, 446, 884, 1013*, 1249, 1384, 1473; Nic., 1013; Peter, 254, 569, 880, 881*, 1013*; Phil., 1473; R., 1238; Ric., 59, 569, 669, 1062, 1083; Sir Ric., 576; Rob., 337; Sam., 974; Sarah, 254, 597*, 598, 881, 953; Stephen, 1013; Thos., 446, 525, 1013, 1384*; W., 772; Wm., 118, 485, 498, 953*, 974, 1502; Wm., earl of Pembroke, 475,

680, 1159; Rev. Wm., 216, 217*; Sir Wm., 927; Lord, 805 n, 806 n, 915, 1035, 1322; *and see* Herbert, Edw.; —, 1015, 1017*, 1032, 1226; fam., 1322; *and see* Harbord

Hercourt, *see* Harcourt

Herde, *see* Heard

Herdman (Hirdeman, Hirdiman, Hurdman), Geo., 1352*; Joan, 1144; Rog., 1404; Thos., 1144; Wm., 1352; —, 1355, 1356; *and see* Hardman

Herebard, *see* Herbert

Hereford, Wm., 311

Hereford [*peerage*](Herford), Edw., Viscount, 1171; Eliz., Viscountess, 1171; Letice, Viscountess, 544; Wal., Viscount, 544, 545 n, 546; countess of, 1148*; earl of, 707 n, 1440, 1476; Lady, 1148*, 1152, 1153, 1154*, 1476; Viscountess, 1152, 1153, 1154, 1170; *and see* Bohun, *passim*; Clare, —; Devereux, Leicester; FitzMilo; FitzWalter, Miles; Lacy, Rog. de; Maunt, Ralph; Newmarch, Sibil de; Plantagenet, Ann; Stafford, Humph.

Heregood, Wm., 1238

Hereward (Herewarde), John, 1259; Wm., 360, 1172

Herford, *see* Harford

Heris, *see* Harris

Heritage, Eliz., 402; Rob., 402

Herle, Sir And., kt., 667; Juliana, 667; *and see* Harley

Herman (Hermo, Hermon), Edw., 1068; John, 1346; —, 1292

Hermington, Adam de, 634

Hermo (Hermon), *see* Herman

Hern (Herne), *see* Hearn

Herney, Mary, 1126*; W. de, 1126

Heron, Mary, 1537; *and see* Hearn

Herretts, Eliz., 641; Simon, 641

Herrick (Heyrick), Eliz., 1336; Sam., 1336; Wm., 1122

Herries, *see* Harris

Herring, John, 485*; Joyce, 485*; Parry, 485; Ric. 485; —, 890; *and see* Harang

Hert, *see* Hart

Hertford, earl of, 502; *and see* Clare, Ric. de; Maunt, Ralph; Seymour, Edw.

Hervey, *see* Harvey

Heryns, Thos., 576

Hesding, Ernulf (Ernulph) de, 690, 769*

Hesketh, Sir R., 1331; (later Juxon), Sir Rob., bt., 804

Heskins (Haskins, Heskyns), Ann, 303*, 304*, 1583; Dan., 1583; Francis, 1583; Jane, 1525; John, 1533; Rev. Jonathan, 619; Joseph, 837; Mary, 303, 937, 1526; Nic., 1525; Ric., 1533; Rob., 937, 1526; Sarah, 837; Wm., 303*, 304, 872; *and see* Hoskins

Hesleham, *see* Haslam

Hetfard, Lebeus, 376

Heth (Hethe), *see* Heath

Hetheway, *see* Hathaway

Heued, *see* Hewett

Hevyn, *see* Heaven

Hewell, Mary, 959; Rob., 959; *and see* Howell

Hewen, *see* Hewens

Hewenhulle, Wal. de, 1238

Hewens (Hewen, Hewings, Huwen), Hannah, 1065; Humph., 1065; John, 1065, 1140; Ric., 1065; Rob., 1150; —, 1074*

Hewer (Huware), Alice, 772; Betty, 510; Cath., 386, 772; Eliz., 752; Francis, 386*, 772; Geo., 1194*, 1351; Giles, 510; Hen., 510; Jeremiah, 772*; John (le), 510*, 1513; Mary, 510*; Ric., 510; Sam., 386; Sarah, 1194; Thos., 339, 752; (or Radbourn), Wm., 891

Hewes, *see* Hughes

Hewett (Ewett, Heued, Hewitt, Huett, Huwet, Huwets), Ant., 1158; Eliz., 55; Geo., 722; Grace, 963; Guy, 1312; Jas., 55; Jane, 731; John, 55, 731, 1160, 1363; R., 1256; Ric., 55; Rob., 1160; Sarah, 1122

Hewings, *see* Hewens

Hewinson, Geo., 984*; Mary, 984; Ric., 984

Hewitt, *see* Hewett

Hewlens, *see* Hewlings

Hewlett (Hewlet, Hulet, Hulett, Hullett, Huwelot, Ulett), Ann(e), 55, 814; Arthur, 133; Benedict, 1027; Betty, 353; Dan., 623, 766, 1438*, 1440; Edw., 1008; Eliz., 133, 353; Esther, 353; Hen., 811; Hester, 814; Jas., 353; Jemima, 353; Job, 353*; John, 353*, 814; Rev. John, 1404; Marg., 1438; Mary, 353, 923; Ric., 55, 814; Susanna, 353; Thos., 353; Wm., 353*, 923*

Hewlings (Hewlens, Hulin, Huling), Ann(e), 107*, 922; Caleb, 107*; Eliz., 105; Francis, 1186; Hannah, 679; Isabella, 107; Jacob, 679*; Jonathan, 922; Mary, 105, 107, 460; Sarah, 679*; Thos., 105*, 107; Wm., 460, 922*; —, 1140

Hews, *see* Hughes

Hewson (Huwesone), John, 413, 1197, 1583; Mary, 413; *and see* Hughesome

Heyden (Heydon), *see* Hayden

Heyes, *see* Hayes

Heysogge, Adam, 1540

Heyley, *see* Hayley

Heylyn, Eliz., 990, 991; John, 990, 991; Dr. John, 990*; Rev. Dr., 991; *and see* Hellen

Heyne (Heynes), *see* Haynes

Heyr, *see* Eyre

Heyrick, *see* Herrick

Heyward, *see* Hayward

Heywood, *see* Haywood

Hiatt, *see* Hyett

Hibbs, Hen., 616

Hiberd (Hybbot), Eliz., 962; Thos., 962; Rev. Thos., 1460

Hichecoke, *see* Hitchcock

Hichman, *see* Hitchman

Hickcock, *see* Hitchcock

Hickes, *see* Hicks

Hickman (Hikeman), Benj., 1047; John, 296; Mary, 296; Thos., 648; Wm., 1478; —, 1017

Hicks (Hickes, Hikes, Hikkes, Hyckes, Hycks), Ann(e), 307, 454, 539, 578, 654, 1111*, 1545; Anne Rachel, 1493; Arthur, 306*, 454, 661, 814;

Rev. Baptist, 571; Sir Baptist, 286, 287*, 288*, 290*, 291, 313, 324*, 1101*, 1288; Betty, 1058; Chas., 308; Chas. Howe, 1492; Christian, 661, 1453; Dan., 283*, 306*, 909, 1450; Deborah, 1167; Edm., 1466; Edw., 597; Eleanor, 1451, 1454; Eliz., 8, 167, 168, 170, 186, 282, 454, 722, 1167*, 1201, 1449*, 1450*, 1451*, 1456*, 1466, 1532; Dame Eliz., 1493*; Geoff., 1061; Geo., 1111*, 1121; Hannah, 170, 1112; Harriott, 168; Heathfield J., 1177; Henrietta Howe, 1492; Henrietta Maria, 1492; (later Hicks Beach), Henrietta Maria, 1005; Hen., 168, 578; Rev. Hen., 288*, 295; Hester, 454; Howe, 263, 422, 667, 1492*, 1493, 1494*; Sir How(e), bt., 713, 1005, 1184, 1493*, 1494*; J., 1220; Jacob, 836; Jas., 8*, 1111; Jane, 170, 1451, 1505, 1507, 1512; Joan (Jone), 578, 1171; John, 306*, 452, 453, 542*, 577, 578*, 654, 808, 891*, 1153*, 1167*, 1169*, 1259, 1302, 1449, 1450*, 1451*, 1487, 1543, 1545, 1547, 1583; Rev. John, 135; Joseph, 308, 1167*; Judith, 307*, 561, 1492; Lady Juliana, 290, 291; Marg., 111, 306, 1290; Lady Maria, 290; Martha, 422, 454, 542*, 578, 654, 1184, 1492*, 1494; Mary, 8, 170*, 295, 438, 453*, 540, 725, 814, 836, 891*, 1153, 1167, 1190, 1193, 1196, 1226, 1450, 1451, 1453*, 1492*, 1494, 1547; Mary Williams, 1492; Mic., 180, 427*, 1492*, 1493; (later Hicks Beach), Mic., 1005; Sir Mic., kt., 1492*, 1493; N., 305; Nat., 279, 282, 539, 1449, 1450*; Newington, 909; Nic., 170*, 305, 306, 307*, 725; Rev. Nic., 305, 453; Ric., 262, 279, 283, 305, 306*, 307*, 308*, 453, 1153*, 1201, 1454, 1505, 1507, 1529, 1532; Rob., 55*, 186, 814, 1201, 1491, 1512, 1528, 1529; Rog., 722; Sam., 836; Sarah, 55, 170, 307, 308*, 1153, 1529; Silvester (Sylvester), 1451, 1543, 1545; Susan, 1494; Susanna, 1492; Susanna Eliz., 422, 1492; Dame Susanna, 1492*; Thos., 159, 167, 168*, 282, 283*, 452, 453*, 454*, 542, 1453, 1532; Rev. Thos., 66, 909; W., 1475; Sir W., 1494*; Weston, 1177; Wm., 100, 111, 283, 308, 836, 1058, 1167*, 1451, 1492, 1493; Rev. Wm., 1346; Sir Wm., bt., 180, 1492*, 1493*, 1494*; Lady, 1493; Mr., 291 n; —, 288, 438, 1020, 1062*, 1176, 1177, 1195*, 1345, 1456, 1476; fam., 159, 179, 286, 305, 452, 453

Hicks Beach, Caroline, 1005; Harriett Victoria, 1005; Heather, 1493; (formerly Hicks), Henrietta Maria, 1005; M., 1005; Sir M. E., 1005; Sir M. Edw., 1005; Sir M. H., bt., 1005; Mic., 1126, 1127; (formerly Hicks), Mic., 1005; Mic. B., 1005; Sir Mic. H., 1126; Sir Mic. Hicks, 1493; Wm. Hicks, 1493

Hide, see Hyde

Hierne, see Hearn

Hieron (Hiron), Betty, 1532; Edith, 660, 1098, 1532*; Eliz., 622, 1570; Giles, 622; John, 622; Kath., 660; Marg., 293, 1570; Martha, 296; Mary, 296, 622, 1532; N., 660; Nat., 660, 1532*; Nic., 1532*, 1570*; Rob., 293, 1532; Sam., 296, 658, 660, 1098, 1532*, 1570; Rev. Sam., 498,

1539; Sarah, 658, 1570*; Thos., 296; Wm., 296, 658; Lieut. Wm., 1532; fam., 864

Hiet (Hiett), see Hyett

Higdon, Rev. Ric., 1513

Higens, see Higgins

Higford (Higforde, Hugford), Anne, 90; Chas., 90; Dorothy (Dorothie), 54, 681; Eliz., 90; Rev. Hen., 27*, 53*, 626; Jas., 54*; John, 27*, 54; Sir John, 681; Kath., 1482; Marg., 54; Thos., 54; Wm., 27*, 90*, 1362; Mr., 27, 89; —, 1362

Higges, see Higgs

Higgins (Hegun, Higens), Abigail, 1453; Ann, 597; Rev. Ant., 770, 798, 1104, 1223; Arabella, 1267; Chas., 112; Edw., 1267; Eleanor, 109; Eliz., 112, 1161, 1162, 1270; Hen., 1315; Imm, 1161*, 1162; Joane, 1161; John, 28*, 109, 542, 1161, 1270, 1277*, 1278, 1315; Jonathan, 110; Lawr., 249; Marg., 1324; Mary, 109, 542, 1161, 1277–8, 1298, 1315; Rev. Obadiah, 1450, 1453, 1456; Ric., 109; Rog., 919; Sarah, 28; Thos., 1161*, 1162*, 1315; Tobias, 1545; Rev. Tobias, 1456; Wm., 1159, 1324; Dr., 405 n; —, 1017, 1161*, 1292; and see Huggins

Higginson (Higgisson), J., 985; John, 842; Joseph, 1282; Joshua, 842; Sophia, 1282; Vertue, 842*; Rev. W. M., 1441; and see Hugginson

Higgs (Higges, Hugges), Agnes, 1422; Amy, 339; Ann(e), 174, 329, 757*, 984, 1111, 1376; Arabella, 1455; Bernard, 329; C., 1226*; Catharina, 1348; Chas., 313, 316, 1376; Dan., 1111*, 1121, 1383, 1551; David, 1121; Eleanor, 1111; Eliz., 317, 329, 1118, 1383, 1384*, 1427; Frances, 317; Geo., 1111; Hannah, 1118, 1384, 1455; Hen., 1111; Jane, 757; Johanna, 1231; Josiah, 1111, 1121, 1384*; John, 1121, 1231, 1376; Lawr., 329; Lazarus, 757; Lewis, 757, 1118*; Mary, 1111*, 1118; Mos(s)es, 757, 1111, 1384, 1385; Nat., 757*; Nic., 1422; Rupertia, 1226; Ruth, 757; Sam., 313, 336, 339*, 1118, 1348; Sarah, 329, 339, 1384; Sarah Ann, 1455; Susanna, 316; Thos., 329*, 339*, 424, 757, 984, 1121, 1403; Rev. Thos., 266; W., 1501*; Wal., 317*; Wm., 174, 757*, 1121, 1427, 1455; fam., 313, 325, 424

Highfield, Edw., 1101

Highnam, Abraham, 1426*; Ann, 1383*; Edith, 1426; Isaac, 1383*; Jacob, 18, 1383, 1384; Jas., 1384; Mary, 18, 1383, 1384

Highway, Hezekiah, 563; John, 562*, 563; Martha, 563; Sarah, 562, 563

Hignell, Ant., 578*; Benj., 578; Betty, 578; Dinah, 578; Eleanor, 578; Eliz., 578*; Esther, 578; Jeremiah, 1116; John, 186*, 578; Mary, 186, 578*, 1116*; Moses, 578; Mordecai, 578*; Sarah, 578, 963; Stephen, 578; Susannah, 578; Thos., 578*, 963*; Wm., 1116*

Hikeman, see Hickman

Hikes (Hikkes), see Hicks

Hilbert, see Hulbert

Hilcot (Huldtcote), Silvester de, 1502

Hilman, see Hillman

Hill, Abraham, 1368; Alice, 744, 937, 1531*;

Allen, 826; Anna, 1532; Ann(e), 270, 329, 550*, 746*, 801, 803, 906, 907, 933, 1316, 1341; Ant., 1405; Benj., 97, 262, 541, 1341*, 1420, 1439; Betsy, 751; Bridget, 97; Chas., 10, 972*, 1427; Dan., 439; Dorothy, 439, 1296, 1297; Edw., 50, 112, 279, 281*, 662*, 1173, 1206, 1296, 1297, 1316*, 1423*; Rev. Edw., 967; Eleanor (Elianor), 227, 281; Eliz., 281, 378, 540*, 541, 543, 550, 880, 903, 930, 972*, 1118, 1161, 1206, 1234*, 1250, 1296*, 1297*, 1508*, 1511, 1532; Francis, 118; Geo., 375*, 659, 906; Rev. H., 1494; Hannah, 661, 803, 905, 972, 1473; Harry, 1413; Hen., 1118; Hester, 176, 972, 1341*, 1365, 1368; Jas., 269, 386, 439, 555, 597, 746, 905*, 907, 933, 1258; Jane, 549, 836, 1118, 1387, 1508, 1511; Jeremiah, 1415*, 1561; Joan, 127, 903; John, 176, 270, 281*, 524, 550*, 597, 623, 659, 714*, 768*, 803, 872, 880*, 903, 930, 965, 972, 1232, 1234*, 1250, 1296*, 1297, 1331, 1418, 1438, 1508; Rev. John, 898; John Why, 1519; Joseph, 269, 270, 439, 1508*; Josiah, 597; Kath., 1413; Lydia, 284; Marg., 118, 262, 269; Maria, 1415; Martha, 10, 1267; Mary, 35, 375*, 386, 524, 540, 548*, 597, 608, 623, 659, 714, 762, 872, 880, 1065, 1296*, 1297, 1341, 1531, 1546, 1561; Moore, 1296*, 1297; Morris, 48; Mountrich, 1413; Rev. Mountrich, 1413; Nat., 555, 836; Phil., 1365; Rebecca, 803; Ric., 262*, 269, 548*, 549*, 611, 662, 684, 762, 930*, 937, 1089, 1267, 1316, 1341*, 1513, 1546*, 1549*; Sir Ric., kt., 1409, 1410, 1420; Rob., 662, 1065; Rev. Rob., 438, 439*, 534, 817; Rowland, 1539; Rev. Rowland, 1539, 1540; Sir Rowland, 816, 817; Sam., 541, 543, 661, 1323, 1388; Sarah, 97, 269*, 375, 550*, 563, 659, 662, 752, 1296, 1316*, 1508; Susanna(h), 549, 611, 1089, 1092; Thos., 97, 127, 176, 227, 269*, 319, 375, 540*, 550*, 608, 659*, 744*, 752, 762, 901, 906, 965, 1289, 1341, 1531*, 1532; Rev. Thos., 1161*; Thos. Dan., 1208; Thos. Rooke Moore, 548; Wal., 1118; Wm., 77, 284, 368, 378, 531, 762, 803*, 903, 969, 1118, 1183, 1186, 1477, 1508, 1511*, 1513; Ensign Wm., 928; Wills, earl of Hillsborough, Viscount Fairford, 588 n; Lord, 1303; —, 404 n, 1020, 1121, 1122, 1238, 1293; fam., 50, 546*: and see Hull

Hiller (Hillar), Margery, 1429; Rob., 1403; Thos., 1289, 1429; Wm., 1429*

Hillersland, Eliz., 194; Providence Potter, 194

Hilley, see Hilly

Hillhouse, Geo., 1415*; Hamell, 1415; Mary, 1415

Hillie, see Hilly

Hillier (Hillierr), Ann, 1112, 1185; Ant., 387; Edm., 510*; Eliz., 510, 749*; Hannah, 387*; J., 1256; Jas., 1112; John, 171, 510*, 748, 749*, 1112, 1185, 1368; Lydia, 1368; M., 1233; Marg., 387; Ric., 387*, 1258; Rob., 608; Sarah, 1112; Susanna, 387; Thos., 752, 1074; —, 1074*; fam., 747

Hillman (Hilman), Anne, 905; Eliz., 843; Hen., 488; John, 843; Josiah, 969; Ric., 843; Thos., 1511; fam., 487

Hillmond, Rob., 1061

Hillsborough, earl of, see Hill, Wills

Hilly (Hilley, Hillie), Ann, 1269; Phil., 1269*; Sarah, 1269; Thos., 1269*; Wm., 1269; —, 1292

Hilpe, John, 1295*, 1308, 1309, 1313; —, 1311, 1313

Hilton, Arthur, 1287; Carew, 1374; Edm. John Scott, 1374; J., 1015; John, 1374; Rev. John, 1184, 1186*

Himes, Cath., 1065

Hinckesman, see Hincksman

Hincks, Mary, 948; Wm., 948

Hincksman (Hinckesman), J., 1064*; Jos., 1064*; Joseph, 1057; Mary, 1057; Nancy, 1057; —, 1064*

Hincler, Mary, 111

Hinde, Ann, 332; Eliz., 1082; Geo., 1003; Jane, 1159; Mary, 1082; Rebecca, 1003; Thos., 332; Wm., 332; —, 1082*

Hine, Alice, 1576; Eliz., 884; Hannah, 818; Hen., 1576; John, 884*; Nic., 818*

Hinman, Rev. John, 764

Hinson, see Hynson

Hinton, Ann(e), 450, 460, 622; Beata, 303; Chris., 303; Edm., 303, 459, 1202; Eliz., 385, 386, 450; Hen., 303; John, 797; Lydia, 622*; Marg., 304; Margery, 62; Mary, 303*, 381*, 386; Mic., 388; Nat., 450*; Ric., 797, 1067*; Sarah, 597; Susanna, 388; T., 1202; Thos., 303*, 304; Wm., 62, 304, 381, 385, 386, 622*, 1012, 1027, 1258; Zecheriah, 597; fam., 301, 459

Hiorns, Eliz., 597; John, 597; Sarah, 597; Wm., 597; —, 1223

Hippesley (Hippisley), Rev. J., 1195, 1226; Jas., 1196; Rev. John, 1189, 1196; Sir John, 1159; Rev. R., 1191; Rev. Ric., 1196; Rev. Rob. Wm., 1189

Hipputt, Wm., 1158

Hirdeman (Hirdiman), see Herdman

Hirler, Rev. Jeremiah, 1545

Hirom, John, 573

Hiron, see Hieron

Hitch, Chas., 754; Marg., 1333; Mary, 1333; Rev. Paul, 754; Wm., 1147, 1333*, 1446

Hitchcock (Hichecoke, Hickcock, Hitchcox), Ann, 296; Rev. J. C., 103; John, 296, 1202; Jonathan, 1244; Matilda, 1202

Hitchings (Hitching, Hitchins), Dan., 991; Eliz., 722, 1488; Hen., 991; Jonathan, 532; Mary, 303, 543*; Ric., 543, 991*; Sarah, 303; Thos., 722, 1323, 1488*; Wm., 284; —, 990, 1064; (or Hutchins), fam., 305 n; and see Hutchins

Hitchman (Hichman), Anne, 1480; Christian, 771; Rev. Edw., 770 771; Eliz., 1272, 1279, 1480; Hercules, 1480; Jane, 597; John, 771*; Judah, 1272; Rob., 771; Thos., 597, 771, 1272*; Wal., 771; —, 1017

Hoare (Hore), Greg. le, 1539; Hen., 1047; Rev. Thos. Mills, 1233; —, 1082

Hoate, John, 948; Mary, 948

Hobbekines, see Hopkins

Hobbes, see Hobbs

Hobbins, Eliz., 1330; John, 1330*; Joseph, 1330*; Mara, 1330; Mary, 1330*; Sarah, 573; Wm., 573

Hobbs (Hobbes), Agnes, 216; Alice, 1325; Anna, 1327; Ann(e), 1325, 1327, 1361; Aqulia, 1159; Benj., 1159; Betty, 77; Cath., 797; David, 398; Edith Maria, 1327; Edw., 397, 1146*, 1324*, 1325*; (or Clarke), Edw., 1326; Eliz., 77, 797*, 1325*, 1326, 1327, 1547; Emy, 472*; Esther, 1455*; Frances, 473; Francis, 1249; Geo., 986, 1450*; Hannah, 397; Henrietta, 1450*; Henrietta Perry, 1455; Hen., 1127, 1159; Jas., 524, 1325*; Jane, 1249*; Joane, 398; John, 77*, 397, 966*, 1046, 1258, 1325*, 1326, 1329, 1361*, 1450*, 1547; Lucy, 1327; Marg., 1325; Martha, 1324*, 1325*; Mary, 397, 797, 966*, 1194, 1324, 1325*, 1450*; Morse Davies, 1324; Nic., 216; Peter, 1325*; Rebecca, 1146; Ric., 398*, 966*, 1428, 1504; Rob., 797*; Sam., 1547; Sarah, 524, 966*, 1250, 1324, 1325*, 1361, 1424, 1450*, 1547; (or Clarke), Sarah, 1326; Sophia, 1327; T., 1027; Thos., 397, 472*, 473, 1301*, 1324, 1325, 1327*, 1424, 1450; Wm., 397, 704, 797, 873, 966, 1149, 1194, 1196, 1250, 1325, 1449, 1450*, 1454, 1455*, 1456; —, 985, 1455, 1456*; (or Clarke), —, 1328*

Hobby, Alice, 709; Ann, 175; Eliz., 174, 741, 1306*; Hen., 174; Jane, 175, 1306; John, 175; Marg., 1306*; Mary, 174, 740*; Sir Ph[il]., 1093; Ric., 1306*, 1459; Sir T., 1093; Thos., 174, 740*, 741; W., 1312; Wm., 175*, 393 n, 707, 709, 741, 1306*

Hobdy, Anne, 1277*; John, 1277

Hobekins, *see* Hopkins

Hobelonde, *see* Hobland

Hobhouse, Sir B., 1419; J. C., Lord Broughton, 1419; John, 1419, 1420; fam., 1419

Hobland (Hobelonde, Hobleone), Gonwold (Gunnilda), 1311, 1314

Hockkys, Rev. Rog., 1147

Hockley (Hockly, Hokkeleye), Anne, 307; Arthur, 1450*; Benj., 307, 1450*; Eliz., 1450*; Joseph (de), 307, 1404; Mary, 1450; Sarah, 1450; Wm., 1450; *and see* Holkeleye

Hoddinott (Hadnock, Hadnot, Hodnot), Ann, 1244, 1534; Gabriel, 1244*; Hen., 1526; Joan, 681; Johanna, 1510; Joseph, 1505, 1510*, 1513; Martha, 1510; Mary, 1244*; Mary Matthews, 1244; Rebekah, 1244; Sam., 1244, 1534

Hodeknas, Wm., 1197

Hoddy (Hodye), Rev. John, 760; Margery, 464; Sir Ric., kt., 464

Hodges, Ann(e), 69, 257*, 538*, 983, 1070*, 1212, 1250; Benj., 1079; Bridget, 1070*; Ant., 257*, 258*, 1226; Barbara, 1361; D., 1196; Danvers, 255, 257*, 258, 1226; Don(ne), 257*, 258*, 1226*; Edith, 1071; Eleanor, 398; Eliz., 257*, 258*, 820, 831*, 983, 1070, 1071*, 1072, 1074, 1079, 1147, 1226, 1228, 1257, 1431; Emma, 1251; Estcourt, 1071, 1074; Frances, 1583; Geo., 1071; Giles, 70, 531, 538, 1053; Grace, 257; Hannah, 550, 1568; Hannah Lane, 194; Hen., 831; Rev. Hen., 438; Hen. Danvers Doughty, 255, 257; Isaac,

1531; Jane, 194*, 842, 1531; John, 69, 194, 258*, 406*, 510, 531, 550*, 842, 1074, 1212*, 1226, 1251, 1583; Rev. John, 406, 1167, 1169; Joyce, 379; Judith, 550; Marg., 69*; Martha, 258, 1510; Martyn, 1250; Mary, 69*, 255, 257, 258, 538, 550; Merrial, 257*, 258; Miles, 1226*; Morrison, 1289; Ric., 258, 398, 538*, 550*, 1226; Rob., 1186, 1213; Sam., 1568*; Sarah, 538*, 1026, 1053, 1212, 1213, 1251, 1359, 1531; Susannah, 907; Thos., 69*, 70, 550, 819, 821, 1026, 1071*, 1074, 1212*, 1513; Thos., high sheriff, 1074; Rev. Thos., 66, 69; W., 820; Rev. Wal., 1072, 1074*; Wm., 190*, 257*, 379, 550*, 907, 983*, 1244*, 1250, 1251, 1289, 1361, 1430, 1431, 1510; Rev. Wm., 783, 1070*, 1071, 1140; Dr., 1359; Mr., 1372; Mrs., 65; Rev., 65, 855; —, 1074*, 1190, 1226; fam., 65, 255*, 1071, 1072, 1074

Hodgeson, *see* Hodgson

Hodgets (or Bayley), —, 1092

Hodgkins (Hotchkins), Alice, 709; Ant., 493; John, 393 n, 709*, 1389; Nat., 1578; Thos., 1289

Hodgson (Hodgeson), Betty, 1401; Chris., 708 n; Eliz., 1529; John, 1401; Phil. Brown, 946; Susannah, 946; Rev. Thos., 946*, 1323

Hodleston, *see* Huddleston

Hodnot, *see* Hoddinott

Hodye, *see* Hoddy

Hoese, *see* Hussey

Hogg, Betty, 1007; Edw., 981*, 1183; Hen., 975; Jas., 981, 1183*; Martha, 981; Mary, 981, 1182, 1183; Rev. Peter, 668*; Sam., 1182; Sarah, 975, 1183; Susanna, 1183; Thos., 410, 975*

Hoggard, Ann, 48; Wm., 48*

Hoghton, *see* Houghton

Hogyn, Wm., 1491; *and see* Huggins

Hoins, Sam., 1499

Hoke, *see* Hook

Hokesforde, John de, 1539; *and see* Oxenford

Hokkeleye, *see* Hockley

Hol, *see* Hole

Holbein, Hans, 220 n, 392 n, 508 n, 719 n, 753

Holbin, Mary, 210; Sam., 212; Thos., 210

Holborow (Holbrow, Holdrow), Anna, 240*, 1144*; Ann(e), 240*, 1136, 1144*, 1248, 1366*; Ant., 1366*; Cath., 1136; Dan., 240, 653*, 758, 1118, 1366; Edw., 182; Eliz., 496, 1136, 1143*, 1144*, 1366*, 1437; Francis, 1118, 1121; Grace, 1138; Hen., 954*; Hester, 910, 911; Isaac, 1248; Jas., 1366; Joan, 496, 701; John, 777, 910, 1136, 1143*, 1144*, 1145-6, 1146, 1147, 1366, 1369; Col. John, 1143; Joseph, 954; Kath., 1366; Martha, 1144; Mary, 653, 758, 777, 911, 954, 1143, 1144, 1146, 1366*; Patience, 182; Rachael, 954; Sam., 240, 496, 701, 1143*; Sarah, 240, 954, 1143*, 1437; Thos., 496, 910*, 911, 1136, 1143, 1144, 1215; Wm., 240*, 496, 777, 1138, 1143, 1144, 1366*, 1369, 1437; Mr., 1215; —, 1139, 1140*, 1147, 1370; fam., 236, 1369

Holbrooke (Holbroke, Holdbrook), Rev. John, 493, 710; Rob., 18

Holbrow, *see* Holborow

Holcombe, Wal. de, 529; fam., 346

Holdare, *see* Holder

Holdbrook, *see* Holbrooke

Holder (Holdare, Houlder), Alice, 1372; Anna, 1234; Ann(e), 1096, 1413; Chas., 1217; Dan., 615*, 616; Diana, 1234; Edw., 1034*, 1234; Ele(a)nor, 903, 1034; Eliz., 543, 623, 666, 950, 1034, 1065, 1100, 1234*, 1235*, 1413; Rev. Fred. Wm., 1485; Hen. le, 1502, 1540; Hester, 543; Jas., 615, 1109; Jane, 906, 1235; Joanna, 616; John, 316, 317, 352, 903, 1034*, 1065, 1096, 1234*, 1235*, 1238, 1307, 1413, 1427, 1437; Kath., 1235; Letitia, 1234*; Louisa Henrietta, 1235; Marg., 352, 1109, 1234; Mary, 615, 1034, 1235, 1413*, 1427; Philippa, 1235; Rob., 1034*, 1109, 1234*; Rev. Rob. Keyse, 1235; Sam., 615, 666*, 887, 1053*, 1109*; Sarah, 514, 666, 1053*; Susannah, 623, 666, 1234; Thos., 514*, 623, 661, 906, 1034, 1053, 1372, 1437; Wm. (le), 543*, 666*, 950, 1034, 1053, 1100, 1234*, 1238, 1372, 1552; Rev. Wm. Chas., 1235; —, 1317; fam., 1237*

Holdey (Houldy), Lydia, 1250; Mary, 973; Ralph, 973; Rob., 1250; Thos., 973

Holdrow, *see* Holborow

Holdship, John, 118; *and see* Hallship

Holdsworth, Rev. Rob., 221; *and see* Oldisworth

Hole (Hol), Ric. de, 1140; Rog. atte, 1339

Holford (Holfred), Anne, 1034; Edw., 1034*; Eliz., 596; Jas., 174; John, 1316; Joseph, 1274; Marg., 906; Mary, 635, 1034, 1316; Peter, 1311; R. S., 1255*, 1257; Ric., 347*, 596, 738; Rob., 1074*; Steyner (Steynor), 493, 634; Susanna(h), 174, 906; Rev. Thos., 1031; Wm., 906; Mr., 1429

Holhurst, Wm. de, 1491

Holiday, *see* Holliday

Holinshed (Holingshead, Hollinshed), —, 251 n, 497, 581 n, 591 n, 1123

Holkeleye (Holkeley), Elenor, 1404; Hen., 1404; —, 1403; *and see* Hockley

Holland (Holloands), Anna, 1276; Ant., 1499; Benj., 1280; Chas., 857; David Hughes, 635, 866; Dorothy, 51, 1499; Eliz., 396, 1161; Francis, 1288; Joan, 683; Joan, countess of Kent, 876; John, 635, 683; John, duke of Exeter, 357, 358; Mary, 803, 866; Phil., 803; R., 1147*; Rebecca (Rebekah), 1147, 1200; Ric., 857, 1161; Rog., 396; Sam., 1275; Rev. Seth, 394; Theophilus, 1275*, 1276*; Thos., 394, 634, 635, 1276; Thos., duke of Surrey, 357, 358, 361; Thos., earl of Kent, 876; Thos. And., 1282; Wm., 51; —, 305 n, 1087; fam., 792, 864

Holland [*peerage*](Hulland), Hen., lord of, 809

Holles (Hollis), Mary, 1159; —, duke of Newcastle, 410

Hollester, *see* Hollister

Holliday (Holiday, Hooleday), Ann(e), 657; Chas., 1079; Deborah, 661*; Edw., 655; Eliz., 1493; John, 657*, 661, 1493, 1574; Marg., 1493; Margery, 655; Mary, 661; N., 1027; Rebecca, 782; Ric., 661; Sam., 750; Thos., 655, 661, 702; W., 1027, 1345; Wm., 661, 782, 1133; —, 1372; *and see* Halliday

Hollington, Rev. W., 848

Hollinshed, *see* Holinshed

Hollis, *see* Holles

Hollister (Hollester), Abigail, 210; Anna, 46, 49; Anne, 46*, 1425; Betty, 1405; Cecilia, 845; Chas., 1405; Edw., 46, 208, 210, 722; Eliz., 46, 1425; Francis, 212; Grace, 46*; Hester, 46*; Hezekiah, 47; Isabell, 47; J., 1169; Jacob, 1425*; Jane, 208; Joane, 1424; John, 47*, 49, 722*, 845, 1169; Luke, 46*, 960; Mark, 46*, 730; Martha, 722; Mary, 46*, 208, 727; Nic., 845; Rachel, 730; Rebekah, 730; Ric., 722*, 1424; Rog., 1169; Sam., 46; Sapin, 212; Stephen, 47, 730*; Thos., 722*; Wm., 46*, 1424*

Holloands, *see* Holland

Hollow, Isabel, 202; Rob., 202; *and see* Hallows; Hellow

Holloway (Hollway, Holway), Ant., 741; Cath., 1326, 1537; Dan., 1576; Edw., 1537; Eliz., 499*, 1326; Jas., 1551; Jeremy, 1554; John, 1177, 1323, 1326; Joseph, 841, 1576; Mary, 996*; Ric., 693; Rob., 499*; Sam., 1537; Thos., 996*, 1195, 1576; W., 1232; Wm., 1326*, 1455*

Hollworthy, Bridget, 43; Thos., 43

Holly, Ann, 728; John 728*; John Hollister, 728*; Sarah, 728

Hollyoke, *see* Holyoak

Holman, Hen., 714; Thos., 714

Holmes (Holme, Home, Homes), Ann, 296; Cathenine [*sic*], 1008; Eleanor, 983; Eliz., 296, 465; Eliz. Jane, 1164; John, 296*, 547, 708 n, 983, 1164*, 1282; Mary, 465*; Ric., 768, 984; Rob., 1008, 1217; Sam., 1186; Sarah, 768; Susanna, 1008; Thos., 465, 1217; Wal., 1415; Rev. Wm., 236, 722; —, 1160, 1282; *and see* Homme

Holsey, *see* Halsey

Holstead (Houldstead), Joseph, 1393, 1397; —, 1404

Holt (Holte), Chas., 643, 891; John, 1258; Leticia, 891; Rog., 1404; Wm., 250, 1404; —, 1403

Holtham (Holtam, Holtom), Ann, 296, 989; Edw., 1390; Eliz., 868, 1389; Giles, 867, 868; Hen., 1388, 1389*; John, 501, 988, 1388, 1389*; Joseph, 1064; Mary, 296, 501*, 867, 1064; Millicent, 868; Oliver, 666; Rebecca, 1389; Rob., 226; Sarah, 226, 666; Thos., 296*, 989; Wm., 501; —, 1392

Holton, Rev. John Reston, 1035; *and see* Halton

Holway, *see* Holloway

Holwell, Sarah, 1214; Thos., 1214; Rev. W., 1313*

Holyoak (Hollyoke), John, 597, 1388

Home (Homes), *see* Holmes

Homme, Ric. de, 1519; Rob. de, 1519; *and see* Holmes

Hompyn (Homypyn), John de, 1491; Wm., 1491

Hondford, *see* Handford

Hondys, *see* Hands

Hone, Anne, 1354; Augusta, 1354; Eliz., 262, 1248, 1494; Geo., 262*; Rev. J. F., 1352; John, 1248*; Rev. John Fred., 1354*; Jonathan, 348; Joseph, 1248; Joseph Terry, 1354; Mary, 262*,

1257; Ric., 262; Sarah, 262, 1248; Wm., 262*, 1248

Honour, Ric., 364*

Honyborne (Honyburn), Rev. John, 1087; Ric., 1519

Honywood, Annabella Christiana, 268; Sir John, 268; Wm., 268

Hood (Hoode), Hester, 174; Thos., 174; Wm., 850, 1447; Rev., 1447

Hook (Hoke, Hooke), Alice, 1010; Anne, 897, 899, 1371, 1395, 1396; Betty, 789; Cecily, 577; Edw., 899*, 1121; Eleanor (Elinour), 897, 1535; Eliz., 354*, 789, 965; Giles, 933; Rev. Hen., 252; Humph., 576, 577, 613, 618, 720; Sir Humph., 618, 720; Jas., 354*; John, 354, 899*, 965, 1238*, 1535; Joseph, 841; Dame Kath., 722; Marg., 898; Mary, 899; Mat., 354*; Phil., 1292; Ric., 1164, 1314, 1395, 1396, 1403, 1539; Rob., 789; Sarah, 933; Thos., 897, 899; Rev. Thos., 696, 1122; Wm., 1010, 1292; —, 897, 1311

Hookham (Hookman), Eliz., 1194; Jas., 1420; Thos., 1194, 1196*

Hooleday, see Holliday

Hooper (Hopere, Hopper), Abigail, 837, 938; Anna, 1243; Ann(e), 254, 276, 871, 923*, 938, 939, 983, 1076*, 1383; Ant., 170; Arthur, 170*, 174, 1175; C., 1186; Dorothy, 731; Edith, 369; Edm., 320; Edw., 276, 923; Eliz., 107, 170*, 276, 338*, 768, 938, 939, 983, 1250, 1499; Frances, 338; Giles, 584; Hannah, 320; Hen., 377, 921, 923*, 1477; Rev. Hen., 266, 462; Hester, 353, 938, 939; Isabel, 107; Jane, 170, 768; Jeremiah, 254*, 275*, 276*, 353; Joan, 923; Johanna, 1383; John, 168, 174, 338, 661, 682, 683, 797, 837, 938, 1250, 1499, 1577; Joseph, 683, 768*, 1243; Kath., 170; Marg., 170, 174, 377; Martha, 254; Mary, 170, 276*, 584*, 797, 822*, 938*, 1043, 1076, 1465; Ric., 107*, 338*, 797, 938, 939, 983*; Rev. Ric., 1387*; Rob., 762, 822*, 1383*; Rog. le, 1259; Sam., 939; Sarah, 174, 338, 550*, 682, 923, 938, 1249, 1465; Thos., 166, 167, 168, 170*, 174*, 731, 760, 822, 871, 923*, 993, 1043, 1076*, 1282, 1383; Wm., 170*, 174, 338, 368, 547, 550, 797*, 873, 938*, 939, 1034*, 1169, 1243, 1249, 1258, 1289, 1465; Mr., 101; —, 154, 1017*, 1317, 1477; —, bishop, 1104, 1123, 1228*, 1232, 1290, 1339, 1351, 1362, 1379, 1392, 1440, 1447, 1456, 1502, 1519

Hopcins, see Hopkins

Hopcutt, Cipprian, 1276; Mary, 1276; Sam., 1276; Thos., 1276*

Hope, Ann(e), 906, 1014, 1016; Benj., 270, 905, 993*; Eliz., 270, 993; Frances, 1279; Giles, 1014*, 1016; John, 715*, 1279, 1289, 1428, 1456; Marg., 270, 905, 993; Mary, 550; Rowland, 1279*; Thos. de, 1314; Wm., 550, 906, 1577; fam., 713

Hopere, see Hooper

Hopkins (Hobbekines, Hobekines, Hopcins, Hopkin, Hopkyns), Alice, 906; Ann(e), 55*, 378*, 730, 735, 777, 811, 971; Ant., 971; Benj., 97, 815, 971; Betty, 107, 173; Blanch, 735;

Bridget, 735; Cecilia, 1447; Chas., 781*, 1339; Chas. Fred., 1366; Dorothy, 340; Edw., 383, 1537; Eliz., 36, 109, 110*, 735*, 919, 1000, 1045, 1222, 1270, 1307*, 1353*, 1354*, 1361, 1454, 1457; Hannah, 1574; Hen., 715; Hester, 777, 1454; Jas., 378, 735*, 1307; Jane, 919; Jeremiah, 777*, 846*, 1354; John, 55, 97, 109*, 110*, 337, 378*, 752, 811*, 906, 913, 1045, 1258, 1307, 1353*, 1354*, 1355, 1361, 1362, 1454, 1574*; Jonathan, 1354; Josiah, 1354; Kath., 1323; Marg., 173; Martha, 777; Mary, 97, 107*, 118, 378, 777, 781*, 1307, 1354, 1457, 1511; Miniet, 1354*; Miriam, 781; Nat., 107*, 110*, 1121; Rachel, 884; Ralph, 1575; Ric., 110*, 884, 1191, 1366*; Rob., 173, 377, 777*, 1511; Sarah, 110, 920, 1354*, 1366*, 1574, 1575; Stephen, 1307, 1537; Susanna, 378*, 715, 777; Thos., 708 n, 730, 735*, 777, 1307*, 1352, 1354*, 1355, 1457; Rev. Thos., 808; W., 1220; Warren, 55*; Wm., 97, 118, 173, 920, 1147, 1168, 1222, 1354, 1460; Rev. Wm., 1270; —, 101, 1323, 1455, 1460, 1478; fam., 101

Hopkinson, Chas., 1046; Edm., 1046*; Eliz., 1046*; Geo., 1046; Geo. Caesar, 479; Col. Geo. Caesar, 1046; Harriet, 1046; Octiavia, 1046

Hopkyns, see Hopkins

Hopley, Abigail, 930*; Eliz., 930; John, 929, 930*

Hopper, see Hooper

Hopson, Edith, 1007, 1008; John, 1008; 1186; Mary, 1008; Solomon, 1186; Wm., 1007*, 1008, 1217

Hopton, Ann(e), 164*, 176, 1181; Dan., 171, 175*, 1181*; Eliz., 163*, 164*, 1290, 1291; Frances, 163, 164, 279; Hen. Cope, 1422; Hester, 1181; Jas., 971; Jeremiah, 164; John, 164*, 971; Rev. John Parsons, 1422; Mary, 164, 171, 631, 1181; Sir Ralph, 6; Ralph, Lord Hopton, 341; Ric., 563, 1181; Sam., 176, 1181; Sarah, 175*, 1181; Thos., 159, 160*, 164; Sir Wal., 761; Wm., 163*, 164*, 563, 631, 761*, 825, 1181, 1186; fam., 163, 278, 825

Hopwood, R., 1419

Horde (Hored), Ann(e), 445, 870, 1226*; Edw., 814; Mary, 422; T., 1226; Thos., 346, 422, 1224, 1226, 1227; —, 1226*

Hore, see Hoare

Hored, see Horde

Horeton, see Horton

Horfield, Ric., 783

Horkins, see Hawkins

Horler, Joan, 498; Lettice, 994; Rev. Jeremiah, 498*, 1552

Horlick (Horlock), Alex., 450; Dan., 450; Hannah, 975; Jas., 975; John, 975; Isaac Webb, 839*, 840; Joseph, 1499; Martha, 450*; Mary, 1499; Peter, 450; Sarah, 450

Horn, see Horne

Hornby (Hornbie), Rev. Hen., 1001; Susanna, 1389; Thos., 1389

Horne (Horn), Arn., 1238; Edm., 643*; J., 1187; John, 1317, 1430, 1540; Sibill, 1431; T., 1238; Thos., 463, 884, 1431*; Rev. Thos., 216; Mr., 643 n; —, 895, 1198*, 1238

Hornedge (Hornidge), John, 854; Rev. Thos., 415
Horner, Amy, 614; Thos., 614
Horniblow, Geo., 1518*; Mary, 1518
Hornidge, see Hornedge
Hornsby, Rev. Geo., 1350, 1351
Horrell (Horrill), Eliz., 1138; Lucy, 730; Rob., 1138; Sam., 1138*; Wm., 730
Horry, John, 1223; Thos., 1223
Horseley, Eliz., 884; Joan, 884; John, 884; Thos., 884
Horseman (Horsman), Ann, 1065; Hen., 1194; Hugh, 1194; Jas., 1194, 1196; Jane, 1194; John, 121; Rev. John, 121; Rebecca, 1194; Rob., 1065; Sam., 288; Thos. de, 1221; Wm., 1196
Horsepol (or Hascombe), Rev. Francis, 1335
Horsforde, John de, 1434
Horsington, Eliz., 932; Wm., 932
Horsler, Mr., 206
Horsman, see Horseman
Horsnayl, Wm., 1519
Horston (Horstone), Eliz., 749; Mary, 633; Ric., 633; Rev. Ric., 748, 749; Thos. (atte), 544 n, 1027; Wal. atte, 1027
Hort, Alice, 541; Amelia, 728; Ann(e), 124, 1405, 1411; Ant., 1412; Bridgett, 1410; Cornelius Grove, 728; Edm., 541*; Eliz., 124*, 1412; Geo., 1549*; Jane, 541*; John, 124*, 541, 1412, 1512; Marg., 124; Mary, 159, 1549; Nat., 541; Thos., 124*, 541, 1405, 1410*, 1412*, 1553; Wm., 124; —, 720; fam., 1420
Horter, Rev. Jeremiah, 1122
Horton (Horeton), Eliz., 452; Geo., 1431; Rev. Humph., 424, 1257; John, 28, 580; Sir John, kt., 579; Mary, 28, 580, 1431; Philipe, 860; Rev. Ric., 668; Thos., 580*; Wm., 860, 1431; fam., 558
Horwell, Rev. Thos., 266
Horwood, Arthur, 1099*, 1100; Chas., 1326, 1327*; Christian, 1326, 1327; Cicilly, 1295; Dan., 1160, 1551; Edw., 1100, 1326*; Eliz., 701; Hen., 703; Hester, 1326*; (or Harwood), Hester, 615; Jane, 1099; John, 701, 1326*; (or Harwood), John, 615*; Mary, 701, 758, 1100, 1116–17, 1326; Nat., 703, 1116, 1117; Nic., 700; Ralph, 959; Ric., 975; Ruth, 975; Sarah, 700, 1326; Thos., 701, 702, 758; Wm., 114; and see Whorwood
Hoschin, see Hoskins
Hosea (Hosy), Alex., 1449*, 1456*; Eliz., 841
Hosford, Olive, 1181; Ric., 1181*
Hosier, Edw., 174; Hannah, 174; John, 174; Margery, 174; Mary, 174
Hoskins (Hoschin, Hoskyns), Alice, 249; Ann(e), 1281, 1282; Ayde, 1282; Betty, 996; Chas., 1282; Rev. Chas., 820; Rev. Chris., 1; Edw., 612, 1169; Eleanor, 249; Eliz., 280*, 715*; Harriet, 280*; Hen., 713; Rev. Hen., 553; Holman, 715*; John, 583, 1169; Kedgwin, 245, 249*; Lewis, 50, 51, 280*, 532, 1258; Mary, 715, 905; Phil., 996; Stephen, 633; Thos., 715, 905, 1281*-2; Wm., 245, 917; Mr., 918; —, 1020; and see Heskins
Hosmer, —, 1039

Hosper, Rev. Thos., 190
Hosy, see Hosea
Hotchkins, see Hodgkins
Hough (Huff), Ann, 846; Jas., 846, 847; Jane, 847, 1117; John, 221, 846; Mary, 847; Mic., 846, 847
Houghton (Hoghton), Ric., 1476; Rev. Thos., 1127; Rev. Wm., 674; —, 1288; and see Haughton
Houlder, see Holder
Houldstead, see Holstead
Houldy, see Holdey
Houly, Eliz., 683; Ralph, 683
Hounsell, Rev. Thos., 427
House, see Howes
Houston, John, 164; Mary, 164
Houwen, John, 1519
Houwse, see Howes
How, see Howe
Howard, Ann, 1485; Lady Dorothy, 1296; Hen., 839, 1312; Lord Hen. Molineux, 927; John, 97, 1201; Kath., 771; Kath., Lady Berkeley, 162; Mary, 97, 1311; Mary, duchess of Norfolk, 1139; P. H., 1403; Phil., duke of Norfolk, 1139; Rob., 97; T., 1485; Thos., 1083; Thos., duke of Norfolk, 162, 1015, 1139, 1296, 1512; Sir W., 1311; Wm., Lord Howard, 878; Mr., 1295; fam., 1311
Howbrook, John, 611; Thos., 611
Howe (How), Anna, 1498; Lady Annabella, 645, 1198, 1497; Bridget(t), 298, 1497, 1498; Chas., 1498; Eliz., 634, 1498; Dame Eliz., 705; Geo., 1498; Hen. Fred., 1198; Isabel, 108; Rev. Jas., 488; Sir Jas., bt., 634, 705; Sir Jo., bt., 298; John, 364*, 643, 766, 830*, 831*, 1132, 1198*, 1497; John, baron Chedworth, 420, 643; John, Viscount Chedworth, 1198; Sir John, 434; John Grubham (Grobham), 645*, 1198, 1497; John Thynne, 1198; Josiah, 832; Lucie, 1497; Mary, 108*, 771, 832; Ric., 108*, 319, 364*, 768, 771; Sir Ric., bt., 366, 367, 688, 1495; Sir Ric., kt., 1492; Ric. Grobham, 1497; Rob., 542; Sarah, 831, 832; Susanna, 1492, 1497; Thos., 108*; Thos. Grobham, 1498; Rev. Thos., 1198; Sir Thos., kt., 766; Wm., 832*, 885, 1498; Lady, 1495; fam., 318
Howell, Abergail, 941; Agnes, 1323; Ann(e), 814, 847, 920, 946, 1413; Betty, 112, 702, 857; Cath., 1425; Chas., 107, 112; David, 941; Edw., 1481; Eliz., 1481; Francis, 702*; Hen., 750, 1551; Hester, 751, 941; Jas., 924*; Jane, 1250*; John, 1, 452, 683*, 847, 918, 920, 924*, 946, 1250*, 1378, 1380; Capt. John, 1413; Joseph, 929, 941; Martha, 702*; Mary, 107, 751, 814, 924, 932, 1481; Maud, 1516; Morgan, 1516; Rev. Morgan Ap, 802; Nic., 1425; Phil., 751*; Ric., 857; S., 1027; Sam., 1021; Sarah, 419, 750, 857, 924; Stephen, 814, 932; T., 1216; T. B., 1380; T. J., 1380; Thos., 814, 932*; (or Powell), Rev. Thos., 1122; Wal., 1481; Wm., 419, 474; —, 915; fam., 885; and see Hewell
Howes (House, Houwes, Hows, Howse), Ann(e), 62*, 509, 517, 526*, 569, 693, 1571; Betty, 64*; Cath., 597; Dan., 946; Edith, 62*, 64; Eleanor,

891, 946; Eliz., 62, 264, 396, 569, 947*, 1076*;
Geo., 1041; Henrietta, 48*; Hen., 264; Hester,
1041; J., 1455*; Jane, 62*; Johanna, 1571; John,
62*, 64*, 138, 296, 431, 510, 569*, 636, 693*,
891, 947*, 986, 1076, 1485; Jonathan, 48*;
Lettice, 800; Marg., 64; Martha, 947; Mary, 48,
296, 431, 597, 947*, 980, 1004*; Mic., 1540;
Ric., 62*, 384, 431, 517, 526*, 597, 800, 980;
Rob., 48, 1350; Sarah, 62*, 947*; Stephen, 1187;
Susanna, 384; Thos., 62, 509, 526*, 568, 569,
597,947*; Rev. Thos., 979*; Wm., 64, 296, 431,
597*, 797, 947, 1004*, 1061; fam., 184, 430,
1501
Howkins, Dan., 1330*; Mary, 1330; Rachel, 1330;
and see Hawkins
Howlett, John, 329; Sarah, 329*; Wm., 329*; Rev.
Wm., 263
Howman, Eliz., 28; Esther, 28; John, 28*; Phil., 28;
Ric., 1334, 1473; Sarah, 1334
Hows (Howse), *see* Howes
Howseman, Ric., 1328
Hoyle, Ann(e), 454, 1548; John, 1016, 1548
Hroald (fl. 918), 649
Huatson, Rev. Miles, 635, 636; Peter, 636; *and see*
Watson
Hubert, bishop, 1419
Huchenson, *see* Hutchinson
Huchones (Huchoun), *see* Hutchins
Huckelbridge, Rebecca, 1412
Hucksall, Geo., 1513
Huckvale, Cuthbert, 1215; John, 1215*
Hudd (Hud), Ch., 1312; Edw., 133; John, 97; Mary,
133; Thos., 97
Huddleston (Hodleston, Huddlestone, Hudlestone),
Ellen, 392, 393 n; Joan, 1501; Dame Johanna,
1475; John, 839; Sir John, kt., 392, 393 n, 638,
709, 1475, 1501; Rev. W., 1356; Rev. Wm., 855;
fam., 392 n
Hudson, Alice, 1488; Anne Maria, 1153; Benj.,
818; Rev. Gil., 1351; Ric., 1362, 1389; Capt.
Ric., 1488; Rev. Ric., 674; —, 1226, 1255
Huett, *see* Hewett
Huff, *see* Hough
Hugford, *see* Higford
Huggen, *see* Huggins
Hugges, *see* Higgs
Huggett, Hannah, 1319; Wm., 1319*, 1457; —,
1322
Huggins (Huggen, Hugin, Hugyn), Abraham, 616*;
Hen., 1422; Isaac, 616; Jacob, 616; John, 1460,
1519; Sam., 1422; Susanna, 616*; Wal., 1519;
Wm., 1519; *and see* Higgins; Hogyn
Hugginson, Rev. Mr., 1441; *and see* Higginson
Hugh, abbot, *see* Bampton, Hugh
Hugh, earl, 1131
Hugh son of Wm. the Norman, *see* FitzWilliam,
Hugh
Hugh son of Reinald, 1227
Hugh (fl. 800), 1287
Hughes (Hewes, Hews, Hughe, Hughs, Huwes),
Abraham, 48, 49; Alice, 736; Rev. And., 430,
431; Anna Maria, 413, 1208; Ann(e), 283*, 431,

464, 797, 815*, 1278; Betty, 746; Bridget, 373;
Cath., 793, 795; Cecilia, 1336; Chas., 49, 430*,
431*, 1514; Rev. Chas., 430*, 431*; David, 634,
635*, 702, 815; Deborah, 1113; Dorcas, 567;
Edw., 795, 815; Eleanor, 736; Eliz., 331, 332,
338*, 373, 385, 413, 796, 923, 1207, 1208, 1514;
Frideswide, 644; Geo., 283, 702*; Grace, 48, 49;
Hannah, 336; Hester, 49; Rev. Hugh, 328; J.,
1312; Jas., 376*, 1477; Jane, 431, 644; Job,
746*; John, 48, 49, 336*, 385, 413, 423, 431,
644, 736, 746, 797, 815, 923, 1069, 1207, 1208,
1388, 1389; Rev. John, 430*, 431, 704; John
Roydon, 332; Joseph, 1238; Marg., 815, 1336;
Martha, 702; Mary, 283*, 385*, 431*, 563, 567,
702, 746, 815, 1473; Mat., 385; Nic., 1278*; R.,
1215; Ric., 563, 793, 1278, 1473, 1474*, 1477;
Rob., 283*, 1207, 1208*, 1526; Rev. Rob., 1065;
Rog., 923; Sam., 702; Sarah, 338, 376, 423, 542,
622; Rev. Simon, 644, 944; Thos., 283*, 331,
332, 385*, 465, 542, 622*, 736, 763, 764, 815,
1208*, 1289; Rev. Thos., 432*, 599, 643*, 644*,
1335; Wal., 1314; Wm., 338*, 423, 464*, 567,
778 n, 796, 797, 1289, 1477; Rev. Wm., 190,
498, 1122, 1336*, 1483; Rev. Mr., 373; —, 1293,
1311; fam., 430, 763
Hughesome, Hen., 1292; *and see* Hewson
Hughs, *see* Hughes
Hugin (Hugyn), *see* Huggins
Hulbert (Hilbert, Hulbard), Ann(e), 129, 1111*;
Betty, 1111; Edw., 847; Eliz., 129; Hannah, 1111;
John, 847, 1493; Mary, 847; Ric., 846, 1031;
Sam., 847; Susan, 1031; Thos., 129, 176, 1111,
1121; —, 1033
Huldtcote, *see* Hilcot
Hulet (Hulett), *see* Hewlett
Hulin (Huling), *see* Hewlings
Hull (Hulle, Hulles, Hulls, Huls), Abigail, 604;
Adam, 1147; Anne, 1468; Ant., 1468; Cath., 296;
Eliz., 608; Hugh, 1422; John, 710*; Jonathan,
296; Judith, 710; Mary, 608, 824; Mic., 824; Nic.
atte, 1491; Rob. atte, 1388, 1552; Rog. atte,
1404, 1440; Thos. (atte), 608, 1034, 1428, 1477;
Wal. atte, 1540; Wm. (de), 1292, 1422; fam.,
440; *and see* Hill
Hulland, *see* Holland [*peerage*]
Hullare, —, 1093
Hulle, *see* Hull
Hullemullc, Ric., 1221
Hulles, *see* Hull
Hullett, *see* Hewlett
Hulls, *see* Hull
Hulme, *see* Hume
Huls, *see* Hull
Humber, Hen., 1048
Humbestone, Eliz., 901
Hume (Hulme), Cath. Eliz., 1303; Geo. Wal., 1303;
Joseph, 1303, 1314; Dr., 327 n
Humfrey (Humfrid, Humfris, Humfry), *see*
Humphrey; Humphreys
Humpage, *see* Humpidge
Humpforson, Ric., 1341
Humpheris, *see* Humphreys

Humphrey, bishop of London, see Henchman
Humphrey (Hunfrid) the chamberlain, 1377
Humphrey (Hunfrid) the cook, 1377
Humphrey (fl. 1086)(Humfrid, Hunfrid), 1119, 1377
Humphreys (Humfrey, Humfrid, Humfris, Humfry, Humpheris, Humphries, Humphris, Humphryes, Humphrys, Umfray), Alice, 637; Ann(e), 213, 846, 1068*, 1499, 1537; Betty, 1200; Chas., 1320; Christian, 97; Edm., 1499*; Edw., 641, 836, 1200, 1499; Eliz., 601*, 637, 693*, 772, 887, 1184, 1267, 1426; Frances, 675; Giles, 1068; Hannah, 60; Hen., 636*, 637; Hester, 637, 1146, 1537; Rev. Hugh, 524; Humph., 1537; Jas., 637, 1200; Jane, 1320; John, 97*, 123, 235, 249, 293, 370, 637*, 693*, 891*, 1016, 1069, 1184, 1267*, 1289, 1320, 1351, 1551; Rev. John, 825; John Joynes, 601; Kath., 1014; Martha, 604, 1426; Mary, 293, 439, 598*, 668, 887, 891, 955, 1181, 1200, 1292, 1302, 1350, 1470, 1537; Sir Orlando, 544; Owner Thos., 339; R., 1092*; Ralph, 1200; Ric., 339, 439, 598*, 1014, 1068, 1092; Rob., 60, 598, 675*; Sam., 887; Sarah, 370, 1350, 1426*; Stephen, 604, 1537; Susanna, 1076; Thos., 249, 515, 601*, 668, 706, 887*, 1068*, 1076, 1146*, 1181, 1184*, 1350*, 1426*; Rev. Thos., 515, 635; Sir W., 547; Welthin, 636; Wm., 213*, 730, 846, 887, 1200, 1320*, 1426, 1470*; Rev., 459; —, 1477
Humpidge (Humpage, Humppidg), Edw., 1215; Mary, 683; Thos., 683*
Hunfrid, see Humphrey
Hungary, queen of, 952
Hunge, Wm. le, 1351
Hungerford, Anna, 509; Ant., 508, 1485; Sir Ant., kt., 367, 370, 507*, 508*, 509*; Bridget, 507, 509; E., 135, 1016; Edm., 1482; Edw., 1482*; Sir Edw., kt., 1133; Eliz., 508, 509; Geo., 1482; Giles, 1407*; J. P., 1339; Jane, 509, 1482, 1483; John, 508, 509, 1339, 1485; Sir John, 509*, 859, 1482*; John P., 1339; John Peach, 19*; Kath., 1482*, 1483; Marg., 1482; Martha, 1407; Mary, 52, 509*, 1407, 1482*; N. Peach, 1339; Susan, 509; T., 1201; Tho(s)., 409, 985; Sir Thos., 507; Sir Wal., kt., 509, 747; Wal., Lord Hungerford, 509; Wm., 1016, 1325; Lady, 1133; —, 1339, 1407, 1480; fam., 1482*, 1485
Hunks, Rob., 255; and see Hanks
Hunsdon, Lord, see Carey, Sir Geo.
Hunt (Hunte), Adam le, 1220, 1335; Rev. Ambrose, 81; Ann(e), 536, 1413; Rev. Ant., 85; B., 1378; Betty, 958; Rev. C., 1362; Dodington, 158, 311, 313, 314, 325, 574; Edm., 1413; Edw., 958*; Eliz., 311, 314, 636*, 730, 815, 1530; Rev. Geo., 427; Hannah, 1493; Rev. Hen., 1460; Hester, 958; J., 1201; Jas., 815; Jane, 683, 815, 1413; Joan, 1525; John, 1196, 1201, 1312, 1389, 1525, 1539*; Rev. John, 1388, 1389; Mary, 203, 958*, 1389; Mat., 958*; Moses, 730; N., 1256; Peter, 1413, 1417; Rev. Ric., 427, 1016, 1147, 1362, 1460; Sam., 203, 1388; Sarah, 1533; Stephen, 1530, 1533*; Thos. (le), 881, 1058, 1196, 1317,

1389; Rev. W., 1460; Wal., 851 n; Wm. (le), 636*, 683, 1069, 1493, 1525; — (le), 986, 1220, 1378
Hunter, Hen., 813; Rev. Wm., 233; (or Perry), fam., 783
Huntesman, Wm., 1355
Huntingdon (Huntington), Anne, 127; Benj., 801; Rev. Dennis, 127, 770; Rev. Frampton, 593*, 596; Hen. of, 355; Rev. R., 1356; Dr. Rob., bishop, 483, 801; Rev. Rob., 802*; Rev. Wm., 126, 127; earl of, see Clinton, Wm.; Lord, 1093
Huntley, Abigail, 669; Alice, 238; Ann(e), 236, 237*, 238*, 1536-7; Bridget, 669; Chas., 669; Constance, 1255*; Edm., 239; Edw., 173, 1100; Eliz., 237*, 238*, 669, 1512; Frances, 237, 238; Sir G., 1256; Geo., 114, 237*, 238, 424, 630*, 631, 1255*, 1512*; Sir Geo., kt., 395, 579*, 628, 630, 631, 1505, 1513; Jas., 579, 669; Rev. Jas., 579; Jane, 395; John, 628, 631*, 669*, 1512; Lois, 173; M., 236; Martha, 669; Mary, 237, 238, 669; Mat., 236, 237*, 238*, 239, 1255; Miles, 667, 669*; Rev. R., 1074; Ric., 236*, 237*, 238*; Rev. Ric., 236*, 237*, 1536; Rose, 238; Sam., 238; Rev. Sam., 239; Sarah, 1536; Sylvester, 237; Thos., 981; W., 1512; Wal., 579; Wm., 173, 239, 785, 986, 1513; Rev. Wykes, 236, 238, 239*; fam., 236*, 628, 1255
Huntley [peerage], Anne, dau. of marquis of, 997; Wm., marquis of, 997
Huntridge, Anne, 467; Francis, 1530; Mary, 1530*
Hunxman, see Hanksman
Hupsman, Rev. Aug. Thos., 161*
Hurcomb, Wm., 1140
Hurd, see Heard
Hurden, Eliz., 202; Thos., 202
Hurdleston, see Hurlston
Hurdman, see Herdman
Hurlock, Rev. Lawr., 27
Hurlston (Hurdleston, Hurlstone), Eliz., 1222*; Joanna, 540, 541; John, 540*, 541, 1222*; Joyce, 541; Rob., 1222; Thos., 1223
Hurn, see Hearne
Hurnall, Eliz., 555*; Jane, 555; John, 555; Thos., 555; and see Hartnell
Hurne, see Hearne
Hurst, Rev. Chas., 704, 1445; Eliz., 138; Rev. Hen., 865, 866, 1221, 1480; Mary, 1480; Rev. Nat., 704; Wal., 138
Hurtnol, see Hartnell
Huseter, Alice, 598; Hugh, 598*
Hussey (Heose, Hoese), Anne, 1051; Constance, 1014; Eliz., 1014, 1051*, 1373; Hen., 1014*, 1051*; Sir Hen., 1014, 1051*; Joan, 1051; Marg., 1051; Mark, 1051; Ric., 1014; Sir Ric., 1373; Vincent, 1373; —, 1017, 1051, 1388
Hutchens, see Hutchins
Hutchenson, see Hutchinson
Hutchins (Huchones, Huchoun, Hutchens), Dorothy, 518; Edith, 1313; Edm., 394, 518, 519; Eliz., 518; Rev. John, 1372; Ric., 518, 1313; Rev. Ric., 691, 692; Wal., 1314; —, 1311; (or Hitchins), fam., 305 n; and see Hitchins

Hutchinson (Huchenson, Hutchenson), Anne, 1543; Eleanor, 1543*; Jas., 1282, 1543; Jasper, 1543; Silvester, 1543*; W., 1127; Wm., 1543*; Rev. Wm., 1543, 1545, 1552

Hutton (Huton), Anne, 330; Esther, 636; Frances, 1089; Jas., 330; John, 1089; Mary, 1412; Nat., 1412*; Rob., 636; Wm., 907

Huware, see Hewer

Huwelot, see Hewlett

Huwen, see Hewens

Huwes, see Hughes

Huwesone, see Hewson

Huwet (Huwets), see Hewett

Huytinge, see Whiting

Hyatt (Hyate), see Hyett

Hybbot, see Hiberd

Hyckes (Hycks), see Hicks

Hycon, Wal., 1388

Hyde (Hide), Geo., 439; Hercules, 439*; Kath., 986; Mary, 397, 439; Ric., 1165; Sir Ric., 986; Rob., 799; Susanna, 439; Thos., 439, 872; Rev. Thos., 534; Wm., 397, 799, 1131, 1165*, 1476; Dr., 1189; Mr., 1165; —, 1476

Hydebury (Ydebury), Alice de, 1074; Ric., 704

Hydon, John, 1493; (or Haddon), —, 1490

Hyett (Hiatt, Hiet, Hiett, Hyate, Hyatt, Hyet, Hyott), A., 1447; Anna, 897; Ann(e), 110, 172, 175, 535, 563, 930, 1103, 1394, 1457; Ant., 141, 1457; B., 1378, 1494; Benj., 113, 114, 115, 263, 275, 667, 684, 713, 855*, 886, 1377; Cath., 333; Chas., 1, 113, 711 n, 971; Cotten, 1273; Dorothy, 786; Edw., 597; Rev. Edw., 1043; Eleanor, 930; Eliz., 623, 786, 884, 1361, 1457; Frances, 1377; Geo., 597*; Giles, 172*; Halsey, 1326; Hannah, 141; Hen., 971, 1447; Jas., 110*, 563*, 786*, 884, 930, 1273, 1326*; Jane, 597; Jeremiah, 1394; John, 110, 175, 176, 265, 333, 535, 623*, 648, 660*, 762, 870, 873*, 897, 1068, 1408; Jonathan, 1530; Jos., 660; Joseph, 1109, 1121; Judith, 953; Lionel, 1457*, 1460; Marg., 338, 563, 873, 1524; Mary, 141, 176, 262, 333, 398, 597*, 623, 636, 660*, 873, 930*, 931, 1326*, 1524, 1530; Nic., 1378; R., 1382, 1447; Ric., 333*, 1521, 1530; Rob., 262, 338, 597, 1351, 1521, 1524*; Rev. Rob., 430; Sam., 873, 1530; Sarah, 1326; Silvester (Sylvester), 873, 1460; Susanna, 338, 1273; Thos., 531, 636, 658, 762, 930*, 931*, 1103, 1162, 1187, 1361, 1457; W., 1187; Watkins, 338; Wm., 338*, 398, 563, 884, 953, 1351, 1521; Mr., 1372, 1378; —, 1317, 1351, 1363, 1378, 1402, 1403, 1460; fam., 275, 482, 684; and see Eyett

Hykedon, Wm., 1420

Hylsley, Thos., 1255; and see Hysley

Hyman, Eleanor, 108; Eliz., 108; John, 108*; Ric., 107, 108*

Hynderlinge, Wm., 1379

Hyndewelle, Edw., 1313

Hynson (Hinson), Ann(e), 116, 1435; Eliz., 115, 116; Mary, 116; Rebecca, 1435*; Thos., 116*, 1435*; Wm., 115, 116*; —, 115, fam., 113

Hyott, see Hyett

Hysley, —, 1475; and see Hylsley

Ibreio, Adelisa de, 667

Icomb (Iccumbe), John de, 1422; Thos. de, 1422*; Wm. de, 1422; fam., 1422

Iddales (Iddols), Martha, 954; Nic., 495, 953, 954

Ifield, Edw., 1097*; Mary, 1097*

Ilchester, earl of, see Strangeways

Iles (Isles), Ann(e), 201, 569, 654, 1006*, 1307; Benj., 1172; Cath., 654; Dan., 1313; Rev. Edw., 78; Eliz., 331, 1006; Esther Windham, 1251; Geo., 18; Rev. Geo., 37, 1349, 1351; Hannah, 1171; J., 1312; Jane, 1006, 1118; John, 652, 654*, 1006, 1119, 1121, 1171*, 1213, 1307, 1511; Joseph, 654; Mary, 654*, 1119, 1171*, 1251; Nat., 1006*; Ric., 1119; Sarah, 1006, 1251; Susannah, 654; Thos., 201*, 654*, 1119*; Rev. Thos., 783, 1251, 1331; Rev. Wm., 569*, 1118*, 1172*, 1224, 1307, 1328, 1551; Winifred, 1307; Mr., 1189; —, 1216, 1455; fam., 649

Illingworth, Rev. Geo., 1349, 1351

Ilmington (Ilmendone), Gil. de, 1431

Imm, Dan., 814; Jas., 1161; Sarah, 814*

Ind, (or Nind), Chris., 1064; Jas., 1258; (or Nind), Mary, 1064; Rob., 97; Sarah, 97; (or Nind), Wm., 1064

Inge (or Joyce), John, 915

Ingelard, John, 1447; —, 1478

Ingles (Inglis), Ann, 1063; Eliz., 1150, 1151; (later Chamberlayne), Hen., 1189, 1195; J., 1447; Jane, 217; John, 522, 1015, 1149, 1150*, 1151*; Rev. John, 216, 217, 1149; —, 1063

Ingoldsby (Ingoldesby), Cath., 1066; Hen., 1066; Jane, 988; Sir Ric., 988; Lieut.-Gen., 1066

Ingoldsthorp, Sir E., 1100; Edm., 1169; Isabel, 1169; Mary, 1169; —, 1169

Ingram (Ingrum), Abigail, 1442; Anne, 1267; Arthur, 1122, 1348; Barbara, 1442; Eliz., 329; Frances, 505; Francis, 505; Jas., 315, 1442; Rev. Dr. Jas., 329, 447, 1442*; John, 182*, 335; Marg., 1442; Sam., 427; Sarah, 182, 1282; Thos., 234, 426, 427*; Wm., 1267, 1282, 1442; Winifred, 315; fam., 232

Inman, Chas., 811*, 815; Eliz., 811, 815; Jane, 815; Martin, 811, 815; Rebekah, 811; —, 1282

Innell, Ann, 204; Jas., 204

Innocent III, pope, 311

Innocent, —, 1092

Innys, And., 1416; Anne, 1416; John, 1417; Martha, 1416; Mary, 1405, 1416

Insall, G., 1276; Ric., 1276, 1289; Sarah, 1276; Wm., 1289; —, 1288

Insula, see Lisle

Inthefelde, see Field

Inthehale, see Hale

Inthehethe, see Heath

Inthehurne, see Hearn

Inthelane, see Lane

Inthelethe, John, 1259

Ions, Rev. Lancelot, 1015

Irby, Augusta Georgina Eliz., 852 n; Cath., 852 n; Charlotte, 852 n; Frances, 852 n; Fred., Lord Boston, 852 n; Hannah, 852 n; Louisa, 852 n; Mary, 852 n; Wm., Lord Boston, 852 n; Wm. Hen., 852 n

Ireland, Ant., 337; Edw., 317, 337*, 611*; Francis, 337; Hester, 329*; John, 55, 337, 398, 542, 611, 954, 1355*; Dr. John, 1088; Martha, 337; Mary, 55, 317, 329, 337, 611*; Nic., 1342; Priscilla, 611; Ralph, 1473; Rebecca, 542; Ric., 329; Sarah, 55, 337, 611*; Susanna, 337; Thos., 55; Wal., 328, 329*, 337; Wm., 542

Iremonger, John, 986

Ireton, Cath., 427, 1003*, 1005*; Hen., 364*, 426, 1003*, 1005

Irish, Eliz., 407; Geo., 407*; John, 176; Sarah, 176

Ironside, see Edmund

Ironside, Jas., 1511

Irvine, Mrs. D'Arcy, 1093

Irving, —, 1455

Isaac (Isaake), Edw., 845, 846, 1118, 1313; Elias, 1119; Eliz., 1119; Grace, 20; Hannah, 756, 1427; Jane, 756, 1119; Jeremiah, 20*; John, 20; Joseph, 756*; Rachel, 20; Sam., 756, 1121; Sarah, 845, 1338; Thos., 20, 756, 1313, 1427; Wm., 1121, 1338*

Isgar (Isger), John, 958; Mary, 418, 958; Nic., 418, 958; Wm., 958

Isles, see Iles

Ithell, Rob., 780

Ivens (Ivin, Ivins, Ivyn), Alice, 1473; Eliz., 1065; John, 1004, 1473; Priscilla, 1004; T., 1092; Thos., 1065; Wm., 1004

Iver, Wal., 1502

Iverei, see Ivory

Ives, John, 318

Ivey (Ivy, Ivye), Ann, 44; Gabriel, 8; Sir Geo., 121; Hugh, 44; John, 1455; Marg., 406; Ric., 8; Thos., 44, 1121

Iveyleafe, see Ivyleafe

Ivin (Ivins), see Ivens

Ivory (Iverei, Ivorey, Ivori, Ivry), Adeline, 263; Jeffry, 1253; Rog. (de), 263, 1032, 1253*, 1474, 1475; —, 1032, 1355

Ivy (Ivye), see Ivey

Ivyleafe (Iveyleafe), Deborah, 8; Ric., 8*, 1085; Sarah, 1085; —, 1087

Ivyn, see Ivens

Izod (Izard, Izode). Agnes, 74; Alice, 1149, 1151; Ann(e), 293, 867; Edw., 867; Eliz., 296, 1150; Esther, 867; H., 1104, 1221; Hen., 867, 1149, 1150*, 1151*, 1335; Rev. Hen., 1104, 1149*, 1151*; J., 1104; Jas., 296; John, 867*, 1103, 1150, 1388; Nathan, 293; Nic., 884; Sarah, 293, 1149, 1151; Thos., 151, 1446; Wm., 74, 293*, 1150*; Rev. Wm., 1388; —, 1150*

Jabel, Hen., 1477

Jack, Eliz., 659; Hopeful, 659

Jackman, Mary, 903; Rev. Thos., 895, 903*; and see Jakeman

Jackson (Jacksons), Adam, 514; Ann(e), 187*, 587, 1409, 1410, 1480, 1481*; Ant., 1481; Benj., 339, 1150, 1151, 1481; Cath., 1415; Chas., 1369; Edw., 1369, 1398; Rev. Edw., 449, 853; Eliz., 489, 832, 1150, 1151, 1263, 1398, 1480*, 1481*; Esther, 514, 1480; Hannah, 1150*, 1151*; Hen.,

827 n; Rev. Hen., 860; Hester, 339; J., 1162; Jas., 339, 796, 1480, 1481; Jane, 679, 1398; John, 187, 568, 946, 1278, 1481*; Rev. John, 1369; Joseph, 1415, 1420, 1480, 1481*, 1555; Rev. Joseph, 488, 489; Kath. Ann, 1410*; Marg., 946; Maria, 1263; Mary, 187, 832, 873, 1150, 1151, 1410*, 1481*; Nic., 1409, 1410*, 1420; Ric., 587, 679, 1150*, 1151*, 1289; Rev. Ric., 678, 679; Rob., 1410*, 1420; Rowland, 1481; Sam., 339, 873; Sarah, 187, 339, 796, 1481; Susanna, 1481; Thos., 187, 868, 1001, 1149, 1150*, 1151*, 1263, 1366, 1480*, 1481*; Wm., 532, 796, 832, 946, 1553, 1554; Rev. Wm., 1482; —, 1288, 1362, 1440; (or Boothe), —, 1150

Jacob (Jacobs), Ann, 388, 1086; Benj., 1281; Betty, 387; Cath., 387; Chris., 1086*; Elisha, 971; Eliz., 1408; Sir Hildebrand, 1227, 1228; Isaac, 388; Joan, 1576; John, 387, 613, 971*, 1407*; Joshua, 1498; Kath., 1111; Marg., 772*; Martha, 33*, 1407; Mary, 1407; Rob., 1576; Rog., 33; Sam., 1408*; Thos., 1111, 1498*; Rev. Thos., 1238; Wm., 661, 772*; fam., 839

Jacovetts, Thos., 862

Jacques (Jaqes), Ann, 258; Edw., 1121; Eliz., 258; Hannah, 258, 730*; John, 258*, 730; Martha, 258; Moses, 258; Ric., 258*; Wm., 258; and see Jakway

Jakeman, Anne, 1389; Marg., 1391; Mary, 1391*; Thos., 1391, 1389*; and see Jackman

Jakway, John, 1146; Sarah, 1146; and see Jacques

James I, 56, 135, 139, 220 n, 230 n, 244, 285, 287*, 288, 324 n, 363, 392, 415, 440, 459, 488, 502, 511, 520, 567, 571, 599, 609, 651 n*, 691 n, 720 n, 748, 783, 802, 829, 838, 860, 864, 894, 913, 943, 1140, 1189, 1196*, 1221, 1228, 1281, 1290, 1293, 1296, 1317, 1329, 1336, 1356, 1369, 1538

James II, 139, 195, 440, 567, 691 n, 865, 1180, 1293, 1367

James, Abraham, 683; Alex., 1323*; Alice, 813, 1556; Anerist, 468; Anna, 583; Anna Jemima, 1007; Ann(e), 247*, 296, 472, 494, 561, 1076*, 1084, 1318, 1319, 1321*, 1323*, 1473; Benj., 468; Betty, 924; C., 1162; Chas., 231, 813*, 1319*, 1321, 1323*; Edith, 1213; Rev. Edm., 593; Edw., 246, 808, 964, 1076*; Rev. Edw. Evans, 1565; Eleanor, 1320; Eliz., 246, 522, 584, 1150, 1151, 1176, 1345, 1535, 1565*; Ellis, 561*; Francis, 247, 1318, 1319, 1323, 1473; Geo., 130, 814, 1175, 1384; Hannah, 584, 1345; Hester, 494, 1176; Rev. Horatio, 1384, 1385; Jane, 246, 814; Jasper, 906; Joan(e), 768*, 1320, 1516; John, 24, 26, 111*, 522, 731*, 924, 1150, 1323, 1565, 1568*; Rev. John, 78, 233, 886, 1221; Joseph, 584*; Joshua, 1420; Leigh, 494; Marg., 24, 873, 1431, 1568*; Margery, 494; Marn, 1162; Mary, 111, 561, 583, 623, 731, 768, 814, 907, 1041, 1318*, 1345, 1384, 1431, 1568, 1572; Morris, 1516; Peter, 924; R., 508; Ric., 97*, 111, 246, 522*, 814, 924, 1041, 1162; Rob., 584, 1031, 1041; Sam., 789, 1175, 1345, 1572; Sarah, 97, 111*, 231*, 683, 924, 1328; Selwyn (Selwin), 531, 1321*, 1323*; Susanna(h), 814,

1318, 1319; Theophilus, 830; Thos., 175, 246*, 494*, 584, 810, 814, 836, 924, 1150, 1213, 1318*, 1320*, 1431, 1513; Rev. Thos., 783; Wm., 110, 111, 231, 246*, 247*, 472*, 623*, 684, 768*, 803, 814, 873, 907, 1007, 1031, 1176*, 1177, 1321, 1323, 1426, 1431, 1565*, 1572*; Rev. Wm., 42, 259, 582, 583*, 619, 829, 830, 1539; —, 1323*, 1381, 1455, 1475; fam., 493, 807

Jamieson, Eliz., 1135

Jane, see Jayne

Janekines, see Jenkins

Janeworth, —, 1069

Jankynes, see Jenkins

Jannen, Emma, 1460

Jannes, see Jayne

Janson (Jansen), Cornelius, 158*, 220 n, 393 n, 791 n*

Janyes, see Jayne

Jaqes, see Jacques

Jarman (Garmyn, Jarmeyn), Rev. Ric., 184; Wm., 1422

Jarratt (Jarrett), Ann, 616; Eliz., 923; Frances, 815; Isaac, 616*; John, 923; Marg., 923*; Margery, 923; Mary, 616*, 923*; Phil., 815, 923*; Thos., 815; Wm., 923

Jarvis (Gerveys, Jervais, Jervis), J., 1195; John, 1081; Joseph, 1584; Rob., 1081; Wm., 1478; —, 565

Jason, Anne, 744; Sir R., 743; Sir Rob., bt., 743*, 744; Sir Warren, bt., 744

Jasper, Alice, 304; Anne, 304; Eliz., 304; Humph., 304*; Thos., 304

Jaunes, see Jayne

Jay (Jaye), Alice, 1174; Anne, 168; Chas., 168*; Eliz., 168*; Francis, 161, 168*, 1174; Martha, 168; Susanna, 1467; Thos., 168, 1467; —, 1282, 1477

Jayne (Jane, Jannes, Janyes, Jaunes, Jaynes), Abel, 731; Alice, 1043, 1504; Cecilia, 731*; Cornelius, 727, 731; Edm., 735; Elinor, 734; Eliz., 731*, 735; Frances, 199; Grace, 721, 727; Hen., 199*, 731, 1154; John, 47, 248, 734, 735*, 1313, 1555; Rev. John, 1323; Rev. Joseph, 13, 1159; Magdalen, 734; Mary, 248*, 735, 1049; Nic., 734; Oscar Wm., 1518; Ric., 1069, 1313; Rob., 884, 1154; Sarah, 199*, 731; T., 1052; Thos., 199*, 1009, 1289; W., 1323; W. H., 1323; Warren, 248, 732, 734*, 1323; Wm., 199, 731*, 734*, 735, 1049*, 1456; Wm. Chas., 1518; —, 1311; fam., 195; and see Jeynes

Jeankes, see Jenkes

Jecock, Ann, 1576; Edw., 1576

Jefferies (Geffreis, Jeffereys, Jefferis, Jefferys, Jeffreys, Jeffries, Jeffris), Abraham, 1086; Amy, 1086; Ann(e), 526*, 726, 934, 1086*, 1411; Cath., 435, 526; Chas., 435; Edm., 1086; Eliz., 212, 429, 526*, 1085, 1086, 1127; Fienneis, 1086; Francis, 1085, 1086*; Geo., 526; Hannah, 1086; Hen., 1270; Rev. Hen. Cha[s]., 651; Isaac, 212, 1086; Israel, 429; Jas., 934*, 1196; Jerome, 575; John, 526*, 611, 924, 1139, 1140; Leonard,

1435; Marg., 526, 1435; Martha, 1085; Mary, 1270*, 1275; Moses, 1086; Nat., 1519*; Paul, 526; Ric., 526*, 1535*; Rob. Cann, 577, 1419; Sam., 611*, 1086, 1270*, 1275*; Rev. Sam., 1333, 1335; Sarah, 611, 846, 1086, 1270, 1275, 1535; Susanna, 526, 1086; Tacey, 10; Thos., 41, 526*, 830, 832, 1085*, 1086, 1087; Wm., 846, 1086, 1361, 1411*, 1460; Mr., 1519; Rev. Mr., 1021; —, 1419, 1519*; fam., 493

Jeffery (Geffray, Geffrey, Jeffray), Hannah, 1383*; Grace, 1383*; John, 1329, 1383*, 1539; Sarah, 1384; Wm., 1292; —, 1195, 1378

Jefferys (Jeffreys, Jeffries, Jeffris), see Jefferies

Jeffray, see Jeffery

Jeffs (Geffe, Geffes), Agnes, 1197; Eliz., 296; Geo., 296; Rob., 1422; Sarah, 296; Wm., 1388, 1422

Jelemay, Wal., 1477

Jelf (Gelfe, Jelfe, Yealfe), Alice, 1271; Ann(e), 465, 1036*; Ant., 682; Dichael [sic], 1289; Eliz., 830*, 832, 1353; Esther, 830; Joan(e), 1036, 1046; John, 175; Rev. John, 214, 465; Judith, 1353; Mary, 175, 465, 1046; Ric., 830*, 832, 1036*; Rog., 1372; Sarah, 830, 832; Thos., 1039, 1046, 1271; Wal., 77; Wm., 857, 1046*; Rev. Wm., 1353*, 1356

Jenens (Jenings), see Jennings

Jenkes (Jeankes), Rev. Ambrose, 1154; Wm., 293

Jenkins (Janekins, Jankynes, Jenkin), Anna, 167*; Anne, 1175, 1275; Ant., 176; Blanch, 812; Cath., 431; Chas., 1275; Rev. Edw. Ap, 802; Eleanor, 922; Eliz., 167*, 543, 1175, 1275*, 1439, 1584; Florence, 1275; Gabriel, 302; Giles, 338*, 703*; Hannah, 539; Hen., 1274; Hester, 1546; Isaac, 302; Isabella, 109; Jas., 1275*; Jane, 703; Jeremiah, 431; John, 100, 683, 1162*, 1174, 1176*, 1177, 1275, 1312; Rev. John, 1346; Jonathan, 338*; Joseph, 338; Marg., 338, 1162; Margery, 1348; Martha, 176; Mary, 100, 539, 550, 683*, 812; Phil., 666, 1355; Phillis, 1157; Ric., 550, 963, 1157, 1275*; Capt. Ric., 1157; Rob., 812*, 1584; Sam., 1323; Sarah, 338*, 543, 666, 683, 1209*, 1275*; Rev. Stivard, 1176, 1177; Thos., 388, 543, 730, 922, 1175*, 1176; W., 1440; Wm., 109, 167*, 730, 812, 922*, 1127, 1209*; Rev. Wm., 619, 1439; Mr., 1516; Rev. Mr., 1053; —, 1323; fam., 1176

Jenkinson, Amelia, 697; Anne Mary, 223; Sir Banks, 695, 1311; Cath., 697; Chas., baron Hawkesbury, 695, 697; Mary, 697; Rob. Banks, 697; Sir Rob., kt., 223, 695, 696*, 697*; Sir Rob. Banks, bt., 697; fam., 695

Jenner, Ann(e), 284, 772, 860, 861*, 862, 1097, 1099, 1184; Anselm, 1182*; Beata, 284,, 862*; Cath., 861*; Dan., 981*; Deborah, 1099*; Editha, 860; Dr. Edw., 1019, 1097*; Eleanor, 141, 861*, 862*; Eliz., 772, 860, 861*, 862*, 1099; Rev. Geo. Chas., 1176, 1177; Hen., 165; Rev. Hen., 1020*, 1176; J., 1052; Jacob, 860; Jas., 772, 861; Jane, 861; John, 141, 772, 859, 860*, 861*, 862*, 1127, 1229, 1258; Marg., 861*; Martha, 861; Mary, 166, 282*, 284, 860*,

861, 862*, 1099, 1127*, 1130, 1229; Nat., 284*;
Ric., 138; Rob., 593, 772*, 861*, 862, 1127,
1184, 1186; Sarah, 165*, 1130; Stephen, 282,
1099*; Rev. Stephen, 161, 164, 165*, 1019,
1020*, 1097, 1177; Susanna(h), 284, 861*;
Thos., 141, 861*, 862, 1182; Rev. Thos., 1423;
Vincent, 1130*; W., 1052; Wm., 860, 861*,
862*; Dr., 1123, 1176; Miss, 1052; —, 1020,
1217, 1256*; fam., 159, 859
Jennevylle, Sir John, kt., 361
Jennings (Jenens, Jenings, Jenyns), Ann(e), 112,
1109, 1268, 1276*; Edw., 1276*, 1289; Eliz.,
1157, 1415; Hen., 716; Rev. Hen., 681, 1034;
Hattil, 1157*; Isabella, 1278; John, 715, 1109;
Rev. John, 288, 674; Marg., 716; Mary, 110, 170,
715*; Rachael, 746; Rebecca, 250; Ric., 110,
111*, 112, 250, 746, 996, 1015; Rev. Ric., 184;
Rob., 1268, 1276*, 1278; Rev. Sam., 689; Sarah,
111; Thos., 170, 715*; Wm., 715, 716, 996,
1061, 1276, 1289*; Rev. Wm., 180, 452, 1233
Jepson, Arthur, 631; Eliz., 631
Jermye, Elenor, 1010
Jerningham (Jernegan), Sir Edw., 671; Dame
Frances, 674; Hen., 324, 875 n; Sir Hen., 671,
674, 1287; Sir Wm., 969; —, 1288; fam., 876,
885
Jervais (Jervis), see Jarvis
Jesop, Wal., 1202
Jesse, Caleb (Cabel), 1488*; Eliz., 1583; Phillis,
1488
Jeynes (Gynes, Jeyne), Alice, 330; Ann(e), 1270*,
1271*, 1288; Edm., 330; Eliza, 1270; Eliz.,
1277; Esther, 1270; Geo., 1270*; J., 1064; John,
1271*, 1278, 1288, 1289*, 1361; Margery,
1270*, 1277, 1289; Martha, 1270; Mary, 330,
1271, 1278*; R., 1312; Ralph, 1288-9; Rev.
Ralph, 798; Rob., 1348; Sam., 1278*, 1289;
Thos., 1270*, 1277, 1282, 1288-9*; Wm.,
1271*, 1289; —, 1288*, 1292, 1381; and see
Jayne
Jobbins (Jobbings, Jobins), Alice, 1529; Ann, 177;
Francis, 700*, 1456, 1529*; Hen., 177*; Jane,
700; Joan, 703; John, 700*, 1529; Mary, 700*,
1529, 1532; Thos., 177, 703; Wm., 1529
Joce, see Joyce
Jocham, Jas., 929*, 933; John, 933; Rebecca,
932-3
Johane, Geof. son of, 1552
Johane, John son of, 1552
John, king, 75, 101, 244, 259, 265 n, 301, 391, 475,
509, 576, 688 n, 717, 771, 869, 927, 985, 1005,
1253*, 1295, 1340, 1455
John, abbot, 605, 708*
John, bishop of London, see Aylmer; King;
Robinson
John, bishop of Worcester, see Alcock; Carpenter
John son of Johane, 1552
John (fl. 1066), 1074
Johns (John), Ann(e), 1209*; Joyce, 765; Mary,
765*; Thos., 765*, 1314; Rev. W., 1217; Rev.
Wm., 630, 1203, 1206, 1209*, 1217; —, 1282,
1455
Johnson (Johnsons, Jonson), Abraham, 1289; Alex.,
919; Alice, 330; Ann(e), 381, 388, 578, 623,
1088, 1445; Rev. Ant., 744; Rev. Baldwin, 635;
Beata, 132*; Betty, 906; Sir Cornelius, 876; E.,
381; Edw., 288, 330, 334*, 1329, 1441; Eliz.,
132, 237, 578*, 1193, 1421, 1441; Hannah, 388,
578; Harman, 1441*; Jas., 221, 302, 716; John,
351, 578*, 623, 1138, 1421, 1473, 1477; Rev.
John, 1392; Jonas, 1088; M., 1447; Marg.,
1421*; Martha, 919; Mary, 46, 256, 334*, 388,
578*, 716; Mat., 304; Nic., 1418; Rev. Ric., 255,
256*, 603; Rev. Rob., 1477; Sam., 906; Rev.
Sam., 370, 373; Sarah, 48, 304, 1138, 1193,
1194, 1474; Susanna(h), 388, 578; T., 237; Thos.,
388, 578, 1193, 1194, 1226, 1228, 1421, 1422;
Wm., 46, 48, 131, 132*, 388, 578, 642, 850,
1088, 1217, 1258, 1421, 1441, 1445*, 1474; Dr.,
21; —, 1441*; fam., 131
Johnston (Johnstoun), Ann, 374; Chris., 374; Edw.,
293*; Eliz., 1244*; Heneretta, 296; Jas., 336*;
Jane, 293, 374, 1244; John, 662*, 1244*; Martha,
336; Mary, 336; Wm., 296, 374
Jolley (Joly), Thos., 693; —, 1477
Jollyff (Jolyf), John, 1370; Wm., 1477
Joly, see Jolley
Jolyf, see Jollyff
Jonas, Eliz., 1499; John, 1499
Jones, Aaron, 442; Abraham, 729, 939; Alice, 207;
Ann(e), 16, 104, 190, 202, 303, 474, 563, 641,
665, 787, 810, 815*, 904*, 923, 974, 1026, 1101,
1271, 1320, 1323, 1511, 1583; Rev. Anselm, 302,
890; Ant., 450; Barbara, 1236; Benj., 104; Rev.
Benj., 886; Betty, 550, 1339; Bluett, 17*; Cath.,
211, 692, 1019, 1162; Ceciley, 569; Chas.
(Chales), 405, 412*, 733*, 808, 831, 904*, 932*,
933, 1371*; Christian, 18, 84; Christiana
Susannah, 731; Dan., 569, 661; Rev. Dan., 1446;
David, 815*, 923, 1289, 1419*, 1427, 1573; Rev.
David, 613, 820; Deborah, 425; Dorothy, 1320;
E., 1312; E. W., 1387; Edith, 429; Edw., 42, 246,
550, 789, 807, 904, 974, 1165, 1236, 1277, 1454,
1473, 1573, 1583*; Rev. Edw., 246, 808, 853; Sir
Edw., kt., 364; Eleanor, 261, 958; Eli, 1511;
Esther, 923, 975, 1328; Rev. Evan, 81; Eliz., 5,
17, 110, 167, 172, 176, 262, 333, 339, 340, 412,
428, 442*, 517, 542, 569, 578, 729, 733, 746,
751, 799, 903, 904*, 906, 922, 932, 957, 1101,
1112, 1165, 1222, 1235, 1377, 1467*, 1490;
Ferd[inand]o, 1467; Fiennis, 1086; Flora L.,
1020; Frances, 1267; Francis, 250, 599, 1515;
Rev. Fulk, 139; Gabriel, 211; Gaddes, 1550*;
Geo., 262, 974, 1583; Rev. Geo., 1228; Geo. Gil.,
641*; Gil., 903*, 1499; Giles, 18; Grace, 1419;
Griffeth, 957*; Rev. Griffith, 1228; H., 1101;
Hannah, 413, 815, 1162, 1347, 1412*, 1454; Sir
Harry, 136; Hen., 143, 167, 731, 1218, 1267,
1268, 1281, 1320*, 1351, 1515*, 1519; Rev.
Hen., 142, 1020, 1267, 1268*, 1290*, 1348,
1504; Sir Hen., 599*; Hester, 584, 845, 846;
Inigo, 349, 363, 663; Isaac, 532, 1415; Rev. J.,
1348; Rev. J. W., 1489*; Jas., 104, 815, 1277;
Rev. Jas., 1043; Jane, 190, 491*, 569, 932, 933,

1086, 1323, 1515; Joan, 939; Job, 789; Jo(h)anna, 104, 807; John, 82, 103, 104*, 172, 176, 202, 250, 261*, 301, 302*, 328, 335, 367, 517, 550, 569, 593, 641, 731, 746, 761, 815, 906*, 907, 920, 922, 923, 1019, 1020, 1039, 1140, 1162, 1168, 1176, 1277, 1287, 1295, 1305, 1309*, 1371, 1377, 1455, 1467*, 1516*; Rev. John, 313, 436, 437, 691, 692, 783, 887, 1222, 1331, 1433; Rev. John Price, 1147; John Turner, 202; John Walker, 1489; Joseph, 104*, 105, 211, 381, 418, 542*, 939; Josiah, 1412, 1415, 1420; Judith, 333, 765, 1279; Kath., 692; Keturah, 413; Leodwick, 1419; Rev. Lewis, 139, 421*, 438; Lucas, 542; Marg., 104*, 105, 636, 641*, 687, 974, 1516; Martha, 413*, 1583; Mary, 82, 104, 111*, 202, 250, 302, 303, 486, 550*, 569, 725, 733*, 815*, 831, 904, 906, 923, 981*, 1101, 1176, 1277*, 1281, 1424*, 1427, 1473*, 1490, 1499, 1550*; Mary Ann, 1489; Matilda, 1519; Mat(t)hea, 1267*, 1268*; Mic., 815; Rev. Mic., 696; Moses, 442*; Nat., 981, 1217; Rev. Nic., 1339, 1482; Noah, 1025; Rev. Parry, 1290; Piercey, 1460; Phil., 731, 922, 1020, 1027; Rev. Phil., 1388, 1392; R., 985, 1312; Rev. Rhees, 798; Rev. Rice, 668; Sir Rice, 599; Ric., 104, 206, 207*, 302, 303, 340*, 486, 599, 665*, 730, 789, 922, 923, 958, 1499, 1513, 1574; Rev. Ric., 739, 1238; Rob., 333, 442, 569, 906, 1490; Rev. Rob., 440, 798, 799; Rog., 1491; Rev. Rog., 1519; Rowland, 175; Roynon, 479*, 807, 808, 810, 927; Rev. Roynon, 103; Sam., 84, 491, 563, 984, 1026*, 1217, 1265, 1292, 1473*; Rev. Sam., 802; Sam. Crowther, 16; Sarah, 261, 335, 381, 573, 731*, 762, 814, 832, 904, 920, 923, 1085, 1573; Rev. Simon, 440, 1372; Rev. Somerset, 53, 1323*, 1381, 1516; Susan, 920; Susanna, 17; Susannah Willett, 1147; T., 1256; Teresa, 733; Thos., 5, 104, 124, 211, 302, 303*, 425, 428, 474, 573*, 636, 683, 687, 733*, 762, 832, 845, 846, 873, 906, 922, 923, 958, 963*, 975, 1085*, 1121, 1162*, 1267, 1305, 1403, 1424, 1552, 1583; Rev. Thos., 935; Trippet, 104; Rev. V., 1127; W., 89, 1160, 1387; Wal., 263, 765; Rev. Wal., 1279, 1348, 1504; Wm., 16, 27, 103, 111*, 147, 175*, 246, 261, 339, 349, 413, 429, 491*, 536, 550, 569, 584, 601, 725, 751*, 760, 761, 765, 787, 814, 832, 872, 904*, 917, 918, 920, 922, 929*, 1019, 1112*, 1121, 1162, 1218, 1258, 1277*, 1289, 1305*, 1320*, 1321, 1339, 1347, 1382, 1386, 1424*, 1499; Rev. Wm., 1329, 1387, 1456, 1482; Younger, 904; Zachariah, 578; Mr., 259, 960, 1189, 1355, 1362, 1420; Mrs., 894*; —, 214, 260, 672, 986*, 1052, 1255, 1256, 1289, 1311*, 1323*, 1428, 1455, 1491, 1501; fam., 259, 301, 779
Jonson, see Johnson
Jordan (Jorden, Jordon, Jortin, Jourdan, Jurda, Jurdan), Ann(e), 193, 234*, 961; Benedick, 193; Cath., 1536; Chris., 1536; Edm., 193; Eliz., 193*, 975; Hannah, 254; Hen., 1292; Hester, 59, 254; Jane, 437; John, 193*, 234*, 254, 670*, 961, 1064, 1226, 1538*; Joseph,, 254; Kath.,

254, 670; Margery, 299; Martha, 335, 975; Mary, 133, 437*; Ric., 133, 299, 437; Rob., 1420; Rog., 1404; Sam., 104, 254; Sarah, 710; Thos., 335, 437*, 661, 975; Wm., 59, 133, 793, 1447, 1460; —, 710, 1068
Jory, Wal., 1356
Joscelyn, see Joslyn
Josephs (Josep), Adam, 1540; Eliz., 1459; Wal., 1540; —, 1017
Josham, Jas., 1413
Joslyn (Joscelyn), Elianor, 962; Sir Rob., kt., 370
Joulins, Mary, 861; Thos., 861
Jourdan, see Jordan
Joy (Joye), John, 1420; Ric., 1227
Joyce (Joce, Joyes), Ann Archer, 996; Eliz. Gandy, 996; Hannah, 118; Hen., 1392; Jas. Archer, 996; (or Inge), John, 915; Sir John, 915; Mary, 118*; Ric., 118*; Wm., 1447; fam., 913
Joye, see Joy
Joyes, see Joyce
Joyner, Ann(e), 417, 419, 906; Edw., 1445; Eliz., 993; Francis, 1187; Hannah, 168; Jas., 417, 419*, 730*; John, 168*; Marg., 730*; Mary, 906; Sam., 419; Sarah, 417, 419, 730; Thos., 730*; Welthin, 417; Wm., 417*, 730*, 906, 993
Joynes (Joyns), Anna Maria, 601*; Ann, 601; Eliz., 601*; Jas., 601; John, 505, 601*, 1063*; Joseph, 601; Sarah, 601; Susan, 1063; Thos., 601*, 948; Wm., 601*
Jubb, Geo., 171
Julius II, pope, 218, 882
Jurdan (Jurda), see Jordan
Jusster, John, 1194
Justice, John, 1061, 1074
Juxon (Juxton), Eliz., 437*; J., 1331; Ric., 436 n; (formerly Hesketh), Sir Rob., bt., 804; Susanna, 437; Thos., 437*; Dr. Wm., archbishop, 436*, 804*, 1331*; Sir Wm., 1055, 1331; Sir Wm., bt., 436*, 437*, 804; fam., 804, 1055

Kante, —, 1328; and see Kent
Kardiff, see Cardiff
Kare, see Care
Karent, see Carent
Karver, see Carver
Kay, see Kays
Kayen, see Cains
Kayfot, John, 1313
Kayleway, fam., 753; and see Kellaway
Kays (Kay, Kayse), Anne, 1371; Rev. J., 1504; John, 1371*; Marg., 814; Ric., 814
Keachment, Frances, 736; Geo., 736*
Keak (Keake), see Keck
Kear (Keare, Kearr, Keir, Kerr), Dan., 339; Edw., 922; Eliz. Ann, 1156; Francis, 1232; Geo., 922; Hen., 924; Joane, 1054; John, 917, 922, 924*; Judith, 1232; Mary, 339, 398, 922; Ric., 339, 398, 399; Rob., 1054; Sam., 922; Sarah, 339; Thos., 922, 924; Dr., 405 n; and see Care; Carr
Kcarby, see Kirby
Keare (Kearr), see Kear
Kearse, Mary, 389; Peter, 389; and see Kersey

Kearsey, *see* Kersey

Keasey, Eliz., 563; John, 563; Ric., 563

Keble (Keeble), A., 595; Edm., 1125; Eleanor, 1127; Eliz., 1125*, 1127; Hen., 1127*; Sir Hen., kt., 568; Jane, 1125; J. P., 1126; John, 661; Rev. John, 427; John Petrie, 1126; Joseph, 398; M., 595; Mary, 569, 797, 1126; Ric., 568*, 569*, 1127; Rob., 706, 793, 797, 1127; Sarah, 398, 1126, 1127; T., 1126, 1127; Thos., 706, 1125*, 1126*, 1127*; Wal., 1126, 1127*; Wm., 1127; —, 1082; fam., 1126

Keck (Keak, Keake, Kecke), A., 1133; And., 1140; Ann, 641; Ant., 640, 641, 986, 1138*, 1153*; Sir Ant., 143, 865 n; Edith, 1182; Eliz., 143, 641, 683; Francis, 1066; Hester, 641; Jas., 1182; John, 850*; Joseph, 641*; Maria, 850; Mary, 640, 641, 1066, 1138*; Rev. N., 1154, 1504; Rob., 641*; Sarah, 640, 641*; Susan, 1153; Wal., 1047; Wm., 641, 683, 850

Kedd, Eliz., 887; Thos., 887

Keddick, Geo., 108*, 109*, 112; Isabella, 112

Kedgwin (Kedgewin), John, 922, 1162; Joyce, 1162; Wm., 923

Kedley (Kidley), Rev. John, 1403, 1404

Kedwards, Jane, 1274; John, 1274; Wm., 1282, 1289

Kee, *see* Keyes

Keeble, *see* Keble

Keech, Anne, 1192; Joseph, 1192*; Mary, 1192*; Sarah, 1192; Wm., 1192*

Keel (Kyll), Rob., 1186; Stephen, 731

Keen (Keene, Kene, Keynne), Ann(e), 296*, 971, 1250; Arabella, 1194; Chas., 658; Charlotte, 658; Dan., 658*, 662; Edw., 924; Eliz., 521, 658; John, 203, 226*, 296*, 450, 1106; Mary, 204, 662, 1106; Ric., 1106; Rob., 1217; Sam., 658, 662; Sarah, 203, 226, 450, 658*, 662; Silas, 1194; Thos., 204, 296*, 1250; Wm., 284, 450, 971*; —, 1069; *and see* Kenn; Kinn

Keepen (Keepin), Ann, 1339; Eliz., 847; John, 17, 1339; Mary, 16; Rob., 16, 847

Keery, John, 660

Kege, Rob., 1404

Keiching, *see* Kitchen

Keining, *see* Kening

Keinton, *see* Keynton

Keir, *see* Kear

Kelham, —, 1092

Kellaway, Capt. Nic., 1158; *and see* Kayleway

Keller, —, 1256

Kellock, Hannah, 133; Wm., 133*

Kelsay, —, 1455

Kelson, Geo., 963*; Jane, 963; Sarah, 963

Kembare, *see* Kimber

Kembe, Wm., 1447; *and see* Kemp

Kemble, Ann(e), 382, 1263, 1289; Ant., 382; Dan., 1263, 1289, 1291; Rev. Dan., 230, 1069, 1263*; Edw., 1263*; Eliz., 171, 938, 1263*, 1376; Hen., 1376, 1377*; John, 938, 1376*; Marg., 230, 1263, 1376; Mary, 1281, 1376*, 1377; Ric., 938; Sarah, 1376; Thos., 71, 230, 382, 938, 1039, 1263*, 1281; Wm., 171, 382, 938*; Mrs., 71, 72; —, 1253, 1362

Kemeseye, John de, 1292

Kemett, *see* Kemmet

Kemeys (Kemis, Kemish), *see* Kemys

Kemmet (Kemett, Kemmett), Eliz., 1266*; Francis, 983; Hester, 1063; J., 1382; John, 339, 983*, 1266; Joseph, 339*; Josias, 1046; Marg., 339; Mary, 339; Thos., 1266*; Wm., 983*, 1266*

Kemp (Kempe), Anne, 47; Sir Benj., bt., 431; Cecilia, 987; Edw., 731; Hester, 47; Sir Nic., kt., 987; Sir Rob., bt., 431; Sarah, 987; Thos., 47*, 731, 923, 1420; Rev. Thos., 431; Miss, 431; —, 1402; —, wife of Sir Rob., 431; *and see* Kembe

Kempson, John, 753; Mary Isabella, 753

Kemys (Kemeys, Kemis, Kemish, Keymis), Ann(e), 613*, 614; Arthur, 614; Barbara, 384; Fortune, 997; Hugh, 1160; J., 1086, 1160; Jane, 384; Joanna, 997; John, 1086, 1160*; Mary, 384; Rog., 613, 614, 1086; Thos., 429; Wm., 613*, 614*, 997; —, 997

Kench, Benj., 953; Mary, 953; Thos., 752, 1016; —, 1015

Kendal (Kendall), John, 262, 1327, 1345; Rebekah, 580; Wm., 580

Kendrick (Kenrick), Rev. Dan., 1335; John, 1333*; Marg., 1333; Ric., 1333; Rob., 1519; Rev. Sam., 802; Sarah, 1333*; Thos., 1333; —, 1519*

Kenelm, [St.], 1220

Kenemsbury, *see* Kimbury

Kenewiek, Nic., 1259

Kening (Keining), Rev. Rob., 839, 840

Kenison, *see* Kennison

Kenn, Sir Chris., 582; Edw., 999; Geo., 999; Isabel, 663; John, 663, 672, 1047; Marg., 582; fam., 663, 870; *and see* Keen; Kinn

Kennedy, Lord, 760

Kennett (Kennet), Dorothy, 1530; Marg., 696; Thos., 696; —, 197, 864 n

Kennison (Kenison), Jas., 578*, 731; Mary, 578

Kenred (Kenrad, Kenric, Kynred), king of Mercia, 271, 1195, 1227, 1447, 1459

Kenrick, *see* Kendrick

Kent, Alice, 1504; Deborah, 976; Eliz., 317, 339; Joanna, 1013; John, 317; Mary, 976; Rev. Ric., 1527, 1539; Rob., 976*; Sam., 339, 1557; Thos., 1047; Rev. Wal., 438; Wm., 1013; *and see* Kante

Kent [*peerage*], Edm., earl of, 876, 1082*; Eliz., countess of, 876; Hen., duke of, 759, 819; Joan, 'fair maid of', 876; John, earl of, 876; *and see* Burgh, Hubert de; Grey, Eliz. *and* Hen.; Holland, Joan *and* Thos.; Woodstock, Edm. of

Kenulf (Kenulph), king of Mercia, 1103, 1220, 1361, 1474, 1475, 1481

Ken'wulph, king of West Saxons, 1461

Kerby, *see* Kirby

Kercheval, *see* Kirchevall

Kerdiff (Kerdyf), *see* Cardiff

Kerkham, *see* Kirkham

Kerle, *see* Kyrle

Kerr, *see* Kear

Kersey (Kearsey), Edw., 906; Eliz., 906; W. W., 1216; *and see* Kearse

Kerver, *see* Carver

Kerwardyn, *see* Carwardine
Kestall, John, 337
Ketelby (Ketilby, Kettelby), And., 1080, 1082*;
Francis, 1082; H., 1082; Hen., 1082; Isabel,
1082*; Jane, 1082*, 1201*; John, 1082; —, 1459
Ketinge, Alice, 1363
Kettelby, *see* Ketelby
Keyes (Kee, Kewys, Key, Keyess, Keys, Keyse),
Ann(e), 716, 1371; Eliz., 397; Gil., 1494; Hen.,
1478; Joan, 906, 1139; Joannah, 397*; John, 397,
654*, 716*, 906, 1139, 1371, 1372; Mary, 789;
Rev. Nic., 1031; Rev. Ric., 114; Rog., 711 n;
Sam., 397; Sarah, 397; Thos., 397*; Rev. Thos.,
80*, 81; Wm., 397, 789*, 1494; fam., 1237
Keylock (Keylocke), Ant., 871; Eliz., 903; Isabel,
871; Jas., 624; Jasper, 903; John, 624; Sarah,
903; Thos., 624, 903*
Keymis, *see* Kemys
Keynes, Ralph, 1032; fam., 1032
Keynton (Keinton), Geo., 729; Kath., 473; Mary,
473*; Sam., 473*; Wm., 729
Keys (Keyse), *see* Keyes
Keyte (Keyt), Agnes, 572; Alice, 296, 572*, 866*;
Ann(e), 296*, 337, 571, 1277; Barbara, 572;
Coventry, 572; Dorothea, 572, 573; Eglantine,
571; Eliz., 296, 571, 572*, 573*; Francis, 571,
572*, 865, 866*; Gil., 572; Hastings, 572; Capt.
Hastings, 1191*; Jane, 572*, 866; John, 571,
572*, 1277; Sir John, 570, 572*; Marg., 572*;
Mary, 572; Ric., 296*, 573; Sam., 296, 573*;
Sarah, 573; Dr. Thos., 572*; Wm., 296, 337, 338,
571*, 572*, 573*; Sir Wm., bt., 570*, 571, 572*;
fam., 54, 570, 864; *and see* Kite
Kibble (Kible), Jas., 203, 448; Jane, 448; John,
567; Mary, 567*; Thos., 130; —, 1126
Kidd, Geo., 847*; Jane, 847; Thos., 847; Wm., 846
Kidderminster, R., abbot, 1475; *and see*
Kittermuster
Kidgell, Kath., 1116; Thos., 1116; Wm., 1116
Kidley, *see* Kedley
Kidman, Geo., 1519
Kidson, *see* Kitson
Kilby, Joan, 517; John, 517*; Marg., 517; Thos.,
517*
Kildermore, Thos., 369*
Kilford, Jane, 1401; Joseph, 1401; Thos., 1401
Kilmister (Kilmaster, Kilminster), Ann, 1030*,
1031; Eliz., 1030*; Hannah, 1031*; Hester, 1030;
Jas., 1030; Jane, 1031; John, 35, 1030*, 1140;
Marg., 35; Martha, 1030*; Mary, 35*; R., 1031;
Rachel, 1031; Ric. (Rd.), 35*, 1031*, 1033; Rob.,
388, 1030*, 1033*; Sarah, 254, 388; Thos., 35;
Wm., 118, 1030*, 1031*, 1033*, 1542; —, 1256
Kilner, Rev. Jas., 459; Mr., 371 n
Kilpeck, Hugh of, 1238
Kimber (Kembare, Kimbare), Edw., 510*; Eliz.,
510*; Hester, 510; John, 510; Mary, 510; Thos.,
510; Tim., 565; Wm., 510*, 1050, 1477, 1502;
—, 1477; fam., 297
Kimble, Ann, 1194; Hannah, 1194; Wm., 1194
Kimbury (Kenemsbury, Kynemersbury), Elgar of,
1380; Phil. de, 1378; Rob. de, 1378

Kimpland, Marg., 1575; Sarah, 1575
Kinard, *see* Kynard
Kindon, Ann, 1566; Geo., 1566; Hen., 1566;
Hester, 1566; Mary, 1566; Sam., 1566*; Thos.,
1566; *and see* Kingdom
Kinemon, Adam., 711 n
King (Kinge, Kings, Kynge), Abigail, 564; Alice,
509, 510, 976; Anna, 1212; Ann(e), 4, 539*, 543,
741, 811, 902, 974, 996, 1004*, 1067, 1101,
1213, 1438*, 1439*, 1509*; Ant., 509, 510*,
813*, 862; Arthur, 174*; Benj., 543, 734*; Cath.,
562*; Chas., 846, 1438, 1509; Chris., 510*,
862*; Lady Conolly, 1417; Dan., 623, 662,
1100*, 1269, 1438, 1440; Edith, 1314; Edm.,
1004*; Edw., 370, 902*, 1004, 1025*, 1027;
Elianor (Eleonor), 261, 1505; Eliz., 170*, 412,
460, 510*, 539*, 541*, 562*, 563*, 622, 624,
734*, 741*, 813, 847, 862, 897, 1025, 1166,
1271, 1399, 1509*; Rev. Erasmus, 635, 639, 640;
Esther, 191; Ezekiel, 1212*, 1213, 1217; Francis
[Frances], 510; Francis, 616; Geo., 846, 996,
1100; Giles, 446; Greg., 2*; Hannah, 623, 847,
1438; Hen. (le), 50, 539, 651, 811*, 815, 1021,
1140, 1399*; Hester, 846; Isabella, 174; J., 1148,
1186; Jas., 249*, 250*, 412, 741, 847; Jane, 382,
510*, 741, 862*, 1004*; John (le), 118, 170*,
174, 175, 202, 261, 284, 532, 539, 558, 561,
562*, 623, 661, 815, 862, 974*, 996, 1020, 1143,
1450*, 1456, 1485, 1509*, 1511, 1512, 1513,
1519; Rev. John, 1166*, 1169, 1505, 1513; John,
bishop, 1067, 1223; Jos., 1139; Joshua, 1438*;
Judith, 539, 974; Marg., 627, 1143, 1271;
Martha, 616, 734, 815, 974*; Mary, 97, 118, 170,
249, 250*, 446, 460, 510*, 539*, 563, 598, 623,
637, 662, 734, 771, 800, 813*, 974, 1004, 1054,
1100*, 1181, 1269, 1438*, 1439, 1509*; Nat.,
541, 563, 564*, 897, 976, 1509*; Rev. Nat.,
1372; Penelope, 907; Sir Peter, 1187; Rebecca,
1450; Ric. (le), 558, 562*, 619, 627, 1006, 1127,
1509; Rob., 598, 771, 772, 996, 1313; Rog.,
1058; Sam., 12, 531*, 541*, 563, 661, 974, 975,
1054, 1100, 1181*, 1438*, 1439*, 1440; Sarah,
170, 284, 537, 561, 813, 996, 1006, 1100, 1212,
1271, 1399, 1438*, 1509; Simon, 191; Susannah,
623*; Syble, 598; Thos., 4, 60, 460, 510*, 526,
531*, 537, 539*, 598*, 627*, 660, 741*, 907,
975, 996, 1100, 1184, 1271*, 1438, 1439*, 1447;
Ursula, 1509; W., 1513; Wal., 734, 800; Wm.
(le), 97, 170*, 174, 175, 446, 532, 563, 633, 847,
943, 944, 1086, 1329, 1335, 1427, 1438*, 1491,
1509; Rev. Wm., 603; Wintle, 1399; Dr., 122; —,
445, 1005, 1017
Kingdom, John, 1289; *and see* Kindon
Kinge, *see* King
Kingescote, *see* Kingscote
Kingford, fam., 484
Kings, *see* King
Kingsbury, Dennis, 1276; Marg., 1276; —, 1282
Kingscote (Kingescote, Kingscot, Kingscott),
Abraham, 775, 776*; Adam, 773*; Aldena, 773*,
776; Alice, 775; Alliday, 776; Anne, 776; Ant.,
773*, 775*, 776*, 1183; Arthur (de), 773*, 776;

Chris., 755, 773*, 775*; Eliz., 755; Ester, 1183; Hen., 776; Joan, 776; John, 773, 1175, 1177; Kath., 776*; Mary, 776*, 963; N., 1083; Nic., 773; Nigel (de), 773*, 775*, 776*, 1083; R., 1083; Ric. (de), 773*, 775*; Rob., 773*, 775, 776*, 909*, 1083*; Rob. Fitzharding, 775; Sarah, 1175*; Thos., 846; Troylus, 776*; W., 1120; Wm., 773*, 775*, 776*; Col., 1083

Kingston (Kingstone, Kyngestone, Kyngston), Sir A., 1147*, 1402*; Ann, 1005; Ant., 606, 879, 1005; Sir Ant., 65, 66, 214, 363, 414, 469, 546, 605, 671, 674, 838, 876, 885, 915, 927, 1005; Edm., 878 n, 1005*; Geo., 760; Sir H., 1039; Howise, 1345; Joan (de), 1102, 1346; Johanna (de), 1345, 1540; John de, 1238, 1313; Mary, 671, 879; N., 1345*; Nic. (de), 1345*, 1346; Sir Nic., 778 n; Ric. (de), 722, 1101; Sir W., 1148, 1312; Wm., 876, 878, 879, 1005*; Sir Wm., kt., 605, 671, 876, 885*; duke of, 627; —, 1312; fam., 878

Kingswood, Rev. Thos., 1238

Kington (Kyngton), Ann, 847; Jane, 847; John, 847; Rob. de, 1314; Simon de, 1314; —, 1311

Kinman (Kinsman), Rev. John, 27; Mr., 28

Kinn, Mary, 96; Sam., 96, 97; and see Keen; Kenn

Kinsman, see Kinman

Kip, —, 119, 134, 359, 392 n, 552, 709, 739, 769, 913, 1494

Kipling, John, 1165; Rev. John, 228, 1163, 1164, 1165; Sarah, 1163, 1164

Kipworth, Wal., 1351

Kirby (Kearby, Kerby, Kirkeby), Alice, 884; Betty, 658, 662; Eliz., 772; John de, 1016, 1197; Martha, 658, 662; Ric., 772; Rowland, 772; Wm., 369, 658, 662, 884, 1505; —, 1227, 1455

Kirchevall (Kercheval), Rev. Dr. John, 859, 860, 861

Kirk (Kirke, Kyrke), Anne, 215; Eliz., 931; Rev. Hen., 674; Rev. Hugh, 696, 1346; Rebekah, 215; Rob., 215*; Thos., 931

Kirkeby, see Kirby

Kirkham (Kerkham), Damaris, 1104; Henrietta, 1149, 1151; Rev. Hen., 865, 895, 1104*, 1149*, 1151*, 1154; Lionel, 1150; Rev. Lionel, 1104*, 1149*, 1151, 1154; Mary, 1149, 1151; N., 1477; Penelope, 1149, 1151; Rev. Rob., 1103, 1104, 1149*, 1151*; Sarah, 1149*, 1151*; —, 1150

Kirkman, Rev. Jas., 1456; Rev. Lionel, 89, 147

Kirkmer, John Joseph, 336

Kirle, see Kyrle

Kirrall, Anne, 431; Jane, 431; John, 431; Capt. John, 431; Mary, 431; Stringer, 431

Kirrington, Ric., 452

Kirwan, Mr., 648 n

Kitchen (Keiching, Kitchin), Ann, 398; Eliz., 543; Esther, 868; Joseph, 398, 543*; Rob., 216, 1405; Thos., 868; Wm., 398; —, 1554

Kite (Kyte), Alice, 1029; Mary, 1029; Ric., 1029; Rob., 1199; Mr., 1029; and see Keyte

Kitley (Kitlee), Eliz., 1583; Sarah, 1583; Wm., 1583

Kitson (Kidson), John, 1576; Rev. R., 1127

Kittermuster, Eliz., 399; Frances, 397; Jas., 399; Thos., 397*; and see Kidderminster

Knaggs, Thos., 812*

Knapp (Knap, Napp), Ann(e), 1108*, 1171; Charity, 18; Edw., 1112*; Eliz., 780, 955*, 1108, 1109*, 1112*; Hester, 1112; John, 1109*, 1490; Mat., 1158; Reg., 1074; Sarah, 1490; Thos., 955*, 1108*, 1112, 1158; Wm., 18, 955*, 1074, 1112, 1171; —, 1020

Knat, Adam, 1404

Knatchbull, Norton, 1420

Knee, Anna, 1528*; Mary, 418; Rob., 1528

Knell (Knelle), Rev. Paul, 744; Rob. de, 1519

Kneller, —, 220 n, 719 n*

Knevet (Knevett, Nevet), Eliz., 559; Joan, Lady Beaumont, 559 n; Mary, 1269; Rev. Ric., 603; Thos., 1269; Sir Wm., kt., 559*

Knight (Knigt, Knyt), Aaron, 176; Ann(e), 46, 175, 507, 975*, 1036, 1193, 1194, 1407*; Betty, 1536; Chas., 1407; Dan., 531, 1136; Rev. Ed., 1092; Edw., 177, 741, 970*, 975*; Eliz., 1136, 1536; Esther, 975*; Francis, 1136; Sir Geo., kt. & bt., 1210; Giles, 751*; Hannah, 1343, 1366, 1536*; Hester, 970*; Jacob, 1407*; Jas., 623, 624, 797*, 1343, 1366, 1536*; Jane, 456, 741, 797*; Joan (Jone), 402, 413; John, 46, 53, 354, 456, 468, 507, 623, 624, 797, 1000, 1025, 1036, 1039, 1193*, 1348, 1368, 1407*; Sir John, kt., 1191, 1407*; Rev. John, 445; Joseph, 175*, 562*, 623, 850, 853; Lydia (Liddy), 538, 751; Marg., 468, 1000; Mary, 176, 177, 354, 468, 562, 934, 1025, 1191, 1368*, 1407, 1418, 1536; Mary Charity, 1412; Mary Compere, 1194; Matilda, 1387; Moses, 537, 538; P., 1136; Patience, 984; Phil., 1292; Rev. R., 1287, 1290; Ric. (le), 468, 1039, 1150*, 1217, 1536; Ric. Widmore, 1194; Rev. Rob., 1290; Sam., 562, 1136; Sarah, 175*, 177, 741, 1536; Simon, 1027; Sophia, 1536; Susannah, 623; Thos., 402, 413, 537, 975, 1038, 1366*, 1368*, 1407; Rev. Thos., 524; Ursula, 1210; Rev. W., 1311; Wal., 177*; Wm., 558, 623*, 753*, 970, 971, 975*, 1039, 1206, 1217, 1368*; Mr., 1420; Rev., 1285*; —, 438, 1195, 1284, 1285, 1311, 1476

Knightly, Mary, 1251; Thos., 1251

Knigt, see Knight

Knipe, Ann, 622; Chas., 622; Eliz., 429; Hen., 429; Jas., 797; Joan, 429; Mic., 429*

Knolles (Knollis, Knollys), see Knowles

Knotsford (Knottesford), Geo., 442*; John, 1139, 1140; Mary, 442; —, 1316

Knott, see Nott

Knottesford, see Knotsford

Knoville (or Onvill), Rog. de, 1237

Knowles (Knolles, Knollis, Knollys), Ann(e), 584, 933; Arthur, 583*; Betty, 564; Bogo, 1238; Eliz., 583, 933*; Rev. Fran., 567; Geo., 563; John, 563, 906, 1208, 1209*; Rev. John, 1428; Joseph, 933*; Leonard, 564; Ric., 563, 583, 584; Rob., 1495; Rev. Rob., 643; Sarah, 1208, 1209; Sybilla, 1495; Rev. Thos., 1502*; Wm., 1209; Rev. Mr., 994; —, 1209; fam., 558, 778

Knox, Geo. Hannah Grogen, 959; Hannah, 959;
    Rev. Hen., 161, 166; Thos. Grogan, 959
Knyfe, Wal. le, 1259
Knyt, see Knight
Kun, Agnes, 1483
Kydun, Nic., 1102
Kyll, see Keel
Kynard (Kinard), Mary, 1427; Matilda, 1233; Nic.,
    1233; Wm., 1427
Kynardesley, Gil. de, 801; —, 915
Kynemersbury, see Kimbury
Kyng—, John, 1404
Kynge, see King
Kyngestone, see Kingston
Kynget, Thos., 1238
Kyngewelle, Rob., 1314
Kyngham, Thos., 1093
Kyngston, see Kingston
Kyngton, see Kington
Kynred, see Kenred
Kynseth, Wal., 1552
Kyntynge, Agnes, 1313
Kyrke, see Kirk
Kyrle (Curll, Kerle, Kirle), Barbara, 875 n, 1235*,
    1236; Eliz., 332; Gabriel, 332; Jas., 1235*, 1236;
    Mary, 176, 749; Ric., 214; Rob., 214; Sir W., 875 n;
    Wm., 176; Col., 915
Kyrrhat, Wm., 188
Kyte, see Kite

La Rose, John, 1272
Lacey (Laci, Lacie), see Lacy
Lack, Rachael, 772; Rob., 772
Lacy (Lacey, Laci, Lacie, Lacye), Agnes de, 1005;
    Ann, 1536; Dan., 1473*; Edw., 1582*; Eleanor,
    1473; Emme(line) (de), 523, 1015; Gil. (de), 638,
    1005, 1015; Hannah, 1582; Hugh, 1005, 1475;
    John, 1536, 1539; Rev. John, 1329; Mary, 1159*;
    Rob., 1475; Rog. (de), 365, 568, 574, 638, 690,
    766, 1005, 1015*, 1091, 1201, 1322*, 1421*, 1475,
    1482, 1518; Rog. de, earl of Hereford, 1482; Sam.,
    1159*, 1160; Sarah, 1582; W. de, 1201*; Wal. (de),
    523, 1016, 1060, 1077*, 1082, 1322*, 1431, 1485;
    — (de), 1091, 1421, 1475*, 1482*; fam., 1043
Ladbrook, Mary, 1391; Susanna, 1391
Ladd, Ann, 847; John, 847
Lady, Edith, 367
Lagraste, Nic., 1314; —, 1311
Laight (Lates, Layght, Layt), Benj., 1272; Edw.,
    1272*; Eliz., 1272*; Francis, 1272; Hester, 1272;
    Rev. J. J., 1220, 1476; John, 1043, 1272*, 1421*;
    Rev. John Jas., 1477; Joseph, 1272*; Lydia,
    1272*; Phil., 1043; Thos., 1272*; Wm., 1272*;
    Withers, 1272; and see Lyte
Lake, Hen., 1138; Rev. John, 808; Wm., 597, 604
Lamb (Lambe), Alice, 540; Ann, 210, 540; Anselm,
    1165; Caroline, 15; Cicely, 727; Esther, 592;
    Francis, 486; Rev. Francis, 486, 1387; Jas., 592;
    John, 540, 543, 555, 727, 746; Jonathan, 542;
    Marg., 542; Mary, 542, 746; Mat., 394; Penelope,
    15; Ric., 15*; Rob., 1065; Thos., 210; Rev.
    Thos., 135, 139, 140; Wm., 897

Lamballe, Dominique, 1088
Lambe, see Lamb
Lambert (Lambard, Lambart), Anne, 428, 796;
    Ant., 186, 429*; Cath., 429; Chas., 907, 1066;
    Edith, 186, 428; Edm. (later Edw.), 533; Eliz.,
    235, 337, 428*, 429; Frances, 1066; Hen., 544,
    546, 547; Joanna, 429; John, 428*; Nixon, 428,
    429; Priscilla, 429; Ric., 533*, 1092; Sabina,,
    429; Stephen, 1574; Thos., 235*; Wm., 1420;
    Rev. Wm., 440, 1335; Winefrid, 533; —, 894,
    1017, 1092
Lambley (Lamly), Ann, 1103; Thos., 850; Wm.,
    1103
Lambrick (Lambric), Betty, 669; Mat., 1217; Sam.,
    669; Wm., 669
Lamburn, Alice, 658; Eliz., 1213; Mat., 1213;
    Thos., 658
Lamly, see Lambley
Lammare, Wm., 1483
Lampitt (Lampet, Lamport), Ann, 1457; Lionel,
    1459; Rev. John, 1031; —, 1460
Lampton, John, 863
Lancaster [peerage], Aveline, countess of, 1120;
    Blanche, duchess of, 1403; Edm., earl of, 869,
    1403; Edw., earl of, 507, 1120; Hen., duke of,
    769*, 1403; Hen., earl of, 769, 1403; Maud,
    countess of, 769; duke of, 507 n; earls of, 1316;
    and see Gaunt, John of
Lance, Betty, 1249; Eliz., 1248*; John, 542; Ric.,
    1249*
Lanceester, —, 1293
Land, Anne, 832, 950; Edw., 442, 505, 832; Eliz.,
    670, 1507; Humph., 670*, 1434; Joan, 1434;
    John, 670, 950; Thos., 670, 1507; Mr., 206; and
    see Londe
Lander (Launder), Francis, 1397; Geo., 973*;
    Mary, 973
Landon, Eliz., 550; Jonathan, 550
Landrake, —, 708
Lane (l'Asne, Lasne, Inthelane), Abigail, 584;
    Abraham, 623; Ann(e), 837, 949, 1400*; Cath.,
    948; Dan., 584*; Rev. Dan., 613; Dinah, 108;
    Edith, 429; Edm., 386; Edw., 111, 425; Eliz., 111,
    295, 466, 468, 486, 1200*, 1389; Emmanuel,
    514*; Esther, 584, 802; Francis, 1164, 1165;
    Hannah, 194, 442; Hen., 335; Hugh, 1043*; Jane,
    77, 110, 349 n, 468, 514; Joan, 1164; John, 76,
    77, 109, 110, 111, 465, 517*, 683*, 803, 835,
    1013, 1165, 1200*, 1259, 1389, 1400; Lettice,
    949; Lydia (Lidia), 803, 1389; Marg., 768;
    Margery, 335; Mary, 77, 111, 768, 802, 803, 814,
    1200, 1372, 1446; Mat., 584; Rebeckah, 468;
    Reg., 708 n; Ric., 335, 360 n, 442, 1013, 1165*;
    Rob., 386; Sam., 442; Sarah, 77, 109, 386;
    Silvester, 584; Susanna(h), 584, 1200; T., 1132;
    Thos., 468, 851, 949, 1078, 1164*, 1200*; Rev.
    Thos., 100, 103, 449; Wal., 335; Wm., 77*, 138,
    188, 429, 466, 483, 484, 517, 670, 687, 768, 788,
    802*, 803*, 814, 837, 948, 949*, 1047, 1200,
    1372, 1390*; Wm. Mayo, 1400*; Mr., 1165; —,
    1017, 1078, 1165, 1355, 1475; fam., 482; and see
    Lone

Laney, —, 1101

Lanfranc, archbishop, 183

Lang (Lange), Edric, 713; Stephen, 1160; W., 1316

Langley (Langele, Langely), Alice, 1082; Christian, 1082, 1351; Edm., duke of York, 1255; Edw., 1082*; Frances, 710; Francis, 1275; Geof. (Jeffery, Jeoffrey) de, 1082*; Isabel, 1082*; J., 1420; John (Johan)(de), 361, 710, 1032, 1033, 1082*; Matilda, 1351; Phil., 710, 1159; Rob. de, 1082; Wal. de, 1082*; Wm., 1082; —, 1082, 1159, 1351, 1392; fam., 365, 833

Langman, Joy, 212; Wm., 212

Langstone, —, 1257

Langton, Eliz., 488, 641; Jo[a]ne, 1554; John, 487, 488; Mary, 151; Nic., 151; Ric., 641; Rev. Wm., 487, 553*, 554*; Wm. Gore, 81, 487, 488; Mr., 553; fam., 487

Lansdown, Ruth, 411; Wm., 411; Lord, see Granville, Geo.

Lanston, Francis, 1517

Lantemersh, John de, 720; Simon, 720

Lapley, Cath., 1108; Clement, 1341, 1342*, 1343; Dan., 1342, 1343; Jas., 1342, 1343, 1537; Joseph, 1340, 1342, 1343; Mary, 35, 1342, 1343, 1537; Ric., 35; Sarah, 1343

Lapthorne, Rev. Ant., 651, 1021

Lapworth, Ann, 569; Cath., 693; Dorothy, 569; Hen., 569; John, 569*; Ric., 569; Thos., 693

Larborde, John, 410

Large, Anne, 861; Frances, 140; Jas. Parker, 1248; Joan, 1481; John, 1481; Joseph, 140; Martha, 1248; Phebe, 1248*; Sam., 1248*, 1258; Sarah, 1248; Susanna, 1248*; Susanna Slatter, 1248

Lark (Larke), Adam, 1027; —, 910 n

Larner, Sarah, 130

Laroche, Dame Eliz. Rachel Ann, 1156; Sir Jas., 49; Sir —, bt., 1156

Larrence, see Lawrence

Larton, John, 701; Mary, 701*; Owen, 701*; Sarah, 33; Wm., 30, 33, 700*, 701

Lasborough (Lasberg, Lasseburgh), Marg. de, 1215; W. de, 1215*; Wm. de, 783

Lascelles, Laur. de, 1033

Laslett, Mr., 1237

l'Asne (Lasne), see Lane

Lasseburgh, see Lasborough

Laston, Thos., 1553

Latch, Dan., 175; John, 175; Ric., 1551; Sarah, 175

Latcham, Chas., 1327; Dorcas, 1327; Eliz., 746; Thos., 746*

Lates, see Laight

Latham, Amy, 693; Anne, 693; Chas., 835; Dorothy, 693; Edw., 660; Farnham, 835; Hester, 693; John, 660, 693*; Judith, 662; Rev. Lawr., 1005; Mary, 660*, 693, 703, 835; Thos., 662; Wm., 660, 693*

Latheburye, Rev. Thos., 1331

Lathropp, Hannah, 412; Ric., 412; Rob., 412

Latimer (Latimore, Latymer), Hannah, 338; Hugh, 221; Jacob, 20; Rev. Jas., 1385; Rob., 338; —, bishop, 197 n, 1423

Latimer [peerage], see Neville, passim

Latner, R., 985; —, 985*

Latymer, see Latimer

Latyn, Mat., 1540

Laud, Jas., 1431; John, 1010

Lauende, Rob. atte, 1127

Laughton, see Lawton

Lauley, see Lawley

Launder, see Lander

Laurence, see Lawrence

Laverick, Victory, 1160

Lavers, 1566

Lavington, Cath., 1019*

Law, Betty, 1576; John, 1289; Rev. Lancelot, 739, 740; Wm., 1289

Lawdy, Sir Ric., 915

Lawford, Ann, 1171; Christian, 1171; Dan., 1171; Rev. Dan., 198; Grace, 1171; John, 45, 1157*, 1554; Rebekah, 1171; Ric., 1171*; Rob., 1171*; Thos., 1171; —, 1160

Lawley (Lauley, Lawly), Jane, 993; Thos., 1583; Rev. Wm. (Willelm), 1132*

Lawrence (Larrence, Laurence, Lawrance), A., 1063; Agnes, 1501; Alice, 1008; Anna, 971*; Ann(e), 116, 374*, 383*, 981, 1063, 1099; Ant., 505, 1057*, 1059*, 1063*, 1064*, 1263*; Rev. Ant. Cocks, 1442; Barrow, 915; Beata, 118*, 1079; Betty, 399; Cath., 64, 1498*; Christian, 1498; Culpeper, 1057, 1263*; Dan., 835, 1007,, 1008*; Dianisia, 261; Dulcibella, 116; Edm., 261, 1498*, 1499, 1502; Edw., 55*, 167, 1098*, 1099, 1501*; Eleanor, 971, 1078, 1324; Eliz., 253, 254, 729, 949, 950, 958, 971, 1025, 1059, 1063, 1088, 1098, 1307, 1350; Frances (Francis), 64, 117*; G., 1101; Geo., 254*, 374, 537, 1098*, 1099, 1350*, 1542; Giles, 1088, 1498, 1542; Guy, 51, 1300, 1329; Rev. Guy, 1300, 1313; Hannah, 317, 1350; Hen., 949, 1064; Hester, 118, 1008; Rev. Hugh, 1504; Isaac, 253, 254, 374, 383; Jabez, 1025; Jas., 399*, 1498*, 1504; Jane, 388, 1099; Joan, 1307, 1498; John, 261, 317, 729*, 800, 949*, 1025, 1057, 1098, 1112, 1323, 1498, 1502; Rev. John, 259, 704*, 1043, 1056*, 1502; Sir John, 1059; Jonathan, 1186; Joseph, 201, 1008, 1027; Littleton, 114, 115, 971, 1501*; Marg., 971*; Martha, 201; Mary, 114, 167, 253, 254, 388, 399, 504, 537, 949, 1007, 1013, 1057, 1063*, 1079*, 1098*, 1396, 1498*; Nic., 1059; Rev. Phil., 630; R., 1061, 1062, 1064; Rebeckah, 505; Ric., 1059*, 1501*, 1502*; Rob., 117, 118, 504, 971, 1057*, 1059*, 1061, 1062*, 1063*, 1064*, 1501*; Rev. Rob., 64, 114*, 117; Sir Rob., 1059; Rob. Colles, 1263; Roger(s), 374, 1057, 1093; Rev. Roger, 696; Sam., 55, 1008, 1013, 1026, 1098, 1307*; Rev. Sam., 785, 1186; Sarah, 55*, 254, 374*, 949, 1008, 1026; Susanna, 261*; T., 1312; Thos., 64, 118*, 958*, 1079, 1112, 1502; W., 1063, 1064, 1078, 1083; W. L., 1061, 1091, 1093; Wal., 1056, 1058, 1059, 1063*, 1064; Wal. Lawr., 1059, 1060, 1442; Wm., 113, 115, 116*, 117, 167*, 253, 254*, 374, 388*, 950*, 971, 981, 1007*, 1057, 1059*, 1078*, 1079,

1098, 1324, 1501*; Wm. Edw., 1501; Dr., 1263; Mr., 1056; Rev., 1042; —, 1059, 1063, 1064, 1154, 1165; fam., 1059*

Lawson, Ann, 539; Eliz., 539; Jas., 754; John, 537, 539; Joseph, 1412; Mary, 754; Nat., 531, 534; Wm., 1415

Lawston, Rob., 1016

Lawton (Laughton), Anne, 1236; Eliz., 1236; John, 398, 1093; Thos., 683, 1236, 1238; —, 1016

Laxly, Ann, 1273

Lay, Anne de la, 1051; Hen. de la, 1051; John, 1481; Kezia, 1481; —, 985; and see Lee; Leigh

Layer, Joseph, 1303

Layght (Layt), see Laight

Layton, see Leighton

Le Neve, —, 515 n

Le Nautre, —, 552

Lea, see Lee

Leach, see Leech

Leaman, Dr. John, 1021

Lear (Leare), Ann., 1575*; Betty, 1159; Geo., 1575; John, 1159*; Ric., 1159; Wm., 212

Lecche (Leche), see Leech

Lechmere (Letchmere), Ant., 1165; Lord, 220 n; —, 1163

Leckhampton, John, 360

Ledbetear, John le, 1238

Leden, Wal. de, 1504

Ledgingham, Jacob, 1250; Jane, 1250; John, 1250

Lediard (Ledyard, Lidiard), Ann Fagg, 1576; Anne, 201, 1576; Deborah, 510; Phil., 510; S. B., 1139; T., 1139*, 1201; Thos., 1576; Wm., 201, 1121

Lee (Lea), Abel, 815*; Alex., 203; Ann(e), 237, 811, 1063; Betty, 1125; Chas. Hen. Dillon, 220; Rev. Chris., 1429; Dan., 803; Dinah, 963; Dorcas, 677; Eliz., 124*, 803; Esther, 1092; Geo., 1092; Geo. Hen., earl of Lichfield, 220; Griffin, 1063, 1064; Hannah, 958; Hen., 236, 237, 238, 1341*; Hester, 815*; J., 1312, 1423; Jas., 124; Joan de, 1015; John, 677, 803, 850, 868; Joseph, 963; Marg., 963; Mark, 811; Mary, 238, 803*, 1330; Ric., 815, 1015, 1063; Sir Ric., kt., 544, 893; Rob., 958; Sarah, 317, 850; Thos. (de), 124*, 317, 803, 1015, 1092*, 1165; Wm., 677, 858, 1415, 1420; —, 1092; and see Lay; Leigh

Leech (Leach, Lecche, Leche), Ann, 339; Ant., 731*; Eliz., 229, 399*, 978; Francis, 1469; Hannah, 339, 1068; Hester, 59; Isaac, 731*; Joan, 731; John (de), 59*, 339, 399*, 568, 791, 1068*; Mary, 59, 399*, 731, 1088; Sam., 229, 339, 731; Sarah, 731; Stephen de, 1197; Thos., 339; Wm., 228, 229*, 399*, 1088; Mrs., 801

Leeke, John, 573; Mary, 573

Leeson, see Lysons

Leet, Christian, 619; S., 619

Leg, see Legg

Lega, see Leigh

Legard, Frances, 409; Sir John, bt., 409

Legate (Legat), Rob. the, 1339; Thos., 1329

Legg (Leg, Legge), Ann, 563*; Chas. Asgill, 1400; Eliz., 563, 564; Geo., 730, 981; John, 564, 730, 1297; Mary, 564, 730, 1068; Nic., 1121, 1297*;

Rosamond, 563; Sam., 563*; Sarah, 563, 730, 1159(?); Thos., 563*, 1140; Wm., 563*, 1159(?), 1420; —, 1052

Leggare, John, 1478

Legge, see Legg

Legh, see Leigh

Leicester [peerage], Marg., countess of, 724; Rob., earl of, 893, 1522; lord of, 1334; and see Cooke, Rob.; Dudley, Rob.; Montfort, Simon de

Leigh (Lega), Alice, 1529; Anne, 23, 25*, 257, 817, 820; Lady Caroline, 25, 36; Cassandra, 23; Cath., 23*; Chas., 23; Lady Dionessa, 842; Eliz., 22, 23*, 130, 408, 817*, 1529; Dame Eliz., 817*; Emma, 23; Geo., 256, 817; Grace, 996; Hen., 23, 440; Hester, 1529; Isabella, 817; Jas., 21*, 23*, 24, 25, 36, 216, 255, 408*; Jas. Hen., 21*, 817; Jane, 1332; Joanna, 22, 23; John, 996, 1538; Rev. John, 128, 130; Marg., 817; Mary, 23*, 24*, 25*, 255, 256, 258, 1014, 1529; Rev. Peter, 258; Peter Neve, 258; Rachel, 23; Rowland, 816; Sir Rowland, 1195; Sam., 1014; Theophilus, 21*, 22*, 23*, 24*, 25*, 130, 255, 817; Rev. Theophilus, 21, 255; Thos., 23*, 816, 817, 820; Rev. Thos., 21*, 255, 817; Sir Thos., 216, 1332; Thos. Chas., Viscount Tracy, 638, 709*, 710*, 1333; Tryphena, 130; W., 1512, 1513; Wm. (de), 21, 22*, 23, 24*, 128*, 817*, 1005, 1529*; Rev. Wm., 24; Sir Wm., kt., 256, 257, 817; Lord, 1332; Mr., 1139; fam., 255, 816, 817; and see Lay; Lee; Leigh; Leys; Lyes

Leighton (Layton), Ann, 584; Eliz., 1510; John, 873; Joseph, 584, 873; Mary, 70*; Ric., 583, 584; Rob., 1510, 1511; Susannah, 583; Thos., 70*; Wm., 70, 584

Leivers, see Lievers

Leland, —, 29, 158, 159, 178, 179, 228, 236, 420, 552, 553, 754, 792, 895, 1120, 1189, 1261, 1287, 1309, 1339, 1345, 1362, 1474, 1475

Lely, —, 349 n, 393n*, 719 n*

Lempster, Jane, 591; Wm., Lord, 591

Lench, Rev. Wm., 1215

Lenard (Lennard), see Leonard

Lennot, Anne, 834, 835; Jonathan, 834, 835; Rob., 834

Lensdin, Eliz., 1338; Sam., 1338

Lenthall (Lenthal), Wm., 255, 1458; —, 546

Leofrice, earl of Mercia, 927

Leolin, prince of Wales, 98

Leon, Agnes, 1148 (?); —, 1148 (?)

Leonard (Lenard, Lennard), Abraham, 932*; Ann, 958*, 1019, 1307*; Betty, 468, 958; Bryan, 932; Edith, 317; Edm., 932; Eliz., 932, 958, 1018; Emma, 932*; Hannah, 1307; Isaac, 211, 1307; John, 468*, 958*, 1018, 1307*; Mary, 468*, 932, 958*, 1018; Oswell, 932; Sam., 419*, 1019*; Sarah, 419, 1018, 1307; Stephen, 317; T., 1195; Thos., 468, 932*, 1307; W., 1312; Wm., 958*, 1307*; —, 1223

Leornare, Nic. le, 1363

Lepegate (Lepeyatt), see Lippiatt

Leslie (Lesley), Chas. Howard, 407; Rev. John, 1482*; —, 1402

Lester (Leyster), Cath., 1330; Malachi, 1330; Thos., 190
Letall, John, 1245
Letchmere, see Lechmere
Lethenard, Joan, 293; John, 293
Lethieulier (Lethifullier), Anne, 11057; Sir John, kt., 1057; Smart, 1064
Lett, Francis, 514; John, 514; Mary, 514*
Lettis, Alice, 1034; Lieut. Ric., 1034
Leuin, see Lewin
Leuric (fl. 1066), 1055, 1077, 1078, 1485
Leutris, Wm., 1038
Levatt, Alice, 1139; John, 1139
Leveridge, see Loveridge
Leversage (Leversegge, Liversage), John, 747; Peter, 1216*, 1217; Mr., 980; fam., 568
Lewellin (Lewelling, Lewelyn), see Llewellin
Lewes, see Lewis
Lewin (fl. 1066)(Leuin), 1032, 1055, 1091, 1482*
Lewin (Lewen, Lewyn, Louwyn), John, 1233; Kath., 489; Ric., 1404; Thos., 489
Lewis (Lewes, Lewys), Abraham, 930; Ambrose, 780, 781; Ann(e), 55, 467*, 598*, 780, 837, 1301*, 1305, 1307, 1413, 1438, 1571; Barbara, 250; Benedicta, 789; Benj., 735*, 1085*, 1573; Betty, 465, 782; Blanch, 250; Chas., 734, 789; Chas. Hanbury, 388; Christian, 1413; Craven, 411; Diana, 1241; Dorcas, 767; Dorothy, 15; Easter, 814; Edm., 543; Edw., 789*; Eleanor, 758, 808*; Eliz., 15, 467, 780*, 796, 814, 1008, 1175, 1316, 1381, 1438, 1571, 1575; Esther, 767; Frances, 734; Francis, 465; Gabriel, 1413; Geo., 250*, 411, 815, 1571*; Giles, 832; Hannah, 735, 1571; Hen., 412, 467, 597, 598*; J., 1312; Jas., 176, 1438; Jane, 735*, 923, 1413; Jenkin, 728; Joan, 83; John, 175, 337, 598*, 782, 814, 846, 1008, 1158*, 1175*, 1236, 1301, 1307, 1571, 1574, 1575*; Rev. John, 582, 767*, 768, 1539; Joseph, 597, 758, 907; Kitty, 1575; Marg., 728; Martha, 781; Mary, 411, 412, 467*, 597, 598, 735*, 789*, 797, 846, 907, 1143*, 1158, 1236, 1438, 1573; Morgan, 411, 1323; Nic., 1243; Obadiah, 923; Rev. Owen, 785; Prudence, 1515; Rasmea, 1236; Rebecca, 780*; Ric., 669, 780*, 1438*; Robert, 976; Sam., 731, 907, 1316, 1420; Sarah, 175, 604, 731, 789, 907, 1038, 1571; T., 1312; Thos., 48, 83*, 721, 780*, 862*, 923*, 1301*, 1307*, 1316*, 1572; Rev. Thos., 674, 829; Tim., 388*; W., 1215, 1216, 1323; Rev. W. P., 1143; Wal., 1370; Wm., 15, 55*, 175, 735, 780, 781, 837, 846, 907*, 923, 963, 1038, 1076, 1217, 1305*, 1348, 1515; Wm. Ebsworth, 598; Rev. Wm. Price, 1143*; —, 1317, 1322, 1381*; fam., 1323
Lewis de Bons, Rev. Peter, 999
Lewkenor (Lukenore), Eleanor, 560; Ric., 863
Lewton (Luton), Ann, 538*, 542; Betty, 1548; Dan., 1548*; Eliz., 213; Hannah, 213; Jas., 213; Jane, 213; John, 213*; Hen., 1583; Sam., 532, 538; Mary, 213, 491, 492*; Sarah, 213; Thos., 532, 538*, 542; Tobias, 491, 492; Wm., 213
Lewyn, see Lewin
Lewys, see Lewis

Leys, Eliz., 409; Evan, 409; Ric., 409; and see Leigh
Leyster, see Lester
Libland, Anne, 193; John, 193
Libby, Mr., 1215
Lichfield (Litchfield), Francis, 1085; Henrietta, 1085; Lady Joan, 913; earl of, see Lee, Geo.
Liddiatt, see Lydiatt
Lidiard, see Lediard
Lidiat, see Lydiatt
Lievers (Leivers), —, 1195, 1196
Lifeley (Liffully, Lifully), Grace, 569; Hen., 569; Mary, 423*; Ric., 423, 425
Ligan (Liggon), see Lygon
Lightbody, Ann, 1320; W., 1320
Lightbourne, Rebecca, 1064*, 1093; Mrs., 1501, 1502
Lightfoot, Anne, 899; Eliz., 898; Esther, 898; Rev. Jas., 1154; John, 1238; Rev. John, 198; Rev. Joseph, 1152, 1154; Rev. Ric., 1147; Sarah, 906; Stephen, 898*, 899, 1039; Wm., 906
Ligon, see Lygon
Lile, see Lisle
Lillington (Lilington), —, 1381*
Lilly, Honora, 289; Rev. Rob., 288, 289; Wm., 288 n
Limas, Ralph de, 1074
Limbrick, Alice, 1484; Anna, 1343*; Ann(e), 524, 1343*; Chas., 1484; Edm., 203; Eliz., 1343*; Hester, 254; Hugh, 1484; Isaac, 1551; Jas., 1484; Jane, 254; Joane, 1551; John, 254*; Joseph, 1343*; Mary, 203, 1343, 1484; Ric., 1343*; Sarah, 1343; Thos., 524, 1484; Wm., 1456; —, 1346
Limesi (Lymeseye), Nic., 1388; Ralph de, 1322
Linch, Ann, 814; Eliz., 1164; Hen., 1164; Jas., 814; John, 814*
Lincoln, Alice, countess of, 638
Linden, see Lyndon
Lindsay, Rev. John, 1228
Linfield, Hester, 1413
Lingen, Ann, 1002*; Blanch, 1002*; Edw., 1002; Eliz., 899, 1002; Frances, 1002; Giles, 899*; Hen., 1002; John, 1002; Marg., 899*; Rachael, 1002; Rob., 1002; Rog., 1002*; T., 1002; Thos., 899*, 1002*; —, 1001
Linke, Ann, 959; Eliz., 1298, 1299; Hester, 1298; Mary, 1298*, 1299, 1301; Ric., 1299; Sarah, 1301; Susan(na), 1298, 1299*; Thos., 959, 1298*, 1299*, 1301; Wm., 1301; —, 1311*, 1312
Linley, Isabel, 124; Martha, 124; Wm., 124
Linnell, John, 1289
Linnet, Wm., 1307
Linton, Eliz., 932; John, 932; Sarah, 932
Lintridge, Wm., 1289
Lippiatt (Lepegate, Lepeyate, Lipyat, Lupeyete, Lypeatt), John, 1307; Matillda, 1314; Ric. atta, 1363(?); Thos., 1312; Wal. atte, 1491; Wm., 1082, 1307; —, 1311
Lippincott, Dame Cath., 435*, 577, 825; Sir H. Cann, 1419; Sir Hen., bt., 435, 577, 825, 1415; Sir Hen. Cann, 1415; Dame Kath., 1415; —, 1419

Lipyat, see Lippiatt

Lisle (de Insula, Lile, Lyle), Florence de, 1014*;
Joan (de), 1014, 1051; John de, 1014, 1051;
Marg. de, 1051; Nic., 1052; R., 1092*; Rob. (de),
1014, 1015; Wal. de, 1014, 1051; Wm. de,
1014*, 1051*; —, 1015, 1051, 1092; fam., 1148

Lisle [peerage], see Talbot, Thos. and —; Warren,
David

Lister, Mary Trye, 1501; T. Y., 1501*

Liston (Listun), Thos., 12, 13; Capt. Thos., 66

Litchfield, see Lichfield

Litsell, Rev. Thos., 1154

Little (Littel), Adam, 587; Alice, 587, 873; Ann(e),
787, 857, 964, 1006; Eleanor, 787; Eliz., 347,
348, 587, 1007; Francis, 1278; Giles, 348; Grace,
1007*, 1172; Jasper, 1510, 1511; John, 347,
587*, 787, 846, 857, 1006, 1007*; Josiah, 347*,
348; Joyce, 984; Marg., 1007; Mary, 587*, 984,
1007; Rob. (le), 581, 964; Sarah, 846*;
Susannah, 587; Thos., 348, 587, 984, 1007*,
1217, 1510, 1511; Wal., 463, 1039; Wm., 857,
873; —, 985*, 1216

Littlecote, Thos. de, 1259

Littlepage, Joseph, 407

Littleton (Lytelton, Lyttleton), Anselm, 872; John,
872; Mary, 830, 873; Rev. Ric., 829, 830; Ruth,
872; Sir Thos., 1421; Wm., 830, 873, 1403;
Lord, 157; Rev., 582

Litton, see Lytton

Livere, John, 1259

Liversage, see Leversage

Living (Lyvynge), John, 1583; Rev. W., 1323

Llen (LLan), Lucy, 633; Humph., 551 n, 552; J.,
1257; Rev. Rob., 551 n, 552, 553; Thos., 551 n*,
552

Llewellyn (Lewellin, Lewelling, Lewelyn,
Llewellin, Llewellying), Anne, 906; Betty, 1427;
Cath., 453; Eliz., 736; Geo., 837; Gil., 1172;
Hannah, 837*; John, 453; Moses, 837; Ric., 736,
1420; Sarah, 837, 1427; W., 1323; Wm., 837,
1427; Rev., 955; —, 906

Llot, Nic., 1513

Lloyd (Lloyde, Loyde), Ann(e), 873, 1435*;
Bridget, 1174; Cove, 1258; Dan., 1539; Edm.,
1435*; Edw., 1303; Eliz., 1174, 1435*, 1437*;
Geo., 619, 770, 985*, 1435*, 1437*; Hannah, 5;
Hen., 1514; Rev. Hen., 1516; Rev. Humph., 328,
579; Jas., 467*, 1200; John, 5, 226, 873, 1201,
1367; Rev. John, 13, 328, 764*, 1367, 1494;
Joseph, 5*; Marg., 1435; Martin, 1258; Mary, 5*,
164, 1174, 1367, 1369; Nat., 1135, 1367, 1472;
(or Floid), Rev. Nic., 1317; Poulden, 1475; Pyrke
Nat., 467; Radagund, 1435*; Rebecca, 1435*;
Ric., 744, 1435; Rev. Ric., 190; Sybill, 1440;
Thos., 1435*; Rev. Thos., 87, 668, 1494; Wal.,
161, 164, 1174; Wm., 221*, 1214, 1435; Rev.
Wm., 221, 606, 607, 1367*, 1368; Wm., bishop,
220; Wm. Freeman, 1135; Dr., 1475*; Mr., 1,
1440; Rev., 328; —, 1177, 1440; (or Floyd), —,
1054; and see Floyd; Lude

Lloyd Baker, see Baker, Thos. John Lloyd and Rev.
Wm. Lloyd

Loader, see Loder

Locett, Edm., 485; Marg., 485

Lock (Locke), Ann, 988; Dorothy, 228, 1165;
Hannah, 751; Hester, 751*; John, 228*, 751, 772,
1165; Joseph, 751*; Mary, 228, 1165; Mat.,
1165; Mic., 413; Phil., 751*; Rachael, 772; Rob.,
751, 772; Sarah, 751, 988, 989; Susannah, 751;
Thos., 988*, 989; Wm., 751; —, 1160; fam., 228

Lockey (Locky), Eliz., 1249; Hopeful(l), 1249,
1258; Joseph, 1249; Mary, 1184*; Rev. R., 1168;
Ric., 1184*, 1255; Wm., 1184

Lockier, see Lockyer

Lockley, Ric., 1509

Lockstone, Mary, 1119; Sampson, 1119

Lockwood, John, 123

Locky, see Lockey

Lockyer (Lockier, Lokier), Deborah, 751; Edw.,
1551; Eliz., 751, 1551; John, 775; Leonard, 775;
Mary, 1531*; Rebecca, 751, 752; Sam., 750;
Thos., 751*, 752; Wm., 749, 1531*

Loder (Loader, Lowder), Ann, 1573*; Beeke, 883;
Chas., 794; Francis, 793, 794*; Hester, 1315;
Jane, 794*; John, 793, 794*, 1126; Rev. John,
793; Lettice, 795; Mary, 883*, 1126; Penelope,
794*; Ric., 1315; Rob., 793*, 794*, 795; Sarah,
1321; Dr. T., 1321; Thos. Edwards, 1573; Wm.,
1003*, 1573; —, 1126; fam., 792*

Lodge (Loge), Dan., 768*; Eliz., 468, 789*; Geo.,
762, 822; Jas., 1401*; Jane, 762, 789, 822; John
of, 1314; Joseph, 789; Rev. Joseph, 198; Marg.,
768; Mary, 306, 307, 608, 822, 1401*; Sarah,
276, 1401; Thos., 608*, 1403; Rev. Thos., 306,
307, 689, 909, 910, 1122; Wm., 276, 468*, 789

Loe, see Lowe

Loge, see Lodge

Loggan, see Loggin

Logger, Thos., 360 n

Loggin (Loggan, Loggins), Anne, 848; Rev. Edw.,
1422; Hannah, 1041; John, 849, 850, 1041, 1422;
Rev. John, 848; Joyce, 1001; Mic., 1376; Muriel,
595; Rev. Rob., 1001; Sarah, 850*; Wm., 849,
1222; Rev. Wm., 848*; —, 401

Lokier, see Lockyer

Lolle, see Lowle

Londe, W., 985; and see Land

London, John, 360 n

Lone, Thos. atte, 1292; and see Lane

Long (Longe), Adam (le), 1074; Alice, 261; And.,
77; Ann(e), 253, 282, 854, 1100, 1167, 1409,
1551, 1573; Ant., 77; Arthur, 1419; Betty, 49,
1231; Calthrop, 842; Cecilia, 1404; Chas., 36,
1344; Chris. (Xr.), 1162; D., 1434; Dan., 36,
1100; Dinah, 1107; Dionysia, 839, 842; Edm.,
77; Edw., 724, 730, 731; Elenor, 77; Eliz., 118*,
138, 229, 253, 261, 348, 587, 832, 1100, 1229*,
1530; Frances, 1231; Francis, 177; Geo., 77, 261,
348, 587*, 854*, 1046, 1098*, 1378; Hannah,
938, 1047; Hen., 177, 1047; Isabella, 587, 854;
Jas., 36, 49; Joane (Jhone, Jone), 77, 676, 1098;
John (le), 36, 49*, 118, 138, 261*, 532, 815*,
938*, 1102, 1187, 1231*, 1313, 1369*, 1409;
Rev. John, 860; Joseph, 36, 211*, 282, 1100;

Joseph Hatton, 1231; Martha, 938; Mary, 36, 77, 177*, 211*, 229, 724, 730, 1511; Nat., 177*, 1369; Nic., 1313; Col. Parker, 1198; Sir Ric., kt., 825; Rob., 282*, 1098; Rog., 229, 676*; Sam., 1168, 1551; Sarah, 77, 261*, 858, 1168; Sarah Neale, 1168; Susannah, 1514; T., 1162; Thos., 118*, 211, 261, 832, 858, 1369, 1514; Wal., 13, 77*, 253, 497, 1530; Sir Wal., 1032; Wm. (de), 229, 261*, 353, 532, 1102, 1107, 1167, 1229*, 1231*, 1258, 1420, 1539, 1573; —, 1020, 1311, 1381; fam., 1232

Longbottom, Jane, 1379; Priscilla, 1379; —, 1379

Longchamp (Longcamp), Geof. de, 766; Isabella, 1401; —, 1401

Longdon (Longden), Dorothy (Dorothn), 1158; Eliz., 811, 813; Giles, 824*; Hester, 703; Rev. J., 1356, 1485; John, 813; Rev. John, 131, 606, 1484, 1485*; Lionel, 1158; Ric., 703; Sarah, 824; Thos., 597; Wm., 811*; Rev. Mr., 1483

Long-Espee (Long Espe, Long Espee), Ela, countess of Salisbury, 690*; Matilda, 1259; Wm., earl of Salisbury, 324, 690*

Longe, see Long

Longeneye, Stephen de, 1292

Longfield, Isabella, 1370; Jeffery, 1370

Longford, Anne, 331*, 1049; Cath., 1501*; Dorothy, 1063; Edith, 1497; Eliz., 331*, 675*, 1501*; Francis, 1029; Geo., 495, 567; Rev. Geo., 495; Hester, 1063; J., 1063; Jane, 331; Jo[a]ne, 1050; John, 240, 331*, 1501; Rev. John, 672*, 675*, 800, 1501; John Trye, 314; Joseph, 1497; Mary, 567, 800, 1029, 1049, 1501; Nic., 1497*, 1501*; Ric., 1049, 1050*, 1501, 1502; Sam., 1361, 1497*; Simon, 1497; Thos., 803, 1049, 1057, 1063*; W., 1063, 1064; Wm., 567, 675, 1057, 1063; Rev. Wm., 1063; Yiddeth, 1497; —, 1063*, 1501

Longmate, —, 996 n

Longmore, —, 1288, 1381*

Longstreth, Ann, 622; Eliz., 622; John, 622*; Judith, 622; Mary, 472; Ric., 472, 622*

Longworth, Rev. R., 1331

Looker, see Luker

Loosby (Lousby), Rev. Edw., 1277, 1290

Lorange, see Loringe

Lord (Lorde), Agnes, 1062; Alice, 1063; Eliz., 203, 1064, 1226; Esther, 1367*; Hen., 1063; Humph., 1063; J., 524; Jas., 1369; John, 430, 689; Rev. John, 1127; Laur., 1226; Martha, 1367; Mary, 1058, 1064*; R., 1064; Rachel, 24; Rob., 1058*, 1064*; Rog., 1367; Thos., 1062*; W., 1061; Wm., 216, 1062, 1063, 1367, 1369; —, 1064*

Loringe (Lorange, Lorrenge, Lorringe), Abigail, 397; Anne, 397, 986; Edw., 397; Eliz., 1471; Frances, 397, 1469; Giles, 16; Hannah, 16; John, 16; Thos., 394, 397*, 986, 1210, 1469, 1471; Capt., 358; fam., 393

Lorymer, John, 1292

Louecok (Louecoke), see Lucock

Louekin, see Loveken

Louel, see Lovell

Louenhulle, John, 1363

Loughborn, —, 1217

Louich, Rob., 1217

Louis XI of France, 852 n

Lousby, see Loosby

Louwyn, see Lewin

Lovecoke, see Lucock

Loveday, Anne, 973*; Esther, 973; Hen., 973*; John, 972, 973*; Mary, 972, 973*; Sarah, 973*; Wm., 972–3*; Dr., 792

Lovegrove, Betty, 1453; John, 1453

Loveken (Louekin), Alice, 1069; —, 1017

Lovel, see Lovell

Lovelace, Lord, 358*

Lovell (Louel, Lovel), Francis, 1015; Francis, Lord Lovel, 1015; Frideswide, 1015; Hen., 778 n; Joan, 1015*; John, 1139; Sir John, 1015*; John, Lord Lovell, 1015*; Lady Marg., 721 n; Maud, 1015; Ric., 111, 1172; Rob., 1455; Susan, 1169; Thos., 836; Thos., Lord Lovell, 721 n; Wm., Lord Lovell, 1015; Lord, 1441; —, 1169, 1455; fam., 1015, 1538

Lovelock, Abraham, 344; Eliz., 124, 125, 846; J., 1256; John, 212; Jonathan, 124, 125; Mary, 344; Ric., 846; Wm., 125

Loveridge (Leveridge, Loverich, Loveridg), Ann(e), 906, 907, 978; Hannah, 978; John, 978*, 1069; Mary, 549; R., 976; Ric., 978; Sarah, 978; Thos., 907; Wm., 549, 906, 907*, 978; —, 1317*

Lovering, Dan., 730; Eliz., 1058; J., 1064*; John, 730, 948*; Mary, 948, 1045; Wm., 1045*, 1058

Lovesey (Lovesy, Luffesey), Ann, 644; Chas., 644, 1075; Eliz., 1075, 1476; John, 644; Judith, 300; Justinian, 569, 1058; Mary, 644; Sarah, 1058; Thos., 1216; Wm., 644

Lovet, Barbara, 904; John, 904; Joseph, 904

Low, see Lowe

Lowder, see Loder

Lowe (Loe, Low), Alice, 1363; Anne, 34, 1455; Edw., 906; Eliz., 1361; Gabriel, 966; Sir Gabriel, kt., 34, 966; John, 296, 906, 1318; Mary, 966; Phillis, 1488; Rebecca, 1490; Ric., 1455, 1488, 1490; Rev. Rog., 1372; Thos., 1361; Tim., 966*; Wm., 348; —, 1455

Lower, Rev. Rob., 1021

Lowle (Lolle), Agnes, 1392; Benj., 1420; John, 1420; Joseph, 1175; Rob., 1175; Rev. Rob., 739, 1177; Sarah, 1175; Stephen, 1175; Rev. Wm., 817

[Lowth], Rob., bishop, 1223

Lowther, Sir John, bt., 771; Kath., 771

Lowton, W. F., 1014

Loxdale, —, 1441

Loyde, see Lloyd

Lucas, Anne, 1464*; Sir Chas., 1197; Edw., 173*; Eliz., 97, 1464; Hen., 97; Jas., 173; Jane, 924; John, 173, 1464*, 1473, 1477; Mary, 173*, 1464*; Rebecca, 1464; Stephen, 1348; Susanna, 1464*; Thos., 97, 924; Wm., 97, 1464; Dr., 327 n; Mr., 327*; —, 1288

Luce, Eliz., 1019; Esther, 1019; Grace, 1344; John, 1019*; Sarah, 1019; Thos., 1019*, 1344

Luckers, see Luker

Luckett, Eliz., 797*; Jas., 796; John, 884; Martha, 796*; Sarah, 636, 884; Thos., 796*, 797; Wm., 636; —, 797

Luckman, Eliz., 598; John, 598; Ric., 598*

Lucock (Louecok, Louecoke, Lovecoke, Lucoke), John, 1074; Nic., 1370; Ric., 1292; Wal., 1404; Wm., 1223, 1363

Lucy, Ann, 1441; Constance, 572, 866; Dorothy, 1372; Eliz., 509; Kath., 1201; Thos., 349, 1016, 1348; Sir Thos., 509, 572, 1372; W., 1016; Sir Wal., kt., 1082; Wm., 1016; —, 1402, 1441

Ludditt, John, 1065

Lude (Luyde), Adam atte, 1491; John de, 1376; Ric. atte, 1428; Wal. de (Ludlow), 1369; and see Lloyd

Luden, Eliz., 534; Wm., 534

Luders, Rev. Alex., 1503; Margaretta Penelope, 1503

Ludgrove, John, 1289

Ludlow, Ann, 388, 1107, 1117; Cath., 1109*; Chris., 1122; Dan., 1109, 1121; Ebenezer, 1109*, 1121; Edw., 976; Eleanor (Elenoer), 1251, 1257; Eliz., 1248*, 1250; Grace, 1252; Hannah, 1117; Jas., 388, 1121, 1546; Jane, 1546; Joan, 1251; John, 1117, 1248*, 1250, 1251*; Joseph, 334, 983; Mary, 334, 677, 757; Rachel, 1109; Sarah, 1257; Thos., 757, 1250, 1251, 1252, 1429; Wal. de, see Lude; Wm., 1107, 1551; Serjt., 1039; —, 328, 1074, 1121, 1123

Luerie (Lueri, Lurei, Lury), Rob. de, 1047; Rog. (de), 643, 667 n, 1032*, 1475; Sir Wm., 707; Earl [sic], 667; —, 1567

Luffe, Jane, 1038; Joseph, 1570; Marg., 1570; Mary, 1038*; Thos., 1038*

Luffesey, see Lovesey

Luffingham, Rev. Jas., 626; Rev. Jonathan, 1084, 1087; Mary, 1084; Rev. Ric., 626; Susannah, 1084; Rev. Wm., 626

Lukenore, see Lewkenor

Luker (Looker, Luckers), Edm., 1307; Eliz., 1497; Hen., 1182; Kath., 641; Mary, 555; Thos., 1499*; Wm., 555*, 1497*

Lumbard, Isaac, 976; Mary, 976

Lumley, Ric., 1140; Ric., earl of Scarborough, 599, 1140; Thos., 599

Lun, see Lunn

Lundberry, Eliz. Leaker, 411

Lunn (Lun, Lunne), Dinah, 486; Christian, 28; Eliz., 149*; John, 28*; Rev. Labeus (Lebbeus), 89, 147, 149*, 1387; Stephen, 486

Lupas, see Lupus

Lupeyete, see Lippiatt

Lupus (Lupas), Hugh, earl of Chester, 1219, 1335; Maud, 1335

Lurei (Lury), see Luerie

Lushington, Thos., 1298*

Lusty, John, 1187; Ric., 1138; Thos., 1146; Wm., 1138

Luther, —, 1154

Luton, see Lewton

Luttrell (Lutrell), Eliz. Jane, 1164; Sir John, 1132

Luxmoore, Dr. John, 1238

Luyde, see Lude

Lyche (or Weyver), Rev. Rob., 1346

Lydall, And., 1224; Anne, 1224; Mary, 1224

Lydian, John, 576

Lydiatt (Liddiatt, Lidiat), John, 1177; Joseph, 77; Sam., 741, 1177; Sarah, 77; Wm., 661

Lyes (Lye), Ann, 641; Hen., 1169; Jane, 1437; John, 641, 1272; Mary, 1272, 1276*; Rev. Nat., 447, 534, 764; Sarah, 1276*; Stephen, 1180; Wm., 1276*, 1437; —, 1494; and see Leigh

Lygon (Ligan, Liggon, Ligon), Arnold, 1101; Sir Arnold, 763; Cath., 330, 591; Eliz., 325, 330; Francis, 1251, 1492, 1494; Geo., 432, 593; Grace, 1251, 1492; Hen., 432; John, 330*, 331, 585 n, 1494; Kath., 595 n, 1492; Marg., 330; Reg., 325, 766; Reg. Pyndar, 766, 767; Ric., 330, 585, 851; Rog., 432, 591, 595 n; Thos., 452; Wm., 451, 764, 1492*, 1494; —, 328 n; fam., 325, 451, 763

Lyle, see Lisle

Lymerick (Lymerik), Eliz., 985; John, 1259; Thos., 985, 1201

Lymeseye, see Limesi

Lynchlade, John de, 1132

Lynde, Edith de la, 1077; Thos. de la, 1077

Lyndon (Linden), Capt. Chas., 1374; Eliz., 1374*; Dr., 327 n; Judge, 1374

Lyne, Cath., 437; Edw., 375*; Frances, 375; Hen., 437, 1494; Jane, 375, 1083; John, 437; Mary, 375; Thos., 1083, 1583

Lyner, John, 1428

Lynett, Johanna, 1139*; John, 1139; Ric., 1139; Rob., 696

Lyngyur, Wm., 1491

Lynscombe, Rev. Wm., 744

Lyons (Lyon), Rev. Ezekiel, 1154; J. W., 1485; Martha, 1582; Priscilla, 1582*; Thos., 1582; Wm., 1582

Lypeatt, see Lippiatt

Lyplofe, Ric., 1061

Lysons (Leeson, Lysane, Lysaune), Anna, 715*; Anna Maria, 714; Arthur, 714; Rev. D., 1031; Dan., 159, 161, 263, 342, 667, 672, 713*, 714*, 715*; Rev. Dan., 1031*; Eliz., 714, 715*; Esther, 715; Jas., 1395, 1402; John, 715*; Josepha Catherina Susanna, 1031; Maria, 715; Mary, 711 n, 714*, 1028, 1512; Matilda, 1016; Priscilla, 715; S., 579 n, 1177, 1512; Rev. S., 1033, 1402; Sam., 357 n, 715, 1005, 1493; Rev. Sam., 342, 713, 1028*, 1031*; Sara(h), 714, 715, 1031; Sylvanus (Silvanus), 711, 714*, 1512; Thos., 714*, 715*, 1016; Wm., 1016, 1395; Rev., 1032 n, 1093; —, 1047, 1123, 1290, 1309, 1385, 1402*; fam., 713, 1032

Lyster, Rev. Rob., 1460

Lysturston, Rev. R., 1460

Lyte, Nic., 655; —, 237; fam., 236; and see Laight

Lytelton (Lyttleton), see Littleton

Lytton (Litton), Anne, 535; Wm., 531*, 535*

Lyvynge, see Living

Mabbett (Mabbatt), Ann(e), 1167, 1168; Joan,

1531; John, 171, 418*, 1167*, 1168, 1169*; Joseph, 1531; Martha, 418; Mary, 171, 418, 1167; Ric., 418*, 1531; Sam., 1531; Thos., 418, 1167; Wm., 1167, 1168; Mr., 1169; —, 1169

Macapen (Maccapen), Eliz., 1272; John, 1289; Thos., 1272

Macaulay (Macauly), Lord, 1160; —, 1198

Maccapen, see Macapen

Mace, Betty, 1013; Eliz., 1421; Francis, 217; Hen., 881; Laur. (Lawr.), 1421*, 1422; Marg., 881; Thos., 881; Wm., 1013; —, 1421

Machen (Machin, Machoun, Machyn, Mechin), Ann(e), 15*, 247, 248, 920*, 978*; Ciscela, 959; Edw., 190, 192*, 247, 248*, 466*, 920*; Rev. Edw., 1228*; Edw. Tomkyns (Tomkins), 188, 192; Eliz., 15*, 17, 466; Emmanuel, 192; Hannah, 192, 1158*; Jas., 549*; John (le), 17, 192*, 336, 700, 978, 1158*, 1401, 1456, 1494; Judith, 192; Marg., 1158; Mary, 15, 192*, 248, 700, 920, 1088, 1255; Ric., 192*, 1088; Rob., 959; Sarah, 247, 549, 700, 1158; Sophia, 1158; Thos., 15*, 159, 188, 276, 959; Wal. le, 1540; Wm., 15, 700*, 978*, 1158*, 1494; —, 1162; fam., 188, 1494

Maci of Mauritania, 1074*

Macie, see Maysey

McKeurtan, Frances, 1250; Jas., 1250

Mackland, Wm., 190

Macknemara, Susanna, 412

Mackworth, fam., 427

Maclaine (Maclane), Gilliam, 1303; Col. Hector, 1303*; Martha, 1303; —, 1311

Macy, see Maysey

Madoc (fl. 1066), 1035

Maddocks (Maddocke, Maddox, Madocke, Madocks, Madox, Maduks), Anselme, 1319*; Bridget, 1318, 1323; Cartwright, 352*; David, 1371; E., 1516; Ed., 1323; Edm., 1319*; Edw., 733, 815; Hannah, 352; Dr. Isaac, bishop, 609; Jane, 854; John, 681, 682, 732, 812, 1319*; Martha, 812; Mary, 353, 1371; Sarah, 815; Thos., 352, 353; Wm., 789, 854; Mr., 157; —, 1322; and see Mattocks

Madrin, Rev. Rob., 878

Maducks, see Maddocks

Magart, Elinor, 1013; Hen., 1013

Magason, Hugh, 481

Maggs, Ann Cox, 1473; John, 1473; Mary, 1473, 1489; Rob., 1473; Sarah, 1473; Wm., 1489

Mahutild, Wal., 1259

Maid, see Mayd

Mail, see Mayall

Mainrearinf, Rev. Thos., 1369

Mainslow, —, 1016

Maisey, see Maysey

Maistres, see Des Maistres

Major, Alice, 1126; Anne, 1126; Eleanor, 338; Eliz., 338; Jane, 505; Rob., 1126*; Toby, 338; Wm., 338, 505

Makepeace, Rev. John, 999

Malbone, Thos., 86

Malcolm, Rev. Wm., 1331

Malden, Geo., Viscount Malden, 325; Mary, 1360; W. de, 1187

Maldson, see Malson

Malemon, Ric., 1477

Maliar, Nic., 1314; —, 1311

Mallard, Allis, 662; Hen., 662

Malle, Wm., 1043

Mallet (Mallett), John, 159, 160, 602, 603, 1018, 1019, 1447; Capt. John, 1018; Mabel, 739, 1019, 1020, 1304; Marg., 1018; Mary, 1018; Nat., 1019, 1305; Sam., 1018, 1304; Thos., 738, 1019*; Rev. Thos. Kennedy, 1161; Ursula, 1305; Rev. W., 1317; Rev. Wm., 1372; —, 154; fam., 603

Mallings, Wm., 644; and see Mallyn

Mallory, Capt. Hen., 928

Mallowes, Marg., 1521

Mallyn, John, 1197; and see Mallings

Malmsbury, Wm. of, 179, 1219

Malpus, Rob., 1350

Malson (Maldson), Eliz., 1395; Hannah, 1395; J., 1403; John, 1396, 1509; Mary, 1395, 1509; Stephen, 1395*; —, 1403*; fam., 1403

Maltar, —, 1311

Maltby (Maltbee), Rev. John, 272*, 273; —, 1257

Maltman, John, 1478

Malton, Cath. de, 617

Maltravers (Mautravers), John, 251, 1020*, 1032, 1139*, 1512; Lord John, 1513; —, 1185*, 1512

Malvern (Malverne), Eliz., 906; Humph., 906; John, 906; (or Parker), Wm., abbot, 684

Maminot, Hugh, 783, 1032, 1121; —, 1032

Man, see Mann

Mancel, see Mansell

Mander (Maunder), Ann, 1208; Eliz., 1330*; Jas., 1208; John, 1330*; Rev. John, 436; Ric., 1330; Sarah, 1330; Thos., 1330*

Mandeville (Mandevil, Maundeuill, Maunduill), Idania, 1404; Isabel, countess of Essex, 1287; Jeffery de, 1295; John, 1404; Wal., 1404; —, 1403; —, earl of Essex, 1287

Mandey, Rob., 1525

Manfield, see Mansfield

Maning, see Manning

Manley (Manly), Eliz., 1064; Rog., 1195; Rev., 1147

Mann (Man, Mans), Ann, 174, 734*, 950; Ant., 1396; Bridget, 1262; Diana, 736; Dinah, 734*; Edw., 110*, 486*; Eliz., 486, 677, 1262, 1263, 1277*; Esther, 1262*; Frances, 247; Geo., 247, 666, 677, 734*, 736, 1277; Hester, 549, 1262; Jas., 608; Jeremiah, 348; John, 174, 611*, 716, 1262*, 1263*, 1269, 1277*, 1289; Marg. (Margarite), 611, 716, 1262, 1263*; Martha, 950; Mary, 595, 608, 611*, 734, 1250, 1263, 1282; Priscilla, 348; Sarah, 666, 1269; Tacey, 734*; Thos., 1250, 1263; Wm., 549, 611, 950, 1262, 1263, 1277, 1289, 1355

Manners (Mannors), Chas., duke of Rutland, 123; Rog., 863

Manning (Maning, Mannings), Ann, 1167, 1337*; Dan., 752, 1101; Deborah, 660; Eliz., 171, 752,

940, 1167; Francis, 1168, 1337*, 1507*–8, 1534;
Giles, 1337*; Grace, 84, 491; Hannah, 84, 491*;
Hen., 940; Hester, 1507; Isaac, 491; Jas., 171*,
752; Joanna, 171*; John, 757, 814; Joyce, 84;
Mary, 84, 171, 442, 1167*, 1168, 1337*; Mary
Dudley, 940; Nic., 84*; Rebekah, 752; Rob.,
1167*; Sam., 84*, 491*, 660; Sam. Dudley, 940;
Sarah, 491, 677, 1307, 1338, 1339; Thos., 84,
171, 442, 491, 677, 1307; Thos. Fielding, 1338*;
Wm., 84, 491, 660; Rev. Wm., 840; Col., 341;
fam., 1337

Mannors, see Manners
Mannye, Sir Ant., kt., 364
Mans, see Mann
Mansell (Mancel, Mansel, Mauncel, Maunsel,
Maunsell), (or Alexander), Alice, 1052*; (or
Alexander), Ambrose, 1052; Ann(e), 989, 1211,
1212, 1269, 1350; (or Alexander), Ant., 1052; (or
Alexander), Cyprian, 1052; Dorothy, 1269;
Edith, 1421*; Edw., 1211, 1212; Sir Edw., bt.,
927, 1220; Eliz., 1421; (or Elysaunder), Hen.,
1051; Jane, 316, 923; Joan(e), 809, 1051; John,
923, 989, 1202, 1350*; Joseph, 1212, 1269;
Leonard, 1413; Marg., 988, 989, 1051, 1215,
1217, 1345*; (or Alexander), Marian, 1052;
Martha, 226; Mary, 989*; (or Alexander), Mary,
1052; Phil., 1051*; Ric., 1269*; Rob., 989*; Rev.
Rob., 1421*; Sam., 316*, 1269; Sarah, 226, 316,
407, 1269; Thos., 809, 988*, 989, 1212, 1413,
1457; (or Alexander), Thos., 1052; Thos., Lord
Mansell, 1382; Rev. Thos., 288; Wal., 313; Wm.,
317, 1051*, 1052*, 1215*, 1217, 1314; Sir Wm.,
1345*; —, 1027, 1104, 1289; fam., 1051, 1052,
1215; (or Alexander), fam., 1052
Mansfield (Manfield), Rev. Edw., 1026; Francis,
797; Capt. Jas. Wm., 1026; John, 131, 133*, 347;
Joseph, 797; Marg., 133*; Rebecca, 347; Sarah,
133; Thos., 797; —, 1027
Mansford, Rev. Thos. de, 184
Mantle, Anne, 821; Mary, 191*; Rev. Ric., 103,
190, 191*; Thos., 193; Rev. Thos., 1, 820, 821
Manwood, John, 475 n
Manygforde, Nichola de, 1292
Mapson, Eliz., 961*; Hen., 961; John, 960, 961;
Mr., 366
Mar, Lord, 1069
Mara, Mabilia de, 1005; Rob. de, 1005; Wm. de,
1005
March (Marche, Merch), Hendery, 921; J., 1516;
Jas., 921; Ric., 1063; Stephen, 1168; Thos.,
1063; Wal. de, 1314; Wm. (de la), 1063, 1172;
and see Murch
March [peerage], see Mortimer, passim
Marchal, see Marshall
Marchant (Marchen, Marchent, Merchant), Aaron,
706; Ant., 1350, 1467*; Eliz., 187*, 706, 1164;
Esther, 348; Hen., 787, 1164; Jane, 1467; John,
187; Jos., 706; Leonard, 187; Mary, 187*, 339,
706; Nic., 339; Ric., 187; Rev. Rob. le, 1013,
1016; Sam., 187; Thos., 187*; Wm., 348,1164,
1200; —. 1064
Marche, see March

Marchen (Marchent), see Marchant
Marcy, see Markey
Marden, W., 1356
Marechal, see Marshall
Mareis (Mareys), see Marsh
Mareschal (Mareshel), see Marshall
Marfilave, Jonathan, 1038
Marflin, John, 959
Marfold, Mark, 841; Mary, 841
Margaret, queen, 570 n
Margetts, Ann-Marg., 1068; Benj., 1196; Eliz.,
1068*; Wm., 1068*
Mariesone, Wal., 1346
Mariet, see Marriott
Marina, John de, 41
Mariot (Marioten), see Marriott
Maris, see Marsh
Mariscall (Marissal), see Marshall
Markeley, see Markley
Markes, Wm., 412
Markey (Marcy), Amey, 1237; Jane, 1166; John,
1166, 1237; Muric [? Maurice], 1404
Markley (Markeley, Markleys), Cicely, 1463; Rev.
Thos., 1463*, 1477
Marklove, Ambrose, 454*, 456*; Ann, 166*; Eliz.,
1101; Hester, 454; Mary, 454; Rob., 166*;
Winifred, 456
Marlborough (Marleberg), Jas., earl of, 842; Ralph
de, 1378; Sibilla de, 1378; countess of, 719 n;
and see Churchill, John
Marle, Edw., 1214; Eliz., 1214; Susan, 1214; Wm.,
1214*
Marleberg, see Marlborough
Marling, N. S., 1216; Nat. Sam., 1185, 1216; S.,
1139; S. S., 1216, 1322*; Sir S. S., bt., 1516;
Messrs., 1139, 1186; Mr., 1215
Marlwood (Morlewode), Wal. (de, of), 1311, 1314
Marmon (Marman, Marmion), Albreda de, 1077,
1431; Jacob, 1576; John, 174*, 660; Rachel, 174;
Ralph, 1316; Rog., 1001; Sarah, 660; —, 1339,
1455
Marner, Phil., 366, 368, 372; —, 1293
Maronne (Marone), Eliz., 45; Grace, 45; John, 45*
Marres, see Marsh
Marriott (Mariet, Mariot, Marioten, Meriot), Ann,
988; Eliz., 988; Hester, 988; Humph., 804; Jane,
988*; John, 437, 987, 988*; Lucy-Ann, 988,
1040; Mary, 501; Matillda, 1440; Ric., 501, 988;
Susanna(h), 437, 1040; Theodosia, 988; Thos.,
988*, 1040; Wm., 988*, 1460; —, 1458, 1460*;
and see Merrett
Marris, see Marsh
Marrowe, Edw., 402; Eliz., 402; Sam., 402
Marsh (Mareis, Mareys, Maris, Marres, Marris,
Mars, Marshe, Marys), Alice, 1302, 1304; Ant.,
1015; Elinor, 714; Eliz., 46, 1108, 1302*; Elliotts,
11; Francis, 575; Rev. Geo., 230; Hen., 1302,
1304, 1305; Hester, 1339; Isaac, 124, 377; J.,
1215; John, 46, 377, 721, 1432; Mary, 124, 1108,
1302, 1305, 1377; Peter la, 1127; Rob. (le), 1302*,
1304*, 1312, 1482, 1483; Thos., 714, 1377; Wm.
(de, le), 1108, 1302*, 1313, 1339, 1346; —, 1091

Marshall (Marchal, Marechal, Mareschal, Mareshel, Mariscall, Marissall, Marshal, Morshall), Adam le, 990; Anna, 143, 1371; Ann(e), 111, 736, 931*, 933; Benj., 890; Caroline, 1490; Rev. Eliezer (Eleazar), 630, 1456; Eliz., 226*, 486, 931, 933; Gef. de, 1402; Geo., 111, 193*, 587; Gunnyld, 1292; Hannah, 561; Isolda, 1313; J., 1402; Jane, 193, 1417; Job, 736; John, 111, 226*, 564, 587, 891, 1371, 1417; Rev. John, 630*; Jonathan, 730; Joseph, 1400; Joshua, 291; Josiah, 106*; Marg., 193, 526, 561; Mary, 106, 194, 931, 932, 933*, 1225, 1416; Lady Maud, 1322; Nic., 1416; Rebecca, 1184, 1344; Ric., 143, 931, 932, 933*; Rog., 1312; Rev. Sam., 1225, 1228; Sarah, 587; Thos. (le), 193*, 469 n, 736, 1102; Rev. Valentine (Valantine), 582, 583, 1344; W., 102; Wal., 111, 561*, 1184; Wm., 194, 226, 232, 526, 587, 927, 931, 932. 933*, 1091; Wm., Earl Marshall, 1512; Wm., earl of Pembroke, 1322; Rev. Wm., 525; Winifred, 106; Dr., 1189; fam., 788

Marsham, fam., 792

Marshe, see Marsh

Marshfield, Jas., 446; Jane, 446; Wm., 446

Marshman, Thos., 814

Marston (Mersshton, Merston), Hen., 950; Hester, 950; John, 950; Rev. John, 315; Mary, 315, 950; Rob. (de), 949*, 950*, 1388; Sarah, 1377; Thos., 950, 1377, 1378; Wm., 950; —, 1177

Marteley, Wm. de, 360

Martell, Adam de, 1198; John, 1038; fam., 643, 1198

Marten, see Martin

Martin, bishop of Gloucester, see Benson

Martin (Marten, Martyn), Agnes, 371; Alice, 250, 980; May, 1410; Ann(e), 221*, 225, 514, 953*, 980*, 1038, 1350, 1386, 1410; Ant., 1465*; Augustine, 256; Rev. Augustin(e), 255, 256*, 257, 817, 1228; Benj., 90, 1473; Chas., 1386; David, 514; Deborah, 215*; Dorothy, 1410; Edith, 208; Eleanor, 4*; Eliz., 215, 220, 221*, 225*, 256, 289, 979, 1473, 1573; Esther, 1354, 1386*, 1410; Francis, 220*, 225*; Geo., 4*, 215*, 256, 531, 843, 1038, 1039*, 1097*, 1490*, 1578; Hannah, 215, 665; Hen., 4*, 215, 250; Hester, 90, 843, 1386; Jas., 1362; Rev. Jas., 1228; Jas. Thos., 1362; Jas. Williams, 1362; Jane, 215, 980*; Jo[a]ne, 1248; John, 256, 289, 371, 386, 514, 531, 857*, 949, 979*, 980*, 1026, 1097, 1194, 1248*, 1289, 1362*, 1386, 1465; Rev. John, 252, 253*, 272, 273, 400, 1441*; John Richmond, 980; Joseph, 815, 1362; Rev. Joseph, 230; Joseph B., 1256; Judith, 256, 1362; Kath., 1235; Marg., 953, 980, 1410, 1465; Martha, 256; Mary, 250, 253, 256*, 257, 857, 979, 980*, 1194, 1214, 1239, 1248, 1354, 1465; Peregrine, 5; R., 272; Rebecca, 256; Ric., 4, 364, 530, 665*, 953*, 979, 980*, 1098, 1439, 1465*; Rob., 979*, 980*; Rog., 1239; Sam., 1505; Sarah, 256*, 665, 1097, 1098*, 1239, 1490; Susannah, 980; Thos., 90, 250*, 980, 1132, 1194, 1386*, 1471; W., 1419; Wm., 208*, 215*, 665, 730, 887*, 1026, 1138,

1214, 1289, 1354*, 1355, 1369, 1386, 1410*, 1471; Mr., 1189, 1440; Mrs., 1237; Rev., 1250; —, 1282, 1288, 1289, 1293, 1311, 1362, 1382, 1386, 1420, 1477; fam., 214, 1362

Marwent, see Morwent

Mary, queen, 53, 180, 184 n, 367, 508, 613, 793, 838, 952, 1123*, 1221, 1287, 1290, 1293, 1309, 1323, 1328, 1369, 1387, 1460, 1482

Mary, queen of Scots, 852 n

Marys, see Marsh

Mascoll, Rev. John, 1385

Masey, see Maysey

Masheder, Wm., 1350

Maskelyne, —, 1255*, 1256

Maslen, Jane, 706; John, 706*; Mary, 706*; Thos., 706

Mason (Masoun, Mayson), Agnes, 1055; Alice, 1270; Ann, 59, 636, 1276, 1446, 1469; Benj., 338, 815, 1543, 1546; Chas., 611, 1049, 1276*; Cornelius, 1037; David, 442; Rev. Dominick, 221; Dorothy, 15; Edith, 204; Edw., 338, 1473; Eleanor, 336; Eliz., 15, 254, 338*, 710, 952, 953, 1063*, 1064, 1276, 1574; Frances, 1276; Rev. Francis, 87; Geo., 15, 660, 953, 1545, 1546; Giles, 1182; Hannah, 710; Hen., 204, 316, 336*; Hester, 1543, 1546*; J., 1148; Jas., 710, 1469; Jeremiah, 662; Joane, 1058; John, 59, 336, 338, 682, 953*, 963, 1058*, 1062, 1064*, 1270, 1446, 1504, 1545, 1546; Jooin, 682; Joseph, 1063, 1545; Kath., 1063; Marg., 1062, 1063; Mary, 338, 442, 611, 953, 963, 1276, 1330, 1473; Nat., 636, 952; Priscilla, 1545; R., 1063*; Rebekah, 1049; Ric., 338, 815, 1062*, 1258, 1330; Rob., 254*, 710, 1055, 1498, 1504; Sara(h), 316, 348, 660, 710, 1182, 1282; T., 985, 1055, 1062; Thos., 348, 1062*, 1063*, 1064, 1276, 1331, 1574; Rev. Thos., 619; Wal., 336; Wm., 1058, 1063*, 1217, 1276, 1289, 1420, 1545, 1546; Rev. Wm., 1543, 1545*, 1546*, 1552; Rev., 1551; —, 1063, 1064*, 1148

Massareane (Mazarine), duchess of, 719 n; Eliz., countess of, 1455

Massenger (Messag), Agnes, 1440; Anna, 1024; Eliz., 972; John, 1024; Joyce, 972; Mary, 972; Rev. Whithastone, 263; Wm., 972*

Massey (Massie), Cath., 947; Col. Edw., 158, 179, 263, 349 n*, 680, 927, 928*, 1035, 1219, 1220, 1238, 1293*, 1323, 1404; Rev. Gil., 121; Rev. Hen., 37, 947*, 1351; Rev. John, 1078; Margery, 1219; Sir Rog., kt., 1219; Susannah, 947; Thos. Ebsworth, 947; fam., 305

Massinberd, Hen., 413

Master (Masters), Alice, 380; Ann(e), 387, 989*, 991*; Bridget, 366, 820; Dan., 387; Edw. (Edv.), 989, 990, 991*; Eliz., 380*, 452, 898, 990, 991*, 1530; Geo., 359 n, 1530; Herb., 990; Dr. Herb., 991; Isabella Marg., 1160; Jas., 387; Jane, 1202*; Johanna, 1201; John, 366; Kath., 130; Mary, 802, 1066; Nat., 452; Rafe, 446; Ric., 364, 990, 1159, 1160, 1201; Dr. Ric., 359, 990; Susannah, 898; T., 990, 1159, 1199, 1201; Thos., 145*, 195, 357, 359*, 363, 364*, 365*, 366, 380*, 396*, 445 n,

806 n, 820*, 898*, 934, 990, 1066, 1159, 1201*;
Wm., 130, 364*, 396; Dr. Wm., 990*; Rev. Wm.,
369, 445, 1238; Sir Wm., kt., 359 n, 364, 366,
369, 380, 802, 990, 1201*; Wm. Chester, 1160;
Winifred, 366, 369; Miss, 1202*; Mr., 989, 990*;
fam., 145, 359, 365*, 430, 445 n, 989, 1256
Maston, Anne, 666; Geo., 666*; Hester, 666*
Mate, Thos., 1226
Matheu (Matheus, Mathew, Mathews, Mathus), see
Matthews
Matilda, queen, 525, 648, 1285, 1287, 1309, 1361,
1381, 1455; and see Maud
Matson (Mattesden, Mattesdene, Mattesdon,
Mattisden), Agnes de, 1102; Ernulph, 1380; Jane,
1398; Joshua, 1398*; Phil. de, 851 n*; Thos. de,
1379; — de, 1378; fam., 255
Mattare, Osbert, 1313
Mattesden (Mattesdene, Mattesdon, Mattisden), see
Matson
Mattocks, Joan, 1171; Rob., 1171*; Wm., 1171;
and see Maddocks
Matthews (Matheu, Matheus, Mathew, Mathews,
Mathus, Matthew), Alice, 1345; Ann(e), 186,
235, 439, 510, 683, 768*, 846, 1013, 1181,
1386; Betty, 847, 1328*; Christian, 683; Clar.,
1460; Clement Lapley, 1340, 1344; Dan., 1433;
Sir David, 1345; Edm., 555; Edw., 439, 636,
1038, 1299*, 1300*, 1341, 1465; Eleanor, 112*;
Eliz., 165, 303, 334, 679, 1038*, 1341*, 1344,
1433; Ellen, 1511; Enock, 1038; Frances, 1465;
Geo., 901, 1511; Giles, 347; Hannah, 636, 683,
1229; Harriet Emma, 1511; Harriet Jane, 1511;
Hen., 768*, 1387; J., 1226; J. D., 1344; Jas.,
683, 1213, 1376; Jane, 47, 186, 555, 901, 1181,
1213, 1343, 1511; John, 138*, 165, 186, 235,
413, 479, 683*, 731, 915, 932*, 1181, 1196,
1341, 1537; Rev. John, 1267, 1290, 1346, 1382;
Joseph, 112, 452, 1340*, 1343*, 1344; Lydia,
1273; Marg., 235; Martha, 1328; (or Page),
Martha, 1471; Mary, 138, 439, 683, 731, 814,
932*, 1038, 1244, 1433*; Moses, 846; Nic.,
1181*; Phil., 991; Rachel, 1340, 1343, 1344;
Ralph, 1273*; Ric., 111, 186*, 303, 683*, 814,
932, 1328, 1343, 1472, 1573; Rob., 138, 1473*,
1477; Rev. Rog., 829; Sam., 1376; Sarah, 138*,
407, 679, 1181, 1213, 1300, 1433*; Stephen
(Steven), 439*, 1013*, 1328; Susanna, 906,
1299, 1300, 1376, 1472; T., 1378; Thos., 138,
510, 679*, 814, 818, 1181, 1186, 1539; Rev.
Thos., 245, 808; Tim., 47; Vincent, 138*; W.,
1519; Wm., 112*, 135, 138, 235*, 691, 768,
820, 847, 906*, 1038*, 1386, 1392, 1433*,
1473; (or Page), Wm., 1471; Rev. Wm., 1433*;
Lieut.-Col., 407; Mr., 894, 929; —, 1017, 1064,
1345*, 1386; fam., 415, 894
Maud, empress, 158, 357, 776, 1219; and see
Matilda
Maudelen, —, chaplain, 358
Maudit, —, lord [of] Hanslape, 1392*
Maul, see Maule
Maulder, see Moulder
Maule (Maul), Eleanor, 399*; Eliz., 1012, 1366;

Emy, 472; John, 1012; Rev. John, 1366; Marg.,
399; Nat., 472; Ric., 399; Wm., 399, 1217
Mauley, Lord de, 1005
Mauncel, see Mansell
Maunche, Stephen le, 1258
Maunder, see Mander
Maundeuill (Maunduill), see Mandeville
Maundy, see Munday
Maunsel (Maunsell), see Mansell
Maunt (Mauntz), Harold (Herold)(de), 1334, 1335;
John de, 1334, 1335; Ralph de, 1334, 1335*;
Ralph (Radulph)(de), earl of Hereford or
Hertford, 1219, 1334, 1335; Wal. de, 1219; Wal.
de, earl of Mauntz, 1335; (or Tracy), Wm., 1334,
1335
Maurice, prince, 6, 806 n, 776, 1293*
Maurice, see Morris
Mautravers, see Maltravers
Mawson, Rev. W., 1289; Rev. Wm., 785
Maxey, Rev. W., 1313
Maxtone, Ric., 530*
Maxwell, Anne, 1360*; Geo., 1362; Capt. Geo.,
1360*; Helen Frances, 1360; Hugh, 1360; Jane
Charlotte, 1360; Rev. Rob., 103; Sam., 1196; W.
G., 1348; Rev. W. G., 1387; Rev. W. Geo., 1387;
Rev. Wm. Geo., 1357, 1360; —, 1361*; fam.,
1362
May (Maye, Mey), Ann, 1244; Betty, 62, 1326;
Chris., 758; Dan., 758; Esther, 703; Hannah, 555;
Hester, 787; Jas., 1326; Jane, 758; John, 60, 369,
703, 1326*, 1328; (or Mayne), Rev. John, 1317;
Jonathan, 62; Mark, 1326; Mary, 1326; Nic.,
1387; Phil., 758; Rob., 555; Sarah, 386, 555,
1326; Simon, 1404; Thos., 2*, 758, 787, 1326;
Wal., 531; Wm., 539, 555, 578*
Mayall (Mail, Mayl, Mayle), Alice, 768; Hen.,
768*; Marg., 550; Phil., 550; Thos., 1282; (or
Heath), Wm., 895
Mayd (Maid, Mayde), Ann, 231; J., 1256; Judith,
1279; Mat(t)hias, 1279*; Nic., 1279; Sam., 1279;
Thos., 1348; Wm., 231, 1244*; Rev. Wm., 230,
231*
Maydegod, Rob., 1197
Maydenstone, Wal. de, bishop, 612, 617, 646, 667,
711, 1312
Maye, see May
Mayer, Thos., 1477; Wm., 1477
Mayfield, Wm., 473
Mayhill, Thos., 1422
Mayle (Mayl), see Mayall
Maylor, Kath., 730; Thos., 730; and see Meyler
Mayn, see Mayne
Maynard, Cath., 220 n; Eliz., 1393; Geo., 658*; Sir
John, 220 n, 1393, 1394; Rob., 1074; Sarah, 658;
Serjt., 1394
Mayne (Mayn), Eliz., 1073; John, 1393; (or Maye),
Rev. John, 1317; —, 1402
Mayo (Mayoe, Mayou, Mayow), Ailward, 1291;
Alis, 173*; Ann, 1395, 1398, 1399, 1400*; B. H.,
1403; Benj., 1393, 1399*; Benj. Harrison, 1400;
Eleanor, 906; Eliz., 173, 832, 884, 1399*; Esther,
1397*; Frances, 884; Hannah, 1400; Hester, 622,

624; Humph., 1534; J., 1404; Jas., 905; Jeremy, 1399; John, 173*, 779, 884*, 906*, 1397, 1399*; Joseph, 1399*; Marg., 907; Martha, 1371; Mary, 215*, 965*, 1371*, 1398, 1399*; R. W., 1403; Rebecca, 1534; Ric., 308, 832; Rob., 1354, 1371, 1397*; Rog., 1478; Ruth, 1399*; Sarah, 1371, 1397, 1533; Sukey, 1400*; Thos., 906*, 965*; Wm., 215*, 622, 624, 906, 1399, 1400*, 1403, 1478, 1533; Rev. Wm., 214, 215, 1395; Rev., 1290

Mayott, Eliz., 1144

Mayou (Mayow), see Mayo

Mays (Mayse), Eliz., 290; John, 428

Maysey (Macie, Macy, Maisey, Masey, Maysie, Mazee, Meisei, Meisie, Meisey, Meysey), A., 985; Ann(e), 201, 1464; Arthur, 1061; Cath., 320; Elianor, 859; Eliz., 1464*, 1526; Jas., 782, 1526; John (de), 112, 201*, 320, 859; Mary, 1464; Priscilla, 782; Radolph, 1007; Thos., 1464*; W., 1063; Wm., 611, 1196, 1329; —, 1064; fam., 859

Mayson, see Mason

Mazarine, see Massareane

Mazee, see Maysey

Meades, see Meads

Meadows (Medows), Augustin, 1519; Francis, 1196; Hen., 818; Patience, 980; Sarah, 818, 980; Thos., 1196; Wm., 226, 980*; —, 1551

Meads (Meades, Medes), Benj., 1391*; John, 868; Mary, 1391*; Phiadlephia [sic], 1391; Ric., 1522; Susannah, 1391; Thos., 868, 1391*

Meakins, see Meekings

Mealing (Mealling), Alice, 510; Ann, 510*, 996; Joan, 569; Ric., 996; Rob., 510; Wm., 510*, 569, 996

Meare, Rev. W., 1362

Mease, Ann, 1229; Rev. H. J., 1233; Rev. Hen., 27, 328, 1229; Rev. John, 1229*, 1233; Mat., 1233

Mechin, see Machen

Medcalfe, see Metcalfe

Medcroft (Medecroft), Wm., 1017, 1259

Medehalle, Humph. de, 1055, 1377

Medes, see Meads

Medlicott (Medicott), Ann, 1250; John, 1258

Medows, see Meadows

Mee, Eliz., 715; Thos., 263, 667

Meek (Meeke), Abigail, 5; Ann(e), 5, 903; Ant., 903*; Francis, 1038; Jane, 468; Rob., 254; Sarah, 1038; Thos., 5, 903

Meekings (Meakins), Ann, 337; Eliz., 337*; John, 337; Thos., 337; Rev. Thos., 76; Wm., 337*, 801

Meisie (Meisei, Meisey), see Maysey

Melcher, Ann, 537; Mary, 537; Rob., 537

Melhent, see Melun

Melhuish (Mellersh, Mellish), Geo., 1233; Hannah, 496*; Jane, 1075; John, 124, 496; Wm., 496

Melksham, W., 1169; —, 1169

Mellersh (Mellish), see Melhuish

Melton, —, abbot, 392; and see Milton

Melun (Melhent), Rob. de, earl of Gloucester, 357; Rob. de, prior and bishop, 1060

Mensier, fam., 867

Mentieth, earls of, 1281

Mercer, Wm., 1058

Merch, see March

Merchant, see Marchant

Meredith (Meredeth), Amy, 488; Ann(e), 52, 190, 191; Cath., 191*; Chas., 488; Deborah, 52; Dionisia, 834; Eliz., 191, 834*, 1054; F., 1317; Geo., 1549; Giles, 1328; Hen., 1549; Rev. Jas., 53, 190*, 191*, 1516; John, 554, 834*, 843*; Rev. John, 840; Lucy Maria, 1306; Martha, 191; Mat., 1306*; Ric., 52; Ensign Rog., 928; Sarah, 1306, 1549*; Symes, 488; Thos. Day, 814; Rev. Tim., 126; Rev. Wm., 745; Mr., 882; —, 1087, 1317; fam., 833

Meredy (or Taylor), Rev. J., 1127

Mereweather, Alworth, 841; John, 841; fam., 838

Merewent, see Morwent

Merewy, Thos., 1363

Merick, see Merrick

Meridew, Madam, 1044

Meriot, see Marriott

Merral (Merrall), Alice, 1278; Dan., 1362; Isaac, 1278*; Sam., 1278*; Sarah, 1278

Merrett (Merret, Merritt), Alice, 1270; Ann, 741; Awdrey (Andriana), 1466*; Barbara, 1270, 1554; Cath., 1271*; Chris., 1466*, 1478; Dr. Chris., 1478; Dan., 974; Eliz., 623, 832, 887, 907, 1186; Geo., 1229; Giles, 677; Hen., 1270*, 1271, 1554, 1563*; Hester, 677; Rev. Jasper, 1513; John, 176, 666, 974, 1132, 1434*, 1513; Joseph, 623; Joyce, 1434; Margery, 1229; Mary, 666, 1181*, 1182, 1270; Nat., 388; Prudence, 666; Ric., 652, 907, 1181*-2, 1211*, 1466*; Sam., 741, 1019; Sarah, 388, 1211, 1270; Stephen, 1181*; T., 1290; Thos., 468*, 666, 1218, 1270, 1271*; Ursula, 660; Wm., 677, 832, 1271*, 1513; —, 1282*, 1289, 1477; and see Marriott

Merrick (Merick, Merricke, Meyrick), Ann(e), 276*, 1508; Betty, 787; Chas., 111; Dan., 541; Rev. Edm., 328, 335; Eliz., 276*, 541; Gilly, 1062; John, 276*, 419, 787; Mary, 844; Ric., 276, 531*, 541*, 884*; Rob., 276*; Sarah, 541; Susanna, 467*; Wm., 276, 463, 467*, 531, 541*, 804*, 907, 1508; —, 1062*, 1064, 1122, 1311

Merriman, see Merryman

Merritt, see Merrett

Merry (Mery), Ann, 1046; G., 1216; Hannah, 803; John, 1046; Joseph, 70; Mary, 70; Rachel, 1046; Thos., 803, 1046; Wm., 1046, 1289

Merryman (Merriman, Myrriman), Ann(e), 1466*, 1467*; Dinah, 1466; Edm., 803*; Eliz., 803*; Hester, 803; Joan, 803; John, 1461, 1466*, 1467*, 1477; Rev. John, 1539; Joseph, 1289; Martha, 803; Mary, 1360*, 1467, 1473; Ric., 803, 1467*; Sarah, 803*; Thos., 803, 1196, 1360*, 1361, 1362, 1461, 1467*, 1477; Wm., 1473, 1477; —, 1386

Mersey, Thos., 1461

Mersshton (Merston), see Marston

Mery, see Merry

Messag, see Massenger

Messeter, Geo., 597

Metcalfe (Medcalfe), Geo., 55*; Mary, 55*; Thos., 55*; Rev. Wm., 252, 449

Methuen, John, 1359; Mary, 1359; Sir Paul, kt., 1359

Mew (Meux, Mewe, Mews), Rev. Dan., 689; Elinor, 681; John, 229; Sir John, 681; Mary, 229; Rev. Sam., 559*; Wm., 1289; Rev. Wm., 559, 560

Mey, see May

Meyler, Rev. T., 1482; and see Maylor

Meyrick, see Merrick

Meysey, see Maysey

Michell (Michel), see Mitchell

Mickleton (Mukeltone), John de, 1431

Mico, Dame Joan, 592; Sir Sam., 592

Middlemore, Anne, 1184; Giles, 1143, 1146*, 1147, 1184; Lydia, 1143; Ric., 1143, 1184; Sarah, 1146*, 1184; Sophia, 1146; Wm., 1184

Middlesex, Anne, countess of, 1390; Leonel (Lionel), earl of, 1390, 1392; Lady Susanna, dau. of Leonel and Anne, 1390; earl of, 1392; and see Cranfield

Middleton, Ann(e), 762, 1426; Edw., 77; Jane, 627; John, 762, 1423; Rev. John, 534; Marg., 77; Rob., 687; Sam., 77; Thos., 1426; Wm., 627

Middleton [peerage], Francis, Lord, 718, 1491; Hen., Viscount, 718, 722*, 833, 834; Lord, 1419, 1423, 1491

Midewint, see Midwinter

Midway, And., 429

Midwinter (Midewint, Mydwynter), Alex., 693; Edith, 38; Edw., 38*, 693; Eliz., 947*; Giles, 693; Hester, 621; John, 38, 320, 693*, 947, 1010, 1197; Joseph, 1499; Marg., 693; Maria, 1499; Mary Eliz., 947; Ric., 1348; Sarah, 320; Rev. Stephen, 621; Wm., 947*

Mifflin (Miflin), Adam, 636; (or Peters), Ant., 679; (or Peters), Frances, 679; Hannah, 636; (or Peters), Isabella, 679; Martha, 706; Rob., 706

Milatt, see Millett

Milborne (Milborn, Milbourn, Milbourne, Milburn, Mylborn), Alex., 1266; Ann, 613; Clayton, 613*; Eliz., 1051; Hen., 613; John, 51*; Mary, 613*; Simon, 1051; Sir Simon, 1422; Susan, 51*; Thos., 51, 1389; —, 1422, 1441

Mildemay, Rob., 1314*

Mile, see Mill

Miles (Myles), Abigail, 1166; Alice, 1118*; Alington, 453*; Rev. Al(l)ington, 452, 453; Ann(e), 229, 303*, 321, 453*, 564, 862, 1075; Armel, 229*; Betty, 321; Dan., 1181; Edm., 1075*; Edw., 321; Eliz., 303, 429, 563*, 564*, 1054, 1118, 1350, 1529; Francis, 884; Hannah, 563, 716; Hen., 862, 922, 923, 1350; Hester, 321, 564; Isabella, 1181, 1350; Joanna, 303; John, 303*, 321, 564, 716*, 1054*, 1217; Joseph, 453, 563; Marg., 303; Mary, 303*, 884, 1181; Nat., 563, 564*, 1000, 1186; P. W. S., 1420; R., 1519; Ric., 1166, 1331; Rob., 884; Sarah, 303*, 716*, 1075, 1350; Thos., 303*, 429, 563, 564, 1118*, 1186, 1350, 1529; Rev. Thos., 1423; Thos. Boteler, 1221; Wm., 114, 1539; —, 1257; fam., 630; and see Mill; Mills

Mill (Mile, Mille, Molendino, Mull, Mulle, Mulne, Mylle), Adam, 1483; Ann, 669; Ant., 677; Dorothea, 68; Dame Dorothy, 66, 67; Edw., 670; Henrietta Margaretta Dorothea, 68; J., 1021; Jane, 670; John (atte), 1074, 1258*; Juliana, 667; Mary, 669, 677, 1021, 1045; Ralph atte, 1074; Ric. atte, 1197, 1519; Sir Ric., bt., 65, 68; Rob. (de), 677, 1127, 1221; Thos., 667*, 668*, 669; W., 1186; Wm., 668*, 669, 1074, 1182; Lady, 65*, 66; fam., 197, 525, 649; and see Miles; Mills

Millar, see Miller

Millard, Ann, 555, 789; Benj., 284, 532*, 542; Dan., 284, 1212, 1551; Edw., 555; Eliner, 644; Eliz., 284, 542, 543, 550, 939, 980, 1138; Giles, 976; Hannah, 1146; Hester, 284, 662, 941, 1547; Isaac, 824; Jas., 1138; Joan, 1144; John, 173, 174, 284*, 304, 543*, 644, 662, 944, 1144, 1146*, 1547*; Joseph, 284, 563, 941, 1146, 1352, 1353; Marg., 662. 939*; Mary, 304, 939, 976, 1146*; Olive, 284; Rebecca, 1146; Ric., 789*; Rob., 550, 939, 1146; Sam., 284; Sarah, 173, 941; Susanna, 304; Thos., 824, 980; Wm., 174, 284, 304, 939*, 1159; —, 1392; and see Miller; Milward

Millaway, Rob., 868

Mille, see Mill

Millechamp (Millecheap, Millenchep), see Millichep

Miller (Millar, Molend, Molendinar, Molendinare, Molendinarius), Alice, 862; Ann, 239, 788; Cath., 1250; Chas., 600, 1217; Dan., 862*; Eliz., 239*, 862, 1085; Geo., 343, 966*; Gil., 1238; Hester, 239*; Isaac, 1339; Jas., 300; Capt. Jas., 1319; Jane, 862*; John, 644, 730, 862, 944*; 1250, 1477; Marg., 879; Martha, 343*, 844; Mary, 300, 730, 844, 862*, 1057, 1064, 1339; Mic., 718, 725, 1420; Nat., 1258; Nic., 1127; Pauncefoot, 239; Phil., 1335; Rachel, 1319; Ric., 239*, 788; Rob., 862; Sarah, 862, 966; Saunderson, 1085; Rev. Saunders Wm., 685; Thos., 343*, 844*, 862, 879*, 1057; Wal., 1314*; Wm., 239*, 879, 1011, 1258, 1519; Mr., 1455; —, 1017; fam., 864; and see Millard; Milner

Milles, see Mills

Millett (Milatt), Alice, 1171; Amey, 1426; Ann(e), 578, 615, 835; Benj., 578; Dan., 1171; Eleanor, 578, 997; Eliz., 604, 1158, 1171*; Frances, 615; Geo., 616; Hannah, 604; Hester, 604, 1171; Isaac, 1171; Jacob, 578, 604*, 1171*; Jane, 615, 616; John, 615, 616, 835; Joseph, 578, 604*, 615*, 1426; Mary, 604*, 615; Thos., 604, 997; Wm., 604*, 615*, 616*

Millichep (Millechamp, Millecheap, Millenchep), Ales, 1028; Rev. Edw., 1028, 1031; Rev. Tim., 424; Rev. W., 1033

Millington, A., 1289; Eliz., 1268; Esther, 368, 381; Francis, 1289; John, 433*, 1268*; Jane, 433*; Jonathan, 368, 386; Mary, 385*, 386, 433, 1268*; Mic., 1268; Patience, 1268*; Ric., 433; Sam., 1268; Stephen, 1268*; Thos., 368, 381*; Wm., 385*

Millinson, Eliz., 378; Thos., 378

Millman, *see* Milman

Mills (Milles), Abraham, 1488; Alice, 423; Anne, 133, 338; Ant., 388; Bridget, 1390; D., 1127; Dan., 448, 666, 880; Deborah, 201; Edw., 64, 338; Eliz. (Elilabeth), 133, 338, 703, 880; Eliz. Cath., 1185; Esther, 133, 880, 1212; Rev. F., 1223; Frances, 338; Rev. Francis, 744; Rev. Fred., 1223; Geo., 1390*; Rev. Giles, 878; Hannah, 1008, 1024, 1025; Hen., 1480, 1511; Hester, 200; Rev. J., 1223; Jas., 1307; Jane, 423, 448; Jasper (Jaspur), 413, 1211, 1214; Job, 1211, 1214; John, 200, 201, 338*, 423*, 624*, 670, 878, 1006, 1047, 1165, 1212, 1217, 1481*; Joseph, 423; Marg., 1165; Martha, 201; Mary, 116, 338*, 423*, 448, 624, 880, 891*, 975, 976, 981*, 1025, 1211, 1214, 1480; Mary Bigland, 1185; Mat., 338, 1389; Rev. Mic., 1480*, 1483; Nat., 1049; Olive, 388; Paul, 423, 891; R., 1216; Ric., 448*, 946, 1025*, 1211, 1214, 1216, 1539; Rosamund, 624; S., 1027; Sam., 703*, 880, 975; Sarah, 880*, 1127*, 1389, 1488; Thos., 133*, 423, 448, 670, 975, 976, 981, 1024, 1389, 1392; Rev. W. Lewis, 1185; Wm., 133*, 259, 338*, 450, 670, 880*, 976, 981, 1008, 1494; fam., 197, 525, 878*; *and see* Miles; Mill

Millsom, *see* Milsom

Millward, *see* Milward

Milly, Geo., 1467; Susanna, 1467

Milman (Millman), Josiah, 308; Wm. Milman Buckle, 336

Milner, Rob., 1033; *and see* Miller

Milo, constable of Gloucester, 424, 581, 878

Milo, earl of Hereford, 711, 713, 925

Milred, bishop, 1502

Milsom (Millsom, Milsam, Milsum), Betty, 1582; David, 8; Eliz., 8; Geo., 846; Hannah, 1582*; Mary, 846; Ric., 1147; Rob., 846, 1582*; Wm., 846

Milson, Chas., 1159; Eliz., 249; John, 249; Mary, 921, 1159; Ric., 921

Milton, Benj., 1348; Betty, 1164; Eliz., 897, 1348; John, 950; Lawr., 1475; Mary, 950, 1234; Ric., 1235; Rob., 660; Sarah, 1164*; Wm., 1164*, 1234; —, 1093; *and see* Melton

Milward (Millward, Mulleward, Mullward, Mulward), A.. 1062; Anne, 1389*; Eugenia, 1504; Jas. le, 1539; John (le), 1033, 1154, 1363; Joseph, 1389; Margerie, 573; Rog. le, 1228; Thos., 544, 1389; Wal. le, 1502; Wm. (le), 573, 1258, 1388, 1389*, 1456, 1539; —, 1017; *and see* Millard

Milwater, Nat., 907

Min, *see* Myn

Mince, Amy, 1192; Anne, 1192*; John, 1192; Mary, 1269*; Ric., 1269*, 1291; Sam., 1192*; Wm., 1192*; —, 1190, 1196

Minchin (Munchyn, Mynchyn), Ann, 1224; Ant., 1016; Eliz., 138; Ellen, 1224; Freame, 412; Hannah, 137, 1429; Humph., 1000; Jeremiah, 1429*; John, 1224*; Marg., 137; Margery, 1429; Mary, 1014; Rachel, 884; Ric., 137, 1016; Ric.

Pat., 137; Rev. Rob., 1016; Sarah, 138*, 1014, 1016; Stephen, 1224, 1227; Thos., 884*, 1014, 1016*, 1429; Wm., 137*, 138*, 1016; —, 1017

Miners, *see* Minors

Mines, Francis, 1362; Rev. Francis, 1362; Misses, 1290

Minett (Minet. Miniet, Mynet, Mynett, Mynetts), Ann(e), 1353, 1361; Betty, 1454; Dan., 284; Eliz., 1353; Francis, 1361; Geo., 671, 677; John, 1217, 1353; Jonathan, 1103; Joseph, 169; Marg., 169; Mary, 1103, 1361; Thos., 1353; Wm., 1333*, 1454, 1504; —, 1148, 1455; fam., 415*

Minnell, Joseph, 1158; Mary, 1158

Minors (Miners, Mynors), Basilia, 1401*; Eliz., 1401; H., 1370*; Hen., 289, 1401; Isabella, 1370, 1401*; John, 296; Rog. de, 1401; Susanna, 296*; Thos., 296*; Wm., 1401; —, 1402

Minshull. Francis, 408*; Marg., 408

Minster, Ellen, 1193; Thos., 1193, 1196

Minterne, Frances, 1267; Hen., 1267

Minty, (or Cooke), Eliz., 1248*; John, 1158; Margery, 496; Mary, 1158; (or Cooke), Rob., 1248; (or Cooke), Sam., 1248*; Thos., 496*, 1158

Mirehouse, Rev. W. S., 1047

Mister (Myster), Chris., 55; Jane, 55; John, 567; Mary, 567

Mitchell (Michel, Michell, Mitchel, Muchele), Abigail, 1007; Adam, 1069; Annabella, 335; Ann(e), 334, 335, 412*; Betty, 1007; Bridget, 669; Chas., 668*, 669, 930, 1007, 1510; Edith, 930; Edw., 328, 334, 335*; Eliz., 335, 841, 951, 1511; Esther, 1007; Hannah, 1007; Hester, 1063; Isabella, 745, 746; Jas., 668*, 669*, 1007*; Rev. Jas., 951*; Jane, 1157; Jeremiah, 347; Jeremy, 347; Jeremy Badger, 347; John, 140*, 335, 412, 563, 668*, 1007*, 1440; Rev. John, 1238; Joseph, 1511*; Rev. Lancelot, 840, 841; Marg., 347, 668; Maria, 1109; Mary, 140, 335*, 668, 1007*; Milles, 1006; Ralph, 1104; Ric., 1069; Sam., 1007*; Rev. Sam., 515, 951; Sarah, 1007, 1510; Syward, 1372; Thos. le, 140, 468, 668, 670, 745, 746, 1007, 1102, 1109*; Wm., 412, 1510; —, 1063, 1402; fam., 311, 667, 778

Mody, *see* Moody

Moels, John de, 1345; Marg. de, 1345; Nic. de, 1345; — de, 1345

Mogge. Geof., 1494; Wm., 1519

Moggridge, John, 546

Mohand (Mohoun, Mohun), *see* Moon

Moire, —, 986

Mole, *see* Moule

Molendinarius (Molend, Molendinar, Molendinare), *see* Miller

Molendino, *see* Mill

Mollineux, *see* Molyneux

Molton, Anselm, 250; *and see* Moulton

Molyneux (Mollineux), Capel, 984; Edw., 124; Eliz., 984*, 1338; Emilia, 984; Lieut.-Gen. Thos., 984*; Major-Gen. Thos., 984; Sir Thos., 1338

Mom'ay, *see* Mom[er]ay

Momelard, Wm., 1477

Mom[er]ay, Wm., 1456

Monce, Wal., 1259

Monck (Monek, Moneke), see Monk

Monesleya, Wm. de, 1091

Money, Wm., 275, 350; fam., 349

Mongondy, Wal., 1292

Monin, Caleb, 758; John, 758

Monk (Monck, Monek, Moneke), Ann, 450; Eliz., 55*; John (le), 1258, 1259; Leonard, 55*; Rog. le, 1385; Wal. (le), 1259, 1313; Wm., 55, 450; Dr., bishop, 1160; and see Moyne

Monmouth, Hen. of, 1217; John de, 244, 732, 1214; John de, bishop, 915; Ric. (de), 1078, 1378; Wihenoc de, 759; duke of, see Scott, Jas.

Monnington, Phebe, 884; Thos., 884

Monox (Monnocks, Monnox), Eliz., 1274; Geo., 366, 368, 383, 1032*; John, 1274; Mary, 370, 383; Thos., 1032; Mr., 369, 370

Monpesson, Thos., 1087

Mons, Rog., 1160

Montacute, see Montague

Montacute [peerage], Ant., Viscount, 691 n, 692; Barbara, Viscountess, 691 n; and see Neville, Isabell and —

Montague (Montacute, Montagu, Mountague), Ann, 352; Chas., 352; Chris., 704; Eliz., 1261; Sir Geo., 1220; Jas., 972*; Sir Jas., 1220; John, 353; John de, earl of Salisbury, 357, 358; Mary, 353; Sarah, 972*; Lady Susan, 1219; Simon, bishop, 1093; —, 705, 1476; fam., 704

Montaigne, —, 230 n

Montar, Dennis (Dyonis), 1292

Montchensy, Joan de, 885; Warine de, 885

Monteath, Rev. Jas., 394; Jas. Stuart, 394

Montefort, see Montfort

Montery, Conde de, 723

Montfort, (Montefort, Mountford), Mabel, 1287; Hen. de, 1047; Simon de, earl of Leicester, 357, 869, 1403; —, 1287; and see Mountford

Montgomery, Rob. de, earl of Shrewsbury, 747; Rog., earl of, 893

Montrose, dukes of, 1281

Moody (Mody, Moodey), Chris., 764, 1513; Eliz., 657, 660, 887; Isabella, 1404; Jas., 657, 1034; Joan, 657, 1073; John, 531, 537, 683, 887, 1034; Mary, 683; Sam., 538; Sarah, 660; Thos., 660; Wm., 660

Moon (Mohand, Mohoun, Mohun), Felix, 845; Geof. de, 1490; Margery le, 1491; Ric., 1491; Sarah, 845; Wm. de, 1086; —, 1478, 1490

Moore (Moor, More), A., 1289; Agnes de la, 1317; Alice atte, 1314; Ann, 1522, 1525; Sir Antonio, 393 n, 791 n; Benj., 1289; Rev. Chas., 929; Christian, 1532; Dan., 976; Edw., 90, 1157, 1390; Eliz., 474*, 666, 930, 1036, 1279; Geo., 1054*, 1279*, 1362; H., 1160; Hannah, 90, 1160; Hester, 1532; J. F., 224*; John (atte), 174, 388, 666, 929, 1027, 1037*, 1038, 1045*, 1121, 1150, 1157, 1279, 1361, 1447, 1518; Rev. John, 85, 840; Rev. Jonathan, 31; Joseph, 1575; Juliana atte, 1314; Marg., 1045, 1361; Mary,

1037, 1038, 1146, 1279*, 1390, 1575; Nat., 1390; Rev. Nat., 1487; Nic., 1045, 1046; Rachel, 1046; Ric., 684, 738, 915, 930, 1257; Rog., 1101; Sam., 1282; Sarah, 1532; Sir T., 393, 590 n; Thos., 474*, 532, 666, 1063, 1407; Rev. Thos., 613; Sir Thos., 1401; Rev. W., 1512*; Wm., 233, 360 n, 474*, 890, 1289, 1363, 1522, 1525, 1532*; Capt. Wm., 537; —, 1061, 1064, 1290, 1311, 1475; fam., 232

Moorton, see Morton

Morande, Wm., 1356

Morbel, Wm., 1502

Morcok, Wm., 1104

More, see Moore

Moreden, Mary, 687; Wm., 687

Morefield, Eliz., 1046; Geo., 1046*; John, 1046

Moreland (Morland), Rev. Ant., 1346; Rev. Thos., 233, 1221, 1477; Rev. Wm., 829

Morell, see Morrell

Moreman, Anne, 837; Joan, 837; Mary, 837; Sarah, 837; Thos., 837

Moren, John, 1053; and see Moring; Moryn

Moreton, see Morton

Morgan, Abigail, 809; Alice, 765, 1317; Ann(e), 442, 467, 472, 473*, 645, 808, 810, 931, 1112, 1175, 1198, 1411, 1576; Anne Maria, 1320; Bridget, 736; Rev. C. H., 1320, 1321, 1323; Chas., 412, 596*, 597, 1576; Rev. Chas., 245, 808; Chas. Tyrrel, 592; Dorothy, 808; Edm., 596*, 1229, 1233; Edw., 596, 736, 765, 1243; Sir Edw., bt., 645, 1198; Eleanor, 248, 808*, 809*, 1415; Eliz., 596*, 814, 861*, 867*, 899, 906, 1112, 1243; Esther, 1019; Eunice, 1415; Evan, 412; Frances Harriett, 1320; Frances Susannah, 1320, 1323; Geo., 473, 807, 809, 921, 1121, 1428; Helen, 1232; Henrietta, 448; Hen., 448, 596, 861*; Hester, 1019, 1112; Rev. Hugh H., 1232; Jas., 473*, 542, 752, 1411; Jane, 111, 563*, 808; Joan, 814; John, 442, 467, 468*, 474, 542, 592*, 736, 815, 899, 922, 931, 963, 1019, 1112, 1175, 1405, 1415; Rev. John, 508; Joseph, 620, 965*, 1112*, 1121; Joshua, 923, 1411; Magdalen, 809; Marg., 1019; Mary, 442, 467, 468, 473, 543, 596*, 620, 730, 808, 906, 1482; Mat., 813; Capt. Mat., 928; Paul, 1323; Phil., 111, 221; Probert, 809; Ric., 87, 536*, 596, 808, 809*, 810, 814; Rev. Ric., 785; Rob., 563*, 592, 593, 596*, 1552; Sam., 213, 543, 1112, 1121; Sarah, 542, 752, 906, 963, 1133; T. H., 1321; Thos., 465, 473, 592, 596, 761*, 808*, 809, 813, 867, 906*, 965, 1112, 1162, 1229*, 1233, 1489; Capt. Thos., 809; Rev. Thos., 328, 1133, 1140, 1147, 1233; Tim., 467; Trevor, 1019*; Wal., 596; Wm., 245, 248*, 523, 563, 730, 808*, 814, 826, 906, 922, 1019, 1140, 1175; Rev. Wm., 547; Col., 1197; Rev. Mr., 929; fam., 807

Morice, see Morris

Moring, Nic., 1048; and see Moren; Moryn

Moris, see Morris

Moriton, see Mortein

Morland, see Moreland

Morlewode, see Marlwood

Morley, Alice, 884, 1454; Edw., 1454; John, 893; Ric., 440; Sarah, 1454*; Stephen, 884, 1454; Thos., 1454; Wm., 1454*; —, 1455

Morman, John, 1202

Morment, Thos., 1238; W., 1238

Morrell (Morell), Hester, 787; Rev. John, 744; Rebecca, 384; Wm., 787; *and see* Murrell

Morrey (Morry), Eliz., 1270; Geo., 1270*; —, 1293

Morris (Maurice, Morice, Moris, Morrice, Morys), Alice, 1258; Ann(e), 455, 641*, 787, 1343, 1458; Cath., 658; Edith, 1259; Edw., 1473; Eliz., 133, 907, 1457, 1526; Ellen, 1400; Esther, 1237; F., 1382; Rev. Geo., 1552; Henrietta, 1400; Hen., 1516; Rev. Hen., 328; Hester, 133; Jas., 304, 338, 931; Jane, 304, 1235*, 1372; Joan, 1371*; John, 48, 71, 72, 74, 131, 133*, 149, 150*, 259, 572, 787, 843*, 907, 931, 1258, 1371, 1378, 1458, 1526; Joseph, 215, 1236*; Martha, 90; Mary, 215, 353, 572, 787, 843*, 931, 933, 1063, 1236, 1237*, 1330, 1400, 1458; Mat., 1315, 1371*; Miles, 1237; Nic., 1363; Rev. Nic., 128; Peter, 658, 1024, 1027; Priscilla, 1327; Ric., 950, 1330; Rob. (le), 71, 402, 449, 1164, 1399, 1400*, 1482; Ruth, 1399; Ruth Mayo, 1400; Sam., 133*, 150, 402; Sarah, 74, 150, 1315, 1458; Susanna, 150, 304; Thos., 90*, 338, 353*, 455*, 641, 797, 884*, 931, 933, 1237*, 1238, 1343, 1372; Rev. Thos., 1356; Ursula, 402; W., 1516; Wm., 843, 848, 850*, 1063, 1064*, 1235*, 1457, 1458; Lieut. Wm., 1327; Rev., 328; —, 414, 927, 1311, 1328, 1362

Morrison (Moryson), Sir C., 1288; Sir Chas., 290 & n; Edm., bishop, 1226; Maria, 290 & n; Lady, 1288

Morry, *see* Morrey

Morse, Abraham, 104, 105; Rev. Abraham, 760*, 761*, 904*; Alice, 922, 1174*; Ann(e), 104, 280*, 388, 760, 1037, 1282, 1453; Ant., 797*; Betty, 1550; Chas., 130; Christian, 1295, 1309; Deborah, 465, 761; Dorothy, 250; Edith, 1453; Edw., 104, 105, 465, 537*, 760, 903; Eleanor, 203*, 1174; Eliz., 99, 170, 283, 724, 904, 1037*, 1250*; Frances, 165; Flo[rence?], 537; Geo., 99, 724, 1037, 1130; Hanna(h), 537*, 1481; Harry, 450; Hen., 1037, 1282; Humph., 1250*; J. Nourse, 894; Rev. Jackman, 103, 104, 105*, 759, 760; Jane, 165, 903, 1037*, 1038; Jasper, 1453; Joan, 471, 797; Joanna, 1174; John, 161, 165*, 170, 203*, 280, 283*, 367, 927, 1037*, 1038, 1073, 1173, 1174*, 1175, 1176*; Rev. John, 214, 760; John Hooper, 1173, 1174*, 1176; John Nourse, 903; Joseph, 1174, 1176, 1197; Marg., 465, 813, 924; Margery, 1481*; Martha, 450, 948*, 1282; Mary, 240, 280, 433, 777, 903, 904, 948, 1130, 1174*; Matthias, 104, 105, 250; Mic., 924; Moses, 813; Nic., 165, 280*, 281*, 537; Ric., 433, 813*, 922; Rob., 388; Rev. Rob., 1519; Sam., 904, 1186; Sarah, 105, 165*, 283, 813; Thos., 165*, 203, 280*, 281*, 433, 471*, 531, 532, 625, 777, 948*, 962, 1054, 1169*, 1174*, 1176, 1550*; W., 1177; Wm., 203*, 240, 283, 388, 463, 524, 777, 1037, 1173, 1174*, 1176,

1481*; Capt., 1169; Mr., 894; —, 463, 1054, 1169*, 1176; fam., 236

Morshall, *see* Marshall

Morson, Chas., 49

Mortein (Moriton), earl of, 816; *and see* Beaufort, Edm.

Mortiboys, Thos., 287 n

Mortimer (Mortymer), Anne, 685, 876; Annora, 1033, 1255; Beatrix, 1253; Cicely de, 1033; Cromwell, 327 n; Edm. (de), 252, 484, 1255; Edm., earl of March, 251, 876; Edw., 685, 986; Edw. (de), earl of March, 643, 1082*; Elianor, countess of March, 876; Eliz., 484*, 986; Hugh (de), 791 n, 1033, 1255; Isabel, 791 n; Je(o)ffry, 876, 1082; Rev. John, 13*, 15, 990, 1372; Marg., 1169; Matilda de, 1255; Rob., earl of March, 1482; Rog. (de, le), 252, 483, 484*, 529, 1082, 1102, 1255*; Rog. (de), earl of March, 643, 876*, 1082; —, 1169, 1255; —, earl of March, 1016; fam., earls of March, 158, 195, 792, 1380, 1485

Morton (Moorton, Moreton, Mortyn), Anna, 550; Dan., 780*; Deborah, 660; Ducy, Lord Ducie, 1139; E., 1456*; Eliz., 49, 203, 1250, 1345; Lady Frances, 1033; Francis, Lord Ducie, 1033; Rev. Gabriel, 1221; Hen. Geo. Francis Reynolds, earl of Ducie, 1344, 1345*, 1455*; Hester, 780; Jas., 1250; John, 793, 836, 1250; Rev. John, 1313; Marg., 780; Mary, 308; Mat., Lord Ducie, 1033*; Mat. Ducie, baron Ducie, 452*, 1346; Nic. de, 1292; Oliver, 1121; Sir Rob., 1491; Sir Rowland, 1275; Sam., 660, 661; Sarah de, 1292; T., 1288; Thos., 660, 1033*, 1491; Rev. Thos., 1062; Wm., 49, 203, 308, 550, 780; Col., 1522; Madam, 1033, 1340; Mr., 918, 1447; —, 1361, 1455, 1456; fam., 546, 792

Mortymer, *see* Mortimer

Mortyn, *see* Morton

Morwent (Marwent, Merewent), Anne, 1053; Joan, 821; John, 1323; Joseph, 1053, 1251, 1396*; Mary, 1251; Rev. Dr. Rob., 525*; Sarah, 1396; Susanna, 930; Thos., 930, 1053*; Wm. (de), 680, 927, 929, 1053

Morwy, John, 1150

Moryn, Alice, 1232, 1233; John, 1361*; Rob., 1232; T., 1477; Wm., 1361; —, 1361; *and see* Moren; Moring

Morys, *see* Morris

Moryson, *see* Morrison

Mose, *see* Moss

Moseley (Mosley), Ann(e), 45*, 296; Eliz., 45, 686, 1181; Ellen Jane, 1515; Isabella, 45; Jas., 1378; John, 1181, 1459; Rev. John 89, 147; Mary, 231; Ric., 231; Rob., 1196; Sarah, 1457; Thos., 45, 296, 1388; Wm., 45, 1457; Rev. Wm., 42, 45*, 685, 686; *and see* Mostley

Mosen, *see* Mosson

Moses, Rev. Wal., 1223

Mosley, *see* Moseley

Moss (Mose, Moso), Eliz., 304; Geo., 960; Hannah, 1384; Isaac, 1172; Joan, 303; John, 1384; John Stone, 303; Margery de, 1120;

Martha, 948; Mary, 948; Rachel, 303; Ric., 1065, 1196; Thos., 303*, 304, 948, 1482; Wm., 302, 303; —, 1475

Mosson (Mosen, Mossum), Ann, 506; Ann Mary, 506; Jas., 506; John, 1196; Mary, 1014*; Ric., 1014; Sarah, 506; Thos., 506; Wm., 506

Mostley, Eliz., 974*; Lieut. John, 974; Rev. John, 974; Rev. Ric., 974; *and see* Moseley

Motley, *see* Mottley

Motloe, *see* Mutlow

Mottesfonte, Wm. de, 1258

Mottley (Motley), Ann, 1164; Jas., 821, 1038*, 1164; Mary, 821, 1038*; Sarah, 821, 1038*; Thos., 1038

Mouget, Rob., 1292

Moul, *see* Moule

Mould, Rev. Jacob, 571, 979; John, 573; Mary, 573, 1459; Sarah, 573; Thos., 573; Rev. Wm., 1459; Rev., 573*

Moulder (Maulder), Ann, 373; Eliz., 130; Humph., 429*; John, 130*, 316*; Joseph, 304; Mary, 304, 429; Ric., 130*; Sarah, 130; Susanna, 130; Thos., 316, 367, 373; Wm., 316; —, 1005

Moule (Mole, Moul), John le, 1317; Joseph, 1289; Rev. Thos., 515

Moulton, Millicent, 1329; W., 1331; Wm., 1329; *and see* Molton

Mount, Caroline, 1005; Chas., 334; Chas. Milman, 334; Wm., 334

Mount Edgecumbe (and Valletort), Geo., earl, 449; Geo., Viscount, 252

Mountague, *see* Montague

Mountene, Chas., 31

Mountford, Rev. Bart., 7, 1428; Edw., 1345; Wm., 1345; *and see* Montfort

Mountjoy, Barbara, 699; Beata, 474; Edm., 1553; Thos., 1486; Wm., 699

Mountnorris, Arthur, earl of, 1172; Lady Cath., 1172

Mountsteven, Rev. Wm., 445, 446

Mousell, Edw., 923; Eliz., 923; Hen., 455*; Martha, 923; Mary, 455; Thos., 923*

Mousto, *see* Mustoe

Mowbray, Aliva, 1253; —, 1239, 1253*; —, duke of Norfolk, 1156; fam., 1253

Mower, Hannah, 563; John, 1213*; Rev. John, 802*, 1539; Sarah, 1213; Ursula, 1213; Wm., 563

Mowtlow, *see* Mutlow

Moxham, Mary, 1326; Ric., 1326*

Moxley, Alex., 734; Jas., 736; Jane, 736; Mary, 736; Phil., 736; Wm., 736

Moye, Mary, 353; Thos., 353

Moyle, John, 550*, 1323

Moyne, Eliz., 1074; Gil. le, 1074; Hen. le, 1074*; Joan le, 1074; Johanna le, 1074*; John le, 1074*; Sir John, 1074; W. le, 1074*; —, 1237; *and see* Monk

Moysey, Jane, 388; John, 388; Susanna, 388

Moystyn, Gen. John, 336

Muchele, *see* Mitchell

Mucklowe, John, 1221

Mudd, Chas., 124; Eliz., 124

Mudwell, Rev. Ric., 586

Muggleton (Mugleton), Thos., 523, 878, 880, 1483

Muggleworth, Rev. Miles, 613

Mugleton, *see* Muggleton

Mukeltone, *see* Mickleton

Mulcot, Rob. de, 1052

Mull (Mulle), *see* Mill

Mulleward, *see* Milward

Mullings, R., 990, 1127 n; Ric., 1187 n

Mullis, Edw., 141, 1012; John, 141; Mary, 141

Mullward, *see* Milward

Mulne, *see* Mill

Mulward, *see* Milward

Mumford, Ann, 850; Jane, 850; John, 850; Ric., 850*; Thos., 71; fam., 764

Munchyn, *see* Minchin

Munday (Maundy), Clynton, 1355; Eliz., 187; Joane, 1054; John, 187; Joseph, 845*; Martha, 845; Sarah, 845*; Tobias, 1054

Munden, Dan., 677; Eliz., 303; Hen. de, 360; Mary, 677; S., 981

Murch, Ann, 1575; Jane, 1575; Thos., 1575; *and see* March

Murdac, Ric., 523

Muridale, Wm., 1388

Murrall, *see* Murrell

Murray (Mury, Murye), Cath., Lady Rollo, 411; Mary, 141; Nic. le, 1379; Wm., 141*; Mr., 590 n

Murrell (Murrall, Murrel), Betty, 906; Eliz., 550; Thos., 547, 906; *and see* Morrell

Mury (Murye), *see* Murray

Musard, Amicia, 876; Asculf (Hascoit), 876*, 878, 1055, 1082*, 1091; Constance, 1082; Joan, 876; John, 876; Marg., 876; Nic., 876*; Ralph, 875, 876*, 1060; Ric., 876; Rob., 876; S., 1082; —, 1201; fam., 875, 1082

Musco, Joseph, 637; Sarah, 637; *and see* Mustoe

Musgrave, Eliz., 1225; Jas., 128*; Mary, 1071; Sam., 1225, 1306; Wm. Jas., 1071; *and see* Musgros; Musgrove

Musgros (Musgrose, Mussegros), Cecily de, 1237; Hawise (Hauise), 1165, 1237, 1238; Hilary de, 1214; Nic., 1491; Ric. de, 1214; Rob., 585; Wm. de, 1214; —, 1237; fam., 275, 785; *and see* Musgrave; Musgrove

Musgrove, Cecilia de, 1238; Dame Cecilia, 1234; Mary, 744; *and see* Musgrave; Musgros

Mussegros, *see* Musgros

Mustoe (Mousto, Musto, Mustow), Ann, 317, 423*, 1058*, 1445; Ant., 317; Eliz., 317; Ferdinando, 1063; John, 423, 1063; Mary, 317; Ric., 317*, 423*; Sarah, 881, 1063; Thos., 881, 1058, 1499; Wm., 1445; —, 1092; *and see* Musco

Mutlow (Motloe, Mowtlow, Mutloe), Ann(e), 934, 1469; Eliz., 1469; Hen., 1469*; Jas., 1039, 1312; Rev. Jas., 820; John, 934, 1468; Lucy, 1468; Mary, 1034, 1469; Mary Ann, 1034; Rev. Wm. Wilton, 1034*

Mydwynter, *see* Midwinter

Myers, Cath., 1231

Myles, *see* Miles

Mylksop, Hen., 1331
Mylborn, *see* Milborne
Mylle, *see* Mill
Myn (Min), Col. Nic., 855; Col., 680, 806 n, 894 n, 1314; Gen., 1293
Mynbridge, —, 1292
Mynchyn, *see* Minchin
Mynde, Rev. Hen., 1404
Mynet (Mynett, Mynetts), *see* Minett
Mynors, *see* Minors
Myrriman, *see* Merryman
Myster, *see* Mister

Nailor, *see* Naylor
Naish, *see* Nash
Nanfan, Giles, 895; Rev. Giles, 269, 993; John, 265, 1288; Mary, 269, 993; R., 1287; —, 1476
Nant, Rev. John, 1539
Naper, (later Dutton), Jas. Lenox, 1066*, 1067, 1068*, 1483; Jas. Lenox Wm., 1067; Jane, 1067*; Wm., 1067
Napp, *see* Knapp
Narroway, Chas., 921; Mary, 921
Nash (Naish, Nasshe), And., 105; Ann, 1185, 1199, 1200, 1272, 1361; Anselm, 104*, 105; Chris., 881; Edw., 435; Eliz., 203, 212, 1181*, 1272; Ester, 1183; F., 1181; Francis, 1181; Geo., 1272; Giles, 560, 1181*, 1182, 1183, 1185, 1512; Hannah, 560; Hugh, 1196; Isaac, 203; J., 1512; Jane, 1200; John, 203*, 212*, 499, 1112, 1121, 1181, 1199, 1201, 1361*, 1512; Joseph Wm., 1272, 1289; Marg., 104, 1112; Mark, 1539; Mary, 104, 203, 1110, 1181; Nehemiah, 1110*; Profet, 549; Rachel, 212; Rose, 105; Sam., 1200; Sarah, 203, 212*, 881, 1182, 1199*, 1200; Slade, 565, 567; Dr T., 1221; Thos. (atte), 212, 1131, 1272, 1552; Rev. Thos., 1494; Wal., 1199*, 1200*; Wm., 1201, 1272; Rev. Dr., 1492; —, 463, 1140, 1380*, 1387, 1494, 1512; fam., 159; *and see* Nayse
Nasmyth, —, 1292
Nason, Rev. Stephen, 400
Nassau, Prince Hen. of, 220 n; Prince Maur. of, 220 n
Nasshe, *see* Nash
Nation, Wm., 815
Nattaber, —, 546
Nayl, John, 1172
Naylor (Nailor), Sir Geo., 1519; Sir Geo., kt., 1218; Hen., 1161; John, 921, 1161, 1563; Marg., 921; Rob., 1423; —, 1160
Nayse, Rev. Urian, 1385; *and see* Nash
Neale (Neal, Neall), Alex., 1548*; Alice, 541; Ann(e), 337, 338, 393 n, 542, 633, 1111, 1427; Ant., 1213; Art., 1312; Benj., 204*, 338*, 1548, 1551; Betty, 174; Cath., 1548*, 1551; Chas., 111*; Rev. Chas., 668, 670; Christian, 175; Dan., 633*, 958*; Eliz., 175, 337, 598*, 670; Esther, 541, 1213; Gabriel, 1548*; Geo., 174, 175, 670*, 958; Grace, 1551; Hannah, 171, 957, 959; Hen., 838; Hester, 393 n; J., 1312; Jas., 958; Jane, 175, 491; Joan, 175; John, 175, 341, 393 n, 541, 555*, 598, 958, 959*, 1140, 1213, 1548*, 1551; Rev.

John, 1163, 1165; John Brown, 1548; Joseph, 338, 959, 1574; Martha, 1213; Mary, 111, 204, 338, 541, 1109, 1213, 1427, 1548; Maur., 1548; Mic., 17, 554; Morris, 1111; Nat., 1213; Nic., 538, 541, 542; Partise, 1548*; Rebecca (Rebeckah), 505, 538; Ric., 491*; Rev. Ric., 802; Rob., 1456; Sam., 598, 948; Sarah, 555, 633*, 958*, 1438, 1548*; Simon, 633, 1438; Susan, 959; Susanna(h), 1213, 1548; Thos., 175*, 337, 505, 541*, 1109, 1217, 1427, 1438*, 1455; W., 1312; Wm., 171, 175*, 337, 554, 598*, 948*, 958, 959, 1438, 1548*, 1551; Rev. Wm., 221, 223; fam., 393*, 525
Neames (Neems, Nemes), Betty, 1537*; Dan., 1537; Thos., 1158; Mrs., 1215
Neast (Nesse, Nest), Ann(e), 1307, 1357; Eliz., 1269*, 1358; Frances, 1269*; John, 611; Mary, 1269; Ric., 1269*, 1358*; Thos., 1355, 1357; Wm., 1269*, 1289, 1358*; Capt. Wm., 1362; —, 1288; fam., 1362
Neat, Emy, 730; Jane, 730; John, 730; Jonathan, 730; Mary, 730; Sarah, 730*; Thos., 730*
Neave (Neve), Rev. Chas., 1105, 1113, 1122
Neccham, Alex., 359
Need, Jas., 906; John, 906
Needham, Rev. And., 180, 181*; Ann(e), 181*; (or Reedham), Margery, 1051; Mary, 181; Sibella, 181; Wm., 181; (or Reedham), Wm., 1051
Neems, *see* Neames
Nelmes (Nelme, Nelms), Alice, 5, 1098; Ann, 1305, 1569; Cath., 781; Edw., 70, 1098*; Eliz., 70, 171*, 442, 904, 1305, 1526*; Ellis, 904; Esther, 486; Francis, 964; Guy, 1019*; Hannah, 902; Hester, 5, 901; Jane, 1098; John (atte), 5*, 161, 165*, 170, 171*, 1154, 1305*, 1526*; Rev. John, 1071; Lydia, 1526, 1569; Marg., 171; Martha, 1098; Mary, 5*, 165*, 1019, 1526; Nic., 442; R., 1238; Ric., 5*, 486*, 781, 1048, 1539, 1569; Rev. Ric., 781*; Rob. atte, 1313; Rog., 902; Sam., 165; Sarah, 170, 442, 741, 1305*; Susannah, 165; Thos., 5, 12, 171*, 741*, 1019, 1305*, 1494; Wm., 165, 171, 901, 902*, 904*, 1526; —, 1238; fam., 159, 1539; *and see* Elmes
Nelson, Eliz., 89, 147; Eliz. Hawkins, 1183; —, 1258
Nelthorpe (Nelthorp), Dame Eliz., 1349, 1350; Sir John, bt., 365, 1082, 1350; Sir Mo(u)ntague, bt., 1349, 1350
Nemes, *see* Neames
Nerot, J., 1323
Nesse (Nest), *see* Neast
Netherton, Alice, 1052; Thos., 1052; Wm., 708 n
Nethewarde, John, 1478
Nettleship (Nettleshipp), Ann, 335*; Mary, 335*; Patience, 335; T., 1519; Thos., 313, 335*; Mr., 327
Neucomen, *see* Newcomen
Neve, *see* Neave
Nevet, *see* Knevet
Neville (Nevil, Nevill, Nevylle), Anne, countess of Salisbury, 763, 1287*; Anne, countess of Warwick, 805; Anne, wife of Richard III, 805,

1287; Rev. Chas., 503; E., Lord Bergavenny, 1177; Eliz., 1328; Eliz., Lady Latimer, 1538; F., 1177; Frances, 520; G., duke of Bedford, 1169; Geo., Lord Latimer, 1538; Isabel, 763, 1287; Isabell, Lady Latimer, 1328; Isabell, Marchioness Montacute, 1169; Ric., 602; Ric., earl of Salisbury, 361, 1287; Ric., earl of Warwick, 244, 805, 1011; Col. Ric., 520; Thos., 1169; —, Lord Latimer, 1328, 1447; —, Marquis Montacute, 1169; fam., 318, 591, 1201, 1287

Nevis, Rev. Mr., 1018

Nevylle, *see* Neville

New, Ann, 744; Anna, 49; Hannah, 744; Rev. Jas., 435, 1553; Joseph, 49; Ric., 744

Newark, Denis [? Denise], 450; Sam., 450; Wm., 450*

Newberry, *see* Newbury

Newburgh (Newborough, Newburg, Neygbrough), Frances, 1046; Hen. de, earl of Warwick, 318; Hugh, 1363; fam., earls of Warwick, 500, 588

Newburgh [*peerage*], Anne, countess of, 1082; Chas., earl of, 1082; Chas., Lord, 363; Jas., earl of, 363, 1082; countess of, 1403; *and see* Ratcliffe, Chas., Jas., *and —*

Newbury (Newberry), John, 1446; Mary, 1446; Wal., 745

Newcastle (Nov. Castr.), W., marquis of, 1339; Wm., earl of, 1339; marquis of, 1336, 1337; *and see* Cavendish, Wm.; Holles, —

Newcombe (Newcomb), John, 1202; Sam., 386; Sarah, 388; Wm., 386, 1202*; Dr. Wm., bishop, 78*, 1078; —, 1064, 1202

Newcomen (Neucomen), Wm., 1314; —, 1311

Newdegate, J., 1331

Newenet, Edith, 1033; Wal., 1033

Newiell, Rowland, 59

Newitt, Thos., 1289

Newland, Eliz., 971; Geo., 970, 971*, 1210; Hen., abbot, 1513; John, abbot, 41; Sarah, 1210

Newman (Neuman, Newema[n]), Abigail, 1470; Agnes la, 1392; Alice, 1063; And. le, 1005; Anna, 1079*; Ann(e), 212, 661, 706, 950, 984, 1480*, 1481; Ant., 1480*; Benj., 611; Comfort, 984; Dan., 150, 660, 764; David, 1355*; Deborah, 598; Edw., 567; Eleanor, 1079; Eliz., 609, 660, 924, 983*, 1064, 1068, 1079, 1470*, 1474, 1480, 1481*; Geo., 660, 983, 1470*; Giles, 598; Grace, 212; Hannah, 764, 924; Harry, 1467; Harvy, 1470; Hen., 1420, 1480; Lieut.-Col. Hen. Wenman, 1303; Hester, 1079; Hugh le, 1392; Jas., 661*, 1480*; Jane, 399, 1298; Joan, 399, 984; John (le), 395 n, 661, 795*, 983*, 984*, 1079, 1388, 1470*, 1473*, 1480, 1502*; Marg., 395 n, 966; Margery, 150; Martha, 486, 795, 1079; Mary, 339, 555, 661, 706, 795, 984, 1079, 1467, 1470*, 1480*; Nat., 1480*; Peter, 567; Philadelphia, 1391; R., 985; Ric., 317, 611*, 984*, 1064, 1298, 1474, 1480*; Ric. Goodenough, 1303; Ric. Newman, 1303; Rob., 611, 795, 950; Sam., 764, 1079*; Sarah, 777, 982–3; Septimus, 150; Susan, 983; Susanna(h), 983, 984, 1473; Thos., 212*, 339, 399*, 486,

677, 706, 764*, 777, 922, 924, 966, 984, 1063, 1068, 1079, 1473; Wm., 486*, 555, 660, 706, 983, 984, 1126, 1140, 1355*, 1363, 1470, 1481; —, 985*, 986, 1062, 1311, 1361, 1475, 1477

Newmarch (Newmarche, Novo Mercato), Bernard de, 925; Hen. de, 1051*; Isabel, 552; Jas. de, 1051*, 1345; Jas., baron Newmarch, 552; Sibil de, countess of Hereford, 925; fam., 552, 1345

Newnham (Newnam), Anne, 1460; W., 1154

Newport, Ann, 730; Dorothy, 730; Edw., 1257; Eleanor, 569; Hen., 569; John, 569; Mary, 569*; Rob., 1126; Susanna, 369; Wm., 730

Newport [*peerage*], Eliz., daughter of Ric., Lord, 1004, 1005; Ric., Lord, 1004*, 1005;

Newsham (Newsum), Giles, 1008; John, 848; Lydia, 1008*; Mary, 1008; Thos., 1008*

Newth, Ann, 542; Betty, 847; Edith, 847; Nat., 842; Sam., 847

Newton, Sir Adam, 324 n; Rev. Benj., 711 n, 1047, 1238; Dorothy, 209; Eleanor, 1575; Eliz., 209, 1399; Gervis, 209; Isaac, 1575; J., 1455; Joan, 1455; John, 1397*, 1399, 1519; Rev. John, 263, 1047, 1238*; Sir John, bt., 205, 206, 209*, 210*; Kizia, 1511; Mary, 906; Dame Mary, 206, 209*; Mic., 206; Owen, 1511; Rob., 1403; Sarah, 1397, 1575; Thos., 209, 906; Wm., 413, 1403; fam., 205

Ney, Rev. Conrad, 791, 793

Neygbrough, *see* Newborough

Niblett (Nibblet, Niblet), Alice, 676*; And., 1130*; Ann(e), 703, 1130, 1182; Dan., 674*, 676*, 677*, 703, 1024*, 1143; Deborah, 676*; Dinah, 752; Eliz., 674, 676*, 693, 796, 1024; Francis, 1102; Gerteres, 703; Jeremiah, 752; Jo[a]ne, 1130; John, 672*, 676*, 796*, 1024, 1130, 1140, 1182; Judith, 676; Martha, 204; Mary, 176, 1008; Miriam, 676; Ric., 176*; Sam., 197, 252, 672, 676*, 677*, 1054, 1130*, 1132, 1451, 1452*, 1456; Sarah, 677, 1452; Stephen, 204; Susannah, 676; Thos., 693; Wm., 676, 677, 1008

Nibley (Nubbeley, Nubbeleye), John de, 1428*

Niceson, *see* Nixon

Nicholas, abbot, 605

Nicholas, bishop of London, *see* Heath

Nicholas (Nicolas, Nycholas), Sir Ambrose, kt., 1067; Ann(e), 536*, 1067*; Bridget, 1027; Edm., 412, 1027; Edw., 412, 1027; Edw. Richmond, 1027; Eliz., 52*; Hannah, 52; Jas., 531, 536*, 540*; Jane, 1082, 1199, 1201; John, 52, 872*; Lewis, 175; Marg., 1201; Martha, 412; Mary, 175, 412, 540*, 872, 1201, 1534*; Millecent, 1534; R., 1063; Ralph, 52*, 826; Reg., 985*, 1032, 1062*, 1063, 1064; Ric., 52, 1522, 1534*; Sarah, 1425; T., 985*, 1064*, 1201*; Thos., 175*, 364, 536, 826, 985, 1062, 1064, 1082*, 1199*, 1201*, 1582; Rev. Tho[s]., 767; Sir Thos., 1067; Wm., 52, 1534*; —, 986, 1064*, 1104, 1282

Nicholls (Nicholes, Nichols, Nickles, Nickols, Nicolls), Ann, 338*; Barbara, 1306; Benj., 835; Cath., 337, 1273; Chas., 1112; Rev. Chris., 1113, 1115, 1122; Dan., 835*, 1306*; Diana, 1573;

Edw., 338, 837, 965*, 1271, 1368, 1488; Rev. Edw., 853; Eleanor, 315, 338; Eliz., 338*, 490, 492*, 835, 996; Esther, 1273; Frances, 1488*; Geo., 490; Greg., 1428; Hannah, 338*; Hen., 843, 996; Hester, 1367; Jas., 490, 492, 996*; Jane, 338, 379*, 996*; Jeremiah, 658; John, 338, 492*, 847, 996*, 1306; Joseph, 329, 338*, 868; Kath., 1273; Marg., 965; Martha, 338, 965, 1488; Mary, 338*, 490*, 491, 846, 847, 996, 1306*; Ralph, 1150; Ric., 337, 338*; Rob., 837, 965, 996*; Sam., 412, 490, 1367, 1488; Sarah, 337*, 542, 996; Susanna, 843; Thos., 338*, 379*, 542*, 996*, 1218, 1306, 1312; Rev. Thos., 1441; Wal., 315, 338*; Wm., 338, 490*, 491, 492*, 846, 965*, 996, 1273*, 1306, 1327, 1428, 1488*; Dr., 492; Mr., 1421; —, 1219, 1351, 1477

Nicholson (Nicolson), Chas., 1127; Rev. Chris. (Xr.), 593, 1127; Rev. Geo., 1385; John, 785; W., bishop, 362, 515 n; Rev. Wm., 394

Nickles (Nickols), see Nicholls

Nicolas, see Nicholas

Nicolls, see Nicholls

Nicolson, see Nicholson

Nightingale, Martha, 906; Wm., 906

Nind (Nynd), Anne, 74; (or Ind), Chris., 1064; Dorothy, 150, 151; Edm., 1467, 1468; Eliz., 74; Hugh Jas., 1467, 1468; Isaac, 74, 1289; Jas., 74*, 1468; John, 150, 1467, 1468*; Lydia, 151; Mary, 74, 1064, 1468; (or Ind), Mary, 1064; Priscilla, 74; Sarah, 1064, 1467*, 1468*; Susanna, 74; Wm., 151*, 1064*, 1468; (or Ind), Wm., 1064; —, 1064*

Nixon (Niceson), Hannah, 174; Hen., 174; Jane, 44; Rob., 44

Noad, Martha, 847; Rachel, 847; Ric., 836; Thos., 847*;

Noble, Eliz., 682; Hen., 682*; Mark, 682*, 1556; Mary, 682; Rob., 1086*; Wm. le, 1519; Mr., 361 n; —, 1064*, 1322

Noel, Lady Anne, 291*; Baptist, 291; Baptist, Lord Noel, 287*; Chas., 291*; Edw., 291; Edw., Lord Noel, 286, 288, 290, 291*; Sir Edw., 291; Eliz., 291; Hen., 291; Lady Juliana, 290; Lady Mary, 291; Lady Penelope, 291*; Lady Rachel, 122; Wriothesley Baptist, earl of Gainsborough, 122; Lord, 288; fam., 286, 864; and see Nowell

Nokes, Mary, 1386; Wm., 1386

Nollekins, —, 379

Norborne, Wal., 1170, 1171

Norbrock, Rev. John, 161

Norden, John, 324

Noreharde, Rob. atte, 1385

Norfolk [peerage], Edw., duke of, 1295; Rog., duke of, 1322; duke of 301 n, 449 n, 955, 1015, 1016, 1441; and see Bigot; Brotherton; FitzAlan, Mary; Howard, Marg., Phil., and Thos.; Mowbray, —

Noris, see Norris

Norman, Wm. son of, 870, 1237

Norman, Ann, 1413; John, 1413; Wm. the, 1237

Normandy, Hen., duke of, 157, 546, 605 n; Rob., duke of, 1403, 1516; duke of, 158

Norris (Noris, Norreyes, Norreys, Norrice, Norrys,

Norys), Alice, 983, 1137; Ann, 654; Cath., 207; Rev. Dan., 1257; Rev. Edw., 1196; Eliz., 79*, 429; Sir Francis, kt., 207; Frideswide, 1015; Rev. Hen., 1257; Hugh, 372; J., 1202*; Joan, 372; John, 79, 138, 388, 429, 983*, 1202, 1476; Rev. John, 1186*; Martha, 79, 138; Mary, 130, 1137; Ric., 130*, 1137*, 1292; Rev. Rob., 1346; Thos., 429, 576; Rev. W., 1186; Wm., 1202; Mrs., 1196; —, 1139, 1288

North (Northe), Anne, 352; Deborah, 931*; Edw., 1016; Jeremiah, 555*; John, 555, 931*; Rev. John, 1115, 1116, 1122; Marg., 813; Mary, 555*, 931, 1115, 1116; Ric., 931*; Rog., 1196; Sam., 555, 1115; Thos., 352, 931*; Wm., 1259

Northalle, Albreda, 1313

Northampton [peerage], Wm., marquis of, 709; and see Compton, passim; Parr, W.; Somerset, Anne

Northcote, John de, 1074; Reg. de, 1074; Ric., 1561

Northe, see North

Northrudynge, Rog. de, 1346

Northumberland [peerage], earl of, 519, 709; and see Dudley, John

Norton, Ann, 789; Cath., 1006; Fortune, 997; Jas., 661*; John, 661; Josias, 727; Judith, 661; Mary, 661; Ric., 661*; Col. Ric., 1322; Susannah, 661; Thos., 789, 997; W., 1291

Norwood (Norwode), Anne, 799; Cath., 395; Chas., 511, 798; Eleanor, 798; Eliz., 799; Francis, 799*; Hen., 798, 799*; Jane, 799; John, 798*; Mary, 799*; Nic., 511; Ralph, 798; Ric., 799*; Rog., 1370; Rev. Thos., 798*, 799*; Wm., 324, 798*, 799*; —, 116

Norys, see Norris

Notelin (Notelyn), see Notlyn

Notervile (Notervyle), —, 1478*

Nothen, Eliz., 800; Lewis, 800

Notlyn (Notelin, Notelyn), Alice, 1139; Hugh (de), 1021, 1139; John, 1139*, 1140

Nott (Knott, Note), Anne, 904; Edw., 298, 906; Geo., 211; John, 837; Rev. John, 1441; Lawr., 169; Lydia, 211; Mary, 169, 609; Ric., 369; Rob., 211; Susanna, 298; Rev. T., 1289; Thos., 768, 904*; and see Nutt

Nottingham, Cecilia, 852 n; Christina, 371; Eliz., 852 n, 1051, 1202, 1238; W. de, 688 n; Sir W., 1378; Wm., 371, 852, 1238; Sir Wm., 365, 367, 444, 1014, 1051*, 1202*; fam., 445

Nouchard, Ralph, 1477

Nourse (Nurse), Ann, 789, 958; Edw., 853, 1380; Elias, 958; Eliz., 900; Geo., 633*; Isabella, 111; John, 716, 789, 958, 1375; Lucy, 900; Marg., 853; Mary, 608, 633, 716, 789, 900*, 901*; Phil., 789*; Sam., 633; Sarah, 633; Thos., 788, 819*, 821; Tim., 895, 896, 900*, 901; Wal., 895, 900*, 901*; Wm., 111, 608, 633*, 754, 1375; Mr., 893, 894, 1189; fam., 819, 894

Nov. Castr., see Newcastle

Novo Mercato, see Newmarket

Nowell, Eliz., 1070*; Wm., 1074; Rev. Wm., 1070, 1074; —, 1074; and see Noel

Nubbeley (Nubbeleye), see Nibley

Nubbery, John, 270
Nugent, Ann, Lady Clare, 507; (later Craggs), Rob., Viscount Clare, 507
Nugutiis, Jerome de, bishop, 838
Nurdin, Eliz., 1146; Wm., 1146*
Nurse, *see* Nourse
Nutt, Ann, 1575; Capt. Geo. Anson, 1085; Joan, 211; John, 211*; Lydia, 1575; Marg., 211*; Mary, 1575*; Mary Tymewell, 1085; Thos., 1575; Wm., 211*; *and see* Nott
Nycholas, *see* Nicholas
Nynd, *see* Nind
Nynge, Wm. le, 1127
Nyvers, John de, 244

Oakes (Okes), Dorothy, 1527, 1533; Eliz., 1527; Hannah, 1535*; Jane, 1533; John, 1522, 1527*; Jonah, 280, 1522, 1527*; Lydia, 280*, 1527; Martha, 1427; Mary, 1527; Sarah, 1527; Thos., 1533*
Oakey (Ockey, Okaye, Okey, Oky), Ann(e), 118*, 505, 803; Ant., 1043; Eliz., 118, 338, 354, 473, 871, 1043; Frances, 338; Hannah, 118; Hen., 338; J., 1387; Jas., 118*, 683*; Jane, 1209; John, 354, 505, 870, 871, 1209, 1217, 1403; Judith, 803; Nat., 505*; Ruth, 683; Sarah, 505*; Thos., 1140; Wm., 118, 473, 683, 803, 1197; —, 1062*, 1063*, 1120, 1317, 1348
Oakley (Ockley, Ocle, Okley), Ann, 1200*; Rev. Chas., 1344; Rev. Chas. Edw., 1455; Chas. Molyneux Edw., 1344; Edw., 1104; Rev. G. E., 1455; Lady Georgiana, 1344; Lady Georgina Mary Louisa, 1455; John, 55, 683, 1200*, 1313; Patience, 1200; Stephen, 1403; Thos., 1008; Vincent, 1016; W. Overbury, 1016; —, 1017, 1148, 1311
Oates, Eliz., 382; John, 369, 382*
Oatridge (Oatridg), Ann, 1127; Dan., 417*, 1243*, 1245, 1255*, 1258; Eliz., 751*; Hannah, 417*, 632; Hen., 1233; J., 1033; Joanna, 417; John, 417*; Marg., 794, 1243; Martha, 417; Mary, 417*, 620, 632, 1029, 1243, 1245*; Miles, 190, 417*, 620, 631, 632; Rob., 417, 793, 794, 1029, 1229; Sarah, 417, 631; Simon, 1243*, 1245, 1255; Thos., 417, 751, 796; fam., 792*, 1255
Obrien (Obrian), Eliz., 1261; Henrietta, 123; Hen. Horatio, Lord Obrian, 123; —, 1261
Oce, Ernesius son of, 1227
Ockell, Eliz., 584; Harry, 584; Hen., 584; Mary, 254; Thos., 254
Ockey, *see* Oakey
Ockford, *see* Okeford
Ockhold (Ockhould), *see* Ockold
Ockland, Chris., 325 n
Ockley, *see* Oakley
Ockold (Ockhold, Ockhould, Ockolde, Ockolt, Okholt), Agnes, 1379*; Ann(e), 1378, 1379; Ant., 880; Cath., 1378, 1379*, 1380; Chas., 1379; Eliz., 1379*; Frances, 1379; Hen., 1375*, 1379*; Joane, 1379; John, 1379*; Judith, 1375*, 1379*; Marg., 1379*; Mary, 1379*; Phil. de, 1379; Priscilla, 1379; Prudence, 1379; R., 1195;

Ric., 1375*, 1379*; Rob., 1379*; Sibilla, 1379*; Tacey, 880; Thos., 1379*; Wm. de, 1379; —, 1378*; fam., 1378, 1379
Ockwell, Ann, 1535; Jeremiah, 1535
Ocle, *see* Oakley
Odell, Rev. John, 435
Odey (Ody), Cath., 1081; Hen., 1314*; Sarah, 598; Thos., 1081; Wm., 598*
Odo, earl of Champagne and Albemarle, 1120
Odo (fl. *c*. 715), 1153, 1285, 1287, 1291
Ody, *see* Odey
Offa, king of Mercia, 680, 717, 1091, 1093, 1386, 1419, 1474, 1481
Offa, governor of East Anglia, 1459
Offer, Jas., 616; Martha, 616; Wm., 616
Offeret, —, 1093
Offley, T., 1015
Ogan, Hen., 1539; Johan, 1539
Ogborne, —, 1311*
Oglander, Rev. John, 840
Oglethorp, Owen, bishop, 1102
Oilei, *see* Doyley
Okaye, *see* Oakey
O'Keasey, Hester, 1470
Okeford (Ockford), Anne, 1547; Chas., 435; Hen., 1547; Thos., 1428; Mr., 1215
Okes, *see* Oakes
Okey, *see* Oakey
Okholt, *see* Ockold
Okley, *see* Oakley
Oky, *see* Oakey
Okyn, Joan, 361; W., 361
Oland (Oweland), Dan., 844; John, 844; Mary, 844; Morris, 727; Wm., 844*
Old, Ann, 1158; Hannah, 1158; John, 1158*
Old House, John of the, 1259
Oldacre, Kinnill, 1154
Oldelonde, *see* Oldland
Oldfield, Eliz., 1109; Geo., 1109
Oldham, Abigail, 1072; Anna, 1072; Christian, 1072; Dan., 1072*; Esther, 1072; Hester, 1072; John, 1072*; Mary, 1072*; Rebecca, 1072; Thos., 496, 1072*; —, 1258
Oldisworth (Oldysworth), Anne, 351; Arnold, 351, 364*; Austin, 595; Dorothy, 351; Edw., 351, 1530; Eliz., 1451*, 1530*; Rev. Giles, 230, 393 n, 771; Jas., 595; Rev. Jas., 595*; Rev. John, 588; Sir Lancelot, kt., 592 n; Marg. (Margarite), 351, 1262, 1263; Mary, 595, 771, 1224, 1262*, 1263*; Muriel, 595; Nic., 588, 1262; Rev. Nic., 230; Rob., 432, 593, 1262, 1530*; Tace, 351; Thos., 351, 592; Wm., 590, 593, 595*, 1451*, 1530; Rev. Wm., 432; fam., 592; *and see* Holdsworth
Oldland (Oldelonde), Ann, 1176; Dan., 1019; Eliz., 172*, 542, 1535; John, 176; Sarah, 176, 1535; T. L., 1020; Thos., 542; W., 1020; Wal. de, 1102; Wm. (de), 172*, 1102, 1176, 1535
Oldmixon, Hannah, 921; John, 921
Oldpen, *see* Owlpen
Oldys, Rev. Ambrose, 891; Cecilia, 891; Wm., 891
Oldysworth, *see* Oldisworth
Olgi, *see* Doyley

Oliff (Oliffe, Olive), *see* Olliff

Oliver, Ant., 406; Isaac, 538; J., 1087; John, 531*, 1334; Joseph, 542; Packer, 279; Ric., 531*; Sarah, 538, 1334

Olliff (Oliff, Oliffe, Olive, Olliffe, Ollive, Ollyffe, Olyve), Ann, 1328; Anna, 317; Beisy [? Betsy], 1360; Bridget, 730; Eliz., 384, 730, 1075; Giles, 1075*, 1078; Hannah, 1045; Jas. Sutton, 1360; John, 730, 1045, 1306; Martha, 1045*; Mary, 384, 388, 1045; R., 1061, 1092; Ralph, 127, 1045*, 1075*, 1078*; Ric., 1078*; Rob., 384*, 1075, 1078*; Sam., 1045*; Thos., 1078; Wm., 317, 388, 1328*; —, 1282

Olney (Ollney), Col., 1190, 1257

Olyve, *see* Olliff

Ombersley, W., 1195

Onion (Onnens), Eleanor, 331; J., 1312; Nat., 388; Sarah, 388*; Thos., 388; Wm., 388; —, 1069

Onslow (Onslowe), Rev. Edw., 1369; Sir Ric., bt., 365, 366

Onvill (or Knoville), Rog. de, 1237

Orange, prince of, 723, 776

Orchard (Orcher), Anne, 1533; Bernard, 1121; Bridget, 1549; Chas., 1546, 1549*, 1550*; Eliz., 1099*, 1550; Grace, 722; Hannah, 1546, 1550; Jas., 1546, 1550*; John, 752, 1551; Mat., 752; Sabina, 752; Sarah, 1099, 1549*, 1550; Thos., 778 n, 1533; Wm., 722, 935, 1099; *and see* Archer

Ordway (Ordewey), Hannah, 296; Hen., 1363; Wm., 296*

Orell, *see* Orrel

Organ, Ann, 939; Chas., 264, 1047; Dan., 264; Edw., 1539; Grace, 746*; Hannah, 746*; Joan, 666; John, 264, 746*, 1539; Jonas, 939; Mary, 264, 746; Moses, 939*; Patience, 939; Sam., 666; Sarah, 264, 1511; Susannah, 939; Wm., 262

Orlebar, Diana, 718, 1419, 1428; Ric., 718, 1419, 1428; —, 1419

Orleton (Orlton), Adam de, bishop, 301, 588 n

Orlidge, Thos., 1218

Orlton, *see* Orleton

Ormerod, Dr., 1321, 1322

Ormond [*peerage*](Ormonde), Jas., duke of, 123, 739 n; *and see* Butler, —; Somerset, Mary

Ormonde and Ossory, Ellen, countess of, 124

Orrel (Orell), John, 1277; —, 1293

Orsborn, *see* Osborne

Orum, Moses, 1258

Osbaldeston (Osbelston, Osburston), Amy, 1051; Rev. Geo., 1221; John, 1051, 1379; Judith, 1379; Sir W., 1016; —, 1378, 1447

Osbarn, *see* Osborne

Osbelston, *see* Osbaldeston

Osbern (Osberne), *see* Osborne

Osborn, bishop of Exeter, *see* FitzOsborne

Osborne (Orsborn, Osbarn, Osbern, Osberne, Osborn, Osburn), Alice, 1532, 1533; Ann(e), 417, 624, 1337, 1495, 1528, 1532; Chas., 1383*; Dan., 1383, 1452*; Dorothy, 1108; Edith, 823; Edw., 847, 1495, 1531; Elias, 83; Eliz., 1337*, 1528*; Frances Reddall, 1337; Francis, 1337; Gil., 1495,

1497*; Rev. Gil., 1495, 1502; Grace, 1250, 1383*, 1497; H., 1185; Hannah, 847, 911; Hester, 1298; Jacob, 624; Jas., 823; Jane, 83; Johane, 82; John, 281, 846, 959, 1502, 1525, 1528*, 1529, 1531; Joseph, 1249, 1337, 1384; Joyce, 1452; Martha, 1300*, 1303, 1531; Mary, 254, 741, 842, 955, 1249, 1250, 1300, 1383*, 1452, 1531*; Nat., 824*, 1337*, 1338, 1339, 1383*; Nat. Ambrose Reddall, 1337; Owen, 254; Phil., 741; R., 1529; Rebecca, 1534; Ric., 281, 779, 911, 1522*, 1524, 1525, 1528, 1531*; Sir Ric., bt., 1495; Rob., 83; Sarah, 281, 824*, 911, 1300, 1337*, 1338, 1452, 1525; Sydenham, 1575; Thos., 501, 841, 842*, 868, 1300, 1337*, 1525, 1531; Rev. Thos., 870; Vertue, 842*; W., 1312; Wal., 236, 417*; Rev. Wal., 1108, 1385; Wm., 83, 99, 910, 955, 959, 1249, 1250, 1298, 1300*, 1303, 1525, 1531*, 1533, 1534; Rev. Wm., 1495*, 1502; —, 1311, 1378, 1401; fam., 779, 823

Osburston, *see* Osbaldeston

Oseland, Hannah, 1384; R. G., 1384; Ric. Grigmond, 1383

Osftor, bishop, 717

Osgood, Eliz., 1110; Rev. John White, 1404; Phil., 1110*

Osgot (fl. 1066), 1077, 1350

Osher, king, 1447, 1502

Osmund, Ric., 362

Osulf (fl. 1066), 1491

Oswald, king of the Northumbrians, 839

Oswald (fl. 1066), 1032

Oswald, Jas., 1556, 1569; Mary, 1569; Sam., 1569; Sarah, 1569

Osward, Rog., 1552

Oswid (fl. 1066), 1082*

Otho, *see* Otto

Ottley, Marg., 1153

Otto son of Thos., 533

Otto (or Otho) son of Wm., 533

Otto, Thos. son of, 533

Otto (or Otho), Wm. son of, 533

Ovard, Ann, 473; Jas., 473

Ovenhill, Mary, 339; Thos., 339

Ovens, Ann, 1325; John, 1325; Wm., 97

Overbury, Ann, 765; Anna, 315; Eliz., 1247; Hannah, 1250; Jane, 369; John, 765, 1258; Joseph, 1247*; Marg., 1351; Nat., 1250; Nic., 1016, 1033; Sir Nic., kt., 230*; R., 1351; Ric., 315; Sir Thos., kt., 230*, 231, 393 n*; W., 1227; Wm., 1258; fam., 864

Overell, widow, 1351

Overthrow, Edw., 787, 873; Sam., 683; Sarah, 873

Overton, Geo., 1160; Wm. (de), 985, 1160

Ovett, Rev. Peter, 619; *and see* Oviatt

Ovey (Ovy), Eliz., 654, 655; John, 654, 655

Oviatt, Blaunche, 675; Peter, 675; *and see* Ovett

Ovy, *see* Ovey

Owe (Eu, Ewe, Ow), Ela de, 690; Fitzosbert, count of Eu, 1322; Sybella de, 690; W. de, 1185*; Wal. de, 690; Wm. de, earl of Salisbury, 525, 690, 807, 1032, 1074*, 1225, 1322*, 1516; counts of, 1322

Oweland, *see* Oland

Owen (Owens), Abraham, 1539; Ann(e), 604, 973; Ant., 1065; Eliz., 334; Emma, 1237; Francis, 334*, 1426; Rev. Francis, 1217; G., 1388; Hannah, 604; Hen., 890; Sir John, bt., 1237; Marg., 328; Mary, 604, 1065, 1426; Dame Mary Frances, 1237; Nic. Owen Smith, 1538*; Ralph, 922; Rob., 329; Sarah, 1009; Thos., 1065*; Rev. Thos., 1422, 1423; Wm., 604*, 1009; Rev. Wm., 973; Dr., 1421; Miss, 1440; Mr., 404 n, 1189; Rev., 952; —, 401, 1218; fam., 885, 1495

Owlpen (Oldpen, Owlepen), Bart., 775, 959

Owner, Joseph, 906; Susan, 906

Oxenford (Oxenforde), Rev. Peter, 184; Rev. Phil., 681; *and see* Hokesforde

Oxenham, Ann, 1306; Jas., 1306; Thos., 1306

Oxford, Edw., earl of, 585; Lord, 1165*

Oyan, John, 1345

Pace (Paice), Alice, 1270; Anne, 904, 907; Betty, 765; Eleanor, 765*; Francis, 904*, 1270; John, 765*; Marg., 830; Mary, 904; Ric., 1127; Sam., 904; Sarah, 765, 831, 907; Susannah, 904; Thos., 765, 895, 904*, 907*; Wm., 765*, 830*, 831; —, 1293

Pacey, Jane, 468; John, 203; Mary, 38, 468, 1511*; Ric., 38; Sarah, 468; Thos., 468*, 1477, 1511; Wal., 468; *and see* Peacy

Pach, *see* Patch

Packer, A., 1064; Alex., 313, 314, 315; Ann(e), 79, 334, 907, 972*, 999, 1276, 1346; Ant., 907; Arthur, 986; Bridget, 972; Cath., 772, 907; Christian, 283; Dan., 419, 550, 907, 969, 972*, 1144, 1403; Dorothy, 315; Edw., 331; Eliz., 314, 331, 473, 907, 972, 1004, 1120, 1231; Francis, 772; Gabriel, 474; Geo., 334, 1155; Hen., 130*, 771, 772*; Isaac, 772; Jane, 771; Joan, 772; John, 79, 175, 283*, 334, 418, 489, 772*, 1279; Jonathan, 474; Joseph, 283*, 334, 623; Kath., 331*; Lodowick, 331*, 334, 1231; Marg., 474*; Mary, 130, 331, 418, 419, 474, 489, 972*, 1144, 1155; Mat., 999*; Ric., 284, 771, 972*; Rob., 1120; Sam., 175, 474, 489*, 907; Sarah, 175, 283, 489*, 772, 937, 972*, 1155; Susan, 331; Thos., 130, 314, 328, 331*, 334, 472, 771*, 772, 937, 972*; Toby, 328; Wm., 472, 473, 489, 972*, 1004, 1276, 1279, 1346; Winifred, 315, 986; Mr., 915; —, 985, 986, 1017, 1292; fam., 313

Packington (Pakington), Frances, 1332; John, 572, 1289; Sir John, bt., 572, 1332; Marg., 572

Padwyn, Rev. Thos., 567

Page (Pagge), Abraham, 1574; Ann, 735*, 974; Chas., 947*; Rev. Chas., 434*, 947; Elinor, 1319; Eliz., 945, 946, 974, 981, 1081, 1470; Dame Frances, 792; Sir Francis, kt., 792; Grace, 945*; Hannah, 945, 946; Hester, 974; Jas., 1473, 1477; Jane, 1127; John, 27, 340*, 945, 947*, 1217, 1331, 1420, 1470; Joseph, 176; Marg., 371; (or Mathews), Martha, 1471; Mary, 176, 339, 340, 835, 862, 1081; Penelope, 947*; Rebekah, 945, 974*; Rev. Reg., 1228; Ric., 945*, 946, 974*; Rob., 371; Sam. Page, 1018; Thos., 884, 945*,

946*, 1319*; Wm., 339, 735*, 814, 862, 981, 1081, 1127, 1132; (or Mathews), Wm., 1471; —, 1017, 1052

Pageham, Thos., bishop, 183

Paget, Ann, 388; Cath., 388; Eliz., 388; Etheldreda, 1068*; Hen., 388; J., 1287, 1288; Jas., 388, 1348; Thos., 388; —, 1476; *and see* Patchet

Pagge, *see* Page

Pagler (Paglor), *see* Pegler

Paice, *see* Pace

Pailin, *see* Paling

Pain (Paine, Pains), *see* Payne

Painter (Payntor), Anne, 384; Christian, 898, 906; Elianor, 904; Eliz., 456; Jane, 212; John, 881; Joyce, 298; Joseph, 212; Martha, 881*; Mary, 456; Phil., 368, 384*; Ric., 298*, 456*; Sarah, 368, 384; Wm., 300, 361, 456, 881*, 904*

Paish (Paysh), Eliz., 524; Frances, 429; Mary, 388; Thos., 388, 429; Wm., 524

Paite, *see* Pates

Pake, Wm., 1460

Pakington, *see* Packington

Palfreyman (Palefrayman), Rudno. (?), 1477; —, 1477

Paling (Pailin), John, 1289; Rev. Wm., 1346

Palling (Pallings, Pawling, Pawlings), Amy, 981; Ann(e), 374, 981*; Beata, 981; Cath., 1; Christiana, 1067; Dinah, 1067*; Edw., 973*, 975, 981*; Eleanor, 973; Eliz., 981*; Francis, 1132; Grace, 973; Hannah, 598; Jane, 1067; Jemima, 981; John, 368*, 374, 969*, 973*, 981*; Mary, 973*, 975, 981*, 1181; Rob., 463, 1067*; Sam., 1112*; Sam. Norris, 1112; Sarah, 368, 374, 973*, 1112*; Thos., 981*; Wm., 969*, 973, 1112, 1181

Palmer (Palmere, Palmore), Alice, 1391, 1542; Ann(e), 38, 212, 489, 831, 923, 1143, 1146, 1227, 1360, 1371; Rev. Ant., 233; Arthur, 212; Benj., 1317; Betty, 38, 489; Bridget, 1070; Chas., 824, 837; Rev. Chas., 853; Deborah, 10; Edith, 1341; Edm., 1012; Edw., 923*, 1542*; Eliz., 84, 923*, 993; Giles, 230 n, 393 n, 831, 887*, 1195; Hannah, 887, 1194, 1276; Hester, 837, 993; Isabell, 1175; Jas., 10, 1372; Jane, 847, 1360*, 1371; Joan, 38; John (le), 38*, 212, 412*, 464, 789, 836, 847*, 887*, 1070, 1175, 1197, 1258, 1329, 1401; Joseph, 847; Joshua, 563; Josiah, 1012*; Judith, 887*; Marg., 1276; Martha, 38; Mary, 38*, 230 n, 295, 412, 824, 887*, 1112, 1371, 1391, 1419; Nic. (le), 213, 1197; Phil., 489*, 1143, 1146, 1371, 1440; Ralph le, 1379; Ric., 38*, 230, 993; Rob., 38, 84, 489, 1542*; Sam., 789; Sarah, 84, 563, 831, 832; Susannah, 837; Thos., 4, 832, 887*, 1276*, 1583; Sir Thos., 878; W., 1227; Wal. (le), 311, 1258; Wm. (le), 38*, 392 n, 831, 847, 887*, 922, 1016, 1112, 1194, 1351, 1360*, 1371*; Rev. Wm., 483, 1341, 1382; —, 393 n, 1017, 1317, 1331; fam., 232, 311, 393 n, 804, 885

Palser, Anne, 1533; Eleanor, 1533; Hugh, 1533*; Hugh Alex., 1533; John, 1539*; Joseph, 1539; Mary, 1533*; Ric., 1533; Rob., 1533; Thos., 1533, 1539

Panckridge (Pancridge), Christian, 138; John, 138; Rob., 186

Panting (Pantin), Ann, 946; Edw., 598; Hannah, 200; J. Wickliffe, 1422; Jas., 203; John, 200; Mary, 1534; Rev. Mat., 432; Rev. Sam., 1534; Sarah, 203; Rev. Thos., 1422; Wm., 1422, 1534; Mr., 1421

Pany, Ric., 1292

Papps, Eliz., 555; Francis, 413, 555

Paradise, Geo., 176; John, 1100, 1101; Mary, 176; —, 1102

Parbery, Mary, 1531

Parcare, see Parker

Parchmenter (Parch.), John, 1428, 1477; —, 1477; and see Parmiter

Pardington, —, 1475

Pardoe (Pardos), John, 948; Mary, 756; Sam., 756

Pardy, Alice, 1270; Comfort, 1275; Eliz., 1275; John, 1275*; Marg., 1275

Pare, John, 407

Parem, see Parham

Parfitt (Parfay, Parfett), Geo., 321; John, 1477; Mary, 413; Wm., 413

Parham (Parem), Ann, 202; Edw., 202; Hen., 304; Ric., 202; Sarah, 203; Wm., 203

Paris, Mat., 707

Parish, John, 611

Park, Abel, 1137; Alice, 1438; Dan. Horwood, 782; Deborah, 1438; Edw., 1438*; Eliz., 1307, 1438, 1439*; Geo., 1438*, 1439; Hannah, 1137, 1438; Jas., 1137; Jane, 1438; John, 1439; Joseph, 1438; Mary, 781, 782, 1438*; Paul, 781; Sarah, 1439; Susannah, 1438; Thos., 1137; Wm., 1438; —, 1455; and see Parkes; Perkes

Parker (Parcare), Adam le, 1420; Alice, 1547; Ann(e), 399, 402, 417, 686, 948, 1050*, 1110, 1425, 1426, 1427, 1433; Arthur, 499*, 1426*; Chas., 616*, 884; Rev. Chas., 685, 686*, 1356; Dan., 343*, 417, 1117, 1171; Rev. Dan., 342*; Deborah, 343; Dinah, 343*; Edith, 1024; Edw., 208*, 412*, 685, 686*, 722, 730, 826, 973, 974, 975, 1050; Rev. Edw., 206; Eleanor, 685; Eliz., 132, 208, 353*, 661, 795, 944, 957, 999, 1171, 1302, 1306, 1389, 1426*, 1427, 1439; Emily, 1415; G., 1172; Geo., 782; Grace, 996; Hannah, 976, 1117; Hen. M., 1415; Hester, 837, 1110; Rev. Humph., 1217; Isaac, 957, 1328, 1426*, 1427; J., 1172; Jacob, 1551; Jas., 417, 661, 1024*, 1235, 1236, 1439*; Jane, 499, 973*, 974, 975*, 976, 1088, 1117, 1454; Job, 1088; John, 132*, 191*, 399, 469, 488, 499, 682, 684, 685*, 686*, 730, 771, 797, 837* 944*, 947, 996, 1050, 1088, 1117*, 1121, 1187, 1302, 1426*, 1427, 1433; Jonathan, 463; Joseph, 208*, 1194; Rev. Lewis, 61; Marg., 685, 1547; Martha, 686, 973, 974; Mary, 191, 208, 417*, 499, 686*, 730, 884, 891, 944*, 973*, 974*, 975, 1050*, 1063, 1110, 1117*, 1236, 1282, 1425*, 1426; Mat., archbishop, 147; Mathias, 1306; Mic., 686; Nic., 1110, 1348; Phil., 1121; Philippa, 1435; Rebecca (Rebekah), 499*, 1088; Ric., 132*, 208*, 993, 1088*; Rob., 999, 1428; Rog., 996; Rev. S.,

1486; Sam., 487; Sarah, 208, 616, 682, 686, 1024, 1050, 1117, 1306, 1425, 1427; Sibill, 191; Susanna, 412, 1050; T., 1052; Tabitha, 1426; Thos., 838*, 853, 891, 948, 973*, 974*, 975*, 976, 1427; Rev. Thos., 132, 275, 350, 853, 1238*; Tim., 1554; W., 1172; Wal., 795, 1435; Wm., 353, 399, 402, 417*, 677, 778 n, 891*, 1050, 1313, 1389, 1425*; (or Malverne), Wm., abbot, 684; Rev. Wm., 1408; Mr., 1080; —, 1455, 1547; —, abbot, 131, 1132

Parkes, Eliz., 335; J., 1064; Jas., 335; John, 335*; Marg., 1061; Mary, 335*; Patience, 335; Rev. Ric., 335, 1356; Wm., 335; —, 1064; and see Park; Perkes

Parkhurst, John, 591 n; John, bishop, 394; —, 404 n

Parkington, Mary, 906

Parkinson, John, 1576; Rev. John, 1335; Mary, 1576; Rev. T., 1043; —, 404 n

Parlow, Benj., 1016

Parlyn (Purlyn), Alice, 738; Jas., 738*; Thos., 738

Parmiter, Hen., 1173*; and see Parchmenter

Parnell (Parnall), Anne, 308; Benj., 1327; Chris., 1305; Edw., 308, 1305*; Hugh, 308, 1305*; John, 1305; Judith, 1305*; Marg., 308; Mary, 308, 573, 1305*; Nic., 308; Sarah, 308; Ursula, 1305*; Wm., 308; Rev. Dr., 1305; and see Purnell

Parr (Parre), Edw., 883, 884; Kath. (Kateryn), queen, 709, 1103, 1159*, 1220*, 1221*; Leger de, 1280; Ric., 883*; W., marquis of Northampton, 1219

Parrett, see Parrott

Parrey, see Parry

Parrott (Parrett), Catherina, 46; Edw., 46; Humph., 274*; John, 735; Mary, 274*; Ric., 706, 1092

Parry (Parrey, Pary), Ann, 353; Benj., 86; Dan., 1200; Dority, 735; Edw., 941*; Eliz., 402, 1074, 1268; Esther, 1200; Hen., 221; Hen., bishop, 324; Hester, 941*; Jas., 815; John, 112, 353, 735, 1007, 1289, 1539; Rev. John, 85, 86*; Joseph, 940, 941*, 1007*, 1317; Lydia, 1007*; Marg., 940; Mary, 86, 941*; (or Perry), Mary, 1489; (or Perry), Mary Kath., 1489; Nancy, 353; Nat., 537; Rebecca, 86*; Rob., 402, 1121; Rev. Rog., 764; Sam., 86; Sarah, 537; Thos., 86, 820, 909, 990, 1268*, 1438; (or Perry), Thos., 1489; Sir Thos., 990; Wal., 735; Wm., 463, 1361; (or Perry), Wm., 1489; (or Perry), Dr. Wm., 1489; —, 1074, 1491*; fam., 400; and see Perry

Parsley, Jas., 1415; Mary, 1415; Patience, 730; Thos., 730, 1420

Parslow (Parslo, Parsloe, Passelewe, Passelow), Abraham, 910, 911; Alice, 419; Ann(e), 166*, 1326; Cath., 284; Dan., 939; Deborah, 623; Edith, 127; Eliz., 176, 633, 939*, 1167, 1168; Geo., 1326*; Giles, 127; Hugh, 1227; John, 50, 166*, 176*, 284, 387, 419, 623, 633, 1168, 1326*; Jonathan, 1217; Joseph, 1307; Judith, 633; Martha, 911; Mary, 387, 623, 939, 1326; Rob., 633; Rog., 633; Sam., 939, 1008; Sarah, 166, 910; Stephen, 939*, 1167*, 1169*; 1169

Parsons (Persones, Pson), Agnes la, 1460; Ailway, 900; Alfred, 1511; And., 815; Ann(e), 375*, 428, 550, 701, 765, 1583; Benj., 550; Betty, 388; Chas., 71, 89, 147, 375*, 764, 765*, 999; Cris., 1055; Dorias, 996; Deborah, 765*; Lieut. Edw., 765; Rev. Edw., 1439; Eliz., 387, 575, 762, 765*, 1386; Geo., 762, 996*; Hester, 1268; Rev. Hugh, 279; Isabella, 1166; J., 1348; Rev. Jas., 252, 567*; Jane, 567, 1439, 1574; John, 71, 72*, 575, 763*, 764*, 765*; Rev. John, 635, 1140, 1335; Marg., 953; Mary, 548*, 765, 996, 1045, 1149, 1151; Mercy, 999; Phil., 137, 1386; Rachel, 1574; Ralph, 372; Ric., 387, 872, 1574*; Rev. Ric., 515, 1045, 1189; Rob. (the), 1074, 1583; Rev. Rob., 534, 953; Simon, 965*; Susan(n)ah, 765*; Thos., 375*, 701; Rev. W., 1289; Wm., 388, 1268; Rev. Wm., 610; Dr., 156, 178, 462, 477, 530, 592; Rev., 639; —, 1292–3, 1378, 1458, 1460

Partridge (Partarridge, Partrich, Partriche, Partrige, P'trich), Alice, 446, 879, 924; Ann(e), 282, 418, 524, 880, 991, 1056; Ant., 879*; Chas., 1420; Dan., 562, 1144, 1145, 1183*; Edw., 465, 924; Eliz., 16, 541, 670, 886, 971, 1144, 1517; Geo., 922; Giles, 418; Hen., 878, 879*, 1083*, 1179, 1419, 1518, 1519; Hester, 879; Jas., 282, 418; Rev. Jas., 1517, 1519; John, 16*, 166*, 282, 524, 531, 537, 670, 683, 880*, 886, 1039, 1144*, 1146, 1147, 1223; Rev. John, 438, 1517*, 1518*, 1519*; Capt. Joseph, 1419; Marg., 1519; Mary, 166, 418, 562, 578, 1517, 1519; Oliver, 799; Rachel, 1144; Rebecca, 1179; Rob., 86, 879, 991; Sam., 1183; Sarah, 880, 1146, 1183; Thos., 879, 921, 1517; Rev. Thos. Esbury, 1370; Wal., 1348, 1491; Wm., 445, 446*, 512, 531*, 541*, 879, 913, 915*, 971, 1144*, 1147, 1258; Mr., 878, 1519; Rev., 959, 1365; —, 1147, 1519*; fam., 779, 878*, 1083, 1519

Pary, see Parry
Pasham, John, 1049; Mary, 1049
Paske, Frances, 32
Pasley, John, 679; Sarah, 679
Passelor, Wal. le, 1033
Passelewe (Passelow), see Parslow
Passemer, Wm., 1102
Passey (Passy), Mary, 1567*; Sam., 1567; Thos., 1567; Thos. Packer, 1567; —, 1361
Passour, Matilda le, 1363; Wal., 1356; —, 1361
Passy, see Passey
Paston (Pastone, Pastons), Ann, 754; Anna Maria, 755; Rev. Benedict, 221; Clement, 753*, 754, 755; Edw., 753*, 754, 1388; Frances, 754, 755*; Jas., 755; John, 754*, 755*, 977; Rev. John, 1388; Mary, 754, 755*; Mary Isabella, 753, 754; Wm. (atte), 753, 754*, 755*, 1460; —, 753
Patch (Pach), Adam, 1314*; Geo., 1130; Jane, 1307; Joseph, 1307; Mary, 1130; —, 1311; and see Path
Patchet, Jane, 1200; John, 1200*; and see Paget
Pate, see Pates
Paternoster, Ralph, 1259
Pates (Paite, Pate), Anne, 315; Barnabas, 335; Cath., 315; Dinah, 70; Edith, 315; Eleanor, 315;

Eliz., 315; Frances, 315, 334*; Jane, 317; John, 315*, 334*, 335*, 1213, 1214; Joseph, 1214; Judith, 315; Lyn(n)ett (Linett), 313, 315*; Marg., 1169; Mary, 334, 335*; R., 1169; Rebekah, 335; Ric., 315*, 317, 325*, 327, 335, 801, 851, 985, 1061, 1122, 1478; Sarah, 1213–14; Thos., 315*, 334, 335*; Wm., 70, 315; fam., 313
Path, John, 368; and see Patch
Patle, Wm. atte, 1187
Patrick, Eliz., 1361; Jas., 1361; Sir Miles, 1122; Ric., 137; W., 1362; Wm., 1289, 1361; —, 1362
Patshall, see Pattshall
Patten (Patyn), Joan, 137; Joanna, 137; John, 137, 138; Judith, 138; Ric., 1221; Rob., 137, 138; —, 1017
Patterson, John, 227; Mary, 1368; Susanna, 227
Pattshall (Patshall), Rev. Thos., 944, 1043
Patty (Paty), Jas., 15; Mary, 15; R., 1016; Ric., 1093, 1195*
Patyn, see Patten
Paul, Cmdr. Alf. John, 1245; Anna, 1508; Ann(e), 1133, 1135*, 1144; Cath., Lady Paul, 1507; Chas. Wm., 1245; Charlotte, 1511; Dean, 1508*; Eliz., 1133, 1135, 1507, 1508; Esther, 1245; Sir G. O., 1139; Geo., 1507; Sir Geo. O., 1027; Hester, 1241*, 1248; Holmin, 1135; Sir J. D., 1027; Sir J. Paul, 1255; Jane, 1184, 1366, 1508; John, 915, 961, 1133, 1241*, 1245, 1248, 1258, 1415; Capt. John, 961, 1133; John Paul, 1245*; Joshua Paul, 1245*; Josiah, 1241, 1248; Lieut. Josiah, 1245; Marg., 1508; Mary, 1135*, 1145, 1214*, 1241*, 1245*; Mat., 546; Nat., 1133*, 1135*, 1136, 1145; Rev. Nic., 619, 621, 1135; Obadiah, 1133*, 1135, 1136, 1512; Onesiphorus, 1133, 1135*, 1366, 1508; Sir Onesiphorus, bt., 1027, 1136, 1184, 1507; Capt. Rob., 1511; Rob. Clark, 1245*; Rob. Snow, 1511*; Sam., 621, 1133, 1139, 1214, 1507; Rev. Sam. Paul, 1245; Sarah, 1135, 1136, 1248, 1257; Susanna, 1133*, 1507; Wm. Matthews, 1255; Messrs., 1256; Mr., 894, 1259 n; —, 1139, 1255, 1256; fam., 159, 894
Paulet, Eleanor, 1431; Sir John, 1431; and see Poulett; Powlett
Pauncefoot (Pauncefoote, Pauncefot, Pauncefote, Pawncefoote), Adamar, 1422; Anne, 978, 992*, 993; Dorothy, 685; Eleanor, 977*, 978*; Eliz., 895, 903, 977, 978*, 997; Esther, 903; Sir Geo., bt., 992; Grimba(u)ld, 684, 977, 978*; Hen., 978, 992; J., 903; Jane, 978; John, 76, 685, 895, 978, 992*, 993; Rev. John, 903*, 1047; Marg., 977; Mary, 674, 977; Poole, 674, 977, 978; Ric., 684, 685; Rob., 978; Sarah, 978*; Sophronia, 76; Wm., 895, 977*, 978*, 992, 993; —, 685, 997; fam., 894
Pauntelegh, Wal. de, 1363
Pavy (Pavey), Ann, 1510; Rev. Briant, 449; John, 97*; Thos., 1510*, 1513; Wm., 97, 1540
Pawling (Pawlings), see Palling
Pawncefoote, see Pauncefoot
Paxford, Ann, 1063; Eliz., 1063; John, 1063; Sarah, 1063; Wm., 818; —, 1063, 1064*

Paxton, Jas., 537
Paye, *see* Baye
Payn, *see* Payne
Paynard, Dan., 307; Eliz., 307*; John, 307*
Payne (Pain, Paine, Pains, Payn), Alice, 1153; Ann(e), 17, 129, 235, 1435; Benj., 1373; Betsey Griffith, 1488; Betty, 777; Capel, 482; Cath., 797, 991, 1135; Chris. Griffith, 1488; Danah, 991; Rev. Dennis, 1423; Dinah, 344; Edith, 1313; Edw., 758; Rev. Edw., 853; Eliz., 235*, 340, 378, 846, 907, 991*, 1575; Ellis, 1573; Frances, 1488*; Francis, 344; Geo., 846; Giles, 907, 1435; Hen., 1153, 1575; Hodgkinson, 377; Isaac, 797, 1488; J., 1154; Jas., 235, 731; Jane, 731, 1024; Jo[a]ne, 1130; John, 264*, 340*, 496, 797, 907, 991*, 1027, 1489; Lieut. John, 1488; John Surman, 340; Joseph, 235*; Rev. Lawr., 1373*; Lucilla, 907; Marg., 1345; Martha, 1488; Mary, 907, 991, 1194, 1438*; Mat., 797; Olive, 264*; Phil., 991; R., 1494; Ric., 129, 264, 340, 1139; Rob., 264, 991, 1130; Rev. Rob., 128, 1339, 1385; Rog., 1232, 1316; Sam., 731; Sarah, 235, 308, 496; Sidham, 1024; Susannah, 731; T. W., 713; Thos., 295, 1194, 1196, 1238, 1345; Dr. W. H., 1216; Wal., 1438*; Wm., 13, 17, 308, 731, 758, 907, 1135*, 1194, 1217, 1314, 1351; Mr., 1538; —, 1027*, 1140, 1316; fam., 482, 1027, 1139
Paynham, —, 1162; *and see* Baynham
Payntor, *see* Painter
Paysh, *see* Paish
Payton (Peyton, Peyvon), Ann, 980; Eliz., 1263*, 1279; Dr. Geo., 1263*; Hen., 980, 1279*, 1289; John, 1263*, 1279*; Mary, 980, 1279; Ric., 1279; Richardson, 1289; Thos., 980; Rev. W., 1127; Rev. Wm., 744*; —, 1044
Peace, Ann, 411; Grace, 683; Jas., 411; Joseph, 411; Marg., 411*; Mat., 411*; Rachel, 411*; Rebecca, 411
Peacey, *see* Peacy
Peach (Peche), Agnes la, 1363(?); Bart., 251; Cath., 657; Christi(a)na, 1369, 1434*; Deborah, 1507*; Edw., 1507*; Eliz., 656*, 660, 1507; John, 657*, 1507*, 1508; M., 660; Marg., 1507*; Mary, 660; N., 1203; Nat., 1139, 1507*, 1511, 1513; S., 660, 1434*; Sam., 619, 649, 656, 660, 960, 962, 1369*, 1434*, 1556; Sam. Peach, 721; Sarah, 657*, 660, 962, 1556; T., 1339; Thos., 19; Wm. Gai(n)sford, 1289, 1507; Mr., 1513; —, 1020, 1139; fam., 649
Peachey (Peache, Peachy), Ann(e), 597, 1077*; Arabella, 598; Emily Mary, 1075; Frances, 338; Isabell Sarah, 1075; Jas., 338; Jane, 1075; John, 597, 598, 1077; Rev. John, 1077; Marg., 1077, 1078*; Mary, 1075, 1077, 1078; Mary Ann, 1501; Ric., 320, 338; Rev. Ric., 445*; Rowena, 1077; Susan, 1501*; Susanna(h), 1077, 1078*; Thos., 1119, 1258; Wm., 1075, 1077*, 1078*, 1501; Wm. Gracchus, 1077; Rev., 1075; —, 1075, 1076
Peachum, Wm., 1201
Peachy, *see* Peachey

Peacy (Peacey), Ann, 948; Eliz., 947*, 1503*; Hannah, 947; John Freeman, 1503; Mary, 948*; Thos., 1503*; Thos. Howes, 947; Wm., 948*, 1503; —, 1504; *and see* Pacey
Pead, Ann(e), 812*, 814; Dan., 175; John, 175, 812, 814; Susanna, 175; Tim., 175
Peak (Peek), Ann, 710; Eliz., 377; Frances, 370, 377; John, 370, 377*, 710*; Mary, 377*; Sarah, 377
Pearce (Pearse, Peirce, Peres, Peris, Pers, Pierce, Piers), Anna, 168; Ann(e), 456, 468, 1006, 1135, 1146*, 1164*, 1367*, 1510, 1529, 1550; Comfort, 1266; Dan., 837, 1131; Dicky, 177; Earl, 1573; Edith, 1164*; Edw., 654*, 741*, 1006; Eleanor, 146; Eliz., 170, 173*, 176*, 654, 741, 786, 924, 1135*, 1163, 1164*, 1266, 1277, 1307, 1534; Francis, 935, 1307*; Geo., 937; Hannah, 170, 1168*; Harry, 1529*; Hen., 10, 229*, 378, 786*, 1160, 1165, 1534, 1584; Hester, 171*, 174; Isaac, 486, 731; J., 1101; Jael, 1534*; Jas., 456*, 797, 1101, 1511; Jane, 304, 1214, 1584; Joan, 229; Joanna, 1344*; John, 170*, 173, 176, 229, 467, 578, 601, 924, 931, 1039, 1104, 1168*, 1289, 1344, 1351, 1510, 1551; John Morse, 173; John Phillips, 170; Joseph, 174, 304, 1164, 1165, 1289, 1307*, 1344*, 1367, 1529, 1539; Lucy, 730; M., 1101; Martha, 176, 456, 1146; Mary, 10, 170, 173*, 229*, 378, 456, 654, 730, 741, 920, 931, 935*, 1088*, 1131, 1508, 1510*, 1534, 1537, 1550; Nat., 1266, 1277; Obadiah Paul, 1135; Rev. Offspring, 1529; Patience, 1534; Priscilla, 1163, 1164, 1511; R., 1186; Ralph, 171*, 741; Ric., 229, 1534*; Rob., 146, 176*, 468, 1534*, 1537; Rose, 937; Sam., 1088*, 1135*, 1513; Sarah, 176, 229*, 456*, 467, 661, 730, 741, 786*, 1146, 1534; Thos., 98, 160, 172, 173*, 174, 229, 730*, 741*, 935, 1121*, 1146, 1164*, 1367*, 1369, 1428, 1508*, 1510*, 1534*; Rev. W., 1043; Wm., 10, 168*, 170, 171, 173, 176, 467*, 473, 537, 661, 730, 1132, 1146*, 1163*, 1164*, 1344, 1367, 1550; Lieut.-Col. Wm., 1164; Rev. Wm., 100, 1164; Wm. Prothero, 1164; Mr., 1512; —, 1018; fam., 228, 1165; *and see* Perys
Peard, Cath., 1231; Matilda, 1231; Oliver, 1231, 1417; *and see* Peart; Pyard
Pearsall, Ann, 793
Pearse, *see* Pearce
Pearson (Peason, Persoun, Pierson), Alice, 1471; Davis, 340; Geo., 1465; Jas., 340; Joannah, 623; Mary, 340, 621*; Nic., 1465*; Phil., 1504; Ralph, 1471; Sam., 1424; Sarah, 1468; Susanna Creswicke, 1424; Thos., 621*, 1477; (or Bilson), Rev. W., 1447; —, 1378
Peart (Pert, Perte), Abigail, 1152; Alex., 1312, 1348, 1382; Anne, 1262; D., 1312; Dan., 1262, 1348, 1382; Hen., 295; Isaac, 765; Laur., 1152; Mary, 1154; Paul, 1063*; Sarah, 765; Thos., 1390; —, 1063, 1288, 1293, 1386; *and see* Peard
Peasley (Peasly), Hester, 48; Joseph, 48*
Peason, *see* Pearson
Pebwall, Tim., 81

Pebworth, Dinah, 1278
Pechar, *see* Pitcher
Peche, *see* Peach
Peck, Francis, 791 n; J., 1054
Peckham, Sir Edw., 651
Pedder, Rev. John, 1502
Pederosse, John, 1058
Pedewardine, Eliz., 1402; —, 1402
Pedhall, Rob., 1289
Pedley, Jane, 1065; Nat., 1065
Pedlingham, Anne, 907; Joseph, 907; R., 1317
Peek, *see* Peak
Peeley, *see* Pelly
Peer, Ann, 677; Ric., 677
Pegg, Sarah, 1159; Wm., 1159
Pegler (Pagler, Paglor, Peglar), Abigail, 564;
    Amelia, 750; Ann(e), 563, 1212*, 1512*, 1576;
    Betty, 174; Caroline, 1212*; Eliz., 217, 563*, 632,
    751, 1510; Esther, 1212; G., 1101; Geo., 632*,
    1511; Hannah, 1007, 1146, 1194; Hen., 1365;
    Hester, 1214, 1365; Howell, 1212*; Humph.,
    1194; Jas., 632, 1007; Jane, 1007; Jeo[?f]., 1140;
    Jeremiah, 750; John, 217, 563*, 632*, 1138*,
    1146, 1147, 1183, 1214*, 1539; John Atwood,
    750; Joseph, 563; Judith, 750; Mary, 632, 1138,
    1183, 1214*; Ric., 203, 1007, 1183*, 1186, 1187,
    1194*; Sam., 174; Sarah, 632, 1007, 1183, 1194*;
    T., 1027; Thos., 632*, 751, 1138, 1212*; Wm.,
    217, 564, 1510; —, 1203, 1369
Peirce, *see* Pearce
Pelie, *see* Pelly
Pell, Rev. John, 696, 700; Mary, 700
Pelly (Peeley, Pelie), Rev. Francis, 1087; Rev. John,
    1430; S., 1078
Pemble, Rev. Wm., 559 n*, 561
Pembridge (Pembruge, Pimbridge), Ant., 856,
    857*; Culpeper, 1263; Edm., 856; Eliz., 1063;
    Eufemia, 1402; Sir Hen., kt., 856; Jane, 856;
    Kath., 856; Rev. Thos., 440, 442, 848, 1221;
    Wm., 856*, 857, 1359*; —, 472, 1402*; fam.,
    392, 546
Pembroke [*peerage*], Hen., earl of, 244; Jaspar, earl
    of, 576; Phil., earl of, 244, 480, 721 n; Ric.
    (Strongbow), earl of, 634 n, 1322; Sir Ric., son
    of Jaspar, earl of, 576; earl of, 707 n, 986, 1219,
    1293; *and see* Herbert, Wm.; Marshall, Wm.;
    Strongbow; Valence, *passim*
Pembruge, *see* Pembridge
Pemerton, Hen., 1063
Pen (fl. 1066), 1077
Pen, *see* Penn
Penbury, —, 1052
Pencutt, Eliz., 38; Rob., 38
Penda, king of Mercia, 649, 839
Penda, Cwichelm son of, 649
Penda, Cynegils son of, 649
Pendarves, Gratiana, 920; Sir Wm., 920
Pendelton, Rev. Hen., 1331
Pendocke, —, 1475
Pendrell, —, 1460
Pendry (Pendrey), Joseph, 1575; Sarah, 1361; Wm.,
    1361*

Penduck, Hester, 1303; Jonathan, 1303
Penell, *see* Pennell
Penger, John, 1011
Pengree, Eliz., 225, 226; Geo., 226; John, 225*
Peniston (Penyston), Dame Eliz., 1262; Letitia,
    1262; Sir Thos., bt., 1262; Madam, 21
Penley, John, 941*; Susannah, 941
Penn (Pen), Geo., 772; Jane, 772; John, 1161*;
    Rev. John, 452, 454, 865; Mary, 847; Philepe,
    1161; Ric., 772; Rob., 847
Pennell (Penell), Edw., 264; John, 1046, 1355;
    Joseph, 73; Marg., 1046
Penneson, *see* Penson
Pennoke, *see* Pynnok
Penny, John, 1146; Rev. Rob., 53, 121*, 452,
    1516*; Sara, 1146
Pennrice, —, 1198; *and see* Penry
Penrose, Rev. Thos., 412
Penry, Anne, 377; Bridget, 377; Rev. Jas., 377; —,
    1020; *and see* Pennrice; Pentry
Pensome (Pensam), Eleanor, 1473; Mary, 611*;
    Philip[?pa], 1473; Thos., 611; Wm., 1473
Penson (Penneson), Betty, 1043; Jane, 1043; John,
    1238, 1493; Mary, 954; Sarah, 611, 1493; Thos.,
    1043*, 1493; Wm., 611
Pentry, Esther, 731; Mary, 731; Thos., 731; *and see*
    Penry
Penyston, *see* Peniston
Percival (Percivall), Sir John, 719 n; Mary, 821
Percy (Percye), Anne, 519; Sir Chas., kt., 519;
    Dame Dorothy, 519; Joseph, 884*; *and see*
    Piercy
Pereman, *see* Perryman
Peres, *see* Pearce
Pereste, Geo., 815
Peret, *see* Perrott
Perey, *see* Perry
Perinchafe (Perinchefe, Perirechief), Rev. John,
    1221; Rev. Ric., 147, 1477
Peris, *see* Pearce
Perkeins, *see* Perkins
Perkes (Perke, Perks), Ant., 336; Chas., 836; Edw.,
    659, 865; Eliz., 1092; Ethelbert, 336*, 1064*;
    Francis, 659; Hen., 1363; Jas., 1064; Joanna,
    336*; Lawr., 336; Martha, 659*; Mary, 659, 836;
    Nat., 659; Rob., 659*; Thos., 864; Rev. Thos.,
    865; Wm., 730; —, 1064; *and see* Park; Parkes
Perkins (Perkeins, Perkines), Alice, 1478; Ann,
    564; Edw., 733*; Eleanor, 983; Eliz., 133, 467,
    564, 899; Geo., 564, 633, 899*; Rev. Geo., 626;
    Hannah, 563; Jane, 983; John, 408, 409, 611,
    881, 978, 1226*; Rev. John, 1228; Marg., 814,
    899; Martha, 408, 409, 1226; Mary, 818; Nat.,
    563*, 564; Sam., 133; Sarah, 611, 881; Thos.,
    467, 814, 818, 1227; Wal., 983*; Wm., 564, 611;
    Sir Wm., 838 n; Mr., 220; —, 1226*, 1447
Perks, *see* Perkes
Perratt (Perret, Perrett), *see* Perrott
Perrie, *see* Perry
Perriman, *see* Perryman
Perrin (Perring, Perryn), Cath., 1096, 1446; Rev.
    Chris., 865; Eliz., 815, 1446; Jane, 815, 1446;

John, 1446; (or York), John, 1194; Martha, 796, 815; Mary, 796, 1446*; Nat., 1539; Ric., 1378, 1446*; Thos., 796, 815, 1446*, 1447; W., 1447; Wm., 296, 815, 1446*

Perrocke, Eliz., 971

Perrott (Peret, Perratt, Perret, Perrett, Perrot), Benedict, 282; Cassandra, 128*; Edm., 531, 538; Edw., 533 n; Eliz., 741; Geo., 758*; Hen., 128; J., 1092; John, 641*, 741, 1016; Martha, 128; Mary, 641*; Miriam, 758; Nic., 1093; Peter, 282; R., 1093; Rebeckah, 282; Ric., 641*. 1089; Sam., 758; Sarah, 641; Rev. Simon, 567; Tho[s]. 128; Wm., 282, 537, 741; fam., 1092

Perry (Perey, Perrie), Anne, 783*, 1159; Dame Anne, 783; Arthur, 542; Benj., 1510, 1511; Eliz., 554, 662, 706, 1046, 1489; Giles, 74, 1046*; Hannah, 658; Hen., 1160, 1489; Hester, 1046; Hugh, 1488, 1521; Joan, 230 n; John, 230 n, 706, 884; Lieut. John, 1027; Joseph, 658, 662; Lucy, 884; Marg., 505, 781; Mary, 74, 542, 662, 1438, 1488, 1489, 1510, 1511; (or Parry), Mary, 1489; (or Parry), Mary Kath., 1489; Mercy, 382; Rev. Mervin, 553, 554; Peter, 505; Rebecca (Rebekah), 560, 781; Ric., 658; Rob., 781*; Rog., 505; Sam., 382, 1489, 1555; Susanna, 298; Thos., 367, 370, 382*, 560, 783, 1438, 1488*, 1489*; (or Parry), Thos., 1489; Tim., 367; Wm., 884, 913; (or Parry), Wm., 1489; (or Parry), Dr. Wm., 1489; (or Hunter), fam., 783; and see Parry; Pirie; Pury

Perryman (Pereman, Perriman), Benj., 846*; Eliz., 963*; Jas., 963; Martha, 846; Mary, 963; Thos., 963*, 1447

Perryn, see Perrin

Pers, see Pearce

Pershore (Pershor, Persore), Rog. de, 1292; Wm., 925

Persones, see Parsons

Persore, see Pershore

Persoun, see Pearson

Pert (Perte), see Peart

Perys, Hen., 1485; Thos., 1348; Wal., 1259; and see Pearce

Pesshoun, Laur., 1491; Reg., 1491; Ric., 1491

Pestell (Pestel), Chas., 988; Eliz., 988; Eliz. Goodwin, 988; Jane, 988; —, 1017

Peter, king of Castile, 361

Peter the Great, king, 1027

Peter, see Petre

Peters, Ann(e), 370, 383; (or Miflin), Ant., 679; Eliz., 786; Frances, 905; (or Miflin), Frances, 679; (or Miflin), Isabella, 679; John, 905, 907; Ric., 786*; Sarah, 786; Thos., 370, 383; Wm., 815*

Petipher, see Pettifer

Petit, see Pettat

Peto (Peyto), Ric., abbot, 605; —, 1392

Petre (Peter), Anne, 1223; Eleonor, 728; Eliz., 728; Geo., 728*; Gwillim, 1102; Martha, 728; Phil., 977; R. J., Lord Petre, 1331; Sir W., 1223, 1331*; Sir Wm., 1223; Lord, 1223; fam., 977

Pettat (Petit, Pettade, Pettit, Petyt), Anne Frances,

1184*; Rev. C. R., 1494; Cath., 1180; Rev. Elias, 1075; Esther, 1180; Jane, 1184*; Rev. John, 1003, 1147, 1179, 1180, 1184*, 1186*, 1494; L. H., 1168; Martha, 1184*, 1494; Mary, 1184*; Rob., 1477; Sophia, 1180; Thos., 1139, 1140, 1180*, 1184*, 1403; Rev. Thos., 1184*; Capt. Thos. John, 1184; Wa[ll]., 1218; Messrs., 1186; —, 1476, 1477; and see Petty

Pettener, Rev. Thos., 525, 526

Pettifer (Petipher, Pettipher), Eliz., 1065; Joseph, 980; Mary, 980; Rob., 1065; Wm., 980*

Pettit, see Pettat

Petty, Anne, 31; Bridget, 330; Rev. Elias, 330; Leon., 31; Rev. Ric., 463*; Wm., 330; Wm., earl of Shelburne, 864 n; and see Pettat

Petyt, see Pettat

Peutris, see Pewtris

Peverell, Thos., bishop, 717; —, 1221

Pew, see Pugh

Pewtris (Peutris, Pewtriss), Betty, 550; Eleanor, 270; Eliz., 270, 993; Esther, 270, 993*; John, 338, 550; Mary, 338; Wm., 270*, 993*

Peyto, see Peto

Peyton (Peyvon), see Payton

Phelip (Phelippes), see Phillips

Phelpes, see Phelps

Phelpots (Phelpotts), see Philpot

Phelps (Phelpes, Philpes, Philps), Abigail, 809, 1398; Anna, 537*, 539; Ann(e), 537*, 632, 1116, 1277*, 1360; Edw., 1277*, 1359*; Eliz., 111, 873, 1277, 1372; Emanuel, 1372; Esther, 535, 543, 1359; F., 1387*; Geo., 713; J. Dela Field, 1215; Jas., 789; Joan, 789; John, 535, 539, 543, 632*, 820, 1116, 1372; John de la Field, 534, 535*; Joseph, 537*; Marg., 632; Mary, 537, 539, 1209, 1277, 1400, 1411*; Millicent, 1359; Nic., 872; Ric., 111, 1502; Rev. Ric., 500; Rob., 1277, 1359*, 1381; Smithsend, 1359; Susannah, 111; Thos., 768, 809, 1372*; Rev. Thos., 500; W. L., 1362; Wm., 873, 1209, 1372*, 1398, 1400, 1403, 1411; Wm. Law, 1360; Mr., 1420; —, 986, 1215, 1293, 1362*; fam., 532; and see Phillips

Philimore, see Phillimore

Philip and Mary, 265 n

Philip of Spain, king, 495

Philip II, king of Spain, 952

Philip (fl. 12th cent.), 1060

Philipe, see Phillips

Philipotts, see Philpot

Philipps (Philips), see Phillips

Phillimore (Philimore), Ann, 284, 1185; D., 1101; Dan., 175, 282, 1098; Eleanor, 282; Eliz., 281, 282*, 1136, 1175; Geo., 175; Hannah, 284; John, 281*, 282*, 1098*; 1185; Josiah, 282; Mary, 281, 282*, 1099, 1185; Rob., 1185; Sam., 282*, 532, 1098, 1136, 1169, 1175, 1185*; Sarah, 1184*, 1185*; Thos., 284, 1184*, 1185*; W., 1101; Wm., 1099*; —, 985, 1102; fam., 278

Phillips (Phelip, Phelippes, Philipe, Philipps, Philips, Phillippes, Phillipps), Ambrose, 1358; Sir Ambrose, kt., 1358; Ann(e), 217, 536, 906, 965, 1157*, 1330, 1430, 1432, 1458, 1463, 1467,

1468*, 1472; Augustin, 531; Benj., 550; Bridget, 789; Coxwell, 1350; David, 522; Edm., 558, 618; Edw., 174, 413, 923*; Eleanor, 898; Eliz., 172*, 413, 473, 541*, 558, 618; Fanny, 1330; Frances, 536*, 796; Francis, 684, 915; Geo., 598*; Giles, 1186; Grace, 1330; H., 1220; Halliday, 1186; Hen., 172; Hester, 172*, 1343; J., 1220; J. W. T., 1220; Jacob, 789; Jas., 172*, 598, 789, 975; Jane, 100, 212, 735, 965, 1358; Jo[a]ne, 789; John, 100, 109, 172, 174, 176, 212, 226, 413, 531*, 536*, 541, 654, 683, 735, 796, 847, 902*, 907, 964, 1024, 1121, 1173, 1179, 1330, 1331, 1343, 1432, 1447, 1458, 1463*, 1468*, 1472*, 1475, 1532*; Rev. John, 909; Sir John, 648, 1256; Judeth, 1320; Kath., 789; Marg., 902, 1472; Marrah, 902; Martha, 789*; Mary, 109, 172, 226, 235, 537, 541, 598, 847, 922, 1050, 1432; Maur., 531, 537, 541*; Moses, 789*; Nat., 1289; Peter, 172; Phil., 1321; Rachel, 1048; Sir R., 1123; Ric., 124, 837, 1330*, 1447; Rev. Ric., 1001; Rob., 250, 789*, 847; Rog., 296; Sam., 1177; Sarah, 217, 654, 781, 1024, 1330*, 1532; Silas, 1172; Rev. Stephen, 198*, 785; Susanna(h), 965, 1468*; T., 1220, 1447; Sir T., bt., 1060, 1202, 1478; Thos., 33, 172*, 217, 598, 731, 781, 898, 965, 1052, 1104, 1382, 1430, 1432, 1467, 1468, 1472; Sir Thos., bt., 990, 1041, 1104, 1153, 1392, 1447, 1460; W., 1402, 1538; Sir W., 1256*; Wm., 235, 250, 473, 789*, 922*, 965*, 1052, 1379, 1432, 1458, 1472; Rev. Wm., 360 n, 370; —, 414, 893, 997, 1016, 1059, 1104, 1226, 1289, 1290, 1402, 1455, 1461, 1475, 1477*; *and see* Phelps
Philpes *see* Phelps
Philpot (Phelpots, Phelpotts, Philipotts, Phillpott, Phillpotts, Philpott, Philpotts), Agnes, 1323*; Alice, 923; Ann, 815; Bridget, 789*; Deborah, 109; Frances, 815; Geo., 109, 1323*; Hester, 939; Isabel, 124; J., 1323; Jas., 923*; John, 815, 1323, 1473; Mary, 923*; Nehemiah, 1455; Ric., 124, 550; Rev. T., 808; Thos., 815; Rev. Thos., 809, 1317; W., 1323; Wm., 789*, 815, 939*, 1323; —, 1323;
Philps, *see* Phelps
Phipes, *see* Phipps
Phippen, Joseph, 1576
Phipps (Phipes, Phippes), Ann(e), 295, 524, 1330, 1518*; Betty, 741; Chas., 1518; Eliz., 1194; Esther, 1518; Rev. Francis, 221; Isaac, 1582; J., 1195; Jas., 741; Jane, 1200; John, 884, 1258, 1330, 1518*; Joseph, 1518; Mary, 295, 524, 1518, 1582, 1584; Mat., 295; Rob., 884; Sarah, 1518, 1584; Thos., 294, 1584; Rev. Thos., 524*, 1217; Wm., 636, 1194; Rev. Wm., 524*, 793; —, 1216
Pichar (Pichard), *see* Pitcher
Pick, Dan., 171, 172*, 1098; Eliz., 170, 308, 455, 456, 781*; Ellen, 1400; Francis, 171, 933, 1399, 1400; Harrison Hugh, 1400; Hester, 1098; Jacob, 456; Jas., 1101; John, 170*, 176, 308, 455*, 781; Joseph, 455*; Marg., 170; Mary, 170, 171, 172, 174, 308, 455, 456, 933, 1399; Ric., 170, 174, 1111; Rob., 781; Sarah, 170, 171; Thos., 170; Wm., 167, 308; Wm. Harrison, 933

Pickerell (Pickerill, Pickernell), Cecily, 1078; Mary, 296; Rob., 296; —, 1370
Pickering, Joseph, 907; Lewis, 907; Rev. Sam., 394; —, 1403
Pickernell, *see* Pickerell
Pickett (Pycot, Pycott), Bart., 459 n; Eliza, 459 n; John, 1576; Rog., 1259; —, 1257
Picking, Wm., 948
Pickthorne, Ric., 907
Pidding, Eliz., 1572*; Rev. Jas., 603*; Jane, 603*; John, 1572*; Thos., 603, 1572
Piddle, —, 1017
Pidgeon, *see* Pigeon
Pierce, *see* Pearce
Piercy, John, 430; *and see* Percy
Pierrepont, Evelyn, 411
Piers, *see* Pearce
Pierson, *see* Pearson
Piff (Pif, Piffe, Pyff), Ann, 587*; Betty, 514, 587; Eliz., 486, 587*; Geo., 514*; Hannah, 587; John, 587*; Joyce, 587; Marg., 587; Mary, 587; Ric., 486, 587; Thos., 587*; Wm., 587*; —, 1195
Pigeon (Pidgeon), Ann, 953; Edw., 1477; John, 953
Pigot (Piggot, Pygotts), Anne, 766, 767; Hen., 93, 766; John, 1123*; Rev. John, 1186; Margery, 767; Wm., 766
Pike (Pyke), Chas., 1243; Charlotte, 1243; Eliz., 676, 1133, 1243, 1252*; Giles, 1244, 1252*, 1258; Hester, 1244; Isaac, 1258; John, 1176*; Kath., 1252; Mary, 1176; Rob., 676; Sarah, 1185, 1243, 1245*; Thos., 1185, 1243, 1245*, 1258; Wal. Wiltshire, 1243; Cmdr. Wal. Wiltshire, 1245; Wm., 1177; Wiltshire Wal., 1258; Capt., 1245; —, 1177
Pikestra, Wal., 1140
Pile, *see* Pill
Pilgrim, John, 410
Pilkington, —, 1195
Pill (Pile, Pyl, Pyle, Pylls), Edm., 1289; Eliz., 1071, 1425; John, 1071*, 1083; Rev. John, 1071, 1385, 1425; Mary, 1083; Ric. atte, 1259; Sam., 1425; Thos., 1425; Rev. Thos., 619*; Wal. (atte), 1313, 1420
Pilman, Eliz., 522; Thos., 522
Pilsworth. Rev. Augustin, 1539; Rev. Chas., 305, 307; Dan., 305*; Rev. Dan., 245, 305, 307*, 808, 809; Rev. Edw., 305*, 307*; Eliz., 307*; Isabella, 307
Pimble, Ric., 1234
Pimbley, John, 550
Pimbridge, *see* Pembridge
Pimbury, Mary, 660*; Ric., 658, 660; Thos., 660
Pin (fl. 1066), 1077
Pinchin (Pinchoun, Pynchonn, Pynchoun), Dan., 254; Elia, 1314; John, 254, 881*; Mary, 254, 881; Phil., 1363; Rob., 1314; Stephen, 1314
Pincott (Pincot, Pinkcot, Pinkett), Anne, 170; Chris., 542; Dan., 542; Eliz., 542; Hen., 1547; Humph., 703; Jas., 542; John, 170; Jonathan, 170; Kath., 1547; Mary, 542, 703; Weekes, 703
Pindar, *see* Pyndar
Pine (Pyn), Ann, 431; Cecilia, 1385; Edw., 431; Ralph, 1385

Pinfold, Ann, 659*; Anna, 1167; Cath., 1167*; Chas., 797; Edw., 652, 655*, 659*, 795, 1025*; Eleanor, 1203, 1210; Eliz., 655, 795, 797, 1167*; Giles, 652, 655, 661*, 1210; J., 1027; Joanna, 659, 797; John, 659, 1025*, 1167*, 1169*; Joseph, 659*, 1025; Judith, 659; Martha, 1025, 1167; Mary, 655, 1167*; Nat., 661; Ric., 655; Sarah, 1025*; Susannah, 661*; Thos., 652, 661*, 1167*; Mr., 1169; —, 1020, 1027; fam., 649*

Pingrey, John, 542; Ric., 542

Pinkcot, see Pincott

Pinker, Hannah, 492; Jas., 211; John, 211*; Mary, 211*; Thos., 492*

Pinkett, see Pincott

Pinkney, Anna Maria, 730; Arthur, 1073; Kath., 1431; Mary, 1073

Pinmore, Edw., 1106; Marg., 1106

Pinnell (Pinnel, Pynel), Eliz., 1100; John, 1172; N., 1101; Nat., 1100; Rog., 1102; Sam., 1539; Sarah, 1100; Thos., 1102, 1377; —, 1102

Pinner, Dan., 1312

Pinney, Alex., 1573*; Esther, 1573; John, 1573; Mary, 1573

Pintches, Wm., 1238

Pipe, Rog., 1218

Pipmash, Joan, 1055; Jo[hn], 1055

Pipon, Jas., 1411; Joshua, 1411

Pirie (Pirye, Pyrie, Pyrry, Pyrye), Benedict atte, 1132; Elia atte, 1392; Elynor, 1317; John (atte), 785, 1132, 1154, 1363; Wm. atte, 1404; and see Perry

Pirke, see Pyrke

Pirye, see Pirie

Piscator, Geof., 1379; and see Fisher

Pistor, John, 1313; Thos., 1313; Wal., 1313; and see Baker

Pitcher (Pechar, Pichar, Pichard), Ann, 1305; Arthur, 735*; Jas., 815*; Jane, 735; Martha, 735*; Mary, 815; Thos., 1312; Wm., 735*, 815, 958, 1301, 1305, 1307*; —, 1311*, 1402

Pitman (Pitiman, Pittman), Ambrose, 1192, 1278*; Anne, 1265, 1278*; Chas., 1415; E., 1196; Eliz., 822*, 1194; Gardner, 822; Grace, 1192; Hannah, 822; John, 1192*, 1194, 1196, 1277, 1555; Joseph, 1192, 1194, 1196; Marg., 1192; Martha, 822; Mary, 1192; Millicent, 1192*; Pebworth, 1278; Phil., 1192*; Capt. Phil., 1327; Priscilla, 822; R., 1227; Ric., 822, 1196; Rob., 1428; Sarah, 1192*, 1194; Thos., 822, 1192*, 1225; Wm., 274, 822*; Zachariah, 822

Pitsbury, Amey, 1004; Ralph, 1004

Pitt (Pitts, Pytt, Pytts), Alice, 224; Ann, 118, 1199, 1441; Cath., 1200; Edith, 510; Edm., 224; Edw., 510; Rev. Edwin, 1129, 1132; Eliz., 856, 872, 1072, 1109, 1247, 1554; Frances, 1266; G., 1220, 1221; Gyles, 1209; Hannah, 1210; Hen., 1200, 1282; Ja., 1201; Jas., 1200, 1201*, 1202*; Rev. Jas., 135, 855, 856; Jane, 1209, 1439, 1475; John, 118, 475, 476, 562, 899, 904*, 906, 1127, 1289; Rev. John, 1323; Jos., 986, 1083; Joseph, 118, 496, 1109, 1127, 1199, 1434; Lawton, 899; Marg., 510; Maria Ann, 1247; Mary, 496, 543,
562, 1019, 1181; Nat., 543, 563; Capt. Nat., 1439; Phylp, 1475; R., 1159; Ric., 872, 1109, 1181; Rog., 530; Rowland, 919; Sam., 1210*; Simon, 1072; Stiles, 1072; Susanna, 446; T., 661; Thos., 446, 510, 906, 964; Wm., 531, 855*, 1210; Wm., earl of Chatham, 403 n; Rev. Mr., 969; —, 1494; — [G. Pitt], Lord Rivers, 1475; — [Jane, wife of G. Pitt], 1220; fam., 1220; and see Putte

Pitthorn, Ant., 787; Betty, 787; Eliz., 787; Mary, 787; Stephen, 787

Pittman, see Pitman

Pitts, see Pitt

Pittway (Pitway), Anne, 1331; Hen., 1331; Wm., 1289

Pius II, pope, 362

Pixell, Rev. Thos., 1423

Plaier, see Player

Plaisher, —, 1455

Plaisted, see Playsted

Planca, Hugh de, 529

Planch, John, 908

Plantagenet, Ann(e), countess of Hereford, 927; Arthur, 885; Edw., duke of Aumerle, 357; Eliz., 885; Isabella, 529; Ric., duke of York, 361; fam., 769

Plassat, Wm., 1074

Platt (Plat), Rev. Chas., 610; Dan., 468; Hen., 464; J., 1201; Jos., 382; Wm., 509

Playche, Adam, 1238

Playdur, Thos. le, 1069

Player (Plaier), Anne, 1084*; Arthur, 9, 487, 489, 1084*, 1159; Dorothy (Dorothe), 489, 1084*; Hannah, 938; Helen, 1084*; Hester, 241; Isabella, 1, 614, 833; John, 1172, 1258; Marg., 489; Mary, 731; Nat., 938; Nic., 1282, 1289; Rob., 241, 731*; Sarah, 1158; Thos., 614, 834; Wm., 612, 614, 833, 834, 1158*; Mr., 1159; —, 1020

Playne, Mary, 1023; Peter, 1023, 1217; Ric., 1023; Mr., 1512

Playsted (Plaisted, Pleystude), Betty, 931*; John (atte), 931*, 1314, 1399; Mary, 1399; Rob. atte, 1420; Thos., 931, 1403; —, 1311

Pleadon, Eliz., 296; John, 296

Plebeien, Jas., 360 n

Pleydell (Pledall, Pledell, Pleydall), Ann, 794; Edw., 794, 1052; Eliz., 58*, 1397*, 1399; Harriot, 523; John, 58, 523, 1397*, 1399; Marg., 1033; Sir Mark Stuart, bt., 523; Mary, 1397, 1400; Ric., 1400; Rob., 56, 57*, 58*, 61*, 63, 678; Rev. Rob., 1206, 1217; Ruth, 1399; Sarah, 1397; Susan(na), 58*; T., 1101; —, 1033*, 1403; fam., 56, 523

Pleystude, see Playsted

Plodde, John atte, 1127

Plokenet (Pluganet), Alan, 1086*; Alice, 1086; Isabella, 1237; fam., 392 n, 1237

Plomer, see Plummer

Plomley, Cath., 1174*, 1175*; Hester, 1175; John, 730, 1175*; Joseph, 1174*, 1175*; Mary, 730

Plott, Cornelius, 1064; John, 985; Marg., 1064; —, 1064

Pluganet, *see* Plokenet

Plummer (Plomer, Plummar), Anne, 1206; Edw. Haynes, 1084; Frances, 655*; Hannah, 535*; Jane, 433; John (le), 433, 530*, 532, 535, 1539; Ric., 655*, 1206; Rob., 1453; Sam., 1539; (or Seaborn), T., 1538; Wm., 532, 535*

Plumstead, Dorothy, 562; Wm., 562

Pocklington, H. S., 1316; —, 1316

Pockridge, John, 662

Pocock (Pucoke), Ann, 616*; Harry, 1338; John, 616; Moses, 616*; Wm., 1363(?); —, 1362

Poel, *see* Pole

Poer, *see* Poore; Power

Pofe, *see* Pope

Poher, *see* Power

Poignard, John, 413

Poilard, *see* Pollard

Point, Thos., 415; Rev. Thos., 415

Pointz, *see* Poyntz

Pole (Poel, Poles, Poll, Pool), A., 1331*; Alice de la, duchess of Suffolk, 648; Ann, 1574; Sir C., 1078, 1223, 1228, 1331; Sir C. Van Notten, bt., 1331; (formerly Van Notten), Chas., 502, 503; Sir Chas., bt., 1222, 1224, 1227, 1502; Edm. de la, 690; Eliz. (de la), 690, 977, 1169, 1328; Sir Giles, kt., 977; Margery, 1082; Mary de la, 1169; Rob., 1016; Thos., 1574; Rev. Thos., 1428; Ursula, 1311; Wal. de la, 1328; Sir Wal. de la, 1169; Wm. (de la), 1328*, 1574; Wm. de la, duke of Suffolk, 648; Mr., 1331; —, 1016, 1223, 1502; *and see* Poole; Powell; Powle

Pollard (Poilard), Adam, 1139; Christian, 1305; John, 412, 1363; Thos., 412*

Pollen, Edw., 905

Polling, John, 111

Pollington, Thos., 919

Polton, *see* Poulton

Polwhele, —, 1069

Pomeroy (Pomeray), Geo., 469; —, 1093

Pomfrey (Pomphrey, Pumfret, Pumfrey, Pumphrey), Barbara, 800; Eliz., 800; Geo., 934; Hester, 934; John, 934; Joseph, 1289; Kath., 1276-7; Mary, 934; Mat., 787, 934*; Phil., 934; Ralph, 800*; Ric., 1276; Rob., 800; Wm., 934; —, 1317

Pons, *see* Poyntz

Ponsonby, Ashley, 1005

Pont de Larch (Pont l'arch, Pontelarch), *see* Pontlarch

Pontes, Gen. Davisies de, 1093

Pontherius, Wal., 1331

Pontifex, Alfred, 1551; Arthur, 1551; Dudley David, 1551; Edm., 1551; Septimus Edm., 1551; Wm. Chas., 1551

Ponting (Pontin, Ponton), Benj., 836; Chas., 174; Eliz., 48, 693; Emma E., 1516; John, 202, 836; Ric., 48*, 836; Rob., 693; Sarah, 174, 202; Thos., 174, 202, 1103; Wm., 174; Mrs., 1103

Pontlarch (Pont de Larch, Pont l'arch, Pontelarch), Juliana, 1148; R., 1476; Rob. de, 885, 1148*; —, 1148

Ponton, *see* Ponting

Pontz, *see* Poyntz

Ponz, Wal. son of, *see* FitzPons

Poole (Pole, Pool, Pulle), Abraham, 872*; Ann(e), 428, 561, 657*, 872, 972, 1048*, 1082; Ant., 973*, 974; Beatrix, 1051; Sir Chas., bt., 1329; D., 1257; Dan., 1454*; Sir Devereux, kt., 1048*; Dorothy, 974, 1048; Edw., 872, 1213; Elinor, 1048*; Eliz., 657, 767, 1031, 1051*; Frances, 1048*; G., 1201; Gil. atte, 1317; Sir Giles, kt., 445, 927, 1027, 1033, 1051*, 1201, 1316; Gyles, 1048; Hannah, 872; Sir H., 1052; Hen., 180, 363, 364*, 428, 767*, 1048; Sir Hen., kt., 445, 459, 525, 574*, 1048*, 1051*, 1082; Isaac, 884; Jane, 657; John, 657, 969, 972*, 973*, 1031*, 1051, 1272, 1316, 1377; Joseph, 580; Judith, 1454*; Julian, 973; Kath., 1051, 1213; Leonard, 1048; Sir Leonard, 1051; Lydia, 580; Marg., 580; Mary, 130*, 412*, 657, 884, 972, 973, 1184, 1454, 1455; Muriel (Murial), 595, 1051; Nat., 561, 580, 1184*; Sir Nevil(l), kt., 301, 364, 393 n, 1048; Penelope, 657; Ralph, 849; Rebecca, 1184; Ric., 297, 444, 1051, 1218, 1538; (or Code), Ric., 1385; Rob., 130*, 198*, 657*; Sam., 412*, 657; Sarah, 130, 972, 973, 1272*; Susannah, 1184; Thos., 124, 363*, 657, 981, 1454, 1455; Sir W., 1082; Wal. de, 1292; Wm. (atte, de), 199, 412*, 657, 884, 1102, 1292, 1324, 1576; Rev. Wm., 524, 579, 580; Sir Wm., 595, 1051; —, 1051; fam., 365, 459, 1256; *and see* Pole; Powle

Poope, *see* Pope

Poore (Poer), John, 409; Lawr. le, 1331; Ric., 753; Sarah, 409*; Col., 806 n; *and see* Power

Pope (Pofe, Poope), Abraham, 412*; Amice, 1404; Ann(e), 728*, 772*; Betty, 1328; Cath., 337; Dennis, 597; Dorothy, 283, 658; Edith, 772; Edw., 177; Rev. Edw., 534; Eliza, 603; Eliz., 337, 422, 429, 436, 518, 728*, 730, 802, 1091; Giles, 1401; Hen., 1311, 1314, 1404; Humph., 772; J., 1202; Jane, 1397; Jerard, 486; Joan, 772; John, 177, 337*, 429, 562, 603, 607, 728*, 990, 1000, 1033, 1216, 1287, 1328*, 1339, 1397*, 1403, 1432; John Pearce, 1173; Joseph, 1403; Joyce, 846; Kath., 728; Lucy (Luce), countess of Downe, 420, 422, 1067; Marg., 486, 1000; Mary, 177, 337, 597, 606, 607*, 1146, 1397; Nat., 1146; Rachael, 1050; Ric. (le), 728*, 730, 1172; Sarah, 429, 1328; Sibilla, 1432; Susanna, 177; Thos., 283*, 337, 658, 728, 772*, 960, 1050; Sir Thos., kt., 436, 518*; Thos., earl of Downe, 420, 422, 1067; W., 985; Wal., 1172; Wm., 337, 412, 485, 1328, 1397; —, 1011, 1311, 1440, 1504; fam., 159, 779

Popham, Alex., 231*; Brilliana, 231; Dorothy, 1265*; E., 1291*; Edw., 1265*; J., 1328; John, 1103; Letitia, 231, 1265; —, 1287, 1289; —, chief justice, 1287; fam., 230

Pople, Thos., 1420

Porer, 985

Porter, Alex., 1331; Alice (Alys), 351, 714, 999; Amy, 1014; Anna, 569; Arthur, 351, 711 n, 714, 999; Brigid, 714; [C]esilly, 714; D., 1331; Eleanor, 1263; Eliz., 569*, 1360, 1426;

Endymion, 287 n; Fredeswid, 999; Hen., 714; Jacob, 569; Jane, 572; John, 569*, 1014, 1268, 1291, 1356, 1426; Joseph, 569; Mary, 569, 999, 1270*; Nic., 714*; Patience, 1268*; Ric., 187*, 864; Rob., 1263, 1268*, 1270*; Rog., 714, 901; Sabina, 187; Sabina Packer, 187; Sam., 569; Sarah, 569, 1342; Tace, 351; Thos., 569, 572, 894; Sir Thos., kt., 351; —, 1288, 1392; fam., 864

[Porteus], Beilby, bishop, 1223

Porthole, W., 1331

Portland, duke of, 365

Portlock, Alice, 304; Eliz., 1487; Esther, 304; John, 304*; Mary, 304*; Thos., 304*

Portman (Portma.), John (le), 1359, 1363, 1372; Rev. Ric., 1357; —, 1362, 1363

Portreue, Cristina, 1292; John, 1292

Portrey, Cath., 249; Chris., 249

Portugal, king of, 952

Pory, Eliz., 437; Rob., 437

Pott (Pots), see Potts

Potter, Rev. And., 415; Ann, 212; Rev. Edw., 1113, 1122; Isabell, 1113; Jas., 399, 1010*, 1063; John, 193, 399, 1401; Joseph, 398*; Lucinda Timbrell, 1063; Mary, 193*, 212, 337, 398*, 399*, 1010, 1401; Meriel, 399; Sam., 212*; Sarah, 399; Thos., 212, 337, 399; Rev. Thos., 829, 1221; Wm., 254, 399*; —, 1063

Potteslip, W., 1476

Pottinger, —, 159

Potts (Pots, Pott), John, 409; Laur., 1526; Sarah, 1526; fam., 220

Pouke, Alice, 1202; J., 1202

Poukethrop (Poukesthrop), Adam de 1363; Ric. de, 1363

Poulden, —, 1475

Poulet, earl, 1156

Poulett, Ann, 614; Lord Giles, 614; Wm., 614; Wm., marquis of Winchester, 614; and see Paulet; Powlett

Poulson, Anne, 337*; Geo., 1412; Ralph, 337*; Wm., 204

Poultney, Edw., 1447

Poulton (Polton, Pulton, Pultone), Agnes de, 1404; Alice, 659; Ann(e), 672*, 675*, 681, 682*, 898; Cath., 974; Dorothy, 682*; Eliz., 612, 672, 675*, 682, 899, 900; Hannah, 974; Hen., 659; J., 1257; Jas., 941*; John (de), 675, 681, 682*, 1350, 1351, 1404, 1481; Marg., 1481; Mary, 127, 675*, 682*, 898, 974; Matilda, 1351; Pauncefoot, 682; Rachel, 941; Ric., 671, 675*, 681, 682*, 898*, 899, 900, 974; Rog. de, 1351; Sam., 672*, 675*; Sarah, 675, 682*, 898; Susannah, 898; T., 1290; Thos., 682*, 685; Rev. Thos., 126, 127*; Ursula, 941*; Wm., 941*, 1481; Rev. Wm., 145; Sir Wm., 612; —, 1221, 1257*, 1293, 1312, 1351, 1402, 1403; fam., 102, 680

Pouton, see Powton

Powder, Eliz., 1427

Powell (Poweal, Powel), Abigail, 109; Alice, 1307*; Ann(e), 109, 192, 231*, 337, 810, 933, 992, 993*, 1076*, 1193, 1444; Ant., 1307*;

Barbara, 1076*; Cath., 1076; Chas., 922, 1578; Dan., 993; David, 1326; Edw., 337, 922*, 1092, 1195; Eleanor, 231; Eliz., 250, 332, 337, 821, 923*, 993, 1053, 1076, 1126, 1193, 1232, 1279, 1397*, 1497; Esther, 1271, 1396; Rev. Evans, 305; Geo., 837; Giles, 1497*, 1501*; Hannah, 467, 837, 1396*; Hen., 1574*; Rev. Howel, 810; Rev. Hugh, 1329; Humph., 250; Rev. J., 1126, 1501; Jas., 484, 933, 1279; Joanna, 1076; John, 337, 484, 550, 821*, 933, 965, 993*, 1064, 1076*, 1121, 1289, 1330, 1356*, 1396*, 1397, 1525, 1539, 1583; Rev. John, 1125, 1335; Sir John, kt., 482*; Jonas, 550*; Joseph, 231, 1397, 1403; Magaretta Maria, 59; Marg., 484, 550; Mary, 250, 841, 842*, 922, 933*, 965*, 1076*, 1326; Sir Nat., bt., 992; Peter, 842; Rachel, 963; Ralph, 337; Rebecca, 366, 367*, 369, 990*; Ric., 192, 450, 836, 922, 923*, 965, 1312, 1444, 1445; Rev. Ric., 305; Rob., 841*, 842*, 843, 1076; Rev. Rog., 332; Sam., 1574; Sarah, 1307, 1574; Stephen, 996; Susanna, 1076; Thos., 48, 367*, 369, 382, 384*, 837, 990, 1150, 1151, 1217, 1397; Rev. Thos., 56, 59, 651; (or Howell), Rev. Thos., 1122; Rev. W., 1504; Wal., 231*; Rev. Wal., 1132; Wm., 36, 109, 231, 274, 531, 550, 730, 963, 965, 993, 1076*, 1109, 1174*, 1193, 1412; Rev. Wm. Fred., 1217; Dr., 467; Rev. Mr., 913; —, 1455; fam., 482, 721; and see Pole; Powle

Power (Poer, Poher, Powers), Chas., 1118; Eliz., 407; Esther, 1210; Hugh (le), 634 n, 1077; Sir Hugh, 634 n; Isabella, 1077; John, 884; Joshua, 1418; Marg., 1077; Mary, 884; Nat., 121, 1108; Penelope, 407; Sarah, 1118, 1418, 1525; Stephen, 1210*; Susanna, 1108; Thos., 407; Wm., 1108; —, 1476; fam., 634 n; and see Poore

Powle (Powles), And., 1154; Cath., 1003, 1005; Eliz., 108, 1003, 1004, 1005; H., 1201; Hen., 364*, 426, 427, 711, 985, 1003*, 1004, 1005*; John, 108*, 1005*; Ric., 1005*; Sir Ric., 1005; Stephen, 108; W., 1201; Wm., 985*, 1005*; fam., 1015; and see Pole; Poole; Powell

Powlett (Powlet), Rychard, 360 n; Wm., 810; and see Paulet; Poulett

Powntney, Rob., 1305; Sarah, 1305–6

Powton (Pouton), Anne, 1278; Edw., 1278*; Eliz., 1278; Isabella, 1278; John, 1278*; Thos., 1278

Poyer, Anne, 781; John, 781

Poyke, Eliz., 906; Hannah, 906; John, 906

Poyner, Edw., 1234, 1238; Laur. (Lawr.), 1382*

Poynter, Martha, 729; Rob., 729*

Poyntz (Pointz, Pons, Pontz), Agnes, 1369; Alice, 32, 997; Ann, 14, 32, 1428; Ant., 1490; Sir Ant., kt., 738; Drew (Drogo), 1225*; Edw., 32; Elianor, 699; Eliz., 14, 31, 32; Hugh (de), 14, 1225; Jane, 1336, 1337, 1338; Joan (Ione), 32, 1539; John, 13, 32, 602, 1366, 1369; Sir John, kt., 13*, 179, 498, 579*, 738; Joseph, 699, 1366; Kath., 602, 737; Mary, 32, 1338; Mat., 30*, 32*, 696; N., 1121; Sir N., 1539; Rev. Newdigate (Newdegate) 19, 1336, 1337, 1338*, 1339; Nic., 13, 14, 32, 738, 997, 1227; Sir Nic., 738, 1428;

Rachel, 32; Rob. (Robard), 14*, 696, 737, 738, 1225; Sir Rob., 265 n*, 737, 738, 1336; Simon (Symon), 1225, 1227*; Sutton, 738 n; Sylvester, 32; Thos., 32; Winifred, 32; —, 1225, 1227*, 1228, 1490, 1491*; fam., 565, 579, 739, 1491

Poythress, Jane, 906; Wm., 906

Pracy, Rob., 1259

Praed, Humph. Mackworth, 1005*; Mary, 1005; fam., 427

Prankerd (Prakhard), Mary, 385; Thos., 385; W., 1312

Pratt (Pratte, Prattes), Abraham, 1009; Agnes, 327; Benj., 342; Edw., 369; Eliz., 1481; Sir Geo., bt., 471; Sir Hen., bt., 369; Isabella, 1485; Jas., 38, 1481; John, 361, 369, 371; Marg., 471; Mary, 471; Rob., 493, 634; Thos., 372; —, widow of Rob., 634

Pratten, Hannah, 1583; Joseph, 1583; Sarah, 1583

Prattes, *see* Pratt

Pray, John, 111; Wm., 111

Predeth, Hannah, 906; Ric., 906

Preece, Alice; Eliz., 194; Greg., *see* Appreece; Jas., 194*; John, 1039; Ric., 906; Sarah, 906; Wm., 194; *and see* Price

Preedon, Hannah, 425; Martha, 425; Ric., 425*; Thos., 425*

Preedy, Rev. Benj., 1460; Rev. Jas., 689; Thos., 1289; W., 1460

Preen, —, 1255

Prelatte, Agnes, 371; Joan, 371; Wm., 361, 371

Prens, *see* Prince

Prentice, Joseph, 1003; Sarah Dallaway, 1003

Prepositus, John, 1127; *and see* Prevost; Pruett; Reeve

Presbury, *see* Prestbury

Prescot (Prescott), Edw., 980; Hannah, 980; Rev. Hen., 1140

Presse, Rev. Simon, 508

Prestbury (Presbury, Prestebur, Prestebury), Ann, 109; Arnold of, 986; Eliz., 107; Hester, 352; John (of), 352*, 986; Joseph, 109*; Phil. of, 986; Ralph of, 986; Rob. (de), 107, 985*, 1370*; Sarah, 352; Thos., 353; Wm. (de), 107, 352, 1404

Prester, John, 922

Preston, Anne, 1466*; Benj., 706*; Edw., 514; Eliz., 514; Jane, 514*; John, 434, 514, 1466*; Mary, 321, 399, 706*; Rob., 399; Thos., 321*, 1227; Wm., 399, 434*, 514, 637*, 1466; —, 1017

Prestwich, Arabella, 1342; Sir Thos., bt., 1342; —, 341

Prettyman, Sir John, kt., 515*; Wm., 515

Prevett, *see* Pruett

Prevost, Sir Geo., 1169; Ven. Sir Geo., bt., 1169; *and see* Prepositus; Pruett

Prevote, *see* Pruett

Prew, Ann, 226; Eliz., 1282; Joseph, 226; Mary, 1282; Ric., 1282; Sarah, 1282

Prewett, *see* Pruett

Price (Pryce), Abigail, 550; Rev. And., 508; Ann(e), 151, 598, 685, 686, 735, 861, 862, 1158;

Bridget, 191; Cath., 526, 862, 1280; Chas., 123, 597; David, 413, 474; Edw., 191, 1553; Eliz., 68, 151, 382, 409, 597, 598, 683, 822, 906, 1510, 1511*; Eliz. Cath., 1281; Even, 761; Frances, 1157; Francis, 274, 409; Geo., 550, 1158*; Capt. Grove, 1237; Rev. Hugh, 432, 853, 1136; Isabella, 686; J., 1154; Jas., 761, 1213; Rev. Jas., 266, 1516; Jas. Mat., 1213; John, 151, 382, 598, 657, 735, 868, 898, 906, 1047, 1103, 1213, 1312, 1366, 1415, 1510, 1511*, 1513, 1529*; Rev. John, 53, 685*, 686*, 727, 1513; John Rob., 1280; Joseph, 1516; Leonard, 706; Lewis, 409; Marg., 706; Mary, 151, 486, 598, 1167, 1415, 1419, 1529; Mary Batt, 1280; Miles, 1213; Morgan, 1047, 1233; Rev. Morgan, 1237; Peter, 1213; Ric., 616, 822, 900*, 1167; Sam., 308; Sarah, 308, 741, 868, 1047, 1136*, 1157, 1213; Stephen, 526, 1213; Susanna(h), 151, 1548; Thos., 409, 597*, 683, 741*, 1031, 1117, 1160, 1312; Major Thos., 68; Rev. Thos., 13, 1317, 1328, 1351; Ursula, 1117; W., 1316; W. P., 1035, 1317; Wal., 861, 862, 1361; Wm., 486, 862*, 986, 1038, 1157, 1419, 1511; Rev. Wm., 770; Mr., 1189; Rev., 1447; —, 414; fam., 346; *and see* Preece

Prichard (Pricherd), *see* Pritchard

Prichet, *see* Pritchett

Prickett, Joan, 111; Joseph, 111; —, 1363; *and see* Pritchett

Prickley (or Harris), fam., 1165

Priday (Priddy, Pridie, Pridy), Eliz., 716; Hannah, 1131; Humph., 1131; John (of), 1131*, 1217; Mary, 716, 1000, 1131; S., 1132; Sam., 1000, 1131, 1334; Sarah, 1131; Thos., 716, 1132; W., 1132; Wm., 1000*, 1131

Pride, Hester, 901; John, 625, 665, 831, 1053; Lawr., 625; Mary, 831; Phil., 1238; Rog., 901; Sarah, 665, 666, 831; Sam., 1289; Simon atte, 1259; Susanna, 1053; Thos., 666, 741, 1147; Wm., 898; fam., 798

Prideaux, Hannah, 1510; Sir John Wilmott, bt., 1510; Neast Greville, 1362

Pridy (Pridie), *see* Priday

Prier, *see* Prior

Priest, Eliz., 199*; Esther, 199; Isaac, 199; Rev. Isaac, 198, 199; Rev. John, 728; Martha, 199*; Mary, 199; Rev. Secundus Isaac, 199; Rev. Simon, 128, 199*; Rev. Mr., 198

Prigg (Prigge), Ann, 18*; Eleanor, 1426; Eliz., 100*, 1426; John, 18, 962, 1009*; Mary, 100*, 1426; Ric., 1424; Rowland, 1489; Sam., 100*, 1426; Sarah, 1426; Thos., 18, 1426*; Rev. Thos., 1423; Wm., 18*, 1009*, 1426*

Prim, Wm., 706

Prince (Prens, Princ, Printz), Adrian, 1187; Ann, 810; Edw., 810; Rev. Edw., 586; Eliz., 317; Hen., 810; John, 317; Joseph, 909; Hester, 317; Mary, 212*; Wm., 212*, 810*

Prinn, *see* Prynne

Print, Anne, 854; Rev. Edw., 579; John, 854; Mary, 854; Wm., 854

Printz, *see* Prince

Prior (Prier, Pryor), Dan., 1429; Edw., 1186; Eliz., 844, 1429; Rev. Gerard, 1044, 1147; Hen., 1289; John, 597, 844; Sarah, 597; Rev. Thos., 351, 415; Wm., 1258; Rev. Wm., 579

Pritchard (Prichard, Pricherd), Abraham, 563, 1118; Alex., 1112; Betty, 1193; Edw., 963; Eliz., 112, 963; Geo., 544, 546, 547; Jas., 789*, 871; Jane, 871, 1112; John, 625, 815, 1112, 1403; Jonathan, 112; Rev. Jonathan, 452, 453; Marg., 1307; Martha, 173; Mary, 741, 789, 1118; Mat., 815; Maur., 963; Rev. Phil., 297; Ric., 250; Rob., 703, 1577; Sarah, 563, 703; Solomon, 1307; Susan Lambert, 544; Thos., 825, 1403; Rev. Thos., 1177; Wal., 815; Rev. Wal., 1348; Wm., 250, 741, 1039, 1118, 1217; Rev. Wm., 173, 739; —, 894; and see Pritchett

Pritchell, Ann, 846; Wm., 846

Pritchett (Prichet), Anne, 1396; Arthur, 703; Joane, 1395*; John, 302; Sarah, 703; Wm., 112, 1395*, 1396; and see Prickett; Pritchard

Proben, see Probyn

Probert (Probit), Dorothy, 808; Eleanor, 809*; Eliz., 1445; Geo., 808; Hen., 809*; John, 768; Joseph, 1445; —, 1386; and see Propert

Probyn (Proben), Anne, 919*, 920; Blanch, 919, 920; Edith, 919; Edm., 1*, 479*, 760, 801, 802, 819, 820*, 913*, 918, 919*, 920*, 921, 922, 1488; Edm. Hopkins, 759; Sir Edm., kt., 759, 819, 920*; Eliz., 906, 919, 920, 1515; Dame Eliz., 920; Eliz. Anne, 920; Frances, 919*, 920, 1488; Hannah, 919, 920; John, 919, 920*; Rev. John, 1; Jonathan, 933; Marg., 919; Mary, 919, 920*; Ric., 921; Sarah, 919, 920, 933; Sophia, 801, 921; Thos., 919; Wm., 919*, 920, 1515; Capt. Wm., 920; Rev. Wm., 820; Mr., 1486; —, 1091, 1491; —, lord chief baron, 913, 919; fam., 1402; and see Provin

Proctor (Prockter, Procter), Agathea, 573; Ann(e), 884, 1282; Eliz., 884*, 1282; Rev. Geo., 1217; Hannah, 90; Jas., 54*, 884, 1361; John, 54, 90, 884*, 1354; M., 1362; Mary, 10, 54, 641, 1354; Ric., 950; Sam., 1354; Sarah, 1354; Thos., 573, 884*; Wm., 10, 641, 1282; —, 1362*

Proger, Ann, 124; Arthur, 124*; Marg., 124

Propert, Judith, 315; and see Probert

Prosser, Ann, 584; Chas., 1236; Edw., 1162; Eliz., 584*, 1162*; Hannah, 584; Rev. Hen., 1460; Jas., 584*; Joan, 1236; John, 730, 734, 923; Joseph, 584; Marg., 352, 727; Mary, 730, 768; Ric., 768; Rog., 727; Sam., 1258; Rev. Theophilus, 788; Thos., 352; Wm., 814; —, 245

Prothero (Protheroe), Hannah, 924; Sir Hen., 1420; Phil., 1420; Ric., 924

Proudfoot, Edm., 407; Eliz., 407

Prout (Proute, Prowte), Ann, 941*; Arthur, 308, 1449, 1450*, 1453*; Cath., 1018, 1434; Christian, 1453; Dan., 1434, 1450; Eliz., 1450; Emanuel, 941; Hannah, 941; Hester, 941, 1434; John, 1139, 1316; Jonathan, 1434; Mary, 1450, 1453; Nebuchadnezzer, 1453; Rebekah, 1434; Rob., 941, 1453*; Sarah, 308, 1450, 1453*; Thos., 941, 1018*; Wallis, 1450; Wm. (le), 941*,

1139, 1215, 1217, 1218; Rev. Wm., 1450*; —, 1456; and see Pruett

Provin, John, 1563; Mary, 1563; and see Probyn

Prowse (Prows, Pruce), Chas., 1093; John, 1194*; Silvester, 1092; Wm., 1194; (or Spruce), —, 1093

Prowte, see Prout

Pruce, see Prowse

Pruen, Eliz., 336*; John, 336*; Sam., 336; Sarah, 336*; Thos., 336*

Pruett (Prevett, Prevote, Prewett), Ann, 958; Eleanor, 957; Eliz., 1106*; John, 957*, 1106; Rev. John, 56; Ric., 1490; Sarah, 957; Thos., 957*, 958*, 1106*; Wm., 957; and see Prepositus; Prevost; Prout

Pryce, see Price

Prynne (Prinn, Prynn), Anne, 330; Eliz., 311, 314*, 315, 330, 574; John, 311, 313, 314*, 315, 1228; Rev. John, 314*; Kath., 314, 315; Mary, 314; Sarah, 314; Wm., 311*, 314*, 317, 328, 330*, 574, 986, 1216; Mr., 158*, 325; fam., 311 n

Pryor, see Prior

Pson, see Parsons

P'trich, see Partridge

Puckmore, Eliz., 550; John, 550*; Mary, 550; Wm., 550, 978

Pucoke, see Pocock

Pudmoor, Ann, 1112; Eliz., 1112; Wm., 1112

Pugh (Pew), Eliz., 48, 388, 1493; Jas., 815; John, 388; Thos., 388; Rev. Thos., 263, 511, 513, 1516; Wm., 48, 1493

Pulestone, Rev. Kenrick, 328, 440

Pulham (Pulm), Geof. (Jeffry), 1074, 1078; Sir John, kt., 1082; Ralph, 1102; W. de, 1201

Pulle, see Poole

Pullen (Pulleine, Pullin, Pulling, Pullings), Ann, 542, 993; Betty, 616, 1328; Edith, 1326; Eliza, 1327; Eliz., 616, 836*, 1325*, 1327*, 1580; Geo., 1580*; Hannah, 616, 1327, 1328; Hester, 1327; Jas., 1326, 1327, 1328, 1384; John, 456, 542, 758, 963, 993, 1327*, 1384, 1549; Jonathan, 1325*; Nat., 1327; Mary, 456, 616, 797, 1325*, 1327*, 1343, 1427; Rev. Ric., 691; Sam., 758; Sarah, 616, 758*, 1327, 1549; Thos., 616, 836, 1325*; Rev. Thos., 691; Rev. W., 1323; Wm., 797*, 1325*, 1327*, 1328*, 1343, 1412, 1427; —, 1328, 1455; fam., 305

Pulley, Ann, 538; Joseph, 531, 538*; Mary, 538*; Morgan, 532

Pullin (Pulling, Pullings), see Pullen

Pulm, see Pulham

Pulton (Pultone), see Poulton

Pumfret (Pumfrey, Pumphrey), see Pomfrey

Punter, Eliz., 1244, 1545; Eunice, 662; Isaac, 662*, 752; Jane, 662*; Joseph, 1244*; Rachel, 1321; Sam., 1160, 1244; Sarah, 662

Purcels, Mr., 965

Purdy, John, 1158; Mary, 1158

Purefoy (Purefoye), Rev. Edw., 142; Col., 928*

Purey, see Pury

Purlewent, Mary, 906

Purlyn, see Parlyn

Purnell (Purnelle), Alice, 1525; Anna, 539; Ann(e), 534, 535, 536*, 537, 538, 539, 621, 936*, 1169, 1343; Chas., 538, 936, 937; Chas. Cooper, 1168; Charlotte Anne, 1168*; Chris., 936*, 1307*; E., 1312; Edith, 938*; Edw., 1305; Eliz., 621, 668, 701, 936; Hester, 936; J., 1369; Jane, 1451; John, 52, 531*, 535, 536*, 537*, 538, 539, 621, 668, 935, 936*, 938, 1343, 1451, 1452, 1525; Capt. John, 701*; Rev. John, 1451; John Bransby, 1168; Joseph, 536, 1304*; Mabel, 1304; Marg., 536; Martha, 536, 936; Mary, 536, 537, 936*, 938; Nat., 535; Olynthya, 1343; Phelps, 1369; Purnell B., 1169; Purnell Bransby, 1168; Rebecca (Rebekah), 936*; Rob., 936*, 938*, 1522*, 1525; Rose, 1168; Sara(h), 936, 1305*, 1343; Susan, 536; T., 1140, 1369; Thos., 531*, 535*, 536*, 936*, 1452; Thos. Purnell, 668; W., 1054*, 1169; Wm., 530, 531*, 535*, 536*, 537*, 539, 701, 936*, 1169, 1343*; Mr., 1452, 1489; Mrs., 1452; —, 1169; fam., 159, 415, 532, 558; *and see* Parnell
Purner, Thos., 1577
Purrock (Purrocke), John, 786*; Mary, 786*; Peregrine, 786, 787*; Wm., 787
Purser, Alice, 573*; Eliz., 573; Hannah, 573; Jane, 573; John, 573*; Joseph, 573; Mary, 573; Rob., 573; Wm., 573*
Purton, Thos., 872
Pury (Purey, Purye), Anne, 466; Barbara, 1235*; Cath., 181; Eliz., 1236*; Sarah, 1235, 1237; Thos., 466, 1233, 1235*, 1236*, 1237; Rev. Thos., 180, 181; fam., 869, 1238; *and see* Perry
Putly, Sarah, 172; Wm., 777
Putot, Wm. de, 833; fam., 833
Putte, Hen. atte, 1335; John atte, 1504; Wm. atte, 1197; *and see* Pitt
Puxton, Eliz., 837; Geo., 837*; Martha, 837; Wm., 837
Pyard, Chris. (Xr.), 1216; J., 1186; *and see* Peard
Pycard, Wm., 1539
Pycot (Pycott), *see* Pickett
Pydus, Hugh, 1539
Pye, Christian, 1351; Edw., 546, 547, 548*; Eliz., 587; Frances, 746; Hester, 746; Marg., 746; Mary, 907, 1195; Rev. Moore, 1539; Philippa, 1195; Rebecca, 1195; Sir Rob., 393; Sam., 587, 746*, 907, 1177; Sophia, 746; Wal., 1378; —, 1351*
Pyff, *see* Piff
Pygges (Pygas, Pyge), J., 1061; Wm., 1292, 1504
Pygotts, *see* Pigot
Pyke, *see* Pike
Pyl (Pyle, Pylls), *see* Pill
Pym, Francis, 309
Pymore, Edw., 1106; Marg., 1106*
Pyn, *see* Pine
Pynchonn (Pynchoun), *see* Pinchin
Pynchpole, W., 1482; Wm., 1482; —, 1482
Pyndar (Pindar), Eliz., 766, 767*; Rev. Martin, 1504; Mic. Gibbons, 176; Reg., 766, 767*; Thos., 766, 767*; Wm., 767
Pynel, *see* Pinnell

Pynnok (Pennoke, Pynnoke, Pynock), Adam, 1539; Alice, 1140; Jas., 1289; Nic., 1259, 1313
Pynsoun, Wm., 1335
Pyrie, *see* Pirie
Pyrke (Pirke), Adam, 1317; Anna, 467; Bridget, 470; Chas., 470, 471; Deborah, 3*, 470; Dorothy, 3, 470*, 471*; Duncomb, 3*, 4, 471; Eliz., 3*, 467, 471*; Hannah, 660; Jane, 3, 1155; Joan, 4; John, 473; Jonathan, 467, 660; Joseph, 1, 463, 469, 479*, 951; Lazarus, 467; Mary, 3*, 467, 471*, 473; Maynard, 470; Nat., 3*, 4, 470*, 1155; Ric., 4, 463, 467*; Rob., 4, 467, 472*; Thos., 3*, 470*, 471*, 473; Mr., 927; fam., 927
Pyrry (Pyrye), *see* Pirie
Pysleye, Wm., 1477
Pytley, Thos., 1559
Pytt (Pytts), *see* Pitt

Quarman, Elinor, 212; Jas., 212*
Quarrel, Geo., 339; Jane, 339; John, 1447
Quarreour, Adam le, 1104
Quene, Rev. Ric., 1388
Quenyld, Ralph, 1150
Quick (Quicke), Jane, 1537; Mrs., 206
Quin, Eliz., 1417
Quincy (Quincey), Rog. de, earl of Winchester, 570; fam., earls of Winchester, 634, 1237*
Quinton (Quintin, Quintine), Ann, 44; Eliz., 1018*; Kath., 343; Mary, 342, 740, 1018; Mic., 44; Theodorea, 1018; Rev. Theophilus, 342, 343, 1020; Wm., 740; Rev. Wm., 1018*, 1020; Rev., 1147

R—ards, Rev. Thos., 1485
Rabskert (or Ramscut), Rev. Ric., 1362
Rachel, Rob., 1013*; Sarah, 1013
Rackley, Sarah, 1010; Thos., 1010
Radbourn (Radburn), Eliz., 891; Frances, 796; Geo., 796; Wm., 891; (or Hewer), Wm., 891
Radcliffe (Radc[l]iffe), Anna Maria, countess of Derwentwater, 691 n; Jas., earl of Derwentwater, 691 n; John, 711 n; Rob., 1180; Rev. Rob., 1180; Thos., 197; *and see* Ratcliffe
Radeforde, *see* Rodford
Radmore, Eliz., 1574; Nat., 1574
Radnor, Hannah, 948; Wm., 948
Radnor [*peerage*], earl of, 994; *and see* Bouverie, Jacob Pleydell *and* Wm.
Radolf, J., 1516
Radulph, earl of Hereford, Harold son of, *see* Sudeley
Radway, Ann(e), 60, 517*; Bridget, 344; Dan., 344; Dorothy, 344; Edith, 388; Eliz., 376, 1350; Frances, 59; Francis, 517, 991, 1350; Giles, 300, 376; Hannah, 429; Hen., 60, 187; Hester, 644; John, 59, 60, 343*, 344, 991; Lydia, 343; Martha, 60, 991; Mary, 59, 321, 343*, 388, 644; Mat., 343*; Mic., 187; Ric., 388*; Rob., 321, 429*, 644; Wm., 59, 64*, 270*, 644, 991*, 1350; Mr., 1351; *and see* Rodway
Rage, Wm. le, 1197
Raglan, Lord, 1073

Ragles, John, 491; Mary, 491
Raikes, Rev. Ric., 855; Rob., 796; Sarah, 796; Wm., 638; fam., 1378
Raine, Rev. Wm., 1441
Rainsford (Raynsford), Ann, 401; Chas., 400; Edm., 1463*; Edw., 1289; Rev. Edw., 1477; Elenor, 401; Eliz., 402*; Em[?ma], 1463; Frauncis, 401; H., 1460; Hen., 400, 401; Sir Hen., kt., 401, 402; Hercules, 401, 402; Wm., 401; —, 1017, 1289
Rainstrop (Rainstorpe), Eliz., 435; John, 435; Mary, 435; Sarah, 435; Wal., 435, 1489; Rev. Wal., 435*; and see Brinstorp
Rainton, Jane, 136; Wm., 136
Raisher, Wm., 70
Raleigh (Ralegh, Ralleigh, Rawleigh), Ant., 990; Cath., 1421; Edm., 990; Edw., 574, 990; Sir Edw., 990; Eliz., 1421; Dame Eliz., 1057; G., 1404; Geo., 990*; Sir Geo., kt., 574, 990; John (de), 990, 1421*; Rose de, 990; Simon, 990, 1402; Thos., 574, 785, 990*; Wal., 990; Sir Wal., kt., 236, 1057; Wm., 785; Lady, 1349; —, 1351, 1402*; fam., 990
Rallings, see Rawlings
Ralph son of Ernald, 1060
Ralph, Simon son of, 1227
Ralph (fl. 11th cent.), 1043, 1077, 1287*, 1421, 1482
Ralph (fl. 12th cent.), 1060
Ralph, Ann, 731; Cath., 1244; Geo., 731; Hester, 1025; John, 1258; Joseph, 1244; Mary, 731; Sarah, 731
Ramell, Thos., 89, 147
Ramscut (or Rabskert), Rev. R., 1362
Ramsden, Sir John, bt., 1341; Marg., 1341
Ramsey, E., 1316; R., 1316
Randall (Randal, Randel, Randell, Randle, Randoll), Alice, 677; Ann(e), 303*, 448, 514, 1081; Benj., 1079; Edw., 448*, 1377; Elisha, 296; Eliz., 303*; Esther, 1079; Fr—, 800; Geo., 1079*; Rev. Giles, 449; Hester, 1079; Rev. Humph., 511; (or Baylis), Jane, 150; Joanh [sic], 1004; John, 303*, 1004*, 1079, 1497*, 1542*; Rev. John, 184, 1328; Joseph, 858; Marg., 118, 448; Martha, 1079*; Mary, 202, 296, 320, 448, 640, 1079, 1081, 1497*, 1542*; Ralph, 202, 800; Susanna, 1004; Thos., 448, 683, 1079*, 1081*; Wm., 118*, 296, 303, 320, 448*, 514, 584, 640, 677, 800, 981
Randolph, prior, 391
Randolph, Brett, 539*; Chas., 1551; Frances, 1551*; Hen. Cater, 1551; Rev. Hen. J., 1551; Jas., 1244; Mary, 539; Dr., 405 n; —, 1455
Randsford (Wranford), Edw., 1289; Nic., 348
Ranger, John, 847
Rannells, Ann(e), 923; Geo., 923*
Ranulf (fl. 1066), 1441
Rapier, Rog., 1438
Rastall (Rastell), see Restell
Rastone, Thos., 906
Ratcliffe (Radcliff, Ratcliff), Abigail, 1031; Anne, 1180; Betsy, 1511; Chas., earl of Newburgh, 364;

Eliz., 1072; Jas., earl of Newburgh, 364; John, 1010; Rev. John, 432*, 1180; Lawr., 884; Mary, 1031, 1180*; Matilda, 1511; Ric., 1180; Rob., 388; Rev. Rob., 1072, 1180*, 1186; Rev. Rog., 432; Sam., 1511; Sarah, 1010; Susanna, 388; Thos., 1010, 1031*; Thos., earl of Sussex, 839; Wm., 1511; —, earl of Newburgh, 1402; and see Radcliffe
Raulings, see Rawlings
Ravenhill, Hannah, 736; Jas. (Jalmes), 917, 923; John, 736, 923; Mary, 923
Ravenswart (fl. 822), 628
Rawes, Rev. Jas., 319*
Rawleigh, see Raleigh
Rawlett, —, 1177
Rawlings (Rallings, Raulings, Rawlins, Rawlyns), Alice, 501; Ann, 231, 1575; Rev. Edm., 500; Eliz., 48, 734, 735; Esther, 734; Francis (Frances), 734*, 736; Frank, 1360*; Geo., 734*, 735*; Jane, 1360*; John, 734, 1360; Rev. John, 37; Rev. Jonathan, 689; Marg., 736; Martha, 735*; Ric., 736, 1389, 1392; Rev. Ric., 668; Sam., 849; Simon, 48; Thos., 231, 500*, 1575*; Rev. Thos., 668, 969*, 1006, 1482; Wm., 500*, 933
Rawlinson, May, 1331
Rawlyns, see Rawlings
Raworth, Thos., 52
Ray (Raye, Rays, Reaey), M., 1420; Mary, 1386; Rob., 1378; Sibilla, 1378*; Wm., 1384, 1386; —, 404 n; and see Rea
Raybon, Rog., 1552
Raye, see Ray
Rayer (Rayeres), Ann, 1153, 1473*; Edw., 1473; Eliz., 1465, 1473; Esther, 1034; H., 1477; John, 1153, 1355*; Ric., 1289; Rob., 1034; Sam., 1473; Sarah, 1153; Wm., 1473; —, 1292
Raymond, Ann(e), 1299, 1300*, 1545; Chas., 1300; Chris., 167, 1545; Dorothy, 167; Eliz., 167, 1299, 1300; Florence, 1299; Geo., 167, 452, 1300*, 1545*; Giles, 167, 1545; Hester, 1299, 1300*; J., 592; Jane, 174; Joan, 1300; Joanna, 171; John, 1300; (later Barker), John, 592; Sir Jonathan, kt., 366; Mary, 167, 1299*, 1300*, 1395*; Phil., 1299, 1303; Sarah, 1300; Sophia, 1303; Thos., 174, 1299; (later Symonds), Thos., 1303; Wm., 167, 171, 1020, 1299*, 1300*, 1303, 1308, 1395*, 1545; Mr., 7; —, 1311; fam., 159
Raynolds (Raynold), see Reynolds
Raynsford, see Rainsford
Rays, see Ray
Razey (Reacy), Ann, 491; Benj., 846; Mary, 846; Rob., 491
Rea, Christiana, 1067; Wm., 1378; and see Ray
Reacy, see Razey
Read (Reade, Rede, Reed, Reid), Abraham, 49; Alice, 1265, 1279; Ann, 108, 276*, 296, 454, 1282; Barbara, 1485; Bart., 1274*; Betty, 789, 815; Cath., 1274, 1348; Dan., 758; David, 394; Rev. Edw., 1485; Eleanor, 395; Eliz., 110, 394, 398, 815, 884, 1027*, 1192, 1237, 1274*, 1279, 1431; Esther, 1212, 1274; Foulke, 1381; Frances,

883; Giles (Gyles), 1363, 1380*, 1381; H., 1387; Hen., 1232, 1329; J., 1221, 1288; Jas., 789, 1212, 1274; Jane, 276, 395; John (de, le), 227, 395, 430, 503, 789, 815, 1061, 1201, 1274, 1281, 1289, 1291, 1333, 1335, 1381, 1420; Sir John, 952; Rev. Jones, 328; Joseph, 1282*; Kath., 1192*, 1380*; Mary, 398, 789, 1274*, 1333; Oliver, 1192*; Peter, 1333*; Philadelphia, 227; R., 1348; Ric., 276*, 395, 1348, 1431*; Rob., 884, 1279; Rog., 708 n; Sam., 431, 1274*; Susanna, 413; Thos., 398, 708 n, 778, 1192, 1237, 1265*, 1279*, 1504; Thos. Yardley, 1274; W., 1195; Wm. (le), 108*, 110, 398, 821, 1027*, 1217, 1288, 1380, 1381, 1513; Rev. Wm., 394; Lady, 952; —, 1052, 1165, 1317, 1361; fam., 1380*, 1381

Reader, Susanna, 1045; *and see* Redare

Ready (Reddy), Alex., 77*, 596, 771, 856, 1125, 1423; (later Colston), Alex., 718; Rev. Alex., 1066; Anne, 856; Edm., 856; Eliz., 77, 276; John, 276; John Chaunler, 432, 1126; Mary, 77, 1125*–6; Sarah, 596; —, 1455

Reaey, *see* Ray

Reave, *see* Reeve

Redare, John le, 1238; *and see* Reader

Reddal (Reddall, Reddell), Ambrose, 216*, 1337; Mary, 1270; Sarah, 1337; Thos., 1289*; Mr., 1056; —, 1064*

Redding (Reding), Wm., 1388; —, prior, 778 n

Reddish (Redish), Edm., 856*; John, 1570, 1571; Nic., 1571; Sam., 1571; Sarah, 1570, 1571*

Reddy, *see* Ready

Rede, *see* Read

Redesdale, Lord, 1104, 1227, 1441, 1476

Redfearn, Ric., 977–8

Reding, *see* Redding

Redish, *see* Reddish

Reece (Rees), Hannah, 762; Rev. Jas., 1441; John, 906; Mary, 1183; Mary Trye, 1501*; Thos., 762*, 1183; Wm., 820; —, 1501

Reed, *see* Read

Reedham, (or Needham), Margery, 1051; (or Needham), Wm., 1051

Reeks, John, 1357

Rees, *see* Reece

Reeve (Reave, Reeves, Reue), Ann, 494; Cath., 978; Dan., 1466; Edm., 1010; Rev. Edw., 1165; Eleanor, 1262; Elena, 1033; Eliz., 715, 746, 1003, 1030*, 1031, 1130; Hannah, 1030; Hester, 978*; Jas., 177, 986; John (le), 385, 494*, 746*, 978*, 1033, 1061, 1456; Joseph, 966, 1262, 1278; Judith, 1466; Juliana, 1033, 1313; Kath., 1130; Marg., 1250*, 1466; Mary, 385, 966*, 1249, 1250; Ralph, 419; Rebecca, 1194; Ric., 1030*, 1031*; Sarah, 419, 1010*, 1035; Thos., 424, 598, 1003, 1015, 1033, 1194; Wal., 1356; Wm., 598, 703, 978, 1030, 1130*, 1249, 1250*, 1348, 1413; —, 1062, 1063, 1064, 1402; *and see* Prepositus

Regerty, —, 1355

Regley, Phil. Reg., 1149, 1151

Regn, Peter, 1404

Regnauld, —, 1392*

Reid, *see* Read

Reilly (Riley), Eglantine, 571; John, 1575; Marg., 1575; *and see* Relly

Reimbald (fl. 11th cent.)(Reinbald, Rembald), 358*, 359, 515, 990

Reinald, Hugh son of, 1227

Reinbald, *see* Reimbald

Relly, Anne, 340; Wm., 340; *and see* Reilly

Reman, Elia, 1540

Rembald, *see* Reimbald

Remington (Remmington), Ann(e), 656; John, 748; Mary, 302, 1509; Ric., 1509*, 1511; Sam., 656, 886, 1513; Thos., 302; fam., 885

Rene, Simon la, 1233

Renfrew, Rob., 538

Rennie (Reynny), Geoc. [?Geof.], 1420; Mr., 1323

Rensham (or Benshire or Benson), Rev. Ric., 1346

Reol, *see* Rowles

Reom, John le, 1218; — le, 1216

Restell (Rastall, Rastell, Restall), A., 1216; Ann, 203; Chris., 1355; Eliz., 610; Esther, 203; Francis, 1356; Isaac, 203*, 1473; John, 609, 610, 1460; Joseph, 203; Mary, 203; Rev. Rob., 1491; —, 1355

Reue, *see* Reeve

Reveley, Eliz., 143; Willey, 143

Revell, Eliz., 1409*, 1420; R., 1420; Rog., 1409

Reymell, R., 1061

Reyner, Hen., 1061; Wal., 1477; Rev. Wm., 1031

Reynny, *see* Rennie

Reynolds (Raynold, Raynolds, Reynald, Reynalds, Reynold, Reynoldes, Reynous), Ann(e), 199, 474, 661, 1471; Bryan, 693*; Cath., 693; Chris., 730; Eliz., 124, 412, 661, 847, 1030; Frances, 661, 1302; Fred., 411; Jo[a]ne, 814; John, 319, 474, 693*, 814; Rev. John, 85, 86, 744; John Bryan, 693; John Knapp, 693; Joyce, 86; Mary, 434, 692, 693, 1302, 1471; Rev. Mic., 764; Rev. Peter, 1127; Ric., 434; Rob., 1302*; Sam., 1030, 1031; Sarah, 411, 693*; Stephen, 389; Thos., 434, 661, 692*, 693, 1471; Rev. Thos., 764; Wm., 124*, 1069, 1447, 1471*, 1477; —, 1017*

Rhese ap Griffeth, prince of Wales, 819

Rhodes, Rev. John, 685; Thos., 1084

Ribble, John, 1110

Ricardo, David, 1536; Fanny, 1536

Ricards, *see* Rickards

Rice, Anna Jemima, 1007; Anne, 1175; Dan., 756; Rev. David, 184; Dorothy, 1003; Rev. E., 1016; Edw., 576*, 1121; Eliz., 1248; Rev. Ephraim, 1174*, 1175, 1177; Hannah, 1008; Rev. Hen., 1012; Hester, 756; Jas., 1174; John, 1008, 1175, 1248, 1539; Martha, 756*; Mary, 699*, 756, 1174, 1282; Methuselem, 1574; Moses, 1289; R., 1216; Ric., 1282; Rev. Ric., 1003, 1483; Rob., 699; Susanna, 1248; Thos., 1026, 1175; Rev. V., 886; Rev. Vincent, 626; Wm., 699*, 1121*; Rev. Mr., 1007; —, 943

Riceards, *see* Rickards

Rich, Anna, 992, 993; Anna-Maria, 298; Anne,

298*, 992, 993, 1497; Ant., 298; Baily, 504; Bridget(t), 298, 1497; Cha[s]., 298; Rev. Chas., 1443; Edw., 298*, 316, 504, 505; Sir Edw., 502; Edw. Gil., 504; Eliz., 298, 504*, 1409; Ewstace, 298; Hen., 298; Jo., 298; John, 298, 1495; Lionel 504*; Lucy, 298; Marg., 316; Martha, 505; Mary, 298, 504*; Nat., 364*; Rev. Pickering, 126; Rob., 298*; Sam., 298, 1409; Rev. Sam., 297, 298, 515*, 579; Sewster, 298; Susanna(h), 129, 298*; Thos., 298*, 738, 992, 1497; Sir Thos., 101; Wm., 298; Madam, 1189*; —, 1078, 1501; fam., 297, 1502
Richard I, 75, 157, 362, 475, 717
Richard II, 153, 244, 265, 297, 305 n, 318, 357, 358*
Richard III, 576, 805, 807, 1369
Richard, abbot, 41, 359, 778
Richard, bishop of Chichester, see Wich
Richard, bishop of London, see Clifford; Terrick
Richard son of Thos., 990
Richards (Richard, Richarde, Richardes), Ann, 584, 731, 1401; Cristina, 1017, 1259; D., 1512*; David, 584; Eliz., 923, 1162, 1464, 1488; Geo., 1162, 1464; Hannah, 662; Jane, 731; John, 662, 923*, 1162, 1488*, 1491; Rev. John, 1249, 1257; Rev. Joseph, 508; Mary, 340, 923, 1354, 1464; Mordecay, 756; Ph[il]., 1127; Rob., 1422; Rev. Rob., 216; Sam., 340, 1108; Sarah, 736; Thos., 662, 731, 736, 923, 1036, 1038, 1354, 1401; W., 1489; Wm., 1491; —, 756
Richardson, Abigail, 1398; Ann(e), 460, 907; Barbara, 898; Rev. Bennet, 808; Conan (Conon), 1262, 1279; Edw., 1262, 1290; Geo., 388; Hen., 1200, 1289; Herbert, 808; Jas., 896, 898, 1200; Jane, 1200; John, 274, 385, 1150, 1282, 1289; Joseph, 907, 1238; Joyce, 1412; Martha, 385; Mary, 460, 1412; Rev. Nic., 1102; Rachel, 385; Ric., 385; Thos., 274, 460, 1412*; Wm., 1398, 1412; —, 214; fam., 1262
Richeman (Richema.), see Richman
Richens, see Richins
Richer, Ranulf, 1091
Riches, Anne, 607; Catharina, 607; John, 607*
Richins (Richens, Ritchens), Ann,, 757; Cath., 569; Drusilla, 1097; John, 757; Rob., 569
Richman (Richema., Richeman, Rychemanes), Isabell, 1172; Juliana, 1348; Thos., 797, 1420
Richmond, Alice, 14; Anne, 1430; Bridget, 1027*; Eliz., 1529; Jas., 1529*; Jane, 1027*; Joanna, 1027*; Mary, 980; (or Webb), Nic., 839; O., 1027*; Olyffe, 1027; Ric., 866, 980; Toby, 14; Wm., 1430; (or Webb), fam., 839
Richmond [peerage], duke of, 765; and see Stuart, Esme
Rick, Styles, 1258
Rickards (Ricards, Riceards, Rycards), Edw., 1328; Eliz., 1101*; John, 174, 658, 1363; Mary, 174, 765, 1490, 1530; Rob., 1101; Sam., 765*; Sarah, 658; Thos., 174, 658, 1490; Wm., 765, 1027
Ricketts (Rickets), Alice, 947*; Ann(e), 752, 931, 1532; Ant., 474; Betty, 947; Cath., 1490; Cath. Eliz., 1231; Chas., 623; Cmdr. Cornwallis, 1231;

Dan., 543; David, 752; Eliza, 1117, 1531; Eliz., 984; Hannah, 947*; Henrietta, 1231; Hen., 1455; Jas., 1532*, 1539; Jane, 752, 947*; Joan, 204; John, 176, 413, 687, 765, 931*, 947, 984, 1289; Rev. John, 204; Kath., 176; Marg., 623; Mary, 339, 845; Dame Rebecca, 1231; Ric., 947*; Rob., 1231; Sir Rob. Tristram, bt., 1231*; Col. St. Vincent Wm., 1231; Sarah, 108, 172, 623*, 984, 1532*; Cmdr. Simpson Hicks, 1231; Stephen, 1117; Thos., 172, 339, 752, 845, 947, 984, 1490, 1532, 1539; Wm., 984*; Cornet Wm. Hamilton, 1231; fam., 415
Riddell (Ridall, Riddall, Riddel, Riddle), Ann, 984; Edw., 984; Eliz., 1415; Hen., 984; Jacob, 1306; John, 1232; Rev. John, 817; Mary, 1232, 1306; Thos., 1232; Thos. Hooper, 1415*
Riddeford (Riddiford), A., 1312; Abraham, 1173
Riddle, see Riddell
Rider, see Ryder
Ridgewall (Ridgewell), Rev. Thos., 681, 682
Ridler, Ann(e), 574, 575, 1206; Barbara, 574, 575; Eliz., 201, 314, 574, 715, 937; Joan(e), 197, 201*, 574; John, 574; Joseph, 1130; Mary, 176, 197, 201, 202, 574*, 575; Nat., 201*, 574*, 575, 659, 1083*, 1216*; Rob., 202, 1206*, 1216; Sam., 659, 1216; Rev. Sam., 449, 574, 1083*; Susanna, 1130; Thos., 151, 201, 314, 575*, 1083; Rev. Thos., 574*; Wal., 197, 201*, 1083*; Wm., 176, 189, 658, 937; —, 1501; (or Gregory), —, 1493
Ridley, Alice, 490; Ann(e), 1546*; Chas., 995; Dan., 1546*; Eliz., 15, 490, 962, 1546*; Rev. Giles, 1177, 1546*; Hester, 490; Jane, 995, 1298, 1300; Jeane, 490; Johane, 962; John, 994*, 1007, 1298, 1300; Mary, 994*, 1007; Nat., 16; Phebe, 1007; Rebecca, 1007; Ric., 416, 489, 490*, 962*; Sarah, 416, 490, 994*, 1007; Susanna, 16; Thos., 15, 490*, 994*, 1007; Rev. Thos., 1223; —, 488; fam., 487
Ridpath, Geo. de, 652; Phil., 652
Righton, Ann, 573; Jas., 217, 573; Sam., 573; Sarah, 217
Rigsby, Eliz., 304; Thos., 304
Riley, see Reilly
Rimel (Rimell, Rymall, Rymell, Rymill), Agnes, 1062; Ann, 1430*, 1459; David, 1459; Eliz., 1459; Hannah, 1459; J., 985; John, 1061, 1062, 1430; Mary, 1459; Sam., 1430; Sarah, 1459; Thos., 1459; Wm., 1062*
Rimer (Rymer), Edw., 660*; J., 661; John, 454; Mary, 454*; Ric., 454*; —, 325 n
Rind, Rob., 1171
Ring, Mary, 413
Rippe (Ripp), Kath., 1295*, 1309; W., 1302; Wm., 1302; —, 1302
Rishton, Dorothy, 1409; Eleanor, 1141*; Hen., 1141*
Ritchens, see Richins
Ritchie, Messrs., 1216
Rivers (River, Rivere, Riviere, Riviers, Ryvers), Dionys de la, 1339; Isabel de la, 1339; Jane, 1219; John de la, 1339*; Sir John de, 1339; Sir

John de la, kt., 1336*; Maur. de la, 1339; Ric. de la, 1491; — de la, 1339, 1491; fam., 553, 823, 1339

Rivers [*peerage*], Geo., Lord, 635, 1221, 1475, 1476, 1477; Ric., Earl, 1334, 1475; Savage, Earl, 1219; Earl, 1219; Lord, 1148, 1220*, 1461, 1475

Riviere (Riviers), *see* Rivers

Rllstrip, *see* Ellstrip

Rivett, T., 1201

Roach (Roch, Roche, Rouch), Ann(e), 307, 703*, 1454; Dan., 703, 1341; Deborah, 1243; Edm., 700, 847; Eleanor, 307*, 308; Eliz., 728, 1454, 1584; Esther, 837; Hannah, 540*, 543, 804; Hen., 1584*; Hester, 1303; Isaac, 837; Jas., 703, 1243; Joan, 124*; John, 283, 804, 1455, 1584; Joseph, 1582*; Josiah, 283*, 543; Martha, 124, 703*, 728; Mary, 124*, 700, 703, 1158; Nat., 1303; Pat., 1243; Rob., 703; Sam., 728*, 837; Sarah, 283*, 1582; Smart, 124*; Thos., 124*; Tim., 1158*, 1303*, 1328; Rev. Wal., 613 n; Wm., 125, 307*, 308, 532, 540, 543, 703*, 1454, 1539, 1576

Roan (Roane, Rone, Rowne), Alice, 1315; Ann, 858; Chas., 686*, 687*; Chris. (Xfus), 1317*; Edw., 514, 858; Eliz., 858; Giles, 587, 858*; Jas., 514; Jane, 686; Jean, 686; Joan, 514; John, 587, 686, 858*, 1315*; Mary, 587; Nic., 1315; Sarah, 587, 687, 1467; —, 1317

Robard, John, 1228; Wm., 1348; *and see* Roberts

Robarts, *see* Roberts

Robbins (Robin, Robins, Robyn, Robynes, Robyns), Agnes, 1379; Ann(e), 369, 496, 846, 854*, 923, 992*, 1075, 1374, 1375; Betty, 846; Cornelius, 496; Dorothy, 854*; Edith, 320; Edw., 1369; Elia, 1331; Eliz., 227, 1065*, 1067; Francis, 227, 1065; Gabriel, 496*; Geo., 211; Giles (Gyles), 320, 1374*; Hannah, 496, 1112; Hen., 992*, 1375; Hester, 961; Humph., 1073; John, 46, 212, 227, 338, 505, 853, 854*, 868, 961*, 962, 1043, 1348, 1504*; Rev. John, 619; Joseph, 320, 388, 433, 846, 1039; Josias, 210*, 212; Marg., 846, 985, 1201, 1348, 1504; Martha, 210; Mary, 46, 227, 320*, 376, 496*, 640, 796, 846, 868, 948, 961, 1037, 1065, 1067; Mat., 320; Penelope, 210; Ralph, 1422; Ric., 320, 338, 675, 853, 868, 923, 985, 992, 993, 1485; Rob., 868; Ruth, 483; Sam., 846, 862, 1065*; Sarah, 46, 320, 961, 1575; Thos., 227, 376, 640, 837, 948, 962, 1067, 1075, 1369, 1433; Rev. Thos., 739, 1335; Wm., 118, 227, 496, 846*, 854*, 868, 948, 1037, 1039, 1112; Mr., 133, 1380; —, 1440; fam., 1378; (or Bocher), fam., 852

Roberdes, *see* Roberts

Roberson, *see* Robertson

Robert, king of Scotland, 1281

Robert, abbot, 359, 502, 708*, 1291

Robert, bishop of London, *see* Lowth

Robert son of Aland, 1221

Robert son of Hardinge, *see* FitzHardinge

Robert, a monk, 390, 394

Roberts (Robarts, Roberdes, Robert, Robertes), Abigail, 164, 668, 831; Alice, 1034, 1359, 1401;

Ann(e), 77, 573, 687, 868, 1080, 1368, 1386*, 1401, 1504; Ant., 1477; Caesar, 1401; Chris., 906; Cox, 333; Edw., 1289, 1368, 1386*; Eleanor, 1165; Eliz., 115, 151*, 227, 249*, 340, 399, 666, 734, 803, 831, 868, 1235, 1303; Geo., 172, 328, 1355, 1428; Rev. Geo., 1387; Giles, 77, 115, 118, 1401*; Rev. Griffin, 1196; Hannah, 15, 661, 996, 1027; Hen., 868*, 1424, 1503; Humph., 1233; Isaac, 150; J., 1082; Jas., 924*, 1473; Rev. Jas. Izod, 1040; Jane, 77*, 227, 818, 924, 1092; Jo., 1034; John, 77*, 249*, 296, 340, 424, 484, 661, 686, 734, 965*, 996, 1080, 1092, 1262, 1290*, 1359, 1386, 1401, 1428*, 1473, 1503*, 1504*; Capt. John, 1424; Rev. John, 1034, 1233, 1387; Joseph, 446, 1040, 1422; Joshua, 947; Kath., 1503*, 1504; Lewis, 670, 672, 674, 675; Marg., 484, 868; Martha, 1027, 1136; Mary, 69, 150*, 296, 446, 468, 686, 687, 906, 965, 1274, 1345, 1424*, 1473, 1503, 1504*; Rev. Maur., 328; Nic., 1393, 1401*; Rev. Ralph, 447; Ric., 150, 151*, 226, 227, 966, 1088, 1345*, 1503*, 1504*; Rev. Ric., 463, 1463, 1477; Rob., 700; Sarah, 172, 264, 296, 333*, 483, 573, 966*, 1027*, 1076; Susanna, 1473; T., 1165; Thos., 69, 264, 333, 399, 468*, 573*, 668*, 670, 687*, 803, 818, 831, 868, 1005, 1025, 1027*, 1076*, 1136, 1233, 1424*, 1425, 1460, 1503, 1504; Rev. Thos., 1154, 1232, 1335; Ursula, 1425; W., 1043, 1093, 1159; Wm., 15, 70, 77, 199, 328, 333*, 666, 895, 966*, 1274*, 1282, 1368; —, 1293, 1378, 1382, 1402, 1428, 1504; fam., 424, 667, 672*, 864, 1428, 1501; *and see* Robard

Robertson (Roberson), Abigail, 660; Ann, 550; Rev. Ant., 511; Hen., 550; John, 660, 1539; Rev. W. H. M., 1329

Robins (Robin), *see* Robbins

Robinson, Adam, 1397; Col. Beverley, 1303*; Dorothy, 1397; Eliz., 489, 867; Hen., 472, 473*; Rev. Hugh, 527, 534; Jacob, 1075; Jane, 5, 472*; Jo., 867; John, 5, 472*, 489, 703*, 1194; John, bishop, 1331*; Joseph, 550; Rev. Joseph, 1348; Mary, 5, 472, 550; Phil., 472*; Sarah, 472*, 1194, 1303; Thos., 1168; Sir W. H., kt., 1303; Mr., 1189; *and see* Robison

Robison, Adam, 965; Mary, 965; *and see* Robinson; Robson

Robotham, Joshua, 1572

Robson, Rev. Wm., 1186; Mr., 1189; —, 1219; *and see* Robison

Robyns (Robyn, Robynes), *see* Robbins

Rocelin, —, 1238

Roch (Roche), *see* Roach

Rochford (Rocheford), Agatha, 1086; Isabell, 1086; Rev. Ralph, 1387

Rock (Roke), John atte, 1372; —, 1372; *and see* Rooke; Ruck

Rockingham [*peerage*], *see* Watson, Cath. *and* Lewis

Rod (Rode), Deborah, 471*; John, 1317; Ric., 1160; Thos., 471*

Rodberg (Rodberge, Rodberghe), *see* Rodborough

Rodborn (Rodbourne), Eliz., 862, 1426; Elner [sic], 489; John, 862; Kath., 862*; Mat., 1426; Rob., 862*

Rodborough (Rodberg, Rodberge, Rodberghe, Rodborow), Agnes, 1027, 1165; Edm. de, 1021; Hugh, 1078; Joan (de), 801, 1027; Matilda de, 1322; John de, 1165*; Miles de, 1322; Ric. de, 1165; Thos. (de), 1027, 1078, 1165, 1217; Wm. de, 1165*

Rodbourne, see Rodborn

Rode, see Rod

Rodemerton, see Rodmerton

Roden, Jenevary, 1108; John, 1108*

Roderick, Rev. David, 1483

Rodey, Geo., 941

Rodford (Radeforde), Edw., 1428; Nic. de, 1428; Thos., 1428*

Rodleye, Hen. de, 1404

Rodman, Eliz., 1159; Geo., 615*; Hannah, 615; John, 616, 702*; Sarah, 702*; Thos., 1159

Rodmerton (Rodemerton), John de, 1258; Rog. de, 360

Rodney, Ellen, 1303; John, 1303; John Stratford, 1303; Lady Louisa, 1303; Maur., 639; Ric. de, 1172; Tollemache Montague Brydges, 1303; Admiral, 932

Rodway, Anna, 1023; Ann(e), 703, 797, 1374*, 1375; Chas., 95, 703, 1536; Dan., 1455*; Deborah, 701*; Edw., 701; Eliz., 701; Esther, 1137; Francis, 991; Giles, 703*; Hester, 701, 1137; Isabell, 1374; Jas., 703*, 797; Joane, 1375; John, 95, 1137, 1374*, 1375; Lydia, 1137; Martha, 701, 703; Mary, 703, 782, 797; Rebecca, 95*; Ric., 1121; Sam., 95*, 1023; Sarah, 703; Susanna, 991; T., 797; Thos., 1373, 1374, 1375*, 1377, 1378; Thos. Wickes, 1513; Wm., 701*, 703, 782, 1374*, 1536; and see Radway

Roe, see Rowe

Roff, Rob., 321; Sabina, 321

Roger, constable of Gloucester, 432

Roger brother of Durand, 1060 n, 1131

Roger, Wal. son of, 1060 n

Rogers (Roger), A., 1519; Abigail, 622*; Alice, 1447; Rev. Ambrose, 1048; And., 1508*; Anna, 204; Ann(e), 18, 204, 370, 383, 407, 456, 504*, 585, 674*, 897*, 972, 1003, 1165, 1498, 1501; Ant., 418, 887, 1098*, 1471*, 1476, 1477, 1498; Croft, 1003; Dennis, 1584; Dennis [?Denise], 319*; Dorothy, 623; Edith, 1197; Edm., 407; Edw., 137, 503, 896, 900, 1048, 1477; Rev. Edw., 1504; Eleanor (Elinor), 32, 674, 977, 1000, 1048, 1471*; Eliz., 65, 66, 137, 334, 337, 383, 418, 503, 505, 622, 674, 896, 897*, 900, 1057, 1244, 1498, 1507; Emela, 1413; E(a)ster, 1412*, 1413; Erasmus, 1513; Francis, 1413; Rev. G. H., 1127; Geo., 18, 204; Giles, 1498, 1501*; Hellen, 503; Hen., 413, 735, 736*; Hester, 1502; Jas., 1508, 1529; Jane, 174; Joane, 398; John, 174, 319, 337, 347, 368, 370, 383*, 430, 502, 504, 585, 671*, 672, 674*, 785, 895, 896, 897*, 924, 1003, 1063, 1165, 1217, 1274, 1345, 1471, 1508; Rev. John, 503, 909, 1102, 1232; Jonathan, 1112; Joseph,

1068; Letitia, 897; Marg., 383, 1098; Mark, 18; Martha, 1068, 1529; Mary, 229, 456, 623, 674*, 736, 887, 974, 1098, 1296, 1311, 1499; Mat., 32; Michah, 412; Nat., 1508; Prudence, 1514, 1515; R., 1064; Rev. R., 334, 346, 1348; Sir R., kt., 1311; Randall, 1415; Rebekah, 334; Ric., 204, 263, 502, 675, 895, 896, 897, 1000, 1062, 1063, 1150, 1151, 1232, 1412, 1413, 1508; Rev. Ric., 504, 667, 785; Sir Ric., kt., 1296; Rob., 18, 505, 972, 1501*, 1502; Rev. Rob., 1238; Sam., 540; Rev. Sam., 56, 800, 1047; Sarah, 543, 897, 1507*, 1508; Thos., 197, 204*, 229, 319*, 334, 368, 383*, 398, 456, 505, 622, 858, 1507*, 1508; Rev. Thos., 622; W., 503*, 1064; Rev. Wal., 1289; Wm., 334, 394, 456, 502, 503*, 504*, 505*, 623, 674, 798, 895, 896*, 897*, 974, 977, 1057, 1064*, 1197, 1501, 1514*, 1515*; Rev. Wm., 56; Dr., 1101; Mr., 894*, 1189; Mrs., 1495; —, 1017, 1043, 1064*, 1165, 1232, 1311; fam., 346, 393, 502, 579, 585, 672, 894, 1477

Roke, see Rock

Rokeley, John, 1092*

Rolby, Adam de, 1201

Rolf (Rolfe), see Rolph

Rolles, see Rowles

Rolleston, Dr., 1228

Rollinson, Martha, 1090; Thos., 1090

Rollo, Rev. Geo., 681; Lady, see Murray, Cath.

Rolls, see Rowles

Rolph (Rolf), Turstin (Turtin) son of, 98, 1162, 1345, 1419

Rolph (Rolf, Rolfe, Rolues, Rolves), Agnes, 1197; Ann, 1427, 1548*; Betty, 1427; Dan., 1427*, 1548*; Edythea, 1519; Eliz., 46; Geo., 46*; Hannah, 1427*; John, 46*, 1348, 1548; Joseph, 1548; Lydia, 1273*; Mary, 1548; Rob., 1440, 1447, 1548*; Sarah, 1548; Susanna, 46*; Thos., 1548*; Wal., 1485; Wm., 1197, 1382; Mr., 1455; —, 1345

Rolt, J., 1485; Sir John, kt., 1485

Rolves (Rolues), see Rolph

Roman (Romaine), Rev. Wm., 1369; Rev. Dr., 987

Rommieu, Ann, 1213*; Eliz., 1213

Romney (Rumney), Eliz., 967; Mary, 1381; Sir W., 1259; Rev. Wm., 1233; Sir Wm., kt., 1239, 1258; —, 1256, 1257*, 1258*

Romzay, —, 1074

Ronalds, Alice, 632; Mary, 632; Ric., 632*

Rone, see Roan

Roo, Rev. Geo., 1477*; and see Rue

Rooke (Rook), Barbara, 247, 513; Chas., 550; Jas., 245, 247*, 513; Major Jas., 732; Major-Gen. Jas., 245; Jane, 247*, 550, 856, 857; John, 235, 1196; Ric., 1223; T. Archdale, 1196; Thos., 856*, 857; and see Rock; Ruck

Rookeby, Thos., 1575

Room, Hannah, 1576

Roos, see Rouse

Roper (Ropier), Ant., 1457, 1460; John, 1440; Mary, 340; Ric., 340; —, 590 n, 1459, 1460

Rose, Alice, 1065, 1227; Ann(e), 217, 601, 800, 1168; Chas., 608*; Chris., 217*, 429; Edm., 235;

Edw., 235, 891; Eliz., 235*, 608*, 1470; Esther, 348; Geo., 1168*; Jas., 258; Jerome, 1228; John, 235, 429, 800*, 868, 1421, 1470*; Joseph, 258; Judith, 258; Marg., 884; Mariam [sic], 1536; Marmaduke, 1265; Mary, 429, 868, 891, 1168, 1421*; Rev. Mat., 424; Miriam, 1168; Ric., 1265, 1421; Rev. Rob., 1441; Sam., 235, 1265; Sarah, 1421; Thos., 235, 601, 868, 884, 1033, 1196; Rev. Thos., 865; Wm., 235, 348, 800, 865, 1065*, 1168, 1421*; —, 1052, 1289; and see Ross; Rouse

Roselarge, M., 1411

Rosen, Thos., 1460

Rosewell, Joan, 210; Joseph, 210*; Stephen, 208; Susanna, 210

Roshall, see Rushall

Rosier (Rossiere), Eliz., 417; Jas., 417; John, 1125

Ross, Arthur, archbishop, 639; Jas., 639; Marg., 639; and see Rose; Rouse

Rosser (Rossor), Edw., 922, 1162; Eliz., 731; Geo., 922*; Mary, 922; Wm., 731, 907

Rossiere, see Rosier

Rossmore, Augusta, baroness Rossmore, 1153; Mary Ann, 1518; Lady, 1153; Lord, 1518

Rossor, see Rosser

Roston, Anne, 902; Edw., 902; Eliz., 902; Wm., 902

Rothery, Anne, 249; Mary, 249; Thos., 249*

Rothes, earl of, 407

Rothwell, Eliz., 1316; Thos., 1316

Rotten (Rotton), Susannah, 660; Rev. Thos., 865; Tim., 660

Roubiliac, —, 852 n

Rouch, see Roach

Rouls, see Rowles

Round, Eliz., 295

Rouse (Roos, Rous, Rufus), Ann, 1305, 1530; Edw., 1331; Eliz., 1524, 1537; Geo., 940; J., 1392; Jas., 1530; Jane, 1524*; John (le), 296, 307, 406*, 1003, 1016, 1093, 1148*, 1195, 1331, 1392, 1530*, 1562; John le, kt., 525; Capt. John, 1555; Joseph, 1331; Juliana le, 667; Lucy, 296; Marg., 406; Mary, 1253, 1524, 1546; Rob., 296*, 1392; Sam., 1305*; Thos., 1524*, 1530*, 1546; Wm., 307, 1392, 1530*; fam., 525, 667; and see Rose; Ross

Rowbery, Caleb, 354

Rowden (Rowdon, Rowdown), Eliz., 421*, 484; Joan, 421*; Mary, 421; Rob., 421*; Rev. Rob., 421*, 1482, 1531; Thos., 421*; Wal., 484

Rowe (Roe), Ann(e), 539, 623*; Betty, 623; Edw., 539; Elenor, 1010; Eliz., 539, 1109; John, 1109; Mary, 539, 1170; Ric., 539, 623*; Rob., 1010, 1170; Sophia, 1367; Thos., 364; Sir Thos., kt., 364, 366, 367, 1126; Wm., 539

Rowill, J., 1055

Rowland, John, 176; Sam., 176*; W., 1369

Rowles (Reol, Rolles, Rolls, Rouls, Rowle), Adam, 1428; Abigail, 70*; Ann(e), 675, 873, 1130; Ant., 633, 1130; Betty, 584; Chas., 70, 677; Chris., 1136; Deborah, 471*; Eliz., 70, 471, 627, 666, 677, 830*; Esther, 677; Frances, 873; Hannah,

832, 1045; Henrietta, 831; Hester, 172; John, 70*, 74, 172, 623, 626, 666*, 675, 677*, 830, 873, 1045; Rev. John, 668, 1147; Kath., 623; Margery, 383; Mary, 69, 70, 172, 383, 471*, 666, 677, 1136, 1155; Ric., 623; Rob., 353, 677*, 1238; Sam., 69*, 1147; Sarah, 584, 677*; Temperance, 832; Thos., 70, 677, 832; Wal., 832; Wm., 383*, 471*, 584, 627, 666, 677*, 830*, 831, 1155; —, 927

Rowne, see Roan

Rowney, fam., 864

Rownton, Marg., 1223

Rowsham, Kath., 818; Sam., 818; Wm., 818

Rowthale (Ruthalle), Alice, 361; John, 361; Marg., 361; Rob., 361; Thos., bishop, 360 n, 361, 362*, 365, 367; and see Rudhall

Royce (Roy's), Rev. D., 1017 n, 1093 n, 1195, 1196, 1197 n, 1228; Rev. David, 1228; John, 1428

Roynon, David, 406; Hannah, 1571; Mary, 1571; Peter, 1571

Roy's, see Royce

Ruck, Ann, 706, 1353; Cath., 315; Edm., 891*; Edw., 706*; Eliz., 636; Emmit, 706; John, 706*; Mary, 706, 891; Ric., 706*; Thos., 706; Wm., 315; fam., 890; and see Rock; Rooke

Rudd, Rev. Rob., 1222, 1223

Ruddall, see Rudhall

Ruddeford, Arabella, 939; Thos., 939

Rudder, Chas., 845*; Chris., 731; Dan., 1368; Eliz., 1368; Hester, 845; John, 1368; Lydia, 1368; Mary, 1368; Ric., 1368; (or Rutter), Rog., 1368; S., 1369; Sam., 1368*; Sarah, 731; Wm., 1368*; —, 1027, 1044, 1120, 1123, 1201, 1220, 1225, 1233, 1284, 1309, 1379, 1381, 1519

Rudge, Aaron, 1168; Ann(e), 368, 1038, 1301; Cath., 468; Dan., 1168; Edith, 1250; Eliz., 465, 468, 906, 939, 1168*, 1399; Esther, 111; Geo., 1399*; Hen., 1036, 1038, 1039; Horatio, 1551; Jas., 467, 939, 1551; Joannah, 465; John, 465, 789, 906, 907, 1250, 1306, 1312; Jonathan, 468*; Joseph, 1250; Marg., 465, 1250; Mary, 468; Nat., 465*; Phil., 906; Rudhall, 939*; S., 1102; Sam., 762; Sarah, 465*, 467; Stephen, 1102; Susanah, 1282; Thos., 111, 463, 465*, 468, 820*, 1186, 1250, 1282, 1289*; Rev. Thos., 619, 674, 820; Wal., 465*; Wm., 1300; Rev., 1372; —, 1228, 1233, 1379

Rudhall (Ruddall), Abraham, 1369; Ford, 1289; —, 990, 1369; and see Rowthale

Ruding, Ann, 257; Clifton, 257; Wal., 257

Rue, Wulfin le, 349*; and see Roo

Rufus, see Rouse

Rugg (Rugge), Ann, 1455; Betty, 1455; Eliz., 1536; John, 1455, 1529, 1535; Lydia, 1529, 1535; Mary, 1529; Ric., 1529, 1535–6; —, 1362

Rumbald (fl. 1086), 1074*

Rumley, Edw., 1575; Mary, 1575

Rumney, see Romney

Rupert, prince, 349 n, 358*, 1293

Rush, Hannah, 891; Mary, 891; Rev. Sam., 878; Thos., 891; —, 1403

Rushall (Roshall), Edw., 437*; Hannah, 437; Jane, 437; John, 437; Mary, 1013; Susanna, 1013; Thos., 1013*; Wm., 1013*; —, 1017

Rushout, Abigail, 220 n; Dame Alice, 224*; Ann, 1227, 1459; Lady Anne, 224*; Arabella, 224, 1227; Cath., 220 n; Eliz., 220, 1227*, 1228; Geo., 1227; Sir J., 1017; Jas., 1227*; Sir Jas., 220 n, 224*, 1227*, 1228*; John, 220 n, 1227*; Sir John, bt., 218, 220*, 221*, 224*, 287, 1227; fam., 218

Russ, Ann, 1084; Ric., 8

Russell (Russel), Alice, 1004; And., 999; Ann(e), 124, 175, 339, 1326*, 1545; Betty, 1427; Cath., 296; Chas., 339, 1361; Edith (Edytha), 1111, 1447; Edw., 729*, 1427; Elianor, 1453; Eliz., 552, 729, 957, 999; Sir F., 1290; Frances, 1010, 1326; Gabriell, 1337*; Geo., 124, 1116, 1336; Giles, 757; Greg., 1498, 1499; Hannah, 16, 598, 1430, 1534; Hen., 339, 948*; Dame Isabel, 552, 554; Henrietta Maria, 1498; Jas., 175*; Jane, 958, 1309, 1336, 1453, 1545*; Jeremiah, 757, 1326*, 1336, 1338, 1545*; John, 360 n, 552, 598, 727, 780, 948, 958, 1010*, 1121, 1159, 1292, 1328, 1336, 1460, 1498, 1502, 1551; Jonathan, 826; Joseph, 1004; Kath., 958, 1337; Marg., 997; Martha, 757, 1111, 1112; Mary, 123, 226, 339, 948*, 1159, 1338, 1361; Sir Maur., kt., 551, 552, 553, 554, 997; Rachel, 1326; Ralph de, 552; Rebecca, 780; Ric., 176, 957*; Rev. Ric., 1404; Rob., 465; Sarah, 176, 1498; Selena, 881; Simon, 1552; Thos., 16, 296*, 598, 826, 881, 1111, 1112, 1326, 1328, 1430, 1450, 1453, 1534, 1545, 1550; Tobias, 1453; Wm., 226, 684, 787, 1011, 1333, 1361*, 1427, 1430, 1450, 1453; Sir Wm., 123; Dr., 327 n; Lord, 1093; —, 1011, 1104, 1122, 1220, 1291, 1293, 1328, 1355, 1458, 1475; fam., 552, 553

Ruthalle, see Rowthale

Ruthey, John, 1139

Rutland, Rev. Edm., 1405*; Kath., 1405; Mrs., 1405

Rutland [peerage], see Manners, Chas.; Somerset, Mary Isabella

Rutter, Ann, 28; Chas., 1334*; Dorothy, 393 n; Rev. Edw., 630; Eleanor, 398; Rev. Ferryman, 500; Hannah, 1334; John, 28, 398, 1334*; Rev. John, 500, 1392; Joseph, 1196; Mary, 176, 398, 1334; Mic., 231, 393 n; Ric., 28, 176, 1196; (or Rudder), Rog., 1368; Rev., 1440; fam., 393 n

Rutty, Dr., 405 n

Rya, Agnes de, 753; Hen. de, 753; Wm. de, abbot, 605

Rycards, see Rickards

Rychemanes, see Richman

Ryder (Rider), Ann(e), 108, 611, 1460; Sir Dudley, 570, 1460*; Edw., 284; Eliz., 831, 872; Geo., 611; Hannah, 109, 284; Hen., 1493; Jas., 133, 831; Jane, 1493; Joan, 465; John, 1493; Mary, 109, 133; Nat., Lord Harrowby, 570, 1460*; Ric., 108, 109*; Sam., 611, 872, 873*; Sarah, 873; Simon, 943; Susanna, 284; Thos., 1403*; Sir W., 1382; Sir Wal., 311; Wm., 109, 465, 1403

Ryeland, see Ryland

Ryez, H., 1475

Ryland (Ryeland), John, 744*; Rev. John, 696; Marg., 744; Mary, 744*; Sam., 744; Thos., 1001*; Rev. W., 1221; —, 1356

Rymall (Rymell, Rymill), see Rimel

Rymer, see Rimer

Rymill, see Rymall

Ryndecombe, Alice, 1292

Rysbrack, —, 119, 224, 497 n

Ryson, Geof., 1258

Ryuet, Rob., 1172

Ryvers, see Rivers

Sabyn, —, 1402

Sachen, Bart., 1313

Sackville, Ann, 1201*; Anne, countess of Dorset, 721 n; Cath., 184, 1201*; Chas., earl of Dorset, 1388*, 1390*; Chas., duke of Dorset, 1388; Eliz., 185, 1201*; Geo. John Fred., duke of Dorset, 1388*, 1389; Hen., 185*, 1201; Lady Isabella, 721 n; Kath., 185; Lady Marg., 721 n; Ric., 184, 1201*; Ric., earl of Dorset, 721 n, 1165; Sir Thos., kt., 183, 184*; —, duchess of Dorset, 1390

Sadds, Mr., 1362

Sadler (Sadleir, Sadlier), Ann, 580, 637*; Ant., 575*, 580*, 637; Cath. Anne, 1138; Eliz., 106*, 450, 799, 800; Geo., 106; Gertrude, 717, 1419; Hannah, 348, 460; Hen., 1138; Jas., 450*, 800*; Jane, 354, 800*; John, 106*, 118*, 348, 450*, 460, 800, 1515; Jonathan, 450; Joseph, 800; Mary, 118*, 637, 799, 800*, 1138, 1515; Ralph, 722, 1361; Sir Ralph, 403, 502, 704, 717, 719, 1350, 1361, 1388, 1419*, 1519; Rev. S. F., 1047; Rev. Sam. Farmer, 1044, 1138*; Sarah, 118, 450, 1515; Thos., 460, 799*, 800; Sir Thos., 717; Tim., 637, 800; Wm., 105, 106, 354*, 450; —, 1282, 1420*

Saffin, Frances, 164; Rev. Ric., 161*, 164

Sagar, Stephen, 392, 708

Sage, Eliz., 730; Hen., 730; John, 1069, 1165, 1225; Martha, 730

Sainer, Joan, 1417

Sainger, see Saniger

St. Amand, Isabel de, 690; barons de, 301

St. Barb, Edith, 560; Hen., 560; Mary, 560

St. Clair (St. Clare), D. L., 1165; Capt. David Latimer, 1164*; Eliz. Isabella, 1164; Isabell de, 1253; Matilda de, 1253

St. Croix, Mary, 1326

St. George, David, 758; Sir Hen., kt., 2

St. John, Dorothy, 1165; John (de), 778, 1053, 1350; Sir John, kt. & bt., 1497; Lucie, 1497; Marg., 1482; Oliver, 364, 368; Oliver, Lord St. John, 1165*; Rev. St. And. [sic], 447; Thos., 663 n; Wm., 429; Lord, 1350; fam., 724

St. Leger, Hen., 334*; John, 334*; Martha, 334; Mary, 334, 692*; Sir W., 1314

St. Loe (St. Loo, Sendlow, Sentlow), Edw., 560; Eliz., 823, 1339; Isabel, 1339; Sir J., kt., 1339; Rev. Sir John, kt., 1337; Sir John, kt., 1160,

1339; Marg., 560*; Sir Wm., kt., 823, 1339; —, 1292; fam., 823

St. Mary (Santemareys), Alice, 1311, 1314

St. Maur, *see* Seymour

St. Philibert (St. Philebert, Sancto Philiberto), Alice, 1126; Hen. de, 599*; John de, 1126*, 1127; Sir John de, 599

St. Valery (St. Vallery, St. Villery, St. Walerick, St. Wallery), Bernard (de), 778 n, 1253; Guy, 1253; Hugh de, 1033; Maud, 1253; Reg. (de), 778, 1033, 1253, 1256; T., 1255, 1256, 1257; Thos. (de), 778 n, 1033, 1253, 1256, 1474; —, 1475*

St. Vincent Ames, Mr., 1420

St. Walerick (St. Wallery), *see* St. Valery

Saintbury (Saintsbury, Seynesbury), Hen., 386, 1217; Rob., 386; Wm. de, 1228

Sake, Reg., 1540

Salcomb (Salcombe), Alice, 1045*; Ann, 1045; Edm., 1045, 1046*; Eliz., 1046; Jas., 787*; John, 1045*; Mary, 787, 1045*; Rach(a)el, 1046*; Ric. de, 1494; Wm., 787, 1045*, 1046*, 1047

Sale, Edw., 70; Mary, 70; Thos., 1388

Salices, *see* Saussay

Saley, *see* Sealey

Salis, Mary, 1518; Ric., 1518

Salisbury [*peerage*], R., Lord, 323 n, 324; earl of, 979, 1139; *and see* Cecil, Rob. *and* Wm.; Long-Espee, Ela *and* Wm.; Montague, John de; Neville, Anne *and* Ric.; Owe, Wm. de;

Sallance, Anne, 107; Thos., 107

Salloway, *see* Salway

Salmon (Salman, Saman), Ann(e), 1299*, 1306*; Chas., 1306; Hen. le, 1485; Jacob, 845*; John, 1299, 1306*, 1331; Joyce, 845; Rob., 1391; Thos. Stokes, 1299, 1306; —, 1020

Salop, Eliz., countess of, 1339

Salperton, Stephen de, 1043

Saltere, Wal., 1477

Saltforde, Thos. de, 1017, 1259

Saltonstall, Eliz., 1033; Sir J., 1033

Salusbury, Rev. John, 400

Salway (Salloway, Solloway), Eliz., 1003*; Mager, 1003; Thos., 1003*; Wm., 1331; Rev. Wm., 593; —, 1331

Saman, *see* Salmon

Sambach, Ann, 1103; Ant., 142; Bridget, 90; John, 90*; Ursula, 90; Wm., 89, 90*, 1103*; widow, 1103; fam., 90

Samford, *see* Sandford

Samme, Mary, 920; Thos., 920

Sampson, Dan., 727, 728; E., 1043; Edw., 99, 718, 721, 722, 724, 725*, 728, 1043; Martha, 724, 728*; John, 724*, 725*, 727*, 728; Mary, 724*, 725*; Ralph, 727, 728; Ric., 1447; Sam., 727

Samuel, bishop of Gloucester, *see* Halifax

Samwaies, Rev. R., 860; Ric., 859

Sancto Mauro, *see* Seymour

Sancto Philiberto, *see* St. Philibert

Sandal *see* Sandell

Sandby, Rev. Chas., 1224, 1228

Sandell (Sandal), Martha, 1575; Thos., 1575; W., 1475; Wm., 1226; —, 1226

Sanders, *see* Saunders

Sanderson, Rev. 1460

Sandford (Samford, Sandiford, Sanford), Anne, 339*, 948, 1145, 1182; Anselm (Anielm, Anselem, Anselme), 280, 1141, 1145*, 1182, 1187; Rev. Anselm, 1145, 1146, 1147; Brian, 1145; Rev. Chas., 103*, 1356; Dorcas, 1182; Dorothy, 280, 1145; Edw., 1187; Elinor, 1145; Eliz., 339*, 1182; Jas., 762; Jane, 948, 1145; Joan, 1145; John, 339*, 948, 1016, 1145*, 1147, 1232; Rev. John, 1147; Margery, 1182; Marie, 1145; Mary, 339, 762, 1145, 1235; R., 1147; Ralph, 1145; Ric. (Rachard), 1145; Rob., 721, 725, 1141*, 1145*, 1147*; Sam., 93, 96; Sarah, 95, 787, 1141*, 1146*; Susanna, 1182; Thos., 339, 1197, 1235; Tobias, 424; W., 93, 1185; Wm., 95, 339, 1145, 1146*, 1182*; Rev. Wm., 56, 691, 692; Rev., 1352; —, 1015, 1141*; fam., 630, 667, 1147, 1195

Sandwigen, Nielsen, 1418; Paa, 1418;

Sandys, Barbara, 875 n, 878, 1485*; Edw., 1485; Edwin, 221; Edwin (Edwyn), bishop, 890, 1223; Eliz., 875 n; Eliz., baroness de la Vine, 328; Rev. Geo., 1460; Rev. Hambury, 252; J. T., 1216; J. Y., 1215; Jane, 328; Dame Marg., 875 n, 880; Mary, 875 n; Dame Mary, 875 n; Miles, 370, 449*, 875 n*, 878*, 1485*; Sir Miles (Myles), kt., 364, 875 n; Ric., 1015; Sam., 449, 876, 878*, 1485*; Thos., Lord Sandys, 1015; Wm., 252*, 449, 875 n*; Sir Wm., kt., 252, 449, 875 n, 876*, 880, 1015; Wm., Lord Sandys, 1015*; Col., 341; Lord, 220 n, 1015*; —, 1015, 1368, 1483; fam., 252*, 875, 876*, 1485; *and see* Sondes

Sanford, *see* Sandford

Saniger (Sainger, Sanigear, Sanger, Senegar, Sonager), Abraham, 542; Cath., 174; Edw., 161, 173*, 176; Eliz., 1159; Esther, 173*; Jane, 173, 958; Rev. John, 1313; Martha, 542; Mary, 176, 542; Maur., 176; Ric., 623; Sarah, 542; Susanna, 173; Thos., 174, 958; Wm., 172, 542*; —, 1069, 1216; fam., 159

Sankey (Sankye), Eleanor, 1062, 1078; Nic., 985; Mr., 1078

Sansom (Sansum), Ann, 703; Edw., 320*; Ephraim, 5, 821; Jas., 5*, 1430; Joanna, 821; Joseph, 542; Marg., 5; Mark [?: wife of Ephraim], 821; Mary, 5, 320, 662*; Thos., 662, 821; Wm., 703

Santemareys, *see* St. Mary

Sapiens, Stephen, 1223; *and see* Wise

Sapton, Alice, 584; Alice Freeme, 584; John, 584

Sapy (Sapye), Alice, 1401; Rob. de, 759, 1217; — de, 1401, 1402*

Saren, Wm., 1197

Sargent (Sargant, Sargeant, Sargeaunt, Sarjaent, Sarjent, Sergeant, Sergeaunt, Sergent, Serjeant, Serjent), Anne, 465, 466*; Rev. Chas., 56; Edw., 466*, 820; Eliz., 240, 332, 466*, 939, 1109, 1401, 1490; Hannah, 1117*, 1401; Hen., 1117; Hester, 768; Isaac, 1384; Isabel, 466; Jane, 499; Joan, 1384; John, 466*, 499, 933, 1112, 1117*, 1177, 1490; Rev. John, 103*, 105; Marg., 110, 895, 903, 1117; Mary, 110, 466*, 939, 1117,

1546; Ric., 110*, 240, 241, 466, 546, 1401; Rob., 466*, 758, 939, 1546*; Sam., 466, 905; Rev. Sam., 903*, 905, 1372*; Sarah, 933, 1117, 1118; Stephen, 768*; Susanna, 1109, 1117; Thos., 332, 465, 1109*, 1176, 1238*, 1401; Rev. Thos., 1121; Wm., 466*, 1117*, 1403; Mr., 894; —, 1177, 1238, 1351; fam., 236, 819, 1176

Sarny, John, 1009

Sarsons, Edm., 337; Frances, 337

Sartain, Anne, 836; John, 836; Susanna, 835; Wm., 835

Sartoris, A., 1226*, 1227

Saul, Rev. Arthur, 488

Saunders (Sanders, Saundres), Abraham, 1413*; Adam, 1027, 1404; Rev. Alex., 129, 302; Ann(e), 202, 884*, 991; Ant., 569; Rev. Ant., 569; Rev. Benj., 582, 583; Cath., 1047, 1243, 1244*; Chas., 1154; Christian, 111, 510; Constantia, 1437; Dan., 1408; Deborah, 202; Dorothea, 898; Dorothy, 58, 1265; Eliz., 111, 491*, 510, 569*, 657, 1408; Erasmus, 224; Rev. Erasmus, 220, 221, 224; Frances, 569; Geof., 1483; Capt. Geo., 1413; Gertrude, 1545, 1546; Hannah, 862, 1321; Hen., 388; Hester, 1053; Jane, 657; John, 111*, 381, 569, 657, 1053, 1054*, 1313, 1533; Dr. John, 58; Rev. John, 37, 722; Joseph, 1311; Rev. Joseph, 1157; M., 1255; Marg., 1243; Maria, 1247; Rev. Mark, 232; Mary, 296, 381, 623*, 660, 1244, 1408, 1413*; Mat., 97*, 660; Mic., 991; Nat., 1244; Peter, 1408*; Ric., 459, 1387, 1545*, 1546; Rev. Ric., 459; Rob., 111*, 1354; Rosa Maria, 1247; Sam., 202, 1243, 1244*, 1258; Sam. Albin, 1247*, 1255; Sarah, 623, 1244*; Susanna (Sussanah), 388, 991; Thos., 111, 569, 623, 657*, 898, 1258, 1321, 1420*, 1437*; Wal., 1317, 1540; Wm., 296, 491, 657, 859, 884, 991, 1053, 1244, 1265*, 1311, 1408; Mr., 870, 1420; —, 202, 1458; fam., 625, 1247

Saussay (Salices, Saussaye), (or Sucia), Wm. de, 1475; —, 1475

Savacre (Savaker), Rev. Edw., 1238; Rev. John, 619; Rev. Ric., 1238

Savage (Savadge), Albert, 862; Alice, 1575; Anna, 1241; Ann(e), 417, 977*, 1165, 1252, 1472, 1517; Chas., 1251*, 1256*; Chris., 977*; Dan., 418*; Dorothy, 1048; Eleanor, 664, 1000, 1165*, 1241; Eliz., 473, 862, 1165, 1241, 1251, 1256*; Francis, 1241, 1243*, 1415; Geo., 102, 479, 664, 672, 713, 1000, 1165; Rev. Geo., 534; Hen., 334*, 473, 1271, 1276; Rev. Hen., 635; Jas., 1248*; Jane, 418, 1248, 1252, 1475; John, 418, 744, 1241, 1245*, 1248, 1251*, 1252*, 1258*, 1517; Rev. John, 1122, 1177, 1258; Sir John, kt., 1048; John Claxton, 1245; Joseph, 418, 419*; Julia Louisa, 1415*; Louisa Walker, 1415; Marg., 1165, 1271; Maria, 1245; Martha, 1000*; Mary, 784, 862, 1073*, 1243, 1251, 1266, 1271, 1276; Maur., 417; Rachel, 1245*; Ric., 1329; Rob. (le), 838, 1047; Rev. Sam., 547, 1266*; Sarah, 418, 419, 1243, 1474; T., 1165; Rev. T., 1165; Theodore, 1248, 1271; Thos., 1276; Rev. Thos., 180, 664, 744, 1000; Thos. Barrow, 1000*; W.,

1073; Wal., 87, 1243; Wm., 703, 731, 784, 1241, 1243*, 1252*, 1473, 1474, 1477; Mr., 288; Rev., 1429; —, 1251; fam., 415, 1256

Savaker, see Savacre

Savory (Savary, Savery, Savoury), Albert, 862; Arabella, 1498; Anne, 1498; Eliz., 1498*; Jas., 1502; Ric., 1498*; Rev. Ric., 259

Sawbridge, John, 1121

Sawyer (Sawier), Eliz., 1086; Jas., 1086*; Wm., 1086; —, 1033

Saxony, Maud, duchess of, 737; duke of, 737

Say (Saye, Sey, Seye), Dianna, 411; Evan, 1505; Rev. Francis, 411; John, 1477; Marg., 1505; Price, 411

Say and Sele, Viscount, see Fiennes, Wm.

Sayer, Charlotte, 1415; Eliz., 881, 1415, 1418; Jarvis, 881; Joan, 524; John, 1415; Rev. John, 1382; Joseph, 524*; Joyce, 1277*; Marg., 1277*; Rog., 1277*; Sam., 1418; and see Sier

Scagrim, Rev. John, 1217

Scales, Eleanor, 1219; Lord, 1219

Scammel, Chas., 1252; Wm., 1252; Rev. Wm., 1257

Scandrett, Joyce, 485; Ric., 485

Scarborough [peerage], Frances, countess of, 599; earl of, 599; and see Lumley, Ric.

Scatley, Ranald of, 1259

Scattergood, Martha, 221*; Rev. Sam., 221*

Schintell, Joane, 809

Schipton, see Shipton

Schireburne, see Sherborne

Scholer, Marg. Barbara, 1193

Scilley, see Silley

Scireford, J., 1092

Scirewold (fl. 1066), 1032*, 1033

Scly, see Sly

Scoll, Mary, 1146

Scoot, Ric., 815; Wm., 815; and see Scott

Scorye (Scory), Ric., 1404; —, bishop, 1059, 1062

Scotford, Sarah, 798; Wm., 598

Scott, Ann(e), 974, 1270*; Eliz., 295, 1129, 1307, 1533; Ellanor, 1419; Grace, 1457*, 1459*; Rev. H. D. Yate, 1317; Hannah, 1330; Hellen, 1419; Hen., 1292; Isaac, 661; Isabel, 446; J., 1074; Jas., duke of Monmouth, 139, 1153–4; Jane, 1459*, 1460; Jane Susanna, 1457, 1459; John, 295, 816, 817, 1129, 1457, 1459; Rev. John, 770, 771, 1074*, 1457*, 1459, 1460; Mary, 771, 1459; R., 259 n; Sam., 974*; Susanna, 1459; Thos., 1330, 1533; Rev. Thos., 1140; W., 1460; Sir W., 1502; Wal., 1477; Wm., 446, 1270, 1307, 1419, 1554; Rev. Wm., 767, 1457, 1459*, 1460; Sir Wm., 1198, 1501; —, Col., 341; and see Scoot

Scr—, Jane, 1175; Thos., 1175

Screen, Arthur, 1019; Rob., 837, 1307; Sarah, 1019

Scrimshire (Skrimshire), E., 1290; Edw., 1348

Scriven (Scryven), Arthur, 963; Betty, 448; Rev. Hen., 635, 1228; Joyce, 731; Rev. Phil., 704; Rev. Ric., 1102; Sam., 448; Thos., 731; Wm., 731

Scroope (Scroop, Scrope, Scrupes), Agnes, 32; Lady Annabella, 645, 1198, 1497; Chas., 32;

Eliz., 1169; Emanuel, earl of Sunderland, 645, 1198, 1497; Thos., Lord Scroop, 1169; (or Crupes), W., 1475

Scruton, Mary, 379*; Ric., 379*

Scryven, see Scriven

Scryvet, Eleanour, 602

Scudamore, Eliz., 471; Frances FitzRoy, 713; Hen., 736; Hen. Blackford, 978; John, 626, 864; Sir John, 785, 1263; Mary, 1263; Radegund, 626; Rowles, 1208, 1420; W., 764; Wm., 1, 471; Mrs., 976; —, 1322; fam., 301 n, 392 n

Scudamore [peerage], Jas., Lord, 713; John, Viscount, 711*, 713*

Scuff, Dorothy, 815; John, 815

Seaborn, Rev. Chris., 696; Dorothy, 1320; Edw., 543; Eliz., 813, 1319*; Francis, 812, 813*, 1320*; Jas., 537; Jane, 284; John, 36; Marg., 36, 812, 813; Mary, 543; Ric., 1319*; Rob., 284; (or Plomer), T., 1538; —, 543

Seagar (Seager, Segar, Segare), Anne, 962; Geof., 1491; Jas., 435, 576; Joan, 1418; John, 48, 95*, 1420*; Ric., 48, 962; Thos., 435*, 1172; Wm., 95

Seal (Seale), Ann, 658; Edm., 845; Esther, 845; Geo., 845*; Rev. John, 342; Sarah, 845; Thos., 658; Rev. Mr., 7

Sealey (Saley, Sealy, Seeley, Sely), John, 1494; Kath., 1389; Rev. Marmaduke, 1122; Thos., 1258, 1420; Wm., 1389; and see Selley

Seaman (Seeman), Eliz., 374; Isaac, 374; John, 970; Rob., 369

Search (Serche), Anne, 945; Rev. John, 783; Rob., 945; Wm., 1202; —, 1312

Searchfield, Rowland, bishop, 567

Sebritt, Thos., 1473

Secker, —, archbishop, 1292

Seckerston, Millicent, 123; Rog., 123

Secole, Ric., 495

Sedgewick (Sedgwick, Selgwick), Rev. John, 198, 689; Obadiah, 1089; Sarah, 1089, 1092

Sedghley, Mary, 953; Thos., 953

Sedgwick, see Sedgewick

See, Rob. atte, 1172

Seed (Seede), Ann, 210, 622; Brice, 206, 210, 622, 1206*; Edw., 204; Eliz., 204; John, 204, 210*; Kath., 208; Martha, 210; Mary, 9; Sarah, 210; Wm., 208, 210*; Mr., 206

Seeley, see Sealey

Seeman, see Seaman

Segar (Segare), see Seager

Segrave, Lord, 1311, 1345, 1455

Seir, see Sier

Selby, Eliz., 388; Hannah, 378; Thos., 388; Wm., 378

Selden (Seldin), Jonas, 210; Martha, 210; Mr., 570 n

Selewine (Selewyne), see Selwyn

Self (Selfe), Ann, 1155; Anna, 1508; Eliz., 373*; John, 373*, 445, 747, 878*, 1508; Capt. John, 1405; Ralph Willet, 373; Sam., 368, 373; Wm., 1270; fam., 365

Selgwick, see Sedgewick

Seller, —, 1293

Sellers, Rev. Thos., 87

Selley (Selly), Edw., 1361; Mary, 584; Ric., 584; Sarah, 1361; and see Sealey

Selman, Edith, 283; John, 283

Seltone, Agnes de, 1069

Selwyn (Selewine, Selewyne, Selvin, Selwin), Albinia, 851, 852 & n*, 853; Albinia, Lady Boston, 852, 854; Anne, 1319; Beata, 132; Cath., 1437; Chas., 852 n; Rev. Chas. Jasper, 180, 221, 852 & n; Deborah, 1396; E., 1027; Eleanor, 280, 1437*; Eliz., 1401; Frances, 852 n; G., 852 n; Geo. Augustus, 852*; Hannah, 854; Hen., 852 & n*, 853, 854; Hen. Chas., 852; Jacob, 1401; Jane, 1182; Jasper, 255, 280, 851, 853, 854*, 1185, 1437*, 1439, 1440, 1512; Rev. Jasper, 66, 1435, 1437*; Joan, 1437*; John, 257, 550, 854, 1401; Col. John, 851*, 852 & n; Judith, 257; Marg., 75, 852 n, 853*, 1000, 1512; Martha, 1396; Mary, 749, 1439; Nic., 1102; R., 1187; Rachel, 1396*; Ric., 1437, 1512; Rob., 1217; Rosamund, 1437; Ruth, 852 n, 854, 1437; Sam., 1396*; Sarah, 280, 1437; Stephen, 1182; Susanna, 1133, 1136*; Theophilus, 853; W., 1139; Wm., 280*, 550, 749, 851, 852 n, 853*, 854*, 1136*, 1137, 1512; Major Gen. Wm., 851, 852, 853; Major Gen., 75, 132, 1000; Mr., 1440*; —, 1139*, 1185, 1190, 1196, 1319; fam., 255, 619, 1185

Sely, see Sealey

Selyman, Rob., 1074

Selyter, Rev. Wm., 691

Semys, see Sims

Sendlow, see St. Loe

Senegar, see Saniger

Senhouse, Ant., 768; Eliz., 768; Mary, 768*; Rev. Peter, 128, 279, 767, 768

Senkenburg, Conrad Jerome, 327 n

Senor, Sir John, 1351; Laur., 1350

Sentlow, see St. Loe

Serche, see Search

Sered, R., 1216

Sergeant (Sergeaunt, Sergent, Serjeant, Serjent), see Sargent

Serlo, abbot, 131, 628

Serlo, dean, 359

Serlo (fl. 12th cent.), 1086

Sermon, see Surman

Serocold, Amy, 1511; Geo. Pearce, 1511

Serrell, Thos., 369

Sessions, Eliz., 526; Jas., 526; Rev. Jas., 525, 526

Setham, John, 778 n

Setton, —, 1460

Seveir, Ann, 1579; Ann Ford, 1579; Ann Munsly, 1579; Fred., 1579; Hannah, 1579*; Jas., 1579*

Sevenhampton, Wm. de, 1061

Sevill, John, 200; Ric., 200; Sam., 200; Scholastica, 200; Wm., 200

Seward (fl. 1066)(Siward), 1016, 1253, 1255, 1351

Seward (Syward), Rev. Chas., 689; Isabell, 1172; Rev. Simon, 1513; Thos., 1223; fam., 495

Sewell, Joan, 204; John, 204*, 1217; Martha, 862; Mary, 204; Thos., 204; Wal., 204; Wm., 862; and see Shewell

Sewy, Nicel, 1385

Sexty, —, 1475
Sey (Seye), *see* Say
Seymour (St. Maur, Sancto Mauro, Seymer, Seymor, Seymore), Alice, 859; Ann(e) (de), 612, 614, 615, 1425, 1427; Dame Anne, 614; Edw., duke of Somerset, 612*, 769, 838; Edw., earl of Hertford, 833; Sir Edw., 493; Elianor de, 859; Fanny, 1247; Geo. Penrose, 1427; Hen., 1160; Sir Hen., 612; Jane, 393 n, 709 n; John (de), 206, 211, 613 & n, 623, 1214; Sir John, kt., 207, 612*, 614*, 615, 1385; Martha (de), 1425, 1427; Mary, 211; Nic. (de, le), 859, 1214, 1217; Sir Nic de, 1080; Price (de), 1425, 1427; Sir Ric., 859; Rog. (de), 1425*, 1427*; Rog. (de), 980, 1217; Sarah, 1425; Sir T., 1055, 1288; Thos. (de), 1425*, 1427*; Thos., Lord Seymour, 1221*, 1475; Sir Thos., 359, 363, 365, 438, 709, 747, 805, 863, 1195, 1219, 1287, 1382, 1476; Sir Wm., 1148; —, 1214, 1420; fam., 393 n, 440, 613, 859
Seynesbury, *see* Saintbury
Seys, Eliz., 1505; Evan, 546*, 1329; John, 1320, 1322; Warren, 1323; Rev. Wm., 1322, 1323*, 1381
Seysel, Edith, 1314
Sezencot (Chesnecot), Maud, 1055; Thos., 1055
Shadwell, Anne, 846; Isabella, 745, 746*; John, 745, 746*; Rev. John, 745; Sam., 846
Shaftesbury, earl of, *see* Cooper, A. A.
Shaftford, Ant., 666; Jane, 666
Shailes, *see* Shayle
Shakel, *see* Shakle
Shakeloke (Shakelók), Ric., 1061; —, 1017
Shakespeare (Shakespear, Shakspeare), Rev. Arthur W., 1385; Betty, 911; Dan., 701; Edw., 911*; John, 967; Kath., 911*; Mary, 967; Sarah, 701, 911; Wm., 910, 911, 1282
Shakle (Shakel), M., 979; Mary, 979; Ric., 979*; Susanna, 979*; Wm., 979*
Shakspeare, *see* Shakespeare
Shalke, Wm., 1370
Shalswell, *see* Shelswell
Shapland, Angel, 844*; Anne, 844; Rev. John, 1287; Joseph, 844; Rev. Joseph, 1281; Mary, 844*; Lieut.-Col. Wm., 1565; —, 844
Shardlow (Sherlow). Rev. R., 1519; Rev. Rob., 1519
Sharington, *see* Sherrington
Sharp (Sharpe). Ann, 138; Edw., 1513; Eliz., 138, 227; Gabriel, 138; Hamlin, 138; Jas., 227; John, 1173, 1175, 1177; Kath., 138; Sarah, 1175; Thos., 138, 1058, 1250; Wm., 1150
Sharples (Sharpell), Ann, 1014; Jas., 1571; Kath., 1014; Marg., 953; Sarah, 1571; Wm., 1014*
Sharrington, *see* Sherrington
Shatford, Jas., 213*; Susanna, 213
Shaw, Alice atte, 1061; Amey, 1222; Ann, 1063, 1270*, 1419; Geo., 1270*; Hannah, 348; John, 111, 1063, 1270; Lieut. John, 1270; Capt. John, 1419*; Marg., 1047; Mary, 1400, 1419; Rev. Rob., 890; Stebbing, 1220, 1238; Thos., 1222, 1400; Rev. Thurston, 1186; Wm., 348, 1047; —, 1401; *and see* Shore

Shayle (Shailes, Sheyle), Ann, 548; Cath., 1029; Chris., 486*; Edw., 1029*; Eliz., 486*; Hen., 486*; Jane, 486; John, 547; Thos., 486*, 548; Wm., 486; fam., 546; *and see* Sheal
Shayler (Shaylor), John, 1195; Thos., 1103, 1197; —, 1103
Sheal, John, 1427; Julinn, 1427; *and see* Shayle
Sheat, Marg., 1442, 1443; Rob., 1442
Sheen (Sheene), Ann, 765; Benj., 1268*; Elinor, 1113; Hester, 1268, 1271; Joseph, 1268, 1271; Mary, 1271; Rebecca, 1268; Sam., 1268; Thos., 1113*; Wm., 765, 1271; Rev. Wm., 1113
Sheepway, *see* Shipway
Shelburne, earl of, *see* Petty, Wm.
Sheldon, Anne, 1152, 1446; E., 1201; Edw., 1201*; Geo., 1421; Gil., bishop, 1223; Hester, 1041; John, 1041; Sir Joseph, 1132; Mary, 142; R., 1447; Ralph, 848*, 1152, 1201, 1421; T., 1421; Thos., 1382*; Wm., 848*, 1201, 1446; Rev. Wm., 184; Rev., 1447; —, 1476; fam., 848, 1447
Shellard (Shelerd), Cath., 1029; Dan., 20; Edw., 1108, 1117, 1121; Rev. Edw., 1029; Edw. Hardwick, 1108; Eliz., 1065, 1108; Hardwick, 1108; Hester, 1117; Jas., 1108; Jane, 20; John, 1108; Rev. John, 1106; Martha, 1117; Mary, 1029; Rachel, 1106; Rob., 1065; Sarah, 1117; Rev. Thos., 1029, 1105, 1329, 1369
Shelswell (Shalswell), Dan., 1065*; Eliz., 1065; Hen., 1065; Martha, 1065
Sheppard (Shepard, Shepde, Shephard, Shepheard, Shepherd, Shepherde, Shephirde, Shephurde), Alice, 714; Ann(e), 93, 653*, 656*, 815, 921, 958, 959; Benj., 881; Cath., 907; E., 1055; Edw., 91, 93*, 651, 1027; Eleanor, 48; Eliza, 653; Eliz., 653*, 1251, 1304*, 1344; Frances, 653*, 656; Gamaliel, 653; Geo., 755*, 1084, 1177*; Hannah, 52, 958; Hen., 1159; Hester, 837; J., 1061; Jas., 958, 959*; John, 48, 424, 902, 906, 1251, 1304*, 1344; Rev. John, 1422; Joseph, 339, 486, 1147; Josiah, 534, 779; Lewis, 921; Marg., 368, 383; Mary, 17, 339, 486, 653*, 755, 837, 1141, 1159, 1304*; Maur., 1476; Nic., 1404; Phil., 93, 383, 424*, 630, 646, 648*, 652, 653*. 1027*; Rev. Phil., 93, 558, 632, 646, 651, 653*, 711 n; Rebecca, 653, 656; Ric., 17, 52; Rev. Ric., 619; Rob. (le), 52*, 815, 1176, 1304, 1540; S., 92, 651; Sam., 52, 91, 93*, 558, 648, 651, 653*, 656*, 657, 660, 907, 1196; Sarah, 653*, 902, 958, 959, 1176*, 1344; Susan, 17; T. Harmer, 1186; Thos. (le), 17, 653, 837, 1176, 1363; Wm. (le), 48, 52*, 683, 714, 1141, 1304, 1513, 1574; —, 1052, 1069, 1093*, 1251, 1370, 1476
Sherborne (Schireburne, Shirebuarn, Shireburn), John, 10; Mary, 10; Nic. de, 1055, 1431; Ric., 1477; Rev. Rob., 1031; —, 1477
Sherborne [*peerage*](Sherborn), Lord (baron), 37, 325, 913*, 915, 1066, 1068, 1069, 1092*, 1093, 1129, 1351*, 1478, 1483; *and see* Dutton, *passim*
Sherby, Geo., 1538; Fr[anci]s, 1538; J., 1538
Sherde, Wm. atte, 1339
Sheridan, Jas. Collier, 1583

Sheriff, Eliz., 398; John, 398*; Kinnard, 398; Ric., 398; Rev. Ric., 1404; Sarah, 398; Wm., 398*

Sherle (Sherley), see Shirley

Sherlow, see Shardlow

Sherman (Shirman), Alice, 34; Anne, 34; Eliz., 1167; Joan, 1216; John, 1455; Ric., 34; Rob., 34; Thos., 34, 1167; Dr., 1554

Shermer (Shermore), see Shurmer

Sherrington (Sharington, Sharrington), Wm., 430, 1078; Sir Wm., 690*; and see Cherington

Sherwin, Rev. Ric., 1102; Rev. Thos., 1102

Sherwood, Ann, 1499; Hester, 1053; John, 1262; Joseph, 1499; Mary, 1262, 1263*; Wm., 1499

Shewell (Shoell, Showell), Eliz., 191, 337, 941; Frances, 941*; Hannah, 941; Jas., 367; Jane, 204, 337; John, 941*; Kateryn, 200; Mary, 337, 413, 941; Rob., 941*; Sam., 337; Thos., 200, 204, 377*, 725, 1216*, 1218; Wal., 1216, 1218; Wm., 1218; —, 1044; fam., 197; and see Sewell

Shewring, Ann, 1071; Dan., 1555; Rob., 1071*

Sheyle, see Shayle

Shield (Shields), John, 74, 1312; Sarah, 74; Wm., 1348

Shill, Ann, 1328; Eliz., 118, 1499; Hen., 1328*; Jas., 1328; John, 118, 716, 1445; Mary, 1328*, 1445; Rob., 1499; Sarah, 1328

Shillain, Dan., 1144; Eliz., 1144; Tobias, 1144

Shillam (Shillum), Christian, 1490; Dan., 1143; Hannah, 810; John, 1250*; Joseph, 810; Judith, 1143*; Mary, 1250; Sam., 1490; Wm., 1490, 1513

Shilling, Capt. And., 866, 867; Damaris, 866, 867

Shillum, see Shillam

Shilton, Eleanor, 1127; Rob., 182; Susanna, 182*

Ship, see Shipp

Shipley, Ar., 1312; Eliz., 837; Joanna, 835; Mary, 837; Sam., 837; Silas, 837; Wm., 837*

Shipman, Alice, 1454; Anne, 1453; Ant., 1516; Chas., 1454; Chris., 1454, 1514; Rev. Edw., 593; Eliz., 1514; Hen., 1453*, 1454*; John, 1454; Rev. John, 593*; Mary, 1453*; T., 1323; Wm., 1454*; and see Chipman

Shipp (Ship), Christian, 1551; Eliz., 499; Hannah, 1551; Joseph, 1551*; Judith, 1086; Mary, 1384; Sam., 1551; Wm., 499, 1086, 1384*; —, 1455

Shipton (Schipton), Abraham, 750; Eliz., 750, 1431; Gil. de, 1074*; John, 1431; Jonathan, 1256; Joseph, 846; Mary, 969*; Rob. de, 1078; Rev. Sam., 1221; Sarah, 846; W. de, 1288; Wal. de, 1292; Wm., 775; —, 1257, 1258

Shipway (Sheepway), Betty, 941; Cath., 181*; Edw., 1026; Eliz., 182, 1504; Hester, 1026; Jane, 182; John, 181*, 182*, 308*, 1026; Mary, 17, 1504*; Rebecca, 308; Ric., 1504*; Rob., 1024*; Sarah, 181, 1024; Susanna, 308, 777; Thos., 124, 308, 958; Wm., 17, 138, 777; —, 1455

Shireburn (Shirebuarn), see Sherborne

Shirley (Sherle, Sherley), Eleanor, 812; Eliz., 368, 437; Frances, 162; Sir Geo., bt., 162; Mary, 368, 386; Ric., 368*, 386, 437; Rob., 884; Sarah, 884; Thos., 230 n; Gen., 1266; Lady, see Berkeley, Frances; Mr., 368; —, 1001

Shirman, see Sherman

Shirugg (Shyrugg), John de, 1428*; Jul., 1428

Sho—, Wm., 919

Shoell, see Shewell

Shoolbred, John, 986

Shoote, see Shute

Shore, Jane, 393 n*; Dame Sarah, 220; Wm., 1227; and see Shaw

Short (Shorte), Darell, 431; Eliz., 573; Geo., 1121*, 1427; Joan, 573; John, 1379, 1573*; Joseph, 1576; Juliana, 1197; Mabell, 1548; Mary, 1427; Ric., 1551; Rob., 573; Sarah, 1548*; Thos., 1197; Wal., 1197, 1379; Wm., 1548*; Dr., 327 n, 558 n; Mrs., 431; —, 1033

Shortman, Abraham, 1086; Ann, 1085; Thos., 1086

Shott, —, 1033

Shough, Rev. Rog., 1372

Showell, see Shewell

Shrapnell, Jas., 537*; Mary, 537, 1101; Mr., 462 n

Shrewsbury, Rev. Thos., 31

Shrewsbury [peerage], Eliz., countess of, 885, 1339; Francis, earl of, 760; Geo., earl of, 1339; John, earl of, 1538*; Marg., countess of, 1100*, 1538*; countess of, 1336; earl of, 1093; Lady, 1538; Lord, 1538*; and see Montgomery, Rob. de; Talbot, passim

Shrieve, Joan, 777; John, 777

Shuckburgh (Shuckborough), Arabella, 818; Chas., 818*; Sir Chas., bt., 816; Sarah, 818

Shuery, Sarah, 258; Thos., 258

Shugar, Ann, 124; Marg., 124; Thos., 124

Shurmer (Shermer, Shermore, Shurmur), Dan., 282; Eliz., 282, 1024; Joane, 1023; John, 282, 653, 794*; Martha, 1024; Mary, 282*, 794, 1024*; Sam., 1024; Sarah, 653, 1509; Tacy, 1024; T., 1512*; Thos., 369, 1023, 1027, 1147, 1509*, 1513; Wm., 1024*; Capt. Wm., 1024

Shute (Shoote), Alice, 14*; Ann, 961; Chris., 1015; Rev. Chris., 960, 961*; Rev. Hen., 1156, 1456; Jonah, 14; Mary, 1576; Sarah, 14; Thos., 14; Rev. Thos., 13, 14*; Wm., 1576; Rev., 1155; fam., 255

Shuter (Shutter), J., 1388; John, 1389*; Mary, 1389*; and see Sutor

Shyrugg, see Shirugg

Siblond (Sibelonde, Siblonde), Rob. (de), 1311, 1314; Rog., 1311, 1314

Sidebottom, Jas., 1104

Sidenham (Sudenham), And., 1455; John, 621, 1101; Mari, 621; Nic., 621

Sidmouth, Lady, 1198

Sier (Seir, Siers), Eliz., 1401; Geo., 550; John, 1393; Joseph, 1401; Sarah, 1100*; Wm., 1100; and see Sayer

Sifford, Mary, 995; Wm., 995, 996

Signett, Ann, 741; Sarah, 741; Wm., 741

Silby, John, 1543; Mary, 1543

Silcocks (Silcoks), Ant., 1171; Eliz., 1515; John, 41, 603, 1170, 1171; Warren, 1515*; —, 1491*

Silley (Scilley, Silly), Alice, 858; Anne, 857; Edw., 857, 1000; Eliz., 857, 1000; Geo., 857*; Giles (Gyles), 857, 858; John, 1000; Mary, 858; Ric., 857, 858*

Silvester (Siluester, Silvister, Sylvester), Benj., 402; Eliz., 1003; Jane, 597; John, 402, 597, 708 n; Mary, 402, 1337; Paul, 597; Ric., 1015, 1329; Thos. Compton, 1389; Wm., 1003, 1388; fam., 1015

Simcox, Rev. Josias, 1392

Simeon (Simeons), see Simmons

Simkins, see Simpkins

Simms, see Sims

Simmons (Simeon, Simeons, Simmond, Simmonds, Simon, Simons, Symon, Symondes, Symonds, Symons), Ann(e), 138, 304, 491, 601, 699, 793, 794, 795, 836*, 1080*, 1299, 1395, 1571; Barbara, 699; Benj., 531; Chas., 137; Rev. Chas., 1513; Christian, 138; Edm., 1080*; Edw., 1080*; Eleanor, 919; Eliz., 563*, 564, 699, 700, 768, 815, 831, 906, 1108, 1150, 1151; Esther, 700; Francis [Frances], 138; G., 1538*; Geo., 815; Hannah, 563*, 1119; Hester, 317, 1425; Jas., 1355, 1571*, 1572*; Jane, 276, 1538; Jeremiah, 831; Jeremy, 831*; Joan, 831, 1130; John, 138, 491, 789, 815*. 919*, 1015, 1102, 1108*, 1121, 1150*, 1151*, 1370; Jonas, 906; Jonathan, 1425; Rev. Jos., 547; Joseph, 354, 563; Kath., 137; Marg., 974; Martha, 1108; Mary, 138*, 354, 442, 701, 730, 920, 1080, 1572; Mat., 699, 700*; Nat., 442, 563, 564, 730*, 1130; Nic., 1460; Ric., 836*, 918, 1069; Sir Ric., 913; Rob., 732, 794*, 1425*; Sam., 317, 531, 563; Sarah, 317, 831, 924, 1199; Stephen, 413, 831, 1130*; T., 1519; Thos., 138*, 317, 601, 768, 920, 1087, 1199, 1299, 1395, 1551; (formerly Raymond), 1303; Rev. Thos., 427, 447, 635, 639; Thos. Powell, 732; Vincent, 138*; W., 1312; Wal., 1370; Wm., 304, 531, 699, 701, 924, 974, 1080*, 1130, 1444; Rev. Wm., 233, 1477; Mr., 1381, 1382; —, 1311, 1381*; fam., 696

Simon, bishop, 717

Simon, bishop of London, see Montague

Simon son of Ralph, 1227

Simons (Simon), see Simmons

Simpkins (Simkins), And., 295; Eliz., 295; Esther, 661*; Frances, 1279; Hester, 1031; Jane, 1031; John, 295*, 661*, 1031; Judith, 1279; Nic., 1279; Ric., 1279*; Thos., 1279

Simpson (Simson), Alice, 597*; Allen, 597; Amy, 996; Eliz., 1175, 1265; Hen., 597*, 1481; Jas., 1265*; Judith, 1265*; Martha, 1106; Mary, 597; Ralph, 1106; Sarah, 124, 597; Wm., 569

Sims (Semys, Simms, Symes, Symmes, Syms), Aaron, 1368; Abigail, 676; Alice, 1100*; Amy (Amii), 554, 614*, 1487*; Ann(e), 612, 614*, 615, 1008, 1206, 1216, 1415; Benj., 1487; Caroline Eliz., 1400; Cath., 931; Eleanor (Elianor), 48, 615; Eliz., 612, 676*, 815, 1487; Frances, 615; Francis, 1206; Giles, 832; Hannah, 1100; Harry, 614*, 615; Hen., 612*, 613, 615; Hester, 677; Jas., 730, 1400; Jane, 612*, 615, 676, 677; John, 614*, 676, 886, 1100*, 1167, 1487; Joseph, 832, 1100*; Mary, 676, 731, 1008, 1400; Nat., 676*; Peregrine, 1397; Ric., 676, 832, 931, 1100, 1214, 1217; Rev. Ric., 1415;

Sarah, 832, 1100, 1167, 1214; Stephen, 1217; Stephens, 1008; Susannah, 612; Thos., 554, 676, 677, 815, 886, 1008, 1274, 1487*; Rev. W., 1447; Wm., 48, 731, 1181; Rev. Wm., 525; fam., 612

Simson, see Simpson

Sinderby, Eliz., 627; Geo., 1403; Hannah, 1400; Joseph, 627; Thos., 1400; —, 1400

Sindry, Eliz., 789; Wm., 789*, 907

Sinetelf, see Sintelf

Singer, W., 1140

Singleton, Rev. Francis, 895, 897; Rev. John, 1539; Laur., 950, 1380; Luke, 950*; Martha, 950; Sarah, 950; Rev. W., 1313; Wm., 1484; fam., 346

Sinor (Synor), John, 734; Ric., 734

Sintelf (Sinetelf), Phil., 985*, 1060

Siricus, archbishop, 1169

Sisil, see Cecil

Sisum, Nic., 1473*

Sitwell, fam., 50

Sivedall, Wm., 900

Siward, see Seward

Sizmore, John, 686; Sarah, 686

Skay, see Skey

Skeate, —, 424

Skelton, Thos., 1243

Skerret, Jas., 976

Skey (Skay), Anna, 455; Ann(e), 1304, 1469; Dorothy, 1268; Eleanor, 455; Eliz., 1304*, 1328; Esther, 455; Frances, 1469; Geo., 1469; Rev. Hen., 455*; Hester, 455*; Joan, 1304; John (le), 1468, 1469, 1540; Mabel, 1304; Rachel, 1304; Rob. (le), 1253, 1328; Simon, 151; Thos., 1269*, 1304*, 1469*; Thomasina, 1269; Wm., 1304*; —, 1020, 1074; fam., 1311

Skidmore, Eliz., 5; Godwin, 5

Skieler, Rev. Thos., 1477

Skillern, Ann, 1473; Isaac, 1473*

Skillicorne (Skillicorn), Eliz., 332; Hen., 327, 332*, 1233; fam., 327

Skinn (Skynn), Edw., 922; Nic., 1475; Wm., 1475; Wr., 1475

Skinner (Skinnar, Skinnere, Skynnar, Skynner), Ann, 904; Elinor (Elner), 637, 900; Rev. Geo., 1147; Hannah, 900; Hen. (le), 1259, 1404; Jane, 904; John (le), 637, 1121, 1392; Marg., 706; Martha, 1514; Mary, 904, 1473; Nat. Cook, 706; Ric., 1514; Rob. le, 1259; Rog., 1388; Stephen, 661, 900*, 904; Thos., 1473; Wal., 1514; Wm., 547, 706, 904*; Rev. Wm., 495; Zacharius, 1109

Skipp (Skip), Geo., 473*; John, bishop, 473; Kath., 473; Mary, 473; Ric., 473, 549; Rob., 549*; T., 1186; Thos., 885; fam., 469, 606, 1186

Skipwith, Ann, 1063; Marg., 664; Sir Wm., 664

Sklater (Sklattare), see Slatter

Skrimshire, see Scrimshire

Skuce (Skuse), Ann, 187*, 1410; Hester, 187; John, 187*; Jonathan, 1410*; Mary, 187; Sam., 1160; Sarah, 837; Thos., 187, 837; Wm., 187*, 837

Skyll, Wm., 1422

Skynn, see Skinn

Skynnar (Skynner), see Skinner

Slade (Sleed), Anne, 757, 758; Cheney, 1367; Cheney Eliz., 1367; Chris., 757*, 758; Eliz., 757; Harcourt Roe, 1367; Hen. Jas., 1367; Hen. Sotheren, 1367; Hester, 758; Admiral Jas., 1367; Louisa Sophia, 1367; Mary, 758, 1112; Moses, 1158; Rev. Ric., 1303, 1313; Rob., 757, 758; Thos., 1112; Wm., 1121; Rev., 1295

Sladen, Abigail, 923; Eliz., 923*; John, 923*; Mary, 923*; Thos., 923

Slatter (Sklattare, Sklater, Slater), Ann, 1473; Rev. Dan., 87; Elias Ball, 1172; Eliz., 235, 336; Frances, 235; Israel, 1473*; John, 235; Rev. John, 1177; Joseph, 1473; Mary, 1225; Susanna, 1248; W., 1027; Wm., 235, 336, 1225, 1477; —, 1477

Slaughter (Sloghter, Slother, Sloughter, Sloughtre, Slouter, Sloutre, Sloutres, Slowghter), Ann(e), 1262, 1290; Bridget, 1467; C., 1091; Chambers, 1016, 1089*, 1092*, 1093; Edm., 1089; Edw., 1467; Eleanor (Elinor), 1090, 1092; Eliz., 1092; Gerard de, 1016; John, 1090*, 1092*, 1093; Margery, 1092; Mary, 1092*, 1467; Paris, 1090, 1092*, 1262; Rob. de, 1016; Sarah, 1089, 1092; Susan, 1092; Susanna, 1089, 1092; T., 1092; Thos., 1016, 1092*, 1093; W., 1093; Wm. (of), 1089, 1091, 1092*; Rev. Wm., 1093; —, 1093, 1292, 1355, 1477; fam., 1015, 1091*, 1092

Sleech, Rob., 369

Sleed, *see* Slade

Slegh, *see* Sly

Sleight, Jane, 1267; Mary, 1267, 1354; Nic., 1267*, 1289*; Sarah, 1267*; Stanby, 1354*; Susanna, 1267*; Wm., 1267*, 1289

Sley (Sleye), *see* Sly

Slimbridge (Slymbrugg), John, 1308; Thos., 1295*; Wm., 1313

Sloghter, *see* Slaughter

Slond, Wm., 615

Sloper, Ann(e), 1243, 1250; Cath., 682; Rev. Chas., 682; Eleanor, 1243; Eliz., 314, 331, 335*, 1243; Geo., 92*; Hen., 1250*; Jane, 337, 682; Joane, 682*; John, 1243*; Joseph, 1243; M., 1257; Mary, 314, 682, 1243; Mat., 1257; Melior, 555; Rob., 77; Sam., 314*, 316*; Sarah, 17, 555; Simon, 13*, 17; Susanna, 314*, 316; Thos., 555*, 682*; Wm., 331, 335*, 337, 682; Mr., 92; fam., 1256

Slother (Sloughter, Sloughtre, Slouter, Sloutre, Sloutres, Slowghter), *see* Slaughter

Slucock, Joseph, 541; Mary, 541

Sly (Scly, Slegh, Sley, Sleye, Slye), Ant., 524*; Elinor, 319; Jane, 1499; John, 1160; Joseph, 320*; Mary, 320, 524, 1542; Phil. le, 1552; Ric., 319; Rob., 320*, 1499, 1542; Sarah, 320*, 1419; Wm., 832

Slydewine, Rob., 1540

Slye, *see* Sly

Slymbrugg, *see* Slimbridge

Slyser, John, 1276; Sarah, 1276

Smalcomb (Smalkomb), Eliz., 1426; Mary, 847, 1426; Sarah, 1426; Thos., 1426

Small (Smale, Smayl), Anne, 378*, 1365; Bridget, 377, 378; Eliz., 654*, 655, 794, 1365*, 1508*; G., 1369; Geo., 365 n, 378*, 654, 655*, 794, 1365*, 1510; Isaac, 368, 378*; J., 1103; Jas., 377, 378*, 794, 1137; Jane, 378, 730; John, 378*, 381, 654*, 655*, 730, 1103, 1365, 1366, 1369*, 1434, 1508*, 1510; John Foyle, 1366; John Lloyd, 1368; Joseph, 565, 654; Marg., 1365; Martha, 1510; Mary, 378*, 654, 655, 1137, 1366; Ric., 1508*; Rob., 1365*; Sam., 1365; Sarah, 655, 1508; Sophia, 1369, 1434; T., 1369; Thos., 971, 1140, 1366, 1369*, 1508*, 1510; Viner, 565; Wm., 1292, 1365*; Mr., 1512; —, 1370, 1401; fam., 365, 649, 1369

Smallbone, Rev. Edw., 817

Smallbrooke (Smallbrook), Anne, 1352; Rev. R., 1502; Thos., 1352

Smalldridge, Eliz., 669; John, 669*

Smallpeece, Edw. Barkman, 332; Geo., 332; Hester, 332*; Jas., 332*; Thos., 332

Smallwell, bishop, 142

Smallwood (Smalwood), Ann, 906; Jas., 530; Thos., 906

Smart (Smert), And., 204; Ann(e), 201, 273, 983, 1514; Baptist, 329, 1466, 1475; Collis, 1466; Eleanor, 1319; Eliz., 112, 1004, 1216; Frances, 1319; Frances Penelope, 1319; Geo., 203, 1039; Rev. Humph., 190; J. C., 1323; Jas., 1319; Rev. Jas., 252; Jas. Campbell, 1319; Jane, 204, 1250; John, 124, 824*, 983*, 1004*, 1319; Josiah, 112*; Martha, 1319; Mary, 112*, 262, 1319, 1514, 1526; Ric., 200*, 526, 1317; Rev. Ric., 272, 273*, 1217; Rob., 1422; Ruth, 124; Sara(h), 112, 201; T., 985; Thos., 200*, 201*, 262, 996, 1287; W., 1475; Wm., 112, 200*, 204, 634, 1319*, 1514*; Dr. Wm., 1466, 1475; Mrs., 1513; —, 1386, 1477; fam., 197

Smayl, *see* Small

Smedley, Eleanor, 1473; John, 1473; Mary, 1473

Smelt, W., 1101; —, 1077

Smert, *see* Smart

Smethyman, Eliz., 167; Rowland, 167

Smily, Hannah, 1418; John, 1418*

Smith (Smyth, Smythe, Smythes): *of London*: Hannah, 1095; Jas., 935; John, 935; Wal., 1095; Mr., 592; fam., 341; *of Nibley*: Anne, 936*; Arabella, 936; Edw., 672, 936; Geo., 935; Grace, 937; John, 41, 414, 527, 778 n, 908, 935*, 936*, 937*, 1101, 1521; Mary, 936, 937, 1185; Thos., 1185; Mr., 153, 156, 157, 158, 159, 179, 277, 278, 451, 452, 533, 576, 602, 612, 720, 757, 745, 773; fam., 748, 778; *generally*: Aaron, 1183, 1369; Abigail, 578, 1166, 1512; Alice (la), 1036, 1146, 1275, 1372, 1460; Ambrose, 804; Ann(e), 111, 171, 176, 211, 386, 399, 540, 542, 549, 550, 555, 623, 660, 715, 722, 725, 731, 749, 762, 797*, 907, 922, 931, 971, 973*, 988, 989*, 996*, 1003, 1068, 1099, 1208, 1298*, 1319, 1334, 1374*, 1376, 1470, 1472, 1525; Anselm, 1130; Ant., 174; Arthur, 962*, 963*; Sir Arthur, 576; B., 1140; Bartlee, 97; Benj., 532, 537, 555, 1535, 1551; Betty, 52, 961, 1298; Blanch, 608; Bridget, 366, 367, 577, 772, 1068; Bromfield, 1531;

Cath., 402; Chas., 386, 656, 749*, 1159, 1298; Rev. Chas., 76*, 440; Chas. Glover, 1250; Chas. R., 1126; Chas. Royd, 1127; Charlotte, 971*; Christiana, 542; Christina la, 1258; Chris., 111, 1411, 1417; Rev. Chris., 400, 402; Damaris, 797; Dan., 172, 1130*, 1160, 1374*, 1584*; Dan. Caple, 811; David, 797*; Deborah, 537, 1271; Dinah, 1159; Dorothy, 600, 1004; Edith, 172, 428*; Edm., 398*, 421, 986, 1471, 1532; Edw. (le), 483, 550, 637, 837, 933, 934, 1063, 1126, 1162, 1282, 1314, 1317, 1531; Rev. Edw., 163*, 165, 562, 630, 631*, 1020; Elen, 1055; Eleanor (Elinor), 421, 1046; Eliz., 16, 95, 111*, 163, 165, 172*, 239, 264, 289, 295, 296, 388, 410*, 537, 541*, 560, 573, 578, 631, 637, 641*, 659*, 683, 715, 718, 750, 782, 811, 872*, 884, 902, 924, 933, 934, 948, 961, 963, 967, 980, 989*, 991*, 1002, 1023, 1162, 1237, 1274, 1275, 1282, 1326, 1374*, 1401, 1419*, 1428, 1431, 1446*, 1529, 1531, 1560*, 1568; Emma, 1211, 1411; Ephraim, 584, 623, 873, 1110, 1112, 1317; Esther, 95, 661; Esther Bart., 1244; Eunicy, 174; Felice de la, 1372; Florence, 718, 1156; Dame Florence, 1156; Frances, 749, 984, 989; Francis, 907, 1481; Geo., 212, 576, 610, 632*, 811, 933*, 934, 989*, 996, 1068*, 1378, 1398*, 1444; Sir Geo. Bromley, bt., 894; Gerald Norton, 1511; Giles, 969, 973*, 988*, 989*, 1002, 1003, 1584*; Hannah, 616, 665*, 757*, 933, 971*, 1003, 1158, 1250, 1270, 1328, 1398, 1446*, 1584; Harry, 1298*; Hen., 212, 510, 531*, 577, 782*, 827, 829*, 884, 923, 996, 1003, 1105, 1112, 1162*, 1211, 1298, 1334, 1470*, 1474, 1512; Dr. Hen., 565; Rev. Hen., 565, 567; Hester, 204, 212, 338, 575, 616, 762, 1250*, 1272, 1275, 1466, 1470; (or Bartholomew), Hester, 1250; Hugh, 534, 1156, 1423; Humph., 678; Rev. Humph., 599, 600*, 678; Isaac, 531*, 541, 996, 1159, 1512, 1539; J., 1140, 1328, 1348, 1411, 1447; Sir J., 1491; Jacob, 1560; Jacob Baker, 1560; Jas., 141*, 388, 659*, 884, 903, 1328, 1374*, 1378, 1411, 1507*, 1512, 1560; Capt. Jas., 1555, 1560; Rev. Jas., 1388; Jane, 264, 295, 410*, 563, 662, 744, 1046, 1098*, 1099*, 1137, 1155, 1156*, 1160, 1166, 1208, 1469, 1481; Jarritt, 1458; Sir Jarrit(t), bt., 98, 718, 1156, 1458; Jeremiah, 1121; Jo[a]ne, 549, 1164; Joanna, 1444; Job, 765; John (le), 10*, 16*, 45, 52*, 111*, 141, 168, 170*, 171, 172, 176, 211*, 264*, 276, 357, 413, 510*, 537, 543*, 575, 584, 608, 632*, 641*, 652, 677, 715*, 716*, 752*, 762*, 846, 886, 924, 934, 961, 962, 967, 971*, 973, 989*, 1000, 1003, 1004*, 1012, 1020, 1036, 1039, 1046*, 1068, 1079, 1121, 1146*, 1150, 1156, 1159, 1174, 1236, 1237, 1250, 1256, 1298, 1314, 1317, 1326*, 1328, 1334, 1374, 1401, 1404, 1418, 1433, 1447, 1466, 1469, 1495, 1530, 1533*; (or Woodward), John, 1288; Sir John, bt., 341, 718*, 722, 725, 1156, 1419, 1423, 1428, 1491*; Rev. John, 432*; Sir John Hugh, bt., 748, 1120, 1160; Jonathan, 660, 1166*, 1334, 1539, 1584; Joseph, 627, 744, 989*, 1247, 1265*, 1307, 1344, 1369; Josiah,

1099; Joyce, 1046*, 1162; Judith, 543; Kath., 289, 338, 740, 1411; Kezia, 1099; Leonard, 661*; Lydia, 1446; M. W., 1475; Marg., 51, 174, 610, 632*, 989, 1121, 1466; Mariah, 577; Mark, 1446*; Martha, 296, 375, 661*, 884, 989, 1003, 1183; Rev. Martin Stafford(e), 370, 855; Mary, 10, 16, 51, 111, 163, 165, 170*, 172, 175*, 264*, 274*, 276, 296*, 317, 375, 398*, 419, 446, 510, 537, 542*, 562, 575, 641*, 656, 659*, 661*, 691, 716, 749, 752, 757, 797, 837*, 866, 884, 886, 907, 924, 930, 938, 971*, 972, 973, 988, 989, 996*, 1004, 1013, 1068*, 1098, 1099, 1105, 1107, 1130*, 1153, 1156, 1159, 1179*, 1236, 1237*, 1247, 1269, 1282, 1327, 1344, 1374*, 1433*, 1446, 1471*, 1507, 1530, 1548, 1562, 1584; Mary Ann, 1473; Mat., 659, 1103, 1137, 1491, 1546; Maur., 172*, 531, 532, 537, 541*; Rev. Maur., 614; Mic., 632; Rev. Miles, 1140; Muriel(l), 988, 989*, 1002; N., 1027; Nat., 88; Nic., 847; Offley, 1525; P., 627; Paul, 1481; Pearce, 627; Peter, 419; Phaliah, 1003; Phil., 111*; Rev. Phil., 840; Poyntes, 837; R., 1447, 1502; Rachel, 891, 1584; Rebekah, 744; Reg. le, 1074; Reuben, 375; Ric. (le), 172, 176, 226, 295, 296*, 352*, 413, 486, 563*, 573, 632, 641*, 661*, 662*, 683, 803, 922*, 930, 972, 973*, 1013, 1039, 1079, 1162, 1250, 1258, 1314, 1374, 1446*, 1447, 1466*, 1470, 1535, 1539; (or Bartholomew), Ric., 1250; Ric. Bart., 1244, 1250; Rev. Ric., 27, 263, 279, 1144; Rob. (le), 10, 51, 264*, 274, 295*, 542, 641, 661, 740, 757*, 772, 902, 989*, 1074, 1086, 1282, 1289, 1314, 1374*, 1388, 1466, 1477; Rev. Rob., 1434; Rev. Rog., 1331; Rowland, 296*; Ruth, 847; S., 1140; Sam., 52, 95, 296*, 342, 540, 542*, 803, 814, 872, 973, 984, 989*, 1002*, 1099, 1112, 1153*, 1265, 1275*, 1374*, 1376, 1470*, 1472*, 1477; Sam., Bennet, 410; Sarah, 16, 52, 141, 165, 167, 170, 212, 226, 264, 296, 352, 419, 460, 510, 584*, 632*, 641, 782*, 872, 903*, 950, 962, 971, 973*, 989*, 996, 1099*, 1112, 1159, 1307, 1326, 1334, 1374, 1398, 1458, 1470, 1471, 1512, 1531*, 1533*, 1546*, 1584; Sarah Bart., 1250; Sawyer, 1028; Rev. Sawyer, 1028, 1031; Simon, 1384; Sophia, 410*; Stephen, 797, 1121; Susanna(h), 45, 264, 296, 542, 716, 948, 989, 1126; Sybil, 614; T., 1140; Tacey, 803; Thos., 18, 51*, 52, 95*, 97, 111*, 165*, 170, 172, 174, 204, 264*, 276, 289, 369, 399, 419*, 428*, 460, 515, 531, 542*, 550, 573, 578, 611, 616, 632, 642, 665*, 678*, 683*, 718, 721, 722, 750, 772*, 782, 797, 833, 834, 872*, 884, 907, 931, 933, 948*, 961, 963, 971, 989*, 991, 1004, 1028, 1155, 1156*, 1158, 1160, 1162, 1172, 1179*, 1236*, 1237*, 1265, 1269, 1270, 1271, 1272, 1275*, 1282*, 1289*, 1298, 1307*, 1326*, 1355, 1362, 1374*, 1447, 1471*, 1473, 1531, 1535*, 1539, 1546*, 1548*, 1568, 1584; Rev. Thos., 508; Utrecia, 866*; Valentine (Volutern), 338*, 394; W., 1102, 1148; Wal., 659*, 1513; Webb, 1023*; Wm., 93, 175, 296*, 317, 360 n, 400, 474, 531, 535, 539, 549, 550, 560, 578, 597, 600, 632*,

641, 659, 660, 661, 716, 741, 748, 772, 797, 814, 847, 872*, 884, 931, 938, 948, 967, 989, 996*, 1013, 1098, 1099*, 1112, 1121, 1130, 1158*, 1164*, 1208, 1217*, 1250, 1274*, 1282, 1298, 1307, 1328, 1334, 1430, 1431, 1446*, 1466, 1529, 1531*, 1568; Rev. Wm., 279, 619, 626, 866, 1147, 1282*, 1335, 1447; Wm. Haris, 1531; Winifred, 600; Zephaniah, 659; Capt., 50; Dr., 327 n, 1101; Mr., 1155, 1440; Mrs., 50; — (le), 430, 797, 1017, 1063, 1064, 1311, 1355, 1423, 1428, 1476, 1477, 1516; (or Woodward), —, 1288; fam., 98, 287, 630, 833, 864; *and see* Faber

Smithelie, Adam de, 1033

Smithfield, Mary, 239; Rosewell, 239

Smithier, John, 184

Smithsend (Smithsed), Alice, 73*; Ann(e), 74*, 1272, 1277; Eliz., 73, 74, 1272, 1381*; Esther, 1359; John, 1359; Mary, 1272, 1381; N., 1381; Nic., 71, 73* 74*, 1272, 1277, 1381*, 1382*; Paulina, 74; Ric., 1277*, 1289; Sarah, 74; Thos., 73, 74*, 1272* 1289; Mr., 1382; —, 1289; fam., 1381*

Smithson, John, 1350; *and see* Faber

Smyth (Smythe, Smythes), *see* Smith

Snailum, Dorothy, 10; Hannah, 10; John, 10; Mary, 10; Mat., 491*; Sarah, 491; Thos., 10, 491

Snedham, Wm. de, 1377, 1378

Snell, Agnes, 1377; Ann, 555; Bennet, 1421; Betty, 824; Chas., 555, 1132; Dorothea, 583; Dorothy, 1132; Frances, 1377*; John, 482, 583, 635; Melior, 555; N., 1323; Peter, 1377*, 1378*; Powell, 65, 66, 67, 482*, 635, 636, 806, 1132*, 1421; Ric., 1292; Rob., 824; Susanna, 806; Sir Thos., kt., 1373*, 1374, 1377*, 1378*; Rev. Vyner, 1377; Wm., 824*; —, 260, 1339; fam., 482*, 890

Snook (Snooke), Anna, 660, 1266; Eliz., 978; Isaac, 1266; Joseph, 1266; Leonard, 978; Rob., 660; Thos., 660; Wm., 660; fam., 232

Snop, —, 1478

Snow, Algar, 1309; Alice, 641; Ann, 1331; Aylward (Ailward), 1285, 1287, 1291, 1309; Geo., 1513; Harriott, 332; Isaac, 818*, 884; John, 641, 1258; Martha, 331, 332; Mary, 884; Rob., 331, 332; Sam., 818; Sarah, 388; T., 1331; Thos., 884; Wm., 641

Snowden, John, 1209; Mary, 1209; Sam., 1209

Snowshil (Snowsell), Anne, 862; Rev. John, 793; Thos., 862

Snyte, Hen., 1539

Soames, Eliz., 875 n; Stephen, 875 n

Sodbury, John, 778 & n; (or Solbury), John, 360

Solars (Solareis, Solariis), *see* Sollars

Solbury (or Sodbury), John, 360

Sole, *see* Soul

Solers, *see* Sollars

Soley, —, 1475

Sollars (Solareis, Solariis, Solars, Solers, Sollace, Sollier, Sollis, Soulier), Alice, 382; And., 367, 369, 382*; Ann, 991, 1402; Cath., 1077; Eleanor, 368, 382*, 975; Eliz., 975; Esau, 388; Isabella

de, 1077, 1431; J., 1092; Jacob, 991; Jas. de, 1077, 1431; Jane, 116; Joan, 1432; John (de), 317, 486, 618, 1061*, 1077*, 1432*; Judith, 388; Juliana, 1077; Marg., 1432*; Martha, 975; Mary, 382, 486, 850; Matilda de, 1011; Ph[il]., 1402; Ric. de, 116*, 1077, 1217; Rob. de, 1061*; Rog. de, 1485; Simon (de), 634 n, 1077, 1431, 1485; Thos. (de), 317, 1485; W. de, 1011; Wal. (de), 1077, 1078, 1402; Wm. (de), 317, 850, 975, 1077*, 1432*, 1476; — (de), 424, 1404, 1432, 1475, 1476*, 1485; fam., 1476

Solloway, *see* Salway

Somer, *see* Somers

Somerford (Sommerford), Bridget, 941; Thos., 940, 941

Somers (Somer, Sommer, Sommers), Alex., 1453; Betty, 1454; Christian, 1453*; Cornwell, 280; Eliz., 1453, 1454; Geo., 1217; Hester, 34; Jane, 1453; Rev. J., 886; John, 34, 1453*, 1551; Rev. John, 259, 261; Joseph, 1539; Lazarus, 1454*; Mary, 555, 1453*; Moses, 1453; Ric., 555*; Sarah, 1453; Thos., 1420; Wm., 1453*, 1454*, 1456; Mrs., 261; —, 1455; *and see* Summers

Somers [*peerage*], Chas., Lord, 519; Lord (baron de), 265, 287; *and see* Cox, Chas.

Somerscales, Anne, 1194; Rev., 1194

Somerset, Ann(e), 754, 977, 978*; Anne, countess of Coventry, 123; Anne, countess of Northampton, 123; Lady Anne, 921; Lord Arthur, 123; Barbara Anne, 1338; C. H., 121; Caroline Frances Eliz., 1338; Cath., duchess of Beaufort, 1172; Charlotte Cicilia Anne, 1338; Chas., 978; Chas., earl of Worcester, 119; Chas., marquis of Worcester, 123; Chas. Noel, duke of Beaufort, 119, 122*, 495, 496; Edw., 123, 754, 977; Edw., earl of Worcester, 119, 921; Edw., earl of Glamorgan, marquis of Worcester, 119; Eliz., 123*, 376, 1338; Eliz., duchess of Beaufort, 1338; Helen, 1338; Henrietta, 123; Hen., 123*; Hen., duke of Beaufort, 119*, 121*, 122*, 123, 496*, 1172, 1338; Hen., earl of Worcester, 119, 732; Hen., marquis of Worcester, 119, 476; Hen. Chas., marquis of Worcester, 121*; Lord John, 978; John Plantagenet Edw. Hen., 1338; Lord John T. H., 1171; Lady Mary, 123; Mary, duchess of Ormonde, 123; Mary Isabella, duchess of Rutland, 123; Wilhelmina Eliz. Sarah, 1171; Wm., earl of Worcester, 119; Lord Wm., 1338; Rev. Wm., 1338; Lord Wm. Geo. Hen., 1338; Mr., 376; —, 753; fam., 119

Somerset [*peerage*], Anne, duchess of, 628; Edw., duke of, 628, 1047, 1054, 1132; Seymour, duke of, 1132; Thos., viscount, 119, 124; Wm., duke of, 123*; *and see* Beaufort, *passim*; Seymour, Edw.

Somerton, John de, 1016

Somerville (Somervile, Summervill), Benj., 595; Chas., 86; Rev. Edw., 85; Frances, 1465; Geo., 184; John, 1465; Rob., 85, 86*; Wm., 85, 86, 595; Rev. Wm., 85, 184; Sir Wm., 85; Lord, 85*; Mr., 287 n; Mrs., 595; —, 1476; fam., 85

Sommer, *see* Somers

Sommerford, *see* Somerford

Sommers, *see* Somers
Somner, *see* Sumner
Sonager, *see* Saniger
Sondes, Kath., Viscountess Sondes, 721 n; Lord, *see* Watson, Edw.; *and see* Sandys
Sone, Wm. le, 1258
Soors, Agnes, 945; Wm., 945
Sothery, Wal. de, 1187
Sottes, John, 1197
Sotton, *see* Sutton
Sotty, T., 1061
Souch, *see* Zouch
Soudby, Eliz., 862; John, 862*
Soudley, Eliz., 517
Soul (Sole, Soule, Souls, Sowle), Ann, 419, 587; Eleanor, 1367; Eliz., 660, 1367*; Francis, 660; John, 419; Mary, 419*, 587, 752; Ric., 419*, 752, 881*; Sam., 1367*, 1369; Sarah, 881, 1367; Wm., 587, 1367; —, 1368
Soulier, *see* Sollars
Souls, *see* Soul
South, Dr., 436
Southam, Eliz., 573; Hannah, 573*; Hester, 573; Mary, 573; Sam., 573; Sarah, 573; Thos., 573*; Thos. Corbett, 1003; —, 1475
Southampton, earl of, *see* FitzWilliam, Wm.
Southby, Ant., 1274; B., 1495; —, 1274
Southcote, John, 1583
Southerland, Hannah, 562; Thos., 562
Southhouse (Southouse), Rev. Mr., 1503, 1504
Southwell, Ann, 723; Cath., 724*; Edw., 719 n*, 721 n*, 723*, 724*; Edw., baron Clifford, 720, 722, 724*; Eliz., 719 n, 723*, 724*; Lady Eliz., 719 n, 721 n, 723, 724; Helena, 719 n, 723, 724; John, 1201; Kath., 719 n*; Mary, 724; Sir R., 719; Ric., 720; Sir Ric., 719 n; Rob., 360 n, 719 n, 723*; Sir Rob., kt., 719 n, 720, 722, 723, 724*; Rupert, 724; Thos., 723; W., 612*; Wm., 612*, 613*, 723; Rev. Rog. de, 1016; Mrs., 719 n; fam., 719
Sowle, *see* Soul
Spackman, Dorothy, 1250; Jane, 1250; Wm., 1250
Span, Eliz., 1302; Wal., 1302*
Sparhawke, *see* Sparrowhawke
Sparkes (Sparks), Ann, 387, 777; Cornelius, 941; Edw., 442; Rev. Edw., 275, 350, 593, 681; Hester, 960*; Jas., 960*; Joseph, 777, 960; Joyce, 1063; Mary, 941, 960; R., 1063*; Ric., 1289, 1494; Sam., 941; Thos., 1306; —, 1063
Sparrow (Sparwe), Anne, 377; Edw., 661; Eliz., 752, 974; John, 97, 659, 974*; Joseph, 752*, 974*; Mary, 800, 974; Nic., 1473; Paul, 1473*; Ric., 752, 1221; Sam., 974*, 1186; Sarah, 974, 1181; Wm., 752, 1181*; Wroten, 377; —ry, 659
Sparrowhawke (Sparhawke), Rev. Wm., 1485; Sir Wm., kt., 1484
Sparry, Humph., 977; John, 871*, 976*; Mary, 976; Rev. Rob., 1020; T., 1381; Wm., 871; *and see* Sperry
Sparwe, *see* Sparrow
Speake (Speke), Sir Geo., 995, 997; Marg., 995, 997

Spear, John, 604; Martha, 604
Speed, —, 1196
Speke, *see* Speake
Spellesbury, *see* Spilsbury
Spenc, *see* Despencer
Spencer (Spenser), Adam, 1239; Alice, 572, 866; And., 399; Ann, 10, 48, 399; Arthur, 337; Constance, 572, 866; Edw., 84; Lord Edw., 1287; Eliz., 48, 796, 1179, 1183, 1239*; Frances, 1551; Francis, 1179, 1183; Giles, 1329; Hugh le, 1017; John, 623*, 624, 1411, 1471; Mary, 337; Mary Ann(e), 1179, 1183; Millicent, 1329; Rev. Oliph Leigh, 1382; Ric., 10*, 1239, 1473; Rob., 1016; Sam., 1179*, 1183*; Sarah, 624, 1179*; Thos., 337*, 399; Wm., 348, 948, 1179, 1239; Sir Wm., bt., 572, 866; —, 1064, 1287, 1288, 1311; fam., 251, 1032, 1047, 1201; *and see* Despencer
Spendelowe, Rev. Chas., 599
Spensator, *see* Despencer
Spense, Thos., 1078
Spenser, *see* Spencer
Sperring, Jas., 413; Mary, 413
Sperry, Dan., 658; Hen., 658; John, 658; Thos., 1289, 1382; —, 1362; *and see* Sparry
Spert, *see* Spirt
Spicer (Spycer, Spycr), Joan, 371; John, 896, 964*, 1292; Juliana, 371; Marg., 371*; Nat., 898; Reg., 371; Rob., 846; Sam., 1279; Wm., 729, 964
Spiers, Alice, 402; Ann, 402*; Eliz., 402; Mary, 402; Ric., 402*; Wm., 402*; fam., 400
Spill, Eleanor, 1009; Eliz., 1009; Thos., 1009*
Spillman (Spilman, Spyleman), Christian, 264*; Eliz., 741; Joan, 741; John(e), 741*, 1027, 1289, 1370; Sir John, kt., 1027; Joyce, 857; Nic., 1027; Ric., 857*; Thos., 264*, 1027; Wm., 741; Mr., 534
Spilsbury (Spellesbury), John, 1289; Warin de, 1447
Spiring, Ann, 1584; Edw., 1584
Spirt (Spert), Mary, 1251; Rob., 1251, 1451; Mr., 1449; Mrs., 1449; —, 1456; *and see* Spuritt
Spofford, Thos., bishop, 1238
Spooner, Eliz., 1444; John, 430
Spragg (Spragge, Sprague), Rev. Dan., 1539; —, 1458, 1460
Sprat (Spratt), Aaron, 1369; Anne, 1163; Dan., 1163; Ruth, 1163; Sam., 1369; Thos., 1163
Spratley, Anne, 729; Kath., 729; Ric., 729*
Spratt, *see* Sprat
Sprigge, Mary, 1336; Wm., 1336
Spring (Sprin), Anne, 1435; Francis, 111, 264; John, 111; Sarah, 111; Wm., 161; Lady, 1435
Springett (Springet), Giles, 1452; Jas., 1452; Sarah, 1452*; Thos., 1452; Wm., 30, 696, 1449, 1456; —, 1456; fam., 696
Sprint, John, 206; Rev. John, 1313; Rev. Wm., 206
Spruce, John, 1088; Mary, 1088*; Ric., 1088; Sarah, 1088; Silvester, 1088*; (or Prows), —, 1093
Spry, Rev. Benj., 1185; Louisa, 1185
Spuritt, Eliz., 1421; Thos., 1421; *and see* Spirt
Spurling, Lucy, 1250
Spycer (Spycr), *see* Spicer

Spye, Ric., 1388
Spyleman, *see* Spillman
Squire (Squires, Squyer), Betty, 1079; Hen., 1456; John, 729; Rev. Rob., 767; Wm., 1079
Stable, John atte, 1502
Stacey, Geo., 597
Stackhouse (Stachhouse), Rev. John, 1351*
Stackmore, Judith, 659
Stafford, Cath., 1296; Dorothy, 1311; Edw., 556, 1311*; Edw., duke of Buckingham, 556*, 559 n, 568, 671, 839, 927, 1011, 1309*; Eleanor, 1265; Frances, 472; Francis, 1265; Hen., 1265; Hen., duke of Buckingham, 1309, 1381; Sir Hen., 1054; Humph., 1011; Humph., earl of Hereford, 927; Humph., duke of Buckingham, 806, 1011*, 1309; Sir Humph., kt., 591; John, 97, 1296*, 1307, 1311; Sir John, kt., 1295, 1296, 1306, 1309, 1311; Marg., 556, 1011*, 1255, 1309; Mary, 1311*; R., 1216; Ric., 472, 1218, 1307; Rog., 1311; Thos., 399, 708; Ursula, 1011, 1311; Wm., 1295, 1311*; —, 1255, 1309, 1311; fam., dukes of Buckingham, 297, 392, 556, 671, 927, 1011*, 1265
Stafford [*peerage*], Ann, countess of, 1439; Ann, Lady, 1309; Edm., earl of, 635; Edm., Lord, 1309; Edw., Lord, 1011, 1295, 1311; Hen., Lord, 556, 839, 927, 1011*, 1216, 1309*, 1311*; Hugh, baron, 559; Hugh, Lord, 1011, 1295, 1309; Humph., Lord, 297; Mary, countess of, 1265; Mary, Lady, 1295–6; Ralph, baron, 556; Ralph, Lord, 1011; Wm., Viscount, 1265; earl of, 1311, 1381; Lord (baron), 287, 1309; Viscount, 1311
Stagges, John le, 1198
Staight, *see* Staite
Stainer, Joan, 1409; Rebecca, 1409; Wm., 1409*
Staite (Staight, Stait, State, Stayt, Stayte, Steight, Steyt, Steyts), Ann(e), 74, 522, 587, 1334, 1465*, 1468*, 1472, 1473, 1474*; Eleanor, 1468, 1472; Eliz., 118, 984, 1468; Fereby, 587*; Hannah, 765; Hen., 90*; J., 1476; Jane, 1518; John, 522, 984, 986, 1465*, 1468*, 1472, 1474; Marg., 765, 1465; Mary, 74*, 522, 898, 1225, 1466, 1468, 1472; Nic., 74*, 765, 898*; Nic. Spicer, 74; Ric., 1474, 1477, 1518; Rob., 522, 1468*, 1472*; Sarah, 90*, 1466; Thos., 86, 1225, 1362*, 1465, 1474, 1477; W., 1475; Wm., 118*, 1225, 1422, 1465*, 1466, 1468*, 1473; Mr., 1226; —, 1422, 1476*, 1477
Stake, R., 1519
Stallard, Ann, 48; Eliz., 48; Hannah, 550; John, 48*; Sarah, 48; Thos., 550
Stamford, Lord, 928*
Stanburn, Wal. de, 1552
Stanby, *see* Stansby
Standfast, Sarah, 727
Standish, Dr. John, 1031
Standley, *see* Stanley
Stanford (Stanforde), Edw., 1265; Eliz., 1265; John, 1313; Kath., 1265; Ric. de, 1314; Wal., 1314
Stanhope, Jane, 158; Sir Miles, 158; Earl, 507 n; Gen., 1532

Stanley (Standley, Stanly), Ann, 1103; Lady Anne, 1219; Ant., 296; Ben., 765; Chas., 765; Eliz., 296; Edw., 400, 1103; Frances, 296, 506; Jas., 506*; John, 339, 778 n, 1354; Martha, 974*; Mary, 339, 765, 797, 1110; Moses, 1103; Naomi, 1103; Ric., 1103; Sam., 797*; Sarah, 1103; Thos., 974*, 976; Rev. Wal., 1238; Wm., 347, 1103; Rev. Wm., 327; Lord, 1538; —, 1064
Stansbury, Eliz., 1576; Serjt.-Major, John, 1576
Stansby (Stanby), Eliz., 118; Wm., 114; Rev. Wm., 118
Stansfield, Ann, 1023; Eliz., 1023; Jas., 1023; Rev. Jas., 1023*, 1513; Mary, 1023; Dr., 1027
Stanshaw (Stanshawe), Gil. de, 1385; Humph., 1120, 1385; Isabella, 1120; J., 1385; John, 1120*, 1385; Nic., 1120; R., 1185; Rob., 1120*, 1185; Thos., 1120*, 1185; —, 1121, 1139, 1491; fam., 696
Stanton, Ann, 1208*; C. Holbrow, 1215, 1369; Chas., 1208, 1215; Edw., 1229; Rev. J., 1216; John (de), 35, 1051; Kath., 1051; Rob., 463; W., 1185, 1216; Rev. W. D., 1185; W. H., 1216*; Wal. J., 1216; Wm., 1208*; Rev. Wm., 573; —, 1489; *and see* Staunton
Stapi, Chrysogon, 1263
Staples, Alex., 1547; Avis, 1547; Eliz., 1547
Stapleton, Joan, 1015; —, 1388, 1392
Starkey, —, 1387
State, *see* Staite
Statherne, *see* Hearne
Staunsted, Wm., 1160
Staunton, Edw., 1233; Rev. John, 1539; Thos. de, 1162; —, 1257; *and see* Stanton
Staure, Wm. de, 244; fam., 927; *and see* Stor; Stour
Staveleye, Nic., 1431
Stawell, Geof., 1490; Geo. de, 1428; Juliana, 1428, 1490; Lady, 1195, 1196; *and see* Stowell
Stayn, Dan., 416; Rob., 416
Stayt (Stayte), *see* Staite
Steavens, *see* Stephens
Stedman (Stedeman), Ann, 118; Geof. le, 1513; Giles, 118*; John, 118, 1251; Mary, 118; Rev. Thos., 1519*; Rev. Wm., 114
Steele (Steel, Steyl), Constant, 1330; Jane, 750; John, 472*, 1172, 1330; Mary, 472*, 922, 924; Ric., 1172; Rob., 413, 1275; Sam., 472, 922*, 924, 1289; Sarah, 385, 474, 1275; Susanna, 472; Thos., 750; Lieut. Thos., 413; Wm., 670, 1275, 1331; Rev. Wm., 674
Steers (Steere), Frances, 1377; Jas., 1377; Rog. le, 1513
Steevens, *see* Stephens
Steight, *see* Staite
Stenard, Wm., 837
Stepham, Ric., 1189, 1196
Stephans, *see* Stephens
Stephen, king, 41, 157, 158, 357, 527, 565, 602, 605, 688, 745, 778, 1005, 1219*, 1253
Stephen son of Odo, 1120
Stephens (Steavens, Steevens, Stephans, Stevenes, Stevens, Stevyns), Abigail, 561, 677; Alice, 1582; Anna, 1103; Ann(e), 47*, 276, 299, 393 n,

474, 560, 561, 611, 747, 826, 906, 1081, 1127, 1150, 1151, 1194*, 1386, 1472; Ant., 1103; Barbara, 137*; Benj., 1477; Betty, 300, 1068; Cath., 146*, 368, 560, 561*, 1004; Chas., 1004*, 1081, 1528; Chris. (Xforus), 1162; Damaris, 810; Dorcas, 567; Dorothy, 1081; Edith, 561; Edm., 1501; Edw., 31, 34, 47*, 141, 231*, 342*, 393 n, 556*, 560*, 561*, 655, 1115*, 1120*, 1122*, 1144, 1385, 1547; Eleanor (Elner), 764, 1127; Eliza, 560; Eliz., 146*, 304, 388, 578, 633, 1004, 1046, 1081, 1199, 1323, 1574; Eugena, 687; Frances, 340, 561; Francis, 354, 561; Geo., 442, 716; Godfrey, 354; Grace, 304, 655; Hanna(h), 561, 637, 765, 1457; Hen., 50, 146*, 559, 561, 626, 687, 748*; 810, 1004*, 1199, 1200*, 1258, 1354, 1385; Rev. Hen., 696, 744; Hester, 34, 986; J., 1215*; Jacob, 567; Jas., 137*, 560*, 644, 743, 744, 814*, 815, 920*, 993, 1150, 1151; Jane, 304, 550, 716, 1004*, 1183, 1200; Joan, 442, 560, 1144; John, 34, 47, 90, 109, 137, 141*, 195, 203*, 304, 321, 393 n, 465*, 637*, 810, 813, 814*, 815, 826*, 880*, 906, 920, 1150, 1172, 1194, 1200*, 1209, 1229, 1259, 1334, 1355, 1385, 1422, 1519, 1575; Rev. John, 767; Jonathan, 611, 1126; Joseph, 542, 578*, 1046*; Rev. Joseph, 1081*; Kath., 561, 826; Marg., 560, 561, 880*, 1547; Mary, 34, 47, 109, 141, 299, 300*, 388, 446, 561, 633, 810, 813, 922*, 988, 1181, 1277, 1354, 1457; Nat., 341, 556, 559*, 560*, 561*, 633, 991, 1385; Nic., 826; Phil., 47, 743, 744; R., 559; Rachael, 578; Rebecca, 203; Ric., 299*, 324, 558, 559*, 560*, 561*, 625, 747, 765*, 991*, 1120, 1171, 1186*, 1189, 1216; Rob., 276, 299, 300*, 560, 561*, 991; Rev. Rob., 56, 558, 559; Sam., 1183*; 1323; Sarah, 47, 164, 304, 377, 465, 542, 561*, 578, 765, 810, 813*, 814*, 815, 988*, 1115–16, 1181*; Stephen, 47*; Susan, 814, 1511; T., 1201, 1215; Tacy, 465; Thos., 146*, 199*, 300, 324, 341*, 393 n, 446, 550, 677, 765, 813*, 826, 922*, 986, 988, 1004, 1068, 1120*, 1122, 1140, 1150, 1181*, 1183, 1199, 1206, 1277*, 1282, 1323, 1457, 1553; Rev. Thos., 603, 1223; Sir Thos., kt., 131, 988*, 1120*; Tim., 377, 388*; W., 985, 1309; Wal., 1554; Wm., 47*, 299, 304*, 542, 660, 810*, 826*, 832, 880, 1150, 1151, 1160, 1282, 1295, 1472*, 1476, 1485, 1501, 1519, 1528; Rev. Wm., 764, 1528, 1539; Sir Wm., kt., 988; Messrs., 1139; —, 1052, 1063, 1092, 1093, 1121, 1132, 1186*, 1190, 1323*, 1447; fam., 114, 195, 389, 393, 556, 747, 1121, 1203
Stephenson (Stevenson), Francis [sic] Marg., 410; Marg., 410; Rob., 410; Rev. Mr., 1217
Sterde, see Sturdy
Sterne, Rev. Joseph, 503
Sternhold, Rob., 101; Thos., 1478; —, 101*
Sterry, Rev. Ant., 1035; Sam., 1401; Thos., 1401
Steuart, see Stuart
Stevens (Stevenes), see Stephens
Stevenson, see Stephenson
Stevyns, see Stephens
Stew, John, 765; Mary, 765; Wm., 765

Steward (Stuard, Styward), And., 295; Mary, 835; Rog. le, 1540; Thos., 835*; Wm., 865; and see Stuart
Steyl, see Steele
Steyt (Steyts), see Staite
Stibbs, John, 211
Stiff, Abraham, 542; Ann, 542; Eliz., 538, 542; Esther, 542, 703; Jacob, 531, 534, 538*, 542*; Martha, 703; Mat., 703; Sam., 284, 703; Thos., 284, 542, 703
Stigand, archbishop, 346, 434, 1232, 1321, 1322*, 1493
Stiles (Style, Styles), Ann, 473, 710*; Caster, 1413; Charlotte Matilda, 1413; Rev. Edw., 1043; Eliz., 70, 74, 485*, 710*, 796; Francis, 339, 1232; Rev. Geo., 483, 485, 586, 1348; Jas., 74; Rev. Jas., 135; Jane, 339, 796; John, 70*, 339, 485, 710*, 891; Joseph, 70, 1232*; Mary, 70, 485, 891, 1232; Ric., 473*; Rog. atte, 1172; Sarah, 473; Thos., 485*; Wm. (atte), 70, 74, 388, 485*, 710, 796*, 797, 1428
Still, Ann, 18; Frances, 1429; Hen., 488; John, 910; Rev. John, 1429; Mary, 18, 995*, 997; Nat., 995*, 997; Philippa, 487; Wm., 18, 910; Rev. Wm., 1429; fam., 487
Stillingfleet, Edw., 221
Stillings, Ant., 413*; Eliz., 413*; Joseph, 413
Stilman, Eliz., 492; John, 1127
Stinchcombe (Stincescombe, Stinchcomb), Arthur, 176; Betty, 703*; Chas., 18*; Dan., 18, 703; Giles, 939; Hester, 18, 173; John, 702; Marg., 455*; Martha, 702; Mary, 18, 455, 703; Mat., 455*; Nat., 1537; Nic., 700, 703; Sarah, 18, 703; Thos., 455*, 702; Wm., 703, 1552; fam., 695
Stirling, Archibald, 408; Marg., 408; Winifred, 106
Stirrey, Rev. Ant., 808
Stoakes, see Stokes
Stobart, Mary, 1271
Stock (Stocks), Ann, 110, 1232; Anna, 308; Chas., 668; Rev. Chas., 384, 668*, 1140; Chr[is]., 296, 992; Rev. Chris., 266; Edw., 858*; Eliza, 992; Eliz., 269, 384, 858, 1549*; Hannah, 522; Jas., 110*; Job, 522, 1289; John, 1232, 1549*, 1551; Rev. John, 266; Rev. John Agg, 1154; John Skinner, 625; Martha, 1549; Mary, 668, 683, 1232; Ric., 683*; Rob., 563; Rev. Rob., 1154; Sarah, 563, 683; Rev. Thos., 668, 704, 1348; Wilkins, 308*; Wm., 1549; and see Stokes; Stooke
Stocker, Justinian, 796; Mrs., 1361
Stockford, Ann, 868; John, 868
Stockham, Caleb, 1217; Thos., 660
Stocking, Jas., 413
Stockman, Rev. Thos., 1539
Stocks, see Stock
Stockwell (Stokwelle), Ann, 543; Dan., 254, 299; Hester, 254, 299; John (de), 299, 1259; Rev. Joseph, 206; Joyce, 298; Mary, 299; Mat., 1217; Phil., 298; Prudence, 298, 299; Ric., 1250; Sam., 543; Susanna, 1250; Thos., 1081; Wm., 1250
Stodard, Rev. Humph., 1020; Rev. Wm., 1177
Stokes (Stoakes, Stoke), Adrian, 1550*, 1551;

Alice, 728, 729, 1431, 1547*; Anna, 729;
Ann(e), 172, 1306, 1547, 1550; Annis, 1550;
Betty, 729*; Christian, 729; Dan., 1547; Deborah
Ellen, 1459; Edw., 728*, 729*, 1451, 1547,
1551; Edw. Wall, 729*; Eleanor, 1451; Eliz., 90*,
172, 331, 729, 1306*, 1409, 1455, 1526, 1547*;
Emily Sarah, 1459; Francis [sic] Elinor, 1459;
Rev. Geo., 328, 331, 335; Grace, 729*; Hen.,
722, 729*, 1385; Hester, 1306; Isabella, 1431,
1451, 1547*; Jas., 102; John, 172, 756*, 1385*,
1547; Joyce, 1547; Kath., 729; Lucy, 895; Marg.,
729, 1409*, 1431; Martha, 335, 756, 1451–2;
Mary, 90, 335, 922, 1547; Mary-Ann, 1575; Reg.
de, 1485; Ric. (de), 1121, 1221, 1385, 1546,
1547, 1551; Rob., 721; Sam., 172, 1451*, 1452,
1547*, 1556; Sarah, 1451*, 1526*, 1550*;
Susanna, 172; T., 1328; Thos., 90*, 172, 922,
1306*, 1312, 1450, 1451*, 1455, 1547, 1550*;
Capt. Thos., 1550*; Wal. de, 1431; Wm., 90,
756, 1250, 1459, 1526*; —, 452, 754, 1122,
1460*; fam., 721; and see Stock: Stooke
Stokesley, John, bishop, 1102
Stokwelle, see Stockwell
Stompe, see Stump
Stone (Ston, Stones, Stoune), Abraham, 84; Alice
de, 775; Anna-Maria, 387; Ann(e), 84, 269, 339,
747, 948*, 1089*, 1090, 1301*, 1338; Benj.,
948*; Betty, 1415; Bridget, 207; Dan., 907;
Dorothy, 563; Edm., 207, 948*; Elena de, 1314;
Eliz., 269, 270, 339, 486, 993, 1086, 1342;
Frances, 84, 891; Francis, 207*, 1086; Geof. atte,
1363; Geo., 1415; Hannah, 564, 1086, 1401;
Hen., 1086; Isabella, 1201; Rev. J., 1101; John,
207, 269, 270, 339, 364*, 369, 384*, 387, 947*,
993, 1003, 1089, 1110, 1150, 1201*, 1289,
1301*, 1401; Rev. John, 1095; Joseph, 891,
1089*; Rev. Joseph, 1089, 1090; Kath., 1089;
Mary, 269, 946, 947*, 948, 993, 1110, 1562;
Matillda atte, 1314; Nic., 290 n; Ric., 266; Rev.
Ric., 1422; Rob. (atte, de), 946*, 1177, 1309,
1420; Rev. St. John, 1095, 1102; Sam., 265, 550,
891; Sarah, 550, 746; Susannah, 946*; Thos.
(de), 339*, 746, 775, 891*, 943, 946, 947*; Capt.
Thos., 1301; W., 1201; Wm. (atte), 269, 375,
387, 486, 550*, 563, 564, 907, 946*, 1087, 1140,
1197, 1201, 1420; Rev. Wm., 266, 435, 1408;
Capt. Wm. Edm., 1562; Mr., 1189; —, 1177,
1311, 1338, 1382; fam., 265, 1176
Stonebridge, John, 1214
Stoneheware, John le, 1372
Stonehouse (Stonhouse), J., 1185*; Rog. de, 1258;
W. de, 1185; Wm. de, 1187, 1494; —, 1139
Stoner, see Stonor
Stones, see Stone
Stonhouse, see Stonehouse
Stonor (Stoner), Ant., 661; Edw., 678; Jas., 661;
John de, 1255; fam., 1255
Stonwell (Stonwelle), John de, 1198*
Stooke, W., 1321; Wm., 1321; and see Stock; Stokes
Stoper, John, 1119
Stopford, Capt. Edw., 1232; Gen. Edw., 1232;
Letitia, 1232

Stor, Thos. atte, 1428; and see Staure; Stour
Stother, Eliz., 679
Stoughton, Eugenia, 920; Geo., 920
Stoune. see Stone
Stour, Stephen, 317; and see Staure; Stor
Stourton, W. de, 1074
Stout, Eliz., 616; Isaac, 211; Mary, 211; Ric., 581;
Stephen, 616*; Susanna, 616
Stouteshull, John de, 1369
Stow (Stowe), Thos. atte, 1428; Wal., 1477; Wm.,
217; —, 358, 1477
Stowell, Lord, 1198*; fam., 1172; and see Stawell
Stracey, Col., 1255
Strachan, Sir Wm., bt., 346, 391, 393, 1289*; fam.,
393; and see Stran
Stradling, Cath., 997; E., 832; Edw., 997; Sarah,
832; and see Stralling
Strafford, Jas., 1196; Ric., 939
Strafford [peerage], Wm., earl of, 644, 1198; earls
of, 643
Straley, Geo., 74; Susanna, 74; Wm., 74*
Stralling, Wm., 1039; —, 1039; and see Stradling
Stran, Rob., 1233; Wal., 1233; and see Strachan
Strang (fl. 1066), 1074
Strange (Straunge), Aaron, 9, 1086; Ann(e), 491,
796, 1086; Bridget, 1199; Dan., 996; E., 1087;
Edm., 797; Edw., 11, 1084; Eliz., 491, 996;
Hannah, 210; Jane, 491; John, 360 n, 796, 861;
Rev. John, 860; Joseph, 212; M., 1087; Marg., 10,
491*; Mary, 48, 212, 491, 1086; Mat., 1086; Mic.,
432, 1199; Moses, 210*; Ric., 491*; Ric. Lee,
48*; Rob., 369; Rob. Harding, 1086; Sarah, 10,
861; Thos., 212*, 363; —, 1339; fam., 251, 1087
Strangeways, Hen. Fox, earl of Ilchester, 255
Strapy, John, 1388
Stratford, Alice, 705; Ann(e), 429, 705*, 832, 854,
1466, 1514; Ant., 1227*, 1228*; Dan., 976;
Edw., 1218; Eleanor, 439; Eliz., 204, 348, 634,
660, 705*, 749, 1229; F. P., 1220, 1475; Rev.
Ferdinando, 1238; Geo., 439*, 705, 1016; Hen.,
634*, 635*, 704, 705*, 1016, 1220*, 1476; Hugh
Stratford, 1232; Humph., 1227; J., 1476; Jane,
677; John, 204*, 348, 634*, 677, 1016*, 1165,
1169, 1220*, 1229, 1232*, 1466*, 1476; Marg.,
705; Mary, 976, 1050, 1229, 1232*; Patience,
939; Ric., 704, 705, 939, 1049; Rob., 677, 1050;
Sam., 1258; Sarah, 281*, 976; Thos., 660, 832,
1217; Rev. Thos., 281*, 749; Valentine, 348; W.,
1227; Wm., 634, 635, 639, 854, 1227; —, 710,
1215, 1220, 1369, 1447, 1477; fam., 634, 704;
and see Strodforde
Strathern, earl of, see Stuart, David
Stratton, Adam de, 1201; Harriett Victoria, 1005;
John, 665*; Mary, 665; Peter de, 1202; Rebekah,
665, 730; Thos., 665, 730; Wal. de, 1202; Lord,
158; —, 1064; and see Stretton
Straunge, see Strange
Street (Strete, Streyt), Anne, 903*; Benj., 903; John
(atte), 786, 903, 1292, 1428; Ric. atte, 1388;
Rob., 98
Strene, Thos., 1494
Strete, see Street

Stretton, Thos., 1420; W., 1201; *and see* Stratton

Streyt, *see* Street

Stringer, Alice, 1137; Anne, 431; Ant., 635, 1055; Eliz., 209*, 464; Francis, 209; Joane, 810, 1024; John, 1431; Mic., 1137, 1023; Rev. N., 1356; Ric., 464; Rev. Ric., 463, 464*; Stephen, 431; Wm., 810; fam., 1027

Strode, Alice de, 1214; Rev. Francis, 1127; R[ichar]d de la, 1214; Simon (atte, de), 1214, 1422; Wal. atte, 1214; *and see* Stroud

Strodforde, Hen. de, 1214, 1215; *and see* Stratford

Strong (Stronge), Eliz., 388*; Mary, 388*; Rob., 225; Thos., 134, 135, 388*; Valentine, 597; —, 1102

Strongbow [Ric. de Clare, earl of Pembroke], 927

Stronge, *see* Strong

Stroud, Edith, 338; Eleanor, 338; Hester, 338; John, 338*, 1012; T., 1288; Thos., 338*, 687, 1348; —, 1476; fam., 80; *and see* Strode

Strype, —, 591 n

Stuard, *see* Steward

Stuart (Steuart), David, earl of Strathern, 1281; Esme, duke of Richmond, 523; Lady Eupheme, 1281; John, Lord Stuart, 341; *and see* Steward

Stubbs (Stubbes, Stubs), Eliz., 1164; Hen., 534; Rev. Hen., 748; Jane, 316*; John, 316, 611, 674, 1164; Rev. John, 128; Mary, 1164; Rev. Rob., 394; Mr., 1165

Stuckey, John, 411; Rev. John, 411

Stuckley, —, 1356;

Studley, fam., 1043

Stukeley, Dr., 355, 357;

Stump (Stompe, Stumpe), Frances, 727; Hen. atte, 1147; Jas., 1342*; John, 170*; Kath., 1342; Mary, 170, 175*, 727; Sarah, 1342; Susanna, 175; Thos., 175*, 727, 1342*; Rev. Thos., 722, 727; Sir W., 1345; Wm., 1345

Sturch, Alice, 1222; Eliz., 1222*; Rob., 1222; Wm., 1222*

Sturdy (Sterde), Edith, 1478; —, 1069

Sturge, Ann, 1384; Eliz., 1453; Hen., 1159; Joseph, 960, 1384; Mary, 1158*; Nathan, 1551; Thos., 1453*; Toby Walker, 1551; Wm., 1159

Sturmy (Sturmie), Alice, 330, 1229; Ann, 332; Cath., 333; Edith, 338; Eleanor, 611; Eliz., 586; Geo., 328, 330*, 332; Hen., 329, 330; Hester, 330, 339; John, 339, 586, 611, 1229*, 1232*; Mary, 333, 611, 1229, 1232*; Susanna, 339; Thos., 338; Toby, 333*; —, 1232, 1477; fam., 1232

Sturt, Humph., 1238

Styles (Style), *see* Stiles

Styward, *see* Steward

Such, Mary, 868; Wm., 868; *and see* Sytche; Zouche

Sucia (or Saussay), Wm. de, 1475

Sudeley (Sudely, Sudleie, Sudley), Bart. de, 1219, 1221, 1474; Eleanor de, 1219; Emma, 1219; Harold de, 1219*, 1220*, 1475; Joan, 1219; John de, 1219*, 1220, 1221*; Margery, 1219; Otwell de, 1219, 1220, 1476

Sudeley [*peerage*](Sudely, Sudley), Arthur, Lord, 1103; John, baron, 1219; Ralph, baron, 1219*;

Lord (baron), 1219, 1477; *and see* Chandos, Jas.; Tracy, C. H. *and* Chas. Hanbury

Sudenham, *see* Sidenham

Sudley (Sudleia), *see* Sudeley

Suffolk [*peerage*], Arabella, countess of, 718, 1419*, 1428; Chas. Wm., earl of, 718; Hen., duke of, 1165; Thos., earl of, 1067; earl of, 177, 1428; Lord, 1419; *and see* Brandon, Chas.; Pole, Alice de la *and* Wm. de la

Suffolk and Bindon [*peerage*], Henrietta, countess of, 123; Hen., earl of 43, 123; Penelope, countess of, 43

Suggestaple, Reg., 1033

Sulewed, Juliana, 1447

Sullivan, Eliz., 124; Honora, 124; Jas., 124; John, 124*

Sumerell, *see* Summerell

Sumerfield, John, 1477

Sumers (Summer), *see* Summers

Summerell (Sumerell), Edw., 730; Jas., 1490; John, 730; Sarah, 1490

Summers (Sumers, Summer), Aaron, 741; Ann, 174, 175*, 555; Betty, 782; Dan., 171; Elias, 1328; Eliz., 175; Esther, 741, 1249*, 1455; Hannah, 1455; Hen., 175; Hester, 836; Jas., 782, 1009, 1169, 1455; Jane, 171; John, 169, 175, 284, 741, 782, 836*, 1455; Rev. John, 42*, 940; Joseph, 846; Mary, 782, 1009*, 1247, 1250, 1257, 1258; Moses, 741; Nat., 782; Olive, 284; Peter, 171*, 175; Rebecca, 782; Rob., 1249, 1250, 1258; Ruth, 836; Sam., 1534; Sarah, 175, 836; Susannah, 940; T., 1456; Thos., 836, 1516; Wm., 174, 868; —, 1551; *and see* Somers

Summerton, Geo., 679*; John, 679; Mary, 679*; Sarah, 679

Summervill, *see* Somerville

Sumner (Somner), Chas., 410; Rev. Hugh, 1485; John, 410; Rev. Wm., 1221

Sumpton, Sarah, 212; Wm., 212

Sunderland, earl of, *see* Scroope

Surman (Sermon, Surmon), Mrs. A., 1422; Anna, 337; Ann(e), 337, 339, 674, 1229, 1346*, 1347*; David, 1346, 1347*; Edw., 872; Eliz., 337, 1229*, 1231*, 1346, 1347*; Giles, 485*; Hannah, 337; Hester, 397, 1347; J., 1348; Jane, 397; John, 394, 789, 1231*, 1232, 1346*, 1347*, 1348*; John Surman, 1402; Marg., 337, 339; Mary, 73, 610, 1229*, 1231*, 1269, 1347*; Phil., 1268*, 1269, 1347, 1362; Ric., 641, 1000; Rob., 569, 1362; Sam., 337; Sarah, 485, 1347; Susann., 1347; Thos., 73, 337, 397, 674, 764, 1229, 1346, 1347*, 1348; Thos. Packer, 1229, 1231*; Ursula, 1268*; Wm., 337*, 339, 397*, 610, 1157, 1229*, 1231*, 1346*, 1347*, 1348*; Wm. Packer, 1346*; Major, 1402; Mr., 1348*; Mrs., 1402; —, 1104, 1292, 1348; fam., 1232, 1348

Surrey, duke of, *see* Holland, Thos.

Sussex, earl of, *see* Ratcliffe, Thos.

Suthinton, Simon, 1456

Suthmor, Edith, 1314

Sutor (Sutore), Ant., 1363; Ric., 1197; *and see* Shuter

Sutton (Sotton), Ann, 175; Arthur, 837; Eleanor, 1073*; Eliz., 1081*; J., 818; Jas., 1073*; John, 175*, 370, 1081*; Rev. John, 56; Laur. de, 1223; Mary, 175; Phil., 789; Philippe, 818; Rev. Prideaux, 27, 89, 147; Ric., 511; Sir Ric., bt., 263, 667, 713; Sarah, 370, 1081*; Thos., 789, 836; Wm., 1081
Suwyk, W. de, 1288
Swain, see Swayne
Swalewe, Ric., 1504
Swan (Swann, Swon), Damaris, 866, 867; Dorothy, 864, 866, 867; Frances, 1116; Ric., 1387; Capt. Ric., 866*, 867*; Sus[an], 867; Wal. le, 1552; Wm., 1348; fam., 863; and see Swayne
Swanley, Ann, 1307; John, 1053, 1244; Mary, 1244, 1307*; Wm., 1307*, 1312
Swann, see Swan
Swatt, Rev. Geo., 764
Swayne (Swain), Christian,931; Eliz., 976; Rev. Geo., 7*, 994, 1423, 1428*; John, 976; Joseph, 743; Sarah, 1424; Thos., 931; Ursula, 548; Wm., 548, 931*; and see Swan
Sweatman, see Sweetman
Sweden, king of, 952
Sweeper, Rev. Wal., 1217
Sweet, Chas., 212; Dorothy, 211; Francis, 429; Hen., 211; Marg., 211; Martha, 429; Sam., 1583; Thos., 211
Sweetman (Sweatman, Swetheman, Swetman), Kath., 797; Mary, 797; Rev. Ralph, 1127; Rev. Thos., 695; Wm., 847; Rev. Wm., 865
Sweetnam, see Swetnam
Swell (Swelle), Adam de, 1228; Joan, 1125*; Juliana de, 1197; Simon of, 1227*; Wal. of, 1227*; Wm., 569
Swetenham, see Swetnam
Swetenote, Joan, 1016; John, 1016
Swetheman, see Sweetman
Swetinge, Juliana, 1258
Swetman, see Sweetman
Swetnam (Sweetnam, Swetenham), Rev. Randall, 1217; Rev. Thos., 571, 1087
Swift, Mary, 118; Mic., 118; Wm., 118; Dean, 177
Swinburn (Swyneborn, Swyneborne), Margery de, 533; Rob. de, 533*; Thos. (de), 533, 1476*; —, 1476
Swinerton, see Swinnerton
Swinford, Cath., 1316; Eliz., 1316; Sir Thos., kt., 1316
Swinnerton (Swinerton), Ann, 1244, 1250; Anna, 1244; Benj., 1250; Eliz., 1244*; Eliz. Rogers, 1244; Geo., 1244*, 1250; Hester, 1244; Jas., 1244; Judith, 1250; Mary, 1244; Rebekah, 1244; Ric., 1244
Swon, see Swan
Swonhunger, John, 775
Swyneborn (Swyneborne), see Swinburn
Swynfen, Rev. John, 93, 95*, 180; Rebecca, 95
Syddal, Elias, 302
Sydney, Algernon, 349 n; Sir Hen., 838
Sydney [peerage], Lord, 1378; and see Townshend, Thos.

Sylvester, bishop of Worcester, see Evesham
Sylvester, see Silvester
Symes (Symmes), see Sims
Symon (Symonds, Symondes, Symons), see Simmons
Syms, see Sims
Synge, Eliz., 959; Geo., bishop, 959
Synor, see Sinor
Syrrell, Rev. Ric., 559
Sytche, John, 1460; and see Such
Syward, see Seward

Tackley, John, 598
Taffley, see Tuffley
Tagg, Mary, 1158; Ric., 1158*
Taggart, Mary, 386; Wm., 386
Taillo, see Tayloe
Tailor (Taillur), see Taylor
Tainton, see Taynton
Talbot (Talbert, Talbott), Caroline Sarah, 1498, 1499; Cecil, 1194; Chas., earl of Shrewsbury, 251; Chas., Lord Chancellor, 134, 640; Eliz., 572*, 759, 885; Eliz., countess of Shrewsbury, 823; Emma Frances, 1499; Emily Sarah, 1499*; Francis, earl of Shrewsbury, 760*; Geo., 638; Geo., earl of Shrewsbury, 407, 823, 1402; Rev. Geo., 640, 642, 1012, 1194; Geo. Gustavus Chetwynd, 1498, 1499; Gil., 819, 1402*; Gil., earl of Shrewsbury, 759; Guenthlien, 819; John, 407, 816, 915; John, earl of Shrewsbury, 574 n, 759 788, 885; Rev. John, 626; Sir John, 330, 572*; Kath., 114; Marg., 330; Ric., 885, 1403, 1431; Rev. Ric., 13, 1388; Rog., 1490; Sherington, 1005; Somes, 691; Thos., 1538*; Thos., Viscount Li(s)le, 185, 885, 1100*, 1538*; Dr., 638; —, 1064, 1148; —, earl of Shrewsbury, 1402; —, Lady Lisle, 1538; fam., 392 n, 574, 759, 788, 792, 915, 1148
Talbot [peerage], Gilbert, Lord, 806; Mary, Countess, 135* 1015; Ric., Lord (baron), 574, 759; Wm., Earl, 1015; Countess, 1016; Earl, 135; Viscountess, 1538
Talboys, Alice, 1251*, 1255; Amy, 1251; Benj., 563, 1251*, 1255; Chas., 1255; Eliz., 1251, 1255*. 1368; Emma, 1251; Josiah, 1368*; Lydia, 1251; Mary, 563, 1251*, 1255; Ric., 1251*, 1255*, 1256*, 1257; Sam., 1251; T., 1257; Thos., 1251, 1255*, 1258; W., 1258; Wm., 1251; —, 1282; fam., 558, 1255
Talman, Wm., 552
Taler (Tallur), see Taylor
Taman, Thos., 1477
Tame, Agnes, 593, 595; Alice, 591, 593, 1255; Cath., 591; Sir E., 1255; Edm., 588, 592, 1011; Sir Edm., kt., 128, 311, 502, 568, 590*, 591, 593, 595*, 678, 1011*, 1101; Sir Edw., 1255; Eliz., 595; Isabel(l), 591, 1255; John, 588*, 590*, 591, 592, 593, 1011; Kath., 595 n; Marg., 591, 1255; —, 361, 1011*, 1198; fam., 588, 591*, 592*, 643*
Tampler, Rob., 814; Susannah, 814
Tamplin, Anne, 812*; Edw., 812*; Eliz., 812; Joseph, 812*; Marg., 812

Tancred, Sir T., 1202

Tancreville, earls of, 952

Tandy (Taundy), John, 1348*; Mary, 703; Nat., 703; Nic., 1382; Wm., 744; —, 1478; *and see* Tanty

Taner, *see* Tanner

Tankerville (or Chamberlayne), Sir Thos., kt., 346

Tanner (Taner, Tannar, Tannare, Tannere), Agnes Louisa, 1489; Alex., 598; Ann(e), 450, 780, 1024, 1117; Arthur, 1117*, 1121; Benj., 730; Cath., 1307; Dan., 1072; David, 1107; Dinah, 1107; Edw., 782; Eliz., 456, 967, 1024, 1072, 1117, 1210; Geo., 456; Hannah, 1214*; Harry, 598; Hen., 1292; Hester, 1117; Jas., 836; John, 781, 782, 1214, 1292, 1302, 1539; Louisa Agnes, 1489; Mark, 211; Mary, 455, 780*, 781*, 836, 1210, 1302, 1511; Nat., 967; Sam., 1024*, 1025; Sarah, 211, 782*; Susanna, 1025; Theophilus, 1307; Thos., 450*, 455, 456, 532, 780, 782, 973, 1024, 1210*, 1313; Wm., 455, 780*, 781*, 1025*, 1107, 1312, 1313, 1323, 1477; —, 325 n, 534 n, 617, 688, 743, 1196, 1205, 1291, 1292; —, bishop, 502

Tanty, Eliz., 316; John, 316*, 317; Wm., 1046; *and see* Tandy

Taplin, Harry, 227

Tappes, Dennis, 791 n

Tarling (Tarlin), Betty, 991; Martha, 1200; Mary, 1200; Thos., 1200*; Wm., 1200; Wm. Borton, 991

Tarlton, Rev. Thos. H., 1217

Tarplett, John, 1003; Susan, 1003

Tarran, Eliz., 984, 1471*; John, 1471*; Mary, 1471*; Mat., 1471; Thos., 1471

Tasker, Edw., 1430; —, 1069

Taswell, Ann, 1327; Dorothy, 1530; Geo., 1327; Lieut.-Col. Geo., 1327; Hen., 1327; Honor, 1327; Rev. Jas., 1530; Rev. W., 1327*; Rev. Wm., 42, 1530, 1539; Mr., 1328

Tattersall, Rev. Jas., 1290*, 1525*; Rev. John, 1525, 1528; Rev. Wm. Dechair, 1521, 1525, 1539

Tatton, Eliz., 1194; Thos., 1194*; —, 1196

Tauley, Hester, 659; Ric., 659

Taundy, *see* Tandy

Taunton, Ann, 868; Chas., 868; Eliz., 701; John, 360; Mat., 701; Sarah, 701

Taus, Wal., 1221

Tavener, Thos., 765

Tawney (Tawny), Edw., 1468; John, 187; Mary, 573; Sam., 187; Thos., 184, 573; Wm., 996; Rev. Wm., 184

Tayer, Anne, 1300; Edw., 16, 1300*; Eliz., 16, 1296; Hester, 1299; John, 962, 1296, 1299, 1300*; Mary, 1300; Sarah, 962, 1296, 1300*; Thos., 1300; —, 1311*; *and see* Theyer

Tayler, *see* Taylor

Taylin, Edw., 989

Tayloe (Taillo), Hest(h)er, 197, 199*; Jas., 1292; John, 197, 200, 1314; Phil., 1292; Rob., 1512*; Susanna, 1025; Thos., 200; W., 197; Wal., 1292; Wm., 199*, 200*, 1025; Mrs., 200; —, 1512*

Taylor (Taillur, Tailor, Taler, Tallur, Tayler,

Taylour), Abel, 270, 993; Amice la, 1363; Ann(e), 45, 290, 293, 295, 636, 812, 846*, 902*, 906*, 907, 958, 959, 963, 1213, 1278, 1304*, 1305, 1330, 1394*, 1413*, 1556, 1560; Benj., 1514; Betty, 906, 933, 1304; (or Emmett), Betty, 64; Chas., 290, 295*; Rev. Chas., 1003; Charlotte, 1415*; Charlotte Ann, 1415; Christian, 1412*; Cyprian, 1153; Dorothy, 974; Edith, 382; Edw., 382, 902*, 907*, 965; Rev. Edw., 1278; Eleanor (Elinor), 683, 906, 1153; Eliz., 17, 45, 111, 133, 141*, 174, 175, 253, 296, 563, 644, 787, 813, 846, 902, 907, 948*, 970, 1071, 1143, 1153, 1300, 1304, 1307, 1330*, 1415, 1514, 1559*; Ellyn, 1121; Emily, 1415; Esther, 446, 1003; Francis, 296, 739; Geo., 84, 683, 812, 846, 1273*, 1275, 1280*; Godfrey, 1035; Grace, 303; Hannah, 253, 539, 907, 1250*; Hen., 922, 1350; Hester, 902*; (or Cradock), Rev. Hum., 767; Humph., 253; Isabella, 38; (or Meredy), Rev. J., 1127; Jas., 174, 235, 636*, 907, 1307, 1331, 1375, 1584; Jane, 38, 293, 846, 948, 963, 1304, 1350; Jemima, 1415; Joan(e), 193, 933; John (le), 45, 60, 79*, 135, 174, 175, 262, 270, 336, 413, 435, 524*, 563*, 636, 683, 741*, 746, 813*, 846, 868, 902*, 906, 907, 922, 923*, 958, 959, 970*, 1030, 1250, 1278*, 1300, 1304, 1305*, 1307, 1312, 1335, 1363, 1410, 1413*, 1415*, 1443, 1445, 1477, 1559; Rev. John, 81, 309, 406, 713, 1143, 1147, 1330*, 1331*, 1477; Jonathan, 906; Joseph, 550, 846; Rev. Joseph, 1556, 1560; Judith, 84; Kezia, 1415; Lydia, 1273; Marg., 413, 572, 1350*; Martha, 813; Mary, 38, 45, 79*, 84, 141, 235, 253, 296, 336*, 343, 386, 446, 472, 524*, 539*, 746, 800, 902*, 923, 933*, 970, 1034, 1207*, 1273, 1278, 1280*, 1394*, 1413, 1546*, 1563; Mic., 413; Mural, 1350; Nathan, 846; Nat., 866; Nic., 296; (or Emmett), Peter, 64; Priscilla, 1307; Rebecca, 644; Rev. Reg., 689; Ric., 38*, 644, 683, 902*, 933*, 948, 958*, 959, 1350; Rev. Ric., 760, 802; Rob., 64, 288, 846, 1218, 1375*, 1472; Rog., 1394*, 1403; Rowland, 303, 386*; Sam., 111, 654, 933, 1350, 1413*, 1551; Sam. Edw., 1415; Sam. Obedias, 1003; Sarah, 45*, 60, 84, 435, 539, 543*, 644, 683, 868, 907, 933*, 995, 1307*, 1376, 1410*, 1413; Simon, 1350; Stephen, 644; Susanna, 290; Thos., 17, 79, 133, 170, 293, 472*, 539*, 654, 868, 902, 906, 933, 963, 1034, 1064, 1153, 1207, 1218, 1250, 1307*, 1312, 1323, 1350*, 1412, 1442, 1546*; Rev. Thos., 406*, 432, 651, 974; Unity, 1305; Ursula, 345; W., 1186; Wal. (le), 338, 933*, 1027, 1258, 1563; Wm., 17, 45*, 64, 84, 118, 141*, 253, 290, 343*, 446, 539*, 543, 572, 787, 800, 815, 825, 846*, 902*, 907, 923, 948*, 995, 1071, 1132, 1153, 1304, 1307*, 1312, 1376, 1394*, 1404, 1415; Wm. Price, 435; —, 1288, 1311, 1472, 1477, 1512; fam., 141, 252, 341

Taynton (Tainton, Tayneton, Teynton), Ann, 1473; Edw., 1100; Hen., 1476; J., 1061; Jane, 814; John (de), 814, 1477*; Jonathan, 1473; Maude of, 1238; Sam., 203; Sarah, 203; T., 1061; W., 985; Mrs., 288; —, 1062, 1237, 1255, 1476, 1477

Tdorndene, *see* Thorndene

Teagle, John, 954; Rachael, 954; *and see* Teakle

Teague, Edw., 1036, 1038*; Eleanor, 1038; Eliz., 1572*; John, 1572*; Mary, 1572; —, 1317

Teague & Co., 913

Teakle (Teekle, Tickell, Tykell, Tykle), Anna, 1054*; Anne, 887; Eliz., 752; Geo., 752; Hannah, 752*; John, 624; Joseph, 624, 887*; Judith, 624; Ric., 1054; Sarah, 624; Stephen, 752*; Susannah, 624; Thos., 672; Wm., 624, 752, 887; —, 1370; fam., 1054; *and see* Teagle

Teal (Teale), Hen., 338; Mary, 660; Sam., 660; Sarah, 338; —, 1201*, 1386

Teast, Dan., 677; Jas., 725; Sidenham, 725; fam., 721; *and see* Test

Tebbat, Isaac, 375; Jacob, 375; Jas., 375; Susanna, 375

Tedder, Joseph, 1412; Mary, 1412; Thos., 1412

Tedinton, Rob. de, 1221

Tedrinton, Ric. de, 1292

Teebay, Geo., 814; Hester, 814

Teekle, *see* Teakle

Telling, Eliz., 597; Isaac, 597; John, 597*; Jacob, 597; Jonathan, 597; Mary, 368, 597*; Wm., 597*

Temes, *see* Timmes

Tempany, Edm., 186

Tempest, Henrietta, 1231; Sir Hen., bt., 894; Col. John Plumbe, 1231

Temple, Ann, 797*; Frances, 1417; J., 1061; Jane, 797; John, 797; Maria Cath., 1417; Nic., 890, 1078, 1350, 1369; R., 1061; Ric., 523; Lieut.-Col. Ric., 1417; Rev. Rob., 503; Sarah, 797; Simon, 797*; Rev. Thos., 233; W., 1043; —, 1475

Tenace, —, 1017

Tennent, Lieut.-Col. Alex., 410

Terberville, *see* Turberville

Teret, *see* Terrett

Ternour, *see* Turner

Terrell (Terrel, Terril, Terrill), Edw., 41, 1554; Francis, 1250; John, 419; Mary, 419, 1250; *and see* Tyrrell

Terrett (Teret, Terret), Ann(e), 112, 191, 686*; Eliz., 960, 1037, 1273*; J., 1290; Jas., 751; Joanna, 112; John, 112*, 191, 682, 920, 1036, 1037*, 1039, 1289*; Joseph, 1273; Mary, 261; Ric., 188*, 191, 1052, 1273*; Sarah, 261, 1036, 1037, 1274*, 1400; Thos., 102, 261, 1036*, 1037*, 1039; W., 1290; Wm., 261, 686*, 960, 1036*, 1274*, 1369, 1400; Winney, 1036*, 1037; Mr., 101; —, 1289

[Terrick], Ric., bishop, 1223

Terril (Terrill), *see* Terrell

Terry, Cath., 412; Rev. Isaac, 13

Test, Alice, 618; Giles, 619; Lawr., 619; Mary, 619; Wm., 618; *and see* Teast

Tetbury (or Walters), Wal. (of), 1256*

Textor, W., 1015; *and see* Weaver; Webber; Webster

Teynton, *see* Taynton

Teysant, Weston, 1491

Thache (Thatch), Abigail, 1048; Mary, 1048; Phil., 347; Rachel, 1048*; Rev. Thos., 275, 350, 1048*, 1186, 1494

Thackham, Rev. Thos., 696

Thackwell, John, 546, 547, 1225*; Mary, 1225; Wm., 1225

Thaidon, *see* Thayden

Thanet [*peerage*], John, earl of, 721 n; Marg., countess of, 721 n; Thos., earl of, 721 n; *and see* Tufton, Thos.

Tharp, Mary, 1003; Wm., 1003

Thatch, *see* Thache

Thatcher, Drummond, 1321; Hannah, 48; Nathan, 48; Peter, 48; Thos., 657

Thawer, John, 813; Marg., 813

Thayden (Thaidon, Theyden), Beatrix, 1015; Hen., 1350; Letitia, 1015*, 1016; Rob. de, 1016; Wm., 1015

Thayer, *see* Theyer

Thelwall, Sir Eubule, 585 n

Theobald, Mary, 883; Thos., 883; *and see* Tibbals

Theyden, *see* Thayden

Theyer (Thayer), Chas., 259 n; Dan., 176; Geo., 1444; John, 259; Mary, 1524*; Ralph, 1444; Ric., 1444*; T., 1197; Thos., 514, 1524*; Wm., 514; —, 259 n; fam., 259; *and see* Tayer

Theyn, Wm., 1314; —, 1311; *and see* Thynne

Thick, —, 1455

Thinne, *see* Thynne

[Thirlby], Thos., bishop, 1331

Thist'le, John de, 1428; Thos., 1428

Thodenham, —, 1093

Thoky, John, 1317

Thokys, Reg., 688

Thomas, archbishop of York, *see* Bayeux

Thomas, bishop, 667

Thomas, bishop of Westminster, *see* Thirlby

Thomas, Otto son of, 533

Thomas, Richard son of, 990

Thomas son of Otto, 533

Thomas (Thomes, Tomas, Tommas, Tommys), Alice, 937; And., 899, 906; Rev. And., 754, 755; Ann(e), 730, 731, 741, 1418*, 1573; Barnabas, 1546*, 1551; Betty, 172; Chas., 250, 492; Christian, 211; Confidence, 276; Edw., 823, 947, 948; Eleanor (Elinor), 661, 1004; Eliz., 172, 474, 731, 741, 746*, 768, 815, 899, 1250, 1401; Ellis, 922; Esther, 474; Francis, 731; Geo., 60, 250, 731, 1418, 1420; Giles, 16; Grace, 746, 937; Hannah, 961; Hester, 660*; Isaac, 768; Jas., 102, 105, 661, 1239, 1250, 1573; Rev. Jas., 547; (formerly Tombs), Mrs. Jenkin, 1005; Joan, 1418; Johanna, 1259; John, 172*, 182, 211, 276*, 413, 446, 474*, 660, 730, 731, 746, 1087, 1146, 1239, 1244, 1365, 1400, 1418*, 1420; Rev. John, 1388; John Byrkyn, 102, 103; Joseph, 746, 1401; Joshua, 660*; Lawr., 1282; Mapson, 960; Margery, 1317; Martha, 1244; Mary, 70, 172, 174, 182, 250, 276, 431, 567, 734*, 922, 1321, 1368, 1542, 1546; Matha [*sic*], 1418; Mawd Parker, 946; Nat., 1250; Paul, 1321; Penelope, 948; Phil., 731; Rachel, 1080; Ric., 70, 924; Sam., 567, 721, 741, 1420*, 1542; Sarah, 172,

250, 823; Susannah, 1365; Rev. T., 1323; Thos., 52, 815, 826, 1016, 1420; Rev. Thos., 779, 1141, 1146, 1318, 1321, 1323; Tim., 696*, 1365*, 1366*, 1368*, 1369; Rev. Wal., 1443; Wm., 174, 660, 730, 734, 741, 746*, 815, 937, 961*, 1004, 1313, 1453; Rev. Wm., 1341, 1346; Mr., 206, 1420; Rev. Mr., 1379; —, 696, 1020, 1061, 1477
Thometrappe, Chris. (Xer), or Thos. Trape, 1346
Thomond, earl of, 43
Thompson (Tompson, Tomson), Anne, 1263; Benj., 1038; Dorothy, 1297; Edw., 1039; Eliz., 212, 611; Isaac, 702; Jas., 212*, 703*; Rev. Jas., 1263; Jane, 76, 210*, 1038*; John, 212, 296, 1297; Rev. Jn., 860; Joseph, 1038, 1182; Mary, 212, 1038*; Mat., 76*; Patience, 702; Ric., 1038*; Rev. Ric., 76*; Sarah, 296, 1038*, 1489; Wm., 210*, 212, 375, 702, 1038*, 1039; Rev., 611; —, 1257, 1489, 1490
Thoms, Ric., 1513
Thoresby, John, 221; John, bishop, 218
Thorn, see Thorne
Thornborough (Thornburgh), Eliz., 1497; Joan, 286 n; John, bishop, 1497; Sir John, 286 n
Thornbury, Rev. Nat., 93; Paul, 921
Thorndell, J., 1064; Joseph, 636*; Sarah, 636*, 1490; Wm., 636; —, 1064
Thorndene (Tdorndene, Thorndon), Gunnilda de, 1502; Ric. de, 1172; Wm. de, 1502
Thorne (Thorn), Abigail, 1152; Alex., 248, 249, 250, 732; Ann, 249; Chris., 248*; Edm., 1463; Edw., 1468*; Eliz., 1282, 1463, 1471; Francis, 1152; Geo., 1220, 1471; Hen., 1468; Rev. Hen., 1463*, 1477; Hester, 1463; Rev. Jas., 678; Joan, 55; John, 1463, 1469; Marg., 1468*; Mary, 248*; Ric., 55, 736; Susannah, 1469; Thos., 736; —, 1092, 1477
Thorner, Anna, 17; John, 17*
Thornett, John, 1222; —, 1223
Thornhill, Avice, 865; John, 765; Ric., 865; Wm., 765
Thorniloe, —, spinster, 393, 394
Thornton, Anne, 899; E., 1203; Eliz., 149; Geo., 47; Jane, 948; Mary, 1167; Rob., 149; Rev. Rob., 899; Wm., 47, 948; Rev. Wm., 1127
Thoroldson, Gislebert, 1419
Thorpe (Thorp), Geo., 172; John, 1024; Sir John, 720*; Rev. John Hersent, 840; Joshua, 1249; Kath., 720; Mary, 172, 1024, 1249; Rebecca, 1249*; Sam., 124; Sarah, 1024, 1249; Wm., 66, 75, 172, 1249; —, 775; fam., 159, 775
Thorstayn, see Thurston
Thressell, see Tressell
Thriftell, Edw., 1420
Throckmorton (Throcmorton, Throgmorton, Throkmorton), Alice, 732, 959; Anna Maria, 755; Anne, 920; Ant., 1333; Baynham, 919, 920; Sir Baynham, kt. & bt., 913, 917, 918, 919, 920*; Cecily, 919, 920; Chris., 1047; Clement, 43; Eliz., 919, 920*, 1431; Geo., 755; Sir Geo., kt., 289, 1430, 1431; Giles, 1355; Isabel, 1355; J., 1052, 1477; John, 1215, 1216, 1218, 1355*; Kath., 289; Lucy, 43; Marg., 634, 1333*; Mary,

920; Nic., 920; Mary, 733, 919, 920*; Myriell, 1170; Nic., 1218; Sir Nic., kt., 732*, 733*; Sir Rob., bt., 508 n, 634, 755; Sir T., 1177; Thos., 634, 920, 1047, 1170, 1238, 1346*, 1355*, 1356*; Sir Thos., kt., 451, 959, 1062*, 1333, 1341*, 1346*, 1355; Sir W., 305, 1063*, 1345, 1504; Wm., 481, 920, 1047, 1062; Sir Wm., kt. & bt., 451, 452, 913, 920, 1059*, 1062*, 1345, 1355, 1356*; Master, 1345; —, 1063*, 1064, 1216, 1345, 1355; fam., 305, 440, 482*, 788, 919, 1340
Thurber, Rev. Wal., 643
Thurloe, (Secretary), 1293*
Thurner, see Turner
Thurston (Thorstayn, Thurstan, Thurstein, Turstane), Ab., 1312; Ann, 1305*; Anna, 1299*; Anselm, 955*; Bethia, 955; Christian, 542; Dan., 1305*; Edw., 1020, 1551; Eliz., 1302*; Geo., 1301; Hannah, 959; Hen., 1069, 1301; Horatius, 1301; Hugh, 1305*; J., 1312; Johanny, 1305; John, 1302, 1305*, 1355, 1477; Judith, 955, 1305; Marg., 1305; Mary, 174, 955, 1299, 1305*, 1307; Nat., 1305*; Ric., 550, 1069, 1313; Rob., 542, 1299*, 1302*, 1307; Sarah, 486, 955*; Thos., 174; Ursula, 1305*; Wm., 486, 550; —, 1311*, 1345; fam., 570
Thynne (Thinne, Thynn), Elinor, 32; Eliz., 699; Francis, 32, 696*, 699; Hannah, 1408; Hen. Fred., 272, 771; Sir Hen. Fred., bt., 273, 770, 771; Jas., 272*, 273, 288, 364, 771, 944; John, 272; Sir John, kt., 126, 271, 272, 778, 1126; (or Bottevyle), Sir John, 769; Kath., 771*; Mary, 273, 771; Penelope, 699; Ric., 696, 699*; Sir T., 1177; Thos., marquis of Bath, 769; Thos., Viscount Weymouth, 126, 272*, 273, 770, 771; Sir Thos., 769, 771; fam., 271; and see Theyn
Tibbals (Tibbells), Eliz., 429; Jane, 429; Sarah, 429*; Wm., 429*; and see Theobald
Tibbet (Tibot), Dan., 287 n; Eliz., 370; Isaac, 370
Tichbourne (Tichborn), Frances, 754, 755; Sir Hen., 754, 755; Mary, 754*
Tickell, see Teakle
Tickner, Edw., 164; Eliz., 164
Tidkin, see Fidkin
Tidman, Ann, 1003; Eliz., 868; Joseph, 1003*; Rob., 868*; Susannah, 868; Thos., 868
Tidmarsh, Anne, 1091; C., 1519; John, 255; Nat., 296; Sam., 26; T., 1093; Thos., 1091*; Rev. Thos., 255; fam., 764
Tiely, see Tiley
Tiff, Ann, 494*; Anna, 494*; Thos., 494*; —, 1148
Tilar (Tiler), see Tyler
Tiley (Tiely, Tilley, Tillie, Tilly, Tily, Tyley), Ann(e), 171, 842, 1338; Betty, 1112; Edith, 994*; Edw., 841, 1554; Eliz., 842, 1110*, 1368; Esther, 1547; Hannah, 1368, 1511; Isabel(la), 1110*; Jas., 1026, 1159, 1513, 1547; Jane, 841; John, 842*, 1112, 1138, 1338; Joseph, 537, 1338*, 1368; Sir Joseph, kt., 537; Lettice, 994; Martha, 844, 845; Mary, 537, 842, 1138, 1159; Mary Ann, 1511; Mic., 1338; Ric., 842; Rob., 844, 845; Sarah, 171, 841, 1026; Sophia, 836;

Susanna(h), 844, 845*, 1338*; Thos., 171, 844, 845*, 1121; Wal., 1511; Wm., 171*, 563*, 836, 1110*, 1121, 1368; —, 1123

Till, Jas., 1345; Mary, 1345; —, 1455

Tilladam (Till-Adam, Till-Adams), Deborah, 540; Eliz., 540; John, 531, 533 n, 540; Joseph, 531, 540*; Martha, 540; Mary, 540; Rob., 739; Thos., 540*, 1405, 1410, 1411

Tiller, Moses, 1169

Tilley (Tillie), see Tiley

Tilling, Ann, 235; Edw., 1481; Eliz., 1481; Jas., 235*; Thos., 1481; Wm., 1481

Tillit, Esther, 1547

Tillotson, —, 1199

Tilly, see Tiley

Tilor, see Tyler

Tily, see Tiley

Timberlake, Hen. Ellerbech, 1084

Timberman, Betty, 1453; Hannah, 1452, 1453; Sam., 1452, 1453

Timbrell (Timbrill, Tymbrell, Tymbrill), Alethia, 374; Amy, 1147*, 1200; Ann(e), 374, 1058, 1472; Eleanor, 1063*; Eliz., 989, 1001, 1063; Hen., 374*, 1200, 1477; Jane, 1473; John, 374, 522*; 986, 1063*, 1200, 1472*, 1477; Joseph, 1058; Judith, 1064; Mary, 374, 522, 1063*, 1064, 1472; Patience, 1064; R., 985, 1063; Rebekah, 1200; Ric., 1061, 1062, 1063*, 1129; Rob., 1063*, 1147*, 1200; Sam., 1058, 1063*, 1064; T., 1063*; Thos., 1001, 1058, 1063*; Wm., 952, 989, 1064, 1473*; —, 986, 1064*, 1092, 1477*; fam., 1093

Timmes (Temes, Timbs, Tymmes, Tyms), Edw., 1222; Eliz., 1222; Francis, 884; John, 1223, 1331, 1491; Wm., 850

Timmins, Jane, 641; Sarah, 641*; Wm., 641

Tindale (Tindall), see Tyndale

Tingle (Tingel), Jas., 472; Joan, 473; Rob., 473; Sarah, 472

Tinker, John, 765; Mary, 765

Tinkler, 1447

Tipins, see Tipping

Tippeler, Susannah, 730; Wm., 730

Tipper (Typper), Anne, 846; Dan., 64; Edw., 846*; Eliz., 846; Hen., 387; Hotson (Hutson), 845*, 846; Jane, 846; John, 846, 928; Mary, 845; Sarah, 846*; Thos., 846; Wm., 845, 846*, 1339; —, 928

Tippett (Tippetts, Tippets, Tippitt), Ann, 212, 541*; Bridget, 835; Eliz., 169, 212; Francis, 212*; Hannah, 538*; Hester, 1241; Jas. Berriman, 541; Jane, 212; Johanna, 624; John, 169, 212, 537, 541*; Josiah, 532, 621; Mary, 541*; Paul Josiah, 1258; Rebecca (Rebeckah), 537, 541; Ric., 531*, 532, 538, 1241; Rob., 169, 624; Sam., 212; Sarah, 212, 538*, 624; Stephen, 212*; Thos., 532, 538*; Wm., 531*, 538*, 835*; fam., 532

Tipping (Tipins), Ann(e), 814, 1144; Eliza, 696; Geo., 696, 814; Sam., 814; Sir Thos., 696

Tippitt, see Tippett

Tiptoft, Eliz., countess of Worcester, 462; John, earl of Worcester, 244, 462

Tirell (Tirrel), see Tyrrell

Tisher, Rebekah, 962*; Thos., 962

Tison, see Tyson

Titian, —, 349 n

Tocknell (Tocknel), Dan., 1140; Geo., 1137, 1508; Jas., 971; Jane, 1137*; Sarah, 1508; Wal., 971

Todd (Tod, Todde, Toddes), Matillda, 1447; Rev. Nic., 1217; Ralph, 1447*; Wm., 1447

Todeford, Hen., 1069

Todeni (Toeni), (or D'Albini), Joan (de), 1014; Marg. de, 618; Ralph de, 570, 678, 1225*, 1421; Ralph, baron de, 618; Rob. de, 753, 1014, 1050, 1051, 1052*; (or D'Albini), Wm. (de), 1014, 1050, 1051

Todington (Tudington), Phil. (de, of), 1220, 1475

Toeni, see Todeni

Tofte, Mary, 994; Capt. Sam., 994*; Sarah, 994; Sybilla, 994

Tofti, earl, 1126

Toghill, Ann, 491; Edw., 555; Eliz., 9; Geo., 9*, 491, 1258; Hester, 1158; Lucy, 491; Martha, 555; Mary, 9, 10; Moses, 491; Sarah, 9*, 10, 11; Stephen, 9*, 555; Susannah, 9*; Thos., 9*, 10, 11; Wm., 1158

Togwell, see Tugwell

Tohpe, see Toppe

Tole (Toll, Tolle), Anne, 1158, 1303; Ashburnham, 1303*; Eliz., 1101*; Joseph, 1158; Sarah, 1158; Thos., 1400

Toller, Ann, 993; Benj., 993; Dinah, 993; Eliz., 993

Tolton, Rev., 848

Tomas, see Thomas

Tombs (Tombes, Tomes), Alex., 454; Alice, 587; Ann(e), 429, 849, 1272*, 1274, 1297*, 1391, 1465*; Bart., 429; Benj., 980; Cath., 235; Edm., 1161; Edw., 693, 862*, 1080; Eleazer, 296; Eliz., 235, 296, 429*, 446, 1200; Esther, 429*; Francis, 587, 1272*, 1274, 1275; Giles, 446*, 526, 1200, 1493; Hannah, 151; Hen., 429*; Hester, 446; Jas., 429*; Jas. Thos., 1005; Jane, 862, 1391; Jo[a]ne, 1465; Joannah, 446; Job, 1493; John, 296*, 386, 429*, 848, 849, 850, 862, 948, 1274, 1391*, 1452*, 1464, 1465*; Joseph, 445; Letitia, 1272; Marg., 454, 611; Mary, 235, 296*, 386, 429*, 446, 526, 849, 862, 980, 1272, 1452; Nic., 1420; R., 1233; Ric., 151*, 296, 1160; Rob., 431; Sarah, 317, 386, 850, 948, 1391*; Thos., 296, 526*, 815, 862, 1297; W., 1202*; Wm., 235*, 317, 429*, 446*, 526, 849, 850, 1465; Winifrede, 693; —, 1005, 1392, 1475; — (later Mrs. Jenkin Thomas), 1005; fam., 444

Tomkins (Tomkyns, Tompkins), Alice, 1080; Allen, 398; Ann(e), 466, 1305; Eliz., 466; Geo., 1418*; Hen., 923; Joan, 398; Rev. John, 421, 422; Joseph, 721; Martha, 1418; Paul, 1305; Ric., 1058, 1477; Rev. Ric., 1080; Sam., 1289, 1312; Sarah, 923; Thos., 466*; Rev. Thos., 1348; Wheeler, 1418; Wm., 398; —, 1092, 1311

Tomlins, Eliz., 924; Mary, 924; Ric., 924; Wm., 924

Tomlinson, Ann, 399, 1418; Eliz., 1418, 1573; Francis, 1418; John, 399, 923, 1573, 1575; Nic., 399; Susanna, 399; Wm., 1418

Tommas (Tommys), *see* Thomas
Tompkins, *see* Tomkins
Tompson (Tomson), *see* Thompson
Toney, Chas., 1518*; Mary, 1518*
Tonge, Hen., 1563; John, 573; Mary, 1563
Tonstall, —, bishop, 305 n
Tooke, *see* Tuck
Tooker, *see* Tucker
Toppe (Tohpe, Topp), Alex., 1337; Dennis, 792; Dorothy, 792; Edw., 1337; Sir F., 1339; Hen., 445 n; Sir J., 1339; John, 1337; Sir John, bt., 19*, 1339; Lingen, 1337; Lady, 19
Topyn, Wm., 1370
Torald, Wal., 1005
Toreigni, Rob. de, 1350; W. de, 1350
Tornor, *see* Turner
Torrent, Rev. Sam., 139
Tosti, earl, 990
Touchet (Touchte), Ric. le, 1102; Thos., Lord Audley, 518
Toule, Wm., 1292
Toulemounde, John, 1292
Toune, John atte 1356
Tour, Wal. le, 1258
Tournay, Rev. Thos., 1552; Wm., 1552
Tourville, Hen., 692
Tovey (Tovay, Tovy), Ann, 598*, 1275; Chas., 686; Comfort, 1275; Edith, 1111; Eliz., 686*; Esther, 598*; Frances, 739; Hen., 27, 598*, 1126; Jane, 1275*; Jo[a]ne, 739; Job, 48; John, 598*, 1121; Luke, 731; Marg., 1276; Mary, 48, 731, 739; Maur., 738, 739; R., 1121*; Ralph, 686*; Ric., 598*, 1111, 1275*; Rob., 731; Rog., 1271; Sarah, 1271; Thos., 1289
Tovi (fl. 1066), 1162, 1185, 1482*
Tovy, *see* Tovey
Tower (Towers), Eliz., 467*, 1549*; Geo., 463; Giles, 463, 467*; Hen., 1549*; Mary, 467, 1549*; Sarah, 467; Wm., 1549
Towgood, Rev. Ric., 206, 1346
Towncell, Magdalen, 669*; Mary, 669; Stephen, 669*
Townend (Townesend, Towneshend, *see* Townsend
Townley, Rob., 74; —, 807
Townsend (Townend, Townesend, Towneshend, Townsende, Townshend), Albinia, 852, 854; Alex., 1127; Anna, 970, 971; Anne, 1006; Ant., 1262; Barbara Charlotte, 1126; Betty, 1010; Chas., Viscount Townshend, 851, 854; Deborah, 1130; Edw., 198, 1507*; Eliz., 202, 378, 429, 969, 971*, 1262*, 1290, 1507, 1530; G., 1196, 1197; Geo., 288, 325, 327, 634, 635, 704, 705, 706*, 944, 1006, 1461, 1477, 1519; Goddard Maria, 1126; Hannah, 948; Hen., 378, 969, 970, 971*; Rev. Hen., 498; Rev. Jas., 1126; Jane, 162, 1348; Joanna, 1433; John (atte), 399*, 601, 807, 1005, 1058, 1126*, 1348, 1437*, 1453*; Jos., 1439; Joseph, 884*; Marg., 584*, 1453; Margery, 300; Mary, 601*, 706, 1046, 1159, 1433; Phil., 584*; R. L., 1403; Ric., 202, 429*, 584, 640, 706, 975, 1226, 1433; Rob., 300; Sir Rog., kt., 162; Sarah, 399, 596, 884, 948, 1300, 1433; Susanna,

348, 1437, 1439; Theyer, 259, 447*, 878; Thos., 348, 596, 706, 851, 852, 854, 891, 948*, 1031, 1189; Thos., Viscount Sydney, 852, 853; Wm., 601, 884, 969, 971*, 1010, 1046, 1062, 1130, 1150, 1433, 1530; Mrs., 969; —, 1061, 1195, 1196, 1362, 1455, 1475, 1519*
Toye (Toy), Edw., 66; Hen., 66, 1378, 1380; Sarah, 69; Rev. Wm., 66, 69
Tracy (Tracey, Traci, Tracie, Trocy), Ann(e), 610, 1267; Anne Maria, 1153; Sir Ant., kt., 1317; Lady Bridget, 595; C. H., Lord Sudeley, 1148*, 1334, 1475, 1476; Chas., 1333; Chas. Hanbury, baron Sudeley, 1333*, 1334; Dodwell, 1064, 1443; Eliz., 79*, 1333, 1476; Ferdinando, 1153*; Grace de, 1335; Hanbury, 1332; Henrietta Susanna, 1153, 1333; Hen. (de), 852 n, 1219, 1262, 1267, 1333; Sir Humph., 684, 1153; J., 1226, 1334*, 1335, 1460, 1476; Jas., 1334; John (de), 487, 1153*, 1154*, 1226*, 1335, 1443; Rev. John, 493*; Sir John, bt., 1190; Sir John, kt., 488, 591, 1153*, 1332, 1333, 1334, 1335*; Lady Juliana, 1190, 1196, 1461; Mary, 114*, 1064*, 1092*, 1093, 1443*; Muriel (Murial), 595, 1051; Nic., 147; Sir P., kt., 1221; Paul, 684, 1154; Sir Paul, bt., 79, 1153, 1154; Sir Paule, kt., 1267; Priscilla, 1262*, 1267; R., 1334; Ralph, 1440; Ric., 1153*, 1334, 1335; Sir Ric., kt., 266, 685, 1153*, 1154; Rob., 493, 494, 634, 1153*, 1154; T., 1092; Thos., 114*, 502, 890, 1064, 1153, 1443; W., 1220; Wm. de, 487, 1092, 1153, 1335*; (formerly Maunt), Wm., 1334, 1335; Sir Wm., 1334; Mrs., 890, 986, 1064*, 1089, 1442; —, 1043, 1219, 1227, 1289, 1334, 1335, 1476*, 1477, 1504; —, judge, 493, 610; Sir —, bt., 1152; fam., 305, 309, 318, 487, 493, 591, 890, 1148, 1288, 1334, 1335*
Tracy [*peerage*](Tracey), Chas., Viscount, 493; Frances, Viscountess, 1332*; Hen., baron, 1334; Hen., Viscount, 1333, 1334; John, Lord (baron), 1153, 1334*; John, Viscount, 709, 710, 1333, 1335*; Rob., baron, 1334; Rob., Viscount, 494, 1335; Thos. Chas., baron, 1334*; Thos. Chas., Viscount, 1332*, 1335*; Wm., baron, 1334; Wm., Viscount, 1332; Lady, 27; Lord, 272, 493, 595, 1051, 1477*; Viscount, 710, 801, 1332; *and see* Leigh, Thos. Chas.
Trafford, Blanch, 814; David, 813*, 814; Eliz., 814*; Jas., 813*, 814*; John, 812*, 813*, 814*; Martha, 812; Mary, 608, 812, 813*, 814; Silvester, 813; Wm., 812*
Trahern, *see* Treherne
Trapp (Trape), Rev. John, 342, 1390, 1392; Rev. Joseph, 342*, 343; Theophilus, 343; Rev. Thos., (or Chris. Thometrappe), 1346; Dr., 1258
Tratman (Trattman), Ann, 172, 176; Chas., 176*; Eliz., 421; Hester, 176; John, 172, 176; Ric., 172; Sarah, 937; Wm., 421; *and see* Trotman
Travell, Rev. F. T., 1067, 1089; Rev. Ferdinando Tracy, 1089, 1090*; Jane, 1067; Martha, 1090; Mr., 1093; *and see* Trevill
Traven, Thos., 1468
Travet, Edm., 1036

Trayhern (Trayhurn), *see* Treherne

Treamon, —, 1017

Trebeck, John, 1140

Tredeag, Mary, 1433

[Tredway?](Trrdway), Tim., 1273

Tree, Ric., 1282

Tregany, Jane, 814; Wm., 814

Trego, Sarah, 1412; Wm., 1412*

Tregoz, —, 1491

Treherne (Trahern, Trayhern, Trayhurn), Ann, 957; Dan., 957; Edw., 957*; Eleanor, 959; Jas., 957*; Jane, 957*; Joseph, 957*; Mary, 957*; Rev. Nat., 1331; Ric., 957*; Sarah, 957*; Thos., 957*; W., 1162; Wm., 957, 959; —, 1312

Trenchard, Dorothy, 1341; Edith, 1341*; Rev. Geo., 1341*, 1346; Jane, 1341*; Miss, 1440

Trenfield, John, 339

Trepet, *see* Trippet

Tressell (Thressell), Jas., 757*; Mary, 757; Miriam, 757

Tresshare, John le, 1127

Trested, Ric., 923

Treuman, *see* Trewman

Trevanion, Lucy, 1276

Trevill (Trevell), And., 1115; Lieut. Peter, 928; *and see* Travell

Trevisa, John, 161;

Trewman (Treuman, Trueman, Truman), Amii, 554; Arthur, 1423, 1425*; Eliz., 1302; John, 15; Jonathan, 1302; Kath., 561; R., 1475; Ric. le, 1447; Sam., 1425*; Rev. Sam., 553, 554*, 561; Wm. (le), 1186, 1447; Rev. Wm., 98, 825; Mr., 1362; —, 1476

Tridelaunde, Wm., 1420

Trigg (Trigge), Abigail, 473; Amey, 930; Benj., 993; Cath., 930; Eliz., 930*; Hannah, 215, 1399; Jas., 1399*; John, 473*, 873, 929, 930*; Mary, 193, 474, 930*; Ric., 193*; Rob., 873; Sam., 473; Sarah, 474; T., 190; Thos., 354, 873, 930*; Wm., 215*, 473, 873, 1403*; —, 927

Trillow (Trillowe), John (de), 1016*, 1082; —, 1017

Trindall, John, 206

Trinder, Ann, 398, 597; Chas., 944; Chris., 234; Dorothy, 569; Edm., 510*; Edw., 597; Eliz., 569, 1111; Hannah, 117; Hen., 64, 984; Jane, 1480*; John, 1111, 1481*; Joseph, 569*; Joyce, 64; Kath., 569*; Marg., 510; Mark, 150; Rev. Mark, 114, 117; Martha, 1481; Mary, 150, 398*, 569, 984; Priscilla, 510*; Rob., 139, 569; Thos., 398, 510, 1480*; Wm., 398*, 1480*; Mr., 63*; Rev. Mr.; fam., 565

Trippet (Trepet, Trippett), Alex., 108; Chas., 106*, 173; Eliz., 106; Joanna, 106; John, 101, 104, 105, 106, 932; Marg., 104, 105; Mary, 106, 173, 932; Ric., 103, 106*

Trissell, Edw., 1559, 1571; *and see* Trussell

Tristram, Alice, 884; Chas., 884; Chas. Kitson, 884; Deborah, 1279; Martha, 1279; Rob., 884; Sarah, 884

Trocy, *see* Tracy

Tropyn, Thos., 576

Trotman, Ann(e), 281*, 283, 703, 958, 1084, 1469, 1472*; Cath., 283; Chas., 281*, 1535; Cisly, 283; Dan., 283, 284, 938*; Dorothy, 117; Edith, 1473; Edm., 117; Edw., 281*, 283*; Eleanor, 279, 281*; Eliz., 419, 541, 632, 830, 1084, 1085, 1167*, 1526; Eliz. Anne, 1085; Emmelina, 1085; Esther, 281*; Fiennes, 721, 1084*, 1085*, 1086; Geo., 176; Geo. Scanderbeg, 1469; Giles, 703; Hannah, 1528; Henrietta, 1085; Hen., 531; Hester, 1083; J., 1064; Jane, 1168, 1472, 1535; Joane, 937; John, 15, 174, 279, 633, 938*, 1086, 1167*, 1169, 1469, 1472*, 1477; Rev. John, 829, 830; John Fiennes, 1085; Lawr. Fiennes, 1085; Lydia, 938, 1168; Marg., 279, 281*, 740; Mary, 227, 542, 938*, 958, 1064, 1086, 1167, 1472; Maur., 1526; Nat., 938; Nic., 281*, 283, 703*; Ric., 283, 1168; Rob., 279, 281*; S., 1087; Sam., 541, 702, 1084, 1168, 1169, 1528; Rev. Sam., 1087; Sarah, 176, 703; Scanderbeg, 1473*; Susanna(h), 1168, 1472; Thos., 227, 530*, 702, 958, 1084*, 1087; Throgmorton, 278, 534; Tim., 542; Wm., 227, 530, 543, 632, 740, 937, 1168*, 1233, 1369, 1472, 1473; Rev., 860; —, 1064*, 1169*, 1232, 1477; fam., 779, 1086; *and see* Tratman

Trott, Martha, 517

Troughton, Benj., 1164*, 1165; Geo., 1477; Joseph, 398; Mary, 1164; Thos., 398; Mr., 1501

Trouncell, Eliz., 907; John, 907

Troy, Isaac, 79*

Troyle, —, 1362

Trrdway, *see* Tredway

Trubie, *see* Truby

Trubody, Hester, 212; Jane, 210; Martha, 11; Thos., 11, 212; Wm., 210

Trubshaw, Rev. John, 1428

Truby (Trubie, Trueby), Edw., 1016*; Giles, 1013, 1016*; John, 296, 1013*, 1016*; Thos., 1013*, 1016; Wm., 1016; —, 1015, 1016, 1017*

True, John, 800; Mic., 517

Trueby, *see* Truby

Truelove, Joseph, 1369

Trueman, *see* Trewman

Trull, Grace, 284; Jas., 284, 542; Ric., 542

Truman, *see* Trewman

Trumbull, Sir Wm., 1070

Trussell, Eliz., 1086; Ric., 1086; Sam., 1086; *and see* Trissell

Trustrum, Elianor, 524; Thos., 524*

Trye, Anne, 665*; Brandon, 314; C. B., 1501*; Cath., 997; Chas. Brandon, 672; Eliz., 331, 663, 664, 800, 1501; Frances, 700; Capt. Hen., 665; Lady Isabella, 664; Rev. J. R., 1494; John, 279, 663*, 664*, 665, 800, 1501; Rev. John, 798, 800*; Marg., 664; Mary, 665*, 800, 1169, 1501; Rawlin (Rawlen), 663, 1169, 1176; Thos., 207, 663, 799; Capt. Thos., 665*; W., 1176; Wm., 166, 314, 331, 663*, 664*, 665*, 671, 672*, 674, 700, 798, 800; —, 997; fam., 663*, 671, 672

Tuck (Tooke, Tucke, Tuke), Anne, 652; Sir Bryan, 1402; Chas., 652; Eliz., 652; Grace, 1250; Hen., 124; J., 1331; John, 13, 1250, 1251, 1256; T., 652; Ursula, 651, 652; Wm., 731

Tuckell, *see* Tuckwell

Tucker (Tooker), Anna, 1489; Anne, 700*, 921, 1244, 1489; Arthur, 1428, 1488, 1489*, 1490; Benj., 212; Charlotte, 1511; Eliz., 1157, 1244, 1488; Frances, 1379*; Francis, 1086*; Grace, 996; Hen., 996, 1086, 1244; Honora, 1580; Jane, 1488; John, 531*, 540, 835*, 921, 1489, 1511, 1580; Jonathan, 834, 835, 1086; Mary, 212, 1489, 1490; Millicent, 1064*; Rev. Nic., 1064*; Obadiah, 835; Ric., 1379; Rob., 612, 613, 1488*, 1489; Sarah, 1488*, 1489; Thos., 700*, 1086, 1157; Rev. Thos., 161; Rev. Tretheway, 272; Dean, 1441; —, 1087

Tuckey (Tuckie), Ann, 846; Hen., 1256; John, 797*, 846; Mary, 797; Rob., 846; Wm., 1078

Tuckwell (Tuckell), Frances, 569*; Humph., 1075, 1125*, 1126; Isabel, 1125, 1126; John, 1126, 1127*; Ric., 569*, 1126; Susannah, 569; Thos., 569*, 1213; W., 1126; Wm., 1125; fam., 1126, 1127; *and see* Tugwell

Tudgey, Rebecca, 1533; Thos., 1533

Tudington, *see* Todington

Tudor, fam., 1156

Tuffley (Taffley, Tuffly), Anne, 423; Betty, 423; Diana, 429; Giles, 348; Hen., 423; John, 320*, 348, 423; Marg., 423; Martha, 348; Mary, 348; Paul, 423*; Rob., 1064; W., 985, 1061; Wm., 429*; —, 1063

Tufton, Lady Cath., 724; Lady Marg., 721 n; Thos., earl of Thanet, 724

Tugwell (Togwell), Ann(e), 182, 1429*; Benj., 262; Betty, 262, 1429*; Edw., 1250, 1258; Esther, 181; Frances, 182; Humph., 182*; John, 1250; Lewen, 181*; Mary, 182*, 1250; Priscilla, 262; Stephen, 1429*; Thos., 181; Wm., 181*, 262, 1258, 1429*; *and see* Tuckwell

Tuke, *see* Tuck

Tully (Tullie), Arthur, 485; Gertrude, 388*; Jane, 388; John, 388*; Rev. John, 1513; Sarah, 485; Susanna, 388; Dr. Thos., 1258; Rev. Wm., 630

Tunnicliff, Eliz. Scott, 1282; Wm. Key, 1282

Tunstan, Ric. son of, 1140

Turbat, *see* Turbot

Turberville (Terberville, Turbervile, Turbervyle, Turbeville, Turbyfield), Ann(e) 1359*; Bethea, 1419; Edm., 1359*, 1419; Eliz., 1152, 1359*; Geo., 1359; John (de), 1078, 1357; Mary, 1359*; Phebe, 1152; Ric., 1152*; Sarah, 1359*; Thos., 467; Wal., 1359; Wm., 1359*, 1362; —, 1293, 1362; fam., 392, 568

Turbot (Turbat), Rev. Wal., 689, 860

Turbyfield, *see* Turberville

Turk, Betty, 317; Chas., 320*; Eliz., 317, 321, 752*, 1542; John, 317, 431; Martha, 317; Mary, 320, 321; Nic., 317, 319*, 320, 321*; Ric., 320, 321, 752*; Sarah, 319, 320, 321*, 431; Thos., 317

Turland, Rev. Francis, 447

Turlington, Thos., 1289

Turner (Ternour, Thurner, Tornor, Turnor, Turnour), Abraham, 66; And., 387; Ann(e), 1026, 1277, 1377; Arthur, 1487*; Barbara, 175; Benedict, 1532; Bethiah, 616; C., 1015; Cath., 379; Chris., 500; Dan., 47*; Deborah, 1209; Edw., 834, 909, 1183, 1289; Rev. Edw., 279, 280, 631, 1177; Edwin, 986; Eliz., 118, 204, 240, 550, 616 (?), 637, 834, 957, 1377*; Frances, 693; Francis, 1422; Grace, 262; Hannah, 47, 637; Hen., 262, 1373, 1377*, 1378; Hester, 280; Jas., 687; Jane, 379, 957; Joan, 262; John, 204, 379, 598, 633, 637*, 687, 797, 870, 1004, 1137, 1289, 1427; John Print, 1377; Rev. John, 252, 379, 1257; Sir John, bt., 341; Joseph, 118, 598, 1183, 1499, 1502; Martha, 948*; Mary, 379, 598*, 631, 633, 641, 702, 797, 1004, 1427, 1487, 1499; Mary Jones, 1487; Ralph, 683, 1477; Ric., 262*, 550, 820, 948, 957*; Rob., 789, 1277; Sabina, 598; Sam., 1112; Sarah, 118, 204*, 1136*, 1487; Simeon, 616*; Simon, 1441; Susannah Jones, 1487; Thos., 175, 641, 762, 948, 957, 1026, 1186, 1258, 1348, 1487*; Rev. Thos., 221, 394, 500, 808, 853; Rev. Thos. Savory, 302; Wm., 175*, 204*, 240, 282, 379*, 693, 702, 1209, 1217, 1258; Lady, 21; —, 1017*, 1311*, 1422, 1580

Turnpenny, Eliz., 730*; John, 730

Turold, Gislebert son of, 890, 1011, 1331

Turser, Wm., 1583

Turstane, *see* Thurston

Turstin (Turtin) son of Rolph (Rolf), 98, 1162, 1345, 1419

Turton, Anne, 1352; Eliz., 1352; Esther, 731; Job, 1352; Rev. John, 1095, 1102; Joseph, 731, 962; Mary, 1352; Rachel, 963; Ric., 1352; Rob., 1352; Sarah, 1352; Wm., 963, 1352*

Turville (Turviles, Turvill), Abigail, 1422; Rev. John, 1362; Wm., 1157

Tustin (Tusten), Ann, 388; Jas., 1169; John, 1477; Joseph, 388; Thos., 1276

Tutt, Eliz., 1085; John, 1085

Tuyles, John, 1404

Twemlow, Joseph, 282; Mary, 282

Twinihoo (Twinihow), *see* Twyniho

Twinning, *see* Twyning

Twinyhow, *see* Twyniho

Twissell (Twysell), Hen., 202; Hugh, 1139; Isabel, 202; John, 202, 1139*; Mary, 202; Rob., 202; Sarah, 202; T., 1216; Rev. Thos., 202*; Wm., 202; —, 1139

Twitty (Twittey), Ann, 1317; Diana, 1275; —, 1316

Twyford, John, 1539

Twynelepypin, Wal., 1258

Twyniho (Twiniho, Twinihow, Twinyhow, Twynihoe, Twynyho), Anne, 1077; Ankaret, 1077; Cath., 1077*; Chris., 1077, 1408; Edith, 1077*; Edw., 1077; Joan, 371; John, 371, 791*, 1077; Rog., 1077; Wm., 1077*; —, 1077, 1078; fam., 792

Twyning (Twinning, Twynning), Joseph, 1483; Rev. Joseph, 1066, 1068, 1069; Rev. Rob., 1031; T., abbot, 1362; Rev. Thos., 969; Wm., 1372

Twynyho, *see* Twyniho

Twysell, *see* Twissell

Tydenham, And., 1456

Tydsale, Rev. J., 1092; R., 1093
Tyers, Ann, 1208*; Jas., 1208*; John, 1208; Sarah, 1208
Tykell (Tykle), see Teakle
Tyler (Tilar, Tiler, Tilor, Tylar, Tylor), Adam, 708 n; Ann, 554; Basil, 1320; Chris., 844; Clement, 1475; Dorothy, 995*–6; Edith, 554, 843; Edw., 550, 843*, 844, 995*, 1584; Eliz., 555, 843*, 844, 1159, 1300*, 1304, 1319; Frances, 555; Geo., 1160; Hannah, 1573, 1584; Hen., 1238; Rev. Hen., 1238; Hester, 171*, 803; Isaac, 554*; Jas., 1551*; Joan, 736; John, 49, 160, 171*, 530, 531, 555*, 736, 803*, 1304*, 1323, 1342*, 1583, 1584*; Jonathan, 614; Joseph, 171; Marg., 171; Mary, 49, 554, 995; Maur., 530; Mic., 1474; Morris, 758; Moses, 758; Nancy, 1159; Nic., 1342; R., 1475; Ric., 160, 171, 1342*; Rev. Ric., 1177; Sam., 1159, 1160; Sarah, 758*, 803, 1299, 1300, 1551, 1573; Thos., 171*, 1127; Wal., 555, 1300; Wm., 250, 555*. 844*, 995, 1159, 1319*, 1323, 1573; —, 995, 1342*; fam., 779
Tyley, see Tiley
Tylor, see Tyler
Tymbrell (Tymbrill), see Timbrell
Tymmes (Tyms), see Timmes
Tyndale (Tindale, Tindall, Tyndal, Tyndall, Tynndale), Aaron, 1167; Anne, 782*; Arthur, 1525; Betty, 1182; Cath., 283; Dan., 284, 937, 938*; Edw., 283, 1153, 1312; Eliz., 1167; Esther, 536; Hannah, 561; Hester, 937; John, 938, 1169; Rev. John, 305, 306*, 938*, 1369; Joseph, 937; Kath., 937; Marg., 284; Mary, 306, 938*; Mat., 1166; Nat., 937; Rebecca, 782; Ric., 937*, 1169*; Rev. Ric., 305; Sam., 1166; Sarah, 282; T., 1311; Thos., 56, 282, 297, 536, 561, 782*, 1169, 1182, 1296, 1313; Wal., 445; Wm., 305* & n, 306*, 307, 1123, 1166, 1169; Rev. Wm., 305, 306, 445*; —, 1169, 1311*, 1388; fam., 305, 1311
Typper, see Tipper
Tyrconnell, earl of, 147; Lord, 89*
Tyrell, see Tyrrell
Tyrer, Eliz., 573; Mary, 573; Rev. Thos., 606, 785; Rev. Mr., 573
Tyringham, Edw., 476*
Tyrone, marquis of, 634
Tyrrell (Tirell, Tirrel, Tyrell), Avery, 596; Chas., 496*; Sir Edw., 665; Eliz., 496*; Mary, 596*, 665; R[ichar]d, 1078; Rev. Ric., 263; S., 1078; Sir Thos., bt., 496; and see Terrell
Tyrwhit, R., 1078
Tysoe, Sam., 980
Tyson (Tison), Lawford, 1299; Mary, 49; Rachel, 1299; Sam., 49, 1299*, 1312; —, 1311
Tyther, Rev. John, 1104

Ueal, see Veale
Uffemore, Nic., 1504
Uggel (Vggel), Wm., 1379
Ulett, see Hewlett
Uley (Ewely, Ewley, Ywelege, Ywly), Peter de, 1369*; Ralph de, 529; —, 1369
Ulf (fl. 1066), 1014, 1050, 1051, 1052

Ulfeg (Ulfegh)(fl. 1066), 819, 870, 1401
Ulfelin (fl. 1066), 1316
Ulgar (fl. 1066), 1237
Ulkinton, Thos., 342
Ulton, —, and wife, 1316
Uluuin (fl. 1066), 1055
Ulvi (fl. 1066), 1015
Umfray, see Humphreys
Underhill, Ann, 1002; Frances, 1002; Geo., 1002*; Hannah, 1002; John, 88, 610, 1279; Kath., 1002*; Mary, 88, 1002; R. de, 1381; Sam., 1251; Sarah, 1251*; Thos., 1001; Wm., 610, 1002*; Rev. Wm., 1177; —, 206, 1292
Underwood (Underwode), Ann, 1236*; Anna Maria, 418; Blanch, 924; Edw., 1489; Hannah, 418; Joan, 906; John, 354, 906, 1579; Mary, 176, 418*, 563, 1236*, 1315, 1489; Mat., 1579; Moses, 1577, 1579; Nat., 418*; Nic., 418; Rebecker, 1579; Rob., 1236; Sam., 176*; Sarah, 176; Thos., 563, 1217, 1236*, 1238*, 1579; W., 1101; Wm., 418, 1236*; —, 1102; —, dean, 791; fam., 415
Unett (Unit), Cath., 265 n; Die [sic], 573; Eliz., 907; Jas., 907; Rev. Lingen, 498; Mary, 573*; Nat., 573*; Rob., 267
Unton, Sir Hen., 591
Unwin, John, 754
Upclive, Wm., 1422
Upcote, Christian de, 1502; John of, 1061
Upediche, Matilda, 1335
Upehulle, see Uphill
Uphatherley, Alisol (Alisot) of, 985*; Hen. of, 985; Thos. of, 985
Uphill (Upehulle, Uppe Hull, Upthehulle, Vppehull, Vppehulle), Alan, 1069; Dulcia, 1428; Ric., 1502; Rob., 1218, 1339; Thos., 1552; Wm., 1351, 1502
Upton, Ann, 1065; Geo., 1331; Rev. Geo., 1223, 1330, 1331; Mary, 1330; Rob., 1065; Wm., 337, 339
Urbane II, pope, 157
Urbran [sic], pope, 1477
Urch, John, 413
Urdle, R[ichar]d, 1082
Ursell, Eliz., 388; Hen., 388*; Mary, 388
Usher, Geo., 1425; John, 1424*; Marie, 1424
Uswold, R., 1186
Uvedale, Rev. Jas., 394, 396; Rob., 394
Uzett, John, 762; Mary, 762

Vachell, Francis, 1005; Sir T., kt., 1005*; Tanfield, 1005*
Vacherel, —, 1093
Vail (Vaile, Vale), Ann, 677; Dan., 677; Eliz., 264, 354, 627; Geo., 677; Hester, 677; Sam., 264, 354; Sarah, 677; W., 1447; Wm., 627
Vaillant, Frances, 1232
Vaisey (Veizey, Vesey, Veyse, Vezey), Abigail, 632; Anne, 1182*; Capel, 676; Eliz., 387*; Frances, 676; Hester, 1181; J., 1255; Mary, 387; Rob., 515; Sam., 1182; Simon, 1181, 1182; Stephen, 1182*; T., 1186; Thos., 387*; W., 1255; Wm., 632, 676*; —, 1017, 1257, 1258

Valander, *see* Vallender
Vale, *see* Vail
Valence (Valencia, Valentia), Aymer de, earl of Pembroke, 574, 885; Joan de, 885; Joan de, countess of Pembroke, 885; Wm. le, 1238; Wm. de, earl of Pembroke, 885, 1148; —, 1148*; fam., earls of Pembroke, 885*
Valentine, Algedus, 1227
Vallender (Valander), Ann(e), 857*, 1316; Benj., 857*; Esther, 858; John, 857; Mary, 857*; Phil., 1034; Thos., 858
Valletort, *see* Mount Edgecumbe
Van Geldar, —, 220 n
Van Leyden, Luca, 591 n
Van Notten, C., 1016; (later Pole), Chas., 502, 503; W., 1078
Vanbrugh (Vanburgh), Sir J., 719; Rev. Rob., 272
Vance, W., 1519
Vanderesch, Jacob, 1299; Mary, 1299
Vandyke, Sir Ant., 591 n; —, 220 n, 719 n*, 875 n
Vangerris, Col., 806 n
Vanlore, Peter, 391
Vannam, Eliz., 186, 1201; Rev. Geo., 186; Jane, 268; John, 191, 268, 1201*; Dr. John, 1201; Rev. John, 184*, 186; Mary, 191; Steven, 191; Dr., 186
Vansittart, Mr., 1378; —, 1378
Vanstone, Dan., 1258; Rev. Thos., 1335
Varnham, Ann, 872; Sarah, 174; Wm., 872
Vassall, Ann, 1119; Laura Ann M., 1119; Leonard, 1119; Sarah, 1119; —, 1120
Vaughan (Vaughane), Anne(e), 4, 1037; Baynham (Beynham), 1036*; Eliz., 1036, 1037, 1129; Frances, 1036; Herburt, 1554; Jas., 1529; Joan(e), 919, 1039; John, 4, 623*, 919, 1035, 1036*, 1037, 1039*, 1372; Jonathan, 4; Martha, 728*; Mary, 4, 5, 204; Nat., 820; Ric., 4*, 5, 1036, 1039*; Rog., 1036; Sarah, 1529; Thos., 204, 1036; Watkin, 1129; Wm., 5; Rev. Wm., 1087; Wm. Gwin, 728*; Mr., 1189; fam., 341, 577, 1039*
Vaulx, Editha, 860; Jas., 860; Philipe, 860
Vavasour, Sir W., 1293*
Veale (Ueal, Veal, Vealle, Veel, Veele, Vele, Vyel, Vyell), Alice, 249, 1345*; Anne, 1536; Cath., 15, 305; Chas., 573; Dorothy, 51, 1084, 1412; Edw., 42; Eliz., 1536; Geof. de, 778 n; Hawise (Howise), 778 n, 1345; John (le), 1311, 1312, 1345; Kath., 42; Mary, 573, 1365, 1525, 1526, 1537; Matilda de, 778 n; Nic. (de), 51*, 625; Peter le, 1345; Sir Peter (de, le), 305, 778 n; Ric., 870; Rob. (de), 778 n, 1311, 1345, 1524, 1551; Sarah, 1536; Thos., 249, 738, 1238, 1525*, 1537, 1552; Col. Thos., 51*; Sir Thos. de, 778 n; W., 1419; Wm., 15, 1084, 1365, 1404, 1524, 1536*, 1537, 1551; Col., 158; —, 1403; fam., 305
Vegler, Eliz., 975*; Geo., 975; Hannah, 975; Leonard, 975; Mary, 975; Ruth, 975
Veizey, *see* Vaisey
Vele, *see* Veale
Ven, *see* Venn
Venables, Anne, 1273; Peter, 1273; Sarah, 1273

Venfield, Giles, 889; John, 234; Ric., 505; Sarah, 118; Thos., 118; —, 1020
Venison, John, 10; Mary, 10; Mic., 10
Venn (Ven, Venne), Ann(e), 264, 701, 938; Arthur, 701*; Dorothy, 832; Eliza, 1529; Esther, 1529; Rev. G., 832; Rev. Geo., 263, 264, 820, 821; Hugh, 1522; John atte, 1428; Joseph, 820; Judith, 821; Martha, 701*; Mary, 701; Rebeckah, 936; Ric., 936, 938; Sir Ric., kt., 1521; Rob., 124*; Thos., 1529*; Wm., 701*; fam., 236
Venour (Venor), Hugh, 1538; John, 1331; —, 1460*
Verdune, —, 1237
Vere, Hor., Lord Vere, 1346; Sir Horatio (Horatius), 451, 1340, 1345, 1346
Vereby, John, 288
Verender (Verinder), Elianor, 450; Sam., 133; Thos., 1217; Wal., 450
Vergo (Virgo), Chas., 1511; John, 174; Joseph, 174; Wm., 174
Verinder, *see* Verender
Vernawls, —, 1186
Verney, Alice, 591, 1255; Esther, 623; Geo., 1255; Greville, Lord Willoughby de Broke, 1328; J., 1256; John, 623*; Marg., 1328; R., 1255; Ric., 1255; Dr. Ric., Lord Willoughby de Broke, 1328; Sir Ric., kt., 591, 1328; Sir T., 1255; Sir Thos., kt., 568, 591; —, 1255; fam., 1255
Vernon, Alice, 1149, 1151, 1282; Ann, 803; Arabella, 224, 1227; Caroline, 233; Chas., 233; Dorothea, 234; Dorothy, 233*, 234; Rev. Edw., 233*, 1388; Eleanor (Elinor), 635*; Eliz., 234, 1045*; Rev. Geo., 233, 234; Hannah, 847; Harriet, 939; Haward, 1045*; Hen., 233; John, 514, 634, 939; Mary, 939, 1045*; Ric., 445*; Rev. Ric., 233, 234, 1149, 1151; Sam., 803; Sarah, 514; Thos., 234, 635*, 1045*, 1227, 1228, 1282; Sir Thos., 224; W. Hughes, 1047; Wm., 847, 1045, 1282; Rev. Wm., 233; Mr., 1189; Rev., 1362; fam., 232, 444
Vernum, Eliz., 229; Sam., 229
Verry (Verrey, Very), Abigail, 1131*; Eliz., 621; Jas., 473, 1131; Joan, 563; John, 563, 623, 1396*; Mary, 1396; Phillis, 871; Rob., 621, 871*, 873; Sam., 623, 873*, 1396; Sibell, 871; Thos., 1131*, 1132
Vertue, —, 864 n
Verulam [*peerage*], Francis, Lord, 323 n*; Lord, 324
Very, *see* Verry
Vescy, Lord, 721 n
Vesey, *see* Vaisey
Vevers, Joseph, 1273; Susannah, 1273; Wm., 1273
Veyayn, Hen. le, 1069; Ric. le, 1069
Veyse, *see* Vaisey
Veysyn, John le, 1483
Vezey, *see* Vaisey
Vggel, *see* Uggel
Vicain, Alice, 1052; Hen., 1052
Vicarage, *see* Vicaridge
Vicaresse, *see* Vickars
Vicaria, *see* Vicary

Vicaridge (Vicarage, Vickaridge), Chas., 818; John, 1268; —, 1293; *and see* Vicary
Vicariis (Vicaris), *see* Vickars
Vicary (Vicaria, Vicory, Vykery), Nic., 1502; Rob., 1504; Wm. le, 1539; —, 1069; *and see* Vicaridge
Vick (Vich), Alice, 923*; Ann(e), 584*, 656; Bridget, 160*; Frances, 656; Grace, 584; Jasper, 923; John, 348, 655, 656*, 923; Marg., 584; Mary, 655, 656*; Rebecca, 651, 656; Ric., 1317; Sarah, 584*; Silvanus, 584*; Stephen, 923; Wm., 584*, 651, 656, 923*, 1217; —, 1455
Vickaridge, *see* Vicaridge
Vickars (Vicaresse, Vicariis, Vicaris), Ann, 398; Hannah, 1503; John, 1503; Mary, 1503; Wm., 398, 1504; —, 1504*
Vicory, *see* Vicary
Vidler, Eliz., 1159*; Mary, 1159; Ric., 1159*
Vigor, Dorothy, 1557; Eliz., 1557; Frances, 1557*; John 1557; Wm., 1555, 1557*
Vickersman, Rob. de, 1476
Villiers (Villars, Villers, Vylers), Alex. de, 507 n; Sir Edw., 475; Nic. de, 507*
Vimpany (Vimpeny), Mary, 731; Wm., 729
Vincent, Eliz., 1389; Sir Francis, bt., 665*; John, 1389; —, 1380
Viner (Vinor, Vyner), Anne, 981, 1305; Benj., 839, 841, 842, 981; Chas., 20*; Eliz., 262, 842; Geo., 981*; Giles, 348; Grace, 20; John, 683, 762, 842; Josiah, 981; Mary, 20, 683, 981; Ric., 20*; Rob., 20*, 981*, 1217, 1305; Sarah, 20; Thos., 262, 353, 842; Rev. Thos., 1104; Wm., 348
Vines (Vyne), Isaac, 1532; Mark, 1539; Mary, 492, 1008, 1532; Peter, 492; Rog. atte, 1385; Sarah, 1532; Thos., 1532, 1539; Wm., 1008
Viney, —, 1047, 1238
Vinor, *see* Viner
Vinot, John, 1372; Thos., 1372
Vinton, Jas., 543; Thos., 543
Vipont, Isabel de, 720 n; Lord Rob. de, 720 n
Virgo, *see* Vergo
Vizard (Vizar, Vizer), Anne, 1166; Arthur, 531, 540, 542, 939, 1539; Edw., 661; Eliz., 939; Hannah, 540*; Hen., 1250; Hester, 661; Isabela, 1166*; Jeremiah, 661*; Jas. Bryan, 1250; John, 537, 540*, 542, 1166*; John [viz. Joan], 542; Martha, 540; Mary, 540; Sarah, 1250; Wm., 1121, 1250; —, 1169, 1512*; fam., 415, 532
Vobes (Vobe), Mary, 1130; Thos., 1006, 1130*; Wal., 1317; Wm., 1317
Voccings, *see* Vokins
Voice, German, 924; Hester, 77; Jo[a]ne, 77; John, 465; Mary, 77; Sarah, 465*; Wm., 77*
Vokins (Voccings, Vokin), Cath., 1004; Hopeful, 368; Wm., 1004; —, 1005, 1257*
Vorst, —, 1093
Vounar, Benedict, 1404
Vowles, Ann, 1427; John, 1427*; Mary, 1423, 1426*; Sam, 1426*; Sarah, 1427
Vppehull (Vppehulle), *see* Uphill
Vychan, Rev. Thos., 760
Vyel (Vyell), *see* Veale
Vykery, *see* Vicary

Vylers, *see* Villiers
Vyll, *see* Fill
Vyne, *see* Vines
Vyner, *see* Viner

Waake, *see* Wake
Waddington (Wadington), Eliz., 983; Sarah, 982–3; Wm., 982–3*; —, 986
Wade, Ann(e), 111, 170*, 604, 620*, 1098; Chas., 735*, 1103; Edw., 47*, 960, 1405; Elinor, 604; Eliz., 111, 731, 812, 1518; Esther, 887; J., 1052; Jas., 811*; Jane, 47, 735; John, 111, 170*, 214*, 503*, 577, 604*, 620, 731, 740, 811, 941, 1228, 1491, 1513; Mary, 112*, 604, 727, 811*, 815; Matillda, 1504; Nic., 1363; Ric., 112, 1098*; Sarah, 170, 620, 731, 735*, 811, 1098*; Thos., 111*, 112*, 214, 463, 604, 620*, 811*, 812, 815; Wilkins, 727*; Wm., 170*, 735*, 1518; Mr., 1512; —, 1501*; fam., 214*
Wadeham, *see* Wadham
Wadeson, J. W., 1216
Wadham (Wadeham), Dorothy, 233 n, 1126; John, 1491; —, 1339
Wadington, *see* Waddington
Wadley (Wadly), Anne, 1268; Bridget, 1268; Dennice, 1481; Edw., 442; Eliz., 442, 907; Jane, 907; John, 907, 1268*; Mary, 1481; Thos., 442*; Wm., 907
Waffaire, Rev. John, 895
Wager, Ric., 317; Wal., 1061*
Wagett, Ric., 316; Sarah, 316
Wagstaffe (Wagstaff), Alice, 1432; Bazel, 683; Eliz., 1432; Frances, 1432; Hen., 856; John, 1289; Marg., 1432; Ric. 1432; Thos., 1432
Waife, John, 666;
Waight, *see* Waite
Wailpy, Rev. Thos., 342
Waine, Ann(e), 38*; Cath., 38; Giles, 38*; John, 38*; Thos., 38; —, 1005
Wainwright, Ann, 1511
Waite (Waight, Wait, Wate, Wayt, Wayte, Weight), Agnes, 1314; And., 1433; Betty, 387, 847; Cath., 954; Chas., 953, 954*; Dan., 1167; Edw., 1167*; Eleanor, 847; Eliz., 730, 1004, 1159, 1167*; Hen., 376; John, 419, 543, 701, 847, 1427; Marg., 1250; Mary, 320, 376, 1439; Nat., 1146*, 1147; Peter, 540; Ric. (atte), 387*, 730, 1356; Rob., 540*; Sam., 1439; Sarah, 540*, 1146, 1159; Thos., 387, 1159; Wm., 376, 730, 847, 1433; —, 1169, 1311
Wake (Waake, Weake), Baldwin, 251 n; Rev. Edw., 21, 255; Hannah, 862; Jane, 398; John, 661; Marg., 661; Martha, 1212; Sam., 862; Wm., 398*, 1212*
Wakefield (Wakfield), Anne, 644; Eliz., 689; Frances, 1016; Hen., bishop, 218, 717, 747; John, 569*, 623, 644, 689; Rev. John, 1016; Mary, 569*, 623, 1043; Peter, 517; Rob., 1015, 1016*, 1043*; Sarah, 517; Susannah, 569; Wm., 146, 176, 1388; —, 1014, 1017, 1221
Wakeham, Ruth, 411; Wm., 411*
Wakeman, Anne, 148, 1278; Bened., 89, 147; Edw.,

148, 1278; Eliz., 1278*; Hen., 71, 72, 89, 147, 148; John, 147, 1237, 1278; John, abbot, 1261; John (or Rob.), bishop, 609; Mary, 148, 1278; Ric., 148; Thos., 1288; W., 1288, 1290; Wm., 1278*, 1290, 1357; Madam, 148; Mr., 147; —, 986, 1288*, 1289, 1293; fam., 147

Wakfield, *see* Wakefield

Walbank (Wallbank), Ann(e), 114, 117; Hester, 253; Mat., 253*; Sam., 114, 579, 1403; Rev. Wm., 449; fam., 252, 649*

Walch (Walche), *see* Walsh

Walcote (Wallecote), John, 1329; Wm. de, 1329

Waldegrave, Jas., earl of, 691 n; Mary, countess of, 691 n

Walden (Walding), Chas., 468; Geo., 5; Joan, 814; Marg., 468; Mary, 468; Rob., 814; Thos., 468

Waldhari (priest, fl. 706), 1227

Walding, *see* Walden

Waldo, Emma, 25; Mary, 25

Waldron (Waldren, Weldron), Chas., 1037; Rev. Francis, 302; Mary, 1510*; Sarah, 1272; Thos., 1289; Wm., 1510*

Waleran (Walerand), *see* Walrond

Wales, Fred., prince of, 1440*; *and see* Rhese; princess of, 1440

Walesworth, Ralph de, 1047; Wm. de, 1047; *and see* Woolworth

Waleys, *see* Wallis

Walford, Ann, 1003*; Edw., 1003*; Elianor, 402; Mary, 402, 1003*; Mat., 1003; Theophilus, 804*; Thos., 818, 1003*; Wm., 402, 804*, 1150

Walker (Walkare, Walkere), Allin, 241*; Ann(e), 124, 295, 450, 756, 1298, 1499; Benj., 18; Charity, 442; Chas., 52, 814, 1542; Rev. Chas., 1102; Dan., 696, 1328; Edw., 296, 1150, 1151; Eliz., 35, 241, 423*, 437*, 758, 814, 891, 1268, 1584; Ezekiel, 1009; Frances, 758; Francis, 1573; Hannah, 550, 1150, 1151, 1278; Hester, 52*, 1009; Isaac, 1258; Rev. J., 1126; Jacob, 1278; Jas., 1356; Rev. Jas., 1127; Jane, 296, 701; Joanna, 413; John, 124, 133, 413, 423*, 550, 701*, 758*, 814, 1009, 1154, 1350, 1543, 1546, 1549*, 1550, 1551; Capt. John, 1562; Rev. John, 442, 1289; Joseph, 35, 423, 891*, 1301; Rev. Joseph, 1076; Joseph Harry, 1542; Joyce, 52, 756*, 1326; Kate, 1542; Mary, 18, 35, 52, 450, 756, 814, 891, 1415, 1542*, 1545, 1549, 1584*; Phil., 1584*; R., 349 n; Rachel, 755; Ralph le, 1027; Rebecca, 1542; Ric. (le), 437, 580, 797*, 1441; Rev. Ric., 328, 754; Rob., 1545*; Sam., 52, 295, 450, 701, 1326, 1328; Sarah, 758, 1009*; Silvester, 701; Thos., 437*, 450*, 756, 796, 891*, 1009*, 1312, 1542*; Toby, 1121; Wm. (le), 755, 756*, 758, 814, 1069, 1268*, 1273, 1362, 1440; Rev. Wm., 124, 128; Rev., 1095; —, 288 n, 1043, 1220

Walkins, Jas., 1551

Walklett, Edw., 795; Mary, 598; Ric., 598

Walkley, Anna Maria, 751; Ant., 1218; Dan., 662, 751; Eliz., 662; Hannah, 1548; Jacob, 1510; John, 1548; Ric., 1396; S., 662; Sam., 662; Susanna, 1548

Wall (Walle, Walls), Ambrose, 412; Caleb, 1073; Cath., 267, 546; Dorothea, 319, 1497; Dorothy, 319, 547*, 548, 1497; Edw., 730; Eliz., 856, 1152; Eliz. Pye, 548; Geof., 1497; Rev. Geo., 259, 713, 856; Capt. Gerard, 1152; Hen., 1020; Rev. Hugh, 685; Jane, 174; Jeffrey, 1497; Rev. Geof. (Jeffrey), 319*, 1497; John, 174, 360 n, 584*, 752, 905, 907, 1280, 1367, 1497; Lieut.-Col. John, 1280; Rev. John, 99, 259, 452, 567, 582, 856*, 1222, 1223; Joseph, 584, 1103; Kath., 548; Lucy, 1497; Marg., 977; Mary, 319, 548, 584*, 687, 730, 752, 907; Penelope, 548; Phil., 584*; Ric., 319, 687; Lieut.-Col. Rob. Martin Popham, 1280; Sarah, 584; Susannah, 1073; Thos., 267, 546*, 547*, 548*, 584*; W., 1103; Wm., 547*, 548*, 584, 977, 1103, 1140, 1497; Mr., 1189; —, 1287; fam., 546, 894

Wallace (Wallas), *see* Wallis

Wallbank, *see* Walbank

Walle, *see* Wall

Wallecote, *see* Walcote

Waller, Edm., 78, 599*, 600, 688, 689; Rev. Harry, 599; Mary, 1088, 1106; Rob., 1106; Tobias, 1106*; Sir W., 1219; Sir Wm., 6, 341, 349 n, 350 n, 1035, 1293*, 1339; Mr., 1350*, 1351*

Walleran, *see* Walrond

Wallery [? St. Valery], —, 1475

Walleye, *see* Whalley

Wallin, *see* Walwyn

Wallington, Alice, 749; Ann(e), 994, 1530; Arnel, 608; Chas., 1530, 1531, 1539; Rev. Chas., 537, 619, 668, 783; Edw., 1525*, 1530; Rev. Hugh, 994*; J., 1169*; Jacob, 531*, 541; John, 227, 532, 749, 1168, 1169, 1531*; Mary, 537, 1530, 1531*; Rev. Mic., 519; Paul, 749; Rebeckah, 655; Ric., 1531*; Rev. Ric., 748, 749, 1543, 1545, 1552; Sam., 531, 532, 1531; Sarah, 994*; Susanna(h), 1525, 1530; Thos., 531, 537; Tim., 531; Walker, 994; Wm., 655, 994, 1177, 1522, 1531*; Rev. Wm., 1477; Mr., 994; fam., 532

Wallis (Waleys, Wallace, Wallas), Betty, 750; Cath., 1108*, 1109; Eliz., 751, 1109; Frances, 1548; Hannah, 1548; Jas., 413, 1105, 1108*, 1109; John, 750, 910, 1534; Joseph, 1121; Kath., 910, 1108*; Kitty, 1108; Marg., 910; Mary, 910, 1535*; Ralph (Rad.), 1101; Rob., 750, 910*, 1535; Sam., 1108; Susannah, 413; T., 1316, 1317; Thos., 730, 1547; Rev. Thos., 1186; Wm., 750, 751, 1535*; Rev. Wm., 840; —, 1092

Walls, *see* Wall

Wallshe, *see* Walsh

Wallwyn, *see* Walwyn

Wally, *see* Whalley

Wallyncote, Rev. Thos., 184

Walmesley, Rev. Hen., 1257

Walpole, H., 1313; Horace, 1380; Sir Rob., 363 n, 1198

Walrond (Waleran, Walerand, Walleran), Alice, 1086; Isabell(a), 1086, 1237; Matilda, 1237; Rob. (de), 244, 420, 612, 1086; —, 1237

Walsh (Walch, Walche, Wallshe, Walshe), Alice, 1202; Edw., 630; Eliz., 576, 1121; Hen., 576,

1120; J., 1101; John (le), 1120, 1121, 1123, 1214, 1217, 1292, 1428, 1490; Sir John, 576*, 1120, 1123*, 1428; Maur. (le), 576, 1120, 1202; Nic., 576, 1120; Ralph, 1490; Wal., 576, 1120; Master, 1121; —, 1121, 1386, 1490*; fam., 1121; *and see* Welch

Walsingham, Augusta Georgina Eliz., 852 n

Walsned, John, 1165

Walter, abbot, 359

Walter, bishop of Worcester, *see* Maydenstone

Walter, sheriff, 301, 1422

Walter *balistarius*, *see* Balistarius

Walter son of Roger, 1060

Walter (? fl. *c.* 1000), 1195

Walters (Walter, Waltres), Ann, 1397, 1409; Chas., 413; Edw., 100, 984, 1397; Eliz., 437, 961, 1157; Geo., 1139; J., 1323; Jane, 3, 463, 469, 1155, 1157*; John, 746, 832, 1015, 1105*, 1112*, 1121, 1329, 1408; Sir John, 437; Lucy, 1153; Marg., 100, 984; Mary, 832, 984, 1105, 1112*, 1155*, 1408; Mat., 1157*; R., 985; Ric., 1378, 1409*; Rowles, 3, 1155*, 1156; Thos., 3, 746, 961, 984, 1155*, 1157*, 1428; (or of Tetbury), Wal., 1256*; Wm., 924*, 1112, 1329, 1408*, 1409*; —, 985*, 986, 1011*, 1160, 1256, 1257; fam., 745, 1160

Walton, H., 1477; John (de), 1292, 1578; John Francis, 1578; Joseph, 305; Judith, 1578; Nic. de, 1292

Waltres, *see* Walters

Walward (fl. 1066), 1077*

Walwyn (Wallin, Wallwyn, Walweyne, Walwin), Alice, 462, 464, 913, 1039, 1401; Edm., 330; Rev. Gabriel, 1404; John, 327, 1229, 1233; Ric., 463, 895, 900; Sibill, 1039; Thos., 467, 468; W., 1039; Wm., 462, 464, 913, 1039; —, 867, 1232, 1401

Wanley (Wansley), And., 1089*, 1090; Anne, 1090; Frances, 1089; Hen., 1037; Humph., 1093; Rob. Bowles, 1090; Wm., 1089, 1090*

Wanswell, —, 1147

Want, Rob., 847; Susannah, 847

Wantner (Wontner), Abel, 943, 1189; Cath., 1473; Edw., 1473; —, 1189

Wanton, W. de, 1147

Wappelegh, Wal. de, 1385

Warbott, Wm., 360 n

Warben, Rev. John, 1006

Warburton, Frances, 535; Wm., 1040; Dr. Wm., bishop, 535

Ward (Warde), Ann(e), 337, 399, 1065; Ant., 473; Barbara, 501; Rev. Bernard John, 1150; Bridget, 962; Rev. Chas. Ric. 1384; Edm., 209; Eliz., 473; Emma E., 1516; Francis, 1417, 1473; Hen., 59, 868; Jane, 1473; John, 337, 473, 551 n, 552, 924, 1065, 1516; Rev. John, 500; Joyce, 337; Mary Sadler, 1516; Ric., 962; Rev. Ric., 1385; Rob., 923, 1516, Rog. le, 1478; Sarah, 980; Thos., 226, 473, 1288; Rev. Thos., 501, 574*; Wm., 337, 399, 980; —, 574

Warder, Ann, 340; Mary, 398; Sarah, 398; Simeon, 398; Thos., 340, 398

Warderobe, Nic., 1540

Ware (Weare, Were), Ann(e), 368, 382, 489, 1029; Edw., 303*; Eliz., 303, 352, 1038; Geo., 382*, 489, 1029; Hen. (atte), 208*, 489, 554*, 1292, 1300*; Jane, 382; Mary, 208*, 382*, 554, 1300*; Penelope, 489, 554; Phil., 208; Ric. (de), 1038, 1331; Rob., lord of, 720*; Sarah, 303; Susanna, 1300*; Thos., 352, 382, 553, 554, 1428; Thos., abbot, 605; Wm., 208, 551 n*, 552, 554; —, 302; fam., 301; *and see* Wyer

Wariner, *see* Warner

Waring (Wearing), Chas., 339; Stephen, 1289; Wm., 623

Warjohn, John, 906

Warkman, Eliz. 1269*; Grace, 1269; Hannah, 1269; Rachel, 1269; Rob., 1269; Thos., 1269*; *and see* Workman

Warlock (Warlick), *see* Worlock

Warmstree (Warmstrey), Rev. Thos., 651

Warne (Warn), Anne, 907*; Edm., 902; Eliz., 206*; J., 1288*; Jas., 905, 1258; John, 902, 905*, 907, 1103; (or Warren), John, 1103; Sarah, 905; Susannah, 907*; Thos., 689, 902, 907*, 1150, 1288; W., 1288; Wm., 905*; —, 1477; (or Warren), —, 1150

Warneford (Warnford), Anne, 880; Rev. Chas., 1001; Edm., 183, 185; Rev. Edw., 1487; Eliz., 185, 970; Rev. Francis, 1422; Hen., 879; Rev. John, 696; Mary, 970; Thos., 879*; Capt., 358; —, 1459

Warner (Wariner, Warnar), Ann(e), 562, 676, 1182; Chas., 463; Christian, 562; Edw., 563, 674, 1438; Eliz., 170, 1208; John (le), 170, 562, 1099, 1136*, 1447; Rev. John, 671 n; Lee, 236*; Marg., 676, 1438; Mary, 562, 563, 920, 1136; R., 1447; Ric., 563, 1218; Rob., 226, 1446*; Sarah, 1099, 1446; T., 1447; Thos., 622, 920, 1121, 1136, 1208*, 1215*, 1447; Wal., 676; Wm., 562, 671 n, 676*, 1099, 1121, 1182, 1215, 1460; —, 1122, 1447; fam., 671, 672

Warnford, *see* Warneford

Warr, Ann, 965; John (de la, le), 903, 965, 1455, 1456; Marg., 965*; Martha, 965; Patience, 903; Reg. le, 1455; Thos., 964, 965*; Wm., 964, 965, 1420; Lord de la, 1456; — de la, 1455; *and see* Delaware

Warrall (Warrell), *see* Worrell

Warren, Ann(e), 48*, 187, 744, 1359; Cath., 744; David, 743, 744*, 1475; David, Lord Lisle, 1539; Dorothea, 68; Edw., 108; Rev. Edw., 147; Eleanor (Elianor), 187, 627; Eliz., 397, 406, 845, 1391; J., 1061; Jane, 1564; Jasper, 187; John, 48*, 110, 744*, 845, 1092, 1149, 1151, 1362*, 1391*, 1469*; (or Warne), John, 1103; Dr. John, bishop, 205; Rev. John, 770, 890, 1217; Joseph, 108; Marg., 1539; Mariana, 245; Mary, 108, 110, 250, 732, 1151, 1277; Ric., 68, 108, 308; Rob., 124, 187*, 1152; Sam., 397; Sarah, 124, 308, 1152; Stephen, 660; Thos., 1149, 1151, 1359, 1362, 1564*; Wm., 245*, 246, 250, 627, 732, 907; —, 1477; (or Warne) —, 1150; fam., 1362, 1475; *and see* Warwin

Warte, Alice, 906; Rob., 906

Warthim, Rev. Phil., 221, 223

Wartnalby, Joseph, 1511

Warwick [*peerage*], Anne, countess of, 591, 634, 1082, 1120, 1348, 1521*; Cicely, duchess of, 318, 805; Geo., earl of, 628, 630; Isabella, countess of, 1082, 1120; John, earl of, 1103, 1195; Ric., earl of, 763, 1082; Walerand, earl of, 805; countess of, 1159; earl of, 318, 500, 592, 1120, 1159, 1287, 1288, 1348, 1382; *and see* Beauchamp, *passim*; Berkeley, Eliz.; Dudley, Ambrose, Anne, *and* —; Neville, Anne *and* Ric.; Newburgh, Hen. de *and* fam.

Warwin, Margery, 1259; *and see* Warren

Waryhulle, Nic. de, 1372

Wasborow (Wasborough, Washborow), Charity, 1409; Cicely (Cicelia), 726*, 727; Edith, 727; Eliz., 727; Hannah, 727; Hen., 613, 726, 727*; John, 726, 727*, 1405, 1409*; Martha, 726; Mary, 727; Sarah, 726, 727*; Thos., 726*, 727*

Wasey, Rev. Geo., 1442

Washborn (Washborne), *see* Washbourne

Washborow, *see* Wasborow

Washbourne (Washborn, Washborne, Washbourn, Washburne, Wassheboure), Agnes, 1432; Ann, 758; Cath., 1432; Eliz., 1432; Joan, 1432; John, 758, 879, 1504, 1563*; Rev. John, 365, 878, 1080; Lydia, 540; Marg., 1432; Mary, 879, 911, 1563*; Nat., 1217; Sarah (Sarr.) de, 1387; Stephen, 911, 1258; Thos., 722; Rev. Tho[s]., 519; Wm., 1432; Dr., 1189; —, 1504; fam., 1092

Washbrook, Eliz., 1065; John, 1065

Washburne, *see* Washbourne

Wasing, Edw., 1431

Wasley, Dan., 398*, 399; John, 399; Mary, 398*, 399*

Wassemers, John, 1456

Wassheboure, *see* Washbourne

Wasteft, T., 1419

Wastfield, Ann, 699; Barbarah, 699; Ric., 699*

Wastin, Geo., 1537

Wate, *see* Waite

Waterford, And., 841*, 843*; Eliz., 841; John, 841, 843; Sarah, 841; Wm., 841

Waterman, Rev. Hugh, 962*; Ric., 1062

Waters, Anne, 329*; Francis, 213; Jas., 1584; Mary, 329, 933; Ric., 933; Rog. atte, 1102; Thos., 329*, 1403; Wm., 933*; —, 1282

Watershipp (Wat'schop), Hugh, 1385; John, 1538

Wathen (Wathan, Wathern, Watthen), Ann Maria, 1511; Anna, 1026, 1532; Ann(e), 35, 1136, 1208*, 1212, 1275, 1532; Cath., 1511; D., 1133, 1140; Edw. Leversage, 1136; Eliz., 1024*, 1133*, 1135, 1138, 1209, 1510, 1511; Eliz. Martha, 1209; Ellen, 1511; Ellen Wood, 1209; Geo., 1136, 1215; Hawtry, 1511; Isabel, 1511; John, 873, 1137*, 1377; John Hayward, 1136; Jonathan, 1209, 1212; Joseph, 49, 1024, 1207, 1208, 1209, 1212*, 1216, 1217, 1511; Joseph Sheppard, 1209; Julia, 1511; Marg., 1136; Marg. Peach, 1511; Mary, 35, 49, 873, 1137, 1510, 1511; N. P., 1511; Nat., 1140; Nat. Peach, 1511;

Obadiah Paul, 1511; Paul, 1139*, 1203, 1215; Peach, 1511; Phil., 1026, 1510; Rebecca, 1137; Sam., 35*, 940, 1133, 1135, 1209*, 1211, 1216, 1275, 1434; Sir Sam., kt., 1136*, 1139, 1511*, 1512; Sarah, 940, 1136, 1138, 1209; Sarah Eliz., 1136; Thos., 661, 1136, 1138*, 1140, 1532; W., 1216; Wm., 662*, 1024*, 1207, 1208, 1377*; Wm. Hen., 1209; —, 1139*, 1203, 1282

Watkins (Watkin, Watkyns), Abraham, 564; Alice, 922; Ann, 200, 541, 1053, 1320, 1575; Benj., 1053*; Betty, 1038; Cath., 203; Christian, 1307; Dorothy, 1320; Edw., 1320; Eleanor, 797; Esther, 538; Eliz., 541, 564, 676, 731, 923, 999, 1515; Evans, 1575; Geo., 677, 1038, 1039; Rev. Giles, 1444; Grace, 435; Rev. Hen., 1223; Isabel(l), 591, 1255; Jas., 339, 933, 1065; Jane, 730; Johanna, 933; John, 200*, 435, 531, 538*, 541*, 615*, 730*, 923, 924*, 1039, 1054, 1092, 1319*, 1320; Rev. John Burton, 840; Lewis, 591, 815; Marg., 1320; Martha, 1037, 1049, 1222; Mary, 52, 924*, 1053*, 1054, 1222; Phil., 676, 1037, 1307; Rebeccah (Rebecka), 133, 1222; Ric., 1130, 1515; Rev. Ric., 230; Rob., 1049; Sam., 999, 1053, 1054, 1211*–12; Sara(h), 133*, 615, 677, 1130, 1211, 1212, 1222*; Susanna(h), 815, 1509; Thos., 531, 730, 1211*, 1319, 1323, 1575; Wm., 52*, 133*, 203, 731, 797, 820, 922, 963, 1037, 1320, 1323, 1378, 1515*, 1516; —, 1132, 1255, 1311

Wats, *see* Watts

Wat'schop, *see* Watershipp

Watson (Watsone), Anne, 621; Cath., 724*, 1265; Cath., countess of Rockingham, 724; Edw., Lord Sondes, 724*; Jas., 1511; Rev. Jas., 691; John, bishop, 1126; Kath., 719 n*; Lewis, earl of Rockingham, 724*; T., 1201; Thos., 1120, 1126, 1201; Wm., 621; —, 1104, 1201*; —, bishop, 1428; *and see* Huatson

Watt (Wattes), *see* Watts

Watteville, Rog. de, 634

Watthen, *see* Wathen

Watts (Wats, Watt, Wattes, Wattis), Alice, 1371; Amelia, 697; Ann(e), 70, 283, 308, 496, 837, 847, 954, 1098, 1212, 1280, 1338, 1453; Arthur, 633*, 1111; Betty, 835; Chas., 133; Dan., 1097; E., 1216; Edith, 496; Edm., 1453; Edw., 175, 837, 954*, 1539; Eliz., 172, 175*, 1117, 1213; Geo., 124, 175*, 496*, 1097*, 1098, 1099*; Hen., 835; Hester, 899; Isabella (Isabelle), 1097, 1099; Jas., 954, 963, 1097*, 1098*, 1099, 1534; Jane, 124, 787, 835, 954, 1111, 1117; Jeffry, 1492; Joanna, 835; John, 133, 172, 175*, 749, 786, 787, 815*, 899, 984, 1062, 1097, 1098, 1117, 1258, 1352, 1371; Rev. John, 1339; Joseph, 1215; Kath., 133; Lydia, 803; Margery, 1339; Mary, 171, 175, 283, 486, 749, 835*, 954, 1097*, 1098, 1117, 1212, 1371, 1492, 1494; Maur., 496; Morris, 1117*; Nat., 496*, 1183, 1211, 1213, 1217; Priscilla, 1183, 1213; R., 1027; Ric., 239, 283, 678, 872, 1213, 1218, 1338*; Rev. Ric. Fowele, 1171; Rob., 486; Ruth, 239; Sam., 847, 1097, 1203, 1212*; Sarah, 70*, 124, 1097, 1211,

1534; Sibil, 907; Stephen, 835*; Susanna, 308; Tabitha, 133; Thos., 70, 121, 124*, 133, 175, 308*, 837, 954, 1117*, 1121; Ursulla, 175; Wm., 308*, 697, 803, 872, 907, 1097, 1117, 1217, 1338, 1371*, 1534*; Mr., 619 n; Rev., 401; —, 1020, 1216, 1455

Waugh, Eliz., 410; John, 410; Joseph, 1415; Joseph Thos., 1415

Wayland (Weyland), Margery, 1120; Ric., 1120; Thos. de, 1120*; Wm. de, 1120

Waynman (Wayneman), R[ichar]d, 1062, 1078; Thos., 1062

Wayt (Wayte), *see* Waite

Weake, *see* Wake

Wealch, *see* Welch

Weale (Weal, Wheale), Ann(e), 270, 549, 871; Eliz., 1273; Hester, 549; Joseph, 549; John, 270*, 549, 762; Margery, 549; Mary, 762; Ric., 111; Thos., 631, 1273*; Wm., 547, 549*, 939; —, 1238, 1289; fam., 546

Wealedarke, Wm., 1289

Weare, *see* Ware

Wearing, *see* Waring

Wearitan (fl. 800), 770

Weaver (Weyver), Ann, 74; Eleanor, 412; Eliz., 906; Hen., 74*; Jane, 1244; Joan, 74, 1389; Joseph, 542*; Mary, 340*, 904, 906, 1065; (or Lyche), Rev. Rob., 1346; Sam., 412; Sarah, 542*; Thos., 1389; Wm., 340, 904, 906, 1065*; —, 1292; (or Baker), —, 1355; *and see* Textor

Weaving, John, 661, 693; Mary, 693; Rob., 693

Webb (Web, Webbe, Werb), A. G., 1328; Abraham, 1415; Adam le, 1346; Alice, 750; Ambrose, 93, 908; Anna, 1244; Anna Maria, 691 n; Ann(e), 18*, 202, 399, 442, 454, 456, 616*, 633, 658, 662, 681*, 682*, 703, 730, 731, 842, 911, 954*, 1014, 1038, 1106*, 1107, 1278, 1413, 1510, 1524*, 1525, 1545; Ant., 316*, 396*, 780; Barbara, 691 n; Rev. Benj., 279*, 470, 1169; Betty, 49, 1200; Brice, 456*, 1303; Cath., 453; Chas., 633, 911, 1153; Christian, 1525; Chris., 842*, 976*, 1545; (or Woolworth), Chris., 530; Dan., 460*, 543, 550, 651, 655, 658, 662*, 730, 750, 938, 1111*, 1121, 1512*, 1535; Deborah, 1209*; Dorothy, 460; E., 970, 1027; Edm., 909, 971*; (or Woolworth), Edm., 529; Edw., 16*, 616, 658, 662*, 748, 749, 750, 781, 909, 910*, 970, 1250, 1512; Rev. Edw., 909; Eleanor, 1108*; Eliz., 17*, 48, 111, 166, 182, 202, 399, 455, 460*, 540*, 658*, 662, 840*, 843, 909, 910*, 931, 938, 948, 955, 967, 976, 1091, 1108, 1174, 1194*, 1206*–7, 1216, 1301, 1326, 1386, 1452, 1512*, 1535, 1580; Frances, 954, 1153*; Francis, 847, 1483; Rev. Francis, 643*, 1484, 1485; Geo., 843, 938*, 1106*, 1107, 1113, 1115, 1405, 1410; Capt. Geo., 1413; Giles, 18, 337; Giles Loringe, 18; Godsall, 1579, 1580*; Grace, 986; Hannah, 171, 1200*, 1452, 1510; Hen., 974*, 1106*, 1111; Hester, 14, 163, 182*, 1525, 1535; Hezekiah, 17*; Isaac, 49, 948, 1488; J., 1328; Jacob, 1488; Jas., 49, 111*, 450* 658; Jane, 316, 910*, 1037, 1083, 1215, 1250*, 1376, 1377, 1566; Jared, 396;

Jasper, 1014; Jeane, 1023; Jo(a)n(e), 450, 543, 847, 971, 1023, 1410, 1483; John (le), 17, 18*, 52, 111, 163, 171, 531, 540, 616*, 631*, 633*, 655, 658*, 661, 662*, 703, 731*, 792, 850, 933*, 970, 1023*, 1153*, 1194, 1196, 1206*, 1209, 1210, 1211*, 1215*, 1216, 1258, 1278, 1301, 1420, 1452*, 1477, 1488, 1512, 1535, 1537, 1539, 1573*; Rev. John, 66, 713, 1012*, 1016, 1266; Sir John, bt., 568*, 690*, 691*, 692*, 693, 792; Jonathan, 1038, 1039; Joseph, 399*, 455, 550, 616; Kath., 1209; King, 460; Kisiah, 1194; Lucia, 453*; Lucy, 843; Luke, 616; Marg., 536, 910*, 1106; Martha, 450, 656, 976, 1106*, 1112, 1113, 1301, 1510; Mary, 5, 16*, 17, 18, 49, 52, 70, 111*, 182, 254, 396*, 453, 460*, 540, 616, 658, 661, 677, 690, 691 & n, 692, 749*, 750, 781*, 843, 850, 910, 933, 938, 939, 1063, 1106, 1111, 1155*, 1160*, 1194*, 1210*, 1211, 1266, 1301, 1325*, 1326, 1344, 1405, 1410, 1413, 1512, 1525, 1573; Matilda le, 1127; N., 1216, 1328; Nancy, 1106; Nat., 460, 536, 656, 658*, 750*, 1106, 1510, 1512*; Nehemiah, 17*; Nic., 52*, 197, 841, 842*, 1174, 1175*, 1176, 1326, 1524, 1525*; (or Richmond), Nic., 839; Obadiah (Obediah), 166, 531, 540, 1413*; Persis, 780; Rachael, 662; Rev. Ralph, 161; Rebecca (Rebeckah), 474, 1107, 1108, 1579*; Ric., 5, 70*, 95*, 111*, 171*, 396*, 454, 658*, 661, 662, 749, 780*, 800, 850, 931*, 967*, 986, 1083, 1091, 1171, 1194, 1206, 1210*, 1250, 1301, 1302, 1328, 1386; (or Woolworth), Ric., 529; Rev. Ric., 1021, 1174; Rob. (le), 17, 202, 399, 452, 453*, 454*, 540, 662, 779, 840*, 955, 1107, 1108, 1216, 1325, 1477, 1522*, 1524*, 1525; S., 970; Sam., 16, 18, 202, 540, 661, 662*, 750, 751, 938*, 969, 974, 1108*, 1112, 1215, 1216*, 1250*, 1278*, 1289, 1420, 1512; Sarah, 460, 540, 651, 656, 658, 731, 750, 847, 910, 954, 970, 971, 1046, 1153, 1181, 1211, 1272, 1326*, 1488; Sergent, 1037; Susanna(h), 454, 662, 731, 910, 1211; T., 1083, 1201*, 1216, 1447; Thos., 5, 48*, 111, 121, 182, 384, 453*, 454, 455*, 460*, 474, 661*, 731, 750, 752, 780, 781*, 910, 939, 970, 1037, 1083*, 1115, 1153, 1155, 1156, 1165, 1175, 1181, 1194, 1203*, 1211*, 1218, 1312, 1344*, 1376, 1377; Tim., 182, 460*, 1200*, 1201; W., 1032, 1187, 1202, 1216; Wal., 909; Wm., 14, 17, 18, 182, 413, 442*, 450, 460, 633, 648, 651, 656*, 681*, 682*, 703, 730, 840*, 843*, 910, 911, 954*, 967, 1106, 1200, 1272, 1326*, 1377, 1420, 1488, 1510*, 1513, 1579, 1580; (or Woolworth), Wm., 529*, 530; Lady, 691; Madam, 949; Mr., 1203; — le, 1174, 1195, 1201, 1301, 1311, 1328, 1339, 1477, 1512*; fam., 452, 630, 671, 690, 691 n, 748*, 779, 1160, 1215, 1216; (or Richmond), fam., 839; (or Woolworth), fam., 530 n; *and see* Weeb

Webber, Ann, 1582; Benedict, 1258; Jas., 1257*; *and see* Textor

Webbley (Webley, Weblie), *see* Weobley

Webster, Cath., 1138; Edw., 1274; Eliz., 536; Frances, 536; Jas., 1138; Rev. Jas., 534, 536*,

1217; John, 1140; Rev. John, 817, 1228; Joseph, 1138; Martha, 1138; Ric., 1138*; Sarah, 536*; Rev. W., 1362; *and see* Textor

Weckys, *see* Wicks

Wedderburn, Lady, 1317

Wedgwood, Joseph, 1420

Wedlock (Widlocke), Betty, 730; Rev. John, 13; Rebekah, 730; Ric., 730; Sarah, 730; Wm., 730

Weeb, Eliz., 660; John, 660; *and see* Webb

Weeks (Weekes, Weekys), *see* Wicks

Weeler, *see* Wheeler

Weerrit, *see* Werrett

Weight, *see* Waite

Weike (Wekys), *see* Wicks

Welch (Wealch, Welche, Welsh, Welsshe), Ann, 388, 1165, 1386*; Edm., 388; Eliz., 204*, 254, 949*; Hannah, 204, 253; Hen., 254; Jas., 254; Jane, 1400; John, 821*, 1025, 1386*, 1388, 1400; Sir John, kt., 621; Kath., 254; Mabel, 621; Marg., 253*; Mary, 821*, 949; Matthias, 204; Ric., 253, 949*; Rob., 1400; Thos., 204; Wal., 1122; Wm. (le), 253*, 949, 1228, 1388, 1400*, 1555; —, 821, 1165, 1494; *and see* Walsh

Weld (Welde), Eliz., 949; John de la, 1120; Margareta, 1466*; Rev. Ralph, 328*; Wm., 1466; —, 1477

Weldron, *see* Waldron

Well, atte, *see* Attwell

Welleford, Ralph of, 1388

Weller, W., 1195*; —, 1196

Welles, *see* Wells

Welley, Alice, 291; Wm., 291

Welling (Wellin), Eliz., 965; Sam., 965; —, 1282

Wellington, Ann, 789*; Francis, 789; Jas., 934; Jane, 789; Sir John de, 778 n; Thos., 789*

Wellman (Welman), Ric., 793, 1126*; Susanna, 1126*; W., 1126

Wells (Welles, Welys), Abigail, 264; Alice, 666; Amy, 1084; Ann, 74; Caleb, 264; Cath., 1334; Chas., 1378; Dan., 1148; Edith, 873; Edw., 543, 871, 872, 873*, 1334; Eliz., 74, 226, 317, 677, 802, 871, 872, 873, 1084; Elp. [*sic*], 1145; Francis, 986, 1031, 1262; Rev. Francis, 865, 986, 1276*, 1289, 1290*; Geo., 20; Grace, 20, 1330; Hannah, 666, 1262*, 1276; Hazlewood, 293; Hen., 334; (or Willis), Rev. Hen., 1369; Hester, 264*; Humph., 1069; Isaac, 264*, 796; Jas., 334, 666, 983*, 984*, 986, 1334; Jane, 334, 854*, 1353; John, 74, 264, 666*, 802*, 881, 983, 1084, 1127, 1148, 1149, 1334, 1373, 1376*, 1377, 1378, 1389; Rev. John, 865, 1084*, 1087; Judith, 1334*; Lucy, 1276; Lydia, 293, 1084*; Marg., 74*, 1000; Margery, 264; Mary, 983, 1000, 1148, 1353, 1458; Mic., 442, 683, 1000*; Nat., 1323; Rachel, 887; Rebecca, 1518; Ric., 334, 802, 818, 1353*; Rev. Ric., 1335; Rob., 74, 983, 984, 1333, 1334; Sam., 871, 872; Sara(h), 486, 543, 677, 983*, 984*, 1276, 1330, 1334, 1376; Silas, 986; Thos., 74*, 226, 586, 1148, 1334*, 1376; Susannah, 1377; T., 1476; Rev. Thos., 66, 447, 982, 985*; Rev. Tobias, 1351; Wal., 677; Wm., 74*, 317, 442, 486, 666, 677, 1000, 1330, 1389,

1458*; Mr., 1378, 1543; —, 986, 1148*, 1165, 1475; fam., 311; *and see* Attwell

Wellstead, Dan., 777; Wm., 1513

Welman, *see* Wellman

Welmore, H[enr]y, 986

Welneforde, Geof. de, 1388

Welsh (Welsshe), *see* Welch

Welyfed, W., 1256

Welys, *see* Welsh

Welywalshe, Ric., 1197

Wemyss (Wemys), Lord, 1154, 1335*

Wemyss and March, earl of, 1153; Lady, 1153

Wenlock, Lord, 1261

Wenman, Ric., 1062; Thos., 546; Wm., 1059, 1062; —, 1062*; fam., 546

Went, Ann(e), 1365, 1367*, 1368*; Hannah, 541; Hester, 1367; John, 541; Mary, 1365, 1368; Nat., 541; Sam., 1365*, 1367*, 1369; Sarah, 1367; Thos., 1365, 1367, 1368*; Wm., 1368; —, 1370

Wentworth, Anne, 643; Eliz., 797; Major-Gen. Hen., 1048; Marg., 1169; Thos., 1169; Thos., Lord Wentworth, 1169*; Sir Wm., 643; Lord, 230, 864, 1169

Weobly (Webbley, Webley, Weblie), Eleanor, 1320*; Eliz., 1320, 1455; Giles, 118; Hannah, 1318–19; Jas., 1455; Jane, 1320*; John, 368; Rob., 1455; Wal., 1319, 1320*, 1322; Wm., 1318*–19, 1320*, 1323; fam., 1322

Werb, *see* Webb

Were, *see* Ware

Werlin, Wm., 1492

Werrett (Weerrit, Wherreat), Eliz., 741; Hester, 702*, 1171; Jane, 741; John, 702, 1171, 1551; Joseph, 1550*, 1551*; Marg., 1550; Ric., 1550; Shadrach, 702*; Thos., 741

Wese, John le, 1539; *and see* Wise

Wesley, Rev. C., 1217; *and see* Westley

Wesson, Ann, 850; David, 1391; John, 850*; Mary, 1391*; Sarah, 850; Thos., 1391

West, Alice, 1033; Alex., 1513; Ann, 492; David, 555; Dyonysia, 83; Edw., 492, 1012; Eliz., 555*, 578, 1386*; Henrietta, 988; Hen., 1033, 1267; Jas., 83*, 420, 864 n*, 987*, 988*; Jane, 555; John, 555, 604, 1014*; John (or Jas.), 988; Jonathan, 1386; Mary, 555, 578*, 1014; Phil., 83*, 555*, 824; Ric., 578; Sarah, 988*; Susanna, 83*; T., 1456; Sir T., 1388; Thos., 1012, 1033; Sir Thos., 1392*; W., 1312; Wm., 1074; —, 1015, 1017*, 1058, 1392

Westal (Westhalle), Luke de, 1422; Wm. de, 533

Westbroke, Nic., 1313

Westbury, Hen., 677; Jane, 881; John, 778 n

Westcombe, —, 1369

Westerdale, Chris. (Xpor), 264, 1234*, 1237, 1238; Eliz., 1234; Hen., 1234; Thos., 264, 1237

Westfaling, —, 1539

Westfield, Ric., 1530; Thos., 1530

Westhalle, *see* Westal

Westhropp, Isaac, 413

Westley, Eliz., 1032; Martha, 659, 661; Thos., 661; Wm., 659, 661; *and see* Wesley

Westmacott, *see* Westmancote

Westman, —, 1052

Westmancote (Westmacott, Westmancot, Westmancott), Cath., 186; Ric., 186; Rog., 944; Sarah, 317; Thos., 944; Wm., 317*

Westmorland [*peerage*], *see* Fane, Francis, Thos., *and* —

Weston (Westone). Agnes de, 1447; Ann, 1273*; Chas., 166*; Eleanor, 256; Eliz., 573, 611; Geo., 163; Harbert, 256; Hen., 1273*; Humph., 980; Jane, 166; John (de, le), 339, 1149, 1150, 1151, 1256, 1258, 1392; Rev. John, 166, 1169; Marg., 997; Mary, 339, 1150, 1151; Mic., 573; Mille [*sic*], 1010; Nat., 256; Rev. Nat., 288; Phil., 166; Ric. de, 1447; Sir Ric., kt., 166, 997; Rob., 758; Sarah, 166; Sir Simon, 1237; Thos., 166, 611, 700, 1361; Wal. de, 1447; Webb, 163; Wm., 758, 1010, 1329; Rev. Wm., 288; Rev. Mr., 287 n; fam., 159

Westripp (or Heyward), Rev. J., 1147

Westroppe, Wm., 1218

Westwood (Westwode), Hugh, 184, 318*, 943, 944, 945, 1031, 1032; Ric., 184; Rob., 430

Wethe, Rob., 1460; Wal., 1460; *and see* Wyth

Wetherall (Wetherell, Wetherill), Rev. Chas., 1399; Hen., 1399; Nat., 986; Rev. Ric., 1393, 1404; fam., 745

Wetherhurde, Cecil[y], 1033; John, 1033

Wetherly, Eliz., 1338*; Lydia, 1338; Thos., 1338*; Wm., 1338

Wetherston, John, 906; Mary, 906

Wetmore (Wettmore), Ann, 1305, 1307; Eliz., 563, 632*, 1025; Hen., 450, 632; Jas., 563, 564; John, 632*, 1025, 1306; Mary, 563, 632*; Rebekah, 1025; Sarah, 563*, 564*, 632*, 1305, 1306*; Thos., 564, 632*, 1305*, 1306*, 1307; Wm., 564*, 632, 1025; —, 1020*; fam., 630; *and see* Whetmore

Wetson, Rev. John, 395

Wettmore, *see* Wetmore

Weykes, *see* Wicks

Weyland, *see* Wayland

Weyman, Ann, 832; John, 264; Mary, 831, 1076; Thos., 831*, 832*; *and see* Wyman

Weymouth [*peerage*]. Viscount, 126*, 272; fam., 271; *and see* Thynne, Thos.

Weyver, *see* Weaver

Whaddon, Ric. de, 1379

Whalley (Walleye, Wally, Whally), Eliz., 837; Jas., 837; Rev. John Sedgewick, 42; T. de, 1061; Rev. T. S., 1491; —, abbot, 708

Wharam, Rob., 409; Sarah, 409

Wharton, Anne, 454; Rev. Mic., 1447; Sam., 1446; Thos., 454; Rev. Tim., 744, 1446, 1447; Mr., 515 n; —, 1368

Wharton [*peerage*], Phil., duke of, 364 n; Lord, 1362

Whatcott (Whatcat, Whatcot), Agnes, 1432; Ann, 884; Hen., 218; Sarah, 226; Thos., 226*; Wm. (de), 884, 1432

Whatley (Whateley), Edw., 1562*; Hester, 1573; Mary, 1562; Rob., 531, 1562; Rog., 531; Thos., 1573; *and see* Wheatly

Wheale, *see* Weale

Wheatcroft, Francis, 226; John, 226; Mary, 226; Mercy, 226; Thos., 226

Wheate, Dame Avice, 793; Frances, 792; Sir Geo., bt., 792, 793; Sir Jacob, bt., 792*, 793; Rev. Sir J. T., 793; Rev. Sir John Thos., bt., 792; Sarah, 165; Thos., 165; *and see* White

Wheatly (Wheateley, Wheatley), Ann, 88; Eleanor, 1431; Eliz., 1470; Esther, 1431; Jervis, 1470; Joseph, 88*, 1430; Marg., 88; Mary, 88; Sam., 88, 1431; Rev. Thos., 1223; *and see* Whatley; Whitley

Wheatstone, Eliz., 1037; *and see* Whetstone

Whecler [? Wheeler], Peter the, 1139

Wheeler (Weeler, Wheelar, Wheeller, Wheler, Wheolar), Alice, 601*; Ann(e), 567, 601, 702, 905, 907, 1038, 1518; Cath., 1004; Chas., 597; Dan., 1367; Edith, 429; Edw., 975*, 1415; Eliz., 597*, 601, 1003, 1367*, 1518; Francis, 857; Rev. Geo., 1072; Gil., 857; Grace, 855; Hen., 273, 378, 1014; Jas., 532, 1367; Jane, 662, 1014, 1363; John, 429, 567*, 597*, 601*, 662, 702, 731, 905, 906, 907*, 1004*, 1367*, 1413; Joseph, 522, 731, 746, 1518; Mary, 52*, 429, 522, 662, 746, 907*, 975*, 1068, 1379; Kath., 662; Lydia, 1272; Peter the, *see* Whecler; Ric. (le), 730, 1038, 1195, 1221, 1272; Rev. Ric., 681; Rob., 1003; Rev. Rog., 263, 853; Sam., 52*; Sarah, 597*, 658, 975, 1278; Tapling, 1518; Thos., 273, 601, 907*, 1014, 1068*, 1379; W., 1027; Wm., 800, 975*; Wm. Webb, 52; —, 272, 1363

Wherreat, *see* Werrett

Whetekyn, Ralph de, 1431

Whetham, Dorothy, 439; Joseph, 439

Whetmore, Sarah, 1019*; Thos., 1019*; daughters of Sarah by former husband, Anne, Hannah, *and* Sarah, 1019; *and see* Wetmore; Whitmore

Whetstone, Joseph, 112*; Mary, 112, 474; Wm., 474*; *and see* Wheatstone

Whidendun (Widendun), Pet. de, 1475; —, 1476; *and see* Whittington

Whillington, *see* Willington

Whillock, Alice, 1153; Eleanor, 1153*; Eliz., 1153; Geo., 1153*; John, 1153

Whinekel, Hen., 1404

Whinfield, *see* Winfield

Whippey, Thos., 1087

Whitaker (Whittacre), Alice, 1275; Anne, 1275*; Diana, 1275; Hen., 1266, 1275*; Joanna, 1159; Stephen, 1159*; Wm., 1408; —, 414, 1387

Whitchurch (Whitechurch, Whytchurch, Whytchyrche, Wytchyrche), Hester, 100; Jane, 1155, 1156*, 1160; John, 927; Joseph, 1155, 1156*, 1160; Mary, 1155*, 1156; Sam., 1460; Wm., 100, 1460; Wm., abbot, 297, 493*, 708; —, 1460

Whitcombe (Whitcomb, Whytecombe, Witcomb, Witcombe), Anne, 854; Betty, 1200; Bridget, 854; Hannah, 1454*; Isabel, 716; Jas., 52*, 1326, 1376*; John (de), 716*, 854*, 1200, 1494; Joyce, 1326; Mary, 52, 716, 1376*; Nat., 52, 1326, 1454; Sarah, 854, 1376; Thos., 854, 1376*; Wm.,

1200, 1376, 1377; Mr., 259; —, 1165, 1455; *and see* Widcombe

White (Whyte, Wight), Adam le, 1314; Alice la, 1239*, 1428, 1535; Alice Talboys, 1239; Ann(e), 296, 317, 336, 409*, 615, 677*, 736*, 777, 803, 921, 923, 929, 975, 1006, 1112, 1117, 1239*, 1307*, 1528; Barbara, 59; Betty, 777, 1384; Cassandra, 25; Cathoren [*sic*], 105; Chas., 677; Rev. Chas., 1290; Christian, 174; Dan., 539, 750, 937*, 1181*, 1424*; Dorothy, 906, 1117; Edith, 1100; Edw., 59, 679, 733, 1099*, 1100, 1515*, 1534; Rev. Edw., 427; Eleanor (Elinor), 736, 803; Eliza, 1117; Eliz., 52*, 273, 419, 677*, 777*, 780, 803, 905*, 975, 979, 1008, 1026*, 1099, 1117, 1118*, 1247, 1384, 1470, 1515, 1528; Francis, 203, 750*; G., 1529; Geo., 111, 386, 677*, 921, 923*, 1029, 1100, 1239*, 1247, 1258, 1403, 1528*; Rev. Geo., 424; Hannah, 677, 891, 1307, 1401, 1424*; Hen., 419, 847, 1117*, 1118, 1121*, 1223, 1384; Henty, 419; Herodias, 1470; Hester, 847; Rev. J., 1258*; Jas., 52, 933*, 1112, 1121, 1258, 1289, 1515*; Jane, 111, 273*, 1008, 1107, 1118, 1239; Joan, 60; John (le), 60*, 105, 111*, 112, 270, 273*, 315, 317, 336, 361, 409, 597*, 641, 677*, 693, 736, 777*, 803, 906, 954*, 975, 980, 993, 1088, 1132, 1243*, 1295, 1307*, 1308, 1314, 1315, 1329, 1401, 1460, 1502, 1525*; 1534; Rev. John, 252, 259, 463, 651, 1239*, 1257, 1258, 1404; John Wight, 1239; Joseph, 803, 847*, 1008; Dr. Joseph, 1218; Lieut. Joseph, 983; Joshua, 905; Marg. (Margareta), 110, 111*, 611, 677, 693*, 847, 933, 937, 1239, 1243*; Martha, 1105, 1117, 1547; Mary, 111*, 235, 273, 486, 597, 677, 722, 736*, 777, 803, 847, 850, 906, 954*, 980, 1029, 1088, 1099, 1100, 1117*, 1118*, 1181, 1212, 1302, 1315, 1371, 1401, 1405, 1515*, 1534; Mat., 815; Miles, 470; Moses, 1534; Naomi, 641; Nat., 1272; Rev. Nat., 1290; Nic., 1107*, 1547; Olive, 1181; Peter, 1258; Phil., 1117, 1118*; Prudence, 1515; Rachel, 1111*; Ric., 110, 111*, 174, 235, 273, 419, 611, 979, 1117, 1181, 1301*, 1528, 1534; Rev. Ric., 929; Ric. Talboys, 1239; Rob., 815, 847, 1111*, 1243, 1314, 1535, 1575; Rog. le, 1329; Sam., 666, 906, 1008, 1239*, 1401, 1403, 1539; Sarah, 112, 143, 203*, 273*, 374, 597*, 679, 683, 796, 857, 923, 1112*, 1117, 1181, 1212, 1371, 1515*; Stephen, 975; Susan, 1301; Susannah, 933, 1302; Thos., 52, 111, 203, 273, 325, 337, 553, 597*, 736*, 803, 850, 857, 923, 983, 1006, 1026*, 1100, 1112*, 1117, 1118, 1121, 1140, 1179, 1185, 1186, 1195, 1212, 1213, 1239, 1258, 1470*; Thos. Colthurst, 1239; Thos. Jacob, 66; Thos. Phillips, 1282; W., 1309; Rev. W. Farren, 1186; Wal., 954, 1121; Wm., 174*, 273, 296, 486, 597, 683*, 777*, 796, 803, 894, 905, 923, 924, 939, 954*, 1292, 1295, 1307, 1312, 1371, 1405, 1455, 1511, 1515*, 1534; Rev. Wm., 1441; Winifred, 1515*; —, 1257*, 1259, 1293, 1311, 1455; fam., 236; *and see* Wheate

Whitechurch, *see* Whitchurch

Whitefield, *see* Whitfield

Whitehall, Rev. John, 1223; Ric., 754

Whitehead (Whitehood), Ann, 1249; Ant., 1555; Edw., 295; Eliz., 132, 962; Geo., 1249*; Gil., 1078; Hen., 962, 1553, 1555; Jas., 1501; Jane, 818; John, 818; Judith, 573; Manasseth, 132; Mary, 573; Sam., 1086; Sarah, 1249, 1282; Rev. W., 1289, 1460; Wm., 573*, 818, 962, 1282*; Mrs., 131

Whitehond, Cristina, 1335

Whitehood, *see* Whitehead

Whitehorn, *see* Whithorne

Whitehouse, John, 167

Whiteing, *see* Whiting

Whitemore, *see* Whitmore

Whiten, Eliz., 1079; Nic. Blount, 1079; *and see* Whiting

Whitesey, Rev. Thos., 342

Whitewood, Eliz., 1567*; John, 836, 1567*; Mary, 1567

Whitfield (Whitefield), And., 1306*, 1307*; Eliz., 1018, 1463; Rev. G., 1027, 1292*; Geo., 1306; Rev. Geo., 1187*; Hester, 1018; John, 1463; Martha, 1307; Mary, 1306, 1307; R., 1312; Rob., 1307; Sam., 1463*; Rev. Sam., 1018*, 1020*; Sarah, 1307; Susan, 1301; Susanna, 1020; Thos., 1018*, 1258; Rev. Thos., 1489, 1516; Wm. de, 265; *and see* Wydefeld

Whitford, Anne, 1153; Eliz., 597; John, 1576; Joseph, 597; Mary, 1153*; Thos., 1153; Wm., 1153*

Whithers, *see* Withers

Whithorne (Whitehorn, Whithorn, Whittorne, Withorne), Anna, 315*; Ann(e), 315, 1376; Conway, 313*, 317, 1270*, 1289; Dr. Conway, 1270; Lieut. Conway, 313 n; Eleanor, 1434; Eliz., 1270*; Geo., 1079; Giles, 641; Hester, 1268; John, 313 n*, 315, 317, 329*, 611, 1163, 1164, 1273*-4, 1434*; Joyce, 317; Kear, 74; Lawr., 1268; M., 611; Marg., 317, 329, 1468; Mary, 329*, 486, 611, 1434; Peter, 611; Ric., 1376*, 1502; Sam., 315*, 317*; Sarah, 317*, 1270*; Wal., 1440; Wm., 74, 486, 1440; fam., 313*; *and see* Whittern

Whiting (Huytinge, Whiteing, Whytinge, Whytynge), Adam, 1339; Ann(e), 1146, 1576; Eliz., 344, 1049; Francis, 797; Rev. Jas., 103; John, 344, 1313; Mary, 343, 923, 1049, 1251, 1576; Nic., 1555; Ric., 1146*; Rob., 1250; Sarah, 1049; Thos., 1576*; Wal., 1197; Wm., 343*, 344, 1049, 1339, 1447; —, 1363; *and see* Whiten

Whitleby, John de, 1485

Whitley, Edm., 1065; John, 387; *and see* Wheatly

Whitmaye, Rev. John, 870

Whitmore (Whitemore), Ann, 399; C. S., 1091, 1092; Cath., 485, 1091; Christian, 858; Cordelia, 1088, 1091; Eliz., 146, 1088, 1091*; Emily Harriett Octavia, 1088; G., 1093; Geo., 485, 1088*, 1091*; Gen. Sir Geo., kt., 1088*; Sir Geo., kt., 1091; Major Geo. St. Vincent, 1088; Hanna(h), 858, 903; Hen., 686; John, 399; Rev. John, 793, 1165; Joseph, 388, 858; Kath., 1088*; Ric., 146, 1088*, 1091*; Sam., 190, 657, 903;

Thos., 858, 1091; W., 1147; Lieut.-Gen. W., 1088; Sir W., 1091; Wm., 687; Lieut.-Gen. Wm., 1088, 1091; Lady, 1088; —, 1091, 1428; fam., 1091; *and see* Whetmore

Whitney, Chas., 540; Eliz., 1423; Francis, 535, 540*; Geo., 540; Mary, 540*; Rob., 540; Susanna, 540; T., 1423; —, 1422

Whitshed, Jas., 364*

Whitson, Alice, 924; John, 917; Wm., 924; Mr., 918

Whittacre, *see* Whitaker

Whittard (Whittarde), Anne, 419; Chas., 911; Ric., 419*; Rev. Ric., 1154; Sarah, 911; Thos., 419*

Whittel, *see* Whittle

Whittern (Whitterne), Ric., 703; Rob., 1498*; Susannah, 703; *and see* Whithorne

Whittick (Whittock, Whittuck), Abraham, 211*; Chas., 1087; John, 205, 211; Joseph, 211; Mary, 211; Sarah, 211; —, 1087

Whittington (Whyttington, Wittington, Wytyndon), Alice, 82, 83, 247; Ann(e), 84, 1155; Cecilia, 1051; Cicely, 801, 1027; Edm., 1273; Eliz., 82*, 209, 977, 1051*, 1236*, 1273; Geo., 82; Guy, 1027; Sir Guy, 801, 1051; Rev. Hugh, 1165; Joan, 1051; John, 81*, 82*, 83, 84, 209, 406, 951, 1051; Kath., 1051; M., 1215; Marg., 1333; Margery, 1032, 1051; Mary, 82; Maud, 1032; Rachel, 81, 82*, 84*; Ric. (Rd.), 82, 920, 1051, 1092; Sir Ric., 1051; Rob., 82*, 1051; Rev. Sam.,, 1236; T., 1032*, 1232; Thos., 80, 81*, 82*, 84*, 801, 977, 1027, 1031*, 1032, 1051*, 1215, 1333; Wm., 80*, 81*, 84, 245*, 247, 248*, 922, 1051*, 1554; Rev. Wm., 1236; Dr., 1123; Mr., 50; Rev., 1043; —, 1039, 1052, 1215; fam., 207, 951*, 1215, 1237; *and see* Whidendun

Whittle (Whittel), Ann, 1046; Geo., 1271*; Phil., 1270*; Sarah, 1271; Wm., 1046

Whittock, *see* Whittick

Whittorne, *see* Whithorne

Whittuck, *see* Whittick

Whitworth, Rob., 792 n, 793 n

Whorwood, Anne, 634; Eliz., 817; Marg., 634; Thos., 634; Wm., 634, 704, 785; Sir Wm., 817; *and see* Horwood

Whyroun, Ric., 1292

Whytchurch (Whytchyrche), *see* Whitchurch

Whyte, *see* White

Whytema[n], Stephen, 1404

Whytecombe, *see* Whitcombe

Whytinge (Whytynge), *see* Whiting

Whyttington, *see* Whittington

Wiannock, —, 1401

Wiatt (Wiat), *see* Wyatt

Wicam, *see* Wickham

[Wich], Ric., bishop, 581 n

Wichell, *see* Witchell

Wichwick, Wm., 1159

Wick (Wickc), *see* Wicks

Wickens, R., 1331; Rev. Rob., 1331

Wickes, *see* Wicks

Wickham (Wicam, Wykeham), Ann, 1109*, 1111, 1426; Ant., 1109, 1111*; Betty, 1112; Edith,

1109*; Eleanor, 1115; Eliz., 1109*; Eliz. Higgs, 1384; Harry, 1383; Hen., 1121, 1424; Hester, 1543*; Jas., 176, 1110*, 1112, 1121*, 1122, 1384; Rev. Jas., 1339; John, 405, 506, 995, 1109*, 1110, 1121, 1426*, 1543, 1551*; John, prior, 1447; Marg., 1109*; Martha, 1426; Mary, 176, 1109, 1110*, 1384, 1424, 1426; Ralph, 616; Ric., 1109, 1110; Rob., 1428; Ruth, 1383*; Sam., 1109, 1110, 1384*; Sarah, 176, 1110, 1384; Thos., 176*, 1109*, 1111; Wm., 176, 1109*, 1121, 1383*; Rev. Wm., 1385; —, 1121, 1122, 1428

Wickliffe, *see* Wycliff

Wicks (Weckys, Weekes, Weeks, Weekys, Weike, Wekys, Weykes, Wick, Wicke, Wickes, Wikes, Wikkys, Wikys, Wiyke, Wyckes, Wyke, Wykes, Wyxe), Aaron, 473, 1510*, 1512; Agnes, 1519; Anna, 970, 971, 1023; Ann(e), 597, 970*, 971, 1244, 1510*, 1512, 1550; Barnard, 1250; Bart., 633; Brice, 937*; Chas., 597; Edm., 529, 908, 969*, 970*, 971; Edw., 19*, 237, 701*, 939, 1306, 1543; Rev. Edw., 1336, 1339*; Eleanor, 1241, 1244, 1543; Eliz., 517, 617, 619, 701*, 703, 937, 970, 971, 1239; Frances, 450; Geo., 970*, 971*, 1212; Hannah, 939; Harriet Barber, 1282; Hen., 59; Hester, 701, 970, 1250; (or Finch), Isaac, 1200; Isabell, 473, 1510; Jane, 1252, 1336; Joan, 744; John (de), 59, 304, 450*, 517, 529*, 619, 621*, 703, 908*, 1244*, 1259, 1404; Rev. John, 613, 619, 621, 1043; Jonathan, 1250; Joseph, 621, 1239, 1241, 1244*; Mary, 621*, 701*, 703, 937, 970, 1306; Mat., 11; Moses, 1244; N., 1147; Nancy, 450; Nat., 1258; Nic., 529, 1336, 1538, 1539; Ric. (de), 701*, 1159, 1404; Rob., 497, 529, 1147, 1159; Sarah, 703, 1212, 1250; (or Finch), Susanna, 1200; Sylvester, 237; T., 1159; Thos., 497, 529, 744, 809*, 1023, 1159; Dr. Thos., 1258; Rev. Thos. C., 1257; Rev. Thos. Croome, 1239; Ursula, 970, 971; Wm., 970*, 1336; Mr., 497 n; —, 1120, 1147, 1312, 1512; fam., 527 n, 530 n, 1147

Wicksey, *see* Wixey

Wicksteed, Thos., 787

Wickwan (Wykewane), Agnes, 1504; W., abbot, 1475

Wickwood, Hannah, 1249; Wm., 1249

Widcombe, Nat., 1551; *and see* Whitcombe

Widder, Rev. Ralph, 147

Widdows (Widdowes), Christian, 225; Thos., 865 n; Wm., 850*

Widendun, *see* Whidendun

Widewesson, Wm., 1491

Widlake, John, 1155

Widlocke, *see* Wedlock

Widmore, N., 1317

Wiett, *see* Wyatt

Wigg, Isaac, 1105

Wiggall, Rob., 450

Wiggan, Rev. Rob., 1348

Wiggeston, *see* Wigston

Wiggett, John, 641

Wiggins, Rog., 1334

Wiggold, Edith, Lady of, 1202
Wight, *see* White
Wigmore, Anne, 344; Dan., 344; Deborah, 841; John, 550; R., 1035; Ric. de, 1035; Thos., 841; Wm., 550; Capt., 469 n*, 928, 929
Wigston (Wiggeston), Christian, 1082; R., 1082; W., 1092
Wikes (Wikkys, Wikys), *see* Wicks
Wilberforce, Mr., 1513
Wilbraham, Edw., 373, 748; John, 1200; Mary, 373
Wilce (Wilse), Ann, 261, 1372, 1401; Eliz., 118; Geo., 1372; Giles, 348; Hannah, 348; Joan, 471; John, 118, 471, 1039*, 1401; Rev. John, 471, 895; Marg., 261, 471; Martha, 348*; Mary, 471; Ric., 1039; Susan, 1038; Thos., 261, 348*, 1038; *and see* Wiles; Wilsie; Wilts
Wilckes, *see* Wilkes
Wilcox (Wilcocks), Ann, 1398; Anselm, 1184*; Chas., 1580*; Edw., 476, 923*; Jane, 923; John, 930, 1398*; Joseph, 302, 1299*; Mary, 923, 930*; Penelope, 1580; Rev. Ralph, 1020; Ric., 923; Sam., 930, 1182, 1184*; Sarah, 923, 930*, 1184*, 1398; Stephen, 929; Susan, 1299; Susanna, 1299; Thos., 923*, 930*, 1044*; Wm., 100, 1020
Wild (Wilde, Wylde), Ann, 659; Eliz., 653*, 1001; Gil., 1160; Hen., 32; Hugh, 1001*, 1002*; Jas., 653*, 659; John, 1002; Rev. Rowland (Rouland), 1191, 1196, 1228; Thos., 1002; Rev. Thos., 1351; Winifred, 32
Wildblood, Rev. Wm., 302
Wilde, *see* Wild
Wildey, fam., 885
Wilding, Francis, 730; John, 1420; Sarah, 730
Wiles, Ric., 1539; *and see* Wilce; Wilsie
Wilford, Thos., 515
Wilkes (Wilcks, Wilks, Wilkys, Wylkes), Ann(e), 111, 133, 339, 490, 542, 1372; Beloved, 7, 36; C. R., 1282; Capel, 133*; Dan., 1372*; Eliz., 225*, 984, 1282, 1421; Ferdinando, 399; Frances, 225, 399; Francis, 771; Rev. Francis, 490*; Giles, 262, 984; Joane, 225; Johanna, 1372; John, 399, 542, 983, 1421*; Rev. John, 1228*; Joseph, 983; Rev. Joseph, 424; Marg., 1064; Mary, 262, 442, 983; Rebeckah, 490*; Ric., 111, 151, 225*; Rev. Ric., 1348, 1382; Rev. Rob., 488, 490*; Sarah, 399, 542, 1361; Susannah, 151; Thos., 225*, 339, 1196, 1361*; Rev. Thos., 713; W., 1064; Wm., 111, 151, 339, 442, 1372; —, 1223
Wilkins (Wilkines, Wylikine, Wylkynes, Wylkyns), Aaron, 187*; Abigail, 563*; Alex., 1194; Alice, 1259; Anna Maria, 1046; Ann(e), 140, 418, 631*, 632*, 858, 1453; Betty, 1143; Cath. Augusta, 1047; Chas., 631; Dan., 1438*; Deborah, 750; Edith, 344, 631, 937; Eleanor, 1243; Eliza, 632; Eliz., 563, 631*, 632*, 750, 858, 1143*; Esther, 1334; Geo., 881; Geo. Chapman, 632; Hester, 937, 1050; J., 1312; Jacob, 1250; Jas., 632, 677, 1396*, 1403, 1453*; Jane, 140, 411; Joan, 187; John, 173, 417*, 563*, 631*, 632*, 677, 858, 937*, 1050, 1127, 1250, 1259, 1331, 1396, 1438; Joseph, 632*, 1143*;

Joshua, 1249, 1258; Josiah, 1250; Margery, 1388; Martha, 418*; Mary, 417, 467, 632*, 858, 1131*, 1143, 1194, 1250*, 1396; Mat., 1243; Moses, 187*; Nat., 418, 632*; Ranulph, 1460; Rebekah, 632; Ric., 1131*; Rob., 750, 1049, 1334, 1519; Sam., 632*, 633; Sarah, 417, 563, 631, 632*, 677, 750; Susannah, 418*, 632; Thos., 140, 187*, 340, 467, 632, 750, 858*, 1194, 1348, 1396, 1513; (or De Winton), Wal., 1047; (later De Winton), Rev. Wal., 1046; Wm., 418*, 632*, 677, 750*, 1131, 1396; —, 1512; fam., 885
Wilkinson, Frances Ann, 1231; Jas., 1486; John, 1289; Mary, 1486, 1497; Rev. Ric., 767; Rev. Thos., 943; Rev. Wm. Denison, 1231
Wilks (Wilkys), *see* Wilkes
Willam, *see* Williams
Willan, Ann, 563; Ric., 563; Mr., 1350
Willdiger, Ann, 175; John, 175
Willes, *see* Willis
Willet, *see* Willett
Willeton, *see* Willington
Willett (Willet, Willetts), Eliz., 368, 1199; Esther, 55; Jane, 376, 1145; John, 366, 376*; Rev. John, 376; Joseph, 55*; Mary, 55*, 1199; Mat., 1527; Peter, 1527; Ralph, 370, 376, 1527, 1528; Rev. Ralph, 366, 368, 651, 1031, 1082, 1141, 1199*, 1257; Rev. Ric., 255; Sam., 1277; Sarah, 1141; Susanna, 376*, 1527, 1528; Thos., 55; Wm., 929, 1527*; Rev., 1423; fam., 747
Willey (Wily), Dan., 887*; Jacob, 542; Mary, 542, 887*; Ric., 887; Thos., 887
William I (the Conqueror), 12, 41, 53, 91, 101, 131, 153, 178, 277, 451, 475*, 481 n, 497*, 525*, 527*, 565, 568, 576, 612 n, 618, 634, 638, 646, 648, 690, 720, 737, 745, 769, 773, 776, 819, 1001, 1050, 1051, 1100, 1131, 1162, 1201, 1287*, 1322, 1335, 1340, 1355, 1455, 1537
William II (Rufus), 318, 527, 1011, 1287, 1309, 1516
William III, 93, 162, 220, 415, 440, 497 n, 723*, 748, 853, 1003, 1093, 1290, 1293, 1428, 1460, 1516; William and Mary, 586, 1186
[William], prince of Orange, 358, 776
William, abbot, 770
William, bishop of Worcester, *see* Lloyd
William, earl, 805
William Leuric (fl. 1066), 798, 1350
William son of Adam, 720
William son of Baderon, *see* FitzBaderon
William son of Faber, 1404
William son of Norman, 870, 1237; his son Hugh, *see* FitzWilliam
William son of Otho, 533
William the Norman, 1237
William, Otto (or Otho) son of, 533
William, vicar of Bisley, 1217
William (fl. 1066), 990
Williams (Willam, Williames, Willyams, Wyllam, Wyllames, Wyllyames), Alice, 1057; Ann(e), 366, 412, 542, 597, 598*, 637, 641*, 642, 700, 729, 736, 800, 813, 922, 1038; Rev. Arnold, 1516; Rev. Basil, 1511; Carew, 1463*; Cecil,

608; Cecilia, 1388; Chas., 642*, 815, 1194, 1323, 1488; Christian, 906; Chris., 10*; Rev. Cooper, 1219; David, 1057, 1463*; Rev. David, 161; Sir David, kt., 744, 1463; Edith, 208; Edw., 296, 386, 468, 608, 868, 924; Rev. Edw., 783, 1147, 1382; Ele(a)nor, 77, 800; Eliz., 212*, 250, 412, 413, 473, 636, 732, 736*, 813, 868, 919, 922, 924, 1152, 1396*, 1454*, 1463, 1484; Esther, 762, 815; Frances, 473, 586; Frances Susannah, 1320, 1323; Francis, 736; G. E., 1027; Geo., 208, 1038, 1152*, 1154; Grace, 1319; Greg., 1388; Griffith, 677; Hannah, 543, 731, 953, 1168; Harriett Mann, 1323; Harritt Maria, 1321; Hen., 541, 731; Hester, 906, 1463, 1476; Hugh, 77; Rev. Hugh, 1348; Isaac, 736, 1289, 1396*, 1403; J., 1055; Rev. J., 1064, 1289; Jas., 250, 736, 934, 1320, 1361, 1403, 1516; Rev. Jas., 511, 802; Jane, 146, 212, 376, 442, 736; John, 50, 55, 337, 442, 531, 550, 597, 622, 635, 636, 637, 640*, 641, 762, 815*, 906, 953, 1004, 1035, 1039, 1097, 1099*, 1139, 1140, 1277, 1278, 1390*, 1551; Rev. John, 534, 1214, 1388, 1513; (or Baker), Rev. John, 1317; Rev. John Hen., 1477; Jonathan, 550; Joseph, 473, 506, 542, 543, 815, 963, 1323, 1454*, 1515; Rev. Joseph, 1454; Lewis, 915, 965; Lucy, 642; Rev. Luke, 328; Magden, 413; Marg., 468, 550, 736, 938, 1064, 1097, 1109, 1153, 1454; Marmaduke, 1109; Martha, 10*; Mary, 55*, 175, 386, 542, 550, 637, 815*, 1099*, 1272, 1282, 1463, 1492, 1573; Merial, 337; Mic., 637; Nat., 212; Peter, 730, 1519; Phil., 412*, 965, 1513; R., 1312; Rev. R., 1127; Rice, 1099; Rev. Rice, 1369; Ric., 212*, 532*, 550*, 637, 736*, 813, 814, 922, 1099*, 1168, 1169, 1282, 1316, 1321, 1477; Lieut. Ric., 206*; Rob., 212, 296, 412, 413, 598, 683, 906*, 1153, 1218, 1258; Rog. 1428; Rev. Rog., 571; S., 1101; Sam., 1099; Sarah, 296, 513, 550, 677, 683, 730, 813, 814, 919, 920, 1099*, 1153, 1194, 1321, 1396, 1472; Sibill, 1319; Simon, 1198; Stephen, 906; Susannah, 906; T., 1320, 1323, 1476; Rev. T., 1421; Tabitha, 1516; Thos., 250, 479, 542, 598, 640, 642*, 744, 800, 922*, 1039, 1099, 1277, 1318, 1320*, 1323, 1396, 1422, 1454, 1463*, 1472, 1473, 1475, 1515, 1575; Rev. Thos., 445, 1161, 1422; W., 1092; Rev. W., 1221; Wal., 920, 1314, 1485; Rev. Wal., 1389; Wm., 55, 124, 146, 212, 376*, 473, 550, 597, 598*, 641*, 700*, 736*, 815, 938, 1194, 1319*, 1323, 1484*, 1485, 1516; Rev. Wm., 72, 586*; Mrs., 918; Rev. Dr., 1214; —, 324, 1017*, 1020, 1064, 1092, 1323, 1355, 1378, 1403, 1441, 1475, 1477*; fam., 1476

Williamson, Alex., 818; Rev. R., 1102
Willing, Wm., 1440
Willington (Whillington, Willeton, Wylington, Wylinton), Geo., 1121; H. de, 1047; Jas., 1418; Joan, 612; John (de), 612, 1047, 1339*, 1552; Sir John de, 511; Margery, 1388; Mary, 1418; Olympias, 1047; R., 1323; Ralph de, 1047*; Wm., 1388; —, 1339; fam., 823, 1047
Willis (Willes, Wylles, Wyllis), Agnes, 1422; Ann,

1298*, 1534; Benj. Wood, 1282; Browne, 221, 242 n; Cath., 373; Charity, 1584; Rev. Chas., 1191; Chris., 1534; Cycely, 686; Rev. Edm., 1385; Edw., 1026*, 1314; Eliz., 611, 731, 1150, 1151, 1418, 1579; Esther, 373; Hannah, 611; Rev. Hen., 184, 1122, 1335, 1385; (or Wells), Rev. Hen., 1369; Hen. Grimston, 1026; J., 677; John, 373, 611*, 632, 687, 731, 1025; Rev. John, 1223; Joseph, 1584; Marg., 611, 1026*, 1191; Marian, 1052; Mary, 373, 1534; Nat., 172; Ric., 1025, 1026*, 1052; Sarah, 632, 677, 1025, 1418; Susan, 1191; Thos., 632*, 686, 1026, 1579, 1581, 1584*; Rev. Thos., 843, 1020, 1298*, 1313, 1392; Wm., 373*, 632, 1420; Rev. Wm., 744*; Rev. Mr., 1150, 1151; —, 156, 763, 1311; and see Wills
Willison, see Wilson
Willobie, see Willoughby
Willoin, Sarah, 1036
Willoughby (Willobie, Willoughbie), Sir Ambrose, kt., 851*, 852; Ann(e), 763, 1195; Benj., 955*; Blanch, 763; Chris., 50, 808, 825; Edw., 763, 1328; Eliz., 763, 1328*; Geo., 1195; H., 1103; Sir H., 1020; Kath., 852 n; R., 1020, 1196; Ric., 1020; Rob., 856; Sarah, 412; Susan, 1169; Thos., 856, 1195*; Wm., 1329; —, 1169; fam., 1328
Willoughby [peerage], Thos., Lord, 838; Wm., Lord, 852 n; Lord, 1381; and see Bertie, Peregrine
Willoughby de Broke [peerage], Rob., Lord, 763, 1328; and see Verney, Greville and Dr. Ric.
Wills, Anne, 261; Rev. Edm., 1383; Eliz., 339; Francis, 336; Giles, 261; Joan, 339; John, 1278; Joseph, 728; Mary, 336, 339; Sarah, 336; Susanna, 1278; Thos., 261, 336, 339*; Wm., 339; —, 288; and see Willis
Willyams, see Williams
Willyson, see Wilson
Wilmot (Wilmott, Wylemot), Anne, 962; Chrysogon, 1263; Dorothy, 42, 98, 99; Edw., 212, 1087; Geo., 212; Jane, 212; Johanna, 933*; John, 933*, 1263; Rev. John, 1346; Marg., 933; Mary, 933; Matillda, 1314; Philippa, 1263*; Ric., 933*; Rob., 933*, 1263; Rev. Rob., 1263; Thos., 473, 962; Mrs., 39, 50; Rev., 1263; —, 1311, 1402, 1404
Wilner, Hester, 1307
Wilse, see Wilce
Wilsha (Wilshere, Wilshire), see Wiltshire
Wilsie, Rev. Thos., 498; and see Wilce; Wiles
Wilson (Willison, Willyson, Wilsone), Alice, 1065, 1276; Ann(e), 637, 814, 895, 1277, 1493, 1499; Bartley, 1499, 1502; Bridget, 320*; Dorothy, 1420; Edw., 296, 1270, 1276*, 1277; Egion, 1420*; Eleanor, 1276*; Eliz., 1273*, 1276, 1409, 1420; Geo., 1372; Rev. Grindal(l), 547*, 1362; Hannah, 1058; Hen., 1493, 1499; John, 320*, 895, 1140, 1273*, 1274, 1417; Rev. John, 142; Joseph, 320, 1091, 1362, 1498, 1499; Joyce, 1268; L., 1434; Marg., 1498; Martha, 1270, 1471; Mary, 320, 1091; Mary Ann, 1417; Miles, 1409*, 1420*; Ric., 320, 814, 1059, 1062, 1274; Rev. Ric., 1165; Rob., 1058, 1498, 1502; Sam.,

440; Dr. Sam., 1276; Sarah, 814, 1274, 1372; Thos., 296, 637, 836, 1065, 1273, 1471; Rev. Thos., 221; W., 1290; Wm., 976, 1268, 1276*, 1499; —, 1198; fam., 440

Wilton (Wylton), Ann, 84; Eliz., 84; H. H., 1440; Jane, 963; John, 660; Mary, 84; Ralph de, 1422; Ric., 212; W. H., 1225; Wm., 84*, 963; Rev. Wm. H., 1228; Rev. Wm. Hen., 1224

Wilts, Dan., 660; Mary, 660*; and see Wilce

Wiltshire (Wilsha, Wilshere, Wilshire, Wiltshere, Wiltshier), Ant., 172; Betty, 172; Cornelius, 1481; Edw. of, 1512; Rev. Hen., 1140; Rev. John, 970; Mary, 172, 1481; Rob., 1307*; Sarah, 172; Thos., 172*, 781, 1218; Wm., 1481; —, 1339

Wily, see Willey

Wimblet, Thos., 868

Wimbow, John, 121

Winch, Hen., 1273

Winchcombe (Winchcomb), Alice, 621*; Ann(e), 618, 620, 621*; Bernard (Barnard), 78, 79; Eliz., 621, 622*, 1028, 1379; Hen., 621*, 1535; Jas., 1203, 1211; John, 621*, 622, 1028, 1211; Mary, 622; Nat., 197, 618, 619, 620; Sarah, 1211, 1522; Thos., 621; Wal., 1028; Wm., abbot, 1461; —, 1027

Winchelsea [peerage], see Finch, —

Winchester, Adam, 641*; Eleanor, 641; Hen., 846; Wm., 641

Winchester [peerage], see Poulett, Wm.; Quincy

Winde (Wind, Wynde), C., 1290*, 1291; Chas., 1262; Dan., 1167; Edith, 1098; Edw., 1167; Humph., 1098; John, 640, 1098, 1167*; Mary, 640, 1098, 1167; Sarah, 316, 1167*; Rev. Wm., 316, 493, 639, 1233; Rev., 493; —, 1289

Winder, Mary, 431; Rev. Mr., 431

Windham, see Wyndham

Windle, Rev. Chris., 198

Window (Windowe, Windows, Wyndow, Wyndowe), Anne, 460, 981, 1214; Dan., 1024; Deborah, 677; Eliz., 873, 974, 1024, 1251; Fream, 1217; Hen., 114, 347, 348*, 575, 1203, 1216; Rev. Hen., 228, 347, 1163, 1165; Jane, 97, 1251; John, 677, 974*; Ric., 460, 1214, 1217; Sarah, 348, 486; Wm., 93, 97, 486, 873, 981, 1251*; fam., 346

Windsor (Winser, Wyndsor), Eliz., 399; Hester, 397, 399; Sam., 397, 399; fam., 648

Windsor [peerage](Windsore, Wyndsore), And., Lord (baron), 91, 525, 646 n, 648; Edw., Lord, 648 n; Thos., Lord, 91, 648; Wm., Lord, 648 n, 651; Lord, 1215

Winfield (Whinfield), Cath., 352; Rev. John, 275, 350, 352, 785; Thos., 577

Wingate, Ann, 1344; Dan., 133; Eleanor, 133, 353; Eliza, 1344; Jane, 133; John, 858, 1344*; Joseph, 133*; Moses, 133; Priscilla, 1344; Wm., 133, 353

Wingfield, Edw. Rhys, 1012; Rev. Wm., 272

Wingod (Wingood, Wynegod), Alice, 768; Avis, 821; Jas., 550; John, 768, 907; Thos., 1540; Wm., 550, 768, 821

Winn, see Wynn

Winnett (Winnat), Eliz., 1213; Jasper, 1213, 1215, 1217; Sophia, 1213; Susannah, 1213

Winniat (Winniate, Winniatt), see Wynniatt

Winning (Wynynge), Matilda, 1317; Sarah, 254; Thos., 254

Winnington, E., 1459; Francis, 1460; Sir T., bt., 1459; —, 1457

Winsemore, see Winsmore

Winser, see Windsor

Winslow, Anne, 883*; John, 883*; Hester, 883*; Thos., 883

Winsmore (Winsemore), Anne, 1192; John, 1192*; Mary, 1192*; R., 1197; Ric., 1192*; Thos., 1192; Wm., 1064

Winsoun (Wynsoun), John, 1363; Ralph, 1150

Winstone (Winston), Albinia, 1156; Ann(e), 204*, 1533; Cath., 203; Dennis [Denise], 1129; Eliz., 1129; Geo., 388, 1129; Giles (Gyles), 1044, 1129; Sir H., 1132*; Hen., 1129; Sir Hen., 533, 1129; Jane, 204; John, 203, 1172; Marg., 1524, 1532; Mary, 388, 1550; P., 1047; Phil., 1044; Ric., 1533*; Sarah, 1522, 1527, 1550; Thos., 204, 264, 999, 1129, 1156, 1160, 1524, 1527, 1532*; W., 1122; (formerly Hayward), W., 1160; Wm., 204*, 1129, 1533, 1550*; Wm. Hayward, 833, 999; Mr., 1160; Mrs., 1160

Winter (Wintour, Wynter, Wyntour), Agnes, 1478; Ann(e), 554*, 723, 921, 929, 1162; Lady Anne, 921; Bridget, 191; Chas., 808; Sir Chas., 806; Editha, 1102; Sir Edw., kt., 576, 720*, 808, 895, 921; Eliza, 920; Eliz., 1494; Frances, 554*; Geo., 191, 552, 553, 554*, 812, 815; Sir Geo., 553; Giles, 788; Hester, 548; John, 552, 553*, 554*, 812, 929; Sir John, kt., 475, 476*, 544, 546*, 720, 759 n*, 805, 806 n*, 893, 928*, 929, 1323, 1404; Marg., 548; Martha, 812*; Mary, 35, 554, 812, 919; Nat., 1494; Ric., 550; Rev. Ric., 1031; Rob., 547, 548*, 1102; Rev. Rog., 1516; Thos., 1112; Wm., 35*, 475, 547*, 548*, 807, 812, 895, 920; Sir Wm., kt., 552, 720*, 805, 808, 893, 919; Lady, 812; Lieut.-Col., 915; —, 1162; fam., 544, 807

Winterbotham, —, 1370

Winterson, Wm., 1176

Wintle, Amy, 871*; Anna, 622; Ann(e), 194, 484*, 1396; Chas., 621, 1265; Durley, 1208; Eliz., 194, 624*, 871, 1399*; Geo., 194*, 932; Jacob, 1396*; Jas., 932, 1399, 1403; Jane, 871, 932, 1400; Joan, 486; John, 105, 264, 486, 822, 871, 931, 1268, 1396, 1400, 1403; Jonathan, 215, 821, 1396*, 1403; Joseph, 484*, 870, 871; Joyce, 822; Mary, 112, 821, 872, 931, 1143, 1396*; Ric., 857, 1396*; Rob., 821, 1403; Rosamund, 621; Rowland, 822; Sam., 215*, 821, 1403; Sarah, 1396, 1399*; Susannah, 821; Thos., 463, 484, 622, 822, 871*, 932, 1399*, 1403; Rev. Thos. Drayton, 1143; Wm., 624*, 871, 872*, 932, 1403; Winifred, 1265; Zachariah (Zechariah), 621*, 624*; —, 105, 1403*; and see Wynell

Winton, see De Winton

Wintour, see Winter

Winwood, Susanna, 1026

Wirlok, see Worlock

Wise (Wisse, Wyse), Ant., 1304; Cath., 389*, 1174;

Edw., 1210, 1304; Eliz., 296, 389, 1446*; Rev. Hen., 1346; Jane, 62*; Joan, 1210; Joanna, 62, 389*; John, 62, 389*, 1325; Mary, 389*; Mat., 1446; Nic. le, 1519; Rob., 296, 922, 1325, 1446*; Sarah, 1304, 1325; Uriah, 1174; Wm., 128, 197, 1210, 1304; fam. 130, 389; *and see* Sapiens; Wese

Wiseman, Edm., 1273*; Lieut. Edm., 1273; Sir Edm., kt., 1273; Mariana, 1273*; Marian Theophila, 1273; Simon, 1257

Wisham, *see* Wysham

Wishonger, Nic., 66

Wisnod (fl. 1066), 1147

Wisse, *see* Wise

Witchell (Wichell), Ann(e), 308*, 938, 1249; Ant., 938; Edw., 938; Eliz., 308*, 954, 1249, 1306*; Esther, 308; Frances, 1529; Hester, 938; Jas., 1249; John, 308*, 938*, 954, 1249; Jonathan, 938, 1535; Jones, 703; Martha, 703; Mary, 308, 703, 938, 1532, 1535; Ric., 1306, 1537; Sam., 305, 308*; Sarah, 308*; Thos., 308*, 1258, 1537; Wm., 701, 703

Witcomb (Witcombe), *see* Whitcombe

Witham, Joseph, 817; —, 817

Withepool (Withepol), Paul, 1015; —, 1441

Wither, *see* Withers

Witherington, Thos., 1282

Witherly, Martha, 728; Rob., 728; Susannah, 721; Thos., 728*

Withers (Whithers, Wither, Wyther, Wythers), Eliz., 937; Hester, 14, 1307; J., 1020; John, 1020; Marg., 1020; Mary, 1431; Phil., 826; Ric., 14; Sam., 1100; T., 1216; Thos., 937, 1307; Rev. Thos., 783; Trubshaw Chas., 1362; W., 1312; Wal., 1121, 1431; Wm., 14, 1110, 1121; (or Wythen), 1311*

Withorne, *see* Whithorne

Witlesey, Wm., bishop, 688, 1542

Witney, J., 1255

Witt, *see* Witts

Wittawar, Wm., 1313

Wittington, *see* Whittington

Witts (Witt, Wytt), Ann, 241, 575; Eliz., 703, 929, 1175; Esther, 399; Rev. F. E., 1090, 1092, 1093, 1154; Rev. Francis Edw., 1090*; Geo., 575; Hen., 575*; Hugh, 1068; Isabella, 703; John, 703*, 929*; Marg., 1090*; Martha, 929; Mary, 399; Rob., 703; Sam., 241, 703; Susannah, 703; Thos., 399, 984, 1164; Wm., 701, 703, 836; Mr. 1093; —, 1148

Wixey (Wicksey, Wixcey), Benj., 1058; Eleanor, 1445; Jas., 1445; Rob., 696

Wiyke, *see* Wicks

Wluvi (fl. 1066), 1074

Wode, atte, *see* Attwood

Wodehouse, Rev. Hen., 748; Wm., 364

Wodema[n], *see* Woodman

Wodemancote, *see* Woodmancote

Woderoue, *see* Woodroff

Wodmancote, *see* Woodmancote

Wodvin, Simon, 1477

Wogan, Eleanor, 1165*; Hen., 1543; John, 1165; Susan, 1165

Wokesey, R., 1074; Ric., 1074*

Wolde, —, 1069

Wolfrig, John, 1187

Wollery, Jane, 1249*; Rebecca, 1249; Thos., 1249*

Wolley, *see* Woolley

Wolnard, —, 704

Wolsey, cardinal, 605 n, 1309

Wolstan, archbishop, 628

Wolstan, bishop, 717, 1132*

Wontner, *see* Wantner

Wood (Woods), A., 233; Alex., 978; Alice, 1051; Ann(e), 904, 965, 976, 1081*, 1091*, 1112, 1138*, 1278, 1279, 1315*, 1316, 1415, 1471*, 1472, 1572; Ant., 1075; Benj., 1144*, 1147, 1289*, 1470*, 1471*; Chas., 631, 1081, 1144; D., 1215; Dinah, 1470*; Dinah Susannah, 1470; Edm., 906, 1081, 1445*; Edw., 636*, 1138, 1140; Eliz., 111, 631, 632*, 963, 965*, 1144, 1168, 1247, 1509; Esther, 317; Geo., 176; Hannah, 336, 473, 542, 636*, 1075*, 1081, 1247; Hen., 1415*; Hester, 904, 906, 1144; Hodges, 884; Humph., 965; Isabella, 1415; Jacob, 1247; Jas., 4, 262*, 336, 632, 696, 965, 1402; Jane, 948; Joan(e), 787, 935, 1279*; John, 4, 148, 370, 413, 419, 542, 632*, 636*, 637, 749, 751, 895, 906, 963, 965*, 976, 999, 1058, 1063, 1075*, 1081*, 1138*, 1144, 1168, 1278, 1279*, 1372, 1400, 1509, 1572*; Rev. John, 1388; Joseph, 787, 904, 906, 1112*, 1121; Judith, 542; Levy, 1513; Marg., 73, 632*, 965, 1433; Martha, 1079, 1400, 1471; Mary, 5, 262, 413, 474, 632, 636*, 751, 906*, 965*, 1075, 1112, 1279, 1433, 1572; Mic., 1051; Penelope, 1149, 1151*; Rebecca, 1144*; Ric., 264, 335, 473, 965, 1433*; Rev. Ric., 1238; Rob., 1405; Ro(w)land, 263, 335, 674; S., 1220; Sam., 904, 906, 1138; Rev. Sam., 1177; Sarah, 336, 542, 632, 637, 1058, 1075, 1247; Susan, 111; Susanna(h), 1470*, 1472; Thos., 5, 111, 336, 473, 474, 637, 803, 935, 1075, 1079, 1091, 1149, 1151, 1168, 1458, 1572; Rev. Thos., 635, 1104, 1149, 1151; Thomasin, 1279; W., 1101; Wm., 4, 133, 317, 336*, 542*, 632*, 904*, 906*, 948*, 965*, 978, 1075*, 1168, 1247*, 1258, 1315, 1316, 1445, 1470*, 1471, 1472, 1505; Rev. Wm., 878; Miss, 1165; —, 142, 259, 346, 893, 1064, 1165, 1256, 1311, 1317, 1378, 1433, 1458, 1475, 1477; fam., 263, 325, 440, 667, 672, 894; *and see* Attwood

Woodall (Woodhall), John, 412; Lydia, 412; Mary, 412; Thos., 412; Rev. Wm., 1217

Woodbury, —, 1122

Woodcock, Jas., 687, 1355; Mary, 858; Thos., 858; Rev. Thos., 674*

Woodcroft, Rev. John, 1017

Wooddeson, Anne, 856; Hen., 856

Woodford, Wentworth, 35

Woodhall, *see* Woodall

Woodham, Eliz., 846*; John, 846; Joseph, 846; Rebekah, 847; Wm., 847

Woodlands (Woodland), John, 778; Ric., 750*; Sarah, 750*; Wm., 750

Woodley, Sarah, 1278; Wm., 1278*

Woodman (Wodema[n]), Ann, 217, 389; Eliz., 1421; Emma, 1404; Hain(e)s, 217, 1421; John, 389*, 1450, 1453; Mary, 633, 1013*, 1453; Phil., 389*, 1013*; Priscilla, 389*; Sam., 633; Thos., 633; —, 1017, 1362; fam., 389*

Woodmancote (Wodemancote, Wodmancote), Peter de, 1381*; Wal. de, 1016

Woodroff (Woderoue, Woodrof, Woodrofe, Woodrofee, Woodroffe, Woodroof, Woodrough, Woodruff), Alice, 815; Ann(e), 1514, 1515; Arthur, 1429*; Blanch, 1514, 1515; Edm., 1514, 1515*, 1516; Eliz., 659, 1515*; Ellen Jane, 1515; Giles, 815; Isaac, 1514; Jas., 1514*, 1515*, 1516; Joan, 1514*; Marg., 1514; Mary, 53, 1514*; Nat., 703; R., 1256; Rebekah, 1429; Rev. Rob., 236; Sir Rob., kt., 53, 463; Susannah, 1514, 1515; Susannah Bland, 1515; Thos., 1514; Wal., 659; Wm. Smallwood, 1514; Mr., 1516; fam., 807

Woods, see Wood

Woodstock, Edm. of, earl of Kent, 876; Eleanor of, duchess of Gloucester, 1309; Thos. de, duke of Gloucester, 244, 927, 1309; —, 1220

Woodwall, Ric., 360 n

Woodward, Acton, 899, 900*; Alice, 280, 1274; Ann(e), 150, 209*, 844, 846, 847, 1250; Benj., 456, 1583; Betty, 844, 845, 1583; Chris., 278, 546, 898, 901*; Capt. Chris., 901; Dan., 1105, 1452*; Dorothy (Dorathy, Dorothea), 209*, 210*, 898, 901; Edw., 293, 296*; Eliz., 209, 293, 296, 844, 867, 1072, 1274*, 1452, 1583; Ferdinando, 844, 845*; Frances, 210; Francis, 206, 209*, 210*; Francis Berkeley, 209; Geo., 906; Gerves, 210; Hannah, 1250; Hen., 760; Hester, 569; J., 1132; Jacob, 1250*; Jas., 845, 847; Jane, 846; John, 84, 206, 209*, 283, 844*, 845, 846, 899, 1072, 1101, 1110, 1250, 1573*; (or Smyth), John, 1288; Jonathan, 280; Joseph, 844*, 846*, 1550*; Rev. Joseph, 1169; Martha, 18; Mary, 9, 150, 209, 283, 844, 845, 847, 901, 1250*, 1548, 1550; Newton, 209*; Prudence, 899; Ralph, 1017; Ric., 150, 210, 296, 708 n, 1101; Rev. Ric., 525; Sam., 9*; Sarah, 283*, 899, 901, 1452*, 1573; Thos., 209, 213*, 218, 296, 845, 867; Rev. Thos., 1392; Wal., 845, 846; Wm., 1274*, 1452, 1548; —, 159, 283, 996, 1074, 1186; (or Smyth), —, 1288; fam., 205, 894

Woolacomb, Rev. John, 1339

Woolams, see Woollam

Woolaston (Woolloston), Foucke, 804; Rob., 778; Susanna, 804

Wooles, Anselm, 873; Hester, 873

Wooley, see Woolley

Woolford, Mr., 1449; Mrs., 1449; —, 1456

Woollam (Woolams, Woollams), And., 1275*; Edw., 706; Eliz., 1275; Esther, 1275; Jane, 706*; Mary, 706; Maurecius, 1150; Thos., 706*; Wm., 744; —, 1150

Woollen, Rev. Thos., 452

Woolley (Wolley, Wooley), Barbara, 1498; Eleanor, 1162*; Eliz., 879*, 1498; Francis, 1010*; Geo., 1162; Jane, 879; John, 1010, 1498*; Joseph, 474,

1162*; Mary, 474; Sarah, 1010; Thos., 1498; Rev. Wm., 878, 879*; —, 1362

Woolloston, see Woolaston

Woolmer, Janet, 744; Thos., 744

Woolmonger, Wm. the, 1253*

Woolnough, Hen., 1120

Woolright, see Woolwright

Woolsworth, see Woolworth

Woolvin, John 699

Woolworth (Woolsworth), Ann, 1534; (or Webbe), Chris., 530; (or Webbe), Edm., 529; John, 1534*; (or Webbe), Ric., 529; Thos., 1534*; W., 1455; Wm., 1455, 1534; (or Webbe), Wm., 529*, 530; —, 1449, 1455; (or Webbe), fam., 530; and see Walesworth

Woolwright (Woolright), Betty, 176*; Emily, 1511; John, 1511; Julia, 1511; Ric., 176, 1539; Thos., 176*; Wilhelmina, 1511; Mr., 1513

Woore, Dan., 550; John, 1289; Mary, 550; Nancy, 550

Woosly, Martha, 826

Wootton (Wooton, Wotton, Woton), Anne, 626; Rev. Benj., 840; Rev. Chris., 696; Deborah, 636*; Joan, 766, 768; John, 1476; Nic. de, 1428*; Rev. Nic., 534; Rev. R. de, 1522; Ralph, 768; (or Culton), Ralph, 768; Ric., 708; Rob. de, 1478; Rev. Thos., 626*; Wm. (de), 360*, 636, 778 n, 1478

Worcester (Wyrcester), Wm. de, 357, 362, 443

Worcester [peerage], countess of, 913, 1516; earl of, 806 n, 915, 1189, 1322, 1516; Lord, 1093, 1516; marquis of, 124, 1121, 1322*, 1516; and see Beauchamp, R.; Somerset, passim; Tiptoft

Worden, Hannah, 1211, 1214; Nat., 1211, 1214

Worgan, Ann, 1400; Dan., 111; Edw., 249*, 921, 922*; Eliz., 248, 249, 922, 1162, 1515*; Hannah, 730, 921, 922; Hen., 249*, 250, 922; Jas., 922, 1162*; Jane, 1162; John, 249, 814, 923*, 1400, 1516; Rev. John Hartland, 1459; Joseph, 1515; Mary, 249, 464, 922, 1162; Mat., 47; Phillippa Challot, 1459; Ric., 105; Sarah, 1515; Thos., 47, 464*, 922, 1162; Wm., 55, 248*, 249, 923*, 1515*; —, 105

Workman (Workeman), Abraham, 782; Anna, 1532; Ann(e), 31, 34, 541, 699*; Bridget, 699; Dan., 543*, 782; Edw., 493, 697; Eliz., 282, 540, 541, 1100; Giles, 541; Rev. Giles, 31*; Hannah, 419, 782; Jas., 537; John, 541*, 699; Rev. John, 1223; Marg., 34, 699; (or Gloucester), Marg., 274; Ric., 31, 34, 419, 699; Rob., 543; Ruth, 842; Sam., 842*; Sarah, 543*; Stephen, 282; Thos., 699*; (or Gloucester), Thos., 274; Wm., 419*, 773; fam., 696; and see Warkman

Worlock (Warlick, Warlock, Wirlok, Worluck), Aaron, 703; Ann, 967; Cath., 1102, 1135, 1136; Eliz., 967, 1346; Hester, 284; Jas., 1133, 1135; Jane, 967*; John, 284, 967*, 1098; Mary, 284, 967*; Ric., 1539; Rob., 967*; Rog., 1346; Sam., 967; Stephen, 967; Susanna, 1098; Thos., 967; Wm., 1133, 1135, 1136; and see Wrilock

Worme, Ric., 761

Wormer, Rob., 797

Wormes, —, 1202

Wornell (Wornehill), Chrr., 985; Mary, 209*; Nic., 209*

Worrell (Warrall, Warrell), Ant., 768; Dan., 768*; Eliz., 1450*; Geo., 191; [?] Joan, 191; John, 1181; Mary, 766, 768*, 1450; Olive, 1181; Sam., 403; Sarah, 1413*, 1450; Susanna, 1413; Thos., 1413, 1450*; [?] Thos., 191; Rev. Thos., 954, 1450; Wm., 191, 1413*, 1450; *and see* Wyrall

Worsfold, John, 1472; Mary, 1472

Worth, Sir Edw., kt., 743

Worthington, Rev. W., 1539

Worthwode, Ric. de, 1102

Wotton (Woton), *see* Wootton

Wranford, *see* Randsford

Wrath or Wriothesley, Eliz., 612; Isabel, 612; Joan, 612; John, 612*

Wren (Wrinn), Edm., 1549; Hester, 204; Jas., 1159; Sarah, 1549; Thos., 204

Wrench, Rev. Elias, 785; Ric., 1313

Wrenshaw, Eliz., 1342; Rob., 1342

Wriggan (Wriggon), Rob., 1291; Rev. Rob., 1382

Wright (Wrighte, Write), Abigail, 5; Alice, 1366; And., 392 n; Ann(e), 412, 433*, 1257; Edm., 348; Edw., 328, 970, 1217; Eliz., 423*, 922, 1344, 1427; Geo., 3, 413, 1100; Harry, 434; Hen., 348; J., 1291; Jane, 348, 922; John, 423, 433, 434, 922, 1366; (or Glover), John, 321; Rev. John, 1228; Kenelm, 764; Mary, 131, 434, 1214, 1421; Nathan, 1344; Nat., 412; Phillis, 434; Rob., 419, 1062, 1366, 1427; Dr. Rob., bishop, 233; Susan, 1100; Thos., 970; Wm., 1064, 1329, 1421*; Rev. Wm., 421, 1329; —, 1062*, 1063, 1064, 1150

Wrilock, Wal., 1201; *and see* Worlock

Wrinn, *see* Wren

Wriothesley or Wrath, Eliz., 612; Isabel, 612; Joan, 612; John, 612*

Write, *see* Wright

Writell, R[ichar]d, 1218

Wrokeshal (Wrokeshull), Sir Geof. de, 778 n; —, 1490

Wroston, fam., 495

Wroths, Sam., 1459

Wroughton, Anne, 1048, 1051; Jas., 364; Sir Wm., kt., 1048, 1051; fam., 495

Wulfric (fl. 1066), 1482*

Wulfrith, archbishop, 1419

Wurfarth, bishop, 1512

Wyatt (Wiat, Wiatt, Wiett, Wyat, Wyett), Amia, 1280; Ann, 1155*, 1330; Cater, 1160; Chas., 1409*; Dan., 204; Eliz., 1155; Frances, 1277; H., 1216; Hen., 1215*, 1216, 1217; John, 204, 1155*, 1156, 1277*, 1280, 1330*; Rev. John, 445*, 691; Lawr., 797; Mary, 1156, 1160, 1277, 1409; Rev. Mic., 1441; Phil., 893; Priscilla, 1209; Ric., 1216; Rev. Ric., 421, 445*; Rev. Wal., 619, 620; Wm., 1277, 1331; Rev. Wm., 691; —, 1160; fam., 688, 1160

Wych, Ric., 1201

Wycherley, Dan., 544

Wyckes, *see* Wicks

Wycliff (Wickliffe), —, 717, 1419

Wydefeld, Wm. de, 1314; *and see* Whitfield

Wydvile, Sir E., 1257

Wye, Ant., 1033; Eliz., 1033; Francis, 909; Humph., 1033; Juliana, 1215*; Marg., 1033; Maud, 1032; Rob., 1031, 1215; T., 1032; Thos., 1032, 1215*; W., 1032, 1033; Rev. W., 1423; Wm., 1031, 1215; Rev. Wm., 1031; —, 1033, 1052, 1215; fam., 301, 1033*, 1203

Wyer, Rev. Dositheus, 1147; *and see* Ware

Wyett, *see* Wyatt

Wyke, *see* Wicks

Wykeham, *see* Wickham

Wykes, *see* Wicks

Wykewane, *see* Wickwan

Wylde, *see* Wild

Wyldefuir, John, 1258

Wylemot, *see* Wilmot

Wyley, John, 864

Wylikine, *see* Wilkins

Wylington (Wylinton), *see* Willington

Wylkes, *see* Wilkes

Wylkyns (Wylkynes), *see* Wilkins

Wyllam (Wyllames), *see* Williams

Wylles (Wyllis), *see* Willis

Wyllyames, *see* Williams

Wylton, *see* Wilton

Wyman, Eliz., 543; John, 760, 761*; Mary, 543*; Thos., 543*; *and see* Weyman

Wymark, Edw., 1140

Wymond, Hugh, 1513; John, 1172, 1379

Wyn, *see* Wynn

Wynde, *see* Winde

Wyndham (Windham), Anne, 765, 919; Chas., 919, 1516; Eleanor, 919; Esther, 1251; Francis, 919; Jane, 919*; John, 704, 919; Rev. John, 704; Mercy, 919; Thos., 765, 913, 919*; Sir Wadham, kt., 704; Wm., 704*, 705; fam., 913, 919

Wyndeley, Rev. Rob., 1228

Wyndow (Wyndowe), *see* Window

Wyndsor, *see* Windsor

Wyndsore, *see* Windsor [*peerage*]

Wynebeke, John, 1329, 1552

Wynegod, *see* Wingod

Wynell (Wynhull), Wal. de, 1440; —, 1403; *and see* Wintle

Wynforton, W., abbot, 1475

Wynhull, *see* Wynell

Wynn (Winn, Wyn, Wynne), Ann. 660, 1389, 1390; Edm., 970; Geo., 660; Lady Henrietta, 123; Hester, 970; John, 1314, 1389*, 1390*; Thos., 970*; Sir Thos., 519; Thos. Duringford, 658; Rev. Wm., 313; Sir Wm. Watkins, bt., 123

Wynniatt (Winniat, Winniate, Winniatt, Wynniat), Ann, 978; Eliz., 978, 1150; Frances, 1150; Hester, 978; Isabel, 1034; Jas., 978*, 1403; John, 548, 978*; Marg., 978; Reg., 1150*; Rev. Reg., 546, 547, 1103, 1104, 1149, 1150*; Ric., 548, 1034; Sarah, 978; Thos., 978, 1150*; Wenman, 546, 1150

Wynnington, Rev. Benj., 184, 185

Wynsoun, *see* Winsoun

Wynter (Wyntour), *see* Winter
Wynyarde, Alice, 238; John, 238
Wynynge, *see* Winning
Wyrall (Wyrhale), Al[i]ce, 191; Anne, 191; Barbara, 192; Bridget, 192*; Cath., 191; Dennis, 191; Edw., 191; Eliz., 191; Geo., 188, 191*, 814; Jenkin, 191; Jeptha(h), 190, 191*, 192*, 193*; John, 814; Jonathan, 192; Lane, 191; Martha, 193; Mary, 191*; Mat., 188; Sarah, 191, 814*; Tace, 191; Wm., 191*; Mr., 188; fam., 188; *and see* Worrell
Wyrcester, *see* Worcester
Wyse, *see* Wise
Wysham (Wisham), Eliz., 1161; Mary, 193, 1161; Ric., 193; Thos., 1161*, 1162; —, 1162
Wyshaud, Peter, 1477
Wytchyrche, *see* Whitchurch
Wytenouz, Wm., 1314
Wyth (Wythe), John, 1504, 1552; Rob., 1292; Thos., 1314; *and see* Wethe
Wythege, Rob., 1331
Wythen (or Wyther), —, 1311*
Wyther (Wythers), *see* Withers
Wytt, *see* Witts
Wytwelle, Geof. de, 1061
Wytyndon, *see* Whittington
Wyxe, *see* Wicks

Yapp, John, 937; Mary, 937
Yardington (Yeardington), Frances, 1463; Hen., 1472, 1477; Jo[a]ne, 1463; Marg., 1472; Susanna, 1463*; Thos., 641, 1463*, 1477; Wm., 1463, 1472; —, 1476
Yardley (Yardly, Yerdeleye), B., 1092; Benj., 1092; Chas., 897; Geo., 897; Rev. Geo., 865, 951*; Mary, 951*; Penelope, 951; Simon de, 1292; —, 1092
Yareforde, John de, 1379
Yarnold, Elisha, 293; John, 1289*; Marg., 293; Thos., 1050
Yarnton (Yearnton), Alice, 1050; Betty, 1050; Eliz., 1049, 1050; John, 1048, 1050*; Mary, 1050; Sarah, 1049, 1050*; Thos., 1049*, 1050*; Rev. Thos., 1050; W., 1052*; Wm., 1050
Yarrow, *see* Yerrow
Yarworth, Eliz., 920, 923; Giles, 923; Hen., 923; Isabella, 922; Jas., 920; Mary, 923; Ric., 922*, 923, 1162; Sarah, 922; Thos., 922; —, 913
Yatcombe, Rob., 722
Yate (Yates, Yeate, Yeates), A., 501; Alice, 501; Anna Maria, 268, 269, 1129; Annabella Christiana, 268*, 269; Anne, 1073, 1458; Arethusa, 820; Barbara, 501; Caroline, 1129; Caroline Eliz., 268, 1315; Cath., 265 n, 266, 267*, 268, 546; Chas., 65, 67, 68*, 265, 268, 295, 820, 1129*, 1132; Dorothy, 470, 471, 1129, 1132; E., 1456; Edw., 1449, 1451; Eleanor, 1431; Eliz., 68*, 262, 268*, 269, 536, 610, 655, 1129*, 1132, 1451, 1459; Esther, 655, 980; Frances, 820*; Francis, 820; Rev. Francis, 1129*, 1132, 1456; Grace, 655; Henrietta, 820, 1129; Henrietta Arabella, 820; Hen., 262*, 980; Rev. Hen. Gorges Dobyns, 266*,

626; Jas., 1529; Jane, 268*, 269; Rev. Job, 1028, 1031; John (atte, de), 65*, 66*, 67, 68, 265*, 266, 268*, 269*, 511, 651, 1102, 1415, 1473; Joseph, 990; Joyce, 68; Kath., 268; Marg., 265 n; Mary, 66, 68*, 262*, 267, 820*, 1129*, 1418, 1431, 1529*; Rev. Mat., 853; Millicent, 295*; Nat., 1129*; Nourse, 819, 820*; Priscilla, 820*; R. G. D., 626; Rice, 265*, 266*, 267*, 268*, 440, 546*, 619; Ric., 3, 65, 67, 68*, 268, 470, 471, 1129; Ric. Gorges, 269; Ric. Gorges Dobyns, 269; Rob., 267; (formerly Dobyns), Rob., 265; Rob. Dobyns, 268, 269*; Rob. Gorges Dobyns, 265, 266*, 268*, 269, 440, 546, 619, 625; Sam., 536, 655*, 1030; Sarah, 151, 232, 262, 655, 1508; Sophia, 1129; T., 1419, 1460; Thos., 151, 262, 265 n, 651, 717, 1431, 1458, 1508; Rev. Thos., 500, 501*; Wal. (atte), 265*, 266*, 267, 268*, 610, 619, 625, 820, 1370; Col. Wal., 546; Wal. Honywood, 266, 268, 546; Wm. (atte), 262*, 267, 295*, 664, 1104, 1129*, 1198, 1232, 1459, 1460; Rev. Wm., 500, 501, 1328, 1458; Mr., 266, 1201; Mrs., 66*; — at, 1402; fam., 65*, 66, 68, 265 n, 268 n, 625, 819, 1543; *and see* Gate
Yateman (Yatman), John, 1127; W. H., 1247; Wm., 900, 1255
Yates, *see* Yate
Yatman, *see* Yateman
Yatton, Rev. Ric., 1404
Ydebury, *see* Hydebury
Yealfe, *see* Jelf
Yeamans (Yeamens), *see* Yeomans
Yeardington, *see* Yardington
Yearnton, *see* Yarnton
Yearp, Joice, 434; Wm., 434
Yearsley, Eliz., 466, 467, 789; Hen., 466*, 467*, 479; John, 789*; Jos., 789; Joseph, 789; Joyce, 789; Mary, 789*; Stephen, 789*
Yeast, Thos., 660
Yeate (Yeates), *see* Yate
Yedith, —, 1033
Yeels (Yeeles), *see* Eyles
Yeend, Eliz., 1348; Frances, 397; Jas., 1348*; John, 74, 397; Mary, 397; Thos., 397
Yells, *see* Eyles
Yelverton, Sir Hen., 560; Marg., 560
Yeme (Yemm), Edm., 536; John, 1039; Marg., 112, 536
Yeomans (Yeamans, Yeamens), Dame Abigail, 1408; Alice, 1343; Ann, 1410; Eliz. Ann(e), 1156, 1157; Eliz. Rachel Ann, 1156; Frances Mackennen, 1156, 1157; Geo., 1386; John, 1156, 1157*, 1343*; Joseph, 161; Marg., 1419; Mary, 1386; Sir Rob., kt. & bt., 1407, 1408, 1419; Sampson, 1410*; Wm., 1156, 1157; Lady, 1408
Yerbury (Yorberry), Jas., 1202; Susanna, 210; Thos., 930; Wm., 210; —, 1202
Yerdeleye, *see* Yardley
Yerrow (Yarrow), Eleanor, 1269; Eliz., 1269; Jonathan, 1269*; Mary, 1269; Sarah, 1269*; —, 1288, 1289
Yewen (Yeuen, Yevens), Hannah, 1368; Joseph, 1186, 1368; —, 1238

Yonge, *see* Young

Yonnes, Rev. John, 1238

Yorberry, *see* Yerbury

York (Yorke), Eliz., 325; Dr. Jas., bishop, 609, 610*; John, 325; (or Perrin), John, 1194; Mary, 276; Phil., earl of Hardwick, 663, 664, 671*, 672*, 674*; Ralph de, 753; Thos., 276, 924; Wm., 1126; fam., 1016, 1380

York [*peerage*], Cicely, duchess of, 252, 791, 792, 1255; Edm., duke of, 1255; Edw., duke of, 195, 807, 893, 1159, 1255; Eliz., wife of Hen. VII, 1580; Jas., duke of, 894 n; Ric., duke of, 252, 876*, 1255; *and see* Plantagenet, Ric.

Young (Yonge, Younge), Adam le, 1102; Ann(e), 1360, 1533; Betty, 543; Chas., 842*, 844*; Dan., 543, 1137; Edw., 344, 353; Eleanor, 1063, 1499; Eliz., 340, 474, 907, 1281; Esther, 1034; Hannah, 434, 442; Hen., 1504; Hester, 276; J., 1404; Jas., 907; Jane, 1534; Jemima, 1444; Rev. Jerome, 802; John, 126, 276, 471, 602, 1082, 1281, 1393, 1399, 1403*, 1498, 1499*; Joseph, 832, 872; Martha, 344; Mary, 261, 344, 442, 471*, 662, 730, 1396; Nash Eliz., 842, 844; Nat., 543, 662; Nic. le, 1447; Ric., 442, 858, 1034, 1187; Rev. Ric., 1228; Rob., 1513, 1533; Sam., 474; Simon, 1498, 1502; Susanna, 1498, 1499; Thos., 276, 344, 434*, 1396, 1444, 1499, 1551; W., 1063; Wal., 1534*; Wm. (le), 261, 276, 442, 499, 730, 1062, 1329, 1534, 1551; Wm. T., 1360; Dr., 364 n; —, 1015, 1016, 1017, 1063*, 1317

Ywelege (Ywly), *see* Uley

Zaneworth, Felicia de, 1485

Zouche (Souch, Zouch), Alice, 859, 988*; Allan la, 1237; Benj., 988; Elinor de la, 1120; Eliz., 989; Eliz. Goodwin, 988; Frances, 989; Francis, 988; Francis Rob., 988*; Goodwin, 988*; John, 988*; Sir John, kt., 162; Marg., 988; Mary, 162, 988, 989; Maud, 1261; Phebe, 988; Ralph le, 688; Thos., 989*; W., Lord Zouch, 1261; Wm. le, 570; Wm., Lord Zouche, 859; Lady, *see* Berkeley, Mary; — (de) la, 1120, 1237; *and see* Such

Zouge, Hen., 1404

—hull, John, 1356

—owles, Thos., 1278; Wm., 1278

INDEX OF PLACES

* An asterisk indicates that the page has more than one reference.

Page-numbers in **bold** type are for the main entry for a parish; the references to the parish on those pages are not analysed further. Places are not indexed when they are named in the text simply to locate other places or for differentiation, are mentioned as at a stated distance, as places to or from which roads and watercourses ran, or as being part of the view, or are included in a peerage title. A few minor place-names are not indexed, such as those of small estates and of fields. Not all minor variations in spelling are shown, but the aim has been to include any variation where to do so might help the user of the index.

Abbenhall (Abbenhull, Abbinhall), *see* Abenhall
Abbey Dore, *see* Dore, Abbey
Abbot's Barton, *see* Barton, Abbot's
Abbots Leigh, *see* Leigh, Abbots
Abbot's Place, in Hartpury, 680
Abbots Wood, in East Dean, 476, 477, 605 n
Abbotside, in Cromhall, 453*, 454
Abenhall (Abbenhall, Abbenhull, Abbinhall, Abinghall), **1–5**, 457, 464, 467, 468, 470*, 479, 605 n, 1403, 1472; *and see* Guns Mill; St. Anthony's Well; Wilderness, the
Aberdare (Aberdear) (Carms., *recte* Glam.), 1174
Abergavenny (Mon.), 113, 714, 1514
Abersenny, near Cray (Brec.), 377
Aberystwyth (Cardig.), 313 n
Abingdon (Abindon) (Berks.), 372, 572; abbey, 518* & n, 519
Abinghall, *see* Abenhall
Ablington, in Bibury, 184*, 185*, 186, 429, 1047
Abloads (Ablodes, Ablonds) Court, in Sandhurst, 131, 350, 853, 1044, 1046*, 1047, 1373
Abnash, *see* Avenis
Abney Park Cemetery, *see* Stoke Newington
Abone (Roman station), 205, 719, 806
Abson (Abston), in Wick and Abson, 726, 1428
Acholt, in Kingswood (formerly Wilts.), 527, 778 n
Acman Street, *see* Akeman Street
Aconbury (Herefs.), nunnery, 1257*
Acton [*unspecified*], 1423, 1455
Acton (Worcs.), 542
Acton [*unspecified*], in Hamfallow or Hinton, 738 n
Acton, Iron (Iorn Acton, Ironacton), **12–18**, 457, 1159; residents, 52*, 265 n, 579, 612, 958, 996*, 1113, 1115, 1306, 1312, 1326, 1327, 1336, 1426, 1452, 1547, 1548*; *and see* Acton Ilger; Chilwood; Latteridge
Acton Ilger, in Iron Acton, 12
Acton Turville (Turvyl Aston), **19–20**, 124, 555, 1339
Addenborough, *see* Attenborough

Adderbury (Oxon.), 891, 1001; *and see* Truckford
Addington (Surr.), 827 n
Adlestrop (Addlestrop), **21–6**, 36, 255, 457
Admington (Adminton), in Quinton, 988*, 989*, 1001, 1002*
Adsett, in Westbury on Severn, 1400, 1401, 1402, 1403
Aedes Brokiane [? Brook House, in Painswick], 290
Africa, 49, 932, 1367; *and see* Alexandria; Algiers; Cape Town; Good Hope, Cape of; Mozambique; Sierra Leone
Ailberton, *see* Aylburton; Elberton
Ailstone (Ayleston), in Atherstone on Stour (Warws.) and Clifford Chambers, 400
Akeman Street (Acman Street, Ikenild Way), 355 n, 427, 1321
Aldborough Hatch, in Ilford (Essex), 393 n
Aldbourne (Aldbourn) (Wilts.), 843; *and see* Upham
Alderley (Alderly), **29–36**, 457, 859, 909, 910; residents, 612, 695, 696*, 967, 1449, 1510, 1521, 1528; *and see* New Mills
Aldermaston (Berks.), 471
Alderton (Aldrinton), **27–8**, 398, 966, 1148, 1287, 1311, 1475, 1504; *and see* Dixton
Aldsworth, **37–8**, 1350*
Alexandria (Alexander) (Egypt), 1026
Algiers, 1281
Aliston, *see* Allaston
Alkerton, in Eastington, 558*, 559, 619, 1006
Alkington, in Berkeley, 154, 159, 160, 161, 170, 171, 173, 175*, 663 n; *and see* Baynham; Blanchworth; Goldwick; Heath, the; Heathfield; Huntingford; Kittsgreen; Michael Wood; Newport; Oakleaze; Rugbag; Swanley; Wick; Woodford
Alkmondesbury, *see* Almondsbury
All Souls College, Oxford, 96, 359 n, 497 n, 651 n, 713 n, 1382*, 1495
Allaston (Aliston, Alliston), in Lydney, 807, 813

Allerton (Yorks. W.R.), 941
Allesley (Warws.), 393 n, 341
Alleston, *see* Alveston (Warws.)
Allington (Wilts.), 311 n
Alliston, *see* Allaston
Allmsbury, *see* Almondsbury
Allstone, *see* Alstone
Allystone, *see* Alveston
Alma (Russia), 1073
Almondsbury (Alkmondesbury, Allmsbury, Almsbury, Aunsbury), **39–49**, 98, 457, 576, 603, 1170, 1327, 1530; Almondsbury Hill, 39, 42; residents, 456, 730*, 731, 833, 961, 963*, 1158, 1426, 1498; *and see* Compton; Compton, Easter; Compton Greenfield; Earthcott, Gaunt's; Ellinghurst; Gumhurn; Hempton; Knole; Over; Patchway; St. Swithin's; Woodlands
Alney (Olney) Island, in Deerhurst, 483
Alney (Olney) Island, in Maisemore, 483
Alresford, New (Hants), 341
Alrington, *see* Alvington
Alscot (Alscoate, Alscote), in Preston on Stour, 987, 988*, 1040, 1441; Alscot House, 987
Alscot (Oxon.), *see* Alvescot
Alstone (Allstone, Alston), in Cheltenham, 325*, 1163; residents, 28, 331, 332, 333*, 334*, 335, 336*, 337*, 338*, 339, 340, 949, 1232
Alstone, in Overbury (Worcs.), 73*
Alton Barnes (Alton) (Wilts.), 879
Altona (Germany), 1067
Alvescot (Alscot) (Oxon.), 136, 220, 600, 1441
Alveston (Allystone), **50–2**, 1405, 1516; residents, 17, 48, 82*, 112, 958, 1020, 1234*, 1297, 1301, 1303, 1306, 1307*, 1326*, 1327*, 1328, 1525; *and see* Earthcott; Grovesend; Woodhouse, the
Alveston (Alleston) (Warws.), 400, 1507
Alvington (Alrington), **53–5**, 205, 457, 806, 807 n, 1111
Amberley, in Minchinhampton, 649
America, 1088
America, Central, *see* Roaton Island
America, North, 1180, 1187, 1303, 1529, 1576; *and see* Boston; Canada; Carolina; Georgia; New England; New York; Newburgh; United States; Virginia
Amiens (France), 1088, 1494
Ampney [*unspecified*], 990, 1202
Ampney, Down, 56, **507–10**, 552 n, 888, 1202, 1482
Ampney brook, 508 n
Ampney Crucis (Amney Crucis, Holy Rood Ampney), **56–60**, 61, 64, 130, 184, 367, 457, 370, 678, 679, 1311, 1345; *and see* Wiggold
Ampney St. Mary or Eastbrook or Ashbrook, 56*, **61–2**, 63, 184, 369, 678; *and see* Chapel, the; Still House, the
Ampney St. Peter or Eastington, 56, **63–4**, 184, 556, 670, 678; *and see* Easington
Ampthill (Beds.), 123
Anderford brook, 478 n
Andoversford, in Dowdeswell, 503, 911, 1056
Angers (Angiers) (France), 136

Anglesey (Monae Insula), 1495
Annandale, *see* Applegarth; Hoddom; Holmains
Anthony, *see* Antony
Antigua (Leeward Islands, West Indies), 407, 1156, 1157, 1316*, 1412
Antony (Anthony) (Cornw.), 1073
Antwerp (Belgium), 305 n*, 1123*
Anwards, in Tidenham, 1320*, 1322
Apperley (Aperley), in Deerhurst, 482, 483, 484, 485*, 486*, 803, 949
Appleby (Westmld.), 720
Applegarth (Applegirth), in Annandale (Scot.), 375
Appleton, in Flitcham wih Appleton (Norf.), 753, 755
Aquae Solis, *see* Bath
Ardingly (Ardingley) (Suss.), 1019
Argoed (Mon.), 809*
Arle, in Cheltenham, 939, 984, 1042; Arle Court, 325, 328 n, 330, 331, 337, 338, 339* 585 & n
Arlingham (Erlingham), **65–70**, 197, 268, 457, 1439, 1440; Arlingham Court, 625; land in, 41, 1054, 1147, 1403; manor, 605 n*, 1538; residents, 3, 172, 265 & n*, 267, 268, 470, 471, 1129, 1201, 1511; *and see* Barrow; Court, the; Milton End; Overton; Puckpool; Slowwe; Southend; Wick
Arlington, in Bibury, 184*, 186, 679, 755
Armagh (Irel.), 1417
Armescote, *see* Armscote
Arms (or Heralds), College (or Office) of (London), 552 n, 1059, 1380
Armscote (Armescote), in Tredington (Worcs.), 989, 1458
Arthingworth (Northants.), 1575
Arundel (Arundell) (Suss.), 1295
Ascott, in Whichford (Warws.), 1002
Ashbrook, *see* Ampney St. Mary
Ashchurch, **71–4**, 457, 586, 1290*, 1348*, 1381, 1382; *and see* Aston on Carrant; Fiddington; Home Downs; Natton; Northway and Newton; Pamington
Ashelworth, *see* Ashleworth
Ashington (Som.), 560
Ashleworth (Ashelworth, Ashlerworth), 41, **75–7**, 442, 682, 684, 687; *and see* Beamonds; High Cross; Knight's Green; Longridge End; Meerend; Nup End; White End; Wickridge
Ashley (Wilts.), 419, 448, 1048
Ashley, in Charlton Kings, 313, 325
Ashmead, in Cam, 277, 283*
Ashridge (Ashrugge) (Herts.), abbey, 709 n
Ashton [*unspecified*] (Northants.), 446
Ashton, Cold (Cold Aston, Coldashton), **80–4**, 457, 555, 846; *and see* Hamswell; Monk Woods; Turners Court
Ashton, Long (Ashton) (Som.), 208, 725, 726, 728, 833, 1120, 1155, 1156, 1160, 1413, 1428, 1458; Ashton Court, 1156
Ashton, Steeple (Steeple Aston, Stepleaston) (Wilts.), 1525, 1537
Ashton Court, *see* Ashton, Long
Ashton Hall, in Ashton with Stodday (Lancs.), 1059

Ashton Keynes (Ashton Kaynes) (Wilts.), 344, 1010, 1083, 1256
Ashton under Hill (Ashton), **89–90**, 150, 174*, 1052, 1287, 1311, 1386*, 1387
Ashwicke (Ashwick), in Marshfield, 839, 840*, 842, 843*, 1524, 1545
Aspley Guise (Aspley Gowiz) (Beds.), 134, 259, 581
Assen [? Aston Ingham (Herefs.)], 789
Aston (Warws.), 656
Aston, in Avening, 91*, 92*, 93, 96, 97*, 341, 648, 1147
Aston, Hanging, see Aston Magna
Aston, Little [? Aston Subedge], 947, 1092
Aston Blank or Cold Aston, **78–9**, 457, 1092*, 1189
Aston Ingham (Herefs.), 467, 659, 789*; and see Assen; Warren, the
Aston Magna (Aston, Eston, Hanging Aston), in Blockley, 218, 220, 225, 226*, 296
Aston on Carrant (Aston), in Ashchurch, 71*, 72*, 397*, 1287, 1289
Aston Rowant (Oxon.), 605 n
Aston Somerville, **85–6**
Aston Subedge, **87–8**, 570, 864 n, 866, 867*, 1430, 1431, 1459; and see Aston, Little
Atcombe Court, in Woodchester, 1511, 1512
Atford, see Atworth
Athelord's Place, see Scarr, the
Atherstone (Great Atherston) (Warws.), 1140
Atherstone on Stour, see Ailstone
Attenborough (Addenborough) (Notts.), 1003
Atworth (Atford), in Bradford on Avon (Wilts.), 496; and see Cottles
Audley End, in Saffron Walden (Essex), 43
Auford, see Ayford
Aunsbury, see Almondsbury
Aust, 50, **98–100**, 457, 717, 1320, 1321; Aust Cliff (Auster Cliff, Austre Clyve), 1345, 1419
Australia, see Brisbane; Queensland
Avenage, see Avenis
Avening (Evening), **91–7**, 457, 1207, 1218; land in, 525, 1512; manor, 648, 653; rector, 341 n, 653, 1029, 1136; residents, 656, 657*, 1137, 1508, 1510; and see Aston; Lowsmoor; Nailsworth; Pimbury; Tingle Stone, the
Avening, in Thornbury, 1312
Avening, in Tortworth, 1345
Avenis (Abnash, Avenage), in Bisley, 197, 204
Avignon (France), 724
Avon rivulet, 91, 341
Avon, river (Bristol Avon), 205, 403, 404
Avon, river (Warwickshire Avon), drowning in, 1358; fishery, 1388
Awre (Awe, Awr), **101–12**, 352, 664 n, 917, 918, 933, 1354; and see Blakeney; Bledisloe; Brims Pill; Etloe; Field House, the; Gatcombe; Hagloe; Hamstalls; Hayes; Hayfield; Millend; Nether Hall; Nibley; Noose, the; Oatfield; Pomerton; Poulton; Sempflye; Wharf, the; Woodend; Woodside, the
Axbridge (Som.), 720

Axminster (Great Axminster) (Som.), 1418
Ayford (Auford, Eyeford), in Marshfield, 839, 845
Aylberton, see Elberton
Aylburton (Ailberton, Aylberton), in Lydney, 55*, 805, 807, 808*, 812, 813*, 814*; and see Hill Common
Aylesmore, in St. Briavels, 245, 733*, 735
Ayleston, see Ailstone
Ayleworth, see Aylworth
Aylton (Herefs.), 993
Aylworth (Ayleworth), in Naunton, 79, 706, 889*, 890*, 944, 1042, 1190
Aynho (Aynhoe) (Northants.), 256

Babington, in Kilmersdon (Som.), 1420
Bachcombe [? Bach in Kimbolton or Bache in Much Cowarne] (Herefs.), 1089
Backhouse, in Bewerley or Bolton Percy (Yorks. W.R.), 1090
Backs [unidentified, ? in Oxenhall], 965*
Baconsthorpe (Bocansthrop) (Norf.), 520
Badbrook, in Stroud, 1037, 1144, 1203, 1215
Badgeworth (Badgworth, Bageworth), **113–18**, 150, 259 n, 457, 511, 585, 587, 640, 1079, 1370, 1494; and see Bentham; Crickley Hill; Greenway, the; Horsebere Bridge; Hunt Court; Shurdington, Little; Witcombe, Little
Badgworth (Badgnorth) (Som.), Badgworth Court, 407
Badminton, Great (Badminton), **119–24**, 125*, 457, 695, 703, 836, 938; and see Great Lodge, the
Badminton, Little, in Hawkesbury, 119, 124, **125**, 695, 696, 697
Badsey (Worcs.), 1274
Bagendon (Baginton, Bagyndene), **126–7**, 362, 431, 1202; and see Barrett's Breach
Bageworth, see Badgeworth
Bagpath, in Newington Bagpath, 1136
Bagstone, in Wickwar, 1345*, 1455
Baise, see Base Court
Baker's Leaze [? in Henbury], 721
Balaklava (Russia), 1073
Balham (Batham), in Streatham (Surr.), 1209
Balling a Gowing, see Balnagown
Balliol (Baliol) College, Oxford, 25, 233 n, 411, 583, 1163, 1355
Ballyn Varwick [? Ballynacarriga] (Irel.), 723
Ballynacarriga, see Ballyn Varwick
Balnagown (Balling a Gowing) (Scot.), 639
Bampton (Oxon.), 373, 795, 1196; and see Cote
Banbury (Banburi) (Oxon.), 311 n, 1189
Bandon, river (Irel.), 723
Bangor (Caern.), 205
Bangor (Cardig.), 1327
Banington, see Langford
Banks Fee or Blanks Fee or Southfield, in Condicote and Longborough, 816, 817
Bannockburn (Scot.), 1011, 1287, 1474
Banwell (Som.), 407; and see St. Georges
Baptist Mills, in St. Philip and St. Jacob, Bristol, 604
Barbados (Barbadoes) (West Indies), 410, 412, 497 n*, 1245, 1281, 1545, 1546

Barcroft Hall, in Whalley (Lancs.), 1559
Bares Court, in Kempsford, 775
Barford [Barford St. John or Barford St. Michael] (Barvard) (Oxon.), 1065
Barkeswell, see Berkswell
Barking (Essex), 1192
Barking (Suff.), 883
Barkley, see Berkeley
Barley Bridge, in Rudford, 1233
Barley Wood, near Wrington (Som.), 1160
Barnes (Surr.), 827 n
Barnesley, see Barnsley
Barnes, Lower, see Barns
Barnet (Mdx.), 1287
Barnet, Chipping (Herts.), 408, 829 n, 1011
Barns (Barnes), Lower, in Kingswood (formerly Wilts.), 1532
Barnsley (Barnesley), **128–30**, 298, 360, 374, 457, 591 n, 761, 1191, 1497; Barnsley Park, 128
Barnstaple (Devon), 1219
Barnwood, **131–3**, 347, 449, 457, 1376, 1377, 1547; Barnwood Court, 1138
Barrett's Breach (Barrow's Bridge), in Bagendon, 126
Barrington (Bernynton) [unspecified], 1059, 1189
Barrington, Great (Barrington), **134–8**, 139, 246, 457, 692, 856, 894
Barrington, Little, 134, **139–41**
Barrow and Barrow Hill, in Arlingham, 65, 66*
Barrow, in Boddington, 228, 229, 1165
Barrow's Bridge, see Barrett's Breach
Barr's Court, in Bitton, 205*, 209
Barton (Herefs.), 1058
Barton, in Temple Guiting, 636*, 638, 639, 640
Barton and Barton Farm, in Cirencester, 365, 387
Barton, Abbot's (Bertona), in Gloucester, 565 n
Barton, King's, manor (Gloucester), 1047, 1377
Barton, King's, hundred, see Barton Regis
Barton End, in Horsley, 748
Barton Regis (King's Barton), manor and hundred (Bristol), 833, 1159*, 1160, 1553
Barvard, see Barford
Base Court (Baise), in Westbury on Severn, 1096
Bath (Aquae Solis) (Som.), 205 , 252; abbey, college, or priory, 80, 838, 1321*, 1322*, 1323; burial, 972, 1185*; death at, 86, 224, 428, 959, 972, 1185*, 1209, 1253*, 1303*, 1338*, 1341, 1360, 1507; military events, 6, 359, 553, 839; residents, 435, 552, 554, 725, 845, 1116*, 1141, 1174, 1318, 1336*, 1427, 1439, 1490, 1552; Brock Street, 1208; St. James's church, 972; and see Walcot
Bath and Wells (Bath, Wells), bishop, 191, 651 n, 838, 1015, 1016, 1056, 1086, 1428*; dean and chapter, 1428
Bath Easton, see Batheaston
Batham, see Balham
Batheaston (Bath Easton) (Som.), 83*, 239, 829 n, 845, 846
Batsford (Battesford), **142–4**, 205, 218, 272, 457, 804, 1077, 1190, 1420

Battersea (Surr.), 827 n
Battesford, see Batsford
Battle (Suss.), 1281; abbey, 101
Battlebridge [unidentified] (Hants), 1538
Baunton (Baudenton), **145–6**, 990, 1201
Baunton Mill, in Cirencester, 1202*
Bayeux (Bayeaux) (Normandy), 525 n
Bayford (Herts.), 779
Baynham, in Alkington, 169
Beach, in Bitton, 81, 82*, 84*, 205, 210, 212*
Beachley, in Tidenham, 53, 98, 1319, 1320, 1321*, 1322*; and see Old Passage Ferry
Beacon Hill, in Standish, 672
Beaconsfield (Bucks.), 599
Beamesley, see Beamsley
Beaminster (Dors.), 1185
Beamonds [? in Ashleworth], 77
Beamsley (Beamesley) (Yorks. W.R.), 867
Bearse, the, in St. Briavels, 479
Beauchamp or Warwick Court, in Fairford, 592
Beaulieu (Boxleau) (Hants), abbey, 707, 869
Beaurepair, in Haresfield, 672
Beauvais (France), 1133
Beauvale, in Greasley (Notts.), 420
Beckford, 71, 89*, **147–51**, 457, 544 n; and see Bengrove; Didcot; Grafton; Tibblestone, the
Beckington (Som.), 412
Beckley (Oxon.), 25
Beddington (Surr.), 420, 827 n
Beddleford [unidentified], in Berkeley, 1098
Bedford (Beds.), 99, 651, 849, 366 n
Bedfordshire, 838; and see Ampthill; Aspley Guise; Bedford; Bletsoe; Dean, Upper; Elstow; Eyworth; Haynes; Henlow; Limbury; Northills; Steppingley; Wood End
Bedminster (Som.), 835, 960, 1185
Bedwyn, Great (Bedwin) (Wilts.), 123*, 1176
Beeks (Bicks), in Marshfield, 839, 840*
Belgium (Belgae), 23, 162; and see Antwerp; Bruges; Brussels; Ghent; Olne; Tournai; Vilvoorde
Bellington, see Billington
Belswardyne (Bells Wardine), in Sheinton (Salop.), 1273
Belton (Lincs.), 448
Belvoir (Belvidere) (Lincs.), priory, 1016, 1043, 1052
Bencombe, in Uley, 1367, 1369
Bengal (India), 187, 697, 974, 1143, 1524
Bengrove, in Beckford, 147, 149
Bengrove, in Sandhurst, 1046
Bennack, see Benwick
Benthall (Salop.), 1274
Bentham, in Badgeworth, 113, 118*, 713
Benwick (Bennack) (Cambs.), 1377
Beoley (Worcs.), 848
Berkeley (Barkley, Berchelai, Berkelie, Berkley, Berkly), 66*, 457, 529, 894 n, 1173, 1176, 1177; abbey, 533, 1101, 1512, 1419; castle, 152, 153*, 157, 158, 159, 330, 529, 530, 628 n, 664, 806 n, 1100*, 1538; hundred, lordship, and manor (Berkeley Harness, Berkeley Hernesse,

Herenesse Nookes), 41, 65, 178, 451, 527, 533, 534, 576, 602, 720, 737*, 738*, 773, 908, 1086, 1100*, 1168, 1368, 1369, 1537*; land in, 778 n, 779, 1145, 1169, 1176, 1521; residents, 98, 108, 497 n, 741*, 825, 826, 963, 1053, 1100, 1312, 1327, 1343, 1512, 1545; *and see* Alkington; Beddleford; Berkeney; Boxtree; Breadstone; Canonbury; Frogpitt; Hamfallow; Hengaston; Hester Hill; Hinton; Hogsdown; Lockfast Bridge; Packington; Phillimore's Bridge; Stock, the
Berkeney [? Berkeley], 107
Berkhamsted (Berkhampsted) (Herts.), 708 n, 709 n
Berkley (Berkly), *see* Berkeley
Berkshire, 359, 962, 986, 1227; *and see under names of separate places*
Berkswell (Barkeswell) (Warws.), 402
Berlin (Berolini) (Germany), 656, 723
Bermingham, *see* Birmingham
Bermondsey (Surr.), 635, 988*, 1327; abbey, 556 n
Bermuda, 607
Bernynton, *see* Barrington
Berolini, *see* Berlin
Berrends (Berring), in Redmarley D'Abitot, 150
Berrington, in Chipping Campden, 287, 288
Berrow (Worcs.), 546
Berry Court estate, *see* Upton-on-Severn
Berry Hill (the Berry), in West Dean, 194, 922*
Berry Towns, *see* Burytown
Bertona, *see* Barton, Abbot's
Berryfield, in Stonehouse, 1185
Berwick St. Leonard (Wilts.), 634, 705
Besika Bay [*unidentified*], 1344
Bessels Leigh (Bessilleleigh, Bessil's Leigh), *see* Leigh, Bessels
Beverston (Beverstone), **178–82**, 324, 720, 773*, 775, 852 n, 894 n, 1184, 1492; residents, 452, 511, 661, 807, 851, 1189
Bevington, in Ham and Stone, 159, 169, 171*, 174*, 175, 1018
Bewdley (Worcs.), 1201
Bewerley, *see* Backhouse
Bexhill (Suss.), 827 n*
Bhurtpore [? Bharatpur] (India), 1023
Bibury, 128, **183–7**, 268, 457, 693, 1189, 1201*, 1343, 1368; Bibury Northumberland and Bibury Osney, 184*; *and see* Ablington; Arlington; Winson
Bibury [*unidentified*], in Hill, 738
Bickmarsh (Warws.), in Welford on Avon, 1392
Bicknor, English, **188–94**, 457, 466, 479, 898, 919; *and see* Braceland; Chapel Hill; Eastbach Court; Stowfield
Bicks, *see* Beeks
Biddestone (Biddeston) (Wilts.), 699
Biddlesden (Bittlesden) (Bucks.), 570, 571
Bidfield, in Bisley or Miserden, 197, 423, 891
Bidford, *see* Marcliff
Bigland, in Cartmel (Lancs.), 1437
Bigs Weir (Bigsware, Bigsweare, Bixwear), in St. Briavels, 245, 246, 247, 513
Bileswike, *see* Bilswick
Billingbear (Billingsbear), in Waltham St. Lawrence (Berks.), 520

Billingshurst (Billinghurst) (Suss.), 920
Billington [? Bellington, in Chaddesley Corbett] (Worcs.), 395 n
Billow, in Breadstone, 177*
Bilswick (Bileswike), in Bristol, 41
Binfield (Berks.), Binfield House, 1320
Binley, in Kingscote, 775
Birdlip, in Brimpsfield, Cowley, and Great Witcombe, 252, 254*, 447, 856, 946, 984, 1380, 1494*; Birdlip Pool, 253
Birlingham (Burlingham) (Worcs.), 1464, 1503
Birmingham (Bermingham) (Warws.), 449, 793 n, 1144, 1169, 1272, 1278, 1352, 1368, 1476, 1576
Birtsmorton (Birts Morton) (Worcs.), 269, 993
Bishampton (Worcs.), 1432
Bishop Sutton, *see* Sutton, Bishop
Bishop's Cleeve, *see* Cleeve, Bishop's
Bishop's Frome, *see* Frome, Bishop's
Bishopstone, in Stapleton, 1160
Bishton, in Tidenham, 1321, 1323
Bisley, **195–204**, 457, 643, 648, 1026, 1214, 1217*, 1218; burial, 880, 1049, 1208, 1209; land in, 1021*, 1051, 1485, 1512; residents, 335, 655, 1006, 1049, 1365; *and see* Avenis; Bidfield; Brown's Hill; Bussage; Catswood; Chalford; Daneway; Ferris Court; Great Common, the; Greys, the; Higgin's Court; Ibnarsh; Lynches, the; Lyppiat, Middle; Lyppiat, Over; Oakridge; Rook Wood; Slad, the; Stean Bridge; Througham; Tunley; Vatch Mill
Bittlesden, *see* Biddlesden
Bitton, 82*, 84*, **205–13**, 457, 527, 612, 833*, 1311, 1384, 1490; *and see* Barr's Court; Beach; Cullyhall; Hanham Abbots and West Hanham; Highfield; Kingswood; Oldland; Upton Cheyney; Weston Court
Bixwear, *see* Bigs Weir
Black Pool stream, *see* Blackpool brook
Blackberry Farm (Blackberries), in Westerleigh, 1424, 1428
Blackhall, in Kings Pyon (King's Peon) (Herefs.), 558
Blackmere [*unidentified*], 251
Blackpool brook (Black Poole stream), 478 n
Blackwell [*unidentified*], 1330
Blackwell Hall, *see* London, buildings
Blackwells End, in Hartpury, 680
Bladon (Blandon) (Oxon.), 295
Blaendyffryn (Bleandyffrin), near Goginan (Cardig.), 1327
Blagrave, in Lambourn (Berks.), 986
Blaisdon (Blaysdon), **214–15**, 465, 605 n*, 821, 1395*; *and see* Spout, the; Stanley
Blaise (Blaize) Castle and Blaise Hill, in Henbury, 718, 719, 1380
Blaize (Blyth's) Bailey, in East Dean, 479
Blaize Castle, *see* Blaise Castle
Blakeney, in Awre, 101*, 102*, 103*, 108*, 110*, 111*, 479; Blakeney Lodge, 810*
Blakeney Walk, in East Dean, 1039
Blanchworth, in Alkington, 159, 173*
Blandon, *see* Bladon

Blanks Fee, *see* Banks Fee

Blaysdon, *see* Blaisdon

Bleandyffrin, *see* Blaendyffryn

Blecheley, *see* Bletchley

Bledington, **216–17**, 1190, 1337

Bledisloe, in Awre, 101, 102, 103; hundred, 102

Blenheim Palace (Blenheim Castle), in Woodstock (Oxon.), 1014

Bletchingdon (Oxon.), 1459

Bletchley (Blecheley) (Bucks.), 843

Bletsoe (Bletshso) (Beds.), 724, 1165

Blisbury (Blisberry), in Ham and Stone, 159, 171

Blisworth (Blissworth) (Northants.), 501

Blithcourt, *see* Bly Court

Blockley (formerly Worcs.), 142, 217, **218–27**, 457, 635, 852 n, 882, 1003, 1393; land in, 1432; peculiar, 438; *and see* Aston Magna; Ditchford; Dorn; Draycott; Northwick; Paxford; Upton Old

Bloors (Bore) Place, in Rainham (Kent), 856

Bluett's Court, in Newnham, 927

Blunsdon (Wilts.), 597; *and see* Burytown

Bly Court (Blithcourt), in Staplehurst (Kent), 44

Bocansthrop, *see* Baconsthorpe

Bockmer (Rockmore), in Medmenham (Bucks.), 1547

Boddington (Bodington, Bodyngton), **228–9**, 482, 587, 854, 1163*, 1165*, 1287, 1291, 1311, 1321, 1336; Boddington Oak, 228; *and see* Barrow; Butler's Court; Haydon; Mordon; Withy Bridge

Bodenham, *see* Meend Park

Bodington, *see* Boddington

Bodleian Library, Oxford, 357, 515 n, 864 n

Bodmin (Cornw.), 876 n

Bodyngton, *see* Boddington

Bold, *see* Bowl Farm

Bollow (Bolley, Botley), in Westbury on Severn, 1396, 1397*, 1399, 1402, 1403, 1404; *and see* Boy's Court

Boloigne, *see* Boulogne

Bologna (Italy), 591 n

Bolton (Lancs.), 1214

Bolton Percy, *see* Backhouse

Bombay (India), 898, 1209, 1321

Boorden and Bourdensfield [*unidentified*, ? in North Nibley], 937, 938

Bootham (Bowtham), in Hatfield (Yorks. W.R.), 409

Bordesley (Boresly), in Redditch (Worcs.), 1368; abbey, 648, 743, 1447, 1539

Bore Place, *see* Bloors Place

Boresley, *see* Bordesley; Boseley

Borneo (East Indies), 1023

Boroughbridge (Yorks. W.R.), 251 n

Borrisbury, *see* Bosbury

Bosbury (Borrisbury) (Herefs.), 1058

Boseley (Boresley, Bosley, Bosteley), in Westbury on Severn, 215, 605 n, 1395, 1401, 1402*

Boston (Mass., U.S.A.), 1180, 1557

Bosworth, Husbands (Leics.), 1157

Botherop, *see* Eastleach Martin

Botley, *see* Bollow

Boughton (Boulton), in St. Johns in Bedwardyne (Worcs.), 257

Boughton House, *see* Bourton House

Boughton Malherbe, *see* Chilston

Boughton Monchelsea, *see* Wierton

Bouldesdon, *see* Boulsdon

Boulogne (Boloigne) (France), 590

Boulsdon (Bouldesdon), in Newent, 893, 894, 904

Boulton, *see* Boughton

Bourdensfield, *see* Boorden

Bourne (Bourn), the, in Stroud, 472, 652, 658, 659, 660*, 1052

Bournstream, in North Nibley, 1522

Bourton [? Boughton] House, in Westbury on Severn, 1393

Bourton (Burton) on the Hill, 218*, **230–1**, 272, 393 n, 457, 771, 882*, 1103, 1193, 1263*, 1331*

Bourton on the Water (Bourton, Burton on the Water), 223, **232–5**, 389*, 457, 1088, 1093*, 1195, 1480; residents, 429, 486, 710, 891, 961, 1092, 1189, 1224, 1478; *and see* Nethercote; Salmonsbury

Boutherop, *see* Eastleach Martin

Boverton (Glam.), 409*

Bowbridge, in Stroud, 1212

Bowden Hall (Bowden Hell), in Upton St. Leonards, 1377, 1378

Bowden Park, in Lacock (Wilts.), 132

Bowl Farm (Bold, Bowlde), in Lower Swell, 1225, 1226

Bowldown, in Lasborough, 783, 784

Bownham's House, in Rodborough, 1507

Bowtham, *see* Bootham

Box (the), in Minchinhampton, 648, 660

Boxleau, *see* Beaulieu

Boxtree, the [? in Berkeley], 170*

Boxwell, **236–41**, 1536; *and see* Leighterton

Boyce, the, in Dymock, 546*, 548

Boyd, river, 6, 205, 487*, 551

Boyfield, *see* Murcott

Boy's Court, in Bollow, 1399

Boyton (Wilts.), 1431*

Braceland, in English Bicknor, 1161

Bracesleigh, *see* Leigh, Brace's

Bradenstoke (Bradestock), in Lyneham (Wilts.), priory, 690, 1120, 1122, 1177, 1339*, 1369

Bradford [? Bradford on Avon (Wilts.)], 1543

Bradford on Avon (Bradford) (Wilts.), 546; *and see* Atworth

Bradley (Bradly), in Wotton under Edge, 1522*, 1526*, 1530*, 1532*, 1537, 1538

Bradley hundred, 1078

Bradon, *see* Braydon

Bradston (Bradstone), in Berkeley, *see* Breadstone

Bradston [? in Tytherington], 1328

Brafferton (Brasserton) Hall (Yorks. N.R.), 1559

Braham Moor, *see* Bramham Moor

Brailes (Brayls) (Warws.), 693, 755

Brailsford (Derb.), 1538

Brainsford, *see* Leigh, Brace's

Brakenbury, *see* Brokenborough

Bramham (Braham) Moor (Yorks. W.R.), 709

Brampton Abbots, *see* Nether Town

Brancaster (Norf.), 1156

Branscombe, *see* Weston, in Branscombe
Bransford, *see* Leigh, Brace's
Brant Broughton, *see* Broughton, Brant
Brasenose (Brazen Nose) College, Oxford, 394 n, 1021, 1497
Brass Mill, in Newent or Taynton, 1233
Brasserton, *see* Brafferton
Braydon (Bradon) (Wilts.), 298
Brayls, *see* Brailes
Braynton, *see* Breinton
Brazen Nose College, *see* Brasenose College
Breaderdine, *see* Bredwardine
Breadstone (Bradston, Bradstone, Bridston), in Berkeley, 154, 159, 161, 1490; residents, 165*, 167, 171*, 172*, 173*, 174*, 176*, 177*, 283, 1526; *and see* Billow
Bream (Breame, Breeme), in Newland, 915, 918, 919*, 922, 923*, 924*, 929; Bream's Lodge, 915, 924; Breams Cross, 922
Breamore (Bremer) (Hants), 628
Breckness (Brecknocks, Brenock) Court, in Newland, 913, 923*
Brecon (Brec.), 1081
Breconshire, 1408*; *and see* Abersenny; Brecon; Cwmdu; Dan-y-parc; Gwernyfed; Madoc, Castle; Pencelli; Trebarried
Bredon (Breedon) (Worcs.), 438, 999, 1266, 1291, 1348, 1387; Bredon Hill, 763, 1293; Bredon's Hardwick, 1381; *and see* Hinchwick; Kinsham; Mitton; Norton
Bredwardine (Breaderdine, Brodwardine) (Herefs.), 898, 1129
Breedon, *see* Bredon
Breeme, *see* Bream
Brees Norton, *see* Norton, Brize
Breinton (Brayntone) (Herefs.), 1058
Bremer, *see* Breamore
Bremhill, *see* Stanley
Brenock Court, *see* Breckness Court
Bretforton (Worcs.), 1432*, 1458*
Brewen, *see* Bruern
Breweshold, in Horfield, 745
Brewood, *see* Engleton
Brickhampton, in Churchdown, 346, 348
Bridg North, *see* Bridgnorth
Bridge Yate, in Siston and Wick and Abson, 6, 1087
Bridge, the [? *recte* the Ridge], in Standish, 1130
Bridgend (Glam.), 453
Bridgend, in Stonehouse, 1185
Bridgnorth (Bridg North) (Salop.), 172, 959; *and see* Cann Hall
Bridgtown, in Stratford-on-Avon (Warws.), 1040*
Bridston, *see* Breadstone
Bridstow, *see* Wilton (Herefs.)
Brighampton [*unidentified*], in Hill, 738
Brimpscomb, *see* Brimscombe
Brimpsfield, **251–4**, 449, 1020, 1172, 1380*, 1485; priory, 251, 252; residents, 798, 875 n, 1139; *and see* Birdlip; Caudle Green; Hazel Hanger Wood; Stoney Hill
Brims Pill, in Awre, 101

Brimscombe (Brimpscomb, Brimscum, Brymscomb), in Stroud, 648, 654*, 656, 659*, 660*, 750, 1024*, 1207*, 1214, 1215, 1216, 1217
Brinkmarsh (Brintmarsh), in Falfield, 1296*, 1297*
Brisbane (Australia), 1354, 1455
Brislington (Bustleton) (Som.), 43
Bristentune (? Ebrington), 570
Bristol (Bristowe, Bryghtstowe):
Bristol, abbey of St. Augustine, 39, 40, 41, 65, 66, 75*, 154*, 178, 393, 405, 451*, 452, 577*, 602*, 603, 721, 737*, 745*, 1101, 1538, 1540
Bristol, bishop: 233 n, 567 n, 1160, 1577; estate, 40, 42, 75*, 76, 451, 452, 577 n, 602, 603, 745*, 869, 870, 1047, 1101, 1502; diocese, chancellor, 682
Bristol, buildings (misc.) & institutions: Colston's School, 1160; Gaunt's hospital, 40; houses, 917, 918; infirmary, 132; lunatic asylum, 1160; Merchant Adventurers, 403, 405, 406; Queen Elizabeth's hospital, 1491; school, 1160; school (bluecoat), 40; St. Augustine's hospital, 1385; workhouse, 1160
Bristol, castle, 1159; castle precincts, 212, 1562, 1567, 1570*, 1572, 1573, 1574; constable, 612, 779, 1296
Bristol, cathedral (college): burial, 205, 532 n, 834, 1338; dean, 255, 258*; dean and chapter, 66, 154, 161, 301, 345, 347, 577*, 737, 785, 1177, 1385, 1539; prebendary, 164, 165, 342, 343, 962
Bristol, churches & parishes, All Saints, 1546; Christ Church, 412, 938, 1575; St. Augustine, 308, 412, 413*, 1410*, 1566; St. Ewen (St. Ewin, St. Owen), 406, 1108; St. George, 211, 213, 1553, 1574, **1577–8**; St. James, 208, 412*, 727, 1412, 1413; St. Mary Port, 411; St. Mary, Redcliff; *see* Redcliff; St. Michael, 412, 729, 1407, 1411; St. Nicholas, 1425, 1574*; St. Paul, 1415, 1455; St. Peter, 833, 1155; St. Philip (St. Phillip) and St. Jacob, 16, 211, 411*, 836, 845, 1156, 1158*, 1159, 1291, 1411, **1553–77**, 1577*, 1578; *and see* Baptist Mills; St. Stephen, 211, 405 n, 412, 730, 731, 736, 1424, 1556, 1561, 1569*; St. Thomas, 52, 1392, 1563; St. Werburgh, 407, 631, 1415; Temple parish, 1575
Bristol, city: alderman, 206*, 618, 720, 725, 917, 1405*, 1419, 1513, 1562, 1564; citizen, 631, 715, 725, 1085; corporation, 40, 42, 532, 533; freeman, 934; Lord Lieutenant, 122, 162; M.P., 724, 920, 1420; magistracy, 1411; mayor, 391, 553, 962, 1405, 1412, 1554*, 1555; recorder, 393 n; sheriff, 619, 1446, 1486, 1488, 1554, 1555, 1563; steward of sheriff's court and deputy town clerk, 199
Bristol, priory of St. James, 833, 1160*; priory of St. Mary Magdalene, 1420*
Bristol, residents: apothecary, 1107*, 1108*, 1411, 1413, 1424, 1426, 1556; apprentices, 819 n; attorney, 1327, 1556; baker, 1526, 1576; banker, 1208; blacksmith, 543, 1584; breeches maker, 1580; brick maker, 1575; brightsmith, 210; butcher, 1574, 1575, 1576; cabinet-maker, 1098; carpenter, 604, 1574; clothworker, 845; cooper,

1583; copper refiner, 1574*; distiller, 1563; engineer, 1583; exciseman, 1574*, 1580; gardener, 1408, 1575, 1583; glass maker (manufacturer), 1566, 1575, 1583; glass-bottle maker, 1568; goldsmith, 1563; grocer, 453, 1159, 1562, 1574; haberdasher, 107, 409, 615, 1575; ironmonger, 1546; joiner, 170, 929; linen draper, 413, 1582; maltster, 336, 1561. 1575*; mariner, 108, 109, 843, 1096, 1109, 1272, 1555, 1571, 1573; mason, 412, 1570; mercer, 100; merchant, 13, 33, 104, 107, 385, 409, 411, 435, 576, 607, 657, 725, 726*, 835, 841, 842*, 843, 919, 932, 937, 962, 970, 988, 990, 991, 1000*, 1109, 1241, 1324*, 1408, 1409, 1410, 1411, 1412, 1413*, 1452, 1487, 1490, 1503, 1507, 1508, 1554, 1555, 1556, 1557, 1561*, 1562, 1569; pewterer, 841, 1175; physician, 1105*, 1407; pump maker, 1575; recruiting officer, 1576; salter (*salorius*), 1337; schoolmaster, teacher, 1158, 1583; shalloon and stuff maker, 1574; shipwright, 728, 736; soapmaker, 83, 746, 1556, 1569; stationer, 725; sugar refiner, 412, 1575; surgeon, 746, 1567*; tiler and painter, 1575; tobacconist, 537; victualler, 727; vintner, 409; wheelwright, 1555; wine cooper, 106, 173, 208, 1325; wine merchant, 1488; woollen draper, 1425; (occupation unstated), 8, 14, 15*, 18, 48, 51, 70, 98, 99, 132, 160, 164, 165*, 167, 171, 247, 249, 250, 306, 308, 406, 409, 448, 456, 489*, 535, 552, 555*, 603, 604, 613, 615, 619, 622, 651, 654, 695 n, 696, 701, 721, 725, 727, 730*, 731, 734, 735, 743, 746, 756, 779, 811, 814, 832, 836, 843, 844, 899, 913, 918, 919, 929, 933*, 955, 960, 962, 963, 967, 981, 997, 1043, 1107, 1109*, 1117*, 1118, 1158, 1175, 1199, 1206, 1210*, 1269, 1280, 1300, 1301, 1302*, 1309, 1318, 1319, 1321, 1322, 1327*, 1350, 1379, 1405, 1408*, 1409*, 1410*, 1411, 1416, 1417, 1418*, 1426, 1427, 1432, 1439, 1450, 1453, 1482, 1486, 1489*, 1491, 1515, 1527, 1550, 1554*, 1555*, 1568, 1569, 1582*, 1583

Bristol, streets &c.: Broadmead, 1123; Corn Street, 407; Queen Square, 1157; Red Lodge, 1408; St. Augustine's Green, 41; St. Michael's Hill, 1304; Temple Street, 1407*; Tucker Street, 206

Bristol, otherwise mentioned: agreement made at, 1100; burial at, 12; civil war, 359 n, 806 n, 1314; communication with, 244; Danish landing at, 497; death at, 15, 306, 1047, 1105, 1235, 1245, 1439; in Domesday, 1419, 1474; gift from, 1295; goods carried to, 444 n, 732; native, 1418; nonconformity, 1123; port or quay, 1418, 553, 720, 1160; visits, 167, 625, 1437

Bristol, *and see* Baptist Mills; Bilswick; Cotham; Hotwells; Kingsdown; Lawfords Gate; Redcliff

Bristol and Birmingham Railway Co., 1169

Bristol and West of England Architectural Society, 1102

Bristol Channel, shipping, 718

Bristowville (Irel.), 1327

Brize Norton, *see* Norton, Brize

Broad Bridge or Broad Barrow Green, *see* Broadbarrow Green

Broad Oak (Broadoak), in Westbury on Severn, 215, 1396, 1397, 1398*, 1400*

Broadbarrow Green (Broad Bridge or Broad Barrow Green), in Haresfield, 672

Broadhinton, *see* Hinton, Broad

Broadoak, *see* Broad Oak

Broadstones (Broadstone), in Staunton, 924

Broadway (Worcs.), 1000, 1052, 1194, 1243, 1432*, 1446, 1447, 1458*; *and see* Middle Hill

Broadwell, 21, **255–8**, 457, 636, 1189, 1195, 1196*, 1225, 1475

Brockenborough, *see* Brokenborough

Brockhampton, in Sevenhampton, 1057, 1059, 1060*, 1061*, 1062*, 1063*, 1064*, 1468

Brockhampton, in Snowshill, 1104*, 1150, 1151

Brockhampton (Rrockhampton), in Southam, 393, 398, 399, 1521

Brockhollands, *see* Brook Hall

Brockrup (Brocktherup, Brockthorp, Brockthrop), *see* Brookthorpe

Brockweir (Brockware, Brockwear, Brockwere, Brockwore, Brookwer), in St. Briavels and Woolaston, 55*, 244, 247, 732, 734*, 735*, 736*

Brockworth (Brokworth), 118*, **259–62**, 348*, 457, 713, 856, 1059, 1376, 1380; manor, 1059; *and see* Cooper's Hill; Droys Court

Broctrop, *see* Brookthorpe

Brodhinton, *see* Hinton, Broad

Brodwardine, *see* Bredwardine

Broken Cross, in Westbury on Severn, 1395

Brokenborough (Brockenborough) (Wilts.), 1070, 1107

Brokenborough (Brakenbury, Brokenborrow, Brokenbrow), in Almondsbury, 40, 41, 42, 1490

Brokesby, *see* Brooksby

Brokworth, *see* Brockworth

Bromesberrow, *see* Bromsberrow

Bromham (Brumham) (Wilts.), 1067

Bromley (Kent), 865

Brompton [*unspecified*], 392 n

Bromsberrow (Bromesberrow, Bromsborowe), **265–70**, 440, 457, 546, 610, 619, 625; Bromsberrow Place, *see* Hook House; *and see* Brookend; Brown's End; Grove House; Russell's End

Bromsberrow (Bromesberrow) Heath, in Dymock, 269

Bromwich, Castle (Warws.), 265

Bromwich, West (Staffs.), 1352

Bromyard (Herefs.), 471, 1058

Brook End, *see* Brookend

Brook Hall [? Brockhollands, in Newland], 250

Brook (Brooke) House, in Old Sodbury, 1119, 1120

Brook House (the Brook, Brookhouse), in Painswick, 973*, 974; *and see* Aedes Brokiane

Brookend (Brook End), in Bromsberrow, 265, 269

Brookhouse, *see* Brook House

Brooksby (Brokesby) (Leics.), 507 n

Brookthorpe (Brockrup, Brocktherup, Brockthorp, Brockthrop, Broctrop, Bruckthrop), 133, **263–4**, 335, 450, 640, 667, 672, 681, 1047, 1218, 1434

Brookwer, *see* Brockweir

Broom (Broome) (Worcs.), 726

Brotherton, see Byram

Broughton (Oxon.), 1040

Broughton, Brant (Lincs.), 536*

Broughton Gifford (Broughton) (Wilts.), 579

Brownings, in Stinchcombe, 1169

Brown's End, in Bromsberrow, 269

Brown's Hill (Brownshill), in Bisley or Painswick, 198, 971, 1127, 1181, 1511

Brown's Mill, see Brownsmill

Brownsend, in Preston, 993

Brownshill, see Brown's Hill

Brownsmill (Brown's Mill), in Ham and Stone, 176, 583

Bruckthrop, see Brookthorpe

Bruern, see Colesborne, Little

Bruern (Brewen) (Oxon.), abbey, 568, 634, 635, 1011*, 1015*, 1055*, 1078, 1092, 1195, 1476, 1501; Bruern Grange, 861; and see Tangley Farm

Bruges (Belgium), 1174

Brumham, see Bromham

Brussels (Belgium), 305 n, 1123

Bruton (Som.), abbey, 747*, 748*, 1440

Bryghtstowe, see Bristol

Brymscomb, see Brimscombe

Buckenham [unspecified] (Norf.), Buckenham Castle, 559 n; Buckenham Hall, 1419

Buckettshill (Buckett's Hill), in Hamfallow, 172

Buckholt, in Cranham, 259, 1380

Buckholt, the, in Frocester, 628

Buckingham (Bucks.), 383

Buckinghamshire, 359, 581 n, 876, 962; and see Beaconsfield; Biddlesden; Bletchley; Bockmer; Buckingham; Chenies; Colnbrook; Eton; Hanslope; Hardmead; Huntercombe; Iver; Lavendon; Notley; Thornton; Weston Underwood

Buckland, 271–4, 457, 1051, 1052*; and see Laverton; Lullyntone

Buckland Newton, see Henley

Bucklebury (Berks.), 1119

Buckover, in Thornbury, 455, 1295, 1303, 1304*, 1307, 1311, 1313, 1314

Budbrooke (Budbrook) (Warws.), 1469

Bulkington (Bulkinton) (Wilts.), 203

Bulley, 275–6, 349, 353*, 1238, 1317, 1238, 1317

Bumpstead (Bumpsted), Steeple (Essex), 1296

Bupton, in Clyffe Pypard (Wilts.), 44

Burclear, see Burghclere

Burford (Oxon.), 217, 372; hospital or priory, 1015, 1068, 1147

Burford (Salop.), see Whitton

Burghclere (Burclear) (Hants.), 1437

Burleigh (Burley), in Minchinhampton, 648, 655*, 657, 660, 661*

Burlingham, see Birlingham

Burrington (Devon), see Palington

Burrington (Som.), 490; and see Langford

Burrows Court, in North Nibley, 170

Bursage, see Bussage

Burscott, see Buscot

Burthorpe, see Eastleach Martin

Burton Dassett, see Northend

Burton, see Bourton on the Hill; Bourton on the Water; Burwarton

Burwarton (Burton) (Salop.), 1002

Bury, in Doynton, 487, 488

Bury Court, in Westbury on Severn, 1394*

Burytown (Berry Towns), in Blunsdon (Wilts.), 1497

Buscot (Burscott) (Berks.), 186, 597, 1199

Bushley (Busley) (Worcs.), 567, 715, 1291; and see Pull

Bussage (Bursage), in Bisley, 197, 204

Bustleton, see Brislington

Butcombe (Som.), 143

Butler's Court, in Boddington, 228, 1164

Butler's Court, in Lechlade, 794, 1229

Buttermere (Buttermore) (Wilts.), 332

Buttersend (Butter's End), in Hartpury, 680

Buttington Tump, in Tidenham, 1321, 1322

Bygrave (Herts.), 501

Byram, in Brotherton (Yorks. W.R.), 1341

Caddecroft (Caddicroft), in Pershore (Worcs.), 572

Caen (Normandy), abbey, 91, 525, 646*, 648, 1027, 1215

Caerleon (Car Lyon, Carleon, Isca) (Mon.), 205 n, 355, 1277

Caernarvonshire, see Bangor

Caerwent (Venta Silurum) (Mon.), 205 n, 1341

Caerwents, see Carway

Cainscross (Caines Cross), in Stonehouse, 1181, 1186, 1217

Cainsham, see Keynsham

Cakebridge (Cake Bridge), in Cheltenham, 983, 984*, 986

Calais (Calays, Calis) (France), 392 n, 804 n, 945, 1136

Calcomb [unidentified], 986

Calcot (Caldecot, Caldicot), in Coln St. Denis, 430*, 1355, 1388

Calcot (Cawkett, Coldcote), in Newington Bagpath, 180, 908, 909

Caldicot (Caldecot) (Mon.), 122, 927

Calis, see Calais

Callecombe, see Cawcombe

Callow, the, in Dymock, 546

Calmsden, in North Cerney, 297, 299

Calne (Wilts.), 829 n, 1170, 1171; and see Derry Hall; Quemerford

Cam (Came, Camme), 160, 277–84, 414, 457, 540, 1166, 1168*, 1169, 1235; land in, 534, 1102*, 1147, 1369; Lower Cam (Nether Town), 277*; manor, 533, 534; residents, 163*, 164, 419, 543, 562, 783, 825, 1019, 1136, 1167*, 1168, 1185, 1206, 1367, 1368, 1437, 1450, 1526*; vicar, 539, 631; and see Ashmead; Churchend; Clingre; Downhouse; Draycott; Halmer; Hengaston; King's Hill; Tilsdown; Upthorpe

Cam, river, 277*

Camberwell (Surr.), 32, 827 n; and see Peckham

Camborne, see Pendarves

Cambrai (Cambray) (France), 921

Cambridge, in Slimbridge, 153, 170, 1096, 1099*, 1100*
Cambridge (Cambs.), 1334; university, 289, 361 n, 534 n, 711 n, 827 n, 1141; *and see* Christ's College; Emmanuel College; Jesus College; King's College; Peterhouse; Queens' College; St. John's College; Trinity College
Cambridgeshire, *see* Benwick; Cambridge; Doddington; Ely; Hatley; Wimblington
Cambuswallace, near Biggar (Scot.), 1562
Camden, *see* Campden
Came, *see* Cam
Camerton (Comerton) (Som.), 743
Camme, *see* Cam
Campden, Chipping (Camden), 220, 272, **285–96**, 311 n, 457, 458, 638 n, 1284, 1331, 1476, 1519; Broad Campden, 287, 296*, 1432; residents, 637, 1153, 1191; *and see* Berrington; Comb, Old; Westington
Campen, *see* Klosterkampen
Canada, 1073; *and see* Nova Scotia
Candaliensis, *see* Kendal
Canford, in Westbury on Trym, 1419
Canford Magna (Cranford, Great Cranford) (Dors.), 568, 690, 691, 692
Cann Hall, in Bridgnorth (Salop.), 485
Canonbury, in Berkeley, 154, 738
Canon's Frome, *see* Frome, Canon's
Canterbury (Kent), 1166; archbishop, 53, 147, 346, 434, 767, 1021, 1031, 1232, 1493, 1516; archbishop, personally, 183, 436*, 804, 1169, 1322; *and see* Dane-John
Canton (China), 1245
Cape Town (South Africa), 1209
Caple, How (Howcaple) (Herefs.), 933
Car Lyon, *see* Caerleon
Cardiff (Cardiffe) (Glam.), 1158, 1381
Cardiganshire, *see* Aberystwyth; Bangor; Blaendyffryn; Gogerddan
Cardinal College [later Christ Church], Oxford, 591 n
Carleon, *see* Caerleon
Carlisle (Carlile) (Cumb.), 359, 708, 1102, 1383
Carmarthenshire, *see* Erw-Wastad; Llanarthney; Llangendeirne; Llansawel; Newcastle Emlyn
Carolina (North America), 875 n
Carrant brook or river, 71, 147, 1387
Carshalton (Surr.), 827 n
Carswalls (Carswells, Caswalls), in Newent, 894*, 977, 978*, 993
Carswell (Berks.), 1495
Cartmel, *see* Bigland
Carway [? Caerwents, in Newent], 899
Cashiobury, *see* Cassiobury
Caslet, *see* Castlett
Cassey Compton, *see* Compton, Cassey
Cassiobury (Cashiobury), in Watford (Herts.), 290 n
Castiard valley, in Flaxley, 605
Castile and Leon, king of, 361
Castillon-la-Bataille (Chastillon) (France), 759
Castle Bromwich, *see* Bromwich, Castle
Castle Combe, *see* Combe, Castle
Castle Dillon, *see* Dillon, Castle

Castle Ditch [lost], in Eastnor (Herefs.), 518, 520
Castle Eaton, *see* Eaton, Castle
Castle End (Castlend), in Lea (Herefs.), 789*
Castle Frome, *see* Frome, Castle
Castle Madoc, *see* Madoc, Castle
Castle Morton, *see* Castlemorton
Castle Town, *see* Castleton; Castletown
Castlemorton (Castle Morton) (Worcs.), 1291
Castlend, *see* Castle End
Castleton (Castle Town), in Sherborne (Dors.), 385
Castletown (Castle Town) (Irel.), 959
Castlett (Caslet, Catteslade), in Guiting Power, 634, 635*, 636, 1263
Caswalls, *see* Carswalls
Catisfield Lodge, in Fareham (Hants), 1245
Catswood (Cattswood), in Bisley, 204*
Catteslade, *see* Castlett
Cattswood, *see* Catswood
Caudle Green, in Brimpsfield, 252, 253, 254*
Causeway (Cawfay), in Radipole (Dors.), 591 n
Cawcombe (Callecombe), in Sevenhampton, 1060
Cawfay, *see* Causeway
Cawkett, *see* Calcot
Cawnpore (Cawnpoore) (India), 1085, 1176
Cayforde, *see* Keyford
Cerney, North, 56, 60, **297–300**, 366, 458, 1028, 1029, 1497; *and see* Calmsden; Woodmancote
Cerney, South (South Sarneye), **301–4**, 369, 458, 1081, 1202; Cerney Wick (Cerney Wyck, Wick), 301, 302*, 304
Chaceley (Chasely) (Worcs.), 336, 1355*; *and see* Corse Lawn; Sandpits
Chaddesley Corbett (Worcs.), 15; *and see* Billington
Chaddington, in Lydiard Tregoze (Wilts.), 14
Chadlington (Oxon.), 1090; *and see* Shadlington
Chailbury (Chalberry), *see* Charlbury
Chalfield, Great (Wilts.), 1200
Chalford, in Bisley (Chalford Bottom, Chalford Hill), 197, 199*, 200*, 201*, 202*, 203, 648, 654, 655, 661*, 1025, 1083
Chalkeley, in Hawkesbury, 695
Châlon-sur-Saône (Chalons) (France), 605 n
Channel, English, 707
Channel Islands, *see* Jersey
Chantry, the, in Lydney, 811*
Chapel, the, in Ampney St. Mary, 62*
Chapel Hill (Mon.), 608
Chapel Hill, in English Bicknor, 188*
Charfield, **305–8**, 453, 458, 938, 1449, 1456, 1538; residents, 780, 938, 1118, 1306, 1327, 1343*, 1344, 1454; *and see* Tafarn-bach inn
Charingworth (Charringworth), in Ebrington, 570*, 573*
Charlbury (Chailbury, Chalberry) (Oxon.), 257, 1543
Charlcombe, *see* Langridge; Lansdown
Charlecote (Warws.), 349, 572, 866
Charleton, *see* Charlton
Charley, in Charnwood Forest (Leics.), 700
Charlton (Kent), 1088, 1345

Charlton (Charleton, Cherlton, Malmsbury Charleton), near Malmesbury (Wilts.), 967, 1253, 1255, 1257*, 1259

Charlton (Charleton), in Henbury, 721, 724, 725, 726*, 728*, 729*

Charlton (Charleton, Cherlton), in Tetbury, 1253, 1255*, 1257, 1259

Charlton Abbots, 79, 257, **309–10**, 335, 891, 1042, 1056, 1057, 1193; *and see* Goldwell

Charlton Kings or Ashley, **311–17**, 324, 458, 1197, 1314; residents, 323 n, 399, 504, 574, 665, 706, 950, 985, 986, 1051*, 1421; *and see* Ashley; Ham

Charnwood Forest, *see* Charley

Charringworth, *see* Charingworth

Chartley (Staffs.), 188, 228

Chasehill, *see* Chaxhill

Chasely, *see* Chaceley

Chaselton, *see* Chastleton

Chastillon, *see* Castillon-la-Bataille

Chastleton (Chaselton) (Oxon.), 883; Chastleton Hill, 437

Chatiscombe, *see* Chettiscombe

Chaulton [*unidentified*], 1322

Chavenage (Shavenage), in Horsley, 50, 95, 97, 343, 556, 747, 1098*

Chaxhill (Chasehill), in Westbury on Severn, 352, 1398*, 1399, 1402, 1403

Cheam (Surr.), 827 n

Chedeston, *see* Chediston

Chedglow (Chedgle), in Crudwell (Wilts.), 1542

Chediston (Chedeston) (Suff.), 829 n

Chedrington, *see* Cherington

Chedworth, **318–21**, 423, 944, 1498, 1542

Cheern, *see* Churn

Chelesworth manor [*unidentified*], 778 n

Chelsea (Great Chelsea) (Mdx.), 537, 1026, 1046, 1059, 1326, 1428

Chelt (Chilt), river or rivulet, 228, 313, 322

Cheltenham, 71, 311*, **322–40**, 458, 869, 1123, 1314, 1478, 1512; death at, 984, 1194, 1232*, 1281*, 1303, 1338*, 1360, 1377*; hundred, 322; manor, 1043, 1123; priory, 325; residents, 74*, 167, 229, 398, 433, 897, 984, 1029, 1077, 1181, 1229, 1231*, 1232, 1238*, 1377, 1464, 1473, 1501, 1503; school, 801, 1029, 1478, 1519; *and see* Alstone; Arle; Cakebridge; Grove Cottage; Harthurstfield; Hewletts; Moors, the; Naunton; Sandford; Westal

Chenies (Cheyney) (Bucks.), 1521

Chepstow (Strigoul, Strigul) (Mon.), 18, 39, 735*, 806 n*, 811, 927, 1097, 1318, 1321, 1322*, 1323, 1513; castle, 1322; priory, 1322, 1323; *and see* Larkfield

Cherington (Chedrington, Cherrington), 34, **341–4**, 529, 556, 659, 1031, 1032, 1138, 1445; *and see* Trull Farm

Cherlton, *see* Charlton

Cherrington, *see* Cherington

Cherry Orchard, in Staunton, 1162

Cheshire, 793 n, 1051, 1069; *and see* Chester; Vale Royal; West Hall

Chester (Ches.), 286, 632, 672, 756, 1069

Chester-le-Street, *see* White Hill

Chesterton, in Cirencester, 365, 367, 1202

Chettiscombe (Chatiscombe), in Tiverton (Devon), 1459

Chew Magna (Som.), 941

Cheyney, *see* Chenies

Chichester (Suss.), 417, 436 n, 453, 1582

Chigwell (Essex), 787, 1415

Chilcompton (Som.), 1580

Childswickham (Childes Wickham, Wickwan), 1152, 1390, **1446–7**, 1016; *and see* Murcot

Chillingham [*unidentified*] (Cornw.), 220 n

Chilston (Chilson), in Boughton Malherbe (Kent), 740

Chilwood, in Iron Acton, 12, 16

China, 1007, 1308; *and see* Canton; Chusan; Macao

Chippenham (Wilts.), 778, 829 n, 1031

Chipping Barnet, *see* Barnet, Chipping

Chipping Campden, *see* Campden, Chipping

Chipping Norton, *see* Norton, Chipping

Chipping Sodbury, *see* Sodbury, Chipping

Chirchamme, *see* Churcham

Chire [*unidentified*], 1401

Chislehampton (Chissel Hampton) (Oxon.), 78

Chislehurst, *see* Scadbury Park

Chissel Hampton, *see* Chislehampton

Chiswick (Mdx.), 410, 807; *and see* Morton Hall

Chosen Hill, *see* Churchdown

Christ Church (Hants), *see* Christchurch

Christ Church (C.C.), Oxford, 572, 1016; alumnus, 342, 395, 849, 1073, 1349, 1390; estate, 13, 37, 142, 216, 349 n, 436*, 507, 508, 634, 638*, 639*, 935, 1227*, 1228*, 1257*, 1295, 1312, 1313, 1351*, 1362*, 1539*; student (fellow), 373, 395, 651 n, 1163, 1300, 1528; *and see* Cardinal College

Christ Church (Surr.), *see* Southwark

Christchurch (Christ Church) (Hants), 671 n

Christchurch (Surr.), *see* Southwark

Christ's College, Cambridge, 113

Christ's Hospital (London), 71, 72

Chudleigh (Devon), 618 n

Church Down, *see* Churchdown

Church End, in Tidenham, 1321, 1323

Church Honeybourne, *see* Poden

Church Icomb, *see* Icomb

Church Langton, *see* Langton, Church

Church Stowe, *see* Stowe, Church

Churcham (Chirchamme), 262, 275, 276, **349–54**, 458, 716, 812, 871, 927, 930, 1404; *and see* Highnam; Over

Churchdown (Church Down), 333, **345–8**, 417, 514, 458, 851, 856, 1130, 1047, 1370, 1493*; Chosen (Churchdown) Hill, 345, 502; *and see* Brickhampton; Hucclecote; Parton; Pirton Court

Churchend, in Cam, 277

Churchend, in Coaley, 414

Churchill (Oxon.), 1085

Churchley, in Wick and Abson, 6

Churn (Cheern, Churne), river, 145, 252 n, 297, 301, 355*, 420, 424, 447, 579

Chusan (China), 1245
Cinderhill, in St. Briavels, 249
Cirencester (Cisseter), 252, **355–88**, 458, 459, 590 n,
    591 n, 792 n, 864 n, 875 n, 881, 1049, 1100;
    abbey, 358, 359, 360, 361, 362, 363; abbey,
    estate, 61, 145, 311, 322 n, 323, 359, 445, 507,
    508, 515*, 523, 585, 617, 990*, 1043, 1052*,
    1074, 1078, 1082*, 1201, 1214, 1350; borough,
    1202; burial, 145, 1368; canal, 792 n; castle,
    357; church, 126, 591 n, 1101, 1284; Cirencester
    Abbey (house), 1159; death at, 393, 784, 940,
    1073; Dyer Street, 357; hospital of St. John,
    estate, 1202; hospital of St. Lawrence, 1202;
    hospital of St. Thomas, 1202; land in, 1201,
    1202; military events, 251, 553, 590, 839, 875,
    1219, 1220, 1293; minister, 163, 991; seven
    hundreds, 371; residents, 129, 130, 145, 171,
    201, 302, 430, 446, 460, 496, 654, 713, 791, 862,
    880, 938, 969*, 983, 985, 990*, 991, 1029, 1050,
    1066, 1080*, 1126, 1132, 1199*, 1200*, 1201*,
    1202, 1255, 1369, 1440, 1474, 1494, 1497, 1508,
    1512, 1530; rural deanery, 360; woollen ind. &
    trade, 588 n, 638 n; and see Barton; Baunton
    Mill; Chesterton; Oakley; Port Farm; Spital Gate;
    Watermoor
Cîteaux (Cisteaux) (France), 605 n
Clacton, Little, see Giddy Hall
Clapham (Surr.), 827 n, 1510
Clapton, in Ham and Stone, 159; residents, 166,
    167, 168, 170*, 172, 174*, 175, 176*, 177, 741,
    958, 1549
Clapton, Upper, see Clopton, in Mickleton
Clapton, Upper, in Hackney (Mdx.), 1193
Clapton on the Hill (Clapton), 217, 232, 233, 235,
    389, 946
Clarendon (Wilts.), Clarendon Park, 1332
Clarkenwell, see Clerkenwell
Claverton (Som.), 834
Clay Hill (Clayhill), in Lechlade, 794*
Clayhunger, see Clehonger
Clayton [unspecified] (Yorks. W.R.), Clayton Hall,
    51
Clearwell (Cleerwell, Clewerwall, Clouerwall,
    Clowerwall), in Newland, 913, 915, 917*, 918;
    residents, 105, 746, 765, 919*, 920*, 921, 922*,
    923*, 924*, 1299, 1395
Clee chase or forest (Cleys) (Salop.), 618 n
Cleerwell, see Clearwell
Cleeve, in Westbury on Severn, 1398*, 1401, 1402,
    1403
Cleeve Hill, see Clevehill
Cleeve, Bishop's (Cleeve), **390–9**, 458, 986, 1043,
    1150, 1151, 1262, 1478*; Cleeve Cloud, 390;
    hundred, 390; residents, 334, 339, 442, 518, 519,
    986, 1210, 1463; and see Gambells;
    Gotherington; Southam; Stoke Orchard;
    Woodmancote
Clehonger (Clayhunger, Cleonger) (Herefs.), 1036,
    1058
Clehongre (Cleihunger), see Clingre
Cleonger, see Clehonger
Clerkenwell (Clarkenwell) (Mdx.), 556, 867

Clevedon (Som.), 1185
Clevehill (Cleeve Hill), in Mangotsfield, 833, 834,
    835
Cleverton, in Lea and Cleverton (Wilts.), 738
Clewerwall, see Clearwell
Cleys, see Clee chase
Clifford (Herefs.), Clifford's Castle, 618, 720 n
Clifford Chambers, **400–2**, 458; and see Ailstone;
    Willicote; Wincot
Clifton (Cliffton), 329, **403–13**, 1401; death at,
    1247, 1338, 1412, 1575; residents, 210, 213, 577,
    730, 1321, 1411, 1412, 1415, 1418, 1488; union
    workhouse, 1160; and see Hotwells; St.
    Vincent's
Climperwell, in Cranham, 332, 449, 605 n
Clingre (Clehongre, Cleihunger, Clinger), in Cam
    and Stinchcombe, 277, 1100, 1169
Cloford (Cloved) (Som.), 614
Clopley, in Sevenhampton, 1061*, 1062*, 1063
Clopton, in Mickleton, 572, 864*, 865; Upper
    Clopton (Upper Clapton), 868
Clouerwall, see Clearwell
Cloved, see Cloford
Cloveshoe (Cloveshoo), in Deerhurst or
    Tewkesbury, 1288, 1419
Clowerwall, see Clearwell
Cloyne (Irel.), 959
Clyffe Pypard, see Bupton
Coaley, 44, **414–19**, 458, 620, 630*, 631, 801,
    1102*, 1507; and see Churchend; Elmcote;
    Greenstreet; Pinnells End
Coalpit Heath, in Westerleigh, 142*
Coat, in Bampton, see Cote
Coat (Cote), in Littleton upon Severn, 578, 1405*,
    1407*, 1408, 1411*, 1420*
Coate (Cote), in Eastleach Martin, 1127
Coates (Cotes), 441, **443–6**, 793 n, 1033, 1051,
    1189, 1202; Coates Wood, 444; and see
    Trewsbury
Coates (Cotes), in Winchcombe, 1474, 1475, 1476
Coberley (Cobberley, Coverle, Cubberley,
    Cuberley), **420–3**, 458, 529, 532 n, 1493, 1531;
    Coberley Court, 420; residents, 484*, 504, 641*,
    684, 800, 1051, 1472*; and see Pinswell; Seven
    Springs
Cobrey (Cowbury), in Walford (Herefs.), 516
Cockbury, in Winchcombe, 1466, 1474, 1476,
    1477
Cockleford, in Elkstone, 579
Cockshoot, in Newnham, 471*, 927
Codrington, in Wapley and Codrington, 32, 495,
    996, 1117*, 1386
Coford [unidentified], 806 n
Cogges (Coggs) (Oxon.), 1146
Colchester (Essex), 718 n
Cold Ashton, see Ashton, Cold
Cold Aston, see Ashton, Cold; Aston Blank
Cold Salperton, see Salperton
Coldashton, see Ashton, Cold
Coldcote, see Calcot
Coldrop (Coldthorp, Coldthrop, Coldthrup), see
    Colethrop

Coleford (Colford), in Newland, 913, 915, 918, 919, 920*, 921*, 922*, 923*, 924*, 1162*; *and see* Edenwall; Poolway; Scowles, the; Whitecliff

Colesborne (Colesbourn, Collesborn), 116, **424–5**, 458, 579, 1059, 1501; *and see* Pinswell; Rapsgate

Colesborne (Colesborn, Colesbourn), Little, or Bruern, in Withington, 424, 1047*, 1501*

Coleshill (Berks.), 471, 523

Colethrop (Coldrop, Coldthorp, Coldthrop, Coldthrup, Colthroop, Colthrope, Coulthrop), in Haresfield, 264, 663 n, 664, 669*, 670, 676*, 677*, 1129, 1130*, 1132*, 1203

Colford, *see* Coleford

Colham (Collum), in Hillingdon (Mdx.), 4

Colkerton (Colkurton), *see* Culkerton

Collesborn, *see* Colesborne

Collingham, *see* Compton, in Collingham

Collingham, South, *see* Columoe

Collopiorum [? Toller Porcorum] (Dors.), 190

Collum, *see* Colham

Coln (Colne), river, 183, 184, 318, 426, 565 n, 588, 592, 1056

Coln Rogers, 429, **432–3**, 583, 1180, 1451*; *and see* Pindrup

Coln St. Aldwyn, 186, 232, 388, **426–9**, 458, 985, 1003, 1005; *and see* Williamstrip

Coln (Colne) St. Denis, 373, 385, **430–1**, 482 n, 458, 1355, 1388; *and see* Calcot

Colnbrook (Colnbrooke) (Bucks.), 278

Colthrooope (Colthrope), *see* Colethrop

Columoe [? South Collingham] (Notts.), 627

Colwall (Colwale) (Herefs.), 1058

Comb (Combe), Old, in Chipping Campden, 287, 1457, 1458*

Comb End (Combend), in Elkstone, 424, 579, 580*, 656, 660

Comb Farm, in Ozleworth, 967

Combe [? Kingcomb, in Weston Subedge], 1430

Combe (Comb, Comba), [*unidentified*], 186, 773, 776

Combe [*unidentified*] (Hants), 401

Combe, Castle (Wilts.), 32, 237

Combe Baskerville, in Icomb, 1016, 1421*, 1422

Comberton, Great (Warws., *recte* Worcs.), 233 n

Comberwood, *see* Cumberwood

Combesend, *see* Coomb's End

Combworth, *see* Cumberwood

Comden, *see* Cowden

Comerton, *see* Camerton

Comney [*unidentified*] (Wilts.), 706

Compton [*unspecified*, Easter Compton or Compton Greenfield], in Almondsbury, 730, 1408, 1419

Compton, in Newent, 894

Compton, in Collingham (Yorks. W.R.), 919

Compton, Cassey (Compton, Little Compton), in Withington, 1495, 1497, 1501*

Compton, Easter, in Almondsbury, 40, 46, 98; *and see* Compton [*unspecified*]

Compton, Little (Compton), **436–7**, 458, 482 n, 518 n, 1355, 1388

Compton, Little, in Withington, *see* Compton, Cassey

Compton, Long (Warws.), 1051

Compton Abdale (Compton, Compton Abdell), 367, **434**, 645, 766, 896, 947, 1042, 1198; *and see* Hampen

Compton Dando (Som.), 1582

Compton Greenfield, in Almondsbury, **435**, 1420; *and see* Compton [*unspecified*]

Compton Murdac, *see* Compton Verney

Compton Scorpion (Compton Scarfen), in Ilmington (Warws.), 230 n

Compton Verney (Compton Murdac) (Warws.), 568, 591

Condicote, **438–9**, 458, 641, 1195; *and see* Banks Fee; Hinchwick

Cone brook, 53

Coneham, in Stonehouse, 1185

Congresbury (Som.), 406

Conington (Cunnington) (Hunts.), 995, 997

Conringham, *see* Corringham

Constance, *see* Coutances

Constantinople (the Porte) (Turkey), 220 n, 224

Cooling (Kent), 1241, 1248

Coombe [*unspecified*], 1201

Coombe (Comb, Coom), in Wotton under Edge, 174, 1524, 1526, 1527, 1528, 1529*, 1533, 1535, 1537

Coomb's End (Combesend), in Old Sodbury, 1115*, 1116

Cooper's Hill (Cowper's Hill), in Brockworth, 259 & n, 261*

Copton, in Preston (Kent), 44

Corfham (Corshum) (Salop.), 618 n

Cork (Irel.), city, 745, 746; county, 413

Cormeilles (Normandy), abbey, 544, 893, 894, 1401

Corndean (Cornden), in Winchcombe, 1057, 1463*, 1471, 1474, 1475, 1476

Cornewell, *see* Cornwell

Cornwall, 7, 707 n, 920;, duchy of, 341; *and see* Antony; Bodmin; Chillingham; Falmouth; Lanner; Pendarves; Pentillie; Port Eliot; St. Erth; St. Ewe; Trerice

Cornwell (Cornewell) (Oxon.), 26, 217, 1262

Corpus Christi College (C.C.C.), Oxford, alumnus, 135, 333, 1200, 1428; estate, 197, 325, 327, 525*, 526, 619, 638*, 639, 801*, 860, 890, 1015, 1043*, 1078, 1092; fellow, 526*, 692, 781, 1315; president, 394 n, 525

Corringham (Corningham) (Essex), 173

Corscombe, *see* Coscombe

Corse (Cors), **440–2**, 458, 482 & n, 1356; Corse Chase, 440; Corse Farm, 440; Corse Wood Hill, 1356; *and see* Oridge; Stainbridge

Corse (Cors) Court, in Tirley, 687, 1353

Corse End, in Hartpury, 680

Corse Lawn, largely in Chaceley (Worcs.), 75, 76, 440*, 1355

Corsham (Wilts.), 129, 1207

Corshum, *see* Corfham

Corstophine (Corstophin) (Scot.), 496

Coscombe (Corscombe, Costcombe), in Stanway, 439, 493, 634, 708 n, 1154
Costessy (Cossey) (Norf.), 875 n
Cote (Coat), in Bampton (Oxon.), 422
Cote, in Eastleach Martin, see Coate
Cote, in Littleton upon Severn, see Coat
Cotes, see Coates
Cotham, in Bristol, 1405, 1420
Cottles, in Atworth (Wilts.), 614; Cottles Farm, 20
Cotysdene, see Cutsdean
Coughton (Warws.), 508 n, 634
Couhull, see Cowhill
Coulthrop, see Colethrop
Court, the, in Arlingham, 65
Court House, in Cromhall, 453
Court House, the, in Newent, 893
Courtbleathing [unidentified] (Mon.), 921
Coutances (Constance) (Normandy), 788, 1384, 1491
Coventry (Warws.), 233 n, 244, 271 n, 393 n*; priory, 848, 927; White Friars, 393 n
Coverall Castle [unidentified] (Salop.), 592
Coverle, see Coberley
Cow... [? Cowarne] (Herefs.), 812
Cowarne, Much, see Bachcombe
Cowbridge (Crowbridge) Park (Glam.), 1306
Cowbury, see Cobrey
Cowcombe, in Minchinhampton, 648, 649
Cowden (Comden) (Kent), 44
Cowhill (Couhull, Cowell), in Oldbury upon Severn, 955, 957*, 1311, 1313*, 1429
Cowley (Couleye), 254, **447–8**, 633, 640, 985, 1217, 1494; residents, 320, 328, 563, 633, 640, 690, 1482, 1531; and see Birdlip; Stockwell
Cowper's Hill, see Cooper's Hill
Cradley (Herefs.), 1058
Cranborne (Cranbourn) (Dors.), priory, 1285, 1291*
Cranbrook (Kent), 44*
Cranford (Mdx.), 163, 366, 455, 1340
Cranford (Great Cranford), see Canford Magna
Cranham, 254, **449–50**, 1499; and see Buckholt; Climperwell; Overtown Farm; Tibboth Farm
Crawless, in Hamfallow, 173*
Crécy (Cressy) (France), 325 n, 326
Creedy [North Creedy, in Sandford, or Lower Creedy, in Upton Helions] (Devon), 725
Crendon, Long, see Notley
Cressy, see Crécy
Cricklade (Wilts.), 510, 793 n, 794, 1070, 1073, 1346; and see Maskelyne's Ham
Crickley Hill, in Badgeworth, 503
Criggion (Crygion) (Mont.), 1373
Crimea (Russia), 1073*
Cromhall (Cromwell, Croomhall), 121, 160, **451–6**, 458, 1324, 1327, 1345*, 1455*; Cromhall Abbots, 41, 451*, 452*, 454; Cromhall Heath, 451; Cromhall Lygon, 451*, 452*; residents, 18, 121, 308*, 955, 1311, 1324, 1327*, 1343, 1344*, 1449, 1450, 1453, 1548, 1551; and see Abbotside; Court House; Whitfield Farm; Woodend; Woodland

Crondall, see Itchell
Crooke's (Crook, Crooks), in Oxenhall, 897, 899*, 964, 965*
Crook's Marsh (Crookmarsh), in Henbury, 721
Croome, Earls (Erls Croome) (Worcs.), 336
Croomhall, see Cromhall
Crowbridge Park, see Cowbridge Park
Crowfield, in Dymock, 546
Crowthorne and Minety hundred, 363
Croydon (Surr.), 827 n, 829 n, 1057; and see Waddon
Crudwell (Wilts.), 375; and see Chedglow
Crygion, see Criggion
Cuba (West Indies), 1303; and see Havana
Cubberley (Cuberley), see Coberley
Cugley, in Newent, 894, 899, 902*, 904*
Culcerton, see Culkerton
Culford, in Newent, 893
Culkerton (Colkerton, Colkurton, Culcerton), in Rodmarton, 778 n, 908, 1028*, 1029*, 1030*, 1032*, 1033*, 1092, 1244, 1328; Culkerton Farm, 1030*
Cullyhall (Culley Hall), in Bitton, 206, 208
Culmington (Culmerton) (Salop.), 618 n
Culver House (Culverhouse), in Minchinhampton, 657, 1508
Culver House, in Newnham, 927
Culverden [unidentified, near Gloucester], 1047*
Culverhouse, see Culver House
Cumberland, 552; and see Carlisle; Esk; Millom; Rottington; Whitehaven
Cumberley [unidentified], 1147
Cumberwood (Comberwood, Combworth), in Tirley, 485, 1352*, 1353*, 1355*, 1356
Cunnington, see Conington
Curbridge, see Witney Park
Custom House, the, see London, buildings
Cutmill (Cutt Mill), in Dymock, 546
Cutsdean (Cotysdene) (Worcs.), 704 n, 1387
Cutt Mill, see Cutmill
Cwmdu (Brec.), 1451

Dagenham (Essex), 1027
Daglingworth (Daglyngworth), 376*, 384, **459–60**, 1201, 1202*
Dalswinton (Scot.), 1360
Dalton (Lancs.), 396
Damsells, in Painswick, 972
Dan-y-parc (Dany Park), near Crickhowell (Brec.), 333
Danby Lodge, in West Dean, 478 n, 479 n
Dane-John, in Canterbury (Kent), 237, 238
Daneway (Danaway, Denway), in Bisley, 197, 201*, 1049, 1050*, 1052; Daneway Bridge, 793 n
Dantesey, see Dauntsey
Dany Park, see Dan-y-parc
Darking, see Dorking
Dartford (Kent), 347; and see Hall Place
Dartmouth (Devon), 1245
Dauntsey (Dantesey) (Wilts.), 508 n
Dauphiné (Dophine) (France), 45
Dawlish (Devon), 639

Day House, in Hill, 168, 176
Day House (Dayhouse), the, in Tidenham, 1320, 1321
Daylesford (Dayleford, Draylesford) (Worcs.), 313 n, 1189
Dean, Forest of, 188*, 244, 458, 461, **475–80**, 605 n, 1039; civil war, 805 n, 806 n, 928; iron, 605 n, 807, 851; officers, 162, 242, 470, 474, 476, 478, 479, 811, 913; produce, 244; *and see* (in East Dean) Abbots Wood; Blakeney Walk; Herbert Lodge; Herbert Walk; Latimer Lodge and Walk; Lea Bailey; Pope's Hill; Ruardean Lodge and Walk; Speech House, the; Yellow Shraf; (in West Dean) Berry Hill; Danby Lodge; Ellwood; Joyford; Parkend; Worcester Lodge and Walk; York Lodge; Yorkley
Dean, Little (Dean Parva, Dene Parva), **469–74**, 605 n*, 925, 928, 929; Little Dean Lodge, 472; Little Dean Walk, 1039; Little Dean's Cross, 472*; residents, 1, 3, 5, 640, 886*, 927, 1155; *and see* Yellow Shraf
Dean, Michel (Michell Dean, Mitchel Dean), *see* Mitcheldean
Dean, Upper (Overdean), in Dean (Beds.), 849
Dean Farm, in Hatherop, 691
Dean stream, 478 n
Deeping Fen (Lincs.), 1027
Deerhurst (Deorhurst, Deorhyrste), 458, **481–6**, 801, 888, 1288, 1291*; Deerhurst Walton (Walton), 421, 482, 483, 486, 1165, 1358; hundred, 481; manor, 585*, 684, 882, 1223, 1331*, 1475*; peculiar, 440; priory, 436, 481 & n; priory estate, 430, 436, 440, 585, 684, 1165*, 1291*, 1331, 1355*, 1356*, 1388*, 1504; *and see* Alney Island; Apperley; Cloveshoe; Oak, the; Plaistow; Wightfield
Deinton, *see* Doynton
Denbighshire, *see* Ruthin
Denchworth (Denworth) (Bucks., *recte* Berks.), 717, 799, 1410
Dene Magna (Michel Dene), *see* Mitcheldean
Dene Parva, *see* Dean, Little
Denmark, 357, 1251
Denny (Dinney, Dunny), in Westbury on Severn, 1402, 1403*
Denton (Lancs.), 1574
Denworth, *see* Denchworth
Deorhurst (Deorhyrste), *see* Deerhurst
Deptford (Depford) (Kent), 1427
Derby (Derb.), 1209
Derbyshire, 459, 660, 876, 1105; *and see* Brailsford; Derby
Derry Hall [? in Calne] (Wilts.), 508 n
Dersley, *see* Dursley
Devizes (Devises) (Wilts.), 654, 864 n, 1006, 1027, 1073*; *and see* New Park
Devon (Devonshire), 687, 994, 1067, 1180, 1367; *and see* Barnstaple; Chettiscombe; Chudleigh; Creedy; Dartmouth; Dawlish; East Down; Exeter; Molland; Netherton; Newtown St. Cyr; Palington; Plymouth; Sedborough; Silverton; Thornbury; Torquay; Totnes; Traymill; Weston, in Branscombe

Deynton, *see* Doynton
Dickler stream, 1225
Didbrook (Didbroke), **493–4**, 637, 707, 708 n, 888, 1519
Didcot, in Beckford, 147*
Didmarton, 416, **495–6**, 1344, 1535; *and see* Woodsha
Dillon (Dilloon), Castle (Irel.), 984, 1338
Dinder (Som.), 1201
Dingestow (Mon.), 920
Dinney, *see* Denny
Dinton (Wilts.), 706
Dirham, *see* Dyrham
Ditchford, in Blockley, 218, 220, 226
Ditchley, in Spelsbury (Oxon.), 1341
Dixton (Mon.), 1161
Dixton, in Alderton, 27, 53, 54, 73, 89, 1287, 1455
Dobuni (Roman province), 355
Docker, near Kendal (Westmld.), 636
Doddington cum Marsh (Duddington Marsh) (Cambs.), 1377
Dodington (Dodrington), 36, 265 n, **497–81**, 529, 840, 888, 1336, 1338*, 1451, 1547; *and see* Dorington
Doncaster (Yorks. W.R.), 1247
Donhead St. Andrew, *see* Ferne House
Donington (Donnington) (Salop.), 1418
Donnington, *see* Donington
Donnington (Herefs.), 270; Donnington Hall, 473
Donnington, in Stow on the Wold, 1194, 1195*, 1196*, 1197*; *and see* Dorington
Door, *see* Dore
Dophine, *see* Dauphiné
Dore (Door), Abbey (Herefs.), 711 n
Doreys, *see* Dureth
Dorington [? Dodington, Donnington, or Dorsington], 1538
Dorking (Darking) (Surr.), 168, 829 n
Dorn, in Blockley, 218, 220, 226, 882, 883
Dorset (Dorsetshire), 190, 359, 534 n, 696, 1059, 1238, 1491; *and see* Beaminster; Canford Magna; Castleton; Causeway; Collopiorum; Cranborne; Hasleborough; Henley, in Buckland Newton; Lyme Regis; Poole; Stalbridge; Stour Provost; Tarrant Hinton; Turnworth; Weymouth; Winfrith Newburgh; Witchington
Dorsington, **500–1**; *and see* Dorington
Dorsington, Little (Warws.), in Welford on Avon, 1392
Doughton (Dufton), in Tetbury, 1243*, 1249, 1251*, 1253, 1255*, 1257, 1259
Dover (Kent), 1027
Dover's Hill, in Weston Subedge, 287
Dowdeswell, **502–6**, 708 n, 888, 1078, 1090, 1445, 1501*, 1502; Lower Dowdeswell, 503; residents, 316, 333, 334*, 393, 585, 671, 977, 1000, 1232*, 1477; Upper Dowdeswell, 502, 503, 504*, 1256, 1501, 1502; *and see* Andoversford; Lower House, the; Pegglesworth; Rossley; Sandywell
Downend (Down End), in Forthampton, 609
Downend (Down End), in Horsley, 748
Downend (Downing), in Mangotsfield, 456, 833

Downesbourn Rous, *see* Duntisbourne Rouse
Downhatherley, *see* Hatherley, Down
Downhouse, in Cam, 280, 281
Downhouse [? in Westbury on Trym], 1415
Downing, in Longney, 831
Downing, in Mangotsfield, *see* Downend
Downington, in Lechlade, 795
Downs, the, in Marshfield, 839
Downton, in Frocester, 1143, 1144
Doynton (Deinton, Deynton), 7, 11, 36, **487–92**, 553*, 555, 888; *and see* Bury; Tracy Park Lodge; Well House
Draicott Cerne, *see* Draycot Cerne
Draiton, *see* Drayton
Draycot (Draicott) Cerne (Wilts.), 1530
Draycot Foliat (Draycott Folliott) (Wilts.), 1116
Draycott, in Blockley, 218*, 220, 226*
Draycott (Dreicote, Draycots Mill), in Cam, 277
Draycott in the Moor (Draycote in the Moors) (Staffs.), 1092
Drayerscourt, *see* Droys Court
Draylesford, *see* Daylesford
Drayton (Draiton) (Oxon.), 311 n
Drayton, West (Drayton) (Mdx.), 220
Dreicote, *see* Draycott, in Cam
Driffield (Dryffeld), **515–17**, 990, 1081, 1202
Droitwich (Worcs.), 680, 1119*, 1360
Droys Court (Drayerscourt), in Brockworth, 259
Drusham, *see* Througham
Dryffeld, *see* Driffield
Dublin (Irel.), 413, 959
Ducklington (Oxon.), 408
Dudbridge (bridge at Dudbrook, Dudefeld), in Rodborough, King's Stanley, and Stonehouse, 1139, 1186, 1187, 1217, 1218; residents, 983, 1023, 1025, 1026, 1137*, 1143, 1187, 1214, 1367, 1439
Duddington Marsh, *see* Doddington cum Marsh
Dudefeld, *see* Dudbridge
Dudstone (Dudston), in Hempsted, 1379
Dufton, *see* Doughton
Dumbleton, 28, 485, **518–22**, 667, 888
Dunesbourn, *see* Duntisbourne
Dunfield (Dunville), in Kempsford, 770
Duni (Dunny), in Minsterworth, 869, 870, 1402
Dunkilns (Dunkley, Dunklins), in St. Briavels, 248, 250
Dunny, in Minsterworth, *see* Duni
Dunny, in Westbury on Severn, *see* Denny
Dunsborne (Dunsborn, Dunsbourne) Rouse, *see* Duntisbourne Rouse
Dunstan [*unidentified*], 467
Duntisbourne (Dunesbourn, Duntesborne) [*unspecified*], 1213, 1482
Duntisbourne Abbots, **523–4**, 878, 1052, 1483, 1485; Duntisbourne Leer, 523, 524; *and see* Nutbeam Farm
Duntisbourne Rouse (Downesbourn Rous, Dunsborn Rouse, Dunsborne Rouse, Dunsbourne Rous, Duntesborne Militis), 200, 384, 524, **525–6**, 575, 649, 667, 1202; *and see* Pinbury
Dunville, *see* Dunfield

Dureth [? Doreys, in Painswick], 387
Durham, *see* Dyrham
Durham (co. Dur.), 144, 191, 361 & n, 1009*, 1559
Durham county, 361 n; *and see* Durham; Heworth; Thornton Hall; Ryton; Westoe; White Hill; Wolsingham
Durrington (Wilts.), 910
Dursley (Dersley), 153, 160, 280, 462, **527–43**, 623, 888, 1097, 1168, 1522; death at, 1097*, 1281; manor, 778, 908*, 1147; residents, 166, 182, 280, 282*, 284, 497, 625, 809, 908*, 938, 939, 970, 971, 976, 1096, 1098, 1140, 1147, 1168*, 1241*, 1302, 1366*, 1440, 1509, 1512, 1525, 1535; rural dean & deanery, 279, 527, 532, 1019; *and see* New Mills; Newhouse; Woodmancote
Dyehouse, the, in Minchinhampton, 655*
Dymock (Dimmock), **544–50**, 605 n*, 611, 888, 894 n, 1189, 1266, 1509; Little Dymock, 546; *and see* Boyce, the; Bromsberrow Heath; Callow, the; Crowfield; Cutmill; Edulus Place; Farm, the; Flaxley tithing; Gamage Hall; Green House, the; Hill Place; Ketford; Leadington; Lintridge; Normans Land; Ockington; Pit Leasow; Ryeland; Ryton; Woodend; Woodfields
Dyrham (Dirham, Durham), 7, 36, 83, 492, **551–5**, 561, 663 n, 723, 747, 823, 888, 1117; *and see* Hinton

Eagleton, *see* Engleton
Earls Croome, *see* Croome, Earls
Earthcott (Yrdcote), in Alveston, 50, 961
Earthcott, Gaunt's, in Almonsdbury, 40, 42, 1202
Easington [? Eastington, or Ampney St. Peter], 366
East Angles, 357, 1459
East Down [*unspecified*] (Devon), 431
East End, in Fairford, 592
East India Co., 455, 473, 1143, 1400, 1576
East Indies, 254, 403 n, 442, 866, 932, 975, 1029, 1085, 1176, 1565; *and see* Borneo; Surinam
Eastbach Court, in English Bicknor, 188, 192*
Eastbrook, *see* Ampney St. Mary
Easter Compton, *see* Compton, Easter
Eastington (Crowthorne and Minety hundred), *see* Ampney St. Peter
Eastington (Estington) (Whitstone hundred), **556–64**, 888, 1097*, 1133, 1138, 1140, 1147, 1440; residents, 105, 282*, 419, 618, 625, 655, 747, 986, 1054, 1184; *and see* Alkerton; Millend; Nastend; Neale's Place; Nupend; Oldbury; Puddleworth; Westend
Eastleach [Eastleach Martin or Eastleach Turville], 691
Eastleach Martin (East Leche St. Martin) or Boutherop (Botherop, Burthorpe), 186, **565–7**, 888, 1127; Burthorpe Farm, 565; *and see* Coate; Fyfield
Eastleach (East Leche) Turville, 482 n, 565, 566, **568–9**, 888
Eastnor (Estnare) (Herefs.), 266, 1058; *and see* Castle Ditch
Easton (Lincs.), 521

Easton, near Wells (Som.), 239
Easton, in Stapleton, 1160
Easton (Eston) Grey (Wilts.), 1070, 1072
Eastwood, in Thornbury, 283, 1304*, 1307*, 1309, 1313, 1343, 1344*
Eastwooodhey, see Woodhey, East
Eatington, Nether, see Thornton
Eaton (Bucks.), see Eton
Eaton, Castle (Wilts.), 771; and see Lus Hill
Eaton, Water (Nunne Eiton), in Latton (Wilts.), 508 n, 862, 1077
Ebernoe (Ebernhoe), in Kirdford (Suss.), 1077*
Eberton, see Ebrington
Ebley (Ebly), in Randwick and Stonehouse, 118, 1006, 1024*, 1026, 1180*, 1183, 1184, 1185, 1186*, 1217, 1507
Ebrington (Eberton), 227, 570-3, 634, 888, 1191, 1277; and see Bristentune; Charingworth; Hidcote Boyce
Ebworth, in Painswick, 970
Eckington (Worcs.), 150
Edenwall, Upper and Lower, in Coleford, 913
Edgbaston (Edgbarston) (Warws.), 977
Edge, the, in Painswick, 975, 976*
Edgeworth (Edgworth), 314, 536, 574-5, 1083; Edgeworth Manor, 1046*; and see Westwood
Edinburgh (Scot.), 410, 639, 811; and see Handerwood
Edington (Wilts.), priory, 599*, 695, 864
Edmonton (Mdx.), 1416
Edmund Hall, see St. Edmund Hall
Edulus Place [? in Dymock], 548
Effington, see Evington
Egcote, see Eycot
Egypt, see Alexandria
Eiton, Nunne, see Eaton, Water
Elberton (Ailberton, Aylberton), 41, 52, 100, 576-8, 962, 720*, 796
Eldersfield (Worcs.), 442, 611, 977*, 1353*, 1354; and see Rue Green
Elkstone (Elkestone, Elstone), 423, 579-80, 660, 888; and see Cockleford; Comb End
Ell brook, 893
Ellinghurst, in Almondsbury, 47
Ellwood (Elwood), in West Dean, 250
Elm Bridge (Elmbridge), in Hucclecote, 346
Elmcote (Hulmancote), in Coaley, 414
Elmeley, see Elmley
Elmestree (Elmstree, Elmtree), in Tetbury, 368, 378, 652, 1080, 1241*, 1247*, 1251, 1256*
Elmley (Elmeley, Elmly Castle) (Worcs.), 784, 1048, 1073, 1219, 1392, 1447
Elmore, 99, 566, 581-4, 713, 869, 888, 1344; Elmore Court, 581; Elmore Court House, 672 n; residents, 105, 666*, 715*, 695, 817, 1236; and see Stone Bench
Elmsett (Suff.), 560
Elmstone Hardwicke (Elmston Hardwick, Elmstone), 398, 585-7, 1052, 1288, 1291; and see Hardwicke; Uckington
Elmstree (Elmtree), see Elmestree
Elstone, see Elkstone

Elstow (Helenstow) (Beds.), abbey, 1186
Elton, in Westbury on Severn, 1238, 1393*, 1394*, 1395*, 1397*, 1399*, 1401, 1402, 1403
Elwood, see Ellwood
Ely (Cambs.), 609, 610*; Isle of, 1377
Emilyn Ukenclet, see Newcastle Emlyn
Emmanuel College, Cambridge, 1028
England, arms of, 361*, 392
Englefield (Berks.), Englefield House, 1344
Engleton (Eagleton), in Brewood (Staffs.), 452
English Bicknor, see Bicknor, English
Englishcombe (Inglescombe) (Som.), 612
Enstone (Enna's Stone) (Oxon.), 512, 1056 n
Epney, in Moreton Valence, 666, 885, 887*
Epsom, see Langley
Ercall, High (Salop.), 1004
Erlingham, see Arlingham
Erls Croome, see Croome, Earls
Ermin (Irmin) Street, 126, 131, 252, 355 n, 459, 1493
Erw-wastad (Erw-Wasted), near Ammanford (Carms.), 409
Escurial, the (Spain), 495
Esk (Cumb.), 1281
Eske [unidentified] (Scot.), 1281
Essex, 838, 977, 1492, 1493, 1494; and see Aldborough Hatch; Audley End; Barking; Bumpstead, Steeple; Chigwell; Colchester; Corringham; Dagenham; Giddy Hall; Gosfield; Harwich; Heydon; Ilford, Little; Layer Marney; Lea, river; Malden; Maylards; Radwinter; Ridley Hall; Ruckholt; Rottenden; Tey, Great; Tilbury; Tillingham; Waltham; Waltham, Great; Waltham Holy Cross; Writtle
Estcourt House (Est Court) and manor, in Shipton Moyne, 784, 1073*, 1074*
Estington, see Eastington
Estnare, see Eastnor
Eston, see Aston Magna
Eston Grey, see Easton Grey
Ethe, see St. Erth
Ethom, see Evesham
Etloe (Etlac, Etloe Duchy), in Awre, 101, 102*, 103, 104, 105, 106*, 107*, 112*, 814
Eton (Eaton) College or School (Bucks.), 147, 393 n, 481 & n, 534 n, 595, 1040, 1528
Euly, see Uley
Evening, see Avening
Evenlode (Evenload) (Worcs.), 1194
Evenlode, river, 21, 216, 218
Evesbatch (Evesvatch) (Herefs.), 265, 267, 268
Evesham (Ethom) (Worcs.), 763, 1040, 1292, 1390, 1458, 1478; abbey of St. Mary, estate, 85, 117, 216*, 232*, 255*, 319, 570, 927, 1016*, 1093*, 1148, 1189, 1194, 1195*, 1196*, 1227*, 1369, 1392*, 1432, 1447, 1459*, 1460, 1475; Cole Street, 1149
Evesvatch, see Evesbatch
Evington (Effington, Yiventon), in Leigh, 801, 1547, 1165
Eweley (Ewley), see Uley
Ewelme (Oxon.), 341

Ewelme, stream, 527, 530
Ewen, in Kemble (Wilts.), 303
Ewyas Harold (Herefs.), 803
Exeter (Exon.) (Devon), 41, 307, 367, 388, 1328, 1424
Exeter College, Oxford, 1180
Exhall (Warws., Barlichway hundred), 1329
Exning (Ixning) (Suff.), 1219
Exton (Rut.), 287 n, 291 n
Eycot (Egcote), in Rendcomb, 1011
Eye (Herefs.), 268
Eyeford, see Ayford
Eyford, 891, 1055*, 1089*, 1090*, 1091, 1093*
Eynsham (Oxon.), abbey, 863*, 1016, 1227, 1253, 1256, 1257*, 1259
Eyworth (Beds.), 995

Fairford (Fayreford), 128, 361, **588–98**, 638 n, 888, 1092, 1209; the Borough, 592; residents, 128, 138, 643, 678, 696, 859, 1125, 1229, 1255, 1262; and see Beauchamp or Warwick Court; East End; Milltown End; Milton
Falaise (Wallison) (Normandy), 432
Falfield (Falefeld, or St. Tyrrel), in Thornbury, 456, 1173*, 1176, 1295, 1304*, 1307, 1309, 1311*, 1313*, 1342*; and see Brinkmarsh; Sundayshill; Whitfield
Falmouth (Cornw.), 1367
Fareham, see Catisfield Lodge
Faringdon (Berks.), 1092
Farleigh, see Farley, in Hardwicke
Farleigh, Monkton (Farley) (Wilts.), priory, 205
Farleigh Hungerford (Farley) (Som., and in error Wilts.), castle, 509, 747, 1407
Farley (Farleigh), in Hardwicke, 663, 664*
Farley, see Farleigh, Monkton; Farleigh Hungerford
Farm Hill (Farmhill), in Stroud, 1006
Farm, the, in Dymock, 899
Farmcote (Farmcoate, Fermecott), in Pinnock and Hyde, 634*, 635*, 637, 705, 854
Farmhill, see Farm Hill
Farmington, **599–601**, 678, 688, 985, 1350
Farnborough (Warws.), 574, 785, 990
Farnham (Surr.), 829 n
Farningham (Farringham) (Kent), 516
Faversham (Feversham) (Kent), 1290, 1530; and see Parry Court Farm
Fayreford, see Fairford
Fécamp (Fescamp, Fiscamp, Fischamp, Montburi Fischamp) (Normandy), abbey, 324, 798, 1068, 1091*, 1093, 1195, 1225, 1227
Feckenham (Worcs.), 992
Felkins, see Filkins
Fermecott, see Farmcote
Ferne House (Ferns), in Donhead St. Andrew (Wilts.), 618
Ferris (Ferrie's) Court, in Bisley, 197, 204*
Fescamp, see Fécamp
Feversham, see Faversham
Fiddington (Fidington), in Ashchurch, 71*, 72, 1287, 1289, 1290, 1381, 1382; residents, 72*, 73*, 74, 484, 686, 1262, 1359

Field (Field's) Court, in Hardwicke, 352, 664, 999*, 1000*
Field House, the, in Awre, 104, 105, 106*, 932
Fields, the (Field Place, Fields Place), in Stroud, 1206, 1208*, 1213, 1215*
Field's Court, see Field Court
Fifield (Oxon.), 77, 256, 565
Fifield, in Eastleach Martin, see Fyfield
Filford, see Vilvoorde
Filkins (Felkins) (Oxon.), 596, 718, 1126
Fillingham (Tillingham) (Lincs.), 1029
Filton, 41, 48, 576, **602–4**, 745, 746, 1383; and see Hay
Firle (Suss.), 921
Fiscamp (Fischcamp), see Fécamp
Fisherwick (Fisherwicke-upon-Trent), near Lichfield (Staffs.), 863, 865
Fishponds, in Stapleton, 1160*
Fladbury, see Throckmorton
Flanders, 136, 285, 431, 532, 599, 638 n, 723, 1174*, 1190, 1512; and see Waal
Flaxley, **605–8**, 888, 1402; abbey, 475, 605; abbey, estate, 1, 65, 66, 214, 469, 477, 544 n, 546, 605, 915, 927, 1039, 1402*; residents, 4, 5, 215*, 473; and see Castiard valley; Grange, the
Flaxley tithing, in Dymock, 546
Flintshire, see Pen-y-Pwlle; St. Asaph
Flitcham with Appleton, see Appleton
Flodden (Scot.), 605 n
Florence (Italy), 1231, 1303
Fontevraud (Fontevrault l'Abbaye) (France), 1256
Ford, in Temple Guiting, 638, 641*
Ford House (the Fordhouse), in Newent, 904
Fort Malborough (India), 1400
Fort William (India), 697
Forthampton (Forth Hampton), 268, 482, **609–11**, 888, 1263; Forthampton Court, 610, 1407*; and see Downend; Lower House; Swailley
Forwood, in Minchinhampton, 97*, 648, 659
Fosse Way, the (Foss Road, Fossway), 78, 145, 220, 252, 318, 346, 355 n, 579, 816, 1195
Fotheringhay (Northants.), college, 481 & n, 544, 893
Fountains Abbey, in Ripon (Yorks. W.R.), 1020
Founteney, see St. Wandrille
Foxcote (Foxcot), in Withington, 1059, 1063, 1495, 1497, 1501*, 1502*
Foxcote, in Ilmington (Warws.), 1432
Framilode (Framlod), in Moreton Valence and Saul, 792 n, 885, 925, 930, 1053, 1054*, 1440; Framilode Mills, 558*
Frampton (Fraunton, Frenlyntone), in Winchcombe, 1465, 1466, 1468, 1473, 1474, 1475, 1476, 1478
Frampton Cotterel (Frampton), 308, **612–16**, 621, 833, 888, 1047, 1428; residents, 17*, 48, 1325*, 1415, 1425, 1453, 1489*; and see Wick Wick
Frampton Mansell (Frampton), in Sapperton, 203, 862, 1032, 1048, 1049*, 1050*, 1051*, 1052*
Frampton on Severn (Frampton), 537, **617–24**, 888, 1102*, 1135, 1440; Frampton Court, 1168; residents, 106, 191, 265 n, 417, 472, 558, 561, 563*, 887, 1096, 1189, 1232, 1437*, 1438, 1439, 1440; and see Frome Bridge; Rosamond's Green

France, 179, 230 n, 534 n, 574 n, 743, 759, 875 n*, 1253, 1303, 1576; arms of, 361*, 392; wars in, &c., 179, 245, 759, 1048, 1303; *and see* Amiens; Angers; Avignon; Beauvais; Boulogne; Calais; Cambrai; Castillon-la-Bataille ; Châlon; Cîteaux; Crécy; Dauphiné; Fontevraud; Gascony; Nantes; Normandy; Orthez; Paris; Pau; Poitiers; Pyrenees; Rushault; St. Florent; Tarbes; Toulouse; Tours; Versailles

France, Petty, *see* Petty France

Fraunton, *see* Frampton

Freechford, *see* Freshford

Frenchay (French Hay) or Froomshaw, in Winterbourne, 1172, 1425, 1487, 1489, 1490*, 1491*

Frenlyntone, *see* Frampton

Freshford (Freechford) (Som.), 1065

Fretherne (Frethern, Frethorn, Frethorne), 618 n, 622, **625–7**, 1045, 1054*, 1183*, 1345, 1440*; Fretherne Cliff, 625; Fretherne Lodge, 625 & n, 627

Fringford (Oxon.), 1059

Frith Farm, *see* Gearing-frith

Frocester (Froster), 414*, 556 n, 562, **628–33**, 888, 1138, 1299, 1307, 1341, 1505; Frocester Court, 579, 628; residents, 106, 163, 395, 417*, 418, 546; *and see* Buckholt, the; Downton

Frog Mill (Frogmill), in Shipton Oliffe or Shipton Solers, 337, 503, 1076*, 1077, 1501

Frogpitt [? in Berkeley], 172*

Frome, *see* Keyford

Frome, Bishop's (Froom) (Herefs.), 615, 1058

Frome, Canon's (Herefs.), 1422

Frome, Castle (Herefs.), 1372

Frome (Froom), river, *see* Stroudwater, river

Frome Bridge (Froombridge), in Frampton on Severn, 623*

Frome Hall, in Rodborough, 1027

Froom, *see* Frome, Bishop's

Froombridge, *see* Frome Bridge

Froomshaw, *see* Frenchay

Furnace, the, in Oxenhall, 964

Furze (Furzy) Hill, in Willersey, 597

Fyfield (Fifield), in Eastleach Martin, 565, 567

Gadlington, *see* Talton

Gainsborough (Lincs.), 167

Gainslow [*unidentified*], near Berwick-upon-Tweed (Northumb.), 852 n, 854

Galway (Irel.), 408

Gamage Hall, in Dymock, 546*

Gambells, in Bishop's Cleeve, 399*

Gambroon [? Jahrom] (Persia), 867

Ganarew (Gannarew) (Herefs.), 539

Ganton (Yorks. E.R.), 409

Garnons, in Mansell Gamage (Herefs.), 1041

Gascony (France), 707

Gatcombe [*unspecified*], 1421*

Gatcombe, in Awre, 101, 102, 110, 111*, 112

Gatcombe Park, in Minchinhampton, 91, 92, 1536

Gatwick, in Westbury on Severn, 1399, 1400

Gaunt's Earthcott, *see* Earthcott, Gaunt's

Gearing-frith [? Frith Farm], in Yate, 1454

Georgia (North America), 1187, 1415

German Spa, the, *see* Spa

Germany, 534 n, 720; *and see* Altona; Berlin; Hamburg; Klosterkampen; Mainz; Minden; Moers; Scurburgh; Spa; Trye; Warburg

Gershill, *see* Gurshill

Ghent (Belgium), 215

Giddinap (Giddiknap), *see* Gydynap

Giddy Hall, in Little Clacton (Essex), 349

Gissing (Norf.), 431

Glamorganshire, 720; *and see* Aberdare; Boverton; Bridgend; Cardiff; Cowbridge; Gower; Llandaff; Llanishen; Llansamlet; Llantwit Fadre; Swansea

Glasbury, *see* Glasherie

Glasgow (Scot.), 583

Glasherie [? Glasbury (Herefs.)], 565 n

Glass House, the, in Newent, 894

Glastonbury (Som.), abbey, 1428

Glench brook, *see* Glynch brook

Gloucester (Glocester, Glocestrensis, Gloster):

Gloucester, abbey of St. Peter, 251 n, 271*, 349, 415, 523, 605 n, 684; estate, 56, 63, 65, 66, 131, 178, 236*, 259, 263*, 277, 301, 349, 365, 400*, 414*, 426*, 432, 449*, 462, 498, 511, 523, 524, 558, 565*, 568, 574, 617 n, 628*, 630, 638, 663, 664, 666*, 680, 681, 688, 696, 743, 769, 770, 785*, 851, 852, 853, 855*, 869*, 885, 908, 909*, 927*, 1005, 1035, 1047, 1054*, 1078, 1101, 1131*, 1132, 1147, 1169, 1185, 1187, 1198, 1201, 1238*, 1350, 1370, 1372*, 1377*, 1378*, 1379, 1380, 1403, 1421, 1440, 1447, 1486; water supply, 851

Gloucester, bishop, 681; estate, 13, 63, 263*, 278, 279*, 301, 302, 360, 370*, 483, 534*, 625 n, 663, 680, 743, 744, 769, 770*, 785, 839*, 853, 855*, 900, 915, 992, 1054, 1078, 1132*, 1169, 1331, 1335, 1348, 1372*, 1373, 1378, 1435, 1440; office, 145, 252, 305, 323 n, 324, 328, 362, 424, 515*, 547, 559 n, 571, 849, 1021, 1104*, 1149*, 1151, 1169, 1187, 1221, 1447; personally, 93, 121, 278, 394 n, 449*, 535, 609* & n, 610, 664, 763, 785, 855, 859, 1101, 1129, 1132, 1160, 1189, 1428, 1502

Gloucester, buildings (misc.) & institutions: Bluecoat hospital, 101; hospital, 1141; hospital of St. Bartholomew, 442, 469, 482 n, 763 n, 766, 893, 925, 1378, 1494, 1502; hospital of St. John, 1005 n; infirmary, 132, 476; school, 993, 1428

Gloucester, castle, 985, 1160; constable, 971

Gloucester, cathedral, 114, 515 n, 592, 627, 1010, 1189, 1379; archdeacon, 532, 536*, 713, 849; dean, 452 n, 625 n, 900, 1016, 1238, 1435, 1440; dean and chapter, 131*, 259, 263*, 275*, 349, 350*, 426*, 432*, 449*, 565, 568, 588, 593, 853*, 1035*, 1047, 1233, 1238, 1317, 1371, 1372, 1378, 1434; prebend, 900, 1502; prebendary or canon, 351, 450, 452 n, 513, 651 n, 1021, 1041, 1180, 1495; school, 464

Gloucester, churches & parishes: St. Catherine, 264, 345, 1379; St. James, 1379; St. John, 975;

St. Mary de Crypt, 77, 713 n, 1180; St. Mary de Lode, 133, 680, 785, 855, 1379; *and see* Longford; St. Michael, 1376, 1379; St. Nicholas, 1186; St. Owen, 581, 711 & n

Gloucester, city: alderman, 351, 513, 535, 682, 783, 992, 1047, 1233, 1365, 1368, 1372, 1494; citizen, 387; corporation (mayor and burgesses), 101, 103, 415, 469, 479, 713, 763, 764, 807, 851, 925, 1186, 1232, 1293, 1378; freeman, 934; High Steward, 162; M.P., 664 n, 852 n, 869, 872, 971, 1035, 1420; mayor (*praetor*), 188, 351, 535, 618, 663 n, 682, 930, 1353, 1379, 1494; sheriff, 930, 1120; town clerk, 1369

Gloucester, civil war, 759 n, 805 n, 806 n, 855, 928, 1197, 1219, 1220, 1238, 1293, 1369, 1404, 1478; siege, 349, 358, 442, 680, 715, 852*,

Gloucester, constable of, 432, 581, 851, 878, 581

Gloucester, diocese, 1189; chancellor, 515 n, 970, 1021, 1045

Gloucester, in Domesday, 792 n, 1138, 1005, 1014, 1287, 1474, 1501, 1512

Gloucester, honour of, 305, 487, 838*, 859, 990, 1032, 1093, 1225*, 1228, 1295, 1311

Gloucester, priory of St. Oswald, 345, 434, 511, 684 n, 785, 869, 870, 889, 890, 1047*, 1078*, 1101, 1323, 1441, 1493, 1494

Gloucester, residents: apothecary, 264, 1268; apprentices, 819 n; attorney, 1053, 1375; baker, 229, 1374, 1377; banker, 252, 870; bellfounder, 1369; builder, 1047; clockmaker, 1182; cordwainer, 761; glover, 353; grocer, 348, 1144; innholder, 1045; ironmonger, 338; maltster, 1235; mason, 66; mercer, 931, 971, 972; solicitor, 1400; surgeon, 1, 1268; surveyor of customs, 931; vintner, 337; wheelwright, 354; occupation unstated, 68, 77, 113, 117, 133*, 169, 197, 262*, 264, 329, 339, 341, 346, 349, 354*, 440, 471, 484, 558, 559 n, 579, 582, 583*, 618, 620, 627, 635, 670, 672, 676, 681, 682*, 683, 684, 687, 688, 696, 713, 738 n, 762, 788, 796, 831, 853, 854*, 857, 870, 872, 930, 931, 935, 972, 975, 984, 997*, 1034, 1035, 1046, 1047*, 1048, 1131, 1144, 1209, 1235, 1244, 1273, 1301, 1316, 1317, 1354, 1374, 1375, 1377*, 1395, 1402, 1433, 1435*, 1437*, 1439*, 1484, 1512, 1530

Gloucester, otherwise mentioned: almshouses, 1478; assizes, 101; coins from, 864 n; death at, 136, 280, 314, 652, 1020, 1139, 1172, 1399; estate or land in, 265, 1021, 1377; fishery, 1309; forest justice seat at, 475; house in, 1044; imprisonment at, 358; iron industry, 851; journey from, 716; native, 1527; Saxon taking of, 553; shops, 1147; walls, 1035; water supply, 851, 1493, 1494; West Bridge, 713 n

Gloucester, *and see* Barton, Abbot's; Kingsholm; Llanthony priory; Longford; Saintbridge; Sheephouse; Sudgrove; Tredworth; Tuffley; Twigworth; Wotton St. Mary

Gloucester and Berkeley Canal, 1054*, 1440

Gloucester and Hereford Canal, 893

Gloucester Hall, Oxford, 251 n, 1478

Gloucestershire, coroner, 55, 106, 217; county gaol, 943; county hospital, 640; deputy lieutenant, 1019, 1042, 1067, 1085, 1536; estates in, 496; Lord Lieutenant, 122, 162, 1170, 1198, 1219; M.P., knight of the shire, 199, 393 n, 359, 1003, 1005, 1066, 1067, 1170, 1171, 1577; militia, 416; resident, 207; sheriff, 188, 269, 289, 301, 349, 482, 547, 664, 891, 896, 980, 997*, 1027, 1055, 1060, 1074, 1082, 1085, 1088, 1091, 1120*, 1160, 1199, 1334*, 1369, 1380, 1385, 1408, 1431

Glympton (Glympton in the Hole) (Oxon.), 165

Glynch (Glench) brook, 265, 440

Goderick (Goderith, Godrich), *see* Goodrich

Godstow (Godstowe), in Wolvercote (Oxon.), abbey, 341, 459*, 1015*, 1255*

Gogerddan (Gogertham), near Aberystwyth (Cardig.), 409

Goldcliff (Mon.), priory, 481 n

Golden Valley, the, in Minchinhampton, 660

Goldwell, in Charlton Abbots, 310

Goldwick, in Alkington, 159, 173*, 1176

Gonerby, Great (Gunwarby) (Lincs.), 209

Good Hope, Cape of, 442

Goodrich (Goderick, Goderith, Godrich, Goodrick) (Herefs.), 605 n, 622, 1528; Castle, 574, 759, 915*; *and see* Mainoaks

Gopshall [*unidentified*], 1214

Gopshill, *see* Gupshill

Gordonstoun (Scot.), 409

Gorsley (Gorsly) Common, in Newent, 894

Gosfield (Essex), Gosfield Hall, 507

Gossington (Gosington), in Slimbridge, 70, 1098, 1100, 1101*

Gotham (Notts.), 1040

Gotheringon (Gutherton), in Bishop's Cleeve, 393, 397, 398*, 399*, 946, 1052, 1345, 1503, 1504

Gower (Gowr) (Glam.), 392, 394

Grafton, in Beckford, 147*, 150*, 151*

Grange, the, in Flaxley, 471, 473, 606

Grange, the, in Kingswood (formerly Wilts.), 779, 781

Grange, the, in Painswick, 1136

Grange, the, in Tetbury, 1241, 1243, 1256*, 1257*

Grange, the, in Westbury on Severn, 1397*, 1402

Grange, the, in Woolaston, 1515, 1516*

Grantham (Lincs.), 910, 1460

Grays, *see* Greys, the

Gray's Inn, *see* London, Inns of Court

Graywell [*unidentified*] (Notts.), 1303

Grease Gate [? in Stroud], 1212

Greasley, *see* Beauvale

Great Common, the, in Bisley, 195

Great Lodge, the, in Great Badminton, 119

Green House (Greenhouse), the, in Dymock, 548*, 549

Green Street, *see* Greenfield; Greenstreet

Greenfield (Greenville), in Watlington (Oxon.), 654, 655

Greenfield near upon Worcestershire [? Green Street, in Ripple, near Upton (Worcs.)], 1267

Greenhouse, in Painswick, 973

Greenhouse, the, *see* Green House, the

Greenstreet (Green Street), in Coaley, 169*, 741

Greenville, *see* Greenfield

Greenway, the, in Badgeworth, 113

Greenwich (Kent), 171*, 656, 1049; East Greenwich, 414, 1074, 1139, 1311, 1440, 1475

Greet (Greote), in Winchcombe, 1219, 1220*, 1221, 1290, 1334, 1474, 1475*, 1477, 1478; residents, 744*, 1386, 1463*, 1464*, 1465*, 1466, 1467*, 1468*, 1469, 1471*, 1472*, 1473, 1474, 1477, 1504

Gregynog, in Tregynon (Mont.), 1333

Grenada (West Indies), 1511

Greote, *see* Greet

Gresham College (London), 271, 1415

Gretton, in Winchcombe, 1219, 1290, 1334, 1474, 1475*, 1476*, 1477, 1478*; residents, 1464*, 1465*, 1466, 1467*, 1468*, 1472*, 1473*

Greys, the (Grays), in Bisley, 197

Grismont, *see* Grosmont

Grittleton (Wilts.), 1258

Grosmont (Grismont, Grosmond) (Mon.), 871, 1452

Grove, in Pembroke (Pemb.), 781

Grove, the, in Painswick, 986

Grove, the, in Taynton, 1237

Grove, the, in Westbury on Severn, 608

Grove Cottage, in Cheltenham, 1231

Grove House, in Bromsberrow, 265

Grove Lays, in Hailes, 710

Grovesend (Grove-end, Grove nen, Grovenend, Grovening), in Alveston, 50*, 52, 615, 1305, 1307

Grovesend, in Olveston, 1019

Gubbshill, *see* Gupshill

Guernevet, *see* Gwernyfed

Guildford (Surr.), 829 n

Guiting (Guyting) [*unspecified*], 1501

Guiting, Temple (Guiting, Upper Guiting), 502, **638–42**, 709 n, 888, 1043, 1078*, 1501; residents, 315, 316, 634, 709 n, 1042, 1043, 1495; *and see* Barton; Ford; Kineton

Guiting (Guyting) brook, 1387

Guiting Power (Lower Guiting, Guiting Poher, Nether Guiting, Guytin, Guyting Poer), **634–7**, 640*, 704, 705*, 888, 1501; Guiting Grange, 482, 635*; *and see* Castlett; Westfield Farm

Gumhurn (Gumbehurne), in Almondsbury, 962*, 963

Guns Mill, in Abenhall, 1

Gunstone, *see* Guston

Gunwarby, *see* Gonerby, Great

Gupshill (Gopshill, Gubbshill, Gupsell), in Tewkesbury, 1266*, 1287, 1288

Gurshill (Gershill), in Lydney, 811

Guston, in Hawkesbury, 695

Gutherton, *see* Gotherington

Guston (Gunstone) (Kent), 898, 900

Guyting (Guytin), *see* Guiting

Gwernyfed (Guernevet, Gwer Newett), near Talgarth (Brec.), 744, 1463

Gydynap (Giddinap, Giddiknap), in Minchinhampton, 655, 658

Hackney (Hacneia) (Mdx.), 58, 592; *and see* Clapton, Upper

Hadham (Herts.), 123

Hagbourne, West (Berks.), 596

Hagloe, in Awre, 101, 102, 104, 105*, 107*, 108*, 109*, 110, 111, 112, 932

Hagpen, *see* Hampen

Hague, the (Netherlands), 723, 1299

Hailes (Hales, Hayles), 334, **707–10**, 1483; abbey, 392, 393 n, 493*, 502, 707, 708, 709, 791; abbey, estate, 493, 634, 688, 816*, 1016, 1020, 1082*, 1148, 1150, 1220, 1225*, 1226*, 1227, 1228*, 1335*, 1475, 1476, 1494, 1519; Hailes Wood and Park, 709, 710; residents, 334, 494; *and see* Grove Lays; Ireley; Millhampost

Hailey (Hayle) (Oxon.), 693

Hailey (Hayley), in Sapperton, 1052*; *and see* Heymond

Haimes (Haims), *see* Haymes

Hales, *see* Hailes

Halesowen (Salop., *recte* Worcs.), 709

Halifax (Yorks. W.R.), 946

Hall End, in Yate, 1543

Hall Place, in Dartford (Kent), 347

Hallen (Hallin), in Henbury, 456

Halmer, 'in Cam' [? Halmore in Hamfallow], 277

Halmore, in Hamfallow, 159, 174*, 176*; *and see* Halmer

Ham [*unspecified*], 986, 1362

Ham (Kent), 1225

Ham, in Charlton Kings, 316*, 317

Ham (Hame, Hamme), in Ham and Stone, 153, 154*, 159*, 160, 530, 738, 1176, 1177*; residents, 161, 168*, 169, 170*, 171, 174*, 175*, 177, 740

Ham [*unidentified*], in Stroud, 202*, 1211; Ham Mill, 1210

Ham and Stone, *see* Bevington; Blisbury; Brownsmill; Clapton; Ham

Ham Fallow, *see* Hamfallow

Hamborough, *see* Hamburg

Hambrook, in Winterbourne, 1172, 1328, 1490*, 1491*

Hamburg (Hamborough, Hamburgh) (Germany), 648, 651, 917, 1505

Hame, *see* Ham, in Ham and Stone

Hamfallow (Ham Fallow), in Berkeley, 161, 175, 1505; *and see* Acton; Buckettshill; Crawless; Halmore; Mobley; Priorswood; Walgaston; Wanswell; Wickselme

Hamme, *see* Ham, in Ham and Stone

Hampen (Hagpen), in Compton Abdale, Sevenhampton, and Shipton, 1064*, 1076, 1077*, 1078*

Hampnett (Hampnet), **643–5**, 944, 945, 1198*

Hampshire (county of Southampton), 122, 168, 475, 620, 986, 993, 1411; *and see* Alresford; Battlebridge; Beaulieu; Breamore; Burghclere; Catisfield Lodge; Christchurch; Combe; Itchell; Mottisfont; New Forest; Odiham; Porchester; Portsmouth; Portswood; Ringwood; Romsey; Somburne; Southampton; Tichborne; Upham; Vyne, the; Wallop, Nether; Winchester; Woodhay, East

Hampstead (Mdx.), 417, 1525
Hampstead, in Old Sodbury, 1120*
Hampton (Hanton) [unspecified], 993
Hampton, see Hempton; Minchinhampton; Shirehampton
Hampton, in Highworth (Wilts.), 905
Hampton, in Minsterworth, 869, 870
Hampton, Great (Hampton) (Worcs.), 1466
Hampton, Meysey (Maysey Hampton), 369, **859–62**, 1311; and see Mayshill
Hampton Bishop (Hamptone) (Herefs.), 1058
Hampton Court (Mdx.), 648
Hampton Court [unidentified] (Radnors.), 1208
Hamstalls, in Awre, 109
Hamswell, in Cold Ashton, 50, 80*, 81
Hanborough, see Handborough
Hanbury (Hanburye) (Worcs.), 1076, 1149, 1151
Handborough (Hanborough) [Church or Long Handborough] (Oxon.), 875 n, 880
Handby Castle, see Hanley Castle
Handerwood, in or near Edinburgh (Scot.), 410
Handley, see Hanley
Hanging Aston, see Aston Magna
Hanham Abbots and West Hanham (Hanham, Hannam), in Bitton, 205*, 206*, 207*, 208, 209, 213*, 665*, 806, 1007, 1582, 1584; Hanham School, 1183
Hankerton (Wilts.), 1031, 1117
Hanley (Handley), in Tidenham, 1320
Hanley, St. Leonard's [? Leonard Stanley], 563
Hanley Castle (Handby Castle, Hanley) (Worcs.), 265 n, 486
Hannington (Wilts.), 794*
Hanslope (Hanslip) (Bucks.), 24
Hanton, see Hampton
Harborough, Market (Leics.), 1336
Hardens [? Hartlands], in Westbury on Severn, 1400
Hardewick, see Hardwicke
Hardmead (Bucks.), 992
Hardwick with Tusmore, see Tusmore
Hardwicke (Hardwick), 314, 563, 583*, 584, **663–6**, 700, 997, 1054, 1132*, 1376; Hardwicke Court (Hardwicke Park Court), 663, 671, 672, 1367; and see Farley; Field Court; Rudge
Hardwicke (Elmstone Hardwicke, Hardewick, Hardwick, Hardwyck), in Elmstone Hardwick, 482, 585, 586, 1165, 1271, 1287, 1291, 1331
Harefield, see Haresfield
Harescombe (Harscombe, Hascomb, Herscomb), 264*, 581, 649, **667–70**, 711 n, 831, 930, 973, 1007, 1047
Harescombe tithing, in Haresfield, 672
Haresfield (Harefield, Harsfield), 665*, **671–7**, 711 n, 969, 1047; Great Haresfield, 1130; residents, 172, 197, 264, 583, 584, 666, 669*, 670*, 985, 997, 1053, 1182, 1274, 1433; and see Beaurepair; Broadbarrow Green; Colethrop; Harescombe tithing; Moat Place; Mount, the; Oakey; Park End; Stars Mead House
Harewood (Harwood) (Yorks. W.R.), 1528
Harford (Hartford), in Naunton, 889, 890*, 891

Harkstead, see Nether Hall
Harnhill, 56, **678–9**, 1202
Harrogate (High Harrogate) (Yorks. W.R.), 1384
Harrow on the Hill (Mdx.), 224; school, 1073
Harrystoke, see Stoke, Harry
Harscombe, see Harescombe
Harsfield, see Haresfield
Hart Barn, see Hartsbarn
Hart Hall [Hertford College], Oxford, 137
Hart Hill, in Hewelsfield, 732
Hartford, see Harford
Harthurstfield (Hathersfield), in Cheltenham, 338*
Hartlands, see Hardens
Hartlebury (Worcs.), 54, 1275; and see Waresley
Hartpury, 77, 442, **680–3**, 997, 1046, 1371; and see Abbot's Place; Blackwells End; Buttersend; Corse End; Lamper's End; Moor End; Morwent; Woolridge Common
Hartsbarn (Hart Barn, Hart's Barn), in Longhope, 466*
Harwich (Essex), 413
Harwood, see Harewood
Hascomb, see Harescombe
Haselbury Bryan or Haselbury Plucknett, see Hasleborough
Haselden (Haseldene), see Hazleton
Haselhouse, see Hazle House
Hasell, see Hazel
Haselton, see Hazleton
Hasfield (Hassefield, Hastfield), 76, 77, 469, 482 & n, 682, **684–7**, 894, 986, 1276, 1352, 1356*; Hasfield Court, 684, 686
Hasilcote, see Hazlecote
Hasilton, see Hazleton
Hasle, see Hazle
Hasleborough [? Haselbury Bryan or Haselbury Plucknett (Dors.)], 413
Hasledon, see Hazleton
Hasleton, see Hazleton
Hassefield (Hastfield), see Hasfield
Hasselton, see Hazleton
Hastings (Suss.), 411, 1247
Hatfield (Herts.), 610
Hatfield (Yorks. W.R.), see Bootham
Hatherley [unspecified], 259 n, 485, 1047
Hatherley, Down (Downhatherley, Hatherley), **511–14**, 786, 888, 1010, 1041, 1044, 1165, 1370
Hatherley, Up (South Hatherley, Up-Atherley, Uphatherley), 348, 800, 985*, **1370**
Hatherop, 129, 369, 565, 568, **690–3**, 792, 1127, 1184; and see Dean Farm; Netherton
Hathersfield, see Harthurstfield
Hatley, East (Cambs.), 411
Havana (the Havannah) (Cuba), 99, 412
Haw (Hawe), the, in Tirley, 398, 482 n, 1291, 1354, 1355*, 1356*; Haw Bridge, 1356
Hawcombe, see Holcombe
Hawe, the, see Haw, the
Hawkesbury, 35, 125*, **694–703**, 1343; Hawkesbury Common, 695; Hawkesbury Upton (Upton), 658, 695*, 696, 697, 701; and see Badminton, Little; Chalkeley; Guston; Hillsley; Holwell;

Inglestone Common; Kilcott; Petty France; Saddlewood; Tresham; Waste, le

Hawling (Halling), 320, 634, **704–6**; *and see* Westfield, the

Hawns, *see* Haynes

Hay, in Filton, 602*

Hay Hill, in Newnham, 927

Hay of Erneseir, the, *see* Hayes chase

Haycroft, *see* High Croft

Haydon (Heydon), in Boddington, 118, 228*, 229, 338, 339, 786, 1163, 1164*, 1165*

Haydon (Essex), *see* Heydon

Hayes, in Awre, 101, 1000

Hayes (Hays), in Newent, 894*

Hayes chase or forest (the Hay of Erneseir) (Salop.), 618 n

Hayfield [? in Awre], 111

Hayle, *see* Hailey

Hayles, *see* Hailes

Hayley, *see* Hailey

Haymes (Haimes, Haims, Heimes, Heines), in Southam, 393, 1150, 1151, 1210, 1471

Haynes (Hawns) (Beds.), 1049

Hays, *see* Hayes

Hayton (Heyton) (Yorks. E.R.), 867

Hayward's End, in Stonehouse, 1185

Haywardsfield (Haywards Field), in Stonehouse, 1185, 1218

Hazel (Hasell, Hazell), in Olveston, 1302; Upper Hazel, 962*

Hazel Hanger Wood, in Brimpsfield, 252

Hazeldon, *see* Hazleton

Hazelhouse, *see* Hazle House

Hazell, *see* Hazel

Hazelor, *see* Upton (Warws.)

Hazle (Hasle), in Ledbury (Herefs.), 520

Hazle House (Haselhouse, Hazelhouse), in Miserden, 878, 880*

Hazlecote (Hasilcote), in Kempsford, 775*

Hazleton (Hasilton, Hasledon, Hasleton, Hasselton), 306, **688–9**, 704, 908, 1328, 1350, 1542

Hazleton (Haselden, Haseldene, Haselton, Hazeldon), in Rodmarton, 778, 1029*, 1030*, 1031, 1032*, 1033*

Heald, the, in Westbury on Severn, 1398*

Heath House, in Stapleton, 1155, 1156*, 1160

Heath, the, in Alkington, 175*, 177*

Heathfield (Hestfield), in Alkington, 167, 170*, 175, 177

Hedecote, *see* Hidcote

Heimes (Heines), *see* Haymes

Helder, den (Netherlands), 1245

Helenstow, *see* Elstow

Helsfred [*unidentified*], 1034

Helsington [*unidentified*] (Salop.), 1437

Hemelhempsted, *see* Hempstead, Hemel

Hemington (Som.), 1052

Hempstead, Hemel (Hemelhempsted) (Herts.), 708 n

Hempsted (Hempstead, Heyhamstede), **711–16**, 1046, 1059; *and see* Dudstone; Newark; Podsmead; Rea, the

Hempton (Hampton), in Almondsbury, 39, 42, 46, 1490, 1491

Henbury, 98*, **717–31**, 1328, 1419*, 1420; residents, 48, 49, 99*, 435*, 792, 963*, 1043, 1106, 1171, 1344, 1412; *and see* Baker's Leaze; Blaise Castle; Charlton; Crook's Marsh; Hallen; Hung Road; King Road; Lamplighters Hall; Northwick; Pen Pole; Redwick; Saltmarsh; Shirehampton; Stowick; Weston; Weston, King's; Weston, Lawrence; Wyck, the

Hencroft [? in Westbury on Trym], 1415

Hendon (Mdx.), 1428

Hengaston, in Berkeley or Cam, 1167*

Henlawe, *see* Henlow

Henleaze, in Westbury on Trym, 1245*

Henley, in Buckland Newton (Dors.), 1525

Henley-in-Arden (Henlyarden) (Warws.), 693

Henley on Thames (Oxon.), 205 n, 355

Henlow (Henlawe) (Beds.), 1059

Henlyarden, *see* Henley-in-Arden

Henton, *see* Hinton, in Oldland; Hinton Charterhouse

Henton Bluet, *see* Hinton Blewett

Heralds, *see* Arms, College of

Herbert Lodge, in East Dean, 479 n

Herbert Walk, in East Dean, 1038

Hereford (Herefs.), 894 n, 1037, 1237, 1287, 1475; bishop, 191, 311, 436, 473, 534, 766, 1056, 1238*, 1258, 1434; bishop, estate, 534 n, 982, 985*, 986, 1059*, 1060*, 1061*, 1062, 1404, 1434; Blackfriars, 325 n; castle, 1060; cathedral, dean and chapter, estate and prebends, 242, 245*, 766, 767*, 805, 808*, 809, 885, 886, 913, 915, 982, 986, 1058, 1061, 1064, 1232, 1404*, 1434*; cathedral, prebendary or canon, 191*, 246; cathedral, precentor, 1039; honour, 581, 678, 1011*, 1214, 1215*, 1216*, 1476; natives, 332, 334, 409, 1525; parish of St. John the Baptist, 1437; priory of St. Peter, 1201*, 1202, 1485; residents, 307, 546, 680, 1183; *and see* Newton; Portfield; Shelwick

Herefordshire, 265, 269, 325 n, 392 n, 475 n, 481 n, 618, 649, 759, 805 n; residents, 190, 268, 278, 350 n, 472, 473, 547, 552, 649, 804 n, 836, 1051, 1359, 1422; *and see under names of separate places*

Herenesse Nooks, *see* Berkeley: hundred

Herscomb, *see* Harescombe

Hertford College, Oxford, 199, 268; *and see* Hart Hall

Hertfordshire, *see* Ashridge; Barnet, Chipping; Bayford; Berkhamsted; Bygrave; Cassiobury; Hadham; Hatfield; Hemel Hempstead; Langley, Kings; St. Albans; Salisbury Hall; Ware

Hester Hill [? in Berkeley], 176

Hestfield, *see* Heathfield

Heston (Mdx.), 164

Hewelsfield (Hewersfield, Huelsfield, Huersfield), 247*, 249, 250*, **732–6**, 805; *and see* Hart Hill; Parsley Hill; Pillston

Hewishfield, *see* Hisefield

Hewletts, in Cheltenham or Prestbury, 1138

Heworth (Heyworth) (co. Dur.), 1198
Heydon (Haydon) (Essex), 875 n
Heydon, in Boddington, see Haydon
Heyhamstede, see Hempsted
Heymond [? recte Hailey, in Sapperton], 1052
Heytesbury (Wilts.), 329
Heythrop (Heythrope) (Oxon.), 1093
Heyton, see Hayton
Heyworth, see Heworth
Hggins, the, see Hoggins, the
Hibernia, see Ireland
Hidcote (Hedecote, Hidecote, Hitcoat, Hithcoat), in
   Mickleton, 863, 864*, 865, 866*
Hidcote Boyce (Hitchcoate, Hithcoat), in
   Ebrington, 570, 572*, 573*
Hied Court, see Hyde, in Minchinhampton
Higgin's Court, in Bisley, 195
High Croft (Haycroft), in Syde, 1083
High Cross, in Ashleworth, 75
High Meadow (Highmeadow), in Staunton, 188,
   806 n, 913, 915, 917*, 920, 921*, 924, 1161*,
   1162*
Highfield, in Bitton, 205
Highfield, in Tetbury, 1255
Highgate (Mdx.), 190, 1282
Highgrove, in St. Briavels, 606
Highleadon (High Leadon, High Leddon,
   Highledon), in Rudford, 683, 894 n, 1035*,
   1316, 1353, 1371; Highleadon Court, 686*; and
   see Leden
Highleigh, see West Hall
Highmeadow, see High Meadow
Highnam, in Churcham, 102, 349*, 350*, 353*,
   354*, 520, 583*, 785, 786*, 787*, 810, 1035;
   Highnam Court, 581; Highnam House, 806 n;
   Highnam Lodge, 786*; and see Linton;
   Vineyard, the
Highworth (Wilts.), 254; and see Hampton
Hilcot (Hillcot), in Withington, 1501*, 1502
Hill, (the), in Painswick, 974*, 1181, 1210, 1211*
Hill (Hull), 154*, 173, 175, 176, 520, **737–41**, 778 n,
   1019*, 1176*, 1177, 1379, 1521; Hill Court, 740,
   1019; and see Bibury; Brighampton; Day House;
   Hisefield; Nupdown; Scotlands; Wickstowe;
   Woodend
Hill, the, in Moreton Valence, 172
Hill Common, the [? in Aylburton], 479
Hill Court [unspecified], 1208
Hill Court (Hillcourt), in Longdon (Worcs.), 965
Hill Court, in Shipton Moyne, 1071
Hill House (Hillhouse), in Mangotsfield, 834
Hill House, in Newnham, 927
Hill House (Hillhouse), in Oxenhall, 965
Hill House, in Rodborough, 1184, 1511
Hill House, in Staunton, 1161*, 1162
Hill House, in Yate, 1546, 1550
Hill Place, in Dymock, 546
Hillcot, see Hilcot
Hillcourt, see Hill Court
Hillery [unidentified], in North Nibley, 936
Hillhouse, see Hill House
Hillingdon, see Colham

Hillington (Norf.), 1409
Hillsley, in Hawkesbury, 35, 695*, 696, 697, 700*,
   701*, 702*
Hilmarton (Wilts.), 1341
Hinchwick, in Bredon (Worcs.) and Condicote, 438
Hinton, in Berkeley, 159, 160*, 161, 165, 169, 170,
   171, 174*, 175*, 176*; and see Acton; Kingshill;
   Middleton; Oldminster; Purton; Riddleford;
   Saniger
Hinton, in Dyrham, 553*
Hinton (Henton), in Oldland, 489
Hinton, Broad (Broadhinton, Brodhinton) (Wilts.),
   1048, 1051
Hinton Blewett (Henton Bluet) (Som.), 614, 1473
Hinton Charterhouse (Henton) (Som.), 690
Hinton on the Green, 86, **742–4**
Hinton Waldrist (Hinton) (Berks.), 794
Hisefield or Hewishfield [unidentified], in Hill, 738
Hitcoat (Hitchcoate, Hithcoat), see Hidcote
Hoarthorns (Whorthorns), in Newland, 194
Hobeland, in Thornbury, 1314
Hocberry (Hockbury), in Rodmarton, 1032
Hockham, Great (Great Hookham) (Norf.), 1149,
   1151
Hoddom (Hoden), in Annandale (Scot.), 1272
Hoggins (Hggins), the, in St. Briavels, 250, 1515
Hogsdown, in Berkeley, 1550
Holborn (London or Mdx.), 764, 1449; Blue Boar
   Inn, 764; St. Andrew's, 1212, 1214, 1478
Holcombe (Hawcombe, Howcombe), in Minchin-
   hampton, Nailsworth, or Woodchester, 648, 651,
   656*, 658, 1510
Holdfast, in Ripple (Worcs.), 1381
Holkham (Norf.), 1066*
Holland, see Netherlands
Hollies (Hollys), the, in Newland, 923
Holm Lacey, see Holme Lacy
Holmains, in Annandale (Scot.), 971
Holme, the, see Kingsholm
Holme Castle, in Tewkesbury, 1287*
Holme Lacy (Holm Lacy, Home Lacey) (Herefs.),
   301 n, 449 n, 711 n
Holt (Holte) (Worcs.), 481, 581 n, 582
Holwell, in Hawkesbury, 35
Holy Brook, in Wick and Abson, 6
Holy Roman Empire, 162
Holy Rood Ampney, see Ampney Crucis
Home Downs, in Ashchurch, 71
Home Lacey, see Holme Lacy
Honduras, Bay of, see Roaton Island
Honeybourne, Church, see Poden
Honibury Bridge, in Winchcombe, 1473
Hook House or Bromsberrow Place, in Broms-
   berrow, 265, 268, 1316
Hookham, Great, see Hockham, Great
Hope and Hope Farm, in Thornbury, 1299, 1311*,
   1313, 1314, 1324, 1343
Hope End (Hopend), in Ledbury (Herefs.), 894
Hopton Castle (Salop.), 163, 290, 592, 657, 761
Horcott (Horcote, Horcutt), in Kempsford, 770, 771
Hordley, see Horley
Horedon, see Horton

Horeham, *see* Horsham

Horewood, *see* Horwood

Horfield, 577, 602*, 603, 604, 721, 731, **745–6**, 961; *and see* Breweshold

Horley (Hordley) (Oxon.), 1207

Hornchurch, *see* Maylards

Horne (Surr.), 829 n

Hornsleasow (Horne's Leasow) Farm, in Stanway, 891

Hornton (Oxon.), 567

Horridge, *see* Oridge

Horse Marley, *see* Horsemarling

Horsebere (Horsebury, Horseperry) Bridge, in Badgeworth, 1493, 1494*

Horsemarling (Horse Marley), in Moreton Valence, 885

Horsemunden, *see* Horsmonden

Horseperry Bridge, *see* Horsebere Bridge

Horsham (Horeham) (Suss.), 380

Horsley, 656, **747–52**, 1138, 1218; *and see* Barton End; Chavenage; Downend; Nailsworth; Nupend; Walford

Horsmonden (Horsemunden) (Kent), 792

Horton (Horedon), **753–8**, 901, 1050, 1490, 1526*; *and see* Horwood

Horwood (Horewood), in Horton, 753

Hospitallers, Knights, *see* Jerusalem

Hotwells (Hot Wells, Hott Wells, Hotwell), in Clifton, 329, 403, 405, 410, 411, 413, 725, 753, 1411, 1412, 1413, 1557

Howcaple, *see* Caple, How

Howcombe, *see* Holcombe

Howle Hill (Howlshill), in Walford (Herefs.), 536

Howley (Howle), in Mitcheldean, 605 n

Howlshill, *see* Howle Hill

Hownhall (Hownell), in Taynton, 1234*, 1237

Hucclecote (in Churchdown), 133*, 346, 348, 398, 1203; *and see* Elm Bridge

Hudnalls, in St. Briavels, 244, 476

Huelsfield (Huersfield), *see* Hewelsfield

Hull, *see* Hill

Hull (Kingston-upon-Hull) (Yorks. E.R.), 413, 1119

Hullasey (Hunlacy), in Rodmarton, 1033

Hullavington (Wilts.), 665, 880

Hulmancote, *see* Elmcote

Humber (Herefs.), 1191

Hung Road (Hungrode), in Henbury, 720, 730

Hungary, 952

Hungrode, *see* Hung Road

Hunlacy, *see* Hullasey

Hunt Court, in Badgeworth, 113, 114, 115

Hunter's Hall, in Kingscote, 775

Huntercombe (Untercomb), in Taplow (Bucks.), 1032

Huntingdon (Hunts.), 1248

Huntingdonshire, *see* Conington; Huntingdon; Staughton, Great; Waresley

Huntingford, in Alkington or Wotton under Edge, 159, 1341*, 1343, 1533, 1537, 1539

Huntley (Huntly), 104, **759–62**, 806 n, 1316, 1393, 1404; *and see* May Hill

Hunwere [*unidentified*], 605 n

Hurley (Hursley) (Berks.), 709, 962*

Hurst (Berks.), 573

Hurst, in Lydney, 807, 808*, 809*

Hurst and Hurst Farm, in Slimbridge, 154, 282, 1095, 1097, 1098, 1100, 1101

Husbands Bosworth, *see* Bosworth, Husbands

Hutton (Som.), 995*, 997

Hwicci (Wicci, Wiccia, Wiccii), kingdom and bishopric, 357, 592 n, 770, 1195, 1502

Hyde, in Minchinhampton, 93, 648, 649, 651, 652*, 661; Hyde (Hied) Court, 655, 657; Upper Hyde, 658, 660

Hyde, in Newnham, 927, 1400*

Hyde Farm, in Prestbury, 985

Hygrove, in Minsterworth, 872

Iberia, *see* Spain

Ibnarsh [? in Bisley], 201

Ichenton, *see* Itchington

Ichull, *see* Itchell

Ickington, *see* Itchington

Icomb, 1092, 1190, 1196, 1197, 1421, **1422–3**; *and see* Combe Baskerville

Icomb (Church Icomb) (Worcs.), 1421, 1422, 1423

Ikenild Way, *see* Akeman Street

Ilford, *see* Aldborough Hatch

Ilford, Little (Essex), 24, 1136*

Ilmington (Warws.), 88, 230 n, 804 n, 1002*; *and see* Compton Scorpion; Foxcote

Ilminster (Som.), 636

India, 352, 697, 1119, 1209, 1282; *and see* Bengal; Bhurtpore; Bombay; Cawnpore; East India Co.; Fort Malborough; Fort William; Lucknow; Madras; Masulipatam

Indies, East and West, *see* East Indies; West Indies

Ingleham Common, *see* Inglestone Common

Inglescombe, *see* Englishcombe

Inglestone (Ingleham) Common, in Hawkesbury, 695

Ingleton (Yorks. W.R.), 1581

Ingst (Inst), in Olveston, 100, 175*, 961, 963*

Inkberrow, *see* Nobury

Inkerman (Russia), 1073

Inst, *see* Ingst

Inwoods, in Stinchcombe, 1169

Iorn Acton, *see* Acton, Iron

Ipswich (Suff.), 1198

Ireland (Hibernia), 723, 1166, 1388, 1486; judges, 143, 177, 570 n, 1029, 1066; residents, 265, 413, 836, 1029, 1066, 1374; viceroy, 162; wars and expeditions, 291, 634, 723, 927; *and see* Armagh; Ballyn Varwick; Bandon, river; Bristowville; Castletown; Cloyne; Cork; Dillon, Castle; Dublin; Galway; Kinsale; Knockmahon; Limerick; Raphoe; Rosmanacher; Rothbride; Waterford

Ireley (Irely), in Hailes, 1465

Irmin Street, *see* Ermine Street

Iron Mills, in Minchinhampton, 650, 658

Ironacton, *see* Acton, Iron

Isbourne (Isborne), river, 493, 1474

Isca, *see* Caerleon

Iscombe, in Painswick, 975
Isis, river, 1056 n; *and see* Thames
Italy, 119, 349 n, 708 n, 876, 1209; *and see*
    Bologna; Florence; Leghorn; Praeneste; Rome
Itchell (Ichull), in Crondall (Hants), 1431
Itchington (Ichenton, Ickington), in Tytherington,
    1309, 1325*, 1328*, 1552
Iver (Bucks.), 1059
Ivy House, in Oxlinch, 1130, 1132
Ivyleafe [? in Siston], 1087
Iwood, in Warbleton (Suss.), 827 n
Ixning, *see* Exning

Jackson's Farm, in Wheatenhurst, 625 n, 1435, 1440
Jahrom, *see* Gambroon
Jamaica (West Indies), 132, 615, 729, 851, 853,
    1097, 1281*, 1299, 1308
James River (Virginia), Warwick in, 539
Jask (Jasques) (Persia), 866
Jersey (Channel Is.), 1411
Jerusalem, Knights Hospitallers of St. John, 131,
    525, 638*, 695, 753, 878, 1005*, 1015, 1032,
    1078, 1082, 1127, 1216; Knights Templars, 634,
    638, 1015, 1032, 1043, 1078*, 1115, 1312, 1475,
    1476, 1501, 1518
Jerviswood [*unidentified*], 406
Jesus College, Cambridge, 1140
Jesus College, Oxford, 113, 311, 313*, 324, 325,
    328*, 518, 519, 585, 1370
Joyford, in West Dean, 194, 922

Keinton, *see* Kyneton, in Thornbury
Keir (Kier) (Scot.), 408
Kellington (Yorks. W.R.), 1430
Kelmarsh (Hants, *recte* Northants.), 875 n
Kelmscott (Kempscot) (Oxon.), 1206
Kelston (Kelveston) (Som.), 9, 211, 839*, 842*
Kemble (Wilts.), 378, 1024, 1028, 1049, 1050*;
    and see Ewen
Kemerton (Kemmerton), 71, 742, **763–5**, 1279,
    1287, 1291, 1311
Kempley (Kempsley), **766–8**; Kempley Court, 993;
    and see Prior's Court; Saywells
Kempscot, *see* Kelmscott
Kempsford, 127, 696, **769–72**, 1125; *and see* Bares
    Court; Dunfield; Hazlecote; Horcott;
    Redecroftes; Whelford
Kempston [*unidentified*], 1147
Kemsing (Kent), 827 n*
Kenchester (Herefs.), 485
Kencott (Kencot) (Oxon.), 595*
Kendal (Candaliensis) (Westmld.), 636
Kenilworth (Kenelworth) (Warws.), 66; priory,
    1016
Kennington (Berks.), 792
Kensdale [*unidentified*] (Glos.), 438 n
Kent, 359 n, 410, 431, 559 n, 688, 853, 897, 917,
    1051, 1082, 1298; *and see under names of
    separate places*
Kentchurch (Herefs.), 626
Kentish Town (Kentesh Town, Kentischtown), in
    St. Pancras (London or Mdx.), 804 n, 1472

Kerries, in Newent, 903
Ketford, in Dymock, 546
Keyford (Cayforde), in Frome (Som.), 371, 1077
Keynsham (Cainsham) (Som.), 488, 1487*; abbey,
    205, 331, 497, 838*
Keynsham, in Woolaston, 1515
Kidderminster (Worcs.), 657, 921, 1137
Kiddington (Oxon.), 223, 726, 1036
Kier, *see* Keir
Kiftsgate hundred, 287 n, 864 n, 867, 1055
Kilcot (Kilcoat), in Newent, 894, 895, 898
Kilcott (Killcott), in Hawkesbury, 695, 696*, 697,
    701, 1529
Kilmersdon, *see* Babington
Kilpeck (Kilpetbeg, Kylpeck) (Herefs.), 392 n,
    1237; priory, 1238*
Kilton (Som.), 615
Kimbolton, *see* Bachcombe
Kimsbury (Kimbury, Kinsbury, Kynsbury), in
    Upton St. Leonards, 1378*, 1380
Kineton (Kyneton, Kyngton, Kynton), in Temple
    Guiting, 637*, 639, 640, 641
King George county (Virginia), 47
King Road, in Henbury, 98
Kingcomb, *see* Combe
Kingeswood (Kingeswode), *see* Kingswood
King's Barton, *see* Barton, King's; Barton Regis
King's College, Cambridge, 410, 534 n, 1040
King's Hall, Oxford, 1021
King's Hill (Kingshill), in Cam, 535*
King's Hill, in Hinton, *see* Kingshill
King's Langley, *see* Langley, King's
King's Lodge, *see* Speech House, the
Kings Lynn, *see* Lynn, Kings
Kings Pyon (King's Peon), *see* Blackhall
Kingscote, 178, 181, 240, **773–7**, 909, 967, 1183,
    1369; *and see* Binley; Hunter's Hall
Kingsdown, near Bristol, 929
Kingsend, in Redmarley D'Abitot, 1352
Kingshill, in Cam, *see* King's Hill
Kingshill (King's Hill), in Hinton, 172
Kingsholm (the Holme), in Gloucester, 1047
Kingston [*unspecified*], 958
Kingston [*unspecified*, ? Kington, in Thornbury], 1300
Kingston (Herefs.), *see* Kingstone
Kingston, in Slimbridge, 1096, 1101
Kingston, in Tidenham, *see* Sedbury
Kingston St. Michael, *see* Kington St. Michael
Kingston upon Thames (Kingston) (Surr.), 827 n,
    829 n
Kingston-upon-Hull, *see* Hull
Kingstone (Kingston) (Herefs.), 1401, 1058
Kingsweston, *see* Weston, King's
Kingswinford (Staffs.), 1568
Kingswood (Kingeswode, Kingeswood, Regis-
    sylva) (formerly Wilts.), 106, 172, 182, 307,
    308*, 529, 702*, 758, **778–82**, 1113, 1343, 1454,
    1512, 1524; abbey, 527, 529, 778*, 779; abbey
    estate, 180, 529, 775, 778, 908*, 909*, 1020,
    1032*, 1033*, 1101, 1255, 1256, 1257*, 1328,
    1539; *and see* Acholt; Barns, Lower; Grange,
    the; Merryford; Nind; Watsome

Kingswood, in Bitton, forest or chase, 12, 29, 50, 205, 527 n, 779, 1159, 1160*

Kington, in Thornbury, 99, 1295, 1309*, 1311, 1313, 1314; residents, 16, 18, 826, 962, 963, 1296, 1297*, 1300*, 1301*, 1302*, 1303*, 1305*, 1306, 1307, 1312; *and see* Kirton

Kington, West (Wilts.), 44

Kington (Kingston) St. Michael (Wilts.), 1437

Kinnersley (Herefs.), 392

Kinsale (Irel.), 723

Kinsbury, *see* Kimsbury

Kinsham (Knisham), in Bredon (Worcs.), 71*, 1464

Kintbury (Kyntbury) (Berks.), 382

Kinton, *see* Kyneton

Kirby, Monks, *see* Newnham Paddox

Kirdford, *see* Ebernoe

Kirkham (Yorks. E.R.), priory, 232

Kirkham Farm, in Upper Slaughter, 1092

Kirtlington, *see* Northbrook

Kirton [Kington or Kyneton], in Thornbury, 826

Kittsgreen (Kitt's Green), in Alkington, 169, 173, 176

Klosterkampen (Campen) (Germany), 58, 410

Knapp, the, in Stroud, 1203, 1215, 1216

Knight's Green, in Ashleworth, 75

Knightswick (Worcs.), 1424

Knisham, *see* Kinsham

Knockmahon (Knockmon) (Irel.), 1495

Knockshinnoch (Knoekshinnock), near Dumfries (Scot.), 896

Knole, in Almondsbury, 40, 43*

Kylpeck, *see* Kilpeck

Kyneton, in Temple Guiting, *see* Kineton

Kyneton (Keinton, Kinton), in Thornbury, 1301, 1302, 1305*, 1312; *and see* Kirton

Kyngton, *see* Kineton

Kynsbury, *see* Kimsbury

Kyntbury, *see* Kintbury

Kynton, *see* Kineton

Lackington, White (Wight Lackington) (Som.), 995

Lacock (Laylock) (Wilts.), 373, 572, 690*, 691, 1253; *and see* Bowden Park

Ladden brook, 12

Lairw [*unidentified*] (Mon.), 1400

Lambeth (London or Surr.), 827 n

Lambourn, *see* Blagrave

Lammas, the, in Minchinhampton, 1247

Lamper's End, in Hartpury, 680

Lamplighters Hall, in Henbury, 1419

Lancashire, 116, 413, 1141, 1342; *and see* Ashton Hall; Barcroft Hall; Bigland; Bolton; Dalton; Denton; Lancaster; Liverpool; Manchester; Ormskirk; Rufford

Lancaster (Lancs.), 819, 869, 1141; duchy of, 392, 695, 732, 759, 1355

Lancaut (Lancaught), 806 n, 1323*, 1516*

Landaff, *see* Llandaff

Landsdown, *see* Lansdown

Langdon, *see* Longdon

Langeley, *see* Langley [*unspecified*]

Langford in Burrington (Banington), near Wrington (Som.), 1107; Langford Court, 42

Langley (Langeley) [*unspecified*], 643 n, 681

Langley, in Epsom or Sanderstead (Surr.), 484

Langley, in Winchcombe, 1471, 1474, 1477

Langley, Kings (Herts.), 829 n

Langridge, in Charlcombe (Som.), 84*, 823

Langston, *see* Llangstone

Langstone, in Llangarron (Herefs.), 3

Langton, Church (Leics.), 1336

Lanishen, *see* Llanishen

Lanlowell, *see* Llanlowell

Lanner (Llanherne) (Cornw.), 618

Lansawell, *see* Llansawel

Lansdown (Landsdown), in Charlcombe (Som.), 6*, 80, 274

Lanthernham, *see* LLantarnam

Lanthony (Lantoney, Lantoni), *see* Llanthony

Lapworth (Warws.), 1275

Larkfield, near Chepstow (Mon.), 1321

Lasborough (Lassborough, Lasseborrow), **783–4**, 908*, 1072, 1215; Lasborough (Loughborough) Park, 909; *and see* Bowldown

Lassington, 442, **785–7**, 1371

Latimer (Latimore) Lodge and Walk, in East Dean, 472, 478 n, 479 n

Latteridge, in Iron Acton, 12

Latton (Wilts.), 1043*; *and see* Eaton, Water

Latvia, *see* Riga

Lausanne (Switzerland), 1193

Lautwitt Vairdre, *see* Llantwit Fardre

Lavendon (Lavenham) (Bucks.), 1051

Laverton, in Buckland, 271, 273*, 274*; *and see* Lullyntone

Lawfords Gate, Bristol, 206

Lay, *see* Ley

Layer Marney (Essex), 518

Layes, the, *see* Leys, the

Laylock, *see* Lacock

Lea (Herefs., partly Glos.), **788–9**; *and see* Castle End

Lea, in Lea and Cleverton (Wilts.), 985; *and see* Cleverton

Lea, river (Essex and Mdx.), 366 n

Lea and Cleverton, *see* Cleverton; Lea

Lea Bailey, in East Dean, formerly in Newland, 477 n, 479, 915

Leach (Leche), river or brook, 37, 565* & n, 643, 791

Leachlade, *see* Lechlade

Leadbury, *see* Ledbury

Leadington (Ledington), in Dymock, 546

Leadon (Leddon), High, *see* Highleadon

Leadon (Leden), river, 349, 546, 680

Leadon (Ledens) Court, in Rudford, 1034

Leafield, *see* Loughborough

Leamington (Lemington) [Leamington Hastings or Leamington Spa] (Warws.), 393 n

Leche, *see* Northleach

Leche, East, *see* Eastleach Martin; Eastleach Turville

Leche, river, *see* Leach

Lechlade (Leachlade, Lechelade, Letchlade), 385, 565 n, 592*, 708 n*, 784, **790–7**, 1126; priory or hospital of St. John, 791, 792, 793; *and see* Butler's Court; Clay Hill; Downington; St. John's Bridge; Thornhill Farm

Leckhampton, 324, 422, 511, **798–800**

Ledbury (Leabury) (Herefs.), 442, 766, 767, 971, 1058, 1272, 1356*; *and see* Hope End; Nether Town

Leden [Highleadon or Upleadon], 1035; *and see* Leadon, river

Ledens Court, *see* Leadon Court

Ledington, *see* Leadington

Ledsham (Yorks. W.R.), 1528

Leeward Islands (West Indies), 209, 497, 724; *and see* Antigua; Montserrat; Nevis; St. Christopher

Legh, High, *see* West Hall

Leghorn (Italy), 632, 1231

Leicester (Leics.), 534 n, 769, 1126, 1336*

Leicestershire, 289, 561, 1358; *and see* Bosworth, Husbands; Brooksby; Charley; Harborough, Market; Langton, Church; Leicester; Shackerstone; Stoughton; Westcoats

Leiden (Leyden) (Netherlands), 327 n

Leigh (the Leigh, Lye, the Lye), 398, 481, 482 & n, 483, 485, **801–3**, 949, 1164, 1165, 1353*; Leigh End, 801; *and see* Evington

Leigh (the) (Wilts.), 1211

Leigh, Abbots (Som.), 1185

Leigh, Bessels (Bessillesleigh, Bessil's Leigh) (Oxon., *recte* Berks.), 255, 1048

Leigh, Brace's (Bracesleigh), in Bransford (Brainsford) (Worcs.), 1089, 1092

Leighterton, in Boxwell, 236*, 237*, 239*, 240

Lemington (Warws.), *see* Leamington

Lemington, Lower (Lemmington), **804**, 1154, 1331

Lemington, Upper, in Todenham, 1329, 1331

Lenchwick (Lench Wick), (Worcs.), 130

Leominster (Herefs.), 1253

Leonard Stanley, *see* Stanley, Leonard

Lescomb Regis, *see* Letcombe Regis

Letchlade, *see* Lechlade

Letcombe (Lescomb) Regis (Berks.), 1231

Lewisham (Kent), 1057

Ley (Lay, Leye), in Westbury on Severn, 471, 605 n, 1393, 1395, 1396, 1397, 1399, 1402, 1403; Lower Ley (Nether Lay, Nether Ley, Netherley), 713, 1401, 1402*, 1404; Over Ley (Overley), 1401, 1402*, 1404

Leyden, *see* Leiden

Leye, *see* Ley

Leys (Layes), the, in Wotton under Edge, 1536

Leyton, *see* Ruckholt

Lichfield (Staffs.), 233 n, 1404

Lidney, *see* Lydney

Lightpill (Light Pill, Lyde Pill), in Rodborough, 1021, 1027

Lilleshall (Lyleshull) (Salop.), priory, 119

Limbrick, *see* Limerick

Limbury (Lymbrey), in Luton (Beds.), 920

Lime Regis, *see* Lyme Regis

Limerick (Limbrick) (Irel.), 1498

Lincoln (Lincs.), 665

Lincoln (Lyncoln) College, Oxford, 469 n, 580, 665

Lincoln's Inn, *see* London, Inns of Court

Lincolnshire, 91, 205, 394 n, 707 n, 1290; *and see* Belton; Belvoir; Broughton, Brant; Deeping Fen; Easton; Fillingham; Gainsborough; Gonerby, Great; Grantham; Lincoln; Skellingthorpe; Spalding; Spilsby; Stoke Rochford; Winterton

Lindridge (Lindrugge) (Worcs.), 391 n

Lineham, *see* Lyneham

Linton, in Highnam, 349 & n, 350*

Linton (Herefs.), 788

Lintridge, in Dymock, 546*, 548; Little Lintridge, 269*

Lippiat, *see* Lypiatt, Over

Lisbon (Portugal), 1292

Lisieux (Liseaux) (Normandy), 783, 1032, 1121

Littlecote, in Ramsbury (Wilts.), 357 n

Littledean, *see* Dean, Little

Littleton, West, **823–4**, 1339*

Littleton upon Severn, 16, 100, 164, **825–6**, 963*, 1295; *and see* Coat

Littleworth, in Minchinhampton, 648, 649, 660

Liverpool (Lancs.), 407, 1320

Livonia, *see* Riga

Llanarmon-yn-Ia, *see* Pen-y-Pwlle

Llanarthney (Llanalthney) (Carms.), 265 n

Llandaff (Landaff) (Glam.), 41, 915*, 1297, 1298*, 1341, 1486

Llandogo (Mon.), 250

Llangardeine, *see* Llangendeirne

Llangarron (Herefs.), 465; *and see* Langstone

Llangendeirne (Llangardeine) (Carms.), 265 n

Llangstone (Langston) (Mon.), 728

Llanherne, *see* Lanner

Llanishen (Lanishen) (Glam.), 1413

Llanllowell (Lanlowell) (Mon.), 1322

Llanrothal, *see* Tregate

Llansamlet (Glam.), 1315

Llansawel (Lansawell) (Carms.), 1007

Llantarnam (Lanternham) (Mon.), 645, 1198

Llanthony (Lanthony, Lantoney, Lantony, Llanthoni) (Mon. and Gloucester), abbey or priory, 259 n, 1060 n; estate, 53*, 101, 134, 139, 259, 301, 424*, 430, 523, 581*, 605 n, 671*, 672, 674, 807, 711, 713*, 851, 878, 890*, 927, 982, 986, 1032, 1033, 1060, 1061, 1062, 1078, 1186, 1187, 1328*, 1348, 1350, 1402, 1404, 1482*

Llantwit Fardre (Lautwitt Vairdre) (Glam.), 1157

Llanvihangel (Llanvihanhill) (Mon.), 919, 922

Llanwenarth (Mon.), 1411

Lockfast Bridge, in Berkeley, 153

Lodge, the [? in Minchinhampton], 660

Lodge, the, in Wotton under Edge, 1535

Lodgemore (Lodgmore), in Stroud, 1006, 1143

Loesmore, *see* Lowsmoor

London, bishop, 305 n, 366, 436, 1102, 1180, 1223*, 1226, 1331*, 1334, 1335

London, buildings (misc.) & institutions: Blackwell Hall, 197, 1342, 1343; Court of Arches, 1021; Custom House, 883; Haberdashers' Co., 101, 103*, 279, 918*, 919; King's Bench, 393; Royal

Exchange, 271; St. James's Palace, Royal Library, 259 n; Swan House, Gray's Inn Lane, 1456; Tower, the, 230 n, 1219

London, cathedral of St. Paul, dean and chapter, 366

London, churches & parishes: All Hallows, Bread Street, 1428; All Hallows, Lombard Street, 72; Allhallows, Staining, 1528; Guildhall chapel, 1428; St. Andrew, Holborn, 1212, 1214; St. Anne, Soho, 336; St. Bride, 891; St. Clement, 521, 665; St. Dunstan, 1321; St. George, Hanover Square, 891; St. George the Martyr, 1049; St. Giles, Cripplegate, 829 n, 1428; St. Helen, 972; St. James, 259 n; St. Lawrence Poultry, 991; St. Martin, Ludgate, 867*; St. Martin in the Fields, 253, 829 n, 984; St. Mary Hault, 534 n; St. Mary le Strand, 375*; St. Marylebone (St. Mary-le-bone), 1524; St. Mildred, 1458; St. Olave, Hart Street, 1249; St. Olave, Old Jewry, 829 n; St. Pancras (St. Pankridge), 811, 1193, 1244; and see Kentish Town and Tottenham Court; St. Sepulchre, 829 n; St. Vedast, Paternoster Lane, 829 n

London, city: alderman (senator), 351, 451, 827, 829 n, 895, 1133, 1521*; chamberlain, 375; citizen, 71, 73, 86*, 239, 269, 290, 313 n, 330, 339, 351, 369, 378, 380, 383, 409, 439, 464, 517, 547, 548*, 625, 631, 639, 701, 725, 796, 867, 879, 891, 923, 974, 1063*, 1064, 1171, 1189, 1190, 1203, 1279, 1360, 1362, 1449, 1461, 1469*, 1524, 1534; lord mayor, 271, 436, 546, 568, 649 n, 717, 1051*, 1239, 1340*, 1394; sheriff, 366, 383, 590, 649 n, 1521

London, Inns of Court: Gray's (Graies) Inn, 561, 717, 738, 1401; Inner Temple, 246, 268, 314, 548, 724, 792, 867, 1201, 1497, 1526; Lincoln's Inn, 311 n, 331, 392, 477 n; Lincoln's Inn, bencher, 311 n, 504, 864 n, 867*, 1266; Lincoln's Inn, member or alumnus, 331, 392, 600, 723, 852 n, 864, 978, 1005, 1029, 1033*, 1174, 1256, 1322, 1343, 1461, 1477, 1508, 1519, 1545; Middle Temple, 22, 257*, 560, 561, 580, 820, 900, 920, 937, 1409; New Inn, 259 n; the Temple, 230 n

London, residents: apothecary, 439, 639; apprentice, 819 n, 1449, 1456; architect, 119; banker, 1171, 1362; brewer, 983; chemist, 1314; clothworker, 1063; coach maker, 787; cooper, 1279; distiller, 269; draper, 376, 602, 1181, 1297; druggist, 336, 1504; dyer, 701; factor, 658, 1214; feltmaker, 1534; fishmonger, 1063; goldsmith, 86, 576, 891, 1064, 1362, 1469; grocer, 409, 796, 935, 974, 1043; joiner, 464; mason (freemason), 134, 135; mercer, 1051, 1189; merchant, 73, 96, 225, 226, 238, 283, 331, 407, 408, 410, 411, 412, 473, 515, 516, 533, 607, 640, 651, 654*, 792 n, 863, 900, 917, 920, 996, 1006, 1166, 1211, 1266, 1408, 1411, 1501, 1505*, 1521, 1524*, 1525; merchant tailor, 378; musician, 1046; needle maker, 923; oilman, 795; physician, 652, 1478; prostitute, 358 n; salter,

1189; sculptor, 291; silk dyer, 701; skinner, 290; stationer, 517, 1469; stockbroker, 1216; surgeon, 880; tallow chandler, 339; Turkey merchant, 1440; vintner, 20; wool merchant, 291, 292; occupation unstated, 43, 93, 106, 116, 125, 135, 167, 187, 210, 220 n, 230 n, 254, 290, 336, 337, 364, 368, 369*, 370, 374, 407, 408*, 440, 534, 540, 562, 565, 590, 592, 638, 658, 665, 678, 702, 730, 739, 743, 747, 768, 779*, 815, 854, 875 n, 901, 917, 935, 944, 970, 990, 994, 1026, 1035, 1062, 1065, 1067, 1097, 1110, 1129, 1140, 1149, 1170, 1179*, 1181, 1183, 1185, 1214, 1229, 1231, 1238, 1265, 1273*, 1277, 1282, 1303, 1322, 1326, 1358, 1359, 1371, 1386, 1400, 1430, 1456, 1458, 1468, 1494, 1512, 1521, 1545, 1554

London, streets &c.: Basing Lane, Aldermary, 1028; Bernard Street, Russell Square, 1377; Bond Street, 1219; Bond Street, New, 1172; Bunhill Fields, 975; Cavendish Square, 1084, 1391; Cheapside, 305 n; Goswell Street, 989; Gracechurch (Grace Church) Street, 795; Great Russell Street, 827 n; Jeffries Square, 412; Lombard (Lumbard) Street, 72; Mortimer Street, Cavendish Square, 1084; New Street Square, 1247; Newgate Street, 1412; Rood Lane, 1043; Silver Street, 827 n; Smithfield, 876, 1401; Soho Square, 368; Southampton Street, 1412; Temple, the, 230 n; Tokenhouse Yard, 1417; Whitehall, 508 n

London, otherwise mentioned: bodies sent to, 358 n; burial, 776, 938, 1212*; death at, 64, 86, 90, 168, 175, 246, 261, 453, 497 n, 620, 631, 632*, 724, 861, 867, 975, 991, 1029, 1247; fire engine from, 1461; journey to, 1186; Knights Templars, 638 n; native, 607; parliament at, 359; road to, 153; Royal Society, 656; trade: 791; traffic to, 793 n; troops from, 1478; wool sent to, 444 n

London, and see Arms, College of; Barking (Essex); Bromley; Charlton (Kent); Christ's Hospital; Dagenham; Deptford; Greenwich; Gresham College; Holborn; Lambeth; Lewisham; Soutwark; Westminster; York House; and places named under Middlesex and Surrey

Lone [unidentified], 684

Long Bridge, the, in Tewkesbury, 1287, 1291, 1293

Long Croft, see Longcroft

Long Hope, see Longhope

Longborough, 36, 256, 257, 439*, **816–18**, 1055, 1193; and see Banks Fee

Longcroft (Long Croft), in Westbury on Severn, 1395*, 1403

Longdon (Langdon) (Worcs.), 422, 611, 1290; and see Hill Court

Longford, in Gloucester, St. Mary de Lode, 514, 950, 1046*

Longford, in Minchinhampton, 648, 1167

Longhope (Long Hope), 214, 215, 353, 466, 474, **819–22**, 1184, 1238; and see Hartsbarn

Longner, see Longnor

Longney, 583, **827–32**, 887; and see Downing; Sten Meadow

Longney Farm, in Newland, 913

Longnor (Longner) (Salop.), Longnor Hall, 1002*

Longridge End, in Ashleworth, 75

Longwood, in Woodmancote in Bishop's Cleeve, 396

Longworth (Berks.), 867

Lorridge (Lorenge, Loridge, Lorringe), in Stinchcombe, 176*, 278, 1101, 1147*

Loughborough (Lovebury in Wychwood), in Leafield (Oxon.), 791

Loughborough Park, see Lasborough

Lower (Lower House) Farm, in Newent, 893

Lower House, in Forthampton, 610

Lower House, the, in Dowdeswell, 505*

Lower Mill, the, in Painswick, 972

Lowerstone, see Stone: Lower Stone

Lowsmoor (Loesmore), in Avening, 92*, 648 n

Lowther (Westmld.), 771

Lubbenham Hall, Thorp, see Thorpe Lubenham Hall

Lucknow (India), 1026

Ludford (Salop.), 999

Ludgershall (Luggershall) (Wilts.), 852 n, 985

Ludlow (Salop.), 782

Luffenham (Leics., recte Rut.), 1336

Luggershall, see Ludgershall

Lugwardine (Herefs.), 395, 1235

Lullyntone [? Laverton, in Buckland], 1519

Lupeyate (Lupyat), see Lypiatt, Lower; Lypiatt, Over

Lurgeshall, see Nutgarshall

Lus Hill (Lyssell), in Castle Eaton (Wilts.), 1435

Lusitani, see Portugal

Luton, see Limbury

Luypyat, see Lypiatt, Lower

Lyddiard Tregoze, see Lydiard Tregoze

Lyde Pill, see Lightpill

Lydiard (Lyddiard) Tregoze (Wilts.), 1497; and see Chaddington

Lydney (Lidney), 242, 732*, 805–15, 894 n, 915, 1035; Lydney Park, 806 n; residents, 102, 475, 546, 552, 720, 733, 919, 921, 932, 1398; and see Allaston; Aylburton; Chantry, the; Gurshill; Hurst; Nass; Newerne; Nursehill; Purton; Rodley; Rodmore; Soilwell; Warren; Whitecross

Lye (the), see Leigh

Lyegrove, in Old Sodbury, 1120

Lyford (Berks.), 1001

Lyleshull, see Lilleshall

Lymbrey, see Limbury

Lyme (Lime) Regis (Dors.), 1409

Lyn Regis, see Lynn, Kings

Lynch brook, 101

Lynches, the, in Bisley, 195

Lyncoln College, see Lincoln College

Lyneham (Lineham) (Oxon.), 217

Lyneham (Wilts.), see Bradenstoke

Lynn, Kings (Lyn Regis) (Norf.), 1334

Lyon-sur-Mer (Lyon) (Normandy), 747 n

Lypiatt (Lypeat, Lypiate, Lypite) [unspecified], 114, 195, 198, 199, 203*, 341, 393 n, 556, 652, 1216

Lypiatt (Luypyat, Lyppiatt), Lower or Nether, in Stroud, 197, 1206, 1207, 1214, 1216, 1217, 1218*

Lypiatt, Middle, in Bisley, 1216

Lypiatt (Over Lippiat, Lupeyate, Lyppiatt), Over or Upper, in Bisley, 199, 1029*, 1032, 1033, 1051*, 1209, 1214, 1215, 1217*, 1218

Lyre (Lyra) (Normandy), abbey, 319, 523, 805, 819, 1322, 1323

Lyssell, see Lus Hill

Maastricht (Mastrick) (Netherlands), 136

Macao (China), 1400

Machynlleth (Machynleth) (Mont.), 1413

Maddersfield, see Madresfield

Madgett (Madgetts, Magett, Magget), in Tidenham, 735, 1319, 1320, 1321, 1323

Madoc, Castle, near Brecon (Brec.), 1136

Madras (Madrass) (India), 975, 1231*, 1327

Madresfield (Maddersfield) (Worcs.), 330, 766

Magdalen College, Oxford, alumnus, 142, 259 n, 346, 431, 497 n, 559 n*, 1019, 1065; estate, 1001, 1095, 1101; fellow, 416, 453, 856; May Day custom, 1095, 1101; organ, 1261; president, 394 n; and see Magdalen Hall

Magdalen Hall, Oxford, 305 n, 671 n

Magett (Magget), see Madgett

Magotsfield, see Mangotsfield

Maidenhead (Berks.), 1033, 1463

Mainoaks (Mannocks), in Goodrich (Herefs.), 352

Mainz (Mentz) (Germany), 739

Maisemore (Maysemore), 77, 99, 587*, 683, 687, 855–8, 1034, 1359; and see Alney, Island; Overton

Malden (Essex), 718 n

Malden (Surr.), 827 n

Malgaresberie, see Maugersbury

Malling Abbey, in West Malling (Kent), 268

Mallswick, see Malswick

Malmesbury (Malmsbury) (Wilts.), 220 n, 349 n, 662, 750, 1024, 1253, 1324, 1383, 1449, 1451; abbey, 648, 825*, 1253, 1322, 1339; school, 1070, 1147

Malmsbury Charlton, see Charlton

Malswick (Mallswick, Maulswick, Mausick), in Newent, 831, 894, 899*, 900, 904*

Malvern [unspecified] (Worcs.), 481 n

Malvern, Great (Worcs.), 767; abbey or priory, 78, 265 n, 565, 827, 829*

Malvern, Little (Worcs.), priory, 420, 421, 440, 889, 1172

Malvern Chase (Worcs.), 265 n

Malvern Hills (Worcs.), 252, 392

Manchester (Lancs.), 1437; Manchester College (later Oxford), 1341

Mangotsfield (Magotsfield, Mangersfield), 45, 833–7, 1159, 1392, 1491; residents, 10, 555, 612, 710, 843, 1113, 1158*, 1307, 1488; and see Clevehill; Downend; Hill House; Moorend; Ridgeway

Mannocks, see Mainoaks

Mansell, see Maunsel

Mansell Gamage, see Garnons

Marburg, see Warburg

Marcle, Little (Herefs.), 992, 993*

Market Harborough, *see* Harborough, Market

Marlborough (Wilts.), 420, 864 n, 1118

Marlcliff (Mart Cleeve), in Bidford (Warws.), 1001

Marlwood (Morlwood), in Thornbury, 1296, 1304, 1305*, 1306, 1307, 1309, 1311

Marsden (Marsdon), in Rendcomb, 1499

Marsh Hill, in Marston Meysey (Wilts.), 861*

Marshfield (Marsfield), 82, 83, 828, **838–47**, 1108, 1112, 1117, 1492; Little Marshfield or Old Marshfield, *see* Westend Town; St. Nicholas, 839; St. Pancras, *see* Westend Town; *and see* Ashwicke; Ayford; Beeks; Downs, the; Meers manor; Oakford; Rocks, the; Westend Town

Marske (Yorks. N.R.), 330, 1089

Marston [*unspecified*] (Wilts.), 1274

Marston, Broad, in Pebworth, 979, 980

Marston, Long or Dry (Marston Sicca), **848–50**, 1041*, 1391

Marston, Priors (Warws.), 560, 1065

Marston Meysey (Marston Maisey, Marston Maysey, Marston Mezey) (Wilts.), 859*, 860*, 862*, 1127*; *and see* Marsh Hill; Marston [*unspecified*]

Marston Moor (Yorks. W.R.), 1366

Mart Cleeve, *see* Marlcliff

Marten Bridge, in North Nibley, 154

Martinique (Martinico) (West Indies), 1231

Maskelyne's Ham, in Cricklade (Wilts.), 367, 369

Mastrick, *see* Maastricht

Masulipatam (Mazulepatam) (India), 974

Matesden, *see* Matson

Mathon (Worcs.), 231

Matson (Matesdon, Mattesden), **851–4**; residents, 75, 133, 255, 749, 798, 886, 887, 950, 974, 1319, 1376, 1380, 1437; *and see* Mudedin

Mattisfort, *see* Mottisfont

Maugersbury (Maugesbury, Malgaresberie), in Stow on the Wold, 640, 1067, 1190*, 1191*, 1194*, 1195*, 1196*, 1197*

Maulswick, *see* Malswick

Maund, *see* Meend Park

Maunsel (Mansell), in North Petherton (Som.), 854

Mausick, *see* Malswick

May (or Yartleton, Yarleton) Hill, in Huntley and Newent, 759, 894, 1233

May Hill, in Westerleigh, *see* Mayshill

Maylards (Maylands), in Hornchurch (Essex), 220 n

Maysey Hampton, *see* Hampton, Meysey

Mayshill, in Meysey Hampton, 141

Mayshill (May Hill, May's Hill), in Westerleigh, 1424, 1425, 1428

Mazulepetam, *see* Masulipatam

Medmenham, *see* Bockmer

Meen Hill, *see* Meon Hill

Meend, Lower, in Ruardean, 250

Meend Park [? Maund, in Bodenham] (Herefs.), 1303

Meerend, in Ashleworth, 75

Meers manor, in Marshfield, 839

Melholme, *see* Millom

Melksham (Milsham) (Wilts.), 377, 781, 1155

Melksham Court, in Stinchcombe, 1169

Mene, *see* Meon

Menevensis, *see* St. Davids

Mentz, *see* Mainz

Meon (Mene), in Quinton, 816 n

Meon (Meen) Hill, in Mickleton and Quinton, 864

Mercia, kingdom and bishopric, 271, 357, 481, 628, 649, 680, 839, 1093, 1131, 1132, 1133, 1138, 1195, 1227, 1253, 1321, 1361, 1386, 1392, 1419*, 1459*, 1502, 1512

Meredith [? in Siston], 1087

Merewent, *see* Morwent

Merriott (Meriolt) (Som.), 1243

Merryford (Mireford), in Kingswood (formerly Wilts.), 778 n

Merton (Surr.), 827 n

Merton College, Oxford, 45, 127, 391*, 591 n*, 961, 990, 1119, 1380, 1382; *and see* St. Alban Hall

Metteliburgi, *see* Middelburg

Meysey Hampton, *see* Hampton, Meysey

Michael Wood (Micklewood) Chase, in Alkington, 159, 305

Michaelstroy, *see* Troy, Mitchel

Mickleton, 634, **863–8**, 951, 980, 1119; *and see* Clopton; Hidcote; Meon Hill

Micklewood, *see* Michael Wood

Middelburg (Metteliburgi) (Netherlands), 1526

Middle Hill, in Broadway (Worcs.), 1041, 1052, 1059, 1432

Middlesex, 91, 864 n, 1281; *and see* Barnet; Chelsea; Chiswick; Clapton, Upper; Clerkenwell; Colham; Cranford; Drayton, West; Edmonton; Hackney; Hampstead; Hampton Court; Harrow on the Hill; Hendon; Heston; Highgate; Holborn; Kentish Town; Lea, river; London, churches; London, streets; Morton Hall; Osterley; Southgate; Stanmore; Stanwell; Stepney; Stoke Newington; Syon; Tottenham Court; Twickenham; Whitechapel; Willesden

Middleton, in Hinton, 171

Midsomer (Midsummer) Norton, *see* Norton, Midsomer

Milborne (Milborn) Port (Som.), 51

Milcote (Milcoat, Milcot, Millcot) (Warws.), 804 n, 850, 863, 988*, 989, 1390, 1391*, 1392*

Mildenhall (Wilts.), 130

Milham Post (Milhampost), *see* Millhampost

Milholme, *see* Millom

Millcot, *see* Milcote

Millend (Millen), in Awre, 112

Millend (Mill End), in Eastington, 558*, 560, 562, 620, 621

Millend, in Newland, 922, 923

Millhampost (Milham Post, Milhampost), in Hailes or Winchcombe, 586, 1229, 1232, 1466, 1475

Millom (Melholme, Milholme) (Cumb.), castle, 392 & n

Milltown End, in Fairford, 592

Milsham, *see* Melksham

Milton [? in Fairford], 135

Milton (Oxon.), 135

Milton Abbotts, *see* Milton Lilbourne

Milton End, in Arlingham, 65, 66

Milton Lilbourne (Milton or Milton Abbotts) (Wilts.), 808

Minchinhampton (Hampton, Minchin Hampton, Minchinghampton), 91*, 525, **646–62**, 1021*, 1027*, 1109, 1138, 1216, 1218*; residents, 97*, 204, 299, 424, 536, 558, 750*, 794, 798, 881, 940*, 1021*, 1025, 1098, 1138, 1433, 1507, 1508*, 1510, 1512; *and see* Amberley; Box, the; Burleigh; Cowcombe; Culver House; Dyehouse, the; Forwood; Gatcombe Park; Golden Valley; Gydynap; Holcombe; Hyde; Iron Mills; Lammas, the; Littleworth; Lodge, the; Longford; Mussilhill; Peaches Farm; St. Chloe; St. Mary Mills; Theescombe; Woefuldane Bottom; Wood House

Minden (Germany), 58, 410

Minsterworth (Ministerworth), 581, **869–73**, 901, 1403; residents, 325, 352, 468, 513, 583, 584, 830, 1098, 1371, 1396, 1403; *and see* Duni; Hampton; Hygrove; Murcott

Mireford, *see* Merryford

Miserden (Miserdine), 254, 339, 348, 449*, 523, **874–81**, 1483; *and see* Bidfield; Hazle House; Slad; Stean Bridge; Sudgrove; Wishanger

Mitcham (Surr.), 827 n*

Mitchel Troy, *see* Troy, Mitchel

Mitcheldean (Dean Michel, Dene Magna, Michel Dene, Michell Dean, Mitchel Dean), 3, 4*, 5, 458, **461–8**, 479, 807, 894, 900, 1238, 1403; *and see* Howley

Mitton, in Bredon (Worcs.), 395, 1380

Moat (Mote), the, in Newent, 898*, 901*

Moat, the, in Sandhurst, 1046

Moat Place, in Haresfield, 671

Mobley, in Hamfallow, 175

Mocksbrook, *see* Mork Brook

Moers, near Wesel (Muers near Wezell) (Germany), 58

Molland (Devon), 755

Monae Insula, *see* Anglesey

Mond Fields [? in Rodborough], 1025

Mongewell (Mungewell) (Oxon.), 856

Monk Woods, in Cold Ashton, 80

Monks Kirby, *see* Newnham Paddox

Monk's Mill, in Wotton under Edge, 1528

Monkton Farleigh, *see* Farleigh, Monkton

Monmouth (Mon.), 136, 245, 805 n, 894 n, 918, 1164, 1515; castle, 759, 819; priory, 759, 819, 1078, 1356; residents, 349, 734, 807, 815, 913, 923, 963, 1341, 1504, 1525

Monmouthshire, 245, 349, 425 n, 475 n, 729, 805 n, 1309, 1323; *and see under names of separate places*

Monnington-on-Wye (Herefs.), 898

Montburi Fischamp, *see* Fécamp

Montgomeryshire, *see* Criggion; Gregynog; Machynlleth; Newtown

Montserrat (Leeward Islands, West Indies), 1472

Moor End, in Hartpury, 680

Moor Hall (Moorehalls, Moorhalls, Morehalls), in Randwick, 1145, 1179*, 1185

Moorend (Morend), in Mangotsfield, 833, 835*

Moorend (More-end), in Slimbridge, 1095, 1096, 1097, 1100

Moorhalls, *see* Moor Hall

Moors (Moores), the, in Cheltenham, 336*

Morcote, *see* Murcott

Morden (Surr.), 827 n

Mordon (Moredon), in Boddington, 228

More-end, *see* Moorend

Morehalls, *see* Moor Hall

Morend, *see* Moorend

Moreslade [*unidentified*], near Gloucester, 1047*

Moreton [*unspecified*] (Herefs.), 332

Moreton (Morton) [*unspecified*] (Staffs.), 452, 1342

Moreton, in Thornbury, *see* Morton

Moreton and Whaddon, prebend, 1434

Moreton in Marsh (Moreton Henmarsh), 218, 230*, **882–4**

Moreton Valence (Morton, Morton Valance), 317, 574 n, 677, **885–7**, 941, 1008, 1131, 1132, 1440; Little Moreton, 885; *and see* Epney; Framilode; Hill, the; Horsemarling

Morewent End, *see* Morwent

Mork, in St. Briavels, 248

Mork Brook (Mocksbrook), in St. Briavels, 248

Morlwood, *see* Marlwood

Mortlake (Surr.), 827 n, 1226

Morton, *see* Moreton Valence

Morton (Staffs.), *see* Moreton

Morton (Moreton), in Thornbury, 1298, 1301, 1302*, 1303, 1304, 1305*, 1307*, 1309, 1311, 1313*, 1314, 1326

Morton, Birts, *see* Birtsmorton

Morton, Castle, *see* Castlemorton

Morton Hall, in Chiswick (Mdx.), 410

Morton Valance, *see* Moreton Valence

Morwent (Merewent, Morewent End), in Hartpury, 680*, 1377

Mote, the, *see* Moat, the

Mottisfont (Mattisfort) (Hants), 68

Mounds Court, in Siston, 1084, 1087

Mount, the, in Haresfield, 672

Mousewell, in Wapley and Codrington, 367

Moys Hill (Moyeshill), in Westbury on Severn, 1395*, 1403

Mozambique, 1245

Muddesley, *see* Mudgley

Mudedin [? Matson], 1035

Mudgley (Muddesley), in Wedmore (Som.), 910

Muers, near Wezell, *see* Moers

Mull, Island of (Scot.), 1303

Mungewell, *see* Mongewell

Murcot, in Childswickham, 1447*

Murcott (Morcote) or Boyfield, in Minsterworth, 869*, 870

Muscovy (Russia), 520

Mussilhill, in Minchinhampton, 653

Mythe (Myth), the, and Mythe Hook, in Tewkesbury, 1285, 1288*, 1289, 1290, 1292*, 1293*, 1361, 1362*; Mythe Bridge, 293, 1356; residents, 986, 1052, 1269*, 1278, 1381

Nabb's End, *see* Newnham: Newnham's Ladder

Nailsworth, in Avening and Horsley, 92, 748, 1512; Nailsworth Hill, 649; residents, 93, 658, 750, 751*, 983, 1140, 1206, 1369, 1508, 1529; *and see* Holcombe

Nantes (France), 1457

Nanton (Nanton-field), *see* Naunton, in Winchcombe

Narford (Norf.), 1424

Nass (Nase, Nast), in Lydney, 349, 733*, 806 n, 807, 808, 810*, 812*, 929

Nastend, in Eastington, 558, 561, 562, 620

Natton, in Ashchurch, 71, 74*, 1287, 1347

Naunton, 706, **889–91**, 952, 1041, 1445, 1478; *and see* Aylworth; Harford

Naunton, in Cheltenham, 325

Naunton (Nanton, Nanton-field, Newton), in Winchcombe, 1334, 1467, 1473, 1474, 1475, 1476, 1478; *and see* Naunton Bampton

Naunton Bampton [? Naunton, in Winchcombe], 1148

Neale's Place, in Eastington, 558

Nempnett Thrubwell, *see* Regilbury

Nether Hall, in Awre, 106

Nether Hall, in Harkstead (Suff.), 1296

Nether Town [? Netherton in Brampton Abbots or Ledbury] (Herefs.), 1504

Nether Town, in Cam, *see* Cam: Lower Cam

Netheravon (Wilts.), 1005

Nethercote, in Bourton on the Water, 232, 1195

Netherlands (Holland, Low Countries), 590; *and see* Hague, the; Helder, den; Leiden; Maastricht; Middelburg; Ryswick

Netherley, *see* Ley

Netherton [*unspecified*] (Devon), 1510

Netherton (Herefs.), *see* Nether Town

Netherton, in Hatherop, 693*

Nettleton (Wilts.), 237, 1300

Neunton, *see* Newnton, Long

Nevis (Leeward Islands, West Indies), 209, 724, 1415

New College, Oxford, 52, 445 n*, 515 n, 838, 840*, 879, 1305, 1451

New England, 208, 1180; *and see* Boston

New Forest (Hants), 122, 475 n

New House, *see* Newhouse, in Stroud

New Inn, *see* London, Inns of Court

New Inn Hall, Oxford, 1458

New Mills, in Alderley, 33

New Mills, in Dursley, 537, 541*

New Mills, in Stroud, 1024

New Park, in Stone, 166, 168, 1174*, 1176, 1177

New Park, in Devizes (Wilts.), 1073*

New Passage, the, in Redwick, 729, 731

New York (North America), 413

Newan, *see* Newerne

Newark (Newark upon Trent) (Notts.), 535, 1015

Newark, in Hempsted, Our Lady's Well, 712

Newarn, *see* Newerne

Newbold on Stour (Newbold), in Tredington (Worcs.), 1392

Newbold Pacey (Warws.), 1432*

Newburgh (N.Y., U.S.A.), 1503

Newbury (Berks.), 1431

Newby Wiske (Yorks. N.R.), 143

Newcastle Emlyn (Emilyn Ukenclet) (Carms.), 325 n

Newcastle-under-Lyme, *see* Seabridge

Newcastle-upon-Tyne (Northumb.), 237, 1198, 1419

Newchurch (Mon.), 1303

Newcombe, in Saintbury, 1041

Newent, 471, 544 n*, **892–907**, 977, 978, 1185; priory, 893; residents, 332, 546, 674, 927, 992, 1238, 1315; *and see* Boulsdon; Brass Mill; Carswalls; Carway; Compton; Court House, the; Cugley; Culford; Ford House; Glass House, the; Gorsley Common; Hayes; Kerries; Kilcot; Lower (Lower House) Farm;; Malswick; May Hill; Moat, the; Okle; Porch House; Porter's Place; Scarr, the; Southend; Stardens; Walden Court; Waterdines; Yartleton manor; Yartleton Woods

Newerne (Newan, Newarn), in Lydney, 811, 812

Newham Quar. in Stinchcombe, 1167

Newhouse [? in Dursley], 539

Newhouse (New House), in Stroud, 1207, 1209*, 1247*

Newington and Newington Butts (Surr.), 827 n, 1327, 1530

Newington Bagpath, 182, 307, 777, **908–11**, 959, 1100; Newington (Newenton, Newinton), 529*, 908*, 909; *and see* Bagpath; Calcot; Nutgarshall; Owlpen

Newland, 242, 249, 605 n, 761, 801, **912–24**, 1066, 1161, 1515; *and see* Bream; Breckness; Brook Hall; Clearwell; Coleford; Hoarthorns; Hollies, the; Lea Bailey; Longney Farm; Millend; Noxon; Owen; Pastor's Hill; Platwell; Redbrook; Scatterford; Scowles, the; Shophouse; Stock, the; Stowe; Wyeseal

Newnham (Newneham), 65, 101, 469, 470, 605 n*, 671, 894 n, **925–34**, 1403, 1404; Newnham's Ladder or Nabb's end, 925; residents, 69, 104, 110, 111, 171, 198, 352, 473*, 474, 548, 623, 887, 915, 1155, 1397*, 1402, 1403; *and see* Bluett's Court; Cockshoot; Culver House; Hay Hill; Hill House; Hyde; Ruddle; Stears

Newnham Paddox, in Monks Kirby (Warws.), 1431

Newnton (Herefs.), *see* Newton, in Hereford

Newnton, Long (Neunton, Newnton) (Wilts.), 1070, 1253, 1529

Newnton Park, *see* Newton St. Loe

Newport (Mon.), 997

Newport, in Alkington, 153, 159, 167, 1538; residents, 163, 166, 169*, 172*, 173*, 175, 176*, 177, 1175, 1176*

Newton [*unspecified*] (Wilts.), 380

Newton, in Ashchurch, *see* Northway and Newton

Newton (Newnton), in Hereford (Herefs.), 471*

Newton, in Rockhampton, 1019*, 1020

Newton, in Tadcaster (Yorks. W.R.), 1193–4

Newton, in Winchcombe, *see* Naunton

Newton, Welsh (Welch Newton) (Herefs.), 1034

Newton St. Loe (Som.), 829 n; Newton (Newnton) Park, 10*

Newtown (Mont.), 1360
Newtown St. Cyr (or Cyres) (Devon), 1169
Nibley, in Awre, 105, 111*, 112
Nibley, in Westerleigh, 12, 1123*, 1425, 1428
Nibley, North (Nibley, Nybley), 154, **935–9**, 1521, 1522, 1538*; Nibley Green, 158, 935, 938, 1538; residents, 41, 281, 362, 533, 538, 543, 552 n, 610, 748, 778, 960, 1185, 1521, 1575; *and see* Boorden; Bournstream; Burrows Court; Hillery; Marten Bridge; Pitt Court; Smart's Green; Snightend; Swinhay; Swynburne Bridge
Nibley Green, *see* Nibley, North
Nimdesfield (Nimpsfield), *see* Nympsfield
Nind, in Kingswood (formerly Wilts.), 781, 937, 1522, 1526, 1527, 1569
Nivelle Tarbes, *see* Tarbes
Nixon, *see* Noxon
Nobury (Norbury), in Inkberrow (Worcs.), 1517
Noose, the, in Awre, 101
Norcott (Northcote), in Preston, 990*
Norfolk, 287 n, 305 n, 729, 754, 876, 885; *and see* Appleton; Baconsthorpe; Brancaster; Buckenham; Costessy; Gissing; Hillington; Hockham, Great; Holkham; Lynn, Kings; Narford; Norwich; Plumstead; Sprowston; Topcroft; Walsingham; Woodrising; Worstead
Norham, *see* Thornton Hall
Norleach, *see* Northleach
Normandy (France), 251, 523, 707, 952, 1538; *and see* Bayeux; Caen; Cormeilles; Coutances; Falaise; Fécamp; Lisieux; Lyon-sur-Mer; Lyre; St. Evroult; St. Wandrille; Ste.-Barbe; Troarn
Normans Land, in Dymock, 965
Norminton [? Normanton, *unidentified*], 1329
Northallerton (Yorks. N.R.), 941
Northampton, 123, 788, 1011, 1085, 1086, 1546
Northamptonshire, 359, 591 n, 605; *and see* Arthingworth; Ashton; Aynho; Blisworth; Fotheringhay; Kelmarsh; Northampton; Paulerspury; Peterborough; Scaldwell; Shrobb Lodge; Stowe, Church; Thornhaugh; Thorp Lubenham Hall; Titchmarsh; Welton
Northbrook, in Kirtlington (Oxon.), 697
Northcote, *see* Norcott
Northend (Nurthen), in Burton Dassett (Warws.), 1329
Northey, in Tetbury, 1265
Northills (Beds.), 829 n
Northleach (Leche, Norleach, North Leach, Northlech, Northleche), 318, 321, 599*, 638 n, 684, **942–8**, 1198*, 1284, 1350*, 1519
Northpetherton, *see* Petherton, North
Northumberland, 305 n; *and see* Gainslow; Newcastle-upon-Tyne; Sutton upon Lown; Thornton Hall
Northumbria, 839
Northway and Newton, in Ashchurch, 71*, 72*, 73, 1387
Northwick, in Henbury, 48*, 721, 722*, 730*, 963
Northwick (Northwycke) and Northwick Park, in Blockley, 218, 220*, 221, 223, 224*, 225, 227, 257, 1459

Northwood (Northwode), in Westbury on Severn, 1396*, 1397*, 1398, 1401, 1402*, 1403, 1404
Northwood Chasteners, *see* Norwood
Northwycke, *see* Northwick
Norton, 77, 118, 346*, 422, 716, 803, **949–50**, 1044, 1047, 1316, 1354; Norton's Court, 949; *and see* Wainload Hill
Norton (Wilts.), 612, 839, 1407*
Norton, in Bredon (Worcs.), 1357, 1358*
Norton (Norton on the Hill), in Weston Subedge, 570, 866, 1430, 1431*; Middle Norton, 1430
Norton, Brize (Brees Norton) (Oxon.), 79
Norton, Chipping (Oxon.), 518, 848, 1458
Norton, Midsomer (Midsummer Norton) (Som.), 1410
Norton, Over (Oxon.), 1226
Norton Malreward (Norton-malereward) (Som.), 554, 1507
Norwich (Norf.), 394 n
Norwood (Northwood Chasteners) (Kent), 798 n
Norwood Park, in Southwell (Notts.), 511
Notgrove, 801, **951–2**, 1015*, 1051, 1501
Notley, in Long Crendon (Bucks.), Notley abbey, 1225, 1228*, 1227*
Nottingham (Notts.), 1460, 1470
Nottinghamshire, 481 n, 890, 894, 1031; *and see* Attenborough; Beauvale; Columoe; Gotham; Graywell; Newark; Norwood Park; Nottingham; Rampton; Stoke
Nova Scotia (Canada), 346, 391
Noverend, *see* Upperend
Noxon (Nixon), in Newland, 923*, 924
Nubdown, *see* Nupdown
Nuneaton (Warws.), 657
Nunne Eiton, *see* Eaton, Water
Nup End, in Ashleworth, 75
Nup-End, in Eastington, *see* Nupend
Nupdown (Nubdown), in Hill and Rockhampton, 741*, 1018*
Nupend (Nup-End), in Eastington, 558*, 562*
Nupend (Nupp End), in Horsley, 748
Nursehill (Nurshill), in Lydney, 809*, 810*
Nurthen, *see* Northend
Nutbeam Farm, in Duntisbourne Abbots, 523
Nutgarshall or Lurgeshall, in Newington Bagpath, 908
Nybley, *see* Nibley, North
Nympsfield (Nimdesfield, Nimpsfield, Nymphsfield), 631, 632, 737*, 972, **940–1**, 1100, 1146, 1379; Nympsfield Park, 1512

Oackley, *see* Oakleaze
Oak, the [? in Deerhurst], 485*
Oakesey, *see* Oaksey
Oakey (Okeys), in Haresfield, 672
Oakford (Okeford), in Marshfield, 839, 844
Oakham (Rut.), 721 n
Oakleaze (Oakley), in Alkington, 164, 171
Oakleaze (Oackley), in Olveston, 961
Oakley, in Alkington, *see* Oakleaze
Oakley, in Cirencester, 365, 366, 525
Oakridge, in Bisley, 197, 201, 202*

Oaksey (Oakesey) (Wilts.), 240, 1029*, 1048
Oatfield, in Awre, 102
Ockington, in Dymock, 546*
Oddington (Odynton), 565 n, **952–3**, 1189, 1224, 1262
Odiham (Hants), 829 n
Odynton, *see* Oddington
Offa's Dyke, 915, 1321
Okeford, *see* Oakford
Okeys, *see* Oakey
Okle (Okle Clifford, Okle Pritchard, and Okle Grandison), in Newent, 894*, 896*, 897*, 900
Old Court, in Stone, 1176
Old Minster, *see* Oldminster
Old Passage ferry, in Beachley, 1322
Oldbury, in Eastington, 418
Oldbury, in Stapleton, 1159, 1160
Oldbury, the, in Tewkesbury, 1285, 1288*, 1290*, 1291
Oldbury House [? in Quedgeley], 999
Oldbury on the Hill, 495, **953–4**, 1450
Oldbury upon Severn (Oldbury, Olbury, Trajectus), in Thornbury, 53, 405, 807 n, **955–9**, 1295, 1309, 1311*, 1312, 1313*, 1321; residents, 18, 173*, 175, 283, 738, 962, 963, 1298*, 1299*, 1301*, 1304*, 1305*, 1306*, 1312; *and see* Cowhill
Oldend (Oldends, Oldings, Ouldings), in Stonehouse, 623, 1143, 1180*, 1183, 1184, 1186
Oldeswelle, *see* Owdeswell
Oldhurst, in Slimbridge, 175
Oldings, *see* Oldend
Oldland, in Bitton, 205*, 206*, 207*, 211, 212, 213; *and see* Hinton
Oldminster (Old Minster), in Hinton, 154, 1099
Oldmixon, in Weston-super-Mare (Som.), 921
Oldpen, *see* Owlpen
Olne (Belgium), 1180
Olney, *see* Alney
Olveston (Olvestone), 50*, 577, **960–3**; residents, 52, 175, 576, 577, 578, 722, 724, 731, 1121, 1300, 1302*, 1307, 1453; *and see* Grovesend; Hazel; Ingst; Oakleaze; Tockington; Woodhouse
Orchard Wyndham (Orchard), in St. Decumans (Som.), 704
Oridge (Horridge), in Corse, 440
Oriel College, Oxford, alumnus, 257, 311 n, 651 n, 1245, 1478; estate, 313, 451, 452, 1065, 1345, 1346; fellow, 1340, 1341*, 1463, 1503; provost, 1072, 1344; *and see* St. Mary Hall
Ormskirk (Lancs.), 829 n
Orthez (Orthes) (France), 1303
Osleworth, *see* Ozleworth
Osney (Oseney), in Oxford, abbey or priory, 37, 183, 184, 1016*, 1033*, 1351*
Osterley Park (Mdx.), 1065
Ouchy (Switzerland), 1194
Ouldings, *see* Oldend
Ouse, Great (Usa), river , 366 n
Outham, in Tidenham, 1321
Over, in Almondsbury, 39, 42, 44, 46, 48*, 49, 98, 1139
Over, in Churcham, 349*, 350*, 352, 353*, 354, 872

Overbury (Worcs.), 868, 1362, 1387*, 1410; *and see* Alstone
Overdean, *see* Dean, Upper
Overley, *see* Ley
Overs, in Siston, 1087
Overton [*unspecified*], 864
Overton, in Arlingham, 65, 66, 70*
Overton, in Maisemore, 855
Overtown (Overton) Farm, in Cranham, 449
Owdeswell (Oldeswelle, Owdswell), in Withington, 1495, 1501*, 1502
Owen [*unidentified*], in Newland, 924
Owlpen (Oldpen, Owlepen), in Newington Bagpath, 908, 909*, 910, 941, **959–60**, 1369*
Owsleworth, *see* Ozleworth
Oxenhall, **964–5**; *and see* Backs; Crooke's; Furnace, the; Hill House; Pella; Sondlow
Oxenton (Oxinton), **965–6**, 1291, 1311, 1348, 1475
Oxford, 286, 529, 643, 793 n*, 891, 1033, 1219, 1220; castle, 889 n; cathedral chapter, 183; death at, 29, 136, 291, 595, 1245, 1430, 1459; residents, 413, 598, 930, 1420; St. Martin's, 1231; St. Thomas's, 1543; theatre, 893; *and see* Osney
Oxford Canal, 793 n
Oxford university, 36, 122, 259 n, 287 & n, 595, 607, 1073; alumnus or graduate, 51*, 306, 334, 361 n, 547, 705, 711 n, 723, 817, 993, 1105, 1380, 1451, 1495, 1546, 1522; Divinity School, 318; estate, 691*, 692, 990, 1016; Physic Garden, 363; professor, 51, 656, 860 n, 861, 1258; vice-chancellor, 52, 1072; *and see* All Souls College; Balliol College; Bodleian Library; Brasenose College; Cardinal College; Christ Church; Corpus Christi College; Exeter College; Gloucester Hall; Hart Hall; Hertford College; Jesus College; King's Hall; Lincoln College; Magdalen College; Magdalen Hall; Manchester; Merton College; New College; New Inn Hall; Oriel College; Pembroke College; Queen's College; St. Alban Hall; St. Bernard's College; St. John's College; St. Mary Hall; St. Mary's College; Trinity College; University College; Wadham College; Worcester College
Oxfordshire, 31, 359, 585, 643 n, 696, 1065, 1069, 1280, 1422, 1441; *and see under names of separate places*
Oxinton, *see* Oxenton
Oxlinch, in Standish, 1131, 1132*; *and see* Ivy House
Ozleworth (Osleworth, Owsleworth, Ozelworth), 529, 908, 910, 954, **966–7**, 1147; *and see* Comb Farm

Packington [? in Berkeley], 176
Padworth (Berks.), 1487
Paganhill (Pagan Hill, Paganhall, Pagenhill, Pakenhill), in Stroud, 1006, 1008, 1026, 1208*, 1212*, 1213, 1214*, 1215, 1216, 1217*, 1218, 1511
Painley (Painsley), near Uttoxeter (Staffs.), 690, 691, 692

Painswick, 574*, 885, **968–76**, 1129, 1218, 1380*; Painswick House, 1377; Painswick Lodge, 831; residents, 52, 113, 378, 482, 659, 676, 684, 761, 950, 1024*, 1208, 1210, 1374, 1484; *and see* Aedes Brokiane; Brook House; Brown's Hill; Damsells; Dureth; Ebworth; Edge, the; Grange, the; Greenhouse; Grove, the; Hill; Iscombe; Lower Mill, the; Paradise; Rock Mill, the; Sheephouse, the; Sheepscombe; Slad; Stroud End; Tocknells; Trillgate; Upper Grange; Well, the; Wick Street

Paken-hill, *see* Paganhill

Palington [? Pavington, in Burrington] (Devon), 1321

Pamington (Paminton, Pannington), in Ashchurch, 71*, 72, 74*, 1287

Pamplona (Pamp-luna) (Spain), 1303

Panclase [*unidentified*] (Mon.), 808

Pandy, *see* Pantee

Pannington, *see* Pamington

Pantee [? Pandy or Panteg] (Mon.), 280

Paradise (Paradice) and Paradise House, in Painswick, 971, 974, 975, 1208, 1209*

Pardon Hill [? in Woolstone], 1503, 1504

Parham (Suss.), 852 n

Paris (France), 591 n*, 656, 1190, 1191, 1443; the Louvre, 852 n; St. Denis (St. Dennis, St. Dyonisius), 1209; abbey of St. Denis, 430*, 436, 481*, 585, 801*, 1165*, 1355*, 1388*, 1475*, 1504

Park End, in Haresfield, 663, 672

Park End, in West Dean, *see* Parkend

Park Hill (formerly Pudhill, Puddhill), in Woodchester, 655, 941, 1510, 1512

Park Mill, in Thornbury, 1306

Park, the [*unidentified*] (Herefs.), 548

Parkend (Park End, Park's End) and Parkend Lodge and Parkend Walk, in West Dean, 250, 924, 1039

Parkham, *see* Sedborough

Parks, the, in Thornbury, 1304*

Parry Court Farm, in Faversham (Kent), 1290

Parsley Hill [*unidentified*, ? in Hewelsfield], 733

Parton, in Churchdown, 346

Parton, in Hinton, *see* Purton

Passenham, *see* Shrobb Lodge

Pastor's Hill (Pastershill), in Newland, 249, 915

Patchway (Petshawe), in Almondsbury, 39, 42, 1490, 1491

Pau (France), 962

Paulerspury (Paulers Perry) (Northants.), 363 n

Pauntley, 951, **976–8**, 1027, 1051*, 1333; Pauntley Court, 754, 760

Pavington, *see* Palington

Paxford (Paxton), in Blockley, 218*, 220, 226*, 227*, 296, 866, 1002, 1330, 1389

Peaches (Peach's) Farm, in Minchinhampton, 649

Peaked (Picked) Elm, in King's Stanley, 1136, 1138*, 1139

Pebworth, 272, 293, 866, **979–80**, 1392; *and see* Marston, Broad; Ullington

Peckham, in Camberwell (Surr.), 1303

Pedington (Peddington), in Stone, 159, 167*, 168*, 170*, 172*, 174*, 176*, 738, 1176

Peers (Piers) Court, in Stinchcombe, 1169

Pegglesworth (Peglesworth, Peggleworth, Pekelworth), in Dowdeswell, 503*, 1471, 1477, 1501*, 1502

Peirsfield, *see* Piercefield

Pekelworth, *see* Pegglesworth

Pella (Pellhall, Pellow), in Oxenhall, 964, 965

Pembridge (Pembruge) (Herefs.), 856

Pembroke, *see* Grove

Pembroke College, Oxford, 313 n, 325, 327, 334, 396, 432, 1097, 1180, 1207, 1519, 1582

Pembrokeshire, 1237; *and see* Grove; St. Davids; St. Ishmael's; Tenby; Wiston

Pen Park (Penpark), in Westbury on Trym, 604, 726*, 727*, 1411, 1419

Pen Pole (Penfold Hill), in Henbury, 1420

Pen-y-Pwlle [? Pen-y-Foel, in Llanarmon-yn-Ia] (Flints.), 249

Penallt (Penalt) (Mon.), 809

Pencelli (Penkelly), near Llanfrynach (Brec.), 975

Pencoed (Mon.), castle, 592 n

Pendarves, in Camborne (Cornw.), 920

Pendock (Worcs.), 687

Pendrop, *see* Pindrup

Penfold Hill, *see* Pen Pole

Pengethly, in Sellack (Herefs.), 732, 1381

Penkelly, *see* Pencelli

Pennebury, *see* Pimbury

Penpark, *see* Pen Park

Pensford (Ponsford) (Som.), 1487

Penthrop, *see* Pindrup

Pentillie Castle, in Pillaton (Cornw.), 1547

Peon, King's, *see* Blackhall

Pershore (Pershor) (Worcs.), 360 n, 695, 829 n, 1262; abbey, 265 n, 447, 481 n, 482, 695, 696*; *and see* Caddecroft

Persia, 867; *and see* Gambroon; Jask

Perton, *see* Purton, in Hinton

Peterborough (Northants.), 609 n

Peterhouse (St. Peter's College), Cambridge, 1367

Petersham (Surr.), 827 n

Peterstow (Herefs.), 104

Petherton, North (Northpetherton) (Som.), 1209*, 1412; *and see* Maunsel

Petropolis, *see* St. Petersburg

Petshawe, *see* Patchway

Petty France, in Hawkesbury, 240, 700*, 756

Phillimore's Bridge, in Berkeley, 154

Picked Elm, *see* Peaked Elm

Piercefield (Peirsfield), near Chepstow (Mon.), 1524

Piers Court, *see* Peers Court

Pierton's Court, *see* Pirton Court

Pill House, in Tidenham, 1320

Pillaton, *see* Pentillie Castle

Pillston [*unidentified*, ? in Hewelsfield], 733

Pimbury (Pennebury), in Avening, 648

Pinbury (Pynbere) and Pinbury Park, in Duntisbourne Rouse, 525, 526, 574, 1051*, 1049

Pinchpool, in Windrush, 1481, 1482

Pindrup (Pendrop, Penthrop), in Coln Rogers, 432

Pinelsend, *see* Pinnells End

Pinkney (Sherston Pinkney), in Sherston (Wilts.), 1431, 1454

Pinnells End (Pinelsend), in Coaley, 414

Pinnock (Pynnock, Pynnocke, Pynock, Pynoke), 493, 494, 638, 706, 708 n, **997**, 1225; Pinnock's Wood, 709; *and see* Farmcote

Pinnockshire (Pynokeshire), lands in, 708 n, 1225*

Pinswell, in Coberley or Colesborne, 420

Pirton (Pierton's, Purton) Court, in Churchdown, 336, 348

Pit Leasow, in Dymock, 546

Pitchcombe, 559 n*, 622, 667, 668, 973, **980-1**, 1144, 1218

Pitcourt, *see* Pitt Court

Pitminster, *see* Poundisford

Pitt Court (Pitcourt), in North Nibley, 938

Plaistow, in Deerhurst, 482, 483, 484*

Plasterwine (Plasterwyne), *see* Plusterwine

Platwell, in Newland, 922

Plimouth, *see* Plymouth

Pluckley, *see* Surrenden-Dering

Plumstead [*unspecified*] (Norf.), 562

Plusterwine (Plasterwine, Plasterwyne), in Woolaston, 1513, 1514*, 1515*, 1516

Plymouth (Plimouth) (Devon), 411, 413, 811, 929, 1301

Podd (Poddesmead), *see* Podsmead

Poden (Powden), in Church Honeybourne (Worcs.), 864 n, 1430

Podsmead (Podd, Poddesmead, Podgemead, Podgmead), in Hempsted, 713, 715*, 886, 1059

Poitiers (Poyters) (France), 179

Polesworth (Polsworth) (Warws.), 401, 1001

Pomerton, in Awre, 102

Ponsford, *see* Pensford

Pontypool (Mon.), 852 n

Pool, *see* Poole; Poole Keynes

Pool (Poole) House, in Wickwar, 1451, 1452, 1455

Pool Hall [*unidentified*] (Mon.), 963

Poole (Pool) (Dors.), 988, 1129, 1231

Poole Court, *see* Pull: Pull Court

Poole Keynes (Pool) (Wilts.), 1266

Poolway, in Coleford, 923

Pope's Hill, in East Dean, 1400

Porch House, in Newent, 893

Porchester (Portchester) (Hants), abbey of Porchester or Southwick (Southwyke), 462

Porshet [*unidentified*] (on the Severn), 955

Port Eliot, in St. Germans (Cornw.), 507

Port Farm, in Cirencester, 375*

Portchester, *see* Porchester

Porte, the, *see* Constantinople

Portefeld, *see* Portfield

Porter's Place, in Newent, 900

Portfield (Portefeld), in Hereford, 1058

Portsmouth (Hants), 409

Portswood (Portswede), in Southampton (Hants), 864 n

Portugal (Lusitani), 23, 723*, 952, 1303; *and see* Lisbon

Postlip (Postlipp, Potteslip), in Winchcombe, 641, 1077, 1334, 1445, 1466*, 1471, 1472, 1474, 1475*, 1476, 1477*; Postlip Hall, 1472

Poulton (Pulton), in Awre, 605 n; Poulton Court, 101, 102, 103, 105

Poultons Hill, in Westbury on Severn, 1395*

Poundisford, in Pitminster (Som.), 614*

Powden, *see* Poden

Powick (Worcs.), 990, 1380

Poynings (Suss.), Poynings Place, 810

Poyters, *see* Poitiers

Praeneste (Italy), 357 n

Praston, *see* Preston (Som.)

Prees (Preece) (Salop.), 1389

Presbury, *see* Prestbury

Prescott (Prescot, Prescote, Prescutt), 399*, **984**, 1153, 1503*, 1504*

Prestbury (Presbury), 315, 860 n, **982-6**, 1058, 1062, 1197, 1276*; manor, 1059*, 1060*, 1062*, 1064*, 1475; Prestbury Park, 983, 984, 985*; residents, 339, 392, 685, 952*, 1090, 1468; *and see* Hewletts; Hyde Farm

Preston (Preston by Cirencester), **989-91**, 1200; *and see* Norcott

Preston (Preston by Ledbury), **992-3**; Preston Court, 992; *and see* Brownsend

Preston (Kent), *see* Copton

Preston (Praston) [? Preston Plucknett] (Som.), 1425

Preston on Stour (Preston upon Avon), 482 n, **987-9**, 1388; *and see* Alscot

Prinknash (Princknash), 469, **994**, 1373*, 1379, **1380**; Prinknash Park, 1377, 1378, 1380

Prior's Court, in Kempley, 766

Priors Marston, *see* Marston, Priors

Priorswood (Prior's Wood), in Hamfallow, 176

Publow (Som.), 1166

Pucclechurch, *see* Pucklechurch

Puckham, in Sevenhampton, 1061*, 1062*, 1063*, 1064*, 1445

Pucklechurch (Pucclechurch), 7, 36, **994-7**, 1085, 1086*, 1423, 1428*; residents, 551 n, 555, 582, 595, 1115

Puckpool, in Arlingham, 65, 69*

Puckrup, in Twyning, 1360, 1362

Puddhill, *see* Park Hill

Puddleworth (Puddle Wharf), in Eastington, 558

Pudhill, *see* Park Hill

Puisy, *see* Pusey

Pull, in Bushley (Worcs.), 1291; Pull (Poole) Court, 283, 482, 565, 585, 609, 610

Pulton, *see* Poulton

Purton (Wilts.), 237, 962

Purton (Parton, Perton), in Hinton, 159, 172, 176, 1097*, 1098, 1099

Purton (Pyrton), in Lydney, 807, 809*, 810*, 1398; Purton Passage, 807, 811*

Purton Court, *see* Pirton Court

Pusey (Puisy) (Berks.), 620

Putloe, in Standish, 625, 1132

Putney (Surr.), 827 n

Pynnock (Pynnocke, Pynock, Pynoke), *see* Pinnock

Pynokeshire, *see* Pinnockshire
Pyon, Kings, *see* Blackhall
Pyrenees (France), 1303
Pyrton, *see* Purton, in Lydney

Quar House (Quarhouse), in Stroud, 202, 1206*, 1216
Quedgeley (Queddesley, Quedgley, Quedgly), 71, 75, 268 n, 852 n, 872, **998–1000**, 1059; Quedgeley Farm, 1000; *and see* Oldbury House; Woolstrop
Queenington, *see* Quenington
Queens' College, Cambridge, 199, 313
Queen's College, Oxford, 22, 190, 230 n, 318, 319*, 502, 723, 943, 944, 1029
Queensland (Australia), 1354
Queinton, *see* Quinton
Quemerford (Somerford), in Calne (Wilts.), 1359
Quenington (Queenington), 429, 596, **1003–5**, 1029; commandery or preceptory, 619 n, 634, 638 n, 753, 1005*, 1078
Quinton (Queinton), 230 n, 393 n, 868, **1001–3**; Lower (Nether) Quinton, 1001*; Upper (Over) Quinton, 1001*; *and see* Admington; Meon; Meon Hill; Radbrook; Wincot

Radbrook, in Quinton, 1001, 1002*
Radford, *see* Rudford
Radipole, *see* Causeway
Radmore, *see* Rodmore, in St. Briavels
Radnor (Radnors.), 829 n
Radnorshire, 919, 1047, 1208; *and see* Hampton Court; Radnor
Radway (Rodway) (Warws.), 1085
Radwinter (Essex), 409
Raggley, *see* Ragley
Raglan (Ragland) (Mon.), 123 *, 459 n, 736; castle, 119, 1322
Ragley (Raggley) (Warws.), 1093, 1148
Raingeworthy, *see* Rangeworthy
Rainham, *see* Bloors Place
Rampton (Notts.), 209
Ramsbury (Wilts.), 1097, 1199; *and see* Littlecote
Ramsgate (Kent), 1072
Randwick (Renwyke), 651, 667, **1006–8**, 1130, 1132, 1182, 1218; *and see* Ebley; Moor Hall; Westrip
Rangeworthy (Raingeworthy, Rangworth, Rangworthy), 18, 36, **1009**, 1085, 1110, 1295, 1312, 1313*, 1521
Ranton (Staffs.), Ranton Abbey, 1171
Raphoe (Irel.), 483, 801
Rapsgate, in Colesborne, 424; hundred, 424
Ratley and Upton, *see* Upton
Ratton Island, *see* Roaton Island
Rea, the, in Hempsted, 713
Reading (Berks.), 573, 793 n, 1186
Red Brook, *see* Redbrook
Red Sea, the, 1321
Redborne, *see* Rodbourne Cheney
Redbrook (Red Brook, Redbrooke), in Newland, 913, 917, 921*, 922*, 923*, 924*, 1524; *and see* Rodrack

Redcliff, in Bristol, St. Mary's, 47, 68, 722, 1185, 1200, 1392, 1557
Redditch, *see* Bordesley
Redecroftes, in Kempsford, 775
Redland, in Westbury on Trym, 1408, 1409, **1416–17**, 1419*, 1489; Redland Court, 1409, 1410*, 1416, 1417, 1420
Redmarley D'Abitot (Redmarley) (Worcs.), 133, 270*, 685, 686, 978*, 993; *and see* Berrends; Kingsend
Redwick, in Henbury, 98, 562, 717, 721, 1419; *and see* New Passage, the
Regilbury (Rochelburgh), in Nempnett Thrubwell (Som.), 605
Regissylva, *see* Kingswood
Reigate (Surr.), 827 n*, 829 n
Rendcomb (Rendcombe), 128*, 311, 361, 367, 591 n, **1009–11**, 1029, 1105, 1352; Little Rendcomb, 1011; *and see* Eycot; Marsden
Renwyke, *see* Randwick
Rhapahanock River (Virginia), 47
Rhyswick, *see* Ryswick
Richmond (Surr.), 827 n*, 829 n, 867, 921
Richmond (Yorks. N.R.), castle, 1219
Riddleford, in Hinton, 176*
Ridford, *see* Rudford
Ridge, the, *see* Bridge, the
Ridge (Rudge), the, in Wotton under Edge, 1366, 1534, 1539
Ridgeway (Rudgeway), in Mangotsfield and Stapleton, 1160
Ridleia, *see* Rodley, in Westbury on Severn
Ridley Hall, in Terling (Essex), 515
Riga (Latvia, Livonia), 1277
Ringwood (Hants), 1251, 1366
Ripon (Yorks. W.R.), 1258, 1384; *and see* Fountains Abbey
Ripple (Worcs.), 879, 1285, 1293, 1353, 1359; *and see* Greenfield; Holdfast
Rissington (Risington) [*unspecified*], 1189, 1482
Rissington, Great (Risendon, Risingdon Magna), 947, **1012–13**, **1014–17**, 1050, 1092
Rissington, Little, **1013**, **1014–17**, 1092*
Rissington, Wick (Wyke Rysingdon), **1014–17**, 1092*, 1195; *and see* Wyke
Roade, the [? in Rodborough], 1024
Roadhouse [? in Rodborough], 1024*
Roadways, the [? in Stroud], 1203
Roaton (Ratton) Island (Bay of Honduras), 1159
Rochelburgh, *see* Regilbury
Rochester (Kent), 1107, 1166
Rock Mill, the, in Painswick, 972, 975
Rockhampton, 739, 778 n, **1018–20**, 1097* & n, 1172, 1176, 1298; residents, 455*, 738, 955, 957, 959, 1304, 1305; *and see* Newton; Nupdown; Sheperdine
Rockmore, *see* Bockmer
Rocks, the, in Marshfield, 839
Rodborn, *see* Rodbourne Cheney
Rodborough, 646, 648, 651*, 973, **1021–7**, 1208, 1218, 1512; residents, 1182, 1507, 1508*, 1510, 1511, 1524, 1538, 203, 447, 657*, 659, 660*,

1133, 1135, 1136, 1137, 1138, 1139; Rodborough
Fort, 1027; *and see* Bownham's House;
Dudbridge; Frome Hall; Hill House; Lightpill;
Mond Fields; Roade, the; Roadhouse;
Rooksmoor; Rownham's; Spilman's Court;
Stringer's; Wallbridge; Woodhouse
Rodbourne Cheney (Redborne, Rodborn,
Rodbourn) (Wilts.), 708 n, 816 n, 824
Rodele, *see* Rodley
Roding, *see* Rottenden
Rodley (Rodleys), in Lydney, 807, 810
Rodley, in Newnham, *see* Ruddle
Rodley (Ridleia, Rodele), in Westbury on Severn,
605 n, 1394*, 1396, 1397*, 1398*, 1399*,
1401*, 1402, 1403*, 1404*; New Weir at, 605 n
Rodmarton, 444, 445 & n, 781, **1028–33**; Rodmarton
Farm, 1030, 1031; *and see* Culkerton; Hazleton;
Hocberry; Hullasey; Tarlton
Rodmore, in Lydney, 55
Rodmore (Radmore), in St. Briavels, 249
Rodrack [? Redbrook, in Newland], 1515
Rodway, *see* Radway
Roel (Rowell), 325, 634, 635, **704–6**, 1006, 1055,
1475
Rolls Court (Rollscourt), in Slimbridge, 1095,
1096*, 1101, 1102
Rolston, *see* Rowlstone
Rome (Italy), 154, 349 n, 590, 875 n; Aventine
Hill, 357 n
Romsey (Rumsey) (Hants), 445; abbey, 1033*
Roncesvalle (Ronces Valles) (Spain), 1303
Ronken, Le [*unidentified*], 605 n
Rook Wood, in Bisley, 201
Rooksmoor (Rooksmore), in Rodborough, 1507
Rorysshe, *see* Ross
Rosamond's Green, in Frampton on Severn, 618
Rosley, *see* Rossley
Rosmanacher (Irel.), 1119
Ross (Rorysshe) (Herefs.), 172, 929, 1058, 1166,
1238
Rossley (Rosley), in Dowdeswell, 503, 1501*
Rosult, *see* Rushault
Rothbride [*unidentified*] (Irel.), 413
Rotherham (Yorks. W.R.), 1486
Rotherhithe (Surr.), 827 n
Rothlain [? Ruthin] (Denb.), castle, 1069
Rottenby, *see* Rottington
Rottenden [? Roding, *unspecified*] (Essex) , 1136
Rottington (Rottenby), in St. Bees (Cumb.), castle,
876
Rowberrow (Roughborough, Rowbarrow) (Som.),
43, 490
Rowell, *see* Roel
Rowgree, *see* Rue Green
Rowlstone (Rolston) (Herefs.), 921
Rownham's, in Rodborough, 1027
Rrockhampton, *see* Brockhampton
Ruardean (Ruerdean, Ruerdeane), 479, 605 n*,
821, **1035–9**; *and see* Meend, Lower; Smither's
Cross Farm; Watercross
Ruardean Lodge and Walk, in East Dean, 478 n,
1039

Ruckholt (Ruckholts), in Leyton (Essex), 792, 1493
Ruddle (Rodley), in Newnham, 927, 929*, 930,
933*
Rudford (Radford, Ridford, Rutford), 686, 714,
904, **1034–5**, 1372; *and see* Barley Bridge;
Highleadon; Leadon Court
Rudge, in Hardwicke, 663, 664*
Rudge, the, in Wotton under Edge, *see* Ridge, the
Rudgeside [*unidentified*] (Wilts.), 975
Rudgeway, *see* Ridgeway
Rue Green (Rowgree), in Eldersfield (Worcs.), 1037
Ruerdean (Ruerdeane), *see* Ruardean
Rufford (Lancs.), 804
Rugbag, in Alkington, 159
Rumsey, *see* Romsey
Ruscombe, in Stroud, 1132, 1181, 1213, 1217
Rushault [? Rosult] (France), 218
Ruslersland [*unidentified*], 270
Russell's End, in Bromsberrow, 265
Russia, 230 n, 1027*, 1067, 1073; *and see* Alma;
Balaklava; Crimea; Inkerman; Muscovy;
St. Petersburg; Sebastopol
Rutford, *see* Rudford
Ruthin (Denb.), 763 n; *and see* Rothlain
Rutland, *see* Exton; Luffenham; Oakham
Rye (Suss.), 1027, 1091, 1190
Rye, in Tirley, 1352, 1355, 1356
Ryeford, in Stonehouse, 1186
Ryeland, in Dymock, 546
Rysingdon, Wyke, *see* Rissington, Wick
Ryswick (Rhyswick) (Netherlands), 497 n
Ryton (co. Dur.), 1367
Ryton, in Dymock, 546

Sadbury, *see* Sodbury
Saddlewood (Seddlewood), in Hawkesbury, 695,
696, 697, 699*
Safford, *see* Salford
Saffron Walden, *see* Audley End
Sages, in Slimbridge, 1095, 1101
Sailsbury Hall, *see* Salisbury Hall
St. Alban Hall [Merton College], Oxford, 559 n
St. Albans (Herts.), 359 n, 988
St. Andrews (Scot.), 635 n
St. Anthony's Well, in Abenhall, 1
St. Arvans, *see* St. Oulard
St. Asaph (Flints.), 41
St. Bees (Cumb.), *see* Rottington
St. Bernard's College [St. John's College], Oxford,
605 n
St. Briavels (St. Breeval), **242–50**, 457, 476, 805,
915; castle, 67, 162, 245, 478, 690, 1039; castle,
constable, 479, 480, 732, 1039; castle, deputy
constable, 470; hundred, 242*, 476, 477 n, 478,
1039; residents, 733, 734, 736, 921; *and see*
Aylesmore; Bearse, the; Bigs Weir; Brockweir;
Cinderhill; Dunkilns; Highgrove; Hoggins;
Hudnalls; Mork; Mork Brook; Rodmore; Stowe;
Willsbury; Wyeseal
St. Chloe (Saint Clear, Saint Low, Saintlieu,
Saintloe, Sinckley), in Minchinhampton, 648,
651*, 1021, 1186, 1505, 1509

St. Christopher (St. Kitts) (Leeward Islands, West Indies), 1180, 1411, 1547

Saint Clear, see St. Chloe

St. Davids (Menevensis) (Pemb.), 93, 142, 144, 392 n, 513, 609, 915, 1041, 1081, 1451

St. Decumans, see Orchard Wyndham

St. Denis (St. Dennis, St. Dyonisius), see Paris, St. Denis

St. Devereux (Sancto Dubbricio) (Herefs.), 1058

St. Domingo, see Santo Domingo

St. Ebrulph, see St. Evroult

St. Edmund Hall (Edmund Hall), Oxford, 1258

St. Erth (Ethe) (Cornw.), 1115

St. Evroult (St. Ebrulph in Utica) (Normandy), abbey, 216, 704, 707, 1103, 1256

St. Ewe (St. Tew) (Cornw.), 369

St. Florent de Saumur (St. Florence de Salurmo) (France), 759

St. Gallen (St. Gall) (Switzerland), 725

St. George, see Bristol, churches

St. Georges (St. Georgis), in Banwell (Som.), 808

St. Germans, see Port Eliot

St. Ishmael's (St. Ismael's) (Pemb.), 1290*

St. James's Palace, see London, buildings

St. John's Bridge, in Lechlade, 791, 792

St. John's College, Cambridge, 410, 1489

St. John's College, Oxford, 136, 411, 436 n, 725, 1486, 1487, 1491; and see St. Bernard's College

St. Johns in Bedwardyne, see Boughton

St. Kitts, see St. Christopher

St. Leonards (Suss.), 1046

St. Leonard's Hanley, see Hanley

Saint Low, see St. Chloe

St. Margaret and St. Barbara, see Ste.-Barbe-en-Auge

St. Mary de Lode, Gloucester, see Longford

St. Mary Hall [Oriel College], Oxford, 122

St. Mary Mills, in Minchinhampton, 648

St. Mary, Redcliff, see Redcliff

St. Marylebone, see London, churches

St. Mary's College, Oxford, 360 n

St. Nicholas, see Marshfield

St. Oswald's priory, see Gloucester, priory

St. Oulard [? St. Arvans] (Mon.), 741

St. Pancras (St. Pankridge), see Kentish Town; London, churches; Westend Town

St. Perre, see St. Pierre

St. Peter's College, Cambridge, see Peterhouse

St. Petersburg (Petropolis) (Russia), 656

St. Philip (St. Phillip) and St. Jacob, see Bristol, churches

St. Pierre (St. Perre) (Mon.), 411, 721

St. Swithin's, in Almondsbury, 40, 435

St. Tew, see St. Ewe

St. Tiriac (St. Trecla), chapel of, in Tidenham, 1322

St. Tyrrel, see Falfield

St. Vincent's Chapel, Rocks, and Well, in Clifton, 404, 405 & n

St. Wandrille (Founteney) (Normandy), abbey, 251

St. Weonards (Herefs.), 921, 922; and see Trippenkennet

Saintbridge (Sendebrugge), in Gloucester and Upton St. Leonards, 1378, 1379

Saintbury (Seyntbury), 876, 988*, 989, **1040–1**, 1052, 1432; and see Newcombe

Ste.-Barbe-en-Auge (St. Margaret and St. Barbara) (Normandy), abbey, 147

Sainthurst, see Sandhurst

Saintlieu (Saintloe), see St. Chloe

Salemansbury, see Salmonsbury

Salford (Safford) (Oxon.), 1067, 1480

Salford (Som.), see Saltford

Salisbury (Sarisburiensis, Sarum) (Wilts.), 130, 260, 412, 753*, 852 n, 1001, 1123, 1185, 1495; bishop, 260, 449, 581, 582; chancellor, 1001; dean, 359, 361 n; prebend and prebendary or canon, 130, 205, 753*, 852 n, 1033*, 1185, 1495

Salisbury (Sailsbury) Hall, in Shenley (Herts.), 1377

Salle, see Saul

Salmonsbury (Salemansbury, Salmenesbury), in Bourton on the Water, 1091; hundred, later Slaughter hundred, 233, 1091*, 1225

Salperton (Cold Salperton), 638, **1042–3**, 1201, 1501

Salt Marsh, see Saltmarsh

Saltford (Salford) (Som.), 995, 996*, 1085

Saltmarsh (Salt Marsh), in Henbury, 717, 720, 721

Saltway, the, 1493

Sancto Dubbricio, see St. Devereux

Sanderstead, see Langley

Sandford (Devon), see Creedy

Sandford (Salop.), Sandford Hall, 725

Sandford (Som.), 165

Sandford, in Cheltenham, 317, 325, 329, 335, 337, 339, 984, 1472

Sandhurst (Sainthurst, Santhurst), 77, 346, 618, 620, 823, 854, **1044–7**, 1138*, 1403; and see Abloads Court; Bengrove; Moat, the; Walleswood; Wallsworth; Willington Court

Sandiwell, see Sandywell

Sandon (Staffs.), 753

Sandpits, in Chaceley (Worcs.) and Tirley, 1352, 1353, 1354, 1355

Sandywell (Sandiwell), in Dowdeswell, 502, 503*, 1057, 1059, 1443*

Saniger, in Hinton, 159, 167, 170, 171, 172*, 173*, 174, 175, 176

Santhurst, see Sandhurst

Santo Domingo (St. Domingo) (West Indies), 1564

Saperton, see Sapperton

Sapina [*unidentified*], in Westbury on Severn, 1401, 1402

Sapperton (Saperton), 444, 793 n, 875 n, 894 n, **1048–52**, 1186; residents, 363, 364, 459, 525, 574, 595, 1027, 1029; and see Frampton Mansell; Hailey

Sarisburiensis, see Salisbury

Sarneye, South, see Cerney, South

Sarsden (Oxon.), 234, 437

Sarum, see Salisbury

Saul (Salle), 584, 625, 887, **1053–4**, 1132*; Saul Farm, 1440*; Saul Lodge, 1053; and see Framilode

Says Farm, in Westerleigh, 1384

Saywells (Saysells), in Kempley, 768

Scadbury Park, in Chislehurst (Kent), 852 n

Scaldwell (Northants.), 4

Scarr, the (or Athelord's Place or Water's End), in Newent, 894*

Scatterford, in Newland, 917

Scotland (North Britain), 410, 583, 633, 639, 652, 885, 985, 1307; and see Applegarth; Balnagown; Bannockburn; Cambuswallace; Corstophine; Dalswinton; Edinburgh; Eske; Flodden; Glasgow; Gordonstoun; Handerwood; Hoddom; Holmains; Keir; Knockshinnoch; Mull; St. Andrews

Scotlands, in Hill, 174, 738

Scowles, the (the Scrowls), in Coleford or Newland, 194

Scurburgh, near Duchland [unidentified] (Germany), 1473

Seabridge, in Newcastle-under-Lyme (Staffs.), 336

Sebastopol (Russia), 1073

Sedborough (Sodborough), in Parkham (Devon), 1090

Sedbury (formerly Kingston), in Tidenham, 1321*, 1322; Sedbury Park, 1321, 1322

Seddlewood, see Saddlewood

Segovia (Spain), 444 n

Seisencote (Seisincot, Seisincote), see Sezincote

Sellack, see Pengethly

Selsley, in King's Stanley, 1140

Selwike, see Shelwick

Selwood (Som. and Wilts.), 496

Sempflye [unidentified], in Awre, 106*

Sendebrugge, see Saintbridge

Serridge, in Westerleigh, 1424

Seven Springs (Seven Wells), in Coberley, 420, 1056

Sevenhampton, 503, 706, 985*, 986, 1042, **1056–64**, 1164, 1263, 1442; and see Brockhampton; Cawcombe; Clopley; Hampen; Puckham; Whitewell

Sevenoaks (Kent), 431

Severn, river: as boundary, 53, 75, 101, 435, 581; banks and flooding, 39, 65, 75, 103, 481 & n, 619 n, 685, 581, 582; bore, 101–2, 582; bridge, 855*; changing course, 101, 617, 805; drowning in, 112, 176, 1054, 1281, 1282; fisheries, 159, 605 n, 713, 870, 1288, 1321, 1323, 1403*, 1516; lot meadows, 684; navigation, 98, 101, 153, 553, 582; passage (crossing, ferry), 50, 53, 65, 98, 582, 625, 738, 807 n*, 925, 955, 1321; places beside, 576, 581; shipwreck in, 101, 955; and see Thames and Severn canal

Seyntbury, see Saintbury

Sezincote (Seisencote, Seisincot, Seisincote), 804, 818, **1055**

Shackerstone (Shakerston) (Leics.), 257

Shadlington [? Chadlington (Oxon.)], 1379

Shakerston, see Shackerstone

Shavenage, see Chavenage

Sheen (Shene) (Surr.), abbey or priory, 318*, 319, 1323; East Sheen, 525

Sheephouse, in Gloucester, 71

Sheephouse (the), in Painswick, 975, 981*

Sheepscombe, in Painswick, 972, 973

Sheinton, see Belswardyne

Shelwick (Selwike), in Hereford, 1058, 1565

Shene, see Sheen

Shenfrith, see Skenfrith

Shenington, **1065**

Shenley, see Salisbury Hall

Sheperdine (Shepardine, Shiperdine), in Rockhampton, 419, 738, 1019*, 1020*, 1309; Sheperdine Pill, 1321

Sheppey (Shepey), Isle of (Kent), 798 n

Shepton Mallet (Som.), 1209

Sherborne (Sherborne, Sherbourne, Shireborne, Shirebourne), 37, 325, 369, 420, 422, 944, **1066–9**, 1092, 1189, 1404, 1482*, 1483

Sherborne (Shireborn) (Dors.), see Castleton

Sherhampton, see Shirehampton

Sherston (Sherston Magna) (Wilts.), 696, 1070; and see Pinkney

Sherthampton, see Shorthampton

Shilton (Oxon., formerly Berks.), 136

Shiperdine, see Sheperdine

Shipston on Stour (Worcs.), 288 n, 1331

Shipton [unspecified], 1351, 1480

Shipton Dovel, see Shipton Moyne

Shipton Moyne (Shipton), 68, 92, **1070–4**, 1251; Shipton Dovel (Dovel), 1072, 1074*; and see Estcourt House; Hill Court

Shipton (Shipton Oliffe and Shipton Solers), 1059*, 1062; Shipton Oliffe, 321, 1060 n, **1075**, 1076*, **1077–8**, 1445; Shipton Solers, 321*, 330, 634 n, 1061, 1075*, **1076–8**, 1445; and see Frog Mill; Hampen

Shireborne (Shireborn, Shireborne, Shirebourne), see Sherborne

Shirehampton (Hampton, Sherhampton, Shirhampton), in Henbury, 49, 727, 728, 729*, 730*, 731*, 1409*, 1411*, 1413*, **1417–19**, 1420*

Shirenewton (Mon.), 945

Shirhampton, see Shirehampton

Shophouse, in Newland, 922*

Shorncote (Shorncott) (Wilts.), 1083, 1202

Shorthampton (Sherthampton) (Oxon.), 257

Shottery, in Stratford-on-Avon (Warws.), 988

Shottesbrooke (Berks.), 985

Shrewsbury (Salop.), 793 n, 1011, 1219

Shrivenham (Shriveham) (Berks.), 660, 994*, 1127, 1298, 1300

Shrobb (Shrobbs) Lodge, in Passenham (Northants.), 1282

Shropshire, 272, 330, 908, 989, 1005, 1337; and see Belswardyne; Benthall; Bridgnorth; Burwarton; Cann Hall; Clee Chase; Corfham; Coverall Castle; Culmington; Donington; Ercall, High; Hayes chase; Helsington; Hopton Castle; Lilleshall; Longnor; Ludford; Ludlow; Prees; Sandford; Shrewsbury; Stanton Lacy; Tunstall; Wem; Whitton; Whixall

Shudeley, see Sudeley

Shurdington (Great Shurdington), 43, 113, 114, 115, 117*, 1059*, **1079**, 1133, 1324, 1370*

Shurdington, Little, in Badgeworth, 113, 132, 1501
Shuthonger, in Twyning, 1360, 1362*
Sibbard [? Sibford Ferris or Sibford Gower, in Swalcliffe (Oxon.)], 1065
Sibland (Sibelond), in Thornbury, 456, 1299, 1303, 1311, 1312, 1314
Siddington (Sidenton, Sodynton-in-the-More, Sodyntune), 708 n, 792 n, 793 n, 1072, **1080–3**, 1202, 1258, 1351; Siddington House, 1082; Siddington St. Mary (Upper Siddington), 990; Siddington St. Peter (Lower Siddington, Siddington Musard), 1033, 1201, 1202; *and see* Tudmoor
Side, *see* Syde
Sidenton, *see* Siddington
Sierford, *see* Syreford
Sierra Leone, 187
Silverton (Devon), 651 n
Simonds Hall, *see* Symond's Hall
Sinckley, *see* St. Chloe
Sinwell, in Wotton under Edge, 1522, 1527*, 1537
Sion, *see* Syon
Sissinghurst (Kent), 44
Siston (Sisson), 747, **1084–7**, 1157; Siston Court, 1085*, 1086; *and see* Bridge Yate; Ivyleafe; Meredith; Mounds Court; Overs; Warmley; Webb's Heath
Sittingbourne (Sittingborn) (Kent), 1298
Skellingthorpe (Skillingthorpe) (Lincs.), 71, 1290
Skenfrith (Shenfrith) (Mon.), 250, 352
Skillingthorpe, *see* Skellingthorpe
Slad, in Miserden or Painswick, 878, 973
Slad (Slade), the, in Bisley or Stroud, 203, 1180, 1209, 1215*
Slaughter, Lower (Nether Slaughter), 146, 232, 233, 399, 818, 1016, **1088**, **1091–3**
Slaughter, Upper (Slaughter), 1067, 1069, **1089–93**, 1262; Manor House, 1092*; *and see* Kirkham Farm
Slaughter hundred, *see* Salmonsbury
Slimbridge (Slymbridge), 1019, **1094–1102**, 1145, 1147; residents, 172, 176, 282, 284*, 353, 373, 474, 537, 622*, 624, 671, 1009, 1189; Slimbridge Warth, 617; *and see* Cambridge; Gossington; Hurst; Kingston; Moorend; Oldhurst; Rolls Court; Sages
Slowwe, in Arlingham, 65, 66, 69*
Slymbridge, *see* Slimbridge
Smart's Green, in North Nibley, 938
Smither's Cross Farm, in Ruardean, 1037
Smow [*unidentified*], 74
Snape (Yorks. N.R.), 1583
Snead Park, *see* Sneyd Park
Snedham, *see* Sneedham
Sneed Park, *see* Sneyd Park
Sneedham (Snedham), in Upton St. Leonards, 1376*, 1378, 1379
Sneyd (Snead, Sneed) Park, in Westbury on Trym, 1409, 1410, 1415*, 1418, 1420*
Snightend (Snighton, Snytend), in North Nibley, 277*, 938
Snowshill, **1103–4**, 1150, 1272; *and see* Brockhampton

Snytend, *see* Snightend
Sodborough, *see* Sedborough
Sodbury (Sadbury) [*unspecified*], 281, 393 n, 576*, 1269
Sodbury, Chipping, **1105–12**, **1119–23**, 1450, 1455; residents, 9, 17, 48, 753, 1115, 1117, 1118, 1119, 1297, 1384*, 1425, 1546*, 1547, 1548, 1550*
Sodbury, Little, **1113**, **1119–23**; rector, 36, 306, 498, 1106, 1107, 1115; residents, 131, 556, 702*, 756*, 757, 1106*, 1115*, 1116, 1117*, 1118*, 1428
Sodbury, Old, 986, 1113, **1113–23**, 1177, 1336; residents, 19, 1107, 1108*, 1110, 1338, 1359, 1545*, 1546, 1549, 1550; *and see* Brook House; Coomb's End; Hampstead; Lyegrove
Sodynton-in-the-More (Sodyntune), *see* Siddington
Soilwell (Soylwell) or Sulla (Sulley, Sully), in Lydney, 246*, 247, 807; Sulla House, 806 n
Somburne [? Somborne (Hants)], 1092
Somerford [*unspecified*], 1199
Somerford (Wilts.), *see* Quemerford
Somerford, Great (Broad Somerford) (Wilts.), 743, 744
Somerford, Little (Somerford) (Wilts.), 1341
Somerford Keynes (Wilts.), 379, 385
Somerset, 359, 552*, 614, 696, 997, 1408, 1564; *and see under names of separate places*
Somerton (Oxon.), 150
Sondlow [*unidentified*, ? in Oxenhall], 964
Sothewyke, *see* Southwick
South Mead, *see* Southmead
Southam, in Bishop's Cleeve, 392*, 393 n, 398*, 399*, 494, 982, 984*, 986, 1206; *and see* Brockhampton; Haymes
Southampton (Southton) (Hants), 328, 401, 1251, 1493; *and see* Portswood
Southampton, county of, *see* Hampshire
Southend, in Arlingham, 66
Southend (Southerns), in Newent, 895, 900
Southfield, in Condicote and Longborough, *see* Banks Fee
Southfield, in Thornbury, 816
Southgate (Mdx.), 990
Southmead (South Mead), in Westbury on Trym, 1191, 1405, 1407*, 1420
Southrop, 889, **1124–7**
Southton, *see* Southampton
Southwark (London or Surr.), 325 n, 410, 607*, 829 n, 937; Christchurch (Christ Church), 829 n; Gleane Alley, 1196; St. John's, 410, 1504; St. Thomas's, 829 n
Southweeke, *see* Southwick
Southwell, *see* Norwood Park
Southwick (Sothewyke, Southweeke), in Tewkesbury, 984, 1262, 1287*, 1288*, 1289, 1292
Southwick (Southwyke) (Hants), *see* Porchester
Southwood, in Wickwar, 1453, 1455
Southwyke, *see* Porchester
Soylwell, *see* Soilwell
Spa (the German Spa) (Germany), 197, 1180
Spain (Iberia), 23, 443 n*, 444 n, 478 n, 723, 952; *and see* Escurial; Pamplona; Roncesvalle; Segovia; Trafalgar; Vigo; Vittoria

Spalding (Lincs.), 1027
Speech House, the (King's Lodge), in East Dean, 478 n, 479 n, 480
Spelsbury (Oxon.), 1480; and see Ditchley
Spetchley (Worcs.), 680
Spilman's Court, in Rodborough, 1027
Spilsby (Lincs.), 852 n
Spital Gate, in Cirencester, 365
Spout, the, in Blaisdon, 215
Sprowston (Norf.), 220 n
Stafford (Staffs.), 95, 817
Staffordshire, 395, 792 n, 793 n, 849; and see Bromwich, West; Chartley; Draycott in the Moor; Engleton; Fisherwick; Kingswinford; Lichfield; Moreton; Painley; Ranton; Sandon; Seabridge; Stafford; Stoke-upon-Trent; Tixall; Tunstall; Uttoxeter; Weston
Staffordshire and Worcestershire Canal, 793 n
Stainbridge (Staynbridge), in Corse, 440
Staintway, see Stantway
Stairs, see Stears
Stalbridge (Dors.), 5
Stancombe (Stancomb), in Stinchcombe, 936*, 937, 1116, 1168, 1169*, 1214, 1216, 1535
Stancombe (Stoncomb) Wood, in Winchcombe, 1473
Standish (Standysch), 534, 565 n, 663*, 696 n, 711 n, 1054*, 1099, **1128–32**, 1218, 1440; residents, 669, 677, 832, 950, 980*, 981*, 1006, 1137, 1181, 1433*, 1437*; Standish Park, 1131; and see Beacon Hill; Bridge, the; Oxlinch; Putloe
Stanley [unspecified], 280, 450, 908
Stanley (Standley), in Blaisdon, 214, 215*
Stanley, in Bremhill (Wilts.), abbey, 1385*
Stanley, in Winterbourne, 1489
Stanley, King's (King Standly, King Stanley), 384, 961, 1021*, 1027, **1133–40**, 1185, 1218; residents, 398, 983, 1006, 1145*, 1182, 1212, 1510*, 1530; Stanley Mills, 1136, 139; and see Dudbridge; Peaked Elm; Selsley
Stanley, Leonard (Stanley, Stanley St. Leonard), 5, 484, 529, 631, **1141–7**, 1183, 1184, 1216, 1218; priory, 65, 66, 278, 414, 497, 532, 558, 1101*, 1146, 1147*, 1369; and see Hanley, St. Leonard's
Stanley Pontlarge (Standley, Standly, Stanley), 708 n, **1148**, 1335*, 1464, 1465*, 1476
Stanmore (Herts., recte Mdx.), 905
Stanshawe (Stanshaw) and Stanshawes Place or Court, in Yate, 1119, 1120, 1451, 1543, 1547, 1550*
Stanton (Staunton) (Kiftsgate hund.), 586, 1103, 1104*, 1132, **1149–51**, 1189
Stanton, near Newland, see Staunton
Stanton (Worcs.), see Staunton
Stanton Drew (Som.), 823
Stanton Lacy (Stanton Lacey) (Salop.), 825
Stanton Prior (Stanton Priors, Stanton Priory) (Som.), 829 n, 1337
Stantway (Staintway), in Westbury on Severn, 1393, 1396*, 1397*, 1398, 1401, 1402*, 1403
Stanway, 684, 1148, **1152–4**, 1190, 1291, 1334, 1335, 1443*, 1476, 1504; Church Stanway, 1153*; Stanway Hall, 1153*, 1154; Wood Stanway, 891, 1152*, 1153*, 1154; and see Coscombe; Hornsleasow; Stanwell; Taddington
Stanwell [? Stanway], 79
Stanwell (Mdx.), 79, 525, 648
Staplehurst (Kent), 44; and see Bly Court
Stapleton, 3, 45, 471, 745, 836, **1155–60**, 1170, 1175, 1427, 1490*, 1554; Stapleton House, 1160; and see Bishopstone; Easton; Fishponds; Heath House; Oldbury; Ridgeway
Stardens, in Newent, 894*, 898, 905
Stares, see Stears
Stars Mead House, in Haresfield, 672
Staughton, Great (Stoughton) (Hunts.), 696
Staunton (Kiftsgate hundred), see Stanton
Staunton (Stanton), near Newland, 478 n, 479 n, 917, 921, 1054, **1161–2**, 1345; and see Broadstones; Cherry Orchard; High Meadow; Hill House
Staunton (Stanton) (Worcs.), 142, 149, 150, 442, 546, 680, 786, 860, 899, 1399*
Staure, see Stears
Staverton, 228*, 397, 482 n, 585, **1163–5**, 1291*, 1355, 1356, 1388; Staverton Court, 1164, 1165; Staverton House, 1164
Staynbridge, see Stainbridge
Stean Bridge (Steanbridge), in Bisley or Miserden, 197, 1214*, 1215, 1217
Stears (Stairs, Stares, Staure), in Newnham, 927, 933, 1401
Stedcote, see Stidcot
Steepingleé, see Steppingley
Steeple Ashton, see Ashton, Steeple
Steeple Bumpstead, see Bumpstead, Steeple
Sten Meadow, in Longney, 827
Stepleaston, see Ashton, Steeple
Stepney (Mdx.), 631*, 1501; and see Whitechapel
Steppingley (Steepingleé) (Beds.), 838
Stidcot (Stedcote), in Tytherington, 1326, 1327*, 1328, 1329
Still House, the, in Ampney St. Mary, 62
Stinchcombe, 50, 166, 277*, 305 n, 536, 561, **1166–9**, 1525; and see Brownings; Clingre; Inwoods; Lorridge; Melksham; Newham Quar; Peers Court; Stancombe
Stock, the [? in Berkeley], 167*, 176
Stock, the, in Newland, 922
Stockton (Wilts.), 1337
Stockwell, in Cowley, 447, 448, 1484
Stodley, see Studley (Oxon.); Studley (Warws.)
Stoke [East Stoke] (Notts.), 325 n
Stoke, Harry (Harrystoke, Stokehenry), in Stoke Gifford, 602*, 1172
Stoke Bishop, in Westbury on Trym, 825, 1405*, 1409*, 1411, 1415*, 1419, 1420*
Stoke by Clare (Stoke Clare) (Suff.), college, 1217
Stoke D'Abernon (Stoke) (Surr.), 665*
Stoke Gifford (Stoke, Stoke Giffard), 41, 603, 1020, 1156, **1170–2**, 1491; residents, 46, 47*, 48*, 122, 509, 612, 615, 720*, 730, 798, 1020, 1158, 1369, 1413*; Stoke House, 1172; and see Stoke, Harry; Tillies Court; Wallscourt

Stoke Lacy (Herefs.), 1279

Stoke Newington (London or Mdx.), Abney Park Cemetery, 1193

Stoke next Guildford (Stoke) (Surr.), 786

Stoke Orchard (Stoke, Stoke Archer), in Bishop's Cleeve, 391 n, 393, 1051, 1287, 1431; residents, 118*, 396, 397, 398*, 399, 1164, 1231, 1232

Stoke Prior (Herefs. or Worcs.), 1290

Stoke Rochford (Lincs.), 834

Stoke-upon-Trent (Stoke) (Staffs.), 325 n

Stoncomb Wood, see Stancombe Wood

Stone, 154, 159, 170, 453, 1097, **1173-7**, 1438, 1546; Lower Stone (Lowerstone), 1018, 1173, 1174, 1175*, 1176; Upper Stone, 1176; and see New Park; Old Court; Pedington; Woodlands

Stone (Kent), 44

Stone Bench, in Elmore, 582

Stonehouse, 1008, 1020, 1072, 1169, **1178-87**, 1218; residents, 77, 95, 112, 560*, 562, 564, 583, 668, 830*, 851, 871, 1006, 1007*, 1008, 1137*, 1143, 1145*, 1146, 1189, 1191, 1433, 1437, 1494, 1508, 1528; and see Berryfield; Bridgend; Cainscross; Coneham; Dudbridge; Ebley; Hayward's End; Haywardsfield; Oldend; Ryeford

Stoneleigh (Warws.), 1332

Stonesfield (Stunsfield) (Oxon.), 357 n

Stoney (Stony) Hill, in Brimpsfield, 253, 254

Stoughton (Leics.), 827 n

Stoughton (Hunts.), see Staughton, Great

Stoulton (Worcs.), 1432

Stour, river, 400*

Stour Provost (Stour Provis) (Dors.), 978

Stourbridge (Worcs.), 857, 1024

Stourden, see Sturden

Stourton (Warws.), 573

Stoutshill, in Uley, 1367, 1369

Stow Nine Churches, see Stowe, Church

Stow on the Wold (Stow, Stow St. Edwards), 640, 1016, 1090, 1092, **1188-97**, 1218, 1474; and see Donnington; Maugersbury

Stowe (Stow) and Stowe Grange, in Newland or St. Briavels, 249, 917, 923*

Stowe, Church (Stow Nine Churches) (Northants.), 607

Stowell, 321, 369, **643-5**, **1198**, 1501, 1542

Stowfield, in English Bicknor, 191

Stowick, in Henbury, 717, 721*, 722, 745

Stratford, Old (Warws.), 1392

Stratford Abbey and Stratford House [? Stratford Park], in Stroud, 618, 1208, 1215

Stratford-on-Avon (Warws.), 66, 400, 849, 988, 1392, 1458; and see Bridgetown; Shottery

Stratton, 366, 459, 990, 1062, 1141, 1145, **1199-1202**, 1256

Streatham (Strentham) (Surr.), 827 n, 829 n, 1460; and see Balham

Stretton on Fosse (Warws.), 218, 295

Strigoul (Strigul), see Chepstow

Stringer's, in Rodborough, 1024, 1026, 1027

Stroat, in Tidenham, 1318, 1321*, 1323

Stroud (Stroude), 195, 1024, 1139, **1203-18**; burial, 1026; residents: apothecary, 204, 1023; butcher,

659; clerk, 204; clothier, 202, 448, 658*, 972, 981, 1024*, 1182; dyer, 1025; millwright, 622; saddler, 1025; victualler, 97; occupation unstated, 202, 203*, 204, 283, 448, 563, 633, 659, 660, 670, 752, 814, 973, 975*, 976, 980, 981*, 1008*, 1024, 1025*, 1026*, 1140, 1143, 1179, 1183*, 1186, 1412, 1413, 1477, 1484, 1512, 1516, 1526; and see Badbrook; Bourne, the; Bowbridge; Brimscombe; Farm Hill; Fields, the; Grease Gate; Ham; Knapp, the; Lodgemore; Lypiatt, Lower; New House; New Mills; Newhouse; Paganhill; Quar House; Roadways, the; Ruscombe; Slad; Stratford Abbey; Stroudwater; Thrupp; Toadsmoor; Whiteshill

Stroud End, in Painswick, 973

Stroudwater (Stroud Water), in Stroud, 638 n, 648, 1115, 1118

Stroudwater (Stroud) Canal, 792 n, 793 n, 1054*, 1187, 1218, 1440*

Stroudwater or Frome, river, 195, 252, 449, 497, 525, 556, 574, 1440*

Studley (Stodley) (Oxon.), priory, 1078, 1238

Studley (Stodley) (Warws.), priory, 1043, 1078, 1238, 1501, 1502

Stunsfield, see Stonesfield

Sturden (Stourden, Sturdon), in Winterbourne, 833, 1486, 1489, 1490, 1491

Stuston (Suff.), 437

Sudeley (Shudely, Sudely, Sudley), 635, 894 n, 1148, **1219-21**, 1334, 1363, 1473, 1475*, 1476, 1477; residents, 309, 361, 596, 634, 641*, 684, 704, 816, 1287, 1335, 1382, 1464*, 1468, 1471*, 1473, 1477, 1501; Sudeley Castle, 27, 1219, 1220, 1473, 1478, 1487; Sudeley Manor, 1471*; and see Wadfield

Sudgrove (Sutgrove), in Gloucester or Miserden, 800, 878, 879, 880*

Sudley, see Sudeley

Suffolk, see Barking; Chediston; Elmsett; Exning; Ipswich; Nether Hall; Stoke by Clare; Stuston; Ubbeston

Sugwas (Suggewas) (Herefs.), 1058

Sulla (Sulley, Sully), see Soilwell

Sundayshill (Sunday Hill), in Falfield, 1307, 1312

Sunninghill (Berks.), 801

Surinam (East Indies), 1303

Surrenden-Dering (Surronden-Dering), in Pluckley (Kent), 723, 724

Surrey, 162, 595, 827 n, 829 n, 997, 1059, 1492, 1493; and see Addington; Balham; Barnes; Battersea; Beddington; Bermondsey; Camberwell; Carshalton; Cheam; Christchurch; Clapham; Croydon; Dorking; Farnham; Guildford; Horne; Kingston upon Thames; Lambeth; Langley; Malden; Merton; Mitcham; Morden; Mortlake; Newington; Peckham; Petersham; Putney; Reigate; Richmond; Rotherhithe; Sheen; Southwark; Stoke D'Abernon; Stoke next Guildford; Streatham; Sutton; Tooting; Waddon; Wandsworth; Wimbledon

Surronden-Dering, *see* Surrenden-Dering

Sussex, 595, 739, 851; *and see* Ardingly; Arundel; Battle; Bexhill; Billingshurst; Chichester; Ebernoe; Firle; Hastings; Horsham; Iwood; Parham; Poynings; Rye; St. Leonards; Telscombe; Trotton; Wadhurst; Warbleton; Winchelsea; Woolbeding; Worth

Sutgrove, *see* Sudgrove

Sutton [*unspecified*], 1250

Sutton (Surr.), 827 n

Sutton, Bishop (Som.), 941

Sutton Benger (Sutton Bangor) (Wilts.), 537

Sutton Bourne [*unidentified*] (Som.), 897

Sutton St. Nicholas (Sutton near Hereford) (Herefs.), 919

Sutton under Brailes (Sutton under Brayles), **1222–3**, 1330, 1331*

Sutton upon Lown [*unidentified*] (Northumb.), 209

Swailley, in Forthampton, 609

Swainswick (Swanswick) (Som.), 311 n; *and see* Tadwick

Swalcliffe (Oxon.), 850; *and see* Sibbard

Swanley, in Alkington, 175, 176

Swansea (Swansey) (Glam.), 169

Swanswick, *see* Swainswick

Sweden, 952

Swell, Lower (Nether Swell, Netherswelle), 79*, 235, 445, 708 n, 816 n, 1017, 1191, 1197, **1224–8**; Swell Wold (Swell Old), 1224, 1226; *and see* Bowl Farm

Swell, Upper, 1000, 1191*, 1192, **1224–8**

Swilgate (Swillyate, Swilyate), river, 585, 982

Swinbrook (Oxon.), 1441*

Swindon (Swyndown), 338, 339, 396, 586, 611, 640, 800, **1229–33**, 1402, 1440; Swindon Hall, 1231

Swindon (Wilts.), 504, 636

Swinford [*unidentified*] (Warws.), 1265

Swinford, Old (Worcs.), 820

Swinhay, in North Nibley, 938

Switzerland, 739; *and see* Lausanne; Ouchy; St. Gallen

Swynburne Bridge, in North Nibley, 154

Swyndown, *see* Swindon

Syde (Side), 523, 878, **1083**; *and see* High Croft

Syenhall [*unidentified*], 1189

Sylva [*unidentified*], 1238

Symond's Hall (Simonds Hall, Symondshall), in Wotton under Edge, 1365, 1524, 1536, 1537*, 1538*, 1539

Syon (Sion) (Mdx.), abbey, 91, 324, 525, 648, 649, 651, 1091, 1225

Syreford (Sierford) and Syreford Farm, in Whittington, 1077, 1445*

Tadcaster, *see* Newton, in Tadcaster

Taddington (Tadington), in Stanway, 1152, 1153*

Tadwick (Tatwick), in Swainswick (Som.), 82

Tafarn-bach inn, in Charfield, 305

Tainton, *see* Taynton

Talton (Gadlington or Talkon), in Tredington (Worcs.), 402

Tangley Farm, in Bruern (Oxon.), 235

Taplow, *see* Huntercombe

Tarbes (Nivelle Tarbes) (France), 1303

Tarlton (Tarleton, Terleton, Torleton), in Rodmarton, 445, 446, 1028*, 1029*, 1030*, 1032*, 1033*, 1049*, 1050*, 1202, 1207

Tarrant Hinton (Dors.), 937

Tatwick, *see* Tadwick

Taunton (Som.), 536, 1321

Taye, Great, *see* Tey, Great

Taynton (Tainton), 133, 466, 821, 894 n, 903, **1233–8**, 1315*, 1317; Great Taynton, 1237*; Little Taynton, 1237*, 1238*; Taynton House, 1235*, 1237; *and see* Brass Mill; Grove, the; Hownhall; Winsford Bridge

Taynton (Oxon.), 136, 856

Teddington (Worcs.), 1051, 1386

Telscombe (Tellescomb) (Suss.), 827 n

Templars, Knights, *see* Jerusalem

Temple, Inner and Middle, the Temple, *see* London, Inns of Court

Temple Guiting, *see* Guiting, Temple

Tenby (Pemb.), 413

Terleton, *see* Tarlton

Terling, *see* Ridley Hall

Tetbury (Tettebury), 372, 534, 778 & n, 1070*, 1147, **1239–59**; residents, 92*, 202, 368, 417, 562, 780, 910, 970*, 1071*, 1185, 1396, 1453; Tetbury Upton (Upton), 1245, 1253*, 1255*, 1257, 1259; Upton Grove, 1247; *and see* Charlton; Doughton; Elmestree; Grange, the; Highfield; Northey

Tew, Great (Oxon.), 401, 1066, 1153

Tewkesbury (Theokesbury), 72, 872, **1260–93**, 1311, 1312, 1334, 1357, 1362, 1381*; abbey, 481 & n, 1285, 1287, 1290; abbey church, 609 n; abbey, estate, 56, 228, 430, 436*, 440, 568, 585, 586, 588, 593, 609, 710, 801, 802, 804*, 833, 838*, 1132*, 1148, 1153*, 1154, 1165*, 1227, 1228, 1285*, 1288*, 1289, 1291*, 1311, 1312*, 1313, 1331*, 1348*, 1355*, 1356, 1362*, 1381*, 1382*, 1387, 1388*, 1402, 1419, 1476, 1504*; battle, 493, 497, 570, 1123; church, 1359, 1381; civil war, 894 n, 1314; death at, 391 n, 940; lordship or manor, 400, 609, 763, 1309, 1348, 1361, 1381*, 1475; residents, 73, 74, 266, 317, 335, 398, 485*, 595, 872, 898, 1352, 1354, 1360, 1382, 1441, 1474; Tewkesbury Lodge, 1265*, 1287*, 1289*; Tewkesbury Park, 1280*, 1281, 1287*, 1288; vicar, 71, 1348*, 1525*; *and see* Cloveshoe; Gupshill; Holme Castle; Long Bridge, the; Mythe, the, and Mythe Hook; Oldbury, the; Southwick

Tey (Taye), Great (Essex), 440

Thames (Thamesis), river, 56, 366 n, 565 n, 791, 793 n, 1027; *and see* Isis

Thames and Severn Canal, 197, 301, 445, 792 & n, 793 n, 1052, 1083, 1218

Theescombe, in Minchinhampton, 648*, 651, 655*, 1127, 1512

Theokesbury, *see* Tewkesbury

Thornbury, 52, 160, 367, 588 n, 839, 955, 957, 1202, **1294–1314**, 1328, 1329; residents, 46*, 455*, 703, 738, 741, 825, 1109, 1325, 1429, 1543; Thornbury Castle, 1309, 1310; Thornbury Park, 1303, 1311, 1313; *and see* Avening; Buckover; Eastwood; Falfield; Hobeland; Hope; Kingston; Kington; Kirton; Kyneton; Marlwood; Morton; Oldbury upon Severn; Park Mill; Parks, the; Sibland; Southfield; Woolford

Thornbury (Devon), 903

Thorndean (Thornden), in Withington, 1501*

Thornhaugh (Thornhough) (Northants.), 768, 1263

Thornhill Farm, in Lechlade, 796

Thornhough, *see* Thornhaugh

Thornton (Bucks.), 496, 665

Thornton, in Nether Eatington (Warws.), 1277

Thornton Hall [? in Norham] (co. Dur., later Northumb.), 330

Thorpe Lubenham Hall (Lubbenham Hall, Thorp) (Northants.), 1232

Thorverton, *see* Traymill

Thraxton, *see* Thruxton

Throckmorton, in Fladbury (Worcs.), 1340

Throp, the, *see* Thrupp

Througham (Drusham, Trowham), in Bisley, 197, 201*, 202, 1214

Thrupp (the Throp, the Thrupp), in Stroud, 1206*, 1207, 1208*, 1209, 1216*

Thruxton (Thraxton) (Herefs.), 1515

Tibberton (Tiberton), 683, 809, 831, 1236, 1238, **1315–17**; Tibberton Court, 1316, 1317, 1369; *and see* Winsford Bridge

Tibblestone (Tibboldstone), the, in Beckford, 147; hundred, 147, 743

Tibboth Farm [*unidentified*, ? in Cranham], 449

Tiberton, *see* Tibberton

Tichborne (Hants), 755

Tidenham (Tiddenham), 736, **1318–23**, 1381; Tidenham House, 1320*, 1323; *and see* Anwards; Beachley; Bishton; Buttington Tump; Church End; Day House, the; Hanley; Madgett; Outham; Pill House; St. Tiriac; Sedbury; Stroat; Tutshill; Wallhope; Wibdon

Tilbury (Tylbury) (Essex), 451, 853

Tillies Court (Tillie Cote), in Stoke Gifford, 1172

Tillingham (Essex), 366

Tillingham (Lincs.), *see* Fillingham

Tilsdown (Tillsdown), in Cam, 535, 536

Tingle Stone, the, in Avening, 92

Tintern (Tinterne, Tinton, Tyntera, Tynterne) (Mon.), 735; abbey, 732, 778*, 1322, 1513

Tirle (Turl) brook, 71, 1387

Tirley (Trinley, Turley) and Haw, 115, 482, 686, 687, 871, 977, 1265, 1291*, **1352–6**; *and see* Corse Court; Cumberwood; Haw, the; Rye; Sandpits; Wigwood Farm

Titchmarsh (Northants.), 1015

Titherington, *see* Tytherington

Tiverton, *see* Chettiscombe

Tixall (Staffs.), 520, 717

Toadsmoor (Toadesmore, Todesmore) and Toadsmoor Bottom, in Stroud, 204, 1210*, 1214*, 1216

Tobago (West Indies), 962, 1109

Tockenham (Tokenham, Tokenham Wick) (Wilts.), 342, 343

Tockington (Tockenton), in Olveston, 45, 49*, 52*, 577, 960*, 961*, 962*, 1018, 1225, 1296, 1307*, 1311

Tocknells, in Painswick, 971

Toddington (Todington, Todynton, Tuddington), 708 n, 709, 866, 1148*, 1221, **1332–5**, 1475; residents, 309, 318, 660, 710, 1153, 1468*

Todenham, **1329–31**; *and see* Lemington, Upper

Todesmore, *see* Toadsmoor

Todington (Todynton), *see* Toddington

Tog Hill, in Wick and Abson, 6

Tokenham, *see* Tockenham

Toller Porcorum, *see* Collioporum

Tong, near Bradford (Yorks. W.R.), Tong Hall, 1231

Tooting (Surr.), 220 n, 827 n

Topcroft (Norf.), 1525

Torleton, *see* Tarlton

Tormarton, 19, 758, 823*, **1336–9**

Torquay (Devon), 1221

Tortworth, 160, 173, 1051*, **1340–6**, 1455, 1512; residents, 52, 305, 308, 810, 920, 959, 1105, 1107, 1108, 1176, 1299, 1304*, 1306, 1333, 1454; Tortworth Court, 1344; *and see* Avening

Totenham Court, *see* Tottenham Court

Totnes (Totness) (Devon), 1115, 1231

Tottenham (Totenham) Court, in St. Pancras (London or Mdx.), 811

Toulouse (France), 1303

Tournai (Tournay) (Belgium), 605 n

Tours (France), 935, 1327

Tower Hill, in Tytherington, 1325

Tower of London, *see* London, buildings

Tracy Park Lodge, in Doynton, 487

Trafalgar (Spain), 1245

Trajectus (Roman station), 53, 205, 405

Traymill (Tremill), in Thorverton (Devon), 667

Trebarried, near Talgarth (Brec.), 728

Tredegar (Mon.), 592

Tredington, 1268, 1287, 1289, 1290*, 1291, **1346–8**, 1356, 1381; residents, 73, 610, 674, 1231, 1382, 1402

Tredington (Worcs.), 989, 1458; *and see* Armscote; Newbold on Stour; Talton

Tredworth, in Gloucester, 852

Tregate (Trigett), in Llanrothal (Herefs.), 1530

Tregynon, *see* Gregynog

Trelough [? Trelleck (Mon.)], 789

Tremill, *see* Traymill

Treowen, in Mitchel Troy (Mon.), 920

Trepenkennet, *see* Trippenkennet

Trerice (Treris, Trerise), in Newlyn (Cornw.), 1297*

Tresham, in Hawkesbury, 36, 241, 695*, 696*, 697, 699*, 701*, 702, 911, 1118 ('Wilts.', in error)

Trewsbury, in Coates, 445

Trier, *see* Trye

Trigett, *see* Tregate

Trillgate (Trillyate, Trillyeat), in Painswick, 970, 971, 972

Trim, *see* Trym

Trinidad (West Indies), 1511

Trinity College, Cambridge, 290, 898

Trinity College, Oxford, 233 n, 287, 295, 363 n, 436, 518 & n, 993, 1145, 1513

Trinley, *see* Tirley

Trippenkennet (Trepenkennet, Tripenkennet), in St. Weonards (Herefs.), 917, 921, 1161

Troarn (Troar, Troarne) (Normandy), priory, 747, 1440

Trotton (Trotten) (Suss.), 560

Trowbridge (Wilts.), 537

Trowham, *see* Througham

Troy, Mitchel (Michaelstroy) (Mon.), 733; *and see* Treowen

Truckford [? Twyford, in Adderbury] (Oxon.), 1084

Trull Farm, in Cherington, 1031, 1033

Trye [? Trier, Germany], 665

Trym (Trim), river, 745

Tuddington, *see* Toddington

Tudmoor, in Siddington, 1083

Tuffley (Tuffliegh, Tufley), in Gloucester, 713, 714, 716, 1377, 1380, 1433; Tuffley Court, 1434

Tunley, in Bisley, 197, 201

Tunstall (Salop., ? *recte* Staffs.), 428

Tupsley (Tuppisley) (Herefs.), 1058

Turkdean, 37, 688, 705, 947, **1349–51**

Turkey, 162, 1073; *and see* Constantinople

Turl brook, *see* Tirle brook

Turley, *see* Tirley

Turners Court, in Cold Ashton, 80

Turnworth (Dors.), 1077

Turvyl Aston, *see* Acton Turville

Tusmore, in Hardwick with Tusmore (Oxon.), 484, 1446

Tutshill, in Tidenham, 1322*

Twickenham (Mdx.), 1440

Twigworth, in Gloucester, 514*, 1046

Twinhoe (Twyniho), in Wellow (Som.), 1077

Twining (Twinning), *see* Twyning

Twyford, *see* Truckford

Twyniho, *see* Twinhoe

Twyning (Twining, Twinning), 1269*, 1287, 1288*, 1291, **1357–63**, 1381, 1419; *and see* Puckrup; Shuthonger

Tylbury, *see* Tilbury

Tyley, in Wotton under Edge, 1367

Tyntera (Tynterne), *see* Tintern

Tytherington (Titherington), 52*, 957, 1029*, 1107, 1311, **1324–9**, 1426*, 1452; *and see* Bradston; Itchington; Stidcot; Tower Hill

Ubbeston (Suff.), 431

Uckington (Hockington, Okynton), in Elmstone Hardwicke, 336, 482 n, 585 & n, 586*, 1165, 1229, 1291, 1355

Ufton (Uffeton) (Warws.), 583

Uley (Euly, Eweley, Ewley, Uly), 1136, 1147, **1365–70**; residents, 203, 419, 496, 576, 696, 720, 747, 783, 955, 1133, 1136, 1137, 1138*, 1437, 1529, 1536; *and see* Bencombe; Stoutshill; Wresden

Ullingswick (Willingswyke) (Herefs.), 449

Ullington, in Pebworth, 979

Uly, *see* Uley

United States of America, 1073, 1119; *and see* America, North; Boston; Newburgh

University College, Oxford, 297*, 799

Unlawater, fishery in the Severn, 1403

Untercomb, *see* Huntercombe

Up-Atherley, *see* Hatherley, Up

Upcote, in Withington, 1061, 1501*

Upham (Hants), 1031

Upham, in Aldbourne (Wilts.), 1431

Uphatherley, *see* Hatherley, Up

Upleadon, 895, 1237, 1238, 1315, **1371–2**; *and see* Leden

Upper Grange, in Painswick, 1208

Upperend (Noverend), in Woolaston, 1514

Upthorpe (Upper Cam, Upthrop), in Cam, 277*, 281, 282*

Upton, *see* Tetbury; Tetbury Upton

Upton [in Hazelor or Ratley and Upton] (Warws.), 220 n, 1066

Upton Bishop (Upton Bishey) (Herefs.), 964, 1058

Upton Cheyney (Upton), in Bitton, 205, 208, 210*

Upton Grove, *see* Tetbury; Tetbury Upton, 1247

Upton Helions, *see* Creedy

Upton Old (Upton Wold), in Blockley, 220*, 224, 225*

Upton Scudamore (Upton Skidmore) (Wilts.), 210

Upton St. Leonards, 131, 259, 367, 511, 583, 1044, 1181, **1373–9**, 1380, 1434*; *and see* Bowden Hall; Kimsbury; Saintbridge; Sneedham; Whitley Court

Upton-on-Severn (Worcs.), 1270, 1293; Berry Court estate, 1291

Upton Skidmore, *see* Upton Scudamore

Upton Wold, *see* Upton Old

Usa, *see* Ouse

Usk (Mon.), priory, 511, 798, 1370

Utica, *see* St. Evroult

Uttoxeter (Staffs.), 549

Val, *see* Waal

Vale Royal (Ches.), 1522

Vatch Mill [? in Bisley], 1211, 1215

Venta Silurum, *see* Caerwent

Vergenia, *see* Virginia

Versailles (France), 1119

Vetelingiana, via, see Watling Street

Victoria, *see* Vittoria

Vigo (Spain), 1528

Vilvoorde (Filford, Vilvord) (Belgium), 305 n, 1123

Vine, the, *see* Vyne, the

Vineyard, the, in Highnam, 349 n

Virginia (Vergenia) (North America), 47, 401, 408, 539, 1170, 1565; *and see* James river; King George County; Rhapahanock River; Williamsburg

Vittoria (Victoria) (Spain), 1303
Vyne (Vine), the, in Sherborne St. John (Hants), 1493

Waal (Val) (Flanders), 431
Waddon (Whaddon), in Croydon (Surr.), 1057
Wadfield and Wadfield Farm, in Sudeley, 706, 1471
Wadham College, Oxford, 233 n, 771, 1093, 1125, 1126*, 1127*, 1190, 1390, 1526
Wadhurst (Suss.), 376*, 431
Wainload Hill, in Norton, 339
Walbridg, see Wallbridge
Walcop, see Wallhope
Walcot, in Bath (Som.), 555
Walcot (Walcott), in Charlbury (Oxon.), 223, 695
Walden, Saffron, see Audley End
Walden Court, in Newent, 894
Wales, 651, 672, 719, 793 n, 806 n, 927, 937, 1123, 1253, 1312, 1321, 1486; Marches of, 230 n, 289; North, 116; South, 428 n, 1356
Walesworth, see Wallsworth
Walford [? in Horsley], 749
Walford (Herefs.), 536, 918*, 920, 1039*, 1235*, 1236; Walford Court, 915; and see Cobrey; Howle Hill
Walforde, see Woolford
Walgaston (Wallgasson), in Hamfallow, 170
Walingoford, see Wallingford
Wallbridge (Walbridg), in Rodborough, 558, 792 n, 793 n, 1006, 1027, 1209, 1211, 1212, 1213
Walles, see Wallscourt
Walleswood [? Wallsworth, in Sandhurst], 1139*
Wallgasson, see Walgaston
Wallhope (Walcop), in Tidenham, 1319, 1323
Wallingford (Walingoford, Walyngford) (Berks.), 707 n, 791, 793 n, 1482; honour of, 341, 612, 816, 1015, 1047, 1350*
Wallison, see Falaise
Wallop, Nether (Hants), 967
Wallscourt (Walles), in Stoke Gifford, 1020
Wallsworth (Walesworth) and Wallsworth Hall, in Sandhurst, 449, 1047*; and see Walleswood
Wally Farm, see Whalley Farm
Walmore (Walmer, Wolmore), in Westbury on Severn, 605 n, 1402, 1403*, 1404
Walmore (Walmore's) Hill, in Westbury on Severn, 1393
Walsingham (co. Dur.), see Wolsingham
Walsingham (Norf.), abbey, 236
Waltham [unspecified] (Essex), 515
Waltham, Great (Much Waltham) (Essex), 281
Waltham Holy Cross (Essex), 1391
Waltham St. Lawrence, see Billingbear
Walton, see Deerhurst: Deerhurst Walton
Walton Cardiff, 74*, 1271*, 1272, 1274, 1287, 1289, 1291, 1311, **1380–2**
Walyngford, see Wallingford
Wanborough (Wanbrough) (Wilts.), 1028, 1432
Wandsworth (Surr.), 827 n*, 829 n
Wanswell, in Hamfallow, 419, 536; Wanswell Court, 52, 159, 165*, 168, 172, 173, 175*

Wapley and Codrington, **1383–5**, 1550; Wapley, 36, 496, 1071, 1110*, 1426*, 1490, 1546; and see Codrington; Mousewell
Warbleton (Suss.), 827 n, 829 n; and see Iwood
Warburg [? recte Marburg] (Germany), 410
Ware (Herts.), 739
Waresley (Waresleie) (Hunts.), 714
Waresley, in Hartlebury (Worcs.), 1368
Warminster (Wilts.), 823
Warmley, in Siston, 1084, 1087
Warren (the Warrens), in Lydney, 246
Warren, the, in Aston Ingham (Herefs.), 789
Warren, the, in Wotton under Edge, 1536
Warwick (Virginia), see James River
Warwick (Warws.), 66, 287, 539, 988, 1119, 1287, 1478, 1522
Warwickshire, 43, 54, 86, 547, 634 n, 804 n, 876, 920, 997, 1223, 1331, 1392; and see under names of separate places
Washbourne (Washborne) [unspecified], 1153, 1504
Washbourne (Washbourn, Washburn), Great, 1051, **1386–7**
Washbourne (Washbourn), Little, **1387**
Waste, Le, in Hawkesbury, 696, 697
Water Eaton, see Eaton, Water
Water's End, see Scarr, the
Watercross (Waters-Cross), in Ruardean, 1038*
Waterdines, in Newent, 904
Waterford (Irel.), 78*, 331, 994, 1078
Watermoor, in Cirencester, 357
Waters-Cross, see Watercross
Watford, see Cassiobury
Watling Street (via Vetelingiana), 366 n
Watlington, see Greenfield
Watsome (Watson), in Kingswood (formerly Wilts.), 308, 781
Weare (Were) (Som.), 720
Webb's Heath, in Siston, 1087
Wedmore, see Mudgley
Week, see Wick, in Alkington
Welch Newton, see Newton, Welsh
Welford (Berks.), see Weston
Welford, in Kempsford, see Whelford
Welford on Avon (Welford, Wellford), 482 n, 1355, **1388–90**, 1391*, 1392*; and see Bickmarsh; Dorsington, Little
Well House, in Doynton, 489
Well, the, in Painswick, 973, 974
Welle, see Wells
Wellesbourne (Wellsborne) Mountford (Warws.), 1149, 1151
Wellford, see Welford on Avon
Wellington (Som.), 1367*
Wellow (Som.), 1407*; and see Twinhoe
Wells (Welle) (Som.), 7*, 237, 392 n, 406, 771, 809, 964, 994, 1408; and see Bath and Wells
Wellsbourne Mountford, see Wellesbourne Mountford
Welsh Newton, see Newton, Welsh
Welton (Northants.), Welton Place, 1184
Wem (Salop.), 1219
Wentworth (Yorks. W.R.), 409; Wentworth Woodhouse, 643

Were, *see* Weare

West Hall (Westhall), in High Legh (Highleigh) (Ches.), 258

West Hood, *see* Westwood

West Indies (Western Islands), 254, 724, 1303, 1564, 1576; *and see* Barbados; Cuba; Grenada; Jamaica; Leeward Islands; Martinique; Santo Domingo; Tobago; Trinidad

West Saxons, king of, 1461

West Town, *see* Westend Town

Westal, in Cheltenham, 325

Westbury [*unspecified*], 652, 975, 1508

Westbury on Severn (Westbury, Westburie in the Forest), 469 n, 759 n, 805 n, 806 n, 870, 890, 925, 928, 929, **1393–1404**; hundred, 242; residents, 70, 175, 215, 352*, 354*, 677, 832*, 871, 930, 931, 933*, 1133, 1299*, 1530; Westbury Court (Westbury House), 1393, 1401, 1404; *and see* Adsett; Base Court; Bollow; Boseley; Bourton House; Broad Oak; Broken Cross; Bury Court; Chaxhill; Cleeve; Denny; Elton; Gatwick; Grange, the; Grove, the; Hardens; Heald, the; Ley; Longcroft; Moys Hill; Northwood; Poultons Hill; Rodley; Sapina; Stantway; Walmore; Walmore Hill

Westbury on Trym (Westbury, Westbury upon Trim), 435, 578, 721*, 728, 730*, 731*, 832, **1405–20**, 1428; college, 195*, 391, 394, 403, 502, 816, 1078, 1217, 1256, 1291, 1350, 1419, 1420, 1501, 1519; *and see* Canford; Downhouse; Hencroft; Henleaze; Pen Park; Redland; Sneyd Park; Southmead; Stoke Bishop

Westcoats [*unidentified*] (Leics.), 257

Westcote (Westcot), 1016, 1189, **1421–2**

Westend, in Eastington, 538

Westend, in Wickwar, 1449, 1450*, 1451*, 1454*, 1455, 1456, 1543

Westend Town (West Town) or Little or Old Marshfield or St. Pancras, in Marshfield, 839

Westerleigh (Westonleigh), **1423–8**; residents, 10, 11, 15, 16*, 100, 308, 489, 994, 995, 1112, 1384, 1452, 1454, 1548; *and see* Blackberry Farm; Coalpit Heath; Mayshill; Nibley; Says Farm; Serridge

Western Islands, *see* West Indies

Westfield, the, in Hawling, 706

Westfield Farm, in Guiting Power, 891

Westhall, *see* West Hall

Westington, in Chipping Campden, 287, 293*

Westminster, abbey, 361 n, 607, 991, 1402; abbey, estate, 228, 230, 440, 481 n, 482*, 585, 684*, 882*, 1223*, 1331*, 1355*; bishop, 1331*; cathedral, 447; chapel of the Broadway, 168; courts, 494, 682, 920, 1463; hospitals, Grey Coat and Blue Coat, 607; parish of St. James, 86, 259 n; parish of St. Margaret, 273; record office, 475; residents, 238, 249, 1049; *and see* London: buildings; London, churches; London, streets

Westminster hundred, 482

Westmorland, 690, 720; *and see* Appleby; Docker; Kendal; Lowther

Westoe (co. Dur.), 409

Weston [? in Welford] (Berks.), 523

Weston [*unspecified*] (Herefs.), 1143, 1146, 1508

Weston (Staffs.), Weston Hall, 166

Weston [? Weston on Avon (Warws.)], 848

Weston (Weston Devon), in Branscombe (Devon), 411

Weston [*unspecified*], in Henbury, 1420

Weston, King's (Kingsweston), in Henbury, 576, 719*, 720, 721*, 722, 723*, 724*, 729*, 807

Weston, Lawrence, in Henbury, 720, 721*, 722, 729

Weston Birt, *see* Westonbirt

Weston Court, in Bitton, 205

Weston Devon, *see* Weston, in Branscombe

Weston Maudit (Weston Mauduyt), in Weston on Avon, 1392*

Weston on Avon, 1388, **1390–2**; *and see* Weston; Weston Maudit; Weston Sands

Weston Sands, in Weston on Avon, 1391*

Weston Subedge. 88, 864 n, 867, 1392, **1430–2**; Weston Park, 1430; *and see* Combe; Dover's Hill; Norton

Weston-super-Mare, *see* Oldmixon

Weston under Penyard (Weston) (Herefs.), 768, 789

Weston Underwood (Bucks.), 755

Westonbirt (Weston, Weston Birt, Westonburt), 757, 1009, 1070, 1074*, 1311, **1429**

Westonleigh, *see* Westerleigh

Westrip, in Randwick, 1181

Westwood (Worcs.), 1332

Westwood (West Hood), in Edgeworth, 575, 1214

Weymouth (Dors.), 1338

Whaddon, 264, 574 n, 711 n, 713, 885, 886, 1181, **1433–4**

Whaddon (Surr.), *see* Waddon

Whaddon (Wilts.), 842

Whalley, *see* Barcroft Hall

Whalley (Wally) Farm, in Whittington, 1445*

Wharf, the, in Awre, 101

Whatley (Wotley) (Som.), 1418

Wheatenhurst (Whitenhurst) or Whitminster, 625 n, 671, 747 n, 831, 1054, 1130, **1435–41**, 1505*; Whitminster Court or House, 1439*, 1440; *and see* Jackson's Farm

Whelford (Welford), in Kempsford, 769, 770

Whichford, *see* Ascott

Whichwood, *see* Wychwood

Whistones (Whitstan) (Worcs.), priory, 1392

Whitbourne (Whitbern) (Herefs.), 1058, 1061

Whitby (Yorks. N.R.), 560, 561

Whitchurch (Warws.), 988

Whitcomb, *see* Witcombe, Little

White Chappel, *see* Whitechapel

White Cliff (White Cleeve), *see* Whitecliff

White Cross, *see* Whitecross

White End, in Ashleworth, 75

White Hill [? in Chester-le-Street] (co. Dur.), 1368

White Lackington, *see* Lackington, White

Whitechapel (White Chappel), in Stepney (London or Mdx.), 1095

Whitecliff (White Cleeve, White Cliff), in Coleford, 811, 923*, 924

Whitecross (White Cross), the, in Lydney, 805
Whitefield, *see* Whitfield; Wightfield
Whitehall, *see* London, streets
Whitehaven (Cumb.), 1437
Whitenhurst, *see* Wheatenhurst
Whiteshill, in Stroud, 1217
Whiteshill, in Winterbourne, 1486
Whitewell, near White Hall Farm, in Seven-
    hampton, 1056 n
Whitfield (Whitefield), in Falfield, 1306, 1307*
Whitfield Farm, in Cromhall, 456
Whithington, *see* Withington
Whitley Court, in Upton St. Leonards, 1373,
    1377*, 1378
Whitley Park, in Wotton under Edge, 159
Whitminster, *see* Wheatenhurst
Whitney (Herefs.), 1423
Whitstan, *see* Whistones
Whitstone hundred, 559
Whittington, 329, 1061, 1077, 1078, **1442–5**; *and
    see* Syreford; Whalley Farm
Whitton (Witton), in Burford (Salop.), 1337*
Whixall (Wixhall) (Salop.), 755
Whorthorns, *see* Hoarthorns
Whyghtfylde, *see* Wightfield
Wibdon (Wibden), in Tidenham, 1318, 1319, 1321
Wicci (Wiccia, Wiccii), *see* Hwicci
Wicelcumbe, *see* Winchcombe
Wiche (Wich) [*unidentified*], 1119, 1153
Wichenford (Wickenford, Witchinford) (Worcs.),
    879, 1360
Wick (Week), in Alkington, 154, 159, 173, 175,
    935, 936, 937, 938*, 1119; Lower Wick, 173*,
    176*; Upper Wick, 176*
Wick, in Arlingham, 66*
Wick, in South Cerney, *see* Cerney, South: Cerney
    Wick
Wick and Abson (Abston, Wick Abston), **6–11**, 36,
    491, 996; Wick, 6, 7, 1119; *and see* Abson;
    Bridge Yate; Churchley; Holy Brook; Tog Hill
Wick Rissington, *see* Rissington, Wick
Wick Street (Wickstreet, Wyke), in Painswick,
    970*, 971, 973, 1210*, 1212, 1213, 1214
Wick Wick (Wickwick), in Frampton Cotterell,
    613*, 614
Wickenford, *see* Wichenford
Wickeridge, *see* Wickridge
Wickes Elm, *see* Wickselme
Wickham, Childes, *see* Childswickham
Wickhamford (Worcs.), 1001
Wickridge (Wickeridge), in Ashleworth, 75, 77,
    685
Wickselme (Wickes Elm, Wicks Elm), in
    Hamfallow, 165*, 174, 175, 281
Wickstowe, in Hill, 738
Wickstreet, *see* Wick Street
Wickwan, *see* Childswickham
Wickwar (Wickware, Wickwarre), 308, 451, 455,
    1122, 1345, **1448–56**, 1527, 1547; residents, 176,
    306, 307, 308*, 700, 1118, 1534, 1535; *and see*
    Bagstone; Pool House; Southwood; Westend
Wickwick, *see* Wick Wick

Widdrington, *see* Wigginton
Widford, **1441**
Widiandun, *see* Withington
Wierton (Wyerton), in Boughton Monchelsea
    (Kent), 992
Wigginton (Widddrington) (Oxon.), 259
Wiggold (Wighall, Wyggold), in Ampney Crucis,
    120, 365, 367, 1201, 1202
Wight, Isle of, *see* Wootton
Wight Lackington, *see* Lackington, White
Wightfield (Whitefield, Whyghtfylde), in
    Deerhurst, 482, 484, 485, 1201
Wigwood (Wynwood) Farm, in Tirley, 1354
Wilderness, the, in Abenhall, 1, 1401
Willersey, **1457–60**; *and see* Furze Hill
Willesden (Mdx.), 89
Williamsburg (Virginia), 1170
Williamstrip (Williamstrop), in Coln St. Aldwyn, 426,
    678, 690, 711 n, 1003*, 1005, 1015, 1066, 1493
Willicote (Wylcotts), in Clifford Chambers, 401,
    989
Willingswyke, *see* Ullingswick
Willington (Willington's) Court (Willington
    House), in Sandhurst, 1044*, 1047*, 1499
Willsbury (Wilsbury), in St. Briavels, 245, 249*,
    250, 923
Wilton (Wilts.), 1219
Wilton, in Bridstow (Herefs.), Wilton Castle, 1263
Wiltshire, 251 n, 302, 359, 496, 770, 778*, 791,
    792*, 986, 1073*, 1258; *and see under names of
    separate places*
Wimbledon (Surr.), 827 n
Wimblington (Cambs.), 1377
Winchcombe (Wicelcumbe, Wincelcumbe,
    Winchcomb, Winchecombe, Wynchcombe), 704 n,
    890 n, 1055, 1196, 1219*, 1220*, **1461–79**,
    1519; abbey of St. Mary, 1474; abbey, estate,
    216*, 309, 438, 558, 570, 688*, 689, 704*, 848,
    863, 864, 1011, 1027, 1055, 1061, 1068*, 1069*,
    1148*, 1149, 1150*, 1198, 1219, 1220, 1221*,
    1361*, 1362*, 1370, 1392, 1447, 1475*, 1476*,
    1481, 1482*, 1501, 1542; The Abbey (Abbey
    House), 1466, 1472, 1475, 1477*; burial, 309,
    891; church, 1221, 1290; in Domesday, 792 n,
    985, 1287; land in, 1195, 1290; residents,
    329, 439, 710, 1061, 1539; *and see* Coates;
    Cockbury; Corndean; Frampton; Greet; Gretton;
    Honibury Bridge; Langley; Millhampost;
    Naunton; Postlip; Stancombe Wood
Winchelsea (Suss.), 1091
Winchester (Winton) (Hants), 876, 1085; bishop,
    394, 525, 599, 638, 855, 859, 1126, 1369;
    cathedral, 366; college (Wykeham's School),
    375, 445 n, 879, 1043*, 1430
Wincot, in Clifford Chambers and Quinton, 400,
    402, 1287
Windesor, *see* Windsor
Windrush (Winrish, Winrush, Wynrich), 232, 601,
    1068*, 1069*, **1480–3**, 1501; *and see* Pinchpool
Windrush, river, 78, 134, 139, 232, 635
Windsor (Windesor) (Berks.), 123, 251, 358 n,
    1253

Winfrith Newburgh (Winfrith) (Dors.), 286
Winkfield (Berks.), 1033
Winniards, *see* Wynyards
Winrish (Winrush), *see* Windrush
Winsford Bridge, in Taynton and Tibberton, 1233
Winson, in Bibury, 183, 184*, 186*, 252, 878, 1485, 1542
Winstone (Winston, Wynstone), 523, 880, 1052, 1092, **1483–5**
Winterbourne (Winterborn, Winterborne, Winterbourn), 41, 603, 1172, 1384, **1486–91**; residents, 18, 47, 554, 582, 835, 1159, 1171, 1547; Winterbourne Court, 1486*, 1488, 1491; Winterbourne Down, 1490, 1491; *and see* Frenchay; Hambrook; Stanley; Sturden; Whiteshill
Winterton (Lincs.), 357 n
Winton, *see* Winchester
Wishanger (Wissinger), in Miserden, 878, 879*, 880, 1083
Wishford, Great (Wishford) (Wilts.), 434, 1497, 1498
Wissinger, *see* Wishanger
Wiston (Pemb.), 1543
Witchampton, *see* Witchington
Witchinford, *see* Wichenford
Witchington [? Witchampton] (Dors.), 10
Witcombe [*unspecified*], 254
Witcombe, Great (Witcomb, Witcombe), 202, 422, **1492–4**, 1498; Witcombe Park, 1184, 1493, 1494; *and see* Birdlip
Witcombe (Whitcomb), Little, in Badgeworth, 114, 118*, 261, 1493, 1494
Withington (Whithington, Widiandun, Wydandun), 319, 424, 502, 689, 716, 1058, 1059, 1077, 1092, **1495–1502**; *and see* Colesborne, Little; Compton, Cassey; Foxcote; Hilcot; Owdeswell; Thorndean; Upcote
Withy Bridge, in Boddington, 228
Witney (Oxon.), 117, 138
Witney Park, in Curbridge (Oxon.), 137
Wittenham, Little (Berks.), 507 n
Witton, *see* Whitton
Wixall, *see* Whixall
Wixford (Warws.), 1329
Wodelond, *see* Woodlands
Woefuldane (Woeful Dane) Bottom, in Minchinhampton, 649
Wolford, Great (Warws.), 572*
Wolford, Little, *see* Woodford, Little
Wollaston, *see* Woolaston
Wolley, *see* Woolley
Wolmore, *see* Walmore
Wolsingham (Walsingham) (co. Dur.), 1070, 1072
Wolstone (Wolston), *see* Woolstone
Wolstrop, *see* Woolstrop
Wolvercote, *see* Godstow
Wolwarde [*unidentified*], 391 n
Wood End, *see* Woodend
Wood End (Woodend), in Bolnhurst (Beds.), 718, 724
Wood House (Woodhouse), in Minchinhampton, 1026

Wood Rising, *see* Woodrising
Wood Stanway, *see* Stanway
Woodchester, 357 n, 648, 651, 1023*, 1138, 1191, 1192, 1218, **1505–13**; manor, 1101, 1133, 1138*, 1139; residents, 44, 284, 503, 655, 656, 659, 1023, 1024, 1133, 1136, 1143, 1183, 1324, 1401; Woodchester Court, 283; Woodchester House, 1513; *and see* Atcombe Court; Holcombe; Park Hill
Woodend (Beds.), *see* Wood End
Woodend, in Awre, 101
Woodend (Wood End), in Cromhall, 452, 453, 454, 1340, 1343, 1345; *and see* Woodland
Woodend (Wood End), in Dymock, 546
Woodend, in Hill, 174, 738*
Woodfields [? in Dymock], 548
Woodford, in Alkington, 159, 167, 168*, 171, 172*, 173, 779, 1173*, 1175*, 1176*, 1342, 1535
Woodford, Little [? *recte* Little Wolford (Warws.)], 437
Woodhay, East (Eastwoodhey) (Hants), 771
Woodhouse, in Minchinhampton, *see* Wood House
Woodhouse, in Olveston, 960
Woodhouse, the, in Alveston, 639*
Woodhouse (the), in Rodborough, 1025, 1027
Woodland [? *recte* Woodend], in Cromhall, 453
Woodlands (Wodelond, Woodland), in Almondsbury, 39, 42, 49, 727, 728, 1491
Woodlands (Woodland), in Stone, 1176
Woodmancote, in Bishop's Cleeve, 334, 393, 396*, 397*, 398, 399*, 984, 1092; *and see* Longwood; Wynyards
Woodmancote, in Dursley, 533*, 534, 535
Woodmancote, in North Cerney, 297*, 299*, 300, 1010
Woodrising (Wood Rising) (Norf.), 719 n, 720
Woodsha [*unidentified*, ? in Didmarton], 496
Woodside, the, in Awre, 108*
Woodstock, *see* Blenheim Palace
Wool Bedding, *see* Woolbeding
Woolaston (Wollaston, Woollaston, Woolloson), 53, 55, 734*, 810, 1322*, 1323*, **1513–16**; High Woolaston, 1516; Woolaston Grange, 1514; *and see* Brockweir; Grange, the; Keynsham; Plusterwine; Upperend
Woolbeding (Wool Bedding) (Suss.), 202
Woolford (Walforde), in Thornbury, 1314
Woolhope (Herefs.), 993
Woollaston, *see* Woolaston
Woolley (Wolley) (Som.), 1439
Woolloson, *see* Woolaston
Woolridge Common, in Hartpury, 680
Woolstone (Wolston, Wolstone), 482 n, 966, 1291, **1503–4**; *and see* Pardon Hill
Woolstrop (Wolstrop), in Quedgeley, 680, 999*, 1000
Wooten (Wooton, Wootton), *see* Wotton St. Mary; Wotton under Edge
Wootton (Wotton) (I.W.), 1159
Wootton Bassett (Wotton Basset) (Wilts.), 678
Worcester (Vigornia) (Worcs.), 251, 359 n, 627, 713 n, 793 n, 864 n, 985, 1475, 1483; bishop,

office or estate, 41, 154*, 158, 183*, 195, 218*, 221, 301, 360 n, 390*, 391*, 403, 426, 717*, 890*, 990, 1011, 1016, 1043, 1078, 1092, 1093, 1104, 1120, 1121, 1132, 1293, 1312*, 1328, 1335, 1339, 1351, 1362, 1392, 1419*, 1420, 1447, 1475, 1495, 1501, 1502, 1542; bishop, personally, 220, 565, 609, 612, 617, 646 n, 667, 688, 707, 711*, 717*, 745, 747, 816, 838, 1407, 1431*, 1432*, 1497; cathedral, abbey, or priory of St. Mary, dean, 436 n, 651 n; cathedral, estate, 183, 390, 391*, 392, 394, 424*, 502, 1120, 1121, 1122, 1123, 1312, 1419, 1422, 1501; cathedral, prebendary, 651 n, 1270; cathedral, prior, 1328, 1335, 1339; church of St. Swithin, 627; city, alderman, 905; civil war, 313 n, 349 n, 380, 420 n, 806 n*, 894 n; diocese, chancellor, 1334, 1367; priory of St. Peter, 1120, 1121, 1502, 1512; residents, 71, 359 n, 393, 485, 585, 872, 1220*, 1221*, 1262, 1263, 1268, 1273, 1365, 1501
Worcester College, Oxford, 1019
Worcester Lodge and Walk, in West Dean, 478 n, 479 n, 922, 1039
Worcestershire, 1191, 1231; land in, 27, 265, 618, 1153, 1380, 1421; residents, 325, 330, 502, 547, 651 n, 1070; sheriff, 571, 572, 1119, 1380, 1447, 1432, 1119, 1380, 1432; *and see under names of separate places*
Wormington, 743, **1517–19**; Wormington Grange, 493, 1387, 1518*
Wormsley (Herefs.), priory, 1033
Worstead (Worsted) (Norf.), 658
Worth (Suss.), 827 n
Wortley (Wortly), in Wotton under Edge, 36*, 779, 1522, 1524, 1528*, 1535, 1536, 1537, 1539
Wotley, *see* Whatley
Wotton, *see* Wootton
Wotton Basset, *see* Wootton Bassett
Wotton St. Mary (Wooton, Wootton), in Gloucester, 133*, 261, 348, 854, 950, 1046, 1377; Wotton Court, 1046
Wotton (Wooten, Wooton) under Edge (Wooton, Wootton, Wotton), 29, 66, 153, 154, 160, 739, 910, 1100, 1102, 1314, 1327, **1520–41**; death at, 1290, 1507; residents, 172, 306, 539, 558, 560, 779*, 780, 910, 935, 937, 994*, 996, 1049, 1167, 1366, 1369, 1452, 1546; *and see* Bradley; Coombe; Huntingford; Leys, the; Lodge, the; Monk's Mill; Ridge, the; Sinwell; Symond's Hall; Tyley; Warren, the; Whitley Park; Wortley
Wraxall, North (Wraxal, North Wrexall) (Wilts.), 845, 1336
Wresden (Wreisden), in Uley, 1365
Wrexall, North, *see* Wraxall
Wrington (Wrinton) (Som.), 1160; *and see* Barley Wood; Langford
Writtle (Essex), 917
Wroxton (Oxon.), 990
Wychwood (Whichwood) (Oxon.), 791; *and see* Loughborough

Wyck, the, in Henbury, 1415
Wydandun, *see* Withington
Wye, river, 188*, 244*, 732*; fisheries, 913, 1321, 1322, 1323; passage, 806 n
Wye Seal, *see* Wyeseal
Wyerton, *see* Wierton
Wyeseal (Wye Seal), in Newland or St. Briavels, 913, 917
Wyggold, *see* Wiggold
Wyke [*unspecified*], 690
Wyke [? Wick Rissington], 1482
Wyke, in Painswick, *see* Wick Street
Wyke Rysingdon, *see* Rissington, Wick
Wykeham's School, *see* Winchester: college
Wylcotts, *see* Willicote
Wynchcombe, *see* Winchcombe
Wynrich, *see* Windrush
Wynstone, *see* Winstone
Wynwood Farm, *see* Wigwood Farm
Wynyards (Winniards), in Woodmancote in Bishop's Cleeve, 399

Yanworth, 636, 688*, 689, 704 n, 1198, 1501, **1542**
Yardington, *see* Yarnton
Yardley (Worcs.), 1472
Yarleton Hill, *see* May Hill
Yarnton (Yardington) (Oxon.), 572, 866
Yartleton Hill, *see* May Hill
Yartleton manor, in Newent, 893
Yartleton Woods, in Newent, 893*
Yate (Yeat), 36, 717, 1105, 1120, 1385, 1419, 1449, 1456, **1543–52**; residents, 17*, 167, 210, 758, 1009*, 1118, 1326, 1336, 1455; Yate House, 1551; *and see* Gearing-frith; Hall End; Hill House; Stanshawe
Yatton Keynell (Wilts.), 653*
Yeat, *see* Yate
Yellow Shraf (Yellow Craft), in East Dean or Little Dean, 478 n
Yeovil (Som.), 939
Yiventon, *see* Evington
York, 409, 413, 532 n, 958, 1488
York House [? in London], 232 n
York Lodge, in West Dean, 478 n, 479 n
York, archbishop, 252, 449, 559 n, 565, 1232, 1370*, 1431, 1441, 1493, 1528
Yorkley, in West Dean, 924
Yorkshire, 58, 88, 271, 754, 793 n
Yorkshire, East Riding, 409; *and see* Ganton; Hayton; Hull; Kirkham
Yorkshire, North Riding, *see* Brafferton; Marske; Newby Wiske; Northallerton; Richmond; Snape; Whitby
Yorkshire, West Riding, 58; *and see* Allerton; Backhouse; Beamsley; Bootham; Borough-bridge; Bramham Moor; Byram; Clayton; Compton; Doncaster; Fountains Abbey; Halifax; Harewood; Harrogate; Ingleton; Kellington; Ledsham; Marston Moor; Newton, in Tadcaster; Ripon; Rotherham; Tong; Wentworth
Yrdcote, *see* Earthcott

INDEX OF OCCUPATIONS AND OFFICES

* An asterisk indicates that the page has more than one reference

With a few exceptions, ecclesiastical offices have been excluded from this index

adjutant-general, 1073
admiral, 866*, 1193*, 1338, 1367; (lord) high
  admiral (of England), 805, 1221; rear admiral,
  1193; vice-admiral,720, 723, 805, 1231, 1245
Admiralty, judge (delegate), 1004, 1198
agent, 55, 796, 867
aide de camp, 974
alderman, see corporation officer or member
almoner, see household, royal
ambassador, 220 n, 224, 434 n, 952; consul, 1308;
  diplomatist, 1123; envoy, 723, 1119; pleni-
  potentiary, 1119
anchor smith, 413
antiquary, 1258; and see historian; topographer
Antiquaries, president of Society of, 988
apothecary, 176, 204, 264, 293, 307, 373, 381, 430,
  439, 541*, 639, 658, 824, 903, 932, 946, 973,
  974, 1023, 1107*, 1108*, 1192, 1210, 1267,
  1273, 1297*, 1413, 1426, 1467, 1529, 1530,
  1556, 1559; apothecary and surgeon, 388, 466,
  896, 947, 948, 1003, 1013, 1268; and see
  druggist; chemist; pharmacist
architect, 332, 1102, 1138*, 1180; architect and
  master builder, 1180
army officer, 317, 411, 657; and see adjutant-
  general; captain (army); captain (militia);
  colonel; commander; cornet; ensign; general;
  lieutenant; major; sergeant
artist, 1262; and see sculptor
assessor, 1317, 1372
astrologer, 288 n
astronomer royal, 656
attorney, see lawyer
attorney general, 324, 341, 634, 663, 704, 785, 852,
  1120, 1215, 1317
auditor, 1312, 1388
author, 567, 1123, 1218, 1258, 1290, 1293, 1323,
  1331, 1403, 1460, 1478*; and see poet

bailiff (baily), 636, 1103, 1132, 1312, 1327, 1348,
  1350, 1351, 1356, 1419, 1469, 1473; and see
  corporation officer; justice
baker, 175, 203, 229, 282*, 368, 412, 413, 455,
  468, 485, 539*, 540, 542*, 653, 658, 661, 706,
  903, 904, 905*, 939, 941, 974, 981, 1138,

  1184, 1210, 1213*, 1271, 1374, 1377, 1465,
  1466*, 1469*, 1470*, 1526, 1576; baker and
  maltster, 1050, 1425; baker and miller, 750,
  1049
banker, 252, 870, 1171, 1208*, 1216, 1303, 1362
barber surgeon, 1271
baron, see Exchequer
barrister, see lawyer
basket maker, 542
bellfounder, 1369
blacksmith, 177, 344, 353, 468, 543, 604, 777, 788,
  911, 923, 1008, 1010*, 1099, 1130, 1159, 1250,
  1473, 1505, 1584; see farrier
blue dyer, see dyer
bone-setter, 1028, 1030
bookseller, 259 n, 1217, 1535
brazier, 335, 381, 1279
breeches maker, 1250, 1580; breeches and glove
  maker, 1250
brewer, 983
bricklayer or brick maker, 337*, 339*, 624, 1575
brightsmith, 210
builder, 1047; master builder, 1180; builder and
  merchant, 1047; builder and surveyor, 1091
burgess, see corporation officer or member;
  parliament
bursar, see university
butcher, 174, 176, 339, 368, 369, 372, 468, 542,
  623*, 633, 659*, 746, 836*, 902, 903*, 905*,
  1008, 1574, 1575, 1576
butler, 660, 741, 922

cabinet maker, 1008, 1098
captain (generally), 50, 66, 99, 134, 136, 358, 431,
  469 n, 537, 665, 701, 740, 759, 809, 852 n, 894 n,
  901, 921, 928*, 929, 1026, 1085*, 1101, 1152,
  1157, 1158, 1169, 1184, 1189, 1231, 1237,
  1303, 1319, 1327, 1338, 1360, 1362, 1368,
  1374, 1383, 1405, 1413*, 1419, 1424, 1439,
  1459, 1466, 1488, 1501, 1550, 1555*, 1562;
  (army), 1562; (militia), 358, 416, 988; (naval),
  208, 413, 496, 866*, 867*, 920, 961, 1024,
  1133, 1164, 1193, 1232, 1245*, 1301, 1344,
  1419, 1511
cardmaker, 381, 538, 540*, 543*, 1531

carpenter, 141, 176, 472, 543*, 604, 750, 898, 902, 905, 923, 974, 975, 1007, 1026, 1098, 1131, 1306, 1331, 1376*, 1390, 1438, 1484, 1489;
house carpenter, 1574; *and see* cabinet maker; ship carpenter; ship's carpenter
carrier, 660, 1024*, 1171
carver, 344, 974, 1146, 1210
castle, constable, 244*, 245, 251*, 252*, 424, 432, 479, 612*, 581, 732, 878, 971, 1039, 1296; deputy constable, 67, 470; governor (keeper), 250, 263, 349 n, 680, 690, 853, 1219*, 1293
catechist, *see* missionary
cementarian [mason], 66
chairman, *see* company chairman
chancellor: of the duchy of Lancaster, 695; *and see* Chancery; Exchequer; university
Chancery: Lord (High) Chancellor (king's chancellor), 134, 358, 570, 571, 640, 663, 718 n, 719 n, 990, 1021, 1226, 1401; master, 1467; master extraordinary, 1444
chandler, 284, 296*, 398, 975, 1206; chandler and mercer, 1206; *and see* tallow chandler
chaplain, *see* household, royal
chemist, 1314; *and see* apothecary; druggist; pharmacist
chief justice, *see* justice
chorister, 1041, 1419
church commmissioner, 1581
clerk, *see* corporation officer: town clerk; county officer; Crown: privy council; parish clerk
clockmaker, 905, 1182, 1211, 1307
cloth drawer, 283, 542, 972; *and see* fine drawer
cloth dresser, 782
clothier, 33, 34, 52, 95*, 96*, 97, 140, 168, 169, 172, 199, 200, 201, 202*, 203*, 204, 282*, 283*, 306*, 308, 366, 368*, 369, 370, 373, 374*, 376, 377, 378*, 383, 387, 448, 450, 453, 456, 472*, 535, 536* 537*, 538*, 540*, 541*, 543, 560*, 562*, 622, 653, 654*, 655*, 657, 658*, 659*, 660*, 661*, 662*, 676*, 700*, 701, 749*, 750*, 751*, 779 & n, 780*, 781*, 782*, 830*, 900, 936, 937*, 938*, 940*, 943*, 967*, 969, 970*, 971*, 972*, 973*, 974*, 975*, 976*, 980*, 981*, 994*, 1006*, 1007*, 1008*, 1021*, 1023*, 1024*, 1025*, 1026*, 1027, 1049*, 1053, 1083, 1096, 1117, 1133*, 1135, 1136*, 1137*, 1138, 1139, 1143, 1144*, 1145*, 1146*, 1167*, 1168, 1179*, 1180*, 1181*, 1182*, 1183*, 1184*, 1185, 1191, 1206*, 1207*, 1209*, 1210, 1211*, 1212*, 1213*, 1214*, 1241, 1244, 1249, 1250, 1256, 1298, 1301, 1304*, 1305, 1324*, 1325*, 1326, 1342*, 1343, 1365*, 1366*, 1367*, 1369*, 1374, 1395, 1437*, 1438*, 1449*, 1450*, 1451, 1454, 1456, 1507*, 1508*, 1509*, 1510*, 1511, 1512*, 1521, 1522*, 1525, 1529, 1531, 1532*, 1533*, 1534*, 1535*, 1536, 1549; clothier and craper, 781
clothing manufacturer, 30*
clothman, 1512
clothworker, 845, 976, 981, 1063
coachmaker, 787
coachman, 124

coalminer, 922
collar maker, 337, 660, 706
collector, *see* customs and excise
colonel, 51, 58, 68, 158, 274, 313 n, 341*, 349, 358, 412, 520, 680, 806 n*, 851, 852 n, 853, 854, 894 n, 915, 927, 928*, 1046, 1083, 1143, 1189, 1190, 1191, 1197*, 1198, 1225, 1231*, 1255, 1293, 1303, 1303*, 1322, 1394, 1402, 1404, 1423, 1522; (of militia), 58, 1031, 1069; colonel commander, 1088; lieutenant colonel (liftinant corranell), 58, 136, 407, 410, 469 n, 915, 928*, 929, 1003, 1164, 1327, 1417, 1529, 1565; (of militia), 268, 1231, 1280*, 1303
commander (army), 24, 776; (militia), 1073; (naval, sea commander), 1073, 1143, 1231*, 1245*, 1418
commissary: *see* Royal Engineers; commissary general, 1303
commissioner, *see* church commissioner; seal, great; seal privy; Treasury
Common Pleas, prothonotary of, 753
company chairman, 1524; company director, 1362, 1524
conservator, *see* forester
constable, *see* castle; parish constable
consul, *see* ambassador
conveyancer, 375
convocation, proctor in, 1029*
cook, 922
cooper, 175, 203, 383, 465, 662, 933, 1279, 1536, 1583; *and see* wine cooper
copper refiner, 1574*
cordwainer (cordiner), 543, 676, 706, 761, 1306; *and see* shoemaker
cornet, 1231
coroner, *see* county officer
corporation officer or member: alderman, 166, 169, 170, 172*, 173, 174*, 175*, 176, 206*, 351, 451, 535, 559, 618, 682, 713, 720, 725, 826, 827, 829 n, 842, 895, 901, 905, 917, 1047, 1121*, 1133, 1233, 1239, 1301, 1306, 1307, 1343, 1353, 1365, 1368, 1372, 1405*, 1419, 1451, 1452, 1494, 1513, 1521*, 1522, 1524, 1532, 1533, 1534, 1554*, 1555*, 1564; bailiff, 1266, 1267*, 1268*, 1270*, 1271*, 1272, 1276*, 1277*, 1278*, 1279*; high bailiff, 1262, 1276, 1472; senior bailiff, 1269; burgess, 288*, 293, 363*, 364*, 1121*, 1259*, 1288*, 1289*, 1450; assistant burgess, 1288*; principal burgess, 1288; chamberlain, 375; lord mayor, 271, 436, 546, 568, 718, 1051*, 1340*, 1394; mayor, 172, 188, 535, 553, 618, 649 n, 663 n, 682, 927, 929, 930*, 931, 933*, 934, 962, 1121, 1265, 1293, 1352, 1353, 1375, 1379, 1405, 1412, 1494, 1524, 1527*, 1530, 1532*, 1533, 1534, 1554*, 1555; member, 1280; (high) steward, 937, 988, 1121, 1312; under steward, 1121; town clerk, 1121, 1266; deputy town clerk, 199
counsellor, *see* Crown: privy counsellor; lawyer
county officer: clerk of the peace, 864; coroner, 55, 99, 106, 217, 343*, 970, 1210; lord lieutenant, 66, 122*, 162*, 1170, 1198, 1219, 1237, 1333;

deputy lieutenant, 67, 68, 268, 614, 1019, 1042, 1046, 1067, 1085, 1164, 1168*, 1185, 1536; receiver (general), 864 n, 985; deputy receiver, 985; (high) sheriff, 3, 71, 199, 269, 289, 325 n, 349, 366, 383, 392, 462, 482, 520, 535, 552, 571, 572, 588, 614, 618*, 619, 649*, 663 n, 664, 879, 891, 896, 930, 980, 988, 997*, 1027, 1055*, 1060*, 1074, 1082, 1085, 1088, 1119, 1120*, 1160, 1199, 1215, 1216, 1239, 1334*, 1337, 1380, 1385, 1401, 1408*, 1422, 1431, 1432, 1434, 1446, 1447, 1474, 1486, 1518, 1521, 1554, 1555, 1563; steward of the sheriff's court, 199
Crown: privy council, clerk of, 560, 561, 718, 723*, 724; privy (or king's) counsellor, 534 n, 695, 959, 1004, 1395; and see seal, great; seal, privy
currier, 465
customs and excise, collector, 1530; exciseman, excise officer, 171, 549, 658, 782*, 837, 847, 907, 939, 958, 1086, 1250, 1326, 1574*, 1580; receiver general, 852 n, 853; solicitor, 561; superviser, surveyor, 931, 1252, 1574
cutler, 657

diplomatist, see ambassador
director, see company director
distiller, 269, 1563
doctor of medicine, of physic, see physician
draper, 307, 376, 602, 1181, 1201, 1268, 1276; and see linen draper; woollen draper
druggist, 106, 336, 1411, 1504; and see apothecary; chemist; pharmacist
dyer, 536, 636, 701, 781, 903, 1275; blue dyer, 1007*; grain dyer, 1211; and see silk dyer

editor and printer, 1440; and see journalist
engineer, 1026, 1356, 1583; and see Royal Engineers
ensign, 411, 928*
envoy, see ambassador
equerry, see household, royal
Exchequer, baron of, 744, 1049, 1349, 1350; chancellor, 440, 585; (lord) chief baron, 482, 483* 713, 819, 910, 920, 1049, 1052, 1521; teller, 851–2
excise, exciseman, see customs and excise
export supervisor, 1573

factor, 197, 658 724, 1214, 1342, 1343
farmer [agricultural], 702, 1459
farmer, queen's, 1132
farrier, 971; and see blacksmith
fellmonger, 384
feltmaker, 1534
fine drawer [? of cloth], 1007
fisher, 1092
fishmonger, 1063, 1473
forester and forest official: conservator, 479; chief forester, 479; forester in fee, 479; gaveller, 479; keeper, 472, 922, 1038, 1559; purveyor, 811; regarder, 105; steward of the swanimote, 479*; surveyor, 811; verderer, 470, 479; lord warden, 476, 479; deputy warden, 479*; wooodward, 479*

founder, 1038
freemason, see mason

gamekeeper, see keeper
gardener, 165, 264, 620, 661, 728, 1159, 1172, 1408, 1575, 1583; and see nurseryman
gaveller, see forester
general, 336, 771, 1088, 1093, 1232, 1245, 1266, 1293, 1303, 1404, 1532; lieutenant general, 984, 1088*; major general, 75, 132, 245, 851, 852, 853, 915, 1000, 1048, 1070, 1073
gentleman, see household, royal: chapel and horse; servant
glass maker or manufacturer, 413, 1566, 1573, 1575, 1583
glass-master, 835
glazier, 924, 1289, 1307
glover, 335, 353, 468, 543, 895, 1250; glover and breeches maker, 1250
gold and silver wire drawer, see wire drawer
goldsmith, 86, 576, 891, 1064, 1362, 1469, 1533, 1534, 1563
governor (keeper), of castle, see castle; of overseas possession, 132, 177, 408*, 497*, 570, 851, 853, 875 n, 1066, 1170; and see school governor
grain dyer, see dyer
great seal, see seal
grocer, 296, 348, 372, 409, 413, 453, 796, 935, 974, 1043, 1144, 1159, 1184, 1193, 1212*, 1213*, 1562, 1574; grocer and tallow chandler, 1184
groom, 174
gunner, master, 682

haberdasher, 107, 369, 409, 615, 1575
hatter, 174, 1534
haven master, 1418*, 1419*
headmaster, see schoolmaster
herald: Chester, 2; Clarenceux king of arms; Garter (principal) king of arms, 630, 631, 1059, 1218; Richmond, 2; Rougedragon, 2; Somerset, 631
historian, 707, 1226; historiographer, 561; and see antiquary; topographer
hosier, 1271, 1278
house carpenter, see carpenter
household, royal: almoner, king's or queen's, 534 n, 1220; bedchamber, lord or gentleman or groom of, 123, 1170*; buckhounds, master of, 986; chambers, messenger of the, 249; chapel royal, gentleman of, 897; chaplain, 1180, 1336, 1528; equerry, 1003; horse, gentleman of, 1003, 1281; king's counting house, comptroller, 1063; maid of honour, 1529; physician, queen's, 359, 990; serjeant at arms, 1316; steward, 798; treasurer, 990; usher, 1059, 1126
housekeeper, 124*, 317, 521, 979, 1116, 1344, 1444
huntsman, 175

innholder, 133, 353, 881, 935, 1045, 1107, 1126, 1175, 1303
ironmonger, 338, 657, 1144, 1546

jester (fool), 177
joiner, 170, 412, 464, 542, 929, 933*, 975, 1184; *and see* cabinet maker; carpenter
journalist, 357; *and see* editor
jurispert, *see* lawyer
justice: judge, 328 n, 429 n, 482, 493, 494, 515, 560, 610, 672, 704, 726, 759, 792, 909, 920, 937, 1049, 1186, 1216, 1374, 1463; Chief Justice (Lord), 29, 34, 35, 570 n, 571, 581, 612, 909, 1015, 1287, 1460; Chief Justice of Chester, 672; Justice of Wales or Welsh Marches, 230 n, 672; Lord Justice of Ireland, 177, 570, 1066; magistrate, justice (conservator) of the peace, or bailiff, 12, 21, 25, 27, 40, 42, 43, 67, 68, 199, 268, 269, 289, 302, 366, 428, 431, 470, 471, 520, 530*, 531*, 532*, 535, 540, 596, 614, 618 n, 654, 817, 838, 854*, 872, 894, 900, 937, 977, 987, 988, 999, 1019, 1023, 1042, 1046, 1066, 1073*, 1085*, 1090, 1091, 1100, 1106, 1141, 1164, 1168*, 1184, 1185, 1206*, 1209, 1215*, 1216*, 1266, 1276*, 1280, 1321, 1344, 1411, 1439, 1494*, 1536*, 1537*, 1550*, 1564; magistrate, chief, of Jersey, 1411; Master of the Rolls, 1003, 1004; recorder, 393 n, 440, 643, 851, 872, 988; senator of College of Justice, Scotland, 410; *and see* Admiralty; Chancery; Exchequer; King's Bench

keeper [gamekeeper or lodgekeeper], 203, 250, 812, 1473; *and see* castle; forester; governor; park keeper; seal, great; seal, privy
King's Bench, Chief Justice of, 737; in Ireland, justice of, 1029
kitchener, 708 n
knight of the shire, *see* parliament

labourer, 1052
lawyer, 865 n, 900, 992, 1121, 1266; attorney at law, 43, 99, 287 n, 375, 479, 621, 655, 682, 930, 931*, 938, 962, 999, 1053, 1130, 1247, 1305, 1327, 1360, 1375, 1383, 1453, 1454, 1469, 1525, 1546, 1556; barrister at law, 199, 228, 257, 265, 268, 504, 561, 592, 600, 625*, 634, 738, 745, 746, 920, 1246, 1298, 1536; counsellor at law, 851, 852 n, 854, 1508; jurispert, 1132; serjeant at law, 393, 500, 546, 560, 570, 625, 688, 1349, 1350, 1394; solicitor, 1245, 1259 n, 1282, 1400, 1472; solicitor in Chancery, 1173, 1174; *and see* justice
leather seller, 1181
lecturer, 98, 1528
lieutenant (generally), 206*, 257, 313 n, 413, 473, 573, 657, 765, 928*, 962, 974, 983, 1023, 1034, 1214, 1245*, 1266, 1270, 1273, 1488; (army), 1532, 1564; (militia), 1537; (naval), 1027, 1107*, 1245, 1281, 1282, 1327, 1400; flag lieutenant, 1245
lieutenant, lord, *see* county officer
lieutenant colonel, *see* colonel
lieutenant general, *see* general
lime burner, 1412
linen draper, 413, 1297, 1582; *and see* draper

lodgekeeper, *see* keeper
lord lieutenant, *see* county officer
lord mayor, *see* corporation officer

magistrate, *see* justice
maid of honour, *see* household, royal
major, 68, 136, 582, 723, 732, 852 n*, 1408
major general, *see* general
maltster, 97, 203, 336*, 338*, 460, 653, 657, 659, 660, 751, 973*, 975, 976, 1026, 1112, 1214, 1235, 1367*, 1409, 1411, 1413, 1455, 1470, 1484*, 1510, 1561, 1575*; maltster and baker, 1050, 1425
marine, paymaster of the, 852 n
mariner, 69, 106, 108, 109, 167, 172, 412*, 583, 623, 729*, 734*, 735, 736, 811, 843, 887*, 931*, 932*, 933, 1054*, 1096, 1109, 1272, 1397*, 1408, 1418*, 1555, 1571, 1573; *and see* midshipman; pilot; sailor; sea-faring man; ship's officer; trowman
mason, 176, 320, 339, 344, 412, 419, 542, 550, 655, 701, 765, 905, 975, 1083, 1158, 1159, 1213, 1489, 1493; freemason, 597, 636, 967, 1570; *and see* cementarian
master, *see* Chancery; gunner; haven master; household, royal: buckhounds; justice: Master of the Rolls; schoolmaster; university: college head; writing master
master builder, *see* builder
mathematician, 10, 70, 1218
mayor, *see* coporation officer
mealman, 77
medical practitioner, *see* bone-setter; physician; surgeon
member, *see* corporation officer or member; parliament
mercer, 100, 166*, 171*, 172*, 173, 174, 175*, 289, 330*, 332, 333, 339, 368, 370, 374, 375, 383, 387, 465*, 466*, 485, 535*, 537*, 540* 541*, 554, 636, 655, 756, 811, 898, 900, 902*, 903, 904, 931, 934, 944, 946, 970, 971, 972*, 973*, 974, 1026, 1180, 1181, 1192*, 1194, 1206, 1210*, 1211, 1212, 1267*, 1279, 1305, 1306, 1452, 1465, 1497, 1525, 1527*, 1530; mercer and chandler, 1206
merchant, 13, 15, 33, 73, 96, 104, 107*, 215*, 226, 238, 283, 291, 293, 307, 331, 352, 371*, 385, 407*, 408, 409, 410*, 411*, 412*, 435, 473, 515, 517, 533, 535, 546, 576, 588, 607*, 640, 648, 651*, 654*, 657, 725, 726*, 728, 835, 841, 842, 843, 863, 900, 917, 919, 920, 929, 931, 932, 937, 945*, 962, 970, 988, 990, 991, 996, 1000, 1006, 1021*, 1025, 1047, 1051, 1069, 1089, 1109, 1166*, 1174*, 1183, 1189, 1211, 1241, 1266, 1280, 1307, 1324*, 1408*, 1409*, 1410, 1411*, 1412*, 1413*, 1419, 1440, 1452, 1457, 1487*, 1488, 1490, 1501, 1503, 1505*, 1507, 1508, 1521, 1524*, 1525*, 1526, 1554*, 1555*, 1556, 1557*, 1561*, 1562, 1564, 1565, 1569; merchant and builder, 1047; *and see* tailor; timber merchant; wool merchant
messenger, *see* household, royal

metaphysician, *see* philosopher
midshipman, 537, 962, 1245, 1344, 1367
militia officers, *see* captain; colonel; lieutenant
miller, 338, 1159*; miller and baker, 750, 1049
millwright, 622
miner, *see* coalminer
missionary, 1187; missionary catechist, 1455
musician, 339, 1046, 1159; *and see* organist

naval officers, *see* admiral; captain; commander; lieutenant
navy, treasurer of, 224
needlemaker, 923
nurseryman, 976; *and see* gardener

oilman, 795
organist, 381, 906, 1101; *and see* musician

packer, 991, 1210
painter and tiler, 1575
parish clerk, 412, 492, 517, 539, 563, 624*, 633, 661*, 685, 715, 765, 780*, 797, 910, 950, 964, 1003, 1007, 1008*, 1025, 1028, 1073, 1079, 1130, 1143, 1168, 1231, 1237, 1328, 1529; *and see* registrar: parish registrar
parish constable, 1519
park keeper, 174
parliament: burgess, 209, 663 n, 664; knight of the shire, 43, 58, 199, 245, 359, 393 n, 502, 612, 614, 784, 913, 1049, 1067*, 1073, 1170, 1334, 1577; member, 136, 358, 697, 723*, 724, 852 n*, 872, 873 n, 920, 971, 988, 1005, 1035, 1066, 1073, 1119, 1216*, 1237, 1280, 1293*, 1334, 1409, 1420*, 1443; speaker of the Commons, 426, 507, 1003, 1458; speaker of the Lords, 1049; usher, 1059
paymaster, *see* marine
periwig maker, 1468
pewterer, 841, 1175
pharmacist, 95, 541*, 849, 1193, 1424; *and see* apothecary; chemist; druggist
philosopher (metaphysician), 1123; natural philosopher, 1218
physician (practitioner of physic), 51, 58, 69, 137, 165, 231, 281, 359, 374, 981, 990, 991, 993, 1053, 1066, 1096, 1097, 1177, 1207, 1209, 1263, 1270, 1276, 1308, 1319, 1320, 1321*, 1407, 1412, 1466, 1494, 1495, 1497*, 1526, 1527, 1531, 1554; itinerant physician, 1177; physician and minister, 981; physician and surgeon, 165, 860 n, 1072; *and see* household, royal
pilot, 1418
plasterer, 922, 924
plenitpotentiary, *see* ambassador
plumber, 412, 1333, 1390; plumber and glazier, 339
poet, 864, 1258
potter, 1573
president, *see* Antiquaries; Royal Society; university: college head
principal, *see* university: college head
printer and editor, 1440
proctor, *see* convocation

professor, 51, 346, 572, 656, 860 n, 861, 953, 1218, 1258, 1415, 1526
prothonotary, *see* Common Pleas
provost, *see* university: college head
provost marshal, 876
pump maker, 1575
purveyor, *see* forester

quartermaster, 412, 473

reader, *see* preacher
rear admiral, *see* admiral
receiver, *see* county officer
receiver general, of prince or barony, 164, 324 n; *and see* customs and excise; county officers
recruiting officer, 1576
regarder, *see* forester
registrar (register), 121, 1189; parish registrar (exact clerk and sworn register), 1130
rope maker, 411
Royal Engineers, commissary of stores, 1564
Royal Society, fellow, 656, 861; president, 723, 864 n, 988

saddle-tree maker, 661, 1531
saddler, 171, 174, 465, 467, 595, 661, 971, 1008, 1025
sailmaker, 1515
sailor, 100, 932, 955; *and see* mariner
salter, 1189
school governor, 1186
schoolmaster, 176, 284, 308, 333, 334, 445 n, 597*, 632, 657, 666, 727, 728, 868, 910, 919, 923, 1008, 1110, 1191, 1282, 1306, 1331, 1374, 1376, 1449, 1456, 1477, 1537, 1583; headmaster, 455, 946, 1258, 1450, 1456; *and see* Sunday school superintendant; teacher; tutor; usher; writing master
schoolmistress, 339
sculptor, 291
sea-faring man, 1273, 1282
seal, great: keeper (lord keeper), 273, 771, 1217; lord commissioner, 865 n, 1394
seal, privy: commissioner, 723; lord privy seal, 361 n
secretary, 122, 123, 164, 361 n, 639, 723, 1209, 1493; *and see* State, secretary of; Treasury
senator, *see* justice
sergeant, 1109; sergeant major, 1576
serjeant at arms, *see* household, royal
serjeant at law, *see* lawyer
servant, 49, 86, 124, 174, 203, 336, 337*, 422, 496, 555, 632, 657, 714, 869, 941*, 1010, 1014, 1068, 1070, 1085, 1086, 1337*, 1343, 1360, 1397, 1443, 1535; 'gentleman', 693; *and see* butler; coachman; cook; groom; housekeeper
shalloon and stuff maker, 1574
shear maker, 658, 781, 939
sheriff: of Queensland, 1354; *and see* county officers
ship carpenter, 604
ship's carpenter, 413
ship's officer, 1143

ship's surgeon, 1097

shipwright, 412, 413, 728, 729, 736, 1397*, 1412

shoemaker, 660, 661, 924, 1210; *and see* cordwainer

shopkeeper, 1099, 1117, 1210

silk dyer, 701

silkman, 367

silkthrowster, 218

skinner, 290

slatter, 1064

smith, *see* anchor smith; blacksmith; brightsmith

soapmaker or soapboiler, 83, 377*, 381, 746, 1512, 1569

solicitor, *see* customs and excise; lawyer

speaker, *see* parliament

State, (principal) Secretary of, 507, 552, 854*, 1070; for Ireland, 723*

stationer, 517*, 725, 1469

staymaker, 658

steward, manorial, 375, 811, 985, 1043, 1061, 1132, 1153, 1256; to noblemen etc., 59, 168, 177, 230 n, 496, 583, 920, 977, 1010, 1019, 1050, 1062 n, 1174, 1334, 1498; *and see* corporation officer; county officer; forester; household, royal

stockbroker, 1216

stone cutter, 174, 175, 922, 923

stuff maker, *see* shalloon and stuff maker

sub centurion (?), 79

sugar refiner, 412, 1575

Sunday school superintendant, 1455

supervisor, *see* customs and excise; exports

surgeon (chirurgeon), 1, 95, 104, 165, 202, 270, 293, 296*, 331, 369, 384, 398, 464, 467, 472, 539, 542*, 620, 624, 653, 658*, 659, 700, 734, 746, 750*, 841, 880, 903, 906, 910, 931*, 988, 1021, 1053, 1097, 1109, 1112, 1123, 1144*, 1181, 1193*, 1208, 1250, 1258, 1266, 1270, 1280, 1282, 1302, 1303, 1437, 1446, 1471*, 1472, 1486*, 1525*, 1530, 1537*, 1567*; surgeon and apothecary, 388, 466, 896, 947, 948, 1003, 1013, 1268; surgeon and physician, 165, 860, 1072; *and see* barber surgeon; bone-setter; ship's surgeon

surveyor, 324, 475, 476*, 985, 1292; land surveyor, 320, 1153*; port surveyor, 1318; surveyor of Crown lands, 1062; surveyor of H.M. gardens and waterworks, 408; *and see* customs and excise; forester

tailor, 338, 412, 660, 945, 1085, 1413; merchant tailor, 378

tallow chandler, 339, 1184, 1331

tanner, 170*, 171*, 174, 211, 455, 812, 903, 905, 933, 1099, 1302, 1307, 1514, 1515

teacher (paedogogus), 1158, 1191; *and see* schoolmaster

teller, *see* Exchequer

tiler and painter, 1575

timber merchant, 1321

tinplate manufacturer, 1053

tobacconist, 537

topographer, 324 n; *and see* antiquary; historian

town clerk, *see* corporation officer

treasurer, prince's, 324 n; *and see* household, royal; navy; Treasury

Treasury, lord commissioner, 724; lord high treasurer, 614; secretary, 988; treasurer, 1219

trowman, 1274

tutor, 1102, 1123, 1489

university, chancellor, 361 n, 990; vice-chancellor, 52, 1072; college bursar, 1127; college head (master, president, principal, provost, or warden), 25, 52, 137, 233, 394 n*, 410, 411, 432, 525, 534 n, 990, 1072, 1127, 1180, 1258, 1305, 1344, 1451; *and see* professor

usher [schoolmaster], 947; *and see* household, royal; parliament; schoolmaster

verderer, *see* forester

vice-admiral, *see* admiral

vice-chancellor, *see* university

victualler, 97, 413, 537, 727, 976, 1146, 1159, 1438

vintner, 20, 337, 409; *and see* wine merchant

waggoner, 658, 1024*

warden, *see* forester; university: college head

watchmaker, 1536; watch and clock maker, 1211

wharfinger, 796

wheelwright, 354, 542, 1031, 1049, 1146, 1213, 1214, 1555

wigmaker, *see* periwig maker

wine cooper, 106, 173, 207, 1325; *and see* cooper

wine merchant, 1488; *and see* vintner

wire drawer, gold and silver, 1531

woodward, *see* forester

wool-man, 945

wool merchant, 286 n, 291, 1255

wool stapler, 373, 446, 657, 780, 972, 990, 1201

woollen draper, 1425; *and see* draper

writing master, 296, 539, 1274, 1535

INDEX OF CAUSES OF DEATH

* An asterisk indicates that the page has more than one reference

accident, 118*
    fall from a horse, 209, 521, 622, 1086, 1290,
      1525, 1536; while hunting, 1388
    struck by a horse, 1131; by a waggon, 1031
childbirth, childbearing, 199, 299, 395, 439, 697,
    900, 949, 1024, 1067, 1076, 1399, 1480, 1489,
    1499 & n
climate of Bengal, 1524
defence, in his own, 1390
disease:
    apoplexy, 267, 1526
    arthritis, 1071, 1451
    atrophy, senile, 1071
    cholera, 1026, 1073
    consumption or phthisis, 23, 73, 136, 409, 640,
      1071, 1527
    dropsy, 58
    dysentery, 58, 1049
    excruciating, 1537
    fever, 1090, 1096, 1097, 1166, 1170, 1191*, 1235,
      1527; and cold, 520; and sore throat, 521
    gangrene (sphakelum), 1190
    incurable, 1430
    lingering, 1131, 1200
    long and painful (or severe or tedious) illness (or
      affliction), 329, 669, 723, 740, 898, 1006,
      1209, 1454
    nervous disorder, 1298

palsy, 130, 494, 1018
plague, 428 n
puerperal fever, 1105
pox (variolae), 1526; smallpox, 136*, 1457,
    1509
short but severe, 1473
sore affliction, 1481, 1507
tedious and painful sickness, 754
violent (and severe) illness (or sickness), 614,
    726
weak and infirm, 919
drowning, 41, 112, 172, 176, 337, 627, 955, 1054*,
    1281, 1282, 1358, 1367, 1459
    shipwreck, 1281
duel, 1214
fire, death in a, 1459
inoculation, 1211
military service, death on, 1245
    in battle, 6, 412
    from wounds received in battle, 58, 410, 1023
murder, 112, 847, 1049, 1117; with poison, 230,
    329
    by rebels, 123, 891
    in mutiny (Indian), 1176
sea, death at, 537, 898, 1023, 1109, 1143, 1245,
    1282, 1316, 1321, 1344, 1511
sudden death, 25, 560, 573, 575, 1214, 1430, 1543,
    1550

blished for the Editor of The History of Gloucestershire compressed December 31st 1803.

Statute Miles 69½ to a Degree.

HEREFORD

MONMOUTH

SOMERSET SHIRE

WILTS

ROSS

NEWENT

GLOUCESTER
Churchdown
Barnwood

MITCHEL DEAN
Longhope
Churcham
Blaisdon
Minsterworth
Westbury

Tuerdean
Abbenhall
English Bicknor
LIT. DEAN

COLEFORD
NEWNHAM
St Bravels

Newland
Clearwell
BLAKENEY
Hewelsfield
Brockweir

Aylburton
Alvington
Woolaston

Berkeley Canal

PAINSWICK
Standish
Pitchcomb
Randwick
STROUD
Rodborough
Chalford

LEONARD STANLEY
MINCHINHAMPTON
Nimpsfield
Avening
Cherington
Beverstone
TETBURY

CHEPSTOW

Tidenham

Sheperdine
Rockhampton
Nibley
South End
WOTTON under Edge
Ozleworth
Boxwell
Weston Birt
Shipton Moign

Oldbury
THORNBURY
Falfield
Tortworth
Chasfield
DURSLEY
Horsley
Kingscot

Aust
Elberton
Cromhall
Long Cross
Alderley
Hawkesbury
Horton
Little Sodbury

New Passage
Northwich Chap.
Olveston
Alveston
Tytherington
WICKWAR
Sweethouse
Hawkesbury Wood

Almondsbury
Knowle
Woodlands
Frampton Cotterel
Yate
SODBURY
Old Sodbury
Acton Turville
London Road
to Oxford 53 Miles

Greenfield
Henbury
Stoke Gifford
Winterbourn
Wapley
Tormarton
to Chippenham & Marlbro
the London Road

Shirehampton
Westbury
Redland
Stapleton
Mangotsfield
Puckle church
Littleton
MARSHFIELD

BRISTOL
Clifton
St George
Hanham
Wick
Deynton
Cold Aston

Oldland Chap.
Hanham
Bitton
N. Stoke
Kilweston
BATH